Baseball America DIRECTORY 2008

YOUR DEFINITIVE GUIDE TO THE GAME

Detailed Information On Baseball In All Leagues At All Levels

MAJORS

MINORS

INDEPENDENT

INTERNATIONAL

COLLEGE

AMATEUR

BASEBALL AMERICA INC. • DURHAM, N.C.

Editor
Will Lingo

Assistant Editors
Ben Badler, Matthew Blood, J.J. Cooper, Matt Eddy, Aaron Fitt, Chris Kline, Josh Leventhal, John Manuel, Nathan Rode, Jim Shonerd

Photo Editor
Nathan Rode

Design & Production
Daniel BeDen, Sara Hiatt, Linwood Webb

Jacket Photos
Erick Aybar by Sports on Film; Theo Epstein by Larry Goren

Cover Design
Linwood Webb

Baseball America

President/Publisher: Lee Folger
Editors in Chief: Will Lingo, John Manuel
Design & Production Director: Sara Hiatt

Distributed by Simon & Schuster
ISBN-10: 1-932391-20-7 ISBN-13: 978-1-932391-20-6

BaseballAmerica.com

TABLE OF CONTENTS

MAJOR LEAGUES

MINOR LEAGUES

STAN DENNY

INDEPENDENT LEAGUES

OTHER LEAGUES & ORGANIZATIONS

WHAT'S NEW IN 2008

TRIPLE-A

FRANCHISE MOVE | Ottawa Lynx (International) become Lehigh Valley IronPigs (Allentown, Pa.)

DOUBLE-A

FRANCHISE MOVE | Wichita Wranglers (Texas) become Northwest Arkansas Naturals (Springdale, Ark.)

LOW CLASS A

NAME CHANGES | Swing of the Quad Cities (Midwest) now known as Quad Cities River Bandits.

SHORT-SEASON

FRANCHISE CHANGES | Mariners add Appalachian League franchise in Pulaski, bringing league to 10 teams.

NAME CHANGES | Casper Rockies (Pioneer) now known as Casper Ghosts. Great Falls White Sox (Pioneer) now known as Great Falls Voyagers.

INDEPENDENT

FRANCHISE CHANGES | American Association adds teams in Grand Prairie, Texas, and Wichita; drops Coastal Bend and St. Joe's franchises. Atlantic League adds team in St. Charles, Md., drops travel team. Can-Am League adds team in Ottawa, drops New Haven County and North Shore franchises. Frontier League's Slippery Rock Sliders moves to Waterford, Mich., and change name to Midwest Sliders. Golden League adds teams in Calgary and Edmonton. Northern League drops teams in Calgary and Edmonton. South Coast League adds team in Jackson, Miss., drops team in Bradenton, Fla.

NAME CHANGES | Fullerton Flyers (Golden) now known as Orange County Flyers.

Baseball america
PROSPECT
HANDBOOK
Franklin Morales of the Colorado Rockies
Clayton Kershaw of the Los Angeles Dodgers
Cameron Maybin of the Florida Marlins
Jay Bruce of the Cincinnati Reds
THE SECRET WEAPON FOR FANTASY LEAGUE SUCCESS!
2008
FOREWORD BY THEO EPSTEIN

USA

Map illustrations by Paul Trap

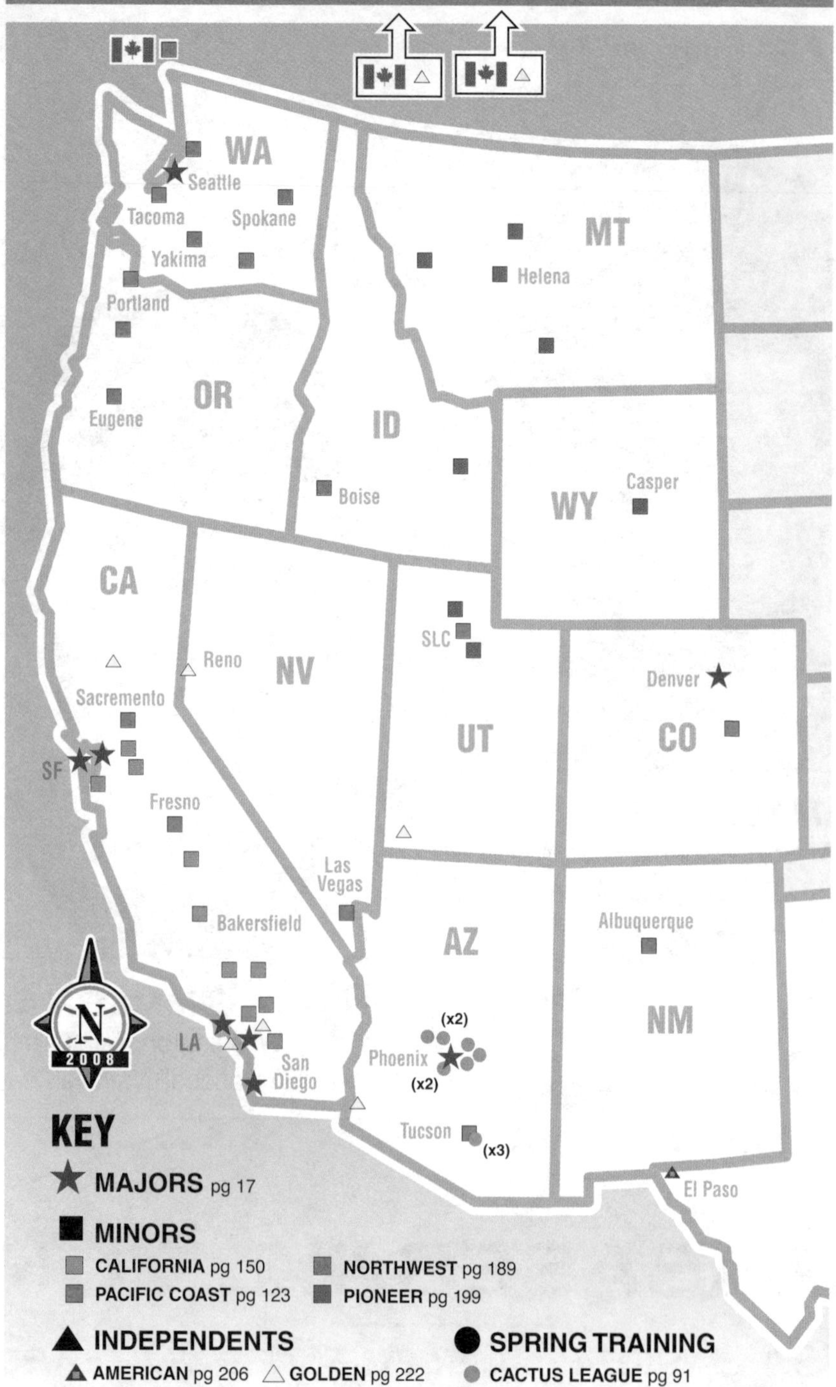

2008
N
ND
Fargo
MN
SD
Minneapolis
Sioux Falls
WI
Milwaukee
Chicago
IA
NE
Des Moines
Omaha
IL
Kansas City
KS
MO
St. Louis
Wichita
KY
Oklahoma City
AR
TN
Amarillo
Memphis
OK
Little Rock
MS
Arlington
Jackson
Alexandria
TX
LA
Houston
New Orleans
San Antonio
MINORS
INTERNATIONAL pg 115
MIDWEST pg 167
PACIFIC COAST pg 123
SOUTHERN pg 139
TEXAS pg 145
KEY
MAJORS pg 17
INDEPENDENTS
AMERICAN pg 206
FRONTIER pg 217
NORTHERN pg 224
SOUTH COAST pg 228
UNITED LEAGUE pg 230

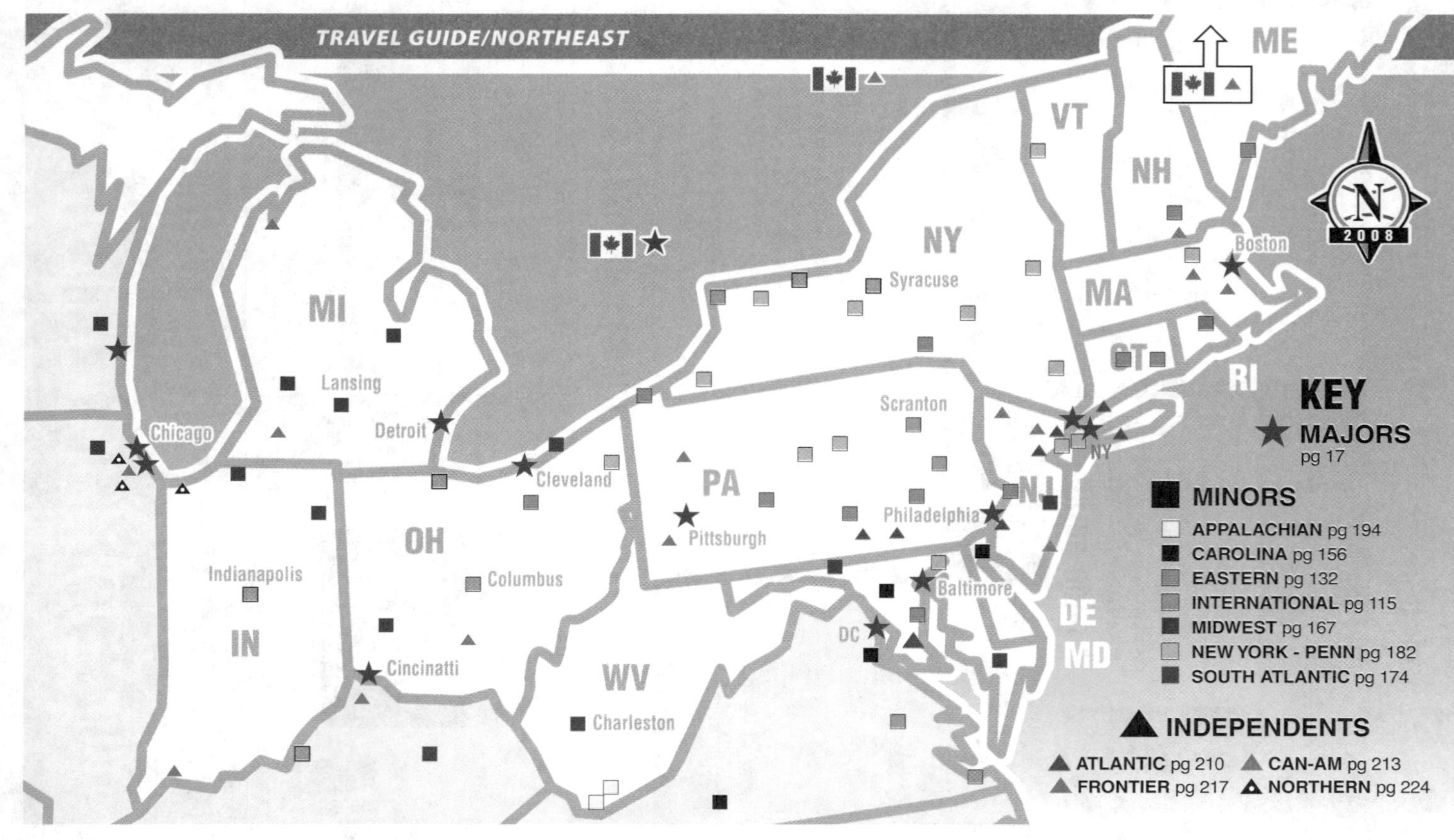
TRAVEL GUIDE/NORTHEAST
MI
Lansing
Detroit
Chicago
IN
Indianapolis
OH
Columbus
Cleveland
Cincinatti
WV
Charleston
PA
Pittsburgh
Scranton
Philadelphia
NY
Syracuse
VT
NH
ME
MA
Boston
CT
RI
NJ
NY
DE
MD
Baltimore
DC
2008
N
KEY
MAJORS pg 17
MINORS
APPALACHIAN pg 194
CAROLINA pg 156
EASTERN pg 132
INTERNATIONAL pg 115
MIDWEST pg 167
NEW YORK - PENN pg 182
SOUTH ATLANTIC pg 174
INDEPENDENTS
ATLANTIC pg 210
CAN-AM pg 213
FRONTIER pg 217
NORTHERN pg 224

BaseBall america®.com
MAJORS ◆ MINORS ◆ PROSPECTS ◆ DRAFT ◆ COLLEGE ◆ HIGH SCHOOL
BaseballAmerica.com
Visit BaseballAmerica.com to get your Baseball America fix every day. You'll find daily coverage of big events like the College World Series and our expansive draft coverage. The site also features signature BA stuff you can't find anywhere else. Here are some things you'll find every day:
Complete minor league statistics
The BA Prospect Hot Sheet
Our weekly Top 25 college rankings
Chats with BA editors
The BA Daily Dish
Our popular "Ask BA" column
900 PROSPECT REPORTS IN ONE PLACE
Second-Season Blues
PROSPECT HOT SHEET
Prospect Hot Sheet
The Prospect Hot Sheet is a weekly snapshot of prospects that are riding the biggest hot streaks. Every Monday during the baseball season BA editors give you the skinny on ten hot prospects that you won't hear about anywhere else. Find out which prospects have the hottest bats and which pitcher's can't be hit in the Prospect Hot Sheet every week at BaseballAmerica.com.
The Baseball America Prospect Report
Baseball America Prospect Report
The BAPR is a free daily e-mail that showcases the best performances from last night's minor league boxscores. It also breaks down players in the offseason as well, highlighting stats from the Arizona Fall League, Mexican League, Puerto Rican League, Venezuelan League and Dominican League.
BLOG
COLLEGE
Three Strikes: April 9
BA.com Blogs
Check our blogs frequently throughout the day for the latest breaking news and opinions about prospects, the draft and college baseball. Leave comments and interact with BA editors and writers as they post.
Subscribe and gain access to premium Baseball America content today.
One year Web-only subscription: $62.00
BaseballAmerica.com
800-845-2726

MAJOR LEAGUES

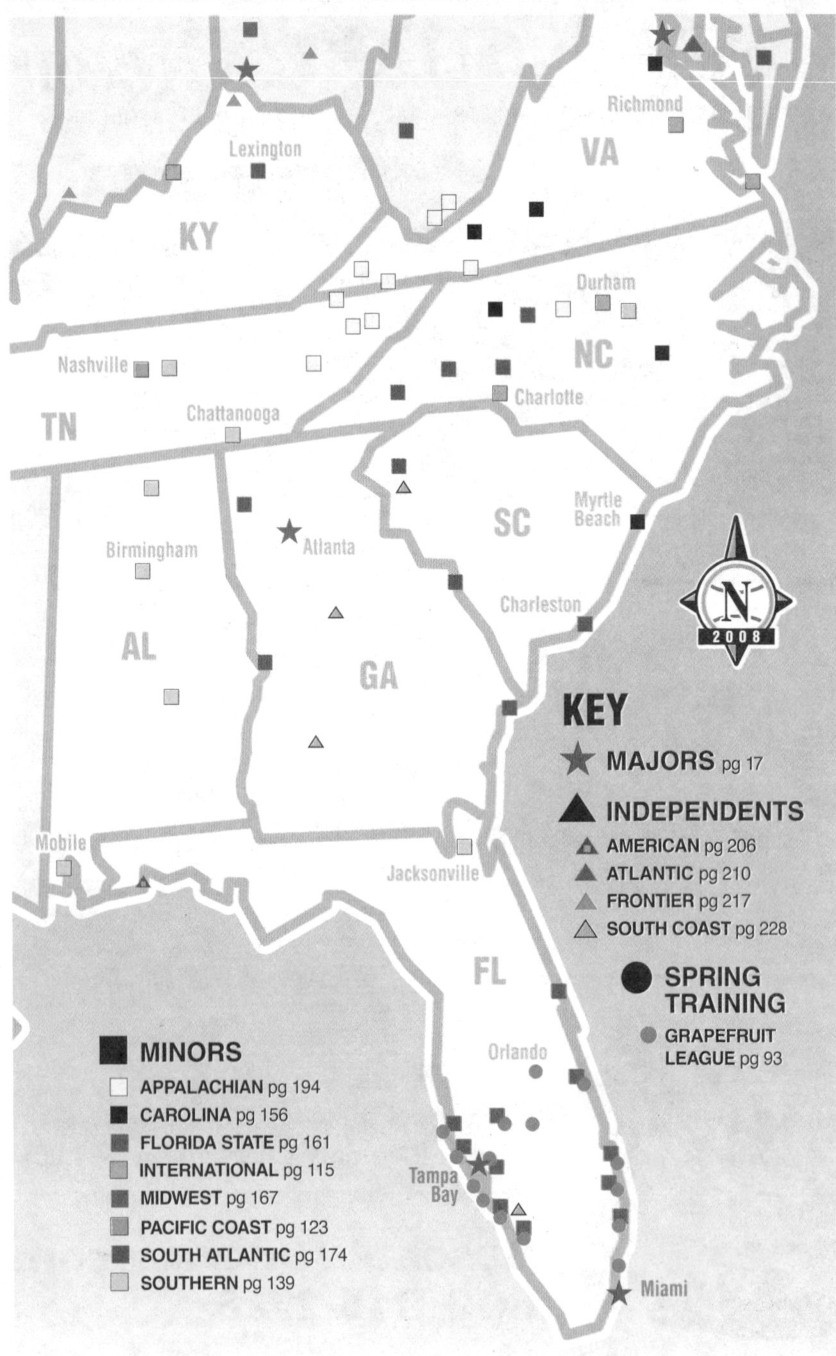
Richmond
VA
Lexington
KY
Durham
NC
Nashville
Charlotte
Chattanooga
TN
Myrtle Beach
SC
Atlanta
Birmingham
Charleston
2008
AL
GA
KEY
MAJORS pg 17
INDEPENDENTS
AMERICAN pg 206
ATLANTIC pg 210
FRONTIER pg 217
SOUTH COAST pg 228
Mobile
Jacksonville
FL
SPRING TRAINING
GRAPEFRUIT LEAGUE pg 93
Orlando
MINORS
APPALACHIAN pg 194
CAROLINA pg 156
FLORIDA STATE pg 161
INTERNATIONAL pg 115
MIDWEST pg 167
PACIFIC COAST pg 123
SOUTH ATLANTIC pg 174
SOUTHERN pg 139
Tampa Bay
Miami

MAJOR LEAGUE BASEBALL

Mailing Address: 245 Park Ave. New York, NY 10167.

Telephone: (212) 931-7800.

Website: www.mlb.com.

Commissioner: Allan H. "Bud" Selig.

President/Chief Operating Officer: Bob DuPuy. **Executive Vice President, Business:** Tim Brosnan. **Executive VP, Labor Relations/Human Resources:** Robert Manfred. **Executive VP, Finance:** Jonathan Mariner. **Executive VP, Administration:** John McHale. **Executive VP, Baseball Operations:** Jimmie Lee Solomon.

Bud Selig

Baseball Operations

Senior Vice President, Baseball Operations: Joe Garagiola Jr.

VP, Baseball Operations/Administration: Ed Burns. **VP, International Baseball Operations/Administration:** Lou Melendez. **VP, Umpiring:** Mike Port. **VP, On-Field Operations:** Bob Watson.

Special Advisor, Baseball Operations: Frank Robinson. **Senior Director, Major League Operations:** Roy Krasik.

Director, Urban Youth Academy: Darrell Miller. **Senior Manager, Minor League Operations:** Sylvia Lind. **Manager, Baseball Operations:** Jeff Pfeifer. **Manager, Dominican Operations:** Ronaldo Peralta. **Senior Specialist, On-Field Operations:** Darryl Hamilton. **Specialist, Major League Operations:** Brian Porter.

Specialist, On-Field Operations: Matt McKendry. **Specialist, Umpiring:** Fred Seymour. **Director, Umpire Administration:** Tom Lepperd.

Director, Umpire Medical Services: Mark Letendre.

Umpiring Supervisors: Rich Garcia, Cris Jones, Jim McKean, Steve Palermo, Rich Rieker, Marty Springstead.

Director, Arizona Fall League: Steve Cobb. **Director, Major League Scouting Bureau:** Frank Marcos. **Assistant Director, Scouting Bureau:** Rick Oliver.

Bob DuPuy

Security

Senior Director, Security: Earnell Lucas.

Senior Manager, Security: Steve Ethier. **Senior Manager, Facility Operations:** Linda Pantell. **Regional Supervisor, Security:** Tom Christopher. **Supervisor, Security Operations:** Nancy Zamudio.

Investigations

Vice President, Investigations: Dan Mullin.

Senior Director, Investigations: George Hanna. **Senior Manager, Investigations:** Leroy Hendricks.

Public Relations

Telephone: (212) 931-7878. **FAX:** (212) 949-5654.

Senior Vice President, Public Relations: Richard Levin. **VP, Public Relations Operations:** Patrick Courtney.

Director, Multicultural/Charitable Communications: Silvia Alvarez. **Senior Manager, Baseball Information:** Rob Doelger. **Managers, Media Relations:** John Blundell, Michael Teevan. **Manager, Business Public Relations:** Kerry Kielar. **Senior Specialist, Business Public Relations:** Daniel Queen. **Specialist, Business Public Relations:** Paige Novack. **Coordinators, Media Relations:** Donald Muller, Sarah Leer. **Senior Administrative Assistant:** Heather Flock. **Administrative Assistant:** Vincent Accardi.

Official Baseball Historian: Jerome Holtzman.

Jimmie Solomon

Club Relations

Senior Vice President, Scheduling/Club Relations: Katy Feeney. **Senior Administrative Assistant, Scheduling/Club Relations:** Raxel Concepcion. **Coordinator, Club Relations:** Andrew Davis.

Senior Vice President, Club Relations: Phyllis Merhige. **Senior Administrative Assistant, Club Relations:** Angelica Cintron. **Administrator, Club Relations:** Julio Torres.

Licensing

Senior Vice President, Licensing: Howard Smith.

VP, Domestic Licensing: Steve Armus. **Vice President, Hard Goods:** Colin Hagen. **Senior Director, Authentics:** Dennis Nolan. **Director, Licensing/Minor Leagues:** Eliot Runyon. **Director, National Retail:** Adam Blinderman. **Director, Gifts/Novelties:** Maureen Mason. **Director, Hard Goods:** Mike Napolitano. **Director, Non-Authentics:** Greg Sim. **Senior Manager, Presence Marketing:** Robin Jaffe. **Senior Manager, Authentics:** Ryan Samuelson.

Publishing and Photographs

Vice President, Publishing/Photographs: Don Hintze. **Editorial Director:** Mike McCormick. **Art Director, Publications:** Faith Rittenberg. **Director, MLB Photographs:** Rich Pilling.

Special Events

Senior Vice President, Special Events: Marla Miller. **Senior Director, Special Events:** Brian O'Gara. **Director, Special**

Events: Eileen Buser. **Senior Manager, Special Events:** Rob Capilli. **Manager, Special Events:** Joe Fitzgerald. **Manager, Special Events:** Jennifer Jacobson.

Broadcasting

Senior Vice President, Broadcasting: Chris Tully. **VP, Broadcast Administration/Operations:** Bernadette McDonald. **VP, Broadcast Business Affairs:** Rob McGlarry. **Senior Director, Distribution Development:** Susanne Hilgefort. **Director, Broadcast Administration/Operations:** Chuck Torres.

Corporate Sales & Marketing

Senior Vice President, Corporate Sales/Marketing: John Brody. **VP, Partnership Marketing:** Jeremy Cohen. **Director, Local Sales:** Joe Grippo. **Director, National Sales:** Ari Roitman. **Manager, Partnership Marketing:** Jean Marie Glenister.

Advertising

Senior Vice President, Advertising/Marketing: Jacqueline Parkes. **Director, Advertising:** Mary Beck. **Senior Director, Research:** Dan Derian. **Research Manager, Advertising:** Marc Beck.

Vice President, Design Services: Anne Occi.

Community Affairs/Educational Programming

Vice President, Community Affairs: Tom Brasuell. **Director, Community Relations:** Celia Bobrowsky.

General Administration

Senior Vice President, Accounting/Treasurer: Bob Clark.

Senior Vice President/General Counsel, Labor Relations: Dan Halem. **Senior VP/General Counsel; Business:** Ethan Orlinsky.

Senior Vice President/General Counsel; BOC: Tom Ostertag. **Senior VP, Finance:** Kathleen Torres.

Vice President, Application Development: Mike Morris. **VP, Deputy General Counsel:** Domna Candido. **VP, Strategic Planning for Recruitment/Diversity:** Wendy Lewis. **VP, Human Resources:** Ray Scott.

Vice President, Deputy General Counsel: Jennifer Simms. **VP, Operations & Tech Support:** Peter Surhoff.

Executive Director, Baseball Assistance Team: Jim Martin. **Senior Director, Office Operations:** Donna Hoder. **Senior Director, Quality Control:** Peggy O'Neill-Janosik.

Director, Recruitment: Francisco Estrada. **Director, Risk Management/Financial Reporting:** Anthony Avitabile. **Senior Manager, Records:** Mildred Delgado.

Manager, Payroll/Pension: Rich Hunt. **Manager, Benefits/HRIS:** Diane Cuddy.

International

Mailing Address: 245 Park Ave., 34th Floor, New York, NY 10167. **Telephone:** (212) 931-7500. **FAX:** (212) 949-5795.

Senior Vice President, International Business Operations: Paul Archey.

Vice President, International Licensing/Sponsorship: Shawn Lawson-Cummings. **VP/Executive Producer:** Russell Gabay. **Tournament Director, World Baseball Classic:** James Pearce. **Director, International Licensing:** Deidra Varona. **Director, International Corporate Marketing and Retail Services:** Jacquelyn Walsh. **Director, Market Development/Communications:** Dominick Balsamo. **VP/Managing Director, MLB Japan:** Jim Small.

Director, China Operations: Michael Marone. **Director, Australian Operations:** Thomas Nicholson. **Director, European Operations:** Clive Russell.

MLB Western Operations

Office Address: 2415 East Camelback Rd., Suite 850, Phoenix, AZ 85016. **Telephone:** (602) 281-7300. **FAX:** (602) 281-7313.

Vice President, Western Operations/Special Projects: Laurel Prieb. **Office Coordinator:** Valerie Dietrich

Major League Baseball Productions

Office Address: 75 Ninth Ave., New York, NY 10011. **Telephone:** (212) 931-7777. **FAX:** (212) 931-7788.

Vice President/Executive In Charge of Production: Dave Gavant. **VP, Programming/Business Affairs:** Elizabeth Scott. **Executive Producer:** David Check. **Director, Operations:** Shannon Valine. **Coordinating Producer:** Adam Schlackman. **Coordinating Producer, Field Production:** Marc Caiafa.

Umpires

Lance Barksdale, Ted Barrett, Wally Bell, C.B. Bucknor, Mark Carlson, Gary Cederstrom, Eric Cooper, Derryl Cousins, Jerry Crawford, Fieldin Culbreth, Phil Cuzzi, Kerwin Danley, Gary Darling, Bob Davidson, Gerry Davis, Dana DeMuth, Laz Diaz, Mike DiMuro, Bruce Dreckman, Doug Eddings, Paul Emmel, Mike Everitt, Andy Fletcher, Marty Foster, Greg Gibson, Brian Gorman, Tom Hallion, Angel Hernandez, Ed Hickox, John Hirschbeck, Bill Hohn, Sam Holbrook, Marvin Hudson, Dan Iassogna, Jim Joyce, Jeff Kellogg, Ron Kulpa, Jerry Layne, Alfonso Marquez, Randy Marsh, Tim McClelland, Jerry Meals, Chuck Meriwether, Bill Miller, Ed Montague, Paul Nauert, Jeff Nelson, Brian O'Nora, Larry Poncino, Tony Randazzo, Ed Rapuano, Rick Reed, Mike Reilly, Charlie Reliford, Jim Reynolds, Brian Runge, Paul Schrieber, Dale Scott, Tim Timmons, Tim Tschida, Larry Vanover, Mark Wegner, Bill Welke, Tim Welke, Hunter Wendelstedt, Joe West, Mike Winters, Jim Wolf, Larry Young.

Events

2008 All-Star Game: July 15 at Yankee Stadium, New York.

2008 World Series: Begins Oct. 22 at ballpark of club whose league wins the 2008 All-Star Game.

AMERICAN LEAGUE

Years League Active: 1901-.

2008 Opening Date: March 31. **Closing Date:** Sept. 28.

Regular Season: 162 games.

Division Structure: East—Baltimore, Boston, New York, Tampa Bay, Toronto. Central—Chicago, Cleveland, Detroit, Kansas City, Minnesota. West—Los Angeles, Oakland, Seattle, Texas.

Playoff Format: Three division champions and second-place team with best record meet in two best-of-five Division Series. Winners meet in best-of-seven League Championship Series.

All-Star Game: July 15, Yankee Stadium, New York (American League vs. National League).

Roster Limit: 25, through Aug. 31 when rosters expand to 40.

Brand of Baseball: Rawlings.

Statistician: MLB Advanced Media, 75 Ninth Ave., 5th Floor, New York, NY 10011.

STADIUM INFORMATION

		Dimensions				
City	Stadium	LF	CF	RF	Capacity	2007 Att.
Baltimore	Camden Yards	333	410	318	48,876	2,164,822
Boston	Fenway Park	310	390	302	33,871	2,970,755
Chicago	U.S. Cellular Field	300	400	335	44,321	2,684,395
Cleveland	Progressive Field	325	405	325	43,863	2,275,912
Detroit	Comerica Park	346	422	330	40,000	3,047,133
Kansas City	Kauffman Stadium	330	400	330	40,529	1,616,867
Los Angeles	Angel Stadium	365	406	365	45,050	3,365,632
Minnesota	Humphrey Metrodome	343	408	327	48,678	2,296,383
New York	Yankee Stadium	318	408	314	57,545	4,271,083
Oakland	McAfee Coliseum	330	400	367	43,662	1,921,844
Seattle	Safeco Field	331	405	326	45,600	2,672,223
Tampa Bay	Tropicana Field	315	407	322	45,200	1,387,603
Texas	Rangers Ballpark in Arlington	334	400	325	49,166	2,353,862
Toronto	Rogers Centre	328	400	328	50,516	2,360,644

NATIONAL LEAGUE

Years League Active: 1876-.

2008 Opening Date: March 30. **Closing Date:** Sept. 28.

Regular Season: 162 games.

Division Structure: East—Atlanta, Florida, New York, Philadelphia, Washington. Central—Chicago, Cincinnati, Houston, Milwaukee, Pittsburgh, St. Louis. West—Arizona, Colorado, Los Angeles, San Diego, San Francisco.

Playoff Format: Three division champions and second-place team with best record meet in two best-of-five Division Series. Winners meet in best-of-seven League Championship Series.

All-Star Game: July 15, Yankee Stadium, New York (American League vs. National League).

Roster Limit: 25, through Aug. 31 when rosters expand to 40.

Brand of Baseball: Rawlings.

Statistician: MLB Advanced Media, 75 Ninth Ave., 5th Floor, New York, NY 10011.

STADIUM INFORMATION

		Dimensions				
City	Stadium	LF	CF	RF	Capacity	2007 Att.
Arizona	Chase Field	330	407	334	48,500	2,325,249
Atlanta	Turner Field	335	401	330	50,528	2,745,207
Chicago	Wrigley Field	355	400	353	38,884	3,252,462
Cincinnati	Great American Ball Park	328	404	325	42,263	2,058,593
Colorado	Coors Field	347	415	350	50,200	2,376,250
Florida	Dolphins Stadium	335	410	345	40,585	1,370,511
Houston	Minute Maid Park	315	435	326	42,000	3,020,405
Los Angeles	Dodger Stadium	330	395	330	56,000	3,857,036
Milwaukee	Miller Park	315	402	315	53,192	2,869,144
New York	Shea Stadium	338	410	338	55,777	3,853,955
Philadelphia	Citizens Bank Park	329	401	330	43,500	3,108,325
Pittsburgh	PNC Park	335	400	335	48,044	1,749,142
St. Louis	Busch Stadium	336	400	335	46,000	3,552,180
San Diego	PETCO Park	334	398	322	42,000	2,790,074
San Francisco	AT&T Park	335	404	307	40,800	3,223,215
Washington	Nationals Park	336	404	335	42,000	1,943,812

Arizona Diamondbacks

Office Address: Chase Field, 401 E. Jefferson St, Phoenix, AZ 85004.
Mailing Address: P.O. Box 2095, Phoenix, AZ 58001.
Telephone: (602) 462-6500. **Fax:** (602) 462-6599.
Website: www.dbacks.com

Ownership

Managing General Partner: Ken Kendrick. **Managing General Partner/CEO:** Jeff Moorad. **General Partners:** Mike Chipman, Dale Jensen, Jeff Royer.

BUSINESS OPERATIONS

Ken Kendrick

President: Derrick Hall. **Executive Assistant to President:** Brooke Mitchell.

Executive Vice President/COO: Tom Garfinkel. **Executive Assistant to Executive VP/COO:** Adriana Fontes. **Special Assistant to President:** Roland Hemond.

Broadcasting

Vice President, Broadcasting: Scott Geyer. **Director, Radio/Broadcast Services:** Leo Gilmartin.

Corporate Partnerships/Marketing

Senior Vice President, Corporate Partnerships/Marketing: Cullen Maxey.

Senior Director, Marketing: Karina Bohn. **Senior Director, Hispanic Marketing/Radio Analyst:** Richard Saenz. **Brand Director:** Doug Alkire. **Director, Business Operations:** Joel McFadden. **Director, Corporate Partnerships:** Tim Emory and Steve Mullins. **Director, Corporate Partnership Alliances:** Judy Olson. **Director, Hispanic Media Sales:** Julie Romero.

Finance/Legal

Executive Vice President/CFO: Tom Harris. **Executive Assistant/Office Manager:** Sandy Cox. **VP, Finance:** Craig Bradley. **VP/General Counsel:** Nona Lee. **Associate General Counsel:** Caleb Jay. **Legal Secretary:** Candace Kerege.

Community Affairs

Senior Vice President, Community Affairs/Ticket Operations: Diane Aguilar. **Director, Community Affairs:** Amy Buchan. **Manager, Community Affairs:** Pete Flocken.

Communications/Media Relations

Telephone: (602) 462-6519. **Fax:** (602) 462-6527.

Vice President, Communications: Shaun Rachau.

Director, Player/Media Relations: Mike McNally. **Director, Cooperate Communications:** Catherine Herman. **Assistant Director, Player/Media Relations:** Aaron Staenberg. **Coordinator, Player/Media Relations:** Lynita Johnson. **Assistant, Player/Media Relations:** Bryan Pelekoudas. **Director, Publications:** Greg Salvatore. **Manager, Publications:** Doug Flanagan.

Stadium Operations

Vice President, Facility/Event Services: Russ Amaral.

Director, Security: Sean Maguire. **Manager, Security:** Greg Green. **Senior Director, Suite/Premium Services:** Diney Ransford. **Director, Building Services:** Jim Hawkins. **Manager, Guest Services/Guest Relations:** Kurt Kleinknecht. **Director, Engineering:** Jim White. **Event Coordinator:** Summer Terrell. **Head Groundskeeper:** Grant Trenbeath. **Official Scorer:** Rodney Johnson.

Manager, Spring Training Operations: Bonnie Faircloth.

Ticketing

Telephone: (602) 514-8400. **Fax:** (602) 462-4141.

Senior Vice President, Community Affairs/Ticket Operations: Dianne Aguilar. **VP, Ticket Sales and Service:** Brent Stehlik. **Senior Director, Season Ticket Services/Ballpark Attractions:** Charlene Vasquez-Inzunza. **Director, Season Tickets:** John Fisher. **Director, Season Ticket Services:** Luis Calderon. **Director, Suite Sales:** Tim Martin. **Director, Group/Inside Sales:** Jeremy Walls. **Director, Premium Seating:** Mike Dunham.

Travel, Clubhouse

Director, Team Travel: Roger Riley. **Visitor Clubhouse:** Bob Doty.

GENERAL INFORMATION

Stadium (year opened): Chase Field (1998).
Home Dugout: Third Base. **Playing Surface:** Grass.
Team Colors: Sedona red, Sonoran sand and black.
Player Representative: Unavailable.

Josh Byrnes

BASEBALL OPERATIONS

Telephone: (602) 462-6500. **Fax:** (602) 462-6425.

Senior Vice President/General Manager: Josh Byrnes.

VP, Special Assistant to GM: Bob Gebhard. **Assistant GM:** Peter Woodfork. **Executive Assistant to GM:** Debra Gallagher. **Manager, Baseball Operations:** Shiraz Rehman. **Assistant, Baseball Operations:** Helen Zelman.

Major League Staff

Manager: Bob Melvin.

Coaches: Bench—Kirk Gibson; Pitching—Bryan Price; Batting—Rick Schu; First Base—Lee Tinsley; Third Base—Chip Hale; Bullpen—Glenn Sherlock.

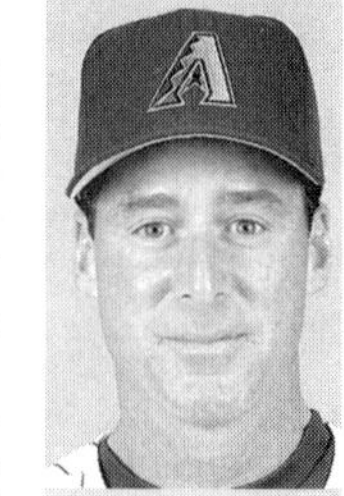

Bob Melvin

Medical, Training

Club Physicians: Dr. Michael Lee, Dr. Roger McCoy. **Head Trainer:** Ken Crenshaw. **Assistant Trainer:** Dave Edwards. **Strength/ Conditioning Coach:** Nate Shaw.

Minor Leagues

Telephone: (602) 462-4400. **Fax:** (602) 462-6421.

Director, Player Development: A.J. Hinch. **Assistant Director, Player Development:** Jeffrey Pickler. **Manager, Minor League Administration:** Susan Webner.

Coordinators: Jack Howell (field), Mel Stottlemyre, Jr. (pitching), Dave Hansen (hitting), Tony Perezchica (infield), Brett Butler (outfield/baserunning), Doug Jones (pitching consultant), Bob Didier (catching). **Tuscon Complex Coordinator:** Bob Bensinger. **Medical Coordinator:** PJ Mainville. **Assistant Medical Coordinator:** Patrick Serbus. **Strength/Conditioning Coordinator:** Brett McCabe. **Dominican Coordinator:** Luis de los Santos.

Farm System

Class	Club	League	Manager	Coach	Pitching Coach
Triple-A	Tucson	Pacific Coast	Bill Plummer	Joel Youngblood	Mike Parrott
Double-A	Mobile	Southern	Hector de la Cruz	Turner Ward	Jeff Pico
High A	Visalia	California	Mike Bell	Rick Burleson	Wellington Cepeda
Low A	South Bend	Midwest	Mark Haley	Francisco Morales	Erik Sabel
Short-season	Yakima	Northwest	Bob Didier	Chris Briones	Dan Carlson
Rookie	Missoula	Pioneer	Audo Vicente	Alan Zinter	Steve Merriman
Rookie	Diamondbacks	Dominican	Unavailable	Unavailable	Unavailable

Scouting

Amateur/International Scouting Telephone: (602) 462-6518. **Fax:** (602) 462-6527.

Professional Scouting Telephone: (602) 462-6557. **Fax:** (602) 462-6425.

Director, Scouting: Tom Allison.

Director, Player Personnel: Jerry Dipoto.

Assistant Director, Scouting/International Supervisor: Chad MacDonald.

Scouting Administrator: Jennifer Blatt. **Assistant to Scouting:** Phil Seibel.

Director, Pacific Rim Operations: Mack Hayashi.

Pro Scouts: Joe Bohringer (De Kalb, IL), Rico Brogna (Woodbury, CT), Bill Earnhart (Point Clear, AL), Jim Marshall (Scottsdale, AZ), Mike Piatnik (Winter Haven, FL), Tim Schmidt (San Bernardino, CA), Mike Sgobba (Scottsdale, AZ), Carlos Gomez (Atlanta, GA), Muzzy Jackson (Key Biscayne, FL), Kevin Jarvis (Franklin, TN).

Crosschecker: Steve Springer (Huntington Beach, CA). **Regional Supervisors:** East—Greg Lonigro (Connellsville, PA), West—Bob Minor (Garden Grove, CA), Central—Steve McAllister (Chillicothe, IL).

Scouts: Shawn Barton (Reading, PA), Ray Blanco (Miami, FL), Darold Brown (Elk Grove, CA) Trip Couch (Sugar Land, TX), Mike Daughtry (St. Charles, IL), Rodney Davis (Glendale, AZ), Jim Dedrick (Davis, CA), Ed Durkin (Clearwater, FL), Ed Gustafson (Spokane, WA), Matt Hass (Cincinnati, OH), Jason Karegeannes (Arlington, TX), Hal Kurtzman (Lake Balboa, CA), T.R. Lewis (Marietta, GA), Howard McCullough (Greenville, NC), Matt Merullo (Madison, CT), Joe Robinson (St. Louis, MO), Luke Wrenn (Lakeland, FL)

Part-Time Scouts: George Swain (Wilmington, NC), Homer Newlin (Tallahassee, FL).

Special Assistant to GM, Latin American Operations: Junior Noboa (Dominican Republic).

International Scouts: Mike Sgobba—Mexico (Scottsdale, AZ); Miguel Nava—Venezuela (Tampa, FL); Jack Pierce (Leon, Mexico); Luis Baez (Santo Domingo, DR).

Part-time International Scouts: Dominican Republic—Gabriel Berroa, José Ortiz, Rafael Mateo, José Ortiz. Nicaragua—José Díaz Perez. Colombia—Julio Sanchez.

Atlanta Braves

Office Address: 755 Hank Aaron Dr, Atlanta, GA 30315.
Mailing Address: P.O. Box 4064, Atlanta, GA 30302.
Telephone: (404) 522-7630. **Fax:** (404) 614-1391.
Website: www.braves.com.

Ownership

Operated/Owned By: Liberty Media.

Chairman Emeritus: Bill Bartholomay. **Chairman/CEO:** Terry McGuirk.

President: John Schuerholz. **Senior Vice President:** Henry Aaron.

Terry McGuirk

BUSINESS OPERATIONS

Executive Vice President, Business Operations: Mike Plant. **VP/General Counsel:** Greg Heller.

Finance

Vice President, Controller: Chip Moore.

Marketing, Sales

Executive Vice President, Sales/Marketing: Derek Schiller. **Executive Director, Marketing:** Gus Eurton. **Senior Director, Ticket Sales:** Paul Adams. **Senior Director, Corporate Sales:** Jim Allen.

Public Relations/Communications

Telephone: (404) 614-1556. **Fax:** (404) 614-1391.

Director, Media Relations: Brad Hainje. **Director, Public Relations:** Beth Marshall.

Publications Manager: Andy Pressley. **Public Relations Manager:** Meagan Swingle. **Senior Coordinator, Media Relations:** Adam Liberman. **Media Relations Coordinator:** Adrienne Midgley.

Stadium Operations

Director, Stadium Operations/Security: Larry Bowman.

Field Director: Ed Mangan. **Director, Game Entertainment:** Scott Cunningham. **PA Announcer:** Casey Motter. **Official Scorers:** Mike Stamus, Jack Wilkinson.

Ticketing

Telephone: (800) 326-4000. **Fax:** (404) 614-2480.

Director, Ticket Operations: Ed Newman.

Travel, Clubhouse

Director, Team Travel/Equipment Manager: Bill Acree.

Visiting Clubhouse Manager: John Holland.

GENERAL INFORMATION

Stadium (year opened): Turner Field (1997).
Home Dugout: First Base. **Playing Surface:** Grass.
Team Colors: Red, white and blue.
Player Representative: Unavailable.

Frank Wren

BASEBALL OPERATIONS

Telephone: (404) 522-7630. **Fax:** (404) 614-3308.

Executive Vice President, General Manager: Frank Wren.

Assistant GM: Bruce Manno. **Executive Assistant:** Melissa Stone.

Major League Staff

Manager: Bobby Cox.

Coaches: Bench—Chino Cadahia; Pitching—Roger McDowell; Batting—Terry Pendleton; First Base—Glenn Hubbard; Third Base—Brian Snitker; Bullpen—Eddie Perez.

Medical, Training

Head Team Physician: Dr. Norman Elliot.

Trainer: Jeff Porter. **Assistant Trainer:** Jim Lovell.

Strength/Conditioning Coach: Frank Fultz.

Bobby Cox

Player Development

Telephone: (404) 522-7630. **Fax:** (404) 614-1350.

Special Assistant to the GM, Player Development: Jose Martinez.

Director, Player Development: Kurt Kemp. **Director, Baseball Administration:** John Coppolella. **Director, International Scouting/Operations:** Johnny Almaraz. **Assistant Director, Player Development:** Matt Price.

Baseball Operations Administrative Assistant: Ronnie Richardson. **Administrative Assistant:** Chris Rice. **Administrative Assistant:** Raquel Davis.

Minor League Field Coordinator: Tommy Shields. **Pitching Coordinator:** Kent Willis. **Hitting Coordinator:** Leon Roberts.

Roving Instructors: Mike Alvarez (pitching), Joe Breeden (catching), Lynn Jones (outfield/base running). **Roving Strength/Conditioning Instructor:** Phil Falco. **Assistant Roving Strength/Conditioning Instructor:** Luckie Dacosta. **Physical Therapist:** Troy Jones

Minor League Equipment Manager: Justin Clift.

Farm System

Class	Farm Club	League	Manager	Coach	Pitching Coach
Triple-A	Richmond	International	Dave Brundage	Chris Chambliss	Guy Hansen
Double-A	Mississippi	Southern	Phillip Wellman	Franklin Stubbs	Derek Botelho
High A	Myrtle Beach	Carolina	Rocket Wheeler	Rick Albert	Bruce Dal Canton
Low A	Rome	South Atlantic	Randy Ingle	Bobby Moore	Jim Czajkowski
Rookie	Danville	Appalachian	Paul Runge	Carlos Mendez	Derrick Lewis
Rookie	Braves	Gulf Coast	Luis Ortiz	Sixto Lezcano	Gabriel Luckert
Rookie	Braves	Dominican	Jose Tartabull	A. Salazar/R. Rosario/T. Herrera	Juan Pablo Rojas

Scouting

Telephone: (404) 614-1359. **Fax:** (404) 614-1350.

Director, Scouting: Roy Clark. **Administrative Assistant, Scouting:** Dixie Keller.

Advance Scout: Bobby Wine (Norristown, PA).

Special Assignment Scouts: Dick Balderson (Englewood, CO), Tim Conroy (Monroeville, PA), Tony DeMacio (Virginia Beach, VA), Jim Fregosi (Tarpon Springs, FL), Duane Larson (Knoxville, TN), Chuck McMichael (Keller, TX).

Professional Scouts: Hep Cronin (Cincinnati, OH), Rod Gilbreath (Lilburn, GA), Lloyd Merritt (Myrtle Beach, SC), John Stewart (Granville, NY), Bob Wadsworth (Westminster, CA).

National Supervisors: Jerry Jordan (Kingsport, TN), Terry R. Tripp (Harrisburg, IL). **Regional Supervisors:** West—Tom Battista (Tustin, CA), Southeast—Paul Faulk (Laurinburg, NC), Northeast—Gene Kerns (Hayerstown, MD), Midwest—Steve Taylor (Shawnee, OK).

Area Supervisors: John Barron (Cameron, TX), Billy Best (Holly Spings, NC), Brian Bridges (Rome, GA), Stu Cann (Bradley, IL), Blaine Clemmens (San Francisco, CA), Ralph Garr (Richmond, TX), Paul Gibson (Center Moriches, NY), Gregg Kilby (Tampa, FL), Chris Knabenshue (Fort Collins, CO), Brian Hunter (Murrieta, CA), Tim Moore (Florence, KY), Bobby Myrick (Colonial Heights, VA), Don Reynolds (Portland, OR), Don Thomas (Geismar, LA), Terry C. Tripp (Raleigh, IL), Gerald Turner (Bedford, TX).

Part-Time Scouts: Hugh Buchanan (Snellville, GA), Joe Caputo (Royersford, PA), Dewayne Kitts (Moncks Corner, SC), George Martin (Altamonte Springs, FL), Abraham Martinez (Santa Isabel, PR), Mike Spiers (San Bernardino, CA), Stan Teem (Ringgold, GA).

International Supervisors: Roberto Aquino (Santo Domingo, Dominican Republic), Phil Dale (Victoria, Australia).

International Scouts: Miguel Alcantara (Dominican Republic), Neil Burke (Australia), Nehomar Caldera (Venezuela), Alberto Cambero (Venezuela), Junior Carrion (Dominican Republic), Jeremy Chou (Taiwan), Carlos Garcia (Colombia), Jose Guzman (Dominican Republic), Duk Lee (Korea), Hiroyuki Oya (Japan), Luis Ortiz (Panama), Johnathan Perez Tejeda (Dominican Republic), Rolando Petit (Venezuela), Maximo Rombley (Dominican Republic), Eduardo Rosario (Venezuela), Manuel Samaniego (Mexico), Miguel Theran (Colombia), Marvin Throneberry (Nicaragua), Carlos Torres (Venezuela).

Baltimore Orioles

Office Address: 333 W. Camden St, Baltimore, MD 21201.
Telephone: (888) 848-BIRD. **Fax:** (410) 547-6272.
E-mail Address: birdmail@orioles.com. **Website:** www.orioles.com.

Ownership

Operated By: The Baltimore Orioles Limited Partnership Inc.
Chairman/CEO: Peter Angelos.

BUSINESS OPERATIONS

Peter Angelos

Vice Chairman, Community Projects/Public Affairs: Thomas Clancy. **Executive Vice President:** John Angelos. **VP/Special Liaison to Chairman:** Lou Kousouris. **General Legal Counsel:** Russell Smouse. **Director, Human Resources:** Lisa Tolson. **Director, Information Systems:** James Kline.

Finance

Vice President/CFO: Robert Ames.

Public Relations/Communications

Telephone: (410) 547-6150. **Fax:** (410) 547-6272.

Director, Communications: Greg Bader. **Director, Media Relations:** Bill Stetka. **Director, Public Affairs:** Monica Pence. **Director, Promotions/Entertainment:** Kristen Schultz.

Ballpark Operations

Director, Ballpark Operations: Roger Hayden. **Manager, Event Operations:** Doug Rosenberger. **Head Groundskeeper:** Nicole Sherry.

PA Announcer: David McGowan. **Official Scorers:** Jim Henneman, Marc Jacobsen.

Ticketing

Telephone: (888) 848-BIRD. **Fax:** (410) 547-6270.

Director, Sales/Fan Services: Neil Aloise. **Assistant Director, Sales:** Mark Hromalik. **Ticket Manager:** Audrey Brown.

Travel/Clubhouse

Traveling Secretary: Phil Itzoe.

Equipment Manager (Home): Jim Tyler. **Equipment Manager (Road):** Fred Tyler. **Umpires, Field Attendant:** Ernie Tyler.

GENERAL INFORMATION

Stadium (year opened): Oriole Park at Camden Yards (1992).
Home Dugout: First Base. **Playing Surface:** Grass.
Team Colors: Orange, black and white.
Player Representative: Unavailable.

Andy MacPhail

BASEBALL OPERATIONS

Telephone: (410) 547-6121. **Fax:** (410) 547-6271.

President, Baseball Operations: Andy MacPhail. **Executive Vice President, Baseball Operations:** Mike Flanagan.

Director, Baseball Administration: Scott Proefrock.

Major League Staff

Manager: Dave Trembley.

Coaches: Bench—Dave Jauss; Pitching—Rick Kranitz; Batting—Terry Crowley; First Base—John Shelby; Third Base—Juan Samuel; Bullpen—Alan Dunn.

Medical, Training

Club Physician: Dr. William Goldiner. **Club Physician, Orthopedics:** Dr. Andrew Cosgarea.

Head Athletic Trainer: Richie Bancells. **Assistant Athletic Trainer:** Brian Ebel. **Strength/Conditioning Coach:** Jay Shiner.

Dave Trembley

Minor Leagues

Telephone: (410) 547-6120. **Fax:** (410) 547-6298.

Director, Minor League Operations: David Stockstill. **Assistant Director, Minor League Operations:** Tripp Norton.

Special Assignment Coach: Brian Graham. **Hitting Coordinator:** Julio Vinas. **Pitching Coordinator:** Dave Schmidt. **Medical Coordinator:** Dave Walker. **Strength/Conditioning Coach:** Joe Hogarty. **Facilities Coordinator:** Jaime Rodriguez. **Camp Coordinator:** Len Johnston.

Roving Instructors: Butch Davis (outfield/baserunning), Alex Arias (infield), Larry Jaster (rehab pitching), Denny Walling (hitting), Don Werner (catching).

Farm System

Class	Farm Club	League	Manager	Coach	Pitching Coach
Triple-A	Norfolk	International	Gary Allenson	Dallas Williams	Larry McCall
Double-A	Bowie	Eastern	Brad Komminsk	Moe Hill	Mike Griffin
High A	Frederick	Carolina	Tommy Thompson	J.J. Cannon	Blaine Beatty
Low A	Delmarva	South Atlantic	Ramon Sambo	Unavailable	Kennie Steenstra
Short-season	Aberdeen	New York-Penn	Gary Kendall	Cesar Devarez	Scott McGregor
Rookie	Bluefield	Appalachian	Orlando Gomez	Jim Saul	Troy Mattes
Rookie	Orioles	Gulf Coast	Jesus Alfaro	Giomar Guevara	Calvin Maduro
Rookie	Orioles	Dominican	Miguel Jabalera	Benny Adames	Robert Perez

Professional Scouting

Telephone: (410) 547-6121. **Fax:** (410) 547-6298.

Director, International Operations: John Stockstill.

Advance Scout: Jim Howard (Clifton Park, NY), Deacon Jones (Sugar Land, TX).

Special Assistant/Director, Professional Scouting: Lee MacPhail IV.

Professional Scouts: Dave Engle (San Diego, CA), Todd Frohwirth (Waukesha, WI), Dave Hollins (Orchad Park, NY), Bruce Kison (Bradenton, FL), Ted Lakas (Worcester, MA), Randy Milligan (Baltimore, MD), Gary Roenicke (Nevada City, CA), Fred Uhlman Sr. (Baltimore, MD).

Amateur Scouting

Telephone: (410) 547-6187. **Fax:** (410) 547-6298.

Director, Amateur Scouting: Joe Jordan.

Scouting Administrator: Marcy Zerhusen.

National Crosschecker: Alan Marr (Sarasota, FL). **Regional Crosscheckers:** East—Nick Presto (Palm Beach Garden, FL), Central—Deron Rombach (Mansfield, TX), West—David Blume (Elk Grove, CA).

Full-Time Scouts: Dean Albany (Baltimore, MD), Keith Connolly (Fair Haven, NJ), Dave Dangler (Camas, WA), Ralph Garr Jr. (Houston, TX), John Gillette (Gilbert, AZ), Troy Hoerner (Gurnee, IL), David Jennings (Daphne, AL), James Keller (Sacremento, CA), Gilbert Kubski (Huntington Beach, CA), John Martin (Tampa, FL), Rich Morales (Indianapolis, IN), Mark Ralston (San Diego, CA), Jim Richardson (Marlow, OK), Mike Tullier (River Ridge, NC), Dominic Viola (Cary, NC).

Dominican Republic Coordinator: Carlos Bernhardt (San Pedro de Macoris, Dominican Republic). **International Scout:** Salvador Ramirez (Dominican Republic).

Boston Red Sox

Office Address: Fenway Park, 4 Yawkey Way, Boston, MA 02215.
Telephone: (617) 226-6000. **Fax:** (617) 226-6416.
Website: www.redsox.com

Ownership

Principal Owner: John Henry. **Chairman:** Thomas Werner. **Vice Chairmen:** David Ginsberg, Phillip Morse.

President/CEO: Larry Lucchino. **Director:** George Mitchell.

BUSINESS OPERATIONS

Larry Lucchino

COO: Mike Dee. **Senior Vice President, Fenway Affairs:** Larry Cancro. **Senior VP, Corporate Relations/Executive Director, Red Sox Foundation:** Meg Vaillancourt. **VP:** Joe McDermott. **Executive Consultant:** Lou Gorman. **Senior Business Analyst:** Tim Zue. **Senior Advisor/Baseball Projects:** Jeremy Klapstein. **Senior Advisor/Strategic Planning:** Michael Porter.

Special Counsel: Bob Thomas. **Vice President, Club Counsel:** Elaine Steward. **VP, Legal Affairs:** Jennifer Flynn.

Finance/Human Resources

Vice President, CFO: Bob Furbush. **VP, Finance:** Steve Fitch. **Director, Finance:** Ryan Oremus. **Payroll Administrator:** Mauricio Rosas. **Accounting Manager:** Cathy Fahy. **Senior Tax Accountant:** Erin Walsh. **Senior Accountant:** Tom Williams. **VP, Human Resources/Office Administration:** Mary Sprong. **Director, Human Resources/Office Administration:** Michelle Julian. **Human Resources Manager:** Patricia Moseley. **Director, Information Technology:** Steve Conley. **Senior Systems Analyst:** Randy George.

Sales/Corporate Marketing/Broadcasting

Senior Vice President, Sales/Marketing: Sam Kennedy. **VP, Corporate Partnerships:** Joe Januszewski. **VP, Marketing:** Adam Grossman. **Director, Client Services:** Troup Parkinson. **Assistant Director, Client Services:** Marcell Saporita. **Manager, Sponsor Services:** Martha Gibbings. **Manager, Club Services:** Carole Alkins. **Manager, Suite Services:** Kim Cameron. **Manager, Community Marketing/Fan Clubs:** Mardi Fuller. **Manager, Advertising Production:** Megan Kaiser.

Vice President, Fenway Enterprises/Broadcasting: Chuck Steedman. **Assistant Director, Fenway Park Enterprises:** Marcita Thompson. **Manager, Fenway Enterprises/Broadcasting:** Colin Burch.

Public/Community Relations

Vice President, Media Relations: John Blake. **VP, Public Affairs:** Susan Goodenow. **Manager, Media Relations:** Pam Ganley. **Coordinator, Baseball Information:** Henry Mahegan. **VP, Publications/Archives:** Dick Bresciani. **Director, Publications:** Debbie Matson.

Business, Ballpark Operations/Development

Senior Vice President, Planning/Development: Janet Smith. **Manager, Planning/Development:** Paul Hanlon. **VP, Business Operations:** Jonathan Gilula. **Director, Security/Emergency Services:** Charles Cellucci. **Director, Facilities Management:** Tom Queenan. **Director, Event Operations:** Jeff Goldenberg. **Director, Grounds:** Dave Mellor. **Director Emeritus, Grounds:** Joe Mooney.

Vice President, Fan Services/Game Entertainment: Sarah McKenna. **Manager, Fan/Neighborhood Services:** Jahaan Blake. **Manager, Entertainment/Special Event Operations:** Dan Lyons. **Manager, Television Production:** John Carter. **Manager, Scoreboard/Video Operations:** Sarah Logan.

PA Announcer: Carl Beane. **Official Scorers:** Charles Scoggins, Mike Shalin, Bob Ellis, Mike Petraglia.

Ticketing Services/Operations

Telephone: 877-REDSOX9. **Fax:** (617) 226-6640.

Vice President/Ticketing: Ron Bumgarner. **Director, Ticketing:** Richard Beaton. **Assistant Director, Ticketing:** Joe Matthews. **Senior Manager, Premium Sales:** Corey Bowdre. **Senior Manager, Ticket Services:** Naomi Calder.

Travel/Clubhouse

Traveling Secretary: Jack McCormick. **Manager, Travel Administration:** Jean MacDougall.

Equipment Manager/Clubhouse Operations: Joe Cochran. **Assistant Equipment Manager:** Edward Jackson. **Visiting Clubhouse Manager:** Tom McLaughlin. **Video Coordinator:** Billy Broadbent.

GENERAL INFORMATION

Stadium (year opened): Fenway Park (1912).
Home Dugout: First Base. **Playing Surface:** Grass.
Team Colors: Navy blue, red and white.
Player Representative: Kevin Youkilis.

Theo Epstein

BASEBALL OPERATIONS

Telephone: (617) 226-6000. **Fax:** (617) 226-6695.

Executive Vice President, General Manager: Theo Epstein. **Assistant GM:** Jed Hoyer.

Vice President, Player Personnel: Ben Cherington. **VP, International Scouting:** Craig Shipley. **Assistant to GM:** Allard Baird. **Special Assistant to GM:** David Howard. **Senior Baseball Operations Advisor:** Bill James. **Director, Baseball Operations:** Brian O'Halloran. **Assistant Director, Baseball Operations:** Zack Scott. **Baseball Operations Executive Assistant:** Erin Cox.

Major League Staff

Manager: Terry Francona.

Coaches: Bench—Brad Mills; Pitching—John Farrell; Batting—Dave Magadan; First Base—Luis Alicea; Third Base—DeMarlo Hale; Bullpen—Gary Tuck.

Terry Francona

Medical/Training

Medical Director: Dr. Thomas Gill. **Team Internist:** Dr. Larry Ronan. **Medical Operations Coordinator:** Jim Rowe.

Head Trainer: Paul Lessard. **Rehab Coordinator/Assistant Trainer:** Mike Reinold. **Assistant Trainer:** Masai Takahashi. **Strength/Conditioning Coach:** Dave Page. **Sports Psychology Coach:** Don Kalkstein. **Rehabilitation Coordinator:** Scott Waugh. **Massage Therapist:** Russell Nua.

Player Development

Telephone: (617) 226-6000. **Fax:** (617) 226-6695.

Director, Player Development: Mike Hazen. **Director, Minor League Operations:** Raquel Ferreira. **Assistant Director, Player Development:** Ethan Faggett. **Assistant, Player Development:** Jared Banner.

Player Development Consultants: Dick Berardino, Tony Cloninger, Dwight Evans, Tommy Harper, Felix Maldonado, Frank Malzone, Carl Yastrzemski.

Manager, Florida Business Operations: Todd Stephenson. **Latin Education Coordinator:** Duncan Webb.

Field Coordinator: Rob Leary. **Roving Instructors:** Bruce Crabbe (infield), Al Nipper (pitching evaluator), Victor Rodriguez (hitting), Ralph Treuel (pitching).

Associate Medical Director/Player Development: Dr. Brian Busconi. **Minor League Athletic Training Coordinator:** Jim Young. **Sport Psychology Coach:** Bob Tewksbury. **Strength/Conditioning Coordinator:** Pat Sandora.

Farm System

Class	Farm Club	League	Manager	Coach(es)	Pitching Coach
Triple-A	Pawtucket	International	Ron Johnson	Russ Morman	Rich Sauveur
Double-A	Portland	Eastern	Arnie Beyeler	Dave Joppie	Mike Cather
High A	Lancaster	California	Chad Epperson	Carlos Febles	TBA
Low A	Greenville	South Atlantic	Kevin Boles	Billy McMillion	Bob Kipper
Short-season	Lowell	New York-Penn	Gary DiSarcina	Luis Lopez	Walter Miranda
Rookie	Red Sox	Gulf Coast	Dave Tomlin	U.L. Washington	Goose Gregson
Rookie	Red Sox	Dominican	Jose Zapata	C. Hernandez/N. Paulino	J.Gonzalez/C. Perez

Scouting

Director, Amateur Scouting: Jason McLeod. **Assistant Scouting Director:** Amiel Sawdaye. **Coordinator, Professional Scouting:** Jared Porter. **Advance Scouting Coordinator:** Ben Crockett.

Advance Scouts: Todd Claus (Wellington, FL), Dana Levangie (East Bridgewater, MA).

Special Assignment Scout: Marc DelPiano (Auburn, NY).

Major League Scouts: Galen Carr (Burlington, VT), Kyle Evans (Boston, MA), Gus Quattlebaum (Long Beach, CA).

Professional Scouts: Jaymie Bane (Riverview, FL), Keith Champion (Ballwin, MO), Dave Klipstein (Roanoke, TX), Bill Latham (Trussville, AL), Curtis Leskanic (Orlando, FL), Jesse Levis (Fort Washington, PA), Joe McDonald (Lakeland, FL), John Sanders (Woodstock, GA), Matt Sczesny (Deer Park, NY), Jerry Stephenson (Fullerton, CA).

National Crosschecker: David Finley (San Diego, CA). **Regional Crosscheckers:** East—Mike Rikard (Durham, NC); Midwest—Danny Haas (Boston, MA); Southeast—Mark Wasinger (El Paso, TX); West—Fred Petersen (Glendale, CA).

Area Scouts: John Booher (Austin, TX), Quincy Boyd (Harrisburg, NC), Chris Calciano (Ocean View, DE), Matt Dorey (Vancouver, WA), Rob English (Duluth, GA), Raymond Fagnant (East Granby, CT), Duane Gustavson (Westerville, OH), Laz Gutierrez (Miramar, FL), Blair Henry (Roseville, CA), Ernie Jacobs (Wichita, KS), Wally Komatsubara (Aiea, HI), Dan Madsen (Murrieta, CA), Matt Mahoney (Scottsdale, AZ), Chris Mears (Lake Villa, IL) Edgar Perez (Vega Baja, PR), Jim Robinson (Arlington, TX), Anthony Turco (Tampa, FL), Danny Watkins (Tuscaloosa, AL), Jim Woodward (Claremont, CA).

Coordinator, Latin American Scouting: John DiPuglia. **Coordinator, Pacific Rim Scouting:** John Deeble. **Coordinator, European Scouting:** Mike Lord

Director, Dominican Operations: Jesus Alou. **Coordinator, Baseball, Scouting Operations:** Manny Nanita.

Chicago Cubs

Office Address: Wrigley Field, 1060 W. Addison St, Chicago, IL 60613.
Telephone: (773) 404-2827. **Fax:** (773) 404-4129.
E-mail Address: cubs@cubs.com
Website: www.cubs.com.

Ownership

Owner: Tribune Co. **Chairman:** Crane Kenney.

BUSINESS OPERATIONS

Mark McGuire

Phone: (773) 404-2827. **Fax:** (773) 404-4111.

Executive Vice President, Business Operations: Mark McGuire. **Executive Coordinator, Business Operations,:** Sarah Poontong.

Accounting

Co-Directors, Finance: Jodi Reischl, Terri Fleischhacker.

Accounting Manager: Mike Van Poucke. **Finance Manager:** Jaime Norton. **Payroll Administrator:** Theresa Bacholzky. **Senior Accountants:** Marian Greene, Aimee Sison.

Human Resources

Senior Director, Human Resources: Jenifer Surma. **Employment Manager:** Marisol Widmayer. **Human Resources Stadium Operations Coordinator:** Danielle Alexa.

Event Operations/Security

Manager, Event Operations/Security: Mike Hill. **Coordinator, Event Operations/Security:** Julius Farrell. **Coordinator, Exterior Operations:** Mary Kusmirek.

Facility Management/Information Technology

Senior Director, Facility Management/Information Technology: Carl Rice. **Information Systems Analyst:** Sean True. **Information Systems Support Specialist:** Lucas Luecke. **Coordinator, Office Services:** Randy Skocz. **Head Groundskeeper:** Roger Baird. **Facility Supervisor:** Bill Scott.

Legal/Community Affairs

Senior Vice President, Community Affairs/General Counsel: Michael Lufrano. **Managers, Community Affairs:** Mary Dosek, Jill Lawlor. **Senior Coordinator, Community Affairs/Neighborhood Relations:** Jennifer Dedes Nowak.

Marketing/Broadcasting

Director, Sales and Promotions: Matthew Wszolek. **Manager, Mezzanine Suites:** Louis Artiaga. **Manager, Special Events/Player Relations/Entertainment:** Joe Rios. **Manager, Sponsorship Sales:** David Knickerbocker. **Senior Account Executive:** Andrea Burke. **Coordinator, Mezzanine Suites:** Jamie Morales. **Coordinator, Special Events/Entertainment:** Katie Marta. **Coordinator, Sponsorship Sales:** Rina Martinez. **Administrative Coordinator, Marketing:** Veronica Lopez.

Media Relations/Publications

Telephone: (773) 404-4191. **Fax:** (773) 404-4129.

Director, Media Relations: Peter Chase. **Assistant Director, Media Relations:** Jason Carr. **Coordinator, Media Services:** Katelyn Thrall. **Assistant, Media Relations:** Dani Holmes. **Director, Publications:** Lena McDonagh. **Manager, Publications:** Jim McArdle. **Publications Editorial Specialist:** Michael Huang. **Senior Graphic Design Specialist:** Juan Alberto Castillo. **Graphic Design Specialist:** Joaquin Castillo. **Photographer:** Stephen Green.

Ticket Operations

Telephone: (773) 404-2827. **Fax:** (773) 404-4014.

Director, Ticket Operations: Frank Maloney.

Assistant Director, Ticket Sales: Brian Garza. **Assistant Director, Ticket Services:** Joe Kirchen. **Vault Room Supervisor:** Cherie Blake. **Coordinator, Ticket Orders:** Jan Jotzat. **Coordinator, Ticket Sales:** Karry Kerness. **Senior Ticket Sales Representative:** Kevin Enerson.

Game Day Operations

Public Address Announcers: Paul Friedman, Wayne Messmer, Michael Terson. **Organist:** Gary Pressy. **Umpires Room Attendant:** Tom Farinella. **Nurse:** Phyllis Donnan. **In-Game Presentation Specialist:** Andie Giafaglione. **Home Clubhouse Manager:** Tom Hellmann. **Visiting Clubhouse Manager:** Michael Burkhart. **Home Clubhouse Assistant:** Gary Stark.

GENERAL INFORMATION

Stadium (year opened): Wrigley Field (1914).
Home Dugout: Third Base. **Playing Surface:** Grass.
Team Colors: Royal blue, red and white.
Player Representative: Unavailable.

Jim Hendry

BASEBALL OPERATIONS

Telephone: (773) 404-2827. **Fax:** (773) 404-4111.

Vice President/General Manager: Jim Hendry.

Assistant GM: Randy Bush. **Director, Baseball Administration:** Scott Nelson. **Senior Advisor:** Billy Williams. **Special Assistants to GM:** Bill Harford, Gary Hughes, Ken Kravec, Ed Lynch, Mike Valarezo, Paul Weaver.

Manager, Baseball Information: Chuck Wasserstrom. **Traveling Secretary:** Jimmy Bank. **Major League Video Coordinator:** Naoto Masamoto. **Executive Assistant to GM:** Hayley DeWitte.

Major League Staff

Manager: Lou Piniella

Coaches: Pitching—Larry Rothschild; Hitting—Gerald Perry; Bench—Alan Trammell; Third Base—Mike Quade; First Base—Mike Sinatro; Bullpen—Lester Strode; Special Assistant—Ivan DeJesus.

Lou Piniella

Medical/Training

Team Physician: Dr. Stephen Adams. **Team Orthopedist:** Dr. Stephen Gryzlo. **Orthopedic Consultant:** Dr. Michael Schafer.

Director, Athletic Training: Mark O'Neal. **Assistant Athletic Trainer:** Ed Halbur. **Strength and Conditioning Coordinator:** Tim Buss.

Player Development

Vice President, Player Personnel: Oneri Fleita.

Field Coordinator: Dave Bialas. **Infield/Bunting Coordinator:** Bobby Dickerson. **Hitting Coordinator:** Dave Keller. **Outfield/Baserunning Coordinator:** Bobby Dernier. **Catching Coordinator:** Casey Kopitzke.

Latin American Field Coordinator: Carmelo Martinez. **Minor League Training Coordinator:** Justin Sharpe. **Assistant, Strength and Conditioning:** Joe Warning. **Assistant Minor League Training Coordinator:** Chuck Baughman. **Manager, Player Development Administration:** Patti Kargakis. **Equipment Manager:** Dana Noeltner.

Farm System

Class	Farm Club	League	Manager	Coach	Pitching Coach
Triple-A	Iowa	Pacific Coast	Pat Listach	Von Joshua	Mike Mason
Double-A	Tennessee	Southern	Buddy Bailey	Barbaro Garbey	Dennis Lewallyn
High Class A	Daytona	Florida State	Jody Davis	Richie Zisk	David Rosario
Low Class A	Peoria	Midwest	Ryne Sandberg	Carmelo Martinez	Rich Bombard
Short-season	Bosie	Northwest	Tom Beyers	Ricardo Medina	Tom Pratt
Rookie	Cubs	Arizona	Franklin Font	Unavailable	Rick Tronerud
Rookie	Cubs I	Dominican	Juan Cabreja	Ramon Caraballo	Leo Hernandez
Rookie	Cubs II	Dominican	Franklin Blanco	Lucerio Vals	Anderson Tavares

Scouting

Telephone: (773) 404-2827. **Fax:** (773) 404-4147.

Director, Amateur/Professional Scouting: Tim Wilken (Dunedin, FL).

Special Assistant to Scouting Director: Steve Hinton (Mather, CA). **Player Development/Scouting Assistant:** Jake Ciarrachi. **Administrative Assistant:** Patricia Honzik.

Major League Scout: Brad Kelley (Phoenix, AZ). **Professional Scouts:** Tom Bourque (Cambridge, MA), Jim Crawford (Madison, MS), Bill Harford (Chicago, IL), Joe Housey (Hollywood, FL), Demie Mainieri (Ft. **Lauderdale, FL), Mark Servais (LaCrosse, WI), Charlie Silvera (Millbrae, CA).**

Special Assignment Scouts: Gene Handley (Newport Beach, CA), Bob Lofrano (Woodland Hills, CA), Glen Van Proyan (Lisle, IL).

National Crosschecker: Sam Hughes (Atlanta, GA). **Crosscheckers:** East—Charles Aliano (Land O'Lakes, FL), Midwest—Steve Riha (Houston, TX), West—Mark Adair (Phoenix, AZ).

Area Scouts: John Bartsch (Rocklin, CA), Billy Blitzer (Brooklyn, NY), Trey Forkerway (Houston, TX), Steve Fuller (Seal Beach, CA), Al Geddes (Canby, OR), Antonio Grissom (Red Oak, GA), Denny Henderson (Orange, CA), Steve McFarland (Scottsdale, AZ), Lukas McKnight (Westfield, NY), Brandon Mozley (Nixa, MO), Rolando Pino (Pembroke Pines, FL), Keith Stohr (Viera, FL), Billy Swoope (Norfolk, VA), Michael Valarezo (Pensacola, FL), Stan Zielinski (Winfeild, IL).

International Scouts: Hector Ortega (Venezuela), Jose Serra (Dominican Republic), Steve Wilson (Asia).

Chicago White Sox

Office Address: 333 W. 35th St., Chicago, IL 60616.
Telephone: (312) 674-1000. **Fax:** (312) 674-5116.
Website: www.whitesox.com.

Ownership

Chairman: Jerry Reinsdorf. **Vice Chairman:** Eddie Einhorn.

Board of Directors: Robert Judelson, Judd Malkin, Robert Mazer, Allan Muchin, Jay Pinsky, Larry Pogofsky, Lee Stern, Sanford Takiff, Burton Ury, Charles Walsh.

Special Assistant to Chairman: Dennis Gilbert. **Assistant to Chairman:** Anita Fasano.

BUSINESS OPERATIONS

Jerry Reinsdorf

Executive Vice President: Howard Pizer.

Senior Director, Information Services: Don Brown. **Senior Director, Human Resources:** Moira Foy. **Administrators, Human Resources:** Leslie Gaggiano, J.J. Krane.

Finance

Senior Vice President, Administration/Finance: Tim Buzard. **Senior Director, Finance:** Bill Waters. **Accounting Manager:** Chris Taylor.

Marketing/Sales

Vice President, Marketing: Brooks Boyer. **Senior Director, Business Development/ Broadcasting:** Bob Grim. **Manager, Scoreboard Operations/Production:** Jeff Szynal. **Director, Game Operations:** Nichole Manning. **Manager, Game Operations:** Amy Sheridan. **Coordinator, Game Operations:** Dan Mielke.

Senior Director, Corporate Partnerships: Jim Muno. **Manager, Corporate Partnerships:** Ryan Gribble, Gail Tucker, Brad Dreher. **Manager, Client Services:** Stephanie Johnson. **Coordinator, Corporate Partnership Services:** Jorie Sax.

Director, Ticket Sales: Tom Sheridan. **Manager, Premium Seating Service:** Deb Theobald. **Senior Director, Community Relations:** Christine O'Reilly. **Director, Mass Communications:** Maggie Luellen. **Manager, Design Services:** Gareth Breunlin. **Senior Coordinator, Design Services:** Matt Peterson. **Manager, Community Relations:** Danielle Disch. **Coordinators, Community Relations:** Stacy Tsihlopoulos, Dane Walkington.

Public Relations

Telephone: (312) 674-5300. **Fax:** (312) 674-5116.

Vice President, Communications: Scott Reifert.

Director, Media Relations: Bob Beghtol. **Director, Public Relations:** Lou Hernandez. **Manager, Media Relations:** Pat O'Connell. **Coordinator, Public Relations:** Marty Maloney. **Coordinator, Media Services:** Vivian Jones.

Stadium Operations

Senior Vice President, Stadium Operations: Terry Savarise. **Senior Director, Park Operations:** David Schaffer. **Senior Director, Guest Services/Diamond Suite Operations:** Julie Taylor. **Head Groundskeeper:** Roger Bossard. **PA Announcer:** Gene Honda. **Official Scorer:** Bob Rosenberg.

Ticketing

Telephone: (312) 674-1000. **Fax:** (312) 674-5102.

Director, Ticket Operations: Mike Mazza. **Manager, Ticket Accounting Administration:** Ken Wisz.

Travel/Clubhouse

Director, Team Travel: Ed Cassin.

Manager, White Sox Clubhouse: Vince Fresso. **Manager, Visiting Clubhouse:** Gabe Morell. **Manager, Umpires' Clubhouse:** Joe McNamara Jr.

GENERAL INFORMATION

Stadium (year opened): U.S. Cellular Field (1991).
Home Dugout: Third Base. **Playing Surface:** Grass.
Team Colors: Black, white and silver.
Player Representative: Unavailable.

Ken Williams

BASEBALL OPERATIONS

Senior Vice President, General Manager: Ken Williams.

VP/Assistant GM: Rick Hahn. **Senior Director, Player Personnel:** David Wilder. **Special Assistants to GM:** Bill Scherrer, Dave Yokam. **Executive Assistant to GM:** Nancy Nesnidal. **Director, Baseball Operations:** Dan Fabian. **Assistant Director, Scouting/Baseball Operations:** Andrew Pinter. **Assistant Director, Baseball Operations:** J.J. Lally.

Major League Staff

Manager: Ozzie Guillen.

Coaches: Bench—Joey Cora; Pitching—Don Cooper; Batting—Greg Walker; First Base—Harold Baines; Third Base—Jeff Cox; Bullpen—Juan Nieves.

Ozzie Guillen

Medical, Training

Senior Team Physician: Dr. Charles Bush-Joseph.

Head Athletic Trainer: Herm Schneider. **Assistant Athletic Trainer:** Brian Ball. **Director, Conditioning:** Allen Thomas.

Player Development

Telephone: (312) 674-1000. **Fax:** (312) 674-5105.

Director, Minor League Instruction: Buddy Bell.

Director, Player Development: Alan Regier.

Director, Minor League Administration: Grace Guerrero Zwit. **Coordinator Minor League Administration:** Kathy Potoski. **Manager, Clubhouse/Equipment:** Dan Flood.

Roving Instructors: Daryl Boston (outfield), Dale Torborg (conditioning coordinator), Kirk Champion (pitching), Jeff Manto (hitting), Art Kusyner (bullpen), John Orton (catching), Manny Trillo (infield). **Coordinator, Minor League Trainers/Rehabilitation:** Scott Takao.

Farm System

Class	Farm Club	League	Manager	Coach	Pitching Coach
Triple-A	Charlotte	International	Marc Bombard	Joe McEwing	Richard Dotson
Double-A	Birmingham	Southern	Carlos Subero	Wes Clements	J.R. Perdew
High A	Winston-Salem	Carolina	Tim Blackwell	Robert Sasser	Brian Drahman
Low A	Kannapolis	South Atlantic	Chris Jones	Andy Tomberlin	Larry Owens
Rookie	Bristol Sox	Appalachian	Bobby Thigpen	Jerry Hairston	Jose Bautista
Rookie	Great Falls	Pioneer	Chris Cron	Ernie Young	Curt Hasler
Rookie	White Sox	Dominican I	Fermin Urbi	Unavailable	Gustavo Martinez
Rookie	White Sox	Dominican II	Nelson Abreu	Unavailable	Jose Betancourt

Scouting

Telephone: (312) 674-1000. **Fax:** (312) 674-5105.

Professional Scouts: Joe Butler (Long Beach, CA), Gary Pellant (Chandler, AZ), Paul Provas (Arlington, TX), Daraka Shaheed (Vallejo, CA), Bill Young (Long Beach, CA), John Tumminia (Newburgh, NY).

Director, Amateur Scouting: Doug Laumann (Florence, KY).

National Crosscheckers: Nathan Durst (Sycamore, IL) Ed Pebley (Brigham City, UT). **Regional Crosscheckers:** Nick Hostetler (East Coast) (Union, KY), Derek Valenzuela (West Coast) (Temecula, CA).

Advisor to Baseball Department: Larry Monroe (Schaumburg, IL).

Area Scouts: Mike Baker (Santa Ana, CA), Alex Cosmidis (Raleigh, NC), Ryan Dorsey (Frederick, MD), Dan Durst (Rockford, IL), Trent Eckstaine (Lemars, IA), Chuck Fox (Summit, NJ), Warren Hughes (Mobile, AL), George Kachigian (Coronado, CA), John Kazanas (Phoenix, AZ), Jeff McKay (Springfield, OR), Jose Ortega (Fort Lauderdale, FL), Clay Overcash (Oologan, OK), Mike Shirley (Anderson, IN), Joe Siers (Wesley Chapel, FL), Kevin Burrell (Sharpsburg, GA), Keith Staab (College Station, TX), Adam Virchis (Modesto, CA), Gary Woods (Solvang, CA).

Part-Time Scouts: Tommy Butler (East Rancho Dominguez, CA), Javier Centeno (Guaynabo, PR), John Doldoorian (Whitinsville, MA), Cade Griffis (Addison, TX), Phil Gulley (Morehead, KY), Jack Jolly (Murfreeboro, TN), Dario Lodigiani (Napa, CA), Jason Morvant (Abbeville, LA), Dave Mumper (Highland Ranch, CO), Glenn Murdock (Livonia, MI), Howard Nakagama (Salt Lake City, UT), Al Otto (Schaumburg, IL), Mike Paris (Boone, IA), Michael Wilder (Oakland, CA).

International Scouts: Ruben Amaro (Weston, FL), Miguel Ibarra (Panama), Marino DeLeon (Dominican Republic), Amador Arias (Venezuela), Jhonny Pantoja (Colombia), Ehire Adrianza (Venezuela), Domingo Toribio (Dominican Republic), Victor Mateo (Dominican Republic).

Cincinnati Reds

Office Address: 100 Main St., Cincinnati, OH 45202.
Telephone: (513) 765-7000. **Fax:** (513) 765-7342.
Website: www.reds.com.

Ownership

Operated by: The Cincinnati Reds LLC.

President/CEO: Robert Castellini. **Executive Assistant to President/CEO:** Tina Tuttle.

Chairman: Joseph Williams Jr. **Vice Chairman/Treasurer:** Thomas Williams. **COO:** Phillip Castellini. **Executive Assistant to COO:** Jodi Czanik. **Secretary:** Christopher Fister.

Robert Castellini

BUSINESS OPERATIONS

Business/Broadcasting Administrator: Ginny Kamp.

Vice President, Business Development: Brad Blettner.

Finance/Administration

Vice President, Finance/CFO: Doug Healy. **VP/General Counsel:** James Marx. **Controller:** Bentley Viator. **Accounting Manager:** Jill Niemeyer. **Director, Human Resources:** Barbara Boles. **Human Resources Generalist:** John Hale. **Employee Benefits Coordinator:** Sara Bowling. **Director, Information Technology:** Brian Keys.

Sales

Senior Director, Ticket Sales: John Davis. **Director, Group Sales:** David Ziegler. **Group Sales Manager:** Ryan Niemeyer. **Suite/Premium Services Manager:** Emily Tincher. **Premium Sales Manager:** Ryan Rizzo. **Premium Sales Coordinator:** Ashley Vella. **Season Sales Manager:** Chris Herrell. **Director, Season/Group Operations:** Pat McCaffrey. **Season Ticket Manager:** Bev Bonavita. **Group Ticket Manager:** Brad Callahan. **Director, Special Events:** Jennifer Green. **Event Services Coordinator:** Kili Hood. **Director, Ticket Client Services:** Craig Warman.

Ticket Operations

Phone: (513) 765-7400.

Director, Ticket Operations: John O'Brien. **Assistant Director, Ticket Operations:** Ken Ayer. **Ticket Operations Administration Manager:** Hallie Kinney.

Communications/Marketing

Vice President, Communications/Marketing: Karen Forgus. **Director, Creative Services/Advertising:** Ralph Mitchell. **Managing Editor:** Jarrod Rollins. **Advertising Coordinator:** Matt Abt. **Senior Graphic Designer:** Lucrecer Braxton. **Senior Director, Entertainment/Events:** Jennifer Berger. **Director, Entertainment/Media Production:** Russ Jenisch. **Media Production Manager:** David Storm. **Public Relations Manager:** Michael Anderson. **Promotional Events/Gameday Operations Manager:** Zach Bonkowski.

Community Relations

Community Fund Executive Director: Charley Frank. **Office Manager:** Teena Schweier. **Outreach/Sponsorship Manager:** Matt Crawford. **Director, Community Relations:** Lorrie Platt. **Program Coordinator:** Casandra Ersel. **Executive Director, Reds Hall of Fame:** Rick Walls. **Operations Manager/Chief Curator:** Chris Eckes. **Education/Programming Manager:** Ken Freeman.

Corporate Sales

Vice President, Corporate Sales: Bill Reinberger. **Assistant, Corporate Sales:** Denise Lockwood. **Corporate Sales Managers:** Christopher Bausano, Dave Collins, Dan Lewis, Mark Scherer. **Broadcast/Affiliates Manager:** Joe Zerhusen. **Corporate Services Managers:** Erin Fischer, Lori Watt. **Trafficking Coordinator:** Brandon Bowman.

Ballpark Operations

Vice President, Ballpark Operations: Declan Mullin.

Director, Ballpark Operations: Mike Maddox. **Ballpark Operations Manager:** Colleen Rodenberg. **Ballpark Operations Superintendent:** Bob Harrison. **Facility/Construction Services Manager:** Kim Hoffa. **Guest Relations Manager:** Jan Koshover. **Manager, Technology Business Center:** Chris Campbell. **Chief Engineer:** Roger Smith. **Assistant Chief Engineer:** Eric Dearing. **Ballpark Operations Administrative Assistant:** Sean Brown.

Head Groundskeeper: Doug Gallant. **Assistant Groundskeeper:** Jon Phelps. **Grounds Supervisor:** Derrick Grubbs. **Director, Safety/Security:** Kerry Rowland. **Switchboard Manager:** Lauren Gaghan. **Switchboard Operator:** Jenny Niehaus.

GENERAL INFORMATION

Stadium (year opened): Great American Ball Park (2003).
Home Dugout: First Base. **Playing Surface:** Grass.
Team Colors: Red, white and black.
Player Representative: Aaron Harang.

Wayne Krivsky

BASEBALL OPERATIONS

Executive Vice President/General Manager: Wayne Krivsky. **Executive Assistant to EVP/GM:** Debbie Bent.

Special Advisor to President/CEO: Walt Jocketty. **Vice President/Assistant General Manager:** Bob Miller. **Assistant GM/Senior Director, Pro Scouting:** Scott Nethery. **Director, Baseball Business Operations:** Dick Williams. **Special Consultant to GM:** Ken Griffey Sr.

Coordinator, Major League Scouting/Video Operations: Nick Krall. **Baseball Operations Assistant:** Jeff Graupe. **Baseball Operations Analyst:** Sam Grossman.

Major League Staff

Manager: Dusty Baker.

Coaches: Bench—Chris Speier; Pitching—Dick Pole; Batting—Brook Jacoby; First Base—Billy Hatcher; Third Base—Mark Berry; Bullpen—Juan Lopez.

Dusty Baker

Player Development

Telephone: (513) 765-7700. **Fax:** (513) 765-7799.

Director, Player Development: Terry Reynolds.

Assistant Director, Player Development: Paul Pierson. **Special Assistant to GM, Player Development:** Ken Parker. **Administration Coordinator, Player Development:** Lois Hudson. **GM, Florida Operations:** Dan Wolfert. **Assistant GM:** Mike Rebok. **Minor League Equipment Manager:** Jonathan Snyder.

Field Coordinator: Freddie Benavides. **Special Assistant, Player Development:** Julio Garcia. **Coordinators:** Ronnie Ortegon (hitting), Bill Doran (infield/baserunning), Mack Jenkins (pitching), Pat Kelly (catching).

Director, Dominican Operations: Mario Soto. **Dominican Academy Director:** Juan Peralta.

Medical Coordinator: Richard Stark. **Medical Administrator:** Mark Schoen. **Strength/Conditioning Coordinator:** Sean Marohn. **Rehab/Physical Therapist:** Andrew McNally.

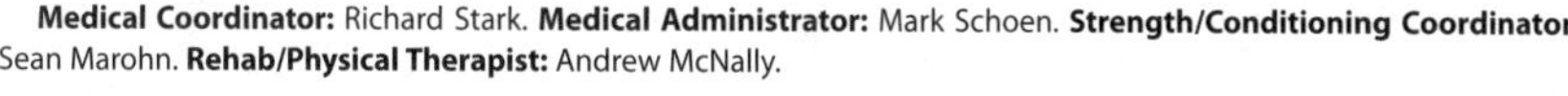

Farm System

Class	Farm Club	League	Manager	Coach	Pitching Coach
Triple-A	Louisville	International	Rick Sweet	Adrian Garrett	Ted Power
Double-A	Chattanooga	Southern	Mike Goff	Jamie Dismuke	Chris Bosio
High Class A	Sarasota	Florida State	Joe Ayrault	Ryan Jackson	Tom Brown
Low Class A	Dayton	Midwest	Donnie Scott	Darren Bragg	Doug Bair
Rookie	Billings	Pioneer	Julio Garcia	Tony Jaramillo	Tom Browning
Rookie	Reds	Gulf Coast	Pat Kelly	Jorge Orta	Rigo Beltran
Rookie	Reds	Dominican	Joel Noboa	Manuel Solano	Unavailable

Scouting

Telephone: (513) 765-7000. **Fax:** (513) 765-7799.

Senior Director, Scouting: Chris Buckley.

Assistant GM/Senior Director, Pro Scouting: Scott Nethery. **Director, Pro Scouting:** J. Harrison. **Senior Special Assistant. to GM/Pro Scout:** Gene Bennett. **Director, Scouting Administration:** Wilma Mann.

Assistant Director, Amateur Scouting: Paul Pierson.

Major League Scout: Butch Baccala.

Professional Scouts: Jeff Morris, John Morris, Ross Sapp, Tom Shafer, Jeff Taylor, Jim Thrift, Lee Tunnell.

Scouting Supervisors: Jason Baker (Rome, NY), Josh Bonifay (Dallas, TX), Jeff Brookens (Chambersburg, PA), Clark Crist (Phoenix, AZ), Rex de la Nuez (Burbank, CA), Jerry Flowers (Baton Rouge, LA), Dan Huston (Bellevue, WA), Mike Keenan (Manhattan, KS), Steve Kring (Charlotte, NC), Mike Misuraca (Pomona, CA), Jeff Morris (Tucson, AZ), Rick Sellers (Remus, MI), Lee Seras (Utica, NY), Tom Shafer (St. Louis, MO), Perry Smith (Charlotte, NC), Tom Wheeler (Martinez, CA), Brian Wilson (Albany, TX), Greg Zunino (Cape Coral, FL).

Part-Time Scouts: George Blackburn (Evans, GA), Mike Brookhart (Greenwood Village, CO), Edwin Daub (Binghamton, NY), Ben Galante (Houston, TX), Jim Grief (Paducha, KY), Bill Killian (Stanwood, MI), Ed Mathes (Wantagh, NY), Denny Nagel (Cincinnati, OH), Marlon Styles (Cincinnati, OH), Mike Wallace (Escondido, CA), John Walsh (Windsor, CT), Roger Weberg (Bemidji, MN), Randy Yamashiro (Pearl City, HI).

Director, Latin America Scouting: Tony Arias. **Director, International Operations:** Jim Stoeckel.

International Scouts: Wellington Alvarado (Dominican Republic), Bill Byckowski (Canada), Oswaldo Alvarez (Mexico), Luis Baez (Dominican Republic) Geronimo Blanco (Colombia), Luis Davalillo (Venezuela), Jose Fuentes (Venezuela), John Gilmore (Pacific Rim), Andres Hiraldo (Dominican Republic), Roberto Morillo (Venezuela), Victor Oramas (Venezuela), Miguel Pol (Domincian Republic), Anibal Reluz (Panama), Maximo Rombley (Dominican Republic), Evereth Velasquez (Venezuela).

Cleveland Indians

Office Address: Progressive Field, 2401 Ontario St, Cleveland, OH 44115.
Telephone: (216) 420-4200. **Fax:** (216) 420-4396.
Website: www.indians.com.

Ownership

Owner, CEO: Lawrence Dolan. **President:** Paul Dolan.

BUSINESS OPERATIONS

Executive Vice President, Business: Dennis Lehman. **Executive Administrative Assistant, Business:** Dru Kosik.

Larry Dolan

Corporate Marketing

Director, Corporate Sales: Matt Brown. **Manager, New Business Development:** Sheff Webb. **Corporate Marketing Account Executives:** Rob Byrne, Bryan Hoffart, Jennifer Horn. **Administrative Assistant, Sales:** Kim Scott.

Finance/Administration

Senior Vice President, Finance/CFO: Ken Stefanov. **Controller:** Sarah Taylor. **Director, Planning, Analysis/Reporting:** Rich Dorffer. **Manager, Accounting:** Karen Menzing. **Manager, Payroll Accounting:** Mary Forkapa. **Retail/Food Service Controller:** Marj Ruhl. **Manager, Spring Training:** Ryan Lantz.

Senior Director, Human Resources/Benefits: Sara Lehrke. **Director, Training/Recruitment:** Susie Downey. **Coordinator, Benefits:** Crystal Basile. **Senior Director, Information Systems:** Dave Powell. **Manager, Systems Development:** Matt Tagliaferri. **Manager, End User Support:** Dan Mendlik. **Network Manager:** Whitney Kuszmaul.

Marketing

Senior Vice President, Sales/Marketing: Vic Gregovits. **Director, Marketing:** Sanaa Julien. **Manager, Broadcasting:** Alex Slemc. **Manager, Promotions:** Jason Kidik. **Manager, Productions:** Justin White. **Manager, In-Game Entertainment:** Annie Merovich. **Coordinator, Special Events:** Kristan Dolan.

Director, Merchandising: Kurt Schloss. **Merchandise Manager:** Karen Fox. **Area Supervisor/Great Northern Manager:** Amy Sawicki. **Analyst, Merchandising/Food Service:** Josh Cramer. **Distribution Center Manager:** Patrick Boyce. **Distribution Center Assistant Manager:** Stephanie Pantea. **Retail/Concession Manager:** Nancy Schneider.

Public Relations, Communications

Telephone: (216) 420-4380. **Fax:** (216) 420-4396.

Vice President, Public Relations: Bob DiBiasio. **Director, Media Relations:** Bart Swain. **Manager, Media Relations/ Administration:** Susie Giuliano. **Manager, Media Relations:** Jeff Sibel. **Manager, Communications/Creative Services:** Curtis Danburg. **Executive Director, Community Outreach:** Jayne Churchmack. **Manager, Community Relations:** Steve Frohwerk. **Coordinator, Community Relations:** Kate Vale.

Stadium Operations

Vice President, Ballpark Operations: Jim Folk.

Director, Facility Maintenance: Chris Donahoe. **Head Groundskeeper:** Brandon Koehnke. **Director, Ballpark Operations:** Jerry Crabb. **Manager, Ballpark Projects:** Jim Goldwire. **Manager, Ballpark Operations:** Brad Mohr.

Ticketing

Telephone: (216) 420-4487. **Fax:** (216) 420-4481.

Director, Ticket Services: Gene Connelly. **Manager, Ticket Services:** Regis Bane. **Manager, Ticket Office:** Ryan Beech. **Manager, Ticket Operations:** Michael Blackert.

Director, Tickets/Premium Sales: Mike Mulhall. **Manager, Customer Service/Sales:** Dave Murray. **Group Sales Manager:** Renee Boerner. **Database Manager:** Dan Foust. **Manager, Premium Services:** Cassy Baskin. **Manager, Premium Seating Development:** Marie Patten. **Manager, Season Ticket Sales:** Nick Arndt.

Travel, Clubhouse

Director, Team Travel: Mike Seghi. **Home Clubhouse/Equipment Manager:** Tony Amato. **Manager, Equipment Acquisition:** Jeff Sipos. **Manager, Video Operations:** Bob Chester. **Video Operations:** Frank Velotta.

GENERAL INFORMATION

Stadium (year opened): Progressive Field (1994).
Home Dugout: Third Base. **Playing Surface:** Grass.
Team Colors: Navy blue, red and silver.
Player Representative: Jake Westbrook.

Mark Shapiro

BASEBALL OPERATIONS

Telephone: (216) 420-4200. **Fax:** (216) 420-4321.

Executive Vice President, General Manager: Mark Shapiro. **Vice President, Baseball Operations:** Chris Antonetti.

Director, Player Personnel: Steve Lubratich. **Director, Baseball Operations:** Mike Chernoff. **Director, Baseball Administration:** Wendy Hoppel. **Sports Psychologist:** Dr. Charles Maher.

Special Assistants, Baseball Operations: Tim Belcher, Jason Bere, Ellis Burks, Robby Thompson.

Director of Latin American Operations: Lino Diaz. **Manager, Baseball Research & Analysis:** Keith Woolner. **Assistant, Baseball Operations:** Andrew Miller. **Executive Administrative Assistant, Baseball Operations:** Marlene Lehky. **Senior Coordinator, Baseball Systems:** Dan Mendlik. **Administrative Assistant, Baseball Operations:** Barbara Lessman.

Eric Wedge

Major League Staff

Manager: Eric Wedge.

Coaches: Bench—Joel Skinner; Pitching—Carl Willis; Batting—Derek Shelton; First Base/Infield—Luis Rivera; Third Base—Jeff Datz; Bullpen—Luis Isaac; Bullpen Catcher—Dan Williams, Dennis Malave.

Medical, Training

Head Team Physician: Dr. Mark Schickendantz.

Director of Medical Services, Head Trainer: Lonnie Soloff. **Assistant Athletic Trainers:** Rick Jameyson, Nick Kenney. **Strength/Conditioning Coach:** Tim Maxey. **Physical Therapy Consultant:** Jim Mehalik.

Player Development

Telephone: (216) 420-4308. **Fax:** (216) 420-4321.

Director, Player Development: Ross Atkins. **Assistant, Player Development:** Meka Asonye.

Advisor, Player Development: Johnny Goryl. **Nutrition Consultant:** Jackie Berning.

Field Coordinator: Dave Hudgens. **Coordinators:** John Couture (mental skills), Bruce Fields (hitting), Jake Beiting (strength/conditioning), Dave Miller (pitching), Ted Kubiak (defense), Gary Thurman (outfield/baserunning).

Field Coordinator, Latin America: Minnie Mendoza.

Farm System

Class	Farm Club	League	Manager	Coach	Pitching Coach
Triple-A	Buffalo	International	Torey Lovullo	Dave Myers	Scott Radinsky
Double-A	Akron	Eastern	Mike Sarbaugh	Lee May Jr.	Tony Arnold
High A	Kinston	Carolina	Chris Tremie	Jon Nunnally	Greg Hibbard
Low A	Lake County	South Atlantic	Aaron Holbert	Jim Rickon	Ruben Niebla
Short-season	Mahoning Valley	New York-Penn	Travis Fryman	Anthony Medrano	Ken Rowe
Rookie	Winter Haven	Gulf Coast	Rouglas Odor	Phil Clark	Steve Lyons
Rookie	Indians	Dominican	Jose Stela	J. Chavez/C. Fermin	Kevin Carcamo

Scouting

Telephone: (216) 420-4309. **Fax:** (216) 420-4321.

Assistant General Manager/Scouting Operations: John Mirabelli.

Director of Scouting: Brad Grant.

Major League Scouts: Jim Benedict, Dave Malpass (Huntington Beach, CA), Don Poplin (Norwood, NC).

Professional Scouts: Tyrone Brooks, Doug Carpenter (North Palm Beach, FL), Pat Murtaugh (Lafayette, IN), Bill Schudlich (Dearborn, MI).

National Crosschecker: Chuck Ricci (Greencastle, PA).

Regional Crosscheckers: Southeast—Scott Barnsby (Brownsboro, AL); West—Paul Cogan (Rocklin, CA); Northeast—Scott Meaney (Apex, NC); Midwest—Matt Ruebel (Oklahoma City, OK).

Full-Time Area Scouts: Steve Abney (Lawrence, KS), Chuck Bartlett, Kevin Cullen, Byron Ewing (Chicago, IL), Cesar Geronimo (Phoenix, AZ), Don Lyle (Sacramento, CA), Bob Mayer (Somerset, PA), Les Pajari (Conroe, TX), Derrick Ross (Olmstead Township, OH), Paul Gillispie (Atlanta, GA), Vince Sagisi (Encino, CA), Greg Smith, Jason Smith (Long Beach, CA), Mike Soper (Tampa, FL), Brent Urcheck (Philadelphia, PA).

Latin American Supervisors: Henry Centeno (Venezuela).

Colorado Rockies

Office Address: 2001 Blake St., Denver, CO 80205.
Telephone: (303) 292-0200. **Fax:** (303) 312-2116.
Website: www.coloradorockies.com.

Ownership

Operated by: Colorado Rockies Baseball Club Ltd.

Vice Chairman/CEO: Charles Monfort. **Vice Chairman:** Richard Monfort. **Executive Assistant to Vice Chairmen:** Patricia Penfold.

BUSINESS OPERATIONS

Charles Monfort

President: Keli McGregor. **Executive Assistant to President:** Terry Douglass. **Senior Vice President, Business Operations:** Greg Feasel. **VP, Human Resources:** Elizabeth Stecklein.

Finance

Senior Vice President/CFO: Hal Roth. **VP, Finance:** Michael Kent. **Senior Director, Purchasing:** Gary Lawrence. **Director, Accounting:** Phil Emerson. **Payroll Administrator:** Juli Daedelow. **Senior Accountant:** Phil Delany. **Accountant:** Laine Campbell.

Marketing/Sales

Senior Director, Corporate Sales: Marcy English-Glasser. **Director, New Partner Development:** Brendan Falvey. **Director, Promotions/Special Events:** Jason Fleming. **Coordinator, Promotions/Special Events:** Liz Coates. **Assistant Director, In-Game Entertainment/Broadcasting:** Kent Krosbakken.

Vice President, Community/Retail Operations: Jim Kellogg. **Managers, Community Affairs:** Dallas Davis, Antigone Vigil. **Manager, Community Fields Program/Historian:** Paul Parker. **Coordinator, Mascot Program:** Brady O'Neill. **Manager, Coors Field Receiving/Distribution Center:** Steve Tomlinson. **Director, Retail Operations:** Aaron Heinrich. **Director, Information Systems:** Bill Stephani. **Senior Director, Advertising/Marketing:** Jill Campbell. **Coordinator, Advertising/Marketing:** Sarah Topf.

Public Relations/Communications

Telephone: (303) 312-2325. **Fax:** (303) 312-2319.

Vice President, Communications/Public Relations: Jay Alves. **Manager, Communications/Public Relations:** Charlie Hepp. **Coordinator, Communications/Public Relations:** Matt Chisholm.

Stadium Operations

Senior Director, Food Service Operations/Development: Albert Valdes. **Vice President, Ballpark Operations:** Kevin Kahn. **Director, Coors Field Administration/Development:** Dave Moore. **Manager, Ballpark Services:** Mary Beth Benner. **Senior Director, Guest Services:** Steven Burke. **Director, Security:** Don Lyon. **Senior Director, Engineering/Facilities:** James Wiener. **Director, Engineering:** Randy Carlill. **Director, Facilities:** Oly Olsen. **Head Groundskeeper:** Mark Razum. **Assistant Head Groundskeeper:** Jose Gonzalez. **PA Announcer:** Reed Saunders. **Official Scorers:** Dave Einspahr, Dave Plati.

Ticketing

Telephone: (303) 762-5437, (800) 388-7625. **Fax:** (303) 312-2115.

Vice President, Ticket Operations/Sales: Sue Ann McClaren. **Senior Director, Ticket Operations/Development:** Kevin Fenton. **Assistant Director, New Business Development:** Todd Thomas. **Director, Ticket Operations/Finances:** Kent Hakes. **Assistant Director, Ticket Operations:** Scott Donaldson. **Manager, Ticket Operations:** Kevin Flood. **Coordinator, Ticket Operations:** Mandy Stecklein. **Representative, Ticket Ops/Spring Training Promotions and Group Sales:** Andy Finley. **Director, Season Tickets/Group Sales:** Jeff Benner. **Manager, Season Tickets:** Farrah Magee. **Supervisor, Outbound Sales:** Matt Haddad. **Coordinator, Group Services:** Cathy Taylor.

Director, Party Facilities/Premier Services, Spring Training Sales/Promotions: Scott Amerman. **Manager, Party Facilities/Premier Services:** Fred Graf. **Director, Ticket Services/Spring Training Business Operations:** Chuck Javernick. **Manager, Ticket Services:** Mariah Davidson.

Travel/Clubhouse

Director, Major League Operations: Paul Egins.

Director, Clubhouse Operations: Keith Schulz. **Assistant to Director, Clubhouse Operations:** Joe Diaz. **Visiting Clubhouse Manager:** Alan Bossart.

GENERAL INFORMATION

Stadium (year opened): Coors Field (1995).
Home Dugout: First base. **Playing Surface:** Grass.
Team Colors: Purple, black and silver.
Player Representative: Unavailable.

Dan O'Dowd

BASEBALL OPERATIONS

Telephone: (303) 292-0200. **Fax:** (303) 312-2320.

Executive Vice President/General Manager: Dan O'Dowd. **Assistant to Executive VP/GM:** Adele Armagost.

VP/Assistant GM: Bill Geivett. **Director, Baseball Operations:** Jeff Bridich. **Manager, Baseball Operations:** Matt Vinnola. **Assistant, Baseball Operations/General Counsel:** Zack Rosenthal.

Special Assistants to GM: Pat Daugherty (Aurora, CO), Dave Holliday (Tulsa, OK), Marcel Lachemann (Penryn, CA), Kasey McKeon (Stoney Creek, NC).

Major League Staff

Manager: Clint Hurdle.

Coaches: Bench—Jamie Quirk; Pitching—Bob Apodaca; Batting—Alan Cockrell; First Base—Glenallen Hill; Third Base—Mike Gallego; Bullpen—Rick Mathews; Bullpen Catcher—Mark Strittmatter; Strength—Brad Andress; Video—Brian Jones.

Medical/Training

Director, Medical Operations: Tom Probst. **Medical Director:** Dr. Thomas Noonan. **Senior Associate Orthopedist:** Dr. Richard Hawkins. **Club Physicians:** Dr. Allen Schreiber, Dr. Douglas Wyland.

Head Athletic Trainer: Keith Dugger. **Assistant Athletic Trainer:** Scott Gehret. **Strength/Conditioning Coordinator:** Brian Jordan. **Rehabilitation Coordinator:** Scott Murayama.

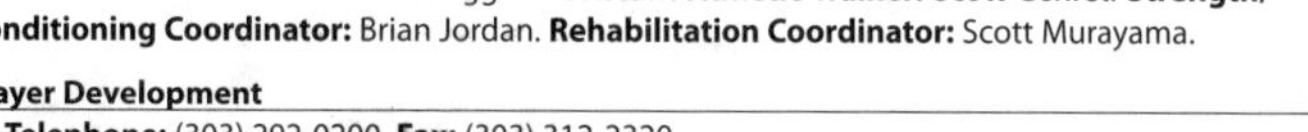
Clint Hurdle

Player Development

Telephone: (303) 292-0200. **Fax:** (303) 312-2320.

Director, Player Development: Marc Gustafson. **Assistant, Player Development:** Walter Sylvester.

Field Coordinator: Ron Gideon. **Roving Instructors:** Rich Dauer (infield), Marv Foley (catching), Trenidad Hubbard (outfield/baserunning), Jim Johnson (hitting), Jim Wright (pitching). **Video Coordinator:** Jimmy Hartley. **Performance Enhancement Coach:** Ronn Svetich. **Equipment Manager:** Jerry Bass.

Cultural Development Coordinator: Dan Pace.

Farm System

Class	Farm Team	League	Manager	Coach	Pitching Coach
Triple-A	Colorado Springs	Pacific Coast	Tom Runnells	Rene Lachemann	Chuck Kniffin
Double-A	Tulsa	Texas	Stu Cole	Dave Hajek	Bo McLaughlin
High A	Modesto	California	Jerry Weinstein	Duane Espy	Butch Hughes
Low A	Asheville	South Atlantic	Joe Mikulik	Houston Jimenez	Doug Linton
Short-season	Tri-City	Northwest	Fred Ocasio	Anthony Sanders	Dave Schuler
Rookie	Casper	Pioneer	Tony Diaz	Kevin Riggs	Eduardo Villacis
Rookie	Rockies	Dominican	Mauricio Gonzalez	Edison Lora	Pablo Paredes
Rookie	Rockies	Venezuela	Maurio Mendez	Unavailable	Unavailable

Scouting

Telephone: (303) 292-0200. **Fax:** (303) 312-2320.

Vice President, Scouting: Bill Schmidt. **Assistant Director, Scouting:** Danny Montgomery. **Manager, Scouting:** Zach Wilson. **Manager, Professional Scouting:** Jon Weil. **Advance Scout:** Chris Warren.

Major League Scouts: Will George (Woolwich Township, NJ). **Professional Scouts:** Jack Gillis (Sarasota, FL), Mike Hamilton (Dallas, TX), Mike Paul (Tucson, AZ).

Special Assignment Scout: Terry Wetzel (Overland Park, KS).

National Crosschecker: Ty Coslow (Louisville, KY).

Scouting Adviser: Dave Snow (Seal Beach, CA).

Full-Time Area Scouts: John Cedarburg (Fort Myers, FL), Scott Corman (Lexington, KY), Dar Cox (Frisco, TX), Mike Ericson (Glendale, AZ), Chris Forbes (Houston, TX), Mike Garlatti (Edison, NJ), Mark Germann (Atkins, IA), Matt Hattabaugh (Westminster, CA), Bert Holt (Visalia, CA), Damon Iannelli (Brandon, MS), Jon Lukens (La Jolla, CA), Alan Matthews (Decatur, GA), Jay Matthews (Concord, NC), Jorge de Posada (Rio Piedras, PR), Ed Santa (Powell, OH), Gary Wilson (Sacramento, CA).

Part-Time Scouts: Steve Bernhardt (Perry Hall, MD), Greg Booker (Elon, NC), Norm DeBriyn (Fayetteville, AR), Brett Evert (Salem, OR), Jeff Hipps (Millbrae, CA), Marc Johnson (Centennial, CO), Bobby Knopp (Phoenix, AZ), Dave McQueen (Bossier City, LA), Greg Pullia (Plymouth, MA).

Director, International Operations: Rolando Fernandez.

Director, Venezuelan Operations: Francisco Cartaya. **Manager, Dominican Republic Operations:** Jhonathan Leyba. **Manager, Pacific Rim Operations:** Ming Harbor.

International Scouts: Phil Allen (Australia), Martin Cabrera (Dominican Republic), Claudino Hernadez (Panama), Martin Jose (Dominican Republic), Carlos Gomez (Venezuela), Orlando Medina (Venezuela), Frank Roa (Dominican Republic).

Detroit Tigers

Office Address: 2100 Woodward Ave, Detroit, MI 48201.
Telephone: (313) 471-2000. **Fax:** (313) 471-2138.
Website: www.tigers.com

Ownership

Operated By: Detroit Tigers Inc. **Owner:** Michael Ilitch.

President, CEO/General Manager: David Dombrowski. **Special Assistant to President:** Al Kaline, Willie Horton. **Executive Assistant to President, CEO/GM:** Marty Lyon. **Senior Vice President:** Jim Devellano.

Mike Ilitch

BUSINESS OPERATIONS

Senior Vice President, Business Operations: Duane McLean. **Executive Assistant to Senior VP, Business Operations:** Peggy Bacarella.

Finance

Vice President/CFO: Stephen Quinn.

Director, Finance: Kelli Kollman. **Manager, Purchasing/Supplier Diversity:** DeAndre Berry. **Accounting Manager:** Sheila Robine. **Financial Analyst:** Kristin Jorgensen. **Accounts Payable Coordinator:** Debbie Sword. **Accounts Receivable Coordinator:** Sharon Szkarlat. **Administrative/Accounting Assistant:** Tracy Rice.

Director, Human Resources: Karen Gruca. **Senior Manager, Payroll Administration:** Maureen Kraatz. **Payroll Administrator:** Mark Cebelak. **Payroll/Human Resources Coordinator:** Maria Delgado. **Internal Auditor:** Scott Calka.

Director, Information Technology: Scott Wruble.

Public/Community Affairs

Vice President, Community/Public Affairs: Elaine Lewis.

Manager, Player Relations, Sports/Youth Programs: Sam Abrams. **Manager, Detroit Tigers Foundation:** Jordan Field. **Manager, Community Affairs:** Alexandrea Thrubis. **Community Affairs Coordinator:** Amy Peterson. **Administrative Assistant:** Audrey Zielinski.

Sales/Marketing

Vice President, Corporate Sales: Steve Harms.

Corporate Sales Manager: Greg Paddock, Zach Wagner, John Wolski. **Sponsorship Services Manager:** Eli Bayless. **Director, Marketing:** Ellen Hill Zeringue. **Marketing Manager:** Ron Wade. **Senior Director, Promotions/In-Game Entertainment:** Joel Scott. **Promotions Coordinator:** Jared Karner.

Vice President, Corporate Suite Sales/Service: Charles Jones. **Director, Suite Sales/Services:** Scot Pett. **Suite Sales/Service Manager:** Amy Howard. **Director, Fantasy Camps:** Jerry Lewis.

Media Relations/Communications

Telephone: (313) 471-2114. **Fax:** (313) 471-2138.

Vice President, Communications: Rob Matwick. **Manager, Baseball Media Relations:** Brian Britten. **Assistant Manager, Baseball Media Relations:** Rick Thompson. **Senior Manager, Broadcasting:** Molly Light.

Ballpark Operations

Vice President, Park Operations: Michael Healy. **Director, Park Operations:** Michael Churchill. **Head Groundskeeper:** Heather Nabozny. **Assistant Groundskeeper:** Gail DeGennaro. **Senior Manager, Park Operations:** Ed Goward. **Event Operations Manager:** Jill Baran. **Park Operations Manager:** Allan Carrise. **Guest Services Manager:** Melissa Ball. **Administrative Coordinator:** Eryka Cheatham. **Scoreboard Operations Manager:** Robb Wilson.

Ticketing

Telephone: (313) 471-2255.

Vice President, Marketing/Ticket Sales: Bob Raymond. **Director, Ticket Sales:** Steve Fox. **Director, Group Sales:** Dwain Lewis. **Senior Director, Ticket Services:** Victor Gonzalez.

Travel/Clubhouse

Traveling Secretary: Bill Brown. **Manager, Home Clubhouse:** Jim Schmakel. **Assistant Manager, Visiting Clubhouse:** John Nelson. **Clubhouse Assistant:** Tyson Steele. **Baseball Video Operations:** Jeremy Kelch. **Assistant, Baseball Video Operations:** Andy Bjornstad.

GENERAL INFORMATION

Stadium (year opened): Comerica Park (2000).
Home Dugout: Third Base. **Playing Surface:** Grass.
Team Colors: Navy blue, orange and white.
Player Representative: Nate Robertson.

Dave Dombrowski

BASEBALL OPERATIONS

Telephone: (313) 471-2000. **Fax:** (313) 471-2099.

General Manager: David Dombrowski.

Vice President/Assistant GM: Al Avila. **VP/Baseball Legal Counsel:** John Westhoff. **VP, Player Personnel:** Scott Reid. **Special Assistant to GM:** Dick Egan. **Director, Baseball Operations:** Mike Smith. **Executive Assistant to VP/Assistant GM, Baseball Legal Counsel:** Eileen Surma.

Major League Staff

Manager: Jim Leyland.

Coaches: Pitching—Chuck Hernandez; Batting—Lloyd McClendon; Infield—Rafael Belliard; First Base—Andy Van Slyke; Third Base—Gene Lamont; Bullpen—Jeff Jones.

Jim Leyland

Medical, Training

Director, Medical Services/Head Athletic Trainer: Kevin Rand. **Assistant Athletic Trainers:** Steve Carter, Doug Teter. **Strength/Conditioning Coach:** Javair Gillett.

Team Physicians: Dr. Michael Workings, Dr. Stephen Lemos. **Team Physician (Florida):** Dr. Louis Saco.

Player Development

Telephone: (863) 686-8075. **Fax:** (863) 688-9589.

Director, Minor League Operations: Dan Lunetta. **Director, Player Development:** Glenn Ezell. **Director, Minor League/Scouting Administration:** Cheryl Evans.

Director, Latin American Scouting: Miguel Garcia. **Director, Dominican Republic Operations:** Ramon Perez. **Director, International Operations:** Tom Moore. **Director, Latin American Player Development:** Manny Crespo.

Minor League Operations Assistant: Avi Becher. **Minor League Operations Administrative Assistant:** Marilyn Acevedo.

Minor League Field Coordinator: Mike Rojas.

Minor League Medical Coordinator: Victor Trasoff-Jilg. **Minor League Strength/Conditioning Coordinator:** Chris Walter.

Roving Instructors: Toby Harrah (hitting), Kevin Bradshaw (infield), Jon Matlack (pitching), Brian Peterson (performance enhancement), Gene Roof (outfield/baserunning).

Farm System

Class	Farm Club	League	Manager	Coach(es)	Pitching Coach
Triple-A	Toledo	International	Larry Parrish	Leon Durham	A.J. Sager
Double-A	Erie	Eastern	Tom Brookens	Glenn Adams	Ray Burris
High A	Lakeland	Florida State	Andy Barkett	Larry Herndon	Joe Coleman
Low A	West Michigan	Midwest	Joe DePastino	Benny Distefano	Alan Mills
Short-season	Oneonta	New York-Penn	Ryan Newman	Luis Quinones	Mark Johnson
Rookie	Lakeland	Gulf Coast	Basilio Cabrera	Garrett Guest	Greg Sabat
Rookie	Tigers	Dominican	Frey Peniche	P. Bautista/R. Martinez	Jose Parra
Rookie	Tigers	Venezuelan	Josman Robles	Jesus Laya	Jorge Cordova

Scouting

Telephone: (863) 413-4112. **Fax:** (863) 413-1954.

Vice President, Amateur Scouting: David Chadd.

Assistant Director, Amateur Scouting: James Orr.

Major League Scouts: Scott Bream (Phoenix, AZ), Al Hargesheimer (Arlington Heights, IL), Jim Olander (Vail, AZ), Mike Russell (Gulf Breeze, FL), Jeff Wetherby (Wesley Chapel, FL).

Advance Scout: Bruce Tanner (New Castle, PA).

National Crosscheckers: Ray Crone (Cedar Hill, TX), Scott Pleis (Tampa, FL). **Regional Crosscheckers:** East—Murray Cook (Orlando, FL), Central—Bob Cummings (Oak Lawn, IL), Midwest—Mike Hankins (Lee's Summit, MO), West—Joe Ferrone (Santa Clarita, CA).

Area Scouts: Grant Brittain (Hickory, NC), Bill Buck (Manassas, VA), Rolando Casanova (Miami, FL), Scott Cerny (Rocklin, CA), Tim Grieve (New Braunfels, TX), Garrett Guest (University Park, FL), Ryan Johnson (Auburn, WA), Tim McWilliam (San Diego, CA), Marty Miller (Chicago, IL), Steve Nichols (Mount Dora, FL), Tom Osowski (Franklin, WI), Jim Rough (Chelsea, AL), Brian Reid (Laveen, AZ), Chris Wimmer (Yukon, OK), Harold Zonder (Louisville, KY).

Director, International Scouting: Tom Moore.

Director, Latin American Development: Manny Crespo. **Director, Latin American Scouting:** Miguel Garcia. **Director, Dominican Operations:** Ramon Perez. **Coordinator, Dominican Academy:** Oliver Arias.

Florida Marlins

Office Address: Dolphin Stadium, 2267 Dan Marino Blvd. Miami, FL 33056.
Telephone: (305) 626-7400. **Fax:** (305) 626-7302.
Website: www.floridamarlins.com.

OWNERSHIP

Owner/CEO: Jeffrey Loria. **Vice Chairman:** Joel Mael.

President: David Samson. **Special Assistants to President:** Andre Dawson, Tony Perez. **Special Assistant to Owner:** Jack McKeon. **Executive Assistant to Owner, Vice Chairman and President:** Beth McConville.

Jeffrey Loria

BUSINESS OPERATIONS

Executive Vice President/CFO: Michel Bussiere. **Senior Vice President, Stadium Development:** Claude Delorme. **Director, Stadium Operations:** Gary Levy.

Director, Human Resources: Ana Hernandez. **Coordinator, Human Resources:** Megan Johansen. **Benefits:** Ruby Mattei. **Supervisor, Office Services:** Karl Heard.

Finance

Senior Vice President, Finance: Susan Jaison. **Controller:** Alina Trigo. **Administrator, Payroll:** Carolina Calderon. **Staff Accountant:** Alina Quiros. **Coordinator, Accounts Payable:** Marva Alexander. **Coordinator, Finance:** Diana Jorge.

Director, Information Technology: David Enriquez. **Manager, Technical Support:** David Kuan. **Network Engineer:** Ozzie Macias. **Manager, Telecommunications:** Sam Mora.

Marketing

Vice President, Marketing: Sean Flynn. **Manager, Retail Operations:** Robyn Feinstein. **Manager, Hispanic Sales:** Juan Martinez. **Manager, Promotions:** Matt Britten. **Coordinator, Marketing:** Boris Menier. **Coordinator, Promotions:** Antonio Torres-Roman. **Coordinator, Mermaids:** Jose Guerrero. **Coordinator, Marlins en Miami:** Marisel Sordo.

Sales

Vice President, New Business Development: Dale Hendricks. **Vice President, Corporate Sales:** Brendan Cunningham. **Manager, Corporate Sales:** Tony Tome. **Manager, Broadcast Sales:** Rick Furr. **Senior Account Executive, Broadcast Sales:** Michael DiLauro. **Coordinators, Corporate Sales:** Sheri Talerico, Christina Brito. **Director, Season/Group Sales:** William Makris. **Director, Customer Service:** Spencer Linden. **Manager, Season/Group Sales:** Marty Mulford. **Senior Account Executive, Groups:** Mario Signorello. **Senior Account Executives:** Sean Flood, Orestes Hernandez.

Media Relations, Communications

Telephone: (305) 626-7492. **Fax:** (305) 626-7302.

Senior Vice President, Communications/Broadcasting: P.J. Loyello. **Director, Media Relations:** Matthew Roebuck. **Administrative Assistant, Media Relations:** Maria Armella. **Director, Broadcast Services:** Suzanne Rayson. **Coordinator, Broadcasting/Media Relations:** Emmanuel Munoz. **Manager, Community Affairs:** Angela Smith. **Assistant, Community Affairs:** Paul Resnick. **Assistant, Player Relations:** Alex Morin.

Executive Director, Marlins Community Foundation: Nancy Olson. **Coordinators, Marlins Community Foundation:** Kelly Schnackenberg, Jeremy Stern.

Stadium Operations

Director, Game Presentation/Events: Larry Blocker. **Manager, Game Presentation/Events:** Eric Ramirez. **Coordinator, Game Presentation/Events:** Edward Limia. **Assistant, Production/Events:** Andrew Resnick. **Director, Creative Services:** Alfred Hernandez. **Manager, Creative Services:** Robert Vigon. **Video Archivist:** Chris Myers. **Mascot:** John DeCicco. **PA Announcer:** Dick Sanford.

Travel, Clubhouse

Senior Director, Team Travel: Bill Beck. **Equipment Manager:** John Silverman. **Assistant Equipment Manager:** Mark Brown. **Visiting Clubhouse Manager:** Bryan Greenberg. **Assistant, Clubhouse/Umpire's Room:** Michael Rock Hughes.

GENERAL INFORMATION

Stadium (year opened): Dolphin Stadium (1993).
Home Dugout: First Base. **Playing Surface:** Grass.
Team Colors: Teal, black, white and silver.
Player Representative: Unavailable.

Larry Beinfest

BASEBALL OPERATIONS

President, Baseball Operations: Larry Beinfest.

Vice President/General Manager: Michael Hill. **Vice President, Player Personnel/Assistant GM:** Dan Jennings. **Special Assistant to GM/Pro Scout:** Orrin Freeman. **General Counsel:** Derek Jackson. **Video Coordinator:** Cullen McRae. **Executive Assistant:** Rita Filbert. **Assistant, Baseball Operations:** Marc Lippman.

Major League Staff

Manager: Fredi Gonzalez.

Coaches: Bench—Carlos Tosca; Pitching—Mark Wiley; Hitting—Jim Presley; First Base/Infield—Andy Fox; Third Base—Bo Porter; Bullpen—Steve Foster; Bullpen Coordinator—Pierre Arsenault.

Fredi Gonzalez

Medical, Training

Team Physician: Dr. **Daniel Kanell. Head Trainer:** Sean Cunningham. **Assistant Trainer:** Mike Kozak. **Director, Strength/Conditioning:** Paul Fournier.

Player Development

Vice President, Player Development and Scouting/Assistant GM: Jim Fleming. **Director, Player Development:** Brian Chattin. **Assistant, Player Development:** Manny Colon.

Field Coordinator: John Pierson. **Coordinators:** Gene Basham (training/rehabilitation), Tarrik Brock (outfield/baserunning), Tim Cossins (catching), John Mallee (hitting), Wayne Rosenthal (pitching), Josh Seligman (Strength/conditioning). **Josue Espada (infield).**

Minor League Equipment Manager: Mark Brown. **Minor League Clubhouse Manager:** Lou Assalone.

Farm System

Class	Farm Club	League	Manager	Coach	Pitching Coach
Triple-A	Albuquerque	Pacific Coast	Dean Treanor	Steve Phillips	Rich Gale
Double-A	Carolina	Southern	Matt Raleigh	Theron Todd	Scott Mitchell
High A	Jupiter	Florida State	Brandon Hyde	Reid Cornelius	Anthony Iapoce
Low A	Greensboro	South Atlantic	Edwin Rodriguez	John Duffy	Jorge Hernandez
Short-season	Jamestown	New York-Penn	Darin Everson	Charlie Corbell, Jr.	Johnny Rodriguez
Rookie	Jupiter	Gulf Coast	Doc Watson	Jeff Schwarz	Cesar Haines
Rookie	Marlins	Dominican	Ray Nunez	Luis Brito	Edison Santana

Scouting

Telephone: (561) 630-1816/Pro (305) 626-7400.

Fax: (561) 775-9935/Pro (305) 626-7294

Director, Scouting: Stan Meek. **Assistant Director, Scouting:** Gregg Leonard. **Assistant, Pro Scouting:** Dan Noffsinger.

Advance Scout: Joel Moeller (San Clemente, CA). **Pro Scouts:** Roger Jongewaard (Fallbrook, CA), Guy Mader (Tewksbury, MA), Phil Rossi (Jessup, PA), Tommy Thompson (Greenville, NC), Michael White (Lakewood Ranch, FL).

National Crosschecker: David Crowson (College Station, TX). **Regional Supervisors:** East—Mike Cadahia (Miami Springs, FL); Central—Ray Howard (Norman, OK); West—Scott Goldby (Yuba City, CA); Canada—Steve Payne (Barrington, RI).

Area Scouts: Matt Anderson (Williamsport, PA), Carlos Berroa (San Juan, PR), Carmen Carcone (GA), Dennis Cardoza (Denton, TX), Robby Corsaro (Victorville, CA), John Hughes (Walnut Creek, CA), Kevin Ibach (Arlington Heights, IL), Kevin Lidle (Lakeland, FL), Joel Matthews (Concord, NC), Tim McDonnell (Westminster, CA), Bob Oldis (Iowa City, IA), Gabe Sandy (Gresham, OR), Scott Stanley (Peoria, AZ), Ryan Wardinsky (Edmond, OK), Mark Willoughby (Hammond, LA).

Director, International Operations: Albert Gonzalez.

International Supervisors: Carlos Acosta (Caracas, Venezuela), Sandy Nin (Santo Domingo, Dominican Republic).

International Scouts: Wilmer Adrian (Caracas, VZ), Wilfredo Blanco (Managua, Nicaragua), Wilmer Castillo (Maracay, VZ), Luis Cordoba (Panama), Rene Garcia (Lara, VZ), Willie Marrugo (Cartagena, Colombia), Alex Martinez (Santo Domingo, DR), Pedro Martinez (Anz, VZ), Domingo Ortega (Santo Domingo, DR).

Houston Astros

Office Address: Minute Maid Park, Union Station, 501 Crawford, Suite 400, Houston, TX 77002.

Mailing Address: P.O. Box 288, Houston, TX 77001.

Telephone: (713) 259-8000. **Fax:** (713) 259-8981.

E-mail Address: fanfeedback@astros.mlb.com. **Website:** www.astros.com.

Ownership

Operated By: McLane Group LP.

Chairman/CEO: Drayton McLane.

Board of Directors: Bob McClaren, G.W. Sanford, Webb Stickney.

Drayton McLane

BUSINESS OPERATIONS

President, Business Operations: Pam Gardner. **Executive Assistant:** Eileen Colgin.

Finance/Human Resources

Senior Vice President, Finance/Administration: Jackie Traywick. **Controller:** Jonathan Germer. **Director, Treasury/Office Services:** Damian Babin. **Senior Accountant:** Abby Price. **Accounts Payable Manager:** Seth Courtney. **Senior Director, Human Resources:** Larry Stokes. **Human Resources Coordinator:** Chanda Lawdermilk. **Director, Payroll/Employee Benefits:** Ruth Kelly. **Manager, Payroll/Benefits:** Jessica Horton. **Benefits Coordinator:** Cyndi Campbell.

Marketing/Sales

Senior Vice President, Premium Sponsorships: Jamie Hildreth. **VP, Sponsorships/Business Development:** John Sorrentino. **VP, Market Development:** Rosi Hernandez.

Senior Director, Marketing: Jennifer Randall. **Assistant Director, Marketing:** Clint Pasche. **Marketing Coordinator:** Mallory Conger. **Assistant Director, Sponsorship Sales:** Chuck Arnold. **Assistant Director, Sponsorship Sales:** Shane Hildreth. **Sponsorship Accounts Manager:** Marisa Lopez. **Market Development Manager:** Celeste Brown. **Graphics Designer:** Chris Garcia.

Public Relations/Communications

Telephone: (713) 259-8900. **Fax:** (713) 259-8981.

Senior Vice President, Communications: Jay Lucas. **Director, Media Relations:** Jimmy Stanton. **Media Relations Managers:** Sally Gunter, Travis Morin. **VP, Community Development:** Marian Harper. **Director, Community Events:** Rita Suchma. **Senior Director, Information Technology/Procurement:** Brad Bourland. **Senior Network Administrator:** Steve Reese. **Network Administrator:** Michael Hovan.

Stadium Operations

Vice President, Ballpark Operations: Bobby Forrest. **VP, Special Events:** Kala Sorenson. **Assistant Director, Engineering:** David McKenzie. **Audio-Visual Coordinator:** Lowell Matheny. **Director, Ballpark Entertainment:** Kirby Kander. **Assistant Director, Ballpark Entertainment:** Brock Jessel. **Director, Broadcast Operations/Affiliate Relations:** Mike Cannon. **Director, Telecommunications/Executive Assistant:** Tracy Faucette.

Director, Customer Service: Michael Kenny. **Assistant Sales Director, Special Events/Conference Center:** Leigh Ann Dawson. **Sales Manager, Special Events:** Valerie Eissler. **Special Events Coordinator:** Katy Walden. **Minute Maid Park Tour Coordinator:** Jordan Green. **Director, Major League Field Operations:** Dan Bergstrom. **Groundskeeper:** Willie Berry. **Second Assistant Groundskeeper:** Kyle Lewis.

PA Announcer: Bob Ford. **Official Scorers:** Rick Blount, Ivy McLemore, Greg Porzucek, Trey Wilkinson.

Ticketing

Telephone: (713) 259-8500. **Fax:** (713) 259-8326.

Director, Ticket Sales: Bill Goren. **Director, Ticket Services:** Brooke Ellenberger. **Director, Ticket Operations:** Marcia Coronado. **Director, Box Office Operations:** Bill Cannon. **Manager, Premium Sales:** Kyle Dawson. **Administrative Assistant, Ticket Sales:** Joannie Cobb. **Senior Account Executive:** Brent Broussard. **Ticket Production Coordinator:** Sandy Luna.

Travel/Clubhouse

Director, Team Travel: Barry Waters.

Equipment Manager: Dennis Liborio. **Assistant Equipment Managers:** Carl Schneider, Sotirios Athanasion. **Visiting Clubhouse Manager:** Steve Perry. **Umpire/Clubhouse Assistant:** Chuck New.

GENERAL INFORMATION

Stadium (year opened): Minute Maid Park (2000).

Home Dugout: First Base. **Playing Surface:** Grass.

Team Colors: Brick red, sand beige and black.

Player Representative: Unavailable.

Ed Wade

BASEBALL OPERATIONS

Telephone: (713) 259-8000. **Fax:** (713) 259-8600.

President, Baseball Operations: Tal Smith. **General Manager:** Ed Wade.

Assistant GM/Baseball Operations: David Gottfried. **Special Assistants to GM:** Jeff Bagwell, Enos Cabell, Matt Galante, Julio Linares, Nolan Ryan. **Director, Research/Analysis:** Charlie Norton. **Assistant Director, Baseball Operations:** Jay Edmiston. **Player Development Coordinator:** Allen Rowin. **Baseball Operations Assistant:** Mike Burns.

Executive Assistant, Major League Operations: Traci Dearing. **Video Coordinator:** Jim Summers.

Major League Staff

Manger: Cecil Cooper.

Coaches: Bench—Jackie Moore; Pitching—Dewey Robinson; Hitting—Sean Berry; First Base—Jose Cruz, Sr.; Third Base—Ed Romero; Bullpen—Mark Bailey; Administrative Coach--Al Pedrique.

Cecil Cooper

Medical, Training

Medical Director: Dr. David Lintner. **Team Physicians:** Dr. Tom Mehlhoff, Dr. Jim Muntz.

Head Trainer: Dave Labossiere. **Assistant Trainer:** Rex Jones. **Strength/Conditioning Coaches:** Dr. Gene Coleman, Nathan Lucero.

Player Development

Telephone: (713) 259-8922. **Fax:** (713) 259-8600.

Assistant GM/Director, Player Development: Ricky Bennett.

Field Coordinator: Tom Wiedenbauer. **Minor League Coordinators:** Orv Franchuk (hitting), Russ Nixon (roving instructor), Britt Burns (pitching), Gary Redus (outfield/baserunning), Danny Sheaffer (catching), Matt Galante/Al Pedrique (infield instructors), Pete Fagan (training/rehabilitation), Mike Smith (strength/conditioning).

Farm System

Class	Farm Club	League	Manager	Coach	Pitching Coach
Triple-A	Round Rock	Pacific Coast	Dave Clark	Ron Jackson	Burt Hooton
Double-A	Corpus Christi	Texas	Luis Pujols	John Tamargo Jr.	Stan Boroski
High A	Salem	Carolina	Jim Pankovits	Keith Bodie	Gary Ruby
Low A	Lexington	South Atlantic	Gregg Langbehn	Stubby Clapp	Charley Taylor
Short-season	Tri-City	New York-Penn	Pete Rancont	Joel Chimelis	Don Alexander
Rookie	Greeneville	Appalachian	Rodney Linares	D.J. Boston	Travis Driskill
Rookie	Astros	Dominican	Rafael Ramirez	Arturo DeFreitas	Hector Eduardo
Rookie	Astros	Venezuela	Omar Lopez	Jesus Aristimuno	Luis Yanez

Scouting

Telephone: (713) 259-8921. **Fax:** (713) 259-8600.

Director, Amateur Scouting: Bobby Heck. **Director, Latin American Scouting:** Felix Francisco. **Director, Pacific Rim Scouting:** Glen Barker. **Director, Major League Scouting:** Fred Nelson.

Major League Scouts: Gene DeBoer (Brandon, WI), Jack Lind (Mesa, AZ), Gordy MacKenzie (Fruitland Park, FL), Walt Matthews (Texarkana, TX), Paul Ricciarini (Pittsfield, MA), Bob Skinner (San Diego, CA). **Professional Scouts:** Brian Johnson (Tucson, AZ), Jeff McAvoy (Palmer, MA), Scipio Spinks (Missouri City, TX), J.D. Elliby (Orlando, FL), Tad Slowik (Arlington Heights, IL).

National Crosschecker: David Post (Canton, GA). **Regional Supervisors:** Midwest—Ralph Bratton (Dripping Springs, TX); West—Doug Deutsch (Costa Mesa, CA); East—Clarence Johns (Tallahassee, FL).

Area Scouts: J.D. Alleva (Charlotte, NC), Keith Bogan (Ridgeland, MS), Jon Bunnell (Tampa, FL), Barry Cheesman (Sarasota, FL), Paul Gale (Keizer, OR), David Kady (Chicago, IL), Joe Graham (Rocklin, CA), Lincoln Martin (Douglasview, GA), Mike Maggart (Penn Yan, NY), Tom McCormack (University City, MO), Rusty Pendergrass (Missouri City, TX), Mark Randall (Edmonton, Alberta, Canada), Mark Ross (Tucson, AZ), Joey Sola (Caguas, PR), Jim Stevenson (Tulsa, OK), Chuck Stone (Moreno Valley, CA), Dennis Twombley (Redondo Beach, CA), Nick Venuto (Massillon, OH).

Senior Advising Scouts: Bob King (La Mesa, CA), Bob Poole (Redwood City, CA), Gene Wellman (Danville, CA).

Coordinator, Venezuela: Pablo Torrealba. **Coordinator, European Scouting:** Mauro Mazzotti.

Kansas City Royals

Office Address: One Royal Way, Kansas City, MO 64129.
Mailing Address: P.O. Box 419969, Kansas City, MO 64141.
Telephone: (816) 921-8000. **Fax:** (816) 924-0347.
Website: www.royals.com

Ownership

Operated By: Kansas City Royals Baseball Club Inc.

Chairman/CEO: David Glass. **President:** Dan Glass. **Board of Directors:** Ruth Glass, Don Glass, Dayna Martz, Julia Kauffman, Herk Robinson.

David Glass

BUSINESS OPERATIONS

Senior Vice President/Business Operations: Kevin Uhlich. **Executive Administrative Assistant:** Cindy Hamilton.

Finance

Vice President, Finance/Administration: Dale Rohr. **Director, Finance:** Joe Kurtzman. **Director, Renovation Accounting/Risk Management:** Patrick Fleischmann. **Manager, Accounting:** Sean Ritchie. **Manager, Ticket Operations/Concessions Accounting:** Tara Madlock. **Accounting Coordinator:** Shelley Wilson.

Senior Director, Payroll/Benefits/Human Resources: Tom Pfannenstiel. **Manager, Human Resources:** Lynne Elder. **Senior Director, Information Systems:** Jim Edwards. **Manager, Programming/Systems Analyst:** Becky Randall. **Manager, Network/Telecommunications:** Scott Novak.

Director, Ticket Operations: Chris Darr. **Coordinators, Ticket Operations:** Betty Bax, Jacque Tschirhart. **Ticket Operations Vault Manager:** Andrew Coughlin.

Communications/Broadcasting

Vice President, Communications/Broadcasting: Mike Swanson. **Director, Broadcast Services/Royals Alumni:** Fred White. **Manager, Radio Network Operations:** Don Free.

Media Relations

Director, Media Relations: David Holtzman. **Manager, Coordinator, Media Services:** Dina Wathan. **Coordinator, Communications/Broadcasting:** Colby Curry.

Publicity/Community Relations

Vice President, Community Affairs and Publicity: Toby Cook. **Senior Director, Publicity:** Lora Grosshans. **Coordinator, Publicity:** Megan Stock. **Administrative Assistant:** Precious Washington. **Senior Director, Royals Charities:** Joy Sedlacek. **Director, Community Outreach:** Betty Kaegel. **Director, Community Relations:** Ben Aken.

Ballpark Operations

Vice President, Ballpark Operations/Development: Bob Rice. **Director, Event Operations/Guest Services:** Chris Richardson. **Manager, Event Operations/Guest Services:** Renee VanLaningham. **Manager, Stadium Tours/Operations:** Morrie Carlson. **Director, Groundskeeping/Landscaping:** Trevor Vance. **Manager, Groundskeeping:** Justin Scott. **Landscape Assistant:** Anthony Bruce. **Director, Stadium Operations:** Rodney Lewallen. **Coordinator, Stadium Operations:** Jermaine Goodwin. **Coordinator Telephone Services:** Kathy Butler. **Coordinator, Mail Services:** Larry Garrett. **Manager, Stadium Services:** Johnny Williams. **Manager, Stadium Engineering:** Todd Burrow.

Sales/Marketing

Vice President, Sales/Marketing: Mark Tilson. **Senior Director, Marketing:** Kim Hillix Burgess. **Director, Marketing:** Curt Nelson. **Director, Game Entertainment:** Chris DeRuyscher. **Manager, Creative Services:** Vic Royal. **Manager, Online/Target Marketing:** Erin Koncak. **Manager, Promotions/Special Events:** Josh Diekmann.

Director, Season Ticket Sales/Royals Lancers: Rick Amos. **Coordinator, Season Tickets:** Mary Lee Martino. **Director, Group Sales/Call Center Operations:** Scott Wadsworth.

Business Development

Vice President, Corporate Alliance: Neil Harwell.

Senior Director, Corporate Sponsorship Sales: Michelle Kammerer. **Senior Director, Corporate Sales:** Mitch Wheeler.

GENERAL INFORMATION

Stadium (year opened): Ewing M. Kauffman Stadium (1973).
Home Dugout: First Base. **Playing Surface:** Grass.
Team Colors: Royal blue and white.
Team Representative: Unavailable.

Dayton Moore

BASEBALL OPERATIONS

Telephone: (816) 921-8000. **Fax:** (816) 924-0347.

Senior Vice President, Baseball Operations/General Manager: Dayton Moore.

VP, Baseball Operations/Assistant GM: Dean Taylor. **Senior Advisor to GM:** Art Stewart, Donnie Williams. **Assistant to GM:** Brian Murphy. **Special Assistant to GM, International Operations:** Rene Francisco. **Special Assistant/Player Personnel:** Louie Medina. **Special Assistants to GM:** Pat Jones, Mike Toomey. **VP, Baseball Operations:** George Brett. **Director, Baseball Operations:** Lonnie Goldberg. **Director, Baseball Administration:** Jin Wong.

Video Coordinator: Mark Topping. **Cultural Development Coordinator:** Colin Gonzales. **Baseball Operations Assistant:** Kyle Vena. **Administrative Assistant:** Emily Penning. **Senior Director, Team Travel:** Jeff Davenport. **Assistant Major League Equipment Manager:** Patrick Gorman. **Visiting Clubhouse Manager:** Chuck Hawke.

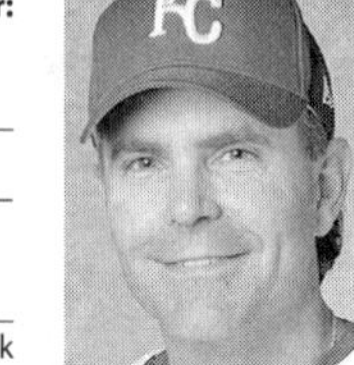

Trey Hillman

Major League Staff

Manager: Trey Hillman.

Coaches: Bench—Dave Owen; Pitching—Bob McClure; Batting—Mike Barnett; First Base—Rusty Kuntz; Third Base—Luis Silverio; Bullpen—John Mizerock.

Medical/Training

Team Physician: Dr. **Steven Joyce. Associate Physicians:** Dr. Tim Badwey, Dr. Mark Bernhardt, Dr. Dan Gurba, Dr. Thomas Phillips, Dr. Charles Rhoades.

Team Chiropractor: Patrick Hammond.

Athletic Trainer: Nick Swartz. **Assistant Athletic Trainers:** Frank Kyte and Jeff Stevenson. **Physical Therapist:** Steve Blum. **Strength/Conditioning Coordinator:** Ty Hill.

Player Development

Telephone: (816) 921-8000. **Fax:** (816) 924-0347.

Director, Player Development: J.J. Picollo. **Assistant Director, Player Development:** Scott Sharp. **Manager, Arizona Operations:** Nick Leto. **Special Assistant to Player Development:** Jack Maloof. **Assistant to Player Development:** John Wathan.

Special Assistant to Player Development/Pitching Coordinator: Bill Fischer. **Field Coordinator:** Doug Sisson. **Assistant Field Coordinator:** Tony Tijerina. **Hitting Coordinator:** Andre David. **Infield Coordinator:** Mark Harris. **Catching Coordinator:** Benny Cadahia. **Roving Coach:** Quilvio Veras.

Strength/Conditioning: Ryan Stoneberg. **Medical Coordinator:** Kyle Turner. **Rehabilitation Cooridnator:** Dale Gilbert. **Rehab Coach:** Carlos Reyes. **Minor League Equipment Coordinator:** Will Simon.

Farm System

Class	Farm Club	League	Manager	Coach	Pitching Coach
Triple-A	Omaha	Pacific Coast	Mike Jirschele	Terry Bradshaw	Tom Burgmeier
Double-A	Northwest Arkansas	Texas	Brian Poldberg	Tommy Gregg	Larry Carter
High A	Wilmington	Carolina	Darryl Kennedy	Nelson Liriano	Steve Luebber
Low A	Burlington	Midwest	Brian Rupp	Ryan Long	Doug Henry
Rookie	Idaho Falls	Pioneer	Jim Gabella	Jon Williams	Jerry Nyman
Rookie	Burlington	Appalachian	Tony Tijerina	Patrick Anderson	Bobby St. Pierre
Rookie	Royals	Arizona	Julio Bruno	Justin Gemoll	Carlos Martinez, Mark Davis
Rookie	Royals	Dominican	Unavailable	Unavailable	Unavailable

Scouting

Telephone: (816) 921-8000. **Fax:** (816) 924-0347.

Senior Director, Scouting: Deric Ladnier. **Assistant Director, Scouting:** Steve Williams. **Manager, Scouting Operations:** Linda Smith.

Professional Scout: Earl Winn (Bowling Green, KY). **Major League Scouts:** Mike Pazik (Bethesda, MD), Gene Watson (Georgetown, Texas). **Advance Scout:** Kelly Heath (Palm Harbor, FL).

National Supervisors: Marty Maier (Chesterfield, MO), Junior Vizcaino (Raleigh, NC), Dennis Woody (Danville, AR). **Regional Supervisors:** John Flannery (Austin, TX), Spencer Graham (Phoenix, AZ), Sean Rooney (Pompton Lake, NJ)

Area Scouts: Jason Bryans (Windsor, Canada), Steve Connelly (Wilson, NC), Sean Gibbs (Canton, GA), Steve Gossett (Fremont, NE), Phil Huttmann (Overland Park, KS), Gary Johnson (Costa Mesa, CA), Ben Jones (Ft. Wayne, IN), Alex Mesa (Miami, FL), Ken Munoz (Phoenix, AZ), Scott Nichols (Richland, MS), Dan Ontiveros (Laguna Niguel, CA), Cliff Pastornicky (Bradenton, FL), John Ramey (Wildomar, CA), Johnny Ramos (Carolina, PR), Scott Ramsay (Fruitland, ID), Brian Rhees (Live Oak, TX), Rick Schroeder (Pleasanton, CA), Max Semler (Lake City, FL), Dennis Sheehan (Glasco, NY), Lloyd Simmons (Oklahoma City, OK).

Latin America Supervisor: Orlando Estevez. **Dominican Republic Academy Administrator:** Pedro Silverio. **Dominican Republic Academy Coordinator:** Victor Baez. **Mexican Scouting Supervisor:** Jose Garcia. **Venezuelan Scouting Supervisor:** Richard Castro.

International Scouts: Salvador Donadelli (Venezuela), Juan Indriago (Venezuela), Joelvis Gonzalez (Venezuela), Juan Lopez (Nicaragua), Fausto Morel (Dominican Republic), Daurys Nin (Dominican Republic), Ricardo Ortiz (Panama), Edis Perez (Dominican Republic), Mike Randall (South Africa), Matthew Sheldon-Collins (Australia), Rafael Vasquez (Dominican Republic).

Los Angeles Angels

Office Address: Angel Stadium of Anaheim, 2000 Gene Autry Way, Anaheim, CA 92806.
Mailing Address: P.O. Box 2000, Anaheim, CA 92803.
Telephone: (714) 940-2000. **Fax:** (714) 940-2205.
Website: www.angelsbaseball.com

Ownership

Owner: Arturo Moreno.
President: Dennis Kuhl.

BUSINESS OPERATIONS

Arte Moreno

Finance/Administration

CFO: Bill Beverage. **Vice President, Finance/Administration:** Molly Taylor. **Controller:** Cris Fisher. **Accountants:** Lorelei Largey, Kylie McManus, Jennifer Whynott. **Assistant, Accounting:** Linda Chubak. **Director, Human Resources:** Jenny Price. **HR Generalist:** Lidia Argomaniz. **Benefits Coordinator:** Tracie Key. **Manager, Information Services:** Al Castro. **Senior Network Engineer:** Neil Farris. **Senior Customer Support Analyst:** David Yun.

Marketing, Corporate Sales

Senior Vice President, Sales/Marketing: John Carpino. **VP, Corporate Sales:** Richard McClemmy. **Corporate Account Executives:** Pennie Contos, Joe Furmanski, Michael Means, Rick Turner, Sabrina Warner. **Corporate Radio Account Executive:** Mike Gullo. **Sponsorship Services Manager:** Cesar Sanchez. **Sponsorship Services Coordinators:** Maria Dinh, Derek Ohta, Jackie Perkins.

Vice President, Marketing/Ticket Sales: Robert Alvarado. **Administrative Assistant, Marketing/Promotions:** Monica Campanis. **Administrative Assistant, Sales:** Pat Lissy. **Sales/Marketing Representative:** Ernie Prukner. **Special Events Representative:** Elaine Lombardi. **Promotions Representative:** Alex Allper. **Ticket Sales Account Executives:** Dan Carnahan, Bryan Lawrence, Carla Enriquez, Jasmin Matthews, Joseph Pinell. **Group Sales Account Executive:** Angel Rodriguez. **Ticket Sales Manager:** Tom DeTemple. **Client Services Manager:** Brian Sanders.

Public/Media Relations, Communications

Telephone: (714) 940-2014. **Fax:** (714) 940-2205.

Vice President, Communications: Tim Mead. **Administrative Assistant:** Jennifer Hoyer.

Director, Communications: Nancy Mazmanian. **Communications/Media Relations Manager:** Larry Babcock. **Media Relations Manager:** Eric Kay. **Manager, Community Development:** Matt Bennett. **Coordinator, Community Relations:** Lindsay McHolm. **Publications Manager:** Doug Ward. **Club Photographers:** Debora Robinson, John Cordes, Bob Binder.

Ballpark Operations/Facilities

Director, Ballpark Operations: Sam Maida. **Director, Facility Services:** Mike McKay. **Event Manager:** Calvin Ching, Manny Almarez.

Manager, Security: Keith Cleary. **Manager, Field/Ground Maintenance:** Barney Lopas. **Assistant Manager, Facility Services:** Linda Fitzgerald. **Maintenance Supervisor:** David Tamblyn. **Purchasing Manager:** Ron Sparks. **Purchasing Assistant:** Suzanne Peters. **Receptionists:** Sandy Sanford, Margie Walsh. **Manager, Entertainment:** Peter Bull. **Associate Producer, Video/Scoreboard Operations:** David Tsuruda. **PA Announcer:** David Courtney.

Ticketing

Manager, Ticket Operations: Sheila Brazelton. **Assistant Ticket Manager:** Susan Weiss. **Ticketing Supervisor:** Ryan Vance. **Ticketing Representatives:** Cyndi Nguyen, Clancy Holligan, Kim Weaver.

Travel, Clubhouse

Traveling Secretary: Tom Taylor. **Clubhouse Manager:** Ken Higdon.
Assistant Clubhouse Manager: Keith Tarter. **Visiting Clubhouse Manager:** Brian Harkins.
Senior Video Coordinator: Diego Lopez. **Video Coordinator:** Ruben Montano.

GENERAL INFORMATION

Stadium (year opened): Angel Stadium of Anaheim (2004).
Home Dugout: Third Base. **Playing Surface:** Grass.
Team Colors: Red, dark red, blue and silver.
Player Representative: Unavailable.

Tony Reagins

BASEBALL OPERATIONS

Vice President, General Manager: Tony Reagins.

Special Assistant to GM, Pro Scouting: Gary Sutherland.

Assistant GM: Ken Forsch. **Special Advisor:** Bill Stoneman. **Administrative Assistant, Scouting/GM:** Kathy Mair.

Major League Staff

Manager: Mike Scioscia. **Coaches:** Bench—Ron Roenicke; Pitching—Mike Butcher; Batting—Mickey Hatcher; First Base—Alfredo Griffin; Third Base—Dino Ebel; Bullpen—Orlando Mercado; Bullpen Catcher—Steve Soliz.

Medical, Training

Medical Director: Dr. **Lewis Yocum. Team Physician:** Dr. Craig Milhouse.

Head Athletic Trainer: Ned Bergert. **Athletic Trainer:** Rick Smith. **Assistant Athletic Trainer:** Adam Nevala. **Physical Therapist:** David Hogarth. **Strength/Conditioning Coach:** Brian Grapes. **Director, Legal Affairs/Risk Management:** David Cohen. **Administrative Assistant:** Chris Titchenal.

Mike Scioscia

Player Development

Telephone: (714) 940-2031. **Fax:** (714) 940-2203.

Director, Player Development: Abe Flores. **Manager, Baseball Operations:** Tory Hernandez. **Director, Arizona Operations:** Eric Blum.

Field Coordinator: Bruce Hines. **Roving Instructors:** Tom Gregorio (catching), T.J. Harrington (strength/conditioning), Geoff Hostetter (training coordinator), Bill Lachemann (catching/special assignment), Rob Picciolo (infield), Kernan Ronan (pitching), Todd Takayoshi (hitting).

Farm System

Class	Farm Club	League	Manager	Coach	Pitching Coach
Triple-A	Salt Lake	Pacific Coast	Bobby Mitchell	Jim Eppard	Erik Bennett
Double-A	Arkansas	Texas	Bobby Magallanes	Eric Owens	Ken Patterson
High A	R. Cucamonga	California	Ever Magallanes	Francisco Matos	Dan Ricabal
Low A	Cedar Rapids	Midwest	Keith Johnson	Damon Mashore	Brandon Emanuel
Rookie	Orem	Pioneer	Tom Kotchman	Brenton Del Chiaro	Zeke Zimmerman
Rookie	Tempe	Arizona	Ty Boykin	Dick Schofield	Trevor Wilson
Rookie	Angels	Dominican	Charlie Romero	Edgal Rodriguez	Santos Alcala

Scouting

Telephone: (714) 940-2038. **Fax:** (714) 940-2203.

Director, Amateur Scouting: Eddie Bane.

Major League Scouts: Marc Russo (Clearwater, FL), Rich Schlenker (Walnut Creek, CA), Jeff Schugel (Denver, CO), Brad Sloan (Brimfield, IL), Dale Sutherland (La Crescenta, CA).

National Crosscheckers: Jeff Malinoff (Lopez, WA), Ric Wilson (Chandler, AZ). **Regional Supervisors:** East—Mike Silvestri (Davie, FL); Midwest—Ron Marigny (New Orleans, LA); West—Bo Hughes (Sherman Oaks, CA).

Area Scouts: Arnold Braithwaite (Steger, IL), Jim Bryant (Chattanooga, TN), John Burden (Fairfield, OH), Tim Corcoran (La Verne, CA), Bobby DeJardin (San Clemente, CA), Demetrius Figgins (Seffner, FL), John Gracio (Mesa, AZ), Kevin Ham (El Paso, TX), Casey Harvie (Lake Stevens, WA), Tom Kotchman (Seminole, FL), Chris McAlphin (Huntersville, NC), Greg Morhardt (So. Windsor, CT), Joel Murrie (Bowling Green, KY), Dan Radcliffe (Green Belt, MD), Scott Richardson (Vacaville, CA), Jeff Scholzen (Hurricane, UT), Rob Wilfong (San Dimas, CA).

International Supervisor: Clay Daniel (Jacksonville, FL).

International Scouts: Felipe Gutierrez (Mexico), Charlie Kim (Seoul, Korea), Alex Messier (Canada), Leo Perez (Dominican Republic), Carlos Porte (Venezuela), Dennys Suarez (Venezuela), Ramon Valenzuela (Dominican Republic), Grant Weir (Australia).

Los Angeles Dodgers

Office Address: 1000 Elysian Park Ave, Los Angeles, CA 90012.
Telephone: (323) 224-1500. **Fax:** (323) 224-1269.
Website: www.dodgers.com

Ownership

Principal Owner/Chairman of the Board: Frank McCourt. **President/Vice Chairman:** Jamie McCourt. **Special Advisor to Chairman:** Tommy Lasorda.

BUSINESS OPERATIONS

Executive Vice President, COO: Dennis Mannion. **Executive VP, CMO:** Dr. Charles Steinberg. **Executive VP, Business Development:** Jeff Ingram.

Senior Vice President, Public Affairs: Howard Sunkin. **Senior VP, General Counsel:** Sam Fernandez.

Frank McCourt

Finance

CFO: Peter Wilhelm.

Director, Accounting: Mike Litvack.

Sales/Advertising/Client Services

Vice President, Sales: Sergio del Prado. **VP, Ticket Sales:** Steve Shiffman. **Director, Sponsorship Sales:** Karen Marumoto. **Director, Premium Seat Sales & Service:** David Siegel.

Communications

Director, Public Relations/Broadcasting: Josh Rawitch. **Assistant Director, Public Relations:** Joe Jareck. **Director, Publications:** Jorge Martin. **Director, Administration, Marketing/Public Relations:** Vanessa Leyvas. **Director, Community Relations:** Don Newcombe.

Stadium Operations

Vice President, Stadium Operations: Lon Rosenberg.

Director, Security: Shahram Ariane. **Facilities Manager:** Mike Grove. **Assistant Director, Stadium Operations/Turf and Grounds:** Eric Hansen.

PA Announcer: Eric Smith. **Official Scorers:** Don Hartack, Ed Munson. **Organist:** Nancy Bea Hefley.

Ticketing

Telephone: (323) 224-1471. **Fax:** (323) 224-2609.

Director, Ticket Operations: Billy Hunter. **Assistant Director, Ticket Operations:** Seth Bluman.

Travel, Clubhouse

Manager, Team Travel: Scott Akasaki.

Home Clubhouse Manager: Mitch Poole. **Visiting Clubhouse Manager:** Jerry Turner. **Advisor, Team Travel:** Billy DeLury.

GENERAL INFORMATION

Stadium (year opened): Dodger Stadium (1962).
Home Dugout: Third Base. **Playing Surface:** Grass.
Team Colors: Dodger blue and white.
Player Representative: Unavailable.

Ned Colletti

BASEBALL OPERATIONS

Telephone: (323) 224-1500. **Fax:** (323) 224-1463.

General Manager: Ned Colletti.

Vice President, Assistant GM: Kim Ng. **VP, Spring Training/Minor League Facilities:** Craig Callan.

Senior Advisor to GM: Bill LaJoie. **Special Assistant, Baseball Operations:** Jose Vizcaino. **Special Assistants to GM:** Mark Weidemaier, Vance Lovelace, Toney Howell, Bill Mueller, Rick Ragazzo. **Assistant Director, Baseball Administration:** Ellen Harrigan. **Coordinator, Minor League Administration:** Adriana Urzua.

Director, Asian Operations: Acey Kohrogi. **Director, International Operations:** Joseph Reaves.

Joe Torre

Major League Staff

Manager: Joe Torre.

Coaches: Bench— Bob Schaefer; Pitching—Rick Honeycutt; Hitting—Mike Easler; First Base—Mariano Duncan; Third Base—Larry Bowa; Bullpen—Ken Howell; Coach--Manny Mota; Special Assignment Coach--Don Mattingly.

Medical/Training

Team Physicians: Dr. Frank Jobe, Dr. Neal ElAttrache, Dr. Ken Landis, Dr. Ralph Gambardella.

Director, Medical Services/Head Trainer: Stan Conte. **Assistant Athletic Trainers:** Todd Tomczyk, Rick Lembo. **Strength/Conditioning Coach:** Brendon Huttman. **Physical Therapist:** Sue Falsone. **Massage Therapist:** Ichiro Tani.

Player Development

Telephone: (323) 224-1431. **Fax:** (323) 224-1359.

Assistant GM, Player Development: De Jon Watson.

Assistant Director, Player Development: Chris Haydock. **Assistant Director, International Player Development:** Luchy Guerra.

Head Minor League Trainer: Greg Harrel

Roving Coordinators: Travis Barbary (catching), David Rivera (rehab), P.J. Carey (field), Rodney McCray (outfield/base running), Matt Martin (infield), Marty Reed (pitching), David Rivera (physical therapy), Gene Clines (hitting).

Training Coordinator: Carlos Olivas. **Director, Campo Las Palmas/Dominican Republic:** Eleodoro Arias. **Field Coordinator:** Antonio Bautista. **Supervisor, Venezuelan Operations:** Camilo Pascual.

Farm System

Class	Farm Team	League	Manager	Coach	Pitching Coach
Triple-A	Las Vegas	Pacific Coast	Lorenzo Bundy	John Moses	Jim Slaton
Double-A	Jacksonville	Southern	John Shoemaker	Luis Salazar	Glenn Dishman
High A	Inland Empire	California	John Valentin	Henry Cruz	Charlie Hough
Low A	Great Lakes	Midwest	Juan Bustabad	Garey Ingram	Danny Darwin
Rookie	Ogden	Pioneer	Mike Brumley	Unavailable	Craig Bjornson
Rookie	Vero Beach	Gulf Coast	Jeff Carter	Kenny Dominguez	Casey Deskins
Rookie	Dodgers	Dominican	Unavailable	Unavailable	Unavailable

Scouting

Assistant GM, Scouting: Logan White.

Director, Amateur Scouting: Tim Hallgren.

Special Advisor, Amateur Scouting/National Crosschecker: Gib Bodet (San Clemente, CA). **National Crosschecker:** Paul Fryer (Calabassas, CA).

Manager, Scouting: Jane Capobianco. **Scouting Coordinator:** Trey Magnuson.

East Coast Supervisor: Marty Lamb (Nicholasville, KY). **Midwest Supervisor:** Gary Nickels (Naperville, IL). **West Coast Supervisor:** Tom Thomas (Phoenix, AZ).

Advance Scouts: Dan Freed, Carl Lowenstein, Al La Macchia, Ron Rizzi.

Area Scouts: Fred Costello (Livermore, CA); Chuck Crim (Santa Clarita, CA); Bobby Darwin (Cerritos, CA); Manny Estrada (Brandon, FL); Scott Hennessey (Jacksonville, FL); Calvin Jones (Highland Village, TX); Henry Jones (Vancouver, WA); Lon Joyce (Spartanburg, SC); John Kosciak (Milford, MA); Dennis Moeller (Birmingham, AL); Matthew Paul (Hermitage, TN); Clair Rierson (Frederick, MD); Chet Sergo (Stoughton, WI); Chris Smith (Montgomery, TX); Brian Stephenson (Chandler, AZ); Mitch Webster (Great Bend, KS).

International Scouts: Ralph Avila (Dominican Republic); Elvio Jimenez (Dominican Republic); Gustavo Zapata (Central America); Rolando Chirino (Curacao); Ezequiel Sepulveda (Dominican Republic); Rafael Rijo (Dominican Republic); Bienvenido Tavarez (Dominican Republic); Wilton Guerrero (Dominican Republic); Keiichi Kojima (Japan); Byung-Hwan An (Korea); Mike Brito (Mexico); Camilo Pascual (Venezuela); Bernardo Torres (Venezuela); Oswaldo Villalobos (Venezuela).

Part-time Scouts: George Genovese, Artie Harris, Luis Faccio, Greg Goodwin.

Milwaukee Brewers

Office Address: Miller Park, One Brewers Way, Milwaukee, WI 53214.
Telephone: (414) 902-4400. **Fax:** (414) 902-4053.
Website: www.brewers.com

Ownership

Operated By: Milwaukee Brewers Baseball Club.
Chairman/Principal Owner: Mark Attanasio.

BUSINESS OPERATIONS

Executive Vice President, Business Operations: Rick Schlesinger. **Executive VP, Finance and Administration:** Robert Quinn Jr. **VP, General Counsel:** Marti Wronski. **Executive Assistant, Business Operations:** Adela Reeve. **Executive Assistant, Ownership Group:** Samantha Ernest.

Mark Attanasio

Finance/Accounting

Vice President, Controller: Joe Zidanic. **Director, Reporting/Special Projects, Finance/Administration:** Steve O'Connell. **Financial Analyst:** Wes Seidel. **Accounting Manager:** Vicki Wise. **Staff Accountant:** Meredith Zaffrann.

Vice President, Human Resources/Office Management: Sally Andrist. **Human Resources Generalist:** Marnie Peterson.

Vice President, Technology/Information Systems: John Winborn. **Network Administrator:** Corey Kmichik. **Systems Support Specialist:** Adam Bauer.

Marketing/Corporate Sponsorships

Vice President, Corporate Marketing: Tom Hecht. **Senior Directors, Corporate Marketing:** Greg Hilt, Jason Hartlund. **Senior Director, Marketing:** Kathy Schwab. **Director, Corporate Marketing:** Dave Tamburrino. **Account Executives, Suites:** Andrew Pauls, Chris Rothwell. **Director, Corporate Suite Services:** Patty Harsch. **Account Coordinators:** David Barnes, Carrie Strueder, Kelly Bigelbach. **Manager, Marketing Promotions:** Caitlin Moyer.

Senior Director, Broadcasting/Entertainment: Aleta Mercer. **Manager, Audio/Video Productions:** Deron Anderson. **Manager, Entertainment/Broadcasting:** Andrew Olson.

Media Relations/Communications

Telephone: (414) 902-4500. **Fax:** (414) 902-4053.

Vice President, Communications: Tyler Barnes. **Director, Media Relations:** Mike Vassallo. **Manager, Media Relations:** John H. Steinmiller. **Coordinator, Media Relations:** Ken Spindler. **Team Photographer:** Scott Paulus. **Community Relations Manager:** Katina Shaw. **Community Relations Assistant:** Erica Bowring. **Manager, Youth Baseball Programs:** Larry Hisle. **President, Brewers Charities:** Lynn Sprangers.

Stadium Operations

Director, Stadium Operations: Bob Hallas. **Manager, Event Services:** Matt Kenny. **Director, Grounds:** Gary Vanden Berg. **Landscape Manager:** Miranda Bintley. **Supervisor, Warehouse:** Patrick Rogo. **Senior Director, Brewers Enterprises:** Wil Gorman. **Administrative Assistant/Miller Park Operations:** Jennacy Cruz. **Receptionist:** Willa Oden. **Mailroom/Receptionist:** Maria Saldana.

PA Announcer: Robb Edwards. **Official Scorers:** Tim O'Driscoll, Wayne Franke.

Ticketing

Telephone: (414) 902-4000. **Fax:** (414) 902-4100.

Vice President, Consumer Marketing: Todd Taylor. **Senior Director, Ticket Sales:** Jim Bathey. **Manager, Group Sales:** Chris Barlow. **Manager, Season Ticket Sales:** Billy Freiss. **Administrative Assistant:** Irene Bolton. **Assistant Director, Ticket Services:** Nancy Jorgensen. **Supervisor, Ticket Phone Center:** Chad Olson. **Senior Account Executives:** Nathan Hardwick, Bill Junker, Kara Kabitzke, Jeff Hibicke, Jason Massopust, Chris Kimball. **Senior Account Executive, Group Sales:** Shaunna Richardson. **Senior Account Executives:** Ben Kaebisch, Jedidiah Justman.

Travel, Clubhouse

Director, Team Travel: Dan Larrea. **Director, Clubhouse Operations/Equipment Manager:** Tony Migliaccio. **Visiting Clubhouse Manager:** Phil Rozewicz. **Assistant, Home Clubhouse:** Jason Shawger.

GENERAL INFORMATION

Stadium (year opened): Miller Park (2001).
Home Dugout: First Base. **Playing Surface:** Grass.
Team Colors: Navy blue, gold and white.
Player Representative: Chris Capuano.

Doug Melvin

BASEBALL OPERATIONS

Telephone: (414) 902-4400. **Fax:** (414) 902-4059.

Executive Vice President, General Manager: Doug Melvin.

VP, Assistant GM: Gord Ash. **Senior Special Assistant to GM/Baseball Operations:** Dan O'Brien.

Director, Administration/Player Development and Scouting: Tom Flanagan. **Manager, Advance Scouting/Baseball Research:** Karl Mueller Coordinator, Baseball Research/Special Projects: Mike Schwartz. **Coordinator, Professional Scouting:** Zack Minasian. **Coaching Assistant/Digital Media Coordinator:** Joe Crawford. **Senior Administrator, Baseball Operations:** Barb Stark.

Major League Staff

Manager: Ned Yost.

Coaches: Bench—Ted Simmons; Pitching—Mike Maddux; Batting—Jim Skaalen; First Base—Ed Sedar; Third Base—Dale Sveum; Bullpen—Bill Castro.

Ned Yost

Medical, Training

Head Team Physician: Dr. William Raasch. **Head Athletic Trainer:** Roger Caplinger. **Assistant Athletic Trainer/Coordinator, Strength and Conditioning:** Dan Wright. **Major League Conditioning Specialist:** Chris Joyner.

Player Development

Special Assistant to GM/Player Development: Reid Nichols (Phoenix, AZ).

Business Manager, Player Development/Minor League Operations: Scott Martens. **Assistant Director, Player Development:** Tony Diggs. **Coordinator, Administration/Player Development:** Mark Mueller.

Field Coordinator: Charlie Greene. **Coordinators:** Frank Neville (medical), Jim Rooney (pitching), Mike Lum (hitting). **Roving Instructors:** Charlie Greene (catching), Garth lorg (roving infield), Ken Berry (roving outfield).

Employee Assistance Coordinator: Tim Hewes.

Equipment Manager: J.R. Rinaldi. **Clubhouse Manager, Arizona:** Matt Bass.

Farm System

Class	Farm Club	League	Manager	Coach	Pitching Coach
Triple-A	Nashville	Pacific Coast	Frank Kremblas	Harry Spilman	Stan Kyles
Double-A	Huntsville	Southern	Don Money	Sandy Guerrero	Chris Hook
High A	Brevard County	Florida State	Mike Guerrero	Corey Hart	Fred Dabney
Low A	West Virginia	South Atlantic	Jeff Isom	Jim Lett	John Curtis
Rookie	Helena	Pioneer	Rene Gonzales	Norberto Martin	Aris Tirado
Rookie	Brewers	Arizona	Tony Diggs	Angel Echevarria	Steve Cline/Jose Nunez

Scouting

Telephone: (414) 902-4400. **Fax:** (414) 902-4059.

Vice President, Special Assistant to GM, Player Personnel: Jack Zdurienick.

Special Assistant to GM/Director, Professional Scouting: Dick Groch (Marysville, MI).

Assistant Director, Amateur Scouting: Tony Blengino. **Coordinator, Administration/Amateur Scouting:** Amanda Kropp.

Professional Scouts: Lary Aaron (Atlanta, GA), Garrett Ball (Milwaukee, WI), Chris Bourjos (Scottsdale, AZ), Brad Del Barba (Ft. Mitchell, KY), Ben McClure (Hummelstown, PA) , Tom Mooney (Pittsfield, MA), Marv Thompson (West Jordan, UT), Tom Wheeler (Martinez, CA), Leon Wurth (Nashville, TN).

Roving Crosschecker: Jeff Cornell (Lee's Summit, MO). **Regional Supervisors:** West—Bruce Seid (Capistrano Beach, CA); Midwest - Ray Montgomery (Pearland, TX); East—Tom McNamara (Lakewood Ranch, FL).

Area Scouts: Josh Belovsky (Orange, CA), Kevin Clouser (Phoenix, AZ), Kevin Ellis (Frisco, TX), Mike Farrell (Indianapolis, IN), Ed Fastaia (Lake Ronkonkoma, NY), Manolo Hernandez (Puerto Rico), Harvey Kuenn, Jr. (New Berlin, WI), Joe Mason (Millbrook, AL), Justin McCray (Davis, CA), Tim McIlvaine (Tampa, FL), Rene Mons (Manchester, NH), Dan Nellum (Crofton, MD), Brandon Newell (Belingham, WA), Doug Reynolds (Tallahassee, FL), Corey Rodriguez (Hermosa Beach, CA), Brian Sankey (Lakeway, TX), Charles Sullivan (Miami, FL).

Part-time Scouts: John Bushart (West Hills, CA), Don Fontana (Pittsburgh, PA), Carmen Fusco (Mechanicsburg, PA), Joe Hodges (Rockwood, TN), Roger Janeway (Englewood, OH), Johnny Logan (Milwaukee, WI), J.R. Salinas (Houston, TX), Brad Stoll (Lawrence, KS).

Latin American Supervisor: Fernando Arango (Davie, FL). **International Scouts:** Jay Lapp (London, Ontario, Canada), Marty Lehn (White Rock, British Columbia, Canada), John Haar (Burnaby, British Columbia, Canada), Mike LaBossiere (Brandon, Manitoba, Canada), J.P. Roy (Saint Nicolas, Quebec, Canada), Fausto Sosa Pena (Dominican Republic), Freddy Torres (Venezuela), Rafael Espinal (Dominican Republic), Jose Guarache (Venezuela), Jose Zambrano (Venezuela).

Minnesota Twins

Office Address: 34 Kirby Puckett Place, Minneapolis, MN 55415.
Telephone: (612) 375-1366. **Fax:** (612) 375-7480.
Website: www.twinsbaseball.com.

Ownership

Operated By: The Minnesota Twins.
Owner: Carl Pohlad.
Chairman, Executive Committee: Howard Fox. **Executive Board:** Carl Pohlad, James Pohlad, Robert Pohlad, William Pohlad, Dave St. Peter.

Carl Pohlad

BUSINESS OPERATIONS

President, Minnesota Twins: Dave St. Peter. **President, Twins Sports Inc.:** Jerry Bell. **Senior Vice President, Business Development:** Laura Day.

New Ballpark Development

Project Manager: John Goeckel. **Director, New Ballpark Development:** Scott O'Connell. **Ballpark Development, Finance/Accounting:** Dan Starkey.

Human Resources/Finance/Technology

Vice President, Human Resources/Diversity: Raenell Dorn. **Payroll Manager:** Lori Beasley. **Benefits Manager:** Leticia Silva. **Workman's Compensation Coordinator:** Tina Flowers.

Senior Vice President, Business Administration: Kip Elliott. **Director, Finance:** Andy Weinstein. **Manager, Ticket Accounting:** Jerry McLaughlin. **Accountant:** Lyndsey Taylor. **Accounts Payable:** Amy Fong-Christianson.

Vice President, Technology: John Avenson. **Director, Information Systems:** Wade Navratil. **Manager, Technology Infrastructure:** Tony Persio. **Technical Services Specialist:** Brent Hildebrandt. **Special Projects Programmer:** Kyle Mai.

Marketing/Broadcasting

Vice President, Marketing: Patrick Klinger. **Director, Advertising:** Nancy O'Brien. **Director, Event Marketing:** Heidi Sammon. **Promotions Coordinator:** Julie Rohloff. **Director, Broadcasting/Game Presentation:** Andy Price. **Radio Network Producer:** Mark Genosky. **Radio Network Studio Host:** Kris Atteberry. **Radio Engineer:** Kyle Hammer.

Corporate Partnerships

Vice President, Corporate Partnerships: Eric Curry. **Senior Manager, Client Services:** Bodie Forsling. **Corporate Partnership Sales/Services Manager:** Jordan Woodcroft. **Corporate Client Services Manager:** Katie Beaulieu. **Corporate Client Services Coordinator:** Paulette Cheatham. **Coordinator, Traffic and Service:** Amy Johnson.

Communications

Telephone: (612) 375-7471. **Fax:** (612) 375-7473.

Director, Baseball Communications: Mike Herman. **Manager, Publications/Media Services:** Molly Gallatin. **Manager, Baseball Communications:** Dustin Morse. **Coordinator, Baseball Communications:** Mitch Hestad.

Public Affairs

Executive Director, Public Affairs/Twins Community Fund: Kevin Smith. **Director, Community Affairs:** Bryan Donaldson. **Manager, Corporate Communications:** Andrea Larson. **Community Fund Coordinator:** Stephanie Johnson. **Community Programs Coordinator:** Josh Ortiz. **Community Relations Coordinator:** Gloria Westerdahl.

Ticketing

Telephone: (612) 338-9467. **Fax:** (612) 375-7464.

Vice President, Ticket Sales/Service: Steve Smith. **Manager, Account Services:** Chris Malek. **Manager, Group Sales Development:** Rob Malec. **Manager, Sales Development:** Eric Hudson. **Manager, Ticket Sales/Service Support:** Beth Vail.

Director, Ticket Operations: Paul Froehle. **Manager, Box Office:** Mike Stiles. **Supervisor, Ticket Office:** Karl Dadenbach. **Manager, Call Center/New Ballpark Migration:** Patrick Forsland.

Stadium Operations

Vice President, Operations: Matt Hoy. **Director, Stadium Operations:** Dave Horsman. **Manager, Stadium Operations:** Dan Smoliak. **Manager, Security:** Dick Dugan. **Manager, Merchandise:** Matt Noll. **PA Announcer:** Adam Abrams. **Equipment Manager:** Rod McCormick. **Visitors Clubhouse:** Troy Matchan. **Manager, Major League Video:** Sean Harlin.

GENERAL INFORMATION

Stadium (year opened): Hubert H. Humphrey Metrodome (1982).
Home Dugout: Third Base. Playing Surface: Field Turf.
Team Colors: Burgundy, navy blue and white.
Team Representative: Unavailable.

Bill Smith

BASEBALL OPERATIONS

Telephone: (612) 375-7484. **Fax:** (612) 375-7417.

Senior Vice President, General Manager: Bill Smith.

Vice President, Player Personnel: Mike Radcliff. **Assistant GM:** Rob Antony. **Senior Advisor to GM:** Terry Ryan. **Special Assistants to GM:** Joe McIlvaine, Tom Kelly. **Director, Baseball Operations:** Brad Steil. **Baseball Operations Assistant:** Joe Pohlad. **Administrative Assistant to GM:** Jack Goin. **Director, Team Travel:** Remzi Kiratli.

Major League Staff

Manager: Ron Gardenhire.

Coaches: Bench—Steve Liddle; Pitching—Rick Anderson; Batting—Joe Varva; First Base—Jerry White; Third Base—Scott Ulger; Bullpen—Rick Stelmaszek.

Ron Gardenhire

Medical, Training

Club Physicians: Dr. Dan Buss, Dr. Vijay Eyunni, Dr. Tom Jetzer, Dr. John Steubs, Dr. Jon Hallberg, Dr. Gustavo Navarrete.

Head Trainer: Rick McWane. **Assistant Trainer:** Dave Pruemer. **Strength/Conditioning Coach:** Perry Castellano.

Player Development

Telephone: (612) 375-7488. **Fax:** (612) 375-7417.

Director, Minor Leagues: Jim Rantz.

Administrative Assistant, Minor Leagues: Kate Townley. **Minor League Field Coordinator:** Joel Lepel.

Farm System

Class	Farm Club	League	Manager	Coach	Pitching Coach
Triple-A	Rochester	International	Stan Cliburn	Riccardo Ingram	Stu Cliburn
Double-A	New Britain	Eastern	Bobby Cuellar	Floyd Rayford	Steve Mintz
High A	Fort Myers	Florida State	Jeff Smith	Jim Dwyer	Eric Rasmussen
Low A	Beloit	Midwest	Nelson Prada	Rudy Hernandez	Gary Lucas
Rookie	Elizabethton	Appalachian	Ray Smith	Jeff Reed	Jim Shellenback
Rookie	Fort Myers	Gulf Coast	Jake Mauer	Milt Cuyler	Ivan Arteaga
Rookie	Twins	Dominican	Julio Paula	Claudio Almonte	Pablo Frias
Rookie	Twins	Venezuela	Asdrubal Estrada	Ramon Borrego	Luis Ramirez

Scouting

Telephone: (612) 375-7525. **Fax:** (612) 375-7417.

Director, Scouting: Deron Johnson (Sacramento, CA)

Special Assignment Scouts: Tom Kelly (Maplewood, MN), Joe McIlvaine (Newton Square, PA).

Major League Scouts: Ken Compton (Cypress, CA), Earl Frishman (Tampa, FL), Bob Hegman (Lee's Summit, MO).

Coordinator, Professional Scouting: Vern Followell (Buena Park, CA). **Pro Scout:** Bill Milos (Crown Point, IN).

Scouting Supervisors: East—Mark Quimuyog (Lynn Haven, FL), West—Sean Johnson (Chandler, AZ), Mideast—Tim O'Neil (Lexington, KY), Midwest—Mike Ruth (Lee's Summit, MO).

Area Scouts: Jeremy Booth (Florence, KY), Billy Corrigan (Tampa, FL) Dan Cox (Santa Ana, CA), JR DiMercurio (Kansas City, MO), Mike Eaglin (Los Angeles, CA), Marty Esposito (Robinson, TX), John Leavitt (Garden Grove, CA), Bill Lohr (Centralia, WA), Hector Otero (Trujillo Alto, CA/Puerto Rico), Jeff Pohl (Evansville, IN), Jack Powell (Sweetwater, TN), Ricky Taylor (Hickory, NC), Jay Weitzel (Salamanca, NY), Ted Williams (Peoria, AZ), John Wilson (Blairstown, NJ), Mark Wilson (Lindstrom, MN).

Coordinator, International Scouting: Howard Norsetter (Australia).

Coordinator, Latin American Scouting: Jose Marzan

International Scouts: Cary Broder (Taiwan), John Cortese (Italy), Glenn Godwin (Europe, Africa), Fred Guerrero (Dominican Republic), Andy Johnson (Europe), David Kim (South Korea), Jose Leon (Venezuela, Panama), Jim Ridley (Canada), Kenny Su (Taiwan), Koji Takahashi (Japan).

New York Mets

Office Address: 123-01 Roosevelt Ave, Flushing, NY 11368.
Telephone: (718) 507-6387. **Fax:** (718) 507-6395.
Website: www.mets.com.

Ownership

Operated By: Sterling Mets LP.
Chairman/CEO: Fred Wilpon; President: Saul Katz; Chief Operating Officer: Jeff Wilpon.
Board of Directors: Fred Wilpon, Saul Katz, Jeff Wilpon, Richard Wilpon, Michael Katz, David Katz, Tom Osterman, Arthur Friedman, Steve Greenberg, Stuart Sucherman.

Fred Wilpon

BUSINESS OPERATIONS

Executive Vice President, Business Operations: David Howard. **Executive VP/General Counsel:** David Cohen.

Finance

CFO: Mark Peskin. **Vice President/Controller:** Lenny Labita. **Assistant Controller:** Rebecca Landau-Mahadeva.

Marketing, Sales

Senior Vice President, Marketing/Communications: David Newman. **Senior Director, Marketing:** Tina Mannix. **Senior Director, Marketing Productions:** Tim Gunkel. **Director, Broadcasting/Special Events:** Lorraine Hamilton. **Director, Marketing Communications:** Jill Grabill. **Director, Community Outreach:** Jill Knee.

Senior Vice President, Corporate Sales/Services: Tom Murphy. **VP, Corporate Sales/ Services:** Paul Asencio. **VP, Venue Services:** Mike Landeen. **Director, Corporate Services:** Jim Plummer. **Director, Corporate Sales/Services:** Greg Stengel. **Director, Suite Sales/Services:** Patrick Jones.

Media Relations

Telephone: (718) 565-4330. **Fax:** (718) 639-3619.
Vice President, Media Relations: Jay Horwitz.
Director, Media Relations: Shannon Forde. **Manager, Media Relations:** Ethan Wilson. **Media Relations Coordinators:** Billy Harner, Valerie Tovar.

Stadium Operations

Vice President, Facilities: Karl Smolarz.
Director, Stadium Operations: Sue Lucchi. **Assistant Stadium Manager:** Mike Dohnert. **Manager, Field Operations:** Bill Deacon.
Senior Director, Information Technology: Joe Milone. **PA Announcer:** Alex Anthony. **Official Scorers:** Bill Shannon, Howie Karpin, Jordan Sprechman, David Freeman, Billy Altman.

Ticketing

Telephone: (718) 507-8499. **Fax:** (718) 507-6369.
Vice President, Ticket Sales/Services: Bill Ianniciello. **Senior Director, Ticket Operations:** Dan DeMato. **Senior Director, Group Sales/Ticket Sales Services:** Tom Fersch. **Director, Ticket Sales Development:** Jamie Ozure. **Director, Ticket Operations:** John Giglio.

Travel, Clubhouse

Clubhouse Manager, Associate Travel Director: Charlie Samuels.
Assistant Equipment Manager: Dave Berni. **Visiting Clubhouse Manager:** Tony Carullo. **Video Editor:** Joe Scarola.

GENERAL INFORMATION

Stadium (year opened): Shea Stadium (1964).
Home Dugout: First Base. **Playing Surface:** Grass.
Team Colors: Blue and orange.
Player Representative: Aaron Heilman.

Omar Minaya

BASEBALL OPERATIONS

Telephone: (718) 565-4315. **Fax:** (718) 507-6391.

Executive Vice President/General Manager: Omar Minaya.

Assistant GM: John Ricco. **VP, Player Development:** Tony Bernazard. **VP, Scouting:** Sandy Johnson. **Special Assistants to GM:** Bryan Lambe, Ramon Pena. **Executive Assistant to GM:** Leonor Barua.

Coordinator, Baseball Operations: Adam Fisher. **Statistical Analyst:** Ben Baumer.

Major League Staff

Manger: Willie Randolph.

Coaches: Bench—Jerry Manuel; Pitching—Rick Peterson; Batting—Howard Johnson; First Base—Tom Nieto; Third Base—Sandy Alomar, Jr.; Bullpen—Guy Conti.

Willie Randolph

Medical, Training

Medical Director: Dr. **David Altchek. Team Physician:** Dr. Struan Coleman.

Head Trainer: Ray Ramirez. **Assistant Trainer:** Mike Herbst.

Coordinator, Strength/Conditioning: Rick Slate.

Player Development

Telephone: (718) 565-4302. **Fax:** (718) 205-7920.

Director, Minor League Operations: Adam Wogan.

Coordinator, Minor League Operations: Jon Miller. **Field Coordinator:** Luis Aguayo. **Coordinator, Instruction/Infield:** Kevin Morgan. **Hitting Coordinator:** Lamar Johnson. **Pitching Coordinator:** Rick Waits. **Catching Coordinator:** Bob Natal. **Outfield/Baserunning/Bunting Coordinator:** Sonny Jackson.

Coordinator, Strength/Conditioning: Jason Craig. **Assistant Coordinator, Strength/Conditioning:** Ken Coward. **Athletic Training Coordinator:** Mark Rogow. **Coordinator, Rehabilitation Pitching:** Randy Niemann. **Coordinator, Rehabilitation:** John Zajac. **Latin American Field Coordinator:** Rafael Landestoy. **Latin American Pitching Coordinator:** Mark Brewer. **Special Consultant:** Al Jackson. **Equipment Manager:** Kevin Kierst. **Assistant Equipment Manager:** Jack Brenner.

Farm System

Class	Farm Club	League	Manager	Coach(es)	Pitching Coach
Triple-A	New Orleans	Pacific Coast	Ken Oberkfell	Jack Voigt	Dan Warthen
Double-A	Binghamton	Eastern	Mako Oliveras	Luis Natera	Ricky Bones
High A	St. Lucie	Florida State	Tim Teufel	M. Hart/J. Fuentes	Dan Murray
Low A	Savannah	South Atlantic	Donovan Mitchell	G. Greer/P. Lopez	Jonathan Hurst
Short-season	Brooklyn	New York-Penn	Edgar Alfonzo	Guadalupe Jabalera	Hector Berrios
Rookie	Kingsport	Appalachian	Nick Leyva	Ryan Ellis	Marc Valdes
Rookie	Mets	Gulf Coast	Unavailable	B. Floyd/T. McCraw	Robert Ellis
Rookie	Mets	Dominican	Liliano Castro	F. Cabrera/L. Rojas	Benjamin Marte
Rookie	Mets	Venezuelan	Leo Hernandez	Y. Garcia/E. Gonzalez	Rafael Lazo

Scouting

Telephone: (718) 565-4311. **Fax:** (718) 205-7920.

Director, Amateur Scouting: Rudy Terrasas. **Assistant, Amateur Scouting:** Elizabeth Gadsden. **Coordinator, Amateur Scouting:** Ian Levin.

Assistant, Professional/International Scouting: Anne Fairbanks.

Advance Scout: Bob Johnson (University Park, FL).

Professional Scouts: Mack Babitt (Richmond, CA), Russ Bove (Longwood, FL), Howie Freiling (Apex, NC), Roland Johnson (Newington, CT), Jerry Krause (Highland Park, IL), Harry Minor (Long Beach, CA), Jim Thompson (Wallingford, PA).

National Crosschecker: David Lakey (Kingwood, TX).

Regional Supervisors: East—Steve Barningham (Land O'Lakes, FL), Midwest—Jeff Edwards (Humble, TX), West—Tim Fortugno (Elk Grove, CA).

Area Supervisors: Mike Brown (Chandler, AZ), Erwin Bryant (Lexington, KY), Larry Chase (Pearcy, AR), Ray Corbett (College Station, TX), Doug Gassaway (Blum, TX), Scott Hunter (Mount Laurel, NJ), Larry Izzo, Jr. (Deer Park, NY), Tommy Jackson (Jupiter, FL), Benny Latino III (Hammond, LA), Steve Leavitt (Huntington Beach, CA), Fred Mazuca (Tustin, CA), Marlin McPhail (Irmo, SC), Les Parker (Hudson, FL), Claude Pelletier (St. Lazare, Quebec) (Canada), Art Pontarelli (Lincoln, RI), Jim Reeves (Camas, WA), Junior Roman (San Sebastian, PR), Doug Thurman (San Jose, CA), Scott Trcka (Hobart, IN), Matt Wondolowski (Washington, DC).

Director, Pacific Rim Scouting: Isao O'Jimi. **Director, International Scouting:** Ismael Cruz. **International Scouts:** Modesto Abreu (Dominican Republic), Robert Alfonzo (Venezuela), Marciano Alvarez (Dominican Republic), Claudio Brito (Dominican Republic), Lionel Chattelle (Germany), David Davalillo (Venezuela), Tony Harris (Australia), Harold Herrera (Colombia), Ivanosky Wong Hurtado (Venezuela), Rafael Arturo Jimenez (Venezuela), Luis Marquez (Venezuela), Kevin Park (S. Korea), Eduardo Urdaneta Reverol (Venezuela), Pablo Garcia Rodriguez (Venezuela), Franklin Taveras (Dominican Republic), Jose Rosario Valdez (Dominican Republic), Marcelino Vallejo (Dominican Republic), Caryl Van Zanten (Netherland Antilles), Victor Hugo Vasquez (Venezuela), Alex Zapata (Panama).

New York Yankees

Office Address: Yankee Stadium, East 161st Street and River Avenue, Bronx, NY 10451.
Telephone: (718) 293-4300. **Fax:** (718) 293-8431.
Website: www.yankees.com

Ownership

Principal Owner: George Steinbrenner.

General Partner/Chairman, Yankee Global Enterprises LLC: Harold Steinbrenner.

Senior Vice President, New York Yankees: Henry Steinbrenner. **Senior VP, New Stadium Public Affairs:** Jennifer Steinbrenner Swindal. **Senior VP, New York Yankees:** Felix Lopez.

George Steinbrenner

BUSINESS OPERATIONS

President: Randy Levine.

COO: Lonn Trost.

Senior Vice President, Marketing: Deborah Tymon. **Senior VP, Strategic Ventures:** Marty Greenspun. **Senior VP, Sponsorship Sales/Service:** Michael Tusiani.

Vice President, Finance: Robert Brown. **VP, Chief Security Officer:** Sonny Hight. **VP, Corporate/Community Relations:** Brian Smith. **VP, Business Development:** Jim Ross.

CFO/Director, Financial Operations: Scott Krug.

Deputy General Counsel/Vice President, Legal Affairs: Alan Chang.

Special Advisory Group: Yogi Berra, Reggie Jackson.

Business Development

Director, Premium Services: Harvey Winston.

Corporate/Community Relations

Director, Latino Affairs: Manny Garcia.

Corporate Sales/Sponsorships

Director, Corporate Sales/Sponsorships: John Penhollow.

Media Relations/Publicity

Telephone: (718) 579-4460. **Fax:** (718) 293-8414.

Senior Media Advisor: Arthur Richman.

Director, Media Relations/Publicity: Jason Zillo. **Managers, Media Relations/Publicity:** Jason Latimer, Michael Margolis. **Coordinators, Media Relations/Publicity:** Loran Moran, Connie Schwab. **Media Advisor, Pacific Rim:** Isao Hirooka. **Administrative Assistant, Media Relations:** Dolores Hernandez.

Office Operations

Director, Human Resources: Lea del Rosario.

Stadium Operations

Senior Director, Stadium Operations: Doug Behar. **Senior Director, Scoreboard/Broadcasting:** Mike Bonner. **Senior Director, Technology:** Mike Lane. **Stadium Superintendent:** Pete Pullara. **Head Groundskeeper:** Dan Cunningham. **Director, Concessions:** Joel White. **Director, Entertainment:** Stanley Kay. **Director, Hospitality:** David Bernstein. **Director, Stadium Tours:** Tony Morante. **PA Announcer:** Bob Sheppard.

Ticketing

Telephone: (718) 293-6000. **Fax:** (718) 293-4841.

Senior Director, Ticket Operations: Irfan Kirimca.

Executive Director, Ticket Operations: Kevin Dart. **Executive Director, Ticket Finance:** Jeff Kline.

Travel, Clubhouse

Traveling Secretary: Ben Tuliebitz.

Home Clubhouse Manager: Rob Cucuzza. **Visiting Clubhouse Manager:** Lou Cucuzza Jr. **Video Operations, Batting Practice Pitcher:** Charlie Wonsowicz.

GENERAL INFORMATION

Stadium (year opened): Yankee Stadium (1923).
Home Dugout: First Base. **Playing Surface:** Grass.
Team Colors: Navy blue and white.
Player Representative: Mike Mussina.

Brian Cashman

BASEBALL OPERATIONS

Telephone: (718) 293-4300. **Fax:** (718) 293-0015.

Senior Vice President/General Manager: Brian Cashman.

Senior VP, Special Advisor: Gene Michael. **VP, Assistant GM:** Jean Afterman. **Special Assistants to GM:** Gordon Blakeley, Stump Merrill.

Director, Quantitative Analysis: Michael Fishman. **Director, Mental Conditioning:** Chad Bohling. **Coordinator, Major League Operations:** Anthony Flynn. **Assistant, Baseball Operations:** Steve Martone. **Systems Architect:** Brian Nicosia. **Administrative Assistant:** Mary Pellino.

Major League Staff

Manager: Joe Girardi.

Coaches: Bench—Rob Thomson; Pitching—Dave Eiland; Batting—Kevin Long; First Base—Tony Pena; Third Base—Bobby Meacham; Bullpen—Mike Harkey.

Joe Girardi

Medical/Training

Team Physician, New York: Dr. Stuart Hershon. **Team Physician, Tampa:** Dr. Andrew Boyer.

Head Trainer: Gene Monahan. **Assistant Trainer:** Steve Donohue. **Strength/Conditioning Coach:** Dana Cavalea. **Director, Mental Conditioning:** Chad Bohling. **Massage Therapist:** Scott Yelin.

Player Development

Telephone: (813) 875-7569. **Fax:** (813) 873-2302.

Senior Vice President, Baseball Operations: Mark Newman. **VP, Player Personnel:** Billy Connors. **Director, Player Development:** Pat Roessler. **Assistant Director, Player Development:** Eric Schmitt. **Administrative Assistant:** Jackie Williams.

Minor League Coordinators: Nardi Contreras (pitching), James Rowson (hitting), Jack Hubbard (outfield), Mick Kelleher (infield), Julio Mosquera (Catching).

Head Trainer: Mark Littlefield. **Coordinator, Strength/Conditioning:** Mike Wickland. **Assistant, Strength/Conditioning:** Javier Alvidrez. **Equipment Manager:** David Hays.

Farm System

Class	Farm Club	League	Manager	Coach	Pitching Coach
Triple-A	Scranton/W.B.	International	Dave Miley	Butch Wynegar	Rafael Chavez
Double-A	Trenton	Eastern	Tony Franklin	Tom Wilson	Scott Aldred
High A	Tampa	Florida State	Luis Sojo	Aaron Ledesma	Greg Pavlick
Low A	Charleston	South Atlantic	Torre Tyson	Greg Colbrunn	Jeff Ware
Short-season	Staten Island	New York-Penn	Pat McMahon	Ty Hawkins	Pat Daneker
Rookie	Tampa	Gulf Coast	Jody Reed	Derek Shumpert	Carlos Chantres
Rookie	Yankees I	Dominican	Julio Valdez	Raul Dominguez	Wilfredo Cordova
Rookie	Yankees II	Dominican	Carlos Mota	Nilson Antigua	Jose Duran

Scouting

Telephone: (813) 875-7569. **Fax:** (813) 873-2302.

Vice President, Scouting: Damon Oppenheimer.

Assistant Director, Amateur Scouting: John Kremer.

Director, Professional Scouting: Billy Eppler. **Assistant Director, Professional Scouting:** Will Kuntz.

Professional Scouts: Ron Brand (Plano, TX), Joe Caro (Tampa, FL), Jay Darnell (San Diego, CA), Bill Emslie (Trinity, FL), Frank Howard (Aldie, VA), Pete Mackanin (Bradenton, FL), Bill Mele (Pittsfield, MA), Tim Naehring (Cincinnati, OH), Greg Orr (Sacramento, CA), Rick Williams (Tampa, FL).

National Crosscheckers: Kendall Carter, Donny Rowland. **Regional Crosscheckers:** East—Brian Barber (Winter Garden, FL); Midwest—Tim Kelly (Pickerington, OH); West—Jeff Patterson (Yorba Linda, CA).

Area Scouts: Mark Batchko (Arlington, TX), Steve Boros (Kingwood, TX), Jeff Deardorff (Clermont, FL), Mike Gibbons (Liberty Township, OH), Matt Hyde (East Boston, Mass.), David Keith (Anaheim, CA), Steve Kmetko (Phoenix, AZ) , Steve Lemke (Geneva, IL), Scott Lovekamp (Lynchburg, VA), Darryl Monroe (Atlanta, GA), Cesar Presbott (Bronx, NY), Stewart Smothers (Los Angeles, CA), D.J. Svihlik (Hoover, AL), Mike Thurman (West Lynn, OR).

Vice President, International Operations: Abel Guerra.

Assistant, International Operations: Alex Cotto. **Latin American Scouting Director:** Carlos Rios Latin American Field Coordinator: Victor Mata Latin Academy, Director of Operations: Martin Valerio. **Latin Academy Operations Manager:** Aniuska Sanchez. **Latin American Scouting Coordinator:** Ricardo Finol. **Dominican Scouting Director:** Ramon Valdivia.

Dominican Scouts: Alfredo Dominguez (San Cristobal), Angel Ovalles (Santo Domingo), Juan Rosario (San Pedro de Macoris), Jose Sabino (Santiago), Raymond Sanchez (Santo Domingo), Sonder Encarnacion, (Santo Domingo), Argenis Paulino, (Santo Domingo).

Venezuelan Scouts: Darwin Bracho (Puerta la Cruz), Jose Gavidea (Caracas), Cesar Suarez (Maracaibo), Hector Rincones (Valencia).

International Scouts: Luis Sierra (Colombia), Lee Sigman (Mexico), Edgar Rodriguez (Nicaragua), Carlos Levy (Panama).

Oakland Athletics

Office Address: 7000 Coliseum Way, Oakland, CA 94621.
Telephone: (510) 638-4900. **Fax:** (510) 562-1633.
Website: www.oaklandathletics.com

Ownership

Co-Owner, Managing Partner: Lewis Wolff.

BUSINESS OPERATIONS

Lew Wolff

President: Michael Crowley. **Executive Assistant to President:** Carolyn Jones.

General Counsel: Steve Johnston. **Senior Counsel:** Neil Kraetsch.

Finance/Administration

Vice President, Finance: Paul Wong.

Director, Finance: Kasey Miraglia. **Payroll Manager:** Kathy Leviege. **Accounting Analyst:** Ling Ding. **Senior Accountant:** Isabelle Mahaffey. **Analyst, Accouting:** Ling Ding. **Specialist, Accounts Receivable:** David Bunnell. **Ticket Accountant:** Scott Zumsteg. **Manager, Human Resources:** Kim Kubo. **Director, Information Systems Manager:** Debbie Dean. **Assistant, Information Systems:** Nathan Hayes. **Coordinator, Office Services:** Julie Vasconcellos. **Executive Office Receptionist:** Maggie Baptist. Travel Specialist: Colleen Osterberg.

Sales/Marketing

Vice President, Sales/Marketing: Jim Leahey.

Director, Corporate Sales: Franklin Lowe. **Corporate Account Managers:** Jill Golden, Susan Weiglein, Matthew Gallagher. **Manager, Marketing/Advertising:** Zachary Glare. **Manager, Creative Services:** Mike Ono. **Advertising, Assistant:** Amy MacEwen. **Manager, Special Events:** Heather Rajeski. **Assistants, Special Events:** Katie Fahy, Jenna Zito. **Manager, Retail Operations:** Brittany Cardinale. **Coordinator, Retail Operations:** Austin Rancadore. **Coordinator, Merchandising:** Mark Spear.

Public Relations/Communications

Telephone: (510) 563-2207. **Fax:** (510) 562-1633.

Vice President, Broadcasting/Communications: Ken Pries. **Director, Public Relations:** Jim Young. **Manager, Baseball Information:** Mike Selleck. **Manager, Media Relations:** Kristy Fick. **Manager, Media Services:** Debbie Gallas. **Team Photographer:** Michael Zagaris. **Director, Community Relations:** Detra Paige. **Manager, Broadcast Services:** Warren Chu. **Assistant, Community Relations:** Erik Farrell.

Director, In-Stadium Entertainment: Troy Smith. **Director, Multimedia Services:** David Don. **Coordinator, Multimedia Services:** Jon Martin. **Coordinator, In-Stadium Entertainment:** Jeff Gass. **PA Announcer:** Roy Steele. **Official Scorers:** Chuck Dybdal, David Feldman, David Bush, Michael Duca.

Stadium Operations

Vice President, Stadium Operations: David Rinetti. **Director, Stadium Operations:** David Avila. **Manager, Stadium Operations:** Paul La Veau. **Manager, Stadium Services:** Randy Duran. **Manager, Stadium Operations Events:** Kristy Ledbetter. **Coordinator, Stadium Operations:** Tara O'Connor. **Stadium Operations Scheduler:** Gabrielle Weems. **Stadium Operations Assistant:** Peter Young. **Head Groundskeeper:** Clay Wood. **Arizona Groundskeeper:** Chad Huss.

Ticketing

Director, Ticket Sales: Todd Santino. **Manager, Ticket Sales:** Brian DiTucci. **Manager, Luxury Suite Sales:** Parker Newton. **Senior Account Manager, Outside Sales:** Phil Chapman, Sean O'Keefe. **Supervisor, Inside Sales:** Aaron Dragomir.

Director, Ticket Operations: Steve Fanelli. **Senior Manager, Ticket Services:** Josh Ziegenbusch. **Manager, Ticket Services:** David Adame. **Manager, Box Office:** Anthony Silva. **Coordinator, Ticket Operations:** Anthony Blue. **Manager, Spring Training Operations/Ticket Services Manager:** Travis LaDolce. **Supervisor, Ticket Services:** Catherine Glazer. **Director, Premium Seating Services:** Dayn Floyd. **Manager, Premium Seating Services:** Susie Weiss..

Travel/Clubhouse

Director, Team Travel: Mickey Morabito. **Equipment Manager:** Steve Vucinich. **Visitors Clubhouse:** Mike Thalblum. **Assistant Equipment Manager:** Brian Davis. **Umpires Assistant:** Matt Weiss. **Clubhouse Assistant:** William Angel. **Supervisor, Arizona Clubhouse:** Jesse Sotomayor. **Manager, Arizona Clubhouse:** James Gibson.

GENERAL INFORMATION

Stadium (year opened): McAfee Coliseum (1968).
Home Dugout: Third Base. **Playing Surface:** Grass.
Team Colors: Kelly green and gold.
Player Representative: Unavailable.

BASEBALL OPERATIONS

Billy Beane

Vice President, General Manager: Billy Beane.

Assistant GM: David Forst. **Director, Player Personnel:** Billy Owens. **Special Assistant to GM:** Randy Johnson. **Executive Assistant:** Betty Shinoda. **Director, Baseball Administration:** Pamela Pitts. **Baseball Operations Analyst:** Farhan Zaidi. **Video Coordinator:** Adam Rhoden.

Major League Staff

Manager: Bob Geren.

Coaches: Bench—Don Wakamatsu; Pitching—Curt Young; Batting—Ty Van Burkleo; First Base—Tye Waller; Third Base—Tony De Francesco; Bullpen—Ron Romanick. **Bullpen Catcher:** Casey Chavez.

Medical, Training

Coordinator, Medical Services: Larry Davis. **Team Physician:** Dr. Allan Pont. **Team Orthopedist:** Dr. John Frazier. **Consulting Orthopedist:** Dr. Thomas Peatman. **Consultant, Internal Medicine:** Dr. Elliott Schwartz.

Arizona Team Physician: Dr. Fred Dicke. **Consulting Orthopedists:** Dr. Doug Freedberg, Dr. Lewis Yocum.

Head Athletic Trainer: Steve Sayles. **Assistant Athletic Trainer:** Walt Horn. **Strength/ Conditioning:** Clarence Cockrell. **Massage Therapist:** Yoshihiro Nishio.

Bob Geren

Player Development

Telephone: (510) 638-4900. **Fax:** (510) 563-2376.

Director, Player Development: Keith Lieppman. **Director, Minor League Operations:** Ted Polakowski.

Roving Instructors: Juan Navarrete (infield), Ron Plaza (infield), Gil Patterson (pitching), Greg Sparks (hitting). **Special Instructor for Scouting/Player Development:** Ruben Escalera.

Medical Coordinator: Jeff Collins. **Strength/Conditioning:** Judd Hawkins.

Farm System

Class	Farm Club	League	Manager	Coach	Pitching Coach
Triple-A	Sacramento	Pacific Coast	Todd Steverson	Brian McArn	Rick Rodriguez
Double-A	Midland	Texas	Webster Garrison	Casey Myers	Scott Emerson
High A	Stockton	California	Darren Bush	Tim Garland	Garvin Alston
Low A	Kane County	Midwest	Aaron Nieckula	Benny Winslow	Donald Schulze
Short-season	Vancouver	Northwest	Rick Magnante	Unavailable	Craig Lefferts
Rookie	Phoenix	Arizona	Ruben Escalera	Marcus Jensen	Jimmy Escalante
Rookie	Athletics I	Dominican	Radames Perez	Juan Dilone	David Brito
Rookie	Athletics II	Dominican	Luis Mateo	Oscar Spencer	Unavailable

Scouting

Telephone: (510) 638-4900. **Fax:** (510) 563-2376.

Director, Scouting: Eric Kubota (Rocklin, CA).

Director, Pro Scouting: Chris Pittaro (Hamilton, NJ).

Major League Advance Scout: Joe Sparks (Phoenix, AZ).

National Crosschecker: Ron Vaughn (Corona, CA). **Western Crosschecker:** Scott Kidd (Los Altos, CA). **Midwest Crosschecker:** Steve Bowden (Houston, TX). **Eastern Crosschecker:** Michael Holmes (Winston Salem, NC).

Pro Scouts: Bryn Alderson (San Francisco, CA), Jeff Bittiger (Saylorsburg, PA), Will Schock (Oakland, CA), Craig Weissmann (San Diego, CA), Mike Ziegler (Orlando, FL).

Area Scouts: Neil Avent (Greensboro, NC), Yancy Ayres (Topeka, KS), Armann Brown (Smyrna, GA), Jermaine Clark (Livermore, CA), Jim Coffman (Portland, OR), Blake Davis (Plano, TX), Rick Magnante (Van Nuys, CA), Eric Martins (Diamond Bar, CA), Kevin Mello (Champaign, IL), Kelcey Mucker (Baton Rouge, LA), Matt Ranson (Nicholasville, KY), Marc Sauer (Cliffwood Beach, NJ), Trevor Schaffer (Belleair, FL), Jeremy Schied (Phoenix, AZ), Rich Sparks (Sterling Heights, MI), J.T. **Stotts (Moorpark, CA).**

Director, Latin American Operations: Raymond Abreu (Santo Domingo, DR). **Coordinator, Latin American Scouting:** Julio Franco (Caracas, VZ).

International Scouts: Ruben Barradas (VZ), Juan Carlos De La Cruz (DR), Angel Eusebio (DR), Andri Garcia (VZ), Matt Higginson (CA), Pablo Marmol (DR), Amaury Reyes (DR), Russell Spear (AU), Oswaldo Troconis (VZ)

Scouting Assistant: Sam Geaney.

Philadelphia Phillies

Office Address: Citizens Bank Park, One Citizens Bank Way, **Philadelphia, PA 19148.**
Telephone: (215) 463-6000.
Website: www.phillies.com.

Ownership

Operated By: The Phillies.
President/CEO: David Montgomery. **Chairman:** Bill Giles.

BUSINESS OPERATIONS

David Montgomery

Senior Vice President/General Counsel: Bill Webb.

Director, Business Development: Joe Giles. **Director, Human Resources:** Terry DeRugeriis.

Finance

Senior Vice President, Business/Finance: Jerry Clothier. **VP, CFO:** John Nickolas. **Director, Payroll Services:** Karen Wright. **Director, Information Systems:** Brian Lamoreaux.

Marketing/Promotions

Senior Vice President, Marketing/Sales: David Buck.

Manager, Client Services/Alumni Relations: Debbie Nocito. **Director, Corporate Partnerships:** Rob MacPherson. **Manager, Advertising Sales:** Scott Nickle, Tom Sullivan. **Director, Advertising Sales:** Brian Mahoney. **Director, Marketing Programs/Events:** Kurt Funk. **Director, Entertainment:** Chris Long.

Manager, Broadcasting: Rob Brooks. **Manager, Advertising/Internet Services:** Jo-Anne Levy-Lamoreaux.

Public Relations/Communications

Telephone: (215) 463-6000. **Fax:** (215) 389-3050.

Vice President, Public Relations: Larry Shenk.

Director, Public Relations: Leigh Tobin. **Manager, Media Relations:** Greg Casterioto. **Coordinator, Media Relations:** Mary Ann Gettis. **Media Relations Assistant:** Kevin Gregg. **Director, Community Relations:** Gene Dias.

Ballpark Operations

Senior Vice President, Operations/Administration: Michael Stiles.

Director, Ballpark Operations: Mike DiMuzio. **Director, Event Operations:** Eric Tobin. **Manager, Concessions Development:** Bruce Leith.

Head Groundskeeper: Mike Boekholder. **PA Announcer:** Dan Baker. **Official Scorer:** Jay Dunn. **Official Scorers:** Bob Kenney, Mike Maconi.

Ticketing

Telephone: (215) 463-1000. **Fax:** (215) 463-9878.

Vice President, Sales/Ticket Operations: John Weber.

Director, Ticket Department: Dan Goroff. **Director, Group Sales:** Kathy Killian. **Director, Ticket Technology/ Development:** Chris Pohl. **Manager, Suite Sales/Services:** Tom Mashek. **Manager, Phone Center:** Phil Feather. **Manager, Club Sales/Services:** Derek Schuster. **Manager, Season Ticket Services:** Mike Holdren.

Travel/Clubhouse

Director, Team Travel/Clubhouse Services: Frank Coppenbarger.

Manager, Visiting Clubhouse: Kevin Steinhour. **Assistant, Home Clubhouse:** Phil Sheridan. **Manager, Equipment and Umpire Services:** Dan O'Rourke.

GENERAL INFORMATION

Stadium (year opened): Citizens Bank Park (2004).
Home Dugout: First Base. **Playing Surface:** Natural Grass.
Team Colors: Red, white and blue.
Player Representative: Unavailable.

Pat Gillick

BASEBALL OPERATIONS

Senior Vice President/General Manager: Pat Gillick.

Assistant GM: Ruben Amaro Jr. **Assistant GM, Scouting/Player Development:** Mike Arbuckle. **Director, Baseball Administration:** Susan Ingersoll Papaneri. **Baseball Information Analyst:** Jay McLaughlin. **Senior Advisor to GM:** Dallas Green. **Special Assistant to GM:** Charley Kerfeld.

Major League Staff

Manager: Charlie Manuel.

Coaches: Dugout—Jimy Williams; Pitching—Rich Dubee; Batting—Milt Thompson; First Base—Davey Lopes; Third Base—Steve J. Smith; Bullpen—Ramon Henderson; Catching—Mick Billmeyer.

Charlie Manuel

Medical/Training

Director, Medical Services: Dr. Michael Ciccotti.

Head Trainer: Scott Sheridan. **Assistant Trainer:** Mark Andersen. **Conditioning Coordinator:** Doug Lien.

Player Development

Telephone: (215) 463-6000. **Fax:** (215) 755-9324.

Director, Minor Leagues: Steve Noworyta.

Assistant Director, Minor League Operations/Florida: Lee McDaniel. **Assistant Director, Minor League Operations:** Mike Ondo. **Director, Latin American Operations:** Sal Artiaga. **Director, Florida Operations:** John Timberlake.

Field Coordinator: Bill Dancy. **Coordinators:** Brian Cammarota (trainers), Mike Compton (catching), Gorman Heimueller (pitching), Dong Lien (conditioning), Don Long (hitting), Jerry Martin (outfield/baserunning).

Farm System

Class	Farm Club	League	Manager	Coach(es)	Pitching Coach
Triple-A	Lehigh Valley	International	Dave Huppert	Gregg Gross	Rod Nichols
Double-A	Reading	Eastern	P.J. Forbes	Frank Cacciatore	Tom Filer
High A	Clearwater	Florida State	Razor Shines	Kevin Jordan	Steve Schrenk
Low A	Lakewood	South Atlantic	Steve Roadcap	Greg Legg	Dave Lundquist
Short-season	Williamsport	New York-Penn	Dusty Wathan	Eric Valent	Bill Bliss
Rookie	Clearwater	Gulf Coast	Roly DeArmas	Luis Melendez	Carlos Arroyo
Rookie	Phillies	Dominican	Domingo Brito	C. Henriquez/C. Mejia	Manny Amador
Rookie	Phillies	Venezuelan	Rafael DeLima	S. Navas/E. Patino	L. Straker/J. Tiamo

Scouting

Telephone: (215) 218-5204. **Fax:** (215) 755-9324.

Director, Scouting: Marti Wolever (Papillion, NE). **Assistant Director, Scouting:** Rob Holiday.

Coordinators, Scouting: Jim Fregosi Jr. (Murrieta, CA), Mike Ledna (Arlington Heights, IL).

Director, Major League Scouting: Gordon Lakey (Barker, TX). **Advance Scout:** Hank King (Limerick, PA).

Director, Professional Scouting: Chuck LaMar (Clearwater, FL). **Professional Scouts:** Sonny Bowers (Hewitt, TX), Ron Hansen (Baldwin, MD), Dean Jongewaard (Fountain Valley, CA), Jon Mercurio (Coraopolis PA), Del Unser (Scottsdale, AZ).

Independent League Coordinator: Mal Fichman (Boise, ID).

Regional Supervisors: Brian Kohlscheen (Central/Norman, OK), John Castleberry (East/High Point, NC), Billy Moore (West/Alta Loma, CA).

Area Scouts: Therron Brockish (Anthem, AZ), Steve Cohen (Spring, TX), Darrell Conner (Riverside, CA), Joey Davis (Rancho Murrieta, CA), Ellis Dungan (Charlotte NC), Tim Kissner (Long Beach, CA), Jerry Lafferty (Kansas City, MO), Chip Lawrence (Palmetto, FL), Paul Murphy (Wilmington, DE), Dave Ryles (Duvall WA), Gene Schall (Harleysville, PA), Paul Scott (Rockwall, TX), Mike Stauffer (Ridgeland, MS), Bob Szymkowski (Chicago, IL), Roy Tanner (North Charleston, SC).

International Supervisor: Sal Agostinelli (Kings Park, NY).

International Scouts: Tomas Herrera (Mexico), Kevin Hooker (Australia), Rick Jacques (Europe), Allan Lewis (Panama, Central America), Jesus Mendez (Venezuela), Wil Tejada (Dominican Republic).

Pittsburgh Pirates

Office Address: PNC Park at North Shore, 115 Federal St, Pittsburgh, PA 15212.
Mailing Address: P.O. Box 7000, Pittsburgh, PA 15212.
Telephone: (412) 323-5000. **Fax:** (412) 325-4412.
Website: www.pirates.com

Ownership

Chairman of the Board: Robert Nutting. **President:** Frank Coonelly.

Board of Directors: Donald Beaver, Kevin McClatchy, G. Ogden Nutting, Robert Nutting, William Nutting, Duane Wittman.

BUSINESS OPERATIONS

GEORGE GOJKOVICH

Frank Coonelly

Finance

Executive Vice President/CFO: Jim Plake.

Controller: David Bowman. **Senior Director, Human Resources:** Pam Nelson Minter. **Senior Director, Information Technology:** Terry Zeigler. **Director, Office Services:** Patti Mistick.

Communications

Telephone: (412) 325-4991. **Fax:** (412) 325-4413.

Senior Director, Communications: Brian Warecki. **Director, Media Relations:** Jim Trdinich. **Manager, Media Services:** Dan Hart.

Community Relations

Vice President, Community/Public Affairs: Patty Paytas.

Director, Diversity Initiatives: Wende Torbert. **Manager, Community Relations:** Michelle Mejia.

Marketing/Sales

Senior Director, Marketing/Ticket Sales: Brian Chiera. **Senior Director, Corporate Partnerships:** Mike Egan.

Director, Alumni Affairs, Promotions/Licensing: Joe Billetdeaux. **Director, Broadcasting:** Marc Garda. **Manager, Special Events:** Christine Serkoch. **Manager, In-Game Entertainment:** Eric Wolff. **Manager, Creative Services:** Alex Moser. **Manager, Promotions/Licensing:** Megan Morris.

Marketing Manager, Advertising/Promotions: Kiley Cauvel.

Stadium Operations

Senior Vice President/General Manager, PNC Park: Dennis DaPra. **Senior Director, Ballpark Operations:** Chris Hunter. **Senior Director, Security/Contract Services:** Jeff Podobnik. **Manager, Security/Service Operations:** Mark Weaver. **Field Maintenance Manager:** Manny Lopez.

Ticketing

Telephone: (800) 289-2827. **Fax:** (412) 325-4404.

Manager, Ticket Services: Dave Wysocki. **Director, Ticket Sales:** Terri Smith. **Director, Ticket Services/Business Development:** Jim Alexander. **Manager, Group Services/Gold Club:** Charlene Cheroke. **Manager, Client Relations:** Jared Kramer.

Travel/Clubhouse

Traveling Secretary: Greg Johnson.

Equipment Manager/Home Clubhouse Operations: Roger Wilson. **Visitors Clubhouse Manager:** Kevin Conrad.

GENERAL INFORMATION

Stadium (year opened): PNC Stadium (2001).
Home Dugout: Third Base. **Playing Surface:** Grass.
Team Colors: Black, gold, red and white.
Player Representative: Paul Maholm.

Neal Huntington

BASEBALL OPERATIONS

Telephone: (412) 325-4743. **Fax:** (412) 325-4414.

Senior Vice President, General Manager: Neal Huntington

VP, General Counsel: Larry Silverman. **Director, Baseball Operations:** Bryan Minniti. **Special Assistants to GM:** Larry Corrigan, Louie Eljaua, Jesse Flores, Jax Robertson, Roy Smith, Doug Strange, Pete Vuckovich. **Senior Advisor:** Chuck Tanner.

Major League Staff

Manager: John Russell.

Coaches: Bench—Gary Varsho; Pitching—Jeff Andrews; Hitting—Don Long; First Base—Lou Frazier; Third Base—Tony Beasley; Bullpen—Luis Dorante.

John Russell

Medical/Training

Medical Director: Dr. Patrick DeMeo. **Team Physician:** Dr. Edward Snell.

Head Athletic Trainer: Brad Henderson. **Assistant Athletic Trainer:** Mike Sandoval. **Strength/Conditioning Coordinator:** Frank Velasquez. **Latin American Strength/ Conditioning Coordinator:** Kiyoshi Momose.

Minor Leagues

Telephone: (412) 325-4737. **Fax:** (412) 325-4414.

Director, Player Development: Kyle Stark.

Minor League Field Coordinator: Jeff Banister. **Advisor, Player Development:** Rich Donnelly. **Outfield/Baserunning Coordinator:** Kimera Bartee. **Pitching Coordinator:** Troy Buckley. **Catching Coordinator:** Brad Fischer. **Infield Coordinator:** Carlos Garcia. **Hitting Coordinator:** Gregg Ritchie.

Latin American Field Coordinator: Euclides Rojas.

Farm System

Class	Farm Club	League	Manager	Coach(es)	Pitching Coach
Triple-A	Indianapolis	International	Trent Jewett	Hensley Meulens	Ray Searage
Double-A	Altoona	Eastern	Tim Leiper	Brandon Moore	Brad Holman
High A	Lynchburg	Carolina	Jeff Branson	Chris Truby	Bob Milacki
Low A	Hickory	South Atlantic	Gary Green	Rudy Pena	Jeff Johnson
Short-season	State College	New York-Penn	Brad Fischer	Sid Bream	Wilson Alvarez
Rookie	Bradenton	Gulf Coast	Tom Prince	Edgar Varela/Woody Huyke	Miguel Bonilla
Rookie	Pirates	Dominican	Ramon Zapata	Cecilio Beltre	R. Carrion/H. Corniel
Rookie	Pirates	Venezuelan	Osmin Melendez	Ivan Colmenares	J. Prieto/D. Urbina

Scouting

Telephone: (412) 325-4738. **Fax:** (412) 325-4414.

Senior Director, Scouting: Greg Smith. **Assistant Director, Scouting:** Joe Delli Carri. **Scouting Administrator:** Sandy Deutsch.

National Supervisors: Jack Bowen (Los Angeles, CA), Jimmy Lester (Columbus, GA).

Regional Supervisors: Rob Guzik (Latrobe, PA), Rodney Henderson (Lexington, KY), Everett Russell (Thibodaux, LA), John Green (Tucson, AZ).

Area Scouts: Rick Allen (Agoura Hills, CA), Matt Bimeal (Overland Park, KS), Sean Campbell (Fresno, CA), Jerome Cochran (Slidell, LA), Steve Fleming (Louisa, VA), Trevor Haley (Richmond, IN), Greg Hopkins (Beaverton, OR), Chris Kline (Rockford, IL), Mike Leuzinger (Mansfield, TX), Darren Mazeroski (Panama City Beach, FL), Bump Merriweather (Glendale, AZ), Buddy Paine (Hartsdale, NY), Joe Salermo (Hallendale Beach, FL), Josh Shaffer (San Diego, CA), Greg Schliz (Greenville, SC).

Part-Time Scouts: Elmer Gray (Pittsburgh, PA), William Price (Austin, TX), Jose Rosario (Bayamon, PR), Bill Sizemore (Sacramento, CA), Troy Williams (Europe).

Director, Latin American Scouting: Rene Gayo.

Supervisors, Dominican Republic: Josue Herrera, Nelson Llenas. **Part-Time Scouts, Dominican Republic:** Marcos Briseno, Ellis Pena.

Supervisor, Venezuela: Rodolfo Petit. **Part-Time Scouts, Venezuela:** Javier Magdaleno, Pablo Csorgi, Charlie Curiel, Johan Hidalgo, Alcides Melendez.

Supervisor, Mexico: Chino Valdez. **Part-Time Scouts, Mexico:** Jose Lavagnino, Alfredo Peralta.

International Scouts: Wilfredo Blanco (Nicaragua), Orlando Covo (Colombia), Daniel Garcia (Colombia), Jose Pineda (Panama), Jesus Valdez (Mexico), Marc Van Zanten (Netherlands Antilles), Darryl Yrausquin (Aruba), Domingo Zabala (Guatemala).

St. Louis Cardinals

Office Address: 700 Clark Street, St. Louis, MO 63102
Telephone: (314) 345-9600. **Fax:** (314) 345-9523
Website: www.stlcardinals.com

Ownership

Operated By: St. Louis Cardinals LLC.

Chairman: Bill Dewitt Jr. **Vice Chairman:** Fred Hanser. **Secretary/Treasurer:** Andrew Baur.

President: Mark Lamping.

Senior Administrative Assistant to Chairman: Grace Pak. **Senior Administrative Assistant to President:** Julie Laningham.

Mark Lamping

BUSINESS OPERATIONS

Senior Vice President, Business Development: Bill Dewitt III.

Vice President, Event Services: Vicki Bryant. **Manager, Event Services:** Missey Tobey. **Director, Government Affairs/ Special Projects:** Ron Watermon. **Director, Human Resources:** Christine Nelson. **Manager, Office Administration/Human Resources Specialist:** Karen Brown.

Finance

Senior Vice President/CFO: Brad Wood.

Director, Finance: Rex Carter. **Supervisor, Ticket Accounting/Reporting:** Michelle Flach. **Senior Accountant:** Tracey Sessions. **Accounting Manager:** John Lowry. **Manager, Payroll & Compliance Reporting:** Shellie Ward.

Marketing/Sales

Senior Vice President, Sales/Marketing: Dan Farrell. **Administrative Assistant, Corporate Sales:** Gail Ruhling.

Vice President, Corporate Sales/Marketing, Stadium Entertainment: Thane van Breusegen. **Director, Target Marketing:** Ted Savage. **Senior Account Executive, Corporate Sales:** Jeff Floerke. **Director, Scoreboard Operations/ Senior Account Executive:** Tony Simokaitis.

Media Relations/Community Relations

Telephone: (314) 345-9600. **Fax:** (314) 345-9530

Director, Media Relations: Brian Bartow.

Assistant Directors, Media Relations: Melody Yount, Jim Anderson. **Director, Publications:** Steve Zesch. **Publication Assistants:** Tom Raber, Larry State.

Vice President/Group Director, Community Outreach/Cardinals Care: Tim Hanser. **Community Relations Specialist:** Jessica Illert. **Youth Baseball Commissioner, Cardinals Care:** Keith Brooks. **Coordinator, Cardinals Care:** Lucretia Payne.

Stadium Operations

Vice President, Stadium Operations: Joe Abernathy. **Administrative Assistant:** Nan Bommarito.

Director, Stadium Operations: Mike Bertani. **Director, Security/Special Services:** Joe Walsh. **Administrative Assistant, Security:** Hope Baker. **Director, Quality Assurance/Guest Services:** Mike Ball. **Manager, Stadium Operations:** Cindy Richards. **Head Groundskeeper:** Bill Findley. **Assistant Head Groundskeeper:** Chad Casella. **PA Announcer:** John Ulett. **Official Scorers:** Gary Muller, Jeff Durbin, Mike Smith

Ticketing

Vice President, Ticket Sales: Joe Strohm. **Director, Ticket Services:** Derek Thornburg. **Manager, Ticket Services:** Brady Bruhn. **Director, Season/Premium Ticket Sales:** Mark Murray. **Manager, Premium Ticket Sales:** Delores Scanlon. **Manager, Season Ticket Services:** Jamie Brickler. **Manager, Season Ticket Sales:** Kristi Mundloch. **Manager, Ticket Technology/Secondary Market:** Jennifer Needham. **Director, Group Sales:** Michael Hall. **Manager, Group Sales:** Mary Clare Bena. **Director, Fan Development/Alumni Relations:** Martin Coco. **Supervisor, Receptionist:** Marilyn Mathews.

Travel/Clubhouse

Traveling Secretary: C.J. Cherre.

Equipment Manager: Rip Rowan. **Assistant Equipment Manager:** Ernie Moore. **Visiting Clubhouse Manger:** Jerry Risch. **Video Coordinator:** Chad Blair.

GENERAL INFORMATION

Stadium (year opened): Busch Stadium (2006).
Home Dugout: First Base. **Playing Surface:** Grass.
Team Colors: Red and white.
Player Representative: Braden Looper.

John Mozeliak

BASEBALL OPERATIONS

Telephone: (314) 345-9600. **Fax:** (314) 345-9525

Vice President, General Manager: John Mozeliak.

Assistant GM: John Abbamondi. **Special Assistants to GM:** Gary LaRocque, Cam Bonifay, Mike Jorgensen, Matt Slater, Alan Benes, Cal Eldred.

Director, Baseball Development: Mike Girsch. **Director, Major League Administration:** Judy Carpenter-Barada. **Coordinator, Baseball Operations/ Professional Scouting:** Matt Carroll.

Major League Staff

Manager: Tony La Russa

Coaches: Bench—Joe Pettini; Pitching—Dave Duncan; Batting—Hal McRae; First Base—Dave McKay; Third Base—Jose Oquendo; Bullpen—Marty Mason.

Tony La Russa

Medical/Training

Medical Advisor: Dr. George Paletta.

Head Trainer: Barry Weinberg. **Assistant Trainer:** Greg Hauck.

Player Development

Telephone: (314) 345-9600. **Fax:** (314) 345-9519

Vice President, Amateur Scouting/Player Development: Jeff Luhnow.

Director, Minor League Operations: John Vuch. **Administrative Assistant:** Lillie Wilson. **Minor League Equipment Manager:** Buddy Bates.

Coordinators: Dyar Miller (pitching), Brent Strom (pitching instructor), Dann Bilardello (catching), Dan Radison (hitting), Tom Spencer (outfield/baserunning).

Farm System

Class	Farm Team	League	Manager	Coach	Pitching Coach
Triple-A	Memphis	Pacific Coast	Chris Maloney	Mark Budaska	Blaise Ilsley
Double-A	Springfield	Texas	Ron Warner	Derrick May	Bryan Eversgerd
High A	Palm Beach	Florida State	Gaylen Pitts	Keith Mitchell	Dennis Martinez
Low A	Quad Cities	Midwest	Steve Dillard	Joe Kruzel	Arthur Adams
Short-season	Batavia	NY-Penn	Mark DeJohn	Jeff Albert	Doug White
Rookie	Johnson City	Appalachian	Joe Almarez	Mike Shildt	Tim Leveque
Rookie	Cardinals	Gulf Coast	Enrique Brito	Ramon Ortiz	Unavailable
Rookie	Cardinals	Dominican	Nelson Norman	Rene Rojas	Unavailable
Rookie	Cardinals	Venezuela	Javier Meza	Unavailable	Dernier Orozco

Scouting

Telephone: (314) 345-9358. **Fax:** (314) 345-9525.

Assistant Scouting Director: Jaron Madison

Director, College Scouting: Dan Kantrovitz. **Amateur Scouting Manager:** Oz Ocampo.

Coordinator, Pro Scouting: Matt Carroll.

Special Assignment Scout: Fred McAlister (Katy, TX).

Professional Scouts: Bruce Benedict (Atlanta, GA), Cam Bonifay (Pfafftown, NC), Mike Jorgensen (Fenton, MO), Marty Keough (Scottsdale, AZ), Gary LaRocque (Browns Summit, NC), Matt Slater (Stevenson Ranch, CA), Mike Squires (Kalamazoo, MI).

National/Regional Supervisors: Chuck Fick (Newbury Park, CA), Joe Rigoli (Parsippany, NJ), Mike Roberts (Hot Springs, AR), Roger Smith (Eastman, GA).

Area Supervisors: Joe Almaraz (San Antonio, TX), Jay Catalano (Joelton, TN), Mike Elias (Houston, TX), Charlie Gonzalez (Weston, FL), Brian Hopkins (Brunswick, OH), Jeff Ishii (Chino, CA), Mike Juhl (Indian Trail, NC), Aaron Krawiec (Gilbert, AZ), Aaron Looper (Shawnee, OK), Scott Melvin (Quincy, IL), Jay North (Vacaville, CA), Koby Perez (North Bergen, NJ), Joel Ronda (Puerto Rico), Anup Sinha (Jupiter, FL), Steve Turco (Clearwater, FL).

Director, International Operations: Moises Rodriguez. **Latin American Supervisor:** Juan Mercado.

International Scouts: Domingo Garcia (Dominican Republic), Jose Gregorio Gonzalez (Venezuela), Carlos Heron (Panama), Neder Horta (Colombia), Rene Rojas (Dominican Republic), Cristino Valdez (Dominican Republic), Crysthiam Blanco (Nicaragua), Fermin Coronel (Curacao).

San Diego Padres

Office Address: Petco Park, 100 Park Blvd, San Diego, CA 92101.
Mailing Address: P.O. Box 122000, San Diego, CA 92112.
Telephone: (619) 795-5000.
E-mail address: comments@padres.com
Website: www.padres.com.

Ownership

Operated By: Padres LP.

Principal Owner/Chairman: John Moores. **Co-Vice Chairmen:** Glenn Doshay, Charles Noell.
CEO: Sandy Alderson. **President/COO:** Dick Freeman.

Sandy Alderson

BUSINESS OPERATIONS

Executive Vice President/Business Operations: Jeff Overton. **Executive VP/General Counsel:** Katie Pothier. **VP, Senior Advisor:** Dave Winfield.

Finance

Executive Vice President/CFO: Fred Gerson. **VP/Controller:** Dan Fumai. **VP/Sales:** Jim Ballweg. **Director, Corporate Sales:** Marty Gorsich. **Director, Information Systems:** Joe Lewis.

Public Relations/Community Relations

Telephone: (619) 795-5265. **Fax:** (619) 795-5266.

Director, Media Relations: Warren Miller. **Manager, Media Relations:** Leah Tobin. **Coordinator, Media Relations:** Bret Picciolo. **Assistant, Media Relations:** Ben Coughlan. **Club Photographer:** Chris Hardy.

Vice President, Community Relations: Michele Anderson. **Director, Padres Foundation:** Sue Botos. **Manager, Community Relations:** Nhu Tran. **Manager, Community Programs:** Rebecca Robinson.

Stadium Operations

Executive Vice President/Ballpark Management; General Manager, Petco Park: Richard Andersen. **VP/Ballpark Operations:** Mark Guglielmo.

Director, Security and Transportation: Ken Kawachi. **Director, Landscape/Field Maintenance:** Luke Yoder. **PA Announcer:** Frank Anthony. **Official Scorers:** Dennis Smythe, Bill Zavestoski.

Ticketing

Telephone: (619) 795-5005. **Fax:** (619) 795-5034.

Executive Director, Ticket Operations: Jim Kiersnowski.

Director, Ticket Sales: Dawson Hughes. **Director, Ticket Customer Services:** Laura Evans.

Travel, Clubhouse

Director, Team Travel/Equipment Manager: Brian Prilaman.

Assistant Clubhouse Manager: Tony Petricca. **Assistant to Equipment Manager:** Spencer Dallin. **Visiting Clubhouse Manager:** David Bacharach.

GENERAL INFORMATION

Stadium (year opened): Petco Park (2004).
Home Dugout: First Base. **Playing Surface:** Grass.
Team Colors: Padres sand, navy blue and sky blue.
Player Representative: Unavailable.

Kevin Towers

BASEBALL OPERATIONS

Telephone: (619) 795-5076. **Fax:** (619) 795-5361.

Executive Vice President/ General Manager: Kevin Towers.

Assistant GM: Fred Uhlman Jr. **Special Assistants to GM/Major League Scouts:** Ken Bracey, Bill Bryk. **Special Assistant, Baseball Operations:** Paul DePodesta. **Director, Baseball Operations:** Jeff Kingston. **Assistant:** Ryan Isaac.

Major League Staff

Manager: Bud Black.

Coaches: Bench—Craig Colbert; Pitching—Darren Balsley; Hitting—Wally Joyner; First Base—Rick Renteria; Third Base—Glenn Hoffman; Bullpen—Darrel Akerfelds.

Bud Black

Medical/Training

Club Physician: Scripps Clinic Medical staff.

Head Trainer: Todd Hutcheson. **Assistant Trainer:** Paul Navarro.

Strength/Conditioning Coach: Jim Malone.

Player Development

Telephone: (619) 795-5343. **Fax:** (619) 795-5036.

Vice President, Scouting/Player Development: Grady Fuson.

Director, Minor League Operations: Mike Wickham. **Coordinator, Latin American Operations:** Juan Lara. **Administrative Assistant, Scouting/Player Development:** Ilana Miller.

Roving Instructors: Mike Couchee (pitching), Tony Muser (hitting), Tom Gamboa (field coordinator), Duffy Dyer (catching), Gary Jones (infield), John Maxwell (trainer coordinator), Dan Morrison (strength/conditioning).

Farm System

Class	Farm Club	League	Manager	Coach	Pitching Coach
Triple-A	Portland	Pacific Coast	Randy Ready	Max Venable	Glenn Abbott
Double-A	San Antonio	Texas	Bill Masse	Terry Kennedy	Steve Webber
High A	Lake Elsinore	California	Carlos Lezcano	Shane Spencer	Wally Whitehurst
Low A	Fort Wayne	Midwest	Doug Dascenzo	Tom Tornincasa	Tom Bradley
Short-season	Eugene	Northwest	Greg Riddoch	Darrell Sherman	Dave Rajsich
Rookie	Padres	Arizona	Jose Flores	Bob Skube	Bronswell Patrick
Rookie	Padres	Dominican	Evaristo Lantigua	J. Mateo/C. Reyes	J.Amancio/C.Hernandez

Scouting

Telephone: (619) 795-5343. **Fax:** (619) 795-5036.

Director, Scouting: Bill Gayton.

Director, Professional/International Scouting: Randy Smith.

Assistant Director, Scouting: Pete DeYoung.

Major League Scouts: Ken Bracey (Dunlap, IL), Ray Crone (Waxahachie, TX), Bill Bryk (Schereville, IL).

Professional Scouts: Chris Gwynn (Alta Loma, CA), Todd Greene (Alpharetta, GA), Van Smith (Belleville, IL), Joe Bochy (Plant City, FL).

National Crosscheckers: Bob Filotei (Mobile, AL), Scott Littlefield (Long Beach, CA).

Area Scouts: Bryan Bealer (Oak Park, CA), Rob Sidwell (Windermere, FL), Rich Bordi (Rohnert Park, CA), Andrew Salvo (Lakebay, WA), Jim Bretz (South Windsor, CT), Lane Decker (Piedmont, OK), Pete DeYoung (Atlanta, GA), David Francia (Dickinson, AL), Brendan Hause (Carlsbad, CA), Tim Holt (Allen, TX), Ash Lawson (Athens, TN), Dave Lottsfeldt (Castle Rock, CO), Jeff Stewart (Normal, IL).

Part-time Scouts: Robert Gutierrez (Carol City, FL), Hank Krause (Akron, IA), Willie Ronda (Las Lomas Rio Piedras, Puerto Rico), Cam Walker (Centerville, IA), Murray Zuk (Souris, Manitoba).

International Scouts: Antonio Alejos (Venezuela), Ysreal Rojas (Dominican Republic), Milton Croes (Aruba), Marical Del Valle (Colombia), Felix Feliz (Dominican Republic), Wellington Herrera (Curacao), Elvin Jarquin (Nicaragua), Yfrain Linares (Venezuela), Victor Magdaleno (Venezuela), Francis Mojica (Dominican Republic), Ricardo Montenegro (Panama), Robert Rowley (Panama), Jose Salado (Dominican Republic), Illich Salazar (Venezuela), Trevor Schumm (Australia).

San Francisco Giants

Office Address: AT&T Park, 24 Willie Mays Plaza, San Francisco, CA 94107.
Telephone: (415) 972-2000. **Fax:** (415) 947-2800.
Website: www.sfgiants.com.

Ownership

Operated By: San Francisco Baseball Associates LP.

President, Managing General Partner: Peter Magowan, Senior General Partner: Sue Burns. **General Partner:** William Neukom. **Special Assistant:** Willie Mays. **Senior Adviser:** Willie McCovey.

BUSINESS OPERATIONS

Executive Vice President/COO: Laurence Baer. **Senior VP, General Counsel:** Jack Bair. **VP, Human Resources:** Joyce Thomas.

Finance

Senior Vice President/CFO: John Yee. **Senior VP/Chief Information Officer:** Bill Schlough. **Director, Information Technology:** Ken Logan. **VP, Administration:** Alfonso Felder. **VP, Finance:** Lisa Pantages.

Marketing/Sales

Senior Vice President, Corporate Marketing: Mario Alioto. **VP, Corporate Sponsorship:** Jason Pearl. **Director, Special Events:** Valerie McGuire.

Senior Vice President, Consumer Marketing: Tom McDonald. **Director, Marketing/Entertainment:** Bryan Srabian.

Vice President, Client Relations: Annemarie Hastings. **VP, Sales:** Jeff Tucker. **Manager, Season Ticket Sales:** Craig Solomon.

Vice President/General Manager, Retail: Connie Kullberg. **Senior Director, Retail:** Derik Landry.

Peter Magowan

Media Relations/Community Relations

Telephone: (415) 972-2448. **Fax:** (415) 947-2800.

Senior Vice President, Communications: Staci Slaughter.

Director, Broadcasting/Media Services: Maria Jacinto. **Director, Media Relations:** Blake Rhodes. **Associate Director, Media Relations:** Jim Moorehead. **Manager, Media Relations:** Matt Hodson. **Hispanic Media Services Coordinator:** Erwin Higueros.

Vice President, Print Publications/Creative Services: Nancy Donati.

Director, Public Affairs: Shana Daum. **Director, Photography/Archives:** Missy Mikulecky.

Ballpark Operations

Senior Vice President, Ballpark Operations: Jorge Costa. **VP, Guest Services:** Rick Mears. **Senior Director, Ballpark Operations:** Gene Telucci.

Director, Housekeeping: Frank Peinado. **Senior Director, Security:** Tinie Roberson. **Head Groundskeeper:** Scott MacVicar.

PA Announcer: Renel Brooks-Moon. **Official Scorers:** Chuck Dybdal, Art Santo Domingo, Al Talboy.

Ticketing

Telephone: (415) 972-2000. **Fax:** (415) 947-2500.

Managing Vice President, Ticket Services/Client Relations: Russ Stanley. **Director, Ticket Services:** Devin Lutes. **Director, Luxury Suites:** Amy Luskotoff. **Manager, Ticket Accounting:** Kem Easley. **Senior Manager, Ticket Operations:** Anita Sprinkles. **Senior Box Office Manager:** Todd Pierce.

Travel/Clubhouse

Coordinator, Team Travel: Michael King. **Coordinator, Organizational Travel:** Mike Scardino.

Home Clubhouse Manager: Miguel Murphy. **Visitors Clubhouse:** Harvey Hodgerney. **Umpires Attendant:** Rob Dean.

GENERAL INFORMATION

Stadium (year opened): AT&T Park (2000).
Home Dugout: Third Base. **Playing Surface:** Grass.
Team Colors: Black, orange and cream.
Player Representative: Randy Winn.

Brian Sabean

BASEBALL OPERATIONS

Telephone: (415) 972-1922. **Fax:** (415) 947-2737.

Senior Vice President, General Manager: Brian Sabean.

Vice President, Player Personnel: Dick Tidrow. **Director, Player Personnel:** Bobby Evans. **Special Assistant to GM:** Felipe Alou. **Senior Advisor, Baseball Operations:** Tony Siegle. **Director, Baseball Operations:** Jeremy Shelley. **Senior Advisors, Player Personnel:** Ron Schueler, Joe Lefebvre. **Executive Assistant to GM:** Karen Sweeney.

Major League Staff

Manager: Bruce Bochy.

Coaches: Bench—Ron Wotus; Pitching—Dave Righetti; Hitting—Carney Lansford; First Base—Roberto Kelley; Third Base—Tim Flannery; Bullpen—Mark Gardner.

Bruce Bochy

Medical/Training

Team Physicians: Dr. Robert Murray, Dr. Ken Akizuki, Dr. Anthony Saglimbeni.

Head Trainer: Dave Groeschner. **Assistant Trainers:** Mark Gruesbeck, Ben Potenziano. **Coordinator, Medical Administration:** Chrissy Yuen.

Player Development

Telephone: (415) 972-1922. **Fax:** (415) 947-2929.

Director, Player Development: Fred Stanley.

Senior Consultants, Player Personnel: Jack Hiatt, Ron Perranoski. **Special Assistants, Player Development:** Joe Amalfitano, Jim Davenport. **Coordinator, Baseball Operations:** Yeshayah Goldfarb.

Director, Arizona Minor League Operations: Alan Lee. **Assistant, Minor League Operations:** Clara Ho. **Arizona Minor League Operations Assistant:** Tyler Holmes.

Coordinator, Minor League Instruction: Shane Turner. **Coordinator, Minor League Pitching:** Bert Bradley. **Coordinator, Minor League Hitting:** Bob Mariano. **Coordinator, Latin American Instruction:** Leo Garcia.

Roving Instructors: Brian Harper (catching), Jose Alguacil (infield), Terry Shumpert (baserunning/outfield), Kirt Manwaring (spring training catching instructor), Lee Smith (pitching), Taira Uematsu (bullpen catcher).

Coordinator, Minor League Trainers: Jay Williams. **Minor League Strength/Rehabilitation Coordinator:** Ben Bush. **Minor League Physical Therapist:** Tony Reale.

Farm System

Class	Farm Club	League	Manager	Coach	Pitching Coach
Triple-A	Fresno	Pacific Coast	Dan Rohn	Jim Bowie	Mike Caldwell
Double-A	Connecticut	Eastern	Bien Figueroa	Victor Torres	Bob Stanley
High A	San Jose	California	Steve Decker	Gary Davenport	Patrick Rice
Low A	Augusta	South Atlantic	Andy Skeels	Lipso Nava	Ross Grimsley
Short-season	Salem-Keizer	Northwest	Tom Trebelhorn	Ricky Ward	Jerry Cram
Rookie	Scottsdale	Arizona	David Machemer	Bert Hunter	Will Malerich
Rookie	Giants	Dominican	Jesus Tavarez	Carlos Valderrama	Marcos Aguasvivas

Scouting

Telephone: (415) 972-1922. **Fax:** (415) 947-2737.

Special Assistant to GM, Scouting: John Barr (Haddonfield, NJ).

Senior Advisor, Scouting: Ed Creech (Moultrie, GA). **Coordinator of Amateur Scouting:** Doug Mapson (Chandler, AZ). **Special Assistants, Scouting:** Matt Nerland (Clayton, CA), Ted Uhlaender (Parshall, CO).

Major League Scouts: Joe DiCarlo (Ringwood, NJ), Lee Elder (Augusta, GA), Stan Saleski (Dayton, OH), Randy Santin (Miami, FL), Paul Turco Sr. (Sarasota, FL), Tom Zimmer (St. Petersburg, FL).

Special Assignment Scouts: Dick Cole (Costa Mesa, CA), Larry Osbourne (Woodstock, GA).

Regional Supervisors: Mideast—Dean DeCillis (Weston, FL), Midwest—Joe Strain (Englewood, CO), East—Paul Turco (Tampa, FL), West—Darren Wittcke (Gresham, OR).

Area Scouts: Ray Callari (Quebec, Canada), Brad Cameron (Los Alamitos, CA), Kevin Christman (Noblesville, IN), Lou Colletti (Elk Grove Village, IL), John DiCarlo (Glenwood, NJ), Chuck Hensley (Erie, CO), Andrew Jefferson (Mobile, AL), Mike Kendall (Rancho Palos Verdes, CA), Tom Korenek (Houston, TX), Felix Negron (Bayamon, PR), Sean O'Connor (Cartersville, GA), Pat Portugal (Wake Forest, NC), John Shafer (Portland, OR), Keith Snider (Stockton, CA), Todd Thomas (Dallas, TX), Glenn Tufts (Bridgewater, MA), Hugh Walker (Jonesboro, AR), Matt Woodward (Vancouver, WA).

Director, Dominican Republic Operations: Pablo Peguero. **Venezuela Supervisor:** Ciro Villalobos. **Special Assignment Scout, Latin America:** Mateo Alou.

International Scouts: Basilio Alvarado (Dominican Republic), Jonathan Arraiz (Venezuela), John Cox (Yucaipa, CA), Philip Elhage (Curacao), Edgar Fernandez (Venezuela), Ricardo Heron (Panama), Ton Hofstede (Holland), Arthur Mari (Netherlands), Juan Marquez (Venezuela), Sebastian Martinez (Venezuela), Daniel Mavarez (Colombia), Francisco Mouet (Mexico), Hector Ortiz (Dominican Republic), Jim Patterson (Australia), Felix Peguero (Dominican Republic), Luis Pena (Mexico), Jesus Stephens (Dominican Republic), Alex Torres (Nicaragua).

Seattle Mariners

Office Address: 1250 First Avenue South, Seattle, WA 98134.
Mailing Address: P.O. Box 4100, Seattle, WA 98194.
Telephone: (206) 346-4000. **Fax:** (206) 346-4400.
Website: www.mariners.com.

Ownership

Board of Directors: Minoru Arakawa, John Ellis, Chris Larson, Howard Lincoln, Wayne Perry, Frank Shrontz, Craig Watjen.

President, Chief Operating Officer: Chuck Armstrong.

Chuck Armstrong

BUSINESS OPERATIONS

Finance

Executive Vice President, Finance/Ballpark Operations: Kevin Mather. **VP, Finance:** Tim Kornegay. **Controller:** Greg Massey. **VP, Human Resources:** Marianne Short.

Marketing, Sales

Executive Vice President, Business/Operations: Bob Aylward. **VP, Corporate Business/ Community Relations:** Joe Chard. **Director, Corporate Business:** Ingrid Russell-Narcisse. **VP, Marketing:** Kevin Martinez. **Director, Marketing:** Gregg Greene. **Senior Director, Merchandise:** Jim La Shell.

Vice President, Sales: Frances Traisman. **Director, Group/Season Ticket Sales:** Bob Hellinger. **Director, Private Suite Sales:** Steve Camp. **Suite Sales:** Moose Clausen, Jill Dahlen.

Baseball Information, Communications

Telephone: (206) 346-4000. **Fax:** (206) 346-4400.

Vice President, Communications: Randy Adamack.

Director, Baseball Information: Tim Hevly. **Manager, Baseball Information:** Jeff Evans. **Coordinator, Baseball Information:** Kelly Munro. **Assistant, Baseball Information:** Fernando Alcala.

Director, Public Information: Rebecca Hale. **Director, Graphic Design:** Carl Morton. **Director, Community Relations:** Gina Hasson. **Manager, Community Programs:** Sean Grindley.

Ticketing

Telephone: (206) 346-4001. **Fax:** (206) 346-4100.

Director, Ticketing/Parking Operations: Malcolm Rogel. **Director, Ticket Services:** Jennifer Sweigert. **Manager, Group/Suite Ticket Services:** Steve Belling. **Manager, Box Office:** Malcolm Rogel.

Stadium Operations

Vice President, Ballpark Operations: Scott Jenkins. **Senior Director, Safeco Field Operations:** Tony Pereira. **Director, Guest Services:** Kathleen Lenihan. **Director, Security:** Jason Weaving. **Director, Events:** Jill Hashimoto.

Vice President, Information Services: Dave Curry. **Director, PBX/Retail Systems:** Oliver Roy. **Director, Procurement:** Sandy Fielder.

Head Groundskeeper: Bob Christofferson. **Assistant Head Groundskeepers:** Tim Wilson, Leo Liebert. **PA Announcer:** Tom Hutyler. **Official Scorer:** Eric Radovich.

Travel, Clubhouse

Director, Team Travel: Ron Spellecy.

Clubhouse Manager: Ted Walsh. **Visiting Clubhouse Manager:** Henry Genzale. **Video Coordinator:** Carl Hamilton.

GENERAL INFORMATION

Stadium (year opened): Safeco Field (1999).
Home Dugout: First Base. **Playing Surface:** Grass.
Team Colors: Northwest green, silver and navy blue.
Player Representative: Unavailable.

Bill Bavasi

BASEBALL OPERATIONS

Executive Vice President, General Manager: Bill Bavasi.

VP, Associate GM: Lee Pelekoudas. **VP, Player Personnel:** Benny Looper. **Special Assistants to GM:** John Boles, Ken Madeja, Dave Wallace. **Director, Baseball Administration:** Jim Na.

Administrator, Baseball Operations: Debbie Larsen.

Major League Staff

Manager: John McLaren.

Coaches: Dugout—Jim Riggleman; Pitching— Mel Stottlemyre; Batting—Jeff Pentland; First Base—Eddie Rodriguez; Third Base—Sam Perlozzo; Bullpen—Norm Charlton.

Medical, Training

Medical Director: Dr. Edward Khalfayan. **Club Physician:** Dr. **Mitchel Storey.**

Head Trainer: Rick Griffin. **Assistant Trainers:** Rob Nodine, Takayoshi Morimoto. **Stength/Conditioning:** Allen Wirtala. **Physical Therapist:** Jason Steere.

John McLaren

Player Development

Telephone: (206) 346-4313. **Fax:** (206) 346-4300.

Director, Player Development: Greg Hunter. **Director, Minor League/Scouting Operations:** Hide Sueyoshi. **Administrator, Player Development:** Jan Plein.

Coordinator, Minor League Instruction: Pedro Grifol. **Trainer Coordinator:** Mickey Clarizio.

Roving Instructors: James Clifford (strength/conditioning), Darrin Garner (infield), Roger Hansen (catching), Jose Castro (hitting), Dave Wallace (pitching), Mike Tosar (outfield/baserunning).

Farm System

Class	Farm Club	League	Manager	Coach	Pitching Coach
Triple-A	Tacoma	Pacific Coast	Darren Brown	Dwight Bernard	Alonzo Powell
Double-A	West Tenn	Eastern	Scott Steinmann	Scott Budner	Phil Plantier
High A	High Desert	California	Jim Horner	Lance Painter	Tommy Cruz
Low A	Wisconsin	Midwest	Terry Pollsreisz	Jaime Navarro	R. Santo Domingo
Short-season	Everett	Northwest	Jose Moreno	Nasusel Cabrera	Henry Cotto
Rookie	Pulaski	Appalachian	Unavailable	Unavailable	Unavailable
Rookie	Peoria	Arizona	Unavailable	Gary Wheelock	Andy Bottin
Rookie	Mariners	Dominican	Raymond Mejia	Franklin Taveras Jr.	Francisco Gerez
Rookie	Mariners	Venezuelan	Russell Vasquez	Jesus Hernandez	W. Oropeza/J. Azuaje

Scouting

Telephone: (206) 346-4000. **Fax:** (206) 346-4300.

Vice President, Scouting: Bob Fontaine. **Administrator, Scouting:** Hallie Larson.

Special Assignments/West Coast Coordinator: Tom Davis. **Advance Scout:** Steve Peck (Phoenix, AZ).

Major League Scouts: Al Gallagher (Arlington, TX), Bob Harrison (Long Beach, CA), Bill Kearns (Milton, MA), John McMichen (Treasure Island, FL), Frank Mattox (Peoria, AZ), Bob Miske (Amherst, NY), Wayne Morgan (Pebble Beach, CA), Bernie Pleskoff (Cave Creek, AZ), Steve Pope (Asheville, NC), Jack Uhey (Ridgefield, WA).

National Coordinators: Rick Ingalls (Long Beach, CA), Steve Jongewaard (Napa, CA), Ron Tostenson (El Dorado Hills, CA). **Territorial Coordinators:** West—Tom Davis (Ripon, CA); Midwest—Mark Lummus (Cleburne, TX); Southeast—John McMichen (Treasure Island, FL); Northeast—Dave May (Wilmington, DE).

Territorial Supervisors: Dave Alexander (Lafayette, IN), Chuck Carlson (Treasure Island, FL), Jim Fitzgerald (Woodinville, WA), Phil Geisler (Mount Horeb, WI), Rob Mummau (Stephens City, VA), Brian Nichols (Taunton, MA), Chris Pelekoudas (Goodyear, AZ), Stacey Pettis (Antioch, CA), Tim Reynolds (Irvine, CA), Alvin Rittman (Memphis, TN), Jack Smitheran (Coto De Caza, CA), Mike Tosar (Miami, FL), Kyle Van Hook (Brenham, TX), Greg Whitworth (Los Angeles, CA), Brian Williams (Cincinnati, OH), Dan Wright (Cave Springs, AR).

Vice President, International Operations: Bob Engle (Tampa, FL).

Coordinator, Special Projects International: Ted Heid (Glendale, AZ), Coordinator, Pacific Rim: Pat Kelly. **Coordinator, Canada/Europe:** Wayne Norton (Port Moody, British Columbia).

Supervisors, International Scouting: Pedro Avila (Venezuela), Emilio Carrasquel (Venezuela), Patrick Guerrero (Dominican Republic), Matt Stark (Mexico), Jamey Storvick (Taiwan), Curtis Wallace (Colombia), Yasushi Yamamoto (Japan).

Tampa Bay Rays

Office Address: Tropicana Field, One Tropicana Drive, St. Petersburg, FL 33705.
Telephone: (727) 825-3242. **Fax:** (727) 825-3111.
Website: www.raysbaseball.com

Ownership

Principal Owner: Stuart Sternberg. **President:** Matt Silverman.

BUSINESS OPERATIONS

Senior Vice President, Administration/General Counsel: John Higgins. **Senior VP, Business Operations:** Brian Auld. **Senior VP/Chief Sales Officer:** Mark Fernandez. **Senior VP, Development/Business Affairs:** Michael Kalt. **Senior Director, Development:** Melanie Lenz.

Stuart Sternberg

Finance

Vice President, Finance: Rob Gagliardi. **Controller:** Patrick Smith. **Supervisor, Accounting:** Sandra Faulkner. **Payroll Supervisor:** Brenda Richardson. **Coordinator, Accounting:** Jill Baetz. **Coordinator, Accounts Payable:** Sam Reams.

Marketing/Community Relations

Vice President, Marketing/Community Relations: Tom Hoof. **Director, Marketing/Promotions:** Brian Killingsworth. **Director, Community Relations:** Suzanne Murchland. **Senior Manager, Community Relations:** Leslie Tieszen. **Manager, Community Relations:** Beth Bohnsack. **Manager, Advertising:** Carey Cox.

Communications/Broadcasting

Vice President, Communications: Rick Vaughn. **Director, Communications:** Chris Costello. **Manager, Communications:** Carmen Molina. **Coordinator, Communications:** Dave Haller. **Senior Director, Broadcasting:** Larry McCabe. **Director, Radio Operations:** Rich Herrera. **Manager, Broadcast Traffic:** Erin Buscemi.

Ticket Sales

Vice President, Sales/Service: Brian Richeson. **Senior Director, Group/Suite Sales:** Clark Beacom. **Director, Season Ticket Sales/Service:** Jeff Tanzer. **Manager, Group Sales:** Chad Collard.

Director, Ticket Operations: Robert Bennett. **Assistant Director, Ticket Operations:** Ken Mallory. **Manager, Home Plate Club:** Craig Champagne. **Administrative Assistant, Fan Development:** Kristi Capone.

Stadium Operations

Vice President, Operations/Facilities: Rick Nafe. **Senior Director, Building Operations:** Scott Kelyman. **Director, Event Operations:** Tom Karac. **Event Manager:** Todd Hardy. **Manager, Audio/Visual Services:** Ron Golick. **Coordinator, Booking Coordinator:** Caren Dana. **Head Groundskeeper:** Dan Moeller.

Vice President, Branding/Fan Experience: Darcy Raymond. **Manager, Fan Experience:** Shannon Poole. **Coordinator, Video:** Jeff Cedarbaum. **Coordinator, Entertainment:** Jamie Patterson.

Travel, Clubhouse

Director, Team Travel: Jeff Ziegler. **Equipment Manager, Home Clubhouse:** Chris Westmoreland. **Assistant Manager, Home Clubhouse:** Jose Fernandez. **Manager, Visiting Clubhouse:** Guy Gallagher. **Video Coordinator:** Chris Fernandez.

GENERAL INFORMATION

Stadium (year opened): Tropicana Field (1998).
Home Dugout: First Base. **Playing Surface:** FieldTurf Duofilament.
Team Colors: Dark blue, light blue, yellow.
Player Representative: Rocco Baldelli.

Andrew Friedman

BASEBALL OPERATIONS

Executive Vice President, Baseball Operations: Andrew Friedman. **Senior VP, Baseball Operations:** Gerry Hunsicker.

Director, Baseball Operations: Dan Feinstein. **Director, International Operations:** Carlos Alfonso. **Director, Major League Administration:** Sandy Dengler. **Senior Baseball Advisor:** Don Zimmer.

Major League Staff

Manager: Joe Maddon.

Coaches: Bench—Dave Martinez; Pitching—Jim Hickey; Batting—Steve Henderson; First Base—George Hendrick; Third Base—Tom Foley; Bullpen—Bobby Ramos; Assistant Major League Coach—Tim Bogar.

Joe Maddon

Medical/Training

Medical Director: Dr. James Andrews. **Medical Team Physician:** Dr. Michael Reilly. **Orthopedic Team Physician:** Dr. Koco Eaton.

Head Athletic Trainer: Ron Porterfield. **Assistant Athletic Trainers:** Paul Harker, Nick Paparesta. **Strength/Conditioning Coach:** Kevin Barr.

Minor Leagues

Telephone: (727) 825-3267. **Fax:** (727) 825-3493.

Director, Minor League Operations: Mitch Lukevics. **Assistant Director, Minor League Operations:** Chaim Bloom. **Administrator, Minor League Operations:** Giovanna Rodriguez.

Field Coordinator: Jim Hoff. **Minor League Coordinators:** Skeeter Barnes (outfield/baserunning), Dick Bosman (pitching), Steve Livesey (hitting), Jamie Nelson (catching), Trung Cao (strength/conditioning), Mark Vinson (rehabilitation/athletic training), Chris Tomashoff (assistant athletic training).

Equipment Manager: Tim McKechney. **Assistant Equipment Manager:** Shane Rossetti.

Farm System

Class	Farm Club	League	Manager	Coach	Pitching Coach
Triple-A	Durham	International	Charlie Montoyo	Gary Gaetti	Xavier Hernandez
Double-A	Montgomery	Southern	Billy Gardner Jr.	Ben Oglivie	Neil Allen
High A	Vero Beach	Florida State	Jim Morrison	Brady Williams	R.C. Lichtenstein
Low A	Columbus	South Atlantic	Matt Quatraro	Ozzie Timmons	Bill Moloney
Short-season	Hudson Valley	New York-Penn	Joe Alvarez	J. Sandberg/M. Johns	Rafael Montalvo
Rookie	Princeton	Appalachian	Joe Szekely	R. Deleon/H. Torres	Marty DeMerritt
Rookie	Rays	Dominican	Manny Castillo	Julio Zorrilla	Darwin Peguero
Rookie	Rays	Venezuelan	Marlon Roche	Wuarner Rincones	Jorge Moncada

Scouting

Telephone: (727) 825-3241. **Fax:** (727) 825-3493.

Scouting Director: R.J. Harrison (Phoenix, AZ).

Administrator, Scouting: Nancy Berry.

Major League Advance Scout: Elanis Westbrooks (Houston, TX).

Professional Scouts: Matt Arnold (Taylor Mill, KY), Bart Braun (Vallejo, CA), Mike Cubbage (Keswick, VA), Larry Doughty (Leawood, KS), Bill Evers (New Port Richey, FL), Gene Glynn (Weseca, MN), Gail Henley (La Verne, CA), Brian Keegan (Matthews, NC), Joe Nigro (Staten Island, NY), Jim Pransky (Davenport, IA), Dave Roberts (Fort Worth, TX).

National Crosschecker: Tim Huff (Cave Creek, AZ). **East Coast Crosschecker:** Kevin Elfering (Wesley Chapel, FL). **Midwest Crosschecker:** Ken Stauffer (Katy, TX). **West Coast Crosschecker:** Fred Repke (Carson City, NV).

Area Scouts: James Bonnici (Davison, MI), Evan Brannon (St. Petersburg, FL), John Ceprini (Massapequa, NY), Tom Couston (Chicago, IL), Carlos Delgado (San Francisco, CA), Rickey Drexler (New Iberia, LA), Jayson Durocher (Cave Creek, AZ), Brian Hickman (Sapulpa, OK), Milt Hill (Cumming, GA), Paul Kirsch (Sherwood, OR), Brad Matthews (Concord, NC), Rob Moen (Playa del Rey, CA), Pat Murphy (Marble Falls, TX), Jake Wilson (Carlsbad, CA), Doug Witt (Brooklyn, MD).

Part-Time Area Scouts: Jack Cressend (Mandeville, LA), Tom Delong (Ocala, FL), Jose Hernandez (Miami, FL), Jim Lief (Wellington, FL), Graig Merritt (Pitts Meadow, Canada), Gil Martinez (San Juan, PR), Casey Onaga (Aiea, HI), Paul Robles (Loomis, CA), Tony Russo (Fayetteville, NC), Donald Turley (Spring, TX).

Director, Venezuelan Operations: Ronnie Blanco. **Director, Dominican Republic Operations:** Eddy Toledo. **Assistant, International Operations:** Nelson Montes de Oca. **Special Assistant, Baseball Operations:** Andres Reiner.

Texas Rangers

Office Address: 1000 Ballpark Way, Arlington, TX 76011.
Mailing Address: P.O. Box 90111, Arlington, TX 76011.
Telephone: (817) 273-5222. **Fax:** (817) 273-5110.
Website: www.texasrangers.com.

Ownership

Owner: Hicks Holdings.
Chairman of the Board: Tom Hicks.

BUSINESS OPERATIONS

Tom Hicks

Executive Vice President, Business Operations: Rick McLaughlin. **Executive VP, Sales/Marketing:** Andy Silverman. **Executive VP, Communications:** Jim Sundberg. **Executive VP, Hicks Holdings LLC:** Casey Shilts. **VP, Hicks Holdings LLC:** Thomas Hicks Jr. **VP, Finance:** Kellie Fischer.

Finance/Accounting

Assistant Vice President, Controller: Starr Pritchard. **Director, Finance:** Donna Kee. **Payroll Manager:** Donna Ebersole. **Senior Staff Accountant:** Paula Murphy. **Staff Accountant, Treasury:** Shannon Garrett.

Human Resources/Legal/Information Technology

Vice President, Human Resources: Terry Turner. **Associate Counsel:** Kate Jett. **Manager, Benefits/Compensation:** Carla Clack. **Supervisor, Staffing/Development:** Shannon Cain.

Assistant Vice President, Information Technology: Mike Bullock. **Manager, IT Systems/Customer Service:** Fred Phillips. **Senior Network Engineers:** Greg Garrison, Erwin Chung.

Business/Event Operations

Vice President, Event Operations/Security: John Hardin. **Senior Director, Customer Service:** Donnie Pordash. **Assistant Director, Security:** Mickey McGovern. **Director, Event Operations:** Danielle Cornwell.

Communications

Phone: (817) 273-5203. **Fax:** (817) 273-5110.

Senior Director, Media Relations: Rich Rice. **Manager, Communications:** Abby Teaf. **Assistant, Media Relations:** Court Berry-Tripp.

Facilities

Assistant Vice President, Facilities Operations: Gib Searight. **Director, Grounds:** Dennis Klein. **Coordinator, Grounds:** Scott Donathan. **Director, Maintenance/MEP:** Mike Call. **Coordinator, Facility Services:** Duane Arber. **Coordinator, General Maintenance:** John Deardorff. **Coordinator, Complex Grounds:** Andrew St. Julian. **Grounds Crew:** Devories Spencer. **Complex Grounds Crew:** Hermillo Chavez, Hipolito Rojas, Jesus Reyes.

Marketing

Vice President, In-Park Entertainment: Chuck Morgan. **VP, External Affairs:** Norm Lyons. **Assistant VP, Marketing:** Kelly Calvert. **Senior Director, Graphic Design:** Rainer Uhlir. **Director, Publications:** Kurt Daniels. **Director, Promotions/Special Events:** Sherry Flow. **Director, Media:** Heidi Benoit. **Director, Hispanic Marketing/Foundation Events:** Karin Morris. **Creative Director, Media:** Rush Olson. **Director, Broadcasting/Promotions:** Angie Swint.

Merchandising

Assistant Vice President, Merchandising: Diane Atkinson. **Senior Manager, Ballpark Retail Operations:** Stephen Moore. **Manager, Warehouse Operations:** Sean Parent. **Retail Manager:** Eric Garcia. **Assistant Retail Manager:** Randy Wolveck. **Grand Slam Store Manager:** John Reneau.

Ticketing

Senior Vice President, Luxury Suite Sales: Paige Farragut. **Senior Director, Ticket Sales:** Ken Troupe. **Senior Director, Baseball Programs/Youth Ballpark:** Breon Dennis. **Director, Inside Sales:** Chip Kisabeth. **Manager, Group Sales:** Pat Harvey. **Manager, Season Tickets:** Troy King. **Database Manager:** Laura O'Brien. **Manager, Nightly Rental Sales Suites:** Heather Hansen. **Coordinator, Premium Services:** Catherine Bartlett. **Manager, Long Term Suite Sales:** Delia Williams.

Director, Ticket Services: Mike Lentz. **Manager, Ticket Operations:** Jordan Jackson. **Coordinator, Season Tickets:** Ben Rogers. **Coordinator, Group Tickets:** Cale Vennum. **Coordinator, Ticket Accounting Administration:** Ranae Lewis.

GENERAL INFORMATION

Stadium (year opened): Rangers Ballpark in Arlington (1994).
Home Dugout: First Base. **Playing Surface:** Grass.
Team Colors: Royal blue and red.
Player Representative: C.J. Wilson.

Jon Daniels

BASEBALL OPERATIONS

Telephone: (817) 273-5222. **Fax:** (817) 273-5285.

General Manager: Jon Daniels.

Assistant GM: Thad Levine. **Senior Advisor, Baseball Operations:** John Hart. **Senior Director, Baseball Operations:** Don Welke. **Special Assistant to GM:** Jay Robertson. **Senior Advisor to GM:** Tom Giordano. **Senior Advisor, Arizona Operations/Pro Scouting:** Mel Didier. **Manager, Baseball Operations:** Jake Krug. **Assistant, Baseball Operations:** Bobby Crook. **Executive Assistant to GM:** Barbara Pappenfus.

Major League Staff

Manager: Ron Washington.

Coaches: Bench—Art Howe; Pitching—Mark Connor; Batting—Rudy Jaramillo; First Base—Gary Pettis; Third Base—Matt Walbeck; Bullpen—Dom Chiti; Special Assignment Coach--Johnny Narron.

Ron Washington

Medical, Training

Team Physician: Dr. Keith Meister. **Team Internist:** Dr. David Hunter. **Head Trainer/Medical Director:** Jamie Reed. **Assistant Trainer:** Kevin Harmon. **Director, Strength/Conditioning:** Jose Vazquez.

Player Development

Telephone: (817) 273-5224. **Fax:** (817) 273-5285.

Director, Player Personnel: Scott Servais.

Director, Minor League Operations: John Lombardo. **Administrative Assistant, Player Development/Scouting:** Margaret Bales. **Assistant, Player Development:** Alex Hicks. **Manager, Cultural Enhancement:** Bill McLaughlin. **Field Coordinator:** Dave Anderson.

Roving Instructors: Rick Adair (pitching), Keith Comstock (rehab pitching coach), Wayne Kirby (baserunning/outfield), Mike Boulanger (hitting), Napoleon Pichardo (strength), Matthew Lucero (medical coordinator), Brian Bobier (rehab coordinator).

Manager, Minor League Complex Operations: Chris Guth. **Assistant Equipment Manager:** Russ Oliver. **Arizona Clubhouse Manager:** Troy Timney.

Farm System

Class	Farm Club	League	Manager	Coach	Pitching Coach
Triple-A	Oklahoma	Pacific Coast	Bobby Jones	Randy Whisler	Andy Hawkins
Double-A	Frisco	Texas	Scott Little	Scott Coolbaugh	Terry Clark
High A	Bakersfield	California	Damon Berryhill	Brant Brown	Dave Chavarria
Low A	Clinton	Midwest	Mike Micucci	Brian Dayett	Danny Clark
Short-season	Spokane	Northwest	Tim Hulett	Hector Ortiz	Mike Anderson
Rookie	Rangers	Arizona	Bill Richardson	Scott Dwyer	J. Perez/J. Carlos Pulido
Rookie	Rangers	Dominican	Jayce Tingler	Guillermo Mercedes	John Burgos

Scouting

Telephone: (817) 273-5277. **Fax:** (817) 273-5285.

Director, Scouting: Ron Hopkins (Seattle, WA).

Director, Pro/International Scouting: A.J. Preller. **Manager, International Operations:** Mike Daly. **Manager, Pro Scouting:** Josh Boyd.

Professional Scouts: Keith Boeck (Chandler, AZ), Scot Engler (Montgomery, IL), Mark Giegler (Brighton, MI), Perry Minasian (Arlington, TX), Gary Rajsich (Arlington, TX).

National Crosschecker: Kip Fagg (Gilbert, AZ). **Central Crosschecker:** Mike Grouse (Olathe, KS). **Eastern Crosschecker:** Doug Harris (Carlisle, PA). **Western Crosschecker:** Kevin Bootay (Sacramento, CA).

Area Scouts: Juan Alvarez (Miami, FL), Russ Ardolina (Rockville, MD), Jim Cuthbert (Chapel Hill, NC), Guy DeMutis (Windermere, FL), Jay Eddings (Sperry, OK), Steve Flores (Temecula, CA), Todd Guggiana (Long Beach, CA), Derek Lee (Frankfurt, IL), Rick Matsko (New Brunswick, NJ), Gary McGraw (Gaston, OR), Butch Metzger (Sacramento, CA), Jon Poloni (Tarpon Springs, FL), Andy Pratt (Scottsdale, AZ), Dustin Smith (Emporia, KS), Randy Taylor (Katy, TX), Frankie Thon (Guaynabo, Puerto Rico), Jeff Wood (Birmingham, AL).

Pacific Rim Director: Jim Colborn.

Latin Coordinator: Manny Batista.

Dominican Program Coordinator: Danilo Troncosco. **International Scouts:** Rafic Saab (Venezuela), Chu Halabi (Curacao), Wilmer Becerra (Venezuela), Jesus Ovalle (Dominican Republic), Rodolfo Rosario (Dominican Republic), Edgar Suarez (Venezuela), Eduardo Thomas (Panama).

Toronto Blue Jays

Office/Mailing Address: 1 Blue Jays Way, Suite 3200, Toronto, Ontario M5V 1J1.
Telephone: (416) 341-1000. **Fax:** (416) 341-1250.
Website: www.bluejays.com.

Ownership

Operated by: Toronto Blue Jays Baseball Club.
Principal Owner: Rogers Communications Inc.

BUSINESS OPERATIONS

President/CEO: Paul Godfrey. **Executive Assistant to the President/CEO:** Julie Stoddart.
Senior Vice President, Stadium Operations: Richard Wong. **VP, Special Projects:** Howard Starkman.

Paul Godfrey

Finance

Vice President, Finance/Administration: John Boots. **Executive Administrative Assistant:** Donna Kuzoff. **Director, Payroll/Benefits:** Brenda Dimmer. **Director, Risk Management:** Suzanne Joncas. **Financial Business Managers:** Leslie Galant-Gardiner, Ela Phillips, Tanya Proctor. **Manager, Ticket Receipts/Vault Services:** Joseph Roach. **Manager, Stadium Payroll:** Sharon Dykstra. **Manager, Human Resources:** Michelle Carter. **Coordinator, Human Resources:** Gurpreet Singh. **Director, Information Technology:** Jacques Farand. **Information Technology Project Manager:** Anthony Miranda.

Marketing/Community Relations

Vice President, Marketing: Laurel Lindsay.
Executive Director, Jays Care Foundation: Danielle Silverstein. **Director, Community Relations:** Michael Volpatti. **Director, Player/Alumni Relations:** Jennifer Santamaria. **Executive Producer, Game Entertainment:** Deb Belinsky.
Vice President, Corporate Partnerships/Business Development: Mark Lemmon. **Director, Business Development:** John Griffin. **Director, Corporate Partnerships:** Robert Mackay. **Director, Partnership Marketing:** Krista Semotiuk.

Communications

Telephone: (416) 341-1301/1302/1303. **Fax:** (416) 341-1250.
Vice President, Communications: Jay Stenhouse.
Manager, Baseball Information: Mal Romanin. **Manager, Communications:** Nadia Flaim. **Coordinator, Baseball Information:** Erik Grosman. **Coordinator, Communications:** Sue Mallabon.

Stadium Operations

Vice President, Stadium Operations/Security: Mario Coutinho. **Executive Assistant, Stadium Operations/Security:** June Sym. **Head Groundskeeper:** Tom Farrell.

Ticketing

Telephone: (416) 341-1234. **Fax:** (416) 341-1177.
Vice President, Ticket Sales/Service: Patrick Elster. **Senior Adviser, Director of Special Projects:** Sheila Stella. **Director, Premium Sales:** Nancy Spotton. **Director, Sales Channel Development:** Shelby Nelson. **Director, Ticket Sales/Service:** Franc Rota. **Director, Ticket System/Box Office:** Doug Barr.

Travel/Clubhouse

Manager, Team Travel: Mike Shaw.
Equipment Manager: Jeff Ross. **Clubhouse Manager:** Kevin Malloy. **Visiting Clubhouse Manager:** Len Frejlich. **Video Operations:** Robert Baumander. **Video Operations Assistant:** Brian Abraham.

GENERAL INFORMATION

Stadium (year opened): Rogers Centre (1989).
Home Dugout: Third base. **Playing Surface:** Field turf.
Team Colors: Blue, silver, graphite, black and white.
Player Representative: Unavailable.

J.P. Ricciardi

BASEBALL OPERATIONS

Senior Vice President, Baseball Operations/General Manager: J.P. Ricciardi.

VP, Baseball Operations/Assistant GM: Alex Anthopoulos. **VP, Baseball Operations/ Assistant GM:** Bart Given. **Assistant GM, Player Personnel:** Tony LaCava. **Special Assistant to GM:** Sal Butera. **Executive Assistant to GM:** Ainsley Doyle. **Executive Assistant, Major League Operations:** Heather Connolly.

Major League Staff

Manager: John Gibbons.

Coaches: Bench—Brian Butterfield; Pitching—Brad Arnsberg; Hitting—Gary Denbo; First Base—Ernie Whitt; Third Base—Marty Pevey; Bullpen—Bruce Walton.

John Gibbons

Medical, Training

Medical Advisor: Dr. Bernie Gosevitz. **Team Physician:** Dr. Ron Taylor.

Head Trainer: George Poulis. **Assistant Trainer:** Dave Abraham. **Strength/Conditioning Coordinator:** Donovan Santas. **Director, Team Safety:** Ron Sandelli.

Player Development

Telephone: (727) 734-8007. **Fax:** (727) 734-8162.

Director, Player Development: Dick Scott.

Director, Employee Assistance Program: Ray Karesky.

Manager, Minor League Operations: Charlie Wilson. **Assistant, Latin American Operations:** Jeff Roemer. **Coordinator, Minor League Administration:** Joanna Nelson. **Administrative Assistant:** Kim Marsh. **Coordinator, Instruction:** Mike Basso.

Roving Instructors: Dane Johnson (pitching), Dwayne Murphy (hitting). **Minor League Coordinators:** Mike Frostad (training & rehab), Bryan King (strength & conditioning), Billy Wardlow (equipment).

Farm System

Class	Farm Team	League	Manager	Coach	Pitching Coach
Triple-A	Syracuse	International	Doug Davis	Al LeBeouf	Rick Langford
Double-A	New Hampshire	Eastern	Gary Cathcart	Ken Joyce	Dave LaRoche
High A	Dunedin	Florida State	Omar Malave	Paul Elliott	Darold Knowles
Low A	Lansing	Midwest	Clayton McCullough	Justin Mashore	Tom Signore
Short-season	Auburn	New York-Penn	Dennis Holmberg	Charlie Poe	Antonio Caceres
Rookie	Gulf Coast	Appalachian	Dave Pano	Danny Solano	Vince Horsman
Rookie	Blue Jays	Dominican 1	Jose Escobar	Emilio De Los Santos	Oswaldo Peraza
Rookie	Blue Jays	Dominican 2	Cesar Martin	Hedbertt Hurtado	Juan Perez

Scouting

Telephone: (416) 341-1115. **Fax:** (416) 341-1245.

Director, Scouting: Jon Lalonde.

Assistant Director, Scouting: Andrew Tinnish.

Professional Scouts: Mike Berger (Oakmont, PA), Tom Clark (Lakeland, FL), Kimball Crossley (Gilbert, AZ), Jim D'Aloia (Lakewood, NJ), Rob Ducey (Tarpon Springs, FL).

National Crosscheckers: Billy Gasparino, Mike Mangan, Tommy Tanous, Marc Tramuta.

Scouting Advisor: Smoke Laval. **Scouting Coordinator:** Ryan Mittleman.

Area Scouts: Chris Becerra (San Francisco, CA), Matt Briggs (Charlotte, NC), Tom Burns (Harrisburg, PA), Dan Cholowsky (Queen Creek, AZ), Joel Grampietro (Tampa, FL), Aaron Jersild (Houston, TX), Steve Miller (Chicago, IL), Ty Nichols (Broken Arrow, OK), Demerius Pittman (Corona, CA), Jorge Rivera (Puerto Nuevo, PR), Carlos Rodriguez (Miami, FL), Tim Rooney (Los Angeles, CA), Rob St. Julien (Lafayette, LA).

Director, Canadian Scouting: Kevin Briand (Etobicoke, ON). **Canadian Scouts:** Don Cowan (Delta, BC), Sean McCann (Toronto, ON), Jean Marc Mercier (Charlesbourg, PQ).

Director, Latin America Operations: Marco Paddy.

International Scouts: Miguel Bernard (Dominican Republic), Robinson Garces (Venezuela), Rafael Moncada (Venezuela), Lorenzo Perez (Dominican Republic), Luis Rodriquez (Panama), Juan Salavarria (Venezuela), Hilario Soriano (Dominican Republic), Greg Wade (Australia).

Washington Nationals

Office Address: 1500 South Capitol St. SE, Washington, DC 20003.
Telephone: (202) 640-7000. **FAX:** (202) 547-0025.
Website: www.nationals.com

Ownership

Managing Principal Owner: Theodore Lerner.

Principal Owners: Annette Lerner, Mark Lerner, Judy Lenkin Lerner, Edward Cohen, Debra Lerner Cohen, Robert Tanenbaum, Marla Lerner Tanenbaum.

BUSINESS OPERATIONS

Stan Kasten

President: Stan Kasten. **Executive Vice President:** Bob Wolfe.

Senior Vice President, Business Affairs: Mike Shapiro. **Senior VP, External Affairs:** Alphonso Maldon Jr. **Senior VP/Chief Marketing Officer:** Tom Ward. **Executive Assistant to President/Executive VP:** Cheryl Stevens.

Legal/Business Affairs

Senior Vice President, Business Affairs: Mike Shapiro. **Director, Ballpark Enterprises:** Heather Westrom. **VP, Club Counsel:** Damon Jones. **Assistant Counsel:** Amy Inlander.

Finance/Human Resources

Senior Vice President/Corporate Controller: Lori Creasy. **Controller:** Ted Towne. **Director, Accounting:** Kelly Pitchford. **Senior Accountants:** Julie Hellmer, Rachel Proctor. **Baseball Analyst:** Michael Page. **Manager, Payroll:** Mario Munoz. **Manager, Payroll (Florida):** Roxanne Earle. **VP, Human Resources:** Bettina Deynes. **Benefits Administrator:** Stephanie Olsen. **Coordinator, Human Resources:** Brenda Ferreira. **Chief Information Officer:** Suzanne Hall. **Director, Information Technology:** Jason Zachariah.

Sales/Marketing

Senior Vice President, Chief Marketing Officer: Tom Ward. **VP, Marketing/Broadcasting:** John Guagliano. **Manager, Database Marketing/Research:** Robert Rardin. **Manager, Promotions/Activations:** Lauren Pober. **Manager, Special Events:** Christine O'Connor. **Coordinator, Creative Services/Publications:** Daniel Kasper. **Production Coordinator:** Kellee Mickens. **Coordinator, Entertainment:** Thomas Davis.

VP, Corporate Partnerships: Tod Rosenweig. **Director, Business Development:** Catherine Silver. **Director, Partnership Services:** Allison Grinham.

Community Relations

Director, Community Relations: Barbra Silva. **Coordinator, Community Relations:** Nadia Wajid. **Senior Vice President, External Affairs/President, Washington Nationals Dream Foundation:** Alphonso Maldon Jr. **Chair, Washington Nationals Dream Foundation:** Marla Tanenbaum. **Managing Coordinator:** Vera Maher.

Media Relations, Communications

Vice President, Communications: Chartese Burnett. **Manager, Communications:** Lisa Pagano. **Senior Director, Baseball Media Relations:** John Dever. **Director, Baseball Media Relations:** Mike Gazda. **Coordinator, Baseball Media Relations:** Bill Gluvna.

Ticketing

Executive Director, Sales: Chris Gargani. **Director, Ticket Sales:** Brian Lowe. **Manager, Inside Sales:** Michael Ragan. **Senior Director, Client Services:** Stacey Marthaler. **Director, Ticket Operations:** Derek Younger. **Manager, Ticket Operations:** Peter Wallace. **Manager, Box Office:** Tyler Hubbard.

Ballpark Operations

Director, Ballpark Operations: Matt Blush. **Director, Security:** Bob Campbell. **Manager, Office Services:** Alberta Fiske. **Manager, Guest Services:** Kynneth Sutton. **Coordinators, Ballpark Operations:** Reemberto Rodriguez, Adam Lasky. **Director, Florida Operations:** Thomas Bell. **Head Groundskeeper:** Larry DiVitto. **Manager, Shipping/Receiving:** Javier Ferreira.

Senior Director, Ballpark District: Gregory McCarthy. **Director, Transportation/Planning:** Francine Waters.

Travel, Clubhouse

Director, Team Travel: Rob McDonald.

Clubhouse Manager: Mike Wallace. **Visiting Clubhouse Manager:** Matt Rosenthal.

GENERAL INFORMATION

Stadium (year opened): Nationals Park (2008).
Home Dugout: First Base. **Playing Surface:** Grass.
Team Colors: Red, white and blue.
Player Representative: Unavailable.

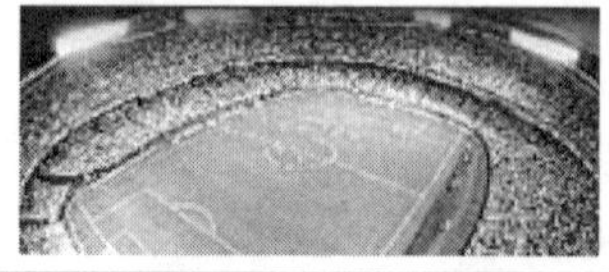

Jim Bowden

BASEBALL OPERATIONS

Vice President/General Manager: Jim Bowden.

Assistant GM/VP, Baseball Operations: Mike Rizzo. **Assistant GM/VP, Player Development:** Bob Boone. **Assistant GM, Baseball Administration:** Squire Galbreath. **Executive Assistant to GM:** Harolyn Cardozo.

Special Assistants to GM: Jose Rijo, Barry Larkin, Moose Stubing.

Video Coordinator: Tom Yost.

Major League Staff

Manager: Manny Acta.

Coaches: Bench—Pat Corrales; Pitching—Randy St. Claire; Hitting—Lenny Harris; First Base—Jerry Morales; Third Base—Tim Tolman; Bullpen—Rick Aponte.

Manny Acta

Medical, Training

Team Physician/Orthopedist: Dr. Benjamin Shaffer. **Team Orthopedist:** Dr. Ed Magur.

Head Trainer: Lee Kuntz. **Assistant Trainer:** Mike McGowen. **Strength/Conditioning Coach:** Kazuhiko Tomooka.

Player Development

Director, Player Development: Bobby Williams. **Assistant Director, Player Development:** Mark Scialabba. **Coordinator, Scouting/Player Development:** Jason Choi.

Assistants, Player Development: Adam Cromie, Ryan Thomas. **Assistant, Statistical Analysis:** Erick Dalton.

Field Coordinator: Jeff Garber. **Roving Coordinators:** Jose Cardenal (outfield/baserunning), Ralph Dickenson (hitting), Steve Gober (training/rehabilitation), Abraham Gonzalez (strength/conditioning), Mark Grater (pitching rehabilitation), Bobby Henley (catching), Devon White (outfield/baserunning), Spin Williams (pitching).

Farm System

Class	Farm Club	League	Manager	Coach(es)	Pitching Coach
Triple-A	Columbus	International	Tim Foli	Rick Eckstein	Steve McCatty
Double-A	Harrisburg	Eastern	John Stearns	Troy Gingrich	Rick Tomlin
High A	Potomac	Carolina	Randy Knorr	Jerry Browne	Randy Tomlin
Low A	Hagerstown	South Atlantic	Darnell Coles	T. Tarasco/S. Mendez	Paul Menhart
Short-season	Vermont	New York-Penn	Ramon Aviles	Jason Camilli	Rusty Meacham
Rookie	Melbourne	Gulf Coast	Bobby Henley	Paul Sanagorski	Franklin Bravo
Rookie	Nationals 1	Dominican	Juan Bernhardt	Elvis Herrera	Manuel Santana
Rookie	Nationals 2	Dominican	Frank Laureano	Soilo Perdoma	Mel Rojas

Scouting

Director, Scouting: Dana Brown. **Assistant Director, Scouting:** Brian Parker.

Assistant, Scouting: Reed Dunn.

Special Assignment/Pro Scouts: Bart Johnson, Bill Singer, Moose Stubing, Jeff Zona.

Advance Scout: Wade Taylor.

National Crosschecker: Ed Durkin. **Regional Crosscheckers:** East—Marteese Robinson; Midwest—Jimmy Gonzales; West—Kris Kline.

Area Scouts: Mike Alberts (Worcester, MA), Anthony Arango (Davie, FL), Steve Arnieri (Barrington, IL), Mark Baca (Temecula, CA), Denis Boucher (Montreal, Quebec), Ryan Fox (Yakima, WA), Bob Hamelin (Concord, NC), Kerrick Jackson (St. Louis, MO), Craig Kornfeld (Rancho Santa Margarita, CA), Bob Laurie (Plano, TX), Eric Robinson (Hiram, GA), Alex Smith (Abingdon, MD), Mitch Sokol (Phoenix, AZ), Paul Tinnell (West Bradenton, FL), Tyler Wilt (Montgomery, TX).

International Scouts: Delvy Santiago (Puerto Rico), Angel Santana (Dominican Republic), Moises De La Mota (Dominican Republic), Rudy Valera (Dominican Republic), Juan Espino (Dominican Republic).

MAJOR LEAGUE SCHEDULES

DRIVING DIRECTIONS

AMERICAN LEAGUE STADIUMS

CAMDEN YARDS, BALTIMORE

From the north and east on I-95, take I-395 (exit 53), downtown to Russell Street; from the south or west on I-95, take exit 52 to Russell Street North.

FENWAY PARK, BOSTON

Massachusetts Turnpike (I-90) to Prudential exit (stay left), right at first set of lights, right on Dalton Street, left on Boylston Street, right on Ipswich Street.

U.S. CELLULAR FIELD, CHICAGO

Dan Ryan Expressway (I-90/94) to 35th Street exit.

JACOBS FIELD, CLEVELAND

From south, I-77 North to East Ninth Street exit, to Ontario Street; From east, I-90/Route 2 west to downtown, remain on Route 2 to East Ninth Street, left to stadium.

COMERICA PARK, DETROIT

I-75 to Grand River exit, follow service drive east to stadium, located off Woodward Avenue.

KAUFFMAN STADIUM, KANSAS CITY

From north or south, take I-435 to stadium exits. From east or west, take I-70 to stadium exits.

ANGEL STADIUM, LOS ANGELES

Highway 57 (Orange Freeway) to Orangewood exit, west on Orangewood, stadium on west side of Orange Freeway.

METRODOME, MINNESOTA

I-35W south to Washington Avenue exit or I-35W north to Third Street exit. I-94 East to I-35W north to Third Street exit or I-94 West to Fifth Street exit.

YANKEE STADIUM, NEW YORK

From I-95 North, George Washington Bridge to Cross Bronx Expressway to exit 1C; Major Deegan South (I-87) to exit G (161st Street); I-87 North to 149th or 155th Streets; I-87 South to 161st Street.

MCAFEE COLISEUM, OAKLAND

From I-880, take either the 66th Avenue or Hegenberger Road exit.

SAFECO FIELD, SEATTLE

I-5 or I-90 to Fourth Avenue South exit.

TROPICANA FIELD, TAMPA BAY

I-275 South to St. Petersburg, exit 11, left onto Fifth Avenue, right onto 16th Street.

RANGERS BALLPARK IN ARLINGTON, TEXAS

From I-30, take Ballpark Way exit, south on Ballpark Way; From Route 360, take Randol Mill exit, west on Randol Mill.

ROGERS CENTRE, TORONTO

From west, take QEW/Gardiner Expressway eastbound and exit at Spadina Avenue, north on Spadina one block, right on Bremner Boulevard. From east, take Gardiner Expressway westbound and exit at Spadina Avenue, north on Spadina one block, right on Bremner Boulevard.

NATIONAL LEAGUE STADIUMS

CHASE FIELD, ARIZONA

I-10 to Seventh Street exit, turn south; I-17 to Seventh Street, turn north.

TURNER FIELD, ATLANTA

I-75/85 northbound/southbound, take exit 246 (Fulton Street); I-20 westbound, take exit 58A (Capitol Avenue); I-20 eastbound, take exit 56B (Windsor Street), right on Windsor Street, left on Fulton Street.

WRIGLEY FIELD, CHICAGO

I-90/94 to Addison Street exit, follow Addison five miles to ballpark. One mile west of Lakeshore Drive, exit at Belmont going northbound, exit at Irving Park going southbound.

GREAT AMERICAN BALL PARK, CINCINNATI

I-75 southbound, take Second Street exit. Ballpark is located off Second Street at Main Street. I-71 southbound, take Third Street exit, right on Broadway. I-75/I-71 northbound, take Second Street exit—far right lane on Brent Spence Bridge. Ballpark is located off Second Street at Main Street.

COORS FIELD, COLORADO

I-70 to I-25 South to exit 213 (Park Avenue) or 212C (20th Street); I-25 to 20th Street, east to park.

DOLPHINS STADIUM, FLORIDA

From south, Florida Turnpike extension to stadium exit; From north, I-95 to I-595 West to Florida Turnpike to stadium exit; From west, I-75 to I-595 to Florida Turnpike to stadium exit; From east, Highway 826 West to NW 27th Avenue, north to Dan Marino Blvd., right to stadium.

MINUTE MAID PARK, HOUSTON

From I-10 East, take Smith Street (exit 769A), left at Texas Ave., 0.6 miles to park at corner of Texas Ave. and Crawford St.; from I-10 West, take San Jacinto St. (exit 769B), right on Fannin St., left on Texas Ave., 0.3 miles to park; From Hwy. 59 North: take Gray Ave./Pierce Ave. exit, 0.3 miles on Gray St. to Crawford St., one mile to park.

DODGER STADIUM, LOS ANGELES

I-5 to Stadium Way exit, left on Stadium Way, right on Academy Road, left to Stadium Way to Elysian Park Avenue, left to stadium; I-110 to Dodger Stadium exit, left on Stadium Way, right on Elysian Park Avenue; US 101 to Alvarado exit, right on Sunset, left on Elysian Park Avenue.

MILLER PARK, MILWAUKEE

From airport/south, I-94 West to Madison exit, to stadium.

SHEA STADIUM, NEW YORK

From Bronx and Westchester, take Cross Bronx Expressway to Bronx-Whitestone Bridge, then take bridge to Whitestone Expressway to Northern Boulevard/Shea Stadium exit. From Brooklyn, take Eastbound BQE to Eastbound Grand Central Parkway. From Long Island, take either Northern State Parkway or LIE to Westbound Grand Central Parkway. From northern New Jersey, take George Washington Bridge to Cross Bronx Expressway. From Southern New Jersey, take any of bridge crossings to Verazzano Bridge, and then take either Belt Parkway or BQE to Grand Central Parkway.

CITIZENS BANK PARK, PHILADELPHIA

From I-95 or I-76, take the Broad Street exit. The ballpark is on on the north side of Pattison Avenue, between 11th and Darien Streets.

PNC PARK, PITTSBURGH

From south, I-279 through Fort Pitt Tunnel, make left off bridge to Fort Duquesne Bridge, cross Fort Duquesne Bridge, follow signs to PNC Park. From north, I-279 to PNC Park (exit 12, left lane), follow directions to parking.

BUSCH STADIUM, ST. LOUIS

From Illinois, take I-55 South, I-64 West, I-70 West or US 40 West across the Mississippi River (Poplar Street Bridge) to Busch Stadium exit. In Missouri, take I-55 North, I-64 East, I-70 East, I-44 East or US 40 East to downtown St. Louis and Busch Stadium exit.

PETCO PARK, SAN DIEGO

Four major thoroughfares feed into and out of downtown in all directions: Pacific Highway, I-5, State Route 163 and State Route 94/Martin Luther King Freeway. Eight freeway interchanges service the area around the ballpark.

AT&T PARK, SAN FRANCISCO

From Peninsula/South Bay, I-280 north (or U.S. 101 north to I-280 north) to Mariposa Street exit, right on Mariposa, left on Third Street. From East Bay (Bay Bridge), I-80/Bay Bridge to Fifth Street exit, right on Fifth Street, right on Folsom Street, right on Fourth Street, continue on Fourth Street to parking lots (across bridge). From North Bay (Golden Gate Bridge), U.S. 101 south/Golden Gate Bridge to Downtown/Lombard Street exit, right on Van Ness Ave., left on Golden Gate Ave., right on Hyde Street and across Market Street to Eighth Street, left on Bryant Street, right on Fourth Street.

NATIONALS PARK, WASHINGTON

From Maryland, use the Beltway, take 295 southbound to the Howard Road exit (3B). Go across the South Capitol Street bridge (north). Turn right on either Potomac Avenue, N Street or M Street (east) toward designated lots and garages. From Virginia, take the 14th Street bridge and merge onto I-395 northbound to the Maine Avenue exit. Follow Maine Avenue until it becomes M Street. Follow M Street across South Capitol Street and turn right on either Van Street or 1st Street SE toward the designated lots and garages. From downtown, take I-395 eastbound to the South Capitol Street exit. Follow South Capitol Street and turn left on M Street then turn right on either Van Street or 1st Street toward designated lots and garages.

SCHEDULES

Bold dates indicate day games. * Games in Japan.

ARIZONA DIAMONDBACKS

CHASE FIELD

Standard Game Times: 6:40 p.m.; Sun. 1:40.

MARCH
31 . . . at Cincinnati

APRIL
2-**3** . . . at Cincinnati
4-5-**6** . . . at Colorado
7-8-**9** . . . Dodgers
11-**12**-**13** . . . Colorado
14-**15**-**16** . . at San Francisco
18-19-**20** . . . San Diego
21-22 . . . San Francisco
23-24 . . . at Dodgers
25-**26**-**27** . . . at San Diego
28-29-**30** . . . Houston

MAY
2-**3**-**4** . . . Mets
5-6-7-**8** . . . Philadelphia
9-**10**-**11** . . . at Cubs
13-14-15 . . . Colorado
16-17-**18** . . . Detroit
20-21-22 . . . at Florida
23-**24**-**25**-**26** . . . at Atlanta
27-28-29 . . . San Francisco
30-31 . . . Washington

JUNE
1 . . . Washington
2-3-**4** . . . at Milwaukee
6-7-**8**-**9** . . . at Pittsburgh
10-11-**12** . . . at Mets
13-14-**15** . . . Kansas City
17-18-**19** . . . Oakland
20-21-**22** . . . at Minnesota
23-24-25 . . . at Boston
27-28-**29** . . . at Florida
30 . . . Milwaukee

JULY
1-2-**3** . . . Milwaukee
4-5-**6** . . . San Diego
8-9-10. . . . at Washington
11-12-**13** . . . at Philadelphia
18-19-**20** . . . Dodgers
21-22-23 . . . Cubs
25-26-**27** . . at San Francisco
28-29-30 . . . at San Diego
31 . . . at Dodgers

AUGUST
1-2-**3** . . . at Dodgers
4-5-**6** . . . Pittsburgh
7-8-**9**-**10** . . . Atlanta
12-13-**14** . . . at Colorado
15-16-**17** . . . at Houston
19-20-21 . . . San Diego
22-23-**24** . . . Florida
25-26-**27** . . . at San Diego
29-30-**31** . . . Dodgers

SEPTEMBER
1-2-**3** . . . St. Louis
5-**6**-**7** . . . at Dodgers
8-9-**10**. . . . at San Francisco
12-13-**14** . . . Cincinnati
15-16-17-18 . . San Francisco
19-20-**21** . . . at Colorado
22-23-24-**25** . . . at St. Louis
26-27-**28** . . . Colorado

ATLANTA BRAVES

TURNER FIELD

Standard Game Times: 7:35 p.m.; Mon./Sat. 7:05; Sun. 1:05.

MARCH
30 . . . at Washington
31 . . . Pittsburgh

APRIL
2-3 . . . Pittsburgh
4-**5**-**6** . . . Mets
7-8-9-**10** . . . at Colorado
11-**12**-**13** . . . at Washington
15-16-17 . . . at Florida
18-**19**-**20** . . . Dodgers
21-22 . . . Washington
23-24 . . . Florida
25-**26**-**27** . . . at Mets
29-**30** . . . at Washington

MAY
2-3-**4** . . . Cincinnati
6-7-**8** . . . San Diego
9-10-**11**-**12** . . at Pittsburgh
13-14-15 . . . at Philadelphia
16-17-**18** . . . Oakland
20-21-22 . . . Mets
23-**24**-**25**-**26** . . . Arizona
27-28-**29** . . . at Milwaukee
30-**31** . . . at Cincinnati

JUNE
1 . . . at Cincinnati
2-3-**4**-5 . . . Florida
6-7-**8** . . . Philadelphia
10-11-**12** . . . at Cubs
13-14-15 . . . at Angels
17-18-**19** . . . at Texas
20-21-**22** . . . Seattle
23-24-**25** . . . Milwaukee
27-**28**-**29** . . . at Toronto

JULY
1-2-3 . . . Philadelphia
4-5-**6** . . . Houston
7-8-9 . . . at Dodgers
11-12-**13** . . . at San Diego
18-19-**20** . . . Washington
21-22-23 . . . at Florida
25-**26**-**27** . . . at Philadelphia
28-29-30-31 . . . St. Louis

AUGUST
1-**2**-**3** . . . Milwaukee
4-5-**6** . . . at San Francisco
7-8-**9**-**10** . . . at Arizona
12-13-14 . . . Cubs
15-16-**17**-**18**. . San Francisco
19-20-21 . . . at Mets
22-**23**-**24** . . . at St. Louis
26-27-28 . . . Florida
29-30-**31** . . . at Washington

SEPTEMBER
1-2-**3** . . . at Florida
4-5-6-**7** . . . Washington
9-10-11 . . . Colorado
12-**13**-**14** . . . at Mets
16-17-18 . . . Philadelphia
19-20-**21** . . . Mets
22-23-24 . . . at Philadelphia
26-27-**28** . . . at Houston

BALTIMORE ORIOLES

ORIOLE PARK AT CAMDEN YARDS

Standard Game Times: 7:05 p.m.; Sat. 4:35; Sun. 1:35.

MARCH
31 . . . Tampa Bay

APRIL
2-3 . . . Tampa Bay
4-5-**6**-7 . . . Seattle
8-9-10. . . . at Texas
11-12-**13** . . . at Tampa Bay
14-15 . . . Toronto
16-17 . . . White Sox
18-19-**20** . . . Yankees
22-23-24 . . . at Seattle
25-26-**27**-**28**. . at White Sox
29-30 . . . Tampa Bay

MAY
1 . . . Tampa Bay
2-**3**-**4** . . . at Angels
5-6-**7** . . . at Oakland
8-9-10-**11** . . at Kansas City
13-**14** . . . Boston
16-17-**18** . . . Washington
20-21-22 . . . at Yankees
23-24-**25** . . . at Tampa Bay
26-27-28 . . . Yankees
30-31 . . . Boston

JUNE
1-2. . . . Boston
3-4-**5** . . . at Minnesota
6-**7**-**8** . . . at Toronto
10-11-12 . . . at Boston
13-14-**15** . . . Pittsburgh
17-18-19 . . . Houston
20-21-**22** . . . at Milwaukee
24-25-**26** . . . at Cubs
27-28-**29** . . . at Washington
30 . . . Kansas City

JULY
1-2-3 . . . Kansas City
4-5-**6** . . . Texas
8-9-10. . . . at Toronto
11-12-**13** . . . at Boston
17-18-19-**20** . . . Detroit
21-22-23-**24** . . . Toronto
25-26-**27** . . . Angels
28-29-**30** . . . at Yankees

AUGUST
1-2-**3** . . . at Seattle
4-5-**6** . . . at Angels
8-9-**10**. . . . Texas
11-12-13-14 . . at Cleveland
15-16-**17** . . . at Detroit
18-19-20 . . . Boston
22-23-**24** . . . Yankees
25-26-27 . . . White Sox
29-30-**31** . . . at Tampa Bay

SEPTEMBER
1-2-**3** . . . at Boston
5-6-7 . . . Oakland
8-9-10-11. . . . Cleveland
12-13-14 . . . Minnesota
16-17-18 . . . at Toronto
19-20-**21** . . . at Yankees
22-23-24 . . . Tampa Bay
26-27-**28** . . . Toronto

BOSTON RED SOX

FENWAY PARK

Standard Game Times: 7:05 p.m.; Sun. 2:05.

MARCH
25-26 . . . * Oakland

APRIL
1-2. . . . at Oakland
4-**5**-**6** . . . at Toronto
8-9-10. . . . Detroit
11-**12**-13 . . . Yankees
14-15 . . . at Cleveland
16-17 . . . at Yankees
18-19-**20**-**21**. . . . Texas
22-23-**24** . . . Angels
25-26-**27** . . . at Tampa Bay
29-30 . . . Toronto

MAY
1 . . . Toronto
2-3-**4** . . . Tampa Bay
5-6-7-8 . . . at Detroit
9-10-11-12. . . at Minnesota
13-**14** . . . at Baltimore
16-**17**-**18**. . . . Milwaukee
19-20-21-**22**. . . Kansas City
23-24-**25** . . . at Oakland
26-27-28 . . . at Seattle
30-31 . . . at Baltimore

JUNE
1-2. . . . at Baltimore
3-4-5 . . . Tampa Bay
6-**7**-**8** . . . Seattle
10-11-12 . . . Baltimore
13-**14**-**15**. . . . at Cincinnati
16-17-**18**. . . at Philadelphia
20-**21**-**22**. . . . St. Louis
23-24-25 . . . Arizona
27-28-**29** . . . at Houston
30 . . . at Tampa Bay

JULY	
1-2	at Tampa Bay
3-**4-5**-6	at Yankees
7-8-**9**	Minnesota
11-12-**13**	Baltimore
18-**19-20**	at Angels
21-22-**23**	at Seattle
25-**26-27**	Yankees
28-29-30	Angels

AUGUST	
1-2-**3**	Oakland
4-5-6	at Kansas City
8-9-**10**-11	at White Sox
12-13-14	Texas
15-16-**17**	Toronto
18-19-20	at Baltimore
22-**23-24**	at Toronto
26-27-**28**	at Yankees
29-30-**31**	White Sox

SEPTEMBER	
1-2-**3**	Baltimore
5-6-**7**	at Texas
8-9-10	Tampa Bay
12-13-**14**	Toronto
15-16-17	at Tampa Bay
19-**20-21**	at Toronto
22-23-24-25	Cleveland
26-27-**28**	Yankees

CHICAGO CUBS

WRIGLEY FIELD

Standard Game Times: 1:20 p.m., 7:05.

MARCH	
31	Milwaukee

APRIL	
2-3	Milwaukee
4-5-6	Houston
7-9-10	at Pittsburgh
11-12-**13**	at Philadelphia
15-16-**17**	Cincinnati
18-19-20	Pittsburgh
21-**22**	Mets
23-**24**	at Colorado
25-26-**27**	at Washington
29-30	Milwaukee

MAY	
1	Milwaukee
2-**3**-4	at St. Louis
5-6-**7**	at Cincinnati
9-10-11	Arizona
12-13-14-**15**	San Diego
16-17-18	Pittsburgh
19-20-21	at Houston
23-24-**25**	at Pittsburgh
26-27-28	Dodgers
29-**30-31**	Colorado

JUNE	
1	Colorado
2-3-4	at San Diego
5-6-7-8	at Dodgers
10-11-**12**	Atlanta
13-**14-15**	at Toronto
17-18-19	at Tampa Bay
20-21-22	White Sox
24-25-**26**	Baltimore
27-28-29	at White Sox
30	at San Francisco

JULY	
1-2-**3**	at San Francisco
4-**5-6**	at St. Louis
8-9-**10**	Cincinnati
11-12-13	San Francisco
18-19-**20**	at Houston
21-22-23	at Arizona
24-**25-26-27**	Florida
28-29-30-**31**	at Milwaukee

AUGUST	
1-2-3	Pittsburgh
4-**5-6**	Houston
8-9-10	St. Louis
12-13-14	at Atlanta
15-16-**17**	at Florida
19-20-**21**	Cincinnati
22-23-24	Washington
25-26-**27**	at Pittsburgh
28-**29-30**-31	Philadelphia

SEPTEMBER	
1-2-3	Houston
5-6-**7**	at Cincinnati
9-10-11	at St. Louis
12-13-**14**	at Houston
16-17-**18**	Milwaukee
19-20-21	St. Louis
22-23-24-25	at Mets
26-**27-28**	at Milwaukee

CHICAGO WHITE SOX

U.S. CELLULAR FIELD

Standard Game Times: 7:05 p.m.; Sat. 6:05; Sun. 1:05.

MARCH	
31	at Cleveland

APRIL	
2-**3**	at Cleveland
4-5-6	at Detroit
7-9-10	Minnesota
11-**12-13**	Detroit
14-**15**	Oakland
16-17	at Baltimore
18-19-**20**	at Tampa Bay
22-23-24	Yankees
25-26-**27-28**	Baltimore
29-**30**	at Minnesota

MAY	
2-**3-4**-5	at Toronto
6-7-**8**	Minnesota
9-10-**11**	at Seattle
12-13-14-15	at Angels
16-17-**18**	at San Francisco
20-21-22	Cleveland
23-**24**-25	Angels
26-27-**28**	at Cleveland
29-30-31	at Tampa Bay

JUNE	
1	at Tampa Bay
3-4-5	Kansas City
6-7-**8**	Minnesota
10-11-**12**	at Detroit
13-14-**15**	Colorado
17-18-**19**	Pittsburgh
20-21-22	at Cubs
24-25-**26**	at Dodgers
27-28-29	Cubs
30	Cleveland

JULY	
1-2	Cleveland
3-4-5-**6**	Oakland
8-9-10	at Kansas City
11-12-**13**	at Texas
18-19-**20**	Kansas City
21-22-**23**	Texas
25-26-**27**	at Detroit
28-29-30-31	at Minnesota

AUGUST	
1-2-**3**	at Kansas City
5-6-7	Detroit
8-9-**10**-11	Boston
12-13-**14**	Kansas City
15-16-**17**	at Oakland
18-19-**20**	Seattle
22-23-**24**	Tampa Bay
25-26-27	at Baltimore
29-30-**31**	at Boston

SEPTEMBER	
1-2-**3**	at Cleveland
5-6-**7**	Angels
8-9-10-11	Toronto
12-13-**14**	Detroit
15-16-17-18	at Yankees
19-20-**21**	at Kansas City
23-24-25	at Minnesota
26-27-**28**	Cleveland

CINCINNATI REDS

GREAT AMERICAN BALL PARK

Standard Game Times: 7:10 p.m.; Sun. 1:15

MARCH	
31	Arizona

APRIL	
2-**3**	Arizona
4-**5-6-7**	Philadelphia
8-9-**10**	at Milwaukee
11-12-**13**	at Pittsburgh
15-16-**17**	at Cubs
18-**19-20**	Milwaukee
21-22	Dodgers
23-**24**	Houston
25-26-**27**	at San Francisco
28-29-**30**	at St. Louis

MAY	
2-3-**4**	at Atlanta
5-6-**7**	Cubs
9-**10-11**	at Mets
12-13-14-15	Florida
16-**17-18**	Cleveland
19-20-21	at Dodgers
22-23-24-**25**	at San Diego
27-28-29	Pittsburgh
30-**31**	Atlanta

JUNE	
1	Atlanta
2-3-4-**5**	at Philadelphia
6-7-**8**-9	at Florida
10-11-12	St. Louis
13-**14-15**	Boston
17-18-**19**	Dodgers
20-21-**22**	at Yankees
24-25-26	at Toronto
27-28-**29**	at Cleveland
30	Pittsburgh

JULY	
1-2	Pittsburgh
3-**4**-5-**6**	Washington
8-9-**10**	at Cubs
11-12-**13**	at Milwaukee
17-18-19-**20**	Mets
21-22-**23**	San Diego
25-26-**27**	Colorado
28-29-30	at Houston

AUGUST	
1-2-**3**	at Washington
4-5-**6**	Milwaukee
7-8-9-**10**	Houston
12-13-14	at Pittsburgh
15-16-**17**	St. Louis
19-20-**21**	at Cubs
22-23-**24**	at Colorado
26-27-**28**	at Houston
29-30-**31**	San Francisco

SEPTEMBER	
2-3-**4**	Pittsburgh
5-6-**7**	Cubs
8-9-**10**	at Milwaukee
12-13-**14**	at Arizona
16-17-18	St. Louis
19-20-**21**	Milwaukee
23-24-25	at Houston
26-27-**28**	at St. Louis

CLEVELAND INDIANS

PROGRESSIVE FIELD

Standard Game Times: 7:05 p.m.; Sun. 1:05.

MARCH	
31	White Sox

APRIL	
2-**3**	White Sox
4-**5-6**	at Oakland
7-8-**9**	at Angels
11-12-**13**	Oakland
14-15	Boston
16-17	Detroit
18-**19-20**	at Minnesota
22-23-24	at Kansas City
25-**26-27**-28	Yankees
29-30	Seattle

MAY	
1	Seattle
2-3-**4**	Kansas City

6-7-**8** . . . . at Yankees
9-10-**11**-12 . . . . Toronto
13-14-**15** . . . . Oakland
16-**17**-**18** . . . . at Cincinnati
20-21-22 . . . . at White Sox
23-24-**25** . . . . Texas
26-27-**28** . . . . White Sox
30-31 . . . . at Kansas City

JUNE

1 . . . . at Kansas City
2-3-4-5 . . . . at Texas
6-7-**8**-9 . . . . at Detroit
10-11-12 . . . . Minnesota
13-14-**15** . . . . San Diego
17-18-19 . . . . at Colorado
20-**21**-**22** . . . . at Dodgers
24-25-26 . . . . San Francisco
27-28-**29** . . . . Cincinnati
30 . . . . at White Sox

JULY

1-2 . . . . at White Sox
4-5-**6** . . . . at Minnesota
8-9 . . . . at Detroit
10-11-12-**13** . . . . Tampa Bay
18-**19**-**20** . . . . at Seattle
21-22-**23** . . . . at Angels
25-26-**27** . . . . Minnesota
28-29-30-**31** . . . . Detroit

AUGUST

1-2-**3** . . . . at Minnesota
4-5-**6** . . . . at Tampa Bay
8-**9**-**10** . . . . at Toronto
11-12-13-14 . . . . Baltimore
15-**16**-**17** . . . . Angels
19-20-**21** . . . . Kansas City
22-23-24 . . . . at Texas
25-26-27 . . . . at Detroit
29-**30**-**31** . . . . Seattle

SEPTEMBER

1-2-**3** . . . . White Sox
5-6-**7** . . . . at Kansas City
8-9-10-11 . . . . at Baltimore
12-13-**14** . . . . Kansas City
15-16-17 . . . . Minnesota
19-20-**21** . . . . Detroit
22-23-24-25 . . . . at Boston
26-27-**28** . . . . at White Sox

COLORADO ROCKIES

COORS FIELD

Standard Game Times: 7:05 p.m.; Sat. 6:05; Sun. 1:05.

MARCH

31 . . . . at St. Louis

APRIL

2-**3** . . . . at St. Louis
4-5-**6** . . . . Arizona
7-8-9-**10** . . . . Atlanta
11-**12**-**13** . . . . at Arizona
15-16-17 . . . . at San Diego
18-19-**20** . . . . at Houston
21-22 . . . . Philadelphia
23-**24** . . . . Cubs
25-26-**27** . . . . at Dodgers
28-29-**30** . . . . at San Francisco

MAY

2-3-**4** . . . . Dodgers
5-6-7-**8** . . . . St. Louis
9-10-**11** . . . . at San Diego
13-14-15 . . . . at Arizona
16-17-**18** . . . . Minnesota
19-20-**21** . . . . San Francisco
23-**24**-**25** . . . . Mets
26-27-28 . . . . at Philadelphia
29-**30**-**31** . . . . at Cubs

JUNE

1 . . . . at Cubs
2-3-**4** . . . . at Dodgers
6-7-**8** . . . . Milwaukee
10-11-**12** . . . . San Francisco
13-14-**15** . . . . at White Sox
17-18-19 . . . . Cleveland
20-21-**22** . . . . Mets
23-24-25 . . . . at Kansas City
27-28-**29** . . . . at Detroit
30 . . . . San Diego

JULY

1-2 . . . . San Diego
3-4-5-**6** . . . . Florida
7-8-9-**10** . . . . at Milwaukee
11-**12**-13 . . . . at Mets
17-18-19-**20** . . . . Pittsburgh
21-22-**23** . . . . Dodgers
25-26-**27** . . . . at Cincinnati
28-29-30 . . . . at Pittsburgh
31 . . . . at Florida

AUGUST

1-2-**3** . . . . at Florida
4-5-6-**7** . . . . Washington
8-9-**10** . . . . San Diego
12-13-**14** . . . . Arizona
15-16-**17** . . . . at Washington
19-20-**21** . . . . at Dodgers
22-23-**24** . . . . Cincinnati
25-26-27 . . . . at San Francisco
29-**30**-**31** . . . . at San Diego

SEPTEMBER

1-**2**-**3** . . . . San Francisco
5-6-**7** . . . . Houston
9-10-11 . . . . at Atlanta
12-13-**14** . . . . Dodgers
15-16-**17** . . . . San Diego
19-20-**21** . . . . Arizona
23-24-25 . . . . at San Francisco
26-27-**28** . . . . at Arizona

DETROIT TIGERS

COMERICA PARK

Standard Game Times: 7:05 p.m.; Sun. 1:05.

MARCH

31 . . . . Kansas City

APRIL

2-**3** . . . . Kansas City
4-5-6 . . . . White Sox
8-9-10 . . . . at Boston
11-**12**-**13** . . . . at White Sox
14-15 . . . . Minnesota
16-17 . . . . at Cleveland
18-**19**-**20**-**21** . . . . at Toronto
22-23-**24** . . . . Texas
25-**26**-27 . . . . Angels
29-30 . . . . at Yankees

MAY

1 . . . . at Yankees
2-3-**4** . . . . at Minnesota
5-6-7-8 . . . . Boston
9-**10**-**11** . . . . Yankees
13-14-**15** . . . . at Kansas City
16-17-**18** . . . . at Arizona
20-21-**22** . . . . Seattle
23-24-**25** . . . . Minnesota
26-27-28 . . . . at Angels
30-**31** . . . . at Seattle

JUNE

1 . . . . at Seattle
2-3-**4** . . . . at Oakland
6-**7**-**8**-9 . . . . Cleveland
10-11-**12** . . . . White Sox
13-**14**-**15** . . . . Dodgers
16-17-**18** . . . . at San Francisco
20-21-**22** . . . . at San Diego
24-25-**26** . . . . St. Louis
27-28-**29** . . . . Colorado
30 . . . . at Minnesota

JULY

1-**2** . . . . at Minnesota
3-**4**-5-**6** . . . . at Seattle
8-9 . . . . Cleveland
10-11-**12**-**13** . . . . Minnesota
17-18-19-**20** . . . . at Baltimore
21-22-**23** . . . . at Kansas City
25-26-**27** . . . . White Sox
28-29-30-**31** . . . . at Cleveland

AUGUST

1-2-**3** . . . . at Tampa Bay
5-6-7 . . . . at White Sox
8-9-**10** . . . . Oakland
11-12-13-**14** . . . . Toronto
15-16-**17** . . . . Baltimore
18-19-20 . . . . at Texas
22-23-**24** . . . . at Kansas City
25-26-27 . . . . Cleveland
29-30-**31** . . . . Kansas City

SEPTEMBER

2-3-4 . . . . Angels
5-**6**-**7** . . . . at Minnesota
8-9-**10** . . . . Oakland
12-13-**14** . . . . at White Sox
15-16-17 . . . . at Texas
19-20-**21** . . . . at Cleveland
22-23-24 . . . . Kansas City
25-26-27-**28** . . . . Tampa Bay

FLORIDA MARLINS

DOLPHINS STADIUM

Standard Game Times: 7:05 p.m.; Sun. 1:05

MARCH

31 . . . . Mets

APRIL

1-2 . . . . Mets
4-5-**6** . . . . Pittsburgh
7-9-10 . . . . at Washington
11-12-**13** . . . . at Houston
15-16-17 . . . . Atlanta
18-19-**20** . . . . Washington
21-22 . . . . at Pittsburgh
23-24 . . . . at Atlanta
25-26-**27** . . . . at Milwaukee
29-30 . . . . Dodgers

MAY

1 . . . . Dodgers
2-3-**4** . . . . San Diego
6-7-8 . . . . Milwaukee
9-10-**11** . . . . at Washington
12-13-14-15 . . . . at Cincinnati
16-17-**18** . . . . Kansas City
20-21-22 . . . . Arizona
23-24-**25** . . . . San Francisco
26-27-28 . . . . at Mets
30-31 . . . . at Philadelphia

JUNE

1 . . . . at Philadelphia
2-3-**4**-5 . . . . at Atlanta
6-7-**8**-9 . . . . Cincinnati
10-11-12 . . . . Philadelphia
13-14-**15** . . . . at Tampa Bay
16-17-18 . . . . at Seattle
20-21-**22** . . . . at Oakland
24-25-**26** . . . . Tampa Bay
27-28-**29** . . . . Arizona
30 . . . . Washington

JULY

1-**2** . . . . Washington
3-4-5-**6** . . . . at Colorado
7-8-**9** . . . . at San Diego
10-11-12-**13** . . . . at Dodgers
18-19-**20** . . . . Philadelphia
21-22-23 . . . . Atlanta
24-**25**-**26**-**27** . . . . at Cubs
28-29-30 . . . . Mets
31 . . . . Colorado

AUGUST

1-2-**3** . . . . Colorado
5-6-**7** . . . . at Philadelphia
8-9-**10** . . . . at Mets
11-12-13-14 . . . . St. Louis
15-16-**17** . . . . Cubs
19-20-**21** . . . . at San Francisco
22-23-**24** . . . . at Arizona
26-27-28 . . . . at Atlanta
29-30-**31** . . . . Mets

SEPTEMBER

1-**2**-**3** . . . . Atlanta
5-6-**7** . . . . at St. Louis
8-9-**10** . . . . at Philadelphia
12-13-**14** . . . . Washington
16-17-18 . . . . Houston
19-20-**21** . . . . Philadelphia
23-24-25 . . . . at Washington
26-**27**-**28** . . . . at Mets

HOUSTON ASTROS

MINUTE MAID PARK

Standard Game Times: 7:05 p.m.; Sat. 6:05; Sun. 1:05.

MARCH
31 . . . at San Diego

APRIL
1-2-**3** . . . at San Diego
4-5-6 . . . at Cubs
7-8-9 . . . St. Louis
11-12-**13** . . . Florida
15-16-**17** . . . at Philadelphia
18-19-**20** . . . Colorado
21-22 . . . San Diego
23-**24** . . . at Cincinnati
25-**26-27** . . . at St. Louis
28-29-**30** . . . at Arizona

MAY
2-3-**4** . . . Milwaukee
6-7-8 . . . Washington
9-10-**11** . . . at Dodgers
12-13-14-**15** at San Francisco
16-17-**18** . . . at Texas
19-20-21 . . . Cubs
22-23-24-**25** . . . Philadelphia
27-28-29 . . . at St. Louis
30-31 . . . at Milwaukee

JUNE
1 . . . at Milwaukee
3-4-5 . . . at Pittsburgh
6-7-**8** . . . St. Louis
10-11-**12** . . . Milwaukee
13-14-**15** . . . Yankees
17-18-19 . . . at Baltimore
20-21-**22** . . . at Tampa Bay
24-25-26 . . . Texas
27-28-**29** . . . Boston
30 . . . Dodgers

JULY
1-2-**3** . . . Dodgers
4-5-**6** . . . at Atlanta
7-8-9 . . . at Pittsburgh
11-12-**13** . . . at Washington
18-19-**20** . . . Cubs
21-22-**23** . . . Pittsburgh
25-26-**27** . . . at Milwaukee
28-29-30 . . . Cincinnati

AUGUST
1-2-**3** . . . Mets
4-**5-6** . . . at Cubs
7-8-9-**10** . . . at Cincinnati
11-12-13-**14** . . . San Francisco
15-16-**17** . . . Arizona
18-19-**20** . . . at Milwaukee
22-23-**24**-25 . . . at Mets
26-27-**28** . . . Cincinnati
29-30-**31** . . . St. Louis

SEPTEMBER
1-2-3 . . . at Cubs
5-6-**7** . . . at Colorado
8-9-10-11 . . . Pittsburgh
12-13-**14** . . . Cubs
16-17-18 . . . at Florida
19-20-**21** . . . at Pittsburgh
23-24-25 . . . Cincinnati
26-27-**28** . . . Atlanta

KANSAS CITY ROYALS

KAUFFMAN STADIUM

Standard Game Times: 7:10 p.m.; Sat. 6:10; Sun. 1:10.

MARCH
31 . . . at Detroit

APRIL
2-3 . . . at Detroit
4-**5-6** . . . at Minnesota
8-9-10 . . . Yankees
11-12-**13** . . . Minnesota
14-**15** . . . at Seattle
16-17 . . . at Angels
18-**19-20** . . . at Oakland
22-23-24 . . . Cleveland
25-26-**27** . . . Toronto
29-30 . . . at Texas

MAY
1 . . . at Texas
2-3-**4** . . . at Cleveland
5-6-7 . . . Angels
8-9-10-**11** . . . Baltimore
13-14-**15** . . . Detroit
16-17-**18** . . . at Florida
19-20-21-**22** . . . at Boston
23-**24-25-26** . . . at Toronto
27-28-29 . . . Minnesota
30-31 . . . Cleveland

JUNE
1 . . . Cleveland
3-4-5 . . . at White Sox
6-7-**8-9** . . . at Yankees
10-11-**12** . . . Texas
13-14-**15** . . . at Arizona
17-18-**19** . . . at St. Louis
20-21-**22** . . . San Francisco
23-24-25 . . . Colorado
27-28-**29** . . . St. Louis
30 . . . at Baltimore

JULY
1-2-3 . . . at Baltimore
4-5-**6-7** . . . at Tampa Bay
8-9-10 . . . White Sox
11-12-**13** . . . Seattle
18-19-**20** . . . at White Sox
21-22-**23** . . . Detroit
24-25-26-**27** . . . Tampa Bay
28-29-**30** . . . at Oakland

AUGUST
1-2-**3** . . . White Sox
4-5-6 . . . Boston
8-9-**10** . . . Minnesota
12-13-**14** . . . at White Sox
15-16-**17** . . . at Yankees
19-20-**21** . . . at Cleveland
22-23-**24** . . . Detroit
25-26-27 . . . Texas
29-30-**31** . . . at Detroit

SEPTEMBER
2-3-4 . . . Oakland
5-6-**7** . . . Cleveland
9-10-**11** . . . at Minnesota
12-13-**14** . . . at Cleveland
15-16-17-**18** . . . Seattle
19-20-**21** . . . White Sox
22-23-24 . . . at Detroit
26-27-**28** . . . at Minnesota

LOS ANGELES ANGELS

ANGEL STADIUM

Standard Game Times: 7:05 p.m.; Sun. 12:35.

MARCH
31 . . . at Minnesota

APRIL
1-2-**3** . . . at Minnesota
4-5-**6** . . . Texas
7-8-**9** . . . Cleveland
11-12-**13** . . . at Seattle
14-**15** . . . at Texas
16-17 . . . Kansas City
18-19-**20** . . . Seattle
22-23-**24** . . . at Boston
25-**26**-27 . . . at Detroit
28-29-30 . . . Oakland

MAY
1 . . . Oakland
2-3-4 . . . Baltimore
5-6-7 . . . at Kansas City
9-10-**11** . . . at Tampa Bay
12-13-14-15 . . . White Sox
16-**17-18** . . . Dodgers
20-21-22 . . . at Toronto
23-**24**-25 . . . at White Sox
26-27-28 . . . Detroit
30-31 . . . Toronto

JUNE
1 . . . Toronto
2-3-**4** . . . at Seattle
6-7-**8** . . . at Oakland
9-10-**11** . . . Tampa Bay
13-14-15 . . . Atlanta
16-17-18 . . . Mets
20-21-**22** . . . at Philadelphia
23-24-25 . . . at Washington
27-28-29 . . . at Dodgers
30 . . . Oakland

JULY
1-**2** . . . Oakland
4-5-**6** . . . Toronto
7-8-9-10 . . . at Texas
11-12-**13** . . . at Oakland
18-**19-20** . . . Boston
21-22-**23** . . . Cleveland
25-26-**27** . . . at Baltimore
28-29-30 . . . at Boston
31 . . . at Yankees

AUGUST
1-**2-3** . . . at Yankees
4-5-**6** . . . Baltimore
8-**9-10** . . . Yankees
12-13 . . . Seattle
15-**16-17** . . . at Cleveland
18-19-20 . . . at Tampa Bay
21-22-23-**24** . . . Minnesota
25-26-27 . . . Oakland
28-29-30-**31** . . . Texas

SEPTEMBER
2-3-4 . . . at Detroit
5-6-**7** . . . at White Sox
8-9-**10** . . . Yankees
11-12-**13**-14 . . . Seattle
16-17-**18** . . . at Oakland
19-20-**21** . . . at Texas
22-23-24-25 . . . at Seattle
26-27-**28** . . . Texas

LOS ANGELES DODGERS

DODGER STADIUM

Standard Game Times: 7:10 p.m.; Fri. 7:40

MARCH
31 . . . San Francisco

APRIL
1-2 . . . San Francisco
4-**5-6** . . . at San Diego
7-8-**9** . . . at Arizona
11-12-**13** . . . San Diego
14-15-16 . . . Pittsburgh
18-**19-20** . . . at Atlanta
21-22 . . . at Cincinnati
23-24 . . . Arizona
25-26-**27** . . . Colorado
29-30 . . . at Florida

MAY
1 . . . at Florida
2-3-**4** . . . at Colorado
5-6-**7** . . . Mets
9-10-**11** . . . Houston
13-14-**15** . . . at Milwaukee
16-**17-18** . . . at Angels
19-20-21 . . . Cincinnati
23-24-**25** . . . St. Louis
26-27-28 . . . at Cubs
29-30-**31** . . . at Mets

JUNE
1 . . . at Mets
2-3-**4** . . . Colorado
5-6-**7**-8 . . . Cubs
10-11-**12** . . . at San Diego
13-**14-15** . . . at Detroit
17-18-**19** . . . at Cincinnati
20-**21-22** . . . Cleveland
24-25-**26** . . . White Sox
27-28-29 . . . Angels
30 . . . at Houston

JULY
1-2-**3** . . . at Houston
4-5-6 . . . at San Francisco
7-8-9 . . . Atlanta
10-11-12-**13** . . . Florida
18-19-**20** . . . at Arizona
21-22-**23** . . . at Colorado
25-26-**27** . . . Washington
28-29-30 . . . San Francisco
31 . . . Arizona

AUGUST
1-2-**3** . . . . Arizona
5-6-**7** . . . . at St. Louis
8-9-**10**. . . . at San Francisco
11-12-13-14 . . Philadelphia
15-16-**17** . . . . . Milwaukee
19-20-**21** . . . . Colorado
22-**23**-**24**-25 at Philadelphia
26-27-28 . . . at Washington
29-30-**31** . . . . . . at Arizona

SEPTEMBER
1-2-3 . . . . San Diego
5-**6**-**7** . . . . Arizona
8-9-10. . . . . . . at San Diego
12-13-**14** . . . . . at Colorado
15-16-17-**18** . . at Pittsburgh
19-20-**21** . . . San Francisco
23-24-25 . . . . . . San Diego
26-27-**28** . . at San Francisco

MILWAUKEE BREWERS

MILLER PARK

Standard Game Times: 7:05 p.m.; Sat. 6:05; Sun. 1:05.

MARCH
31 . . . . at Cubs

APRIL
2-3. . . . . at Cubs
4-5-6 . . . . . . San Francisco
8-9-**10**. . . . . Cincinnati
11-**12**-**13** . . . . at Mets
15-16-**17** . . . . . at St. Louis
18-**19**-**20** . . . . at Cincinnati
21-**22** . . . . St. Louis
23-**24** . . . . . . Philadelphia
25-26-**27** . . . . Florida
29-30 . . . . at Cubs

MAY
1 . . . . at Cubs
2-3-**4** . . . . at Houston
6-7-8 . . . . at Florida
9-**10**-**11**-12 . . . . . St. Louis
13-14-**15** . . . . Dodgers
16-**17**-**18** . . . . . . at Boston
20-21-22 . . . . at Pittsburgh
23-24-**25**-**26** at Washington
27-28-**29** . . . . Atlanta
30-31 . . . . Houston

JUNE
1 . . . . Houston
2-3-**4** . . . . Arizona
6-7-**8** . . . . at Colorado
10-11-**12** . . . . . at Houston
13-14-**15** . . . . . . Minnesota
17-18-**19** . . . . Toronto
20-21-**22** . . . . . . Baltimore
23-24-**25** . . . . . . at Atlanta
27-28-**29** . . . . at Minnesota
30 . . . . at Arizona

JULY
1-2-**3** . . . . at Arizona
4-5-6 . . . . Pittsburgh
7-8-9-**10** . . . . Colorado
11-12-**13** . . . . Cincinnati
18-**19**-**20** . . at San Francisco
21-22-23-24 . . . . at St. Louis
25-26-**27** . . . . Houston
28-29-30-**31** . . . . Cubs

AUGUST
1-**2**-**3** . . . . at Atlanta
4-5-**6** . . . . . . at Cincinnati
8-9-**10**-**11** . . . . Washington
12-13-**14** . . . . at San Diego
15-16-**17** . . . . . at Dodgers
18-19-**20** . . . . Houston
22-23-**24** . . . . . . Pittsburgh
26-27 . . . . at St. Louis
29-30-**31** . . . . at Pittsburgh

SEPTEMBER
1-2-3 . . . . Mets
4-5-6-**7** . . . . San Diego
8-9-**10**. . . . . Cincinnati
11-12-**13**-**14** at Philadelphia
16-17-**18** . . . . at Cubs
19-20-**21** . . . . at Cincinnati
23-24-25 . . . . . . Pittsburgh
26-**27**-**28** . . . . Cubs

MINNESOTA TWINS

HUBERT H. HUMPHREY METRODOME

Standard Game Times: 7:10 p.m.; Sat. 6:10; Sun 1:10.

MARCH
31 . . . . Angels

APRIL
1-2-**3** . . . . Angels
4-**5**-6 . . . . Kansas City
7-9-10. . . . . . at White Sox
11-12-**13** . . . at Kansas City
14-15 . . . . at Detroit
16-17 . . . . Tampa Bay
18-**19**-**20** . . . . . . Cleveland
22-23-**24** . . . . . at Oakland
25-26-**27** . . . . at Texas
29-**30** . . . . White Sox

MAY
2-3-**4** . . . . Detroit
6-7-**8** . . . . . . at White Sox
9-10-11-12. . . . . Boston
13-14-**15** . . . . Toronto
16-17-**18** . . . . . at Colorado
19-20-21-**22** . . . . Texas
23-24-**25** . . . . . . at Detroit
27-28-29 . . . at Kansas City
30-31 . . . . Yankees

JUNE
1-2. . . . . Yankees
3-4-**5** . . . . Baltimore
6-7-**8** . . . . at White Sox
10-11-12 . . . . . at Cleveland
13-14-**15** . . . . at Milwaukee
17-18-**19** . . . . . Washington
20-21-**22** . . . . Arizona
24-25-**26** . . . . at San Diego
27-28-**29** . . . . . . Milwaukee
30 . . . . Detroit

JULY
1-**2**. . . . . Detroit
4-5-**6** . . . . Cleveland
7-8-**9** . . . . at Boston
10-11-**12**-**13** . . . at Detroit
18-19-**20** . . . . Texas
21-22-**23** . . . . . at Yankees
25-26-**27** . . . . at Cleveland
28-29-30-31 . . . . White Sox

AUGUST
1-2-**3** . . . . Cleveland
4-5-**6** . . . . at Seattle
8-9-**10**. . . . . at Kansas City
11-12-**13** . . . . Yankees
15-**16**-**17** . . . . Seattle
18-19-**20** . . . . Oakland
21-22-23-**24**. . . . at Angels
25-26-**27** . . . . . . at Seattle
28-29-30-**31** . . . at Oakland

SEPTEMBER
2-3-4 . . . . at Toronto
5-**6**-**7** . . . . Detroit
9-10-**11**. . . . . . . Kansas City
12-13-14 . . . . . at Baltimore
15-16-17 . . . . at Cleveland
18-19-20-**21** . . at Tampa Bay
23-24-25 . . . . . . White Sox
26-27-**28** . . . . . Kansas City

NEW YORK METS

SHEA STADIUM

Standard Game Times: 7:10 p.m.; Sun. 1:10.

MARCH
31 . . . . at Florida

APRIL
1-2. . . . . at Florida
4-**5**-**6** . . . . at Atlanta
8-9-10. . . . . . Philadelphia
11-**12**-**13**. . . . . Milwaukee
15-16-17 . . . . . Washington
18-**19**-20 . . . at Philadelphia
21-**22** . . . . at Cubs
23-24 . . . . . at Washington
25-**26**-**27** . . . . Atlanta
28-29-**30** . . . . . . Pittsburgh

MAY
2-**3**-**4** . . . . at Arizona
5-6-**7** . . . . at Dodgers
9-**10**-**11**. . . . . . . Cincinnati
12-13-14-**15** . . Washington
16-17-18 . . . . . at Yankees
20-21-22 . . . . . . at Atlanta
23-**24**-**25** . . . . at Colorado
26-27-28 . . . . Florida
29-30-**31** . . . . Dodgers

JUNE
1 . . . . Dodgers
2-3-**4** . . . . at San Francisco
5-6-7-**8** . . . . . at San Diego
10-11-**12** . . . . Arizona
13-14-**15** . . . . Texas
16-17-18 . . . . . . at Angels
20-21-**22** . . . . . at Colorado
23-24-25 . . . . Seattle
27-**28**-**29** . . . . Yankees
30 . . . . at St. Louis

JULY
1-2-3 . . . . at St. Louis
4-5-**6**-7 . . . . at Philadelphia
8-9-**10**. . . . . San Francisco
11-**12**-13 . . . . Colorado
17-18-19-**20**. . at Cincinnati
22-23-**24** . . . . Philadelphia
25-26-**27** . . . . St. Louis
28-29-30 . . . . . . at Florida

AUGUST
1-2-**3** . . . . at Houston
5-6-**7** . . . . San Diego
8-9-**10**. . . . . Florida
12-13-14 . . . at Washington
15-16-**17**-**18**. . at Pittsburgh
19-20-21 . . . . Atlanta
22-23-**24**-25 . . . . . Houston
26-27 . . . . . at Philadelphia
29-30-**31** . . . . . . at Florida

SEPTEMBER
1-2-3 . . . . . . at Milwaukee
5-**6**-**7** . . . . . . Philadelphia
9-10 . . . . Washington
12-**13**-**14**. . . . . Atlanta
15-16-17-18 . at Washington
19-20-**21** . . . . . . at Atlanta
22-23-24-25 . . . . Cubs
26-**27**-**28**. . . . . Florida

NEW YORK YANKEES

YANKEE STADIUM

Standard Game Times: 7:05 p.m.; Sat.-Sun. 1:05.

MARCH
31 . . . . Toronto

APRIL
2-3. . . . . Toronto
4-**5**-**6**-7 . . . . . . Tampa Bay
8-9-10. . . . . at Kansas City
11-**12**-13 . . . . . . at Boston
14-15 . . . . . . at Tampa Bay
16-17 . . . . Boston
18-19-**20** . . . . at Baltimore
22-23-24 . . . . at White Sox
25-**26**-**27**-28. . at Cleveland
29-30 . . . . Detroit

MAY
1 . . . . Detroit
2-3-**4** . . . . Seattle
6-7-**8** . . . . Cleveland
9-**10**-**11**. . . . . . . at Detroit
12-13-14-**15**. . at Tampa Bay
16-17-18 . . . . Mets
20-21-22 . . . . . . Baltimore
23-24-**25** . . . . Seattle
26-27-28 . . . . at Baltimore
30-31 . . . . . . at Minnesota

JUNE
1-2. . . . . at Minnesota

3-4-**5** . . . Toronto
6-7-**8**-**9** . . . Kansas City
10-11-12 . . . at Oakland
13-14-**15** . . . at Houston
17-18-**19** . . . San Diego
20-21-**22** . . . Cincinnati
24-25-26 . . . at Pittsburgh
27-**28**-**29** . . . at Mets
30 . . . Texas

JULY

1-2 . . . Texas
3-**4**-**5**-6 . . . Boston
8-**9** . . . Tampa Bay
11-**12**-**13** . . . at Toronto
18-**19**-**20** . . . Oakland
21-22-**23** . . . Minnesota
25-**26**-**27** . . . at Boston
28-29-**30** . . . Baltimore
31 . . . Angels

AUGUST

1-**2**-**3** . . . Angels
4-5-6-7 . . . at Texas
8-**9**-**10** . . . at Angels
11-12-**13** . . . at Minnesota
15-16-**17** . . . Kansas City
19-20-21 . . . at Toronto
22-23-**24** . . . at Baltimore
26-27-**28** . . . Boston
29-30-**31** . . . Toronto

SEPTEMBER

2-3-4 . . . at Tampa Bay
5-6-**7** . . . at Seattle
8-9-**10** . . . at Angels
12-13-**14** . . . Tampa Bay
15-16-17-18 . . . White Sox
19-**20**-**21** . . . Baltimore
23-24-25 . . . at Toronto
26-**27**-**28** . . . at Boston

OAKLAND ATHLETICS

MCAFEE COLISEUM

Standard Game Times: 7:05 p.m.; Sat.-Sun. 1:05.

MARCH

25-26 . . . * Boston

APRIL

1-2 . . . Boston
4-**5**-**6** . . . Cleveland
8-9-10 . . . at Toronto
11-12-**13** . . . at Cleveland
14-**15** . . . at White Sox
16-17 . . . Seattle
18-**19**-**20** . . . Kansas City
22-23-**24** . . . Minnesota
25-26-**27** . . . at Seattle
28-29-30 . . . at Angels

MAY

1 . . . at Angels
2-3-**4** . . . Texas
5-6-**7** . . . Baltimore
9-10-**11** . . . at Texas
13-14-**15** . . . at Cleveland
16-17-**18** . . . at Atlanta
19-20-**21** . . . Tampa Bay
23-24-**25** . . . Boston
27-28-**29** . . . Toronto
30-31 . . . at Texas

JUNE

1 . . . at Texas
2-3-**4** . . . Detroit
6-7-**8** . . . Angels
10-11-12 . . . Yankees
13-14-**15** . . at San Francisco
17-18-**19** . . . at Arizona
20-21-**22** . . . Florida
24-25-**26** . . . Philadelphia
27-28-**29** . . . San Francisco
30 . . . at Angels

JULY

1-**2** . . . at Angels
3-4-5-**6** . . . at White Sox
7-8-9-**10** . . . Seattle
11-12-**13** . . . Angels
18-**19**-**20** . . . at Yankees
21-22-**23** . . . at Tampa Bay
25-**26**-**27** . . . Texas
28-29-**30** . . . Kansas City

AUGUST

1-2-**3** . . . at Boston
4-5-6-7 . . . at Toronto
8-9-**10** . . . at Detroit
12-13-**14** . . . Tampa Bay
15-16-**17** . . . White Sox
18-19-**20** . . . at Minnesota
21-22-23-**24** . . . at Seattle
25-26-27 . . . at Angels
28-29-30-**31** . . . Minnesota

SEPTEMBER

2-3-4 . . . at Kansas City
5-6-7 . . . at Baltimore
8-9-**10** . . . at Detroit
11-12-**13**-**14** . . . Texas
16-17-**18** . . . Angels
19-**20**-**21** . . . Seattle
22-23-**24** . . . at Texas
26-27-**28** . . . at Seattle

PHILADELPHIA PHILLIES

CITIZENS BANK PARK

Standard Game Times: 7:10 p.m.; Fri. 7:40

MARCH

31 . . . Washington

APRIL

2-**3** . . . Washington
4-**5**-**6**-**7** . . . at Cincinnati
8-9-10 . . . at Mets
11-12-**13** . . . Cubs
15-16-**17** . . . Houston
18-**19**-20 . . . Mets
21-22 . . . at Colorado
23-**24** . . . at Milwaukee
25-26-**27** . . . at Pittsburgh
29-30 . . . San Diego

MAY

1 . . . San Diego
2-3-**4** . . . San Francisco
5-6-7-**8** . . . at Arizona
9-**10**-**11** . . . at San Francisco
13-14-15 . . . Atlanta
16-17-**18** . . . Toronto
19-20-21 . . . at Washington
22-23-24-**25** . . . at Houston
26-27-28 . . . Colorado
30-31 . . . Florida

JUNE

1 . . . Florida
2-3-4-**5** . . . Cincinnati
6-7-**8** . . . at Atlanta
10-11-12 . . . at Florida
13-**14**-**15** . . . at St. Louis
16-17-**18** . . . Boston
20-21-**22** . . . Angels
24-25-**26** . . . at Oakland
27-28-29 . . . at Texas

JULY

1-2-3 . . . at Atlanta
4-5-**6**-7 . . . Mets
8-9-**10** . . . St. Louis
11-12-**13** . . . Arizona
18-19-**20** . . . at Florida
22-23-**24** . . . at Mets
25-**26**-**27** . . . Atlanta
29-30-31 . . . at Washington

AUGUST

1-2-**3** . . . at St. Louis
5-6-**7** . . . Florida
8-9-**10** . . . Pittsburgh
11-12-13-14 . . . at Dodgers
15-**16**-**17** . . . at San Diego
19-20-21 . . . Washington
22-**23**-**24**-25 . . . Dodgers
26-27 . . . Mets
28-**29**-**30**-31 . . . at Cubs

SEPTEMBER

1-2-3 . . . at Washington
5-**6**-**7** . . . at Mets
8-9-**10** . . . Florida
11-12-**13**-**14** . . . Milwaukee
16-17-18 . . . at Atlanta
19-20-**21** . . . at Florida
22-23-24 . . . Atlanta
26-27-**28** . . . Washington

PITTSBURGH PIRATES

PNC PARK

Standard Game Times: 7:05 p.m.; Sun. 1:35.

MARCH

31 . . . at Atlanta

APRIL

2-3 . . . at Atlanta
4-5-**6** . . . at Florida
7-9-10 . . . Cubs
11-12-**13** . . . Cincinnati
14-15-16 . . . at Dodgers
18-**19**-**20** . . . at Cubs
21-22 . . . Florida
23-24 . . . St. Louis
25-26-**27** . . . Philadelphia
28-29-**30** . . . at Mets

MAY

1-2-**3**-**4** . . . at Washington
6-7-**8** . . . San Francisco
9-10-**11**-**12** . . . Atlanta
13-14-**15** . . . at St. Louis
16-**17**-**18** . . . at Cubs
20-21-22 . . . Milwaukee
23-24-**25** . . . Cubs
27-28-29 . . . at Cincinnati
30-31 . . . at St. Louis

JUNE

1-2 . . . at St. Louis
3-4-5 . . . Houston
6-7-**8**-**9** . . . Arizona
10-11-**12** . . . Washington
13-14-**15** . . . at Baltimore
17-18-**19** . . . at White Sox
20-21-**22** . . . Toronto
24-25-26 . . . Yankees
27-28-**29** . . . Tampa Bay
30 . . . at Cincinnati

JULY

1-2 . . . at Cincinnati
4-5-**6** . . . at Milwaukee
7-8-9 . . . Houston
11-12-**13** . . . St. Louis
17-18-19-**20** . . . at Colorado
21-22-**23** . . . at Houston
24-25-26-**27** . . . San Diego
28-29-30 . . . Colorado

AUGUST

1-**2**-**3** . . . at Cubs
4-5-**6** . . . at Arizona
8-9-**10** . . . at Philadelphia
12-13-14 . . . Cincinnati
15-16-**17**-**18** . . . Mets
19-20 . . . at St. Louis
22-23-**24** . . . at Milwaukee
25-26-**27** . . . Cubs
29-30-**31** . . . Milwaukee

SEPTEMBER

2-3-**4** . . . at Cincinnati
5-6-**7** . . . at San Francisco
8-9-10-11 . . . at Houston
12-13-**14** . . . St. Louis
15-16-17-**18** . . . Dodgers
19-20-**21** . . . Houston
23-24-25 . . . at Milwaukee
26-27-**28** . . . at San Diego

ST. LOUIS CARDINALS

BUSCH STADIUM

Standard Game Times: 7:10 p.m.; Sun. 1:15.

MARCH

31 . . . Colorado

APRIL

2-**3** . . . Colorado
4-**5**-**6** . . . Washington

7-8-9 . . . at Houston
10-11-**12-13** at San Francisco
15-16-**17** . . . Milwaukee
18-**19-20** . . . San Francisco
21-**22** . . . at Milwaukee
23-24 . . . at Pittsburgh
25-**26-27** . . . Houston
28-29-**30** . . . Cincinnati

MAY

2-**3**-4 . . . Cubs
5-6-7-**8** . . . at Colorado
9-**10-11**-12 . . . at Milwaukee
13-14-**15** . . . Pittsburgh
16-**17-18** . . . Tampa Bay
19-20-21 . . . at San Diego
23-24-**25** . . . at Dodgers
27-28-29 . . . Houston
30-31 . . . Pittsburgh

JUNE

1-2 . . . Pittsburgh
3-4-5 . . . at Washington
6-7-**8** . . . at Houston
10-11-12 . . . at Cincinnati
13-**14-15** . . . Philadelphia
17-18-**19** . . . Kansas City
20-**21-22** . . . at Boston
24-25-**26** . . . at Detroit
27-28-**29** . . . at Kansas City
30 . . . Mets

JULY

1-2-3 . . . Mets
4-**5-6** . . . Cubs
8-9-**10** . . . at Philadelphia
11-12-**13** . . . at Pittsburgh
17-18-**19-20** . . . San Diego
21-22-23-24 . . . Milwaukee
25-26-**27** . . . at Mets
28-29-30-31 . . . at Atlanta

AUGUST

1-2-**3** . . . Philadelphia
5-6-**7** . . . Dodgers
8-9-10 . . . at Cubs
11-12-13-14 . . . at Florida
15-16-**17** . . . at Cincinnati
19-20 . . . Pittsburgh
22-**23-24** . . . Atlanta
26-27 . . . Milwaukee
29-30-**31** . . . at Houston

SEPTEMBER

1-2-**3** . . . at Arizona
5-6-**7** . . . Florida
9-10-11 . . . Cubs
12-13-**14** . . . at Pittsburgh
16-17-18 . . . at Cincinnati
19-20-21 . . . at Cubs
22-23-24-**25** . . . Arizona
26-27-**28** . . . Cincinnati

SAN DIEGO PADRES

PETCO PARK

Standard Game Times: 7:05 p.m.; Sun. 1:05

MARCH

31 . . . Houston

APRIL

1-2-**3** . . . Houston
4-**5-6** . . . Dodgers
7-8-9 . . . at San Francisco
11-12-**13** . . . at Dodgers
15-16-17 . . . Colorado
18-19-**20** . . . at Arizona
21-22 . . . at Houston
23-24 . . . San Francisco
25-**26-27** . . . Arizona
29-30 . . . at Philadelphia

MAY

1 . . . at Philadelphia
2-3-**4** . . . at Florida
6-7-**8** . . . at Atlanta
9-10-**11** . . . Colorado
12-13-14-**15** . . . at Cubs
16-17-**18** . . . at Seattle
19-20-21 . . . St. Louis
22-23-24-**25** . . . Cincinnati
27-28-**29** . . . Washington
30-**31** . . . at San Francisco

JUNE

1 . . . at San Francisco
2-3-4 . . . Cubs
5-6-7-**8** . . . Mets
10-11-**12** . . . Dodgers
13-14-**15** . . . at Cleveland
17-18-**19** . . . at Yankees
20-21-**22** . . . Detroit
24-25-**26** . . . Minnesota
27-28-**29** . . . Seattle
30 . . . at Colorado

JULY

1-2 . . . at Colorado
4-5-**6** . . . at Arizona
7-8-**9** . . . Florida
11-12-**13** . . . Atlanta
17-18-**19-20** . . . at St. Louis
21-22-**23** . . . at Cincinnati
24-25-26-**27** . . . at Pittsburgh
28-29-30 . . . Arizona

AUGUST

1-2-**3** . . . San Francisco
5-6-**7** . . . at Mets
8-9-**10** . . . at Colorado
12-13-**14** . . . Milwaukee
15-**16-17** . . . Philadelphia
19-20-21 . . . at Arizona
22-**23-24** . . . at San Francisco
25-26-**27** . . . Arizona
29-**30-31** . . . Colorado

SEPTEMBER

1-2-3 . . . at Dodgers
4-5-6-**7** . . . at Milwaukee
8-9-10 . . . Dodgers
11-12-13-**14** . . . San Francisco
15-16-**17** . . . at Colorado
19-20-**21** . . . at Washington
23-24-25 . . . at Dodgers
26-27-**28** . . . Pittsburgh

SAN FRANCISCO GIANTS

AT&T PARK

Standard Game Times: 7:15 p.m.; Sun. 1:05

MARCH

31 . . . at Dodgers

APRIL

1-2 . . . at Dodgers
4-5-6 . . . at Milwaukee
7-8-9 . . . San Diego
10-11-**12-13** . . . St. Louis
14-**15-16** . . . Arizona
18-**19-20** . . . at St. Louis
21-22 . . . at Arizona
23-24 . . . at San Diego
25-26-**27** . . . Cincinnati
28-29-**30** . . . Colorado

MAY

2-3-**4** . . . at Philadelphia
6-7-**8** . . . at Pittsburgh
9-**10-11** . . . Philadelphia
12-13-14-**15** . . . Houston
16-17-**18** . . . White Sox
19-20-**21** . . . at Colorado
23-24-**25** . . . at Florida
27-28-29 . . . at Arizona
30-**31** . . . San Diego

JUNE

1 . . . San Diego
2-**3-4** . . . Mets
6-7-**8**-9 . . . at Washington
10-11-**12** . . . at Colorado
13-14-**15** . . . Oakland
16-17-**18** . . . Detroit
20-21-**22** . . . at Kansas City
24-25-26 . . . at Cleveland
27-28-**29** . . . at Oakland
30 . . . Cubs

JULY

1-2-**3** . . . Cubs
4-5-**6** . . . Dodgers
8-9-**10** . . . at Mets
11-12-13 . . . at Cubs
18-**19-20** . . . Milwaukee
22-23-**24** . . . Washington
25-26-**27** . . . Arizona
28-29-30 . . . at Dodgers

AUGUST

1-2-**3** . . . at San Diego
4-5-**6** . . . Atlanta
8-9-**10** . . . Dodgers
11-12-13-**14** . . . at Houston
15-16-**17-18** . . . at Atlanta
19-20-**21** . . . Florida
22-**23-24** . . . San Diego
25-26-27 . . . Colorado
29-30-**31** . . . at Cincinnati

SEPTEMBER

1-2-**3** . . . at Colorado
5-6-**7** . . . Pittsburgh
8-9-**10** . . . Arizona
11-12-13-**14** . . . at San Diego
15-16-17-18 . . . at Arizona
19-20-**21** . . . at Dodgers
23-24-25 . . . Colorado
26-27-**28** . . . Dodgers

SEATTLE MARINERS

SAFECO FIELD

Standard Game Times: 7:05 p.m.; Sun. 1:05.

MARCH

31 . . . Texas

APRIL

1-2 . . . Texas
4-5-**6**-7 . . . at Baltimore
8-9-**10** . . . at Tampa Bay
11-12-**13** . . . Angels
14-**15** . . . Kansas City
16-17 . . . at Oakland
18-19-**20** . . . at Angels
22-23-24 . . . Baltimore
25-26-**27** . . . Oakland
29-30 . . . at Cleveland

MAY

1 . . . at Cleveland
2-3-**4** . . . at Yankees
5-6-7-8 . . . Texas
9-10-**11** . . . White Sox
12-13-**14** . . . at Texas
16-17-**18** . . . San Diego
20-21-**22** . . . at Detroit
23-24-**25** . . . at Yankees
26-27-28 . . . Boston
30-**31** . . . Detroit

JUNE

1 . . . Detroit
2-3-**4** . . . Angels
6-**7-8** . . . at Boston
9-10-**11** . . . at Toronto
13-14-**15** . . . Washington
16-17-18 . . . Florida
20-21-**22** . . . at Atlanta
23-24-25 . . . at Mets
27-28-**29** . . . at San Diego
30 . . . Toronto

JULY

1-2 . . . Toronto
3-**4-5-6** . . . Detroit
7-8-9-**10** . . . at Oakland
11-12-**13** . . . at Kansas City
18-**19-20** . . . Cleveland
21-22-**23** . . . Boston
25-**26-27** . . . at Toronto
28-29-30-31 . . . at Texas

AUGUST

1-2-**3** . . . Baltimore
4-5-**6** . . . Minnesota
7-8-9-**10** . . . Tampa Bay
12-13 . . . at Angels
15-**16-17** . . . at Minnesota
18-19-**20** . . . at White Sox
21-22-23-**24** . . . Oakland
25-26-**27** . . . Minnesota
29-**30-31** . . . at Cleveland

SEPTEMBER

1-2-**3** . . . at Texas
5-6-**7** . . . Yankees
9-**10** . . . Texas
11-12-**13**-14 . . . at Angels
15-16-17-**18** . . . at Kansas City
19-**20**-**21** . . . at Oakland
22-23-24-25 . . . Angels
26-27-**28** . . . Oakland

TAMPA BAY RAYS

TROPICANA FIELD

Standard Game Times: 7:10 p.m.; Sun. 1:40.

MARCH

31 . . . at Baltimore

APRIL

2-3 . . . at Baltimore
4-5-**6**-7 . . . at Yankees
8-9-**10** . . . Seattle
11-12-**13** . . . Baltimore
14-15 . . . Yankees
16-17 . . . at Minnesota
18-19-**20** . . . White Sox
22-23-24 . . . Toronto
25-26-**27** . . . Boston
29-30 . . . at Baltimore

MAY

1 . . . at Baltimore
2-3-**4** . . . at Boston
6-7-8 . . . at Toronto
9-10-**11** . . . Angels
12-13-14-**15** . . . Yankees
16-**17**-**18** . . . at St. Louis
19-20-**21** . . . at Oakland
23-24-**25** . . . Baltimore
26-27-**28** . . . Texas
29-30-31 . . . White Sox

JUNE

1 . . . White Sox
3-4-5 . . . at Boston
6-7-**8** . . . at Texas
9-10-**11** . . . at Angels
13-14-**15** . . . Florida
17-18-19 . . . Cubs
20-21-**22** . . . Houston
24-25-**26** . . . at Florida
27-28-**29** . . . at Pittsburgh
30 . . . Boston

JULY

1-2 . . . Boston
4-5-**6**-**7** . . . Kansas City
8-**9** . . . at Yankees
10-11-12-**13** . . . at Cleveland
18-19-**20** . . . Toronto
21-22-**23** . . . Oakland
24-25-26-**27** . . . at Kansas City
28-29-**30** . . . at Toronto

AUGUST

1-2-**3** . . . Detroit
4-5-**6** . . . Cleveland
7-8-9-**10** . . . at Seattle
12-13-**14** . . . at Oakland
15-16-**17** . . . at Texas
18-19-20 . . . Angels
22-23-**24** . . . at White Sox
26-27-28 . . . Toronto
29-30-**31** . . . Baltimore

SEPTEMBER

2-3-4 . . . Yankees
5-**6**-**7** . . . at Toronto
8-9-10 . . . at Boston
12-13-**14** . . . at Yankees
15-16-17 . . . Boston
18-19-20-**21** . . . Minnesota
22-23-24 . . . at Baltimore
25-26-27-**28** . . . at Detroit

TEXAS RANGERS

RANGERS BALLPARK IN ARLINGTON

Standard Game Times: 7:05 p.m.; Sun. 1:05.

MARCH

31 . . . at Seattle

APRIL

1-2 . . . at Seattle
4-5-**6** . . . at Angels
8-9-10 . . . Baltimore
11-12-**13** . . . Toronto
14-**15** . . . Angels
16-17 . . . at Toronto
18-19-**20**-**21** . . . at Boston
22-23-**24** . . . at Detroit
25-26-**27** . . . Minnesota
29-30 . . . Kansas City

MAY

1 . . . Kansas City
2-3-**4** . . . at Oakland
5-6-7-8 . . . at Seattle
9-10-**11** . . . Oakland
12-13-**14** . . . Seattle
16-17-**18** . . . Houston
19-20-21-**22** . . at Minnesota
23-24-**25** . . . at Cleveland
26-27-**28** . . . at Tampa Bay
30-31 . . . Oakland

JUNE

1 . . . Oakland
2-3-4-5 . . . Cleveland
6-7-8 . . . Tampa Bay
10-11-**12** . . . at Kansas City
13-14-**15** . . . at Mets
17-18-**19** . . . Atlanta
20-21-**22** . . . at Washington
24-25-26 . . . at Houston
27-28-29 . . . Philadelphia
30 . . . at Yankees

JULY

1-2 . . . at Yankees
4-5-**6** . . . at Baltimore
7-8-9-10 . . . Angels
11-12-**13** . . . White Sox
18-19-**20** . . . at Minnesota
21-22-**23** . . . at White Sox
25-**26**-**27** . . . at Oakland
28-29-30-31 . . . Seattle

AUGUST

1-2-3 . . . Toronto
4-5-6-7 . . . Yankees
8-9-**10** . . . at Baltimore
12-13-14 . . . at Boston
15-16-17 . . . Tampa Bay
18-19-20 . . . Detroit
22-23-24 . . . Cleveland
25-26-27 . . . at Kansas City
28-29-30-**31** . . . at Angels

SEPTEMBER

1-2-**3** . . . Seattle
5-6-**7** . . . Boston
9-**10** . . . at Seattle
11-12-**13**-**14** . . . at Oakland
15-16-17 . . . Detroit
19-20-**21** . . . Angels
22-23-**24** . . . Oakland
26-27-**28** . . . at Angels

TORONTO BLUE JAYS

ROGERS CENTRE

Standard Game Times: 7:07 p.m.; Sat. 4:07; Sun. 1:07.

MARCH

31 . . . at Yankees

APRIL

2-3 . . . at Yankees
4-**5**-**6** . . . Boston
8-9-10 . . . Oakland
11-12-**13** . . . at Texas
14-15 . . . at Baltimore
16-17 . . . Texas
18-**19**-**20**-**21** . . . Detroit
22-23-24 . . . at Tampa Bay
25-26-**27** . . . at Kansas City
29-30 . . . at Boston

MAY

1 . . . at Boston
2-**3**-**4**-5 . . . White Sox
6-7-8 . . . Tampa Bay
9-10-**11**-12 . . . at Cleveland
13-14-**15** . . . at Minnesota
16-17-**18** . . . at Philadelphia
20-21-22 . . . Angels
23-**24**-**25**-**26** . . Kansas City
27-28-**29** . . . at Oakland
30-31 . . . at Angels

JUNE

1 . . . at Angels
3-4-5 . . . at Yankees
6-**7**-**8** . . . Baltimore
9-10-**11** . . . Seattle
13-**14**-**15** . . . Cubs
17-18-**19** . . . at Milwaukee
20-21-**22** . . . at Pittsburgh
24-25-26 . . . Cincinnati
27-**28**-**29** . . . Atlanta
30 . . . at Seattle

JULY

1-2 . . . at Seattle
4-5-**6** . . . at Angels
8-9-10 . . . Baltimore
11-**12**-**13** . . . Yankees
18-19-**20** . . . at Tampa Bay
21-22-23-**24** . . . at Baltimore
25-**26**-**27** . . . Seattle
28-29-**30** . . . Tampa Bay

AUGUST

1-2-3 . . . at Texas
4-5-6-7 . . . Oakland
8-**9**-**10** . . . Cleveland
11-12-13-**14** . . . at Detroit
15-16-**17** . . . at Boston
19-20-21 . . . Yankees
22-**23**-**24** . . . Boston
26-27-28 . . . at Tampa Bay
29-30-**31** . . . at Yankees

SEPTEMBER

2-3-4 . . . Minnesota
5-**6**-**7** . . . Tampa Bay
8-9-10-11 . . . at White Sox
12-13-**14** . . . at Boston
16-17-18 . . . Baltimore
19-**20**-**21** . . . Boston
23-24-25 . . . Yankees
26-27-**28** . . . at Baltimore

WASHINGTON NATIONALS

NATIONALS PARK

Standard Game Times: 7:05 p.m.; Sun. 1:35

MARCH

30 . . . Atlanta
31 . . . at Philadelphia

APRIL

2-**3** . . . at Philadelphia
4-**5**-**6** . . . at St. Louis
7-9-10 . . . Florida
11-**12**-**13** . . . Atlanta
15-16-17 . . . at Mets
18-19-**20** . . . at Florida
21-22 . . . at Atlanta
23-24 . . . Mets
25-26-**27** . . . Cubs
29-**30** . . . Atlanta

MAY

1-2-**3**-**4** . . . Pittsburgh
6-7-8 . . . at Houston
9-10-**11** . . . Florida
12-13-14-**15** . . . at Mets
16-17-**18** . . . at Baltimore
19-20-21 . . . Philadelphia
23-24-**25**-**26** . . . Milwaukee
27-28-**29** . . . at San Diego
30-31 . . . at Arizona

JUNE

1 . . . at Arizona
3-4-5 . . . St. Louis
6-7-**8**-9 . . . San Francisco
10-11-**12** . . . at Pittsburgh

13-14-**15** . . . . . . at Seattle
17-18-**19** . . . . at Minnesota
20-21-**22** . . . . Texas
23-24-25 . . . . Angels
27-28-**29** . . . . . . Baltimore
30 . . . . at Florida

JULY

1-**2** . . . . at Florida
3-**4**-5-**6** . . . . . at Cincinnati

8-9-10 . . . . .Arizona
11-12-**13** . . . . Houston
18-19-**20** . . . . . . at Atlanta
22-23-**24** . . at San Francisco
25-26-**27** . . . . . at Dodgers
29-30-31 . . . . Philadelphia

AUGUST

1-2-**3** . . . . Cincinnati
4-5-6-**7** . . . . . . at Colorado

8-9-**10**-**11** . . . at Milwaukee
12-13-14 . . . . Mets
15-16-**17** . . . . . . .Colorado
19-20-21 . . . at Philadelphia
22-**23**-**24** . . . . at Cubs
26-27-28 . . . . Dodgers
29-30-**31** . . . . Atlanta

SEPTEMBER

1-2-3 . . . . . . Philadelphia

4-5-6-**7** . . . . at Atlanta
9-10 . . . . at Mets
12-13-**14** . . . . . . at Florida
15-16-17-18 . . . . Mets
19-20-**21** . . . . . . San Diego
23-24-25 . . . . Florida
26-27-**28** . . . at Philadelphia

SPRING TRAINING

ARIZONA CACTUS LEAGUE

ARIZONA DIAMONDBACKS

Major League Club

Complex Address (first year): Tucson Electric Park (1998), 2500 Ajo Way, Tucson, AZ 85713. **Telephone:** (520) 434-1400. **FAX:** (520) 434-1443. **Seating Capacity:** 11,000. **Location:** I-10 to exit 262 (Park Street) or 263 (Kino Street), south to Ajo Way, left (east) on Ajo Way to park.

Hotel Address: JW Marriott Starr Pass Resort, 3800 W. Starr Pass Blvd., Tucson, AZ 85745. **Telephone:** (520) 792-3500.

Minor League Clubs

Complex Address: Kino Veterans Memorial Sportspark, 3600 S. Country Club, Tucson, AZ 85713. **Telephone:** (520) 434-1400. **FAX:** (520) 434-1443. **Hotel Address:** The Hotel Arizona, 181 W. Broadway, Tucson, AZ 85701. **Telephone:** (520) 624-8711.

CHICAGO CUBS

Major League Club

Complex Address (First Year): HoHoKam Park (1979), 1235 N. Center St., Mesa, AZ 85201. **Telephone:** (480) 668-0500. **FAX:** (480) 668-4541. **Seating Capacity:** 12,632. **Location:** Main Street (U.S. Highway 60) to Center Street, north 1 1/2 miles on Center Street.

Hotel Address: Best Western Dobson Ranch Inn, 1666 S. Dobson Rd., Mesa, AZ 85202. **Telephone:** (480) 831-7000.

Minor League Clubs

Complex Address: Fitch Park, 160 E. Sixth Place, Mesa, AZ 85201. **Telephone:** (480) 668-0500. **FAX:** (480) 668-4501. **Hotel Address:** Best Western Mezona, 250 W. Main St., Mesa, AZ 85201. **Telephone:** (480) 834-9233.

CHICAGO WHITE SOX

Major League Club

Complex Address (first year): Tucson Electric Park (1998), 2500 E. Ajo Way, Tucson, AZ 85713. **Telephone:** (520) 434-1300. **FAX:** (520) 434-1151. **Seating Capacity:** 11,000. **Location:** I-10 to exit 262 (Park Street) or 263 (Kino Street), south to Ajo Way, left (east) on Ajo Way to park.

Hotel Address: Doubletree Guest Suites, 6555 E. Speedway Blvd., Tucson, AZ 85710. **Telephone:** (520) 721-7100.

Minor League Clubs

Complex Address: Same as major league club. **Hotel Address:** Ramada Palo Verde, 5251 S. Julian Dr., Tucson, AZ 85706. **Telephone:** (520) 294-5250.

COLORADO ROCKIES

Major League Club

Complex Address (first year): Hi Corbett Field (1993), 3400 E. Camino Campestre, Tucson, AZ 85716. **Telephone:** (520) 322-4500. **Seating Capacity:** 8,655. **Location:** I-10 to Broadway exit, east on Broadway to Randolph Park.

Hotel Address: Hilton Tucson East, 7600 Broadway, Tucson, AZ 85710.

Minor League Clubs

Complex Address: Same as major league club. **Hotel Address:** Randolph Park Hotel & Suites, 102 N. Alvernon, Tucson, AZ 85711. **Telephone:** (520) 795-0330.

KANSAS CITY ROYALS

Major League Club

Complex Address (first year): Surprise Stadium (2003), 15946 N. Bullard Ave., Surprise, AZ 85374. **Telephone:** (623) 266-8800. **FAX:** (623) 266-8012. **Seating Capacity:** 10,700. **Location:** I-10 West to Route 101 North, 101 North to Bell Road, left on Bell for five miles, stadium on left.

Hotel Address: Wingate Inn & Suites, 1188 N. Dysart Rd., Avondale, AZ 85323. **Telephone:** (623) 547-1313.

Minor League Clubs

Complex: Same as Major League club. **Hotel Address:** Quality Inn, 16741 N. Greasewood St., Surprise, AZ 85374. **Telephone:** (623) 583-3500.

LOS ANGELES ANGELS

Major League Club

Complex Address (first year): Tempe Diablo Stadium (1993), 2200 W. Alameda, Tempe, AZ 85282. **Telephone:** (480) 858-7500. **FAX:** (480) 438-7583. **Seating Capacity:** 9,785. **Location:** I-10 to exit 153B (48th Street), south one mile on 48th Street to Alameda Drive, left on Alameda.

Minor League Clubs

Complex Address: Tempe Diablo Minor League Complex, 2225 W. Westcourt Way, Tempe, AZ 85282. **Telephone:** (480) 858-7555.

Hotel Address: Extended Stay America, 3421 E. Elwood Street, Phoenix, AZ 85040. **Telephone:** (602) 438-2900.

MILWAUKEE BREWERS

Major League Club

Complex Address (first year): Maryvale Baseball Park (1998), 3600 N. 51st Ave., Phoenix, AZ 85031. **Telephone:** (623) 245-5555. **FAX:** (623) 245-5580. **Seating Capacity:** 9,000. **Location:** I-10 to exit 139 (51st Ave.), north on 51st Ave.; I-17 to exit 202 (Indian School Road), west on Indian School Road.

Hotel Address: Holiday Inn Express-Tempe, 5300 S. Priest Dr., Tempe, AZ 85283. **Telephone:** (480) 820-7500.

Minor League Clubs

Complex Address: Maryvale Baseball Complex, 3805 N. 53rd Ave., Phoenix, AZ 85031. **Telephone:** (623) 245-5600. **FAX:** (623) 245-5607. **Hotel Address:** Same as major league club.

OAKLAND ATHLETICS

Major League Club

Complex Address (first year): Phoenix Municipal Stadium (1982), 5999 E. Van Buren, Phoenix, AZ 85008. **Telephone:** (602) 225-9400. **FAX:** (602) 225-9473. **Seating Capacity:** 8,500. **Location:** I-10 to exit 153 (48th Street), HoHoKam Expressway to Van Buren Street (U.S. Highway 60), right on Van Buren, park two miles on right.

Hotel Address: Doubletree Suites Hotel, 320 N. 44th St., Phoenix, AZ 85008. **Telephone:** (602) 225-0500.

Minor League Clubs

Complex Address: Papago Park Baseball Complex, 1802 N. 64th St., Phoenix, AZ 85008. **Telephone:** (480) 949-5951. **FAX:** (480) 945-0557. **Hotel Address:** Extended Stay America, 4357 East Oak Street, Phoenix, AZ 85008 Telephone: (602) 225-2998

SAN DIEGO PADRES

Major League Club

Complex Address (first year): Peoria Sports Complex (1994), 8131 W. Paradise Lane, Peoria, AZ 85382. **Telephone:** (623) 486-7000. **FAX:** (623) 486-7154. **Seating Capacity:** 10,000. **Location:** I-17 to Bell Road exit, west on Bell to 83rd Ave.

Hotel Address: La Quinta Inns and Suites, 16321 N. 83rd Avenue Peoria, AZ 85382. **Telephone:** (623) 487-1900

Minor League Clubs

Complex Address: Same as Major League club.

Hotel Address: The Country Inn and Suites, 20221 N. 29th Avenue, Phoenix, AZ 85027. **Telephone:** (623) 879-9000.

SAN FRANCISCO GIANTS

Major League Club

Complex Address (first year): Scottsdale Stadium (1981), 7408 E. Osborn Rd., Scottsdale, AZ 85251. **Telephone:** (480) 990-7972. **FAX:** (480) 990-2643. **Seating Capacity:** 11,500. **Location:** Scottsdale Road to Osborne Road, east on Osborne 1/2 mile.

Hotel Address: Hilton Garden Inn Scottsdale Old Town, 7324 East Indian School Rd., Scottsdale, AZ 85251. **Telephone:** (480) 481-0400.

Minor League Clubs

Complex Address: Indian School Park, 4415 N. Hayden Road at Camelback Road, Scottsdale, AZ 85251. **Telephone:** (480) 990-0052. **FAX:** (480) 990-2349.

Hotel Address: Days Inn, 4710 N. Scottsdale Rd., Scottsdale, AZ 85351. **Telephone:** (480) 947-5411.

SEATTLE MARINERS

Major League Club

Complex Address (first year): Peoria Sports Complex (1993), 15707 N. 83rd Ave., Peoria, AZ 85382. **Telephone:** (623) 776-4800. **FAX:** (623) 776-4829. **Seating Capacity:** 10,000. **Location:** I-17 to Bell Road exit, west on Bell to 83rd Ave.

Hotel Address: LaQuinta Inn & Suites, 16321 N. 83rd Ave., Peoria, AZ 85382. **Telephone:** (623) 487-1900.

Minor League Clubs

Complex Address: Peoria Sports Complex (1993), 15707 N. 83rd Ave., Peoria, AZ 85382. **Telephone:** (602) 412-9000. **FAX:** (602) 412-9382. **Hotel Address:** Hampton Inn, 8408 W. Paradise Lane, Peoria, AZ 85382. **Telephone:** (623) 486-9918.

TEXAS RANGERS

Major League Club

Complex Address (first year): Surprise Stadium (2003), 15754 N. Bullard Ave., Surprise, AZ 85374. **Telephone:** (623) 266-8100. **FAX:** (623) 266-8120. **Seating Capacity:** 10,714. **Location:** I-10 West to Route 101 North, 101 North to Bell Road, left at Bell for seven miles, stadium on left.

Hotel Address: Windmill Suites at Sun City West, 12545 W. Bell Rd., Surprise, AZ 85374. **Telephone:** (623) 583-0133.

Minor League Clubs

Complex Address: Same as major league club.

Hotel Address: Hampton Inn, 2000 N. Litchfield Rd., Goodyear, AZ 85338. **Telephone:** (623) 536-1313; Holiday Inn Express, 1313 N. Litchfield Rd., Goodyear, AZ 85338.

FLORIDA/GRAPEFRUIT LEAGUE

ATLANTA BRAVES

Major League Club

Stadium Address (first year): Champions Park (1998), The Ballpark at Disney's Wide World of Sports Complex, 700 S. Victory Way, Kissimmee, FL 34747. **Telephone:** (407) 939-2200. **Seating Capacity:** 9,500. **Location:** I-4 to exit 25B (Highway 192 West), follow signs to Magic Kingdom/ Wide World of Sports Complex, right on Victory Way.

Hotel Address: World Center Marriott, World Center Drive, Orlando, FL 32821. **Telephone:** (407) 239-4200.

Minor League Clubs

Complex Address: Same as major league club. **Telephone:** (407) 939-2232. **FAX:** (407) 939-2225. **Hotel Address:** Marriot Village at Lake Buena Vista, 8623 Vineland Ave., Orlando, FL 32821. **Telephone:** (407) 938-9001.

BALTIMORE ORIOLES

Major League Club

Complex Address (first year): Fort Lauderdale Stadium (1996), 1301 NW 55th St., Fort Lauderdale, FL 33309. **Telephone:** (954) 776-1921. **FAX:** (954) 776-9116. **Seating Capacity:** 8,340. **Location:** I-95 to exit 32 (Commercial Blvd.), West on Commercial, right on Orioles Blvd. (NW 55th Street), stadium on left.

Hotel Address: Sheraton Suites, 555 NW 62nd St., Fort Lauderdale, FL 33309. **Telephone:** (954) 772-5400.

Minor League Clubs

Complex Address: Twin Lakes Park, 6700 Clark Rd., **Sarasota, FL 34241. Telephone:** (941) 923-1996. **FAX:** (941) 922-3751. **Hotel Address:** Ramada Inn Limited, 5774 Clark Rd., Sarasota, FL 34233. **Telephone:** (941) 921-7812; Americinn, 5931 Fruitville Rd., Sarasota, FL 34232. **Telephone:** (941) 342-8778.

BOSTON RED SOX

Major League Club

Complex Address (First year): City of Palms Park (1993), 2201 Edison Ave., **Fort Myers, FL 33901. Telephone:** (239) 334-4799. **FAX:** (239) 332-8105. **Seating Capacity:** 7575. **Location:** I-75 to exit 138, four miles west to Fowler St., left on Fowler to Edison Ave., right on Edison Ave., park on right.

Hotel Address: Homewood Suites Hotel, 5255 Big Pine Way, Fort Myers, FL 33907. **Telephone:** (239) 275-6000.

Minor League Clubs

Complex Address: Red Sox Minor League Complex, 4301 Edison Ave., Fort Myers, FL 33916. **Telephone:** (239) 334-4799. **FAX:** (239) 332-8107. **Hotel Address:** Ambassador Hotel, 2500 Edwards Dr., Fort Myers, FL 33901. **Telephone:** (239) 337-0300.

CINCINNATI REDS

Major League Club

Complex Address (first year): Ed Smith Stadium (1998), 1090 N. Euclid Ave., Sarasota, FL 34237. **Telephone:** (941) 955-6501. **FAX:** (941) 955-6365. **Seating Capacity:** 7,500. **Location:** I-75 to exit 39, west on Fruitville Road (Route 780) for four miles, right on Tuttle.

Hotel Address—Staff: Marriott Residence Inn, 1040 University Pkwy., Sarasota, FL 34234. **Telephone:** (941) 358-1468. **FAX:** (941) 358-0850.

Players: Wellesley Inn, 1803 N. Tamiami Trail, Sarasota, FL 34234. **Telephone:** (941) 366-5128. **FAX:** (941) 953-4322.

Minor League Clubs

Complex Address: Same as major league club. **Hotel Address:** Holiday Inn, 7150 N. Tamiami Trail, Sarasota, FL 34243. **Telephone:** (941) 355-2781.

CLEVELAND INDIANS

Major League Club

Complex Address (first year): Chain O' Lakes Park (1993), Cypress Gardens Blvd. at U.S. 17, Winter Haven, FL 33880. **Telephone:** (863) 293-5405. **FAX:** (863) 291-5772. **Seating Capacity:** 7,000. **Location:** U.S. 17 (3rd Street) south through Winter Haven to Cypress Gardens Boulevard.

Hotel Address: Holiday Inn, 1150 Third St. SW, Winter Haven, FL 33880. **Telephone:** (863) 294-4451.

Minor League Clubs

Complex Address/Hotel: Same as major league club.

DETROIT TIGERS

Major League Club

Complex Address (first year): Joker Marchant Stadium (1946), 2301 Lakeland Hills Blvd., Lakeland, FL 33805. **Telephone:** (863) 686-8075. **FAX:** (863) 688-9589. **Seating Capacity:** 9,000. **Location:** I-4 to exit 19 (Lakeland Hills Boulevard), left 1 1/2 miles.

Hotel Address: Holiday Inn Lakeland Hotel and Conference Center, 3260 Hwy. 98 N., Lakeland, FL 33805. **Telephone:** (863) 688-8280.

Minor League Clubs

Complex/Hotel Address: Tigertown, 2125 N. Lake Ave., Lakeland, FL 33805. **Telephone:** (863) 686-8075. **FAX:** (863) 688-9589.

FLORIDA MARLINS

Major League Club

Complex Address (first year): Roger Dean Stadium (1998), 4751 Main St., Jupiter, FL 33458. **Telephone:** (561) 775-1818.

Seating Capacity: 7,000.

Location: I-95 to exit 83, east on Donald Ross Road for one mile to Central Blvd, left at light, follow Central Boulevard to circle and take Main Street to Roger Dean Stadium.

Hotel Address: Hampton Inn, 401 RCA Blvd., Palm Beach Gardens, FL 33410. **Telephone:** (561) 625-8880. **FAX:** (561) 625-6766.

Minor League Clubs

Complex Address: Same as major league club. **Hotel Address:** Fairfield Inn, 6748 W. Indiantown Rd., Jupiter, FL 33458. **Telephone:** (561) 748-5252.

HOUSTON ASTROS

Major League Club

Complex Address (first year): Osceola County Stadium (1985), 631 Heritage Park Way, Kissimmee, FL 34744. **Telephone:** (321) 697-3150. **FAX:** (321) 697-3199. **Seating Capacity:** 5,300. **Location:** From Florida Turnpike South, take exit 244, west on U.S. 192, right on Bill Beck Boulevard; From Florida Turnpike North, take exit 242, west on U.S. 192, right on Bill Beck Blvd.; From I-4, take exit onto 192 East for 12 miles, stadium on left; From 17-92 South, take U.S. 192, left for three miles.

Hotel Address: Reunion Resort & Club, 1000 Reunion Way, Reunion, Florida 34747. **Telephone:** 407-662-1000. **Fax:** 407-662-1111

Minor League Clubs

Complex Address: 1000 Bill Beck Blvd., Kissimmee, FL 34744. **Telephone:** (321) 697-3100. **FAX:** (321) 697-3195. **Hotel Address:** Same as major league club.

LOS ANGELES DODGERS

Major League Club

Complex Address (first year): Holman Stadium (1948). **Seating Capacity:** 6,500. **Location:** Exit I-95 to Route 60 East, left on 43rd Avenue, right on 26th Street.

Hotel Address: Dodgertown, 4001 26th St., Vero Beach, FL 32960. **Telephone:** (772) 569-4900. **FAX:** (772) 567-0819.

Minor League Clubs

Complex/Hotel Address: Same as major league club.

MINNESOTA TWINS

Major League Club

Complex Address (first year): Lee County Sports Complex/Hammond Stadium (1991), 14100 Six Mile Cypress Pkwy., Fort Myers, FL 33912. **Telephone:** (239) 768-4282. **FAX:** (239) 768-4211. **Seating Capacity:** 7,905. **Location:** Exit 21 off I-75, west on Daniels Parkway, left on Six Mile Cypress Parkway.

Hotel Address: Clarion Hotel, 12635 Cleveland Ave., Fort Myers, FL 33907. **Telephone:** (239) 936-4300.

Minor League Clubs

Complex Address/Hotel: Same as major league club.

NEW YORK METS

Major League Club

Complex Address (first year): St. Lucie Sports Complex/Tradition Field (1987), 525 NW Peacock Blvd., Port St. Lucie, FL 34986. **Telephone:** (772) 871-2100. **FAX:** (772) 878-9802. **Seating Capacity:** 7,000. **Location:** Exit 121C (St. Lucie West Boulevard) off I-95 , east 1/4 mile, left onto NW Peacock Boulevard.

Hotel Address: Spring Hill Suites, 2000 NW Courtyard Circle, Port St. Lucie, FL 34986. **Telephone:** (772) 871-2929.

Minor League Clubs

Complex Address: Same as major league club. **Hotel Address:** Holiday Inn, 10120 South Federal Hwy., Port St. Lucie, FL 34952. **Telephone:** (772) 337-2200.

NEW YORK YANKEES

Major League Club

Complex Address (first year): Legends Field (1996), One Steinbrenner Dr., **Tampa, FL 33614. Telephone:** (813) 875-7753. **FAX:** (813) 673-3199. **Seating Capacity:** 10,000. **Location:** I-275 to Martin Luther King, west on Martin Luther King to Dale Mabry.

Hotel Address: Radisson Bay Harbor Inn, 770 Courtney Campbell Causeway, Tampa, FL 33607. **Telephone:** (813) 281-8900.

Minor League Clubs

Complex Address: Yankees Player Development/ Scouting Complex, 3102 N. **Himes Ave., Tampa, FL 33607. Telephone:** (813) 875-7569. **FAX:** (813) 873-2302. **Hotel Address:** Holiday Inn Express, 4732 N. **Dale Mabry, Tampa, FL 33614.**

PHILADELPHIA PHILLIES

Major League Club

Complex Address: Bright House Networks Field (2004), 601 N. Old Coachman Rd., Clearwater, FL 33765. **Telephone:** (727) 467-4457. **FAX:** (727) 712-4498. **Seating Capacity:** 8,500. **Location:** Route 60 West, right on Old Coachman Road, ballpark on right after Drew Street.

Hotel: None.

Minor League Clubs

Complex Address: Carpenter Complex, 651 N. Old Coachman Rd., Clearwater, FL 33765. **Telephone:** (727) 799-0503. **FAX:** (727) 726-1793. **Hotel Addresses:** Hampton Inn, 21030 U.S. Highway 19 North, Clearwater, FL 34625. **Telephone:** (727) 797-8173; Econolodge, 21252 U.S. Hwy. 19, Clearwater, FL 34625. **Telephone:** (727) 799-1569.

PITTSBURGH PIRATES

Major League Club

Stadium Address (first year): McKechnie Field (1969), 17th Ave. West and Ninth Street West, Bradenton, FL 34205. **Seating Capacity:** 6,562. **Location:** U.S. 41 to 17th Ave, west to 9th Street.

Complex/Hotel Address: Pirate City, 1701 27th St. E., Bradenton, FL 34208. **Telephone:** (941) 747-3031. **FAX:** (941) 747-9549.

Minor League Clubs

Complex/Hotel Address: Same as major league club.

ST. LOUIS CARDINALS

Major League Club

Complex Address (first year): Roger Dean Stadium (1998), 4795 University Dr., Jupiter, FL 33458. **Telephone:** (561) 775-1818. **FAX:** (561) 799-1380. **Seating Capacity:** 6,864. **Location:** I-95 to exit 58, east on Donald Ross Road for 1/4 mile.

Hotel Address: Embassy Suites, 4350 PGA Blvd., Palm Beach Gardens, FL 33410. **Telephone:** (561) 622-1000.

Minor League Clubs

Complex: Same as major league club. **Hotel:** West Palm Beach Marriott, 630 Clearwater Rd., **West Palm Beach, FL 33401. Telephone:** (561) 833-1234.

TAMPA BAY RAYS

Major League Club

Stadium Address (first year): Progress Energy Park/ Home of Al Lang Field (1998), 180 Second Ave. SE, St. Petersburg, FL 33701. **Telephone:** (727) 825-3137. **FAX:** (727) 825-3167. **Seating Capacity:** 6,438. **Location:** I-275 to exit 23A, left on First Street South to Second Avenue South, stadium on right.

Complex/Hotel Address: Raymond A. Naimoli Complex, 7901 30th Ave. N., St. Petersburg, FL 33710. **Telephone:** (727) 384-5517.

Minor League Clubs

Complex/Hotel Address: Same as major league club.

TORONTO BLUE JAYS

Major League Club

Stadium Address (first year): Knology Park (1977), 373 Douglas Ave. #A, Dunedin, FL 34698. **Telephone:** (727) 733-9302. **Seating Capacity:** 5,509. **Location:** From I-275, north on Highway 19, left on Sunset Point Road for 4 miles, right on Douglas Avenue, stadium one mile on right.

Minor League Clubs

Complex Address: Bobby Mattick Training Center at Englebert Complex, 1700 Solon Ave., Dunedin, FL 34698. **Telephone:** (727) 743-8007. **Hotel Address:** Red Roof Inn, 3200 U.S. 19 N., Clearwater, FL 34684. **Telephone:** (727) 786-2529.

WASHINGTON NATIONALS

Major League Club

Complex Address (first year): Space Coast Stadium (2003), 5800 Stadium Pkwy., Viera, FL 32940. **Telephone:** (321) 633-9200. **Seating Capacity:** 8,100. **Location:** I-95 southbound to Fiske Blvd. (exit 74), south on Fiske/ Stadium Parkway to stadium; I-95 northbound to State Road #509/Wickham Road (exit 73), left off exit, right on Lake Andrew Drive; turn right on Stadium Parkway, stadium is 1/2 mile on left.

Hotel Address: Melbourne Airport Hilton, 200 Rialto Place, Melbourne, FL 32901. **Telephone:** (321) 768-0200.

Minor League Clubs

Complex Address: Carl Barger Complex, 5600 Stadium Pkwy., Viera, FL 32940. **Telephone:** (321) 633-8119. **Hotel Address:** Imperial Hotel & Conference Center, 8298 N. Wickman Rd., Viera, FL 32940. **Telephone:** (321) 255-0077.

MEDIA
INFORMATION

LOCAL MEDIA INFORMATION

AMERICAN LEAGUE

BALTIMORE ORIOLES

Radio Announcers: Joe Angel, Jim Hunter, Fred Manfra. **Flagship Station:** WHFS-FM (105.7).

TV Announcers: Jim Hunter, Fred Manfra, Jim Palmer, Buck Martinez. **Flagship Station:** Mid-Atlantic Sports Network (MASN).

Newspapers, Daily Coverage (*national/beat writers): Baltimore Sun (*Dan Connolly, Jeff Zerbiec), Washington Post (Marc Carig, *Dave Sheinin). **MLB.com:** Spencer Fordin.

BOSTON RED SOX

Radio Announcers: Joe Castiglione, Dave O'Brien, Glenn Geffner Flagship Station: WRKO (680 AM).

TV Announcers: Don Orsillo, Jerry Remy, Tina Cervasio. **Flagship Station:** New England Sports Network (regional cable).

Spanish Radio Announcers: Uri Berenguer, Juan Carlos Baez. **Flagship Station:** WROL (950 AM)

Newspapers, Daily Coverage (*national/beat writers): Boston Globe (Gordon Edes, *Nick Cafardo), Boston Herald (Jeff Horrigan, Tony Massarotti, Michael Silverman), Providence Journal (Steve Krasner, Sean McAdam), Worcester Telegram & Gazette (Bill Ballou, Phil O'Neill), Hartford Courant (Jeff Goldberg, Paul Doyle). **MLB.com:** Ian Browne.

CHICAGO WHITE SOX

Radio Announcers: Chris Singleton, Ed Farmer. **Flagship Station:** WMVP/ESPN Radio 1000-AM.

TV Announcers: Ken Harrelson, Darrin Jackson. **Flagship Stations:** WGN TV-9, WCIU-TV, Comcast Sports Net (regional cable).

Newspapers, Daily Coverage (*national/beat writers): Chicago Sun-Times (Joe Cowley), Chicago Tribune (Mark Gonzales), Arlington Heights Daily Herald (Scot Gregor), Daily Southtown (Nate Whalen). **MLB.com:** Scott Merkin.

CLEVELAND INDIANS

Radio Announcers: Tom Hamilton, Mike Hegan. **Flagship Station:** WTAM 1100-AM.

TV Announcers: Rick Manning, Matt Underwood. **Flagship Station:** SportsTime Ohio.

Newspapers, Daily Coverage (beat writers): Cleveland Plain Dealer (Paul Hoynes), Lake County News-Herald (Jim Ingraham), Akron Beacon-Journal (Sheldon Ocker), Canton Repository (Andy Call). **MLB.com:** Anthony Castrovince.

DETROIT TIGERS

Radio Announcers: Dan Dickerson, Jim Price. **Flagship Station:** WXYT 1270-AM.

TV Announcers: Rod Allen, Mario Impemba. **Flagship Station:** Fox Sports Net Detroit (regional cable).

Newspapers, Daily Coverage (beat writers): Detroit Free Press (John Lowe, Jon Paul Morosi), Detroit News (Tom Gage), Oakland Press (Jim Hawkins), Booth Newspapers (Danny Knobler). **MLB.com:** Jason Beck.

KANSAS CITY ROYALS

Radio Announcers: Ryan Lefebvre, Denny Matthews. **Kansas City affiliate:** WHB 810-AM.

TV Announcers: Bob Davis, Paul Splittorff. **Flagship Stations:** Royals Sports Television Network.

Newspapers, Daily Coverage (beat writers): Kansas City Star (Bob Dutton). **MLB.com:** Dick Kaegel.

LOS ANGELES ANGELS

Radio Announcers: Rory Markas, Terry Smith. **Spanish**— Jose Mota. **Flagship Station:** ESPN Radio 710-AM, AM 830 (Spanish).

TV Announcers: Rex Hudler, Steve Physioc. **Flagship Stations:** FSN West (regional cable).

Newspapers, Daily Coverage (*national/beat writers): Los Angeles Times (Mike DiGiovanna), Orange County Register (Bill Plunkett), Riverside Press Enterprise (Matt Hurst), San Gabriel Valley Tribune/LA News Group (Doug Padilla). **MLB.com:** Mike Scarr.

MINNESOTA TWINS

Radio Announcers: Herb Carneal, John Gordon, Dan Gladden. **Flagship Station:** KSTP-1500.

TV Announcers: Bert Blyleven, Dick Bremer. **Flagship Station:** Fox Sports Net North.

Newspapers, Daily Coverage (beat writers): St. Paul Pioneer Press (Jason Williams), Minneapolis Star Tribune (LaVelle Neal). **MLB.com:** Kelly Thesier.

NEW YORK YANKEES

Radio Announcers: John Sterling, Suzyn Waldman.

Flagship Station: WCBS 880-AM.

TV Announcers: John Flaherty, Joe Girardi, Kim Jones, Michael Kay, Al Leiter, Bobby Murcer, Paul O'Neill, Ken Singleton.

Flagship Stations: YES Network (Yankees Entertainment & Sports).

Newspapers, Daily Coverage (beat writers): New York Daily News (Mark Feinsand), New York Post (George King), New York Times (Tyler Kepner), Newark Star-Ledger (Ed Price), The Bergen Record (Pete Caldera), Newsday (Jim Baumbach), Hartford Courant (Dom Amore), The Journal News (Pete Abraham). **MLB.com:** Brian Hoch.

OAKLAND ATHLETICS

Radio Announcers: Vince Cotroneo, Ray Fosse, Ken Korach. **Flagship Station:** FREE FM 106.9, KYCY AM 1550

TV Announcers: Ray Fosse, Tim Roye, Glen Kuiper. **Flagship Stations:** KICU, FOX Sports Net Bay Area (regional cable).

Newspapers, Daily Coverage (*national/beat writers): San Francisco Chronicle (*John Shea, Susan Slusser), Oakland Tribune (Josh Suchon), Contra Costa Times (*Rick Hurd), San Jose Mercury News (*Dan Brown), Sacramento Bee (Paul Gutierrez), Santa Rosa Press Democrat (Jeff Fletcher). **MLB.com:** Mychael Urban.

SEATTLE MARINERS

TV/Radio Announcers: Mike Blowers, Dave Niehaus, Rick Rizzs, Dave Simms

Flagship Stations: KOMO 1000-AM (radio), FOX Sports Net Northwest (TV).

Newspapers, Daily Coverage (*national/beat writers): Seattle Times (Geoff Baker, *Larry Stone), Seattle Post-Intelligencer (John Hickey), Tacoma News Tribune (Larry LaRue), The Everett Herald (Kirby Arnold), Kyodo News (Keizo Konishi), Daily Sports (Nobuyuki Kobayashi), Nikkan Sports (Mamoru Shikama). **MLB.com:** Corey Brock.

TAMPA BAY RAYS

Radio Announcers: Andy Freed, Dave Wills. **Flagship Station:** WHNZ 1250 AM.

TV Announcers: Dewayne Staats, Joe Magrane. **Flagship Stations:** FSN FLORIDA (regional cable), PAX-TV.

Newspapers, Daily Coverage (beat writers): St. Petersburg Times (Marc Topkin), Tampa Tribune (Marc Lancaster), Bradenton Herald (Roger Mooney), Port Charlotte Sun-Herald (John Fineran), Lakeland Ledger (Dick Scanlon), Sarasota Herald-Tribune (Dennis Maffezoli). **MLB.com:** Bill Chastain.

TEXAS RANGERS

Radio Announcers: Eric Nadel, Victor Rojas; Spanish—Eleno Ornelas, Jose Guzman. **Flagship Station:** KRLD 1080-AM, KESS 1270-AM (Spanish).

TV Announcers: Josh Lewin, Tom Grieve. **Flagship Stations:** KDFI, KDFW, Fox Sports Southwest (regional cable).

Newspapers, Daily Coverage (beat writers): Dallas Morning News (Evan Grant, Richard Durrett), Fort Worth Star-Telegram (Kathleen O'Brien, Jan Hubbard). **MLB.com:** T.R. Sullivan.

TORONTO BLUE JAYS

Radio Announcers: Jerry Howarth, Warren Sawkiw, Mike Wilner. **Flagship Station:** THE FAN 590-AM.

TV Announcers: Rogers SportsNet—Jamie Campbell, Pat Tabler, Rance Mulliniks, Darrin Fletcher. TSN—Rod Black, Pat Tabler. **Flagship Stations:** Rogers SportsNet, The Sports Network.

Newspapers, Daily Coverage (*national/beat writers): Toronto Sun (Mike Rutsey, *Bob Elliott, Mike Ganter), Toronto Star (Geoff Baker, *Richard Griffin, Alan Ryan, Mark Zwolinski), Globe and Mail (Larry Millson, *Jeff Blair), National Post (John Lott). **MLB.com:** Jordan Bastian.

NATIONAL LEAGUE

ARIZONA DIAMONDBACKS

Radio Announcers: Greg Schulte, Tom Candiotti, Jeff Munn, Spanish—Miguel Quintana, Oscar Soria, Richard Saenz. **Flagship Stations:** KTAR 620-AM, KSUN 1400-AM (Spanish).

TV Announcers: Daron Sutton, Mark Grace, Greg Schulte, Joe Garagiola, Matt Williams. **Flagship Stations:** KTVK-TV 3, FSN Arizona (regional cable).

Newspapers, Daily Coverage (beat writers): Arizona Republic (Bob McManaman), East Valley Tribune (Jack Magruder), Arizona Daily Star, Tucson Citizen (Ken Brazzle). **MLB.com:** Steve Gilbert.

ATLANTA BRAVES

Radio Announcers: Skip Caray (approx. **110 games), Pete Van Wieren (162 games).**

Flagship Station: WGST 640-AM & 94.9 FM The Bull

TV Announcers: TBS—Chip Caray & TBD

Fox Sports Net South and SportSouth -Joe Simpson and Jon Sciambi.

Flagship Stations: TBS (national cable); Fox Sports Net South, SportSouth (regional cable).

Newspapers, Daily Coverage (*national/beat writers): Atlanta Journal-Constitution (*Carroll Rogers, Dave O'Brien), Morris News Service (*Travis Haney). **MLB.com:** Mark Bowman.

CHICAGO CUBS

Radio Announcers: Pat Hughes, Ron Santo. **Flagship Station:** WGN 720-AM.

TV Announcers: Len Kasper, Bob Brenly. **Flagship Stations:** WGN Channel 9 (national cable), Comcast Sports Net Chicago (regional cable), WCIU-TV Channel 26.

Newspapers, Daily Coverage (*national/beat writers): Chicago Tribune (*Phil Rogers, Paul Sullivan), Chicago Sun-Times (Unavailable), Arlington Heights Daily Herald (Bruce Miles), Daily Southtown (Jeff Vorva). **MLB.com:** Carrie Muskat.

CINCINNATI REDS

Radio Announcers: Marty Brennaman, Thom Brennaman, Jeff Brantley, Joe Nuxhall. **Flagship Station:** WLW 700-AM.

TV Announcers: George Grande, Chris Welsh, Thom Brennaman, Jeff Brantley. **Flagship Station:** FSN Ohio (regional cable).

Newspapers, Daily Coverage (beat writers): Cincinnati Enquirer (John Fay), Cincinnati Post (C. Trent Rosecrans), Dayton Daily News (Hal McCoy), Columbus Dispatch (Jim Massie). **MLB.com:** Mark Sheldon.

COLORADO ROCKIES

Radio Announcers: Jack Corrigan, Jeff Kingery. **Flagship Station:** KOA 850-AM.

TV Announcers: Drew Goodman, George Frazier, Jeff Huson. **Flagship Stations:** KWGN, 2, WB, FSN Rocky Mountain (regional cable).

Newspapers, Daily Coverage (beat writers): Rocky Mountain News (*Tracy Ringolsby, Jack Etkin), Denver Post (Troy Renck, Patrick Saunders). **MLB.com:** Thomas Harding.

FLORIDA MARLINS

Radio Announcers: Dave Van Horne, Roxy Bernstein.

Spanish: Felo Ramirez, Yiky Quintana.

Flagship Stations: WQAM 560-AM, WQBA 1140-AM (Spanish).

TV Announcers: Tommy Hutton, Rich Waltz.

Flagship Stations: FSN Florida, Sun Sports (regional cable).

Newspapers, Daily Coverage (*national/beat writers): Miami Herald (Clark Spencer), Fort Lauderdale Sun-Sentinel (*Mike Berardino, Juan Rodriguez), Palm Beach Post (Joe Capozzi). Spanish—El Nuevo Herald (Jorge Ebro). **MLB.com:** Joe Frisaro

HOUSTON ASTROS

Radio Announcers: Brett Dolan, Milo Hamilton, Dave Raymond; Spanish—Francisco Ernesto Ruiz, Alex Trevino. **Flagship Stations:** KTRH 740-AM, KLAT 1010-AM (Spanish).

TV Announcers: Bill Brown, Jim Deshaies. **Flagship Station:** Fox Sports Net (regional cable).

Newspapers, Daily Coverage (beat writers): Houston Chronicle (Jesus Ortiz, Brian McTaggart), The Herald Coaster (Bill Hartman). **MLB.com:** Alyson Footer, Jim Molony.

LOS ANGELES DODGERS

Radio Announcers: Vin Scully, Rick Monday, Charley Steiner, Jerry Reuss; Spanish—Jaime Jarrin, Fernando Valenzuela, Pepe Yniguez. **Flagship Stations:** KFWB 980-AM, KWKW 1330-AM (Spanish).

TV Announcers: Vin Scully, Steve Lyons, Charley Steiner. **Flagship Stations:** KCAL 9, Fox Sports Net Prime Ticket (regional cable).

Newspapers, Daily Coverage (*national/beat writers): Los Angeles Times (Steve Henson), South Bay Daily Breeze (Bill Cizek), Los Angeles Daily News (Tony Jackson), Orange County Register (Al Balderas), Riverside Press-Enterprise (Diamond Leung). Spanish—La Opinion (Carlos Alvarado). **MLB.com:** Ken Gurnick.

MILWAUKEE BREWERS

Radio Announcers: Bob Uecker, Jim Powell. **Flagship Station:** WTMJ 620-AM.

TV Announcers: Bill Schroeder, Brian Anderson. **Flagship Station:** Fox Sports Net North.

Newspapers, Daily Coverage (beat writers): Milwaukee Journal Sentinel (Tom Haudricourt, Rick Braun), Wisconsin State Journal (Vic Feuerherd), Capital Times (Dennis Semrau). **MLB.com:** Adam McCalvy.

NEW YORK METS

Radio Announcers: Howie Rose, Tom McCarthy, Ed Coleman. **Flagship Station:** WFAN 660-AM.

TV Announcers: Gary Cohen, Keith Hernandez, Ron Darling, Ralph Kiner, Kevin Burkhardt. **Flagship Stations:** CW11-TV, Sports Net New York (regional cable).

Newspapers, Daily Coverage (*national/beat writers): New York Times (*Murray Chass, *Jack Curry, Ben Shpigel), New York Daily News (*Bill Madden, *John Harper, Adam Rubin), New York Post (*Joel Sherman, *Jay Greenberg, Mark Hale), Newsday (*Johnette Howard, *Ken Davidoff, Dave Lennon), Newark Star-Ledger (*Dan Graziano, Don Burke), The Bergen Record (*Bob Klapisch, *Adrian Wojnarowski, Steve Popper), The Journal News (John Delcos). **MLB.com:** Marty Noble.

PHILADELPHIA PHILLIES

Radio Announcers: Larry Andersen, Scott Franzke, Harry Kalas, Gary Matthews. **Flagship Stations:** WPHT 1210-AM.

TV Announcers: Larry Andersen, Harry Kalas, Gary Matthews, Chris Wheeler. **Flagship Stations:** WPSG CW 57, Comcast SportsNet (regional cable).

Newspapers, Daily Coverage (*national/beat writers): Philadelphia Inquirer (Todd Zolecki, *Jim Salisbury), Philadelphia Daily News (*Paul Hagen, Marcus Hayes), Bucks County Courier Times (Randy Miller), Delaware County Times (Dennis Deitch), Wilmington News-Journal (Scott Lauber). **MLB.com:** Ken Mandel.

PITTSBURGH PIRATES

Radio Announcers: Steve Blass, Greg Brown, Lanny Frattare, Bob Walk, John Wehner. **Flagship Station:** WPGB 104.7 FM.

TV Announcers: Steve Blass, Greg Brown, Lanny Frattare, Bob Walk, John Wehner. **Flagship Station:** Fox Sports Net Pittsburgh (regional cable).

Newspapers, Daily Coverage (beat writers): Pittsburgh Post-Gazette (Dejan Kovacevic), Pittsburgh Tribune-Review (Rob Biertempfel), Beaver County Times (John Perrotto). **MLB.com:** Jenifer Langosch.

ST. LOUIS CARDINALS

Radio Announcers: Mike Shannon, John Rooney. **Flagship Station:** KTRS 550-AM.

TV Announcers: Joe Buck , Al Hrabosky, Dan McLaughlin, Rick Horton, Jay Randolph. **Flagship Stations:** KSDK Channel 5, Fox Sports Midwest (regional cable).

Newspapers, Daily Coverage (beat writers): St. Louis Post-Dispatch (Joe Strauss, Rick Hummel, Derrick Goold), Belleville, Ill., News-Democrat (Joe Ostermeier, David Wilhelm). **MLB.com:** Matthew Leach.

SAN DIEGO PADRES

Radio Announcers: Ted Leitner, Jerry Coleman Flagship Station: XX Sports Radio 105.7 FM /1090-AM.

TV Announcers: Matt Vasgersian, Mark Grant, Tony Gwynn. **Flagship Station:** Channel 4 San Diego (cable).

Newspapers, Daily Coverage (beat writers): San Diego Union-Tribune (Tom Krasovic, Bill Center), North County Times (Shaun O'Neill, John Maffei). **MLB.com:** Lyle Spencer.

SAN FRANCISCO GIANTS

Radio Announcers: Mike Krukow, Duane Kuiper, Jon Miller, Greg Papa, Dave Flemming. **Flagship Station:** KNBR 680-AM (English); KLOK-1170 AM (Spanish).

TV Announcers: FSN Bay Area—Mike Krukow, Duane Kuiper; KTVU-FOX 2—Jon Miller, Mike Krukow, Duane Kuiper, Greg Papa. **Flagship Stations:** KTVU-FOX 2, FSN Bay Area (regional cable).

Newspapers, Daily Coverage (*national/beat writers): San Francisco Chronicle (Henry Schulman, *John Shea), Media News Group (Andrew Baggarly), Santa Rosa Press Democrat (Jeff Fletcher). **MLB.com:** Unavailable.

WASHINGTON NATIONALS

Radio Announcers: Charlie Slowes, Dave Jageler. **Flagship Station:** Washington Post Radio (WTOP 1500-AM, 107.7 FM).

TV Announcers: Bob Carpenter, Don Sutton. **Flagship Station:** Mid-Atlantic Sports Network (MASN).

Newspapers, Daily Coverage (beat writers): Baltimore Sun (Jeff Barker, Dan Connolly), The Free-Lance Star (Todd Jacobson), Washington Post (Barry Svrluga, Dave Sheinin), Washington Times (Mark Zuckerman, Ken Wright). Washington Examiner (John Keim, Rick Snider). **MLB.com:** Bill Ladson.

NATIONAL MEDIA INFORMATION

BASEBALL STATISTICS

ELIAS SPORTS BUREAU INC.

Official Major League Statistician

Mailing Address: 500 Fifth Ave., Suite 2140, New York, NY 10110. **Telephone:** (212) 869-1530. **Fax:** (212) 354-0980. **Website:** www.esb.com.

President: Seymour Siwoff.

Executive Vice President: Steve Hirdt. **Vice President:** Peter Hirdt. **Data Processing Manager:** Chris Thorn.

MAJOR LEAGUE BASEBALL ADVANCED MEDIA

Official Minor League Statistician

Mailing Address: 75 Ninth Ave., New York, NY 10011. **Telephone:** (212) 485-3444. **Fax:** (212) 485-3456.

Director, Minor League Baseball Advanced Media: Misann Ellmaker. **Deputy Project Manager, Minor League Baseball Advanced Media:** Nathan Blackmon. **Senior Project Manager, Minor League Baseball Advanced Media:** Sammy Arena. **Senior Editorial Producer:** Jason Ratliff. **Senior Manager, Statistics Operations:** Chris Lentine. **Senior Reporter:** Jonathan Mayo. **Reporters:** Kevin Czerwinski, Lisa Winston.

STATS Inc.

Mailing Address: 8130 Lehigh Ave., Morton Grove, IL 60053**. Telephone:** (847) 583-2100. **Fax:** (847) 470-9140. **Website:** biz.stats.com.

Chief Executive Officer: Gary Walrath. **Executive Vice Presidents:** Steve Byrd, Robert Schur. **Director, Sales:** Jim Capuano, Greg Kirkorsky. **Director, Marketing:** Walter Lis. **Director, Sports Operations:** Allan Spear. **Manager, Baseball Operations:** Jeff Chernow.

TELEVISION NETWORKS

ESPN/ESPN2

- Sunday Night Baseball
- Monday Night Baseball
- Wednesday Night Baseball
- Opening Day, Holiday Games
- Spring Training Games
- Baseball Tonight
- Home Run Derby, All-Star Game Programming

Mailing Address, ESPN Connecticut: ESPN Plaza, Bristol, CT 06010. **Telephone:** (860) 766-2000. **Fax:** (860) 766-2213.

Mailing Address, ESPN New York Executive Offices: 77 W. 66th St., New York, NY, 10023. **Telephone:** (212) 456-7777. **Fax:** (212) 456-2930.

President, ESPN/ABC Sports: George Bodenheimer.

Executive Vice President, Administration: Ed Durso.

Executive VP, Content: John Skipper. **Executive VP, Studio/Remote Production:** Norby Williamson.

Senior VP, Programming/Acquisitions: Len DeLuca. **VP, Programming:** Mike Ryan.

Senior VP/Executive Producer, Remote Production: Jed Drake. **Senior Coordinating Producer, Remote Production:** Tim Scanlan. **Coordinating Producer, Remote Production:** Matt Sandulli.

Senior VP/Managing Editor, Studio Production: Mark Gross. **Senior Coordinating Producer, Baseball Tonight:** Jay Levy.

Senior VP, Communications: Chris LaPlaca. **VP, Communications:** Mike Soltys. **VP, Communications:** Diane Lamb. **Associate Manager:** Nate Smeltz.

ESPN CLASSIC, ESPNEWS

Vice President, Programming/Acquisitions: John Papa.

ESPN INTERNATIONAL, ESPN DEPORTES

Executive Vice President/Managing Director, ESPN International: Russell Wolff.

Senior VP, ESPN Radio and ESPN Deportes: Traug Keller.

General Manager, ESPN Deportes: Lino Garcia.

Senior VP, International Production, ESPN Classic/ESPNEWS: Jodi Markley. **Vice President, International Production/Operations:** Chris Calcinari.

MAJOR LEAGUES

FOX SPORTS

- Saturday Game of the Week
- All-Star Game
- National League Championship Series
- World Series

Mailing Address, Los Angeles: Fox Network Center, Building 101, Fifth floor, 10201 West Pico Blvd., Los Angeles, CA 90035. **Telephone:** (310) 369-6000. **Fax:** (310) 969-6700.

Mailing Address, New York: 1211 Avenue of the Americas, 20th Floor, New York, NY 10036. **Telephone:** (212) 556-2500. **Fax:** (212) 354-6902. **Website:** www.foxsports.com.

Chairman, Chief Executive Officer, Fox Sports Television Group: David Hill. **President/Executive Producer:** Ed Goren. **Executive Vice President, Production/Coordinating Studio Producer:** Scott Ackerson. **Executive VP, Production and Field Operations/Senior Producer:** Bill Brown. **Executive VP, Programming/Production:** George Greenberg. **Senior VP, Research/Programming:** Bill Wanger. **Coordinating Producer, MLB on Fox:** Pete Macheska. **Lead Game Director:** Bill Webb. **Studio Producer, MLB on Fox:** Gary Lang. **Studio Director, MLB on Fox:** Bob Levy.

Senior VP, Communcations: Lou D'Ermilio. **VP, Communications:** Dan Bell. **Director, Communications:** Tim Buckman. **Communications Manager:** Ileana Pena.

Broadcasters: Kenny Albert, Thom Brennaman, Joe Buck, Mark Grace, Joe Girardi, Eric Karros, Kevin Kennedy, Josh Lewin, Tim McCarver, Matt Vasgersian, Jeanne Zelasko.

TURNER SPORTS

- American League/National League Division Series
- American League Championship Series
- Sunday Game of the Week

Mailing Address: 1015 Techwood Drive, Atlanta, GA 30318. **Telephone:** (404) 827-1700. **Fax:** (404) 827-1339. **Website:** www.tbs.com.

Coordinating Producer: Glenn Diamond. **Directors:** Lonnie Dale, Renardo Lowe. **Executive Producer:** Jeff Behnke. **Senior Producer:** Howard Zalkowitz.

FOX SPORTS NET

- Regional Coverage

Mailing Address: 10201 W. Pico Blvd., Building 103, Los Angeles, CA 90035. **Telephone:** (310) 369-1000. **Fax:** (310) 969-6049.

President, Chief Executive Officer/Fox Sports Television Group: David Hill. **President, Fox National Cable Networks:** Bob Thompson. **President, Fox Regional Cable Sports Networks:** Randy Freer. **President, Advertising Sales, Fox Cable Networks:** Lou LaTorre. **Executive VP, Programming/Production:** George Greenberg. **Senior VP, Production/Executive Producer, Event Coverage:** -Doug Sellers. **Director, Communications:** Justin Simon. **Senior Publicist:** Emily Corliss.

OTHER TELEVISION NETWORKS

ABC SPORTS

Mailing Address: 47 W. 66th St., New York, NY 10023. **Telephone:** (212) 456-7777. **Fax:** (212) 456-4317.

President, ABC Sports: George Bodenheimer. **President:** George Bodenheimer. **Senior Vice President, Programming:** Loren Matthews.

CBS SPORTS

Mailing Address: 51 W. 52nd St., New York, NY 10019. **Telephone:** (212) 975-5230. **Fax:** (212) 975-4063.

President, CBS Sports: Sean McManus. **Executive VP/Executive Producer:** Tony Petitti. **Senior Vice Presidents, Programming:** Mike Aresco, Rob Correa. **Vice President, Communications:** Leslie Anne Wade.

CNN SPORTS

Mailing Address: One CNN Center, Atlanta, GA 30303. **Telephone:** (404) 878-1600. **Fax:** (404) 878-0011.

Vice President, Production: Jeffrey Green.

HBO SPORTS

Mailing Address: 1100 Avenue of the Americas, New York, NY 10036. **Telephone:** (212) 512-1000. **Fax:** (212) 512-1751.

President, HBO Sports: Ross Greenburg.

NBC SPORTS

Mailing Address: 30 Rockefeller Plaza, Suite 1558, New York, NY 10112. **Telephone:** (212) 664-2014. **Fax:** (212) 664-6365.

Chairman, NBC Sports: Dick Ebersol. **President, NBC Sports:** Ken Schanzer.

Vice President, Sports Communications: Mike McCarley.

ROGERS SPORTSNET (Canada)

Mailing Address: 333 Bloor St. East, Toronto Ontario M4W 1G9. **Telephone:** (416) 332-5600. **Fax:** (416) 332-5629. **Website:** www.sportsnet.ca.

President, Rogers Media: Tony Viner. **President, Rogers Sportsnet:** Doug Beeforth. **Vice President, Communications:** Jan Innes. **Director, Communications/Promotions:** Dave Rashford.

THE SPORTS NETWORK (Canada)

Mailing Address: Bell Globemedia Inc., 9 Channel Nine Court, Scarborough, Ontario M1S 4B5. **Telephone:** (416) 332-5000. **Fax:** (416) 332-4337. **Website:** www.tsn.ca

Executive Producer, News: Marc Milliere. **President, TSN:** Phil King. **Executive Producer:** Jim Marshall. **VP, Programming and Production:** Rick Chisholm, VP, Marketing: Adam Ashton. **Communications Director:** Andrea Goldstein. **Executive Producer, tsn.ca:** Mike Day.

RADIO NETWORKS

ESPN RADIO

- Game of the Week
- Sunday Night Baseball
- All-Star Game
- Division Series
- League Championship Series
- World Series

Address: ESPN Plaza, 935 Middle St., Bristol, CT 06010. **Telephone:** (860) 766-2000, (800) 999-9985. **Fax:** (860) 589-5523. **Website:** espnradio.espn.go.com/espnradio/index.

General Manager, ESPN Radio Network: Bruce Gilbert. **Senior Director, Operations:** Keith Goralski. **Senior Director, Programming:** Peter Gianesini. **Senior Director, Marketing/Integration:** Freddy Rolon. **Executive Producer, Remote Broadcasts:** John Martin. **News Editor:** Peter Ciccone. **Program Directors:** Justin Craig, Louise Cornetta, Larry Gifford, David Zaslowsky. **Chief Engineer:** Tom Evans. **Administrative Coordinator:** Janet Alden. **VP, Sports, ABC Radio Network and VP/Affiliate Relations:** T.J. Lambert.

Executive Producer, Major League Baseball on ESPN Radio: John Martin.

Commentators: Dan Shulman, Dave Campbell, Jim Durham, Dave Barnett, Harold Reynolds, Jon Miller, Joe Morgan, Joe D'Ambrosio.

MLB ADVANCED MEDIA MULTIMEDIA

Mailing Address: 75 Ninth Ave., New York, NY 10011. **Telephone:** (212) 485-3444. **Fax:** (212) 485-3456. **E-Mail Address:** radio@mlb.com. **Website:** www.mlb.com.

Senior Vice President, Multimedia/Distribution: Joe Inzerillo. **VP/Executive Producer, Content:** Jim Jenks. **Senior Director, Production:** Daria Debuono. **Director, Remote Programming:** Mike Siano. **Director, Studio Programming:** Richard Bush. **Video Acquisition:** Stephanie Gentile. **Audio Acquisition:** Scott Majeska.

Talent: Harold Reynolds, John Marzano, Billy Sample, Hal Bodley, Seth Everett, Vinny Micucci, Casey Stern, Ed Randall, Jim Salisbury, Peter McCarthy, Noah Coslov.

XM SATELLITE RADIO

- 24-hour MLB Home Plate channel (baseball talk)
- MLB live play-by-play for spring training, regular season, playoffs, World Series
- MLB En Espanol channel (Spanish language play-by-play and baseball talk)

Mailing Address: 1500 Eckington Place NE, Washington, DC 20002. **Telephone:** (202) 380-4000. **Fax:** 202-380-4500. **E-Mail Address:** mlb@xmradio.com. **Website:** www.xmradio.com.

Executive Vice President, Programming: Eric Logan. **Vice President, Talk Programming:** Kevin Straley. **Senior VP, Corporate Communications:** Nathaniel Brown. **VP, Corporate Affairs:** Chance Patterson. **Director, MLB Programming:** Chuck Dickemann. **Executive Producer, MLB Home Plate Channel:** Matt Fishman. **Commentators:** Joe Castellano, Rob Dibble, Kevin Kennedy, Ronnie Lane, Buck Martinez, Mark Patrick, Billy Ripken, Cal Ripken Jr., **Charley Steiner, Chuck Wilson.**

SPORTING NEWS RADIO NETWORK

Mailing Address: 1935 Techny St., Suite 18, Northbrook IL 60062. **Telephone:** (847) 509-1661. **Producers Line:** (800) 224-2004. **Fax:** (847) 509-1677. **Website:** www.sportingnewsradio.com.

President: Clancy Woods. **Executive Vice President, Sales:** John Coulter. **Acting Director, Affiliate Relations:** Ryan Williams. **Program Director:** Matt Nahigian. **Sports Director:** Randy Merkin. **Executive Producer:** Jen Williams.

SPORTS BYLINE USA

Mailing Address: 300 Broadway, Suite 8, San Francisco, CA 94133. **Telephone:** (415) 434-8300. **Guest Line:** (800) 358-4457. **Studio Line:** (800) 878-7529. **Fax:** (415) 391-2569. **E-Mail Address:** alex@sportsbyline.com. **Website:** www.sportsbyline.com.

President: Darren Peck. **Executive Producer:** Alex Murillo.

NEWS ORGANIZATIONS

ASSOCIATED PRESS

Mailing Address: 450 W. **33rd St., New York, NY 10010. Telephone:** (212) 621-1630. **Fax:** (212) 621-1639. **Website:** www.ap.org.

Sports Editor: Terry Taylor. **Deputy Sports Editor:** Ben Walker. **Sports Photo Editor:** Mike Feldman. **Baseball Writers:** Ron Blum, Mike Fitzpatrick.

BLOOMBERG SPORTS

Address: 731 Lexington Ave., New York, NY 10022. **Telephone:** (212) 617-2301. **Fax:** (917) 369-5633.

Sports Editor: Jay Beberman. **Deputy Sports Editor:** Mike Sillup. **Baseball Writer:** Danielle Sessa.

CANADIAN PRESS

Mailing Address, Toronto: 36 King St. **Mailing Address, Montreal:** 215 Saint-Jacques St., **Suite 100, Montreal,** Quebec H2Y 1M6. **Telephone:** (416) 507-2154 (Toronto), (514) 985-7240 (Montreal). **Fax:** (416) 507-2074 (Toronto), (514) 282-6915 (Montreal). **E-Mail Address:** sports@cp.org.

Sports Editor: Neil Davidson. **Baseball Writer, Toronto:** Shi Davidi. **Baseball Writer, Montreal:** Bill Beacon.

CBS SPORTSLINE.com

Mailing Address: 2200 W. **Cypress Creek, Fort Lauderdale, FL 33309. Website:** cbs.sportsline.com.

Senior Writer: Scott Miller.

ESPN.com

Mailing Address: ESPN Plaza, Bristol, CT 06010. **Telephone:** (860) 766-2000.

Editor-In-Chief: Neal Scarborough. **Executive Editor:** Len Lampugnale. **Deputy Editor:** David Kull.

ESPN/SPORTSTICKER

Mailing Address: ESPN Plaza, Building B, Fourth Floor, Bristol, CT 06010. **Telephone:** (860) 766-1899. **Fax:** (800) 336-0383. **E-Mail Address:** newsroom@sportsticker.com.

General Manager: Jim Morganthaler. **News Director:** Chris Bernucca. **Baseball Editor:** Jim Keller. **Manager, Customer Marketing/Communications:** Lou Monaco.

Senior Bureau Manager: Michael Walczak. **Bureau Managers:** Tom Diorio. **Associate Bureau Manager:** Ian Anderson. **Programmer Analysts:** John Foley, Walter Kent. **Historical Consultant:** Bill Weiss.

FOX SPORTS.com

Mailing Address: 1440 Sepulveda Blvd., Los Angeles, CA. **Telephone:** (310) 444-8000. **Fax:** (310) 444-8180. **Website:** www.msn.foxsports.com.

Senior Vice President/General Manager: Ross Levinsohn.

MLB ADVANCED MEDIA (MLB.COM)

Office Address: 75 Ninth Ave., 5th Floor, New York, NY 10011**. Telephone:** (212) 485-3444. **Fax:** (212) 485-3456.

Chief Executive Officer: Bob Bowman.

Vice President, Marketing: Kristen Fergason. **VP, Ticketing:** Heather Benz. **VP, Human Resources:** Leslie Knickerbocker. **Senior VP/Chief Technical Officer:** Joe Choti. **Senior VP, Corporate Communications:** Jim Gallagher. **Executive VP, E-Commerce and Sponsorships:** Noah Garden. **Executive VP/Editor-In-Chief, mlb.com:** Dinn Mann. **VP, Design:** Deck Rees.

Senior VP/General Counsel: Michael Mellis, Executive VP, Business: George Kliavkoff.

SI.com

Mailing Address: 1271 Avenue of the Americas, 32nd Floor, New York, NY 10020. **Telephone:** (212) 522-1212. **Fax:** (212) 467-0339.

Managing Editor: Paul Fichtenbaum.

PRESS ASSOCIATIONS

BASEBALL WRITERS' ASSOCIATION OF AMERICA

Mailing Address: P.O. Box 610611, Bayside, NY 11361. **Telephone:** (718) 767-2582. **Fax:** (718) 767-2583. **E-Mail Address:** bbwaa@aol.com.

President: Bob Dutton (Kansas City Star). **Vice President:** David O'Brien (Atlanta Journal-Constitution). **Secretary/Treasurer:** Jack O'Connell (BBWAA). **Board of Directors:** Bob Elliott (Toronto Sun), Paul Hoynes (Cleveland Plain Dealer), Tracy Ringolsby (Rocky Mountain News), Phil Rogers (Chicago Tribune).

NATIONAL COLLEGIATE BASEBALL WRITERS ASSOCIATION

Mailing Address: 2201 Stemmons Fwy., 28th Floor, Dallas, TX 75207. **Telephone:** (214) 753-0102. **Fax:** (214) 753-0145. **E-Mail Address:** bo@big12sports.com.

Executive Director, Newsletter Editor: Bo Carter (Big 12 Conference).

NEWSPAPERS/PERIODICALS

USA TODAY

Mailing Address: 7950 Jones Branch Dr., McLean, VA 22108. **Telephones/Baseball Desk:** (703) 854-5286, 854-5954, 854-3706, 854-3744, 854-3746. **Fax:** (703) 854-2072. **Website:** www.usatoday.com.

Publishing Frequency: Daily (Monday-Friday).

Baseball Editors: Peter Barzilai, Gabe Lacques, Matt Cimento, John Tkach. **Baseball Columnist:** Hal Bodley. **Baseball Writers:** Mel Antonen, Rod Beaton, Mike Dodd, Gary Graves, Jorge Ortiz.

THE SPORTING NEWS

Mailing Address: 10176 Corporate Square Dr., Suite 200, St. Louis, MO 63132. **Telephone:** (314) 997-7111. **Fax:** (314) 993-7726. **Website:** www.sportingnews.com.

Publishing Frequency: Weekly.

Senior Vice President/Editorial Director: John Rawlings. **Executive Editor:** Bob Hille. **Managing Editor:** Stan McNeal. **Senior Writer:** Ken Rosenthal. **Senior Editor:** Tom Gatto. **Senior Photo Editor:** Paul Nisely.

SPORTS ILLUSTRATED

Mailing Address: 1271 Avenue of the Americas, New York, NY 10020. **Telephone:** (212) 522-1212. **Fax, Editorial:** (212) 522-4543. **Fax, Public Relations:** (212) 522-0747. **Website:** www.si.com.

Publishing Frequency: Weekly.

Managing Editor: Terry McDonnell. **Senior Editor:** Larry Burke. **Associate Editor:** B.J. **Schecter. Senior Writer:** Tom Verducci. **Staff Writer:** Danny Habib. **Writers/Reporters:** Albert Chen, Melissa Segura

Vice President, Communications: Art Berke.

USA TODAY SPORTS WEEKLY

Mailing Address: 7950 Jones Branch Dr., McLean, VA 22108. **Telephone:** (800) 872-1415, (703) 854-6319. **Fax:** (703) 854-2034. **Website:** www.usatoday.com.

Publishing Frequency: Weekly.

Managing Editor: Monte Lorell. **Senior Editor:** Lee Ivory. **Senior Assignment Editor:** Tim McQuay. **Baseball Editors:** Peter Barzilai, Steve Borelli, Gabe Laques. **Baseball Writers:** Steve DiMeglio, Bob Nightengale, Paul White.

STREET AND SMITH'S SPORTS BUSINESS JOURNAL

Mailing Address: 120 W. Morehead St., Suite 310, Charlotte, NC 28202. **Telephone:** (704) 973-1400. **Fax:** (704) 973-1401. **Website:** www.sportsbusinessjournal.com.

Publishing Frequency: Weekly.

Publisher: Richard Weiss. **Editor-in-chief:** Abraham Madkour. **Managing Editor:** Ross Nethery.

ESPN THE MAGAZINE

Mailing Address: 19 E. 34th St., Seventh Floor, New York, NY 10016. **Telephone:** (212) 515-1000. **Fax:** (212) 515-1290. **Website:** www.espn.com.

Publishing Frequency: Bi-weekly.

Executive Editor: Sue Hovey. **Senior Editors:** Jon Scher, Ed McGregor. **Senior Writers:** Jorge Arangure Jr., Jeff Bradley, Tim Keown, Tim Kurkjian, Buster Olney. **Associate Editors:** Ian Gordon, Matt Meyers. **Writer/Reporter:** Amy Nelson. **Photo Editor:** Catriona Ni Aolain. **Photo Operations Coordinator:** Tricia Reed. **Manager, Communications:** Ellie Seifert.

BASEBALL AMERICA

Address: 201 West Main St., Suite 201, Durham, NC 27702. **Mailing Address:** P.O. Box 2089, Durham, NC 27702. **Telephone:** (919) 682-9635. **Fax:** (919) 682-2880.

Publishing Frequency: Bi-weekly.

President/Publisher: Lee Folger. **Editors In Chief:** Will Lingo, John Manuel. **Managing Editor:** J.J. Cooper. **Executive Editor:** Jim Callis.

BASEBALL DIGEST

Mailing Address: 990 Grove St., Evanston, IL 60201. **Telephone:** (847) 491-6440. **Fax:** (847) 491-6203. **E-Mail Address:** bkuenster@centurysports.net. **Website:** www.centurysports.net/baseball.

Publishing Frequency: Monthly, April through January.

Publisher: Norman Jacobs. **Editor:** John Kuenster. **Managing Editor:** Bob Kuenster.

COLLEGIATE BASEBALL

Mailing Address: P.O. Box 50566, Tucson, AZ 85703. **Telephone:** (520) 623-4530. **Fax:** (520) 624-5501. **E-Mail Address:** editor@baseballnews.com. **Website:** www.baseballnews.com.

Publishing Frequency: Bi-weekly, January-June; September, October.

Publisher: Lou Pavlovich. **Editor:** Lou Pavlovich Jr.

JUNIOR BASEBALL MAGAZINE

Mailing Address: P.O. Box 9099, Canoga Park, CA 91309. **Telephone:** (818) 710-1234. **Customer Service:** (888) 487-2448. **Fax:** (818) 710-1877. **E-Mail Address:** editor@juniorbaseball.com. **Website:** www.juniorbaseball.com.

Publishing Frequency: Bi-monthly.

Publisher/Editor: Dave Destler. **Publishing Director:** Dayna Destler.

SPORTS ILLUSTRATED FOR KIDS

Mailing Address: 1271 Avenue of the Americas, Third Floor, New York, NY 10020. **Telephone:** (212) 522-1212. **Fax:** (212) 522-0120. **Website:** www.sikids.com.

Publishing Frequency: Monthly.

Publisher: Dave Watt. **Managing Editor:** Neil Cohen. **Deputy Managing Editor:** Bob Der. **Senior Editors:** Michael Northrop, Justin Tejada.

BASEBALL ANNUALS

ATHLON SPORTS BASEBALL

Mailing Address: 220 25th Ave. N., Suite 200, Nashville, TN 37203. **Telephone:** (615) 327-0747. **Fax:** (615) 327-1149. **E-Mail Address:** editor@athlonsports.com. **Website:** www.athlonsports.com.

President/CEO: Chuck Allen. **Managing Editor:** Charlie Miller. **Senior Editor:** Rob Doster. **Editor:** Mitch Light. **Website Editor:** Bill Trocchi.

LINDY'S BASEBALL/LINDY'S FANTASY BASEBALL

Mailing Address: DMD Publications, 2100 Centennial Drive, Suite 100, Birmingham, AL 35216. **Telephone:** (205) 871-1182. **Fax:** (205) 871-1184. **E-Mail Address:** lindy@lindyssports.com. **Website:** www.lindyssports.com.

Publisher: Lindy Davis Jr. **Senior Editor:** Shane O'Neill. **Art Director:** Ginny O'Neill.

SPORTING NEWS BASEBALL YEARBOOK/SPORTING NEWS FANTASY BASEBALL

Mailing Address: 120 West Morehead St., Suite 230, Charlotte, NC 28202. **Telephone:** (704) 973-1575. **Fax:** (704) 973-1576. **E-Mail Address:** annuals@streetandsmiths.com. **Website:** www.streetandsmiths.com.

Publisher: Mike Kallay. **Editor:** Scott Smith.

SPRING TRAINING YEARBOOK ONLINE

Mailing Address: Vanguard Publications, P.O. Box 667, Chapel Hill, NC 27514. **Telephone:** (919) 967-2420. **Fax:** (919) 967-6294. **E-Mail Address:** vanguard3@mindspring.com. **Website:** www.springtrainingmagazine.com.

Publisher: Merle Thorpe. **Editor:** Myles Friedman.

BASEBALL ENCYCLOPEDIAS

THE ESPN BASEBALL ENCYCLOPEDIA

Mailing Address: Sterling Publishing, Co. Inc., 387 Park Ave. South, New York, NY 10016. **Telephone:** (212) 633-3516. **Fax:** (212) 633-3327. **E-Mail Address:** ggillette@247baseball.com. **Editors:** Pete Palmer, Gary Gillette.

THE SPORTS ENCYCLOPEDIA: BASEBALL

Mailing Address: St. Martin's Press, 175 Fifth Ave., New York, NY 10010. **Telephone:** 646-307-5565. **E-Mail Address:** joseph.rinaldi@stmartins.com. **Website:** www.stmartins.com.

Authors: David Neft, Richard Cohen, Michael Neft. **Editor:** Marc Resnick.

TOTAL BASEBALL

Mailing Address: SportClassic Books, Sport Media Publishing, 55 Mill St.-Building 5, Suite 240, Toronto, Ontario MSA 3C4. **Telephone:** (416) 466-0418. **Fax:** (416) 466-9530. **E-Mail Address:** info@sportclassicbooks.com. **Website:** www.sportclassicbooks.com.

Editors: John Thorn, Phil Birnbaum, Bill Deane.

HOBBY PUBLICATIONS

BECKETT MEDIA

Beckett Baseball Collector

Mailing Address: 4635 McEwen Road., Dallas, TX 75244. **Telephone:** (972) 991-6657, (800) 840-3137. **Fax:** (972) 991-8930. **Website:** www.beckett.com.

CEO: Peter Gudmundsson. **COO:** Margaret Steele. **Vice President, Sales/Marketing:** Mike Obert. **Associate Publisher:** Tracy Hackler. **Editor:** Kevin Haake. **Price Guide Editor:** Brian Fleischer.

F+W PUBLICATIONS

Fantasy Sports/Sports Collectors Diegest/Tuff Stuff

Mailing Address: 4700 E. Galbraith Road, Cincinnati, OH 45236. **Telephone:** (715) 445-2214. **Fax:** (715) 445-4087. **Websites:** www.fantasysportsmag.com, www.sportscollectorsdigest.com, www.tuffstuff.com.

President, Magazine Division: David Blansfield.

Editor, Fantasy Sports: Greg Ambrosius. **Editor, Sports Collectors Digest:** T.S. O'Connell. **Editor, Tuff Stuff:** Scott Kelnhofer.

TEAM PUBLICATIONS

SCOUT PUBLISHING

Diehard (Boston Red Sox), Indians Ink (Cleveland Indians), Inside Pitch (New York Mets), Pinstripes Plus (New York Yankees)

Mailing Address: 1916 Pike Place, Suite 12-250, Seattle, WA 98101. **Telephone:** (888) 979-0979. **Fax:** (206) 267-4050.

Managing Editor, Diehard: Jerry Beach. **Publisher/Editor In Chief, Indians Ink:** Frank Derry. **Publisher/ Managing Editor, Inside Pitch:** Bryan Hoch. **Publisher, Pinstripes Plus:** Patrick Teale.

VINE LINE

(Chicago Cubs)

Mailing Address: Chicago Cubs Publications, 1060 W. Addison St., Chicago, IL 60613. **Telephone:** (773) 404-2827. **Fax:** (773) 404-4758. **E-Mail Address:** vineline@cubs.com. **Managing Editor:** Lena McDonagh. **Editor:** Jim McArdle.

YANKEES MAGAZINE

(New York Yankees)

Mailing Address: Yankee Stadium, Bronx, NY 10451. **Telephone:** (718) 293-4300. **Publisher/Director, Publications and Media:** Mark Mandrake. **Associate Director:** Alfred Santasiere. **Senior Editor:** Michael Margolis. **Photography Editor:** Ariele Goldman.

OUTSIDE PITCH

(Baltimore Orioles)

Mailing Address: P.O. Box 27143, Baltimore, MD 21230. **Telephone:** (410) 234-8888, (800) 342-4737. **Fax:** (410) 234-1029. **Website:** www.outsidepitch.com. **Publisher:** David Simone. **Editor:** David Hill.

REDS REPORT

(Cincinnati Reds)

Mailing Address: Columbus Sports Publications, P.O. Box 12453, Columbus, OH 43212. **Telephone:** (614) 486-2202. **Fax:** (614) 486-3650. **Publisher:** Frank Moskowitz. **Editor:** Mark Schmetzer. **Managing Editor:** Mark Rae.

GENERAL INFORMATION

MAJOR LEAGUE BASEBALL PLAYERS ASSOCIATION

Mailing Address: 12 E. 49th St., 24th Floor, New York, NY 10017. **Telephone:** (212) 826-0808. **FAX:** (212) 752-4378. **E-Mail Address:** feedback@mlbpa.org. **Website:** www.mlbplayers.com.

Year Founded: 1966.

Executive Director: Donald Fehr.

Chief Operating Officer: Gene Orza. **General Counsel:** Michael Weiner. **Assistant General Counsel:** Doyle Pryor, Robert Lenaghan, Jeff Fannell.

Special Assistants to Executive Director: Bobby Bonilla, Phil Bradley, Steve Rogers, Allyne Price.

Managing Officer: Martha Child. **Manager, Financial Operations:** Marietta DiCamillo. **Contract Administrator:** Cindy Abercrombie. **Accounting Assistants:** Terri Hinkley, Yolanda Largo. **Administrative Assistants:** Virginia Carballo, Aisha Hope, Melba Markowitz, Sharon O'Donnell, Lisa Pepin. **Receptionist:** Rebecca Rivera.

Director, Business Affairs/Licensing: Judy Heeter. **General Manager, Licensing:** Richard White. **Director, Communications:** Greg Bouris. **Assistant General Counsel, Licensing:** Evie Goldstein. **Category Director, Interactive Games:** John Olshan. **Communications Manager:** Chris Dahl. **Category Director, Trading Cards/Collectibles:** Evan Kaplan. **Category Manager, Apparel/Novelties:** Nancy Willis. **Manager, Player Trust:** Melissa Persaud. **Administrative Manager:** Heather Gould. **Program Coordinator:** Hillary Falk. **Licensing Assistant:** Eric Rivera. Manager, Office Services: Victor Lugo. Executive Secretary/Licensing: Sheila Peters.

Executive Board: Player representatives of the 30 major league clubs.

MLBPA Representatives: Tony Clark, Mark Loretta. **MLBPA Alternate Representatives:** Ray King, Craig Counsell.

SCOUTING

MAJOR LEAGUE BASEBALL SCOUTING BUREAU

Mailing Address: 3500 Porsche Way, Suite 100, Ontario, CA 91764. **Telephone:** (909) 980-1881. **FAX:** (909) 980-7794.

Year Founded: 1974.

Director: Frank Marcos. **Assistant Director:** Rick Oliver. **Office Coordinator:** Debbie Keedy. **Administrative Assistant:** Ana Melendez.

Board of Directors: Ed Burns (Major League Baseball), Dave Dombrowski (Tigers), Bob Gebhard (Diamondbacks), Roland Hemond (White Sox), Frank Marcos (MLBSB), Omar Minaya (Mets), Randy Smith (Padres), Art Stewart (Royals), Kevin Towers (Padres).

Scouts: Rick Arnold (Spring Mills, PA), Matt Barnicle (Huntington Beach, CA), Andy Campbell (Chandler, AZ), Mike Childers (Lexington, KY), Craig Conklin (Cayucos, CA), Dan Dixon (Temecula, CA), Jim Elliott (Winston-Salem, NC), Brad Fidler (Douglassville, PA), Art Gardner (Walnut Grove, MS), Rusty Gerhardt (New London, TX), Dennis Haren (San Diego, CA), Chris Heidt (Cherry Valley, IL), Don Jacoby (Winter Haven, FL), Don Kohler (Asbury, NJ), Mike Larson (Waseca, MN), Johnny Martinez (Overland Park, KS), Wayne Mathis (Cuero, TX), Junie Melendez (Toledo, OH), Paul Mirocke (Lutz, FL), Carl Moesche (Gresham, OR), Tim Osborne (Woodstock, GA), Gary Randall (Rock Hill, SC), Willie Romay (Miami Springs, FL), Kevin Saucier (Pensacola, FL), Harry Shelton (Ocoee, FL), Pat Shortt (South Hempstead, NY), Craig Smajstrla (Pearland, TX), Christie Stancil (Raleigh, NC), Ed Sukla (Irvine, CA), Doug Takarawa (Fountain Valley, CA), Jim Walton (Shattuck, OK).

Supervisor, Canada: Walt Burrows (Brentwood Bay, B.C.). **Canadian Scouts:** Curtis Bailey (Red Deer, Alberta), Jason Chee-Aloy (Toronto, Ontario), Bill Green (Vancouver, B.C.), Andrew Halpenny (Winnipeg, Manitoba), Ian Jordan (Kirkland, Quebec), Ken Lenihan (Bedford, Nova Scotia), Dan Mendham (Dorchester, Ontario), Todd Plaxton (Saskatoon, Sask.), Jasmin Roy (Longueuil, Quebec), Bob Smyth (Ladysmith, B.C.), Tony Wylie (Anchorage, AK).

Supervisor, Puerto Rico: Pepito Centeno (Cidra, PR).

PROFESSIONAL BASEBALL SCOUTS FOUNDATION

Mailing Address: 9665 Wilshire Blvd., Suite 801, Beverly Hills, CA 90212. **Telephone:** (310) 858 1935. **FAX:** (310) 246-4862. **E-Mail Address:** hitter19@aol.com. **Website:** www.professionalbaseballscoutsfoundation.com.

Chairman: Dennis Gilbert. **Director:** Cindy Picerni.

Board of Directors: Bill Gayton, Pat Gillick, Derrick Hall, Roland Hemond, Gary Hughes, Lisa Jackson, Tommy Lasorda, J.J. Lally, Roberta Mazur, Harry Minor, Bob Nightengale, Tracy Ringolsby, Dale Sutherland, Kevin Towers, Dave Yoakum, John Young.

SCOUT OF THE YEAR FOUNDATION

Mailing Address: P.O. Box 211585, West Palm Beach, FL 33421. **Telephone:** (561) 798-5897, (561) 818-4329. **FAX:** (561) 798-4644. **E-Mail Address:** bertmazur@aol.com.

President: Roberta Mazur. **Vice President:** Tracy Ringolsby. **Treasurer:** Ron Mazur II.

Board of Advisers: Joe L. Brown, Bob Fontaine, Pat Gillick, Roland Hemond, Gary Hughes, Tommy Lasorda, Allan Simpson, Ron Shapiro, Ted Spencer, Bob Watson.

UMPIRES

WORLD UMPIRES ASSOCIATION

Mailing Address: P.O. Box 394, Neenah, WI 54957. **Telephone:** (920) 969-1580. **FAX:** (920) 969-1892. **E-Mail Address:** worldumpiresassn@aol.com. **Website:** www.worldumpires.com.

Year Founded: 2000.

President: John Hirschbeck. **Vice President:** Tim Welke. **Secretary/Treasurer:** Jeff Nelson. **Labor Counsel:** Joel Smith. **Administrator:** Phil Janssen.

PROFESSIONAL BASEBALL UMPIRE CORPORATION

Office Address: 201 Bayshore Dr. SE, St. Petersburg, FL 33701. **Mailing Address:** P.O. Box A, St. Petersburg, FL 33731. **Telephone:** (727) 822-6937. **Fax:** (727) 821-5819.

President: Pat O'Conner. **Treasurer/Executive Vice President:** Tim Purpura. **Secretary/VP, Legal Affairs/General Counsel:** Scott Poley. **Special Assistant, PBUC:** Lillian Patterson. **Special Assistant to President:** Mike Fitzpatrick.

Executive Director, PBUC: Justin Klemm (Branchburg, NJ). **Chief, Instruction/Field Evaluator:** Mike Felt (Lansing, MI). **Field Evaluators/Instructors:** Jorge Bauza (San Juan, PR), Dennis Cregg (Webster, MA), Larry Reveal (Chesapeake, VA), Andy Shultz (Philadelphia).

HARRY WENDELSTEDT UMPIRE SCHOOL

Mailing Address: 88 S. St. Andrews Dr., Ormond Beach, FL 32174. **Telephone:** (386) 672-4879. **FAX:** (386) 672-3212. **E-Mail Address:** admin@umpireschool.com. **Website:** www.umpireschool.com.

Operators: Harry Wendelstedt, Hunter Wendelstedt.

JIM EVANS ACADEMY OF PROFESSIONAL UMPIRING

Mailing Address: 200 South Wilcox St., #508, Castle Rock, CO 80104. **Telephone:** (303) 290-7411. **E-Mail Address:** jimsacademy@earthlink.net. **Website:** www.umpireacademy.com.

Operator: Jim Evans.

TRAINERS

PROFESSIONAL BASEBALL ATHLETIC TRAINERS SOCIETY

Mailing Address: 400 Colony Square, Suite 1750, 1201 Peachtree St., Atlanta, GA 30361. **Telephone:** (404) 875-4000. **FAX:** (404) 892-8560. **E-Mail Address:** rmallernee@mallernee-branch.com. **Website:** www.pbats.com.

Year Founded: 1983.

President: Jamie Reed (Texas Rangers). **Secretary:** Richie Bancells (Baltimore Orioles). **Treasurer:** Jeff Porter (Atlanta Braves). **American League Head Athletic Trainer Representative:** Kevin Rand (Detroit Tigers). **American League Assistant Athletic Trainer Representative:** Steve Carter (Detroit Tigers). **National League Head Athletic Trainer Representative:** Roger Caplinger (Milwaukee Brewers). **National League Assistant Athletic Trainer Representative:** Rex Jones (Houston Astros).

General Counsel: Rollin Mallernee.

MUSEUMS

BABE RUTH BIRTHPLACE

Office Address: 216 Emory St., Baltimore, MD 21230. **Telephone:** (410) 727-1539. **FAX:** (410) 727-1652. **E-Mail Address:** info@baberuthmuseum.com. **Website:** www.baberuthmuseum.com.

Year Founded: 1973.

Executive Director: Mike Gibbons. **Curator:** Shawn Herne.

Museum Hours: April-September, 10 a.m.-6 p.m (10 a.m.-7:30 p.m. for Baltimore Orioles home games); October-March, Tuesday-Sunday, 10 a.m.-5 p.m. (10a.m.-8 p.m. for Baltimore Ravens home games).

CANADIAN BASEBALL HALL OF FAME AND MUSEUM

Museum Address: 386 Church St., St. Marys, Ontario N4X 1C2. **Mailing Address:** P.O. Box 1838, St. Marys, Ontario N4X 1C2. **Telephone:** (519) 284-1838. **FAX:** (519) 284-1234. **E-Mail Address:** baseball@baseballhalloffame.ca. **Website:** www.baseballhalloffame.ca.

Year Founded: 1983.

President/CEO: Tom Valcke. **Director, Operations:** Scott Crawford. **Curator:** Carl McCoomb.

Museum Hours: May—weekends only; June 1-Oct. 8—Daily, 10:30-4p.m.

FIELD OF DREAMS MOVIE SITE

Address: 28963 Lansing Rd., Dyersville, IA 52040. **Telephone:** (888) 875-8404. **FAX:** (319) 875-7253. **E-Mail Address:** shoelessjoe@fieldofdreamsmoviesite.com. **Website:** www.fieldofdreamsmoviesite.com.

Year Founded: 1989.

Manager, Business/Marketing: Betty Boeckenstedt.

Hours: April-November, 9 a.m.-6 p.m.

LEGENDS OF THE GAME BASEBALL MUSEUM

Address: 1000 Ballpark Way, Suite 400, Arlington, TX 76011. **Telephone:** (817) 273-5600. **FAX:** (817) 273-5093. **E-Mail Address:** museum@texasrangers.com. **Website:** http://museum.texasrangers.com.

Director: Amy Polley.

Hours: April-September, game days/Texas Rangers, 9 a.m.-7:30 p.m.; non-game days, Mon.-Sat., 9 a.m.-4 p.m., Sunday 11 a.m.-4 p.m.; October-March, Tues.-Sat., 10 a.m.-4 p.m.

LITTLE LEAGUE BASEBALL MUSEUM

Office Address: 525 Route 15 S., Williamsport, PA 17701. **Mailing Address:** P.O. Box 3485, Williamsport, PA 17701. **Telephone:** (570) 326-3607. **FAX:** (570) 326-2267. **E-Mail Address:** museum@littleleague.org. **Website:** www.littleleague.org/museum.

Year Founded: 1982.

Director: Janice Ogurcak. **Administrative Assistant:** Adam Thompson.

Museum Hours: Memorial Day-Labor Day, 10 a.m.-7 p.m. (Sun., noon-7 p.m.); Labor Day-Memorial Day, Mon., Thurs. and Fri., 10 a.m.-5 p.m., Sat. noon-5 p.m., Sun. noon-4 p.m.

LOUISVILLE SLUGGER MUSEUM AND FACTORY

Office Address: 800 W. Main St., Louisville, KY 40202. **Telephone:** (502) 588-7228. **FAX:** (502) 585-1179. **Website:** www.sluggermuseum.org.

Year Founded: 1996.

Executive Director: Anne Jewell.

Museum Hours: Mon.-Sat., Jan. 2-Dec. 23, 9 a.m.-5 p.m,; Sunday (April-November), noon-5p.m.

THE NATIONAL PASTIME: MUSEUM OF MINOR LEAGUE BASEBALL

(Under Development)

Museum Address: 175 Toyota Plaza, Suite 300, Memphis, TN 38103. **Telephone:** (901) 722-0207. **FAX:** (901) 527-1642. **E-Mail Address:** dchase@memphisredbirds.com. **Website:** www.memphisredbirds.com/autozone_park/museum.html.

Founders: Dean Jernigan, Kristi Jernigan.

Executive Director: Dave Chase.

NATIONAL BASEBALL HALL OF FAME AND MUSEUM

Address: 25 Main St., Cooperstown, NY 13326. **Telephone:** (888) 425-5633, (607) 547-7200. **FAX:** (607) 547-2044. **E-Mail Address:** info@baseballhalloffame.org. **Website:** www.baseballhalloffame.org.

Year Founded: 1939.

Chairman: Jane Forbes Clark. **Vice Chairman:** Joe Morgan. **President:** Dale Petroskey. **VP, Marketing:** Sean Gahagan. **VP, Development, Greg Harris. VP, Communications/Education:** Jeff Idelson. **VP/Chief Curator:** Ted Spencer. **Curator, Collections:** Peter Clark. **Librarian:** Jim Gates. **Controller:** Fran Althiser. **Director, Communications:** Brad Horn.

Museum Hours: Memorial Day Weekend-Labor Day, 9 a.m.-9 p.m.; remainder of year, 9 a.m.-5 p.m. Open daily except Thanksgiving, Christmas, New Year's Day.

2008 Hall of Fame Induction Ceremonies: July 27.

NEGRO LEAGUES BASEBALL MUSEUM

Mailing Address: 1616 E. 18th St., Kansas City, MO 64108. **Telephone:** (816) 221-1920. **FAX:** (816) 221-8424. **E-Mail Address:** nlmuseum@hotmail.com. **Website:** www.nlbm.com.

Year Founded: 1990.

Chairman: Buck O'Neil. **President:** Mark Bryant.

Executive Director: Don Motley. **Marketing Director:** Bob Kendrick. **Curator:** Raymond Doswell.

Museum Hours: Tues.-Sat. 9 a.m.-6 p.m.; Sun. noon-6 p.m. Closed Monday.

NOLAN RYAN FOUNDATION AND EXHIBIT CENTER

Mailing Address: 2925 S. Bypass 35, Alvin, TX 77511. **Telephone:** (281) 388-1134. **FAX:** (281) 388-1135. **Website:** www.nolanryanfoundation.org.

Hours: Mon.-Sat. 9 a.m.-4 p.m.

TED WILLIAMS MUSEUM and HITTERS HALL OF FAME

Mailing Address: 2455 N. Citrus Hills Blvd., Hernando, FL 34442. **Telephone:** (352) 527-6566. **FAX:** (352) 527-4163. **E-Mail Address:** twm@tedwilliamsmuseum.com. **Website:** twmuseum.com.

Executive Director: Dave McCarthy. **Director, Operation:** Mike Colabelli.

Museum Hours: Tues.-Sun., 10 a.m.-4 p.m.

RESEARCH

SOCIETY FOR AMERICAN BASEBALL RESEARCH

Mailing Address: 812 Huron Rd. **E., Suite 719, Cleveland, OH 44115. Telephone:** (216) 575-0500. **FAX:** (216) 575-0502. **Website:** www.sabr.org.

Year Founded: 1971.

President: Dick Beverage. **Vice President:** Bill Nowlin. **Secretary:** Neil Traven. **Treasurer:** F.X. **Flinn. Directors:** Fred Ivor-Campbell, Tom Hufford, Paul Hirsch, Andy McCue.

Executive Director: John Zajc. **Membership Services Associate:** Eileen Canepari. **Director, Publications:** Jim Charlton.

ALUMNI ASSOCIATIONS

MAJOR LEAGUE BASEBALL PLAYERS ALUMNI ASSOCIATION

Mailing Address: 1631 Mesa Ave., Suite B, Colorado Springs, CO 80906. **Telephone:** (719) 477-1870. **FAX:** (719) 477-1875. **E-Mail Address:** postoffice@mlbpaa.com. **Website:** www.baseballalumni.com.

President: Brooks Robinson. **Chief Executive Officer:** Dan Foster. **Board of Directors:** Sandy Alderson, John Doherty, Denny Doyle, Brian Fisher, Jim "Mudcat" Grant, Rich Hand, Jim Hannan (chairman), Jim Poole, Steve Rogers, Will Royster, Jose Valdivielso, Fred Valentine (vice chairman).

Legal Counsel: Sam Moore. **Vice President, Player Appearances:** Chris Torgusen. **VP, Special Events:** Geoffrey Hixson. **Director, Administration:** Blaze Bautista. **Special Events Coordinator:** Mike Groll. **Youth Baseball Coordinator:** Derek Mayfield.

ASSOCIATION OF PROFESSIONAL BALL PLAYERS OF AMERICA

Mailing Address: 1820 W. Orangewood Ave., Suite 206, Orange, CA 92868. **Telephone:** (714) 935-9993. **FAX:** (714) 935-0431. **E-Mail Address:** ballplayersassn@aol.com. **Website:** www.apbpa.org.

Year Founded: 1924.

President: Roland Hemond. **First Vice President:** Tal Smith. **Second VP:** Dick Wagner. **Secretary/Treasurer:** Dick Beverage. **Administrative Assistant:** Patty Helmsworth.

Directors: Sparky Anderson, Mark Grace, Tony Gwynn, Orel Hershiser, Whitey Herzog, Tony La Russa, Tom Lasorda, Brooks Robinson, Nolan Ryan, Tom Seaver.

BASEBALL ASSISTANCE TEAM (BAT)

Mailing Address: 245 Park Ave., 31st Floor, New York, NY 10167. **Telephone:** (212) 931-7822, (212) 931-7823. **FAX:** (212) 949-5433.

Year Founded: 1986.

President, Chief Executive Officer: Ted Sizemore. **Vice Presidents:** Frank Torre, Greg Wilcox, Earl Wilson. **Chairman:** Bobby Murcer.

Executive Director: James Martin. **Secretary:** Thomas Ostertag. **Treasurer:** Jonathan Mariner. **Consultant:** Sam McDowell.

MINOR LEAGUE BASEBALL ALUMNI ASSOCIATION

Mailing Address: P.O. Box A, St. Petersburg, FL 33731. **Telephone:** (727) 822-6937. **FAX:** (727) 821-5819. **E-Mail Address:** alumni@minorleaguebaseball.com. **Website:** www.milb.com.

Manager, Exhibiton Services/Alumni Association: Noreen Brantner.

MINISTRY

BASEBALL CHAPEL

Mailing Address: P.O. Box 302, Springfield, PA 19064. **Telephone:** (610) 690-2474. **E-Mail Address:** office@baseballchapel.org. **Website:** www.baseballchapel.org.

Year Founded: 1973.

President: Vince Nauss.

Director, Hispanic Ministry: Rich Sparling. **Director, Ministry Operations:** Robe Crose. **Director, Chapel Staff:** Wayne Beilgard. **Director, Player Relations:** Steve Sisco.

Board of Directors: Don Christenson, Dave Dravecky, Greg Groh, Dave Howard, Chuck Murphy, Vince Nauss, Bill Sampen, Tye Waller, Walt Wiley.

TRADE/EMPLOYMENT

BASEBALL WINTER MEETINGS/THE BASEBALL TRADE SHOW

Mailing Address: P.O. Box A, St. Petersburg, FL 33731. **Telephone:** (727) 822-6937, (727) 456-1718. **FAX:** (727) 825-3785. **Website:** www.baseballtradeshow.com

Manager, Exhibition Services: Noreen Brantner.

2008 Convention: Dec. 8-11, Las Vegas.

PROFESSIONAL BASEBALL EMPLOYMENT OPPORTUNITIES

Mailing Address: P.O. Box A, St. Petersburg, FL 33731. **Telephone:** (866) 937-7236. **FAX:** (727) 821-5819. **E-Mail Address:** info@pbeo.com. **Website:** www.pbeo.com.

Contact: Scott Kravchuk.

BASEBALL CARD MANUFACTURERS

DONRUSS/PLAYOFF

Mailing Address: 2300 E. Randol Mill, Arlington, TX 76011. **Telephone:** (817) 983-0300. **FAX:** (817) 983-0400. **Website:** www.donruss.com.

Marketing Manager: Scott Prusha.

GRANDSTAND CARDS

Mailing Address: 22647 Ventura Blvd., #192, Woodland Hills, CA 91364. **Telephone:** (818) 992-5642. **FAX:** (818) 348-9122. **E-Mail Address:** gscards1@pacbell.net. **Website:** www.grandstandcards.com.

MULTIAD SPORTS

Mailing Address: 1720 W. Detweiller Dr., Peoria, IL 61615. **Telephone:** (800) 348-6485, ext. **5111. FAX:** (309) 692-8378. **E-Mail Address:** bjeske@multiad.com. **Website:** www.multiad.com/sports.

TOPPS

Mailing Address: One Whitehall St., New York, NY 10004. **Telephone:** (212) 376-0300. **FAX:** (212) 376-0573. **Website:** www.topps.com.

UPPER DECK

Mailing Address: 5909 Sea Otter Place, Carlsbad, CA 92008. **Telephone:** (800) 873-7332. **FAX:** (760) 929-6548. **E-Mail Address:** customer_service@upperdeck.com. **Website:** www.upperdeck.com.

MINOR LEAGUE BASEBALL

NATIONAL ASSOCIATION OF PROFESSIONAL BASEBALL LEAGUES

Office Address: 201 Bayshore Dr. SE, St. Petersburg, FL 33701. **Mailing Address:** P.O. Box A, St. Petersburg, FL 33731. **Telephone:** (727) 822-6937. **Fax:** (727) 821-5819. **Website:** www.milb.com.

Year Founded: 1901.

President, Chief Executive Officer: Pat O'Conner.

Vice President: Stan Brand (Washington, D.C.).

Treasurer, Chief Operating Officer/Executive VP: Tim Purpura.

Pat O'Conner

Executive Assistant to President: Mary Wooters.

Senior Vice President: John Cook.

Vice President Legal Affairs/General Counsel: Scott Poley. **Administrator, Legal Affairs:** Sandie Olmsted. **Special Counsel:** George Yund (Cincinnati, OH).

Special Assistant to President: Mike Fitzpatrick.

Executive Director, Baseball Operations: Tim Brunswick.

Director, Media Relations: Jim Ferguson. **Associate Director, Media Relations:** Steve Densa.

Director, Business/Finance: Eric Krupa. **Assistant Director, Business/Finance:** Jonathan Shipman. **Manager, Accounting:** Jeff Carrier.

Director, Information Technology: Rob Colamarino.

Official Statistician: Major League Baseball Advanced Media, 75 Ninth Ave., New York, NY 10011. **Telephone:** (212) 485-3444.

2008 Winter Meetings: Las Vegas, December 8-11.

AFFILIATED MEMBERS/COUNCIL OF LEAGUE PRESIDENTS

TRIPLE-A

League	President	Telephone	Fax Number
International	Randy Mobley	(614) 791-9300	(614) 791-9009
Mexican	Plinio Escalante	011-52-555-557-1007	011-52-555-557-1007
Pacific Coast	Branch Rickey	(719) 636-3399	(719) 636-1199

DOUBLE-A

League	President	Telephone	Fax Number
Eastern	Joe McEacharn	(207) 761-2700	(207) 761-7064
Southern	Don Mincher	(770) 321-0400	(770) 321-0037
Texas	Tom Kayser	(210) 545-5297	(210) 545-5298

HIGH CLASS A

League	President	Telephone	Fax Number
California	Joe Gagliardi	(408) 369-8038	(408) 369-1409
Carolina	John Hopkins	(336) 691-9030	(336) 691-9070
Florida State	Chuck Murphy	(386) 252-7479	(386) 252-7495

LOW CLASS A

League	President	Telephone	Fax Number
Midwest	George Spelius	(608) 364-1188	(608) 364-1913
South Atlantic	Eric Krupa	(727) 456-1420	(727) 499-6853

SHORT-SEASON

League	President	Telephone	Fax Number
New York-Penn	Ben Hayes	(727) 821-7000	(727) 822-3768
Northwest	Bob Richmond	(208) 429-1511	(208) 429-1525

ROOKIE ADVANCED

League	President	Telephone	Fax Number
Appalachian	Lee Landers	(704) 873-5300	(704) 873-4333
Pioneer	Jim McCurdy	(509) 456-7615	(509) 456-0136

ROOKIE

League	President	Telephone	Fax Number
Arizona	Bob Richmond	(208) 429-1511	(208) 429-1525
Dominican Summer	Orlando Diaz	(809) 532-3619	(809) 532-3619
Gulf Coast	Tom Saffell	(941) 966-6407	(941) 966-6872
Venezuela Summer	Saul Gonzalez	011-58-41-24-0321	011-58-41-24-0705

NATIONAL ASSOCIATION BOARD OF TRUSTEES

TRIPLE-A

At-large: Ken Young (Norfolk). **International League:** Mike Tamburro (Pawtucket). **Pacific Coast League:** Sam Bernabe, vice chairman (Iowa). **Mexican League:** Gabriel Escalante (Campeche).

DOUBLE-A

Eastern League: Joe Finley, chairman (Trenton). **Southern League:** Frank Burke (Chattanooga). **Texas League:** Bill Valentine (Arkansas).

CLASS A

California League: Tom Volpe (Stockton). **Carolina League:** Chuck Greenberg (Myrtle Beach). **Florida State League:** Ken Carson, secretary (Dunedin). **Midwest League:** Dave Walker (Burlington). **South Atlantic League:** Alan Stein (Lexington).

SHORT-SEASON

New York-Penn League: Bill Gladstone (Tri-City). **Northwest League:** Bob Beban (Eugene).

ROOKIE

Appalachian League: Mitch Lukevics (Princeton). **Pioneer League:** Dave Baggott (Ogden). **Gulf Coast League:** Bill Smith, Twins.

PROFESSIONAL BASEBALL PROMOTION CORPORATION

Office Address: 201 Bayshore Dr. SE, St. Petersburg, FL 33701. **Mailing Address:** P.O. Box A, St. Petersburg, FL 33731. **Telephone:** (727) 822-6937. **Fax/Marketing:** (727) 894-4227. **Fax/Licensing:** (727) 825-3785.

President: Pat O'Conner.

Chief Operating Officer/Executive VP: Tim Purpura.

Secretary/Vice President, Leagal Affairs/General Counsel: D. Scott Poley. **Senior Vice President, Business Operations:** John Cook. **Executive Director, Baseball Operations:** Tim Brunswick. **Director, Branded Properties:** Brian Earle. **Executive Director, Sales/Marketing:** Rod Meadows. **Director, Information Technology:** Rob Colamarino. **Director, Media Relations:** Jim Ferguson.

Director, Licensing: Tina Gust. **Director, Accounting:** Jonathan Shipman. **Associate Director, Media Relations:** Steve Densa. **Senior Assistant Director, Special Operations:** Kelly Ryan. **Assistant Director, Special Operations:** Scott Kravchuk. **Senior Manager, Sales/Marketing:** Melissa Keilen. **Manager, Special Operations:** Casey Boudrot. **Manager, Exhibition Services:** Noreen Brantner. **Manager, Accounting:** Jeff Carrier. **Manager, Sponsor Relations:** Nicole Ferro. **Manager, Contracts:** Jeannette Machicote. **Manager, Team Relations:** Mary Marandi. **DAP Manager, Durham Operations:** Jill Rusinko. **Manager, Trademarks:** Bryan Sayre. **Assistant to Marketing Director, Sponsorship Development:** Heather Raburn. **Assistant/Special Operations:** Darryl Henderson. **Administrative Assistant:** Peter Martinez.

PROFESSIONAL BASEBALL UMPIRE CORPORATION

Office Address: 201 Bayshore Dr. SE, St. Petersburg, FL 33701. **Mailing Address:** P.O. Box A, St. Petersburg, FL 33731. **Telephone:** (727) 822-6937. **Fax:** (727) 821-5819.

President: Pat O'Conner.

Treasurer/Executive Vice President: Tim Purpura. **Secretary/Vice President, Leagal Affairs/General Counsel:** D. Scott Poley. **Special Assistant, PBUC:** Lillian Patterson. **Special Assistant to President:** Mike Fitzpatrick.

Executive Director, PBUC: Justin Klemm (Branchburg, NJ). **Chief, Instruction/Field Evaluator:** Mike Felt (Lansing, MI).

Field Evaluators/Instructors: Jorge Bauza (San Juan, PR), Dennis Cregg (Webster, MA), Larry Reveal (Chesapeake, VA), Andy Shultz (Philadelphia).

GENERAL INFORMATION

	Regular Season				All-Star Games	
	Teams	Games	Opening Day	Closing Day	Date	Host
International	14	144	April 3	Sept. 1	*July 16	Louisville
Pacific Coast	16	144	April 3	Sept. 1	*July 16	Louisville
Eastern	12	142	April 3	Sept. 1	July 16	New Hampshire
Southern	10	140	April 3	Sept. 1	July 14	Carolina
Texas	8	140	April 3	Sept. 1	June 25	Springfield
California	10	140	April 3	Sept. 1	#June 24	Myrtle Beach
Carolina	8	140	April 4	Sept. 1	#June 24	Myrtle Beach
Florida State	12	140	April 3	Aug. 31	June 14	Brevard County
Midwest	14	140	April 3	Sept. 1	June 17	Great Lakes
South Atlantic	16	140	April 3	Sept. 1	June 17	Greensboro
New York-Penn	14	76	June 17	Sept. 6	Aug. 19	Tri-City
Northwest	8	76	June 17	Sept. 3	None	
Appalachian	10	68	June 17	Aug. 26	None	
Pioneer	8	76	June 17	Sept. 5	None	
Arizona	9	56	June 22	Aug. 31	None	
Gulf Coast	16	56/60	June 17	Aug. 27	None	

*Triple-A All-Star Game. #California League vs. Carolina League

INTERNATIONAL LEAGUE

TRIPLE-A

Office Address: 55 South High St., Suite 202, Dublin, Ohio 43017.
Telephone: (614) 791-9300. **Fax:** (614) 791-9009.
E-Mail Address: office@ilbaseball.com. **Website:** www.ilbaseball.com.

Years League Active: 1884-present.

President/Treasurer: Randy Mobley

Randy Mobley

Vice Presidents: Harold Cooper, Dave Rosenfield, Tex Simone.

Assistant to the President: Chris Sprague. **Corporate Secretary:** Max Schumacher.

Directors: Bruce Baldwin (Richmond), Don Beaver (Charlotte), Joe Finley (Lehigh Valley), George Habel (Durham), Joe Napoli (Toledo), Bob Rich Jr. (Buffalo), Dave Rosenfield (Norfolk), Jeremy Ruby (Scranton/Wilkes-Barre), Ken Schnacke (Columbus), Max Schumacher (Indianapolis), Naomi Silver (Rochester), John Simone (Syracuse), Mike Tamburro (Pawtucket), Gary Ulmer (Louisville).

Office Manager: Gretchen Addison.

Division Structure: North—Buffalo, Lehigh Valley, Pawtucket, Rochester, Scranton/Wilkes-Barre, Syracuse. West—Columbus, Indianapolis, Louisville, Toledo. South—Charlotte, Durham, Norfolk, Richmond.

Regular Season: 144. **2008 Opening Date:** April 3. **Closing Date:** Sept. 1.

All-Star Game: July 16 at Louisville (IL vs. Pacific Coast League).

Playoff Format: South winner meets West winner in best of five series; wild card (non-division winner with best winning percentage) meets North winner in best of five series. Winners meet in best of five series for Governors' Cup championship.

Triple-A Championship Game: Sept. 16, Oklahoma City (IL vs. Pacific Coast League).

Roster Limit: 24. **Player Eligibility:** No restrictions.

Official Baseball: Rawlings ROM-INT.

Umpires: Scott Barry (Quincy, MI), Damien Beal (Fultondale, AL), Jason Bradley (Blackshear, GA), John Brammer, (Benbrook, TX), Fran Burke, Charlotte, NC), Kevin Causey (Chesterfield, VA), Chris Conroy (North Adams, MA), Adam Dowdy (Bloomington, IL), Jason Dunn (Savannah, TN), Mike Estabrook (Boynton Beach, FL), Chad Fairchild (Sarasota, FL), Rob Healey (Warwick, RI), James Hoye (North Royalton, OH), Adrian Johnson (Houston, TX), Brian Kennedy (Clermont, FL), Jason Klein (Orange, CT), Todd Paskiet (Sarasota, FL), Pete Pedersen (Orlando, FL), Brian Reilly (Lansing, MI), R.J. Thompson (Jonesborough, TN), David Uyl (Shorewood, IL), Andy Vincent (Simsburg, CT).

STADIUM INFORMATION

			Dimensions				
Club	Stadium	Opened	LF	CF	RF	Capacity	2007 Att.
Buffalo	Dunn Tire Park	1988	325	404	325	18,150	572,635
Charlotte	Knights Stadium	1990	325	400	325	10,002	311,119
Columbus	Cooper Stadium	1977	355	400	330	15,000	507,155
Durham	Durham Bulls Athletic Park	1995	305	400	327	10,000	520,952
Indianapolis	Victory Field	1996	320	402	320	14,500	586,785
*Lehigh Valley	Coca-Cola Park	2008	336	400	325	8,1000	126,894
Louisville	Louisville Slugger Field	2000	325	400	340	13,131	653,915
Norfolk	Harbor Park	1993	333	410	338	12,067	464,034
Pawtucket	McCoy Stadium	1946	325	400	325	10,031	613,065
Richmond	The Diamond	1985	330	402	330	12,134	342,090
Rochester	Frontier Field	1997	335	402	325	10,840	473,288
Scranton/WB	Lackawanna County Stadium	1989	330	408	330	10,982	580,908
Syracuse	Alliance Bank Stadium	1997	330	400	330	11,671	380,152
Toledo	Fifth Third Field	2002	320	412	315	8,943	590,159

*Franchise played in Ottowa last year.

BUFFALO BISONS

Office Address: 275 Washington St., Buffalo, NY 14203.
Telephone: (716) 846-2000. **Fax:** (716) 852-6530.
E-Mail address: info@bisons.com. **Website:** www.bisons.com.
Affiliation (first year): Cleveland Indians (1995). **Years in League:** 1886-90, 1912-70, 1998-

OWNERSHIP, MANAGEMENT

Operated By: Rich Products Corp.

Principal Owner, President: Robert Rich Jr. **President, Rich Entertainment Group:** Melinda Rich. **President, Rich Baseball Operations:** Jon Dandes. **Vice President/Treasurer:** David Rich. **VP/Secretary:** William Gisel.

VP/General Manager: Mike Buczkowski. **VP, Finance:** Joseph Segarra. **Corporate Counsel:** Raquel Bonventre, William Grieshober. **Director, Sales:** Christopher Hill. **Director, Stadium Operations:** Tom Sciarrino. **Controller:** Kevin Parkinson. **Senior Accountants:** Rita Clark, Nicole Winiarski. **Accountant:** Amy Delaney. **Human Resource Specialist:** Pat De'Aeth. **Manager, Ticket Operations:** Mike Poreda. **Director, Public Relations:** Brad Bisbing. **Director, Game Day Entertainment/Promotions Coordinator:** Matt LaSota. **Sales Coordinator:** Cindy Smith. **Account Executives:** Mark Gordon, Jim Harrington, Amanda Kolin, Geoff Lundquist, Margaret Martello, Burt Mirti, Frank Mooney, Anthony Sprague. **Manager, Merchandise:** Kathleen Wind. **Manager, Office Services:** Margaret Russo. **Executive Assistant:** Tina Sarcinelli. **Community Relations:** Gail Hodges. **Director, Food/Beverages:** John Rupp. **Assistant Concessions Manager:** Roger Buczek. **General Manager, Pettibones Grill:** Robert Free. **Head Groundskeeper:** Dan Blank. **Chief Engineer:** Pat Chella. **Home Clubhouse/Baseball Operations Coordinator:** Scott Lesher. **Visiting Clubhouse Manager:** Dan Brick.

FIELD STAFF

Manager: Torey Lovullo. **Coach:** Dave Myers. **Pitching Coach:** Scott Radinsky. **Trainer:** Jeff Desjardins.

GAME INFORMATION

Radio Announcers: Ben Wagner, Duke McGuire. **No of Games Broadcast:** Home-72, Road-72. **Flagship Station:** WWKB-1520.

PA Announcer: Jon Summers. **Official Scorers:** Mike Kelly, Kevin Lester.

Stadium Name: Dunn Tire Park. **Location:** From north, take I-190 to Elm Street exit, left onto Swan Street. From east, take I-190 West to exit 51 (Route 33) to end, exit at Oak Street, right onto Swan Street. From west, take I-190 East, exit 53 to I-90 North, exit at Elm Street, left onto Swan Street. **Standard Game Times:** 7:05 p.m., **1:**05 Sunday Ticket Price Range: $5-18.

Visiting Club Hotel: Adams Mark Hotel, 120 Church St, Buffalo, NY 14202. **Telephone:** (716) 845-5100. Hyatt Hotel, 2 Fountain Plaza, Buffalo, NY 14202. **Telephone:** (716) 856-1234.

CHARLOTTE KNIGHTS

Office Address: 2280 Deerfield Dr., Fort Mill, SC 29715.
Telephone: (704) 357-8071. **Fax:** (704) 329-2155.
E-Mail address: knights@charlotteknights.com. **Website:** www.charlotteknights.com.
Affiliation (first year): Chicago White Sox (1999). **Years in League:** 1993-

OWNERSHIP, MANAGEMENT

Operated by: Knights Baseball, LLC.

Principal Owners: Bill Allen, Don Beaver.

Vice President/General Manager: Dan Rajkowski. **Director, Group Sales:** Thomas Lee. **Director, Media Relations:** John Agresti. **Director, Creative Services:** Mike Riviello. **Director, Broadcasting/Team Travel:** Matt Swierad. **Director, Corporate Accounts:** Chris Semmens. **Operations Manager:** Mark McKinnon. **Business Manager:** Michael Sanger. **Promotions Coordinator:** Drew Tyler. **Sales Executive:** Heath Dillard. **Group Event Coordinators:** Chris Petot, Jacob Giles, Ali White. **Box Office Coordinator:** Meredith Storrie. **Director of Merchandise:** Becka Leveille. **Head Groundskeeper:** Eddie Busque. **Assistant Groundskeeper:** Greg Burgess. **Clubhouse Manager:** Dan Morphis. **Manager of Media Relations:** Patrick Starck. **Director, Community Relations:** Tim O'Reilly. **Marketing Assistant:** Chris Inklebarger. **Executive Assistant to the General Manager:** Julie Clark. **Office Manager:** Jastina Patterson.

FIELD STAFF

Manager: Marc Bombard. **Coach:** Joe McEwing. **Pitching Coach:** RIchard Dotson. **Trainer:** Scott Johnson. **Strength/Conditioning:** Chad Efron.

GAME INFORMATION

Radio Announcer: Mike Pacheco, Matt Swierad. **No of Games Broadcast:** Home-72 Road-72. **Flagship Station:** WFNA 1660-AM.

PA Announcer: Ken Conrad. **Official Scorers:** Sam Copeland, Jack Frost, Brent Stastny.

Stadium Name: Knights Stadium. **Location:** Exit 88 off I-77, east on Gold Hill Road. **Ticket Price Range:** $7-12.

Visiting Club Hotel: Comfort Suites, 10415 Centrum Parkway, Pineville, NC 28134. **Telephone** 704-540-0559.

COLUMBUS CLIPPERS

Office Address: 1155 W. Mound St, Columbus, OH 43223.
Telephone: (614) 462-5250. **Fax:** (614) 462-3271.
E-Mail address: info@clippersbaseball.com. **Website:** www.clippersbaseball.com.
Affiliation (first year): Washington Nationals (2007). **Years in League:** 1955-70, 1977-

OWNERSHIP, MANAGEMENT

Operated By: Columbus Baseball Team Inc.

Principal Owner: Franklin County, Ohio. **Board of Directors:** Tom Fries, Wayne Harer, Thomas Katzenmeyer, David Leland, Cathy Lyttle, Bob Milbourne, Richard Smith.

President, General Manager: Ken Schnacke. **Assistant GM:** Mark Warren. **Director, Stadium Operations:** Steve Dalin. **Director, Ticket Operations:** Scott Ziegler. **Director, Marketing:** Mark Galuska. **Assistant Director, Marketing:** Ty Debevoise. **Director, Broadcasting:** Scott Leo. **Director, Communications/Media Relations:** Joe Santry. **Director, Merchandising:** Krista Oberlander. **Director, Finance:** Bonnie Badgley. **Director, Group Sales:** Ben Keller. **Assistant Director, Group Sales:** Brett Patton. **Assistant Director, Communications:** Chris Anders. **Assistant Director, Media Relations:** Anthony Slosser. **Assistant to GM:** Kelly Ryther. **Administrative Assistant, Tickets:** Ashley Alexander. **Administrative Assistant, Marketing:** Paula Knudsen. **Director, Multimedia:** Rich Hanchette. **Assistant Director, Multimedia:** Yoshi Ando. **Clubhouse Manager:** J.J. Thomas. **Administrative Assistants:** Eddie Langhenry, Brittany White.

FIELD STAFF

Manager: Tim Foli. **Hitting Coach:** Rick Eckstein. **Pitching Coach:** Steve McCatty. **Trainer:** Mike Quinn.

GAME INFORMATION

Radio Announcer: Scott Leo, Randy Rhinehart. **No of Games Broadcast:** Home-72, Road-72. **Flagship Station:** WKVO 1580-AM.

PA Announcer: Rich Hanchette. **Official Scorer:** Unavailable.

Stadium Name: Cooper Stadium. **Location:** From north/south, I-71 to I-70 West, exit at Mound Street. From north/south, I-71 to I-70 West, exit at Mound Street. From west, I-70 East, exit at Broad Street, east to Glenwood, south to Mound Street. From east, I-70 West, exit at Mound Street. **Ticket Price Range:** $6-10.

Visiting Club Hotel: Holiday Inn, 7007 N. High St., Columbus, OH 43085. Telephone: (614) 436-0700. Sheraton Suites, 201 Hutchinson Ave., Columbus, OH 43235. **Telephone:** (614) 781-7316. Holiday Inn, 175 Hutchinson Ave., Columbus, OH 43235. **Telephone:** (614) 431-4457.

DURHAM BULLS

Office Address: 409 Blackwell St., Durham, NC 27701.
Mailing Address: P.O. Box 507, Durham, NC 27702.
Telephone: (919) 687-6500. **Fax:** (919) 687-6560.
Website: www.durhambulls.com
Affiliation (first year): Tampa Bay Devil Rays (1998). **Years in League:** 1998-

OWNERSHIP, MANAGEMENT

Operated By: Capitol Broadcasting Company, Inc.
President, CEO: Jim Goodmon.
Vice President: George Habel.

General Manager: Mike Birling. **Assistant GM:** Jon Bishop. **Account Executive, Sponsorships:** Cameron Knowles, Chris Overby, Neil Solondz, Gregg Van Leuven. **Coordinator, Sponsorship Services:** Allison Phillips. **Director, Media Relations/Promotions:** Matt DeMargel. **Coordinator, Multimedia:** Ari Ecker. **Assistant, Media Relations and Promotions:** Matt Koizim. **Director, Ticketing:** Tim Season. **Supervisor, Ticket Operations:** Ben DuGoff. **Business Development Coordinators:** Rich Brady, Mike Miller, Jacob Powers, Mary Beth Warfford. **Group Sales Assistants:** Todd Crowell, Jen Ferrell. **GM, Concessions:** Jamie Jenkins. **Assistant GM, Concessions:** Tammy Scott. **Head Groundskeeper:** Scott Strickland. **Manager, Business:** Rhonda Carlile. **Supervisor, Accounting:** Theresa Stocking. **Security:** Ed Sarvis. **Box Office Sales:** Jerry Mach. **Office Manager:** Leanne Jones. **Manager, Home Clubhouse:** Colin Saunders.

FIELD STAFF

Manager: Charlie Montoyo. **Coach:** Gary Gaetti. **Pitching Coach:** Xavier Hernandez. **Trainer:** Jimmy Southard.

GAME INFORMATION

Radio Announcers: Steve Barnes, Neil Solondz, Ken Tanner. **No. of Games Broadcast:** Home-72, Road-72. **Flagship Station:** WCMC 99.9 FM.

PA Announcer: Tony Riggsbee. **Official Scorer:** Brent Belvin.

Stadium Name: Durham Bulls Athletic Park. **Location:** From Raleigh, I-40 West to Highway 147 North, exit 12B to Willard, two blocks on Willard to stadium. From I-85, Gregson Street exit to downtown, left on Chapel Hill Street, right on Mangum Street. **Standard Game Times:** 7 p.m., Sunday 5 p.m. **Ticket Price Range:** $5-8.

Visiting Club Hotel: Durham Marriot at the Civic Center, 201 Foster St., Durham, NC 27701. **Telephone:** (919) 768-6000.

INDIANAPOLIS INDIANS

Office Address: 501 W. Maryland Street, Indianapolis, IN 46225.
Telephone: (317) 269-3542. **Fax:** (317) 269-3541.
E-Mail address: indians@indyindians.com. **Website:** www.indyindians.com.
Affiliation (first year): Pittsburgh Pirates (2005). **Years in League:** 1963, 1998-

OWNERSHIP, MANAGEMENT

Operated By: Indians Inc.

President/Chairman of the Board: Max Schumacher.

VP/General Manager: Cal Burleson. **Assistant GM:** Randy Lewandowski. **Director, Marketing:** Chris Herndon. **Director, Operations:** Jamie Mehringer. **Director, Tickets:** Matt Guay. **Manager, Stadium Operations:** Mark Anderson. **Director, Facility Maintenance:** Tim Hughes. **Assistant Director, Facility Maintenance:** Allan Danehy. **Office Manager:** Julie Fischer. **Director, Business Operations:** Brad Morris. **Director, Facilities:** Bill Sampson. **Head Groundskeeper:** Joey Stevenson. **Administrative Assistant:** Stu Tobias. **Manager, Community Relations:** Ryan Bowman. **Manager, Marketing:** Autumn Gaslor. **Director, Merchandising:** Mark Schumacher. **Manager, Media Relations:** Matt Segal. **Manager, Database/Information Technology:** Anthony Veach. **Senior Executive, Ticket Sales:** Chad Bohm. **Ticket Sales Executives:** Drew Heincker, Jonathan Howard, Scott McCauley, Keri Oberting, Matt Wilkinson. **Manager, Ticket Services: Bryan Spisak. Manager, Ticket/Premium Services:** Kerry Vick. **Director, Broadcasting:** Howard Kellman. **Executives, Sponsorship Sales:** Meagan Gonser, Bob Woelfel. **Director, Corporate Development:** Bruce Schumacher. **Coordinator, Sponsorship Sales:** Joel Zawacki. **Home Clubhouse Manager:** Steve Humphrey. **Visiting Clubhouse Managers:** Bob Martin, Jeremy Martin.

FIELD STAFF

Manager: Trent Jewett. **Hitting Coach:** Hensley Meulens. **Pitching Coach:** Ray Searage. **Trainer:** Jose Ministral. **Strength/Conditioning Coach:** Mubarak Malik.

GAME INFORMATION

Radio Announcer: Howard Kellman, Scott McCauley. **No. of Games Broadcast:** Home-72, Road-72. **Flagship Station:** WXLW 950-AM.

PA Announcer: Bruce Schumacher. **Official Scorers:** Bill McAfee, Gary Johnson, Kim Rogers.

Stadium Name: Victory Field. **Location:** I-70 to West Street exit, north on West Street to ballpark. I-65 to Martin Luther King and West Street exit, south on West Street to ballpark. **Standard Game Times:** 7:15 p.m., 2 p.m. on Wed./Sun. **Ticket Price Range:** $9-13.

Visiting Club Hotel: Holiday Inn Express, 410 South Missouri Street, Indianapolis, IN 46225. **Telephone:** (317) 822-6400. Courtyard by Marriott, 510 W. Washington St., Indianapolis, IN 46204. **Telephone:** (317) 635-4443.

LEHIGH VALLEY IRONPIGS

Office Address: 1050 IronPigs Way/P.O. Box 90220, Allentown, PA 18109
Telephone: (610) 435-3001. **Fax:** (610) 435-3088.
E-Mail address: info@ironpigsbaseball.com. **Website:** www.ironpigsbaseball.com.
Affiliation (first year): Philadelphia Phillies (2008). **Years in League:** 2008-

OWNERSHIP, MANAGEMENT

Ownership: Gracie Baseball LP,

President: Chuck Domino.

General Manager: Kurt Landes. **Asst. GM, Marketing:** Danny Tetzlaff. **Asst. GM, Ticketing:** Howard Scharf. **Director, Stadium Operations:** Tom Kulczewski. **Director, Media Relations:** Matt Provence. **Manager, Media Relations:** Jon Schaeffer. **Director, Community Relations:** Sarah Marten. **Director, Merchandise:** Janine Kurpiel. **Manager, Merchandise:** Julie Rowan. **Director, Ticket Sales:** Scott Hodge. **Director, Ticket Operations:** Amy Schoch. **Director, Group Sales:** Don Wilson. **Director, Marketing:** Ron Rushe. **Director, Marketing Services:** Christa Linzey. **Manager, Marketing Services:** Andy Hein. **Director, Creative Services:** Matt Zidik. **Director, Promotions:** Lindsey Knupp. **Director, Special Events:** Mary Nixon. **Director, Food/Beverage:** Richard Heimberg. **Manager, Food/Beverage:** Alex Rivera. **Director, Finance:** Heather Dillon. **Manager, Finance:** Michelle Valkovek. **Director, Administration:** Robin Hill. **Marketing Managers:** Corey Bugno, Matt Glass, Brandon Kelly, Josh LaBarba. **Manager, Ticket Operations:** Erin Owens. **Tickets/Group Representatives:** Mark Anderson, Ryan Contento, Scott Evans, Jim Kelly, Jason Kettering, Katrina Lerch, Bryan Schuster, Brandon Smith. **Account Executives:** Sheila Musselman, Leigh Anne Whitelatch. **Field Operations:** Bill Butler.

FIELD STAFF

Manager: Dave Huppert. **Hitting Coach:** Greg Gross. **Pitching Coach:** Rod Nichols. **Trainer:** Unavailable.

GAME INFORMATION

Radio Announcers: Matt Provence, Jon Schaeffer. **No. Games Broadcast:** 144 (72 Home; 72 Away). **Flagship Radio Station:** WXLV 90.3 FM. **Television Station:** TV2. **Television Announcers:** Mike Zambelli, Ricky Bottalico, Matt Provence. **No. Games Televised:** 72 Home. **PA Announcer:** Tim Chorones. **Official Scorers:** Jack Logic, David Sheriff.

Stadium Name (year opened): Coca-Cola Park (2008)

Location: Take U.S. 22 to exit for Airport Road South. Head south, make right on American Parkway. Left into stadium.

Standard Game Times: 7:05 p.m.; Sun. 1:35 p.m. (April-May), 5:35 p.m. (June-August).

Visiting Club Hotel: Hotel Bethlehem (437 Main Street, Bethlehem, PA 18018). **Telephone:** (610) 625-5000

LOUISVILLE BATS

Office Address: 401 E. Main St, Louisville, KY 40202.

Telephone: (502) 212-2287. **Fax:** (502) 515-2255.

E-Mail address: info@batsbaseball.com. **Website:** www.batsbaseball.com.

Affiliation (first year): Cincinnati Reds (2000). **Years in League:** 1998-

OWNERSHIP, MANAGEMENT

Chariman: Dan Ulmer Jr. **Board of Directors:** John Hillerich, Edward Glasscock, Gary Ulmer, Roberts Stallings, Kenny Huber, Steve Trager, J. Michael Brown.

Vice President/GM: Dale Owens. **Assistant GM/Director, Marketing:** Greg Galiette. **Director, Stadium Operations:** Scott Shoemaker. **Director, Ticket Sales:** James Breeding. **Director, Baseball Operations:** Earl Stubblefield. **Controller:** Michele Anderson. **Manager, Tickets:** George Veith. **Director, Public Relations:** Megan Dimond. **Director, Group Sales:** Bryan McBride. **Director, Broadcasting:** Jim Kelch. **Director, Suite Level Services:** Kerri Ferrell. **Senior Account Executive:** Hal Norwood. **Assistant Director, Public Relations:** Nick Evans. **Asst. Director, Stadium Operations:** Doug Randol. **Account Executive:** Matt Andrews. **Account Executives:** Evan Patrick, Justin Seamon, Curtis Cunningham, Josh Hargreaves, Jason Abraham, Sarah Nordman, Tony Brown. **Asst. Manager, Tickets:** Kyle Reh. **Stadium Operations:** Brian Tabler. **Community Relations:** Jodi Tischendorf. **Groundskeeper:** Tom Nielsen.

FIELD STAFF

Manager: Rick Sweet. **Hitting Coach:** Adrian "Smokey" Garrett. **Pitching Coach:** Ted Power. **Trainer:** Chris Lapole.

GAME INFORMATION

Radio Announcers: Jim Kelch, Matt Andrews. **No. of Games Broadcast:** Home-72, Road-72. **Flagship Station:** WKRD 790-AM.

PA Announcer: Charles Gazaway. **Official Scorer:** Ken Horn. **Organist:** Bob Ramsey.

Stadium Name: Louisville Slugger Field. **Location:** I-64 and I-71 to I-65 South/North to Brook Street exit, right on Market Street, left on Jackson Street; stadium on Main Street between Jackson and Preston. **Ticket Price Range:** $5-10.

Visiting Club Hotel: Galt House Hotel, 140 North Fourth Street, Louisville, KY 40202. **Telephone:** (502) 589-5200.

NORKFOLK TIDES

Office Address: 150 Park Ave, Norfolk, VA 23510.

Telephone: (757) 622-2222. **Fax:** (757) 624-9090.

E-Mail Address: receptionist@norfolktides.com. **Website:** www.norfolktides.com.

Affiliation (first year): Baltimore Orioles (2007). **Years in League:** 1969-

OWNERSHIP, MANAGEMENT

Operated By: Tides Baseball Club Inc.

President: Ken Young.

General Manager: Dave Rosenfield. **Assistant GM:** Ben Giancola. **Business Manager:** Mike Giedlin. **Director, Media Relations:** Ian Locke. **Director, Community Relations:** Heather McKeating. **Director, Ticket Operations:** Gretchen Todd. **Business Manager:** Mike Giedlin. **Director, Group Sales:** Dave Harrah. **Director, Stadium Operations:** Mike Zeman. **Manager, Merchandising:** Mandy Cormier. **Assistant Director, Stadium Operations:** Mike Cardwell. **Manager, Group Sales:** Stephanie Brammer. **Executives, Corporate Sponsorships/Promotions:** Jonathan Mensink, Sarah Heth. **Director, Ticket Operations:** Gretchen Todd. **Box Office Manager:** Linda Waisanen. **Event Staff Manager:** Deirdre Zimmerman. **Administrative Assistant:** Stefanie Cola. **Head Groundskeeper:** Kenny Magner.

FIELD STAFF

Manager: Gary Allenson. **Coach:** Dallas Williams. **Pitching Coach:** Larry McCall. **Trainer:** Mark Shires.

GAME INFORMATION

Radio Announcers: Bob Socci, Pete Michaud. **No. of Games Broadcast:** Home-72, Road-72. **Flagship Station:** ESPN 1310-AM.

PA Announcers: John Lewis, Jack Ankerson, Don Bolger. **Official Scorers:** Dave Lewis, Mike Holtzclaw.

Stadium Name: Harbor Park. **Location:** Exit 9, 11A or 11B off I-264, adjacent to the Elizabeth River in downtown Norfolk. **Ticket Price Range:** $9.50-11.

Visiting Club Hotel: Sheraton Waterside, 777 Waterside Dr, Norfolk, VA 23510. **Telephone:** (757) 622-6664.

PAWTUCKET RED SOX

Office Address: One Ben Mondor Way, Pawtucket, RI 02860.
Mailing Address: P.O. Box 2365, Pawtucket, RI 02861.
Telephone: (401) 724-7300. **Fax:** (401) 724-2140.
E-Mail Address: info@pawsox.com. **Website:** www.pawsox.com.
Affiliation (first year): Boston Red Sox (1973). **Years in League:** 1973-.

OWNERSHIP, MANAGEMENT

Operated by: Pawtucket Red Sox Baseball Club, Inc.

Chairman: Ben Mondor. **President:** Mike Tamburro.

Vice President/General Manager: Lou Schwechheimer. **VP, Chief Financial Officer:** Matt White. **VP, Sales/Marketing:** Michael Gwynn. **VP, Stadium Operations:** Mick Tedesco. **VP, Public Relations:** Bill Wanless. **Director, Community Relations:** Jeff Bradley. **Manager, Sales:** Augusto Rojas. **Director, Ticket Operations:** Diane Silveira. **Manager, Finance:** Kathryn Tingley. **Director, Merchandising:** Eric Petterson. **Director, Media Services:** Jeff Ouimette. **Director, Concession Services:** Jim Hogan. **Director, Corporate Services:** Frank Quinn. **Director, Warehouse Operations:** Dave Johnson. **Facility Operations:** Kevin Galligan Director, Group Sales: Bill Crawford. **Gameday Statistician/Account Executive:** Stephen Acciardo. **Account Executive:** Mike Abramson. **Administrative Assistant:** Becky Berta. **Head Groundskeeper:** Matt McKinnon. **Director of Security:** Rick Medeiros. **Executive Chef:** Ken Bowdish.

FIELD STAFF

Manager: Ron Johnson. **Coach:** Russ Morman. **Pitching Coach:** Rich Sauveur. **Trainer:** Greg Barajas.

GAME INFORMATION

Radio Announcer: Dan Hoard, Steve Hyder. **No. of Games Broadcast:** Home-72, Away-72. **Flagship Station:** WHJJ 920-AM.

PA Announcer: Jim Martin. **Official Scorer:** Bruce Guindon.

Stadium Name: McCoy Stadium. **Location:** From north, 95 South to exit 2A in Massachusetts (Newport Ave.), follow Newport Ave. for 2 miles, right on Columbus Ave., follow one mile, stadium on right. From south, 95 North to exit 28 (School Street), right at bottom of exit ramp, through two sets of lights, left onto Pond Street, right on Columbus Ave., stadium entrance on left. From west (Worcester), 295 North to 95 South and follow directions from north. From east (Fall River), 195 West to 95 North and follow directions from south. **Standard Game Times:** 7 p.m.; Sat. 6, Sun. 1. **Ticket Price Range:** $6-10.

Visiting Club Hotel: Comfort Inn, 2 George St., Pawtucket, RI 02860. **Telephone:** (401) 723-6700.

RICHMOND BRAVES

Office Address: 3001 N. Boulevard, Richmond, VA 23230.
Mailing Address: P.O. Box 6667, Richmond, VA 23230.
Telephone: (804) 359-4444. Fax: (804) 359-0731.
E-Mail Address: info@rbraves.com. Website: www.rbraves.com .
Affiliation (first year): Atlanta Braves (1966). **Years in League:** 1884, 1915-17, 1954-64, 1966-

OWNERSHIP, MANAGEMENT

General Manager: Bruce Baldwin. **Assistant General Manager:** Bill Blackwell. **Office Manager:** Joanne Curnutt. **Receptionist:** Janet Zimmerman. **Manager, Stadium Operations:** Ryan Stoltenberg. **Manager, Field Maintenance:** Gerry Huppman. **Manager, Public Relations:** John Emmett. **Assistant Manager, Promotions/Entertainment:** Noir Fowler. **Manager, Corporate Sales:** Ben Terry. **Manager, Ticket Operations:** Mike Castle. **Assistant Manager, Ticket Operations:** Jason Hasty. **Corporate Sales Representatives:** Lisa Howell, Jared Johnson.

FIELD STAFF

Manager: Dave Brundage. **Coach:** Chris Chambliss. **Pitching Coach:** Guy Hansen. **Trainer:** Mike Graus.

GAME INFORMATION

Radio Announcers: Robert Fish, Sean Robertson. **No of Games Broadcast:** Home-72 Road-72. **Flagship Station:** WRNL 910-AM.

PA Announcer: Mike Blacker. **Official Scorers:** Gary Criswell, Rusty Gold.

Stadium Name: The Diamond. **Location:** Exit 78 (Boulevard) at junction of I-64 and I-95, follow signs to park. **Ticket Price Range:** $5-12.

Visiting Club Hotel: Quality Inn, 8008 W. Broad St, Richmond, VA 23230. **Telephone:** (804) 346-0000.

ROCHESTER RED WINGS

Office Address: One Morrie Silver Way, Rochester, NY 14608.
Telephone: (585) 454-1001. **Fax:** (585) 454-1056, (585) 454-1057.
E-Mail Address: info@redwingsbaseball.com. **Website:** www.redwingsbaseball.com.
Affiliation (first year): Minnesota Twins (2003). **Years in League:** 1885-89, 1891-92, 1895-.

OWNERSHIP, MANAGEMENT

Operated by: Rochester Community Baseball.

Chairman, Chief Operating Officer: Naomi Silver. **President, Chief Executive Officer:** Gary Larder.

General Manager: Dan Mason. **Assistant GM:** Will Rumbold. **Controller:** Darlene Giardina. **Head Groundskeeper:** Gene Buonomo. **Director, Media/Public Relations:** Chuck Hinkel. **Director, Corporate Development:** Nick Sciarratta. **Group/Picnic Director:** Parker Allen. **Director, Promotions:** Matt Cipro. **Director, Ticket Operations:** Rob Dermody. **Director, Production:** Jeff Coltoniak. **Director, Merchandising:** Barbara Moore. **Director, Human Resources:** Paula LoVerde. **Account Executive:** Jeff Cogan, Bob Craig. **Assistant Director, Groups/Picnics:** Zach Holmes. **Executive Secretary:** Ginny Colbert. **Director, Food Services:** Jeff Dodge. **Manager, Catering:** Courtney Trawitz. **Manager, Concessions:** Jeff DeSantis. **Business Manager, Concessions:** Dave Bills. **Clubhouse Operations:** Terry Costello.

FIELD STAFF

Manager: Stan Cliburn. **Coach:** Ricardo Ingram. **Pitching Coach:** Stu Cliburn. **Trainer:** Tony Leo.

GAME INFORMATION

Radio Announcers: Joe Altobelli, Josh Whetzel. **No. of Games Broadcast:** Home-72, Away-72. **Flagship Stations:** WHTK 1280-AM, WYSL 1040-AM.

PA Announcer: Kevin Spears. **Official Scorer:** Warren Kozereski.

Stadium Name: Frontier Field. **Location:** I-490 East to exit 12 (Brown/Broad Street) and follow signs. I-490 West to exit 14 (Plymouth Ave.) and follow signs. **Standard Game Times:** 7:05 p.m., Sun 1:35. **Ticket Price Range:** $5.50-9.50

Visiting Club Hotel: Crown Plaza, 70 State St., Rochester, NY 14608. **Telephone:** (585) 546-3450.

SCRANTON/WILKES-BARRE YANKEES

Office Address: 235 Montage Mountain Rd, Moosic, PA 18507.
Telephone: (570) 969-2255. **Fax:** (570) 963-6564.
E-Mail address: info@swbyankees.com. **Website:** www.swbyankees.com.
Affiliation (first year): New York Yankees (2007). **Years in League:** 1989-

OWNERSHIP, MANAGEMENT

Operated By: Mandalay Baseball Properties.

Executive Vice President/COO: Jeremy Ruby. **Vice President, Marketing Services:** Jon Stephenson. **Director, Accounting:** Paul Chilek. **Director, Finance:** Donna Kunda. **Director, Corporate Partnerships:** Jason Tribbet, Mike Trudnak. **Play Ball/Sponsor Service Manager:** Mike Cummings. **Sponsor Service Managers:** Jeff Verklan, Angela Wright. **Senior Director, Ticket Sales:** Ryan Limburg. **Manager, Sales/Marketing:** Josh Katyl. **Corporate Marketing Managers:** Tim Connell, Mark Schueler, Dave Walsh. **Senior Group Sales Manager:** Raquel Bonventre. **Group Sales Coordinators:** Brandon Lawrence, Andrew Reichert. **Customer Account Managers:** Janice Matacic, Steve Vasilenko. **Director, Ticket Operations:** Jeff Weinhold. **Box Office Manager:** Ann Marie Nocera. **Director, Operations:** Curt Camoni. **Head Groundskeeper:** Steve Horne. **Assistant Groundskeeper:** Bill Casterline. **Office Manager:** Kelly Byron. **Director, Broadcasting/Media Relations:** Mike Vander Wood. **Director, Merchandise:** Karen Healey. **Director, Game Entertainment:** Barry Snyder.

FIELD STAFF

Manager: Dave Miley. **Coach:** Butch Wynegar. **Pitching Coach:** Rafael Chaves. **Trainer:** Darren London. **Coach:** Alvaro Espinoza.

GAME INFORMATION

Radio Announcer: Mike Vander Wood. **No of Games Broadcast:** Home-72 Road-72. **Flagship Station:** WICK 1340-1400 AM.

PA Announcer: Johnny Davies. **Official Scorers:** Jeep Fanucci, Bob McGoff.

Stadium Name: PNC Field. **Location:** I-81 to exit 182 (Davis Street/Montage Mountain Road), take Montage Mountain Road one mile to stadium. **Ticket Price Range:** $8-10.

Visiting Club Hotel: Radisson at Lackawanna Stadium, 700 Lackawanna Ave, Scranton, PA 18503. **Telephone:** (570) 342-8300.

SYRACUSE CHIEFS

Office Address: One Tex Simone Dr., Syracuse, NY 13208.

Telephone: (315) 474-7833. **Fax:** (315) 474-2658.

E-Mail Address: baseball@syracusechiefs.com. **Website:** www.syracusechiefs.com.

Affiliation (first year): Toronto Blue Jays (1978). **Years in League:** 1885-89, 1891-92, 1894-1901, 1918, 1920-27, 1934-55, 1961-.

OWNERSHIP, MANAGEMENT

Operated by: Community Owned Baseball Club of Central New York, Inc.

Chairman: Charles Rich. **President:** Ron Gersbacher. **Vice President:** Patricia Campbell. **VP/Treasurer:** Anton Kreuzer. **VP/COO:** Anthony Simone. **General Manager:** John Simone. **Assistant GM, Business:** Don Lehtonen. **Director, Group Sales:** Victor Gallucci. **Director, Operations:** H.J. Refici. **Director, Corporate Sales/Public Relations:** Andy Gee. **Director, Promotions:** Mike Voutsinas. **Director, Merchandising:** Wendy Shoen. **Director, Ticket Office:** Nick Pelkey. **Team Historian:** Ron Gersbacher. **Administrative Assistant:** Sarah Reynolds. **Receptionist:** Priscilla Venditti. **Field Maintenance:** Wes Ganobcik.

FIELD STAFF

Manager: Doug Davis. **Coach:** Al LeBoeuf. **Pitching Coach:** Rick Langford. **Trainer:** Jon Woodworth.

GAME INFORMATION

Radio Announcer: Bob McElligott. **No. of Games Broadcast:** Home-72, Away-72. **Flagship Station:** WHEN Sportsradio 620-AM, NOVA 105.1-FM.

PA Announcer: Brent Axe. **Official Scorer:** Paul Fairbanks, Tom Leo.

Stadium Name: Alliance Bank Stadium. **Location:** New York State Thruway to exit 36 (I-81 South), to 7th North Street exit, left on 7th North, right on Hiawatha Boulevard. **Standard Game Times:** 7 p.m., Sun. 6. **Ticket Price Range:** $6-9.

Visiting Club Hotel: Ramada Inn, 1305 Buckley Rd., Syracuse, NY 13212. **Telephone:** (315) 457-8670.

TOLEDO MUD HENS

Office Address: 406 Washington St, Toledo, OH 43604.

Telephone: (419) 725-4367. **Fax:** (419) 725-4368.

E-Mail address: mudhens@mudhens.com. **Website:** www.mudhens.com.

Affiliation (first year): Detroit Tigers (1987). **Years in League:** 1889, 1965-

OWNERSHIP, MANAGEMENT

Operated By: Toledo Mud Hens Baseball Club, Inc.

Chairman, President: Michael Miller. **Vice President:** David Huey. **Secretary/Treasurer:** Charles Bracken. **General Manager/Executive Vice President:** Joseph Napoli. **Assistant GM/Director, Marketing, Advertising, Sales:** Scott Jeffer. **Assistant GM/Director, Corporate Partnerships:** Neil Neukam. **Assistant GM, Ticket Sales/Operations:** Erik Ibsen. **CFO:** Pam Alspach. **Manager, Promotions:** JaMay Edwards. **Director, Public/Media Relations:** Jason Griffin. **Director, Ticket Sales/Services:** Thom Townley. **Accounting:** Sheri Kelly, Brian Leverenz. **Manager, Gameday Operations:** Greg Setola. **Manager, Groups Sales:** Brian Perkins. **Manager, Box Office Sales:** Justin Morelli. **Manager, Community Relations:** Cheri Pastula. **Corporate Sales Associate:** Ed Sintic. **Season Ticket/Group Sales Associates:** Chris Hole, Mike Keedy, Frank Kristie, Kyle Moll, John Mulka, Nathan Steinmetz, Eric Tomaszewski. **Season Ticket Service Coordinator:** Jessica Aten. **Manager, Video Board Operations:** Mike Ramirez. **Graphic Designer:** Dan Royer. **Manager, Souvenir Sales:** Craig Katz. **Assistant Manager, Souvenir Sales:** Heidi Srock. **Manager, Ballpark Operations:** Ken Westenkirchner. **Office Manager:** Carol Hamilton. **Executive Assistant:** Tracy Evans. **Turf Manager:** Jake Tyler. **Assistant Turf Manager:** Kyle Leppelmeier.

FIELD STAFF

Manager: Larry Parrish. **Coach:** Leon Durham. **Pitching Coach:** A.J. **Sager. Trainer:** Matt Rankin.

GAME INFORMATION

Radio Announcers: Frank Gilhooley, Jim Weber, Jason Griffin. **No of Games Broadcast:** Home-72 Road-72. **Flagship Station:** WLQR 1470-AM.

PA Announcer: Kevin Mullan. **Official Scorers:** Jeff Businger, Ron Klenfelter, Guy Lammers.

Stadium Name: Fifth Third Field. **Location:** From Ohio Turnpike 80/90, exit 54 (4A) to I-75 North, follow I-75 North to exit 201-B, left onto Erie Street, right onto Washington Street. From Detroit, I-75 South to exit 202-A, right onto Washington Street. From Dayton, I-75 North to exit 201-B, left onto Erie Street, right on Washington Street. From Ann Arbor, Route 23 South to I-475 East, I-475 east to I-75 South, I-75 South to exit 202-A, right onto Washington Street. **Ticket Price Range:** $9.

Visiting Club Hotel: Park Inn, 101 North Summit, Toledo, OH 43604. **Telephone:** (419) 241-3000.

PACIFIC COAST LEAGUE

PACIFIC COAST LEAGE

TRIPLE-A

Mailing Address: 1631 Mesa Ave., Suite A, Colorado Springs, CO 80906.

Telephone: (719) 636-3399. **Fax:** (719) 636-1199.

E-Mail Address: office@pclbaseball.com. **Website:** www.pclbaseball.com.

President: Branch Rickey.

Vice President: Don Logan (Las Vegas).

Branch Rickey

Directors: Don Beaver (New Orleans), Sam Bernabe (Iowa), Dave Chase (Memphis), Chris Cummings (Fresno), Dave Elmore (Colorado Springs), Kirby Schlegel (Tacoma), Don Logan (Las Vegas), Jay Miller (Round Rock), Larry Miller (Salt Lake), Bill Shea (Omaha), Scott Pruitt (Oklahoma), Merritt Paulson (Portland), Art Savage (Sacramento), John Traub (Albuquerque), Glenn Yaeger (Nashville), Stuart Katzoff (Tucson).

Vice President, Business Operations: George King. **Director, Administration:** Melanie Fiore. **Operations Assistant:** John Meyer.

Division Structure: American Conference—Northern: Iowa, Memphis, Nashville, Omaha. **Southern:** Albuquerque, New Orleans, Oklahoma, Round Rock. **Pacific Conference—Northern:** Colorado Springs, Portland, Salt Lake, Tacoma. **Southern:** Fresno, Las Vegas, Sacramento, Tucson.

Regular Season: 144 games. **2008 Opening Date:** April 3. **Closing Date:** Sept. 1.

All-Star Game: July 16 at Louisville (PCL vs. International League).

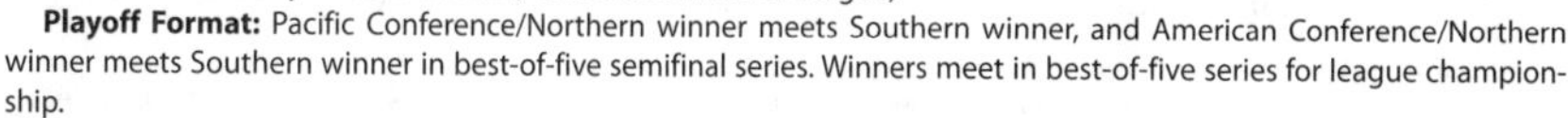

Playoff Format: Pacific Conference/Northern winner meets Southern winner, and American Conference/Northern winner meets Southern winner in best-of-five semifinal series. Winners meet in best-of-five series for league championship.

Triple-A Championship Game: Sept. 18, Oklahoma City (PCL vs. International League).

Roster Limit: 24. **Player Eligibility Rule:** No restrictions.

Brand of Baseball: Rawlings ROM.

Umpires: Dan Bellino (Crystal Lake, IL), Cory Blaser (Westminster, CO), Angel Campos (San Bernadino, CA), Scot Chamberlain (Strawberry Plains, TN), Delfin Colon (San Juan, Puerto Rico), John Coons (Streator, IL), Robert Drake (Mesa, AZ), Stephen Fritzoni (Hesperio, CA), Chris Griffith (Justin, TX), Chris Guccione (Brighton, CO), Jason Kiser (Columbia, MO), Brian Knight (Helena, MT), Barry Larson (Hayden, ID), Jeff Laiter (Gresham, OR), Eric Loveless (Layton, UT), Jeff Macias (Phoenix, AZ), Jonathan Merry (Dahlonega, GA), Casey Moser (Iowa Park, TX), Michael Muchlinski (Ephrata, WA), Shawn Rakos (Orting, WA), Travis Reininger (Brighton, CO), D.J. Reyburn (Nashville, TN), Mark Ripperger (Carlsbad, CA), Will Robinson (Savannah, GA), Todd Tichenor (Holcomb, KS), Chris Tiller (Bullard, TX), Jake Uhlenhopp (Phoenix, AZ), Garrett Watson (Las Vegas, NV).

STADIUM INFORMATION

			Dimensions				
Club	**Stadium**	**Opened**	**LF**	**CF**	**RF**	**Capacity**	**2007 Att.**
Albuquerque	Isotopes Park	2003	340	400	340	13,279	563,686
Colorado Springs	Security Service Field	1988	350	410	350	8,400	274,408
Fresno	Chukchansi Park	2002	324	402	335	12,500	520,093
Iowa	Principal Park	1992	335	400	335	11,000	576,310
Las Vegas	Cashman Field	1983	328	433	328	9,334	371,676
Memphis	AutoZone Park	2000	319	400	322	14,200	633,129
Nashville	Herschel Greer Stadium	1978	327	400	327	10,700	411,959
New Orleans	Zephyr Field	1997	333	405	332	10,000	368,210
Oklahoma	AT&T Bricktown Ballpark	1998	325	400	325	13,066	529,690
Omaha	Johnny Rosenblatt Stadium	1948	332	408	332	24,000	326,627
Portland	PGE Park	1926	319	405	321	19,810	388,963
Round Rock	The Dell Diamond	2000	330	400	325	10,000	662,595
Sacramento	Raley Field	2000	330	405	325	14,111	710,235
Salt Lake	Franklin Covey Field	1994	345	420	315	15,500	466,123
Tacoma	Cheney Stadium	1960	325	425	325	9,600	345,538
Tucson	Tucson Electric Park	1998	340	405	340	11,000	270,853

ALBUQUERQUE ISOTOPES

Office Address: 1601 Avenida Cesar Chavez SE, Albuquerque, NM 87106.
Telephone: (505) 924-2255. **Fax:** (505) 242-8899.
E-Mail address: info@albuquerquebaseball.com. **Website:** www.albuquerquebaseball.com.
Affiliation (first year): Florida Marlins (2003). **Years in League:** 1972-2000, 2003-

OWNERSHIP, MANAGEMENT

President: Ken Young. **Secretary/Treasurer:** Emmett Hammond. **General Manager:** John Traub. **Assistant General Manager, Sales/Marketing:** Nick LoBue. **Director, Box Office/Retail Operations:** Chrissy Baines. **Director, Sales/ Promotions:** Adam Beggs. **Director, Media Relations:** Steve Hurlbert. **Director, Stadium Operations:** Bobby Atencio. **Manager, Suite Relations:** Paul Hartenberger. **Season Ticket/Group Sales Representatives:** Eddie Enriquez, Justin Sommer, Jordan Gillum, Jacob Smith. **Corporate Sales Executive:** Ryan Scherling. **Community Relations/ Marketing Coordinator:** Amanda Martinez. **Coordinator Sponsorships/Promotions:** Lauren Farris. **Bookkeeper:** Cynthia DiFrancesco. **Assistant Director, Retail Operations:** Kara Hayes. **Stadium Operations Assistant:** Chris Taylor. **Assistant Director, Box Office Operations:** Ben Zalewski. **Head Groundskeeper:** Jarad Alley. **Home Clubhouse Manager:** Jonathan Sanchez. **Visiting Clubhouse Manager:** Rick Pollack. **Office Manager:** Susan Martindale. **Ovations Foodservice Concession Manager:** Mike Enostrosa. **Ovations Foodservice Catering Manager:** Sheryl Duran. **Ovations Office Manager:** Jen Stevens.

FIELD STAFF

Manager: Dean Treanor. **Coach:** Steve Phillips. **Pitching Coach:** Rich Gale. **Trainer:** Steve Miller.

GAME INFORMATION

Radio Announcer: Robert Portnoy. **No. of Games Broadcast:** Home-72 Road-72. **Flagship Station:** KNML 610-AM.

PA Announcer: Stu Walker. **Official Scorers:** Gary Herron, John Miller.

Stadium Name: Isotopes Park. **Location:** From 1-25, exit east on Avenida Cesar Chavez SE to University Boulevard. From I-40, exit south on University Boulevard SE to Avenida Cesar Chavez. **Standard Game Times:** 7:05 p.m., 6:35 Sunday. **Ticket Price Range:** $5-20.

Visiting Club Hotel: MCM Elegante, 2020 Menaul NE, Albuquerque, NM 87107. **Telephone:** (505) 884-2511.

COLORADO SPRINGS SKY SOX

Office Address: 4385 Tutt Blvd, Colorado Springs, CO 80922.
Telephone: (719) 597-1449. **Fax:** (719) 597-2491.
E-Mail address: info@skysox.com. **Website:** www.skysox.com.
Affiliation (first year): Colorado Rockies (1993). **Years in League:** 1988-

OWNERSHIP, MANAGEMENT

Operated By: Colorado Springs Sky Sox Inc.

Principal Owner: David Elmore.

President/General Manager: Tony Ensor. **Senior Vice President, Marketing:** Rai Henniger. **Asst. GM/Director, Sales:** Jeff Windle. **Asst. GM/Director, Public Relations:** Mike Hobson. **General Manager/Diamond Creations:** Don Giuliano. **Director, Broadcast Operations:** Dan Karcher. **Director, Promotions:** Matt Person. **Accountant:** Kelly Hanlon. **Director, Ticket Sales:** Whitney Shellem. **Director, Community Relations:** Ira Liebman. **Director, Group Sales:** Adam Sciorsci. **Asst. Director, Group Sales:** Keith Hodges. **Group Sales/Ticket Operations:** Chip Dreamer. **Group Sales Manager:** Brien Smith. **Special Events Manager:** Chad Miller. **Graphics Manager/Merchandise:** Erin Eads. **Head Groundskeeper:** Steve DeLeon. **Administrative Assistant:** Marianne Paine. **Home Clubhouse Manager:** Ricky Grima. **Visiting Clubhouse Manager:** Steve Martin. **Marketing Representatives:** Jim Aborn, Nick Armstrong, Jon Eddy, Amy Fortman, Greg Ralph, David Rose, Justin Rosenberg.

FIELD STAFF

Manager: Tom Runnells. **Coach:** Rene Lachemann. **Pitching Coach:** Chuck Kniffin. **Trainer:** Heath Townsend.

GAME INFORMATION

Radio Announcer: Dan Karcher, Ira Liebmann. **No. of Games Broadcast:** Home-72 Road-72. **Flagship Station:** KZNT 1460-AM.

PA Announcer: Chip Dreamer. **Official Scorer:** Marty Grantz, Rich Wastler.

Stadium Name: Security Service Field. **Location:** I-25 South to Woodmen Road exit, east on Woodmen to Powers Boulevard, right on Powers to Barnes Road. **Standard Game Times:** 7:05 p.m.; Sun. 1:05. **Ticket Price Range:** $5-11.

Visiting Club Hotel: La Quinta Inn, Garden of the Gods, 4385 Sinton Rd., Colorado Springs, CO 80907. **Telephone:** (719) 528-5060.

FRESNO GRIZZLIES

Office Address: 1800 Tulare St, Fresno, CA 93721.
Telephone: (559) 320-4487. **Fax:** (559) 264-0795.
E-Mail address: info@fresnogrizzlies.com. **Website:** www.fresnogrizzlies.com.
Affiliation (first year): San Francisco Giants (1998). **Years in League:** 1998-

OWNERSHIP, MANAGEMENT

Operated By: Fresno Baseball Club, LLC.

Executive Vice Presidents: Andrew Stuebner, Mike Maiorana. **VP, Operations:** Garret Fahrmann. **VP, Tickets:** Tom Backemeyer. **VP, Marketing:** Scott Carter. **Director, Community Relations:** Danielle Cabral. **Director, Entertainment/ Publications:** Krista Boyd. **Director, Business Development:** Josh Phanco. **Director, Event Opearations:** Jason Hannold. **Director, Finance:** SuSin Correa. **Director, Group Sales:** Shaun Northup. **Director, Inside Sales:** Derek Franks. **Director, Marketing/Corporate Partnerships:** Jeff Benton. **Director, Mascot Relations/Corporate Sales:** Brad Collins. **Director, Media/Public Relations:** Paul Kennedy. **Director, Sponsorship Services:** Michelle Sanchez. **Director, Special Events:** Andrew Melrose. **Director, Stadium Operations:** Harvey Kawasaki. **Director, Tickets:** Paul Zilm. **Account Executives:** Freddie Dominguez Jr., Ray Ortiz. **Manager, Corporate Accounts/Special Events:** Courtney Jantz. **Corporate Partnership Executive:** Jon DeChambeau. **Finance Managers:** Murray Shamp, Karen Thomas, Monica De La Cerda. **Group Sales Manager:** Peter Marthedal. **Group Sales Account Executive:** Ryan Stos. **Merchandise Managers:** Mia Flores, Stephanie Harman. **Operations Managers:** Ira Calvin. **Manager, Sponsorship Services:** Meredith Peyton. **Manager, Ticket Sales:** Sebastian Biagioni. **Seating Coordinator:** Ashley Tennel. **Community Relations Coordinator:** Daniel Newman. Receptionist: DeeAnn Hernandez.

FIELD STAFF

Manager: Dan Rohn. **Coach:** Jim Bowie. **Pitching Coach:** Mike Caldwell. **Trainer:** Anthony Reyes.

GAME INFORMATION

Radio Announcer: Doug Greenwald. **No of Games Broadcast:** Home-72 Road-72. **Flagship Station:** 790-AM ESPN2.

Official Scorer: Unavailable.

Stadium Name: Chukchansi Park. **Location:** From 99 North, take Frsno Street exit, left on Fresno Street, left on Inyo or Tulare to stadium. From 99 South, take Fresno Street exit, left on Fresno Street, right on Broadway to H Street. From 41 North, take Van Ness exit toward Fresno, left Van Ness, left on Inyo or Tulare, stadium is straight ahead. From 41 South, take Tulare exit, stadium is located at Tulare and H Streets, or take Van Ness exit, right on Van Ness, left on lyno or Tulare, stadium is straight ahead. **Ticket Price Range:** $5-15.

Visiting Club Hotel: Radisson Hotel Fresno, 2233 Ventura St, Fresno, CA 93721. **Telephone:** (559) 441-2931.

IOWA CUBS

Office Address: One Line Dr, Des Moines, IA 50309.
Telephone: (515) 243-6111. **Fax:** (515) 243-5152.
E-Mail address: info@iowacubs.com. **Website:** www.iowacubs.com.
Affiliation (first year): Chicago Cubs (1981). **Years in League:** 1969-

OWNERSHIP, MANAGEMENT

Operated By: Raccoon Baseball Inc.

Chairman, Principal Owner: Michael Gartner. **Executive Vice President:** Michael Giudicessi.

President, General Manager: Sam Bernabe. **Vice President/Assistant GM:** Jim Nahas. **VP, CFO:** Sue Tollefson. **VP/Director, Stadium Operations:** Tom Greene. **VP/Director, Broadcast Operations:** Deene Ehlis. **Director, Media Relations:** Jeff Lantz. **Coordinator, Public Relations:** Andrea Breen. **Director, Logistics:** Scott Sailor. **Group Sales Coordinators:** Kenny Houser, Lindsay Cox. **Director, Sales:** Rich Gilman. **Director, Luxury Suites:** Brent Conkel. **Ticket Office Manager:** Katie Hogan. **Manager, Stadium Operations:** Jeff Tilley. **Assistant Manager, Stadium Operations:** Janelle Videgar. **Corporate Sales Executives:** Mark Dempsey, Melanie Doser, Nate Teut. **Corporate Relations:** Red Hollis. **Head Groundskeeper:** Chris Schlosser. **Director, Merchandise:** Amber Gartner. **Coordinator, Merchandise:** Rick Giudicessi. **Accountant:** Lori Auten. **Manager, Cub Club:** Bob Thormeier. **Director, Information Systems:** Larry Schunk. **Office Manager:** Betsy Duncan. **Landscape Coordinator:** Shari Kramer.

FIELD STAFF

Manager: Pat Listach. **Coach:** Von Joshua. **Pitching Coach:** Mike Mason. **Trainer:** Matt Johnson.

GAME INFORMATION

Radio Announcer: Deene Ehlis. **No of Games Broadcast:** Home-72 Road-72. **Flagship Station:** KXNO 1460-AM.

PA Announcers: Geoff Conn, Mark Pierce. **Official Scorers:** Dirk Brinkmeyer, Brian Gibson, Mike Mahon.

Stadium Name: Principal Park. **Location:** I-80 or I-35 to I-235, to Third Street exit, south on Third Street, left on Line Drive. **Standard Game Times:** 7:05 p.m.; **12:**05; 1:05 Sundays. **Ticket Price Range:** $6-11.

Visiting Club Hotel: Valley West Inn, 3535 Westown Pkwy, West Des Moines, IA 50266. **Telephone:** (515) 225-2524.

LAS VEGAS 51S

Office Address: 850 Las Vegas Blvd. North, Las Vegas, NV 89101.
Telephone: (702) 386-7200. **Fax:** (702) 386-7214.
E-Mail address: info@lv51.com. **Website:** www.lv51.com.
Affiliation (first year): Los Angeles Dodgers (2001). **Years in League:** 1983-.

OWNERSHIP, MANAGEMENT

Operated By: Stevens Baseball Group.

CEO: Derek Stevens. **President, General Manager:** Don Logan. **Executive Vice President:** Allen Taylor. **Assistant GM/VP, Marketing:** Chuck Johnson. **VP, Sales/Marketing:** Mike Hollister. **VP, Ticket Operations:** Mike Rodriguez. **VP, Operations/Security:** Nick Fitzenreider. **Special Assistant to GM:** Bob Blum. **Director, Business Development:** Derek Eige. **Director, Broadcasting:** Russ Langer. **Manager, Community Relations:** Larry Brown. **Manager, Baseball Administration:** Denise Korach. **Media Relations Director:** Jim Gemma. **Administrative Assistants:** Pat Dressel, Michelle Taggart. **Managers, Corporate Marketing:** Erik Eisenberg, Isaiah Flynn, Melissa Harkavy, Bruce Simons. **Merchandise Coordinator:** Ashley Reese. **Sponsorship Services Manager:** William Graham. **Interns:** Brad Burton, Matthew Simons, Julius Wood. **Operations Manager:** Chip Vespe.

FIELD STAFF

Manager: Lorenzo Bundy. **Hitting Coach:** Unavailable. **Pitching Coach:** Jim Slaton. **Trainer:** Greg Harrel.

GAME INFORMATION

Radio Announcer: Russ Langer. **No. of Games Broadcast:** Home-72 Road-72. **Flagship Station:** Fox Sports Radio 920-AM.

PA Announcer: Dan Bickmore. **Official Scorer:** Mark Wasik.

Stadium Name: Cashman Field. **Location:** I-15 to U.S. 95 exit (downtown), east to Las Vegas Boulevard North exit, one-half mile north to stadium. **Standard Game Time:** 7:05 p.m. **Ticket Price Range:** $8-13.

Visiting Club Hotel: Golden Nugget Hotel & Casino, 129 Fremont Street, Las Vegas, NV 89101. **Telephone:** (702) 385-7111.

MEMPHIS REDBIRDS

Office Address: 175 Toyota Plaza, Suite 300, Memphis, TN 38103.
Telephone: (901) 721-6000. **Fax:** (901) 842-1222.
Website: www.memphisredbirds.com
Affiliation (first year): St. Louis Cardinals (1998). **Years in League:** 1998-

OWNERSHIP, MANAGEMENT

Operated By: Memphis Redbirds Baseball Foundation, Inc. **Founders:** Dean Jernigan, Kristi Jernigan.

President/General Manager: Dave Chase. **Senior Vice President, Sales:** Pete Rizzo. **Vice President, Community Relations:** Reggie Williams. **Director of Baseball Operations:** Tony Martin. **Director of Marketing:** Jason Potter. **Controller:** Garry Condrey. **Accounting Specialist:** Leslie Wilkes. **Manager, Ticket Sales:** Ryan Thompson. **Media Relations Manager:** Kyle Parkinson. **Manager, Ticket Operations:** Mark Anderson. **Marketing Coordinator:** Harrison Lampley. **Event Sales Coordinator:** Devyn Parkinson. **Graphics Coordinator:** Allison Rhoades. **Coordinator, Premium Seats/Foundation Services:** Kela Jones. **Programs Coordinator:** Corey Gillum. **Mascot Coordinator:** Chris Pegg. **Retail Supervisor:** Starr Taiani. **Senior Account Executive:** Rob Edgerton. **Account Executives:** Mindy Campbell, Terry Colbert. **Sales Coordinator:** Katie Reid. **Executive Assistant:** Cindy Compton. **Senior Ticket Sales Executive:** Lisa Shurden. **Ticket Sales Executives:** Adam Shelton, Valerie Hight. **Office Coordinator:** Linda Smith. **Head Groundskeeper:** Ed Collins. **Chief Engineer:** Danny Abbott. **Maintenance:** Spencer Shields.

FIELD STAFF

Manager: Chris Maloney. **Coach:** Mark Budaska. **Pitching Coach:** Blaise Ilsley. **Trainer:** Chris Conroy.

GAME INFORMATION

Radio Announcer: Steve Selby. **No of Games Broadcast:** Home-72 Road-72. **Flagship Station:** WHBQ 560-AM.

PA Announcer: Tim Van Horn. **Official Scorer:** J.J. Guinozzo.

Stadium Name: AutoZone Park. **Location:** North on I-240, exit at Union Avenue West, one and half mile to park. **Standard Game Times:** 7:05 p.m.; Saturday 6:05; Sunday 2:05. **Ticket Price Range:** $5-17.

Visiting Club Hotel: Sleep Inn at Court Square, 40 N. Front, Memphis, TN 38103. **Telephone:** (901) 522-9700.

NASHVILLE SOUNDS

Office Address: 534 Chestnut Street, Nashville, TN 37203.
Telephone: (615) 242-4371. **Fax:** (615) 256-5684.

E-Mail address: info@nashvillesounds.com. **Website:** www.nashvillesounds.com
Affiliation (first year): Milwaukee Brewers (2005). **Years in League:** 1998-

OWNERSHIP, MANAGEMENT

Operated By: AmeriSports LLC.
President/Owner: Al Gordon.
General Manager: Glenn Yaeger. **Assistant GM, Operations:** Joe Hart. **Assistant GM, Ticket Sales/Marketing:** Brandon Vonderharr. **Assistant GM, Communications/Baseball Operations: Doug Scopel. Assistant GM, Sponsorship Sales:** Jason Bennett. **Assistant GM:** Chris Snyder. **Director, Accounting:** Barb Walker. **Director, Ticketing:** Ricki Schlabach. **Director, Food/Beverage:** Mark Lawrence. **Director, Stadium Operations:** Nick Barkley. **Director, Broadcasting:** Chuck Valenches. **Asst. Director, Food/Beverage:** P.J. Harrison. **Manager, Community Relations:** Amy Smith. **Manager, Food/ Beverage:** Cameron Claiborne. **Manager, Entertainment:** Buddy Yelton. **Manager, Promotions/Marketing:** Kali Mork. **Manager, Sales:** Andrew Chelton, Becky Davis. **Director, Faith Nights:** Ryan Bennett. **Office Manager:** Sharon Ridley. **Head Groundskeeper:** Peter Lockwood. **Clubhouse Manager:** J.R. Rinaldi, Thomas Miller, Peter Thomashefski.

FIELD STAFF

Manager: Frank Kremblas. **Coach:** Harry Spilman. **Pitching Coach:** Stan Kyles. **Trainer:** Jeff Paxson. **Strength/ Conditioning Coach:** Nigel Price.

GAME INFORMATION

Radio Announcer: Chuck Valenches. **No of Games Broadcast:** Home-72 Road-72. **Flagship Station:** WNSR 560-AM.
PA Announcer: Eric Berner. **Official Scorers:** Eric Jones, Trevor Garrett.
Stadium Name: Herschel Greer Stadium. **Location:** I-65 to Wedgewood exit, west to Eighth Avenue, right on Eighth to Chestnut Street, right on Chestnut. Standard Game Times: 6 p.m. (April, Aug.), 7 p.m. (May-July); Wed. noon; Sat. 6, Sun. 2 (April-May), 6 (June-Sept.). **Ticket Price Range:** $6-10.
Visiting Club Hotel: Holiday Inn Select, 2613 West End Ave, Nashville, TN 37203. **Telephone:** (615) 327-4707.

NEW ORLEANS ZEPHYRS

Office Address: 6000 Airline Dr, Metairie, LA 70003.
Telephone: (504) 734-5155. **Fax:** (504) 734-5118.
E-Mail address: zephyrs@zephyrsbaseball.com. **Website:** www.zephyrsbaseball.com.
Affiliation (first year): New York Mets (2007). **Years in League:** 1998-

OWNERSHIP, MANAGEMENT

Operated By: New Orleans Zephyrs Baseball Club, LLC.
Managing Partner/President: Don Beaver. **COO/Executive Director:** Ron Maestri. **General Manager:** Mike Schline. **Director, Community Relations:** Marc Allen. **Director, Broadcasting/Team Travel:** Tim Grubbs. **Director, Operations:** Todd Wilson. **Director, Marketing/Special Events:** Jaime Burchfield. **Director, Ticket Operations:** Kathy Kaleta. **Director, Finance:** Kim Topp. **Promotions, Director:** Jessica DeOro. **Director, Media Relations:** Kevin Maney. **Group Sales Director:** Leah Rigby. **Group Sales Representatives:** Jordan Price, Lindsey Rall. **Corporate Sales Executive:** Melissa Mahony. **Merchandise Manager:** Dan Zajac. **Head Groundskeeper:** Thomas Marks. **Assistant Groundskeeper:** Craig Shaffer. **Maintenance Coordinator:** Bill Rowell. **Assistant Director, Operations:** Brandon Thomas. **Media Relations Assistant:** Dave Sachs. **Ticket Operations Assistant:** Katie Bonaccorso. **Receptionist:** Susan Hirar. **Director of Operations, Messina's Inc.:** George Messina. **Administrative Assistant, Messina's Inc.:** Priscilla Arbello. **Catering Manager, Messina's Inc.:** Kristen Wahl. **Conncessions Manager, Messina's Inc.:** Darin Yuratich.

FIELD STAFF

Manager: Ken Oberkfell. **Coach:** Jack Voigt. **Pitching Coach:** Dan Warthen. **Trainer:** Brian Chicklo. **Strength Coach:** Ken Coward.

GAME INFORMATION

Radio Announcers: Tim Grubbs, Ron Swoboda. **Color Analyst/Speakers Bureau:** Ron Swoboda. **No. of Games Broadcast:** Home-72 Road-72. **Flagship Station:** WIST 690-AM.
PA Announcer: Doug Moreau. **Official Scorer:** J.L. Vangilder.
Stadium Name: Zephyr Field. **Location:** I-10 West toward Baton Rouge, exit at Clearview Pkwy (exit 226) and continues south, right on Airline Drive (U.S. 61 North) for 1 mile, stadium on left. From airport, take Airline Drive (U.S. 61) east for 4 miles, stadium on right. **Standard Game Times:** 7 p.m.; Sat. 6; Sun. 2. **Ticket Price Range:** $6-10.
Visiting Club Hotel: Best Western-St. Christopher, 114 Magazine St., New Orleans, LA 70130. **Telephone:** (504) 648-0444.

OKLAHOMA REDHAWKS

Office Address: 2 S. Mickey Mantle Dr, Oklahoma City, OK 73104.
Telephone: (405) 218-1000. **Fax:** (405) 218-1001.
E-Mail address: info@oklahomaredhawks.com. **Website:** www.oklahomaredhawks.com.

Affiliation (first year): Texas Rangers (1983). **Years in League:** 1963-1968, 1998-

OWNERSHIP, MANAGEMENT

Operated By: Oklahoma Baseball Club LLC.

Principal Owner: Robert Funk. **Managing General Partner:** Scott Pruitt.

Executive Director: John Allgood. **CFO:** Steve McEwen. **Director, Public Relations/Assistant to Managing General Partner:** Holly McGowen. **Director, Facility Operations:** Harlan Budde. **Director, Operations:** Mike Prange. **Director, Sponsorships:** Mark Pritchard. **Director, Multimedia Sales:** David Patterson. **Director, Special Events:** Mary Ramsey. **Senior Accountant:** Nicole Wise. **Promotions Manager:** Brandon Baker. **Ticket Operations Manager:** Armando Reyes. **Account Executives:** Jason Black, Lisa Ptak, Andrew Barton, Rusty Wiley, Jeff Hawkins Erich Wendt. **Group Sales Account Executives:** Megan Morgan, Larissa Wolfe. **Clubhouse Manager:** Russ Oliver. **Head Groundskeeper:** Monte McCoy.

FIELD STAFF

Manager: Bobby Jones. **Coach:** Randy Whisler. **Pitching Coach:** Andy Hawkins. **Trainer:** Lee Slagle.

GAME INFORMATION

Radio Announcer: Jim Byers. **No of Games Broadcast:** Home-72 Road-72. **Flagship Station:** KEBC 1340 AM.

PA Announcer: Matt Gierat. **Official Scorers:** Mike Treps, Justin Tinder.

Stadium Name: AT&T Bricktown Ballpark. **Location:** Near interchange of I-235 and I-40, take Lincoln exit off I-40 to Reno, west on Reno to ballpark.. **Standard Game Times:** 7:05 p.m.; Sunday 2:05 (April-May), 7:05 (June-August). **Ticket Price Range:** $6-15.

Visiting Club Hotel: Courtyard Oklahoma City Downtown/Bricktown, 2 West Reno Ave., Oklahoma City, OK 73102. **Telephone:** (405) 235-2780.

OMAHA ROYALS

Office Address: Rosenblatt Stadium, 1202 Bert Murphy Ave, Omaha, NE 68107.

Telephone: (402) 734-2550. **Fax:** (402) 734-7166.

E-Mail address: info@oroyals.com. **Website:** www.oroyals.com.

Affiliation (first year): Kansas City Royals (1969). **Years in League:** 1998-

OWNERSHIP, MANAGEMENT

Operated By: Omaha Royals Limited Partnership.

Principal Owners: William Shea, Warren Buffett, Walter Scott.

President: Alan M. Stein. **General Manager:** Martie Cordaro. **VP, Baseball Operations:** Kyle Fisher. **Assistant GM, Group Sales:** Eric Leach. **Director, Marketing:** Rob Crain. **Director, Broadcasting:** Mark Nasser. **Director, Media Relations:** Kevin McNabb. **Director, Community Relations:** Lesley Crutcher. **Director, Ticket Operations:** Jeff Gogerty. **Merchandise Manager:** Jason Kinney. **Group Sales Executives:** Paul Hammes, Adam Kelly, Andrea Stava. **Corporate Sales Executive:** Michael Jermain. **Adminstrative Assistants:** Kay Besta, Lois Biggs. **Marketing/Community Relations Intern:** Ty Cobb. **Group Sales Intern:** Nick Bates. **Ticket Operations Intern:** James Jensen. **Head Groundskeeper:** Jesse Cuevas. **General Manager, CenterPlate Concessions:** Ryan Slane.

FIELD STAFF

Manager: Mike Jirschele. **Coach:** Terry Bradshaw. **Pitching Coach:** Tom Burgmeier. **Trainer:** Unavailable.

GAME INFORMATION

Radio Announcers: Mark Nasser, Kevin McNabb. **No of Games Broadcast:** Home-72 Road-72. **Flagship Station:** News Talk 1420-AM.

PA Announcers: Paul Cohen, Craig Evans, Bill Jensen. **Official Scorers:** Frank Adkisson, Kent Poncelow, Ryan White.

Stadium Name: Rosenblatt Stadium. **Location:** South off I-80 on 13th Street. **Ticket Price Range:** $6-10. **Standard Game Times:** Monday-Thursday, 6:35 p.m. (April-May), 7:05 p.m. (June-August); Friday/Saturday, 7:05 p.m.; Sunday, 1:35 p.m. **Visiting Club Hotel:** Holiday Inn at Ameristar, 2202 River Rd, Council Bluffs, IA 51501. **Telephone:** (712) 322-5050.

PORTLAND BEAVERS

Office Address: 1844 SW Morrison, Portland, OR 97205.

Telephone: (503) 553-5400. **Fax:** (505) 553-5405.

E-Mail address: info@pgepark.com. **Website:** www.portlandbeavers.com.

Affiliation (first year): San Diego Padres (2001). **Years in League:** 1903-1917, 1919-72, 1978-1993, 2001-

OWNERSHIP, MANAGEMENT

Operated By: Shortstop, LLC.

President/GM: Merritt Paulson. **VP, Business Development/Broadcasting:** Ryan Brach. **VP, Baseball Operations/Communications:** Chris Metz. **VP, Operations:** Ken Puckett. **Senior Advisor:** Jack Cain. **Senior Director, Ticket Sales:** Joe Cote. **Senior Director, Business Operations/Marketing:** Cory Dolich. **Senior Director, Finance/Human Resources:** Martin Harvey. **Director, Corporate Partnerships:** Rick Barr. **Director, Ticket Operations:** Ben Hoel. **Director,**

Promotions: Jadira Ruiz. **Director, Community Outreach:** Keri Stoller. **Senior Manager, Season Ticket Accounts:** Dan Zusman. **Manager, Group Sales:** Ashley Bedford. **Managers, Partner Services:** Amy Lilly, Suzy Stride. **Manager, Corporate Partnerships:** Nate Liberman. **Corporate Ticket Sales Account Executive:** Brian Pollard. **Manager, Housekeeping:** Brian Kennedy. **Manager, Facility Maintenance:** Dave Tankersley. **Manager, Guest Services:** Andrea Tolonen. **Manager, Creative Services:** Ryan Wantland. **Coordinator, Media Relations:** Marc Kostic. **Coordinator, Ticket Sales Coordinator/Executive Assistant:** Patti Peters. **Account Executives, Group Ticket Sales:** Erin Andrews, Alison Mathes, Kyle Veach. **Account Executives, Corporate Ticket Sales:** Tim Hagerty, Nick Jensen. **Senior Accounting Clerk:** Penny Bishop. **Receptionist/Office Manager:** Jeanne Nichols. **Head Groundskeeper:** Jesse Smith. **Home Clubhouse Manager:** Shane Hickenbottom. **Visiting Clubhouse Manager:** Tyler Neves.

FIELD STAFF

Manager: Randy Ready. **Coach:** Max Venable. **Pitching Coach:** Glenn Abbott. **Trainer:** Unavailable.

GAME INFORMATION

Radio Announcer: Rich Burk. **No. of Games Broadcast:** Home-72 Road-72. **Flagship Station:** KKAD 1550-AM.

PA Announcer: Mike Stone. **Official Scorer:** Blair Cash.

Stadium Name: PGE Park. **Location:** I-450 to West Burnside exit, SW 20th Street to park. **Standard Game Times:** 7:05 p.m.; **Sun. 2:**05. **Ticket Price Range:** $8-14.

Visiting Club Hotel: Doubletree Hotel-Portland Lloyd Center, 1000 NE Multnomah, Portland, OR 97232. **Telephone:** (503) 281-6111.

ROUND ROCK EXPRESS

Office Address: 3400 East Palm Valley Blvd., Round Rock, TX 78664.
Telephone: (512) 255-2255. **Fax:** (512) 255-1558.
E-Mail Address: info@rrexpress.com. **Website:** www.roundrockexpress.com
Affiliation (first year): Houston Astros (2005). **Year in League:** 2005-

OWNERSHIP, MANAGEMENT

Operated By: Ryan Sanders Baseball, LP.

Principal Owners: Eddie Maloney, Jay Miller, Nolan Ryan, Reese Ryan, Reid Ryan, Don Sanders, Brad Sanders, Bret Sanders.

President: Jay Miller. **Vice President, General Manager:** Dave Fendrick. **Controller:** Debbie Coughlin. **Director, Communications:** Avery Holton. **Director, Community Relations:** Heather Tantimonaco. **Director, Ballpark Entertainment:** Clint Musslewhite. **Director, Merchandising (Ryan-Sanders Baseball):** Brooke Milam. **Director, Ticket Operations:** Ross Scott. **Director, United Heritage Center:** Scott Allen. **Director, Special Events:** Laura Whatley. **Director, Group Sales:** Henry Green. **Director, Sales:** Gary Franke. **Director, Marketing Development:** Gregg Miller. **Account Executives:** Brent Green, Richard Tapia. **Receptionist:** Wendy Gordon. **Field Superintendent:** Brad Detmore. **Director, Broadcasting:** Mike Capps. **Clubhouse Manager:** Kenny Bufton. **Visiting Clubhouse Manager:** Kevin Taylor. **Assistant Manager, The Railyard Retail Store:** Nikki Lopez, Debbie Goodman. **Director, Stadium Operations:** Mark Maloney. **Director, Stadium Maintenance:** Aurelio Martinez. **Housekeeping:** Ofelia Gonzalez.

FIELD STAFF

Manager: Dave Clark. **Coaches:** Ron Jackson, Burt Hooton. **Trainer:** Mike Freer.

GAME INFORMATION

Radio Announcer: Mike Capps. **No. of Games Broadcast:** Home-72 Road-72. **Flagship Station:** 1530-AM.

PA Announcer: Clint Musslewhite. **Official Scorer:** Tommy Tate, Avery Holton.

Stadium Name: The Dell Diamond. **Location:** Take I-35 North to Exit 253 (Highway 79 East/Taylor). Highway 79 east for 31/2 miles. Stadium on left. **Standard Game Times:** 7:05 p.m., 2:05. Ticket Price Range: $5-12.

Visiting Club Hotel: Hilton Garden Inn, 2310 N IH-35, Round Rock, TX 78681. **Telephone:** (512) 341-8200.

SACRAMENTO RIVER CATS

Office Address: 400 Ballpark Dr, West Sacramento, CA 95691.
Telephone: (916) 376-4700. **Fax:** (916) 376-4710.
E-Mail address: info@rivercats.com. **Website:** www.rivercats.com.
Affiliation (first year): Oakland Athletics (2000). **Years in League:** 1903, 1909-11, 1918-60, 1974-76, 2000-

OWNERSHIP, MANAGEMENT

Operated By: Sacramento River Cats Baseball Club, LLC.

CEO: Art Savage. **President, General Manager/COO:** Alan Ledford. **Executive Vice Presidents:** Bob Hemond, Warren Smith. **Vice President, Finance/Project Development:** Jeff Savage. **General Counsel:** Matthew Re. **Executive Assistant:** Gay Caputo. **Senior VP/CFO:** Dan Vistica. **Manager, Financial Reporting/Controls:** Stan Kelly. **Senior Accounting/IT Support:** Jess Olivares. **Accounting Clerk:** Madeline Forma. **Financial Consultant:** Jeff Savage.

Assistant GM/Director, Media Relations: Gabe Ross. **Coordinator, Media/Community Relations:** Jimmy Spencer. **Vice President, Corporate Partnerships/Broadcasting:** Darrin Gross. **Director, Corporate Partnership:** Scott Druskin. **Director, Corporate Services:** Jennifer Maiwald. **Account Executive, Corporate Partnerships:** Kevin Hilton. **Coordinators, Corporate Services:** Kris Stringfellow, Delia Estrada, Kacie McDaniel. **Manager, Luxury Suites:** Ryan Von Sossan. **Administrative Assistant:** Jamie Easterly. **VP, Ticket Sales/Marketing:** Ripper Hatch. **Director, Ticket Sales:** Chad Collins. **Director, Ticket Operations:** Steve Hill. **Senior Manager, Special Projects:** Jennifer Maxwell. **Manager, Group Sales:** Creighton Kahoalii. **Manager, Inside Sales:** Chris Dreesman. **Manager, Ticket Operations:** Jennifer Tokuyama. **Senior Coordinator, Ticket Services:** Matt Togami. **Managers, Season Ticket Accounts:** Scott Kemp, Christi Lorenson. **Senior Group Event Executive:** Jamie Free. **Group Event Executives:** Melanie Levy, Andrew Halford, Ross Johnson. **Account Executives, Corporate Sales:** Hovik Khosrovian, Bryan Iredell, Steve Gracio, Mike Luevano. **Vice President/Chief Marketing Officer:** Andy Fiske. **Senior Manager, Marketing:** Danna Bubalo. **Manager, Creative Production:** Mark Matus. **Creative Department Graphic Artist:** Mike Villareal. **Coordinator, Website Research:** Brent Savage. **Senior Director, Community Relations:** Tony Asaro. **VP, Stadium Operations/Special Events:** Matt Larose. **Senior Director, Operations:** Matt Thomas. **Manager, Grounds:** Dave Vander Heyden. **Senior Coordinator, Event Services:** Carla Mosher. **Coordinator, Stadium Operations:** Mario Constancio. **Coordinator, Guest Services:** Kaitlyn Couch. **Receptionist:** Valerie Vander Heyden. **Engineer:** Javier Navarro. **Day Porter:** Alexandra Ortiz. **Manager, Field Events/Entertainment:** Stephanie Spees. S**enior Coordinator, Operations:** Whitney Tool. **Coordinator, Field Events/Entertainment:** Sarah Perkovich. **Chief Engineer:** Shaun Meyer. **On Deck Shop Manager:** Jamie Von Sossan. **Coordinator, Merchandise:** Daniel Fenstermaker.

FIELD STAFF

Manager: Todd Steverson. **Hitting Coach:** Brian McArn. **Pitching Coach:** Rick Rodriguez. **Trainer:** Brad LaRosa.

GAME INFORMATION

Radio Announcers: Johnny Doskow, Jose Reynoso. **No. of Games Broadcast:** Home-72 Road-72. **Flagship Station:** KTKZ 1380-AM, KCFA 106.1-FM (Spanish).

PA Announcer: Mark Standriff. **Official Scorers:** Brian Berger, Ryan Bjork, Mark Honbo.

Stadium Name: Raley Field. **Location:** I-5 to Business-80 West, exit at Jefferson Boulevard. **Standard Game Time:** 7:05 p.m. **Ticket Price Range:** $5-18.

Visiting Club Hotel: Holiday Inn, Capitol Plaza, 300 J St., Sacramento, CA 95814. **Telephone:** (916) 446-0100.

SALT LAKE BEES

Office Address: 77 W. 1300 South, Salt Lake City, UT 84115.
Mailing Address: P.O. Box 4108, Salt Lake City, UT 84110.
Telephone: (801) 325-BEES. **Fax:** (801) 485-6818.
E-Mail Address: info@slbees.com. **Website:** www.slbees.com.
Affiliation (first year): Los Angeles Angels (2001). **Years in League:** 1915-25, 1958-65, 1970-84, 1994-.

OWNERSHIP, MANAGEMENT

Operated by: Larry H. Miller Baseball Inc.

Principal Owner: Larry Miller.

President: Randy Rigby. **Senior Vice President, Business Operations/CFO:** Robert Hyde. **Senior VP, Broadcasting:** Chris Baum. **Senior VP, Facilities:** Scott Williams. **Vice President/General Manager:** Marc Amicone. **Vice President, Finance:** John Larson. **Senior VP, Sales/Marketing:** Jim Olson. **VP, Communications:** Linda Luchetti. **VP, Marketing:** Eric Schulz. **Senior VP, Strategic Partnerships/Advertising:** Mike Snarr. **Assistant GM, Director, Corporate Sales:** Brad Tammen. **Controllers:** Travis Court, Nathan Kenyon. **Director, Ticket Sales:** Casey Patterson. **Director, Broadcasting:** Steve Klauke. **Communications Coordinator:** Hannah Lee. **Box Office Manager:** Laura Russell. **Corporate Sponsorship Executive:** Derek Cullimore. **Ticket/Group Sales Executive:** Brian Prutch. **Ticket Sales Executives:** Rob Long, Ryan O'Connor. **Team Photographer:** Brent Asay. **Director, Events/Booking:** Mark Powell. **Vice President, Public Safety:** Jim Bell. **Vice President, Food Services:** Mark Stedman. **Concession Manager:** Dave Dalton.

FIELD STAFF

Manager: Bobby Mitchell. **Coach:** Jim Eppard. **Pitching Coach:** Charles Nagy. **Trainer:** Armando Rivas.

GAME INFORMATION

Radio Announcer: Steve Klauke. **No. of Games Broadcast:** Home-72, Away-72. **Flagship Station:** ESPN 1230-AM.

PA Announcer: Jeff Reeves. **Official Scorers:** Howard Nakagama, Chuck Scale.

Stadium name: Franklin Covey Field. **Location:** I-15 North/South to 1300 South exit, east to ballpark at West Temple. **Standard Game Times:** 7 p.m., 6:30 (April-May); Sun. 2. **Ticket Price Range:** $7-22.

Visiting Club Hotel: Sheraton City Centre, 150 W. 500 South, Salt Lake City, UT 84101. **Telephone:** (801) 401-2000.

TACOMA RAINIERS

Office Address: 3560 Bridgeport Way West, University Place, WA 98466
Stadium Address: 2502 S. Tyler St., Tacoma, WA 98405.
Telephone: (253) 752-7707, (800) 281-3834. **Fax:** (253) 752-7135.
Website: www.tacomarainiers.com.
Affiliation: Seattle Mariners (1995). **Years in League:** 1904-1905, 1960-

OWNERSHIP, MANAGEMENT

Operated by: Schlegel Sports.

Owners: Bob Schlegel, Kirby Schlegel, Nick Lachey. **President:** Mike McCall. **Board of Directors:** Bob Schlegel, Kirby Schlegel, Nick Lachey, Mike McCall.

Team President: Aaron Artman. **Executive Vice President:** Rebecca King. **Administrative Assistant:** Patti Stacy. **VP, Corporate Sales:** Brian Simpson. **VP, Operations:** Dave McKenna. **VP, Ticket Sales:** Chip Maxon. **Director, Corporate Partner Services:** Jocelyn Hill. **Corporate Partner Services Coordinator:** Kari Hockett. **Director, Ticket Sales:** Shane Santman. **Corporate Sales Managers:** Brett Breece, Josh Baker, Matthew Barron. **Group Event Managers:** Chris Aubertin, Beth Mager, Lindsay Enger. **Director, Customer Service/Special Projects:** Annie Shultz. **Merchandise Manager:** Kacy Roe. **Director, Special Events:** Alyson Jones. **Director, Marketing/Community Development:** Josie Wilkes. **Director, Media Development:** Geoff Corkum. **Director, Game Entertainment:** Danah Wietry. **Director, Finance:** Eric Scott. Head Groundskeeper: Ryan Schutt. **Maintenance Supervisor:** Jim Smith. **Home Clubhouse Manager**: Jeff Bopp. **Visiting Clubhouse Manager:** Rich Arneson.

FIELD STAFF

Manager: Daren Brown. **Coach:** Alonzo Powell. **Pitching Coach:** Dwight Bernard. **Trainer:** Tom Newberg.

GAME INFORMATION

Radio Broadcaster: Mike Curto. **No. of Games Broadcast:** Home-72, Away-72. **Flagship Station:** KHHO 850-AM.

PA Announcer: Craig Sullivan. **Official Scorekeepers:** Gary Brooks, Micahel Jessee.

Stadium Name: Cheney Stadium. **Location:** From I-5, take exit 132 (Highway 16 West) for 1.2 miles to 19th Street East exit, right on Tyler St for 1/3 mile. **Standard Game Times:** 7 p.m.; Sun., 1:35. **Ticket Price Range:** $6-9.

Visiting Club Hotel: Unavailable.

TUCSON SIDEWINDERS

Office Address: 2500 E. Ajo Way, Tucson, AZ 85713.
Mailing Address: P.O. Box 27045, Tucson, AZ 85726.
Telephone: (520) 434-1021. **Fax:** (520) 889-9477.
E-Mail address: mail@tucsonsidewinders.com. **Website:** www.tucsonsidewinders.com.
Affiliation (first year): Arizona Diamondbacks (1998). **Years in League:** 1969-

OWNERSHIP, MANAGEMENT

Operated By: SK Baseball.

Previous Owner/Consultant: Jay Zucker.

General Manager: Rick Parr. **Assistant GM:** Sean Smock. **Director, Group Sales:** Brian Moss. **Director, Media Relations:** Landon Q. Vincent. **Director, Broadcasting:** Ryan Radtke. **Director, Promotions/Community Relations:** Naomi Proano. **Director, Stadium Operations:** Matthew Burke. **Director, Ticket Operations:** Brad Hudecek. **Director, Inside Sales:** Sandy Davis. **Director, Merchandising:** Kimberly Levin. **Account Executive:** Dan Izzo. **Group Sales Coordinator:** Pam Dunlap. **Administrative Assistant/Director, Game Day Staff:** Debbie Clark. **Home Clubhouse Manager:** James Cameron. **Visiting Clubhouse Manager:** Chris Rasnake. **Head Groundskeeper:** Chris Bartos.

FIELD STAFF

Manager: Bill Plummer. **Coach:** Joel Youngblood. **Pitching Coach:** Mike Parrott. **Trainer:** Greg Barber. **Strength/ Conditioning:** Kyle Barbour.

GAME INFORMATION

Radio Announcer: Ryan Radtke. **No of Games Broadcast:** Home-72 Road-72. **Flagship Station:** Unavailable.

PA Announcer: Dale Lopez. **Official Scorer:** Unavailable.

Stadium Name: Tucson Electric Park. **Location:** From Northwest, I-10 to Ajo exit, east on Ajo to stadium. From southeast, I-10 to Palo Verde exit, north to Ajo, west to stadium. **Standard Game Times:** 7 p.m.; 6:30 p.m. (April-May); Sun. 6. **Ticket Price Range:** $6-9.

Visiting Club Hotel: Holiday Tuscon Airport North, 4550 S. Palo Verde Blvd., Tucson, AZ 85714. **Telephone:** (520) 746-1161.

EASTERN LEAGUE

DOUBLE-A

Office Address: 30 Danforth St., Suite 208, Portland, ME 04101.
Telephone: (207) 761-2700. **Fax:** (207) 761-7064.
E-Mail Address: elpb@easternleague.com. **Website:** www.easternleague.com.

Years League Active: 1923-.

President, Treasurer: Joe McEacharn.

Vice President, Secretary: Charles Eshbach.

Vice President: Chuck Domino.

Assistant to President: Bill Rosario.

Joe McEacharn

Directors: Greg Agganis (Akron), Lou DiBella (Connecticut), Bill Dowling (New Britain), Charles Eshbach (Portland), Joe Finley (Trenton), Chuck Greenberg (Altoona), Michael Reinsdorf (Harrisburg), Arthur Solomon (New Hampshire), Craig Stein (Reading), Hank Stickney (Erie), Mike Urda (Binghamton), Ken Young (Bowie).

Division Structure: Northern—Binghamton, Connecticut, New Britain, New Hampshire, Portland, Trenton. Southern—Akron, Altoona, Bowie, Erie, Harrisburg, Reading.

Regular Season: 142 games. **2008 Opening Date:** April 3. **Closing Date:** Sept. 1.

All-Star Game: July 16 at New Hampshire.

Playoff Format: Top two teams in each division meet in best-of-five series. Winners meet in best-of-five series for league championship.

Roster Limit: 24. **Player Eligibility Rule:** No restrictions.

Brand of Baseball: Rawlings ROM-EL.

Umpires: Lance Barrett (Burleson, TX), Mark Buchanan (Glendale, AZ), Darren Budahn (Milwaukee, WI), Jon Byrne (Thornlie, WA), Victor Carapazza (Palm Harbor, FL), Johnathan Conrad (Phoenix, AZ), Derek Crabill (Wonder Lake, IL), Timothy Daub (Catonsville, MD), Shaun Francis (Cohoes, NY), Matthew Hensel (Monroe, CT), Cory Hinga (Schoolcraft, MI), Douglas Levy (Sharon, MA), Mark Lollo (New Lexington, OH), Grant Menke (North Bethesda, MD), Bradley Purdom (Bend, OR), Christopher Schultz (Henderson, NV), John Tumpane (Oak Lawn, IL), Chad Whitson (Dublin, OH).

STADIUM INFORMATION

			Dimensions				
Club	**Stadium**	**Opened**	**LF**	**CF**	**RF**	**Capacity**	**2007 Att.**
Akron	Canal Park	1997	331	400	337	9,097	355,376
Altoona	Blair County Ballpark	1999	325	405	325	7,210	356,339
Binghamton	NYSEG Stadium	1992	330	400	330	6,012	230,053
Bowie	Prince George's Stadium	1993	309	405	309	10,000	287,098
Connecticut	Thomas J. Dodd Memorial Stadium	1995	309	401	309	6,695	195,235
Erie	Jerry Uht Park	1995	312	400	328	6,000	220,401
Harrisburg	Commerce Bank Park	1987	335	400	335	6,300	229,241
New Britain	New Britain Stadium	1996	330	400	330	6,146	341,816
New Hampshire	MerchantsAuto.com Stadium	2005	326	400	306	6,500	371,710
Portland	Hadlock Field	1994	315	400	330	7,368	421,368
Reading	FirstEnergy Stadium	1951	330	400	330	9,000	466,385
Trenton	Mercer County Waterfront Park	1994	330	407	330	6,440	412,312

AKRON AEROS

Office Address: 300 S Main St, Akron, OH 44308.
Telephone: (330) 253-5151. **Fax:** (330) 253-3300.
E-Mail address: info@akronaerons.com. **Website:** www.akronaerons.com.
Affiliation (first year): Cleveland Indians (1989). **Years in League:** 1989-

OWNERSHIP, MANAGEMENT

Operated By: Akron Professional Baseball, Inc.

Principal Owners: Mike Agganis, Greg Agganis.

Executive Vice President/General Manager: Jeff Auman. **CFO:** Bob Larkins. **Director, Corporate Sales/Public Relations:** Ken Fogel. **Director, Ticket Operations:** Kim Fogel. **Director, Ticket Sales:** Keith Solar. **Senior Account Representative, Group Sales:** Thomas Craven. **Account Representative, Ticket Sales:** Ross Swaldo. **Director, Field/Facility Maintenance:** Shaun Card. **Office Manager:** Arlene Vidumansky. **Box Office Manager:** Cathy Peto. **Media Relations Coordinator:** Rob Sinclair. **Merchandising Coordinator:** Jason Vaughan. **Consultant, Field/Facility Operations:** Matt Duncan. **Clubhouse/Equipment Manager:** Ben Boggess. **Aerofare General Manager:** Bob Jankowski. **Aerofare Assistant General Manager:** Brad Strobl. **Aerofare Suites/Picnics Supervisor:** Molly Taylor.

FIELD STAFF

Manager: Mike Sarbaugh. **Coach:** Lee May Jr. **Pitching Coach:** Tony Arnold. **Trainer:** Mike Salazar.

GAME INFORMATION

Radio Announcers: Jim Clark, Rob Sinclair. **No of Games Broadcast:** Home-71 Road-71. **Flagship Station:** Sports Radio 1350-AM.

PA Announcer: Joe Jastrzemski, Joe Dunn. **Official Scorer:** Roger Grecni.

Stadium Name: Canal Park. **Location:** From I-76 East or I-77 South, exit onto Route 59 East, exit at Exchange/Cedar, right onto Cedar, left at Main Street. From I-76 West or I-77 North, exit at Main Street/Downtown, follow exit onto Broadway Street, left onto Exchange Street, right at Main Street. **Ticket Price Range:** $8-10.

Visiting Club Hotel: Radisson Hotel Akron Centre, 20 W. Mill St, Akron, OH 44308. **Telephone:** (330) 384-1500.

ALTOONA CURVE

Office Address: Blair County Ballpark, 1000 Park Avenue, Altoona, PA 16602.
Mailing Address: P.O. Box 1029, Altoona, PA 16603.
Telephone: (814) 943-5400. **Fax:** (814) 942-9132.
E-Mail Address: frontoffice@altoonacurve.com. **Website:** www.altoonacurve.com.
Affiliation (first year): Pittsburgh Pirates (1999). **Years in League:** 1999-

OWNERSHIP, MANAGEMENT

Operated By: Curve Baseball LP.

President, Managing Partner: Chuck Greenberg. **General Manager:** Todd Parnell. **Associate GM/Senior Director, Ticketing:** Jeff Garner. **Senior Director, Marketing:** Rick Janac. **CFO:** John Donley. **Director, Broadcasting/Communications:** Jason Dambach. **Director, Community Relations:** Elsie Zengel. **Director, Merchandising:** Ben Rothrock. **Director, Sports Turf Management:** Patrick Coakley. **Director, Ballpark Operations:** Kirk Stiffler. **Director, Box Office Operations:** Dave Villiotti. **Director, Finance:** Jen Margroum. **Director, Promotions:** Matt Hoover. **Executive Producer, In-Game Entertainment:** John Foreman. **Director, Ticket Sales:** Denny Watson. **Director, Human Resources:** John Palilla. **Producer, In-Game Entertainment:** Ken Mountain. **Ticket Sales Associates:** Chris Keefer, Kerri McEachern, Mike Pence, Brian Stefan, Scott Walker. **Media Relations/Broadcasting Assistant:** Dan Zangrilli. **Administrative Assistant:** Carol Schmittle. **Accounting Specialist:** Tara Figard. **Assistant Sports Turf Manager:** Lisa Guinivan.

FIELD STAFF

Manager: Tim Leiper. **Coach:** Brandon Moore. **Pitching Coach:** Brad Holman. **Trainer:** Thomas Pribyl.

GAME INFORMATION

Radio Announcer: Jason Dambach, Dan Zangrilli. **No. of Games Broadcast:** Home-71 Road-71. **Flagship Station:** WHPA 93.5-FM.

PA Announcer: Rich DeLeo. **Official Scorer:** Ted Beam.

Stadium Name: Blair County Ballpark. **Location:** Located just off the Frankstown Road Exit of I-99. **Standard Game Times:** 7:05 p.m., 6:35 (April-May); Sun. 6:05, 3:05 (April-May). **Ticket Price Range:** $5-14.

Visiting Club Hotel: Ramada Altoona, Route 220 and Plank Road, Altoona, PA 16602. **Telephone:** (814) 946-1631.

BINGHAMTON METS

Office Address: 211 Henry St, Binghamton, NY 13901.
Mailing Address: P.O. Box 598, Binghamton, NY 13902.
Telephone: (607) 723-6387. **Fax:** (607) 723-7779.
E-Mail address: bmets@bmets.com. **Website:** www.bmets.com.
Affiliation (first year): New York Mets (1992). **Years in League:** 1923-37, 1940-63, 1966-68, 1992-

OWNERSHIP, MANAGEMENT

Principal Owners: Bill Maines, David Maines, George Scherer, Michael Urda.

General Manager: Scott Brown. **Assistant GM:** Jim Weed. **Director, Stadium Operations:** Richard Tylicki. **Director, Ticket Operations:** Jason Hall. **Special Event Coordinators:** Heith Tracy-Bronson, Connor Gates, Bob Urda. **Ticket Office Manager:** Casey Both. **Scholastic Programs Coordinator:** Lou Ferraro. **Community Relations Coordinator:** Nancy Wiseman. **Office Manager:** Rebecca Brown. **Merchandising Manager:** Lisa Shattuck. **Broadcasting Director:** Robert Ford. **Sports Turf Manager:** Stephen Wiseman.

FIELD STAFF

Manager: Max Oliveras. **Coach:** Luis Natera. **Pitching Coach:** Ricky Bones.

GAME INFORMATION

Radio Announcer: Robert Ford. **No. of Games Broadcast:** Home-71 Road-71. **Flagship Station:** WNBF 1290-AM.
PA Announcer: Unavailable. **Official Scorer:** Unavailable.
Stadium Name: NYSEG Stadium. **Location:** I-81 to exit 4S (Binghamton), Route 11 exit to Henry Street. **Standard Game Times:** 7:05 p.m., 6:35 (April-May); Sun. 1:05. **Ticket Price Range:** $8-9.
Visiting Club Hotel: Best Western, 569 Harry L Drive, Johnson City, NY 13790. **Telephone:** (607) 729-9194.

BOWIE BAYSOX

Office Address: Prince George's Stadium, 4101 NE Crain Hwy, Bowie, MD 20716.
Telephone: (301) 805-6000. **Fax:** (301) 464-4911.
E-Mail address: info@baysox.com. **Website:** www.baysox.com.
Affiliation (first year): Baltimore Orioles (1993). **Years in League:** 1993-

OWNERSHIP, MANAGEMENT

Owned By: Bowie Baysox Baseball Club LLC.
President: Ken Young.
General Manager: Brian Shallcross. **Assistant GM:** Phil Wrye. **Director, Marketing:** Sean Ream. **Director, Communications:** Ryan Roberts. **Director, Field/Facilit Operations:** Matt Parrott. **Promotions Manager:** Lauren Phillips. **Marketing Assistant:** Lindsay Johnson. **Communications Assistant:** Tom Sedlacek. **Account Executives:** Stephen Toutsis, Brandan Kaiser. **Sponsorship Account Coordinator:** Anthony Williams. **Group Events Managers:** Kari Fredriksen, Chris Rogers, Jacob Stettes, Joseph Machion. **Group Events Coordinator:** Tyson Heck. **Box Office Director:** Charlene Fewer. **Box Office Coordinator:** Anthony Kerere. **Manager, Stadium Operations:** Rick Wade. **Director, Gameday Personnel:** Darlene Mingioli. **Clubhouse Manager:** Milton Miles. **Office Manager:** Leslie McClain. **Bookkeeper:** Carol Terwilliger.

FIELD STAFF

Manager: Brad Komminsk. **Coach:** Moe Hill. **Pitching Coach:** Mike Griffin. **Trainer:** Joe Benge.

GAME INFORMATION

Radio Announcer: Steven Smith. **No. of Games Broadcast:** Home-71 Road-0. **Flagship Station:** WRGW.
PA Announcer: Adrienne Roberson. **Official Scorer:** Jeff Hertz.
Stadium Name: Prince George's Stadium. **Location:** 1/4 mile south of U.S. 50/RT. 301 Interchange in Bowie.
Standard Game Times: 7:05 p.m; Sun. 2:05 (April-May), 6:05 (June-Sept.) **Ticket Price Range:** $6-14.
Visiting Club Hotel: Best Western Annapolis, 2520 Riva Rd, Annapolis, MD 21401. **Telephone:** (410) 224-2800.

CONNECTICUT DEFENDERS

Office Address: 14 Stott Ave, Norwich, CT 06360.
Telephone: (860) 887-7962. **Fax:** (860) 886-5996.
E-Mail address: info@ctdefenders.com. **Website:** www.ctdefenders.com.
Affiliation (first year): San Francisco Giants (2003). **Years in League:** 1995-

OWNERSHIP, MANAGEMENT

Operated By: Navigators Baseball LP.
President/Managing Partner: Lou DiBella.

General Manager: Charlie Dowd. **Controller:** John Cunningham. **Director, Corporate Sales:** Johnny Gill. **Director, Group Sales:** Brendon Porter. **Group Sales Representatives:** Steve Given, Lindsay Carroll. **Director, Sales:** Andy Pappas. **Director, Merchandise/Concessions:** Shannon Johnson. **Box Office Manager:** Tony Scott. **Director, Media/Broadcasting:** Brian Irizarry. **Head Groundskeeper:** Mike Cannistra. **Assistant Groundskeeper:** Mike Foley. **Accounts Payable:** Tammy Nolin. **Office Manager:** Michelle Savage.

FIELD STAFF

Manager: Bienvenido Figueroa. **Coach:** Victor Torres. **Pitching Coach:** Bob Stanley. **Trainer:** Dustin Luepker.

GAME INFORMATION

Radio Announcers: Brian Irizarry. **No of Games Broadcast:** Home-71 Road-71. **Flagship Station:** WICH 1310-AM.

PA Announcer: Ed Weyant. **Official Scorer:** Chris Cote.

Stadium Name: Sen. Thomas J. Dodd Memorial Stadium. **Location:** I-395 to exit 82, follow signs for Dodd Stadium. **Standard Game Times:** 6:35 p.m.; Sunday, 1:05. **Ticket Price Range:** $7-10.

Visiting Club Hotel: Comfort Inn Mystic, 48 Whitehall Avenue, Mystic, CT 6355. **Telephone:** (860) 572-8531.

ERIE SEA WOLVES

Office Address: 110 E. 10th St, Erie, PA 16501.

Telephone: (814) 456-1300. **Fax:** (814) 456-7520.

E-Mail address: seawolves@seawolves.com. **Website:**www.seawolves.com.

Affiliation (first year): Detroit Tigers (2001). **Years in League:** 1999-

OWNERSHIP, MANAGEMENT

Operated By: Mandalay Baseball Properties.

Principal Owners: Hank Stickney, Ken Stickney, Peter Gruber, Paul Schaeffer.

General Manager: John Frey. **Assistant GM/Sales:** Mike Uden. **Assistant GM/Marketing:** Rob Magee. **Director, Ticket Sales:** Joe Etling. **Senior Ticket Sales Executive/Suite Coordinator:** Becky Obradovic. **Director, Finance:** Bernadette Mulvihill. **Director, Operations/Concessions:** Ragen Walker. **Director, Media Relations:** Greg Gania. **Box Office Manager/Merchandising:** Mark Pirrello. **Operations Manager:** Eric Phillips. **Marketing/Promotions Manager:** Carol Trumbo.

FIELD STAFF

Manager: Tom Brookens. **Coach:** Glen Adams. **Pitching Coach:** Ray Burris. **Trainer:** Chris McDonald. **Strength/Conditioning:** Steve Chase.

GAME INFORMATION

Radio Announcer: Greg Gania. **No. of Games Broadcast:** Home-71 Road-71. **Flagship Station:** WFNN 1330-AM.

PA Announcer: Bob Shrieve. **Official Scorer:** Les Caldwell.

Stadium Name: Jerry Uht Park. **Location:** U.S. 79 North to East 12th Street exit, left on State Street, right on 10th Street. **Standard Game Times:** 7:05 p.m., 6:35 (April-May); Sun. 1:05. **Ticket Price Range:** $5-12.

Visiting Club Hotel: Avalon Hotel, 16 W. 10th St, Erie, PA 16501. **Telephone:** (814) 459-2220.

HARRISBURG SENATORS

Office Address: Commerce Bank Park, City Island, Harrisburg, PA 17101.

Mailing Address: P.O. Box 15757, Harrisburg, PA 17105.

Telephone: (717) 231-4444. **Fax:** (717) 231-4445.

E-Mail address: hbgsenator@aol.com. **Website:** www.senatorsbaseball.com.

Affiliation (first year): Washington Nationals (2005). **Years in League:** 1924-35, 1987-

OWNERSHIP, MANAGEMENT

Operated By: Senators Partners, LLC.

President: Michael Reinsdorf.

Vice President, Operations: Bill Davidson. **General Manager:** Randy Whitaker. **Assistant GM, Business Operations:** Mark Clarke. **Director, Facilities Operations:** Tim Foreman. **Director, Concessions Operations:** Steve Leininger. **Director, Community Relations/Customer Service:** Emily Winslow. **Ticket Sales Manager:** Jon Tapper. **Ticket Sales Executives:** Kristal Narkiewicz, Jessica Snader. **Director, Group Sales:** Brian Egli. **Director, Picnic Operations:** Melissa Altemose. **Director, Broadcasting/Media Relations:** Terry Byrom. **Assistant, Broadcasting/Media Relations:** Dan Watson. **Bookkeeper:** Donna Demczak. **Interns:** Andy Brooks, Noel Vega, Jessica Kauffman, Kristine Erskine, Shawna Ott, Amber Zeigler, Matt Brightbill, Shane Thornton, Emily Myers, Jonathan Boles, Josh Giffin.

FIELD STAFF

Manager: John Stearns. **Coach:** Tony Gingrich. **Pitching Coach:** Rick Tomlin. **Trainer:** Beth Jarrett.

GAME INFORMATION

Radio Announcer: Terry Byrom, Don Watson. **No. of Games Broadcast:** Home-71 Road-71. **Flagship Station:** 1460-

AM.

PA Announcer: Chris Andree. **Official Scorer:** Unavailable.

Stadium Name: Commerce Bank Park. **Location:** I-83, exit 23 (Second Street) to Market Street, bridge to City Island. **Ticket Price Range:** $3-9.

Visiting Club Hotel: Radisson Penn Harris Hotel, 1150 Camp Hill Bypass, Camp Hill, PA 17011. **Telephone:** (717) 763-7117.

NEW BRITAIN ROCK CATS

Office Address: 230 John Karbonic Way, New Britain, CT 06051.
Mailing Address: P.O. Box 1718, New Britain, CT 06050.
Telephone: (860) 224-8383. **Fax:** (860) 225-6267.
E-Mail address: rockcats@rockcats.com. **Website:** www.rockcats.com.
Affiliation (first year): Minnesota Twins (1995). **Years in League:** 1983-

OWNERSHIP, MANAGEMENT

Operated By: New Britain Baseball Club Inc.

Principal Owners: Bill Dowling, Coleman Levy. **President, CEO:** Bill Dowling.

Chairman of the Board: Coleman Levy.

Vice President/General Manager: John Willi. **Vice President:** Evan Levy. **Assistant GM/Sales:** Ricky Ferrell. **Director, Broadcasting:** Jeff Dooley. **Director, Ticket Operations:** Marissa Farris. **Coordinator, Promotions/Group Sales:** Kim Pizighelli. **Director, Media Relations:** Robert Dowling. **Director, Corporate Sales:** Andres Levy. **Senior Account Executive:** Jonathan Lissitchuk. **Stadium Operations Coordinator:** Mike Mariano. **Account Executive/Sales:** Evan Paradis. **Marketing Coordinator:** Lori Soltis. **Corporate Sales Manager:** Kate Baumann. **Controller:** Paula Perdelwitz. **Concessionaire:** Chris Coonrad.

FIELD STAFF

Manager: Bobby Cuellar. **Coach:** Floyd Rayford. **Pitching Coach:** Steve Mintz. **Trainer:** Chad Jackson.

GAME INFORMATION

Radio Announcer: Dan Lovallo. **No. of Games Broadcast:** Home-71 Road-71. **Flagship Station:** WDRC 1360-AM.

PA Announcer: Unavailable. **Official Scorer:** Ed Smith.

Stadium Name: New Britain Stadium. **Location:** From I-84, take Route 72 East (exit 35 of Route 9 South (exit 39A), left at Ellis Street (exit 25), left at South Main Street, stadium one mile on right. From Route 91 or Route 5, take Route 9 North to Route 71 (exit 24), first exit. **Ticket Price Range:** $5-12.

Visiting Club Hotel: Holiday Inn Express, 120 Laning St, Southington, CT 06489. **Telephone:** (860) 276-0736.

NEW HAMPSHIRE FISHER CATS

Office Address: 1 Line Dr., Manchester, NH 3101.
Telephone: (603) 641-2005. **Fax:** (603) 641-2055.
E-Mail address: info@nhfishercats.com. **Website:** www.nhfishercats.com.
Affiliation (first year): Toronto Blue Jays (2004). **Years in League:** 2004-

OWNERSHIP, MANAGEMENT

Operated By: Triple Play LLC.

Owner/Managing Partner: Art Solomon. **Owner/Minority Partner:** Drew Weber.

President/General Manager: Rick Brenner. **Vice President, Business Operations:** Tim Restall. **Executive Director, Sales:** Mike Ramshaw. **Corporate Controller:** Cindy Garron. **Director, Public Affairs:** Danielle Matteau. **Director, Media Relations:** Mike Murphy. **Director, Ticket Sales:** Dennis Meehan. **Director, Group Sales:** Erik Lesniak. **Head Turf Manager:** Eric Blanton. **Director, Stadium Operations:** Ross Rodriguez. **Merchandise Manager:** Kaitlyn Tomasello. **Marketing Manager/Ticket Sales Account Executive:** Michaela Sweet. **Community Relations Manager/Ticket Sales Account Executive:** Morgan Crandall. **Production Manager:** Jason Mason. **Production Manager Assistant:** Stephanie Cohen. **Ticket Sales Account Executives:** Brian Cronin, Stephanie Livoli, Mike Murphy, Jeremy Roop, Mike Tarleton, Justin Smith. **Office Manager/Ticket Sales Account Executive:** Kathryn Mitchell. **Stadium Operations Assistant:** Matt Moore. **Senior Assistant:** Whitney McKeon. **Assistant:** Pat Lewis. **Director, Media Relations:** Bob Lipman. **Media Relations Assistant:** Tim Hough. **Clubhouse Attendant:** Nick Botelho. **Clubhouse Assistants:** Brian Devlin, Michael Brown.

FIELD STAFF

Manager: Gary Catchcart. **Coach:** Ken Joyce. **Pitching Coach:** Dave LaRoche. **Trainer:** Voon Chong.

GAME INFORMATION

Radio Announcer: Bob Lipman, Mike Murphy. **No of Games Broadcast:** Home-71 Road-71. **Flagship Station:** WGIR 610-AM.

PA Announcer: John Zahr. **Official Scorers:** Chick Smith, Pete Dupuis, Greg Royce.

Stadium Name: MerchantsAuto.com Stadium. **Location:** From I-93 North, take I-293 North to exit 5 (Granite Street), right on Granite Street, right on South Commerical Street, right on Line Drive. **Ticket Price Range:** $4-12.

Visiting Club Hotel: Comfort Inn, 298 Queen City Ave, Manchester, NH 03102. **Telephone:** (603) 668-2600.

PORTLAND SEA DOGS

Office Address: 271 Park Ave, Portland, ME 04102.
Mailing Address: P.O. Box 636, Portland, ME 04104.
Telephone: (207) 874-9300. **Fax:** (207) 780-0317.
E-Mail address: seadogs@seadogs.com. **Website:** www.seadogs.com.
Affiliation (first year): Boston Red Sox (2003). **Years in League:** 1994-

OWNERSHIP, MANAGEMENT

Operated By: Portland, Maine Baseball, Inc.

Principal Owner, Chairman: Daniel Burke.

President, General Manager: Charles Eshbach. **Executive Vice President:** John Kameisha. **VP:** Jim Heffley. **Assistant GM, Public Relations:** Chris Cameron. **Assistant GM, Sales/Promotions:** Geoff Iacuessa. **Director, Group Sales:** Corey Thompson. **Director, Ticketing:** Dave Strong. **Assistant Director, Ticketing:** Liz Riley. **Director, Video Operations:** Todd Jamison. **Director, Boradcasting:** Mike Antonellis. **Director, Food Services:** Mike Scorza. **Asstistant Director, Food Services:** Greg Moyes. **Office Manager:** Judy Bray. **Administrative Assistants:** Kelsey Albair, Matt Combra, Ryan Durrell, Nick Fox, Tom Gauthier, Jessica Johnson, Rachel Masse, Mike Mestieri, Dan Vassallo, Lyndsay Woods, Jack Yerxa. **Clubhouse Managers:** Craig Candage Sr., Craig Candage Jr., Rick Goslin. **Head Groundskeeper:** Rick Anderson.

FIELD STAFF

Manager: Arnie Beyeler. **Coach:** Dave Joppie. **Pitching Coach:** Mike Cather. **Trainer:** Brad Pearson.

GAME INFORMATION

Radio Announcer: Mike Antonellis. **No. of Games Broadcast:** Home-71 Road-71. **Flagship Station:** WBAE 1490-AM.

PA Announcer: Dean Rogers. **Official Scorer:** Thom Hinton.

Stadium Name: Hadlock Field. **Location:** From South, I-295 to exit 5, merge onto Congress Street, left at St. John Street, merge right onto Park Ave. From North, I-295 to exit 6A, right onto Park Ave. **Ticket Price Range:** $4-9.

Visiting Club Hotel: Clarion Hotel, 1230 Congress St, Portland, ME 04102. **Telephone:** (207) 774-5611.

READING PHILLIES

Office Address: Route 61 South/1900 Centre Ave., Reading, PA 19601.
Mailing Address: P.O. Box 15050, Reading, PA 19612.
Telephone: (610) 375-8469. **Fax:** (610) 373-5868.
E-Mail Address: info@readingphillies.com. **Website:** www.readingphillies.com.
Affiliation (first year): Philadelphia Phillies (1967). **Years in League:** 1933-35, 1952-61, 1963-65, 1967-.

OWNERSHIP, MANAGEMENT

Operated By: E&J Baseball Club, Inc.

Principal Owner: Craig Stein.

President: Chuck Domino.

General Manager: Scott Hunsicker. **Assistant GM:** Ashley Forlini. **Director, Stadium Operations/Concessions:** Andy Bortz. **Director, Sales:** Joe Bialek. **Director, Baseball Operations/Merchandise:** Kevin Sklenarik. **Director, Communications:** Rob Hackash. **Director, Ticket Operations:** Mike Becker. **Director, Group Sales:** Mike Robinson. **Controller:** Kristyne Haver. **Corporate Sales/Graphic Artist/Game Entertainment:** Matt Jackson. **Client Relationship Manager/Ticket Manager:** Josh Holly. **Group Sales Managers:** Holly Frymer, Brian Babik. **Client Relationship Managers:** Chris McConney, Matt Hoffmaster, Adam Lanzendorfer, Curtis Burns. **Group Sales Manager:** Tim McGee. **Operations/Concessions Assistant:** Tim Martino. **Head Groundskeeper:** Dan Douglas. **Office Manager:** Deneen Giesen. **Video Director:** Andy Kauffman.

FIELD STAFF

Manager: P.J. **Forbes. Coach:** Frank Cacciatore. **Pitching Coach:** Tom Filer. **Trainer:** Unavailable.

GAME INFORMATION

Radio Announcers: Steve Degler, Kale Beers. **No. of Games Broadcast:** Home-71, Away-71. **Flagship Station:** ESPN 1240-AM.

PA Announcer: Dave Bauman. **Official Scorer:** Josh Leiboff, Paul Jones, Dick Shute, BJ Spiegelmeyer, Brian Kopetsky, John Gump.

Stadium Name: FirstEnergy Stadium. **Location:** From east, take Pennsylvania Turnpike West to Morgantown exit, to 176 North, to 422 West, to Route 12 East, to Route 61 South exit. From west, take 422 East to Route 12 East, to Route 61 South exit. From north, take 222 South to Route 12 exit, to Route 61 South exit. From south, take 222 North to 422 West, to Route 12 East exit at Route 61 South. **Standard Game Times:** 7:05 p.m., Mon.-Thurs. (April-May) 6:35; Sun. 1:05. **Ticket**

Price Range: $5-10.

Visiting Club Hotel: Days Inn, 910 Woodland Ave., Wyomissing PA 19610. Telephone: (610) 375-1500.

TRENTON THUNDER

Office Address: One Thunder Rd, Trenton, NJ 08611.
Telephone: (609) 394-3300. **Fax:** (609) 394-7666.
E-Mail address: fun@trentothunder.com. **Website:** www.trentonthunder.com.
Affiliation (first year): New York Yankees (2003). **Years in League:** 1994-

OWNERSHIP, MANAGEMENT

Operated By: Garden State Baseball, LLP.

General Manager/COO: Brad Taylor. **Assistant GM:** Greg Coleman. **Vice President, Marketing:** Eric Lipsman. **Director, Finance:** Jeff Kluge. **Director, Ticket Operations:** Matt Pentima. **Director, Merchandising:** Joe Pappalardo. **Director, Broadcasting:** Steve Rudenstein. **Director, Stadium Operations:** Ryan Crammer. **Director, Group Sales:** Brian Cassidy. **Director, Public Relations:** Bill Cook. **Executive Director, Ticket Sales:** Jason Schubert. **Assistant Director, Ticket Sales:** Patience Purdy. **Production Manager:** Mark Zangara. **Baseball Operations/Accounting Manager:** Jeff Hurley. **Ticket/Events Coordinators:** Ross Mehalko, Adam Smedberg, Matt Schwartz, David Kuhn, Stephanie Bissell. **Director, Food/Beverages:** Kevin O'Byrne. **Office Manager:** Kathy Gallagher. **Media Relations/Broadcasting Assistant:** Josh Landsburg. **Stadium Operations Assistant:** Steve Brokowsky. **Merchandise Assistant:** Caitlin Hyde. Ticket Assistants: Erin Leigh. **Interns:** Evan Cheresnick, Hardik Parikh, Stacy Dichter, Adam Mamawala, Gabby Peck, Kristin Marie Grey, Joe Haubrich, Zach Bright, Charlie Betcher, Allison Berkley. **Home Clubhouse Manager:** Tom Kackley. **Visiting Clubhouse Manager:** John Annis. **Head Groundskeeper:** Bob Shinn.

FIELD STAFF

Manager: Tony Franklin. **Coach:** Tom Wilson. **Pitching Coach:** Scott Aldred. **Trainer:** Tim Lentych. **Strength/Conditioning:** Lee Tressel.

GAME INFORMATION

Radio Announcer: Steve Rudenstein, Josh Landsburg. **No. of Games Broadcast:** Home-71 Road-71. **Flagship Station:** WBUD 1260-AM.

PA Announcer: Bill Bromberg. **Official Scorer:** Jay Dunn, Greg Zak.

Stadium Name: Samuel L. Plumeri Sr. Field at Mercer County Waterfont Park. **Location:** From I-95, take Route 1 North to Route 29 South, stadium entrance just before tunnel. From NJ Turnpike, take Exit 7A and follow I-195 West. Road will become Rte. 29. Follow through tunnel and ballpark is on left. **Standard Game Times:** 7:05 p.m.; Sat. 1:05 (April); Sun 1:05. **Ticket Price Range:** $5-10.

Visiting Club Hotel: Unavailable.

SOUTHERN LEAGUE

DOUBLE-A

Mailing Address: 2551 Roswell Rd., Suite 330, Marietta, GA 30062.
Telephone: (770) 321-0400. **Fax:** (770) 321-0037.

E-Mail Address: soleague@earthlink.net. **Website:** www.southernleague.com.

Years League Active: 1964-.

President: Don Mincher.

Don Mincher

Vice President: Steve DeSalvo.

Directors: Peter Bragan Jr. (Jacksonville), Steve Bryant (Carolina), Frank Burke (Chattanooga), Steve DeSalvo (Mississippi), Tom Dickson (Montgomery), Doug Kirchhofer (Tennessee), David Freeman (West Tenn), Jonathan Nelson (Birmingham), Miles Prentice (Huntsville), Bill Shanahan (Mobile).

Vice President, Operations: Lori Webb. **Director of Marketing/Media Relations:** Joe Barbieri.

Division Structure: North—Carolina, Chattanooga, Huntsville, Tennessee, West Tenn. South—Birmingham, Jacksonville, Mississippi, Mobile, Montgomery.

Regular Season: 140 games (split schedule). **2008 Opening Date:** April 3. **Closing Date:** Sept. 1.

All-Star Game: July 14 at Carolina.

Playoff Format: First-half division winners meet second-half division winners in best-of-five series. Winners meet in best-of-five series for league championship.

Roster Limit: 24. **Player Eligibility Rule:** No restrictions.

Brand of Baseball: Rawlings.

Umpires: Unavailable.

STADIUM INFORMATION

			Dimensions				
Club	**Stadium**	**Opened**	**LF**	**CF**	**RF**	**Capacity**	**2007 Att.**
Birmingham	Regions Park	1988	340	405	340	10,800	280,171
Carolina	Five County Stadium	1991	330	400	330	6,500	273,198
Chattanooga	AT&T Field	2000	325	400	330	6,362	242,104
Huntsville	Joe W. Davis Municipal Stadium	1985	345	405	330	10,200	164,079
Jacksonville	Baseball Grounds of Jacksonville	2003	321	420	317	11,000	396,012
Mississippi	Trustmark Park	2005	337	332	400	7,416	246,674
Mobile	Hank Aaron Stadium	1997	325	400	310	6,000	232,235
Montgomery	Montgomery Riverwalk Stadium	2004	335	402	332	7,000	311,872
Tennessee	Smokies Park	2000	330	400	330	6,000	258,121
West Tenn	Pringles Park	1998	310	395	320	6,000	113,351

BIRMINGHAM BARONS

Office Address: 100 Ben Chapman Dr., Hoover, AL 35244.
Mailing Address: P.O. Box 360007, Birmingham, AL 35236.
Telephone: (205) 988-3200. **Fax:** (205) 988-9698.
E-Mail Address: barons@barons.com. **Website:** www.barons.com.
Affiliation (first year): Chicago White Sox (1986). **Years in League:** 1964-65, 1967-75, 1981-

OWNERSHIP, MANAGEMENT

Principal Owners: Don Logan, Jeff Logan, Stan Logan.

General Manager: Jonathan Nelson. **Assistant General Manager:** Michael Pepper. **Director, Stadium Operations:** James Young. **Director, Broadcasting:** Curt Bloom. **Director, Media Relations:** Justin Firesheets. **Director, Sales/Marketing:** Bill Adema. **Director, Promotions/Tickets:** Jeremy Neisser. **Director, Community Relations:** Brian Hudson. **Community Relations Coordinator:** Kyle Krebs. **Corporate Event Planners:** Casey Odom, Jonathan Howe. **Community Group Ticket Representative:** Charlie Santiago. **General Manager, Grand Slam Catering:** Eric Crook. **Director, Catering:** Taylor Youngson. **Office Manager:** Kecia Braswell. **Accountant:** Jo Ann Bragan. **Interns:** Matt McCoy, Blair Hayes, Jennifer Allen, Haddon Mackie, Chris Huggins. **Head Groundskeeper:** Steve Hamilton.

FIELD STAFF

Manager: Carlos Subero. **Coach:** Wes Clements. **Pitching Coach:** J.R. Pedrew. **Trainer:** Joe Geck. **Strength/Conditioning:** Raymond Smith.

GAME INFORMATION

Radio Announcer: Curt Bloom. **No of Games Broadcast:** Home-70 Road-70. **Flagship Station:** Unavailable.

PA Announcer: Allan Guenther. **Official Scorer:** Grant Martin.

Stadium Name: Hoover Metropolitan Stadium. **Location:** I-459 to Highway 150 (exit 10) in Hoover. **Standard Game Times:** 7:05 p.m.; Sun. 2:05 (First Half), 5:05 (Second Half). **Ticket Price Range:** $6-12.

Visiting Club Hotel: Riverchase Inn, 1800 Riverchase Dr, Birmingham, AL 35244. **Telephone:** (205) 985-7500.

CAROLINA MUDCATS

Office Address: 1501 N.C. Hwy. 39, Zebulon, NC 27597.
Mailing Address: P.O. Drawer 1218, Zebulon, NC 27597.
Telephone: (919) 269-2287. **Fax:** (919) 269-4910.
E-Mail Address: muddy@gomudcats.com. **Website:** www.gomudcats.com.
Affiliation (first year): Florida Marlins (2003). **Years in League:** 1991-.

OWNERSHIP, MANAGEMENT

Operated by: Carolina Mudcats Professional Baseball Club Inc.

Principal Owner: Steve Bryant.

General Manager: Joe Kremer. **Assistant GM:** Eric Gardner. **Office Manager:** Jackie DiPrimo. **Director, Broadcasting:** Patrick Kinas. **Directors, Stadium Operations:** Robert Slaughter, Eric Morgan. **Director, Marketing:** Alexandra Briley. **Director, Food/Beverage:** Zia Torabian. **Assistant Director, Food/Beverage:** Alan Hinnant. **Director, Community Relations:** Lindsay Wiener. **Merchandise Manager:** LuAnne Reynolds. **Coordinator, Multi-Media Productions:** Aaron Bayles. **Director, Tickets:** Rachel Burke. **Ticket Sales Associate:** Adrian Bridges. **Corporate Sales Representative:** Ricky Ray. **Director, Group Sales:** Haig Lea. **Group Sales Associates:** Kaitlin Brunner, Chris Signorelli, Josh Bridges. **Director, Fundraising:** Macy Dykema. **Assistant Director, Fundraising:** Corey Bass. **Head Groundskeeper:** John Packer. **Director, Special Events:** Nathan Priddy.

FIELD STAFF

Manager: Matt Raleigh. **Coach:** Theron Todd. **Pitching Coach:** Scott Mitchell. **Trainer:** Ben Heimos.

GAME INFORMATION

Radio Announcer: Patrick Kinas. **No. of Games Broadcast:** Home-70, Away-70. **Flagship Stations:** WDOX-AM 570; WKXU-FM 102.5.

PA Announcer: Dave Slade. **Official Scorer:** Tim Ryan.

Stadium Name: Five County Stadium. **Location:** From Raleigh, U.S. 64 East to 264 East, exit at Highway 39 in Zebulon. **Standard Game Times:** 7:15 p.m.; Sat. 6:15; Sun. 2. **Ticket Price Range:** $5-9.

Visiting Club Hotel: Best Western Raleigh North, 2715 Capital Blvd., Raleigh, NC 27604. **Telephone:** (919) 872-5000.

CHATTANOOGA LOOKOUTS

Office Address: 201 Power Alley, Chattanooga, TN 37402.
Mailing Address: P.O. Box 11002, Chattanooga, TN 37401.
Telephone: (423) 267-2208. **Fax:** (423) 267-4258.
E-Mail Address: lookouts@lookouts.com. **Website:** www.lookouts.com.
Affiliation (first year): Cincinnati Reds (1988). **Years in League:** 1964-65, 1976-.

OWNERSHIP, MANAGEMENT

Operated By: Scenic City Baseball LLC.

Principal Owner: Daniel Burke, Frank Burke, Charles Eshbach.

President/General Manager: Frank Burke. **Assistant GM:** John Maedel. **Director, Business Administration/ Executive Assistant:** Debby Kennedy. **Director, Group Sales:** Bill Wheeler. **Director, Merchandising/Marketing:** Chrysta Jorgensen. **Director, Media Relations:** Peter Intza. **Director, Ticketing Operations:** Luis Gonzalez. **Director, Concessions:** Steve Sullivan. **Director, Broadcasting:** Larry Ward. **Head Groundskeeper:** Bo Henley. **Director, Stadium Operations:** Alex Vaughn. **Director, Business Administration/Accounting:** Brian Eshbach. **Assistant Director, Broadcasting:** Will Poindexter. **Assistant Director, Ticket Operations:** Kat Hauschild. **Assistant Director, Concessions:** John Quirk. **Ticketing Assistant:** Matt St. Charles.

FIELD STAFF

Manager: Mike Goff. **Coach:** Jamie Dismuke. **Pitching Coach:** Chris Bosio. **Trainer:** Ryuji Araki.

GAME INFORMATION

Radio Announcers: Larry Ward, Will Poindexter. **No. of Games Broadcast:** Home-70 Road-70. **Flagship Station:** WDOD 1310-AM.

PA Announcer: John Maedel. **Official Scorers:** Wirt Gammon, Andy Paul.

Stadium Name: AT&T Field. **Location:** From I-24, take U.S. 27 North to exit 1C (4th Street), first left onto Chestnut Street, left onto Third Street. **Ticket Price Range:** $4-8.

Visiting Club Hotel: Holiday Inn, 2345 Shallowford Rd, Chattanooga, TN 37412. **Telephone:** (423) 855-2898.

HUNTSVILLE STARS

Office Address: 3125 Leeman Ferry Rd., Huntsville, AL 35801.
Mailing Address: P.O. Box 2769, Huntsville, AL 35804.
Telephone: (256) 882-2562. **Fax:** (256) 880-0801.
E-Mail Address: info@huntsvillestarts.com. **Website:** www.huntsvillestars.com.
Affiliation (first year): Milwaukee Brewers (1999). **Years in League:** 1985-

OWNERSHIP, MANAGEMENT

Operated By: Huntsville Stars LLC.

President: Miles Prentice.

General Manager: Buck Rogers. **Director, Broadcasting:** Brett Pollock. **Office/Parking Manager:** Earl Grilliot. **Director, Broadcasting:** Brett Pollock. **Director, Field Maintenance:** Lane Oglesby. **Director, Media/Public Relations:** Brian Massey. **Director, Merchandising:** Tyler Ericson. **Director, Promotions/Community Relations:** Matt Price. **Director, Stadium Operations:** Paul Westbrook. **Director, Ticketing:** Eric Laue. **Ticket Sales Associate:** Kylee Hanish. **Ticket Sales Associate:** Alicia English.

FIELD STAFF

Manager: Don Money. **Coach:** Sandy Guerrero. **Pitching Coach:** Chris Hook.

GAME INFORMATION

Radio Announcers: Brett Pollock. **No. of Games Broadcast:** Home-70, Away-70.

PA Announcers: Todd Blass, J.J Lewis. **Official Scorer:** Don Rizzardi.

Stadium Name: Joe W. Davis Municipal Stadium. **Location:** I-65 to I-565 East, south on Memorial Parkway to Drake Avenue exit, right on Don Mincher Drive. **Ticket Price Range:** $5-8.

Visiting Club Hotel: La Quinta Inn, 3141 University Dr, Huntsville, AL 35805. **Telephone:** (256) 533-0756.

JACKSONVILLE SUNS

Office Address: 301 A. Philip Randolph Blvd., Jacksonville, FL 32202.
Mailing Address: P.O. Box 4756, Jacksonville, FL 32201.
Telephone: (904) 358-2846. **Fax:** (904) 358-2845.
E-Mail Address: info@jaxsuns.com. **Website:** www.jaxsuns.com.
Affiliation (seventh year): Los Angeles Dodgers (2001). **Years In League:** 1970-.

OWNERSHIP, MANAGEMENT

Operated by: Baseball Jax Inc.

Principal Owner, Chairman of the Board: Peter Bragan Sr. **Madame Chairman:** Mary Frances Bragan. **President/ General Manager:** Peter Bragan Jr.

Assistant GM: Brad Rodriguez. **Director, Ticket Operations:** Jane Carole Bunting. **Director, Broadcasting/Media Relations:** J.P. Shadrick. **Director, Community Relations:** Katherine Jeschke. **Director, Field Operations:** Ed Attalla. **Director, Food/Beverage/Sponsorship Sales:** Chris Peters. **Director, Merchandise:** Victoria Eure. **Director, Sales/ Promotions:** Casey Nichols. **Director, Stadium Operations:** Matt Glancy. **Office Manager:** Barbara O'Berry. **Director, Video Services:** David Scheldorf. **Manager, Box Office:** Amy DeLettre. **Director, Group Sales:** Meghan Clark. **Group Sales Associate:** Kathleen Parker. **Assistant GM, Ballpark Foods/Finance:** Mitch Buska. **Business Manager:** Craig Barnett. **Administrative Assistants:** Charles Smith, Joe Vitale, Kim Watson. **Administrative Receptionist:** Theresa Viets.

FIELD STAFF

Manager: John Shoemaker. **Coach:** Luis Salazar. **Pitching Coach:** Glenn Dishman. **Trainer:** Carlos Olivas.

GAME INFORMATION

Radio Announcer: J.P. Shadrick. **No. of Games Broadcast:** Home-70, Away-70. **Flagship Station:** WFXJ 930-AM.

PA Announcer: John Leard. **Official Scorer:** Jason Eliopulos.

Stadium Name: The Baseball Grounds of Jacksonville. **Location:** I-95 South to Martin Luther King Parkway exit, follow Gator Bowl Blvd. around Alltel Stadium; I-95 North to Exit 347 (Emerson Street), go right to Hart Bridge Expressway, take Sports Complex exit, left at light to stop sign, take left and follow around Alltel Stadium; From Mathews Bridge, take A. Philip Randolph exit, right on A. Philip Randolph, straight to stadium. **Standard Game Times:** 7:05 p.m., Wed. 1:05, Sun. 3:05/5:05. **Ticket Price Range:** $5.50-19.50.

Visiting Club Hotel: Hyatt Regency Jacksonville Riverfront, 225 Coastline Dr., Jacksonville, FL 32202. **Telephone:** (904) 633-9095.

MISSISSIPPI BRAVES

Office Address: Trustmark Park, 1 Braves Way, Pearl, MS 39208.
Mailing Address: P.O. Box 97389, Pearl, MS 39288.
Telephone: (601) 932-8788. **Fax:** (601) 936-3567.
E-Mail Address: mississippi.braves@turner.com. **Website:** www.mississippibraves.com.
Affiliation (first year): Atlanta Braves (2005). **Years in League:** 2005-

OWNERSHIP, MANAGEMENT

Operated By: Atlanta National League Baseball Club Inc.

General Manager: Steve DeSalvo. **Assistant GM:** Jim Bishop. Ticket Manager Bob Askin. Merchandise Manager: Sarah Banta. **Advertising/Design Manager:** Brian Byrd. **Facility Maintenance Manager:** Greg Craddock. **Community Relations Manager:** Lisa Dunn. **Sales Associate:** Brian Emory. **Head Chef:** Tina Funches. **Sales Associate:** Sean Guillotte. **Suites/Catering Manager:** Debbie Herrington. **Stadium Operations Manager:** Colby Johnson. **Special Events Manager:** Georganna Keenum. **Assistant Restaurant Manager:** Jack McGill. **Promotions/Entertainment Manager:** Brian Prochilo. **Concessions Manager:** Jim Rawson. **Office Administrator:** Christy Shaw. **Public Relations Manager:** Nicholas Skinner. **Restaurant Manager:** Gene Slaughter. **Director, Field/Facility Operations:** Matt Taylor.

FIELD STAFF

Manager: Phillip Wellman. **Coach:** Franklin Stubbs. **Pitching Coach:** Derek Botelho. **Trainer:** Ricky Alcantara.

GAME INFORMATION

Radio Announcer: Unavailable. **No. of Games Broadcast:** Home-70 Road-70. **Flagship Station:** Unavailable.

PA Announcer: Derrel Palmer. **Official Scorer:** Butch Raley.

Stadium Name: Trustmark Park. **Location:** I-20 to exit 48/Pearl (Pearson Road). **Ticket Price Range:** $5-12.

Visiting Club Hotel: America's Best Inns & Suites, 1003 Treetops Boulevard, Flowood, MS 39232. **Telephone:** (601) 933-0066.

MOBILE BAYBEARS

Office Address: Hank Aaron Stadium, 755 Bolling Bros. Blvd., Mobile, AL 36606.
Telephone: (251) 479-2327. **Fax:** (251) 476-1147.
E-Mail Address: baybears@mobilebaybears.com. **Website:** www.mobilebaybears.com.
Affiliation (first year): Arizona Diamondbacks (2007). **Years in League:** 1966, 1970, 1997-

OWNERSHIP, MANAGEMENT

Operated by: HWS Baseball Group.

Principal Owner: Mike Savit.

President/COO: Bill Shanahan. **Vice President/General Manager:** Travis Toth. **Assistant GM, Finance:** Betty Adams.

Assistant GM, Ticket Operations: Jeff Long. **Assistant GM, Promotions/Corporate Sales:** Mike Callahan. **Director, Operations:** John Hilliard. **Head Groundskeeper:** Daniel Ruggiero. **Director, Community Relations/Merchandising:** Cindy Guay. **Stadium Operations Manager:** Jonathan Nobles. **Audio/Visual Director:** Ari Rosenbaum. **Sales/Youth Programs:** Lloyd Meyers. **Sales Representatives:** Cary Jones, Chad Hoerner. **Clubhouse Manager:** Rick Schweitzer. **Stadium Operations Assistant:** Wade Vadakin. **Internet Liaison/Team Chaplain:** Lorin Barr. **Interns:** Sarah Martin, Brian Vesely, Amy Byrd.

FIELD STAFF

Manager: Hector De La Cruz. **Coach:** Turner Ward. **Pitching Coach:** Jeff Pico. **Trainer:** James Ready. **Strength/Conditioning:** Brian Melton.

GAME INFORMATION

Radio Announcer: Wayne Randazzo. **No. of Games Broadcast:** Home-70, Away-70. **Flagship Station:** Comcast Channel 19.

PA Announcers: Jason Taylor, Matt McCoy, Mary Booth. **Official Scorers:** Kevin Beasley, Matthew Hicks, Randy Peters. **tadium Name:** Hank Aaron Stadium. **Location:** I-65 to exit 1 (Government Blvd. East), right at Satchel Paige Drive, right at Bolling Bros. Boulevard. **Standard Game Times:** 7:05 p.m.; Sun. 6:05, 2:05 (April-May). **Ticket Price Range:** $5-10.

Visiting Club Hotel: Riverview Plaza, 64 S. Water St., Mobile, AL 36602. **Telephone:** (251) 438-4000.

MONTGOMERY BISCUITS

Office Address: 200 Coosa St., Montgomery, AL 36104.
Telephone: (334) 323-2255. **Fax:** (334) 323-2225.
E-Mail address: info@biscuitsbaseball.com. **Website:** www.biscuitsbaseball.com.
Affiliation (first year): Tampa Bay Rays (2004). **Years in League:** 1965-1980, 2004-

OWNERSHIP, MANAGEMENT

Operated By: Montgomery Professional Baseball LLC.

Principal Owners: Tom Dickson, Sherrie Myers.

General Manager: Greg Rauch. **Director, Sponsorships/Marketing:** Marla Terranova. **Marketing Assistants:** Helena Ballard, April Catarella, Jim Tocco. **Sponsorship Service Representative:** Erin Tracy. **Box Office Manager:** Jason Benton. **Box Office Assistant:** Alyson Smith. **Season Ticket Coordinator/Head Concierge:** Kent Rose. **Director, Operations:** Steve Blackwell. **Group Sales Representatives:** Justin Buschman, Michael Davis, Lance Fischel. **Director, Food Service:** Jason Wilson. **Assistant Director, Food Service:** Ben Blankenship. **Catering Supervisor:** Adam Curley. **Business Manager:** Linda Fast. **Assistant Manager, Business:** Tranitra Babers. **Retail Manager:** Monte Meyers. **Office Manager:** Bill Sisk.

FIELD STAFF

Manager: Billy Gardner Jr. **Coach:** Ben Oglivie. **Pitching Coach:** Neil Allen. **Trainer:** Joel Smith.

GAME INFORMATION

Radio Announcer: Jim Tocco. **No of Games Broadcast:** Home-70 Road-70. **Flagship Station:** WLWI 1440-AM.

PA Announcer: Rick Hendrick. **Official Scorer:** Kyle Kreutzer.

Stadium Name: Montgomery Riverwalk Stadium. **Location:** I-65 to exit 172, east on Herron Street, left on Coosa Street. **Ticket Price Range:** $7-11.

Visiting Club Hotel: La Quinta Inn, 128 Eastern Blvd, Montgomery, AL 36117. **Telephone:** (334) 271-1260.

TENNESSEE SMOKIES

Office Address: 3540 Line Drive, Kodak, TN 37764.
Telephone: (865) 286-2300. **Fax:** (865) 523-9913.
E-Mail Address: info@smokiesbaseball.com. **Website:** www.smokiesbaseball.com.
Affiliation (first year): Chicago Cubs (2007). **Years in League:** 1964-67, 1972-

OWNERSHIP, MANAGEMENT

Operated By: SPBC LLC.

President: Doug Kirchhofer.

General Manager: Brian Cox. **Assistant GM:** Jeff Shoaf. **Director, Stadium Operations:** Bryan Webster. **Director, Community Relations:** Lauren Chesney. **Director, Communications/Media Relations:** Jon Zeitz. **Director, Ticket Operations:** Kamryn Hollar. **Director, Food/Beverage:** Tony DaSilveira. **Director, Marketing Development:** Rennie Leon. **Director, Client Services:** Ryan Cox. **Director, Field Operations:** Bob Shoemaker. **Director, Group Sales:** Ryan Koehler. **Group Sales Representatives:** Dan Blue, Matt Strutner, Allison Swafford, Chad Cartner. **Business Manager:** Suzanne French. **Merchandise Manager:** Mark French. **Operations Assistants:** Elizabeth Ann Flynn, Michael Kann, Paul Reynolds, Walter Sullins. **Administrative Assistants:** Tolena Trout, Jana Bray.

FIELD STAFF

Manager: Buddy Bailey. **Hitting Coach:** Barbaro Garbey. **Pitching Coach:** Dennis Lewallyn. **Trainer:** Nick Frangella.

GAME INFORMATION

Radio Announcer: Mick Gillispie. **No. of Games Broadcast:** Home-70 Road-70. **Flagship Station:** WNML 99.1-FM/990-AM.

PA Announcer: George Yardley. **Official Scorers:** Jeff Muir, Jack Tate.

Stadium Name: Smokies Park. **Location:** I-40 to exit 407, Highway 66 North. **Standard Game Times:** 7:15 p.m., **Sun. 5. Ticket Price Range:** $5-10.

Visiting Club Hotel: Days Inn-Exit 407, 3402 Winfield Dunn Pkwy, Kodak, TN 37764. **Telephone:** (865) 933-4500.

WEST TENN DIAMOND JAXX

Office Address: 4 Fun Place, Jackson, TN 38305.

Telephone: (731) 988-5299. **Fax:** (731) 988-5246.

E-Mail Address: fun@diamondjaxx.com. **Website:** www.diamondjaxx.com.

Affiliation (first year): Seattle Mariners (2007). **Years in League:** 1998-.

OWNERSHIP, MANAGEMENT

Operated by: Lozinak Baseball Properties LLC.

General Manager: Jeff Parker. **Director, Operations:** Robert Jones. **Director, Broadcasting/Media Relations:** Ron Potesta. **Director, Ticketing/Merchandise/Publications:** Liz Malone. **Director, Group Sales:** Jason Compton. **Manager, Community Group Sales:** David Madison. **Turf Manager:** Nash Jimenez. **Manager, Sales/Advertising:** Erica Davidson. **Clubhouse Manager:** Bradley Arnold.

FIELD STAFF

Manager: Scott Steinmann. **Coach:** Phil Plantier. **Pitching Coach:** Scott Budner. **Trainer:** Jeremy Clipperton.

GAME INFORMATION

Radio Announcer: Ron Potesta. **No. of Games Broadcast:** Home-70, Away-70. **Flagship Station:** WNWS 101.5-FM.

PA Announcer: Dan Reaves. **Official Scorer:** Tracy Brewer.

Stadium Name: Pringles Park. **Location:** From I-40, take exit 85 South on F.E. Wright Drive, left onto Ridgecrest Road. **Standard Game Times:** 7:05 p.m.; Sun 1:05. **Ticket Price Range:** $4.50-$9.

Visiting Club Hotel: Doubletree Hotel, 1770 Hwy. 45 Bypass, Jackson, TN 38305. **Telephone:** (731) 664-6900.

TEXAS LEAGUE

TEXAS LEAGUE OF PROFESSIONAL BASEBALL CLUBS

DOUBLE-A

Mailing Address: 2442 Facet Oak, San Antonio, TX 78232.

Telephone: (210) 545-5297. **Fax:** (210) 545-5298.

E-Mail Address: texasleague@sbcglobal.net. **Website:** www.texas-league.com.

Years League Active: 1888-1890, 1892, 1895-1899, 1902-1942, 1946-.

President, Treasurer: Tom Kayser.

Tom Kayser

Vice President: Matt Gifford. **Corporate Secretary:** J. J. Gottsch .

Directors: Jon Dandes (Northwest Arkansas)*, J.J. Gottsch (Corpus Christi), Mike Lamping (Springfield), Chuck Lamson (Tulsa), Scott Sonju (Frisco), Miles Prentice (Midland), Bill Valentine (Arkansas), Burl Yarbrough (San Antonio).

Division Structure: North—Arkansas, Northwest Arkansas, Springfield, Tulsa. South—Corpus Christi, Frisco, Midland, San Antonio.

Regular Season: 140 games (split schedule). **2008 Opening Date:** April 3. **Closing Date:** Sept. 1.

All-Star Game: June 25 at Springfield.

Playoff Format: First-half division winners play second-half division winners in best-of-five series. Winners meet in best-of-five series for league championship.

Roster Limit: 24. **Player Eligibility Rule:** No restrictions.

Brand of Baseball: Rawlings.

Umpires: Aaron Banks (Olathe, KS), Steve Barga (Castle Rock, CO), Clint Fagan (Tomball, TX), Tyler Funneman (Wildwood, IL), Mike Jarboe (La Crescenta, CA), Brad Lawhead (Pueblo West, CO), Mike Lusky (Baldwin Park, CA), Jason Millsap (Bryan, TX), T. J. Newport (Kalamazoo, MI), Brett Robson (Thornlie, West Australia, AU), Brian Sinclair (Lakewood, CO), Dixon Stureman (San Martin, CA).

STADIUM INFORMATION

			Dimensions				
Club	**Stadium**	**Opened**	**LF**	**CF**	**RF**	**Capacity**	**2007 Att.**
Arkansas	Dickey-Stephens Park	2007	332	400	330	7,000	372,475
Corpus Christi	Whataburger Field	2005	325	400	315	7,500	479,289
Frisco	Dr Pepper Ballpark	2003	330	410	322	10,000	545,421
Midland	Citibank Ballpark	2002	330	410	322	6,669	270,331
Northwest Arkansas	Arvest Ballpark	2008	325	400	325	6,500	*113,368
San Antonio	Nelson Wolff Municipal Stadium	1994	310	402	340	6,200	277,150
Springfield	John Q. Hammons Field	2003	315	400	330	8,458	460,063
Tulsa	Drillers Stadium	1981	335	390	340	11,003	296,017

*Team played in Wichita in 2007.

ARKANSAS TRAVELERS

Office Address: Dickey-Stephens Park, 400 West Broadway, North Little Rock, AR 72114.

Mailing Address: P.O. Box 55066, Little Rock, AR 72215.

Telephone: (501) 664-1555. **Fax:** (501) 664-1834.

E-Mail address: travs@travs.com. **Website:** www.travs.com.

Affiliation (first year): Los Angeles Angels (2001). **Years in League:** 1966-

OWNERSHIP, MANAGEMENT

President: Bert Parke.

Executive Vice President/COO: Bill Valentine. **General Manager:** Pete Laven. **Director, Media Relations/ Broadcasting:** Phil Elson. **Assistant GM/Tickets:** David Kay. **Director, Food/Beverage:** Kody LaFollett. **Director, In-Game Entertainment:** Tommy Adam. **Director, Suite Operations:** Jill McIlroy. **Director, Merchandise:** Alex Raley. **Administrative Assistant:** Nicole Ammann. **Office Manager/Account Executive:** Heather Massey. **Park Superintendent:** Greg Johnston. **Assistant Park Superintendent:** Reggie Temple. **Turf Manager:** Mark Brown. **Restaurant Manager:** Karen O'Keefe. **Bookkeeper:** Nena Valentine.

FIELD STAFF

Manager: Bobby Magallanes. **Batting Coach:** Eric Owens. **Pitching Coach:** Ken Patterson. **Trainer:** Brian Reinker. **Strength/Conditioning:** Mike Sigmund.

GAME INFORMATION

Radio Announcer: Phil Elson. **No. of Games Broadcast:** Home-70 Road-70. **Flagship Station:** KWBF 101.1-FM.

PA Announcer: Unavailable. **Official Scorers:** Tim Cooper, Doug Crise, Mike Garrity.

Stadium Name: Dickey-Stephens Park. **Location:** I-30 to Broadway exit. Proceed west to ballpark, located at Broadway Avenue and the Broadway Bridge. **Standard Game Time:** 7:10 p.m. **Ticket Price Range:** $3-10.

Visiting Club Hotel: LaQuinta-North Little Rock, 4100 E. McCain Blvd., North Little Rock, AR 72117. **Telephone:** (501) 758-8888.

CORPUS CHRISTI HOOKS

Office Address: 734 East Port Ave, Corpus Christi, TX 78401.

Telephone: (361) 561-4665. **Fax:** (361) 561-4666.

E-Mail Address: info@cchooks.com. **Website:** www.cchooks.com.

Affiliation (fourth year): Houston Astros (2005). **Years in League:** 1958-59, 2005-

OWNERSHIP, MANAGEMENT

Operated By: Ryan-Sanders Baseball.

Principal Owners: Eddie Maloney, Reese Ryan, Reid Ryan, Nolan Ryan, Brad Sanders, Bret Sanders, Don Sanders.

CEO: Reid Ryan. **CFO:** Reese Ryan. **COO:** Jay Miller.

President: J.J. Gottsch. **Vice President, Sales/Marketing:** Ken Schrom. **General Manager:** Michael Wood. **Director, Communications:** Matt Rogers. **Director, Broadcasting/Media Relations:** Matt Hicks. **Director, Sponsor Services:** Elisa Macias. **Director, Ballpark Entertainment:** Seamus Gallivan. **Director, Retail:** Brooke Milam. **Director, Group Sales:** Adam Nuse. **Account Executive:** Andy Steavens. **Box Office Manager:** Matt Boland. **Controller:** Christy Lockard. **Head Groundskeeper:** Garrett Reddehase. **Stadium Maintenance:** Leslie Hitt, Mark Rushton. **Clubhouse Manager:** Brad Starr. **Receptionist:** Ann Loberg.

FIELD STAFF

Manager: Luis Pujols. **Coaches:** John Tamargo Jr. **Pitching Coach:** Stan Boroski. **Trainer:** Jamey Snodgrass.

GAME INFORMATION

Radio Announcers: Matt Hicks. **No of Games Broadcast:** Home-70 Road-70. **Flagship Station:** News Radio 1360 KKTX-AM.

PA Announcer: Seamus Gallivan. **Official Scorer:** Unavailable.

Stadium Name: Whataburger Field. **Location:** I-37 to end of interstate, left at Chaparral, left at Hirsh Ave. **Ticket Price Range:** $5-12.

Visiting Club Hotel: Omni Hotel, 900 N. Shoreline Dr., Corpus Christi, TX 78401. **Telephone:** (361) 886-3553.

FRISCO ROUGH RIDERS

Office Address: 7300 RoughRiders Trail, Frisco, TX 75034.
Telephone: (972) 731-9200. **Fax:** (972) 731-5355.
E-Mail Address: info@ridersbaseball.com. **Website:** www.ridersbaseball.com.
Affiliation (first year): Texas Rangers (2003). **Years in League:** 2003-.

OWNERSHIP, MANAGEMENT

Operated by: Mandalay Sports Entertainment.

President/General Manager: Scott Sonju. **Executive Assistant/Office Manager:** Penny Martin. **Accounting/HR Manager:** Dustin Alban. **Senior Vice President:** Michael Byrnes. **VP, Corporate Partnerships:** Andrew Kahn. **Director, Partner Services:** Scott Burchett. **Partner/Event Services Coordinator:** Kristin Russell. **Graphic Design Coordinator:** Erik Davila. **Suites/Events Coordinator:** Megan Langwell. **Director, Partner/Community Relations:** Michael Davidow. **Director, Community Development:** Mara Simon-Meyer. **Senior Director, Group Sales:** Jenna Snider. **Ticket Operations Managers:** Mac Amin, Shannon Muller. **Sales/Marketing Coordinator:** Meghan Burkett. **Corporate Marketing Managers:** Justin Ramquist, Jared Venia, Mark Playko, Jordan King, Erich Dietz, Chris Sorrels, Bradford Lacy, Matthew Hernandez. **Director, Inside Sales/Customer Service:** Jay Lockett. **Senior Group Sales Coordinator:** Ryan Bippert. **Group Sales Coordinators:** Anthony Hunt, Joey Schumacher, Will LoVerde, Eric Rowley, Allison Cloud. **Director, Game Entertainment:** Gabriel Wilhelm. **Director, Operations:** Michael Poole. **Director of Maintenance:** Alfonso Bailon. **Assistant Director, Maintenance:** Gustavo Bailon. **Head Groundskeeper:** David Bicknell. **Operations Manager:** Scott Arnold. **Baseball Operations Manager:** Brian SanFilippo.

FIELD STAFF

Manager: Scott Little. **Coach:** Scott Coolbaugh. **Pitching Coach:** Terry Clark. **Trainer:** Jason Roberts.

GAME INFORMATION

Broadcaster: Scott Garner. **No. of Games Broadcast:** Home-70, Away-70. **Radio Station:** Unavailable.

PA Announcer: John Clemens. **Official Scorers:** Kenny King, Lary Bump.

Stadium Name: Dr Pepper Ballpark. **Location:** Dallas North Tollway to State Highway 121. **Standard Game Times:** 7 p.m., Sun. 6. **Ticket Price Range:** $7-15.

Visiting Club Hotel: ExtendedStay Deluxe Plano/Legacy Area, 2900 North Dallas Tollway. **Telephone:** (972) 378-9978.

MIDLAND ROCKHOUNDS

Office Address: 5514 Champions Dr., Midland, TX 79706.
Telephone: (432) 520-2255. **Fax:** (432) 520-8326.
Website: www.midlandrockhounds.org.
Affiliation (first year): Oakland Athletics (1999). **Years in League:** 1972-.

OWNERSHIP, MANAGEMENT

Operated By: Midland Sports, Inc.

Principal Owners: Miles Prentice, Bob Richmond. **President:** Miles Prentice.

Executive Vice President: Bob Richmond. **General Manager:** Monty Hoppel. **Assistant GM:** Jeff VonHolle. **Assistant GM, Marketing/Tickets:** Jamie Richardson. **Director, Broadcasting/Publications:** Bob Hards. **Executive Director, Timeout Sports Inc.:** Dave Baur. **Concessions Assistant:** Edwin White. **Assistant GM, Facilities Manager:** Ray Fieldhouse. **Media Relations/IT Director:** Greg Bergman. **Director, Group Sales:** Jeremy Lukas. **Director, Business Operations:** Eloisa Galvan. **Head Groundskeeper:** Eric Ferland. **Assistant Groundskeeper:** Chris Mills. **Director, Ticket Operations:** Michael Richardson. **Customer Service/Advertising Director:** Michael Fitts. **Sales Representative:** Harold Fuller. **Director, Team/Community Relations:** Kyle Pierce. **Administrative Assistants:** John Conners, David Hutfles, Jason Tarnowski.

FIELD STAFF

Manager: Webster Garrison. **Hitting Coach:** Casey Myers. **Pitching Coach:** Scott Emerson. **Trainer:** Justin Whitehouse.

GAME INFORMATION

Radio Announcer: Bob Hards. **No. of Games Broadcast:** Home-70, Away-70. **Flagship Station:** KCRS 550-AM.

PA Announcer: Kevin Porter. **Official Scorer:** Paul Burnett.

Stadium Name: Citibank Ballpark. **Location:** From I-20, exit Loop 250 North to Highway 191 intersection. **Standard Game Times:** 7 p.m., 6:30 (April-May, August); Sun. 4, 6 (June-Aug.). **Ticket Price Range:** $5-9.

Visiting Club Hotel: Clarion Hotel and Suites, 4300 W. Hwy. 80, Midland, TX 79703. **Telephone:** (432) 697-3181.

NORTHWEST ARKANSAS NATURALS

Office Address: 3000 S. 56th Street, Springdale, AR 72762.
Mailing Address: P.O. Box 6817, Springdale, AR 72766.
Telephone: (479) 927-4900. **Fax:** (479) 756-8088.
E-Mail Address: info@nwanaturals.com. **Website:** www.nwanaturals.com.
Affiliation (first year): Kansas City Royals (1995). **Years in League:** 1987-

OWNERSHIP, MANAGEMENT

Principal Owner: Rich Products Corp.

Chairman: Robert Rich Jr. **President/Rich Entertainment:** Melinda Rich. **President/Rich Baseball:** Jon Dandes.

General Manager: Eric Edelstein. **Assistant GM:** Justin Cole. **Business Manager:** Anna Whitham. **Marketing/PR Manager:** Frank Novak. **Stadium Operations Manager:** Monty Sowell. **Merchandise Coordinator/Account Executive:** Morgan Smith. **Broadcaster:** Steven Davis. **Account Executive/Ticket Sales Coordinator:** Dustin Dethlefs. **Account Executives:** Brian Nickerson, Andrew Thaxton, Ryan Ritchie, Chantelle Abbott. **Game Day Operations Associate:** Kim Christie. **PR/Marketing Associate:** Josh Castillo. **Stadium Operations Associate:** Corey Whorton. **Field Operations Coordinator:** Josh Anderson. **Clubhouse Manager:** Danny Helmer.

FIELD STAFF

Manager: Brian Poldberg. **Hitting Coach:** Tommy Gregg. **Pitching Coach:** Larry Carter. **Trainer:** Chris DeLucia

GAME INFORMATION

Radio Announcers: Steven Davis. **No. of Games Broadcast:** Home-70, Away-70. **Flagship:** KURM 790 AM.

PA Announcer: Unavailable. **Official Scorer:** Unavailable.

Stadium Name: Arvest Ballpark. **Location:** I-540 to U.S. 412 West (Sunset Ave). Left on 56th St. **Standard Game Times:** 7 p.m.; 7:30 p.m. Friday; 4 p.m. Sunday. **Visiting Club Hotel:** Holiday Inn Springdale; 1500 S. 48th St., Springdale, AR 72762. **Telephone:** (479) 751-8300.

SAN ANTONIO MISSIONS

Office Address: 5757 Hwy. 90 W, San Antonio, TX 78227.
Telephone: (210) 675-7275. **Fax:** (210) 670-0001.
E-Mail address: sainfo@samissions.com. **Website:** www.samissions.com.
Affiliation (first year): San Diego Padres (2007). **Years in League:** 1888, 1892, 1895-99, 1907-42, 1946-64, 1968-

OWNERSHIP, MANAGEMENT

Operated By: Elmore Sports Group. **Principal Owner:** David Elmore.

President: Burl Yarbrough. **General Manager:** David Gasaway. **Assistant GMs:** Jeff Long, Jeff Stewart. **Director, Accounting:** Debra Zepeda-Banda. **Field Superintendent:** Karsten Blackwelder. **Director, Media Relations:** Mickey Holt. **Director, Marketing:** Rudy Vasquez. **Manager, Group Sales:** Bill Gerlt. **Director, Box Office:** Tiffany Johnson. **Director, Stadium Operations:** Jesse Perez. **Account Executives:** George Levandoski, Royce Hickman, John Hernandez, Stu Paul, Mac Simmons. **Office Manager:** Delia Rodriguez. **Clubhouse Operations:** Matt Martinez, Jim Vasaldua.

FIELD STAFF

Manager: Billy Masse. **Coach:** Terry Kennedy. **Pitching Coach:** Steve Webber. **Trainer:** Wade Yamasaki.

GAME INFORMATION

Radio Announcers: Roy Acuff, Stu Paul. **No of Games Broadcast:** Home-70 Road-70. **Flagship Station:** KKYX 680-AM.

PA Announcer: Stan Kelly. **Official Scorer:** David Humphrey.

Stadium Name: Nelson W. Wolff Municipal Stadium. **Location:** From I-10, I-35, or I-37, take U.S. 90 West to Callaghan Road exit, stadium on right. **Ticket Price Range:** $4-9.

Visiting Club Hotel: Quality Inn and Suites, 9522 Brimhall Rd, San Antonio, TX 78254. **Telephone:** (210) 372-9900.

SPRINGFIELD CARDINALS

Office Address: 955 East Trafficway, Springfield, MO 65802.
Telephone: (417) 863-2143. **Fax:** (417) 863-0388.
E-Mail address: springfield@stlcardinals.com. **Website:** www.springfieldcardinals.com.
Affiliation (first year): St. Louis Cardinals (2005). **Years in League:** 2005-

OWNERSHIP, MANAGEMENT

Operated By: St. Louis Cardinals.

Vice President/General Manager: Matt Gifford. **VP, Baseball/Business Operations:** Scott Smulczenski. **VP, Sales/Marketing:** Kirk Elmquist. **VP, Facility Operations:** Bill Fischer. **Operations Manager:** Ron Henderson. **Box Office Manager:** Angela Deke. **Public Relations Manager/Broadcaster:** Mike Lindskog. **Public Relations Coordinator:** Becky Ziegler. **Senior Account Executive:** Dan Reiter. **Group Sales Coordinator:** Kate Mata. **Account Executives:** Jenny Barlow, Becky Bowles, Dan Kreigshauser, Duane Miller, Megan Welch. **Visual Marketing Specialist:** Jacob Neimeyer. **Ticket Sales:** Jared Nevins, Christine Weyler. **Head Groundskeeper:** Brock Phipps. **Assistant Groundskeeper:** Aaron Lowrey.

FIELD STAFF

Manager: Ron Warner. **Hitting Coach:** Derrick May. **Pitching Coach:** Bryan Eversgerd. **Trainer:** Jay Pierson.

GAME INFORMATION

Radio Announcer: Rob Evans. **No of Games Broadcast:** Home-70 Road-70. **Flagship Station:** JOCK 98.7-FM.

PA Announcer: Kevin Howard. **Official Scorer:** Unavailable.

Stadium Name: Hammons Field. **Location:** Highway 65 to Chestnut Expressway exit, west to National, south on National, west on Trafficway. **Standard Game Time:** 7:10 p.m. **Ticket Price Range:** $6-24.50.

Visiting Club Hotel: University Plaza Hotel, 333 John Q. Hammons Parkway, Springfield, MO 65806. **Telephone:** (417) 864-7333.

TULSA DRILLERS

Office Address: 4802 E. 15th St, Tulsa, OK 74112.
Telephone: (918) 744-5998. **Fax:** (918) 747-3267.
E-Mail Address: mail@tulsadrillers.com. **Website:** www.tulsadrillers.com.
Affiliation (first year): Colorado Rockies (2003). **Years in League:** 1933-42, 1946-65, 1977-

OWNERSHIP, MANAGEMENT

Operated By: Tulsa Baseball Inc.

Principal Owner/President: Chuck Lamson. **Vice President:** Went Hubbard.

General Manager: Mike Melega. **Assistant GM:** Jason George. **Bookkeeper:** Cheryll Couey. **Director, Ticket Sales:** Mark Hilliard. **Director, Operations:** Peter McAdams. **Director, Public/Media Relations:** Brian Carroll. **Manager, Promotions/Merchandise:** Tom Jones. **Manager, Group Ticket Sales:** Brandon Shiers. **Group Ticket Sales Assistant:** Geoff Beatty. **Operations Assistant:** Mark Rasmussen. **Ticket Sales Assistant:** Kyle Manigold. **Promotions/Merchandise Assistant:** Michael Taranto. **Head Groundskeeper:** Gary Shepherd. **Assistant Groundskeeper:** Logan Medlock. **Home Clubhouse Attendant:** Unavailable. **Visiting Clubhouse Attendent:** Unavailable.

FIELD STAFF

Manager: Stu Cole. **Coach:** Dave Hajek. **Pitching Coach:** Bo McLaughlin. **Trainer:** Austin O'Shea. **Strength Coach:** Tyler Christiansen.

GAME INFORMATION

Radio Announcer: Mark Neely. **No. of Games Broadcast:** Home-70 Road-70. **Flagship Station:** KTBZ 1430-AM.

PA Announcer: Kirk McAnany. **Official Scorers:** Bruce Howard, Duane DaPron.

Stadium Name: Drillers Stadium. **Location:** Three miles north of I-44 and 1.5 miles south of I-244 at 15th Street and Yale Avenue. **Standard Game Times:** 7:05 p.m.; Sun. 2:05. **Ticket Price Range:** $6-12.50.

Visiting Club Hotel: Southern Hills Marriott, 1902 E. 71st St., Tulsa, OK 74136. **Telephone:** (918) 493-7000.

CALIFORNIA LEAGUE

HIGH CLASS A

Office Address: 2380 S. Bascom Ave., Suite 200, Campbell, CA 95008.
Telephone: (408) 369-8038. **Fax:** (408) 369-1409.
E-Mail Address: cabaseball@aol.com. **Website:** www.californialeague.com.

Years League Active: 1941-1942, 1946-.

President/Treasurer: Joseph M. Gagliardi.

Vice President: David Elmore (Inland Empire). **Corporate Secretary:** John Oldham.

Directors: Bobby Brett (High Desert), Peter Carfagna (Lancaster), David Elmore (Inland Empire), D.G. Elmore (Bakersfield), Gary Jacobs (Lake Elsinore), Michael Savit (Modesto), Tom Seidler (Visalia), Hank Stickney (Rancho Cucamonga), Tom Volpe (Stockton), Jim Weyermann (San Jose).

League Administrator: Kathleen Kelly. **Director, Umpire Development:** John Oldham. **League Historian:** Chris Lampe.

Division Structure: North—Bakersfield, Modesto, San Jose, Stockton, Visalia. South—High Desert, Inland Empire, Lake Elsinore, Lancaster, Rancho Cucamonga.

Regular Season: 140 games (split schedule). **2008 Opening Date:** April 3. **Closing Date:** Sept. 1.

Joe Gagliardi

Playoff Format: Six teams. First-half winners in each division earn first-round bye; second-half winners meet wild cards with next best overall records in best-of-three quarterfinals. Winners meet first-half champions in best-of-five semifinals. Winners meet in best-of-five series for league championship.

All-Star Game: June 24 at Myrtle Beach (California League vs. Carolina League).

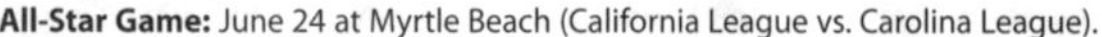

Roster Limit: 25 active. **Player Eligibility Rule:** No more than two players and one player/coach on active list may have more than six years experience.

Brand of Baseball: Rawlings.

Umpires: Unavailable.

STADIUM INFORMATION

			Dimensions				
Club	Stadium	Opened	LF	CF	RF	Capacity	2007 Att.
Bakersfield	Sam Lynn Ballpark	1941	328	354	328	4,200	78,888
High Desert	Mavericks Stadium	1991	340	401	340	3,808	117,262
Inland Empire	Arrowhead Credit Union Park	1996	330	410	330	5,000	174,152
Lake Elsinore	The Diamond	1994	330	400	310	7,866	231,063
Lancaster	Clear Channel Stadium	1996	350	410	350	4,500	125,353
Modesto	John Thurman Field	1952	312	400	319	4,000	158,936
Rancho Cucamonga	The Epicenter	1993	335	400	335	6,615	290,843
San Jose	Municipal Stadium	1942	340	390	340	4,000	171,028
Stockton	Banner Island Ballpark	2005	300	399	326	5,200	218,497
Visalia	Recreation Park	1946	320	405	320	1,647	83,452

BAKERSFIELD BLAZE

Office Address: 4009 Chester Ave., Bakersfield, CA 93301.
Mailing Address: P.O. Box 10031, Bakersfield, CA 93389.
Telephone: (661) 716-4487. **Fax:** (661) 322-6199.
E-Mail Address: blaze@bakersfieldblaze.com. **Website:** www.bakersfieldblaze.com.
Affiliation: Texas Rangers (2005). **Years In League:** 1941-42, 1946-75, 1978-79, 1982-

OWNERSHIP, MANAGEMENT

Principal Owner: Bakersfield Baseball Club LLC.

General Manager: Shawn Schoolcraft. **Director, Food/Beverage:** Brandon Caudill. **Manager, Community Relations:** Alicja Burnette. **Head Groundskeeper:** Tim Martin. **Clubhouse Manager:** Mike Marshment.

FIELD STAFF

Manager: Damon Berryhill. **Coach:** Brant Brown. **Pitching Coach:** Dave Chavarria. **Trainer:** Jeff Bodenhammer.

GAME INFORMATION

Radio: None.

PA Announcer: Mike Cushine. **Official Scorer:** Tim Wheeler.

Stadium Name: Sam Lynn Ballpark. **Location:** Highway 99 to California Avenue, east three miles to Chester Avenue, north two miles to stadium. **Standard Game Time:** 7:30 p.m. **Ticket Price Range:** $5-9.

Visiting Club Hotel: Days Inn, 818 Real Road, Bakersfield, CA 93309.. **Telephone:** (661) 324-6666.

HIGH DESERT MAVERICKS

Office Address: 1200 Stadium Way, Adelanto, CA 92301.
Telephone: (760) 246-6287. **Fax:** (760) 246-3197.
E-Mail Address: mavsinfo@hdmavs.com. **Website:** www.hdmavs.com.
Affiliation (first year): Seattle Mariners (2007). **Years in League:** 1991-

OWNERSHIP, MANAGEMENT

Operated By: High Desert Mavericks Inc.

Principal Owner: Bobby Brett.

Brett Sports COO: Andy Billig. **President:** Brent Miles. **Vice President/General Manager:** Derrel Ebert. **Assistant General Manager/Sponsorships:** Tim Altier. **Director,Ticket Sales:** CJ Loper. **Director, Group Sales:** Eric Jensen. **Account Executive/Director, Broadcasting:** Alex Freedman. **Controller:** Robin Buckles. **Director, Concessions:** Larry Cummins.

FIELD STAFF

Manager: Jim Horner. **Coach:** Tommy Cruz. **Pitching Coach:** Lance Painter.

GAME INFORMATION

Radio Announcer: Alex Freedman. **No of Games Broadcast:** Home-70 Road-70. **Flagship Station:** KRAK 960-AM.

PA Announcer: Ernie Escajieda. **Official Scorer:** Bob Witt.

Stadium Name: Mavericks Stadium. **Location:** I-15 North to Highway 395 to Adelanto Road. **Ticket Price Range:** $6-8.

Visiting Club Hotel: Ramada Inn, I-15 and Palmdale Road, Victorville, CA 92392. **Telephone:** (760) 245-6565.

INLAND EMPIRE 66ERS

Office Address: 280 South E St., San Bernardino, CA 92401.
Telephone: (909) 888-9922. **Fax:** (909) 888-5251.
Website: www.ie66ers.com
Affiliation (first year): Los Angeles Dodgers (2007). **Years in League:** 1941, 1987-.

OWNERSHIP, MANAGEMENT

Operated by: Inland Empire 66ers Baseball Club of San Bernardino.

Principal Owners: David Elmore, Donna Tuttle.

Owner/President: Dave Elmore. **Owner/Chairman:** Donna Tuttle. **General Manager:** Loren Foxx. **Vice President:** Paul Stiritz. **Vice President, Business Development:** Dave Oldham. **CFO:** Ana Gonzalez. **Director, Broadcasting:** Mike Saeger. **Director, Corporate Communications:** Laura Tolbirt. **Director, Food/Beverage:** Joe Hudson. **Manager, Stadium Operations:** Ryan English. **Director, Entertainment:** Raj Narayanan. **Director, Mascot Operations:** Raymond Anaya. **Manager, Group Hospitality/Client Sevices:** Jessica Scott. **Asistant Director, Broadcasating:** Luke Foth. **Account Executives:** Matt Koehn, Ryan Wilson. **Account Executive/Administrative Assistant:** Hannah Woolverton. **Head Groundskeeper:** Dan Mudd.

FIELD STAFF

Manager: John Valentin. **Coach:** Henry Cruz. **Pitching Coach:** Charlie Hough. **Trainer:** Yosuke Nakajima.

GAME INFORMATION

Radio Announcer: Mike Saeger, Luke Foth. **Flagship Station:** KCAA 1050-AM.

PA Announcer: J.J. Gould. **Official Scorer:** Josh Rawtich.

Stadium Name: Arrowhead Credit Union Park. **Location:** From south, I-215 to 2nd Street exit, east on 2nd, right on G Street; from north, I-215 to 3rd Street exit, left on Rialto, right on G Street. **Standard Game Times:** 7:05 p.m.; Sun. (April-May) 2:05, (July-Aug.) 6:05. **Ticket Price Range:** $5-9.

Visiting Club Hotel: Clarion Hotel, 295 North E Street, San Bernandino, CA 92401. **Telephone:** (909) 381-5288.

LAKE ELSINORE STORM

Office Address: 500 Diamond Dr, Lake Elsinore, CA 92530.

Mailing Address: P.O. Box 535, Lake Elsinore, CA 92531.

Telephone: (951) 245-4487. **Fax:** (951) 245-0305.

E-Mail Address: info@stormbaseball.com. **Website:** www.stormbaseball.com.

Affiliation (first year): San Diego Padres (2001). **Years in League:** 1994-

OWNERSHIP, MANAGEMENT

Operated By: Storm LP.

Principal Owner: Gary Jacobs.

President: Dave Oster. **Vice President/General Manager** Chris Jones. **Assistant: GM:** Tracy Kessman. **Assistant GM/Director, Sales:** Allan Benavides. **Director, Broadcasting:** Sean McCall. **Director, Media Relations:** Steve Smaldone. **Senior Graphic Designer:** Mark Beskid. **Director, New Business:** Dave Endress. **Director, Food/Beverage:** Arjun Suresh. **Director, Merchandising:** Donna Grunow. **Assistant Director, Merchandising:** Kyle Hanrahan. **Director, Business Administration:** Corrine Roberge. **Assistant Director, Business Administration:** Christina Conlon. **Director, Ticket Operations:** Ruli Garcia. **Director, Ticket Sales:** Joe Menez. **Director, Mascot Operations:** Patrick Gardenier. **Director, Game Operations:** Matt Dompe. **Assistant Director, Group Sales:** Dave McCrory. **Account Executive:** Rick Riegler. **Ticket Sales Executives:** Robert Gillet, Michael Festa. **General Manager, Storm Entertainment:** Bruce Kessman. **Director, Stadium Operations:** Matt Thompson. **Assistant Director, Stadium Operations:** Roberto Cabrera. **Director, Finance:** Laurie Barron. **Executive Chef:** Steve Bearse. **Event Coordinator:** Kim Johnson. **Head Groundskeeper:** Chris Ralston. **Assistant Groundskeeper:** Peter Hayes. **Office Manager:** Jennifer Trammell.

FIELD STAFF

Manager: Carlos Lezcano. **Coach:** Shane Spencer. **Pitching Coach:** Wally Whitehurst.

GAME INFORMATION

Radio Announcer: Sean McCall. **No. of Games Broadcast:** Home-70 Road-70. **Flagship Station:** San Diego 1700 AM.

PA Announcer: Joe Martinez. **Official Scorer:** Lloyd Nixon.

Stadium Name: The Diamond. **Location:** From I-15, exit at Diamond Drive, west one mile to stadium. **Standard Game Times:** 7:08 p.m.; Wed. 6:08; Sun. 2:08 (first half), 6:08 (second half). **Ticket Price Range:** $7-10.

Visiting Club Hotel: Lake Elsinore Hotel and Casino, 20930 Malaga St, Lake Elsniore, CA 92530. **Telephone:** (951) 674-3101.

LANCASTER JETHAWKS

Office Address: 45116 Valley Central Way, Lancaster, CA 93536.

Telephone: (661) 726-5400. **Fax:** (661) 726-5406.

E-Mail Address: info@jethawks.com. **Website:** www.jethawks.com.

Affiliation (first year): Boston Red Sox (2007). **Years in League:** 1996-.

OWNERSHIP, MANAGEMENT

Operated By: Hawks Nest LLC.

President: Peter Carfagna Sr. **Senior Vice President:** Pete Carfagna.

General Manager: Brad Seymour. **Assistant GM:** Derek Sharp. **Director, Group Ticket Sales:** Jeff Stewart. **Director, Stadium Operations:** John Laferney. **Director, Promotions:** Jeremy Castillo. **Director, Broadcasting/Media Relations:** Jeff Lasky. **Director, Community Relations:** Will Murphy. **Director, Food/Beverage:** Stephen Toth. **Account Executive:** Trent Wondra. **Office Administrator:** Michelle Seymour. **Office/Merchandising Assistant:** Larry Brady.

FIELD STAFF

Manager: Chad Epperson. **Coach:** Carlos Febles. **Pitching Coach:** Unavailable. **Trainer:** Jon Jochim.

GAME INFORMATION

Radio Announcer: Jeff Lasky. **No. of Games Broadcast:** Home-70, Away-70. **Flagship Station:** KTPI 1340-AM.

PA Announcer: Fred Jaramillo. **Official Scorer:** David Guenther.

Stadium Name: Clear Channel Stadium. **Location:** Highway 14 in Lancaster to Avenue I exit, west one block to stadium. **Standard Game Times:** 7 p.m.; Sat., 5 (April-June); Sun. 2 (April–June), 5 (June-Sept.). **Ticket Price Range:** $6-12.

Visiting Club Hotel: Best Western Antelope Valley Inn, 44055 North Sierra Hwy., Lancaster, CA 93534. **Telephone:** (661) 948-4651.

MODESTO NUTS

Office Address: 601 Neece Dr., Modesto, CA 95351.
Mailing Address: P.O. Box 883, Modesto, CA 95353.
Telephone: (209) 572-4487. **Fax:** (209) 572-4490.
E-Mail Address: fun@modestonuts.com. **Website:** www.modestonuts.com.
Affiliation (first year): Colorado Rockies (2005). **Years in League:** 1946-64, 1966-.

OWNERSHIP, MANAGEMENT

Operated by: HWS Group IV.

Principal Owner: Mike Savit.

President: Bill Shanahan. **Vice President:** Michael Gorrasi. **General Manager:** Alex Schwerin. **Marketing/Community Relations Manager:** Samantha Sabarese. **Director, Tickets:** Tyler Richardson. **Accounting/HR Manager:** Debra Baucom. **Director, Media Services:** Grant Boring. **Director. Group Sales:** Eric Rauber. **Director, Food/Beverage:** Ed Mack. **Director, Stadium Operations:** Anthony DeGrande. **Office Manager:** Julia Hensen.

FIELD STAFF

Manager: Jerry Weinstein. **Coach:** Duane Espy. **Pitching Coach:** Butch Hughes. **Trainer:** Chris Strickland.

GAME INFORMATION

Radio Announcer: Unavailable. **No. of Games Broadcast:** Home-50, Away-50. **Flagship Station:** KESP 970-AM.

PA Announcer: Unavailable. **Official Scorer:** Unavailable.

Stadium Name: John Thurman Field. **Location:** Highway 99 in southwest Modesto to Tuolomne Boulevard exit, west on Tuolomne for one block to Neece Drive, left for 1/4 mile to stadium. **Standard Game Times:** 7:05 p.m.; Sun. 1:05 (April-June), 6:05 (July-Aug.). **Ticket Price Range:** $5-10.

Visiting Club Hotel: Ramada Inn, 2001 W. Orangeburg Ave., Modesto, CA 95350. **Telephone:** (209) 521-9000.

RANCHO CUCAMONGA QUAKES

Office Address: 8408 Rochester Ave., Rancho Cucamonga, CA 91730.
Mailing Address: P.O. Box 4139, Rancho Cucamonga, CA 91729.
Telephone: (909) 481-5000. **Fax:** (909) 481-5005.
E-Mail Address: info@rcquakes.com. **Website:** www.rcquakes.com.
Affiliation (first year): Los Angeles Angels (2001). **Years in League:** 1993-

OWNERSHIP, MANAGEMENT

Operated By: Valley Baseball Inc.

Owners: Henry Stickney, Scott Ostlund, Charles Buquet.

Executive Vice President/General Manager: Gerard McKearny. **VP, Operations/Asst. GM:** Matt Blankenheim. **VP, Ticket Operations:** Kyle Schoonover. **Director, Finance:** Joanne Araiza. **Director, Entertainment:** Jonathan Mercier. **Director, Broadcasting/Media Relations:** Jeff Levering. **Director, Group Services/Guest Relations:** Linda Rathfon. **Director, Food/Beverage:** Joe Henderson. **Director, Marketing:** Kevin Shaw. **Community Relations Manager:** Ashley Cordero. **Ticket Office Manager:** Rachel Barker. **Director, Inside Sales:** Matt Bumpass. **Food Operations Managr:** Mike Liotta. **Corporate Partners Account Executives:** William Esterline, Lauren Voors. **Group Sales Representatives.:** Megan De La Hoya, Matt Dedeluk, Ryan Eifler. **Corporate Sponsorship Services Representative:** Alison Dahlgren. **Group Sales Representative:** Jan Selasky.

FIELD STAFF

Manager: Ever Magallanes. **Coach:** Francisco Matos. **Pitching Coach:** Dan Ricabal. **Trainer:** Eric Munson.

GAME INFORMATION

Radio Announcer: Jeff Levering.

PA Announcer: Unavailable. **Official Scorer:** Unavailable.

Stadium Name: The Epicenter. **Location:** I-10 to I-15 North, exit at Foothill Boulevard, left on Foothill, left on Rochester to Stadium. **Standard Game Times:** 7:05 p.m.; Sun. 2:05 (April-July), 5:05 (July-Sept.). **Ticket Price Range:** $8-12.

Visiting Club Hotel: Best Western Heritage Inn, 8179 Spruce Ave, Rancho Cucamonga, CA 91730. **Telephone:** (909) 466-1111.

SAN JOSE GIANTS

Office Address: 588 E. Alma Ave., San Jose, CA 95112.
Mailing Address: P.O. Box 21727, San Jose, CA 95151.
Telephone: (408) 297-1435. **Fax:** (408) 297-1453.
E-Mail Address: info@sjgiants.com. **Website:** www.sjgiants.com.
Affiliation (first year): San Francisco Giants (1988). **Years in League:** 1942, 1947-58, 1962-76, 1979-.

OWNERSHIP, MANAGEMENT

Operated by: Progress Sports Management.
Principal Owners: Heidi Stamas, Richard Beahrs, Rich Kelley.
President, CEO: Jim Weyermann.

Vice President/General Manager: Mark Wilson. **VP, Marketing/Public Affairs:** Juliana Paoli. **Assistant GM:** Zach Walter. **Director, Player Relations:** Linda Pereira. **Director, Stadium Operations:** Lance Motch. **Director, Group Sales:** Ainslie Reynolds. **Controller:** Cami Yuasa. **Manager, Marketing/Public Affairs:** Mandy Stone. **Manager, Ticket Services:** Katherine Krassilnikoff. **Assistant Manager, Box Office:** Tyler Weyermann. **Ticket Sales Account Executives:** Laura Miller, Taylor Haynes, Adam Hensleigh. **Radio Broadcaster/Baseball Operations:** Joe Ritzo. **International Relations Executive:** Kaz Sekine. **Merchandise Intern:** Reiko Jinno..

FIELD STAFF

Manager: Steve Decker. **Coach:** Gary Davenport. **Pitching Coach:** Pat Rice. **Trainer:** Yukiya Oba.

GAME INFORMATION

Radio Broadcaster: Joe Ritzo. **No. of Games Broadcast:** Home-70, Away-70. **Station:** www.sjgiants.com.
PA Announcer: Russ Call. **Official Scorers:** Michael Melligan, Luke Fortier.

Stadium Name: Municipal Stadium. **Location:** South on I-280: Take the 10th/11th Street Exit. Turn right on 10th Street. Turn left on Alma Street. North on I-280: Take the 10th/11th Street Exit. Turn left on 10th Street. Turn Left on Alma Street**.** **Standard Game Times:** 7 p.m.; Sat. 5 (6 after July 5); Sun. 2 (5 after June 8). **Ticket Price Range:** $6-14.

Visiting Club Hotel: Pruneyard Plaza, 1995 S. Bascom Ave., Campbell, CA 95008. **Telephone:** (408) 559-4300.

STOCKTON PORTS

Office Address: 404 W. Fremont St, Stockton, CA 95203.
Telephone: (209) 644-1900. **Fax:** (209) 644-1931.
E-Mail Address: info@stocktonports.com. **Website:** www.stocktonports.com.
Affiliation (first year): Oakland Athletics (2005). **Years in League:** 1941, 1946-72, 1978-

OWNERSHIP, MANAGEMENT

Operated By: 7th Inning Stretch LLC.

President/General Manager: Pat Filippone. **Assistant GM, Tickets:** Luke Reiff. **Director, Broadcasting/Public Relations:** Zack Bayrouty. **Director, Marketing:** Eron Zehavi. **Director, Group Sales:** Ben Carr. **Director, Finance:** Jason Steffens. **Senior Account Executive:** John Watts. **Community Relations Manager:** Danielle Alt. **Stadium Operations Manager:** Travis McPherson. **Box Office Manager:** Justin Gray. **Inside Sales Manager:** Jeff Kaminski. **Group Sales Account Executives:** Jennifer Norris, Tim Pasisz. **Special Events Account Executive:** Kyle DeWitt. **Food/Beverage Service Provider:** Ovations. **Front Desk:** Deborah Auditor.

FIELD STAFF

Manager: Darren Bush. **Coach:** Tim Garland. **Pitching Coach:** Garvin Alson. **Trainer:** Brian Thorson.

GAME INFORMATION

Radio Announcer: Zack Bayrouty. **No of Games Broadcast:** Home-70, Away-70. **Flagship Station:** Unavailable.
PA Announcer: Unavailable. **Official Scorer:** Paul Muyskens.

Stadium Name: Banner Island Ballpark. **Location:** From I-5/99, take Crosstown Freeway (Highway 4) exit El Dorado Street, north on El Dorado to Freemont Street, left on Freemont. **Standard Game Times:** 7:05 p.m.; Sun. 2:05 first half, 6:05 second half. **Ticket Price Range:** $5-15.

Visiting Club Hotel: Best Western Waterloo, 4219 East Waterloo Road, Stockton CA 95215. **Telephone:** (209) 931-3131.

VISALIA OAKS

Office Address: 440 N. Giddings St, Visalia, CA 93291.
Telephone: (559) 625-0480. **Fax:** (559) 739-7732.
E-Mail Address: oaksbaseball@hotmail.com. **Website:** www.oaksbaseball.com.
Affiliation (first year): Arizona Diamondbacks (2007). **Years in League:** 1946-62, 1968-75, 1977-

OWNERSHIP, MANAGEMENT

Operated By: Top of the Third Inc.

Principal Owners: Kevin O'Malley, Tom Seidler.

President/General Manager: Tom Seidler. **Executive Assistant:** Jennifer Pendergraft. **Sales Manager/Legal Counsel:** Liz Martin. **Director, Broadcasting:** Josh Rogol. **Manager, Media Relations:** Dan Besbris. **Head Groundskeeper:** Tom Drietz. **Ballpark Operations Manager:** Dan Sprung. **Ticket Manager:** Mike Candela. **Marketing Coordinator:** Stephanie Skulstad. **Group Coordinator:** Pamela Lott. **Marketing Intern:** Maureen Shanahan.

FIELD STAFF

Manager: Mike Bell. **Coach:** Rick Burleson. **Pitching Coach:** Wellington Cepeda. **Trainer:** Ryan DiPanfilo. **Strength/ Conditioning:** Josh Cuffe.

GAME INFORMATION

Radio Announcers: Josh Rogel/Dan Besbris. **No. of Games Broadcast:** Home-70, Away-70. **Flagship Station:** KJUG 1270-AM.

PA Announcer: Unavailable. **Official Scorer:** Harry Kargenian.

Stadium Name: Recreation Park. **Location:** From highway 99, take 198 East to Mooney Boulevard exit, left at second signal on Giddings; four blocks to ballpark. **Standard Game Times:** Mon.-Sat. 7:05 p.m.; Sun., 1:05 (first half), 7:05 (second half). **Ticket Price Range:** $5-15.

Visiting Club Hotel: Lamp Liter Inn, 3300 W Mineral King Ave, Visalia, CA 93291. **Telephone:** (559) 732-4511.

CAROLINA LEAGUE

HIGH CLASS A

Office Address: 1806 Pembroke Rd., Greensboro, NC 27408.
Mailing Address: P.O. Box 9503, Greensboro, NC 27429.
Telephone: (336) 691-9030. **Fax:** (336) 691-9070.

E-Mail Address: office@carolinaleague.com. **Website:** www.carolinaleague.com.

Years League Active: 1945-.

President/Treasurer: John Hopkins.

John Hopkins

Vice Presidents: Art Silber (Potomac), Calvin Falwell (Lynchburg). **Corporate Secretary:** Ken Young (Frederick).

Directors: Mike Dee (Salem), Calvin Falwell (Lynchburg), Chuck Greenberg (Myrtle Beach), Dave Ziedelis (Frederick), Cam McRae (Kinston), Jack Minker (Wilmington), Billy Prim (Winston-Salem), Art Silber (Potomac).

Administrative Assistant: Marnee Larkins.

Division Structure: North—Frederick, Lynchburg, Potomac, Wilmington. South—Kinston, Myrtle Beach, Salem, Winston-Salem.

Regular Season: 140 games (split schedule). **2008 Opening Date:** April 4. **Closing Date:** Sept. 1.

All-Star Game: June 24 at Myrtle Beach. (Carolina League vs. California League).

Playoff Format: First-half division winners play second-half division winners in best-of-five series; if a team wins both halves, it plays a wild card (team with next-best record). Division series winners meet in best-of-five series for Mills Cup.

Roster Limit: 25 active. **Player Eligibility Rule:** No age limit. No more than two players and one player/coach on active list may have six or more years of prior minor league service.

Brand of Baseball: Rawlings.

Umpires: Matthew Abbott (Zanesville, OH). Gerard Ascani (Metairie, LA), William Best (Midlothian, VA). Jason Cooksey (Florence, SC). Anthony Johnson (McComb, MS). Jonathan Saphire (Centerville, OH). Chris Segal (Burke, VA). David Soucy (Glastonbury, CT).

STADIUM INFORMATION

			Dimensions				
Club	Stadium	Opened	LF	CF	RF	Capacity	2007 Att.
Frederick	Harry Grove Stadium	1990	325	400	325	5,400	283,065
Kinston	Grainger Stadium	1949	335	390	335	4,100	115,195
Lynchburg	City Stadium	1940	325	390	325	4,000	164,413
Myrtle Beach	BB&T Coastal Federal Field	1999	325	405	328	4,324	215,059
Potomac	Pfitzner Stadium	1984	315	400	315	6,000	165,000
Salem	Salem Memorial Stadium	1995	325	401	325	6,300	258,469
Wilmington	Frawley Stadium	1993	325	400	325	6,532	306,430
Winston-Salem	Ernie Shore Field	1956	325	400	325	6,000	161,180

FREDERICK KEYS

Office Address: 21 Stadium Dr, Frederick, MD 21703.
Telephone: (301) 662-0013. **Fax:** (301) 662-0018.
E-Mail address: info@frederickkeys.com. **Website:** www.frederickkeys.com.
Affiliation (first year): Baltimore Orioles (1989). **Years in League:** 1989-

OWNERSHIP, MANAGEMENT

Ownership: Maryland Baseball Holding LLC.

President: Ken Young. **General Manager:** Dave Ziedelis. **Assistant GM, Marketing:** Keri Scrivani. **Assistant GM, Operations:** Branden McGee. **Assistant GM, Sales:** Deanna Davis. **Director, Public Relations:** Adam Pohl. **Box Office Manager:** Adam Weaver. **Assistant Director, Marketing:** Jennifer Smoral. **Account Managers:** Christian Amorosi, Tara Reedy, Mike Rosenow, Jeff Wiggins, Quinn Williams, Steve Young. **Head Groundskeeper:** Kyle Slaton. **Public Relations Assistant:** Towney Godfrey. **Sales Coordinator:** Katy Finchman. **Stadium Operations Assistant:** David Garvey. **Clubhouse Operations Assistant:** Kenny Collopy. **Finance Manager:** Tami Hetrick. **Office Manager:** Barb Freund. **Ovations General Manager:** Anita Clarke.

FIELD STAFF

Manager: Tommy Thompson. **Coach:** J.J. Cannon. **Pitching Coach:** Blaine Beatty. **Trainer:** Trek Schuler. **Strength/Conditioning Coach:** Derek Soloway.

GAME INFORMATION

Radio: None.

PA Announcer: Andy Redmon. **Official Scorers:** Dennis Hetrick, George Richardson.

Stadium Name: Harry Grove Stadium. **Location:** From I-70, take exit 54 (Market Street), left at light. From I270, take exit 32 (I-70 Baltimore/Hagerstown) towards Baltimore (I-70), to exit 54 at Market Street. **Ticket Price Range:** $8-11.

Visiting Club Hotel: Comfort Inn, 7300 Executive Way, Frederick, MD 21701. **Telephone:** (301) 668-7272.

KINSTON INDIANS

Office Address: 400 East Grainger Avenue, Kinston, NC 28501.
Mailing Address: P.O. Box 3542, Kinston, NC 28502.
Telephone: (252) 527-9111. **Fax:** (252) 527-0498.
E-Mail Address: info@kinstonindians.com. **Website:** www.kinstonindians.com.
Affiliation (first year): Cleveland Indians (1987). **Years in League:** 1956-57, 1962-74, 1978-

OWNERSHIP, MANAGEMENT

Operated by: Slugger Partners LP.

Principal Owner/Chairman: Cam McRae.

General Manager: Shari Massengill. **Assistant GM:** Janell Bullock. **Director, Broadcasting/Public Relations:** Chris Hemeyer. **Director, Sales/Promotions:** Venika Streeter. **Director, Food/Beverage:** Tony Patterson. **Head Groundskeeper:** Tommy Walston. **Clubhouse Operations:** Robert Smeraldo. **Team Photographer:** Carl Kline.

FIELD STAFF

Manager: Chris Tremie. **Coach:** Jon Nunnally. **Pitching Coach:** Greg Hibbard. **Trainer:** Chad Wolfe.

GAME INFORMATION

Radio Announcer: Chris Hemeyer. **No. of Games Broadcast:** Home-70, Away-70. **Flagship Station:** WRNS 960-AM.

PA Announcer: Unavailable. **Official Scorer:** Unavailable.

Stadium Name: Grainger Stadium. **Location:** From west, take U.S. 70 Business (Vernon Avenue), left on East Street; from east, take U.S. 70 West, right on Highway 58, right on Vernon Avenue, right on East Street. **Standard Game Times:** 7 p.m., Sun. 2. **Ticket Price Range:** $4-7.

Visiting Club Hotel: Hampton Inn, Highway 70 Bypass, Kinston NC 28504. **Telephone:** (252) 523-1400.

LYNCHBURG HILLCATS

Office Address: Lynchburg City Stadium, 3180 Fort Ave, Lynchburg, VA 24501.
Mailing Address: P.O. Box 10213, Lynchburg, VA 24506.
Telephone: (434) 528-1144. **Fax:** (434) 846-0768.
E-Mail address: info@lynchburg-hillcats.com. **Website:** www.lynchburg-hillcats.com.
Affiliation (first year): Pittsburgh Pirates (1995). **Years in League:** 1966-

OWNERSHIP, MANAGEMENT

Operated By: Lynchburg Baseball Corp.

President: Calvin Falwell.

General Manager: Paul Sunwall. **Assistant GM:** Ronnie Roberts. **Head Groundskeeper/Sales:** Darren Johnson. **Director, Broadcasting/Publications:** Scott Bacon. **Director, Food/Beverage:** Jason Wells. **Ticket Manager:** Joe Rixon. **Director, Information Technology:** Andrew Chesser. **Office Manager:** Diane Tucker.

FIELD STAFF

Manager: Jeff Branson. **Coach:** Chris Truby. **Pitching Coach:** Bob Milacki. **Trainer:** Bryan Housand. **Strength/ Conditioning Coach:** Derek Frankllin.

GAME INFORMATION

Radio Announcer: Scott Bacon, Aaron Canada. **No. of Games Broadcast:** Home-70 Road-70. **Flagship Station:** WKDE 105.5-FM.

PA Announcer: Chuck Young. **Official Scorer:** Malcolm Haley, Chuck Young.

Stadium Name: Calvin Falwell Field at Lynchburg City Stadium. **Location:** U.S. 29 Business South to Lynchburg City Stadium (exit 6). U.S. 29 Business North to Lynchburg City Stadium (exit 4). **Ticket Price Range:** $5-8.

Visiting Club Hotel: Best Western, 2815 Candlers Mountain Rd, Lynchburg, VA 24502. **Telephone:** (434) 237-2986.

MYRTLE BEACH PELICANS

Office Address: 1251 21st Ave. N, Myrtle Beach, SC 29577.

Telephone: (843) 918-6002. **Fax:** (843) 918-6001.

E-Mail Address: info@myrtlebeachpelicans.com. **Website:** www.myrtlebeachpelicans.com.

Affiliation (first year): Atlanta Braves (1999). **Years in League:** 1999-

OWNERSHIP, MANAGEMENT

Operated By: Myrtle Beach Pelicans LP

President/Managing Partner: Chuck Greenberg.

G.E.R.T.: Todd Parnell. **General Manager:** North Johnson. **Assistant GM, Director, Ticket Sales:** Derrick Martin. **Director, Field Operations:** Chris Ball. **Director, Broadcasting/Communications:** Jon Laaser. **Assistant Director, Broadcasting/Communications:** Bret Lasky. **Director, Promotions:** Maggie Neil. **Box Office Manager:** Josh Holley. **Ticketing Associate:** Jim Fleming. **Ticket Sales Associates:** Derrick Nunziante, Lynn Huber, Jeremy Pryce. **Community Relations Manager:** Julie Borshak. **Facility Operations Manager:** Mike Snow. **Producer, In-Game Entertainment:** Jake White. **Director, Merchandise:** Richard Graves. **Director, Finance:** Anne Frost. **Director, Sponsorship Sales:** Carol McGraw. **Sponsorship Sales Associate:** Matt Hewitt. **Accounting Assistant:** Michelle Moody. **Golf/Hospitality Marketing Specialist:** Mike Browne. **GM/Ovations Catering:** Shane Mabry. **Administrative Assistant:** Shellene May. **Clubhouse Manager:** Eric Wilson.

FIELD STAFF

Manager: Rocket Wheeler. **Coach:** Rick Albert. **Pitching Coach:** Bruce Dal Canton. **Trainer:** Ricky Alcantara.

GAME INFORMATION

Radio Announcers: Jon Laaser, Bret Lasky. **No. of Games Broadcast:** Home-70, Road-70. **Flagship Station:** ESPN Radio 93.9-FM/93.7-FM/1050-AM.

PA Announcer: Mike Browne. **Official Scorer:** Dave Binder.

Stadium Name: BB&T Coastal Federal Field. **Location:** U.S. Highway 17 Bypass to 21st Avenue North, 1/2 mile to stadium. **Standard Game Times:** 7:05 p.m.; Sun. 3:05/6:05. **Ticket Price Range:** $7-9.

Visiting Club Hotel: Holiday Inn Express-Broadway at the Beach, U.S. Highway 17 Bypass & 29th Avenue North, Myrtle Beach, SC 29578. **Telephone:** (843) 916-4993.

POTOMAC NATIONALS

Office Address: 7 County Complex Ct., Woodbridge, VA 22192.

Mailing Address: P.O. Box 2148, Woodbridge, VA 22195.

Telephone: (703) 590-2311. **Fax:** (703) 590-5716.

E-Mail Address: info@potomacnationals.com. **Website:** www.potomacnationals.com.

Affiliation (first year): Washington Nationals (2005). **Years in League:** 1978-

OWNERSHIP, MANAGEMENT

Operated By: Potomac Baseball LLC.

Principal Owner: Art Silber. **President:** Lani Silber Weiss. **Senior Vice President:** Bobby Holland.

General Manager: Jonathan Griffith. **Assistant GM, Marketing/Media:** Anthony Opperman. **Director, Ticket Operations:** Douglas McConnell. **Director, Stadium Operations:** Carter Buschman. **Assistant Director, Stadium Operations:** Ryan Johnston. **Head Groundskeeper:** Mike Lundy. **Director, Group Sales:** John LeGacy. **Group Sales Account Executive:** Andrew Stinson. **Public Relations Manager:** Susanna Hall. **Assistant Director, Promotions/ Broadcasting:** Chris Fisher.

FIELD STAFF

Manager: Randy Knorr. **Coach:** Jery Browne. **Pitching Coach:** Randy Tomlin. **Trainer:** Sean Wayne.

GAME INFORMATION

Radio Announcer: Anthony Opperman. **No. of Games Broadcast:** Home-70 Road-70. **Flagship:** www.potomacnationals.com.

PA Announcer: Chris Fisher. **Official Scorer:** David Vincent.

Stadium Name: G. Richard Pfitzner Stadium. **Location:** From I-95, take exit 158B and continue on Prince William Parkway for five miles, right into County Complex Court. **Standard Game Times:** 7:05 p.m.; Sat. 6:35; Sun. 1:05 (April-May), 6:05 (June-Sept.). **Ticket Price Range:** $7-13.

Visiting Club Hotel: Holiday Inn Quantico Center, 3901 Fettler Park Dr., Dumfries, VA 22026. **Telephone:** (703) 441-9001.

SALEM AVALANCHE

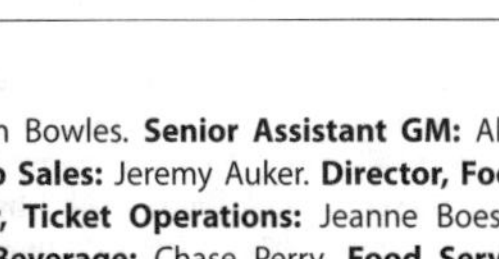

Office Address: 1004 Texas St., Salem, VA 24153.
Mailing Address: P.O. Box 842, Salem, VA 24153.
Telephone: (540) 389-3333. **Fax:** (540) 389-9710.
E-Mail Address: info@salemavalanche.com. **Website:** www.salemavalanche.com.
Affiliation (first year): Houston Astros (2003). **Years in League:** 1968-

OWNERSHIP, MANAGEMENT

Operated By: Carolina Baseball, LLC/Fenway Sports Group.

President: Mike Dee.

Vice President/General Manager: John Katz. **VP/Director, Finance:** Brian Bowles. **Senior Assistant GM:** Allen Lawrence. **Assistant GM, Sales/Marketing:** Josh Eagan. **Assistant GM, Group Sales:** Jeremy Auker. **Director, Food/Beverage:** Scott Burton. **Head Groundskeeper:** Tracy Schneweis. **Director, Ticket Operations:** Jeanne Boester. **Assistant Director, Group Sales:** Jeremy Long. **Assistant Director, Food/Beverage:** Chase Perry. **Food Service Manager:** Giles Cochran. **Corporate Sales Manager:** Steve Lawhorn. **Broadcasting/Media Relations:** Jason Benetti. **Special Events/Office Manager:** Kelly Surber. **Account Executives:** Chris Byrne, Steven Elovich, Ashby Knack. **Clubhouse Manager:** Tom Wagner.

FIELD STAFF

Manager: Jim Pankovits. **Coach:** Keith Bodie. **Pitching Coach:** Gary Ruby. **Trainer:** Eric Montague.

GAME INFORMATION

Radio Announcer: Jason Benetti. **No. of Games Broadcast:** Home-70 Road-70. **Flagship Station:** WFIR 960-AM.

PA Announcer: Unavailable. **Official Scorer:** Billy Wells.

Stadium Name: Lewis-Gale Medical Center Field at Salem Memorial Baseball Stadium. **Location:** I-81 to exit 141 (Route 419), follow signs to Salem Civic Center Complex. **Standard Game Times:** 7:07 p.m.; Sat. 6:07; Sun. 2:07 (April-June 15), 6:07 (June 16-Sept.) **Ticket Price Range:** $7-8.

Visiting Club Hotel: Comfort Inn Airport, 5070 Valley View Blvd, Roanoke, VA 24012. **Telephone:** (540) 527-2020.

WILMINGTON BLUE ROCKS

Office Address: 801 S. Madison St., Wilmington, DE 19801.
Telephone: (302) 888-2015. **Fax:** (302) 888-2032.
E-Mail Address: info@bluerocks.com. **Website:** www.bluerocks.com.
Affiliation (first year): Kansas City Royals (2007). **Years in League:** 1993-.

OWNERSHIP, MANAGEMENT

Operated by: Wilmington Blue Rocks LP.

Honorary President: Matt Minker. **President:** Tom Palmer.

General Manager: Chris Kemple. **Assistant GM:** Andrew Layman. **Director, Broadcasting/Media Relations:** John Sadak. **Assistant Director, Broadcasting/Media Relations:** Mark Kasubinski. **Director, Merchandise:** Jim Beck. **Merchandise Assistant:** Bill Kinney. **Director, Promotions:** Kevin P. Linton. **Director, Marketing:** Mark Vanderhaar. **Marketing Assistants:** Corey Wolfe, Kyle Love. **Director, Community Relations:** Dave Arthur. **Community Relations Assistant:** Walt Meredith. **Director, Sales/Ticket Operations:** Jared Forma. **Ticket Manager:** John Kramer. **Group Sales Associates:** Kristi Pooler, Bill Levy, Stefani DiChiara. **Ticket Office Assistants:** Greg Matthews, Joe Fargnoli. **Director, Field Operations:** Steve Gold. **Director, Finance:** Denis Weigert. **Video Production Assistant:** Atlee McHeffey. **Office Manager:** Julie Gross.

FIELD STAFF

Manager: Daryl Kennedy. **Coach:** Nelson Liriano. **Pitching Coach:** Steve Luebber. **Athletic Trainer:** David Iannicca.

GAME INFORMATION

Radio Announcers: John Sadak, Mark Kasubinski. **No. of Games Broadcast:** Home-70, Away-70. **Flagship Station:**

WWTX 1290-AM.

PA Announcer: Kevin Linton. **Official Scorers:** E.J. Casey, Dick Shute, Adam Kamras.

Stadium Name: Judy Johnson Field at Daniel S. Frawley Stadium. **Location:** I-95 North to Maryland Ave. (exit 6), right onto Maryland Ave., right on Read Street, right on South Madison Street to ballpark; I-95 South to Maryland Ave. (exit 6), left at Martin Luther King Blvd., right on South Madison Street. **Standard Game Times:** 7:05 p.m., 6:35 (April-May); Sat. 6:05; Sun. 1:35. **Ticket Price Range:** $4-9.

Visiting Club Hotel: Quality Inn-Skyways, 147 N. DuPont Hwy., New Castle, DE 19720. **Telephone:** (302) 328-6666.

WINSTON-SALEM WARTHOGS

Office Address: 401 Deacon Blvd, Winston-Salem, NC 27105.
Mailing Address: P.O. Box 4488, Winston-Salem, NC 27115.
Telephone: (336) 759-2233. **Fax:** (336) 759-2042.
E-Mail Address: warthogs@warthogs.com. **Website:** www.warthogs.com.
Affiliation (first year): Chicago White Sox (1997). **Years in League:** 1945-

OWNERSHIP, MANAGEMENT

Operated By: Sports Menagerie.

Co-Owners: Billy Prim, Andrew Filipowski. **President:** Guy Schuman.

General Manager: Ryan Manuel. **CFO:** Kurt Gehsmann. **Director, Broadcasting/Media Relations:** Ed Collari. **Director, Merchandise:** Amy Newman. **Director, Community Relations:** Trey Kalny. **Director, Ticketing:** Brian Shollenberger. **Director, Operations:** Cass Ferguson. **Director, Group Sales:** Jerry Shadley. **Account Executives:** Sarcanda Bellissimo, Shaun McElhinny. **Office Manager:** Amanda Elbert. **Head Groundskeeper:** Doug Tanis. **Assistant to the General Manager:** David Beal. **Interns:** Devin Bedwell, Katie Green, David Roach, Jason Wilford. **Home Clubhouse Manager:** Roger O'Dell. **Visitor Clubhouse Manager:** Rob Pellucia.

FIELD STAFF

Manager: Tim Blackwell. **Coach:** Robert Sasser. **Pitching Coach:** Brian Drahman. **Trainer:** Josh Fallin.

GAME INFORMATION

Radio Announcer: Ed Collari. **No. of Games Broadcast:** Home-70 Road-70. **Flagship:** www.warthogs.com.

PA Announcer: Larry Berry. **Official Scorer:** Unavailable.

Stadium Name: Ernie Shore Field. **Location:** I-40 Business to Cherry Street exit, north through downtown, right on Deacon Boulevard, park on left. **Ticket Price Range:** $6.50-8.50.

Visiting Club Hotel: Holiday Inn Hanes, 2008 S. Hawthorne Rd, Winston-Salem, NC 27103. **Telephone:** (336) 765-6670.

FLORIDA STATE LEAGUE

HIGH CLASS A

Street Address: 115 E. Orange Ave., Daytona Beach, FL 32114.
Mailing Address: P.O. Box 349, Daytona Beach, FL 32115.
Telephone: (386) 252-7479. **Fax:** (386) 252-7495.
E-Mail Address: fslbaseball@cfl.rr.com. **Website:** www.floridastateleague.com.

Chuck Murphy

Years League Active: 1919-1927, 1936-1941, 1946-.

President, Treasurer: Chuck Murphy.

Vice Presidents: Ken Carson (Dunedin), Paul Taglieri (St. Lucie).

Corporate Secretary: David Hood.

Directors: Brian Barnes (Jupiter), Ken Carson (Dunedin), Craig Callan (Vero Beach), Shawn Geinett (Palm Beach), Marvin Goldklang (Fort Myers), Dan Wolfert (Sarasota), Ron Myers (Lakeland), Bill Papierniak (Daytona), Kyle Smith (Brevard County), Vance Smith (Tampa), Paul Taglieri (St. Lucie), John Timberlake (Clearwater).

Office Secretary: Peggy Catigano.

Division Structure: East—Brevard County, Daytona, Jupiter, Palm Beach, St. Lucie, Vero Beach. West—Clearwater, Dunedin, Fort Myers, Lakeland, Sarasota, Tampa.

Regular Season: 140 games (split schedule). **2008 Opening Date:** April 3. **Closing Date:** Aug. 31.

All-Star Game: June 14 at Brevard County.

Playoff Format: First-half division winners meet second-half winners in best-of-three series. Winners meet in best-of-five series for league championship.

Roster Limit: 25. **Player Eligibility Rule:** No age limit. No more than two players and one player-coach on active list may have six or more years of prior minor league service.

Brand of Baseball: Rawlings.

Umpires: Jason W. Arends (Marion, IA), Sean M. Barber (Lakeland, FL) Matthew A. Cunningham (Carmel, IN), Andrew S. Dudones (Lakeland, FL), Hal H. Gibson III (Mayfield, KY), Jeffrey C. Gosney (Newark OH), Adam C. Hamari (Marquette, MI), Christopher W. Hamner (Richmond, VA), Kellen Levy (Portland, OR), Bradley M. Myers (Holland, OH), Joe A. Rackley (Webster, TX), Anthony N. West (Joliet, IL).

STADIUM INFORMATION

				Dimensions			
Club	Stadium	Opened	LF	CF	RF	Capacity	2007 Att.
Brevard County	Space Coast Stadium	1994	340	404	340	7,500	83,954
Clearwater	Bright House Networks Field	2004	330	400	330	8,500	166,359
Daytona	Jackie Robinson Ballpark	1930	317	400	325	4,000	146,195
Dunedin	Knology Park	1977	335	400	315	6,106	48,326
Fort Myers	William H. Hammond Stadium	1991	330	405	330	7,500	115,647
Jupiter	Roger Dean Stadium	1998	330	400	325	6,871	82,386
Lakeland	Joker Marchant Stadium	1966	340	420	340	7,100	48,653
Palm Beach	Roger Dean Stadium	1998	330	400	325	6,871	77,805
St. Lucie	Tradition Field	1988	338	410	338	7,500	100,646
Sarasota	Ed Smith Stadium	1989	340	400	340	7,500	38,313
Tampa	Legends Field	1996	318	408	314	10,386	123,829
Vero Beach	Holman Stadium	1953	340	400	340	6,500	46,989

BREVARD COUNTY MANATEES

Office Address: 5800 Stadium Pkwy., Suite 101, Viera, FL 32940.
Telephone: (321) 633-9200. **Fax:** (321) 633-4418.
E-Mail Address: info@spacecoaststadium.com. **Website:** www.manateesbaseball.com.
Affiliation (first year): Milwaukee Brewers (2005). **Years in League:** 1994-

OWNERSHIP, MANAGEMENT

Operated By: Central Florida Baseball Group LLC.
Director, Stadium Operations: Kyle Smith. **Business Operations Manager:** Kelley Wheeler.

FIELD STAFF

Manager: Mike Guerrero. **Coach:** Corey Hart. **Pitching Coach:** Fred Dabney. **Trainer:** Tommy Craig. **Strength/Conditioning:** Nick Miller.

GAME INFORMATION

PA Announcer: J.C. Meyerholz. **Radio:** None.
Official Scorer: Ron Jernick.

Stadium Name: Space Coast Stadium. **Location:** I-95 North to Wickham Rd. (exit 191), left onto Wickham, right at traffic circle onto Lake Andrew Drive for 1 1/2 miles through the Brevard County government office complex to the four-way stop, right on Stadium Parkway. Space Coast Stadium 1/2 mile on the left. I-95 South to Rockledge exit (exit 195), left onto Stadium Parkway. Space Coast Stadium is 3 miles on right. **Standard Game Times:** 7 p.m.; Sat. 6; Sun. 1. **Ticket Price Range:** $6-7.

Visiting Club Hotel: Imperial's Hotel & Conference Center, 8928 N. Wickham Rd, Viera, FL 32940. **Telephone:** (321) 255-0077.

CLEARWATER THRESHERS

Office Address: 601 N. Old Coachman Rd, Clearwater, FL 33765.
Telephone: (727) 712-4300. **Fax:** (727) 712-4498.
Website: www.threshersbaseball.com.
Affiliation (first year): Philadelphia Phillies (1985). **Years in League:** 1985-.

OWNERSHIP, MANAGEMENT

Operated by: Philadelphia Phillies.
Chairman: Bill Giles. **President:** David Montgomery.

Director, Florida Operations/General Manager: John Timberlake. **Assistant Director, Florida Operations:** Lee McDaniel. **Business Manager:** Dianne Gonzalez. **Assistant GM/Director, Sales:** Dan McDonough. **Assistant GM/Ticketing:** Jason Adams. **Director, Merchandising:** Carrie Adams. **Group Sales:** Dan Madden, Bobby Mitchell. **Ballpark Operations:** Jay Warren. **Ticket Manager:** Kevin Brahm. **Maintenance Coordinator:** Cory Sipe. **Manager, Food/Beverage:** Brad Dudash. **Office Manager:** De De Angelillis. **Head Groundskeeper:** Opie Cheek.

FIELD STAFF

Manager: Razor Shines. **Coach:** Kevin Jordan. **Pitching Coach:** Steve Shrenk. **Trainer:** Ichiro Kitano.

GAME INFORMATION

Radio: None.
PA Announcer: Don Guckian. **Official Scorer:** Larry Wiederecht.

Stadium Name: Bright House Networks Field. **Location:** U.S. 19 North and Drew Street in Clearwater. **Standard Game Times:** 7 p.m.; Sun. 1. **Ticket Price Range:** $4-9.

Visiting Club Hotel: Buena Vista Hotel, 21252 U.S. 19 N., Clearwater, FL 33765. **Telephone:** (727) 796-3165.

DAYTONA CUBS

Office Address: 105 E. Orange Ave, Daytona Beach, FL 32114.
Telephone: (386) 257-3172. **Fax:** (386) 257-3382.
E-Mail Address: info@daytonacubs.com. **Website:** www.daytonacubs.com.
Affiliation (first year): Chicago Cubs (1993). **Years in League:** 1920-24, 1928, 1936-41, 1946-73, 1977-87, 1993-

OWNERSHIP, MANAGEMENT

Operated By: Big Game Florida LLC.
Principal Owner/President: Andrew Rayburn.

General Manager: Bill Papierniak. **Assistant GMs:** Brady Ballard, Tom Denlinger. **Director, Sales:** Rick Polster. **Director, Broadcasting/Media Relations:** Derek Ingram. **Director, Stadium Operations:** J.R. Laub. **Director, Tickets:**

Eric Freeman. **Director, Groups:** Brandon Greene. **Director, Food/Beverage:** Josh Lawther. **Manager, Special Events/ Group Sales:** Laura Landry. **Office Manager:** Tammy Devine.

FIELD STAFF

Manager: Jody Davis. **Coach:** Richie Zisk. **Pitching Coach:** Dave Rosario. **Trainer:** Bob Grimes.

GAME INFORMATION

Radio Announcer: Derek Ingram. **No. of Games Broadcast:** Home-70, Road-70. **Flagship Station:** WELE 1380-AM.

PA Announcer: Tim Lecras. **Official Scorer:** Lyle Fox.

Stadium Name: Jackie Robinson Ballpark. **Location:** I-95 to International Speedway Blvd. Exit (Route 92), east to Beach Street, south to Magnolia Ave., east to ballpark; A1A North/South to Orange Ave., west to ballpark. **Standard Game Time:** 7:05 p.m. **Ticket Price Range:** $6-10.

Visiting Club Hotel: Unavailable.

DUNEDIN BLUE JAYS

Office Address: 373-A Douglas Ave., Dunedin, FL 34698.

Telephone: (727) 733-9302. **Fax:** (727) 734-7661.

E-Mail Address: feedback@dunedinbluejays.com. **Website:** www.dunedin-bluejays.com.

Affiliation (first year): Toronto Blue Jays (1987). **Years in League:** 1978-79, 1987-

OWNERSHIP, MANAGEMENT

Operated by: Toronto Blue Jays.

General Manager: Jason Diplock. **Assistant GM:** Jared Gates. **Senior Consultant:** Ken Carson. **Community Relations Manager:** Janette Donoghue. **Manager, Ticket Operations:** Michael Nielsen. **Administrative Assistant:** Manda Minch. **Account Executives:** Kevin Schildt, Cameron O'Connell, Kathi Wiegand. **Office Manager:** Karen Howell. **Interns:** Tony Penna, Jacob Karr, Ben Jewett, Alan Borock. **Head Groundskeeper:** Budgie Clark. **Assistant Groundskeeper:** Patrick Skunda. **Clubhouse Managers:** Adelis Barious, Freddy Mcdina.

FIELD STAFF

Manager: Omar Malave. **Coach:** Paul Elliott. **Pitching Coach:** Darold Knowles. **Trainer:** Andrew Muccino.

GAME INFORMATION

Radio: None.

PA Announcer: Dave Bell. **Official Scorer:** Josh Huff.

Stadium Name: Kronology Park. **Location:** From I-275, north on Highway 19, left on Sunset Point Rd. for 4 1/2 miles, right on Douglas Ave., stadium is 1/2 mile on right. **Standard Game Times:** 7 p.m.; Sun. 1. **Ticket Price Range:** $5-7.

Visiting Club Hotel: Comfort Inn Countryside, 26508 U.S. 19 N., Clearwater, FL 33761. **Telephone:** (727) 796-1234.

FORT MYERS MIRACLE

Office Address: 14400 Six Mile Cypress Pkwy, Fort Myers, FL 33912.

Telephone: (239) 768-4210. **Fax:** (239) 768-4211.

E-Mail Address: miracle@miraclebaseball.com. **Website:** www.miraclebaseball.com.

Affiliation (first year): Minnesota Twins (1993). **Years in League:** 1926, 1978-87, 1991-

OWNERSHIP, MANAGEMENT

Operated By: Greater Miami Baseball Club LP.

Principal Owner/Chairman: Marvin Goldklang. **CEO:** Mike Veeck. **President:** Linda McNabb.

General Manager: Steve Gliner. **Director, Business Operations:** Suzanne Reaves. **Director, Sales/Marketing:** Terry Simon. **Director, Promotions:** Gary Sharp. **Director, Ticket Sales:** Matt Bomberg. **Manager, Food/Beverage:** Kris Koch. **Account Executive/Merchandise Manager:** Justin Stecz. **Community Relations Coordinator:** Sean Fox. **Assistant, Food/Beverage:** Mike Petrillo. **Administrative Assistants:** Alyssa Benolkiin, David Hermann. **Customer Relations Associates:** Nancy Rowe, Sue Pinola. **Head Groundskeeper:** Keith Blasingim.

FIELD STAFF

Manager: Jeff Smith. **Coach:** Jim Dwyer. **Pitching Coach:** Eric Rasmussen. **Trainer:** Larry Bennese.

GAME INFORMATION

Radio Announcer: Sean Fox. **No. of Games Broadcast:** Home-70, Road-70. **Flagship Station:** ESPN 770-AM.

PA Announcer: Gary Sharp. **Official Scorer:** Unavailable.

Stadium Name: William H. Hammond Stadium. **Location:** Exit 131 off I-75, west on Daniels Parkway, left on Six Mile Cypress Parkway. **Standard Game Times:** 7 p.m.; Sun. 1. **Ticket Price Range:** $5-7.

Visiting Club Hotel: Fairfield Inn by Marriot, 7090 Cypress Terrace, Fort Myers, FL 33907. **Telephone:** (239) 437-5600.

JUPITER HAMMERHEADS

Office Address: 4751 Main Street, Jupiter, FL 33458.
Telephone: (561) 775-1818. **Fax:** (561) 691-6886.
E-Mail Address: f.desk@rogerdeanstadium.com. **Website:** www.jupiterhammerheads.com.
Affiliation (first year): Florida Marlins (2002). **Years in League:** 1998-

OWNERSHIP, MANAGEMENT

Owned By: Florida Marlins. **Operated By:** Jupiter Stadium Ltd.

General Manager, JSL: Joe Pinto. **Executive Assistant:** Carol McAteer.

GM, Jupiter Hammerheads: Brian Barnes. **Assistant GM, Jupiter Hammerheads:** Shawn Gelnett. **Director, Sales/Marketing:** Jennifer Brown. **Merchandise Manager:** Stephanie Glavin. **Stadium Building Manager:** Jorge Toro. **Facility Operations Manager:** Marshall Jennings. **Assistant Facility Operations Managers:** Karsten Blackwelder, Johnny Simmons. **Office Manager:** Chris Tunno. **Ticket Manager:** Joe Schuler. **Stadium/Event Operations Manager:** Bryan Knapp. **Marketing Sales Executives:** Lisa Fegley, Brad Hofmeister, Selena Samios. **Customer Service Representative:** Bob Mee.

FIELD STAFF

Manager: Brandon Hyde. **Coach:** Anthony Iapoce. **Pitching Coach:** Reid Cornelius. **Trainer:** Unavailable.

GAME INFORMATION

Radio: None.

PA Announcers: John Frost, Dick Sanford. **Official Scorer:** Brennan McDonald.

Stadium Name: Roger Dean Stadium. **Location:** I-95 to exit 83, east on Donald Ross Road for 1/4 mile. **Standard Game Times:** 7:05 p.m.; Sat. 6:05; Sun. 1:05 (April-May), 6:05 (June-Aug.). **Ticket Price Range:** $6.50-8.50.

Visiting Club Hotel: Comfort Inn & Suites Jupiter, 6752 West Indiantown Rd, Jupiter, FL 33458. **Telephone:** (561) 745-7997.

LAKELAND FLYING TIGERS

Office Address: 2125 N. Lake Ave., Lakeland, FL 33805.
Mailing Address: P.O. Box 90187, Lakeland, FL 33804.
Telephone: (863) 686-8075. **Fax:** (863) 688-9589.
Website: www.lakelandflyingtigers.com.
Affiliation (first year): Detroit Tigers (1967). **Years in League:** 1919-26, 1953-55, 1960, 1962-64, 1967-.

OWNERSHIP, MANAGEMENT

Operated by: Detroit Tigers, Inc.

Principal Owner: Mike Ilitch. **President:** David Dombrowski. **Director, Florida Operations:** Ron Myers.

General Manager: Zach Burek. **Administration/Operations Manager:** Shannon Follett. **Ticket Operations:** Ryan Eason. **Merchandising/Concessions:** Elise Aronson. **Head Groundskeeper:** Bryan French.

FIELD STAFF

Manager: Andy Beckett. **Coach:** Larry Herndon. **Pitching Coach:** Joe Coleman. **Trainer:** Dustin Campbell.

GAME INFORMATION

Radio: None.

PA Announcer: Shari Szabo. **Official Scorer:** Sandy Shaw.

Stadium Name: Joker Marchant Stadium. **Location:** Exit 33 on I-4 to 33 South, 1 1/2 miles on left. **Standard Game Times:** 7 p.m.; Sat. 6; Sun. 1 (April), 6 (May-Aug.). **Ticket Price Range:** $4-6.

Visiting Club Hotel: Howard Johnson Inn ExecutiveCenter, 3311 US Highway 98 North, Lakeland, FL 33805. **Telephone:** (863) 688-7972.

PALM BEACH CARDINALS

Office Address: 4751 Main Street, Jupiter, FL 33458.
Telephone: (561) 775-1818. **Fax:** (561) 691-6886.
E-Mail address: f.desk@rogerdeanstadium.com. **Website:** www.palmbeachcardinals.com.
Affiliation (first year): St. Louis Cardinals (2003). **Years in League:** 2003-

OWNERSHIP, MANAGEMENT

Owned By: St. Louis Cardinals. **Operated By:** Jupiter Stadium Ltd.

General Manager, JSL: Joe Pinto. **Executive Assistant:** Carol McAteer.

GM, Palm Beach Cardinals: Chris Easom. **Assistant GM:** Brian Barnes. **Director, Sales/Marketing:** Jennifer Brown. **Merchandise Manager:** Stephanie Glavin. **Stadium Building Manager:** Jorge Toro. **Facility Operations Managers:**

Karsten Blackwelder, Johnny Simmons. **Office Manager:** Chris Tunno. **Ticket Manager:** Joe Schuler. **Stadium/Event Operations Manager:** Bryan Knapp. **Marketing Sales Executives:** Lisa Fegley, Brad Hofmeister, Selena Samios. **Customer Service Representative:** Bob Mee.

FIELD STAFF

Manager: Gaylen Pitts. **Coach:** Derrick May. **Pitching Coach:** Derek Lilliquist. **Trainer:** Allen Thompson.

GAME INFORMATION

Radio: None.

PA Announcers: John Frost, Dick Sanford. **Official Scorer:** Lou Villano.

Stadium Name: Roger Dean Stadium. **Location:** I-95 to exit 83, east on Donald Ross Road for 1/4 mile. **Standard Game Times:** 7:05 p.m.; Sat. 6:05; Sun. 1:05 (April-May), 6:05 (June-Aug.). **Ticket Price Range:** $6.50-8.50.

Visiting Club Hotel: Comfort Inn & Suites Jupiter, 6752 West Indiantown Rd, Jupiter, FL 33458. **Telephone:** (561) 745-7997.

ST. LUCIE METS

Office Address: 525 NW Peacock Blvd., Port St. Lucie, FL 34986.
Telephone: (772) 871-2100. **Fax:** (772) 878-9802.
Website: www.stluciemets.com.
Affiliation (first year): New York Mets (1988). **Years in League:** 1988-

OWNERSHIP, MANAGEMENT

Operated by: Sterling Mets LP.

Chairman: Fred Wilpon. **President:** Saul Katz. **Senior Executive Vice President/COO:** Jeff Wilpon.

Director, Florida Operations/General Manager: Paul Taglieri. **Assistant Director, Florida Operations/Assistant General Manager:** Traer Van Allen. **Manager, Food/Beverage Operations:** Brian Paupeck. **Manager, Sales/Ballpark Operations:** Ryan Strickland. **Ticketing/Merchandise Coordinator:** Erin Rescigno. **Office Assistant:** Cynthia Gaumond. **Staff Accountant:** Paula Andreozzi. **Administrative Assistants:** Matt Gagnon, Natalie Deem. **Head Groundskeeper:** Tommy Bowes. **Clubhouse Manager:** Jack Brenner.

FIELD STAFF

Manager: Tim Teufel. **Coach:** Mike Hart, Joel Fuentes. **Pitching Coach:** Dan Murray. **Trainer:** Ruben Barrera.

GAME INFORMATION

Radio: None.

PA Announcer: Matt Gagnon. **Official Scorer:** Bob Adams.

Stadium Name: Tradition Field. **Location:** Exit 121 (St. Lucie West Blvd.) off I-95, east 1/2 mile, left on NW Peacock Blvd. **Standard Game Times:** 7 p.m.; Sat. 6; Sun. 5. **Ticket Price Range:** $4-6.

Visiting Club Hotel: Holiday Inn, 10120 S. Federal Hwy., Port St. Lucie, FL 34952. **Telephone:** (772) 337-2200.

SARASOTA REDS

Office Address: 2700 12th St., Sarasota, FL 34237.
Mailing Address: 1090 N. Euclid Ave, Sarasota, FL 34237.
Telephone: (941) 365-4460. **Fax:** (941) 365-4217.
E-Mail Address: sarasotaredsinfo@reds.com. **Website:** www.sarasotareds.com.
Affiliation (first year): Cincinnati Reds (2005). **Years in League:** 1927, 1961-65, 1989-

OWNERSHIP, MANAGEMENT

Operated By: Cincinnati Reds LLP.

General Manager, Florida Operations/Sarasota Reds: Dan Wolfert. **Assistant GM:** Mike Rebok. **Manager, Sales/Marketing:** Gary Saunders. **Ticket Manager:** Barbara Robinson. **Florida Operations Staff Administrator:** Eric Jordan. **Administrative Assistants:** Bobby Basham, Nick Jarosh, Logan Lykins. **Equipment Manager:** Jon Snyder. **Head Groundskeeper:** Gene Egan. **Clubhouse Manager:** Joe Salomone.

FIELD STAFF

Manager: Joe Ayrault. **Coach:** Ryan Jackson. **Pitching Coach:** Tom Brown. **Athletic Trainer:** Tomas Vera.

GAME INFORMATION

Radio: None.

PA Announcer: Alex Topp. **Official Scorer:** Phil Denis, Howard Spungen, David Taylor.

Stadium Name: Ed Smith Stadium. **Location:** I-75 to exit 210, three miles west to Tuttle Ave., right on Tuttle 1/2 mile to 12th Street, stadium on left. **Standard Game Times:** 7 p.m.; Sat. 6; Sun. 1. **Ticket Price Range:** $5-6.

Visiting Club Hotel: AmericInn and Suites, 5931 Fruitville Rd, Sarasota, FL 34232. **Telephone:** (941) 342-8778.

TAMPA YANKEES

Office Address: One Steinbrenner Dr., Tampa, FL 33614.

Telephone: (813) 875-7753. **Fax:** (813) 673-3174.

E-Mail Address: vsmith@yankees.com.

Affiliation (first year): New York Yankees (1994). **Years in League:** 1919-27, 1957-1988, 1994-

OWNERSHIP, MANAGEMENT

Operated by: New York Yankees LP.

Principal Owner: George Steinbrenner.

General Manager: Vance Smith. **Assistant GM:** Julie Kremer. **Director, Stadium Operations:** Dean Holbert. **Director, Sales/Marketing:** Howard Grosswirth. **Director, Ticket Sales:** Brian Valdez. **Head Groundskeeper:** Ritchie Anderson.

FIELD STAFF

Manager: Luis Sojo. **Coach:** Aaron Ledesma. **Pitching Coach:** Greg Pavlick. **Trainer:** Kris Russell. **Strength/Conditioning:** Jay Signorelli.

GAME INFORMATION

Radio: None.

PA Announcer: Steve Hague. **Official Scorer:** Unavailable.

Stadium Name: Legends Field. **Location:** I-275 to Martin Luther King, west on Martin Luther King to Dale Mabry. **Standard Game Times:** 7 p.m.; Sun. 1. **Ticket Price Range:** $3-5.

Visiting Club Hotel: Holiday Inn Express, 4732 N. Dale Mabry Hwy., Tampa, FL 33614. **Telephone:** (813) 877-6061.

VERO BEACH DEVIL RAYS

Office Address: 4101 26th St, Vero Beach, FL 32960.

Mailing Address: P.O. Box 2887, Vero Beach, FL 32961.

Telephone: (772) 569-4900. **Fax:** (772) 567-0819.

E-Mail Address: info@vbdrays.com. **Website:** www.vbdrays.com.

Affiliation (first year): Tampa Bay Devil Rays (2007). **Years in League:** 1980-

OWNERSHIP, MANAGEMENT

Operated By: Los Angeles Dodgers.

President: Martin Greenspun. **VP Spring Training/Minor League Facilities:** Craig Callan

Co-General Managers: Shawn Marette, Katie Siegfried. **Operations Manager:** Brian Barlow. **Office Manager:** Ed Callahan. **Head Groundskeeper:** Steve Carlsward. **Manager, Concessions/Souvenirs:** John Gordon. **Clubhouse Manager:** Joe Harry. **Visiting Clubhouse Manager:** Geoff Freedman.

FIELD STAFF

Manager: Jim Morrison. **Coach:** Brady Williams. **Pitching Coach:** R.C. Lichtenstein. **Trainer:** Unavailable.

GAME INFORMATION

PA Announcer: Joe Sanchez. **Official Scorer:** Randy Phillips.

Stadium Name: Holman Stadium. **Location:** I-95 to Route 60 East, left on 43rd Avenue, right on Aviation Boulevard. **Ticket Price Range:** $5-6.

Visiting Club Hotel: Best Western Vero, 8797 20th Street, Vero Beach FL 32966. **Telephone:** (772) 567-8321.

MIDWEST LEAGUE

LOW CLASS A

Office Address: 1118 Cranston Rd., Beloit, WI 53511.
Mailing Address: P.O. Box 936, Beloit, WI 53512.
Telephone: (608) 364-1188. **Fax:** (608) 364-1913.
E-Mail Address: mwl@midwestleague.com. **Website:** www.midwestleague.com.
Years League Active: 1947-.
President, Treasurer: George Spelius.

George Spelius

Vice President: Ed Larson. **Legal Counsel/Secretary:** Richard Nussbaum.

Directors: Jason Freier (Fort Wayne), Tom Barbee (Cedar Rapids), Lew Chamberlin (West Michigan), Dennis Conerton (Beloit), Tom Dickson (Lansing), David Heller (Quad Cities), Joe Kernan (South Bend), Gary Mayse (Dayton), Paul Schnack (Clinton), William Stavropoulos (Great Lakes), Rocky Vonachen (Peoria), Dave Walker (Burlington), Mike Woleben (Kane County), Rob Zerjav (Wisconsin).

League Administrator: Holly Voss.

Division Structure: East—Dayton, Fort Wayne, Lansing, South Bend, Great Lakes, West Michigan. West—Beloit, Burlington, Cedar Rapids, Clinton, Kane County, Peoria, Quad Cities, Wisconsin.

Regular Season: 140 games (split schedule). **2008 Opening Date:** April 3. **Closing Date:** Sept. 1.

All-Star Game: June 17 at Great Lakes (Midland, Mich.).

Playoff Format: Eight teams qualify. First-half and second-half division winners and wild-card teams meet in best-of-three quarterfinal series. Winners meet in best-of-three series for division championships. Division champions meet in best-of-five final for league championship.

Roster Limit: 25 active. **Player Eligibility Rule:** No age limit. No more than two players and one player-coach on active list may have more than five years experience.

Brand of Baseball: Rawlings ROM-MID.

Umpires: Unavailable.

STADIUM INFORMATION

			Dimensions				
Club	**Stadium**	**Opened**	**LF**	**CF**	**RF**	**Capacity**	**2007 Att.**
Beloit	Pohlman Field	1982	325	380	325	3,500	82,819
Burlington	Community Field	1947	338	403	318	3,200	66,857
Cedar Rapids	Veterans Memorial Stadium	2002	315	400	325	5,300	173,219
Clinton	Alliant Energy Field	1937	335	390	325	4,000	116,261
Dayton	Fifth Third Field	2000	338	402	338	7,230	585.348
Fort Wayne	Memorial Stadium	1993	330	400	330	6,516	237,966
Great Lakes	Dow Diamond	2007	332	400	325	5,200	324,564
Kane County	Philip B. Elfstrom Stadium	1991	335	400	335	7,400	468,869
Lansing	Oldsmobile Park	1996	305	412	305	11,000	341,746
Peoria	O'Brien Field	2002	310	400	310	7,500	259,784
Quad Cities	John O'Donnell Stadium	1931	343	400	318	4,024	148,773
South Bend	Coveleski Regional Stadium	1987	336	405	336	5,000	149,281
West Michigan	Fifth Third Ballpark	1994	317	402	327	10,051	377,412
Wisconsin	Fox Cities Stadium	1995	325	400	325	5,500	197,511

BELOIT SNAPPERS

Office Address: 2301 Skyline Dr., Beloit, WI 53511.
Mailing Address: P.O. Box 855, Beloit, WI 53512.
Telephone: (608) 362-2272. **Fax:** (608) 362-0418.
E-Mail Address: snappy@snappersbaseball.com. **Website:** www.snappersbaseball.com.
Affiliation (first year): Minnesota Twins (2005). **Years in League:** 1982-.

OWNERSHIP, MANAGEMENT

Operated by: Beloit Professional Baseball Association Inc.
Chairman: Dennis Conerton. **President:** Marcy Olsen.
General Manager: Jeff Vohs. **Assistant General Manager:** Riley Gostisha. **Director, Media and Community Relations/Marketing:** Erik VanDyck. **Director, Ticket Operations/Merchandise:** Matt Bosen. **Director, Corporate Sales/Promotions:** Dan Showman.

FIELD STAFF

Manager: Nelson Prada. **Hitting Coach:** Rudy Hernandez. **Pitching Coach:** Gary Lucas. **Trainer:** Alan Rail.

GAME INFORMATION

Radio Announcer: Jason Lamar. **No. of Games Broadcast:** 22. **Flagship Station:** WTJK 1380-AM.
PA Announcer: Unavailable. **Official Scorer:** Rob Lucas.
Stadium Name: Pohlman Field. **Location:** I-90 to exit 185-A, right at Cranston Road for 1 1/2 miles; I-43 to Wisconsin 81 to Cranston Road, right at Cranston for 1 1/2 miles. **Standard Game Times:** 7 p.m., 6:30 (April-May); Sun. 2. **Ticket Price Range:** $6-8.
Visiting Club Hotel: Econo Lodge, 2956 Milwaukee Rd., Beloit, WI 53511. **Telephone:** (608) 364-4000.

BURLINGTON BEES

Office Adwdress: 2712 Mt. Pleasant St, Burlington, IA 52601.
Mailing Address: P.O. Box 824, Burlington, IA 52601.
Telephone: (319) 754-5705. **Fax:** (319) 754-5882.
E-Mail Address: staff@gobees.com. **Website:** www.gobees.com.
Affiliation (first year): Kansas City Royals (2001). **Years in League:** 1962-.

OWNERSHIP, MANAGEMENT

Operated By: Burlington Baseball Association Inc.
President: Dave Walker.
General Manager: Chuck Brockett. **Assistant GM, Baseball Operations/Radio Broadcaster:** Randy Wehofer. **Asst. GM, Sales/Marketing:** Jared Schjei. **Director, Group Outings:** Whitney Henderson. **Director, Tickets/Merchandise:** Kourtney Kelso. **Groundskeeper:** T.J. Brewer.

FIELD STAFF

Manager: Brian Rupp. **Coach:** Ryan Long. **Pitching Coach:** Doug Henry. **Athletic Trainer:** Yoshi Kitaura.

GAME INFORMATION

Radio Announcer: Randy Wehofer. **No. of Games Broadcast:** Home-70, Away-70. **Flagship Station:** NewsRadio KBUR 1490-AM.
PA Announcer: Nathan McCoy. **Official Scorer:** Scott Logas.
Stadium Name: Community Field. **Location:** From U.S. 34, take U.S. 61 North to Mt. Pleasant Street, east 1/8 mile. **Standard Game Times:** M-F: 6:30 p.m. (1st half), 7:00 p.m. (2nd half), Sat. 6:30 p.m., Sun. 2:00 p.m. **Ticket Price Range:** $4-7.
Visiting Club Hotel: Pzazz Best Western FunCity, 3001 Winegard Dr, Burlington, IA 52601. **Telephone:** (319) 753-2223.

CEDAR RAPIDS KERNELS

Office Address: 950 Rockford Rd. SW, Cedar Rapids, IA 52404.
Mailing Address: P.O. Box 2001, Cedar Rapids, IA 52406.
Telephone: (319) 363-3887; 1-800-860-3609. **Fax:** (319) 363-5631.
E-Mail Address: kernels@kernels.com. **Website:** www.kernels.com.
Affiliation (first year): Los Angeles Angels (1993). **Years in League:** 1962-.

OWNERSHIP, MANAGEMENT

Operated by: Cedar Rapids Ball Club Inc.
President: Tom Barbee.

General Manager: Jack Roeder. **Chief Financial Officer:** Doug Nelson. **Director, Operations:** Scott Wilson. **Director, Broadcasting:** John Rodgers. **Director, Communications:** Andrew Pantini. **Sports Turf Manager:** Jesse Roeder. **Director, Ticket/Group Sales:** Andrea Murphy. **Director, Finance/Human Resources:** Charlie Patrick. **Entertainment Manager/Sales:** Sonya Masse. **Stadium Operations Manager:** Seth Dohrn. **Customer Services/Suites Manager/Sales:** Jessica Fergesen. **Concessions Manager:** Dave Soper. **Receptionist:** Marcia Moran.

FIELD STAFF

Manager: Keith Johnson. **Hitting Coach:** Damon Mashore. **Pitching Coach:** Brandon Emanuel. **Trainer:** Dan Nichols. **Strength Coach:** Adam Wagner.

GAME INFORMATION

Radio Announcer: John Rodgers. **No. of Games Broadcast:** Home-70, Away-70. **Flagship Stations:** KMRY 1450-AM.

PA Announcer: Dale Brodt. **Official Scorers:** Unavailable.

Stadium Name: Veterans Memorial Stadium. **Location:** From I-380 North: Take the Wilson Ave. exit. Turn left on Wilson Ave. After the railroad tracks, turn right on Rockford Road. Proceed 0.8 miles, stadium is on your left. From I-380 South: exit at First Avenue. Proceeed to Eighth Avenue (first stop sign) and turn left. Stadium entrance is 0.1 miles on your right (before tennis courts). **Standard Game Times:** April: 6:30 p.m Mon.-Fri., 2 p.m. Sat.-Sun; May: 6:30 p.m., 2 p.m. Sun; June-August: 7 p.m., 2 p.m. Sun. **Ticket Price Range:** $6-9.

Visiting Club Hotel: Best Western Cooper's Mill, 100 F Ave. NW, Cedar Rapids, IA 52405. **Telephone:** (319) 366-5323.

CLINTON LUMBERKINGS

Office Address: Alliant Energy Field, 537 Ball Park Drive, Clinton, IA 52732.

Mailing Address: P.O. Box 1295, Clinton, IA 52733.

Telephone: (563) 242-0727. **Fax:** (563) 242-1433.

E-Mail Address: lumberkings@lumberkings.com. **Website:** www.lumberkings.com.

Affiliation (first year): Texas Rangers (2003). **Years in League:** 1956-.

OWNERSHIP, MANAGEMENT

Operated By: Clinton Baseball Club Inc.

Chairman: Don Roode. **President:** Paul Schnack. **General Manager:** Ted Tornow. **Assistant GM:** Nate Kreinbrink. **Director, Operations:** Justin Sampson. **Director, Media Relations:** Dave Lezotte.

FIELD STAFF

Manager: Mike Micucci. **Coach:** Brian Dayett. **Pitching Coach:** Danny Clark. **Trainer:** Jacob Newburn.

GAME INFORMATION

Radio Announcer: Gary Determan, Dave Lezotte. **No. of Games Broadcast:** Home-70, Away-70. **Flagship Station:** KROS 1340-AM.

PA Announcer: Brad Seward. **Official Scorer:** Tom Whaley.

Stadium Name: Alliant Energy Field. **Location:** Highway 67 North to Sixth Avenue North, right on Sixth, cross railroad tracks, stadium on right. **Standard Game Times:** 7 p.m. (Mon.-Sat.); 2.pm. (Sun.). **Ticket Price Range:** $5-7.

Visiting Club Hotel: Super 8 Motel, 1711 Lincoln Way, Clinton, IA 52732. **Telephone:** (563) 242-8870.

DAYTON DRAGONS

Office Address: Fifth Third Field, 220 N. Patterson Blvd, Dayton, OH 45402.

Mailing Address: P.O. 2107, Dayton, OH 45401.

Telephone: (937) 228-2287. **Fax:** (937) 228-2284.

E-Mail Address: dragons@daytondragons.com. **Website:** www.daytondragons.com.

Affiliation (first year): Cincinnati Reds (2000). **Years in League:** 2000-.

OWNERSHIP, MANAGEMENT

Operated By: Dayton Professional Baseball LLC./Mandalay Baseball Properties. **Owners:** Hank Stickney, Ken Stickney, Peter Guber, Paul Schaeffer, Earvin "Magic" Johnson, Archie Griffin.

President: Robert Murphy. **Executive Vice President:** Eric Deutsch. **VP, Accounting/Finance:** Mark Schlein. **Executive VP/General Manager:** Gary Mayse. **VP, Sponsorships:** Jeff Webb. **Director, Sponsor Services:** Brad Eaton. **Director, Entertainment:** Shari Sharkins. **Director, Marketing:** Jim Francis. **Director, Media Relations:** Unavailable. **Director, Ticket Sales:** Jeff Stewart. **Box Office Manager:** Sally Ledford. **Marketing Managers:** Brandy Abney, Chris Hart, Kevin Johnson, Laura Rose, Clint Taylor, Emilee Verrengia. **Senior Operations Director:** Joe Eaglowski. **Facilities Operations Manager:** Joe Elking. **Baseball Operations Manager:** John Wallace. **Director, Operations:** Andrew Ottmar. **Head Groundskeeper:** Dan Ochsner.

FIELD STAFF

Manager: Donnie Scott. **Hitting Coach:** Darren Bragg. **Pitching Coach:** Doug Bair. **Trainer:** Jimmy Mattocks.

GAME INFORMATION

Radio Announcers: Unavailable. **No. of Games Broadcast:** Home-70, Away-70. **Flagship Station:** WING 1410-AM ESPN Radio.

PA Announcer: Unavailable. **Official Scorers:** Matt Lindsay, Jim Scott.

Stadium Name: Fifth Third Field. **Location:** I-75 South to downtown Dayton, left at First Street; I-75 North, right at First Street exit. **Ticket Price Range:** $7-13.25.

Visiting Club Hotel: Comfort Inn, 7125 Miller Lane, Dayton, OH 45414. **Telephone:** (937) 890-9995.

FORT WAYNE WIZARDS

Office Address: 1616 E. Coliseum Blvd, Fort Wayne, IN 46805.
Telephone: (260) 482-6400. **Fax:** (260) 471-4678.
E-Mail Address: info@fortwaynewizards.com. **Website:** www.fortwaynewizards.com.
Affiliation (first year): San Diego Padres (1999). **Years in League:** 1993-.

OWNERSHIP, MANAGEMENT

Operated By: Hardball Capital.

Owners: Jason Freier, Chris Schoen.

General Manager: Mike Nutter. **Assistant GM, Business Operations:** Brian Schackow. **Senior Assistant GM:** David Lorenz. **Director, Community/Media Relations/Account Executive:** Jared Parcell. **Director, Graphic Design:** Tony Desplaines. **Director, Ticket Operations:** Patrick Ventura. **Director, Group Sales:** Brad Shank. **Director, Broadcasting:** Mike Maahs. **Group Sales Representatives:** Brent Harring, Matt Huffman, Kyle Kiffner, Justin Shurley. **Director, Marketing and Promotions:** Chris Watson. **Office Manager:** Cathy Tinney.

FIELD STAFF

Manager: Doug Dascenzo. **Hitting Coach:** Tom Tornincasa. **Pitching Coach:** Tom Bradley. **Trainer:** JoJo Tarantino.

GAME INFORMATION

Radio Announcer: Kent Hormann, Mike Maahs. **No. of Games Broadcast:** Home-70, Away-70. **Flagship Station:** WKJG 1380-AM.

PA Announcer: Jim Shovlin. **Official Scorers:** Unavailable.

Stadium Name: Memorial Stadium. **Location:** Exit 112A (Coldwater Road South) off I-69 to Coliseum Blvd., left to stadium. **Ticket Price Range:** $6.50-9.

Visiting Club Hotel: Econolodge, 1734 W. Washington Center Rd., Fort Wayne, IN 46818. **Telephone:** (260) 489-5554.

GREAT LAKES LOONS

Office Address: 825 East Main St., Midland, MI 48640.
Mailing Address: P.O. Box 365, Midland, MI 48640.
Telephone: (989) 837-2255. **Fax:** (989) 837-8780.
E-Mail Address: info@loons.com. **Website:** www.loons.com.
Affiliation (first year): Los Angeles Dodgers (2007). **Years in League:** 2007.

OWNERSHIP, MANAGEMENT

Operated By: Michigan Baseball Foundation.

Founder/Foundation President: William Stavropoulos.

President/General Manager: Paul Barbeau. **Assistant GM, Ticket Sales:** Scott Litle. **Assistant GM, Marketing/Promotions:** Chris Mundhenk. **Assistant GM, Finance:** Tammy Brinkman. **Assistant GM, Retail/Guest Services:** Ann Craig. **Director, Broadcast/Media Relations:** Brad Golder. **Director, Business Operations:** Patti Tuma. **Director, Food/Beverage:** Nick Kavalauskas. **Director, Production:** Chirs Lones. **Director, Special Events:** Dave Gamola. **Director, Sponsorships:** Karrie Sells. **Director, Stadium Operations:** Greg Kigar. **Head Groundskeeper:** Matt McQuaid. **Catering/Kitchen Services Manager:** Shantel Johnson-Lawson. **HR/Business Manager, Food/Beverage:** Alyson Schafer. **Marketing Manager:** Ben Gurnee. **Promotions Manager:** Linda Uliano.

Field Staff

Manager: Juan Bustabad. **Pitching Coach:** Danny Darwin. **Hitting Coach:** Garey Ingram. **Trainer:** Dan Christoffer. **Strength Coach:** Unavailable.

GAME INFORMATION

Radio Announcer: Brad Golder. **No. of Games Broadcast:** Home-70, Away-70. **Flagship Station:** WYLZ I00.9-FM.

PA Announcer: Jerry O'Donnell. **Official Scorer:** Unavailable.

Stadium Name: Dow Diamond. **Location:** I-75N to US-10 W. Take the M-20/US10 Business exit on the left toward downtown Midland. Merge onto US-10 W/MI-20 W (also known as Indian St.). Turn left onto State Street. The entrance to the stadium is located at the intersection of Ellsworth and State Streets. **Standard Game Times:** 7:05 p.m.; Sun. 3:05. **Ticket Price Range:** $6-8.50.

Visiting Club Hotel: Holiday Inn of Midland, 1500 W. Wackerly Street, Midland, MI 48640. **Telephone:** (989) 631-4220.

KANE COUNTY COUGARS

Office Address: 34W002 Cherry Lane, Geneva, IL 60134.
Telephone: (630) 232-8811. **Fax:** (630) 232-8815.
E-Mail Address: info@kanecountycougars.com. **Website:** www.kccougars.com.
Affiliation (first year): Oakland Athletics (2003). **Years in League:** 1991-.

OWNERSHIP, MANAGEMENT

Operated By: Cougars Baseball Partnership/American Sports Enterprises, Inc. **President:** Mike Woleben. **Vice President:** Mike Murtaugh. **Vice President/General Manager:** Jeff Sedivy. **Assistant GMs:** Curtis Haug, Jeff Ney. **Special Assistant to GM:** Rich Essegian. **Business Manager:** Mary Almlie. **Controller:** Doug Czurylo. **Finance/Accounting Manager:** Lance Buhmann. **Administrative Assistant:** Kathy Sfondeles. **Director, Food/Beverage:** Mike Klafehn. **Concession Supervisor:** Bill Gentzler. **Personnel Supervisor:** Rob Newlin. **Catering Manager:** Sheila Savage: Staium Maintenance Supervisor: Jeff Snyder. **Accounting Clerk/Merchandise:** Katie Doyle. **Head Groundskeeper:** John Pawlik. **Director, Security:** Dan Klinkhamer. **Media Relations Coordinator:** Shawn Tourney. **Manager, Advertising Placement:** Bill Baker. **Design/Graphics:** Emmet Broderick, Todd Koenitz. **Director, Ticket Operations:** Amy Mason. **Manager, Business Development:** Amy Seipp.

FIELD STAFF

Manager: Aaron Nieckula. **Coach:** Benny Winslow. **Pitching Coach:** Don Schuze. **Trainer:** Nate Brooks.

GAME INFORMATION

Radio Announcer: Jeff Hem. **No. of Games Broadcast:** Home-70, Away-70. **Flagship Station:** WBIG 1280-AM.
PA Announcer: Kevin Sullivan. **Official Scorer:** Bill Baker.
Stadium Name: Philip B. **Elfstrom Stadium. Location:** From east or west, I-88 (Ronald Reagan Memorial Tollway) to Fansworth Avenue North exit, north five miles to Cherry Lane, left into stadium complex; from northwest, I-90 to Randall Road South exist, south to Fabyan Parkway, east to Kirk Road, north to Cherry Lane, left into stadium complex. **Standard Game Times:** 6:30 p.m.; Sat., 6 p.m.; Sun., 2 p.m. **Ticket Price Range:** $8-12.
Visiting Club Hotel: Best Western Naperville, 1617 Naperville Rd, Naperville, IL 60563. **Telephone:** (630) 505-0200.

LANSING LUGNUTS

Office Address: 505 E. Michigan Ave, Lansing, MI 48912.
Telephone: (517) 485-4500. **Fax:** (517) 485-4518.
E-Mail Address: info@lansinglugnuts.com. **Website:** www.lansinglugnuts.com.
Affiliation (first year): Toronto Blue Jays (2005). **Years in League:** 1996-.

OWNERSHIP, MANAGEMENT

Operated By: Take Me Out to the Ballgame LLC.
Principal Owners: Tom Dickson, Sherrie Myers.
General Manager: Pat Day. **Assistant GM:** Nick Grueser. **Director, Food Service:** Dave Parker. **Director, Box Office/Retail:** Jeffrey Jaworski. **Director, Operations/Head Groundskeeper:** Matt Anderson. **Director, Catering:** Denise Davis. **Marketing Manager:** Justin Furr. **Corporate Sales Manager:** Jim LaPorte. **Sponsorship Service Representative:** Diane Bollom. **Business Manager:** Heather Viele. **Media Relations:** Brad Tillery.

FIELD STAFF

Manager: Clayton McCullough. **Coach:** Justin Mashore. **Pitching Coach:** Tom Signore. **Trainer:** Bob Tarpey.

GAME INFORMATION

Radio Announcer: Brad Tillery. **No of Games Broadcast:** Home-70, Away-70. **Flagship Station:** WQTX 92.1-FM.
Official Scorer: Seth Van Hoven; Dave Schaberg.
Stadium Name: Oldsmobile Park. **Location:** I-96 East/West to U.S. 496, exit at Larch Street, north of Larch, stadium on left. **Ticket Price Range:** $7-9.
Visiting Club Hotel: Holiday Inn South, 6820 South Cedar, Lansing, MI 48911. **Telephone:** (517) 694-8123.

PEORIA CHIEFS

Office Address: 730 SW Jefferson, Peoria, IL 61602.
Telephone: (309) 680-4000. **Fax:** (309) 680-4080.
E-Mail Address: feedback@chiefsnet.com. **Website:** www.peoriachiefs.com.
Affiliation (first year): Chicago Cubs (2005). **Years in League:** 1983-.

OWNERSHIP, MANAGEMENT

Operated By: Peoria Chiefs Community Baseball Club LLC.

President: Rocky Vonachen. **Vice President/General Manager:** Ralph Converse. **Vice President, Sales:** Joe Wagoner. **Broadcast/Media Manager:** Nathan Baliva. **Manager, Ticket Sales:** Eric Obalil. **Director, Guest Services/Account Executive:** Howard Yates. **Manager, Box Office:** Ryan Sivori. **Entertainment/Events Manager:** Camden Linstead. **Corporate Sales Account Executive:** John Jackson. **Head Groundskeeper:** Noel Brusius.

FIELD STAFF

Manager: Ryne Sandberg. **Hitting Coach:** Ricardo Medina. **Pitching Coach:** Rich Bombard. **Trainer:** Kelly Vanhove.

GAME INFORMATION

Radio Announcer: Nathan Baliva. **No. of Games Broadcast:** Home-70, Away-70. **Flagship Station:** WOAM 1350-AM.

PA Announcer: Unavailable. **Official Scorer:** Brandon Thome.

Stadium Name: O'Brien Field. **Location:** From South/East, I-74 to exit 93 (Jefferson Street), continue one mile, stadium is one block on left. From North/West, I-74 to Glen Oak Exit. Turn right on Glendale which turns into Kumpf Blvd. Turn right on Jefferson, stadium on left. **Standard Game Times:** 7 p.m., 6:30 (April-May, after Aug. 22); Sat. 6:30; Sun. 2. **Ticket Price Range:** $6-10.

Visiting Club Hotel: Super 8-Peoria, 1816 W. War Memorial Dr., Peoria, IL 61614. **Telephone:** (309) 698-8074.

QUAD CITIES RIVER BANDITS

Office Address: 209 S. Gaines St., Davenport, IA 52802.
Mailing Address: P.O. Box 3496, Davenport, IA 52808.
Telephone: (563) 324-3000. **Fax:** (563) 324-3109.
E-Mail Address: bandit@riverbandits.com. **Website:** www.riverbandits.com.
Affiliation (first year): St. Louis Cardinals (2005). **Years in League:** 1960-.

OWNERSHIP, MANAGEMENT

Operated by: Main Street Iowa.

Vice President, Main Street Baseball: Kirk Goddman. **General Manager:** Ben Burke. **Assistant GM, Corporate Sales:** Cory Howerton. **Assistant GM, Fan Experience:** Keith Lucier. **Director, Corporate Sales:** Shannon Mandsager. **Director, Broadcasting/Media Relations:** Ben Chiswick. **Director, Community/Client Relations:** Stefanie Brown. **Director, Baseball Operations:** Bob Evans. **Director, Food and Beverage:** James Falconer. **Manager, Corporate Marketing:** Jeff Koenig. **Ticker Manager:** Nick Harvey. **Head Groundskeeper/Stadium Operations:** Ben Kratz.

FIELD STAFF

Manager: Steve Dillard. **Hitting Coach:** Joe Kruzel. **Pitching Coach:** Arthur "Ace" Adams. **Trainer:** Manabu Kuwazuru.

GAME INFORMATION

Radio Announcer: Ben Chiswick. **No. of Games Broadcast:** Home-70, Away-70. **Flagship Station:** WKBF 1270-AM.

PA Announcer: Unavailable. **Official Scorer:** Unavailable.

Stadium Name: John O'Donnell Stadium. **Location:** From I-74, take Grant Street exit left, west onto River Drive, left on South Gaines Street; from I-80, take Brady Street exit south, right on River Drive, left on South Gaines Street. **Standard Game Times:** 7 p.m., 6:30 (April); Sun. 1. **Ticket Prices:** $5-12.

Visiting Club Hotel: Clarion Hotel, 5202 Brady St., **Davenport, IA 52806. Telephone:** (563) 391-1230.

SOUTH BEND SILVER HAWKS

Office Address: 501 W. South St, South Bend, IN 46601.
Mailing Address: P.O. Box 4218, South Bend, IN 46634.
Telephone: (574) 235-9988. **Fax:** (574) 235-9950.
E-Mail Address: hawks@silverhawks.com. **Website:** www.silverhawks.com.
Affiliation (first year): Arizona Diamondbacks (1997). **Years in League:** 1988-

OWNERSHIP, MANAGEMENT

Operated By: South Bend Professional Baseball Club LLC.

President: Joe Kernan.

Vice President, Baseball Operations: John Baxter. **Director, Finance:** Cheryl Carlson. **Director, Sales/Marketing:** Amy Hill. **Director, Stadium Operations:** Peter Argueta. **Marketing Manager:** Jeff Scholfield. **Group Sales Manager:** James McAvoy. **Box Office Manager:** Kirk Venderlic. **Sales Manager:** Terry Coleman. **Account Manager:** Jon Lies. **Account Manager:** Jackie Batteast. **Corporate Sales:** Rita Baxter. **Head Groundskeeper:** Joel Reinebold.

FIELD STAFF

Manager: Mark Haley. **Hitting Coach:** Francisco Morales. **Pitching Coach:** Erik Sabel. **Trainer:** Brian Czachowski.

Strength Coach: Vaughn Robinson.

GAME INFORMATION

Radio: None.

Stadium Name: Stanley Coveleski Regional Stadium. **Location:** I-80/90 toll road to exit 77, take US 31/33 south to South Bend to downtown (Main Street), to Western Avenue, right on Western, left on Taylor. **Ticket Price Range:** $5-7.

Visiting Club Hotel: Quality Inn, 515 Dixie Way North, South Bend, IN 46637. **Telephone:** (574) 272-6600.

WEST MICHIGAN WHITECAPS

Office Address: 4500 West River Dr., Comstock Park, MI 49321.
Mailing Address: P.O. Box 428, Comstock Park, MI 49321.
Telephone: (616) 784-4131. **Fax:** (616) 784-4911.
E-Mail Address: playball@whitecaps-baseball.com. **Website:** www.whitecapsbaseball.com.
Affiliation (first year): Detroit Tigers (1997). **Years in League:** 1994-.

OWNERSHIP, MANAGEMENT

Operated By: Whitecaps Professional Baseball Corp.

Principal Owners: Denny Baxter, Lew Chamberlin.

President: Scott Lane. **Vice President, Whitecaps Professional Baseball:** Jim Jarecki. **VP, Sales:** Steve McCarthy. **Director, Outside Events:** Matt Costello. **Director, Food/Beverage:** Matt Timon. **Director, New Business Development:** Dan McCrath. **Manager, Marketing:** Mickey Graham. **Promotions Coordinator:** Brian Oropallo. **Manager, Public Relations:** Jamie Farber. **Coordinator, Media Relations:** Ryan Alexander. **Box Office Manager:** Meghan Brennan. **Groundskeeper:** Greg Salyer. **Manager, Facility Maintenance:** John Passarelli. **Director, Ticket Sales:** Chad Sayen.

FIELD STAFF

Manager: Joe DePastino. **Hitting Coach:** Benny Distefano. **Pitching Coach:** Alan Mills. **Trainer:** Eric Hall.

GAME INFORMATION

Radio Announcer: Dave Skoczen. **No. of Games Broadcast:** Home-70, Away-70. **Flagship Station:** WBBL 1340-AM.

PA Announcers: Mike Newell, Bob Wells. **Official Scorers:** Mike Dean, Don Thomas.

Stadium Name: Fifth Third Ballpark. **Location:** U.S. 131 North from Grand Rapids to exit 91 (West River Drive). **Ticket Price Range:** $5-10.

Visiting Club Hotel: Days Inn Express-GR North, 358 River Ridge Dr. NW, Walker, MI 49544. **Telephone:** (616) 647-4100.

WISCONSIN TIMBER RATTLERS

Office Address: 2400 N. Casaloma Dr, Appleton, WI 54913.
Mailing Address: P.O. Box 7464, Appleton, WI 54912.
Telephone: (920) 733-4152. **Fax:** (920) 733-8032.
E-Mail Address: info@timberrattlers.com. **Website:** www.timberrattlers.com.
Affiliation (first year): Seattle Mariners (1993). **Years in League:** 1962-.

OWNERSHIP, MANAGEMENT

Operated By: Appleton Baseball Club Inc.

Chairman: Craig Dickman.

President, General Manager: Rob Zerjav. **Director, Operations:** Justin Johnson. **Team Operations:** Scott Moudry. **Controller:** Cathy Spanbauer. **Director, Community/Media Relations:** Nikki Becker. **Director, Promotions:** Angie Ceranski. **Manager, Merchandise/Internet Specialist:** Jay Grusznski. **Director, Ticket Sales:** Aaron Hahn. **Group Sales:** Heidi Jett, Brandon Goebel. **Box Office Manager:** Darren Shimanski. **Corporate Sales:** Scott Moudry, Diann Spataro. **Manager, Corporate Sales:** Chris Mehring. **Groundskeeper:** Eddie Warczak.

FIELD STAFF

Manager: Terry Pollreisz. **Coach:** Rafael Sonto Domingo. **Pitching Coach:** Jamie Navarro. **Trainer:** Matt Toth.

GAME INFORMATION

Radio Announcer: Chris Mehring. **No. of Games Broadcast:** Home-70, Away-70. **Flagship Station:** WJMQ 92.3-FM.

PA Announcer: Joe Dotterweich. **Official Scorer:** Jay Grusznski.

Stadium Name: Fox Cities Stadium. **Location:** Highway 41 to Highway 15 (00) exit, west to Casaloma Drive, left to stadium. **Standard Game Times:** 7:05 p.m., 6:35 (April-May); Sat. 6:35; Sun. 1:05. **Ticket Price Range:** $5-8.50.

Visiting Club Hotel: Microtel Inn & Suites, 321 Metro Dr, Appleton, WI 54913. **Telephone:** (920) 997-3121.

SOUTH ATLANTIC LEAGUE

LOW CLASS A

Office Address: 111 Second Avenue NE, Suite 335, St. Petersburg, FL 33701.

Mailing Address: 111 Second Avenue NE, Suite 335, St. Petersburg, FL 33701.

Telephone: (727) 456-1240. **Fax:** (727) 499-6853.

E-Mail Address: office@saloffice.com. **Website:** www.southatlanticleague.com.

Eric Krupa

Years League Active: 1904-1964, 1979-.

President/Secretary-Treasurer: Eric Krupa.

First Vice President: Chip Moore (Rome). **Second Vice President:** Craig Brown (Greenville).

Directors: Don Beaver (Hickory), Cooper Brantley (Greensboro), Craig Brown (Greenville), Peter Carfagna (Lake County), Joseph Finley (Lakewood), Marvin Goldklang (Charleston), David Heller (Columbus), Sean Henry (Asheville), Alan Levin (West Virginia), Tom Volpe (Delmarva), Chip Moore (Rome), Rich Neumann (Hagerstown), Chris Flannery (Augusta), John Simmons (Savannah), Brad Smith (Kannapolis), Alan Stein (Lexington).

Division Structure: North—Delmarva, Greensboro, Hagerstown, Hickory, Lake County, Lakewood, Lexington, West Virginia. South—Asheville, Augusta, Charleston, Columbus, Greenville, Kannapolis, Rome, Savannah.

Regular Season: 140 games (split schedule). **2008 Opening Date:** April 3. **Closing Date:** Sept. 1.

All-Star Game: June 17 at Greensboro.

Playoff Format: First-half and second-half division winners meet in best-of-three semifinal series. Winners meet in best-of-five series for league championship.

Roster Limit: 25 active. **Player Eligibility Rule:** No age limit. No more than two players and one player-coach on active list may have more than five years of experience.

Brand of Baseball: Rawlings.

Umpires: Unavailable.

STADIUM INFORMATION

				Dimensions			
Club	**Stadium**	**Opened**	**LF**	**CF**	**RF**	**Capacity**	**2007 Att.**
Asheville	McCormick Field	1992	328	402	300	4,000	164,910
Augusta	Lake Olmstead Stadium	1995	330	400	330	4,322	177,780
Charleston	Joseph P. Riley Jr. Ballpark	1997	306	386	336	5,800	284,718
Columbus	Golden Park	1951	330	415	330	5,000	71,809
Delmarva	Arthur W. Perdue Stadium	1996	309	402	309	5,200	220,219
Greensboro	NewBridge Bank Park	2005	322	400	320	7,599	441,106
Greenville	West End Field	2006	310	400	302	5,000	339,356
Hagerstown	Municipal Stadium	1931	335	400	330	4,600	146,763
Hickory	L.P. Frans Stadium	1993	330	401	330	5,062	170,000
Kannapolis	Fieldcrest Cannon Stadium	1995	330	400	310	4,700	114,140
Lake County	Classic Park	2003	320	400	320	7,273	330,352
Lakewood	FirstEnergy Park	2001	325	400	325	6,588	442,256
Lexington	Applebee's Park	2001	320	401	318	6,033	385,506
Rome	State Mutual Stadium	2003	335	400	330	5,100	232,674
Savannah	Historic Grayson Stadium	1941	290	410	310	8,000	91,722
West Virginia	Appalachian Power Park	2005	330	400	320	4,300	248,766

ASHEVILLE TOURISTS

Office Address: McCormick Field, 30 Buchanan Place, Asheville, NC 28801.
Telephone: (828) 258-0428. **Fax:** (828) 258-0320.
E-Mail Address: info@theashevilletourists.com. **Website:** www.theashevillet-ourists.com.
Affiliation (first year): Colorado Rockies (1994). **Years in League:** 1976-.

OWNERSHIP, MANAGEMENT

Operated By: Palace Baseball.

Executive Director: Mike Bauer. **General Manager:** Larry Hawkins. **Assistant GM:** Chris Smith. **Director, Media Relations:** Bill Ballew. **Director, Marketing/Merchandise:** Jodee Ciszewski. **Box Office Manager:** Jodee Ciszewski. **Head Groundskeeper:** Mike Friel. **Office Manager:** Unavailable. **Corporate Sales Managers:** Andy Kroeger, Patrick Spence.

FIELD STAFF

Manager: Joe Mikulik. **Coach:** Houston Jimenez. **Pitching Coach:** Doug Linton. **Trainer:** Chris Dovey.

GAME INFORMATION

Radio: None.

PA Announcer: Rick Diggler. **Official Scorer:** Mike Gore.

Stadium Name: McCormick Field. **Location:** I-240 to Charlotte Street South exit, south one mile on Charlotte, left on McCormick Place. **Ticket Price Range:** $6-10.

Visiting Club Hotel: Quality Inn, 1 Skyline Drive, Arden, NC 28704.

AUGUSTA GREENJACKETS

Office Address: 78 Milledge Rd., Augusta, GA 30904.
Mailing Address: P.O. Box 3746, Augusta, GA 30914.
Telephone: (706) 736-7889. **Fax:** (706) 736-1122.
E-Mail Address: info@greenjacketsbaseball.com. **Website:** www.greenjacketsbaseball.com.
Affiliation (first year): San Francisco Giants (2005). **Years in League:** 1988-.

OWNERSHIP, MANAGEMENT

Owners: Baseball Enterprises, LCC

Operated By: Ripken Professional Baseball.

General Manager: Nick Brown. **Assistant GM:** Tom D'Abruzzo. **Director, Stadium Operations:** David Ryther. **Director, Ticket Sales:** Chris Demake. **Corporate Partnership Manager:** Patrick McMaster. **Account Executives:** Adam English, Jonathan Pribble, Josh McDaniel, Chris Lieberman, Kyle Coppess. **Marketing Coordinator:** Alex Rata. **Game Entertainment Coordinator:** Stephanie Bindewald. **Bookkeeper:** Debbie Whisenant. **Box Office Coordinator:** Gary Olson. **Broadcaster/Media Relations:** Nick Barrale.

FIELD STAFF

Manager: Andy Skeels. **Coach:** Lipso Nava. **Pitching Coach:** Ross Grimsley. **Trainer:** Eric Ortega.

GAME INFORMATION

Radio Announcer: Nick Barrale. **No of Games Broadcast:** Home-70 Road-70. **Flagship Station:** WRDW 1630-AM.

PA Announcer: Scott Skaden. **Official Scorer:** Unavailable.

Stadium Name: Lake Olmstead Stadium. **Location:** I-20 to Washington Road exit, east to Broad Street exit, left on Milledge Road. **Standard Game Times:** Mon.-Sat.: 7:05 p.m.; Sun. 2:05. **Ticket Price Range:** $5-10.

Visiting Club Hotel: Fairfield Inn by Marriott, 201 Boy Scout Rd, Augusta, GA 30909. **Telephone:** (706) 733-8200.

CHARLESTON RIVERDOGS

Office Address: 360 Fishburne St., Charleston, SC 29403.
Mailing Address: P.O. Box 20849, Charleston, SC 29413.
Telephone: (843) 723-7241. **Fax:** (843) 723-2641.
E-Mail Address: admin@riverdogs.com. **Website:** www.riverdogs.com.
Affiliation (first year): New York Yankees (2005). **Years in League:** 1973-78, 1980-.

OWNERSHIP, MANAGEMENT

Operated by: The Goldklang Group/South Carolina Baseball Club LP.

Principal Owners: Marv Goldklang, Mike Veeck, Bill Murray, Gene Budig.

General Manager: Dave Echols. **Assistant GMs:** Andy Lange, Jim Pfander. **Media Relations:** Andy Solomon. **Business Manager:** Dale Stickney. **Director, Special Events:** Melissa McCants. **Director, Food/Beverage:** Wil Lindsay. **Assistant Director Food/Beverage:** Mike DeNicola. **Sales Managers:** Jake Terrell, Mike Petrini. **Office Manager:** Kristal Lessington.

Director, Community Relations: Lavon Alls. **Director, Sales:** Harold Craw. **Director, Merchandise:** Mike DeAntonio. **Box Office Manager:** Noel Blaha. **Head Groundskeeper:** Mike Williams. **Assistant Groundskeeper:** Brian Soukup.

FIELD STAFF

Manager: Torre Tyson. **Coach:** Greg Colbrunn. **Pitching Coach:** Jeff Ware. **Trainer:** Scott DiFransico.

GAME INFORMATION

Radio Announcer: Josh Mauer. **No. of Games Broadcast:** Home-70, Away-70. **Flagship Station:** WTMZ 910-AM.

PA Announcer: Ken Carrington. **Official Scorer:** Chuck Manka.

Stadium Name: Joseph P. **Riley Jr. Ballpark. Location:** From U.S. 17, take Lockwood Drive North, right on Fishburne Street. **Standard Game Times:** 7:05 p.m., Sun. 4:05. **Ticket Price Range:** $5-10.

Visiting Club Hotel: Best Western, 250 Spring St., Charleston, SC 29403. **Telephone:** (843) 722-4000.

COLUMBUS CATFISH

Office Address: Golden Park, 100 Fourth St, Columbus, GA 31901.

Telephone: (706) 571-8866. **Fax:** (706) 571-9984.

E-Mail Address: mail@columbuscatfish.com. **Website:** www.columbuscatfish.com.

Affiliation (first year): Tampa Bay Rays (2007). **Years in League:** 1991-.

OWNERSHIP, MANAGEMENT

Operated By: Main Street Baseball LLC.

Owner: David Heller.

General Manager: Ken Clary. **Public Relations Manager:** Joey Zehner. **Ticket Manager:** Jessica Stremming. **Head Groundskeeper:** Ben Heiple. **Concessions/Stadium Ops Manager:** Tim Gaines.

FIELD STAFF

Manager: Matt Quatraro. **Coach:** Ozzie Timmons. **Pitching Coach:** Bill Moloney. **Trainer:** Nick Medina.

GAME INFORMATION

Radio: None.

PA Announcer: Steve Thiele. **Official Scorer:** Brian Evans.

Stadium Name: Golden Park. **Location:** I-85 South to exit 7 (Manchester Expressway), right on Manchester Expressway for one mile, left on Veterans Parkway into South Commons Complex. **Standard Game Times:** 7 p.m.; Sun. 2 (April-June 15), 6 (after June 15). **Ticket Price Range:** $4-15.

Visiting Club Hotel: Quality Inn of Phenix City, 1700 US Hwy 280 Bypass, Phenix City, AL 36867. **Telephone:** (334) 298-9321.

DELMARVA SHOREBIRDS

Office Address: 6400 Hobbs Rd, Salisbury, MD 21804.

Mailing Address: P.O. Box 1557, Salisbury, MD 21802.

Telephone: (410) 219-3112. **Fax:** (410) 219-9164.

E-Mail Address: information@theshorebirds.com. **Website:** www.theshorebirds.com.

Affiliation (first year): Baltimore Orioles (1997). **Years in League:** 1996-.

OWNERSHIP, MANAGEMENT

Operated By: 7th Inning Stretch, LLP.

Directors: Tom Volpe, Pat Filippone.

General Manager: Chris Bitters. **Assistant GM/Director, Corporate Sales:** Jimmy Sweet. **Director, Community Relations:** Aubrey Pfau. **Ticket Office Manager:** Peter Frikker. **Director, Stadium Operations:** Jonathan Blair. **Head Groundskeeper:** Dave Super. **Assistant Groundskeeper:** Caroline Beauchamp. **Director, Marketing:** Brian Patey. **Director, Ticket Operations:** Randy Atkinson. **Group Sales Manager:** Evan Wagner. **Group/Ticket Sales Managers:** Robert Sheuermann, David Bledsoe, Jonathan Patrick, Brandon Berns. **Accounting Manager:** Gail Potts. **Office Manager:** Tracy Schmidt.

FIELD STAFF

Manager: Ramon Sambo. **Coach:** Ryan Minor. **Pitching Coach:** Kennie Steenstra. **Trainer:** Pat Wesley. **Strength Coach:** Ken Conner.

GAME INFORMATION

Radio Announcer: Randy Scott. **No of Games Broadcast:** Home-70 Road-70. **Flagship Station:** WTGM 960-AM.

PA Announcer: Jim Whittemore. **Official Scorer:** Gary Hicks.

Stadium Name: Arthur W. Perdue Stadium. **Location:** From U.S. 50 East, right on Hobbs Road; From U.S. 50 West, left on Hobbs Road. **Standard Game Times:** 7:05 p.m. **Ticket Price Range:** $4-12.

Visiting Club Hotel: Best Value Inn, 2625 N. Salisbury Blvd, Salisbury, MD 21801. **Telephone:** (410) 742-7194.

GREENSBORO GRASSHOPPERS

Office Address: 408 Bellemeade St., Greensboro, NC 27401.
Telephone: (336) 268-2255. **Fax:** (336) 273-7350.
E-Mail Address: info@gsohoppers.com. **Website:** www.gsohoppers.com.
Affiliation (first year): Florida Marlins (2003). **Years in League:** 1979-.

OWNERSHIP, MANAGEMENT

Operated By: Greensboro Baseball LLC.

Principal Owners: Cooper Brantley, Wes Elingburg, Len White.

President, General Manager: Donald Moore. **Vice President, Baseball Operations:** Katie Dannemiller. **CFO:** Jimmy Kesler. **Assistant GM/Head Groundskeeper:** Jake Holloway. **Assistant GM/Sales, Marketing:** Tim Vangel. **Director, Community Relations/Game Promotions:** Kerry Kelly. **Director, Creative Services/Media Relations:** Amanda Williams. **Director, Ticketing:** Kate Barnhill. **Director, Merchandise:** Yunhui Harris. **Director, Group Sales:** Todd Olson. **Group Sales Associate:** Ben Kramer. **Executive Assistant:** Rosalee Brewer. **Assistant Groundskeeper:** Brandon Hobbs. **Assistant Director, Stadium Operations:** Hudson Callaway. **Director, Special Events/Hoppin' Fun:** Allison Moore. **Sales Associate:** Brian Lee.

FIELD STAFF

Manager: Edwin Rodriguez. **Hitting Coach:** Jorge Hernandez. **Pitching Coach:** John Duffy. **Athletic Trainer:** James Stone.

GAME INFORMATION

Radio Announcer: Andy Durham. **No. of Games Broadcast:** Home-70, Away-0. **Flagship Station:** WPET 950-AM.

PA Announcer: Unavailable. **Official Scorer:** Paul Wirth.

Stadium Name: NewBridge Bank Park. **Location:** From I-85, take Highway 220 South (exit 36) to Coliseum Blvd; continue on Edgeworth Street, ballpark at corner of Edgeworth and Bellemeade Streets. **Ticket Price Range:** $6-9.

Visiting Club Hotel: Ramada Inn Conference Center/Coliseum, 2003 Athena Ct., Greensboro, NC 27407. **Telephone:** (336) 294-9922.

GREENVILLE DRIVE

Office Address: 945 South Main St, Greenville, SC 29601.
Telephone: (864) 240-4500. **Fax:** (864) 240-4501.
E-Mail Address: info@greenvilledrive.com. **Website:** www.greenvilledrive.com.
Affiliation (first year): Boston Red Sox (2005). **Years in League:** 2005-.

OWNERSHIP, MANAGEMENT

Operated By: RB3 LLC.

Co-Owner/President: Craig Brown. **General Manager:** Mike deMaine. **Senior Vice President, Customer Development:** Nate Lipscomb. **Director, Finance:** Cathy Boortz. **Director, Ticket Operations:** Adam Sadler. **Director, Group Sales:** Andy Paul. **Director, Marketing Services:** Mike Bonasia. **Director, Ballpark Operations:** Blake Wilson. **Director, Media Relations:** Eric Jarinko. **Director, Merchandise:** Renee Allen. **Food/Beverage Manager:** Jeff Cirelli. **Sponsor Services Manager:** Jackie Schetter. **Producer, Game Entertainment:** Jeremiah Drew. **Corporate Marketing Managers:** Cazzie Blocker, Paul Ortenzo. **Group Events Coordinator:** Mary Kovarik. **Head Groundskeeper:** Ray Sayre.

FIELD STAFF

Manager: Kevin Boles. **Hitting Coach:** Billy McMillon. **Pitching Coach:** Bob Kipper. **Head Trainer:** Paul Buchheit.

GAME INFORMATION

Radio: None.

PA Announcer: Joe Trusty. **Official Scorer:** Sanford Rogers.

Stadium Name: West End Field. **Location:** From south: I-85N to exit 42 toward downtown Greenville, turn left onto Augusta Road, stadium is two miles on the left. **From north:** I-85S to I-385 toward Greenville, turn left onto Church Street, turn right onto University Ridge. **Standard Game Times:** 7p.m.; Sun. 2. **Ticket Price Range:** $5-8.

Visiting Club Hotel: Confort Inn & Suites, 831 Congaree Road, Greenville, SC 29607. **Telephone:** (864) 288-6221.

HAGERSTOWN SUNS

Office Address: 274 E. Memorial Blvd., Hagerstown, MD 21740.
Telephone: (301) 791-6266. **Fax:** (301) 791-6066.
E-Mail Address: info@hagerstownsuns.com. **Website:** www.hagerstownsuns.com.
Affiliation (First-Year): Washington Nationals (2007). **Years in League:** 1993-.

OWNERSHIP, MANAGEMENT

Operated by: Mandalay Baseball Properties.

Principal Owners: Peter Guber, Paul Schaeffer, Hank Stickney, Ken Stickney.

General Manager: Will Smith. **Assistant GM:** C.J. Johnson. **Director, Business Operations:** Carol Gehr. **Director, Stadium Operations/Head Groundskeeper:** Blake Bostelman. **Director, Group Sales:** Drew Himsworth. **Director, Food/Beverage:** Unavailable. **Director, Promotions/Special Events:** Joel Pagliaro. **Director, Ticket Sales/Merchandise:** Jason Bucur. **Director, Media Relations/Broadcasting:** Ryan Mock. **Interns:** Louis Wright III, Justin Murphy, Rusty Jagoe. **Clubhouse Manager:** Cliff Eiland.

FIELD STAFF

Manager: Darnell Coles. **Hitting Coach:** Tony Tarrasco. **Pitching Coach:** Paul Menhart. **Coach:** Sergio Mendez. **Trainer:** Atsushi Torrida

GAME INFORMATION

Radio Announcer: Ryan Mock. **No. of Games Broadcast:** Home-70, Away-70. **Flagship Station:** Cool 95.9-FM

PA Announcer: Unavailable. **Official Scorer:** Chris Spaid.

Stadium Name: Municipal Stadium. **Location:** Exit 32B (U.S. 40 West) on I-70 West, left at Eastern Boulevard; Exit 6A (U.S. 40 East) on I-81, right at Eastern Boulevard. **Standard Game Times:** 7:05 p.m., **6:**35 (April-May); Sun. 1:35, 5:35 (July-Sept.). **Ticket Price Range:** $5-13.

Visiting Club Hotel: Clarion Hotel & Conference Center, 901 Dual Hwy., Hagerstown, MD 21740. **Telephone:** (301) 733-5100.

HICKORY CRAWDADS

Office Address: 2500 Clement Blvd. NW, Hickory, NC 28601.
Mailing Address: P.O. Box 1268, Hickory, NC 28603.
Telephone: (828) 322-3000. **Fax:** (828) 322-6137.
E-Mail Address: crawdad@hickorycrawdads.com. **Website:** www.hickorycrawdads.com.
Affiliation (first year): Pittsburgh Pirates (1999). **Years in League:** 1952, 1960, 1993-.

OWNERSHIP, MANAGEMENT

Operated by: Hickory Baseball Inc.

Principal Owners: Don Beaver, Luther Beaver, Charles Young.

President: Don Beaver. **General Manager:** Mark Seaman. **Assistant GM:** Charlie Downs. **Director, Group Sales:** Mark Parker. **Director, Ticket Operations:** Tony Iliano. **Director, Promotions:** Joe Arnstein. **Director, Broadcasting:** Landon Sears. **Sales Representatives:** Matt Carter, Ashley Cline, Kent Barlow, Thomas LaVerde.

FIELD STAFF

Manager: Gary Green. **Coach:** Rudy Pena. **Pitching Coach:** Jeff Johnson. **Trainer:** Jared Destro.

GAME INFORMATION

Radio Announcer: Landon Sears. **No. of Games Broadcast:** Home-70, Away-70. **Flagship Station:** WMNC 92.1-FM.

PA Announcers: JuJu Phillips, L.A. **Freeman. Official Scorer:** Gary Olinger.

Stadium Name: L.P. **Frans Stadium. Location:** I-40 to exit 123 (Lenoir North), 321 North to Clement Blvd., **left for 1/2 mile. Standard Game Times:** 7 p.m., **6:**30 (April-May); Sun. **5, 2 (April-May).**

Visiting Hotel: Quality Inn & Suites, 1725 13th Ave. Dr. NW, Hickory, NC 28601. **Telephone:** (828) 431-2100.

KANNAPOLIS INTIMIDATORS

Office Address: 2888 Moose Rd., Kannapolis, NC 28083.
Mailing Address: P.O. Box 64, Kannapolis, NC 28082.
Telephone: (704) 932-3267. **Fax:** (704) 938-7040.
E-Mail Address: info@intimidatorsbaseball.com. **Website:** www.intimidatorsbaseball.com.
Affiliation (first year): Chicago White Sox (2001). **Years in League:** 1995-.

OWNERSHIP, MANAGEMENT

Operated by: Smith Family Baseball Inc.

President: Brad Smith.

Vice President, Sales: Tim Mueller. **General Manager:** Randy Long. **Director, Stadium Operations/Head Groundskeeper:** Jason Londeree. **Director, Food/Beverage:** Brad Baranowski. **Director, Ticket Sales:** Jason Bright. **Director, Group Sales:** Greg Pizzuto. **Director, Broadcasting/Media Relations:** Dan Bumpus.

FIELD STAFF

Manager: Chris Jones. **Coach:** Andy Tomberlin. **Pitching Coach:** Larry Owens. **Trainer:** Chris McKenna. **Strength/ Conditioning Coach:** Jeremie Imbus

GAME INFORMATION

Radio Announcer: Unavailable. **No. of Games Broadcast:** Home-70, Away-70. **Flagship:** www.intimidatorsbaseball.com.

PA Announcer: Shea Griffin. **Official Scorer:** Unavailable.

Stadium Name: Fieldcrest Cannon Stadium. **Location:** Exit 63 on I-85, west on Lane Street to Stadium Drive. **Standard Game Times:** 7:05 p.m., Sun. 5:05. **Ticket Price Range:** $3-8.

Visiting Club Hotel: Fairfield Inn by Marriott, 3033 Cloverleaf Pkwy., Kannapolis, NC 28083. **Telephone:** (704) 795-4888.

LAKE COUNTY CAPTAINS

Office Address: Classic Park, 35300 Vine Street, Eastlake, OH 44095-3142.
Telephone: (440) 975-8085. **Fax:** (440) 975-8958.
E-Mail Address: kevinb@captainsbaseball.com. **Website:** www.captainsbaseball.com.
Affiliation (first year): Cleveland Indians (2003). **Years in League:** 2003-.

OWNERSHIP, MANAGEMENT

Chairman, Secretary/Treasurer: Peter Carfagna. **Vice Chairman:** Rita Carfagna. **Vice President:** Ray Murphy. **Senior Vice President:** Pete Carfagna. **Executive Assistant to Chairman:** Sherry Carbeck.

General Manager: Kevin Brodzinski. **Assistant GM:** Paul Siegwarth. **Director, Suite/Electronic Media Sales:** Gary Thomas. **Senior Director, Corporate Sales/Marketing:** Neil Stein. **Gameday Entertainment/Corporate Advertising:** Dan Burr. **Senior Director, Season Ticket Sales:** Matt Phillips. **Senior Director, Group Sales:** Jeff Hull. **Director, Sports Turf Operations:** Greg Elliott. **Senior Director, Community/Media Relations:** Craig Deas. **Manager, Promotions/ Graphic Design:** Jonathan Levey. **Director, Captains Concessions:** Adam New. **Director, Finance:** Jen Doan. **Manager, Ticket Office:** Jen Yorko. **Manager, Corporate Sales:** Justin Hukill. **Account Representative, Group Sales:** Jim Carfagna, Amy Gladieux. **Manager, Merchandise:** Kelli Ashline.

FIELD STAFF

Manager: Aaron Holbert. **Coach:** Jim Rickon. **Pitching Coach:** Ruben Niebla. **Trainer:** Jeremy Heller.

GAME INFORMATION

Radio Announcers: Craig Deas, Kevin Rhomberg. **No. of Games Broadcast:** Home-70, Away-70. **Flagship Station:** WELW 1330-AM.

PA Announcer: Ray Milavec. **Official Scorer:** Fred Heyer.

Stadium Name: Classic Park. **Location:** From Ohio State Route 2 East, exit at Ohio 91, go left and the stadium is 1/4 mile north on your right. From Ohio State Route 90 East, exit at Ohio 91, go right and the stadium in approximately five miles north on your right. **Standard Game Times:** 7:05 p.m.; Wed. 12:05 (April-July); Sat. 7:05 (April-July); Sun. 1:05. **Ticket Price Range:** $6-9.

Visiting Club Hotel: Unavailable.

LAKEWOOD BLUECLAWS

Office Address: 2 Stadium Way, Lakewood, NJ 08701.
Telephone: (732) 901-7000. **Fax:** (732) 901-3967.
E-Mail Address: info@blueclaws.com. **Website:** www.blueclaws.com.

Affiliation: Philadelphia Phillies (2001). **Years In League:** 2001-.

OWNERSHIP, MANAGEMENT

Operated by: American Baseball Company LLC.

President: Joseph Finley. **Partners:** Joseph Caruso, Lewis Eisenberg, Joseph Plumeri, Craig Stein.

General Manager: Geoff Brown. **Assistant GM, Operations:** Brandon Marano. **Assistant GM, Sales:** Rich Mozingo. **Accounting Controller:** Bob Halsey. **Director, Community Relations:** Jim DeAngelis. **Director, Promotions:** Hal Hansen. **Director, Marketing:** Mike Ryan. **Marketing Manager:** Zack Rosenberg. **Director, Business Development:** Mike Leonard. **Director, Ticket Sales:** Dan DeYoung. **Box Office Manager:** Rebecca Ramos. **Ticket Sales Manager:** Kate Hannam. **Corporate Sales Manager:** Joe Pilon. **Director, Group Sales:** Jim McNamara. **Group Sales Managers:** Ray Mencke, Tracy Davis. **Director, New Client Development:** Mike Van Hise. **Special Events Managers:** Lisa Carona, Steve Farago. **Media Relations Manager:** Brendan Burke. **Merchandise Manager:** Mark Euler. **Director, Food/Beverage**

Services: Chris Tafrow. **Executive Chef:** Sandy Cohen. **Concessions Manager:** Brendan Geary. **Concourse Manager:** Scott Braden. **Head Groundskeeper:** Ryan Radcliffe. **Home Clubhouse Manager:** Russ Schaefer. **Visiting Clubhouse Manager:** Tom Germano.

FIELD STAFF

Manager: Steve Roadcap. **Coaches:** Greg Legg. **Pitching Coach:** Dave Lundquist. **Trainer:** Mickey Kozack.

GAME INFORMATION

Radio Announcers: Brendan Burke, Alex Gyr. **No. of Games Broadcast:** Home-70, Away-70. **Flagship Station:** WOBM 1160-AM.

PA Announcer: Kevin Clark, Mike Gavin. **Official Scorer:** Joe Bellina.

Stadium Name: FirstEnergy Park. **Location:** Route 70 to New Hampshire Ave., north on New Hampshire for 2 1/2 miles to ballpark. **Standard Game Times:** 7:05 p.m., 6:35 (April-May); Sun. 1:05, 5:05 (July-Aug.). **Ticket Prices:** $6-9.

Visiting Team Hotel: Quality Inn of Tom's River, 815 Route 37 West, Tom River, NJ 08755. **Telephone:** (732) 341-3400.

LEXINGTON LEGENDS

Office Address: 207 Legends Lane, Lexington, KY 40505.
Telephone: (859) 252-4487. **Fax:** (859) 252-0747.
E-Mail Address: webmaster@lexingtonlegends.com.
Website: www.lexingtonlegends.com.
Affiliation (first year): Houston Astros (2001). **Years in League:** 2001-

OWNERSHIP, MANAGEMENT

Operated By: Ivy Walls Management Company.

President/Chief Operating Officer: Alan Stein. **General Manager:** Andy Shea. **Assistant GM:** Luke Kuboushek. **Vice President, Facilities:** Gary Durbin. **Director, Stadium Operations/Human Resource Manager:** Shannon Kidd. **Business Manager:** Jeff Black. **Financial Assistant:** Micci Murrell. **Director, Marketing:** Seth Poteat. **Director, Ticket Operations:** Beth Ann Goldenberg. **Director, Broadcasting/Media Relations:** Rob Gidel. **Account Executive:** Ron Borkowski. **Senior Group Sales Representatives:** Justin Ball, David Barry. **Group Sales Representative:** Scott Tenney. **Executive Assistant/ Community Relations:** Emily Crumrine. **Promotions Coordinator:** Mario Anderson. **Head Groundskeeper:** Chris Pearl. **Facility Specialist:** Steve Moore. **Facility Assistant/Clubhouse Manager:** Greg Wood. **Receptionist:** Beverly Howard.

FIELD STAFF

Manager: Gregg Langbehn. **Coach:** Stubby Clapp. **Pitching Coach:** Charley Taylor. **Trainer:** J.D. **Shields.**

GAME INFORMATION

Radio Announcer: Rob Gidel. **No of Games Broadcast:** Home-70 Road-70. **Flagship Station:** WLXG 1300-AM.

PA Announcer: Unavailable. **Official Scorer:** Rob Gidel.

Stadium Name: Applebee's Park. **Location:** From I-64/75, take exit 113, right onto North Broadway toward downtown Lexington for 1.2 miles, past New Circle Road (Highway 4), right into stadium, located adjacent to Northland Shopping Center. **Standard Game Times:** 7:05 p.m.; 6:35 p.m., Mon.-Thurs. (April-May); Sun. 2:05 (April-May), 6:05 (June-Aug.). **Ticket Price Range:** $4-16.50.

Visiting Club Hotel: Ramada Inn and Conference Center, 2143 N. Broadway, Lexington, KY 40505. **Telephone:** (859) 299-1261.

ROME BRAVES

Office Address: State Mutual Stadium, 755 Braves Blvd., Rome, GA 30161.
Mailing Address: P.O. Box 5515, Rome, GA 30162.
Telephone: (706) 368-9388. **Fax:** (706) 368-6525.
E-Mail Address: rome.braves@turner.com. **Website:** www.romebraves.com.
Affiliation (first year): Atlanta Braves (2003). **Years in League:** 2003-.

OWNERSHIP, MANAGEMENT

Operated By: Atlanta National League Baseball Club Inc.

General Manager: Michael Dunn. **Assistant GM:** Jim Jones. **Director, Stadium Operations:** Eric Allman. **Director, Ticket Sales:** Erin White. **Director, Food/Beverage:** Dave Atwood. **Manager, Community Relations:** Rachel Rogers. **Administrative Manager:** Libby Simonds. **Account Representatives:** Doug Bryller, John Layng. **Head Groundskeeper:** Mike Hurd. **Retail Manager:** Starla Roden. **Operations Manager:** Terry Morgan.

FIELD STAFF

Manager: Randy Ingle. **Coach:** Bobby Moore. **Pitching Coach:** Jim Czajkowski. **Trainer:** Chas Hall.

GAME INFORMATION

Radio Announcer: Randy Davis, Josh Caray. **No. of Games Broadcast:** Home-70, Away-70. **Flagship Station:** WLAQ 1410-AM.

PA Announcer: Eddie Brock. **Official Scorer:** Ron Taylor.

Stadium Name: State Mutual Stadium. **Location:** I-75 North to exit 190 (Rome/Canton), left off exit and follow Highway 411/Highway 20 to Rome, right at intersection on Highway 411 and highway 1 (Veterans Memorial Highway), stadium is at intersection of Veterans Memorial Highway and Riverside Parkway. **Ticket Price Range:** $4-10.

Visiting Club Hotel: Days Inn, 840 Turner McCall Blvd, Rome, GA 30161. **Telephone:** (706) 295-0400.

SAVANNAH SAND GNATS

Office Address: 1401 E. Victory Dr., Savannah, GA 31404.

Mailing Address: P.O. Box 3783, Savannah, GA 31414.

Telephone: (912) 351-9150. **Fax:** (912) 352-9722.

E-Mail Address: info@sandgnats.com. **Website:** www.sandgnats.com.

Affiliation (first year): New York Mets (2007). **Years in League:** 1904-1915, 1936-1960, 1962, 1984-

OWNERSHIP, MANAGEMENT

Operated By: Rickshaw Baseball.

Owner/President: John Simmons.

General Manager: Bradley Dodson. **Assistant GM/Director, Sales:** Unavailable. **Director, Stadium Operations:** Unavailable. **Director, Client Services/Promotions:** Lauren Povia. **Director, Media Relations/Creative Services:** Mike Passanisi. **Senior Account Executive, Tickets:** Jeff Bierly. **Head Groundskeeper:** Andy Rock. **Ticketing Director:** Unavailable. **Account Executive, Tickets:** Benton Roark. **Account Executive, Tickets:** Pat Shaw. **Director, Finance:** Tasha Drain. **Media Relations Assistant:** Matt Pedersen. **Promotions/Client Services Assistant:** Sarah King. **Box Office Assistant:** Justin Scariato. **Video Production Assistant:** Unavailable.

FIELD STAFF

Manager: Donovan Mitchell. **Hitting Coach:** George Greer. **Pitching Coach:** Jonathan Hurst. **Coach:** Pedro Lopez. **Trainer:** Matt Thayer. **Strength/Conditioning:** Nick Wright.

GAME INFORMATION

Radio Announcer: Mike Passanisi. **No. of Games Broadcast:** Home-70, Away-0. **Flagship:** www.sandgnats.com.

PA Announcer: Unavailable. **Official Scorer:** Michael MacEachern.

Stadium Name: Historic Grayson Stadium. **Location:** I-16 to 37th Street exit, left on 37th, right on Abercorn Street, left on Victory Drive; From I-95 to exit 16, east on 204, right in Victory Drive, Stadium is on right in Daffin Park.. **Standard Game Times:** 7:00 p.m.; Sun. 2:00. **Ticket Price Range:** $7-10.

Visiting Club Hotel: Best Western, 45 Eisenhower Drive, Savannah, GA 31406. **Telephone:** (912) 355-1000.

WEST VIRGINIA POWER

Office Address: 601 Morris St, Suite 201, Charlestown, WV 25301.

Telephone: (304) 344-2287. **Fax:** (304) 344-0083.

E-Mail Address: team@wvpower.com. **Website:** www.wvpower.com.

Affiliation (first year): Milwaukee Brewers (2005). **Years in League:** 1987-.

OWNERSHIP, MANAGEMENT

Operated By: Palisades Baseball.

Principal Owner: Alan Levin.

Executive Vice President: Andy Milovich. **General Manager:** Ryan Gates. **Assistant GM:** Joe Payne. **Director, Group Sales:** Jeremy Taylor. **Director, Tickets:** Mike Link. **Director, Marketing:** Kristin Call. **Director, Promotions:** Dan Helm. **Director, Merchandise/Client Services:** Jillian Heeren. **Director, Concessions:** Greg Ledger. **Operations Manager:** Ben Sanger. **Accountant:** Kim Hill. **Receptionist:** Terri Byrd. **Director, Catering:** Shawn Huffman. **Box Office Manager:** Dan Cudoc.

FIELD STAFF

Manager: Jeff Isom. **Coach:** Jim Lett. **Pitching Coach:** John Curtis. **Trainer:** Jeremy Herniman.

GAME INFORMATION

Radio Announcer: Andy Barch. **No. of Games Broadcast:** Home-70, Away-70. **Flagship Station:** WSWW 1490-AM.

PA Announcer: Donald Cook. **Official Scorer:** Lee France.

Stadium Name: Appalachian Power Park. **Location:** I-77 South to Capitol Street exit, left on Lee Street, left on Brooks Street. **Standard Game Times:** 7:05 p.m.; Sun. 2:15 (April-May), 5:05 (June-Sept.) **Ticket Price Range:** $6-8.

Visiting Club Hotel: Ramada Plaza Hotel, Second Av./B St., S. Charleston, WV 25303. **Telephone:** (304) 744-4641.

NEW YORK-PENN LEAGUE

SHORT-SEASON

Mailing Address: One Progress Plaza, 200 Central Ave., Suite 2300, St. Petersburg, FL 33701.

Telephone: (727) 576-6300. **Fax:** (727) 822-3768.

Website: www.newyork-pennleague.com.

Years League Active: 1939-.

President: Ben Hayes.

Ben Hayes

President Emeritus: Bob Julian.

Vice President: Sam Nader (Oneonta). **Treasurer:** Jon Dandes (Jamestown).

Directors: Tim Bawmann (Lowell), Steve Cohen (Brooklyn), Jon Dandes (Jamestown), Jeff Eiseman (Aberdeen), Tom Ganey (Auburn), Bill Gladstone (Tri-City), Jeff Goldklang (Hudson Valley), Chuck Greenberg (State College), CJ Knudsen (Vermont), Alan Levin (Mahoning Valley), Sam Nader (Oneonta), Brian Paris (Batavia), Ken Stickney (Staten Island), Paul Velte (Williamsport).

League Administrator: Debbie Carlisle. **League Historian:** Charles Wride.

Division Structure: McNamara—Aberdeen, Brooklyn, Hudson Valley, Staten Island. Pinckney—Auburn, Batavia, Jamestown, Mahoning Valley, State College, Williamsport. Stedler—Lowell, Oneonta, Tri-City, Vermont.

Regular Season: 76 games. **2008 Opening Date:** June 17. **Closing Date:** Sept. 6.

All-Star Game: Aug. 19 at Tri-City. **Hall of Fame Game:** Tri-City vs. Oneonta, July 26 at Cooperstown.

Playoff Format: Division winners and wild-card team meet in best-of-three semifinals. Winners meet in best-of-three series for league championship.

Roster Limit: 30 active, but only 25 may be in uniform and eligible to play in any given game. **Player Eligibility Rule:** No more than four players 23 or older; no more than three players on active list may have four or more years of prior service.

Brand of Baseball: Rawlings.

Umpires: Unavailable.

STADIUM INFORMATION

			Dimensions				
Club	**Stadium**	**Opened**	**LF**	**CF**	**RF**	**Capacity**	**2007 Att.**
Aberdeen	Ripken Stadium	2002	310	400	310	6,000	241,215
Auburn	Falcon Park	1995	330	400	330	2,800	66,222
Batavia	Dwyer Stadium	1996	325	400	325	2,600	44,270
Brooklyn	KeySpan Park	2001	315	412	325	7,500	294,972
Hudson Valley	Dutchess Stadium	1994	325	400	325	4,494	153,697
Jamestown	Russell E. Diethrick Jr. Park	1941	335	410	353	3,324	48,305
Lowell	Edward LeLacheur Park	1998	337	400	302	5,000	198,453
Mahoning Valley	Eastwood Field	1999	335	405	335	6,000	129,601
Oneonta	Damaschke Field	1906	350	406	350	4,200	49,118
State College	Medlar Field at Lubrano Park	2006	328	403	322	5,412	151,394
Staten Island	Richmond County Bank Ballpark	2001	325	400	325	6,500	164,207
Tri-City	Joseph L. Bruno Stadium	2002	325	400	325	5,000	136,809
Vermont	Centennial Field	1922	330	405	323	4,400	90,311
Williamsport	Bowman Field	1923	345	405	350	4,200	70,884

ABERDEEN IRONBIRDS

Office Address: 873 Long Drive, Aberdeen, MD 21001.
Telephone: (410) 297-9292. **Fax:** (410) 297-6653.
E-Mail Address: info@ironbirdsbaseball.com. **Website:** www.ironbirdsbaseball.com.
Affiliation (first year): Baltimore Orioles (2002). **Years in League:** 2002-.

OWNERSHIP, MANAGEMENT

Operated By: Ripken Professional Baseball LLC.
Principal Owner: Cal Ripken Jr. **Co-Owner/Executive Vice President:** Bill Ripken. **VP:** Jeff Eiseman.
General Manager: Aaron Moszer. **Assistant GM:** Jon Peterson. **Director, Sales:** Lev Shellenberger. **Director, Ticket Operations:** Brad Cox. **Director, Retail Merchandising:** Don Eney. **Director, Facilities:** Tom Boehl. **Head Groundskeeper:** Chris Walsh.

FIELD STAFF

Manager: Gary Kendall. **Coach:** Cesar Devarez. **Pitching Coach:** Scott McGregor. **Trainer:** Aaron Scott.

GAME INFORMATION

Radio Announcer: Unavailable. **No. of Games Broadcast:** Home-38, Away-38. **Flagship Station:** WAMD 970-AM.
PA Announcer: Andrew Holly. **Official Scorer:** Joe Stetka.
Stadium Name: Ripken Stadium. **Location:** I-95 to exit 85 (Route 22), west on 22 West, right onto Long Drive. **Ticket Price Range:** $5-14.
Visiting Club Hotel: Unavailable.

AUBURN DOUBLEDAYS

Office Address: 130 N. Division St., Auburn, NY 13021.
Telephone: (315) 255-2489. **Fax:** (315) 255-2675.
E-Mail Address: ddays@auburndoubledays.com. **Website:** www.auburndoubledays.com.
Affiliation (first year): Toronto Blue Jays (2001). **Years in League:** 1958-80, 1982-.

OWNERSHIP, MANAGEMENT

Operated by: Auburn Community Non-Profit Baseball Association Inc.
President: Tom Ganey.
General Manager: Carl Gutelius. **Assistant GM:** Kevin Breen. **Head Groundskeeper:** Rich Wild. **Director, Media/Public Relations:** Unavailable.

FIELD STAFF

Manager: Dennis Holmberg. **Coach:** Charles Poe. **Pitching Coach:** Antonio Caceres. **Trainer:** Daniel McIntosh.

GAME INFORMATION

Radio Announcer: Unavailable. **No of Games Broadcast:** Home-38 Away-38. **Flagship Station:** WAUB 1590-AM.
PA Announcer: Unavailable. **Official Scorer:** Unavailable.
Stadium Name: Falcon Park. **Location:** I-90 to exit 40, right on Route 34 for 8 miles to York Street, right on York, left on North Division Street. **Standard Game Times:** 7 p.m.; Sat.-Sun. 6. **Ticket Price Range:** $4-7.
Visiting Club Hotel: Inn at the Fingerlakes, 12 Seminary Ave., Auburn, NY 13021. **Telephone:** (315) 253-5000.

BATAVIA MUCKDOGS

Office Address: Dwyer Stadium, 299 Bank St, Batavia, NY 14020.
Telephone: (585) 343-5454. **Fax:** (585) 343-5620.
E-Mail Address: info@muckdogs.com. **Website:** www.muckdogs.com.
Affiliation (first year): St. Louis Cardinals (2007). **Years in League:** 1939-53, 1957-59, 1961-.

OWNERSHIP, MANAGEMENT

Operated By: Genesee County Baseball Club.
General Manager: David Wellenzohn. **Clubhouse Operations:** Tony Pecora.

FIELD STAFF

Manager: Mark DeJohn. **Coach:** Jeff Albert. **Pitching Coach:** Doug White. **Trainer:** Unavailable.

GAME INFORMATION

Radio Announcer: Unavailable. **No. of Games Broadcast:** Home-38 Away-12. **Flagship Station:** WBTA 1490-AM.

PA Announcer: Unavailable. **Official Scorer:** Unavailable.

Stadium Name: Dwyer Stadium. **Location:** I-90 to exit 48, left on Route 98 South, left on Richmond Avenue, left on Bank Street. **Standard Game Times:** 7:05 p.m.; **Sun. 1:**05. **Ticket Price Range:** $4-6.

Visiting Club Hotel: Days Inn of Batavia, 200 Oak St., Batavia, NY 14020. **Telephone:** (585) 343-1440.

BROOKLYN CYCLONES

Office Address: 1904 Surf Ave, Brooklyn, NY 11224.

Telephone: (718) 449-8497. **Fax:** (718) 449-6368.

E-Mail Address: info@brooklyncyclones.com. **Website:** www.brooklyncyclones.com.

Affiliation (first year): New York Mets (2001). **Years in League:** 2001-.

OWNERSHIP, MANAGEMENT

Managing Member: Fred Wilpon.

Senior Executive Vice President/COO: Jeff Wilpon.

General Manager: Steve Cohen. **Assistant GM:** Kevin Mahoney. **Manager, Media Relations:** Dave Campanaro. **Manager, Brooklyn Baseball Gallery/Community Relations:** Elizabeth Lombardi. **Manager, Graphics:** Kevin Jimenez. **Manager, Operations:** Vladimir Lipsman. **Manager, Tickets:** Mark Cole. **Administrative Assistant/Community Relations:** Sharon Lundy. **Manager, Ticket Sales:** Will Gahagan. **Account Executive:** Ricky Viola. **Bookkeeper:** Tatiana Kanevsky. **Head Groundskeeper:** Kevin Ponte.

FIELD STAFF

Manager: Edgar Alfonzo. **Hitting Coach:** Guadalupe Jabalera. **Pitching Coach:** Hector Berrios.

GAME INFORMATION

Radio Announcer: Warner Fusselle. **No. of Games Broadcast:** Home-38, Away-38. **Flagship Station:** WKRB 90.3-FM.

PA Announcer: Dave Freeman. **Official Scorer:** Rose DeInnocentis.

Stadium Name: KeySpan Park. **Location:** Belt Parkway to Cropsey Ave. South, continue on Cropsey until it becomes West 17th St.; continue to Surf Ave., stadium on south side of Surf Ave. By subway, west/south to Stillwell Ave./Coney Island station. **Ticket Price Range:** $6-16.

Visiting Club Hotel: Staten Island Hotel, 1415 Richmond Ave, Staten Island, NY 10314. **Telephone:** (718) 698-5000.

HUDSON VALLEY RENEGADES

Office Address: Dutchess Stadium, Route 9D, Wappingers Falls, NY 12590.

Mailing Address: P.O. Box 661, Fishkill, NY 12524.

Telephone: (845) 838-0094. **Fax:** (845) 838-0014.

E-Mail Address: gadesinfo@hvrenegades.com. **Website:** www.hvrenegades.com.

Affiliation (first year): Tampa Bay Devil Rays (1996). **Years in League:** 1994-.

OWNERSHIP, MANAGEMENT

Operated by: Keystone Professional Baseball Club Inc.

Principal Owner: Marv Goldklang. **President:** Jeff Goldklang.

General Manager: Eben Yager. **Assistant GM:** Corey Whitted. **Director, Food Services/Sales Manager:** Joe Ausanio. **Director, Media Relations:** Rick Kubitschek. **Director, Sales/Marketing:** Jack Weatherman. **Director, Ticket Operations:** Michael Branda. **Group Sales Manager:** Marie Moffatt. **Ticket Sales Account Manager:** Kristen Huss. **Community Relations Specialist:** Bob Outer. **Director, Business Operations:** Vicky DeFreese. **Director, Special Events/Renegades Charitable Foundation:** Rick Zolzer. **Director, Mascots:** Lisa Weatherman. **Pitch-for-kids Fund, Director of Operations:** Eddie Cunningham. **Merchandise Manager/Community Relations:** Jillian Hoffman. **Director, Stadium Operations:** Tom Hubmaster. **Head Groundskeeper:** Evan Bardua. **Clubhouse Manager:** Anthony Dunnagan.

FIELD STAFF

Manager: Joe Alvarez. **Coaches:** Jared Sandberg, Michael Johns. **Pitching Coach:** Rafael Montalvo. **Trainer:** Jeff Dill.

GAME INFORMATION

Radio Announcer: Sean Ford. **No. of Games Broadcast:** Home-38, Away-38. **Flagship Stations:** WBNR 1260-AM/WLNA 1420-AM.

PA Announcer: Rick Zolzer. **Official Scorers:** Zach Finnelstein, Jeff Cohen.

Stadium Name: Dutchess Stadium. **Location:** I-84 to exit 11 (Route 9D North), north one mile to stadium. **Standard Game Times:** 7:05 p.m.; Sun. 5:05.

Visiting Club Hotel: Ramada Inn, 20 Schuyler Blvd. and Route 9, Fishkill, NY 12524. **Telephone:** (845) 896-4995.

JAMESTOWN JAMMERS

Office Address: 485 Falconer St, Jamestown, NY 14701.
Mailing Address: P.O. Box 638, Jamestown, NY 14702.
Telephone: (716) 664-0915. **Fax:** (716) 664-4175.
E-Mail Address: email@jamestownjammers.com. **Website:** www.jamestownjammers.com.
Affiliation (first year): Florida Marlins (2002). **Years in League:** 1939-57, 1961-73, 1977-.

OWNERSHIP, MANAGEMENT

Operated By: Rich Baseball Operations.
President: Robert Rich Jr.
Cheif Operating Officer: Jonathon Dandes.
General Manager: Matthew Drayer. **Assistant GM:** George Sisson. **Director, Baseball Operations:** Scott Eddy. **Head Groundskeeper:** Jamie Bloomquist.

FIELD STAFF

Manager: Darin Everson. **Coach:** Johnny Rodriguez. **Pitching Coach:** Charlie Corbell. **Trainer:** Josh Seligman.

GAME INFORMATION

Radio: Unavailable.
PA Announcer: Unavailable. **Official Scorer:** Unavailable.
Stadium Name: Russell E. Diethrick Jr. Park. **Location:** From I-90, south on Route 60, left on Buffalo Street, left on Falconer Street. **Standard Game Times:** 7:05 p.m.; Sun. 6:05. **Ticket Price Range:** $4.50-7.
Visiting Club Hotel: Red Roof Inn, 1980 Main St., Falconer, NY 14733. **Telephone:** (716) 665-3670.

LOWELL SPINNERS

Office Address: 450 Aikens St, Lowell, MA 01854.
Telephone: (978) 459-2255. **Fax:** (978) 459-1674.
E-Mail Address: generalinfo@lowellspinners.com. **Website:** www.lowellspinners.com.
Affiliation (first year): Boston Red Sox (1996). **Years in League:** 1996-.

OWNERSHIP, MANAGEMENT

Operated By: Diamond Action Inc.
Owner/CEO: Drew Weber.
Vice President/General Manager: Tim Bawmann. **VP, Business Operations:** Brian Lindsay. **VP, Corporate Communications:** Jon Goode. **Controller:** Priscilla Harbour. **Director, Stadium Operations:** Dan Beaulieu. **Director, Facility Management:** Gareth Markey. **Director, Media Relations:** Jon Shestakofsky. **Director, Merchandising:** Jeff Cohen. **Director, Ticket Group Sales:** Jon Healy. **Director, Ticket Operations:** Justin Williams. **Head Groundskeeper:** Jeff Paolino. **Clubhouse Manager:** Del Christman.

FIELD STAFF

Manager: Gary DiSarcina. **Hitting Coach:** Luis Lopez. **Pitching Coach:** Walter Miranda.

GAME INFORMATION

Radio Announcer: Unavailable. **No. of Games Broadcast:** Home-38 Away-38. **Flagship Station:** WCAP 980-AM.
PA Announcer: George Brown. **Official Scorers:** David Rourke, Bob Ellis.
Stadium Name: Edward A. LeLacheur Park. **Location:** From Route 495 and 3, take exit 35C (Lowell Connector), follow connector to exit 5B (Thorndike Street) onto Dutton Street, left onto Father Morrissette Boulevard, right on Aiken Street. **Standard Game Times:** 7:05 p.m.; Sat.-Sun. 5:05. **Ticket Price Range:** $3.50-7.50.
Visiting Club Hotel: Doubletree Inn, 50 Warren St, Lowell, MA 01852. **Telephone:** (978) 452-1200.

MAHONING VALLEY SCRAPPERS

Office Address: 111 Eastwood Mall Blvd, Niles, OH 44446.
Mailing Address: 111 Eastwood Mall Blvd, Niles, OH 44446.
Telephone: (330) 505-0000. **Fax:** (303) 505-9696.
E-Mail Address: info@mvscrappers.com. **Website:** www.mvscrappers.com.
Affiliation (first year): Cleveland Indians (1999). **Years in League:** 1999-.

OWNERSHIP, MANAGEMENT

Operated By: Palisades Baseball Ltd.
Managing General Partner: Alan Levin.

Executive Vice President: Andy Milovich. **General Manager:** Dave Smith. **Assistant GM:** Jordan Taylor. **Director, Finance:** Debbie Primmer. **Director, Stadium Operations:** Dan Stricko. **Director, Ticket Operations:** Andrea Zagger. **Director, Client Services/Merchandising:** Stephanie Fife. **Director, Promotions:** Billy Richards. **Senior Corporate Sales Executive:** Matt Thompson. **Ticket Sales Representatives:** Brad Ludwig, Marc Means, Al Macias. **Director, Concessions:** Brad Hooser. **Administrative Assistant:** Trish Trill.

FIELD STAFF

Manager: Travis Fryman. **Coach:** Anthony Medrano. **Pitching Coach:** Ken Rowe. **Trainer:** Unavailable.

GAME INFORMATION

Radio Announcer: Marc Means. **No. of Games Broadcast:** Home-38, Away-38. **Flagship Station:** WNIO 1390-AM.

PA Announcer: Unavailable. **Official Scorer:** Craig Antush.

Stadium Name: Eastwood Field. **Location:** I-80 to 11 North to 82 West to 46 South; stadium located behind Eastwood Mall. **Ticket Price Range:** $7-9.

Visiting Club Hotel: Days Inn & Suites, 1615 Liberty St., Girard, OH 44429. **Telephone:** (330) 759-9820

ONEONTA TIGERS

Office Address: 95 River St, Oneonta, NY 13820.
Telephone: (607) 432-6326. **Fax:** (607) 432-1965.
E-Mail Address: naderas@telenet.net. **Website:** www.oneontatigers.com.
Affiliation (first year): Detroit Tigers (1999). **Years in League:** 1966-

OWNERSHIP, MANAGEMENT

Operated By: Oneonta Athletic Corp.

President, General Manager: Sam Nader. **Assistant GM/Director, Operations:** Bob Zeh. **Controller:** Sidney Levine. **Director, Media/Public Relations:** Alice O'Conner. **Director, Marketing/Merchandising:** Suzanne Longo. **Director, Special Projects:** Mark Nader. **Director, Food Services:** Brad Zeh.

FIELD STAFF

Manager: Ryan Newman. **Coach:** Luis Quinones. **Pitching Coach:** Mark Johnson. **Trainer:** Tyler Depew.

GAME INFORMATION

Radio: None.

PA Announcer: John Horne. **Official Scorer:** Tom Heitz.

Stadium Name: Damaschke Field. **Location:** Exit 15 off I-88. **Standard Game Times:** 7 p.m.; Sun. 6. **Ticket Price Range:** $5-7.

Visiting Club Hotel: Super 8 Motel, 4973 St Hwy 23, Oneonta, NY 13820. **Telephone:** (607) 432-9505.

STATE COLLEGE SPIKES

Office Address: Medlar Field, Lubrano Park, University Park, PA 16802.
Telephone: (814) 272-1711. **Fax:** (814) 272-1718.
Website: www.statecollegespikes.com
Affiliation (first year): Pittsburgh Pirates (2007). **Years in League:** 2006-.

OWNERSHIP, MANAGEMENT

Operated By: Curve Baseball LP.

President, Managing Partner: Chuck Greenberg.

General Manager: Rick Janac. **Associate GM/Senior Director, Ticketing:** Jeff Garner. **Cheif Financial Officer:** John Donley. **Director, Community Relations:** Elsie Zengel. **Director, Human Resources:** John Palilla. **Director, Merchandising:** Ben Rothrock. **Sports Turf Manager:** Matt Neri. **Manager, Stadium Operations:** Dan Petrazzolo. **Director of Finance:** Jen Margroum. **Director, Ticket Sales:** Chris Phillips. **Box Office Manager:** Ethan Stewart-Smith. **Director, Promotions:** Matt Hoover. **Executive Producer, In-Game Entertainment:** John Foreman. **Ticket Sales Associates:** Dan Granville, Andy Stephenson, Brian Murphy. **Executive Producer, In-Game Entertainment:** John Foreman. **Administrative Assistant, Office Manager:** Rani Poague. **Manager, Community Relations/Promotions:** Jennifer Orlando. **Assistant Sports Turf Manager:** Shaun Meredith. **Manager, Off the Rack Outfitters:** Claire Martin.

FIELD STAFF

Manager: Brad Fischer. **Hitting Coach:** Sid Bream. **Pitching Coach:** Wilson Alvarez. **Trainer:** Mike Zalno.

GAME INFORMATION

Radio Announcer: Steve Jones. **No of Games Broadcast:** Home-38 Road-38. **Flagship Station:** WZWW 95.3-FM.

PA Announcer: Dean Devore. **Official Scorer:** Dave Baker.

Stadium Name: Medlar Field at Lubrano Park. **Location:** From west, U.S. 322 to Mount Nittany Expressway, I-80 to exit 158 (old exit 23/Milesburg), follow Route 150 South to Route 26 South. From east, I-80 to exit 161(old exit 24/Bellefonte) to Route 26 South or U.S. 220/I-99 South. **Standard Game Times:** 7:05 p.m., Sun. 6:05. **Ticket Price Range:** $6-14.

Visiting Club Hotel: Ramada Conference Center State College, 1450 Atherton St., State College, PA 16801. **Telephone:** (814) 238-3001

STATEN ISLAND YANKEES

Stadium Address: 75 Richmond Terrace, Staten Island, NY 10301.
Telephone: (718) 720-9265. **Fax:** (718) 273-5763.
E-Mail Address: siyanks@siyanks.com. **Website:** www.siyanks.com.
Affiliation (first year): New York Yankees (1999). **Years in League:** 1999-.

OWNERSHIP, MANAGEMENT

Operated by: Mandalay Baseball Properties.
Principal Owners: Staten Island Minor League Holdings LLC.
President: Joseph Ricciutti.

Executive Vice President, General Manager: Jane Rogers. **VP, Community/Media Relations:** John Davison. **VP, Ticket Sales:** Jason Cohen. **Directors, Corporate Partnerships:** Matt Slatus, Bob Gearing. **Director, Entertainment:** Mike d'Amboise. **Finance Manager:** Wayne Seguin. **Manager, Sponsorship Services:** Heidi Silber. **Ticket Manager:** Matt Gulino. **Marketing/Sales Coordinator:** Samantha DiTata. **Corporate Marketing Managers:** Katie Grenda, Domenick Loccisano. **Group Sales Coordinators:** Steve Greenblatt, Christopher Feller, Ryan Hewitt, Matt Schulman. **Customer Account Managers:** Skip Russell, Andrea Blann. **Director, Stadium Operations:** Robert Brown. **Manager, Stadium Operations:** Pete Derwin. **Office Manager:** Rebekah Overholser. **Maintenance Worker:** Nick Pinto. **Groundskeeper:** Aaron Madill.

FIELD STAFF

Manager: Pat McMahon. **Coaches:** Ty Hawkins, Victor Valencia. **Pitching Coach:** Pat Daneker. **Trainer:** Steve Kramer.

GAME INFORMATION

Radio Announcer: Unavailable. **No. of Games Broadcast:** Home-38, Away-38. **Flagship Station:** Unavailable.
PA Announcer: Unavailable. **Official Scorer:** Unavailable.

Stadium Name: Richmond County Bank Ballpark at St. **George. Location:** From I-95, take exit 13E (1-278 and Staten Island), cross Goethals Bridge, stay on I-278 East and take last exit before Verrazano Narrows Bridge, north on Father Cappodanno Boulevard, which turns into Bay Street, which goes to ferry terminal; ballpark next to Staten Island Ferry Terminal. **Standard Game Times:** 7:00 p.m.; Sun 2. **Ticket Price Range:** $9-11.

Visiting Club Hotel: The Navy Lodge, 408 North Path Rd., Staten Island, NY 10305. **Telephone:** (718) 442-0413.

TRI-CITY VALLEYCATS

Office Address: Joseph L. Bruno Stadium, 80 Vandenburgh Ave, Troy, NY 12180.
Mailing Address: P.O. **Box 694, Troy, NY 12181.**
Telephone: (518) 629-2287. **Fax:** (518) 629-2299.
E-Mail Address: info@tcvalleycats.com. **Website:** www.tcvalleycats.com.
Affiliation (first year): Houston Astros (2001). **Years in League:** 2002-.

OWNERSHIP, MANAGEMENT

Operated By: Tri-City ValleyCats Inc.
Principal Owners: Martin Barr, John Burton, William Gladstone, Rick Murphy, Alfred Roberts, Stephen Siegel.
President: William Gladstone.

Vice President, General Manager: Rick Murphy. **Assistant GM:** Vic Christopher. **Senior Advisors:** William Rowan, Buddy Caruso. **Ticket/Merchandise Manager:** Liz Litsch. **Stadium Operations Manager:** Scott Obergefell. **Community Relations Manager:** Chris Turner. **Account Executives:** Ryan Burke, Keith Sweeney, Mike Wiseman, Matt Callahan. **Bookkeeper:** Gene Gleason.

FIELD STAFF

Manager: Pete Rancont. **Coach:** Joel Chimelis. **Pitching Coach:** Don Alexander. **Trainer:** Brian Baca.

GAME INFORMATION

Radio Announcer: Dan Flanagan. **No. of Games Broadcast:** Home-38, Away-38. **Flagship Station:** WVCR 88.3-FM.
PA Announcer: Anthony Pettograsso. **Official Scorer:** William Rowan.

Stadium Name: Joseph L. **Bruno Stadium. Location:** From north, I-87 to exit 7 (Route 7), go east 1½ miles to I-787 South, to Route 378 East, go over bridge to Route 4, right to Route 4 South, one mile to Hudson Valley Community College campus on left. From south, I-87 to exit 23 (I-787), I-787 north six miles to exit for Route 378 east, over bridge to Route 4, right to Route 4 South, one mile to campus on left. From east, Massachusetts Turnpike to exit B-1 (I-90), nine miles to Exit 8 (Defreestville), left off ramp to Route 4 North, five miles to campus on right. From west, I-90 to exit 24 (I-90 East), I-90 East for six miles to I-787 North (Troy), 2.2 miles to exit for Route 378 East, over bridge to Route 4, right to Route 4 south for one mile to campus on left. **Standard Game Times:** 7 p.m.; Sun. 5. **Ticket Price Range:** $5-10.

Visiting Club Hotel: Days Inn, 16 Wolf Rd, Albany, NY 12205. **Telephone:** (518) 459-3600.

VERMONT LAKE MONSTERS

Office Address: 1 King Street Ferry Dock, Burlington, VT 05401.
Telephone: (802) 655-4200. **Fax:** (802) 655-5660.
E-Mail Address: mail@vermontlakemonsters.com. **Website:** www.vermontlakemonsters.com.
Affiliation (first year): Washington Nationals (2005). **Years in League:** 1994-.

OWNERSHIP, MANAGEMENT

Operated by: Vermont Expos Inc.
Principal Owner, President: Ray Pecor.
General Manager: C.J. Knudsen. **Assistant GM:** Nate Cloutier. **Operations Manager:** Sander Falzone. **Director, Community Relations/Promotions:** Melissa Gagne. **Director, Finance:** Florianne Irwin. **Director, Media Relations:** Paul Stanfield. **Director, Concessions:** Dan Keogh. **Director, Stadium Operations:** Jim O'Brien.
Director, Special Projects: Onnie Matthews. **Clubhouse Operations:** Phil Schelzo.

FIELD STAFF

Manager: Ramon Aviles. **Hitting Coach:** Jason Camilli. **Pitching Coach:** Rusty Meacham.

GAME INFORMATION

Radio Announcers: Dave Koehn, George Commo. **No. of Games Broadcast:** Home-38, Away-38. **Flagship Station:** The Zone 96.7-FM/960-AM.
PA Announcer: Rich Haskell. **Official Scorer:** Ev Smith.
Stadium Name: Centennial Field. **Location:** I-89 to exit 14W, right on East Avenue for one mile, right at Colchester Avenue. **Standard Game Times:** 7:05 p.m.; Sun. 5:05. **Ticket Price Range:** $5-8.
Visiting Club Hotel: University Inn & Suites, 5 Dorset St., South Burlington, VT 05403. **Telephone:** (802) 863-5541.

WILLIAMSPORT CROSSCUTTERS

Office Address: Bowman Field, 1700 W. Fourth St, Williamsport, PA 17701.
Mailing Address: P.O. Box 3173, Williamsport, PA 17701.
Telephone: (570) 326-3389. **Fax:** (570) 326-3494.
E-Mail Address: mail@crosscutters.com. **Website:** www.crosscutters.com.
Affiliation (first year): Philadelphia Phillies (2007). **Years in League:** 1968-72, 1994-.

OWNERSHIP, MANAGEMENT

Operated By: Geneva Cubs Baseball Inc.
Principal Owners: Paul Velte, John Schreyer. **President:** Paul Velte. **Vice President:** John Schreyer.
Vice President, General Manager: Doug Estes. **Vice President, Marketing/Public Relations:** Gabe Sinicropi. **Director, Concessions:** Bill Gehron. **Director, Ticket Operations/Community Relations:** Sarah Budd. **Director, Client Services:** Jenny Hoover. **Head Groundskeeper:** Melissa Ward.

FIELD STAFF

Manager: Dusty Wathan. **Coach:** Eric Valent. **Pitching Coach:** Bill Bliss.

GAME INFORMATION

Radio Announcer: Adam Marco. **No. of Games Broadcast:** Home-38, Away-38. **Flagship Station:** WLYC 1050-AM.
PA Announcer: Rob Thomas. **Official Scorer:** Ken Myers.
Stadium Name: Bowman Field. **Location:** From south, Route 15 to Maynard Street, right on Maynard, left on Fourth Street for one mile. From north, Route 15 to Fourth Street, left on Fourth. **Ticket Price Range:** $4.50-7.
Visiting Club Hotel: Best Western, 1840 E. Third St, Williamsport, PA 17701. **Telephone:** (570) 326-1981.

NWL NORTHWEST LEAGUE OF PROFESSIONAL BASEBALL

NORTHWEST LEAGUE

SHORT-SEASON

Office Address: 910 Main St., Suite 351, Boise, ID 83702.
Mailing Address: P.O. Box 1645, Boise, ID 83701.
Telephone: (208) 429-1511. **Fax:** (208) 429-1525.
E-Mail Address: bobrichmond@att.net. **Website:** www.northwestleague.com.
Years League Active: 1954-.
President, Treasurer: Bob Richmond.
Vice President: Brent Miles. **Corporate Secretary:** Jerry Walker (Salem-Keizer).
Directors: Bob Beban (Eugene), Bobby Brett (Spokane), Peter Carfagna (Everett), Jake Kerr (Vancouver), Mike McMurray (Yakima), Brent Miles (Tri-City), Jerry Walker (Salem-Keizer), Neil Leibman (Boise).
Administrative Assistant: Rob Richmond.
Division Structure: East—Boise, Spokane, Tri-City, Yakima. West—Eugene, Everett, Salem-Keizer, Vancouver.
Regular Season: 76 games. **2008 Opening Date:** June 17. **Closing Date:** Sept. 3.
Playoff Format: Division winners meet in best-of-five series for league championship.
All-Star Game: None.
Roster Limit: 30 active, 35 under control. **Player Eligibility Rule:** No more than three players on active list may have four or more years of prior service.
Brand of Baseball: Rawlings.
Umpires: Unavailable.

Bob Richmond

STADIUM INFORMATION

			Dimensions				
Club	**Stadium**	**Opened**	**LF**	**CF**	**RF**	**Capacity**	**2007 Att.**
Boise	Memorial Stadium	1989	335	405	335	4,500	102,878
Eugene	Civic Stadium	1938	335	400	328	6,800	134,949
Everett	Everett Memorial Stadium	1984	330	395	330	3,682	106,683
Salem-Keizer	Volcanoes Stadium	1997	325	400	325	4,100	118,722
Spokane	Avista Stadium	1958	335	398	335	7,162	192,021
Tri-City	Dust Devils Stadium	1995	335	400	335	3,730	75,308
Vancouver	Nat Bailey Stadium	1951	335	395	335	6,500	126,491
Yakima	Yakima County Stadium	1993	295	406	295	3,000	70,117

BOISE HAWKS

Office Address: 5600 N. Glenwood St., Boise, ID 83714.
Telephone: (208) 322-5000. **Fax:** (208) 322-6846.
Website: www.boisehawks.com.
Affiliation (first year): Chicago Cubs (2001). **Years in League:** 1975-76, 1978, 1987-.

OWNERSHIP, MANAGEMENT

Operated by: Boise Baseball LLC.
CEO: Neil Leibman.
President/General Manager: Todd Rahr. **Assistant GM/Director, Business Operations:** Dina Duncan. **Director, Facility Oversight/GM Home Plate Food Services:** Roger Inwards. **Creative Services Manager:** Ken Hyde. **Ticket Sales Manager:** Andy Simon. **Sponsorship Sales Manager:** Pete Korstad. **Client Services Manager:** Kelly Kerkvliet. **Stadium Operations Manager:** Jeff Israel. **Accountant:** Joe Austin.

FIELD STAFF

Manager: Tom Beyers. **Hitting Coach:** Ricardo Medina. **Pitching Coach:** Tom Pratt. **Trainer:** Anthony Sanderson.

GAME INFORMATION

Radio Announcer: Mike Safford. **No. of Games Broadcast:** Home-38, Away-38. **Flagship Station:** KTIK 1350-AM.
PA Announcer: Unavailable. **Official Scorer:** Unavailable.
Stadium Name: Memorial Stadium. **Location:** I-84 to Cole Road, north to Western Idaho Fairgrounds at 5600 North Glenwood Street. **Standard Game Time:** 7:15 p.m. **Ticket Price Range:** $5-10.
Visiting Club Hotel: Owyhee Plaza Hotel, 1109 Main St., Boise, ID 83702. **Telephone:** (208) 343-4611.

EUGENE EMERALDS

Office Address: 2077 Willamette St, Eugene, OR 97405.
Mailing Address: P.O. Box 5566, Eugene, OR 97405.
Telephone: (541) 342-5367. **Fax:** (541) 342-6089.
E-Mail Address: ems@go-ems.com. **Website:** www.go-ems.com.
Affiliation (first year): San Diego Padres (2001). **Years in League:** 1955-68, 1974-.

OWNERSHIP, MANAGEMENT

Operated By: Elmore Sports Group Ltd.
Principal Owner: David Elmore.
President, General Manager: Bob Beban. **Assistant GMs:** Bryan Beban, Nathan Skalsky. **Director, Business Operations:** Eileen Beban. **Director, Food Services:** Phil Bopp. **Director, Tickets/Special Events:** Geoff Weatherbie. **Director, Stadium Operations:** David Puente. **Director, Media Relations:** Bryan Beban. **Grounds Superintendent:** Joe Johannsen.

FIELD STAFF

Manager: Greg Riddoch. **Coach:** Darrell Sherman. **Pitching Coach:** Dave Rajsich. **Trainer:** Nate Stewart.

GAME INFORMATION

Radio Announcer: Unavailable. **No. of Games Broadcast:** Home-38, Away-38. **Flagship Station:** KPNW 1120-AM.
PA Announcer: Unavailable. **Official Scorer:** George McPherson.
Stadium Name: Civic Stadium. **Location:** From I-5, take I-105 to Exit 2, stay left and follow to downtown, cross over Ferry Street Bridge to Eighth Avenue, left on Pearl Street, south to 20th Avenue. **Ticket Price Range:** $5.50-9.
Visiting Club Hotel: Shilo Inn Eugene/Springfield, 3350 Gateway Street, Springfield, OR 97477. **Telephone:** (541) 747-0332.

EVERETT AQUASOX

Mailing Address: 3802 Broadway, Everett, WA 98201.
Telephone: (425) 258-3673. **Fax:** (425) 258-3675.
E-Mail Address: aquasox@aquasox.com. **Website:** www.aquasox.com.
Affiliation (first year): Seattle Mariners (1995). **Years in League:** 1984-.

OWNERSHIP, MANAGEMENT

Operated by: Famiglia II.
President: Peter Carfagna. **Vice President, Baseball Operations:** Pete Carfagna.
General Manager: Brian Sloan. **Assistant GM:** Cathy Bierman. **Director, Broadcasting/Corporate Sales:** Pat Dillon. **Director, Ballpark Operations:** Jason Jarett. **Director, Ticket Services:** Scott Gray. **Director, Food/Beverage:** Todd

Holterhoff. **Director, Accounting:** Teresa Sarsted. **Account Representative:** Rick O'Connor. **Technology Specialist:** Matt Nystrom

FIELD STAFF

Manager: Jose Moreno. **Hitting Coach:** Henry Cotto. **Pitching Coach:** Nasusel Cabrera. **Trainer:** Spyder Webb.

GAME INFORMATION

Radio Announcer: Pat Dillon. **No. of Games Broadcast:** Home-38, Away-38. **Flagship Station:** KRKO 1380-AM.

PA Announcer: Tom Lafferty. **Official Scorer:** Pat Castro.

Stadium Name: Everett Memorial Stadium. **Location:** I-5, exit 192. **Standard Game Times:** 7:05 p.m., Sun. 1:05. **Ticket Price Range:** $7-15.

Visiting Club Hotel: Best Western Cascadia Inn, 2800 Pacific Ave., Everett, WA 98201. **Telephone:** (425) 258-4141.

SALEM-KEIZER VOLCANOES

Street Address: 6700 Field of Dreams Way NE, Keizer, OR 97303.

Mailing Address: P.O. Box 20936, Keizer, OR 97307.

Telephone: (503) 390-2225. **Fax:** (503) 390-2227.

E-Mail Address: probasebal@aol.com. **Website:** www.volcanoesbaseball.com.

Affiliation (first year): San Francisco Giants (1997). **Years in League:** 1997-.

OWNERSHIP, MANAGEMENT

Operated By: Sports Enterprises Inc.

Principal Owners: Jerry Walker, Bill Tucker.

President, General Manager: Jerry Walker. **Vice President, Operations:** Rick Nelson. **Corporate Sponsorships/ Business Operations:** Greg Stone. **Coporate Sponsorships:** Jerry Howard. **Media Relations:** Rick Nelson. **Director, Community Relations:** Robin Barney. **Corporate Ticket Sales:** Greg Herbst. **Director, Merchandising/Ticket Office Operations:** Bea Howard.

FIELD STAFF

Manager: Tom Trebelhorn. **Coach:** Ricky Ward. **Pitching Coach:** Jerry Cram. **Trainer:** Unavailable.

GAME INFORMATION

Radio Announcer: Unavailable. **No. of Games Broadcast:** Home-38, Away-38. **Flagship Station:** Unavailable.

PA Announcer: Bill Post. **Official Scorer:** Dawn Hills.

Stadium Name: Volcanoes Stadium. **Location:** I-5 to exit 260 (Chemawa Road), west one block to Stadium Way NE, north six blocks to stadium. **Standard Game Times:** 6:35 p.m.; Fri-Sat. 7:05; Sun. 5:05. **Ticket Price Range:** $7-11.

Visiting Club Hotel: Comfort Suites, 630 Hawthorne Ave. SE, Salem, OR 97301. **Telephone:** (503) 585-9705.

SPOKANE INDIANS

Office Address: Avista Stadium, 602 N. Havana, Spokane, WA 99202.

Mailing Address: P.O. Box 4758, Spokane, WA 99220.

Telephone: (509) 535-2922. **Fax:** (509) 534-5368.

E-Mail Address: mail@spokaneindiansbaseball.com. **Website:** www.spokaneindiansbaseball.com.

Affiliation (first year): Texas Rangers (2003). **Years in League:** 1972, 1983-

OWNERSHIP, MANAGEMENT

Operated By: Longball Inc.

Principal Owners: Bobby Brett, J.B. **Brett.**

President: Andrew Billig.

Vice President, General Manager: Chris Duff. **Senior VP:** Otto Klein. **VP, Tickets:** Josh Roys. **Assistant GM:** Lesley DeHart. **Assistant GM, Promotions:** Sarah Cislo. **Director, Sponsorhips:** Matt Almond. **Director, Stadium Operations:** Manny Boralessa. **Sales Support Director:** Stacey Dacar. **Group Sales Coordinators:** Jason O'Polka, Moira Mis. **Senior Account Executive:** Ryan Donckers. **Coordinator, Promotions:** Nikki Stokes. **CFO:** Greg Sloan. **Director, Accounting:** Renee Stearnes. **Director, Public Relations:** Keenan Bowen. **Manager, Ticket Office:** Briana K'Burg. **Head Groundskeeper:** Unavailable. **Assistant Director, Stadium Operations:** Larry Blummer.

FIELD STAFF

Manager: Tim Hulett. **Coach:** Hector Ortiz. **Pitching Coach:** Unavailable. **Trainer:** Unavailable.

GAME INFORMATION

Radio Announcer: Bob Robertson. **No. of Games Broadcast:** Home-38, Away-38. **Flagship Station:** 790 The FAN.

PA Announcer: Unavailable. **Official Scorer:** Unavailable.

Stadium Name: Avista Stadium at the Spokane Fair and Expo Center. **Location:** From west, I-90 to exit 283B (Thor/ Freya), east on Third Avenue, left onto Havana. From east, I-90 to Broadway exit, right onto Broadway, left onto Havana.

Standard Game Time: 6:30 p.m. **Ticket Price Range:** $4-9.

Visiting Club Hotel: Mirabeau Park Hotel & Convention Center, N. 1100 Sullivan Rd, Spokane, WA 99037. **Telephone:** (509) 924-9000.

TRI-CITY DUST DEVILS

Office Address: 6200 Burden Blvd., Pasco, WA 99301.

Telephone: (509) 544-8789. **Fax:** (509) 547-9570.

E-Mail Address: info@dustdevilsbaseball.com. **Website:** www.dustdevilsbaseball.com.

Affiliation (first year): Colorado Rockies (2001). **Years in League:** 1955-1974, 1983-1986, 2001-.

OWNERSHIP, MANAGEMENT

Operated by: Northwest Baseball Ventures.

Principal Owner: George Brett.

President: Brent Miles. **Vice President/General Manager:** Monica Ortega. **VP, Business Operations:** Tim Gittel. **Assistant GM, Operations:** Garrett Flowers. **Director, Season Tickets:** Matt Nash. **Director, Sponsorships:** Kelli Walter. **Group Sales Coordinator:** Jesse Robinson. **Account Executive:** Josh Alfrey. **Head Groundskeeper:** Michael Angel.

FIELD STAFF

Manager: Freddie Ocasio. **Coach:** Anthony Sanders. **Pitching Coach:** Dave Schuler. **Trainer:** Andy Stover.

GAME INFORMATION

Radio Announcer: Mike Boyle. **No. of Games Broadcast:** Home-38, Away-38. **Flagship Station:** ESPN 960-AM.

PA Announcer: Patrick Harvey. **Official Scorer:** Tony Wise.

Stadium Name: Dust Devils Stadium. **Location:** I-182 to exit 9 (Road 68), north to Burden Blvd., **right to stadium. Standard Game Time:** 7:15 p.m. **Ticket Price Range:** $4-9.

Visiting Club Hotel: Red Lion Hotel-Columbia Center, 1101 N. Columbia Center Blvd., Kennewick, WA 99336. **Telephone:** (509) 783-0611.

VANCOUVER CANADIANS

Office Address: Nat Bailey Stadium, 4601 Ontario St., Vancouver, British Columbia V5V 3H4.

Telephone: (604) 872-5232. **Fax:** (604) 872-1714.

E-Mail Address: staff@canadiansbaseball.com. **Website:** www.canadiansbaseball.com.

Affiliation (first year): Oakland Athletics (2000). **Years in League:** 2000-.

OWNERSHIP, MANAGEMENT

Operated by: Vancouver Canadians Professional Baseball LLP.

Principal Owners: Jake Kerr, Jeff Mooney. **President:** Andy Dunn.

General Manager: Andrew Seymour. **Vice President, Stadium Operations:** Delany Dunn. **Senior Director, Sales/Marketing:** Graham Wall. **Director, Media Relations/Broadcast:** Rob Fai. **Director of Ticketing:** Jason Takefman. **BBQ/Group Ticket Manager:** Spiro Khouri. **Assistant Ticket Manager:** Allan Bailey. **Ballpark Operations Manager:** JC Fraser. **Sales/Marketing Administrator:** Cynthia Wildman. **Outside Sales/Marketing Rep:** Stephen Hopkins. **Financial Controller:** Delores Sebellin. **Concessions Director:** Roy Lake. **Clubhouse Manager:** Glenn Hall.

FIELD STAFF

Manager: Rick Magnante. **Coach:** Unavailable. **Pitching Coach:** Craig Lefferts. **Trainer:** Travis Tims.

GAME INFORMATION

Radio Announcer: Rob Fai. **No. of Games Broadcast:** Home-38, Away-38. **Flagship Station:** The Team 1040-AM.

PA Announcer: Don Andrews. **Official Scorer:** Pat Karl.

Stadium Name: Nat Bailey Stadium. **Location:** From downtown, take Cambie Street Bridge, left on East 25th Ave./King Edward Ave., right on Main Street, right on 33rd Ave., right on Ontario St. to stadium. From south, take Highway 99 to Oak Street, right on 41st Ave., left on Main Street to 33rd Ave., right on Ontario St. to stadium. **Standard Game Times:** 7:05 p.m., Sun. 1:05. **Ticket Price Range:** $9-20.

Visiting Club Hotel: Accent Inns, 10551 Edwards Dr., Richmond, B.C. V6X 3L8. **Telephone:** (604) 273-3311.

YAKIMA BEARS

Office Address: 8 N. 2nd St., Yakima, WA 98901.
Mailing Address: P.O. Box 483, Yakima, WA 98907.
Telephone: (509) 457-5151. **Fax:** (509) 457-9909.
E-Mail Address: info@yakimabears.com. **Website:** www.yakimabears.com.
Affiliation (first year): Arizona Diamondbacks (2001). **Years in League:** 1955-66, 1990-.

OWNERSHIP, MANAGEMENT

Operated by: Short Season LLC.
Managing Partners: Mike McMurray, Mike Ellis, Josh Weinman, Myron Levin.
President: Mike McMurray.
General Manager: K.L. **Wombacher. Assistant GM, Sales:** Aaron Arndt. **Assistant GM, Operations:** Broc Arndt. **Director, Food and Beverage:** Jared Jacobs. **Director, Ticket Operations:** Tom Gross. **Director, Group Sales:** Unavailable. **Office Manager:** Lauren Wombacher. **Head Groundskeeper:** Bill Brown. **Administrative Assistants:** Kristin Sheldon, Bo Hubbard, Ryan Coffey.

FIELD STAFF

Manager: Bob Didier. **Coach:** Chris Briones. **Pitching Coach:** Dan Carlson. **Trainer:** Mark Ryan.

GAME INFORMATION

Radio Announcer: Randy Brochu. **No. of Games Broadcast:** Home-38, Away-38. **Flagship Station:** KUTI 1460-AM.
PA Announcer: Todd Lyons. **Official Scorer:** Mike McMurray.
Stadium Name: Yakima County Stadium. **Location:** I-82 to exit 34 (Nob Hill Boulevard), west to Fair Avenue, right on Fair, right on Pacific Avenue. **Standard Game Times:** 7:05 p.m., Sun. 5:35. **Ticket Price Range:** $4.50-8.50.
Visiting Club Hotel: Best Western Ahtanum Inn, 2408 Rudkin Rd., Union Gap, WA 98903. **Telephone:** (509) 248-9700.

APPALACHIAN LEAGUE

ROOKIE ADVANCED

Mailing Address: 283 Deerchase Circle, Statesville, NC 28625.
Telephone: (704) 873-5300. **Fax:** (704) 873-4333.
E-Mail Address: appylg@hughes.net. **Website:** www.appyleague.com.

Lee Landers

Years League Active: 1921-25, 1937-55, 1957-.

President, Treasurer: Lee Landers. **Corporate Secretary:** Jim Holland (Princeton).

Directors: Ricky Bennett (Greeneville), Greg Hunter (Pulaski), Mitch Lukevics (Princeton), J.J. Picollo (Burlington), Alan Regier (Bristol), Len Johnston (Bluefield), Jeff Luhnow (Johnson City), Kurt Kemp (Danville), Adam Wogan (Kingsport), Jim Rantz (Elizabethton).

League Administrator: Bobbi Landers.

Division Structure: East—Bluefield, Burlington, Danville, Princeton, Pulaski. **West—Bristol, Elizabethton, Greeneville, Johnson City, Kingsport.**

Regular Season: 68 games. **2008 Opening Date:** June 17. **Closing Date:** Aug. **26.**

All-Star Game: None.

Playoff Format: Division winners meet in best-of-three series for league championship.

Roster Limit: 35 active. **Player Eligibility Rule:** No more than two years of prior minor league service.

Brand of Baseball: Rawlings.

Umpires: Unavailable

STADIUM INFORMATION

			Dimensions				
Club	**Stadium**	**Opened**	**LF**	**CF**	**RF**	**Capacity**	**2007 Att.**
Bluefield	Bowen Field	1939	335	400	335	2,250	28,895
Bristol	DeVault Memorial Stadium	1969	325	400	310	2,000	20,768
Burlington	Burlington Athletic Stadium	1960	335	410	335	3,000	33,060
Danville	Dan Daniel Memorial Park	1993	330	400	330	2,588	42,016
Elizabethton	Joe O'Brien Field	1974	335	414	326	1,500	30,134
Greeneville	Pioneer Park	2004	331	400	331	2,400	51,425
Johnson City	Howard Johnson Field	1956	320	410	320	2,500	21,101
Kingsport	Hunter Wright Stadium	1995	330	410	330	2,500	34,301
Princeton	Hunnicutt Field	1988	330	396	330	1,950	26,882
Pulaski	Calfee Park	1935	335	405	310	2,500	—

BLUEFIELD ORIOLES

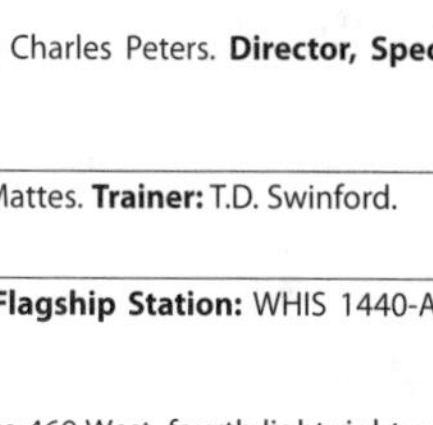

Office Address: Stadium Drive, Bluefield, WV 24701.
Mailing Address: P.O. Box 356, Bluefield, WV 24701.
Telephone: (276) 326-1326. **Fax:** (276) 326-1318.
E-Mail Address: babybirds1@comcast.net. **Website:** www.bluefieldorioles.com.
Affiliation (first year): Baltimore Orioles (1958). **Years in League:** 1946-55, 1957-.

OWNERSHIP, MANAGEMENT

Operated By: Adam Shaffer.
Director: Len Johnston (Baltimore Orioles).
Vice President: Cecil Smith. **Secretary:** M.K. Burton. **Counsel:** David Kersey.
President: George McGonagle. **General Manager:** Michael Showe. **Controller:** Charles Peters. **Director, Special Projects:** Tuillio Ramella.

FIELD STAFF

Manager: Orlando Gomez. **Coach:** Jim Saul, Len Johnston. **Pitching Coach:** Troy Mattes. **Trainer:** T.D. Swinford.

GAME INFORMATION

Radio Announcer: Buford Early. **No. of Games Broadcast:** Home-34 Road-34. **Flagship Station:** WHIS 1440-AM/ WTZE 1470-AM.
PA Announcer: Buford Early. **Official Scorer:** Unavailable.
Stadium Name: Bowen Field. **Location:** I-77 to Bluefield exit 1, Route 290 to Route 460 West, fourth light right onto Leatherwood Lane, left at first light, past Chevron station and turn right, stadium 1/4 mile on left. **Ticket Price Range:** $3.50.
Visiting Club Hotel: Holiday Inn Bluefield, 3350 Big Laurel Highway. U.S. 460, Bluefield, WV 24701. **Telephone:** (304) 325-6170.

BRISTOL WHITE SOX

Office Address: 1501 Euclid Ave., Bristol, VA 24201.
Mailing Address: P.O. Box 1434, Bristol, VA 24203.
Telephone: (276) 494-1786. **Fax:** (276) 669-7686.
E-Mail Address: brisox@btes.tv. **Website:** www.bristolsox.com.
Affiliation (first year): Chicago White Sox (1995-). **Years in League:** 1921-25, 1940-55, 1969-.

OWNERSHIP, MANAGEMENT

Owned by: Chicago White Sox.
Operated by: Bristol Baseball Inc.
Director: Alan Regier (Chicago White Sox).
President: Mahlon Luttrell. **Vice Presidents:** Lynn Armstrong, Perry Hustad.
General Manager: Mahlon Luttrell. **Treasurer:** Dorothy Cox. **Secretary:** Bentley Hudgins.

FIELD STAFF

Manager: Bobby Thigpen. **Hitting Coach:** Jerry Hairston. **Pitching Coach:** Jose Bautista. **Trainer:** Cory Barton. **Conditioning Coach:** Matt Stennis.

GAME INFORMATION

Radio: None.
PA Announcer: Chuck Necessary. **Official Scorer:** Allen Shepherd.
Stadium Name: DeVault Memorial Stadium. **Location:** I-81 to exit 3 onto Commonwealth Ave., right on Euclid Ave. for 1/2 mile. **Standard Game Time:** 7 p.m. **Ticket Price Range:** $3-5.
Visiting Club Hotel: Howard Johnson, 2221 Euclid Ave, Bristol VA 24201. **Telephone:** (276) 669-7171.

BURLINGTON ROYALS

Office Address: 1450 Graham St., Burlington, NC 27217. **Mailing Address:** P.O. Box 1143, Burlington, NC 27216.
Telephone: (336) 222-0223. **Fax:** (336) 226-2498.
E-Mail Address: info@burlingtonroyals.com. **Website:** www.burlingtonroyals.com.
Affiliation (first year): Kansas City Royals (2007). **Years in League:** 1986-.

OWNERSHIP, MANAGEMENT

Operated by: Burlington Baseball Club Inc.

Director: J.J. Picollo (Kansas City Royals). **President:** Miles Wolff. **Vice President:** Dan Moushon.

General Manager: Steve Brice. **Assistant GM:** Matt Schweitzer. **Director, Stadium Operations:** Mike Thompson.

FIELD STAFF

Manager: Tony Tijerina. **Hitting Coach:** Patrick Anderson. **Pitching Coach:** Bobby St. Pierre. **Trainer:** Unavailable.

GAME INFORMATION

Radio Announcer: Unavailable. **No. of Games Broadcast:** Home-34, Away-34. **Flagship:** www.burlingtonroyals.com. **PA Announcer:** Bradford Hines. **Official Scorer:** Bob Lowe.

Stadium Name: Burlington Athletic Stadium. **Location:** I-40/85 to exit 145, north on Route 100 (Maple Avenue) for 1 1/2 miles, right on Mebane Street for 1 1/2 miles, right on Beaumont, left on Graham. **Standard Game Time:** 7 p.m. **Ticket Price Range:** $3-8.

DANVILLE BRAVES

Office Address: Dan Daniel Memorial Park, 302 River Park Dr., Danville, VA 24540.

Mailing Address: P.O. Box 378, Danville, VA 24543.

Telephone: (434) 797-3792. **Fax:** (434) 797-3799.

E-Mail Address: info@dbraves.com. **Website:** www.dbraves.com.

Affiliation (first year): Atlanta Braves (1993). **Years in League:** 1993-.

OWNERSHIP, MANAGEMENT

Operated by: Atlanta National League Baseball Club Inc.

Director: Kurt Kemp (Atlanta Braves).

General Manager: David Cross. **Assistant GM:** Bob Kitzmiller. **Operations Manager:** Kyle Mikesell. **Head Groundskeeper:** Richard Gieselman.

FIELD STAFF

Manager: Paul Runge. **Hitting Coach:** Carlos Mendez. **Pitching Coach:** Derrick Lewis. **Athletic Trainer:** Eric Malek.

GAME INFORMATION

Radio Announcer: Nick Pierce. **No. of Games Broadcast:** Home-34, Away-0. **Flagship Station:** WMNA 106.3-FM.

PA Announcer: Jay Stephens. **Official Scorer:** Mark Bowman.

Stadium Name: American Legion Field Post 325 Field at Dan Daniel Memorial Park. **Location:** U.S. 29 Bypass to River Park Drive/Dan Daniel Memorial Park exit; follow signs to park. **Standard Game Times:** 7 p.m., Sun. 4. **Ticket Price Range:** $3.50-6.50.

Visiting Club Hotel: Innkeeper-West, 3020 Riverside Dr., Danville, VA 24541. **Telephone:** (434) 799-1202.

ELIZABETHTON TWINS

Office Address: 300 West Mill Street, Elizabethton, TN 37643

Stadium Address: 208 N. Holly Lane, Elizabethton, TN 37643.

Mailing Address: 136 S. Sycamore St., Elizabethton, TN 37643.

Telephone: (423) 547-6441. **Fax:** (423) 547-6442.

E-Mail Address: etwins@charterinternet.com. **Website:** www.elizabethtontwins.com.

Affiliation (first year): Minnesota Twins (1974). **Years in League:** 1937-42, 1945-51, 1974-.

OWNERSHIP, MANAGEMENT

Operator: City of Elizabethton.

Director: Jim Rantz (Minnesota Twins).

President: Harold Mains.

General Manager: Mike Mains. **Assistant GM/Clubhouse Operations:** David McQueen. **Head Groundskeeper:** David Nanney.

FIELD STAFF

Manager: Ray Smith. **Coach:** Jeff Reed. **Pitching Coach:** Jim Shellenback. **Trainer:** Ryan Headwall.

GAME INFORMATION

Radio Announcer: Jay Santose . **No. of Games Broadcast:** Home-34, Away-6. **Flagship Station:** WBEJ 1240-AM.

PA Announcer: Tom Banks. **Official Scorer:** Bill Crow.

Stadium Name: Joe O'Brien Field. **Location:** I-81 to Highway I-26, exit at Highway 321/67, left on Holly Lane. **Standard Game Time:** 7 p.m. **Ticket Price Range:** $3-5.

Visiting Club Hotel: Holiday Inn, 101 W. Springbrook Dr., Johnson City, TN 37601. **Telephone:** (423) 282-4611.

GREENEVILLE ASTROS

Office Address: 135 Shiloh Rd., Greeneville, TN 37743.
Mailing Address: P.O. Box 5192, Greeneville, TN 37743.
Telephone: (423) 638-0411. **Fax:** (423) 638-9450.
E-Mail Address: info@greenevilleastros.com. **Website:** www.greenevilleastros.com .
Affiliation (first year): Houston Astros (2004). **Years in League:** 2004-.

OWNERSHIP, MANAGEMENT

Operated by: Houston Astros Baseball Club.
Director: Ricky Bennett (Houston Astros).
General Manager: David Lane. **Assistant GM:** Hunter Reed. **Director of Marketing/Media Relations:** Hunter Reed. **Head Groundskeeper:** Unavailable. **Clubhouse Operations:** Unavailable.

FIELD STAFF

Manager: Rodney Linares. **Pitching Coach:** Travis Driskill. **Hitting Coach:** DJ Boston. **Trainer:** Unavailable.

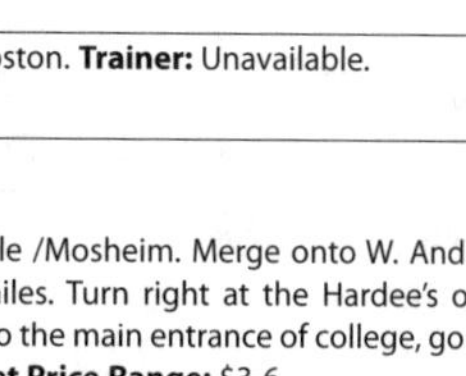

GAME INFORMATION

Radio: None.
PA Announcer: Stephen Pugh. **Official Scorer:** Johnny Painter.
Stadium Name: Pioneer Park. **Location:** Take I-81 to exit 23 toward Greeneville /Mosheim. Merge onto W. Andrew Johnson Highway (U.S. 11E North/Tennessee 34 East) and continue for 16.6 miles. Turn right at the Hardee's onto Tusculum Boulevard for 0.9 miles, Tusculum College campus on right. Turn right into the main entrance of college, go left onto Shiloh Road for 0.3 mile. **Standard Game Times:** 7 p.m.; Sat. and Sun. 6. **Ticket Price Range:** $3-6.
Visiting Club Hotel: The Jameson Inn, 3160 E. Andrew Johnson Hwy., Greeneville, TN 37743. **Telephone:** (423) 638-7511.

JOHNSON CITY CARDINALS

Office Address: 111 Legion St., Johnson City, TN 37601.
Mailing Address: P.O. Box 179, Johnson City, TN 37605.
Telephone: (423) 461-4866. **Fax:** (423) 461-4864.
E-Mail Address: info@jccardinals.com. **Website:** www.jccardinals.com.
Affiliation (first year): St. Louis Cardinals (1975). **Years in League:** 1911-13, 1921-24, 1937-55, 1957-61, 1964-.

OWNERSHIP, MANAGEMENT

Operated by: Johnson City Sports Foundation Inc.
President: Mark Fox.
Director: John Vuch (St. Louis Cardinals).
General Manager: Chuck Arnold. **Assistant GM:** Andy Barnett. **Clubhouse Operations:** Unavailable. **Groundskeeper:** Mike Whitson.

FIELD STAFF

Manager: Joe Almaraz. **Coach:** Unavailable. **Pitching Coach:** Unavailable. **Trainer:** Unavailable.

GAME INFORMATION

Radio: None.
PA Announcer: Unavailable. **Official Scorer:** Unavailable.
Stadium Name: Howard Johnson Field at Cardinal Park. **Location:** I-181 to exit 32, left on East Main, through light onto Legion Street. **Standard Game Time:** 7 p.m. **Ticket Price Range:** $3-5.
Visiting Club Hotel: Holiday Inn, 101 W. Springbrook Dr., Johnson City, TN 37601. **Telephone:** (423) 282-4611.

KINGSPORT METS

Office Address: 800 Granby Rd, Kingsport, TN 37660.
Mailing Address: P.O. Box 1128, Kingsport, TN 37662.
Telephone: (423) 378-3744. **Fax:** (423) 392-8538.
E-Mail Address: info@kmets.com. **Website:** www.kmets.com.
Affiliation (first year): New York Mets (1980). **Years in League:** 1921-25, 1938-52, 1957, 1960-63, 1969-82, 1984-.

OWNERSHIP, MANAGEMENT

Operated By: S&H Baseball LLC..
Director: Adam Wogan (New York Mets).
President: Rick Spivey. Vice President: Steve Harville. **VP/General Manager:** Roman Stout. **Accountant:** Bob Dingus.

Director, Concessions: Teresa Haywood. **Head Groundskeeper:** Josh Warner. **Clubhouse Attendant:** Travis Baker

FiELD STAFF

Manager: Nick Leyva. **Pitching Coach:** Marc Valdes. **Hitting Coach:** Ryan Ellis. **Trainer:** Deb Iwanow. **Strength/ Conditioning Coach:** Troy Fassbender.

GAME INFORMATION

Radio: None.

PA Announcer: Don Spivey. **Official Scorer:** Eddie Durham.

Stadium Name: Hunter Wright Stadium. **Location:** I-81 to I-181 North, exit 1 (Stone Drive), left on West Stone Drive (U.S. 11W), right on Granby Road. **Ticket Price Range:** $3-5.

Visiting Club Hotel: The Jameson Inn, 3004 Bays Mountain Plaza, Kingsport, TN 37660. **Telephone:** (423) 282-4611.

PRINCETON DEVIL RAYS

Office Address: Hunnicutt Field, Old Bluefield Rd, Princeton, WV 24740.

Mailing Address: P.O. Box 5646, Princeton, WV 24740.

Telephone: (304) 487-2000. **Fax:** (304) 487-8762.

E-Mail Address: raysball@citlink.net. **Website:** www.princetondevilrays.com.

Affiliation (first year): Tampa Bay Devil Rays (1997). **Years in League:** 1988-.

OWNERSHIP, MANAGEMENT

Operated By: Princeton Baseball Association Inc.

Director: Mitch Lukevics (Tampa Bay Rays).

President: L. Mori Williams.

General Manager: Jim Holland. **Director, Stadium Operations:** Mick Bayle.

FIELD STAFF

Manager: Joe Szekely. **Hitting Coach:** Rafael Deleon. **Pitching Coach:** Marty DeMerritt. **Coach:** Hector Torres. **Trainer:** Scott Thurston.

GAME INFORMATION

Radio Announcer: Rich Bogard. **No. of Games Broadcast:** Away-34. **Flagship Station:** WAEY 1490-AM.

PA Announcer: Unavailable. **Official Scorer:** Bob Redd.

Stadium Name: Hunnicutt Field. **Location:** Exit 9 off I-77, U.S. 460 West to downtown exit, left on Stafford Drive, stadium located behind Mercer County Technical Education Center. **Standard Game Times:** 7 p.m., Sun 4 p.m. **Ticket Price Range:** $3-5.

Visiting Club Hotel: Days Inn, I-77 and Ambrose Lane, Princeton, WV 24740. **Telephone:** (304) 425-8100.

PULASKI MARINERS

Mailing Address: P.O. Box 676, Pulaski, VA 24301.

Telephone: (540) 980-1070. **Fax:** (540) 980-1850.

E-Mail Address: wayne.carpenter101@comcast.net.

Affiliation (first year): Seattle Mariners (2008). **Years in League:** 1946-50, 1952-55, 1957-58, 1969-77, 1982-92, 1997-2006, 2008-

OWNERSHIP, MANAGEMENT

Operated By: Pulaski Baseball Inc.

Director: Greg Hunter (Seattle Mariners).

President: Wayne Carpenter.

General Manager: Tom Compton. **Assistant GM:** Marty Gordon.

FIELD STAFF

Manager: Unavailable. **Hitting Coach:** Unavailable. **Pitching Coach:** Unavailable. **Trainer:** Unavailable.

GAME INFORMATION

Radio: None.

PA Announcer: Andy French. **Official Scorer:** Edgar Williams.

Stadium Name: Calfee Park. **Location:** Interstate 81 to Exit 89-B (Route 11), north to Pulaski, right on Pierce Avenue. **Standard Game Times:** 7 p.m. **Ticket Price Range:** $4-6.

Visiting Club Hotel: Unavailable.

PIONEER LEAGUE

ROOKIE ADVANCED

Office Address: 157 S. Lincoln Ave., Spokane, WA 99201.
Mailing Address: P.O. Box 2564, Spokane, WA 99220.
Telephone: (509) 456-7615. **Fax:** (509) 456-0136.

E-Mail Address: fanmail@pioneerleague.com. **Website:** www.pioneerleague.com.

Jim McCurdy

Years League Active: 1939-42, 1946-.

President/Secretary-Treasurer: Jim McCurdy.

Vice President: Mike Ellis (Missoula).

Directors: Dave Baggott (Ogden), Mike Ellis (Missoula), D.G. Elmore (Helena), Kevin Greene (Idaho Falls), Kevin Haughian (Casper), Jeff Katofsky (Orem), Vinny Purpura (Great Falls), Jim Iverson (Billings).

Administrative Assistant: Teryl MacDonald.

Division Structure: North—Billings, Great Falls, Helena, Missoula. South—Casper, Idaho Falls, Ogden, Orem.

Regular Season: 76 games (split schedule). **2008 Opening Date:** June 17. **Closing Date:** Sept. 5.

Playoff Format: First-half division winners meet second-half division winners in best-of-three series. Winners meet in best-of-three series for league championship.

All-Star Game: None.

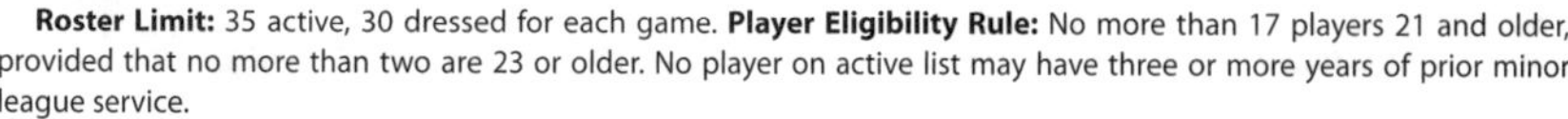

Roster Limit: 35 active, 30 dressed for each game. **Player Eligibility Rule:** No more than 17 players 21 and older, provided that no more than two are 23 or older. No player on active list may have three or more years of prior minor league service.

Brand of Baseball: Rawlings.

Umpires: Unavailable.

Great Falls has changed their name to Great Falls Voyagers, Casper are now the Casper Ghosts

Age Limits do not apply for 2008 (for all leagues)

STADIUM INFORMATION

			Dimensions				
Club	**Stadium**	**Opened**	**LF**	**CF**	**RF**	**Capacity**	**2007 Att.**
Billings	Cobb Field	1948	335	405	325	4,000	95,309
Casper	Mike Lansing Field	2002	355	400	345	2,500	45,354
Great Falls	Legion Park	1956	335	414	335	3,800	107,045
Helena	Kindrick Field	1939	335	400	325	1,700	39,396
Idaho Falls	Melaleuca Field	1976	340	400	350	3,400	104,960
Missoula	Ogren Park at Allegiance Field	2004	309	398	287	3,500	86,881
Ogden	Lindquist Field	1997	335	396	334	5,000	130,266
Orem	Home of the Owlz	2005	305	408	312	4,500	109,125

BILLINGS MUSTANGS

Office Address: Dehler Park, 2611 Ninth Avenue North, Billings, MT 59101.
Mailing Address: P.O. Box 1553, Billings, MT 59103-1553.
Telephone: (406) 252-1241. **Fax:** (406) 252-2968.
E-Mail Address: mustangs@billingsmustangs.com. **Website:** www.billingsmustangs.com .
Affiliation (first year): Cincinnati Reds (1974). **Years in League:** 1948-63, 1969-

OWNERSHIP, MANAGEMENT

Operated By: Billings Pioneer Baseball Club Inc.
President: Woody Hahn.
General Manager: Gary Roller. **Assistant GM:** Matt Bender. **Director, Stadium Operations:** Chris Marshall. **Director, Field Maintenance:** John Barta. **Director, Clubhouse Operations:** Zachary Haden.

FIELD STAFF

Manager: Julio Garcia. **Coach:** Tony Jaramillo. **Pitching Coach:** Tom Browning.

GAME INFORMATION

Radio Announcer: Unavailable. **No. of Games Broadcast:** Home-38, Away-38. **Flagship Station:** KBUL 970-AM.
PA Announcer: Kyle Riley. **Official Scorer:** Phil Sites.
Stadium Name: Dehler Park. **Location:** I-90 to North 27th Street exit, north to Ninth Avenue North. **Standard Game Times:** 7:05 p.m.; Sun. 4:05. **Ticket Price Range:** $3-9.
Visiting Club Hotel: Rimrock Inn, 1203 North 27th Street, Billings, MT 59101. **Telephone:** (406) 252-7107.

CASPER GHOSTS

Office Address: 330 Kati Lane, Casper, WY 82601.
Mailing Address: P.O. Box 1293, Casper, WY 82602.
Telephone: (307) 232-1111. **Fax:** (307) 265-7867.
E-Mail Address: homerun@casperrockies.com. **Website:** www.casperrockies.com.
Affiliation (first year): Colorado Rockies (2001). **Years in League:** 2001-.

OWNERSHIP, MANAGEMENT

Operated by: Casper Professional Baseball Club LLC.
Principal Owner, CEO: Kevin Haughian.
Operator/Director, Operations: Seth Mathews. **Operator/Corporate Sales/Marketing:** Matt Warneke.

FIELD STAFF

Manager: Tony Diaz. **Coach:** Duane Espy. **Pitching Coach:** Eduardo Villacis. **Trainer:** Billy Whitehead.

GAME INFORMATION

Radio Announcer: Tim Ray. **No. of Games Broadcast:** Home-38, Away-38. **Flagship Station:** KVOC 1230-AM.
PA Announcer: Unavailable. **Official Scorer:** Unavailable.
Stadium Name: Mike Lansing Field. **Location:** I-25 to Poplar Street exit, north on Poplar Street, right into Crossroads Park. **Standard Game Times:** 7:05 p.m., Sun. 4:05. **Ticket Price Range:** $7.50-9.
Visiting Club Hotel: Parkway Plaza, 123 West E St., Casper, WY 82601. **Telephone (307) 235-1777.**

GREAT FALLS VOYAGERS

Office Address: 1015 25th St. N, Great Falls, MT 59401.
Mailing Address: P.O. Box 1621, Great Falls, MT 59403.
Telephone: (406) 452-5311. **Fax:** (406) 454-0811. **Toll Free:** (877) 815-1950
E-Mail Address: voyagers@gfvoyagers.com. **Website:** www.gfvoyagers.com .
Affiliation (first year): Chicago White Sox (2003). **Years in League:** 1948-1963, 1969-.

OWNERSHIP, MANAGEMENT

Operated By: Great Falls Baseball Club, Inc. **President:** Vinney Purpura. **General Manager:** Jim Keough. **Head Groundskeeper:** Billy Chafin. **Office Manager:** Christine Oxley. **Marketing Executive/Stadium Operations Manager:** Bob Pinski.

FIELD STAFF

Manager: Chris Cron. **Hitting Coach:** Ernie Young. **Pitching Coach:** Curt Hasler. **Trainer:** Kevin Pillifant. **Conditioning:** Jeremie Imbus.

GAME INFORMATION

Radio Announcer: Unavailable. **No. of Games Broadcast:** Home-38, Away-38. **Flagship Station:** KMON 560-AM.

PA Announcer: Tim Paul. **Official Scorer:** Mike Lewis.

Stadium Name: Centene Stadium located at Legion Park. **Location:** From I-15 to exit 281 (10th Ave. S), left on 26th, left on Eighth Ave. North, right on 25th, ballpark on right, past railroad tracks. **Ticket Price Range:** $5-8.

Visiting Club Hotel: Mid Town Motel, 526 Second Ave. N, Great Falls, MT 59401. **Telephone:** (406) 453-2411.

HELENA BREWERS

Office Address: 1300 N. Ewing, Helena, MT 59601.
Mailing Address: P.O. Box 6756, Helena, MT 59604.
Telephone: (406) 495-0500. **Fax:** (406) 495-0900.
E-Mail Address: info@helenabrewers.net. **Website:** www.helenabrewers.net.
Affiliation (first year): Milwaukee Brewers (2003). **Years in League:** 1978-2000, 2003-.

OWNERSHIP, MANAGEMENT

Operated by: Helena Baseball Club LLC.

Principal Owner: D.G. Elmore.

General Manager: Paul Fetz. **Assistant GM:** Nick Bowsher. **Director, Tickets:** Nick Bowsher. **Director, Broadcasting/ Media Relations:** Unavailable.

FIELD STAFF

Manager: Rene Gonzales. **Batting Coach:** Norberto Martin. **Pitching Coach:** Aris Tirado. **Trainer:** Aaron Hoback.

GAME INFORMATION

Radio Announcer: Unavailable. **No. of Games Broadcast:** Home-38, Away-38. **Flagship Station:** KCAP 1340-AM.

PA Announcer: Randy Bowsher. **Official Scorer:** Kevin Higgens.

Stadium Name: Kindrick Field. **Location:** Cedar Street exit off I-15, west to Main Street, left at Memorial Park. **Standard Game Time:** 7:05 p.m. **Ticket Price Range:** $6-8.

Visiting Club Hotel: Unavailable

IDAHO FALLS CHUKARS

Office Address: 568 W. Elva, Idaho Falls, ID 83402.
Mailing Address: P.O. 2183, Idaho, ID 83403.
Telephone: (208) 522-8363. **Fax:** (208) 522-9858.
E-Mail Address: chukars@ifchukars.com. **Website:** www.ifchukars.com.
Affiliation (first year): Kansas City Royals (2004). **Years in League:** 1940-42, 1946-

OWNERSHIP, MANAGEMENT

Operated By: The Elmore Group. **Principal Owner:** David Elmore. **President, General Manager:** Kevin Greene. **Assistant General Manager, Merchandise:** Marcus Loyola. **Director, Concessions:** Unavailable. **Director, Public Relations:** Andrew Daugherty. **Head Groundskeeper:** Jon Clark.

FIELD STAFF

Manager: Jim Gabella. **Hitting Coach:** Jon Williams. **Pitching Coach:** Jerry Nyman. **Trainer:** Unavailable.

GAME INFORMATION

Radio Announcers: John Balginy, Jim Garshow, Steven Davis. **No. of Games Broadcast:** Home-38 Road-38. **Flagship Station:** KUPI 980-AM.

Official Scorer: John Balginy.

Stadium Name: Melaleuca Field. **Location:** I-15 to West Broadway exit, left onto Memorial Drive, right on Mound Avenue, 1/4 mile to stadium. **Standard Game Times:** 7:15 p.m., Sun. 4. **Ticket Price Range:** $6-9.

Visiting Club Hotel: Guesthouse Inn & Suites, 850 Lindsay Blvd, Idaho Falls, ID 83402. **Telephone:** (208) 522-6260.

MISSOULA OSPREY

Office Address: 412 W. Alder St, Missoula, MT 59802.
Telephone: (406) 543-3300. **Fax:** (406) 543-9463.
E-Mail Address: info@missoulaosprey.com. **Website:** www.missoulaosprey.com.
Affiliation (first year): Arizona Diamondbacks (1999). **Years in League:** 1956-60, 1999-.

OWNERSHIP, MANAGEMENT

Operated By: Mountain Baseball LLC.
President: Mike Ellis. **Executive Vice President:** Judy Ellis.
VP/General Manager: Matt Ellis. **VP, Finance/Merchandising:** Shelly Ellis. **GM, Ogren Park at Allegiance Field:** Jared Amoss. **Assistant GM:** Rod Austin. **Assistant GM:** Jeff Griffin. **Office Administrator:** Nola Hunter. **Concession Manager:** Byron Dike. **Stadium Operations Intern:** Unavailable. **Promotions/PR Intern:** Unavailable.

FIELD STAFF

Manager: Audo Vincente. **Hitting Coach:** Alan Zinter. **Pitching Coach:** Steve Merriman. **Trainer:** Atsu Takei. **Strength/ Conditioning:** Unavailable.

GAME INFORMATION

Radio Announcer: Ben Catley. **No. of Games Broadcast:** Home-38, Away-38. **Flagship Station:** KLCY 930-AM.
PA Announcer: Patrick Nicklay. **Official Scorer:** David Kinsey.
Stadium Name: Ogren Park at Allegiance Field. **Location:** 700 Cregg Lane. **Directions:** Take Orange Street to Cregg Lane, west on Cregg Lane, stadium west of McCormick Park. **Standard Game Times:** 7:05 p.m.; Sun 5:05 p.m. **Ticket Price Range:** $4-10.
Visiting Club Hotel: Mountain Valley Inn, 420 W. Broadway, Missoula, Mt. 59802. **Telephone:** (406) 728-4500

OGDEN RAPTORS

Office Address: 2330 Lincoln Ave, Ogden, UT 84401.
Telephone: (801) 393-2400. **Fax:** (801) 393-2473.
E-Mail Address: homerun@ogden-raptors.com. **Website:** www.ogden-raptors.com.
Affiliation (first year): Los Angeles Dodgers (2003). **Years in League:** 1939-42, 1946-55, 1966-74, 1994-

OWNERSHIP, MANAGEMENT

Operated By: Ogden Professional Baseball, Inc. **Principal Owners:** Dave Baggott, John Lindquist. **Chairman, President:** Dave Baggott. **General Manager:** Joey Stein. **VP/Director, Marketing:** John Stein. **Controller:** Carol Spickler. **Head Groundskeeper:** Ken Kopinski. **Director, Merchandising:** Geri Kopinski.

FIELD STAFF

Manager: Mike Brumley. **Hitting Coach:** Henry Cruz. **Pitching Coach:** Craig Bjornson. **Trainer:** Peter Hite.

GAME INFORMATION

Radio Announcer: Eric Knighton. **No. of Games Broadcast:** Home-38, Away-38. **Flagship Station:** 1490 AM KOGN.
PA Announcer: Pete Diamond. **Official Scorer:** Dennis Kunimura.
Stadium Name: Lindquist Field. **Location:** I-15 North to 21th Street exit, east to Lincoln Avenue, south three blocks to park. **Standard Game Times:** 7 p.m ., Sun. 1**. Ticket Price Range:** $6-9.
Visiting Club Hotel: Hotel Ben Lomond, 2510 Washington Blvd., Ogden, UT 84401. **Telephone:** (801) 627-1900.

OREM OWLZ

Office Address: 970 W. University Parkway, Orem, UT 84058.
Telephone: (801) 377-2255. **Fax:** (801) 377-2345.
E-Mail Address: fan@oremowlz.com. **Website:** www.oremowlz.com.
Affiliation (first year): Los Angeles Angels (2001). **Years in League:** 2001-.

OWNERSHIP, MANAGEMENT

Operated By: Bery Bery Gud To Me LLC.
Principal Owner: Jeff Katofsky.
General Manager: Aaron Wells. **Assistant GM (Public Relations):** Sarah Hansen. **Assistant GM (Sales):** Blake Buswell. **Director of Baseball Operations/Clubhouse Manager:** Brett Crane. **Director, Ticketing:** Landen Garner.

FIELD STAFF

Manager: Tom Kotchman. **Coach:** Brent Del Chiaro. **Pitching Coach:** Zeke Zimmerman. **Trainer:** Dan Nichols.

GAME INFORMATION

Radio Announcer: Matt Gittins. **No. of Games Broadcast:** Home-38, Away-38. **Flagship Station:** Unavailable.
PA Announcer: Lincoln Fillmore. **Official Scorer:** Unavailable
Stadium Name: Home of the Owlz. **Location:** Exit 269 (University Parkway) off I-15 at Utah Valley University campus. **Ticket Price Range:** $4-9.
Visiting Club Hotel: Provo Days Inn, 1675 N. 200 West, Provo, UT 84604. **Telephone:** (801) 375-8600.

ARIZONA LEAGUE

ROOKIE

Office Address: 910 Main St., Suite 351, Boise, ID 83702.
Mailing Address: P.O. Box 1645, Boise, ID 83701.
Telephone: (208) 429-1511. **Fax:** (208) 429-1525. **E-Mail Address:** bobrichmond@att.net.
Years League Active: 1988-.
President/Treasurer: Bob Richmond.
Vice President: Oneri Fleita (Cubs). **Corporate Secretary:** Ted Polakowski (Athletics).
Administrative Assistant: Rob Richmond.
Division Structure: None.
Regular Season: 56 games (split schedule). **2008 Opening Date:** June 22. **Closing Date:** Aug. 30.
Standard Game Times: 10:30 a.m.; night games, 7 p.m.
Playoff Format: First-half winner meets second-half winner in one-game championship.
All-Star Game: None.
Roster Limit: 35 active. **Player Eligibility Rule:** No more than 12 players 20 or older, no more than four players 21 or older, and no more than four players of any age not selected in 2007 first-year draft. A maximum of four foreign players not subject to the draft playing in the United States for the first time are exempt from the age limits.
Brand of Baseball: Rawlings.

Clubs	Playing Site	Manager	Coach	Pitching Coach(es)
Angels	Angels minor league complex, Tempe	Ty Boykin	Dick Schofield	Trevor Wilson
Athletics	Papago Park Baseball Complex, Phoenix	Ruben Escalera	Marcus Jensen	Jimmy Escalante
Brewers	Maryvale Baseball Complex, Phoenix	Tony Diggs	Angel Echevarria	Steve Clline/Jose Nunez
Cubs	Fitch Park, Mesa	Franklin Font	Desi Wilson	Rick Tronerud
Giants	Giants Baseball Complex, Scottsdale	Dave Machemer	Bert Hunter	Will Malerich/Brian Cooper
Mariners	Peoria Sports Complex	Andy Bottin	Eddie Menchaca	Gary Wheelock
Padres	Peoria Sports Complex	Jose Flores	Bronswell Patrick	Bob Skube
Rangers	Surprise Recreation Campus	Bill Richardson	Josue Perez	Carlos Pulido/Scott Dwyer
Royals	Surprise Recreation Campus	Julio Bruno	Justin Gemoll	Mark Davis/Carlos Martinez

GULF COAST LEAGUE

ROOKIE

Office Address: 1503 Clower Creek Dr., Suite H-262, Sarasota, FL 34231.
Telephone: (941) 966-6407. **Fax:** (941) 966-6872.
Years League Active: 1964-.
President/Secretary-Treasurer: Tom Saffell.
First Vice President: Steve Noworyta (Phillies). **Second Vice President:** Jim Rantz (Twins).
Administrative Assistant: Bill Ventolo.
Division Structure: East—Cardinals, Dodgers, Marlins, Mets, Nationals. North—Blue Jays, Braves, Indians, Phillies, Tigers, Yankees. South—Orioles, Pirates, Reds, Red Sox, Twins.
Regular Season: North: 60 games; East/South: 56 games. **2008 Opening Date:** June 19. **Closing Date:** Aug. 27.
Playoff Format: Division winner with best regular season winning percentage meets wild card team in one-game playoff. Remaining two division winners meet in one-game playoff. Playoff winners advance to best-of-three championship series.
Roster Limit: 35 active, but only 30 eligible for each game. **Player Eligibility Rule:** No age restriction limits. No player who has two or more years of prior minor league and/or major league service time can participate.
Brand of Baseball: Rawlings.

Clubs	Playing Site	Manager	Coach(es)	Pitching Coach
Blue Jays	Mattick Training Center, Dunedin	Clayton McCullough	Danny Solano	Vince Horsman
Braves	Disney's Wide World of Sports, Orlando	Luis Oritz	Sixto Lezcano	Gabe Luckert
Cardinals	Cardinals Complex, Jupiter	Enrique Brito	Unavailable	Ramon Ortiz
Dodgers	Dodgertown, Vero Beach	Jeff Carter	Kenny Dominguez	Casey Deskins
Indians	Chain O'Lakes Park, Winter Haven	Rouglas Odor	Phil Clark	Steve Lyons
Marlins	Roger Dean Complex, Jupiter	Doc Watson	Andy Haines	Jeff Schwartz
Mets	St. Lucie Sports Complex, St. Lucie	Juan Lopez	Unavailable	Unavailable
Nationals	Carl Barger Baseball Complex, Melbourne	Bobby Henley	Paul Sanagorski	Franklin Bravo
Orioles	Twin Lakes Park, Sarasota	Jesus Alfaro	Giomar Guevara	Calvin Maduro
Phillies	Carpenter Complex, Clearwater	Roly deArmas	Luis Melendez	Carlos Arroyo
Pirates	Pirate City Complex, Bradenton	Tom Prince	E. Varela/W. Huyke	Miguel Bonilla
Reds	Ed Smith Complex, Sarasota	Pat Kelly	Ricardo Cuevas	Ramon Ortiz
Red Sox	Red Sox Minor League Complex	Dave Tomlin	U.L. Washington	Goose Gregson
Tigers	Tigertown, Lakeland	Basilio Cabrera	Garrett Guest	Greg Sabat
Twins	Lee County Complex, Fort Myers	Nelson Prada	M. Cuyler/J. Mauer	Ivan Arteaga
Yankees	Yankee Complex, Tampa	Jody Reed	Unavailable	Unavailable

INDEPENDENT
LEAGUES

AMERICAN ASSOCIATION

Office Address: 1415 Hwy. 54 West, Suite 210, Durham, NC 27707.
Telephone: (919) 401-8150. **FAX:** (919) 401-8152. **Website:** www.americanassociationbaseball.com.
Year Founded: 2006.
Commissioner: Miles Wolff. **President:** Dan Moushon.
Administrative Assistant: Jason Deans. **Director, Umpires:** Kevin Winn.
Division Structure: North--Lincoln, St. Paul, Sioux City, Sioux Falls, Wichita. South--El Paso, Fort Worth, Grand Prairie, Pensacola, Shreveport.
Regular Season: 96 games (split schedule). **2008 Opening Date:** May 7. **Closing Date:** Aug. **23.**
All-Star Game: July 22 at St. Paul (North Division vs. South Division).
Playoff Format: First-half division winners and second-half division winners in best-of-five series. Winners meet in best-of-five series for league championship.
Roster Limit: 22. **Player Eligibility Rule:** Minimum of five first-year players, maximum of four veterans with at least four years of professional experience.
Brand of Baseball: Rawlings.
Statistician: PA SportsTicker, 55 Realty Drive, Cheshire, CT 06410.

STADIUM INFORMATION

			Dimensions				
Club	**Stadium**	**Opened**	**LF**	**CF**	**RF**	**Capacity**	**2007 Att.**
El Paso	Cohen Stadium	1990	340	410	340	9,725	155,651
Fort Worth	LaGrave Field	2002	325	400	335	5,100	177,894
Grand Prairie	AirHogs Stadium	2008					—
Lincoln	Haymarket Park	2001	335	395	325	4,500	190,873
Pensacola	Pelican Park	1991	320	390	320	2,500	78,755
St. Paul	Midway Stadium	1982	320	400	320	6,069	288,171
Shreveport	Fair Grounds Field	1986	330	400	330	4,500	53,107
Sioux City	Lewis and Clark Park	1993	330	400	330	3,630	88,408
Sioux Falls	Sioux Falls Stadium	1964	312	410	312	4,029	120,536
Wichita	Lawrence-Dumont Stadium	1934	344	401	312	6,055	—

EL PASO DIABLOS

Office Address: 9700 Gateway North Blvd., **El Paso, TX 79924.**
Telephone: (915) 755-2000. **Fax:** (915) 757-0681.
E-mail Address: info@diablos.com. **Website:** www.diablos.com
Managing Partner: Mark Schuster.
General Manager: Matt LaBranche. **Director, Sponsorships:** Bernie Ricono. **Manager, Media/Community Relations:** Adriana Ruiz. **Director, Marketing/Promotions:** Holly McWatters. **Director, Group Sales:** Jeff Hoover. **Box Office Manager:** Steve Martinez. **Account Executives:** Nicole Barela, Donna Blair, Champ Hernandez. **Business Manager:** Pat Hofman.
Manager: Butch Henry. **Coach:** David McWatters, Ryan Medrano.

GAME INFORMATION

Radio Announcer: Jon Barr. **Games Broadcast:** 96. **Flagship Station:** ESPN Radio 1380-AM. **Webcast Address:** www.diablos.com.
Stadium Name: Cohen Stadium. **Location:** I-10 to U.S. 54 (Patriot Freeway), east to Diana exit to Gateway North Boulevard.
Standard Game Times: Monday-Saturday - 7:05 PM, Sunday - 5:05 PM.
Visiting Club Hotel: Howard Johnson Express Inn, 500 Executive Center Blvd., El Paso, TX 79902. **Telephone:** (915) 532-8981.

FORT WORTH CATS

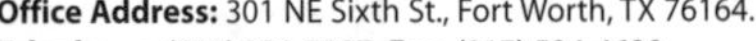

Office Address: 301 NE Sixth St., Fort Worth, TX 76164.
Telephone: (817) 226-2287. **Fax:** (817) 534-4620.
E-Mail Address: info@fwcats.com. **Website:** www.fwcats.com.
Principal Owner/CEO: Carl Bell.
President/COO: John Dittrich.
Executive Vice President/General Manager: John Bilbow. **Account Executive:** Dick Smith. **VP, Special Projects:** Maury Wills. **VP, Communications:** David Hatchett. **Assistant VP, Communications:** Emil Moffatt. **Business Manager:** Lois Dittrich. **Stadium Operations:** Steven Ballard. **Director, Community Relations/Promotions:** Cody Crume.

Merchandise Manager: Andrea Dailey. **Baseball Operations:** Ryan Carlock. **Director, Ticket Operations:** Alexis Arteaga. **Ticket Operations:** Jeff Meyers. Account Executives: Dave Moharter, Reg Robbins.

Director, Player Personnel/Manager: Chad Tredaway. **Coaches:** Wayne Terwilliger, James Frisbie, Heath Autrey. **Head Athletic Trainer:** Kenny Shuman.

GAME INFORMATION

Radio Announcers: Emil Moffatt, David Hatchett. **No. of Games Broadcast:** 96. **Flagship Station:** KHFX 1460-AM. **Webcast Address:** www.fwcats.com.

Stadium Name: LaGrave Field. **Location:** From 1-30, take 1-35 North to North Side Drive exit, left (west) off exit to Main Street, left (south) on Main, left (east) onto NE Sixth Street.

Standard Game Times: 7:05 p.m.; Sunday 2:05 p.m.

Visiting Club Hotel: Unavailable.

GRAND PRAIRIE AIRHOGS

Office Address: 1600 Lone Star Parkway, Grand Prairie, TX 75050

Phone: (972) 504-9383. **Fax:** (972) 504-2288

Website: www.airhogsbaseball.com

President: Mark Schuster.

VP/General Manager: Dave Burke. **VP, Sales:** Greg Lynch. **Assistant General Managers:** Matt Barry, Tim Savona. **Group Sales Executives:** Tiffany Dilworth, Sara Heisig, Ryan Lewis. **Account Executive:** Sam Ward. **Media Relations Manager:** Alan Barr. **Director, Food/Beverage:** Sander Stotland.

Manager: Pete Incaviglia.

GAME INFORMATION

Stadium Name: Ballpark of Grand Prairie. **Location:** From I-30, take Beltline Road exit going north. Once on Beltline Road (1/2 mile), take Lone Star Park entrance (gate #2) towards the stadium.

Standard Game Times: 7:05 pm.

Visiting Club Hotel: Unavailable.

LINCOLN SALTDOGS

Office Address: 403 Line Drive Circle, Suite A, Lincoln, NE 68508.

Telephone: (402) 474-2255. **Fax:** (402) 474-2254.

E-Mail Address: info@saltdogs.com. **Website:** www.saltdogs.com.

Owner: Jim Abel. **President:** Charlie Meyer.

Vice President/General Manager: Tim Utrup. **Assistant GM/Director, Sales/Marketing:** Bret Beer. **Director, Broadcasting/Communications:** Bill Doleman. **Director, Merchandising/Promotions:** Anne Duchek. **Director, Ticketing:** Toby Antonson. **Director, Stadium Operations:** Josh Jorgensen. **Assistant Director, Stadium Operations:** Dave McCoy. **Account Executives:** Dave Aschwege, Scott Mauser. **Office Manager:** Jeanette Eagleton. **Athletic Turf Manager:** Josh Klute. **Assistant Turf Managers:** Jared Hertzel, Jen Roeber.

Manager: Tim Johnson. **Coaches:** Mike Garcia, Jim Haller, Brett Kim, Mike Workman.

GAME INFORMATION

Radio Announcer: Bill Doleman. **No. of Games Broadcast:** 96. **Flagship Station:** KFOR 1240-AM. **Webcast Address:** www.kfor1240.com.

Stadium Name: Haymarket Park. **Location:** I-80 to Cornhusker Highway West, left on First Street, right on Sun Valley Boulevard, left on Line Drive.

Standard Game Times: 7:05 p.m.; Sunday, 2:05 p.m., 6:05 p.m.

Visiting Club Hotel: Holiday Inn Downtown, 141 N. Ninth St., Lincoln, NE 68508. **Telephone:** (402) 475-4011.

PENSACOLA PELICANS

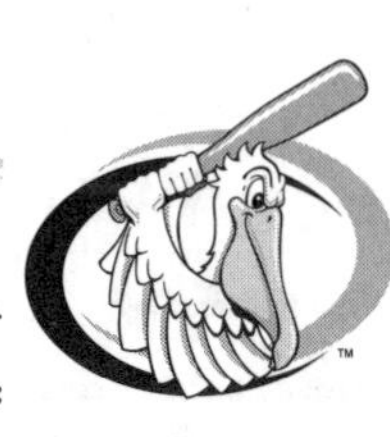

Office Address: 4920 North Davis Highway, Pensacola, FL 32503.

Telephone: (850) 934-8444. **Fax:** (850) 791-6256.

E-Mail Address: info@pensacolapelicans.com. **Website:** www.pensacolapelicans.com.

Owners: Quint Studer, Rishy Studer. **President:** Rishy Studer. **Chief Executive Officer:** Quint Studer.

General Manager: Talmadge Nunnari. **Assistant General Manager/ Emerald Diamond Director:** Gary Colon. **Chief Financial Officer:** Bess Abernathy. **Media Relations Director:** Jason Libbert. **Ticketing/Merchandise Director:** Shelley Welch. **Community Relations Director:** Carrie Smith. **Stadium Operations/Sales Executive:** Mike Coziahr. **Media Relations Assistant/Sales Executive:** Paul Chestnutt. **Group Sales Executive:** Conley Jones. **Promotions Coordinator:**

Tim Mulroy.

Manager: Mac Seibert. **Coach:** Hunter Vick.

GAME INFORMATION

Radio Announcer: Paul Chestnutt. **No. of Games Broadcast:** 96. **Flagship Station:** WNRP 1620-AM. **Webcast Address:** www.pensacolapelicans.com.

Stadium Name: Pelican Park. **Location:** On the campus of University of West Florida. From I-10 West, north on Davis Highway (SR 291) to exit 13, left on University Parkway, right on Campus Drive, stadium 1/2 mile on right.

Standard Game Times: 6:35 p.m.; Saturday-Sunday, 6:05 p.m.

Visiting Club Hotel: Microtel Inn & Suites, 8001 Lavelle Way, Pensacola, FL 32526. **Telephone:** 850-941-8902.

ST. PAUL SAINTS

Office Address: 1771 Energy Park Dr., St. Paul, MN 55108.

Telephone: (651) 644-3517. **Fax:** (651) 644-1627.

E-Mail Address: funsgood@saintsbaseball.com. **Website:** www.saintsbaseball.com.

Principal Owners: Marv Goldklang, Mike Veeck, Bill Murray. **Chairman:** Marv Goldklang. **President:** Mike Veeck. **Executive Vice President/General Manager:** Derek Sharrer. **Executive Vice President:** Tom Whaley. **Assistant GM:** Dan Lehv. **Vice President Customer Service/Community Partnerships:** Annie Huidekoper. **Director, Corporate Sales:** Scott Bush. **Director, Promotions/Merchandise:** Scott Riley. **Director, Ticket Sales:** Matt Teske. **Director, Special Events:** Amy Heimer. **Group/Season Ticket Sales Manager:** Mike Nachreiner. Technology Manager/Group Ticket Sales: Jeremy Loosbrock. Ticket Sales Representative: Erin Luehti. Ticket Sales Representative: Marc Elliot. Coordinator, Comm. Partnerships/Marketing Assistant: Aleda Jordan. Director, Food/Beverage: Curtis Nachtsheim. Business Manager: Leesa Anderson. Director, Stadium Operations: Bob Klepperich. Groundskeeper: Connie Rudolph.

Manager: George Tsamis. **Coaches:** Lamarr Rogers, TJ Wiesner.

GAME INFORMATION

Radio Announcer: Sean Aronson. **No. of Games Broadcast:** 96. **Flagship Station:** Relevant Radio 1330-AM. **Webcast Address:** www.saintsbaseball.com.

Stadium Name: Midway Stadium. **Location:** From I-94, take Snelling Avenue North exit, west onto Energy Park Drive.

Standard Game Times: 7:05 p.m., Sunday, 1:05 p.m.

Visiting Club Hotel: Crowne Plaza-St. Paul Riverfront, 11 East Kellogg Blvd., St. Paul, MN 55101. **Telephone:** (651) 292-1900.

SHREVEPORT SPORTS

Office Address: 2901 Pershing Blvd, Shreveport, LA 71109.

Telephone: (318) 636-5555. **Fax:** (318) 636-5670.

Website: www.shreveportsports.com.

Owner: Gary Elliston.

General Manager: Terri Sipes. **VP, Business Development:** Michael Beasley. **Stadium/Field Operations:** Bobby Entrekin. **Director, Media/Community Relations:** Dave Nitz. **Account Executive:** Adam Delatte.

Manager: Terry Bevington. **Coaches:** Eddie Gerald, Bert Snow.

GAME INFORMATION

Radio Announcer: Dave Nitz. **No. of Games Broadcast:** 96. **Flagship Station:** KWKH 1130-AM. **Webcast Address:** www.shreveportsports.com.

Stadium Name: Fair Grounds Field. **Location:** Hearne Avenue (U.S. 171) exit off I-20 at Louisiana State Fairgrounds.

Standard Game Times: Monday-Saturday - 7:05 PM, Sunday - 2:05 PM.

Visiting Club Hotel: Unavailable.

SIOUX CITY EXPLORERS

Office Address: 3400 Line Drive, Sioux City, IA 51106.

Telephone: (712) 277-9467. **Fax:** (712) 277-9406.

E-Mail Address: siouxcityxs@yahoo.com. **Website:** www.xsbaseball.com.

President: John Roost.

General Manager: Shane M. **Tritz. Assistant GM:** Luke Nielsen. **Box Office/ Promotions Coordinator:** Ashley Schroenrock.

Field Manager/Player Procurement Director: Les Lancaster. **Coaches:** Billy Williams, Jim Allen.

GAME INFORMATION

Radio Announcer: Chris Varney. **No. of Games Broadcast:** 96. **Flagship Station:** KSCJ 1360-AM. **Webcast Address:** www.xsbaseball.com.

Stadium Name: Lewis and Clark Park. **Location:** I-29 to Singing Hills Blvd. North, right on Line Drive.

Standard Game Times: 7:05 p.m. (Monday - Saturday) 5:05 p.m. (Sunday)

Visiting Club Hotel: Best Western City Centre, 130 Nebraska St., Sioux City, IA 51106. **Telephone:** (712) 277-1550.

SIOUX FALLS CANARIES

Office Address: 1001 N. West Ave., Sioux Falls, SD 57104.

Telephone: (605) 333-0179. **Fax:** (605) 333-0139.

E-Mail Address: info@canariesbaseball.com. **Website:** www.canariesbaseball.com.

Operated by: Sioux Falls Canaries Professional Baseball Club, LLC.

President: John Kuhn.

General Manager: Matt Hansen. **Assistant GM/Groundskeeper:** Larry McKenney. **VP, Group/Ticket Sales:** Chris Schwab. **Director, Media/Public Relations:** Matt Meola. **Director, Food/Beverage:** Bill Sedelmeier. **Group Sales Executive:** Rustin Buysse. **Director, Promotions:** Nate Welch. **Event Coordinator/Account Executive:** Mallory Selway. **Office Manager:** Peggy Ashdown.

Manager: Steve Shirley. **Coaches:** Benny Castillo, Mike Meyer.

GAME INFORMATION

Radio Announcer: Matt Meola. **No. of Games Broadcast:** 96. **Flagship Station:** KWSN 1230-AM. **Webcast Address:** www.kwsn.com.

Stadium Name: Sioux Falls Stadium. **Location:** I-29 to Russell Street, south one mile, right on West Avenue.

Standard Game Times: 7:05 p.m., Sunday, 2:05 p.m.

Visiting Club Hotel: Staybridge Suites, 2505 S. Carolyn Avenue, Sioux Falls, SD 57106. Telephone: (605) 361-2298.

WICHITA WINGNUTS

Office Address: 300 South Sycamore, Wichita, KS 67213.

Telephone: (316) 264-4625. **Fax:** (316) 264-3037.

Website: www.wichitawingnuts.com.

Owners: Horn Chen, Steve Ruud, Dan Waller, Gary Austerman, Nick Easter, **Nate Robertson, Chris Presson, Josh Robertson.**

President: Chris Presson. **Senior Vice-President:** Joel Lomurno.

General Manager: Josh Robertson. **General Manager Corporate Sales Baseball:** Bob Flanagan. **General Manager Corporate Sales Hockey:** Matt Brokaw. **General Manager Group Sales:** Joe Greene. **Director, Ticket Sales/ Merchandise:** Sally Knofflock. **Director, Community Relations:** Amy Wilds. **Director, Broadcast:** Steve Schuster. **Directors, Finance:** Kay Brown, Vicki Lehrman. **Corporate Sales Associates:** Ben Keiter, Josh Roehr. **Staff Assistants:** Jeremy Mock, Kip Smith. **Director, Stadium Operations:** Jeff Kline. **Director, Operations, NBC World Series:** Jerry Taylor. Clubhouse Manager: Brad Brungart.

Manager: Kash Beauchamp. **Coach:** Luke Robertson.

GAME INFORMATION

Radio Announcer: Steve Schuster. **Games Broadcast:** KGSO 1410-AM. **Webcast Address:** www.wichitawingnuts.com or www.kgso.com.

Stadium Name: Lawrence-Dumont Stadium. **Location:** 135 North to Kellogg (54) West. Take Seneca Street exit North to Maple. Go East on Maple to Sycamore. Stadium is located on corner of Maple and Sycamore.

Standard Game Times: 7:05 p.m.; Sunday, 4:05 p.m.

Visiting Club Hotel: Unavailable.

ATLANTIC LEAGUE

Mailing Address: 401 N. Delaware Ave. Camden, NJ 08102.

Telephone: (856) 541-9400. **FAX:** (856) 541-9410.

E-Mail Address: info@atlanticleague.com Website: www.atlanticleague.com.

Year Founded: 1998.

Chief Executive Officer/Founder: Frank Boulton.

Vice Presidents: Peter Kirk, Steven Kalafer.

Executive Director: Joe Klein.

Directors: Marc Berson (Newark), Frank Boulton (Long Island), Mary Jane Foster (Bridgeport), Steve Kalafer (Somerset), Peter Kirk (Lancaster, Camden,York, Southern Maryland).

League Operations Latin Coordinator: Ellie Rodriguez.

Director, Baseball Administration: Patty MacLuckie

Division Structure: Liberty Division–Bridgeport Bluefish, Camden Riversharks, Long Island Ducks, Southern Maryland Bluecrabs. Freedom Division—Lancaster Barnstormers, Newark Bears, Somerset Patriots, York Revolution.

2008 Opening Date: April 25.

Closing Date: Sept. 21.

Regular Season: 140 games (split schedule) First half ends July 6. Second half begins July 8.

All-Star Game: July 16 at Somerset.

Playoff Format: First-half division winners meet second-half winners in best-of-three series. Winners meet in best-of-five final for league championship.

Roster Limit: 25. **Eligibility Rule:** No restrictions.

Brand of Baseball: Rawlings.

Statistician: SportsTicker, ESPN Plaza—Building B, Bristol, CT 06010.

STADIUM INFORMATION

			Dimensions				
Club	Stadium	Opened	LF	CF	RF	Capacity	2006 Att.
Bridgeport	The Ballpark at Harbor Yard	1998	325	405	325	5,300	193,096
Camden	Campbell's Field	2001	325	405	325	6,425	253,013
Lancaster	Clipper Magazine Stadium	2005	372	400	300	6,000	370,076
Long Island	Citibank Park	2000	325	400	325	6,002	419, 150
Newark	Bears & Eagles Riverfront Stadium	1999	302	394	323	6,201	178, 132
Somerset	Commerce Bank Ballpark	1999	317	402	315	6,100	362,585
*Southern Maryland	Regency Stadium	2008	305	400	320	6,000	—
York	Sovereign Bank Stadium	2007	300	400	325	5,500	218,826

*Expansion Team

BRIDGEPORT BLUEFISH

Office Address: 500 Main St., Bridgeport, CT 06604.

Telephone: (203) 345-4800. **FAX:** (203) 345-4830.

Website: www.bridgeportbluefish.com.

Operated by: Get Hooked, LLC. **Management Board:** Michael Kramer, Jack McGregor, Thomas D'Addario, Thomas Kushner, Thomas Schneider, Mary-Jane Foster.

Chairmen: Michael Kramer, Jack McGregor. **Chief Executive Officer:** Mary-Jane Foster. **General Manager:** Todd Marlin. **Assistant General Manager:** Joe Izzo. **Sales Manager:** Todd Marlin. **Senior Account Executive:** John Harris. **Account Executives:** Dave Linardy. **Director, Marketing:** Todd Marlin. **Box Office:** Rob Finn. **Group Sales:** Nick Razzette, Larry Stewart, Karen Luciano, Tom Healy. **Media Relations Manager:** Nick Razzette. **Stadium Operations:** Tom Healy. **Merchandise Manager:** Kelly Ball

Assistant,Finance: Barbara Prato. **Business Manager:** Ellen Broedlin.

Manager: Tommy John. **Coach:** Unavailable. **Pitching Coach:** Unavailable. **Trainer:** Unavailable.

GAME INFORMATION

Radio Announcer: Jeff Holtz. **No. of Games Broadcast:** Unavailable. **Flagship Station:** WVOF 88.5-FM. **PA Announcer:** Bill Jensen. **Official Scorer:** Rick Cohen.

Stadium Name: The Ballpark at Harbor Yard. **Location:** I-95 to exit 27, Route 8/25 to exit 1. **Standard Game Times:** 7:05 p.m.; Sunday, 2:05 p.m.

Visiting Club Hotel: Holiday Inn Bridgeport, 1070 Main St., Bridgeport, CT 06604. Telephone: (203) 334-1234.

CAMDEN RIVERSHARKS

Office Address: 401 N. Delaware Ave., Camden, NJ 08102. **Telephone:** (856) 963-2600. **FAX:** (856) 963-8534. **E-Mail Address:** riversharks@riversharks.com. **Website:** www.riversharks.com.

Operated by: Camden Baseball, LLC

Principal Owners: Frank Boulton, Peter Kirk. **President:** Jon Danos. **Senior Vice President:** Brad Sims. **Controller:** Emily Merrill

General Manager: Adam Lorber. **Assistant General Manager:** Kristen Simon. **Director, Corporate Partnerships:** Joel Seiden. **Director, Business Development:** Stu Cohen. **Director, Group Events:** Bob Nehring. **Director, Finance:** Bryan Humphreys. **Director, Marketing:** Natalie Filomeno. **Facilities Manager:** Barry Huver. **Group Account Manager:** Nikki Varoutsos. **Group Account Manager:** Jeremy VanEtten. **Corporate Partnerships Manager:** Elizabeth Stevenson. **Corporate Partnerships Manager:** Bill DeGeorge. **Community Relations Assistant:** Dolores Rozier. **Groundskeeper:** Kevin Moses. **Office Manager:** Cheryl Parker.

Director, Baseball Operations: David Keller. **Manager:** Joe Ferguson. **Pitching Coach:** Dick Such. **Hitting Coach:** Unavailable. **Trainer:** Unavailable.

GAME INFORMATION

Radio: Rowan Radio, WGLS-FM. **PA Announcer:** Kevin Casey. **Official Scorer:** Dick Shute.

Stadium Name: Campbell's Field. **Location:** From Philadelphia, right on Sixth Street, right after Ben Franklin Bridge toll booth, right on Cooper Street until it ends at Delaware Ave. From Camden, I-676 to exit 5B, follow signs to field. **Standard Game Times:** Weekdays- 7:05 p.m., Saturdays- 5:05 p.m., Sundays- 1:05 p.m. Gates open one hour prior to game time.

Visiting Club Hotel: Holiday Inn, Route 70 and Sayer Avenue, Cherry Hill, NJ 08002. **Telephone:** (856) 663-5300.

LANCASTER BARNSTORMERS

Office Address: 650 North Prince St., Lancaster, PA 17603. **Telephone:** (717) 509-4487. **FAX:** (717) 509-4486. **E-Mail Address:** info@LancasterBarnstormers.com. **Website:** www.LancasterBarnstormers.com

Operated by: Lancaster Baseball Club, LLC. **Principal Owners:** Opening Day Partners. **President:** Jon Danos. **Senior Vice President:** Brad Sims. **Controller:** Emily Merrill. **General Manager:** Kevin Cummings. **Assistant General Manager:** Vince Bulik. **Director, Marketing/Public Relations:** Adam Aurand. **Director, Stadium Operations:** Don Pryer. **Director, Finance:** Barbara Wert. **Director, Premium Account Services:** Kaye Willis. **Creative Services Manager:** Brad Jagielski. **Community Relations Manager:** Kevin Manno. **Ticket Operations Manager:** Maureen Wheeler. **Assistant Director, Stadium Operations:** Jeffrey Daws. **Marketing/Public Relations Assistant:** Pamela Denlinger. **Corporate Partnerships Associates:** Robert Ford, Kristin Lovelace, Richard Molina, Brian Radle. **Group Events Coordinators:** Sean Dougherty, Michael Minney, Lindsay Minnich, Jonathan Naff, Benjamin Peifer. **Customer Service Specialists:** Dana Mundey, Emily Reinbold. **Administrative Assistant:** Susan Shue. **Centerplate General Manager (Concessions/Merchandise):** Josh Leatherman. **Centerplate Merchandise Manager (Merchandise):** John Farrell.

Senior Vice President, Baseball Operations: Keith Lupton. **Manager:** Von Hayes. **Pitching Coach:** Rick Wise. **Coach:** Sam Snider. **Trainer:** Unavailable

GAME INFORMATION

Radio Announcer: Dave Collins. **No. of Games Broadcast:** Home-70, Away-70. **Flagship Station:** WLPA 1490-AM. **PA Announcer:** John Witwer. **Official Scorer:** Joel Schreiner

Stadium Name: Clipper Magazine Stadium. **Location:** From Route 30, take Fruitville Pike or Harrisburg Pike toward downtown Lancaster, stadium at intersection of Prince Street and Harrisburg Pike. **Standard Game Times:** 7:05 p.m., Sun. 1:35 p.m.

Visiting Club Hotel: Sleep Inn, 314 Primose Lane, Mountville, Pa., 17554. **Telephone:** (717) 285-2500

LONG ISLAND DUCKS

Mailing Address: 3 Court House Dr., Central Islip, NY 11722.

Telephone: (631) 940-3825. **FAX:** (631) 940-3800.

E-Mail Address: info@liducks.com. **Website:** www.liducks.com.

Operated by: Long Island Ducks Professional Baseball, LLC.

Principal Owner, Chief Executive Officer: Frank Boulton. **Owner/Senior Vice President, Baseball Operations:** Bud Harrelson.

General Manager: Michael Pfaff. **Assistant GMs:** Doug Cohen, Alex Scannella. **Director, Group Sales:** Bill Harney.

Director, Administration: Gerry Anderson. **Director, Operations:** Russ Blatt. **Manager, Box Office:** Ben Harper. **Manager, Promotions:** Morgan Tranquist. **Manager, Media Relations:** Mike Solano. **Manager, Merchandise:** Anthony Barberio. **Manager, Facilities:** Chris Gee. **Manager, Ticket Sales:** Brad Kallman. **Manager, Community Relations:** Katie Capria. **Coordinator, Administration:** Stephanie Valentinetti. **Account Executive, Group Sales:** John Wolff. **Head Groundskeeper:** Brad Keith. **Clubhouse Manager:** Rich Jensen.

Manager: Dave LaPoint Coaches: Bud Harrelson, Kevin Baez. **Trainers:** Tony Amin, Adam Lewis, Dorothy Pitchford.

GAME INFORMATION

Radio Announcers: Chris King, Mike Solano, David Weiss. **No. of Games Broadcast:** 140 on www.liducks.com. **Flagship Station:** TBA. **PA Announcer:** Bob Ottone. **Official Scorers:** Joe Donnelly, Red Foley.

Stadium Name: Citibank Park. **Location:** Southern State Parkway east to Carleton Avenue North (exit 43 A), right onto Courthouse Drive, stadium behind federal courthouse complex. **Standard Game Times:** 7:05 p.m.; 6:35 p.m. Sunday, 1:35/5:05.

Visiting Club Hotel: Radisson Hotel MacArthur Airport. 1730 North Ocean Avenue, Holtsville NY 11742. **Telephone:** (631) 758-2900 Fax: (631) 758-2612.

NEWARK BEARS

Office Address: 450 Broad St., Newark, NJ 07102.
Telephone: (973) 848-1000. **FAX:** (973) 621-0095.
Website: www.newarkbears.com.
Operated by: NB Baseball LLC. **Owner:** Marc Berson.
General Manager: John Brandt. **Assistant GM:** Jim Cerny. **Controller:** Ken Bossart.
Director, Ticket Sales: Kevin Gattie. **Director, Corporate Sponsorships:** Michael Luteran. **Director, Marketing:** Michael Collazo. **Manager, Media Relations:** Andres Mendez. **Manager, Community Relations:** Stu Smilowitz. **Head Groundskeeper:** Carlos Arocho.

Manager: Wayne Krenchicki. **Pitching Coach:** Steve Foucault. **Hitting Coach:** Ryan Jones.

GAME INFORMATION

Radio Announcer: Jim Cerny. **No. of Games Broadcast:** Home-70, Away-70. **Flagship Station:** WSOU-89.5 FM. **PA Announcer:** Steve Boland. **Official Scorer:** Kim DeRitter.

Stadium Name: Bears & Eagles Riverfront Stadium. **Location:** Garden State Parkway North/South to exit 145 (280 East), to exit 15; New Jersey Turnpike North/South to 280 West, to exit 15A. **Standard Game Times:** 7:05 p.m ., Saturday 6:05 p.m., Sunday 1:35 p.m.

Visiting Club Hotel: TBD.

SOMERSET PATRIOTS

Office Address: One Patriots Park, Bridgewater, NJ 08807. **Telephone:** (908) 252-0700. **FAX:** (908) 252-0776. **Website:** www.somersetpatriots.com.

Operated by: Somerset Patriots Baseball Club, LLC. **Principal Owners:** Steve Kalafer, Jack Cust, Byron Brisby, Don Miller. **Chairman:** Steve Kalafer. **President, General Manager:** Patrick McVerry. **Senior VP, Marketing:** Dave Marek. **VP, Assistant General Manager:** Rob Lukachyk. **Vice President, Public Relations:** Marc Russinoff. **Vice President, Ticketing:** Bryan Iwicki. **Head Groundskeeper:** Ray Cipperly. **Director, Group Sales:** Matt Kopas. **Director, Sales:** Kevin Forrester. **Director, Operations:** Tim Ur. **Corporate Marketing Manger:** Mike Desmond. Group Sales: Adam Cobb, Robert Crossman, Ian Haggerty. **Account Executive:** Mark Burgoon, Don Walters. **Ticket Sales Manager:** Adam Lifson. **Executive Assistant to GM:** Michele DaCosta. Controller: Ron Schultz. **Accountants:** Stephanie Diez, Tom Unchester. **Receptionist:** Lorraine Ott. **GM, Centerplate:** Mike McDermott. **Director, Player Procurement:** Brett Jodie. **Groundskeeper:** Dan Purner.

Manager: Sparky Lyle. **Pitching Coach:** Brett Jodie. **Hitting Coach:** Kevin Dattola. **Trainer:** Ryan McMahon.

GAME INFORMATION

Radio Announcer: Brian Bender. **No. of Games Broadcast:** Home-70, Away-70. **Flagship Station:** WCTC 1450-AM. **PA Announcer:** Paul Spychala. **Official Scorer:** John Nolan.

Stadium Name: Commerce Bank Ballpark. **Location:** Route 287 North to exit 13B/Route 287 South to exit 13 (Somerville Route 28 West); follow signs to ballpark. **Standard Game Times:** 7:05 p.m.; Sunday, 1:35 p.m. **Visiting Club Hotel:** Somerset Ramada, 60 Cottontail Lane, Somerset, NJ 08873. **Telephone:** (732) 560-9880.

SOUTHERN MARYLAND BLUE CRABS

Office Address: 3200 Crain Highway, Suite 203, Waldorf, MD 20603

Telephone: (301) 638-9788. **Fax:** (301) 638-9877.

E-Mail Address: info@somdbluecrabs.com. **Website:** www.somdbluecrabs.com

Principal Owners: Opening Day Partners, LLC and Brooks Robinson. **Chairman:** Peter Kirk. **President:** Jon Danos. **Senior Vice President:** Brad Sims. **Controller:** Emily Merrill.

General Manager: Mark Vinyard. **Assistant GM:** Chris Allen. **Senior Director of Marketing:** Andy Frankel. **Director of Corporate Partnerships:** Bill Snitcher. **Ticket Sales and Group Events Account Manager:** Crystal Martinez. **Marketing Assistant:** Kim Hedden. **Administrative Assistant/Special Projects:** Autumn Boyd. **Box Office Manager:** Carrine Cole. **Centerplate General Manager-Concessions:** Darren Hubbard.

Manager: Butch Hobson. **Pitching Coach:** Andre Rabouin. **Bench Coach:** Andy Etchebarren.

GAME INFORMATION

Radio: Unavailable.

Stadium: Regency Furniture Stadium. **Standard Game Times:** 2:05 p.m., **Sun:** 2:05 p.m.

Visiting Team Hotel: La Quinta Inn, 11770 Business Park Dr., Waldorf, MD, 20601. **Telephone:** (301) 645-0022.

YORK REVOLUTION

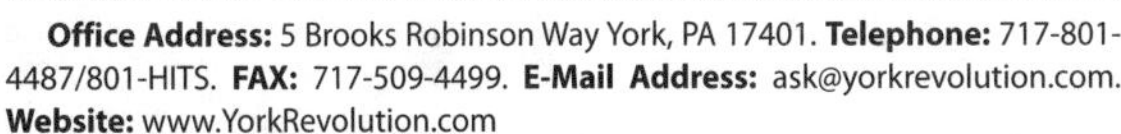

Office Address: 5 Brooks Robinson Way York, PA 17401. **Telephone:** 717-801-4487/801-HITS. **FAX:** 717-509-4499. **E-Mail Address:** ask@yorkrevolution.com. **Website:** www.YorkRevolution.com

Operated by: *York Professional Baseball Club, LLC.*

Principal Owners: Opening Day Partners. **President:** Jon Danos. **Senior Vice President:** Brad Sims. **Controller:** Emily Merrill. **General Manager:** Matt O'Brien. **Assistant General Manager:** Neil Fortier. **Finance Director:** Lori Brunson. **Ticket Sales Director:** Joe Charles. **Marketing/Promotions Director:** Greg Vojtanek. **Community Marketing Manager:** Ed Moran. **Corporate Sales Managers:** John Gibson, Mary Beth Hare. **Client Services Associate:** Miranda Malkemes. **Facility Operations Manager:** Josh Brown. **Group Events Manager:** Michelle Gemmill. **Group Events Coordinators:** Dan App, Lisa Howell. **Customer Service Manager:** Jen Kester. **Ticket Sales/Service Coordinator:** Geneva Sease. **Box Office Manager:** Cindy Burkholder. **Administration Assistant:** Jordan Carr. **Head Groundskeeper:** Brandon Putman. **Centerplate General Manager (Concessions/Merchandise):** Travis Johnson.

Baseball Operations Director: Adam Gladstone. **Manager:** Chris Hoiles. **Pitching Coach:** Tippy Martinez.

GAME INFORMATION

Radio Announcer: Darrell Henry. **No. of Games Broadcast:** 140. **Flagship Station:** WSBA 910-AM. **PA Announcer:** Al Rose. **Official Scorer:** Brian Wisler.

Stadium Name: Sovereign Bank Stadium. **Location:** Take Route 30 West to North George Street. Turn left onto North George Street. Follow that straight for four lights, Sovereign Bank Stadium is on left. **Standard Game Times:** 7:07 p.m.; Sunday, 5:07 p.m.

Visiting Club Hotel: The Yorktowne Hotel, 48 E Market St. York, PA 17401. **Telephone:** 717-848-1111.

CAN-AM LEAGUE

Office Address: 1415 Hwy. 54 West, Suite 210, Durham, NC 27707.

Telephone: (919) 401-8150. **Fax:** (919) 401-8152. **Website:** www.canamleague.com.

Year Founded: 2005.

Commissioner: Miles Wolff. **President:** Dan Moushon.

Administrative Assistant: Jason Deans. **Director, Umpires:** Kevin Winn.

Division Structure: None.

Regular Season: 94 games (split schedule). **2008 Opening Date:** May 22. **Closing Date:** Sept 1.

Playoff Format: First and second-half winners meet two teams with best overall records in best-of-five series. Winners meet in best-of-five series for league championship.

Roster Limit: 22. **Eligibility Rule:** Minimum of five first-year players; maximum of four veterans with at least four years of professional experience.

Brand of Baseball: Rawlings.

Statistician: PA SportsTicker, 55 Realty Drive Cheshire, CT 06410.

STADIUM INFORMATION

			Dimensions				
Club	**Stadium**	**Opened**	**LF**	**CF**	**RF**	**Capacity**	**2007 Att.**
Atlantic City	Bernie Robbins Stadium	1998	313	410	312	5,500	134,900
Brockton	Campanelli Stadium	2002	340	404	320	4,750	157,462
Nashua	Holman Stadium	1937	307	401	315	4,375	57,975
New Jersey	Yogi Berra Stadium	1998	308	398	308	3,784	89,385
Ottawa	Lynx Stadium	1993	325	404	325	10,332	—
Quebec	Stade Municipal de Quebec	1938	315	385	315	4,800	138,376
Sussex	Skylands Park	1994	330	392	330	4,300	85,126
Worcester	Hanover Insurance Park-Fitton Field	1905	361	417	307	3,000	116,712

ATLANTIC CITY SURF

Office Address: 545 North Albany Avenue, Atlantic City, NJ 08401.

Telephone: (609) 344-8873. **Fax:** (609) 344-7873.

E-Mail: info@acsurf.com. **Website:** www.acsurf.com.

Owner: Mark Schuster.

President: Chris Carminucci. **Vice President:** Ryan Conley. **Director, Operations:** Hoffman Wolff. **Director, Sales:** Kerry Pritchard. **Director, Food/Beverage:** Sander Stotland. **Manager, Community Relations:** Barry Kraus.

Manager: Cecil Fielder. **Coaches:** J.C. Huguet, Brian Rodaway.

GAME INFORMATION

Announcer (Webcast): Matt Martucci. **No. of Games Broadcast:** 94. **Webcast Address:** www.acsurf.com.

Stadium Name: Bernie Robbins Stadium. **Location:** From Points South (Ocean City, Cape May): Take the Garden State Parkway North to Exit 38 (Atlantic City Expressway East), AC Expressway to Exit 2 (Rt. 40/322). Take Rt. 40/322 East for 1 1/2 miles to the ballpark. From the West: Take AC Expressway East to Exit 2 and follow directions from the south above. From the North: Take the Garden State Parkway South to Exit 38 (Atlantic City Expressway East). Follow directions from the South above (AC Expressway Exit 38).

Standard Game Times: 7:05 p.m.; May 26, 6:30 p.m.; May 28, June 11, July 16, July 30: 11:00 a.m.

Visiting Club Hotel: Comfort Inn Victorian, 6817 Black Horse Pike, West Atlantic City, NJ 08234. **Telephone:** (609) 646-8880.

BROCKTON ROX

Office Address: One Feinberg Way, Brockton, MA 02301

Telephone: (508)559-7000. **Fax:** (508)587-2802.

E-Mail: roxrock@brocktonrox.com. **Website:** www.brocktonrox.com

Principal Owner: Van Schley. **President:** Jack Yunits. **Executive Vice President:** Michael Canina.

General Manager: Brian Voelkel. **Director, Food/Beverage:** Steve Bowker. **Client Services Manager:** Allison Gemelli. **Director, Promotions/Merchandise:** Bailey Frye. **Director, Media Relations/Broadcasting:** Matt Futrell. **Group Sales Representative:** Chris Corbett, Loretta Sullivan. **Community Relations/Sales:** Terri Kuskoski. **Receptionist:** Me'Shay Hurt. **Bookkeeper:** Mary Scarlett. **Groundskeeper:** Tom Hassett.

Manager: Chris Miyake. **Coaches:** Ryan Kane, John Kelly. **Trainer:** Lauren Eck.

GAME INFORMATION

Radio Announcer: Matt Futrell. **No. of Games Broadcast:** 94. **Flagship Station:** WXBR 1460-AM. **Webcast Address:**

www.brocktonrox.com.

Stadium Name: Campanelli Stadium. **Location:** Route 24 North/South to Route 123 east, stadium is two miles on right.

Standard Game Times: Monday/Saturday: 6:05 p.m.; Tuesday-Friday 7:05 p.m.; Sunday (May/June), 1:05 p.m. (July/August), 5:05 p.m.

Visiting Club Hotel: Holiday Inn Brockton, 195 Westgate Drive, Brockton, MA 02301. **Telephone:** (508) 588-6300.

NASHUA PRIDE

Office Address: 67 Amherst St., Nashua, NH 03064.

Telephone: (603) 883-2255. **Fax:** (603) 883-0880.

E-Mail Address: info@nashuapride.com. **Website:** www.nashuapride.com.

Operated by: Nashua Pride Baseball, LLC.

Principal Owner: John Stabile. **COO:** Jim Stabile

General Manager/VP, Baseball Operations: Chris Hall. **Assistant General Manager:** Courtney Hollis. **Director, Sales:** Cliff Jacques. **Director, Baseball Administration:** Beverly Taylor. **Manager, Media/Community Relations:** Nick Travalini. **Group Sales Manager:** Shaela Walsh.

Manager: Rick Miller. **Coach:** Richie Hebner.

GAME INFORMATION

Stadium Name: Historic Holman Stadium. **Location:** Route 3 to exit 7E (Amherst Street), stadium one mile on left.

Standard Game Times: 7:05 p.m.; Sunday, 5:05 p.m.

Visiting Club Hotel: Radisson-Nashua Hotel, 11 Tara Boulevard, Nashua, **NH 03062. Telephone:** (603) 888-9970.

NEW JERSEY JACKALS

Office Address: One Hall Dr., Little Falls, NJ 07424.

Telephone: (973) 746-7434. **Fax:** (973) 655-8006.

E-Mail Address: info@jackals.com. **Website:** www.jackals.com.

Operated by: Floyd Hall Enterprises, LLC.

Chairman: Floyd Hall. **President:** Greg Lockard.

General Manager: Larry Hall. **Business Manager:** Jennifer Fertig. **Director, Ticket Operations:** Pierson Van Raalte. **Director, Group Sales:** Sue Beck. **Facilities Manager:** Aldo Licitra. **Concessions Manager:** Michele Guarino. **Clubhouse Manager:** Wally Brackett.

Manager: Joe Calfapietra. **Coaches:** Bryan Gaal, Ed Ott, Ani Ramos.

GAME INFORMATION

Announcer (Webcast): Joe Ameruoso. **No. of Games Broadcast:** 94. **Webcast Address:** www.jackals.com.

Stadium Name: Yogi Berra Stadium. **Location:** Route 80 or Garden State Parkway to Route 46, take Valley Road exit to Montclair State University.

Standard Game Times: 7:05 p.m.; Sunday, 5:05 p.m.

Visiting Club Hotel: Ramada Inn, 130 Rte. 10 West, East Hanover, NJ 07936. **Telephone:** (973) 386-5622.

OTTAWA RAPIDS

Office Address: 300 Coventry Rd., Ottawa, Ontario K1K4P5.

Telephone: 613-747-5969. **Fax:** 613-747-0003

Email: info@baseballottawa.com. **Website:** www.baseballottawa.com.

Operated by: Ottawa Pro Baseball, Inc.

General Manager: Don Charrette. **Director, Sales:** Francois Marchand. **Office Administrator:** Lorraine Charrette. **Account Executive:** Richard Poulin. **Director, Marketing:** Angela Thompson. **Head Groundskeeper:** Josh Teuscher.

Manager: Ed Nottle. **Coach:** Mike Kusiewicz.

GAME INFORMATION

Stadium: Ottawa Stadium. **Location:** Hwy. 417 to Vanier Parkway exit. Vanier Parkway north ° mile to Coventry Rd. Turn right to stadium.

Standard Game Times: 7:05 p.m; Sunday, 1:05 p.m.

Visiting Club Hotel: Chimo Hotel. 119 Joseph Cyr Rd., Ottawa, Ontario K1K 3P5. **Telephone:** (613)744-1060.

QUEBEC CAPITALES

Office Address: 100 Rue du Cardinal Maurice-Roy, Quebec City, Quebec G1K8Z1.
Telephone: (418) 521-2255. **Fax:** (418) 521-2266.
E-Mail Address: baseball@capitalesdequebec.com. **Website:** www.capitalesdequebec.com.
Owner/President: Miles Wolff

General Manager: Alex Harvey. **Vice-President:** Michel Laplante, Stephane Dionne. **Sales Director:** Maxime Lamarche. **Promotions Director:** Guillaume Lamb. **Media Relations Director:** Pier-Luc Nappert. **Sales Representatives:** Jean-Philippe Auger, Jean Marois.

Manager: Michel Laplante. **Coaches:** Stephane Dionne, Patrick Scalabrini.

GAME INFORMATION

Radio Announcers: Jacques Doucet, Francois Paquet. **No. of Games Broadcast:** 94. **Flagship Station:** Info 800-AM. **Webcast Address:** www.info800.ca.

Stadium Name: Stade Municipal de QuÈbec. **Location:** Highway 40 to Highway 173 (Centre-Ville) exit 2 to Parc Victoria.

Standard Game Times: 7:05 p.m.; Sunday, 1:05 p.m.

Visiting Club Hotel: Hotel du Nord, 640 St. Vallier Ouest, Quebec City, QC G1N1C5. **Telephone:** (418) 522-1554.

SUSSEX SKYHAWKS

Office Address: 94 Championship Place Suite 11, Augusta, NJ 07822.
Telephone: (973) 300-1000. **Fax:** (973) 300-9000.
E-Mail Address: info@sussexskyhawks.com. **Website:** www.sussexskyhawks.com.
Operated By: Sussex Professional Baseball, LLC.
President: Larry Hall.

General Manager: Ben Wittkowski. **Director, Corporate Sales:** Herm Sorcher. **Director, Corporate Partnerships:** Matt Millet. **Director, Ticket Sales/Operations:** Seth Bettan. **Group Sales Representatives:** Corinne Oravits, Amy Rude. **Concessions Manager:** Matt Myers. **Facility Manager:** Aldo Licitra.

Manager: Hal Lanier. **Coaches:** Brooks Carey, Dave Cash.

GAME INFORMATION

Television: Channel 10 Sussex County. **No. of Broadcasts:** 10 Games.

Stadium Name: Skylands Park. **Location:** From New Jersey, I-80 to exit 34B (Rt. 15 N) to Route 565; From Pennsylvania, I-84 to Route 6 to Route 206 North to Route 565 East. **Standard Game Times:** 7:05 p.m.; Saturday, 5:05 p.m.; Sunday, 2:05 p.m.

Visiting Club Hotel: Ramada Inn, 130 Rte. 10 West, East Hanover, NJ 07936.
Telephone: (973) 386-5622.

WORCESTER TORNADOES

Office Address: 303 Main St., Worcester, MA 01613.
Telephone: (508) 792-2288. **Fax:** (506) 926-3662.
E-Mail Address: info@worcestertornadoes.com. **Website:** www.worcestertornadoes.com.

President/General Manager: RC Reuteman. **Director, Community Relations:** Rich Gedman. **Director, Sales:** Dave Peterson. **Director, Broadcasting:** Jeremy Lechan. **Director, Community Affairs/Education:** Dave Smith. **Office Manager:** Sandie Rousseau.

Director, Group Sales: Miriam Hyder. **Ticket Manager:** Alise Wales Controller: Anne Thebeau. **Director, Stadium Operations:** Chris Leach

Manager: Rich Gedman. **Coaches:** Bob Ojeda, Barry Glinski, Dave Smith.

GAME INFORMATION

Radio Announcer: Jeremy Lechan. **No. of Games Broadcast:** 94. **Flagship Station:** WTAG 580-AM. **Webcast Address:** www.worcestertornadoes.com.

Stadium Name: Hanover Insurance Park at Fitton Field. **Location:** I-290 to exit 11 College Square, right on College Street, left on Fitton Avenue.

Standard Game Times: 6:05pm Mon-Sat (May-June) 7:05 p.m. Mon-Sat (July-August); 1:05 p.m. Sunday

Visiting Club Hotel: Hampton Inn, 110 Summer St., Worcester, MA 01609. **Telephone:** (508)754-0400.

FRONTIER LEAGUE

Office Address: 408 W. U.S. Hwy 40, Suite 100, Troy, IL 62294.

Mailing Address: P.O. Box 62, Troy, IL 62294.

Telephone: (618) 667-8000. **FAX:** (618) 667-8524.

E-Mail Address: office@frontierleague.com. **Website:** www.frontierleague.com.

Year Founded: 1993.

Commissioner: Bill Lee. **Chairman:** Chris Hanners (Chillicothe).

President: Rich Sauget (Gateway). **Vice President:** John Swiatek (Washington). **Corporate Secretary/Treasurer:** Bob Wolfe. **Legal Counsel/Deputy Commissioner:** Kevin Rouch. **Deputy Commissioner, Development:** Leo Trich.

Director, Operations: Steve Gomric

Directors: Dan Brennan (Windy City), Clint Brown (Florence), Bill Bussing (Evansville), Kurt Carlson (Rockford), Erik Haag (Southern Illinois), Chris Hanners (Chillicothe), Rob Hilliard (Midwest), Steve Malliet (River City), Joe Rosenhagen (Kalamazoo), Rich Sauget (Gateway), John Swiatek (Washington), Leslye Wuerfel (Traverse City).

Division Structure: East—Chillicothe, Florence, Kalamazoo, Midwest, Traverse City, Washington West—Evansville, Gateway, River City, Rockford, Southern Illinois, Windy City

Regular Season: 96 games. **2008 Opening Date:** May 21. **Closing Date:** Sept. 3.

All-Star Game: July 16 at Traverse City.

Playoff Format: Division winners and two remaining teams with the best overall regular season records meet in best-of-five semifinal series. Winners meet in best-of-five series for league championship.

Roster Limit: 24. **Eligibility Rule:** Minimum of 10 first-year players; maximum of seven players with one year of professional experience, maximum of two players with two years of experience and maximum of three players with three or more years of experience. No player may be 27 prior to Jan. 1 of current season.

Brand of Baseball: Wilson.

Statistician: SportsTicker, 55 Reality Drive, Suite 200, Cheshire, CT 06410

STADIUM INFORMATION

			Dimensions				
Club	**Stadium**	**Opened**	**LF**	**CF**	**RF**	**Capacity**	**2007 Att.**
Chillicothe	V.A. Memorial Stadium	1954	328	400	325	4,000	84,383
Evansville	Bosse Field	1915	315	415	315	5,181	131,707
Florence	Champion Window Field	2004	325	395	325	4,200	99,333
Gateway	GCS Ballpark	2002	318	385	301	6,500	196,134
Kalamazoo	Homer Stryker Field	1995	306	400	330	4,806	54,950
River City	T.R. Hughes Ballpark	1999	320	382	299	4,989	100,556
Rockford	Road Ranger Stadium	2006	315	380	312	4,056	113,930
So. Illinois	Rent One Park	2007	325	400	330	4,500	259,392
Traverse City	Wuerfel Park	2006	320	400	320	4,600	206,102
Washington	Falconi Field	2002	325	400	325	3,200	155,894
Windy City	Hawkinson Ford Field	1999	335	390	335	4,000	81,586

CHILLICOTHE PAINTS

Office Address: 59 N. Paint St., Chillicothe, OH 45601.

Telephone: (740) 773-8326. **FAX:** (740) 773-8338.

E-Mail Address: paints@bright.net. **Website:** www.chillicothepaints.com.

Operated by: Chillicothe Paints Professional Baseball Association, Inc.

Principal Owner: Chris Hanners. **President:** Shirley Bandy.

Vice President, General Manager: Bryan Wickline. **Director, Baseball Operations:** Mark Mason. **Stadium Superintendent:** Jim Miner. **Director, Finance:** Maleine Davis. **Director, Sales/Marketing:** John Wend. **Administrative Assistant:** Christina Diehl. **Director, Group Sales:** Greg Bigam. **Director, Operations:** Adam Dettwiller. **Special Events Coordinator:** Greg Bigam. **Head Groundskeeper:** Jim Miner.

Field Manager: Mark Mason. **Coach:** Marty Dunn. **Trainer:** Jeremy Dicus.

GAME INFORMATION

Radio Announcers: Ryan Mitchell, Greg Bigam. **No. of Games Broadcast:** Home-48, Away-48. **Flagship Station:** WXIZ 100.9-FM. **PA Announcer:** John Wend. **Official Scorer:** Aaron Lemaster.

Stadium Name: V.A. Memorial Stadium. **Location:** Route 23 to Bridge Street, west on Route 35, north on Route 104. Standard Game Times: 7:05 p.m.; Sunday, 6:05 p.m.

Visiting Club Hotel: Comfort Inn, 20 N. Plaza Blvd., Chillicothe, OH 45601. **Telephone:** (740) 775-3500.

EVANSVILLE OTTERS

Operated by: Evansville Baseball, LLC.

President: Bill Bussing. **Senior Vice President:** Pat Rayburn.

Vice President, General Manager: Deana Johnson. **Senior Account Manager:** Liam Miller

Director, Operations: Scott Trible. **Ticket Manager:** Ali Chesnut. **Account Manager:** Casie Williams. **Account Manager:** Brandon McClish. **Account Manager:** Jason Troop. **Office Manager:** Curt Stewart.

Manager/Director, Baseball Operations: Jason Verdugo. **Coaches:** Brendan Sagara, Bobby Bell, Bill McKeon. **Trainer:** Unavailable.

GAME INFORMATION

Radio Announcer: Jason Troop. **No. of Games Broadcast for 2008:** Home-51, Away-45. **Flagship Station:** WUEV 91.5-FM. **PA Announcer:** Unavailable. **Official Scorer:** Unavailable.

Stadium Name: Bosse Field. **Location:** U.S. 41 to Lloyd Expressway West(IN-62), Main St. Exit, Right on Main St., ahead 1 mile to Bosse Field. **Standard Game Times:** 7:05 p.m.; Sunday, 6:05 p.m.

Visiting Club Hotel: Executive Inn Downtown, 600 Walnut Drive, Evansville, IN 47708. **Telephone:** 812-424-8000.

FLORENCE FREEDOM

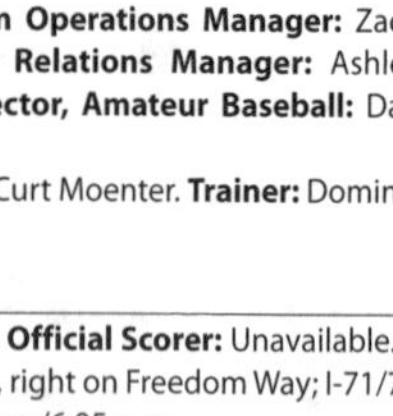

Office Address: 7950 Freedom Way, Florence, KY 41042.

Telephone: (859) 594-4487. **FAX:** (859) 594-3194.

E-Mail Address: info@florencefreedom.com. **Website:** www.florencefreedom.com.

Operated by: Canterbury Baseball, LLC.

President: Clint Brown. **General Manager:** Kari Rumfield Controller: Dave Flischel. **Director, Promotions:** Kevin Schwab. **Box Office Manager:** Sarah Straughn. **Stadium Operations Manager:** Zach Prehn. **Senior Account Executive:** Elizabeth Quatman. **Account Executive/Media Relations Manager:** Ashley Thompson. **Account Executive:** Kyle Gehring. **Head Groundskeeper:** Lyle Travis. **Director, Amateur Baseball:** Dan Guttridge.

Baseball Operations/Manager: Jamie Keefe. **Coach:** Jason Graham. **Pitching Coach:** Curt Moenter. **Trainer:** Dominic Favia.

GAME INFORMATION

Radio: 106.7 WNKR. **Radio Broadcaster:** Roger Redmon. **PA Announcer:** Unavailable. **Official Scorer:** Unavailable.

Stadium: Champion Window Field. **Location:** I-71/75 South to exit 180, left onto US 42, right on Freedom Way; I-71/75 North to exit 180. **Standard Game Times:** 7:05 p.m.; **Saturday 6:**05 p.m. **Sunday 2:**05 p.m./6:05 p.m.

Visiting Club Hotel: Wildwood Inn

GATEWAY GRIZZLIES

Mailing Address: 2301 Grizzlie Bear Blvd., Sauget, IL 62206.

Telephone: (618) 337-3000. **FAX:** (618) 332-3625.

E-Mail Address: grizzlies@accessus.net. **Website:** www.gatewaygrizzlies.com.

Operated by: Gateway Baseball, LLC.

Managing Officer: Richard Sauget. **General Manager:** Tony Funderburg. **Assistant GM:** Steven Gomric. **Director, Group Sales:** Jason Murphy. **Stadium Operations:** Brent Pownall. **Media Relations Director/Events Coordinator:** Jeff O'Neill. **Director, Corporate Sales:** C.J. **Hendrickson. Director, Mechandise/Ticket Sales Associate:** Gina Perschbacher. **Head Groundskeeper/Corporate Sales Associate:** Craig Kuhl. **Broadcaster/Corporate Sales Associate:** Joe Pott. **Director, Ticket Sales:** Will Myers. **Director, Guest Relations:** Evan Bolesta. Director, Promotions: Adam Cooper. Interns: Justin Shackil, Erin Nolan, Elyse Morris, Isaac Cox, Bryan Gegg, Nicholas Griggs, Megan Kramper.

Manager: Phil Warren. **Pitching Coach:** Randy Martz. **Bench Coach:** Darin Kinsolving

Trainer: Geof Manzo. **Clubhouse Manager:** Mike Sartore

GAME INFORMATION

Radio Announcer: Joe Pott. **No of Games Broadcast:** Home-51, Away-45.Flagship Station: Unavailable.

PA Announcer: Tom Calhoun. **Official Scorer:** Jim Powers.

Stadium Name: GCS Ballpark. **Location:** I-255 at exit 15 (Mousette Lane). **Standard Game Times:** 7:05 p.m.; Sunday, 6:05 p.m./3:05 p.m.

Visiting Club Hotel: Ramada Inn, 6900 N. Illinois St., Fairview Heights, IL 62208. **Telephone:** (618) 632-4747

KALAMAZOO KINGS

Mailing Address: 251 Mills St., Kalamazoo, MI 49048.
Telephone: (269) 388-8326. **FAX:** (269) 388-8333.
Website: www.kalamazookings.com.
Operated by: Team Kalamazoo, LLC.

Owners: Bill Wright, Mike Seelye, Pat Seelye, Joe Rosenhagen, Ed Bernard, Scott Hocevar. **Vice President /General Manager/Managing Partner:** Joe Rosenhagen. **Fundraising Coordinator:** Sara Krebill. **Community Relations:** Chris Peake.

Director, Baseball Operations/Field Manager: Fran Riordan. **Pitching Coach:** Joseph Thomas.

GAME INFORMATION

Radio Announcers: Unavailable. **No. of Games Broadcast:** Home-54, Away-42.

Flagship Station: ESPN 1660-AM. **PA Announcers:** Jim Lefler. **Official Scorer:** Jason Zerban. **Stadium Name:** Homer Stryker Field. **Location:** I-94 to Sprinkle Road (exit 80), north on Sprinkle Road, left on Business Loop I-94, left on Kings Highway, right on Mills Street. **Standard Game Times:** 7:05 p.m.; Sunday, 2:05 p.m.

Visiting Club Hotel: Red Roof Inn, 5425 W. Michigan Ave., Kalamazoo, MI 49009. **Telephone:** (269)375-7400.

MIDWEST SLIDERS

Team Name: Midwest Sliders
Mailing Address: 315-130 North Telegraph Road, Waterford, MI 48328. **Telephone:** 248-681-0700.
E-mail Address: info@cruisersbaseball.com. **Web Site:** www.cruisersbaseball.com
Operated By: Baseball Heroes of Oakland County, LP
President/Director, Team Personnel: Rob Hilliard
Manager/Director, Player Development: Eric Coleman. **Coaches:** Cory Domel, Chris Barney.

RIVER CITY RASCALS

Office Address: 900 TR Hughes Blvd., O'Fallon, MO 63366.
Telephone: (636) 240-2287. **FAX:** (636) 240-7313.
E-Mail Address: info@rivercityrascals.com. **Website:** www.rivercityrascals.com.

Operated by: PS&J Professional Baseball Club LLC. **Owners:** Tim Hoeksema, Jan Hoeksema, Fred Stratton, Anne Stratton, Pam Malliet, Steve Malliet, Michael Veeck.

President: Steve Malliet. **Assistant General Manager:** Chris Franklin. **Business Manager:** Tammie Hopkins. **Director, Ticket Sales:** Zach Ziler. **Director, Broadcasting:** Josh Anderson. **Director, Stadium Operations:** Matt Vertin. **Head Groundskeeper:** Chris Young. **Group Sales Executives:** Kyle Wicks. **General Manager, Aramark Sports/Entertainment Services:** Mark Duffy.

Team Manager: Toby Rumfield. **Pitching Coach:** Steve Brook.

GAME INFORMATION

Radio Announcer: Josh Anderson. **No. of Games Broadcast:** Home-51, Away-46. **Flagship Station:** KSLQ 104.5-FM. **PA Announcer:** Unavailable. **Official Scorer:** Unavailable.

Stadium Name: T.R. **Hughes Ballpark. Location:** I-70 to exit 219, north on T.R. Hughes Road, follow signs to ballpark. **Standard Game Times:** 7:05 p.m.; Sunday, 6:05 p.m.

Visiting Club Hotel: Holiday Inn Select, 4341 Veterans Memorial Parkway St.Peters, MO 63376 .
Telephone: 636-925-1500.

ROCKFORD RIVERHAWKS

Office Address: 4503 Interstate Blvd., **Loves Park, IL 61111.**
Telephone: (815) 885-2255. **FAX:** (815) 964-2462.
E-Mail Address: playball@rockfordriverhawks.com . **Website:** www.rockfordriverhawks.com.

Owners: Dennis Arouca, Kurt Carlson, Dave Ciarrachi, Jim Ciarrachi, Nick Belleson, Brian McClure. **Managing Partner:** Dave Ciarrachi.

General Manager: Josh Olerud. **Assistant GM:** Todd Fulk. **Director, Broadcasting/Media Relations:** Bill Czaja. **Director, Marketing/Promotions:** Marshall Mackinder. **Director, Sales:** Dan Macdonald. **Director, Community Relations/Merchandising:** Erin Columbi. **Director, Tickets/Finance:** Brad Sholes. **Director, Group Sales:** Jim Ciarrachi. **Head Groundskeeper:** Travis Stephen.

Manager: Bob Koopmann. **Coaches:** J.D. Arndt, Sam Knaack. **Trainer:** Jim Halpin.

GAME INFORMATION

Radio Announcer: Bill Czaja. **No. of Games Broadcast:** Home-51, Away-45. **Flagship Station:** WNTA, 1330-AM. **PA Announcers:** Scott Bentley, Brett Myhers. **Official Scorer:** TBA.

Stadium Name: Road Ranger Stadium. **Location:** I-90 to Riverside Boulevard exit, east to Interstate Drive, left on Interstate Drive. **Standard Game Times:** 7:05 p.m.; Sunday, 6:05 p.m.

Visiting Club Hotel: TBA.

SOUTHERN ILLINOIS MINERS

Office Address: 3000 West BeYoung, Marion, IL 62959

Mailing Address: Rent One Park, 1000 Miners Drive, Marion, IL 62959

Telephone: (618) 998-8499. **Fax:** (618) 969-8499

E-Mail Address: info@southernillinoisminers.com. **Website:** www.southernillinoisminers.com

Operated by: Southern Illinois Baseball Group.

Vice President: Erik Haag. **General Manager:** Tim Arseneau. **Team Merchandise:** Derek Garber. **Director, Media Relations/Broadcasting:** Scott Gierman. **Director, Sales/Marketing:** Brad Grenoble. **Bookeeper:** Sarah Hagler. **Director, Production:** Chris Hagstrom. **Corporate Sales Director:** Barry Katz. **Group Sales Executive:** Casey Law. **Account Executive:** Brad Cleveland. **Account Executive/Bullpen Coach:** Sean Patrick. **Director, Stadium Operations:** Billy Peterman. **Operations/Team Merchandise:** Jeff Pink.

Manager: Mike Pinto. **Pitching Coach:** Brad Hall. **Coaches:** Bart Zeller, Ralph Santana, Sean Patrick.

GAME INFORMATION

Radio Announcer: Scott Gierman. **No. of Games Broadcast:** 96. **Flagship Station:** 97.7 WQUL-FM

Stadium Name: Rent One Park. **Location:** US 57 to Route 13 East, right at Halfway Road to Fairmont Dr.

Standard Game Times: 7:05 p.m.; Sunday, 2:05 p.m.

Visiting Club Hotel: Econo Lodge, 1806 Bittle Place, Marion, IL 62959

TRAVERSE CITY BEACH BUMS

Office Address: 333 Stadium Dr., Traverse City, MI 49684.

Telephone: (231) 943-0100. **FAX:** (231) 943-0900.

E-Mail Address: info@tcbeachbums.com. **Website:** www.traversecitybeachbums.com.

Operated by: Traverse City Beach Bums, LLC. **Managing Partners:** John Wuerfel, Leslye Wuerfel, Jason Wuerfel.

President/CEO: John Wuerfel. **General Manager:** Leslye Wuerfel. **Vice President:** Jason Wuerfel.

Director, Sales/Marketing: Jeremy Crum. **Director, Promotions/Community Relations:** Michele LeMieux. **Director, Concessions:** Juli Babcock. **Director, Merchandise:** Scott McDowell. **Director, Ticketing:** Nick Jacqmain. **Director, Media/Broadcasting:** Tim Calderwood.

Manager: Jonathan Cahill. **Hitting Coach:** Jason Wuerfel. **Pitching Coach:** John Sexton. **Clubhouse Manager:** Denny Dame. **Trainer:** Brian Rosenau.

GAME INFORMATION

Radio Announcer: Tim Calderwood. **No. of Games Broadcast:** Home-54, Away-42. **Flagship Stations:** WFCX 94.3-FM , The FOX; WFDX 92.5-FM. **PA Announcer:** Tim Moeggenberg. **Official Scorer:** Greg Rosinski.

Stadium Name: Wuerfel Park. **Location:** 3 miles south of the Grand Traverse Mall just off US-31 and M-37 in Chums Village.-Stadium is visible from the highway (Or north of US 31 and M-37 Chums Corner intersection) Turn-west on Chums Village Drive, north on Village Park Drive, right on Stadium Drive. **Standard Game Times:** 7:05 p.m.; Sunday, 6:05 p.m.

Visiting Club Hotel: Days Inn & Suites of Traverse City.

WASHINGTON WILD THINGS

Office Address: One Washington Federal Way, Washington, PA 15301.
Telephone: (724) 250-9555. **FAX:** (724) 250-2333.
E-Mail Address: info@washingtonwildthings.com . **Website:** www.washingtonwildthings.com.

Owned by: Sports Facility, LLC. **Operated by:** Washington Frontier League Baseball, LLC.

Managing Partner: John Swiatek.

President/Chief Executive Officer: John Swiatek. **General Manager:** Ross Vecchio. **Director, Marketing:** Christine Blaine. **Director. Stadium Operations:** Steve Zavacky. **Sponsorship Account Executive:** Greg Thompson. **Box Office Manager:** Joe Traynor. **Merchandise Manager:** Dee Lober. **Concessions Manager:** Joe Pagano. **Ticket Account Executives:** David Shrader, Dan Wolkiewicz, Ashlee Nichol, Phil Dillon, Peter Barakat

Manager: Greg Jelks. **Coach:** Bob Bozzuto. **Pitching Coach:** Unavailable. **Trainer:** Bobby Smith.

GAME INFORMATION

Radio Announcer: Bob Gregg. **No. of Games Broadcast:** Home-50, Away-45. **Flagship Station:** WJPA 95.3-FM . **PA Announcer:** Bill DiFabio. **Official Scorer:** Scott McGuinness. **Stadium Name:** Location: I-70 to exit 15 (Chestnut Street), right on Chestnut Street to Washington Crown Center Mall, right at mall entrance, right on to Mall Drive to stadium. **Standard Game Times:** 7:05 p.m.; Sunday, 6:35 p.m.

Visiting Club Hotel: Unavailable.

WINDY CITY THUNDERBOLTS

Office Address: 14011 South Kenton Ave., Crestwood, IL 60445-2252.

Telephone: (708) 489-2255. **FAX:** (708) 489-2999. **E-Mail Address:** info@wcthunderbolts.com. **Website:** www.wcthunderbolts.com.

Owned by: Crestwood Professional Baseball, LLC.

General Manager: Steve Tahsler. **Assistant GM:** Mike Lucas. **Director, Sales:** Pete Kelly. **Director, Community Relations/Group Sales:** Tom Linehan. **Director, Stadium Operations:** Bob Weiss. **Director, Fundraising/Head Groundskeeper:** Mike VerSchave. **Office Manager:** Robbin Zaffino.

Manager: Brian Nelson. **Pitching Coach:** Jim Miksis. **Hitting Coach:** Kevin Wilson. **Bench Coach:** Mike Kashirsky. **Trainer:** Unavailable.

GAME INFORMATION

Radio Announcer: Unavailable. **No. of Games Broadcast:** 96. **Flagship Station:** TBA.

PA Announcer: Unavailable. **Official Scorer:** Jason Collins.

Stadium Name: Standard Bank Stadium. **Location:** I-294 to S. Cicero Ave., exit (Route 50), south for 1 1/2 miles, left at Midlothian Turnpike, right on Kenton Ave.; I-57 to 147th Street, west on 147th to Cicero, north on Cicero, right on Midlothian Turnpike, right on Kenton. **Standard Game Times:** 7:05 p.m.; Sunday, 6:05 p.m.

Visiting Club Hotel: Georgio's Comfort Inn, 8800 W. 159th St., Orland Park, IL 60462. **Telephone:** (708) 403-1100. **Fax:** (708) 403-1105.

GOLDEN LEAGUE

Office Address: 7080 Donlon Way, Suite 109, Dublin, CA 94568.

Telephone: (925) 226-2889. **FAX:** (925) 226-2891.

E-mail Address: info@goldenbaseball.com. **Website:** www.goldenbaseball.com.

Founded: 2005.

CEO: David Kaval. **President:** Amit Patel. **Commissioner/Chief Marketing Officer:** Kevin Outcalt. **Director, Operations:** Curt Jacey

League Historian/Secretary: Bill Weiss.

Supervisor, Officials: Ron Barnes. **Director, Baseball Operations:** Stephen Bedford.

Division Structure: North: Edmonton, Calgary, Chico, Reno South: Long Beach, Orange County, St. **George, Yuma.**

Regular Season: 88 games. **2008 Opening Date:** May 22. **Closing Date:** Aug. **31.**

All-Star Game: July 15th versus United League All-Stars in San Angelo, Texas.

Playoff Format: First- and second-half winners of each division meet in four team playoffs with best of five semi final and Championship series.

Roster Limit: 22. **Eligibility Rules:** No minimum number of rookies, age limit of 28 as of Jan. 1 unless player has MLB, AAA, AA, or former GBL experience.

Brand of Baseball: Spalding TF PRO.

Statistician: SportsTicker, ESPN Plaza—Building B, Bristol, CT 06010.

STADIUM INFORMATION

			Dimensions				
Club	**Stadium**	**Opened**	**LF**	**CF**	**RF**	**Capacity**	**Attendance**
*Calgary	Foothills Stadium	1966	345	400	325	8,000	71,363
Chico	Nettleton Stadium	1997	330	405	330	4,400	69,330
*Edmonton	TELUS Field	1995	340	420	420	9,200	82,414
Long Beach	Blair Field	1958	348	400	348	3,500	50,791
Orange County	Goodwin Field	1992	330	400	330	3,500	36,526
Reno	Peccole Park	1994	340	401	340	3,000	50,330
St.George	Bruce Hurst Field	1994	340	390	335	3,000	23,870
Yuma	Desert Sun Stadium	1969	335	410	335	7,100	54,818

*Franchises played in Northern League in 2007.

CALGARY VIPERS

Address: 2255 Crowchild Trail NW, Calgary, Alberta, Canada T2M4S7.

Telephone: (403) 277-2255

E-Mail Address: py@calgaryvipers.com. **Website:** www.calgaryvipers.com.

President/Chief Operating Officer: Peter Young. **Box Office Manager:** Riley Anderson. **Facilities Director:** Rick Penner. **Senior Accountant:** John Kirkbride. **Director, Absolute Baseball Academy:** Neil Gidney. **Media Relations:** Patrich Haas. **Admiistrative Assistance:** Jaylene Church

Manager: Mike Busch. **Coach:** Morgan Burkhart. **Coach:** Darryl Brinkley. **Coach:** Carlos Duncan. **Pitching Coach:** unavailable.

GAME INFORMATION

Radio Announcer: Patrick Haas. **No. of Games Broadcast:** Home-44 Away-44. **Flagship Station:** AM 770 CHQR. **PA Announcer:** Kramer. **Official Scorer:** Darcy Leitz/Gord Siminon.

Stadium Name: Foothills Athletic Park.

Standard Game Times: 7:05 p.m., Sat. 5:05 Sun. 1:35.

Visiting Club Hotel: Unavailable

CHICO OUTLAWS

Office Address: 555 Main St., Suite 200, Chico, CA 95928.

Telephone: (530) 345-3210.

E-Mail Address: bob@goldenbaseball.com. **Website:** www.chicooutlawsbaseball.com .

President: Bob Linscheid. **General Manager:** Becca Hoffer. **Director, Public Relations/ Broadcasting:** Rory Miller. **.**

Manager: Jon Macalutas. **Hitting Coach:** Chris Corso. **Pitching Coach:** Reece Borges.

GAME INFORMATION

Radio Announcer: Unavailable. **No. of Games Broadcast:** Home-44, Away-44. **Flagship Station:** KPAY 1290-AM.

PA Announcer: Rory Miller. **Official Scorer:** Unavailable.

Stadium Name: Nettleton Stadium. **Location:** California 99 North to California 32 West/East Eighth Street, right on

Main Street, left on West First Street; stadium at 400 West First Street. **Standard Game Times:** 7:05 p.m., **Sun. 1:**05.

Visiting Club Hotel: Feather Falls Casino & Lodge, #3 Alverda Drive, Oroville, CA 95966. **Telephone:** (530) 533-3885.

EDMONTON CRACKERCATS

Address: 10233-96 Avenue, Edmonton, Alberta, Canada T5K0A5
Telephone: (780) 423-2255
E-Mail Address: teaminfo@crackercats.ca. **Website:** www.crackercats.ca
Owner: Dan Ohrlich. **Vice-President:** Erica Cruise.
Manager: Brent Bowers. **Coach:** Unavailable. **Pitching Coach:** Unavailable.

GAME INFORMATION

Radio Announcer: Al Coates. **No. of Games Broadcast:** Home-44 Away-44. **Flagship Station:** Unavailable.

PA Announcer: Unavailable. **Official Scorer:** Al Coates.

Stadium Name: Telus Field. **From North:** 101st Street to 96th Ave. Left on 96th, 1 block East. From South: Take Calgary Trail North to Queen Elizabeth Hill, make a right across Walterdale Bridge, and then a right on 96th Avenue.

Standard Game Times: 7:05 p.m., Sun. 1:35.

Visiting Club Hotel: Sutton Place Hotel. 10235-101st Street, Edmonton, Alberta, Canada T5J3E9 (780) 428-7111.

LONG BEACH ARMADA

Office Address: 4720 E. Los Coyotes Diagonal, Long Beach, CA 90815
Telephone: (562) 434-7161
E-Mail Address: sbash@goldenbaseball.com. **Website:** www.longbeacharmada.com .
President/General Manager: Steve Bash. **Office Manager:** Doug Cowgill.
Manager: Steve Yeager. **Coach:** Chris Wakeland. **Pitching Coach:** Bob Welch.

GAME INFORMATION

Radio Announcer: Unavailable. **Webcast Address:** www.longbeacharmada.com .

PA Announcer: Unavailable fficial Scorer: Unavailable.

Stadium Name: Blair Field. **Location:** From Orange County, take 405 North to Seventh Street/22 West, right at Park Avenue. From Los Angeles, take 405 South to Lakewood Boulevard South, go to traffic circle and get on Pacific Coast Highway South, right on Ximeno, left on 10th Street; park at intersection of 10th Street and Park Avenue. **Standard Game Times:** 7:05 p.m.; **Sunday, 1:**05 p.m.

Visiting Club Hotel: Unavailable.

ORANGE COUNTY FLYERS

Office Address: 2461 E. Orangethorpe, Suite 102, Fullerton, CA 92831.
Telephone: (714) 526-8326.
E-Mail Address: jgurney@orangecountyflyers.com. **Website:** www.orangecountyflyers.com
President: Alan Mintz. **GM:** Justin Gurney.
Manager: Gary Carter. **Coach:** Unavailable. **Pitching Coach:** Unavailable.

GAME INFORMATION

Radio: FM 90.1 KBPK; www.SportsNetUSA.net. **PA Announcer:** Unavailable. **Official Scorer:** Unavailable

Stadium Name: Goodwin Field. **Location:** From Orange Freeway, take Yorba Linda Blvd. Exit, west on Yorba Linda, left on Associated Road to parking lot G. **Standard Game Times:** 7:05 p.m.; **Sunday, 1:**05 p.m.

Visiting Club Hotel: Holiday Inn Express - Placentia, 118 E Orangethorpe Ave, Placentia, CA 92870 714-528-7778.

RENO SILVER SOX

Office Address: 205 Redfield Parkway, Suite 201, Reno NV 89509.
Telephone: (775) 348-7769.
E-Mail Address: renoinfo@goldenbaseball.com . **Website:** www.renosilversox.com.
General Manager: Curt Jacey. **Director, Sales/Marketing:** Judy Crilley. **Director, Operations:** John Rice. **Director, Tickets Sales:** Unavailable. **Director, Public Relations/Broadcasting:** Unavailable.
Manager: Jeffrey Leonard. **Coach:** Unavailable. **Pitching Coach:** Unavailable.

GAME INFORMATION

Radio: Unavailable. **PA Announcer:** Unavailable. **Official Scorer:** Unavailable.

Stadium Name: Peccole Park. **Location:** Take 395 North, exit at I-80 West, exit at Virginia Street, right (north) on Virginia, right on Ninth Street/Evans Avenue, park on left. **Standard Game Times:** 7:05 p.m.; **Sunday, 1:**05 p.m.

Visiting Club Hotel: Unavailable

ST. GEORGE ROAD RUNNERS

Office Address: 216 W. St. George Blvd, Suite A, St. George, Utah 84770.
Telephone: (435) 673-5333.
E-Mail Address: rberry@goldenbaseball.com.
Website: www.stgeorgeroadrunners.com.
General Manager: Rick Berry. **Sales Executive:** Gary Webster.
Office Manager: Unavailable.
Manager: Cory Snyder. **Pitching Coach:** Mark Woodyard Hitting Coach: Unavailable

GAME INFORMATION

Radio Announcer: John Potter. **No. of Games Broadcast:** Home-44, Away-44. **Flagship Station:** 1210 AM ESPN

PA Announcer: Ed Rogers. **Official Scorer:** Jeff Clough.

Stadium Name: Bruce Hurst Field. **Location:** 225 South 700 East Saint George, UT Standard Game Times: 7:05 p.m.

Visiting Club Hotels: Budget Inn & Suites, Comfort Suites, Holiday Inn, Ramada Inn, and Hilton Garden Inn all in St. George, Utah.

YUMA SCORPIONS

Address: 1280 W. Desert Sun Dr., Yuma, AZ 85366.
Telephone: (928) 257-4700.
E-Mail Address: jmatlock@goldenbaseball.com. **Website:** www.yumascorpions.com.
General Manager: Mike Marshall. **Vice President, Sales:** Jason Matlock. **Director, Promotions/Marketing :** Glenn Dobson. **Office Manager:** Christina Kitchen.
Manager: Mike Marshall. **Coach:** Henry Calderon. **Pitching Coach:** unavailable.

GAME INFORMATION

Radio Announcer: Unavailable. **No. of Games Broadcast:** Away-44. **Flagship Station:** KBLU 560-AM. **PA Announcer:** Virgil Tudor. **Official Scorer:** Greg Abbott

Stadium Name: Desert Sun Stadium. **Location:** From I-8, take Fourth Avenue or 16th Street exit to Avenue A.
Standard Game Times: 7:05 p.m., **Sun. 1:**05.

Visiting Club Hotel: Best Western Inn Suites 1450 Castle Dome Ave. Yuma, AZ. (928) 783-4776.

NORTHERN LEAGUE

Office Addresses: 80 South Eighth Street, Suite 4920, Minneapolis, MN 55402
Telephone: 612-338-9097 Fax: 612-338-9098
Email: commissioner@northernleague.com or baseballoperations@northernleague.com
Website: www.northernleague.com
Founded: 1993
Commissioner: Clark Griffith. **Director, Baseball Operations:** Harry Stavrenos
Directors: John Ehlert (Kansas City), Rich Ehrenreich (Schaumburg), John Costello (Joliet), Sam Katz (Winnipeg), Timothy Haffner (Gary), Bruce Thom (Fargo).
Office addresses: 80 South Eighth Street, Suite 4920, Minneapolis, MN 55402
Telephone: 612-338-9097 Fax: 612-338-9098
Regular Season: 96 games (full-season format). **2008 Opening Date:** May 15. **Closing Date:** August 31.
All-Star Game: July 8 at Winnipeg.
Playoff Format: Top four teams meet in best-of-five semifinal series. Winners meet in best-of-five series for the league championship.
Brand of Baseball: Rawlings
Statistician: PA SportsTicker, Cheshire, CT 06410

STADIUM INFORMATION

			Dimensions				
Club	**Stadium**	**Opened**	**LF**	**CF**	**RF**	**Capacity**	**2007 Att.**
Fargo-Moorhead	Newman Outdoor Field	1996	318	400	314	4,513	170,122
Gary	U.S. Steel Yard	2003	320	400	335	6,139	166,338
Joliet	Silver Cross Field	2002	330	400	327	4,616	184,611
Kansas City	Community America Ballpark	2003	300	396	328	4,365	289,162
Schaumburg	Alexian Field	1999	355	400	353	7,048	206,749
Winnipeg	CanWest Global Park	1999	325	400	325	7,481	300,938

FARGO-MOORHEAD REDHAWKS

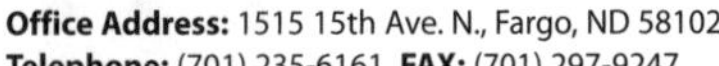

Office Address: 1515 15th Ave. N., Fargo, ND 58102.
Telephone: (701) 235-6161. **FAX:** (701) 297-9247.
E-Mail Address: redhawks@fmredhawks.com. **Website:** www.fmredhawks.com.
Operated by: Fargo Baseball, LLC.
President: Bruce Thom. **Executive Vice President:** Brad Thom.
General Manager: Josh Buchholz. **Assistant General Manager:** Megan Salic. **Senior Accountant:** Sue Wild. **Director, Stadium Operations:** Eric Jorgenson. **Director, Ticket Sales:** Michael Larson. **Director, Group Sales:** Karl Hoium. **Director, Food/Beverage:** Sean Kiernan. **Head Groundskeeper:** Matt Wallace.
Manager/Director, Player Procurement: Doug Simunic. **Assistant Director, Player Procurement/Consultant:** Jeff Bittiger. **Pitching Coach:** Steve Montgomery. **Coaches:** Bucky Burgau, Robbie Lopez. **Trainer:** Mike Bogenreif. **Clubhouse Operations:** Derek Rice.

GAME INFORMATION

Radio Announcers: Scott Miller, Maury Wills. **No. of Games Broadcast:** Home-48, Away-48. **Flagship Station:** WDAY 970-AM. **PA Announcer:** Erick Johnson. **Official Scorer:** Rob Olson.
Stadium Name: Newman Outdoor Field. **Location:** I-29 North to exit 67, right on 19th Ave. North, right on Albrecht Boulevard. **Standard Game Times:** 7 p.m.; Saturday 6 p.m.; Sunday, 1 p.m.
Visiting Club Hotel: Comfort Inn West, 3825 9th Ave. SW, Fargo, ND 58103. **Telephone:** (701) 282-9596.

GARY RAILCATS

Office Address: One Stadium Plaza, Gary, IN 46402.
Telephone: (219) 882-2255. **FAX:** (219) 882-2259.
E-Mail Address: info@railcatsbaseball.com Website: www.railcatsbaseball.com.
Operated by: SouthShore Baseball, LLC. **Chairman:** George Huber. **Vice President, General Manager:** Bill Terlecky. **Director, Media Relations/Broadcasting:** Tom Nichols. **Assistant General Manager/Sales/Marketing:** Mike Smith. **Assistant General Manager/Business Operations:** Becky Kremer. **Director, Marketing Communications:** Jahi Garrett. **Director, Facility:** Jim Kerr. **Group Sales Manager:** Jim Rice. **Director, Merchandise/Baseball Operations:** Cydni

Johnson. **Community Relations Manager:** Maribeth Sarnecki. **Sports Turf Manager:** Mitch McClary. **Ticket Sales Executive/Media Assistant:** Aaron Pineda. **Ticket Sales Specialists:** Laura Blakeley, Adam Harris, Chris Nunley, Tony Wiedman. **Executive Assistant:** Arcella Moxley.

Manager: Greg Tagert. **Coaches:** Jamie Bennett, Joe Gates.

GAME INFORMATION

Radio Announcer: Tom Nichols. **No. of Games Broadcast:** Home-48, Away-48. **Flagship Station:** WEFM 95.5-FM.

Stadium Name: U.S. Steel Yard. **Location:** I-80/94 to Broadway Exit (Exit 10). North on Broadway to Fifth Avenue. East one block to stadium. **Standard Game Times:** 7 p.m.; **Saturday, 6 p.m.; Sunday, 2 p.m.**

Visiting Club Hotel: Majestic Star Casino Hotel, 1 Buffington Harbor Dr., Gary, IN 46406. **Telephone:** (219) 977-9999.

JOLIET JACKHAMMERS

Office Address: 1 Mayor Art Schultz Dr., Joliet, IL 60432.

Telephone: (815) 726-2255. **Fax:** (815) 726-9223.

E-Mail Address: info@jackhammersbaseball.com.

Website: www.jackhammerbaseball.com.

Operated by: Joliet Professional Baseball Club, LLC.

Chairman: Peter Ferro. **Vice Chairman:** Charles Hammersmith. **Chief Exectutive Officer/General Counsel:** Michael Hansen. **Chief Financial Officer/President:** John Costello.

Executive Vice President/General Manager: Kelly Sufka. **Assistant General Manager:** Kyle Kreger. **Director of Corporate Partnerships:** Victoria Loughrey. **Box Office Manager:** Ryan Harris. **Ticket Sales Representatives:** Mike Evans, Jeremy Timm, Joe Verschueren. **Radio Broadcaster/Media Relations:** Jon Versteeg. **Community Sales/ Promotions Manager:** Sarah Grady. **Head Groundskeeper:** Nick Hill. **Director, Accounting/Human Resources:** Tammy Harvey. **Administrative Assistant/Team Travel Coordinator:** Sonja Little.

Manager: Wally Backman. **Coach:** Larry Olenberger.

GAME INFORMATION

Radio Announcers: Jon Versteeg and Bryan Dolgin. **No of Games Broadcast:** Home-48, Away-48. **Flagship Station:** WJOL, 1340-AM.

Stadium Name: Silver Cross Field. **Location:** I-80 to Chicago Street/Route 53 North exit, go 1/2 mile on Chicago Street, right on Washington Street to Jefferson Street/U.S. 52, right on Jefferson, ballpark on left. **Standard Game Times:** 7:05 p.m. Tues: 6:05 p.m. Sunday: 2:05/5:05 p.m.

KANSAS CITY T-BONES

Office Address: 1800 Village West Pkwy., Kansas City, KS 66111.

Telephone: (913) 328-2255. **FAX:** (913) 328-5652. **E-Mail Address:** batterup@tbones-baseball.com. **Website:** www.tbonesbaseball.com.

Operated By: T-Bones Baseball Club, LLC; Ehlert Development. **Owner, President:** John Ehlert.

Vice President: Adam Ehlert. **Vice President/General Manager:** Rick Muntean. **Assistant GM:** Chris Browne. **Director, Merchandise:** Laura Hayes. **Director, Community Relations:** Janet Lindsay. **Director, Media Relations:** Tommy Thrall. **Director, Promotions:** Colin Aldrich. **Director, Ticket Operations:** Brandon Smith. **Head Groundskeeper:** Don Frantz. **Bookkeeper:** Theresa Bird. **Box Office Manager:** Sarah Keel. **Sales Executive:** Eric Marshall.

Manager: Andy McCauley. **Coach:** Tim Doherty. **Pitching Coach:** Marty Kenney. **Trainer:** Josh Adams.

GAME INFORMATION

Radio Announcer: Tommy Thrall. **No. of Games Broadcast:** Home-48, Away-48. **Flagship Station:** WDAF 1660am. **Official Scorer:** Louis Spry.

Stadium Name: Community America Ballpark. **Location:** State Avenue West off I-435, corner of 110th and State Avenue. **Standard Game Times:** 7:05 p.m.; Sunday, 5:05.

Visiting Club Hotel: Hyatt Crown Center.

SCHAUMBURG FLYERS

Office Address: 1999 S. Springinsguth Rd., Schaumburg, IL 60193.

Telephone: (847) 891-2255. **FAX:** (847) 891-6441.

E-Mail Address: info@flyersbaseball.com. **Website:** www.flyersbaseball.com.

Principal Owners: Richard Ehrenreich, John E. **Hughes, Mike Conley. Managing Partner:** Richard Ehrenreich.

Vice President / Sales: Rick Rungaitis. **General Manager:** Morgan West. **Assistant GM/Director, Group Sales:** Scott Boor. **Assistant GM/Manager, Business Development:** Aaron Studebaker. **Director, Corporate Sales:** Steve Sullivan. **Director, Media/Community Relations:** Sarah Eichenberger. **Director, Ticket Operations:** Carly Tracey. **Director, Graphics/Publications:** Sarah Prange. **Account Executive:** Robert Heck. **Group Sales Associate:** Ray Gross. **Head**

Groundskeeper: Nathan Bradley. **Medical Director:** Tony Garofalo.

Manager: Steve Maddock. **Coach:** Tom Waelchli.

GAME INFORMATION

Radio Announcer: Unavailable. **No. of Games Broadcast:** Home-48, Away-48. **Flagship Station:** flyersbaseball.com. **PA Announcer:** Unavailable. **Official Scorer:** Mark Madorin.

Stadium Name: Alexian Field. **Location:** From north, I-290 to Elgin-O'Hare Expressway (Thorndale), west on expressway to Irving Park Road exit, left on Springinsguth under expressway, stadium on left; From south, U.S. 20 West (Lake Street) to Elgin-O'Hare Expressway (Thorndale), east on expressway, south on Springinsguth Road. **Standard Game Times:** 7:05 p.m.; Saturday, 6:20 p.m.; Sunday, 1:20 p.m.

Visiting Club Hotel: Unavailable.

WINNIPEG GOLDEYES

Office Address: One Portage Ave. E., Winnipeg, Manitoba R3B 3N3.

Telephone: (204) 982-2273. **FAX:** (204) 982-2274.

E-Mail Address: goldeyes@goldeyes.com. **Website:** www.goldeyes.com.

Operated by: Winnipeg Goldeyes Baseball Club, Inc.

Principal Owner, President: Sam Katz.

General Manager: Andrew Collier. **Director, Sales/Marketing:** Dan Chase. **Director, Communications:** Jonathan Green. **Director, Promotions:** Barb McTavish. **Director, Group Sales:** Regan Katz. **Account Representatives:** Paul Duque, Paul Edmonds, Dave Loat, Darren McCabe, Dennis McLean, Scott Taylor. **Director, Merchandising:** Carol Orchard. **Controller:** Judy Jones. **Facility Manager:** Scott Horn. **Administrative Assistants:** Bonnie Alavrez, Angela Sanche. **Head Groundskeeper:** Don Ferguson.

Manager/Director, Player Procurement: Rick Forney. **Coaches:** Rudy Arias, Tom Vaeth. **Pitching Coach:** Rich Hyde. **Trainer:** Brad Shaw.

GAME INFORMATION

Radio Announcer: Paul Edmonds. **No. of Games Broadcast:** Home-48, Road-48.

Flagship Station: CFRW 1290-AM. **PA Announcer:** Ron Arnst. **Official Scorer:** Steve Eitzen.

Stadium Name: CanWest Global Park. **Location:** Pembina Highway (Route 75), east on River Ave., north on Main Street, east on Water Ave. **Standard Game Times:** 7:05 p.m.; **Sunday, 1:**35 p.m.

Visiting Club Hotel: The Marlborough, 331 Smith St., Winnipeg, Manitoba R3B 2G9. **Telephone:** (204) 942-6411.

UNITED LEAGUE

Office Address: 920 North Sugar Road, Suite #10, Edinburg, Texas 78541. **Telephone:** (800) 930-8189 Ext. 100. **Fax:** (888) 803-6517.

E-mail Address: info@unitedleague.org. **Website:** www.unitedleague.org

Founded: 2006.

Founder/CEO: Brad Wendt.

Principal, League Properties: Gary Wendt.

League President/Executive General Manager: Craig Brasfield.

Executive General Manager, Sales/Marketing: Mike Babcock.

Chief Administrative Officer: Helen Forte.

Administrative Officer: Susan Knob. **Director, Group Sales, Rio Grande Valley:** Cory Dirksen. **Director, Accounting:** Merci Oubre. **Director, Communications:** Eileen Wright. **Director, Food/Beverage:** John Ciarrachi. **Director, Media Relations:** Danny Garza. **Director, Umpires:** Woodie Belle.

Regular Season: 90 games, split-season. **2008 Opening Date:** May 13. **Closing Date:** Aug. 17.

Playoff Format: Top four teams meet in best of three series. Winners meet in best of three championship series.

All-Star Game: July 15 at San Angelo vs. Golden League All-Stars.

Roster Limit: 24

Eligibility Rules: None.

Brand of Baseball: Spalding.

Statistician: PA Sportsticker

STADIUM INFORMATION

			Dimensions				
Club	**Stadium**	**Opened**	**LF**	**CF**	**RF**	**Capacity**	**2007 Att.**
Alexandria	Bringhurst Field	1933	315	385	315	3,200	71,204
Amarillo	Dilla Villa	1956	330	420	330	7,500	153,262
Edinburg	Edinburg Stadium	2001	325	400	325	5,500	85,556
Laredo	Veterans Field	1950	320	400	340	5,000	57,908
Harlingen	Harlingen Field	1950	330	400	330	4,500	74,663
San Angelo	Foster Field	2000	325	405	325	4,000	106,411

ALEXANDRIA ACES

Office Address: 1 Babe Ruth Drive; Alexandria, LA 71301

Telephone: (800) 930-8189 Ext 200. **Fax:** (888) 480-2794.

E-mail Address: aces@unitedleague.org. **Website:** www.myacesbaseball.com

General Manager: Chet Carey. **Assistant GM:** Andrew Aguilar. **Office Manager:** Merci Oubre. **Director, Stadium Operations:** Jodie White. **Director, Ticket/Group Sales:** Amy Dox. **Director, Food Services:** Grady Welch. **Director, Special Projects:** Ricky Doyle. **Head Groundskeeper:** John Hickman. **Clubhouse Operations:** Ricky Doyle, Jr. **Visiting Clubhouse Manager:** Eric Doyle.

Manager/Director Player Personnel: Ricky VanAsselberg. **Coach:** Dusty Vercher. **Team Doctor:** Dr. **Chris Rich. Trainers:** Chuck Estave, Jeff Hammond.

GAME INFORMATION

Radio Announcer: Lyn Rollins. **No. of Games Broadcast:** 90. **Website:** www.myacesbaseball.com

PA Announcer: Rich Dupree. **Music Coordinator:** Kenneth Strother. **Scoreboard/Message Center Operator:** Josh Dupree. **Official Scorer:** Jim Smilie.

Stadium: Bringhurst Field. **Standard Game Time:** 7:05 p.m.; Sundays, 5:05 p.m.

Visiting Club Hotel: Rodeway Inn, 2211 N. MacArthur Drive, Alexandria, LA 71303. **Phone:** (318) 484-9530.

AMARILLO DILLAS

Office Address: 801 S Polk Amarillo, TX 79106.

Telephone: (806) 342-0400. **Fax:** (806) 342-0407.

E-mail Address: mlee@unitedleague.org. **Website:** www.amarillodillasbaseball.com.

General Manager: Mark Lee. **Director, Marketing/Sales:** Rhonda Dittfurth. **VP, Marketing/Promotions:** Johnny Leigh. **Director, Sales/Stadium Operation:** Marcus Langford. **Director, Sales/Head Groundskeeper:** Brett Myers. **Office Manager/Ticket manager:** Jaylin Henderson.

Manager: Brady Bogart. **Coaches:** Unavailable.

GAME INFORMATION

Radio Announcer: Ben Miller. **No. of Games Broadcast:** 90. **PA Announcer:** Joe Frank Wheeler. **Official Scorer:** Wade Coulter.

Standard Game Time: 7:05 p.m. **Visiting Club Hotel:** La Kiva Hotel, 2501 I–40 East, Amarillo, TX 79104, (806) 379-6555.

EDINBURG COYOTES

Office Address: 920 North Sugar Road; Edinburg, TX 78541. **Telephone:** (800) 930-8189 Ext 400. **Fax:** (888) 480-2794.

E-mail Address: edinburgcoyotes@unitedleague.org. **Website:** www.edinburgcoyotes.com

General Manager: Tuffy Martinez. **Assistant General Manager/Director, Sales:** Omar Ortiz. **Director, Community Relations/Group Sales:** Annalisa Limas. **Director, Game Operations/Asst. Director, Sales:** Ben De La Paz. **Director, Stadium Operations/Clubhouse Manager:** Jarod Hickle. **Director, Food/Beverage:** Isaac Briones. **Director, Media Relations:** Danny Garza. **Office Manager:** Lupita Gomez

Manager/Director Player Personnel: Vince Moore. **Trainer:** Unavailable

GAME INFORMATION

Radio Announcer: Ben De La Paz. **No. of Games Broadcast:** 90. **Website:** www.edinburgcoyotes.com

PA Announcer: Unavailable. **Official Scorer:** Unavailable.

Stadium: Edinburg Stadium. **Standard Game Time:** 7:05 p.m.

Visiting Club Hotel: Unavailable.

HARLINGEN WHITEWINGS

Office Address: 1216 Fair Park Blvd, Harlingen, TX 78550. **Telephone:** (956) 412-WING (9464). **Fax:** (956) 412-9479.

E-mail Address: dkost@unitedleague.org. **Website:** www.whitewingsbaseball.com.

Vice President, Baseball Operations/General Manager: Dave Kost. **Assistant General Manager, Sales/Marketing:** Fernando Toledo. **Assistant General Manager, Baseball Operations:** Heath Brown. **Director, Ticket Operations:** Dan Ramirez. **Director, Media Operations/Broadcasting:** Jonah Goldberg. **Director, Community Relations/Guest Services:** Noel Espinosa. **Office Manager/Corporate Relations:** Beverly Woodward.

Manager: Alan Gallagher. **Trainer:** Unavailable.

GAME INFORMATION

Radio Announcer: Jonah Goldberg. **No. of Games Broadcast:** 90. **Flagship Station:** Unavailable. **PA Announcer:** Unavailable. **Official Scorer:** Unavailable.

Standard Game Time: 7:05 p.m. **Visiting Club Hotel:** Harlingen Hotel/Event Center.

LAREDO BRONCOS

Office Address: 2200 Santa Maria, Laredo, TX 78040. **Mailing Address:** P.O. Box 2836, Laredo, TX 78044. **Telephone:** (800) 930-8189 Ext. 600. **Fax:** (888) 480-2810.

E-mail Address: jmelendez@unitedleague.org. **Website:** www.laredobroncos.com.

General Manager: Jose Melendez. **Assistant General Manager/Operations:** Albert Herrera. **Director, Community Relations:** Doug Robinson. **Director, New Business Development:** Jon Hinkel.

Manager/Director Player Personnel: Dan Shwam. **Coach:** John Hinkel. **Trainers:** Ernst Feisner, JoJo Villareal.

GAME INFORMATION

Radio Announcer: Unavailable. **No. of Games Broadcast:** 90 . **Website:** www.laredobroncos.com.

PA Announcer: Chema Guevara. **Official Scorer:** Gable Blakely.

Stadium: Veterans Field. **Standard Game Time:** 7:35 p.m.

Visiting Club Hotel: Unavailable.

SAN ANGELO COLTS

Office Address: 1600 University, San Angelo, TX 76951.
Telephone: (325) 942-6587. **Fax:** (325) 947-9480.
E-mail Address: mbabcock@unitedleague.org. **Website:** www.sanangelocolts.com.

General Manager: Mike Babcock. **Assistant General Manager:** Mary Larson. **Stadium Superintendent:** Joe Stapp. **Director, Business Operations:** Ken Franz. **Director, Sales:** Rob Gusick. **Director, Media Operations/Broadcasting:** Frank Mentesana. **Office Manager:** Lea Self.

Manager/Director, Player Personnel: Doc Edwards. **Trainers:** Randy Matthews, Joe Briley.

GAME INFORMATION

Radio Announcer: Frank Mentesana. **No. of Games Broadcast:** 100. **Flagship Station:** KCLL-100.1 FM. **PA Announcer:** Jeremy Bryant. **Official Scorer:** Bill Mahr. **Standard Game Time:** 7:05 p.m. **Visiting Club Hotel:** Best Western.

CONTINENTAL LEAGUE

Office Address: 16633 Dallas Parkway, Suite 600, Addison, TX 751.

Telephone: (214) 234-0018. **Fax:** (972)-588-3363

Website: www.cblproball.com.

Chief Executive Officer/President: Ron Baron.

Director, League Operations/Communications: Bob Ibach. **Director, Marketing:** Laura Keith. **Director, Team Relations:** Jay Johnstone.

Year Founded: 2007.

Regular Season: 72 games. **2008 Opening Date:** May 23. **Closing Date:** August 17.

All-Star Game: July 8.

Playoff Format: Top two teams (best-of-five series).

Roster Limit: 25.

Team Owners: Larry Faulkner (McKinney), Frank Snyder (Texarkana), Ron Baron (Corpus Christi), Local Investor Group (Houston-Bay Area Toros);

Official Baseball: Unavailable. **Statistician:** Unavailable

SOUTH COAST LEAGUE

Telephone: (478) 314-7251 Fax: (478) 314-7252.

Website: www.southcoastleague.com. **E-Mail:** info@southcoastleague.com.

Chief Executive Officer: Jamie Toole. **Chief Development Officer:** JD Hardin.

Vice President, Sales/Marketing: Steven Tricarico. **Vice President, South Carolina Operations:** Garrett Ball. **Director, Baseball Operations:** James Gamble. **Coordinator, Operations:** Chris Deines. **Director, Umpires:** Cord Coslor.

League Founded: 2007

Member Clubs: Aiken (S.C.) Foxhounds, Bradenton (Fla.) Juice, Charlotte County (Fla.) Redfish, Jackson (MS), Macon (Ga.) Music, South Georgia Peanuts. **Roster Limit:** 21.

Player Eligibility Rule: No age limit. Any player age 27 or older must receive league office approval prior to signing.

Regular Season: 80 games. **2008 Opening Date:** May 15. **Closing Date:** Aug. **15.**

All-Star Game: No game scheduled.

Playoffs: Two teams qualify, first-half and second-half winners. In case of a tie, or if the same team wins both halves of the season, a wild card will be awarded to the team with the second-best overall winning percentage. Championship is a best-of-three series.

Official Baseball: Spalding.

Official Statistician: Howe Sportsdata/SportsTicker.

STADIUM INFORMATION

			Dimensions				
Club	**Stadium**	**Opened**	**LF**	**CF**	**RF**	**Capacity**	**2007 Att.**
Aiken	Roberto Hernandez Stadium	2004	330	400	330	2,000	42,225
Bradenton	Robert C. Wynn Field	1967	330	405	330	1,500	27,999
Charlotte County	Charlotte County Stadium	1987	334	410	334	5,321	58,444
Jackson	Smith-Willis Field	1975	330	400	330	5,200	—
Macon	Luther Williams Field	1929	335	405	335	4,000	73,655
South Georgia	Paul Eames Stadium	1993	310	300	335	3,500	49,353

INTERNATIONAL

AMERICAS

MEXICO

MEXICAN LEAGUE

Member, National Association

NOTE: The Mexican League is a member of the National Association of Professional Baseball Leagues and has a Triple-A classification. However, its member clubs operate largely independent of the 30 major league teams, and for that reason the league is listed in the international section.

Mailing Address: Angel Pola No. 16, Col. Periodista, CP 11220, Mexico, D.F. **Telephone:** (52) 555-557-1007. **Fax:** (52) 555-395-2454. **E-Mail Address:** oficina@lmb.com.mx. **Website:** www.lmb.com.mx.

Years League Active: 1955-.

President: Plinio Escalante Bolio. **Operations Manager:** Nestor Alba Brito.

Division Structure: North—Aquascalientes, Laguna, Monclova, Monterrey, Puebla, San Luis, Saltillo, Tijuana. South—Angelopolis, Campeche, Mexico City, Minatitlan, Oaxaca, Tabasco, Veracruz, Yucatan.

Regular Season: 110 games (split-schedule). **2008 Opening Date:** March 18. **Closing Date:** July 27.

All-Star Game: May 31, site unavailable.

Playoff Format: Top six teams in each division qualify; first- and second-place teams in each division receive first-round byes. First, second and semifinal rounds are best-of-seven series; division champions meet in best-of-seven series for league championship.

Roster Limit: 28. **Roster Limit, Imports:** 6.

PIRATAS DE CAMPECHE

Office Address: Unidad Deportiva 20 de Noviembre, Local 4, CP 24000, Campeche, Campeche. **Telephone:** (52) 981-816-2116. **Fax:** (52) 981-816-3807. **E-Mail Address:** Unavailable. **Website:** www.piratasdecampeche.com.mx.

President: Gabriel Escalante Castillo. **General Manager:** Maria del Socorro Morales.

Manager: Manual Cazarin.

DORADOS DE CHIHUAHUA

Office Address: Blvd. Juan Pablo II No. 4506, Col. Aeropuerto CP 31380. **Telephone:** (52) 614-459-0317. **Fax:** (52) 614-459-0336. **E-Mail Address:** Unavailable. **Website:** www.tunerosdeslp.com.

President: Marcelo de los Santos. **General Manager:** Leonardo Clayton Rodriguez.

Manager: Dan Firova.

VAQUEROS LAGUNA

Office Address: Juan Gutenberg s/n, Col. Centro, CP 27000, Torreon, Coahuila. **Telephone:** (52) 871-718-5515. **Fax:** (52) 871-717-4335. **E-Mail Address:** unionlag@prodigy.net.mx. **Website:** www.clubvaqueroslaguna.com.

President: Carlos Gomez del Campo. **General Manager:** Carlos de la Garza.

Manager: Fernando Elizardo.

DIABLOS ROJOS DEL MEXICO

Office Address: Av. Cuauhtemoc #451-101, Col. Narvarte, CP 03020, Mexico DF. **Telephone:** (52) 555-639-8722. **Fax:** (52) 555-639-9722. **E-Mail Address:** diablos@sportsya.com. **Website:** www.diablos.com.mx.

President: Roberto Mansur Galán. **General Manager:** Eduardo de la Cerda.

Manager: Marco Antonio Vazquez.

ACEREROS DE MONCLOVA

Office Address: Cuauhtemoc #299, Col. Ciudad Deportiva, CP 25750, Monclova, Coahuila. **Telephone:** (52) 866-636-2334. **Fax:** (52) 866-636-2688. **E-Mail Address:** acererosdelnorte@prodigy.net.mx. **Website:** www.acereros.com.mx.

President: Donaciano Garza Gutierrez. **General Manager:** Victor Favela Lopez.

Manager: Unavailable.

SULTANES DE MONTERREY

Office Address: Av. Manuel Barragan s/n, Estadio Monterrey, Apartado Postal 870, Monterrey, Nuevo Leon, CP 66460. **Telephone:** (52) 818-351-0209. **Fax:** (52) 818-351-8022. **E-Mail Address:** sultanes@sultanes.com.mx. **Website:** www.sultanes.com.mx.

President: José Maiz García. **General Manager:** Roberto Magdaleno Ramírez.

Manager: Bernardo Tatis.

TECOLATES DE NUEVO LAREDO

Office Address: Calle Manuel Madrigal y Juan de la Barrera, Colonia Heroes, Aguascalientes, Aguascalientes, CP 20250. **Telephone:** (52) 449-970-4585. **E-Mail Address:** rieleros@lmb.com.mx. **Website:** www.rielerosdeaguascalientes.com.

President: Jean Paul Mansur Beltran. **General Manager:** Carlos Hernandez.

Manager: Alex Taveras.

GUERREROS DE OAXACA

Office Address: Privada del Chopo #105, Fraccionamiento El Chopo, CP 68050, Oaxaca, Oaxaca. **Telephone:** (52) 951-515-5522. **Fax:** (52) 951-515-4966. **E-Mail Address:** guerreros@infosel.net.mx. **Website:** www.guerrerosdeoaxaca.com.

President: Vicente Pérez Avellá Villa. **General Manager:** Jose Diaz del la Vega.

Manager: Homer Rojas Villarreal.

PETROLEROS DE MINATITLAN

Club Information Unavailable.

Manager: Edgar Castro.

PERICOS DE PUEBLA

Office Address: Calle Paseo de las Fuentes, #13 Col Arboledas de Guadelupe, CP 72210, Puebla, Puebla. **Telephone:** (52) 222-236-3313. **Fax:** (52) 222-236-2906. **E-Mail Address:** oficina@pericosdepuebla.com.mx. **Website:** www.pericosdepuebla.com.mx.

President: Hassan Taja Abraham. **General Manager:** Francisco Minjarez Garcia.

Manager: Unavailable.

TIGRES DE QUINTANA ROO

Office Address: Calle Paseo de las Fuentes, #13 Col. Arbodedas de Guadelupe, CP 72210, Puebla, Puebla. **Telephone:** (52) 222-236-4909. **Fax:** (52) 222-234-0192. **E-Mail Address:** tigres@tigrescapitalinos.com.mx. **Website:** www.tigresdemexico.com.mx.

President: Cuauhtémoc Rodriguez. **General Manager:** Iram Campos Lara.

Manager: Unavailable.

SARAPEROS DE SALTILLO

Office Address: Blvd. Nazario Ortiz Esquina con Blvd. Jesus Sanchez, CP 25280, Saltillo, Coahuila. **Telephone:** (52) 844-416-9455. **Fax:** (52) 844-439-1330. **E-Mail Address:**

aley@grupoley.com. **Website:** www.saraperos.com.mx.

President: Juan Manuel Ley. **General Manager:** Eduardo Valenzuela Guajardo.

Manager: Derek Bryant.

OLMECAS DE TABASCO

Office Address: Explanada de la Ciudad Deportiva, Parque de Beisbol Centenario del 27 de Febrero, Col. Atasta de Serra, CP 86100, Villahermosa, Tabasco. **Telephone:** (52) 993-352-2787. **Fax:** (52) 993-352-2788. **E-Mail Address:** olmecastab@prodigy.net.mx. **Website:** www.olmecasde-tabasco.com.mx.

President: Raul Gonzalez Rodriguez. **General Manager:** Luis Guzman Ramos.

Manager: Mario Mendoza Aizpuro.

POTROS DE TIJUANA

Office Address: Blvd. Insurgentes 17017-21, Colonia Los Alamos, Tijuana, Baja California, Mexico 22320. **Telephone:**(52) 664-621-3787. **Fax:** (52) 664-621-3883. **E-Mail Address:** potros@potrosdetijuana.com. **Website:** www.potrosdetijuana.com.

President: Belisario Cabrera. **General Manager:** Raul Cano.

Manager: Domingo Rivera.

ROJOS DEL AGUILA DE VERACRUZ

Office Address: Av. Jacarandas s/n, Esquina España, Fraccionamiento Virginia, CP 94294, Boca del Rio, Veracruz. **Telephone:** (52) 229-935-5004. **Fax:** (229) 935-5008. **E-Mail Address:** rojosdelaguila@terra.com.mx. **Website:** www.aguiladeveracruz.com.

President: Jose Antonio Mansur Beltran. **General Manager:** Carlos Nahun Hernandez.

Manager: Juan Jose Pacho Burgos.

LEONES DE YUCATAN

Office Address: Calle 50 #406-B, Entre 35 y 37, Col. Jesus Carranza, CP 97109, Merida, Yucatán. **Telephone:** (52) 999-926-3022. **Fax:** (52) 999-926-3631. **E-Mail Addresses:** leonesy@sureste.com. **Website:** www.leonesdeyucatan.com.mx.

President: Gustavo Ricalde Durán. **General Manager:** Jose Rivero.

Manager: Lino Rivera.

MEXICAN ACADEMY

Rookie Classification

Mailing Address: Angel Pola No. 16, Col. Periodista, CP 11220, Mexico, D.F. **Telephone:** (52) 555-557-1007. **Fax:** (52) 555-395-2454. **E-Mail Address:** mbl@prodigy.net.mx. **Website:** www.lmb.com.mx.

Member Clubs: Celaya, Guanajuato, Queretaro, Salamanca.

Regular Season: 50 games. **2008 Opening Date:** Oct. 9. **Closing Date:** Dec. 21.

DOMINICAN REPUBLIC

DOMINICAN SUMMER LEAGUE

Member, National Association

Rookie Classification

Mailing Address: Calle Segunda No. 64, Reparto Antilla, Santo Domingo, Dominican Republic. **Telephone/Fax:** (809) 532-3619. **Website:** www.dominicansummerleague.com. **E-Mail Address:** ligadeverano@codetel.net.do.

Years League Active: 1985-.

President: Freddy Jana. **Administrative Assistant:** Orlando Diaz.

2008 Member Clubs/Participating Organizations: Angels, Astros, Athletics I, Athletics II, Blue Jays, Braves I, Braves II, Cardinals, Cubs, Diamondbacks, Dodgers I, Dodgers II, Giants, Indians I, Indians II, Mariners, Marlins, Mets, Nationals, Orioles, Padres, Phillies, Pirates, Rangers, Reds, Red Sox, Rockies, Royals, Tigers, Twins, White Sox, Yankees I, Yankees II.

Regular Season: 70-72 games, depending on divisions. **2008 Opening Date:** June 4. **Closing Date:** Aug. 24.

Playoff Format: Six divisions; two division champions with best winning percentages receive first-round byes. Four teams meet in best-of-three quarterfinals; winners and division champions with first-round byes meet in best-of-three semifinals; winners meet in best-of-five series for league championship.

Roster Limit: 35; 30 active. **Player Eligibility Rule:** No more than eight players 20 or older and no more than two players 21 or older. At least 10 players must be pitchers. No more than four years of prior service, excluding Rookie leagues outside the U.S. and Canada.

VENEZUELA

VENEZUELAN SUMMER LEAGUE

Member, National Association

Rookie Classification

Mailing Address: C.C. Caribbean Plaza Modulo 8, P.A. Local 173-174, Valencia, Carabobo, Venezuela. **Telephone:** (58) 241-824-0321, (011) 58-241-824-0980. **Fax:** (58) 241-824-0705. **Website:** www.vsl.com.ve.

Years League Active: 1997-.

Administrator: Saul Gonzalez Acevedo. **Coordinator:** Ramon Feriera.

2008 Member Clubs: Aguirre, Cagua, Ciudad Alienza, San Joaquin, Troconero 1, Tronconero 2, Universidad, Venoco 1, Venoco 2. **Participating Organizations:** Astros, Blue Jays, Mariners, Marlins, Mets, Orioles, Phillies, Pirates, Reds, Red Sox, Rockies, Twins.

Regular Season: 60 games. **2008 Opening Date:** May 16. **Closing Date:** Aug. 28.

Playoffs: Best-of-three series between top two teams in regular season.

Roster Limit: 35; 30 active. **Player Eligibility Rule:** No player on active list may have more than three years of minor league service. Open to players from all Latin American Spanish-speaking countries except the Dominican Republic and Puerto Rico.

ASIA

CHINA

CHINA BASEBALL ASSOCIATION

Mailing Address: 5, Tiyuguan Road, Beijing 100763, Peoples Republic of China. **Telephone:** (011-86) 10-85826002. **Fax:** (011-86) 10-85825994. **E-Mail Address:** chinabaseball2008@yahoo.com.cn.

Years League Active: 2002-.

Chairman: Hu Jian Guo. **Vice Chairmen:** Tom McCarthy, Shen Wei. **Executive Director:** Yang Jie. **General Manager, Marketing/Promotion:** Lin Xiao Wu.

Member Clubs: Beijing Tigers, China Hopestars, Guangdong Leopards, Shanghai Eagles, Sichuan Dragons, Tianjin Lions.

Regular Season: 30 games.

Playoff Format: Top two teams meet in best-of-five series for league championship.

Import Rule: Three players on active roster.

JAPAN

Mailing Address: Imperial Tower, 14F, 1-1-1 Uchisaiwai-cho, Chiyoda-ku, Tokyo 100-0011. **Telephone:** 03-3502-0022. **Fax:** 03-3502-0140.

Commissioner: Yasuchika Negoro.

Executive Secretary: Kazuo Hasegawa. **Executive Director:** Kunio Shimoda. **Director, Baseball Operations:** Nobby Ito. **Public Relations Director:** Minoru Hirata..

Japan Series: Best-of-seven series between Central and Pacific League champions, begins Nov. 1 at home of Central League club.

All-Star Series: July 31 at Kyocera Dome, Osaka; Aug. 1 at Yokohama Stadium.

Roster Limit: 70 per organization (one major league club, one minor league club). Major league club is permitted to register 28 players at a time, though just 25 may be available for each game.

Roster Limit, Imports: Four in majors (no more than three position players or pitchers); unlimited in minors.

CENTRAL LEAGUE

Mailing Address: Asahi Bldg. 3F, 6-6-7 Ginza, Chuo-ku, Tokyo 104-0061. **Telephone:** 03-3572-1673. **Fax:** 03-3571-4545.

President: Hajime Toyokura.

Secretary General: Hideo Okoshi. **Planning Department:** Masaaki Nagino. **Public Relations:** Kazu Ogaki.

Regular Season: 144 games. **2008 Opening Date:** March 28. **Closing Date:** Sept. 24.

Playoff Format: Second-place team meets third-place team in best-of-three series. Winner meets first-place team in best-of-five series to determine league's representative in Japan Series.

CHUNICHI DRAGONS

Mailing Address: Chunichi Bldg. 6F, 4-1-1 Sakae, Naka-ku, Nagoya 460-0008. **Telephone:** 052-261-8811. **Fax:** 052-263-7696. **Chairman:** Bungo Shirai. **President:** Junnosuke Nishikawa. **General Manager:** Kazumasa Ito. **Field Manager:** Hiromitsu Ochiai.

2008 Foreign Players: Rafael Cruz, Tomas de la Rosa, Lee Byung Kyu, Tyrone Woods, Chen Wei Yin.

HANSHIN TIGERS

Mailing Address: 2-33 Koshien-cho, Nishinomiya-shi, Hyogo-ken 663-8152. **Telephone:** 0798-46-1515. **Fax:** 0798-46-3555. **Chairman:** Tsuneaki Miyazaki. **President:** Nobuo Minami. **Field Manager:** Akinobu Okada.

2008 Foreign Players: Scott Atchison, Lew Ford, Ryan Vogelsong, Jeff Williams.

HIROSHIMA TOYO CARP

Mailing Address: 5-25 Motomachi, Naka-ku, Hiroshima 730-8508. **Telephone:** 082-221-2040. **Fax:** 082-228-5013. **President:** Hajime Matsuda. **General Manager:** Kiyoaki Suzuki. **Field Manager:** Marty Brown.

2008 Foreign Players: Ben Kozlowski, Colby Lewis, Victor Marte, Alex Ochoa, Scott Seabol, Mike Schultz. **Coach:** Jeff Livesey.

TOKYO YAKULT SWALLOWS

Mailing Address: Shimbashi MCV Bldg. 5F, 5-13-5 Shimbashi, Minato-ku, Tokyo 105-0004. **Telephone:** 03-5470-8915. **Fax:** 03-5470-8916. **Chairman:** Sumiya Hori. **President:** Tadashi Suzuki. **General Manager:** Kesanori Kurashima. **Field Manager:** Shigeru Takada.

2008 Foreign Players: Dicky Gonzalez, Aaron Guiel, Adam Riggs, Daniel Rios, Lim Chang Yong.

YOKOHAMA BAYSTARS

Mailing Address: Kannai Arai Bldg, 7F, 1-8 Onoe-cho, Naka-ku, Yokohama 231-0015. **Telephone:** 045-681-0811. **Fax:** 045-661-2500. **Chairman:** Kiyoshi Wakabayashi. **President:** Kuniaki Sasaki. **Field Manager:** Akihiko Oya.

2008 Foreign Players: Larry Bigbie, J.J. Furmaniak, Travis Hughes, Matt White, Dave Williams, Mike Wood. **Coach:** John Turney.

YOMIURI GIANTS

Mailing Address: Otemachi Nomura Bldg., 7F, 2-1-1 Otemachi, Chiyoda-ku, Tokyo 100-8151. **Telephone:** 03-3246-7733. **Fax:** 03-3246-2726. **Chairman:** Takuo Takihana. **President:** Tsunekazu Momoi. **General Manager:** Hidetoshi Kiyotake. **Field Manager:** Tatsunori Hara.

2008 Foreign Players: Adrian Burnside, Chiang Chien-ming, Luis Gonzalez, Seth Greisinger, Marc Kroon, Alex Ramirez, Lee Seung-Yeop.

PACIFIC LEAGUE

Mailing Address: Asahi Bldg. 9F, 6-6-7 Ginza, Chuo-ku, Tokyo 104-0061. **Telephone:** 03-3573-1551. **Fax:** 03-3572-5843.

President: Tadao Koike. **Secretary General:** Shigeru Murata. **General Affairs Director:** Shiromitsu Hanai. **Administration:** Kazuo Nakano.

Regular Season: 144 games. **2008 Opening Date:** March 20. **Closing Date:** Oct. 1.

Playoff Format: Second-place team meets third-place team in best-of-three series. Winner meets first-place team in best-of-five series to determine league's representative in Japan Series.

CHIBA LOTTE MARINES

Mailing Address: 1 Mihama, Mihama-ku, Chiba-shi, Chiba-ken 261-8587. **Telephone:** 043-296-1450. **Fax:** 043-296-7496. **Chairman:** Takeo Shigemitsu. **President:** Ryuzo Setoyama. **Field Manager:** Bobby Valentine.

2008 Foreign Players: Winston Abreu, Benny Agbayani, Jose Ortiz, Brian Sikorski, Wu Szu Yo, Julio Zuleta. **Coaches:** Frank Ramppen, Lyle Yates. **Minor League Manager:** Lenn Sakata.

FUKUOKA SOFTBANK HAWKS

Mailing Address: Fukuoka Yahoo! Japan Dome, Hawks Town, Chuo-ku, Fukuoka 810-0065. **Telephone:** 092-844-1189. **Fax:** 092-844-4600. **Chairman:** Masayoshi Son. **President:** Kazuhiko Kasai. **General Manager:** Sadaharu Oh. **Field Manager:** Sadaharu Oh.

2008 Foreign Players: Rick Guttormson, D.J. Houlton, C.J. Nitkowski, Michael Restovich, Jason Standridge, Yang Yao-hsun.

HOKKAIDO NIPPON HAM FIGHTERS

Mailing Address: 1 Hitsujigaoka, Toyohira-ku, Sapporo 062-8655. **Telephone:** 011-857-7786. **Fax:** 011-857-3900. **Chairman:** Hiroji Okoso. **President:** Junichi Fujii. **General Manager:** Masao Yamada. **Field Manager:** Masataka Nashida.

2008 Foreign Players: Ryan Glynn, Mitch Jones, Terrmel Sledge, Brian Sweeney.

ORIX BUFFALOES

Mailing Address: Dojima Grand Bldg., 8F, 1-5-17 Dojima, Kita-ku, Osaka 530-0003. **Telephone:** 06-4799-6688. **Fax:** 06-4799-6711. **Chairman:** Yoshihiko Miyauchi. **General Manager:** Katsuhiro Nakamura. **Field Manager:** Terry Collins.

2008 Foreign Players: Alex Cabrera, Tom Davey, Greg LaRocca, Tuffy Rhodes. **Coaches:** Mike Brown, Jon Debus.

SAITAMA SEIBU LIONS

Mailing Address: 2135 Kami-Yamaguchi, Tokorozawa-shi, Saitama-ken 359-1189. **Telephone:** 04-2924-1155. **Fax:** 04-2928-1919. **President:** Shinji Kobayashi. **Field Manager:** Hisanobu Watanabe.

2008 Foreign Players: Hiram Bocachica, Craig Brazell, Alex Graman, Matt Kinney, Hsu Ming-chieh.

TOHOKU RAKUTEN GOLDEN EAGLES

Mailing Address: 2-11-6 Miyagino, Miyagino-ku, Sendai-shi, Miyagi-ken 983-0045. **Telephone:** 022-298-5300. **Fax:** 022-298-5360. **Chairman:** Hiroshi Mikitani. **President:** Toru Shimada. **Field Manager:** Katsuya Nomura.

2008 Foreign Players: Lin En-yu, Jose Fernandez, Domingo Guzman, Rick Short, Lin Ying-chieh.

KOREA

KOREA BASEBALL ORGANIZATION

Mailing Address: 946-16 Dokokdong, Kangnam-gu, Seoul, Korea. **Telephone:** (02) 3460-4632. **Fax:** (02) 3460-4639.

Years League Active: 1982-.

Website: www.koreabaseball.com.

Commissioner: Shin Sang-woo. **Secretary General:** Ha Il-sung. **Deputy Secretary General:** Lee Sang-il.

Division Structure: None.

Regular Season: 126 games. **2008 Opening Date:** Unavailable.

Playoffs: Third- and fourth-place teams meet in best-of-three series; winner advances to meet second-place team in best-of-five series; winner meets first-place team in best-of-seven Korean Series for league championship.

Roster Limit: 26 active through Sept. 1, when rosters expand to 31. **Imports:** Two active.

CENTENNIAL INVESTMENT

Centennial Investment purchased the club formerly known as the Hyundai Unicorns, but had not worked out any details about the club's operation by press time. The club is expected to play in Seoul.

DOOSAN BEARS

Mailing Address: Chamsil Baseball Stadium, 10 Chamsil-1 dong, Songpa-ku, Seoul, Korea 138-221. **Telephone:** (02) 2240-1777. **Fax:** (02) 2240-1788. **Website:** www.doosan-bears.com. **President:** Kim Jin. **General Manager:** Kim Seung-young. **Manager:** Kim Kyung-Moon.

HANHWA EAGLES

Mailing Address: 22-1 Youngjeon-dong, Dong-ku, Daejeon, Korea 300-200. **Telephone:** (042) 637-6001. **Fax:** (042) 632-2929. **Website:** www.hanwhaeagles.co.kr. **President:** Lee Kyung-jae. **General Manager:** Song Kyu-Soo. **Manager:** Kim In-sik.

KIA TIGERS

Mailing Address: 266 Naebang-dong, Seo-ku, Gwangju, Korea 502-807. **Telephone:** (062) 370-1895. **Fax:** (062) 525-5350. **Website:** www.kiatigers.co.kr. **President:** Cho Nam-hong. **General Manager:** Jeong Jae-kong. **Manager:** Seo Jung-hwan.

LG TWINS

Mailing Address: Chamshil Baseball Stadium, 10 Chamshil 1-dong, Songpa-ku, Seoul, Korea 138-221. **Telephone:** (02) 2005-5760-5. **Fax:** (02) 2005-5801. **Website:** www.lgtwins.com. **President:** Kim Young-soo. **General Manager:** Kim Yeong-joong. **Manager:** Kim Jae-park.

LOTTE GIANTS

Mailing Address: 930 Sajik-dong Dongrae-Ku, Pusan, Korea, 607-120. **Telephone:** (051) 505-7422. **Fax:** 51-506-0090. **Website:** www.lotte-giants.co.kr. **President:** Ha Young-chul. **General Manager:** Lee Sang-koo. **Manager:** Jerry Royster.

SAMSUNG LIONS

Mailing Address: 184-3, Sunhwari-jinrliangyun, Kyungsan, Kyungsan, Kyungsangbuk-do, Korea 712-830. **Telephone:** (053) 859-3114. **Fax:** (053) 859-3117. **Website:** www.samsunglions.com. **President:** Kim Eung-yong. **General Manager:** Kim Jae-ha. **Manager:** Sun Dong-yeol.

SK WYVERNS

Mailing Address: 8 San, Moonhak-dong, Nam-ku, Inchon, Korea 402-070. **Telephone:** (032) 422-7949. **Fax:** (032) 429-4565. **Website:** www.skwyvers.com. **President:** Shin Young-chul. **General Manager:** Myung Young-chul. **Manager:** Kim Sung-keun.

TAIWAN

CHINESE PROFESSIONAL BASEBALL LEAGUE

Mailing Address: 2F, No. 32, Pateh Road, Sec. 3, Taipei, Taiwan. **Telephone:** 886-2-2577-6992. **Fax:** 886-2-2577-2606. **Website:** www.cpbl.com.tw.

Years League Active: 1990-.

Commissioner: Shou-Po Chao. **Secretary General:** Wayne Lee.

Member Clubs: Brother Elephants (Taipei), China Trust

Whales (Chiayi City), President Lions (Tainan), Sinon Bulls (Taichung), La New Bears (Kaohsiung), Cobras (Taipei).

Regular Season: 100 games. **2008 Opening Date:** Unavailable.

Playoffs: Second- and third-place teams meet in best-of-seven series; winner advances to meet first-place team in best-of-seven championship series.

Import Rule: Only three import players may be active, and only two may be on the field at the same time.

EUROPE

HOLLAND

DUTCH MAJOR LEAGUE

Mailing Address: Koninklijke Nederlandse Baseball en Softball Bond (Royal Dutch Baseball and Softball Association), Postbus 2650, 3430 GB Nieuwegein, Holland. **Telephone:** 31-(0) 30-751-3650. **FAX:** 31-30-751-3651. **Website:** www.knbsb.nl.

President: Hans Meijer.

ADO

Mailing Address: Dr. G. Knuttlepark 93, 2552 LK Den Haag. **Telephone:** +31 (0) 64-583-7439. **Website:** www.svado.nl.

ALMERE '90

Mailing Address: B.S.C. Almere '90, Postbus 1076, 1300 BB Almere. **Telephone:** +31 (0) 36-549-9540. **Website:** www.almere90.nl.

AMSTERDAM PIRATES

Mailing Address: Postbus 8862, 1006 JB Amsterdam. **Telephone:** +31 (0) 20-612-6969. **Website:** www.amsterdampirates.nl.

HCAW

Mailing Address: Mr. Cocker HCAW, Postbus 1321, 1400 BH Bussum. **Telephone:** +31 (0) 35-693-1430. **Website:** www.hcaw.nl.

HOOFDDORP PIONIERS

Mailing Address: Postbus 475, 2130 AL Hoofddorp. **Telephone:** +31 (0) 23-561-3557. **Website:** www.hoofddorp-pioniers.nl.

KINHEIM

Mailing Address: Gemeentelijk Sportpark, Badmintonpad, 2023 BT Haarlem. **Telephone:** +31 (0) 23-526-0021. **Website:** www.kinheim.net.

NEPTUNUS

Mailing Address: Familiestadion Sportclub Neptunus, Abraham van Stolkweg 31, 3041 JA Rotterdam. **Telephone:** +31 (0) 10-462-5859. **Website:** www.neptunussport.com.

RCH PINGUINS

Mailing Address: Mediamonks RCH, Kantine "De Kuil", Ringvaartlaan 2, 2103 XW Heemstede. **Telephone:** +31 (0) 23-528-4388. **Website:** www.rch-pinguins.nl.

SPARTA/FEYENOORD

Mailing Address: Postbus 9211, 3007 AE Rotterdam. **Telephone:** +31 (0) 10-479-0483. **Website:** www.sparta-feyenoord.nl.

ITALY

SERIE A

Mailing Address: Federazione Italiana Baseball Softball, Viale Tiziano 74, 00196 Roma, Italy. **Telephone:** 39-06-36858376. **FAX:** 39-06-36858201. **Website:** www.fibs.it.

President: Riccardo Fraccari.

AVIGLIANA

Mailing Address: Via San Pietro 3, 10051 Avigliana. **Telephone:** 39-011-932-7774. **Website:** www.aviglianabaseball.com.

President: Antonio Carbone. **Manager:** Gian Mario Costa.

BOLOGNA

Mailing Address: Piazzale Atleti Azzurri d'Italia, 40122 Bologna. **Telephone:** 39-051-479618. **FAX:** 39-051-554000. **E-Mail Address:** fortitudobaseball@tin.it. **Website:** www.fortitudobaseball.com.

President: Marco Macchiavelli. **Manager:** Marco Nanni.

GODO

Mailing Address: Viale Baracca 17 48010 Godo di Russi (Ravenna). **Telephone:** 39-0544-414352. **E-Mail Address:** baseball-godo@libero.it. **Website:** www.baseball-godo.com.

President: Claudio Banchi. **Manager:** Mauro Mazzotti.

GROSSETO

Mailing Address: Via Papa Giovanni XXIII, 58100 Grosseto. **Telephone:** 39-0564-494149. **E-Mail Address:** info@bbcgrosseto.it. **Website:** www.bbcgrosseto.it.

President: Claudio Banchi. **Manager:** Mauro Mazzotti.

NETTUNO

Mailing Address: Via Borghese Scipione, 00048 Nettuno (Roma). **Telephone:** 39-06-9854966. **E-Mail Address:** web@nettunobaseball.net. **Website:** www.nettunobaseball.net.

President: Augusto Spigoni. **Manager:** Ruggero Bagialemani.

PARMA

Mailing Address: Via Donatore 4, Collecchio, 43044 Parma. **Telephone:** 39-0521-774-301. **E-Mail Address:** info@parmabaseball.it. **Website:** www.parmabaseball.it.

President: Rossano Rinaldi. **Manager:** Gilberto Gerali.

RIMINI

Mailing Address: Via Monaco 2, 47900 Rimini. **Telephone:** 39-0541-741761. **E-Mail Address:** info@baseballrimini.com. **Website:** www.baseballrimini.com.

President: Cesare Zangheri. **Manager:** Michele Romano.

SAN MARINO

Mailing Address: Via Piana 37, 47031 Republic of San Marino. **Telephone:** 39-0549-901412. **FAX:** 39-0549-901757. **E-Mail Address:** info@sanmarinobaseball.com. **Website:** www.sanmarinobaseball.com.

President: Paolo Achilli. **Manager:** Doriano Bindi.

WINTER BASEBALL

CARIBBEAN BASEBALL CONFEDERATION

Mailing Address: Frank Feliz Miranda No. 1 Naco, Santo Domingo, Dominican Republic. **Telephone:** (809) 381-2643. **Fax:** (809) 565-4654.

Commissioner: Juan Francisco Puello. **Secretary:** Benny Agosto.

Member Countries: Dominican Republic, Mexico, Puerto Rico, Venezuela.

2009 Caribbean Series: Mexicali, Mexico, Feb. 1-7.

DOMINICAN LEAGUE

Office Address: Estadio Quisqueya, 2da. Planta, Ens. La Fe, Santo Domingo, D.N., Dominican Republic. **Mailing Address:** Apartado Postal 1246, Santo Domingo, D.N., Dominican Republic. **Telephone:** (809) 563-5085. **Fax:** (809) 567-5720. **E-Mail Address:** info@besiboldominicano.com. **Website:** www.lidom.com.

Years League Active: 1951-.

Commisioner: Porfirio Veras Mercedes. **Administrator:** Marcos Rodríguez. **Public Relations Director:** Jorge Torres.

Regular Season: 50 games. **2008-09 Opening Date:** Oct. 16. **Closing Date:** Jan. 13.

Playoff Format: Top four teams meet in 18-game round-robin. Top two teams advance to best-of-nine series for league championship. Winner advances to Caribbean Series.

Roster Limit: 30. **Imports:** 7.

AGUILAS CIBAENAS

Office Address: Estadio Cibao, Apartado 111, Santiago, Dom. Rep. **Mailing Address:** Calle 3, No. 16, Reparto Oquet, Santiago, Dom. Rep.. **Telephone:** (809) 575-8250. **Fax:** (809) 575-0865. **E-Mail Address:** info@lasaguilas.com. **Website:** www.lasaguilas.com.

President: Winston Llenas. **General Manager:** Reynaldo Bisono. **Manager:** Felix Fermin.

AZUCAREROS DEL ESTE

Mailing Address: Estadio Francisco Micheli, La Romana, Dom. Rep. **Telephone:** (809) 556-6189. **Fax:** (809) 550-1550. **E-Mail Address:** azucareros@verizon.net.do. **Website:** www.lostorosdeleste.com.

President: Francisco Micheli. **General Manager:** Jean Giraldi. **Manager:** Carlos Tosca.

ESTRELLAS DE ORIENTE

Office Address: Estadio Tetelo Vargas, San Pedro de Macoris, Dom. Rep. **Telephone:** (809) 246-4077. **Fax:** (809) 529-3618. **E-Mail Address:** info@estrellasdeoriente.com. **Website:** www.estrellasdeoriente.com.

President: Miguel Feris Iglesias. **General Manager:** Jose Mallen. **Manager:** Arturo DeFreites.

LEONES DEL ESCOGIDO

Office Address: Estadio Quisqueya, Ens. la Fe, Apartado Postal 1287, Santo Domingo, Dom. Rep. **Telephone:** (809) 562-6715. **Fax:** (809) 567-7643. **E-Mail Address:** info@escogido.com. **Website:** www.escogido.com.

President: Julio Hazim Risk. **General Manager:** Mario Soto. **Manager:** Donny Scott.

GIGANTES DEL CIBAO

Office Address: Estadio Julian Javier, San Francisco de Macoris, Dom. **Rep. Telephone:** (809) 566-1730. **Fax:** (809) 472-3504. **Website:** www.gigantesdelcibao.com.

President: Alberto Genao. **General Manager:** Patrick Guerrero. **Manager:** Mike Rojas.

TIGRES DE LICEY

Office Address: Estadio Quisqueya, Apartado Postal 1321, Santo Domingo, Dom. Rep. **Telephone:** (809) 567-3090. **Fax:** (809) 542-7714. **E-Mail Address:** fernando.ravelo@codetel.net.do. **Website:** www.licey.com.

President: Jose Manuel Busto. **General Manager:** Fernando Ravelo. **Manager:** Tim Tolman.

MEXICAN PACIFIC LEAGUE

Mailing Address: Av. Insurgentes No. 847 Sur, Interior 402, Edificio San Carlos, Col. Centro, CP 80120, Culiacan, Sinaloa. **Telephone:** (52) 667-761-2570. **Fax:** (52) 667-761-2571. **E-Mail Address:** ligadelpacifico@ligadelpacifico.com.mx. **Website:** www.ligadelpacifico.com.mx.

Years League Active: 1958-.

President: Renato Vega Alvarado. **General Manager:** Oviel Dennis Gonzalez.

Regular Season: 68 games. **2008-09 Opening Date:** Oct. 16. **Closing Date:** Jan. **10.**

Playoff Format: Six teams advance to best-of-seven quarterfinals. Three winners and losing team with best record advance to best-of-seven semifinals. Winners meet in best-of-seven series for league championship. Winner advances to Caribbean Series.

Roster Limit: 30. **Imports:** 5.

AGUILAS DE MEXICALI

Mailing Address: Estadio De Beisbol De La Cd. Deportiva, Calz. Cuautemoc s/n, Las Fuentes Mexicali, Baja, CA, Mexico. **Telephone:** (52) 686-567-0040. **Fax:** (52) 686-567-0095. **E-Mail Address:** aguilas2@telnor.net. **Website:** www.aguilasdemexicali.com.mx.

President: Dio Alberto Murillo. **General Manager:** Antonio Castro. **Manager:** Bobby Magallanes.

ALGODONEROS DE GUASAVE

Mailing Address: Obregon No. 43, CP 81000, Guasave, Sinaloa, Mexico. **Telephone:** (52) 687-872-2998. **Fax:** (52) 687-872-1431. **E-Mail Address:** algodon@prodigy.net.mx. **Website:** www.clubalgodoneros.com.mx.

President: Fausto Perez. **General Manager:** Luis Carlos Joffroy. **Manager:** Tim Johnson.

CANEROS DE LOS MOCHIS

Mailing Address: Francisco I. Madero No. 116 Oriente, CP 81200, Los Mochis, Sinaloa, Mexico. **Telephone:** (52) 668-815-0005. **Fax:** (52) 668-812-6740. **E-Mail Address:** verdes@prodigy.net.mx. **Website:** www.verdes.com.mx.

President: Mario Lopez Valdez. **General Manager:** Carlos Soto Castro. **Manager:** Marco Antonio Vazquez.

MAYOS DE NAVOJOA

Mailing Address: Antonio Rosales No. 102, E/Pesqueira Y no Reeleccion, CP 85830, Navojoa, Sonora, Mexico. **Telephone:** (52) 642-422-1433. **Fax:** (52) 642-422-8997. **E-Mail Address:** mayosbeisbol@mayosbeisbol.com. **Website:** www.mayosbeisbol.com.

President: Victor Cuevas Garibay. **General Manager:** Victor Cuevas. **Manager:** Mauricio Zazueta.

NARANJEROS DE HERMOSILLO

Mailing Address: Blvd. Solidaridad s/n, Estadio Hector Espino, E/Jose S. Healey Y Blvd., Luis Encinas, CP 83188, Hermosillo, Sonora, Mexico. **Telephone:** (52) 662-260-6932. **Fax:** (52) 662-260-6931. **E-Mail Address:** webmaster@naranjeros.com.mx. **Website:** www.naranjeros.com.

President: Enrique Mazon Rubio. **General Manager:** Arturo Leon Lerma. **Manager:** Lorenzo Bundy.

TOMATEROS DE CULIACAN

Street Address: Av. Alvaro Obregon 348 Sur, CP 8000, Culiacan, Sinaloa, Mexico. **Telephone:** (52) 667-712-2446. **Fax:** (52) 667-715-6828. **E-Mail Address:** tomateros@infosel.com.mx. **Website:** www.tomateros.com.mx.

President: Juan Manuel Ley Lopez. **General Managers:** Jaime Blancarte. **Manager:** Marco Antonio Guzman.

VENADOS DE MAZATLAN

Mailing Address: Gutierrez Najera No. 821, CP 82000, Mazatlan, Sinaloa, Mexico. **Telephone:** (52) 669-981-1710. **Fax:** (52) 669-981-1711. **E-Mail Address:** club@venadosdemazatlan.com.mx. **Website:** www.venadosdemazatlan.com.mx.

President: José Luis Martínez Moreno. **General Manager:** Jesus Valdez. **Manager:** Juan Jose Pacho.

YAQUIS DE OBREGON

Mailing Address: Guerrero y Michoacan, Estadio de Beisbol Tomas Oroz Gaytan, CP 85130, Ciudad Obregon, Sonora, Mexico. **Telephone:** (52) 644-413-7766. **Fax:** (52) 644-414-1156. **E-Mail Address:** clubyaquisdeobregon@yaquisdeobregon.com.mx. **Website:** www.yaquisdeobregon.com.mx.

President: Luis Alfonso Lugo Platt. **General Manager:** Rene Arturo Rodriguez. **Manager:** Homar Rojas.

PUERTO RICAN LEAGUE

Office Address: Avenida Munoz Rivera 1056, Edificio First Federal, Suite 501, Rio Piedras, PR 00925. **Mailing Address:** P.O. Box 191852, San Juan, PR 00019. **Telephone:** (787) 765-6285, 765-7285. **Fax:** (787) 767-3028. **Website:** www.hitboricua.com.

Years League Active: 1938-2007. Suspended play for 2007-08 season; scheduled to resume play in 2008-09.

President: Joaquin Monserrate Matienzo. **Executive Director:** Benny Agosto.

Regular Season: 42 games. **2008-09 Opening Date:** Nov. 11. **Closing Date:** Jan. **22.**

Playoff Format: Top four teams meet in best-of-seven semifinal series. Winners meet in best-of-nine series for league championship. Winner advances to Caribbean Series.

Roster Limit: 30. **Imports:** 5.

ATENIENSES DE MANTAI

Mailing Address: Direccion Postal Box 1155, Manati, PR 00674. **Telephone:** (787) 854-5757. **Fax:** (787) 854-6767.

President: Tony Valentin.

CRIOLLOS DE CAGUAS

Mailing Address: P.O. Box 1415, Caguas, PR 00726. **Telephone:** (787) 258-2222. **Fax:** (787) 743-0545.

President/General Manager: Frankie Thon.

GIGANTES DE CAROLINA

Mailing Address: Roberto Clemente Stadium, P.O. Box 366246, San Juan, PR 00936. **Telephone:** (787) 765-1152. **Fax:** (787) 765-2965.

President: Benjamin Rivera. **General Manager:** Angel Roman.

INDIOS DE MAYAGUEZ

Mailing Address: 3089 Marina Station, Mayaguez, PR 00681. **Telephone:** (787) 834-5211. **Fax:** (787) 834-7480.

President/General Manager: Ruben Escalera.

LEONES DE PONCE

Mailing Address: P.O. Box 363148, San Juan, PR 00936. **Telephone:** (787) 848-0150. **Fax:** (787) 848-8884.

President/General Manager: Ramon Conde.

LOBOS DE ARECIBO

Mailing Address: Unavailable. **Telephone:** (787) 315-1003. **Fax:** (787) 816-0456.

President/General Manager: Candy Maldonado.

VENEZUELAN LEAGUE

Mailing Address: Avenida Casanova, Centro Comercial "El Recreo," Torre Sur, Piso 3, Oficinas 6 y 7, Sabana Grande, Caracas, Venezuela. **Telephone:** (58) 212-761-6408. **Fax:** (58) 212-761-7661. **Website:** www.lvbp.com.

Years League Active: 1946-.

President: Ramon Guillermo Aveledo. **General Manager:** Jose Domingo Alvarez.

Division Structure: East—Caracas, La Guaira, Magallanes, Oriente; West—Aragua, Lara, Pastora, Zulia.

Regular Season: 62 games. **2008-09 Opening Date:** Oct. 18. **Closing Date:** Jan. **15.**

Playoff Format: Top two teams in each division, plus a wild-card team, meet in 16-game round-robin series. Top two finishers meet in best-of-seven series for league championship. Winner advances to Caribbean Series.

Roster Limit: 26. **Imports:** 7.

AGUILAS DEL ZULIA

Mailing Address: Avenida 8 con Calle 81, Urb. Santa Rita, Edificio Las Carolinas, Mezzanine Local M-3, Maracaibo, Zulia, Venezuela. **Telephone:** (58) 261-798-0541. **Fax:** (58) 261-798-0579. **Website:** www.aguilas.com.

President: Lucas Rincon Colmenares. **General Manager:** Luis Rodolfo Machado. **Manager:** Stan Cliburn.

BRAVOS DE MARGARITA

Mailing Address: Unavailable. **Telephone:** (58) 295-263-6316. **Fax:** (58) 295-263-4418.

President: Tobias Carrero. **General Manager:** Ruben Mijares. **Manager:** Phil Regan.

CARDENALES DE LARA

Mailing Address: Av. Rotaria, Estadio Antonio Herrera Gutiérrez, Barquisimeto, Lara, Venezuela. **Telephone:** (58) 251-442- 8321. **Fax:** (58) 251-442-1921. **E-Mail Address:** administrator@cardenalesdelara.com. **Website:** www.cardenalesdelara.com.

President: Adolfo Alvarez. **General Manager:** Humberto Oropeza. **Manager:** Luis Sojo.

CARIBES DE ORIENTE

Mailing Address: Avenida Estadio Alfonso Carrasquel, Oficina Caribes de Oriente, Centro Comercial Novocentro, Piso 2, Local 2-4, Puerto la Cruz, Anzoategui, Venezuela. **Telephone:** (58) 281-266-2536. **Fax:** (58) 281-267-2972. **E-Mail Address:** caribes@telcel.net.ve. **Website:** www.caribesbbc.com.

President: Aurelio Fernandez Concheso. **Vice President:** Pablo Ruggeri. **Manager:** Marco Davilillo.

LEONES DE CARACAS

Mailing Address: Av. Francisco de Miranda, Centro Seguros la Paz, Piso 4, ofc. 42-C, La California Norte.

Telephone: (58) 212-761-3211. **Fax:** (58) 212-761-3211. **E-Mail Address:** contacto@leones.com. **Website:** www.leones.com.

President: Ariel Pratt Pinedo. **General Manager:** Oscar Prieto. **Manager:** Carlos Hernandez.

NAVEGANTES DEL MAGALLANES

Mailing Address: Centro Comercial Caribbean Plaza, Modulo 8, Local 173, Valencia, Carabobo, Venezuela. **Telephone:** (58) 241-824-0980. **Fax:** (58) 241-824-0705. **E-Mail Address:** magallanes@magallanesbbc.com.ve. **Website:** www.magallanesbbc.com.ve.

President: Jorge Latouche. **General Manager:** Juan Castillo. **Manager:** Al Pedrique.

TIBURONES DE LA GUAIRA

Mailing Address: 4ta., Avienda Urb. Los Palos Grandes, Torre Seguros Altamira, 1er. Piso, Officinas C, D y E, Caracas, Venezuela. **Telephone:** (58) 212-284-4456. **Fax:** (58) 212-286-8373. **E-Mail Addres:** prensa@tiburonesdelaguiara.com.ve. **Website:** www.tiburonesdelaguaira.com.ve.

President: Francisco Arocha. **Vice President, General Manager:** Alejandro Herrera. **Manager:** Julio Vina.

TIGRES DE ARAGUA

Mailing Address: Estadio Jose Perez Colmenares, Calle Campo Elias, Barrio Democratico, Maracay, Aragua, Venezuela. **Telephone:** (58) 243-554-4134. **Fax:** (58) 243-553-8655. **E-Mail Address:** tigres@telcel.net.ve. **Website:** www.tigresdearagua.net.

President, General Manager: Rafael Rodriguez Rendon. **Manager:** Buddy Bailey.

COLOMBIAN LEAGUE

Office/Mailing Address: Unavailable. **Telephone:** Unavailable.

Website: www.teamrenteria.com.

Regular season: 65 games. **2008 Opening Date:** Oct. 28. **Closing Date:** Jan. 12.

Active Teams: Barranquilla, Cartagena, Monteria, Sincelejo.

Playoff Format: Top two teams meet in best-of-seven finals for league championship.

NICARAGUAN LEAGUE

Office Address/Mailing Address: Managua de Canal 2, Casa 1013 en Bolonia, Managua, Nicaragua. **Telephone:** (011) 505-266-1009. **Website:** www.lnbp.net.

President: Enrique Gasteazoro. **Vice President:** Eduardo Ureuyo.

Regular Season: 40 games. **2008 Opening Date:** Dec. 1. **Closing Date:** Jan. 16.

Active Teams: Boer, Leon, Chinandega, San Fernando.

Playoff Format: Top two teams meet in best-of-seven finals for league championship.

DOMESTIC WINTER LEAGUES

ARIZONA FALL LEAGUE

Mailing Address: 2415 E. Camelback Road, Suite 850, Phoenix, AZ 85016. **Telephone:** (602) 281-7250. **Fax:** (602) 281-7313. **E-Mail Address:** afl@mlb.com. **Website:** www.mlb.com.

Years League Active: 1992-.

Operated by: Major League Baseball.

Executive Director: Steve Cobb. **Seasonal Assistant:** Joan McGrath.

Teams: Mesa Solar Sox, Peoria Javelinas, Peoria Saguaros, Phoenix Desert Dogs, Scottsdale Scorpions, Surprise Rafters.

2008 Opening Date: Unavailable. Play usually opens in early October.

Playoff Format: Division champions meet in one-game championship.

Roster Limit: 30. Players with less than one year of major league service are eligible, with one foreign player and one player below the Double-A level allowed per team.

HAWAII WINTER BASEBALL

Mailing Address: 1000 Bishop St., Suite 904, Honolulu, HI 96813. **Telephone:** (808) 973-7247. **Fax:** (808) 973-7117. **E-Mail Address:** info@hawaiiwinterbaseball.com. **Website:** www.hawaiiwinterbaseball.com.

Years League Active: 1993-97; 2006-

Chairman/CEO: Duane Kurisu. **President:** Hervy Kurisu. **Vice President/Director, Operations:** Clyde Nekoba.

Teams: Honolulu Sharks, North Shore Honu, Waikiki Beach Boys, West Oahu Canefires.

2008 Opening Date: Unavailable. Play usually opens in late September.

MINOR LEAGUE SCHEDULES

TRIPLE-A

INTERNATIONAL LEAGUE

BUFFALO

APRIL
3-4-5-6 . . . . at Norfolk
7-8-9-10 . . . . at Richmond
11-12-13-14. . . . . Toledo
15-16-17-18. . . .Syracuse
19-20-21 . . . . at Pawtucket
22-23-24-25 at Scranton/WB
26-27 . . . . . . .Pawtucket
28-29 . . . . . Scranton/WB

MAY
1-2-3-4 . . . . . . Charlotte
5-6-7-8 . . . . . . at Syracuse
9-10-11-12. . . at Rochester
13-14-15-16. . .Pawtucket
17-18-19-20 Lehigh Valley
22-23-24-25 . . at Columbus
26-27-28-29 . . . . .at Toledo
30-31 . . . . Columbus

JUNE
1-2. . . . . Columbus
3-4-5-6 . . . . . . Rochester
7-8-9 . . . . . . at Pawtucket
10-11-12-13 at Lehigh Valley
14-15-16-17. . . . Durham
19-20-21-22 . . .at Louisville
23-24-25-26 . at Indianapolis
27-28-29 . . . Scranton/WB
30 . . . . . . at Scranton/WB

JULY
1 . . . . at Scranton/WB
2-3. . . . . Rochester
4-5. . . . . at Rochester
6-7. . . . . .Syracuse
8-9. . . . . at Syracuse
10-11-12-13. . . Louisville
17-18-19-20. . . Richmond
21-22-23-24. . . . .Norfolk
25-26-27-28 . . .at Charlotte
29-30-31 . . . . . .at Durham

AUGUST
1 . . . . .at Durham
2-3. . . . . .Syracuse
4-5-6-7 . . . . Indianapolis
8-9-10-11. . at Lehigh Valley
14-15 . . . . Rochester
16-17 . . . . . . .Pawtucket
18-19-20-21 Lehigh Valley
22-23 . . . . at Syracuse
24-25 . . . . at Scranton/WB
26-27-28 . . . Scranton/WB
29-30 . . . . . . at Pawtucket
31 . . . . at Rochester

SEPTEMBER
1 . . . . at Rochester

CHARLOTTE

APRIL
3-4-5-6 . . . . . at Columbus
7-8-9-10 . . . . . . .at Toledo
11-12-13-14. . . Columbus
15-16-17-18 Scranton/WB
19-20-21 . . . . at Richmond
22-23 . . . . .at Durham
25-26-27 . . . . . . Durham
28-29-30 . . . . . . .Norfolk

MAY
1-2-3-4 . . . . at Buffalo
5-6-7-8 . . . at Scranton/WB
9-10-11-12. . . . . . Toledo
13-14-15-16. . . . Syracuse
17-18 . . . . at Durham
20-21 . . . . Durham
22-23-24-25 at Lehigh Valley
26-27-28-29 . . at Rochester
30-31 . . . . Richmond

JUNE
1-2. . . . . Richmond
3-4-5-6 . . . . . .Pawtucket
7-8. . . . . .at Durham
10-11-12-13 . . . . at Norfolk
14-15-16-17 . . at Richmond
19-20-21-22 Lehigh Valley
23-24-25-26. . . . .Norfolk
27-28 . . . . at Richmond
29-30 . . . . at Norfolk

JULY
1-2-3 . . . . .at Durham
4-5. . . . . Durham
6-7-8-9 . . . . . . Rochester
10-11-12-13. . . Richmond
17-18-19-20 . . . at Louisville
21-22-23-24 . at Indianapolis
25-26-27-28. . . . . Buffalo
29-30-31 . . . . . Louisville

AUGUST
1 . . . . Louisville
2-3. . . . . Durham
4-5-6-7 . . . . . . at Syracuse
8-9-10-11. . . . at Pawtucket
12-13 . . . . Richmond
15-16-17-18 . . . . at Norfolk
19-20-21-22. Indianapolis
23-24-25-26. . . . .Norfolk
27-28 . . . . at Richmond
29-30 . . . . .at Durham
31 . . . . Durham

SEPTEMBER
1 . . . . Durham

COLUMBUS

APRIL
3-4-5-6 . . . . . . Charlotte
7-8-9-10 . . . . . . Durham
11-12-13-14 . . .at Charlotte
15-16-17-18 . . . .at Durham
19-20 . . . . . Indianapolis
22-23 . . . . .at Toledo
24-25 . . . . Toledo
26-27-28 . . . . . at Louisville
29-30 . . . . . at Indianapolis

MAY
1-2-3-4 . . . .Lehigh Valley
5-6-7-8 . . . . . . Rochester
9-10-11-12. at Lehigh Valley
13-14-15-16 . . at Rochester
17-18 . . . . Toledo
19-20 . . . . .at Toledo
22-23-24-25. . . . . Buffalo
26-27-28-29. . . Louisville
30-31 . . . . at Buffalo

JUNE
1-2. . . . . at Buffalo
3-4-5-6 . . . . . . at Syracuse
7-8. . . . . .at Toledo
10-11-12-13. . . .Syracuse
14-15 . . . . . Indianapolis
16-17 . . . . . at Indianapolis
19-20-21-22 . . at Pawtucket
23-24-25-26 at Scranton/WB
27-28-29 . . . Indianapolis
30 . . . . Toledo

JULY
1-2-3 . . . . Toledo
4-5. . . . . .at Toledo
6-7-8-9 . . . . at Indianapolis
10-11-12-13 Scranton/WB
17-18-19-20. Indianapolis
21-22-23-24. . .Pawtucket
25-26-27-28 . . . . at Norfolk
29-30-31 . . . . at Richmond

AUGUST
1 . . . . at Richmond
2-3. . . . . Louisville
4-5-6-7 . . . . .Norfolk
8-9-10-11. . . . . .at Louisville
12-13 . . . . . at Indianapolis
15-16-17-18. . . Louisville
19-20-21-22. . . Richmond
23-24-25-26 . . . at Louisville
27-28-29 . . . . . . .at Toledo
30-31 . . . . Toledo

SEPTEMBER
1 . . . . Toledo

DURHAM

APRIL
3-4-5-6 . . . . .at Toledo
7-8-9-10 . . . . at Columbus
11-12-13-14 Scranton/WB
15-16-17-18. . . Columbus
19-20-21 . . . . . . at Norfolk
22-23 . . . . Charlotte
25-26-27 . . . . . at Charlotte
28-29-30 . . . . . Richmond

MAY
1-2-3-4 . . . at Scranton/WB
5-6-7-8 . . . . . at Pawtucket
9-10-11-12. . . . .Syracuse
13-14-15-16. . . . . Toledo
17-18 . . . . Charlotte
20-21 . . . . .at Charlotte
22-23-24-25 . . at Richmond
26-27-28-29 . . . . at Norfolk
30-31 . . . . . . .Pawtucket

JUNE
1-2. . . . . .Pawtucket
3-4-5-6 . . . . . . Richmond
7-8. . . . . Charlotte
10-11-12-13 . . at Rochester
14-15-16-17 . . . . at Buffalo
19-20-21-22. . . . .Norfolk
23-24-25-26 Lehigh Valley
27-28 . . . . at Norfolk
29-30 . . . . at Richmond

JULY
1-2-3 . . . . Charlotte
4-5. . . . . .at Charlotte
6-7-8-9 . . . . .Norfolk
10-11-12-13. . . Rochester
17-18-19-20 . . . at Syracuse
21-22-23-24 at Lehigh Valley
25-26-27-28. . . Louisville
29-30-31 . . . . Buffalo

AUGUST
1 . . . . .Buffalo
2-3. . . . . .at Charlotte
4-5-6-7 . . . . . at Richmond
8-9-10-11 . . . . Richmond
13-14 . . . . .Norfolk
15-16-17-18 . at Indianapolis
19-20-21-22 . . .at Louisville
23-24-25-26. Indianapolis
27-28 . . . . at Norfolk
29-30 . . . . Charlotte
31 . . . . .at Charlotte

SEPTEMBER
1 . . . . at Charlotte

INDIANAPOLIS

APRIL
3-4-5-6 . . . . . at Pawtucket
7-8-9-10 . . . . . at Syracuse
11-12-13-14. . . . .Norfolk
15-16-17-18. . .Pawtucket
19-20 . . . . at Columbus
22-23-24-25. . . Louisville
26-27-28 . . . . .at Toledo
29-30 . . . . Columbus

MAY
1-2-3-4 . . . . at Norfolk
5-6-7-8 . . . . . at Richmond
9-10-11-12. . Scranton/WB
13-14-15-16. . . Richmond
17-18 . . . . at Louisville
20-21 . . . . Louisville
22-23-24-25 at Scranton/WB
26-27-28-29 at Lehigh Valley
30-31 . . . . Toledo

JUNE
1-2. . . . . Toledo
3-4-5-6 . . . .Lehigh Valley
7-8. . . . . .at Louisville
10-11-12-13 . . . . .at Toledo
14-15 . . . . at Columbus
16-17 . . . . Columbus
19-20-21-22. . . Rochester
23-24-25-26. . . . . Buffalo

27-28-29 . . . . at Columbus
30 . . . . at Louisville

JULY

1-2-3 . . . . at Louisville
4 . . . . Louisville
5 . . . . at Louisville
6-7-8-9 . . . . . . Columbus
10-11-12-13. . . . . Toledo
17-18-19-20 . . at Columbus
21-22-23-24. . . Charlotte
25-26-27-28. . . .Syracuse
29-30-31 . . . . . . .at Toledo

AUGUST

1-2-3 . . . . Toledo
4-5-6-7 . . . . at Buffalo
8-9-10-11. . . . at Rochester
12-13 . . . . Columbus
15-16-17-18. . . . Durham
19-20-21-22 . . .at Charlotte
23-24-25-26 . . . .at Durham
27-28-29-30. . . Louisville
31 . . . . at Louisville

SEPTEMBER

1 . . . . at Louisville

LEHIGH VALLEY

APRIL

3-4-5-6 . . . at Scranton/WB
7-8-9-10 . . . . at Pawtucket
11-12-13-14. . . Richmond
15-16-17-18. . . . . Toledo
19-20-21-22 . . . at Syracuse
23-24-25 . . . . at Rochester
26-27 . . . . Rochester
29-30 . . . . Syracuse

MAY

1-2-3-4 . . . . . at Columbus
5-6-7-8 . . . . .at Toledo
9-10-11-12. . . . Columbus
13-14-15-16. . . . .Norfolk
17-18-19-20 . . . . at Buffalo
22-23-24-25. . . Charlotte
26-27-28-29. Indianapolis
30-31 . . . . at Louisville

JUNE

1-2. . . . . at Louisville
3-4-5-6 . . . .at Indianapolis
7-8-9 . . . . Rochester
10-11-12-13. . . . .Buffalo
14-15-16-17. . .Pawtucket
19-20-21-22 . . .at Charlotte
23-24-25-26 . . . .at Durham
27-28-29 . . . . . .Syracuse
30 . . . . at Rochester

JULY

1 . . . . at Rochester
2-3. . . . . Scranton/WB
4-5. . . . . at Pawtucket
6-7-8-9 . . . . . . Louisville
10-11-12-13 . . . at Syracuse
17-18-19-20 Scranton/WB
21-22-23-24. . . . Durham
25-26-27-28 . . at Richmond
29-30-31 . . . . . . at Norfolk

AUGUST

1 . . . . at Norfolk
2-3-4 . . . . Rochester
5-6-7 . . . . at Rochester
8-9-10-11 . . . . . .Buffalo
14-15 . . . . at Scranton/WB
16-17 . . . . . Scranton/WB
18-19-20-21 . . . . at Buffalo
22-23 . . . . at Scranton/WB
24-25-26-27. . .Pawtucket
28-29-30 . . . . . .Syracuse
31 . . . . at Pawtucket

SEPTEMBER

1 . . . . at Pawtucket

LOUISVILLE

APRIL

3-4-5-6 . . . . . . at Syracuse
7-8-9-10 . . at Scranton/WB
11-12-13-14. . .Pawtucket
15-16-17-18. . . . .Norfolk
19-20 . . . . .at Toledo
22-23-24-25 . at Indianapolis
26-27-28 . . . . . Columbus
29-30 . . . . Toledo

MAY

1-2-3-4 . . . . . at Richmond
5-6-7-8 . . . . at Norfolk
9-10-11-12. . . . Richmond
13-14-15-16 Scranton/WB
17-18 . . . . . Indianapolis
20-21 . . . . . at Indianapolis
22-23-24-25 . . . . .at Toledo
26-27-28-29 . . at Columbus
30-31 . . . . .Lehigh Valley

JUNE

1-2. . . . . . .Lehigh Valley
3-4-5-6 . . . . Toledo
7-8. . . . . Indianapolis
10-11-12-13 . . at Pawtucket
14-15-16-17 . . at Rochester
19-20-21-22. . . . .Buffalo
23-24-25-26. . . Rochester
27-28-29 . . . . .at Toledo
30 . . . . Indianapolis

JULY

1-2-3 . . . . . Indianapolis
4 . . . . at Indianapolis
5 . . . . Indianapolis
6-7-8-9 . . . at Lehigh Valley
10-11-12-13 . . . . at Buffalo
17-18-19-20. . . Charlotte
21-22-23-24. . . .Syracuse
25-26-27-28 . . . .at Durham
29-30-31 . . . . . at Charlotte

AUGUST

1 . . . . .at Charlotte
2-3. . . . . at Columbus
4-5-6-7 . . . . Toledo
8-9-10-11 . . . . Columbus
13-14 . . . . .at Toledo
15-16-17-18 . . at Columbus
19-20-21-22. . . . Durham
23-24-25-26. . . Columbus
27-28-29-30 . at Indianapolis
31 . . . . Indianapolis

SEPTEMBER

1 . . . . Indianapolis

NORFOLK

APRIL

3-4-5-6 . . . . Buffalo
7-8-9-10 . . . . . Rochester
11-12-13-14 . at Indianapolis
15-16-17-18 . . . at Louisville
19-20-21 . . . . . . Durham
23-24 . . . . Richmond
25-26-27 . . . . at Richmond
28-29-30 . . . . . at Charlotte

MAY

1-2-3-4 . . . . Indianapolis
5-6-7-8 . . . . . . Louisville
9-10-11-12. . . at Pawtucket
13-14-15-16 at Lehigh Valley
17-18 . . . . at Richmond
20-21 . . . . Richmond
22-23-24-25. . . .Syracuse
26-27-28-29. . . . Durham
30-31 . . . . at Syracuse

JUNE

1-2. . . . . at Syracuse
3-4-5-6 . . . at Scranton/WB
7-8. . . . . at Richmond
10-11-12-13. . . Charlotte
14-15-16-17 Scranton/WB
19-20-21-22 . . . .at Durham
23-24-25-26 . . . at Charlotte
27-28 . . . . Durham
29-30 . . . . Charlotte

JULY

1-2-3 . . . . Richmond
4-5. . . . . at Richmond
6-7-8-9 . . . . . . .at Durham
10-11-12-13. . .Pawtucket
17-18-19-20 . . at Rochester
21-22-23-24 . . . . at Buffalo
25-26-27-28. . . Columbus
29-30-31 . . .Lehigh Valley

AUGUST

1 . . . . .Lehigh Valley
2-3. . . . . Richmond
4-5-6-7 . . . . . at Columbus
8-9-10-11. . . . . . .at Toledo
13-14 . . . . .at Durham
15-16-17-18. . . Charlotte
19-20-21-22. . . . . Toledo
23-24-25-26 . . . at Charlotte
27-28 . . . . Durham
29-30 . . . . Richmond
31 . . . . at Richmond

SEPTEMBER

1 . . . . at Richmond

PAWTUCKET

APRIL

3-4-5-6 . . . . Indianapolis
7-8-9-10 . . .Lehigh Valley
11-12-13-14 . . .at Louisville
15-16-17-18 . at Indianapolis
19-20-21 . . . . . . .Buffalo
23-24-25 . . . . . .Syracuse
26-27 . . . . at Buffalo
28-29-30 . . . . at Rochester

MAY

1-2-3-4 . . . . . . at Syracuse
5-6-7-8 . . . . Durham
9-10-11-12. . . . . . .Norfolk
13-14-15-16 . . . . at Buffalo
17-18-19-20 at Scranton/WB
22-23-24-25. . . Rochester
26-27-28-29 Scranton/WB
30-31 . . . . .at Durham

JUNE

1-2. . . . . .at Durham
3-4-5-6 . . . . . . .at Charlotte
7-8-9 . . . . .Buffalo
10-11-12-13. . . Louisville
14-15-16-17 at Lehigh Valley
19-20-21-22. . . Columbus
23-24-25-26. . . Richmond
27-28-29 . . . . at Rochester
30 . . . . at Syracuse

JULY

1 . . . . at Syracuse
2-3. . . . . Syracuse
4-5. . . . . . .Lehigh Valley
6-7-8-9 . . . . . at Richmond
10-11-12-13 . . . . at Norfolk
17-18-19-20. . . . . Toledo
21-22-23-24 . . at Columbus
25-26-27-28 . . . . .at Toledo
29-30-31 . . . . . Rochester

AUGUST

1 . . . . Rochester
2-3. . . . . . . Scranton/WB
4-5-6-7 . . . at Scranton/WB
8-9-10-11 . . . . Charlotte
12-13 . . . . . Scranton/WB
14-15 . . . . at Syracuse
16-17 . . . . at Buffalo
19-20-21 . . . . . .Syracuse
22-23 . . . . . . at Rochester
24-25-26-27 at Lehigh Valley
29-30 . . . . .Buffalo
31 . . . . . . .Lehigh Valley

SEPTEMBER

1 . . . . .Lehigh Valley

RICHMOND

APRIL

3-4-5-6 . . . . . . Rochester
7-8-9-10 . . . . .Buffalo
11-12-13-14 at Lehigh Valley
15-16-17-18 . . at Rochester
19-20-21 . . . . . Charlotte
23-24 . . . . at Norfolk
25-26-27 . . . . . . .Norfolk
28-29-30 . . . . . .at Durham

MAY

1-2-3-4 . . . . . . Louisville
5-6-7-8 . . . . Indianapolis
9-10-11-12. . . .at Louisville
13-14-15-16 . at Indianapolis
17-18 . . . . .Norfolk
20-21 . . . . at Norfolk
22-23-24-25. . . . Durham
26-27-28-29. . . .Syracuse
30-31 . . . . .at Charlotte

JUNE

1-2. . . . . .at Charlotte
3-4-5-6 . . . . .at Durham

7-8 . . . . Norfolk
10-11-12-13 Scranton/WB
14-15-16-17 . . . Charlotte
19-20-21-22 . . . at Syracuse
23-24-25-26 . . at Pawtucket
27-28 . . . . Charlotte
29-30 . . . . Durham

JULY
1-2-3 . . . . at Norfolk
4-5 . . . . Norfolk
6-7-8-9 . . . . . Pawtucket
10-11-12-13 . . . at Charlotte
17-18-19-20 . . . . at Buffalo
21-22-23-24 at Scranton/WB
25-26-27-28 Lehigh Valley
29-30-31 . . . . . Columbus

AUGUST
1 . . . . Columbus
2-3 . . . . at Norfolk
4-5-6-7 . . . . Durham
8-9-10-11 . . . . . at Durham
12-13 . . . . at Charlotte
15-16-17-18 . . . . . Toledo
19-20-21-22 . . at Columbus
23-24-25-26 . . . . . at Toledo
27-28 . . . . Charlotte
29-30 . . . . at Norfolk
31 . . . . Norfolk

SEPTEMBER
1 . . . . Norfolk

ROCHESTER

APRIL
3-4-5-6 . . . . . at Richmond
7-8-9-10 . . . . . . at Norfolk
11-12-13-14 . . . . Syracuse
15-16-17-18 . . . Richmond
19-20-21 . . at Scranton/WB
23-24-25 . . . Lehigh Valley
26-27 . . . . at Lehigh Valley
28-29-30 . . . . . Pawtucket

MAY
1-2-3-4 . . . . at Toledo
5-6-7-8 . . . . . at Columbus
9-10-11-12 . . . . . . Buffalo
13-14-15-16 . . . Columbus
17-18-19-20 . . . at Syracuse
22-23-24-25 . . at Pawtucket
26-27-28-29 . . . Charlotte
30-31 . . . . . Scranton/WB

JUNE
1-2 . . . . Scranton/WB
3-4-5-6 . . . . at Buffalo
7-8-9 . . . . at Lehigh Valley
10-11-12-13 . . . . Durham
14-15-16-17 . . . Louisville
19-20-21-22 . at Indianapolis
23-24-25-26 . . . at Louisville
27-28-29 . . . . . Pawtucket
30 . . . . Lehigh Valley

JULY
1 . . . . Lehigh Valley
2-3 . . . . at Buffalo
4-5 . . . . Buffalo
6-7-8-9 . . . . . . at Charlotte
10-11-12-13 . . . . at Durham
17-18-19-20 . . . . . Norfolk
21-22-23-24 . . . . . Toledo
25-26 . . . . at Scranton/WB
27-28 . . . . . Scranton/WB
29-30-31 . . . . at Pawtucket

AUGUST
1 . . . . at Pawtucket
2-3-4 . . . . at Lehigh Valley
5-6-7 . . . . . Lehigh Valley
8-9-10-11 . . Indianapolis
12-13 . . . . Syracuse
14-15 . . . . at Buffalo
16-17 . . . . at Syracuse
19-20-21 . . at Scranton/WB
22-23 . . . . Pawtucket
24-25 . . . . at Syracuse
26-27 . . . . Syracuse
29-30 . . . . . Scranton/WB
31 . . . . Buffalo

SEPTEMBER
1 . . . . Buffalo

SCRANTON/WB

APRIL
3-4-5-6 . . . . Lehigh Valley
7-8-9-10 . . . . . Louisville
11-12-13-14 . . . at Durham
15-16-17-18 . . at Charlotte
19-20-21 . . . . . Rochester
22-23-24-25 . . . . . Buffalo
26-27 . . . . at Syracuse
28-29 . . . . at Buffalo

MAY
1-2-3-4 . . . . Durham
5-6-7-8 . . . . . . Charlotte
9-10-11-12 . . at Indianapolis
13-14-15-16 . . . at Louisville
17-18-19-20 . . Pawtucket
22-23-24-25 . Indianapolis
26-27-28-29 . . at Pawtucket
30-31 . . . . . . at Rochester

JUNE
1-2 . . . . at Rochester
3-4-5-6 . . . . Norfolk
7-8-9 . . . . Syracuse
10-11-12-13 . . at Richmond
14-15-16-17 . . . . at Norfolk
19-20-21-22 . . . . . Toledo
23-24-25-26 . . . Columbus
27-28-29 . . . . . . at Buffalo
30 . . . . Buffalo

JULY
1 . . . . Buffalo
2-3 . . . . . . at Lehigh Valley
4-5 . . . . Syracuse
6-7-8-9 . . . . at Toledo
10-11-12-13 . . at Columbus
17-18-19-20 at Lehigh Valley
21-22-23-24 . . . Richmond
25-26 . . . . Rochester
27-28 . . . . at Rochester
29-30-31 . . . . . at Syracuse

AUGUST
1 . . . . at Syracuse
2-3 . . . . at Pawtucket
4-5-6-7 . . . . . . Pawtucket
8-9-10 . . . . Syracuse
12-13 . . . . . . at Pawtucket
14-15 . . . . . Lehigh Valley
16-17 . . . . at Lehigh Valley
19-20-21 . . . . . Rochester
22-23 . . . . . Lehigh Valley
24-25 . . . . Buffalo
26-27-28 . . . . . . at Buffalo
29-30 . . . . . . at Rochester
31 . . . . at Syracuse

SEPTEMBER
1 . . . . at Syracuse

SYRACUSE

APRIL
3-4-5-6 . . . . . . Louisville
7-8-9-10 . . . Indianapolis
11-12-13-14 . . at Rochester
15-16-17-18 . . . . at Buffalo
19-20-21-22 Lehigh Valley
23-24-25 . . . . at Pawtucket
26-27 . . . . . Scranton/WB
29-30 . . . . at Lehigh Valley

MAY
1-2-3-4 . . . . . . Pawtucket
5-6-7-8 . . . . Buffalo
9-10-11-12 . . . . . at Durham
13-14-15-16 . . . at Charlotte
17-18-19-20 . . . Rochester
22-23-24-25 . . . . at Norfolk
26-27-28-29 . . at Richmond
30-31 . . . . Norfolk

JUNE
1-2 . . . . Norfolk
3-4-5-6 . . . . . . Columbus
7-8-9 . . . . at Scranton/WB
10-11-12-13 . . at Columbus
14-15-16-17 . . . . . at Toledo
19-20-21-22 . . . Richmond
23-24-25-26 . . . . . Toledo
27-28-29 . . at Lehigh Valley
30 . . . . Pawtucket

JULY
1 . . . . Pawtucket
2-3 . . . . at Pawtucket
4-5 . . . . . . at Scranton/WB
6-7 . . . . at Buffalo
8-9 . . . . Buffalo
10-11-12-13 Lehigh Valley
17-18-19-20 . . . . Durham
21-22-23-24 . . . at Louisville
25-26-27-28 . at Indianapolis
29-30-31 . . . Scranton/WB

AUGUST
1 . . . . Scranton/WB
2-3 . . . . at Buffalo
4-5-6-7 . . . . . . Charlotte
8-9-10 . . . . at Scranton/WB
12-13 . . . . . . at Rochester
14-15 . . . . Pawtucket
16-17 . . . . Rochester
19-20-21 . . . . at Pawtucket
22-23 . . . . Buffalo
24-25 . . . . Rochester
26-27 . . . . . . at Rochester
28-29-30 . . at Lehigh Valley
31 . . . . Scranton/WB

SEPTEMBER
1 . . . . Scranton/WB

TOLEDO

APRIL
3-4-5-6 . . . . Durham
7-8-9-10 . . . . . Charlotte
11-12-13-14 . . . . at Buffalo
15-16-17-18 at Lehigh Valley
19-20 . . . . Louisville
22-23 . . . . Columbus
24-25 . . . . . . at Columbus
26-27-28 . . . Indianapolis
29-30 . . . . at Louisville

MAY
1-2-3-4 . . . . . . Rochester
5-6-7-8 . . . . Lehigh Valley
9-10-11-12 . . . . at Charlotte
13-14-15-16 . . . . at Durham
17-18 . . . . . . at Columbus
19-20 . . . . Columbus
22-23-24-25 . . . Louisville
26-27-28-29 . . . . . Buffalo
30-31 . . . . . at Indianapolis

JUNE
1-2 . . . . at Indianapolis
3-4-5-6 . . . . . . at Louisville
7-8 . . . . Columbus
10-11-12-13 . Indianapolis
14-15-16-17 . . . . Syracuse
19-20-21-22 at Scranton/WB
23-24-25-26 . . . at Syracuse
27-28-29 . . . . . Louisville
30 . . . . at Columbus

JULY
1-2-3 . . . . . . at Columbus
4-5 . . . . Columbus
6-7-8-9 . . . . Scranton/WB
10-11-12-13 . at Indianapolis
17-18-19-20 . . at Pawtucket
21-22-23-24 . . at Rochester
25-26-27-28 . . . Pawtucket
29-30-31 . . . Indianapolis

AUGUST
1-2-3 . . . . . at Indianapolis
4-5-6-7 . . . . . . at Louisville
8-9-10-11 . . . . . . Norfolk
13-14 . . . . Louisville
15-16-17-18 . . at Richmond
19-20-21-22 . . . . at Norfolk
23-24-25-26 . . . Richmond
27-28-29 . . . . . Columbus
30-31 . . . . . . at Columbus

SEPTEMBER
1 . . . . at Columbus

MINOR LEAGUES

PACIFIC COAST LEAGUE

ALBUQUERQUE

APRIL

3-4-5-6 . . . . at Omaha
7-8-9-10 . . . . .at Iowa
11-12-13-14. . .Oklahoma
15-16-17-18 . . .at Memphis
19-20-21-22. . . Nashville
24-25-26-27 . . at Oklahoma
28-29-30. . . . . Las Vegas

MAY

1 . . . . Las Vegas
2-3-4-5 . . . . Tucson
6-7-8-9 . . . . . . at Salt Lake
10-11-12-13 at Colo. Springs
15-16-17-18. . . . .Omaha
19-20-21-22. .Round Rock
23-24-25-26 .at New Orleans
27-28-29-30. . . Nashville
31 . . . . Memphis

JUNE

1-2-3 . . . . Memphis
5-6-7-8 . . . . . . at Nashville
9-10-11-12. . .Round Rock
13-14-15-16. . . . .Omaha
17-18-19-20 . . .at Memphis
21-22-23-24. . . . . . Iowa
26-27-28-29 . . . . . .at Iowa
30 . . . . at Round Rock

JULY

1-2-3 . . . . . at Round Rock
4-5-6 . . . . . New Orleans
7-8-9-10 . . . . at Oklahoma
11-12-13-14. . . . . . Iowa
18-19-20-21 .at New Orleans
22-23-24-25. .Sacramento
26-27-28-29. . . . . Fresno
30-31 . . . . at Portland

AUGUST

1-2. . . . . at Portland
3-4-5-6 . . . . at Tacoma
8-9-10-11 . . . .Oklahoma
12-13-14-15 . . . . at Omaha
16-17-18-19. . . Memphis
20-21-22-23-24. . . . .New Orleans
25-26-27-28 . . . at Nashville
29-30-31 . . . at Round Rock

SEPTEMBER

1 . . . . at Round Rock

COLORADO SPRINGS

APRIL

3-4-5-6 . . . . at Tucson
7-8-9-10 . . . . .at Las Vegas
11-12-13-14. . . . .Tacoma
15-16-17-18. . . .Portland
19-20-21-22 . . . . at Tacoma
24-25-26-27. .Sacramento
28-29-30 . . . . . at Nashville

MAY

1 . . . . at Nashville
2-3-4-5 . . . . . .at Memphis
6-7-8-9 . . . . .Round Rock
10-11-12-13 Albuquerque
15-16-17-18 . . . . .at Fresno
19-20-21-22 . at Sacramento
23-24-25-26. . . . .Tacoma
27-28-29-30 . . . at Salt Lake
31 . . . . .Sacramento

JUNE

1-2-3 . . . . . .Sacramento
5-6-7-8 . . . . . . .Salt Lake
9-10-11-12. . . . . .at Fresno
13-14-15-16 . . . . at Tucson
17-18-19-20. . . .Salt Lake
21-22-23-24. . . . . Fresno
26-27-28-29 . . . at Portland
30 . . . . at Tacoma

JULY

1-2-3 . . . . at Tacoma
4-5-6 . . . . Las Vegas
7-8-9-10 . . . at Sacramento
11-12-13-14. . . . . Fresno
18-19-20-21 . . . at Portland
22-23-24-25. New Orleans
26-27-28-29. . .Oklahoma
30-31 . . . . at Iowa

AUGUST

1-2. . . . . at Iowa
3-4-5-6 . . . . at Omaha
8-9-10-11 . . . . . Portland
12-13-14-15. . . . . Tucson
16-17-18-19 . . . at Salt Lake
20-21-22-23-24. Las Vegas
25-26-27-28. . . . . Tucson
29-30-31 . . . . .at Las Vegas

SEPTEMBER

1 . . . . .at Las Vegas

FRESNO

APRIL

3-4-5-6 . . . . . . at Portland
7-8-9-10 . . . . . . at Tacoma
11-12-13-14. . . . . Tucson
15-16-17-18. . . . .Tacoma
19-20-21-22 . . . . at Tucson
24-25-26-27 . . . at Salt Lake
28-29-30. . . . . Iowa

MAY

1 . . . . Iowa
2-3-4-5 . . . . .Omaha
6-7-8-9 . . . .at New Orleans
10-11-12-13 . . at Oklahoma
15-16-17-18 Colo. Springs
19-20-21-22. . . .Salt Lake
23-24-25-26 . . .at Las Vegas
27-28-29-30. . . . .Tacoma
31 . . . . Tucson

JUNE

1-2-3 . . . . Tucson
5-6-7-8 . . . . at Tacoma
9-10-11-12. . Colo. Springs
13-14-15-16. . . . Portland
17-18-19-20 . at Sacramento
21-22-23-24 at Colo. Springs
26-27-28-29. . . Las Vegas
30 . . . . at Tucson

JULY

1-2-3 . . . . at Tucson
4-5-6 . . . . . .Sacramento
7-8-9-10 . . . . . . Portland
11-12-13-14 at Colo. Springs
18-19-20-21. . . . .Salt Lake
22-23-24-25 . at Round Rock
26-27-28-29 at Albuquerque
30-31 . . . . Memphis

AUGUST

1-2. . . . . Memphis
3-4-5-6 . . . . . . Nashville
8-9-10-11. . . . . at Salt Lake
12-13-14-15 . . . at Portland
16-17-18-19. . . Las Vegas
20-21-22-23-24. . . . . Sacramento
25-26-27-28 . . .at Las Vegas
29-30-31 . . . at Sacramento

SEPTEMBER

1 . . . . at Sacramento

IOWA

APRIL

3-4-5-6 . . . . .Round Rock
7-8-9-10 . . .Albuquerque
11-12-13-14 . . . at Nashville
15-16-17-18 .at New Orleans
19-20-21-22. . .Oklahoma
24-25-26-27. . . Memphis
28-29-30 . . . . . . .at Fresno

MAY

1 . . . . .at Fresno
2-3-4-5 . . . . at Sacramento
6-7-8-9 . . . . .Tacoma
10-11-12-13. . . .Portland
15-16-17-18 . at Round Rock
19-20-21-22 . . . . at Omaha
23-24-25-26. . .Oklahoma
27-28-29-30. . . Memphis
31 . . . . at Nashville

JUNE

1-2-3 . . . . at Nashville
5-6-7-8 . . . . at Omaha
9-10-11-12. . . .at Memphis
13-14-15-16. . . Nashville
17-18-19-20. New Orleans
21-22-23-24 at Albuquerque
26-27-28-29 Albuquerque
30 . . . . .Omaha

JULY

1-2-3 . . . . .Omaha
4-5-6 . . . . . . at Oklahoma
7-8-9-10 . . . .Round Rock
11-12-13-14 at Albuquerque
18-19-20 . . . . . Nashville
22-23-24-25 . . . . at Tucson
26-27-28-29 . . .at Las Vegas
30-31 . . Colorado Springs

AUGUST

1-2. . . . Colorado Springs
3-4-5-6 . . . . . . .Salt Lake
8-9-10-11. . . at Round Rock
12-13-14-15. New Orleans
16-17-18-19 .at New Orleans
20-21-22-23-24at Oklahoma
25-26-27-28 . . .at Memphis
29-30-31. . . . . . .Omaha

SEPTEMBER

1 . . . . .Omaha

LAS VEGAS

APRIL

3-4-5-6 . . . . . . .Salt Lake
7-8-9-10 . . . Colo. Springs
11-12-13-14 . at Sacramento
15-16-17-18 . . . at Salt Lake
19-20-21-22. .Sacramento
24-25-26-27. . . . Portland
28-29-30 . . at Albuquerque

MAY

1 . . . . at Albuquerque
2-3-4-5 . . . . at Round Rock
6-7-8-9 . . . . . . Memphis
10-11-12-13. . . Nashville
15-16-17-18 . . . at Portland
19-20-21-22 . . . . at Tacoma
23-24-25-26. . . . . Fresno
27-28-29-30 . . . . at Tucson
31 . . . . at Portland

JUNE

1-2-3 . . . . at Portland
5-6-7-8 . . . . Tucson
9-10-11-12. . . . .Portland
13-14-15-16 . . . at Salt Lake
17-18-19-20. . . . .Tacoma
21-22-23-24 . . . . at Tucson
26-27-28-29 . . . . .at Fresno
30 . . . . .Salt Lake

JULY

1-2-3 . . . . .Salt Lake
4-5-6 . .at Colorado Springs
7-8-9-10 . . . . Tucson
11-12-13-14. . . . .Tacoma
18-19-20-21 . at Sacramento
22-23-24-25. . . . .Omaha
26-27-28-29. . . . . . Iowa
30-31 . . . . . . at Oklahoma

AUGUST

1-2. . . . . at Oklahoma
3-4-5-6 . . . .at New Orleans
8-9-10-11 . . .Sacramento
12-13-14-15 . . . . at Tacoma
16-17-18-19 . . . . .at Fresno
20-21-22-23-24at Colo. Springs
25-26-27-28. . . . . Fresno
29-30-31 . . . Colo. Springs

SEPTEMBER

1 . . . . . Colorado Springs

MEMPHIS

APRIL
3-4-5-6 . . . . . at Oklahoma
7-8-9-10 . . .at New Orleans
11-12-13-14. . . . .Omaha
15-16-17-18 Albuquerque
19-20-21-22 . at Round Rock
24-25-26-27 . . . . . . at Iowa
28-29-30 . . . . . .Salt Lake

MAY
1 . . . . .Salt Lake
2-3-4-5 . Colorado Springs
6-7-8-9 . . . . . .at Las Vegas
10-11-12-13 . . . . at Tucson
15-16-17-18. . .Oklahoma
19-20-21-22 . . . at Nashville
23-24-25-26. . . Nashville
27-28-29-30 . . . . . . at Iowa
31 . . . . . . at Albuquerque

JUNE
1-2-3 . . . . at Albuquerque
5-6-7-8 . . . . .Round Rock
9-10-11-12. . . . . . . Iowa
13-14-15-16 . at Round Rock
17-18-19-20 Albuquerque
21-22-23-24 . . . at Nashville
26-27-28-29. New Orleans
30 . . . . Nashville

JULY
1-2-3 . . . . Nashville
4-5-6 . . . . at Omaha
7-8-9-10 . . .at New Orleans
11-12-12-13. . . . .Omaha
18-19-20-21 . . at Oklahoma
22-23-24-25. . . .Portland
26-27-28-29. . . . .Tacoma
30-31 . . . . .at Fresno

AUGUST
1-2. . . . . .at Fresno
3-4-5-6 . . . . at Sacramento
8-9-10-11 . . New Orleans
12-13-14-15. .Round Rock
16-17-18-19 at Albuquerque
20-21-22-23-24. . at Omaha
25-26-27-28. . . . . . Iowa
29-30-31 . . . . .Oklahoma

SEPTEMBER
1 . . . . .Oklahoma

NASHVILLE

APRIL
3-4-5-6 . . . .at New Orleans
7-8-9-10 . . . . at Oklahoma
11-12-13-14. . . . . . Iowa
15-16-17-18. . . . .Omaha
19-20-21-22 at Albuquerque
24-25-26-27 . . . . at Omaha
28-29-30 . . . Colo. Springs

MAY
1 . . . . . Colorado Springs
2-3-4-5 . . . . . . .Salt Lake
6-7-8-9 . . . . at Tucson
10-11-12-13 . . .at Las Vegas
15-16-17-18. New Orleans
19-20-21-22. . . Memphis
23-24-25-26 . . .at Memphis
27-28-29-30 at Albuquerque
31 . . . . Iowa

JUNE
1-2-3 . . . . Iowa
5-6-7-8 . . . .Albuquerque
9-10-11-12. . . at Oklahoma
13-14-15-16 . . . . . . at Iowa
17-18-19-20. . .Oklahoma
21-22-23-24. . . Memphis
26-27-28-29 . at Round Rock
30 . . . . .at Memphis

JULY
1-2-3 . . . . . . .at Memphis
4-5-6 . . . . . .Round Rock
7-8-9-10 . . . . . . at Omaha
11-12-13 . . . New Orleans
18-19-20 . . . . .at Iowa
22-23-24-25. . . . .Tacoma
26-27-28-29. . . .Portland
30-31 . . . . . at Sacramento

AUGUST
1-2. . . . . . . at Sacramento
3-4-5-6 . . . . .at Fresno
8-9-10-11 . . . . . . Omaha
12-13-14-15. . .Oklahoma
16-17-18-19 . at Round Rock
20-21-22-23-24. . . Round Rock
25-26-27-28 Albuquerque
29-30-31 . . .at New Orleans

SEPTEMBER
1 . . . . .at New Orleans

NEW ORLEANS

APRIL
3-4-5-6 . . . . . . Nashville
7-8-9-10 . . . . . Memphis
11-12-13-14 . at Round Rock
15-16-17-18. . . . . . Iowa
19-20-21-22 . . . . at Omaha
24-25-26-27. .Round Rock
28-29-30 . . . . . . .at Tacoma

MAY
1 . . . . .at Tacoma
2-3-4-5 . . . . . . at Portland
6-7-8-9 . . . . Fresno
10-11-12-13. .Sacramento
15-16-17-18 . . . at Nashville
19-20-22 . . . . at Oklahoma
23-24-25-26 Albuquerque
27-28-29-30. .Round Rock
31 . . . . at Round Rock

JUNE
1-2-3 . . . . . at Round Rock
5-6-7-8 . . . . . . .Oklahoma
9-10-11-12. . . . . .Omaha
13-14-14-15-16 . . . .at Okla.
17-18-19-20 . . . . . . at Iowa
21-22-23-24. . . . .Omaha
26-27-28-29 . . .at Memphis
30 . . . . .Oklahoma

JULY
1-2-3 . . . . .Oklahoma
4-5-6 . . . . at Albuquerque
7-8-9-10 . . . . . Memphis
11-12-12-13 . . . at Nashville
18-19-20-21 Albuquerque
22-23-24-25 at Colo. Springs
26-27-28-29 . . . at Salt Lake
30-31 . . . . .Tucson

AUGUST
1-2. . . . . Tucson
3-4-5-6 . . . . . . Las Vegas
8-9-10-11. . . . .at Memphis
12-13-14-15 . . . . . .at Iowa
16-17-18-19. . . . . . Iowa
20-21-22-23-24. . . . . . . at Albuquerque
25-26-27-28 . . . . at Omaha
29-30-31 . . . . . Nashville

SEPTEMBER
1 . . . . Nashville

OKLAHOMA

APRIL
3-4-5-6 . . . . . . Memphis
7-8-9-10 . . . . . Nashville
11-12-13-14 at Albuquerque
15-16-17-18. .Round Rock
19-20-21-22 . . . . . . at Iowa
24-25-26-27 Albuquerque
28-29-30 . . . . . at Portland

MAY
1 . . . . at Portland
2-3-4-5 . . . . at Tacoma
6-7-8-9 . . . . .Sacramento
10-11-12-13. . . . . Fresno
15-16-17-18 . . .at Memphis
19-20-22 . . . New Orleans
23-24-25-26 . . . . . . at Iowa
27-28-29-30 . . . . at Omaha
31 . . . . .Omaha

JUNE
1-2-3 . . . . .Omaha
5-6-7-8 . . . .at New Orleans
9-10-11-12. . . . Nashville
13-14-14-15-16. . New Orl.
17-18-19-20 . . . at Nashville
21-22-23-24. .Round Rock
27-28-28-29 . . . . at Omaha
30 . . . . . . .at New Orleans

JULY
1-2-3 . . . . .at New Orleans
4-5-6 . . . . Iowa
7-8-9-10 . . .Albuquerque
11-12-13-14 . at Round Rock
18-19-20-21. . . Memphis
22-23-24-25 . . . at Salt Lake
26-27-28-29 at Colo. Springs
30-31 . . . . Las Vegas

AUGUST
1-2. . . . . Las Vegas
3-4-5-6 . . . . Tucson
8-9-10-11. . at Albuquerque
12-13-14-15 . . . at Nashville
16-17-18-19. . . . .Omaha
20-21-22-23-24. . . . Iowa
25-26-27-28 . at Round Rock
29-30-31 . . . . . .at Memphis

SEPTEMBER
1 . . . . .at Memphis

OMAHA

APRIL
3-4-5-6 . . . .Albuquerque
7-8-9-10 . . . .Round Rock
11-12-13-14 . . .at Memphis
15-16-17-18 . . . at Nashville
19-20-21-22. New Orleans
24-25-26-27. . . Nashville
28-29-30 . . . at Sacramento

MAY
1 . . . . at Sacramento
2-3-4-5 . . . . .at Fresno
6-7-8-9 . . . . . . .Portland
10-11-12-13. . . . .Tacoma
15-16-17-18 at Albuquerque
19-20-21-22. . . . . . Iowa
23-24-25-26 . at Round Rock
27-28-29-30. . .Oklahoma
31 . . . . at Oklahoma

JUNE
1-2-3 . . . . . . at Oklahoma
5-6-7-8 . . . . Iowa
9-10-11-12. .at New Orleans
13-14-15-16 at Albuquerque
17-18-19-20 . at Round Rock
21-22-23-24 .at New Orleans
27-28-28-29. . .Oklahoma
30 . . . . .at Iowa

JULY
1-2-3 . . . . .at Iowa
4-5-6 . . . . Memphis
7-8-9-10 . . . . . Nashville
11-12-12-13 . . .at Memphis
18-19-20-21. .Round Rock
22-23-24-25 . . .at Las Vegas
26-27-28-29 . . . . at Tucson
30-31 . . . . .Salt Lake

AUGUST
1-2. . . . . .Salt Lake
3-4-5-6 . Colorado Springs
8-9-10-11. . . . . at Nashville
12-13-14-15 Albuquerque
16-17-18-19 . . at Oklahoma
20-21-22-23-24. Memphis
25-26-27-28. New Orleans
29-30-31 . . . . .at Iowa

SEPTEMBER
1 . . . . .at Iowa

PORTLAND

APRIL
3-4-5-6 . . . . Fresno
7-8-9-10 . . . . Sacramento
11-12-13-14 . . . at Salt Lake
15-16-17-18 at Colo. Springs
19-20-21-22. . . . Salt Lake
24-25-26-27 . . .at Las Vegas
28-29-30 . . . . . Oklahoma

MAY
1 . . . . Oklahoma
2-3-4-5 . . . . New Orleans
6-7-8-9 . . . . at Omaha
10-11-12-13 . . . . . . at Iowa
15-16-17-18. . . Las Vegas
19-20-21-22. . . . Tucson
23-24-25-26 . . . at Salt Lake
27-28-29-30. . Sacramento
31 . . . . Las Vegas

JUNE
1-2-3 . . . . Las Vegas
5-6-7-8 . . . . at Sacramento
9-10-11-12. . . .at Las Vegas
13-14-15-16 . . . . .at Fresno
17-18-19-20. . . . . Tucson
21-22-23-24 . . . . at Tacoma
26-27-28-29 Colo. Springs
30 . . . . at Sacramento

JULY
1-2-3 . . . . . at Sacramento
4-5-6 . . . . Tacoma
7-8-9-10 . . . . . . .at Fresno
11-12-13-13 . . . . at Tucson
18-19-20-21 Colo. Springs
22-23-24-25 . . . at Memphis
26-27-28-29 . . . at Nashville
30-31 . . . . . Albuquerque

AUGUST
1-2. . . . . . . Albuquerque
3-4-5-6 . . . . . Round Rock
8-9-10-11. . at Colo. Springs
12-13-14-15. . . . . Fresno
16-17-18-19 . . . . at Tucson
20-21-22-23-24. . . Tacoma
25-26-27-28. . . . Salt Lake
29-30-31 . . . . . . at Tacoma

SEPTEMBER
1 . . . . at Tacoma

ROUND ROCK

APRIL
3-4-5-6 . . . . at Iowa
7-8-9-10 . . . . . . at Omaha
11-12-13-14. New Orleans
15-16-17-18 . . at Oklahoma
19-20-21-22. . . Memphis
24-25-26-27 .at New Orleans
28-29-30 . . . . Tucson

MAY
1 . . . . Tucson
2-3-4-5 . . . . . . Las Vegas
6-7-8-9 .at Colorado Springs
10-11-12-13 . . . at Salt Lake
15-16-17-18. . . . . . Iowa
19-20-21-22 at Albuquerque
23-24-25-26. . . . . Omaha
27-28-29-30 .at New Orleans
31 . . . . New Orleans

JUNE
1-2-3 . . . . . New Orleans
5-6-7-8 . . . . . .at Memphis
9-10-11-12. at Albuquerque
13-14-15-16. . . Memphis
17-18-19-20. . . . . Omaha
21-22-23-24 . . at Oklahoma
26-27-28-29. . . Nashville
30 . . . . Albuquerque

JULY
1-2-3 . . . . . Albuquerque
4-5-6 . . . . at Nashville
7-8-9-10 . . . . at Iowa
11-12-13-14. . . Oklahoma
18-19-20-21 . . . . at Omaha
22-23-24-25. . . . . Fresno
26-27-28-29. . Sacramento
30-31 . . . . at Tacoma

AUGUST
1-2. . . . . at Tacoma
3-4-5-6 . . . . . . at Portland
8-9-10-11 . . . . Iowa
12-13-14-15 . . .at Memphis
16-17-18-19. . . Nashville
20-21-22-23-24 at Nashville
25-26-27-28. . . Oklahoma
29-30-31 . . . Albuquerque

SEPTEMBER
1 . . . . Albuquerque

SACRAMENTO

APRIL
3-4-5-6 . . . . at Tacoma
7-8-9-10 . . . . . at Portland
11-12-13-14. . . Las Vegas
15-16-17-18. . . . . Tucson
19-20-21-22. . .at Las Vegas
24-25-26-27 at Colo. Springs
28-29-30 . . . . Omaha

MAY
1 . . . . Omaha
2-3-4-5 . . . . Iowa
6-7-8-9 . . . . . at Oklahoma
10-11-12-13 .at New Orleans
15-16-17-18. . . . Salt Lake
19-20-21-22 Colo. Springs
23-24-25-26 . . . . at Tucson
27-28-29-30. . . at Portland
31 . . . .at Colorado Springs

JUNE
1-2-3 . .at Colorado Springs
5-6-7-8 . . . . Portland
9-10-11-12. . . . . at Tucson
13-14-15-16. . . . . Tacoma
17-18-19-20. . . . . Fresno
21-22-23-24 . . . at Salt Lake
26-27-28-29. . . . . Tucson
30 . . . . Portland

JULY
1-2-3 . . . . Portland
4-5-6 . . . . .at Fresno
7-8-9-10 Colorado Springs
11-12-13-14 . . . at Salt Lake
18-19-20-21. . . Las Vegas
22-23-24-25 at Albuquerque
26-27-28-29 . at Round Rock
30-31 . . . . Nashville

AUGUST
1-2. . . . . Nashville
3-4-5-6 . . . . . . Memphis
8-9-10-11. . . . .at Las Vegas
12-13-14-15. . . . Salt Lake
16-17-18-19. . . . . Tacoma
20-21-22-23-24. . .at Fresno
25-26-27-28 . . . . at Tacoma
29-30-31 . . . . Fresno

SEPTEMBER
1 . . . . Fresno

SALT LAKE

APRIL
3-4-5-6 . . . . . .at Las Vegas
7-8-9-10 . . . . . . at Tucson
11-12-13-14. . . . Portland
15-16-17-18. . . Las Vegas
19-20-21-22 . . . at Portland
24-25-26-27. . . . . Fresno
28-29-30 . . . . . at Memphis

MAY
1 . . . . at Memphis
2-3-4-5 . . . . . . at Nashville
6-7-8-9 . . . . Albuquerque
10-11-12-13. . Round Rock
15-16-17-18 . at Sacramento
19-20-21-22 . . . . .at Fresno
23-24-25-26. . . . Portland
27-28-29-30 Colo. Springs
31 . . . . at Tacoma

JUNE
1-2-3 . . . . at Tacoma
5-6-7-8 .at Colorado Springs
9-10-11-12. . . . . . Tacoma
13-14-15-16. . . Las Vegas
17-18-19-20 at Colo. Springs
21-22-23-24. . Sacramento
26-27-28-29 . . . . at Tacoma
30 . . . . .at Las Vegas

JULY
1-2-3 . . . . . . .at Las Vegas
4-5-6 . . . . Tucson
7-8-9-10 . . . . Tacoma
11-12-13-14. . Sacramento
18-19-20-21 . . . . .at Fresno
22-23-24-25. . . Oklahoma
26-27-28-29. New Orleans
30-31 . . . . at Omaha

AUGUST
1-2. . . . . at Omaha
3-4-5-6 . . . . at Iowa
8-9-10-11 . . . . . . Fresno
12-13-14-15 . at Sacramento
16-17-18-19 Colo. Springs
20-21-22-23-24. . . Tucson
25-26-27-28 . . . at Portland
29-30-31 . . . . . . at Tucson

SEPTEMBER
1 . . . . at Tucson

TACOMA

APRIL
3-4-5-6 . . . . . Sacramento
7-8-9-10 . . . . Fresno
11-12-13-14 at Colo. Springs
15-16-17-18 . . . . .at Fresno
19-20-21-22 Colo. Springs
24-25-26-27 . . . . at Tucson
28-29-30 . . . New Orleans

MAY
1 . . . . New Orleans
2-3-4-5 . . . . . . Oklahoma
6-7-8-9 . . . . at Iowa
10-11-12-13 . . . . at Omaha
15-16-17-18. . . . . Tucson
19-20-21-22. . . Las Vegas
23-24-25-26 at Colo. Springs
27-28-29-30. . . . .at Fresno
31 . . . . Salt Lake

JUNE
1-2-3 . . . . Salt Lake
5-6-7-8 . . . . Fresno
9-10-11-12. . . . at Salt Lake
13-14-15-16 . at Sacramento
17-18-19-20 . . .at Las Vegas
21-22-23-24. . . . Portland
26-27-28-29. . . . Salt Lake
30 . . . . Colorado Springs

JULY
1-2-3 . . Colorado Springs
4-5-6 . . . . at Portland
7-8-9-10 . . . . . at Salt Lake
11-12-13-14 . . .at Las Vegas
18-19-20-21. . . . . Tucson
22-23-24-25 . . . at Nashville
26-27-28-29 . . . at Memphis
30-31 . . . . . . Round Rock

AUGUST
1-2. . . . . Round Rock
3-4-5-6 . . . . Albuquerque
8-9-10-11. . . . . . at Tucson
12-13-14-15. . . Las Vegas
16-17-18-19 . at Sacramento
20-21-22-23-24 . at Portland
25-26-27-28. . Sacramento
29-30-31 . . . . . . Portland

SEPTEMBER
1 . . . . Portland

TUCSON

APRIL
3-4-5-6 . Colorado Springs
7-8-9-10 . . . . . . Salt Lake
11-12-13-14 . . . . . at Fresno
15-16-17-18 . at Sacramento
19-20-21-22. . . . . Fresno
24-25-26-27. . . . . Tacoma
28-29-30 . . . at Round Rock

MAY
1 . . . . at Round Rock
2-3-4-5 . . . at Albuquerque
6-7-8-9 . . . . . . Nashville
10-11-12-13. . . Memphis
15-16-17-18 . . . . at Tacoma
19-20-21-22 . . . at Portland
23-24-25-26. . Sacramento
27-28-29-30. . . Las Vegas
31 . . . . at Fresno

JUNE
1-2-3 . . . . at Fresno
5-6-7-8 . . . . . . at Las Vegas
9-10-11-12. . . Sacramento
13-14-15-16 Colo. Springs
17-18-19-20 . . . at Portland
21-22-23-24. . . Las Vegas
26-27-28-29 . at Sacramento
30 . . . . Fresno

JULY
1-2-3 . . . . Fresno
4-5-6 . . . . at Salt Lake
7-8-9-10 . . . . . at Las Vegas
11-12-13-13. . . . Portland
18-19-20-21 . . . . at Tacoma
22-23-24-25. . . . . . Iowa
26-27-28-29. . . . . Omaha
30-31 . . . . . at New Orleans

AUGUST
1-2. . . . . . . at New Orleans
3-4-5-6 . . . . . at Oklahoma
8-9-10-11 . . . . . . Tacoma
12-13-14-15 at Colo. Springs
16-17-18-19. . . . Portland
20-21-22-23-24 at Salt Lake
25-26-27-28 at Colo. Springs
29-30-31 . . . . . . Salt Lake

SEPTEMBER
1 . . . . Salt Lake

DOUBLE-A

EASTERN LEAGUE

AKRON

APRIL
3-4-5-6 . . . . . at Harrisburg
7-8-9 . . . . . at Binghamton
10-11-12-13. . . . . . Bowie
14-15-16 . . . Binghamton
17-18-19-20 . . . . . at Bowie
21-22-23 . . . . . . at Altoona
24-25-26-27. . Harrisburg
29-30 . . . . Erie

MAY
1 . . . . Erie
2-3-4 . . . . at Bowie
5-6-7-8 . . . . Altoona
9-10-11. . . . . . . Trenton
13-14-15 . . . . . . at Altoona
16-17-18 . . . . . . at Reading
19-20-21-22. . . . Altoona
23-24-25-26. . . . . . . Erie
27-28-29 . . . . at Harrisburg
30-31 . . . . Bowie

JUNE
1 . . . . Bowie
3-4-5 . . at New Hampshire
6-7-8 . . . . at Portland
10-11-12 . New Hampshire
13-14-15 . . . . . . Portland
17-18-19 . . . . at Bowie
20-21-22 . . . . . . at Reading
23-24-25-26. . . . . . Bowie
27-28-29 . . . . . . Reading
30 . . . . at Erie

JULY
1-2-3 . . . . at Erie
4-5-6-7 . . . . at Binghamton
8-9-10. . . . . Bowie
11-12-13-14 . . . . at Reading
17-18-19-20. . . . . . . Erie
21-22-23-24 . . . . at Altoona
25-26-27 . . . Binghamton
28-29-30-31 . . . . Erie

AUGUST
1-2-3 . . . . . . Harrisburg
4-5-6 . . . . at Altoona
7-8-9-10 . . . . . . at Trenton
12-13-14. . . . Connecticut
15-16-17. . . . New Britain
19-20-21 . . . at Connecticut
22-23-24 . . . at New Britain
26-27-28. . . . . . Altoona
29-30-31 . . . . at Erie

SEPTEMBER
1 . . . . at Erie

ALTOONA

APRIL
3-4-5-6 . . . . Reading
7-8-9 . . . . Trenton
11-12-13 . . . . . . at Reading
14-15-16 . . . . at Trenton
17-18-19-20. . . . . . . Erie
21-22-23 . . . . Akron
24-25-26-27 . . . . . . at Erie
29-30 . . . . . . Harrisburg

MAY
1 . . . . Harrisburg
2-3-4 . . . . Erie
5-6-7-8 . . . . at Akron
9-10-11-12. . . . . at Reading
13-14-15. . . . . Akron
16-17-18 . . . . at Harrisburg
19-20-21-22 . . . . . at Akron
23-24-25-26. . . . Trenton
27-28-29 . . . . at Bowie
30-31 . . . . at Erie

JUNE
1 . . . . at Erie
3-4-5 . . . . . . New Britain
6-7-8 . . . . . . Connecticut
10-11-12 . . . at New Britain
13-14-15 . . . at Connecticut
17-18-19 . . . . . . Reading
20-21-22. . . . . Bowie
23-24-25-26 . at Binghamton
27-28-29 . . . . at Bowie
30 . . . . Binghamton

JULY
1-2-3 . . . . . Binghamton
4-5-6-7 . . . . . Harrisburg
8-9-10. . . . . at Trenton
11-12-13-14 . . . . at Erie
17-18-19-20. . Harrisburg
21-22-23-24. . . . . . Akron
25-26-27 . . . . at Harrisburg
28-29-30-31 . . . . at Trenton

AUGUST
1-2-3 . . . . Bowie
4-5-6 . . . . Akron
7-8-9-10 . . . . at Harrisburg
12-13-14 . . . . . . at Portland
15-16-17 at New Hampshire
19-20-21 . . . . . . Portland
22-23-24 . New Hampshire
26-27-28 . . . . at Akron
29-30-31 . . . . . . Reading

SEPTEMBER
1 . . . . Reading

BINGHAMTON

APRIL
3-4-5-6 . . . . Trenton
7-8-9 . . . . Akron
10-11-12-13 . . . . . . at Erie
14-15-16 . . . . at Akron
17-18-19-20. . . . Portland
21-22-23 . . . . . . Trenton
24-25-26-27 . . . at Portland
29-30 . . . . . . New Britain

MAY
1 . . . . New Britain
2-3-4 . . . . . . Connecticut
5-6-7-8 . . . . at Reading
9-10-11 . . . . at Connecticut
13-14-15. . . . New Britain
16-17-18. . . . . Erie
19-20-21-22 . at Connecticut
23-24-25-26. . . . Reading
27-28-29 . . . . . . at Portland
30-31 . . . . . at Connecticut

JUNE
1 . . . . at Connecticut
3-4-5 . . . . . . at Harrisburg
6-7-8 . . . . . . New Britain
10-11-12. . . . Harrisburg
13-14-15 . . . at New Britain
17-18-19 . . . . Erie
20-21-22 . . . . . . at Trenton
23-24-25-26. . . . Altoona
27-28-29 . . . . Connecticut
30 . . . . at Altoona

JULY
1-2-3 . . . . at Altoona
4-5-6-7 . . . . Akron
8-9-10. . . . . at Connecticut
11-12-13-14 . . . . at Trenton
17-18-19-20. . Connecticut
21-22-23-24 . . . . . . at Erie
25-26-27 . . . . at Akron
28-29-30-31. . Connecticut

AUGUST
1-2-3 . . . . . at New Britain
4-5-6 . . . . at Bowie
7-8-9-10 . New Hampshire
12-13-14. . . . . . Reading
15-16-17 . . . . at Bowie
19-20-21 . New Hampshire
22-23-24. . . . . Bowie
26-27-28 at New Hampshire
29-30-31 . . . at New Britain

SEPTEMBER
1 . . . . at New Britain

BOWIE

APRIL
3-4-5-6 . . . . Erie
7-8-9 . . . . Reading
10-11-12-13 . . . . . at Akron
14-15-16 . . . . at Erie
17-18-19-20. . . . . . Akron
21-22-23 . . . at Connecticut
24-25-26-27 . . . . . . at New Hampshire
29-30 . . . . Portland

MAY
1 . . . . Portland
2-3-4 . . . . Akron
5-6-7-8 . . . . at New Britain
9-10-11 . . . . at Portland
13-14-15 . . . . Erie
16-17-18 . . . . Connecticut
19-20-21-22 . . . . . . at Erie
23-24-25-26. . . . . . . New Hampshire
27-28-29 . . . . . . Altoona
30-31 . . . . at Akron

JUNE
1 . . . . at Akron
3-4-5 . . . . Reading
6-7-8 . . . . . . at Harrisburg

10-11-12 . . . . . .at Reading
13-14-15 . . . . Harrisburg
17-18-19 . . . . .Akron
20-21-22 . . . . . .at Altoona
23-24-25-26 . . . . . at Akron
27-28-29 . . . . . . Altoona
30 . . . . at Harrisburg

JULY

1-2-3 . . . . . . at Harrisburg
4-5-6-7 . . . . Erie
8-9-10. . . . . at Akron
11-12-13-14 . . at Harrisburg
17-18-19-20. . . . Reading
21-22-23-24. . Harrisburg
25-26-27 . . . . at Erie
28-29-30-31. . New Britain

AUGUST

1-2-3 . . . . .at Altoona
4-5-6 . . . . . Binghamton
7-8-9-10 . . . . New Britain
12-13-14 . . . . . . at Trenton
15-16-17 . . . Binghamton
19-20-21 . . . . . .at Reading
22-23-24 . . .at Binghamton
26-27-28 . . . . . . Trenton
29-30-31 . . . . at Harrisburg

SEPTEMBER

1 . . . . at Harrisburg

CONNECTICUT

APRIL

3-4-5-6 . . New Hampshire
7-8-9 . . . . Portland
10-11-12-13 . . . . . . at New Hampshire
14-15-16 . . . . . at Portland
17-18-19-20. . . . Reading
21-22-23 . . . . .Bowie
25-26-27 . . . . . .at Reading
29-30 . . . . Trenton

MAY

1 . . . . Trenton
2-3-4 . . . . .at Binghamton
5-6-7-8 . . . . . at Harrisburg
9-10-11. . . . Binghamton
13-14-15 at New Hampshire
16-17-18 . . . . at Bowie
19-20-21-22. Binghamton
23-24-25-26. . Harrisburg
27-28-29 . . . at New Britain
30-31 . . . . . Binghamton

JUNE

1 . . . . Binghamton
3-4-5 . . . . Trenton
6-7-8 . . . . .at Altoona
10-11-12 . . . . . .at Trenton
13-14-15 . . . . . . Altoona
17-18-19 at New Hampshire
20-21-22 . . . . New Britain
23-24-25-26. . . . Portland
27-28-29 . . .at Binghamton
30 . . . . . New Hampshire

JULY

1-2-3 . . . New Hampshire
4-5-6-7 . . . . at New Britain
8-9-10. . . . . Binghamton
11-12-13-14. . . . . . .New Hampshire
17-18-19-20 . at Binghamton
21-22-23-24 . . . at Portland
25-26-27 . . . . New Britain
28-29-30-31 . at Binghamton

AUGUST

1-2-3 . . at New Hampshire
4-5-6 . . . . Trenton
7-8-9-10 . . . . . .Portland
12-13-14 . . . . at Akron
15-16-17 . . . . at Erie
19-20-21 . . . . .Akron
22-23-24 . . . . Erie
25-26-27-28 . . . .at Reading
29-30-31 . . . . . . at Trenton

SEPTEMBER

1 . . . . at Trenton

ERIE

APRIL

3-4-5-6 . . . . at Bowie
7-8-9 . . . . . . at Harrisburg
10-11-12-13. Binghamton
14-15-16 . . . . .Bowie
17-18-19-20 . . . .at Altoona
21-22-23 . . . . at Harrisburg
24-25-26-27. . . . Altoona
29-30 . . . . at Akron

MAY

1 . . . . at Akron
2-3-4 . . . . .at Altoona
5-6-7-8 . . . . Trenton
9-10-11. . . . . Harrisburg
13-14-15 . . . . at Bowie
16-17-18 . . .at Binghamton
19-20-21-22. . . . . .Bowie
23-24-25-26 . . . . . at Akron
27-28-29 . . . . . . Reading
30-31 . . . . Altoona

JUNE

1 . . . . Altoona
3-4-5 . . . . at Portland
6-7-8 . . at New Hampshire
10-11-12 . . . . . .Portland
13-14-15 . New Hampshire
17-18-19 . . .at Binghamton
20-21-22 . . . . at Harrisburg
23-24-25-26 . . . . at Trenton
27-28-29 . . . . Harrisburg
30 . . . . .Akron

JULY

1-2-3 . . . . .Akron
4-5-6-7 . . . . at Bowie
8-9-10. . . . . .at Reading
11-12-13-14. . . . Altoona
17-18-19-20 . . . . . at Akron
21-22-23-24. Binghamton
25-26-27 . . . . .Bowie
28-29-30-31 . . . . . at Akron

AUGUST

1-2-3 . . . . Reading
4-5-6 . . . . Harrisburg
7-8-9-10 . . . . . .at Reading
12-13-14 . . . . New Britain
15-16-17 . . . .Connecticut
19-20-21 . . . at New Britain
22-23-24 . . . at Connecticut
26-27-28 . . . . Harrisburg
29-30-31 . . . . .Akron

SEPTEMBER

1 . . . . .Akron

HARRISBURG

APRIL

3-4-5-6 . . . . .Akron
7-8-9 . . . . Erie
10-11-12-13 . . . . at Trenton
14-15-16 . . . . . .at Reading
17-18-19-20. . . . . . .New Hampshire
21-22-23 . . . . Erie
24-25-26-27 . . . . . at Akron
29-30 . . . . .at Altoona

MAY

1 . . . . .at Altoona
2-3-4 . . . . Reading
5-6-7-8 . . . . .Connecticut
9-10-11 . . . . at Erie
13-14-15 . . . . . . Reading
16-17-18 . . . . . . Altoona
19-20-21-22 . at New Britain
23-24-25-26 . at Connecticut
27-28-29 . . . . .Akron
30-31 . . . . .at Reading

JUNE

1 . . . . .at Reading
3-4-5 . . . . . Binghamton
6-7-8 . . . . .Bowie
10-11-12 . . .at Binghamton
13-14-15 . . . . at Bowie
17-18-19 . . . . . . Trenton
20-21-22 . . . . Erie
23-24-25-26 . . . .at Reading
27-28-29 . . . . at Erie
30 . . . . .Bowie

JULY

1-2-3 . . . . .Bowie
4-5-6-7 . . . . . . .at Altoona
8-9-10. . . . . . New Britain
11-12-13-14. . . . . .Bowie
17-18-19-20 . . . .at Altoona
21-22-23-24 . . . . . at Bowie
25-26-27 . . . . . . Altoona
28-29-30-31 . . . . Reading

AUGUST

1-2-3 . . . . at Akron
4-5-6 . . . . at Erie
7-8-9-10 . . . . . . Altoona
12-13-14 at New Hampshire
15-16-17 . . . . . at Portland
19-20-21 . . . . . . at Trenton
22-23-24 . . . . . .Portland
26-27-28 . . . . at Erie
29-30-31 . . . . .Bowie

SEPTEMBER

1 . . . . .Bowie

NEW BRITAIN

APRIL

3-4-5-6 . . . . . . .Portland
8-9. . . . . New Hampshire
11-12-13 . . . . . at Portland
14-15-16 at New Hampshire
17-18-19-20. . . . Trenton
21-22-23 . . . . . . Reading
24-25-26-27 . . . . at Trenton
29-30 . . . . .at Binghamton

MAY

1 . . . . .at Binghamton
2-3-4 . . . New Hampshire
5-6-7-8 . . . . .Bowie
9-10-11-12. . . . . . . at New Hampshire
13-14-15 . . .at Binghamton
16-17-18 . . . . . .Portland
19-20-21-22. . Harrisburg
23-24-25-26 . . . at Portland
27-28-29 . . . .Connecticut
30-31 . . . . Trenton

JUNE

1 . . . . Trenton
3-4-5 . . . . .at Altoona
6-7-8 . . . . .at Binghamton
10-11-12. . . . . . Altoona
13-14-15 . . . Binghamton
17-18-19 . . . . . at Portland
20-21-22 . . . at Connecticut
23-24-25-26. . . . . . .New Hampshire
27-28-29 at New Hampshire
30 . . . . .at Reading

JULY

1-2-3 . . . . .at Reading
4-5-6-7 . . . . .Connecticut
8-9-10. . . . . . at Harrisburg
11-12-13-14. . . . Portland
17-18-19-20 . . . . . . at New Hampshire
21-22-23-24. . . . Reading
25-26-27 . . . at Connecticut
28-29-30-31 . . . . . at Bowie

AUGUST

1-2-3 . . . . . Binghamton
4-5-6 . . . New Hampshire
7-8-9-10 . . . . at Bowie
12-13-14 . . . . at Erie
15-16-17 . . . . at Akron
19-20-21 . . . . Erie
22-23-24 . . . . .Akron
25-26-27-28 . . . at Portland
29-30-31 . . . Binghamton

SEPTEMBER

1 . . . . Binghamton

NEW HAMPSHIRE

APRIL

3-4-5-6 . . . . at Connecticut
8-9. . . . . at New Britain
10-11-12-13. .Connecticut
14-15-16 . . . . New Britain
17-18-19-20 . . at Harrisburg
21-22-23 . . . . . at Portland
24-25-26-27. . . . . .Bowie
29-30 . . . . Reading

MAY

1 . . . . Reading
2-3-4 . . . . . . at New Britain
5-6-7-8 . . . . at Portland
9-10-11-12. . . New Britain
13-14-15 . . . .Connecticut
16-17-18 . . . . at Trenton
20-21-22 . . . . . . .Portland
23-24-25-26 . . . . . at Bowie
27-28-29 . . . . . . at Trenton
30-31 . . . . Portland

JUNE
1-2 Portland
3-4-5 Akron
6-7-8 Erie
10-11-12 at Akron
13-14-15 at Erie
17-18-19 Connecticut
20-21-22 Portland
23-24-25-26 at New Britain
27-28-29 New Britain
30 at Connecticut

JULY
1-2-3 at Connecticut
4-5-6-7 Trenton
8-9-10 at Portland
11-12-13-14 at Connecticut
17-18-19-20 New Britain
21-22-23-24 Trenton
25-26-27 at Reading
28-29-30-31 Portland

AUGUST
1-2-3 Connecticut
4-5-6 at New Britain
7-8-9-10 at Binghamton
12-13-14 Harrisburg
15-16-17 Altoona
19-20-21 at Binghamton
22-23-24 at Altoona
26-27-28 Binghamton
29-30-31 at Portland

SEPTEMBER
1 at Portland

PORTLAND

APRIL
3-4-5-6 at New Britain
7-8-9 at Connecticut
11-12-13 New Britain
14-15-16 Connecticut
17-18-19-20 at Binghamton
21-22-23 New Hampshire
24-25-26-27 Binghamton
29-30 at Bowie

MAY
1 at Bowie
2-3-4 at Trenton
5-6-7-8 New Hampshire
9-10-11 Bowie
13-14-15 at Trenton
16-17-18 at New Britain
20-21-22 at New Hampshire
23-24-25-26 New Britain
27-28-29 Binghamton
30-31 at New Hampshire

JUNE
1-2 at New Hampshire
3-4-5 Erie
6-7-8 Akron
10-11-12 at Erie
13-14-15 at Akron
17-18-19 New Britain
20-21-22 at New Hampshire
23-24-25-26 at Connecticut
27-28-29 Trenton
30 at Trenton

JULY
1-2-3 at Trenton
4-5-6-7 Reading
8-9-10 New Hampshire
11-12-13-14 at New Britain
17-18-19-20 Trenton
21-22-23-24 Connecticut
25-26-27 at Trenton
28-29-30-31 at New Hampshire

AUGUST
1-2-3 Trenton
4-5-6 at Reading
7-8-9-10 at Connecticut
12-13-14 Altoona
15-16-17 Harrisburg
19-20-21 at Altoona
22-23-24 at Harrisburg
25-26-27-28 New Britain
29-30-31 New Hampshire

SEPTEMBER
1 New Hampshire

READING

APRIL
3-4-5-6 at Altoona
7-8-9 at Bowie
11-12-13 Altoona
14-15-16 Harrisburg
17-18-19-20 at Connecticut
21-22-23 at New Britain
25-26-27 Connecticut
29-30 at New Hampshire

MAY
1 at New Hampshire
2-3-4 at Harrisburg
5-6-7-8 Binghamton
9-10-11-12 Altoona
13-14-15 at Harrisburg
16-17-18 Akron
20-21-22 Trenton
23-24-25-26 at Binghamton
27-28-29 at Erie
30-31 Harrisburg

JUNE
1 Harrisburg
3-4-5 at Bowie
6-7-8 at Trenton
10-11-12 Bowie
13-14-15 Trenton
17-18-19 at Altoona
20-21-22 Akron
23-24-25-26 Harrisburg
27-28-29 at Akron
30 New Britain

JULY
1-2-3 New Britain
4-5-6-7 at Portland
8-9-10 Erie
11-12-13-14 Akron
17-18-19-20 at Bowie
21-22-23-24 at New Britain
25-26-27 New Hampshire
28-29-30-31 at Harrisburg

AUGUST
1-2-3 at Erie
4-5-6 Portland
7-8-9-10 Erie
12-13-14 at Binghamton
15-16-17-18 Trenton
19-20-21 Bowie
22-23-24 at Trenton
25-26-27-28 Connecticut
29-30-31 at Altoona

SEPTEMBER
1 at Altoona

TRENTON

APRIL
3-4-5-6 at Binghamton
7-8-9 at Altoona
10-11-12-13 Harrisburg
14-15-16 Altoona
17-18-19-20 at New Britain
21-22-23 at Binghamton
24-25-26-27 New Britain
29-30 at Connecticut

MAY
1 at Connecticut
2-3-4 Portland
5-6-7-8 at Erie
9-10-11 at Akron
13-14-15 Portland
16-17-18 New Hampshire
20-21-22 at Reading
23-24-25-26 at Altoona
27-28-29 New Hampshire
30-31 at New Britain

JUNE
1 at New Britain
3-4-5 at Connecticut
6-7-8 Reading
10-11-12 Connecticut
13-14-15 at Reading
17-18-19 at Harrisburg
20-21-22 Binghamton
23-24-25-26 Erie
27-28-29 at Portland
30 Portland

JULY
1-2-3 Portland
4-5-6-7 at New Hampshire
8-9-10 Altoona
11-12-13-14 Binghamton
17-18-19-20 at Portland
21-22-23-24at New Hampshire
25-26-27 Portland
28-29-30-31 Altoona

AUGUST
1-2-3 at Portland
4-5-6 at Connecticut
7-8-9-10 Akron
12-13-14 Bowie
15-16-17-18 at Reading
19-20-21 Harrisburg
22-23-24 Reading
26-27-28 at Bowie
29-30-31 Connecticut

SEPTEMBER
1 Connecticut

SOUTHERN LEAGUE

BIRMINGHAM

APRIL
3-4-5-6-7 Tennessee
8-9-10-11-12at Chattanooga
14-15-16-17-18 Mississippi
19-20-21-22-23 at West Tenn
24-25-26-27-28 Mont
30 Mobile

MAY
1-2-3-4 Mobile
5-6-7-8-9 at Montgomery
10-11-12-13-14 West Tenn
15-16-17-18-19at Jacksonville
21-22-23-24-25 at Huntsville
26-27-28-29-30 Jax
31 at Mississippi

JUNE
1-2-3-4 at Mississippi
5-6-7-8-9 Montgomery
11-12-13-14-15 at Carolina
17-18-19-20-21-22 Jax
24-25-26-27-28-29 at Miss
30 Mobile

JULY
1-2-3 Mobile
4-5-6-7 at Huntsville
8-9-10-11-12 Carolina
16-17-18-19-20 at Mont
22-23-24-25-26 Miss
27-28-29-30-31 at West Tenn

AUGUST
1-2-3-4-5 Chattanooga
6-7-8-9-10 Montgomery
12-13-14-15-16at Tennessee
18-19-20-21-22 Huntsville
23-24-25-26-27 at Jax
28-29-30-31 at Mobile

SEPTEMBER
1 at Mobile

CAROLINA

APRIL
3-4-5-6-7 at Mobile
9-10-11-12-13 Mont
14-15-16-17-18 at Jacx
19-20-21-22-23 Tennessee
24-25-26-27-28 at Chatt
29-30 West Tenn

MAY
1-2-3 West Tenn
5-6-7-8-9 at Jacksonville
10-11-12-13-14 Chatt
15-16-17-18-19 at Huntsville
21-22-23-24-25 Jax
26-27-28-29-30at Tennessee
31 at Montgomery

JUNE
1-2-3-4 at Montgomery
6-7-8-9-10 Jacksonville

11-12-13-14-15Birmingham
17-18-19-20-21-22. at Chatt
24-25-26-27-28-29 .Hunts
30 . . . . at Jacksonville

JULY

1-2-3 . . . . . at Jacksonville
4-5-6-7 . . . . . .Tennessee
8-9-10-11-12 at Birmingham
16-17-18-19-20at Mississippi
22-23-24-25-26 Huntsville
27-28-29-30-31. . . . . Jax

AUGUST

1-2-3-4-5. . . . at Tennessee
6-7-8-9-10 . . . . . . Mobile
12-13-14-15-16 at West Tenn
18-19-20-21-22. . . . .Miss
23-24-25-26-27 at Huntsville
28-29-30-31. . .Tennessee

SEPTEMBER

1 . . . . .Tennessee

CHATTANOOGA

APRIL

3-4-5-6-7. . at Montgomery
8-9-10-11-12 Birmingham
14-15-16-17-18 at Huntsville
19-20-21-22-23. . . Mobile
24-25-26-27-28. . Carolina
30 . . . . .at Mississippi

MAY

1-2-3-4 . . . . .at Mississippi
5-6-7-8-9. . . . .Tennessee
10-11-12-13-14. .at Carolina
15-16-17-18-19 Mississippi
21-22-23-24-25 at West Tenn
26-27-28-29-30. . . . Mont
31 . . . . .Huntsville

JUNE

1-2-3-4 . . . . . .Huntsville
5-6-7-8-9. . . . at Tennessee
11-12-13-14-15 at West Tenn
17-18-19-20-21-22 . .Caro
24-25-26-27-28-29. . . at Jax
30 . . . . .West Tenn

JULY

1-2-3 . . . . .West Tenn
4-5-6-7 . . . . .at Mississippi
8-9-10-11-12 . .Huntsville
16-17-18-19-20. . at Mobile
22-23-24-25-26 West Tenn
27-28-29-30-31at Mississippi

AUGUST

1-2-3-4-5. . .at Birmingham
6-7-8-9-10. . . .Tennessee
12-13-14-15-16 at Huntsville
18-19-20-21-22. . . . . Jax
23-24-25-26-27 at Tennessee
28-29-30-31. . .Huntsville

SEPTEMBER

1 . . . . .Huntsville

HUNTSVILLE

APRIL

3-4-5-6-7. . . . Mississippi
9-10-11-12-13. at West Tenn
14-15-16-17-18. . . . Chatt
19-20-21-22-23at Mississippi
24-25-26-27-28. . . . . Jax
30 . . . . . . at Montgomery

MAY

1-2-3-4 . . . at Montgomery
5-6-7-8-9. . . . . . . Mobile
10-11-12-13-14 at Tennessee
15-16-17-18-19. . Carolina
21-22-23-24-25. . . . Birm
26-27-28-29-30. . at Mobile
31 . . . . . . at Chattanooga

JUNE

1-2-3-4 . . . at Chattanooga
5-6-7-8-9. . . . .West Tenn
11-12-13-14-15. . . . .at Jax
17-18-19-20-21-22. West Tenn
24-25-26-27-28-29at Carolina
30 . . . . at Tennessee

JULY

1-2-3 . . . . . . at Tennessee
4-5-6-7 . . . . Birmingham
8-9-10-11-12at Chattanooga
16-17-18-19-20 Tennessee
22-23-24-25-26. .at Carolina
28-29-30-31 Montgomery

AUGUST

1-2-3-4-5. . . . Mississippi
6-7-8-9-10 . . . at West Tenn
12-13-14-15-16. . . . . Chattanooga
18-19-20-21-22. . . . . . . at Birmingham
23-24-25-26-27. . Carolina
28-29-30-31 at Chattanooga

SEPTEMBER

1 . . . . at Chattanooga

JACKSONVILLE

APRIL

3-4-5-6-7. . . . .West Tenn
9-10-11-12-13 at Tennessee
14-15-16-17-18. . Carolina
19-20-21-22-23. . . at Mont
24-25-26-27-28 at Huntsville
30 . . . . .Tennessee

MAY

1-2-3-4 . . . . . .Tennessee
5-6-7-8-9. . . . . . Carolina
10-11-12-13-14. . at Mobile
15-16-17-18-19. . . . Birm
21-22-23-24-25. .at Carolina
26-27-28-29-30. . . . at Birm
31 . . . . Mobile

JUNE

1-2-3-4 . . . . Mobile
6-7-8-9-10 . . . . .at Carolina
11-12-13-14-15 Huntsville
17-18-19-20-21-22. . at Birm
24-25-26-27-28-29 . Chatt
30 . . . . Carolina

JULY

1-2-3 . . . . Carolina
4-5-6-7 . . . . at Mobile
8-9-10-11-12 . Mississippi
16-17-18-19-20 at West Tenn
22-23-24-25-26. . . Mobile
27-28-29-30-31 . .at Carolina

AUGUST

1-2-3-4-5. . . . . . . Mobile
6-7-8-9-10 . . . at Mississippi

MISSISSIPPI

APRIL

3-4-5-6-7. . . . at Huntsville
9-10-11-12-13 . . . Mobile
14-15-16-17-18. . . . at Birm
19-20-21-22-23 Huntsville
24-25-26-27-28. . at Mobile
30 . . . . Chattanooga

MAY

1-2-3-4 . . . . Chattanooga
5-6-7-8-9. . . . at West Tenn
10-11-12-13-14. . . . Mont
15-16-17-18-19. . . at Chatt
20-21-22-23-24 at Tennessee
26-27-28-29-30 West Tenn
31 . . . . Birmingham

JUNE

1-2-3-4 . . . . Birmingham
5-6-7-8-9. . . . . . at Mobile
11-12-13-14-15 Tennessee
17-18-19-20-21-22. at Mont
24-25-26-27-28-29 . Birm
30 . . . . . . at Montgomery

JULY

1-2-3 . . . . at Montgomery
4-5-6-7 . . . . Chattanooga
8-9-10-11-12 at Jacksonville
16-17-18-19-20. . Carolina
22-23-24-25-26. . . . at Birm
27-28-29-30-31. . . . Chatt

AUGUST

1-2-3-4-5. . . . at Huntsville
6-7-8-9-10 . . Jacksonville
12-13-14-15-16. . at Mobile
18-19-20-21-22. .at Carolina
23-24-25-26-27. . . Mobile
28-29-30-31. . . West Tenn

SEPTEMBER

1 . . . . .West Tenn

MOBILE

APRIL

3-4-5-6-7. . . . . . Carolina
9-10-11-12-13 at Mississippi
14-15-16-17-18 West Tenn
19-20-21-22-23. . . at Chatt
24-25-26-27-28 Mississippi
30 . . . . . . .at Birmingham

MAY

1-2-3-4 . . . .at Birmingham
5-6-7-8-9. . . . at Huntsville
10-11-12-13-14. . . . . Jax
16-17-18-19-20 at West Tenn
21-22 . . . . at Montgomery
23-24-25 . . . Montgomery
26-27-28-29-30 Huntsville
31 . . . . at Jacksonville

JUNE

1-2-3-4 . . . . at Jacksonville
5-6-7-8-9. . . . Mississippi
11-12-13 . . at Montgomery
14-15 . . . . . Montgomery
17-18-19-20-21-22. . at Tenn
24-25-26-27-28-29 . Mont
30 . . . . . . .at Birmingham

JULY

1-2-3 . . . . .at Birmingham
4-5-6-7 . . . . Jacksonville
8-9-10-11-12at Montgomery
16-17-18-19-20. . . . Chatt
22-23-24-25-26. . . . . at Jax
27-28-29-30-31 Tennessee

AUGUST

1-2-3-4-5. . . at Jacksonville
6-7-8-9-10 . . . . .at Carolina
12-13-14-15-16 Mississippi
18-19-20-21-22 West Tenn
23-24-25-26-27at Mississippi
28-29-30-31. Birmingham

SEPTEMBER

1 . . . . Birmingham

MONTGOMERY

APRIL

3-4-5-6-7. . . Chattanooga
9-10-11-12-13. . .at Carolina
14-15-16-17-18 at Tennessee
19-20-21-22-23 Jacksonville
24-25-26-27-28. . . . at Birm
30 . . . . .Huntsville

MAY

1-2-3-4 . . . . . .Huntsville
5-6-7-8-9. . . Birmingham
10-11-12-13-14at Mississippi
15-16-17-18-19 Tennessee
21-22 . . . . Mobile
23-24-25 . . . . at Mobile
26-27-28-29-30. . . at Chatt
31 . . . . Carolina

JUNE

1-2-3-4 . . . . Carolina
5-6-7-8-9. . .at Birmingham
11-12-13 . . . . Mobile
14-15 . . . . at Mobile
17-18-19-20-21-22 . .Miss
24-25-26-27-28-29 at Mobile
30 . . . . Mississippi

JULY

1-2-3 . . . . . . Mississippi
4-5-6-7 . . . . . at West Tenn
8-9-10-11-12 . . . . Mobile
16-17-18-19-20. . . . Birm
22-23-24-25-26 at Tennessee
28-29-29-30-31 at Huntsville

AUGUST

1-2-3-4-5. . . . . West Tenn
6-7-8-9-10 . . at Birmingham
12-13-14-15-16. . . . . at Jax
18-19-20-21-22 Tennessee
23-24-25-26-27 at West Tenn
28-29-30-31. . Jacksonville

SEPTEMBER

1 . . . . Jacksonville

TENNESSEE

APRIL

3-4-5-6-7 . . . at Birmingham
9-10-11-12-13 Jacksonville
14-15-16-17-18. . . . Mont
19-20-21-22-23. . at Carolina
24-25-26-27-28 West Tenn
30 . . . . at Jacksonville

MAY

1-2-3-4 . . . . at Jacksonville
5-6-7-8-9 . . at Chattanooga
10-11-12-13-14 Huntsville
15-16-17-18-19 . . . at Mont
20-21-22-23-24 Mississippi
26-27-28-29-30. . Carolina
31 . . . . at West Tenn

JUNE

1-2-3-4 . . . . . at West Tenn
5-6-7-8-9. . . Chattanooga
11-12-13-14-15at Mississippi
17-18-19-20-21-22 Mobile
24-25-26-27-28-29at West Tenn
30 . . . . Huntsville

JULY

1-2-3 . . . . Huntsville
4-5-6-7 . . . . at Carolina
8-9-10-11-12 . . West Tenn
16-17-18-19-20 at Huntsville
22-23-24-25-26. . . . Mont
27-28-29-30-31 . . at Mobile

AUGUST

1-2-3-4-5. . . . . . Carolina
6-7-8-9-10 . at Chattanooga
12-13-14-15-16. . . . Birm
18-19-20-21-22. . . at Mont
23-24-25-26-27. . . . Chatt
28-29-30-31 . . . . at Carolina

SEPTEMBER

1 . . . . at Carolina

WEST TENN

APRIL

3-4-5-6-7 . . . at Jacksonville
9-10-11-12-13 . Huntsville
14-15-16-17-18. . at Mobile
19-20-21-22-23. . . . Birm
24-25-26-27-28 at Tennessee
29-30 . . . . at Carolina

MAY

1-2-3 . . . . at Carolina
5-6-7-8-9. . . . Mississippi
10-11-12-13-14. . . . at Birm
16-17-18-19-20. . . Mobile
21-22-23-24-25. . . . Chatt
26-27-28-29-30at Mississippi
31 . . . . Tennessee

JUNE

1-2-3-4 . . . . . . Tennessee
5-6-7-8-9 . . . . at Huntsville
11-12-13-14-15. . . . Chatt
17-18-19-20-21-22 at Hunts
24-25-26-27-28-29 . Tenn
30 . . . . . . at Chattanooga

JULY

1-2-3 . . . . at Chattanooga
4-5-6-7 . . . . Montgomery
8-9-10-11-12 . at Tennessee
16-17-18-19-20. . . . . Jax
22-23-24-25-26. . . at Chatt
27-28-29-30-31. . . . Birm

AUGUST

1-2-3-4-5. . at Montgomery
6-7-8-9-10 . . . . Huntsville
12-13-14-15-16. . Carolina
18-19-20-21-22. . at Mobile
23-24-25-26-27. . . . Mont
28-29-30-31 . . at Mississippi

SEPTEMBER

1 . . . . at Mississippi

TEXAS LEAGUE

ARKANSAS

APRIL

3-4-5 . . . . Midland
6-7-8 . . . . Frisco
10-11-12 . . . . . at Midland
13-14-15 . . . . at Frisco
17-18-19-20 NW Arkansas
21-22-23-24 . . . . . . at Tulsa
25-26-27-28 at NW Arkansas
29-30 . . . . Tulsa

MAY

1-2. . . . . Tulsa
3-4-5-6 . . . . . at Springfield
7-8-9-10 . . . . at Tulsa
12-13-14-15. . Springfield
16-17-18-19 NW Arkansas
21-22-23 . . at Corpus Christi
24-25-26 . . . at San Antonio
28-29-30. . Corpus Christi
31 . . . . San Antonio

JUNE

1-2. . . . . . . San Antonio
4-5-6-7 . . . at NW Arkansas
8-9-10-11. . . . at Springfield
12-13-14-15. . . . . Tulsa
16-17-18-19. . Springfield
20-21-22-23 at NW Arkansas
26-27-28 . . . . . . Midland
29-30 . . . . Frisco

JULY

1 . . . . Frisco
3-4-5 . . . . at Midland
6-7-8 . . . . at Frisco
10-11-12-13. . . . . . Tulsa
14-15-16-17 at NW Arkansas
18-19-20-21. . . . . . Tulsa
22-23-24 . . . . at Springfield
25-26-27-28 . . . . . . at Tulsa
29-30-31 . . . . Springfield

AUGUST

1-2-3-4 . . . . NW Arkansas
6-7-8 . . . . at Corpus Christi
9-10-11. . . . at San Antonio
13-14-15 . . Corpus Christi
16-17-18 . . . San Antonio
19-20-21-22 . . . . . . at Tulsa
23-24-25 . . . . at Springfield
26-27-28-29 NW Arkansas
30-31 . . . . . . Springfield

SEPTEMBER

1 . . . . Springfield

CORPUS CHRISTI

APRIL

3-4-5 . . . . Tulsa
6-7-8 . . . . . NW Arkansas
10-11-12 . . . . at Tulsa
13-14-15 . . at NW Arkansas
17-18-19-20. . . . . . Frisco
21-22-23-24. . . . Midland
25-26-27-28 . . . . . at Frisco
29-30 . . . . at Midland

MAY

1-2. . . . . at Midland
3-4-5-6 . . . . San Antonio
7-8-9-10 . . . . Frisco
12-13-14-15 . at San Antonio
16-17-18-19 . . . at Midland
21-22-23 . . . . . . Arkansas
24-25-26 . . . . Springfield
28-29-30 . . . . . at Arkansas
31 . . . . at Springfield

JUNE

1-2. . . . . at Springfield
4-5-6-7 . . . . Midland
8-9-10-11 . . San Antonio
12-13-14-15 . . . . . at Frisco
16-17-18-19 . at San Antonio
20-21-22-23 . . . . . at Frisco
26-27-28 . . . . Tulsa
29-30 . . . . . NW Arkansas

JULY

1 . . . . NW Arkansas
3-4-5 . . . . at Tulsa
6-7-8 . . . . at NW Arkansas
10-11-12-13. . . . . Frisco
14-15-16-17 . . . at Midland
18-19-20-21. . . . . Frisco
22-23-24 . . . at San Antonio
25-26-27-28. . . . Midland
29-30-31 . . . San Antonio

AUGUST

1-2-3-4 . . . . . . at Midland
6-7-8 . . . . Arkansas
9-10-11. . . . . Springfield
13-14-15 . . . . . at Arkansas
16-17-18 . . . . at Springfield
19-20-21-22. . . . Midland
23-24-25 . . . San Antonio
26-27-28-29 . . . . . at Frisco
30-31 . . . . . at San Antonio

SEPTEMBER

1 . . . . at San Antonio

FRISCO

APRIL

3-4-5 . . . . . . at Springfield
6-7-8 . . . . at Arkansas
10-11-12 . . . . Springfield
13-14-15 . . . . . Arkansas
17-18-19-20at Corpus Christi
21-22-23-24. San Antonio
25-26-27-28 Corpus Christi
29-30 . . . . . at San Antonio

MAY

1-2. . . . . . . at San Antonio
3-4-5-6 . . . . Midland
7-8-9-10 . . at Corpus Christi
12-13-14-15 . . . at Midland
16-17-18-19. San Antonio
21-22-23 . . . . at Tulsa
24-25-26 . . at NW Arkansas
28-29-30 . . . . Tulsa
31 . . . . NW Arkansas

JUNE

1-2. . . . . . . NW Arkansas
4-5-6-7 . . . . at San Antonio
8-9-10-11 . . . . . Midland
12-13-14-15 Corpus Christi
16-17-18-19 . . . at Midland
20-21-22-23 Corpus Christi
26-27-28 . . . . at Springfield
29-30 . . . . at Arkansas

JULY

1 . . . . at Arkansas
3-4-5 . . . . . . Springfield
6-7-8 . . . . Arkansas
10-11-12-13at Corpus Christi
14-15-16-17. San Antonio
18-19-20-21at Corpus Christi
22-23-24 . . . . . at Midland
25-26-27-28. San Antonio
29-30-31 . . . . . . Midland

AUGUST

1-2-3-4 . . . . at San Antonio
6-7-8 . . . . at Tulsa
9-10-11 . . . at NW Arkansas
13-14-15 . . . . Tulsa
16-17-18 . . . NW Arkansas
19-20-21-22 . at San Antonio
23-24-25 . . . . . at Midland
26-27-28-29 Corpus Christi
30-31 . . . . Midland

SEPTEMBER

1 . . . . Midland

MIDLAND

APRIL
3-4-5 . . . . at Arkansas
6-7-8 . . . . . .at Springfield
10-11-12 . . . . . .Arkansas
13-14-15 . . . . Springfield
17-18-19-20 . at San Antonio
21-22-23-24at Corpus Christi
25-26-27-28. San Antonio
29-30 . . . . Corpus Christi

MAY
1-2. . . . . . Corpus Christi
3-4-5-6 . . . . at Frisco
7-8-9-10 . . .at San Antonio
12-13-14-15. . . . . .Frisco
16-17-18-19 Corpus Christi
21-22-23 . . at NW Arkansas
24-25-26 . . . . .at Tulsa
28-29-30 . . . NW Arkansas
31 . . . . Tulsa

JUNE
1-2. . . . . Tulsa
4-5-6-7 . . .at Corpus Christi
8-9-10-11. . . . . . . at Frisco
12-13-14-15. San Antonio
16-17-18-19. . . . . .Frisco
20-21-22-23. San Antonio
26-27-28 . . . . . at Arkansas
29-30 . . . . . .at Springfield

JULY
1 . . . . .at Springfield
3-4-5 . . . . .Arkansas
6-7-8 . . . . . . Springfield
10-11-12-13 . at San Antonio
14-15-16-17 Corpus Christi
18-19-20-21 . at San Antonio
22-23-24 . . . . .Frisco
25-26-27-28at Corpus Christi
29-30-31 . . . . at Frisco

AUGUST
1-2-3-4 . . . Corpus Christi
6-7-8 . . . . at NW Arkansas
9-10-11 . . . . .at Tulsa
13-14-15 . . . NW Arkansas
16-17-18 . . . . Tulsa
19-20-21-22at Corpus Christi
23-24-25 . . . . .Frisco
26-27-28-29. San Antonio
30-31 . . . . at Frisco

SEPTEMBER
1 . . . . at Frisco

NW ARKANSAS

APRIL
3-4-5 . . . . .at San Antonio
6-7-8 . . . .at Corpus Christi
10-11-12 . . . San Antonio
13-14-15 . . Corpus Christi
17-18-19-20 . . . at Arkansas
21-22-23-24. . Springfield
25-26-27-28. . . .Arkansas
29-30 . . . . . .at Springfield

MAY
1-2. . . . . . . .at Springfield
3-4-5-6 . . . . Tulsa
7-8-9-10 . . . . Springfield
12-13-14-15 . . . . . .at Tulsa
16-17-18-19 . . . at Arkansas
21-22-23 . . . . . . Midland
24-25-26 . . . . .Frisco
28-29-30 . . . . . at Midland
31 . . . . at Frisco

JUNE
1-2. . . . . at Frisco
4-5-6-7 . . . . . . .Arkansas
8-9-10-11. . . . . . . .at Tulsa
12-13-14-15 . .at Springfield
16-17-18-19. . . . . . Tulsa
20-21-22-23. . . .Arkansas
26-27-28 . . . at San Antonio
29-30 . . . .at Corpus Christi

JULY
1 . . . . . . .at Corpus Christi
3-4-5 . . . . . San Antonio
6-7-8 . . . . Corpus Christi
10-11-12-13 . .at Springfield
14-15-16-17. . . .Arkansas
18-19-20-21 . .at Springfield
22-23-24 . . . . Tulsa
25-26-27-28. . Springfield
29-30-31 . . . . .at Tulsa

AUGUST
1-2-3-4 . . . . . . at Arkansas
6-7-8 . . . . Midland
9-10-11. . . . . .Frisco
13-14-15 . . . . . at Midland
16-17-18 . . . . at Frisco
19-20-21-22. . Springfield
23-24-25 . . . . .at Tulsa
26-27-28-29 . . . at Arkansas
30-31 . . . . Tulsa

SEPTEMBER
1 . . . . Tulsa

SAN ANTONIO

APRIL
3-4-5 . . . . .NW Arkansas
6-7-8 . . . . Tulsa
10-11-12 . . at NW Arkansas
13-14-15 . . . . .at Tulsa
17-18-19-20. . . . Midland
21-22-23-24 . . . . . at Frisco
25-26-27-28 . . . at Midland
29-30 . . . . .Frisco

MAY
1-2. . . . . .Frisco
3-4-5-6 . . .at Corpus Christi
7-8-9-10 . . . . . . Midland
12-13-14-15 Corpus Christi
16-17-18-19 . . . . . at Frisco
21-22-23 . . . . Springfield
24-25-26 . . . . . .Arkansas
28-29-30 . . . .at Springfield
31 . . . . at Arkansas

JUNE
1-2. . . . . at Arkansas
4-5-6-7 . . . . .Frisco
8-9-10-11. .at Corpus Christi
12-13-14-15 . . . at Midland
16-17-18-19 Corpus Christi
20-21-22-23 . . . at Midland
26-27-28 . . . NW Arkansas
29-30 . . . . Tulsa

JULY
1 . . . . Tulsa
3-4-5 . . . . at NW Arkansas
6-7-8 . . . . .at Tulsa
10-11-12-13. . . . Midland
14-15-16-17 . . . . . at Frisco
18-19-20-21. . . . Midland
22-23-24 . . Corpus Christi
25-26-27-28 . . . . . at Frisco
29-30-31 . .at Corpus Christi

AUGUST
1-2-3-4 . . . . .Frisco
6-7-8 . . . . . . Springfield
9-10-11. . . . . . .Arkansas
13-14-15 . . . .at Springfield
16-17-18 . . . . . at Arkansas
19-20-21-22. . . . . .Frisco
23-24-25 . .at Corpus Christi
26-27-28-29 . . . at Midland
30-31 . . . . Corpus Christi

SEPTEMBER
1 . . . . Corpus Christi

SPRINGFIELD

APRIL
3-4-5 . . . . .Frisco
6-7-8 . . . . Midland
10-11-12 . . . . at Frisco
13-14-15 . . . . . at Midland
17-18-19-20. . . . . . Tulsa
21-22-23-24 at NW Arkansas
25-26-27-28 . . . . . .at Tulsa
29-30 . . . . .NW Arkansas

MAY
1-2. . . . . . .NW Arkansas
3-4-5-6 . . . . . . .Arkansas
7-8-9-10 . . at NW Arkansas
12-13-14-15 . . . at Arkansas
16-17-18-19. . . . . . Tulsa
21-22-23 . . . at San Antonio
24-25-26 . .at Corpus Christi
28-29-30 . . . San Antonio
31 . . . . . . Corpus Christi

JUNE
1-2. . . . . . Corpus Christi
4-5-6-7 . . . . .at Tulsa
8-9-10-11 . . . . .Arkansas
12-13-14-15 NW Arkansas
16-17-18-19 . . . at Arkansas
20-21-22-23 . . . . . .at Tulsa
26-27-28 . . . . .Frisco
29-30 . . . . Midland

JULY
1 . . . . Midland
3-4-5 . . . . at Frisco
6-7-8 . . . . at Midland
10-11-12-13 NW Arkansas
14-15-16-17 . . . . . . .at Tulsa
18-19-20-21 NW Arkansas
22-23-24 . . . . . .Arkansas
25-26-27-28 at NW Arkansas
29-30-31 . . . . . at Arkansas

AUGUST
1-2-3-4 . . . . Tulsa
6-7-8 . . . . . at San Antonio
9-10-11 . . .at Corpus Christi
13-14-15 . . . San Antonio
16-17-18 . . Corpus Christi
19-20-21-22 at NW Arkansas
23-24-25 . . . . . .Arkansas
26-27-28-29. . . . . . Tulsa
30-31 . . . . at Arkansas

SEPTEMBER
1 . . . . at Arkansas

TULSA

APRIL
3-4-5 . . . .at Corpus Christi
6-7-8 . . . . . at San Antonio
10-11-12 . . Corpus Christi
13-14-15 . . . San Antonio
17-18-19-20 . .at Springfield
21-22-23-24. . . .Arkansas
25-26-27-28. . Springfield
29-30 . . . . at Arkansas

MAY
1-2. . . . . at Arkansas
3-4-5-6 . . . at NW Arkansas
7-8-9-10 . . . . . .Arkansas
12-13-14-15 NW Arkansas
16-17-18-19 . .at Springfield
21-22-23 . . . . .Frisco
24-25-26 . . . . . . Midland
28-29-30 . . . . at Frisco
31 . . . . at Midland

JUNE
1-2. . . . . at Midland
4-5-6-7 . . . . . Springfield
8-9-10-11 . .NW Arkansas
12-13-14-15 . . . at Arkansas
16-17-18-19 at NW Arkansas
20-21-22-23. . Springfield
26-27-28 . .at Corpus Christi
29-30 . . . . . at San Antonio

JULY
1 . . . . .at San Antonio
3-4-5 . . . . Corpus Christi
6-7-8 . . . . . San Antonio
10-11-12-13 . . . at Arkansas
14-15-16-17. . Springfield
18-19-20-21 . . . at Arkansas
22-23-24 . . at NW Arkansas
25-26-27-28. . . .Arkansas
29-30-31 . . .NW Arkansas

AUGUST
1-2-3-4 . . . . .at Springfield
6-7-8 . . . . .Frisco
9-10-11. . . . . . . Midland
13-14-15 . . . . at Frisco
16-17-18 . . . . . at Midland
19-20-21-22. . . .Arkansas
23-24-25 . . .NW Arkansas
26-27-28-29 . .at Springfield
30-31 . . . . at NW Arkansas

SEPTEMBER
1 . . . . at NW Arkansas

HIGH CLASS A

CALIFORNIA LEAGUE

BAKERSFIELD

APRIL
3-4-5-6 . . . . San Jose
7-8-9 . . . . at Stockton
10-11-12-13 . . . at San Jose
14-15-16 . . .Rancho Cuca.
17-18-19-20. . . Lancaster
22-23-24 . . at Rancho Cuca.
25-26-27-28 . at High Desert
29-30 . . . . .Modesto

MAY
1 . . . . .Modesto
2-3-4 . . . . at Visalia
6-7-8 . . . . at Modesto
9-10-11. . . . . . .Stockton
12-13-14-15. .High Desert
16-17-18-19 . . .at Lancaster
21-22-23-24. . . . . Visalia
25-26-27 . .at Inland Empire
28-29-30-31 . . . . . at Visalia

JUNE
2-3-4-5 . . . . . . .Stockton
6-7-8-9 . . . . . . at San Jose
10-11-12 . . . . . at Stockton
13-14-15 . . . . . . San Jose
16-17-18 . . Inland Empire
19-20-21 . . . . . .Modesto
26-27-28-29 . . . . . at Visalia
30 . . . . San Jose

JULY
1-2-3 . . . . San Jose
4-5-6-7 . . . at Lake Elsinore
8-9-10-11 . . . . .Stockton
12-13-14 . . . . at Visalia
16-17-18 . . . . . at Modesto
19-20-21 . . . . Visalia
22-23-24 . . . . . at San Jose
25-26-27 . . . . . at Stockton
29-30-31 . . . . Visalia

AUGUST
1-2-3 . . . . .Lake Elsinore
5-6-7 . . . . . . .at Lancaster
8-9-10. . . . . . . at Modesto
11-12-13 . . . . . .Stockton
14-15-16 . . . . . .Modesto
17-18-19 . . . . . at Stockton
20-21-22 . . . . . Lancaster
23-24-25 . . .Lake Elsinore
27-28-29 . . . . at Visalia
30-31 . . . . .Modesto

SEPTEMBER
1 . . . . .Modesto

HIGH DESERT

APRIL
3-4-5-6 . . . . . . Lancaster
7-8-9 . . . . at Rancho Cuca.
10-11-12-13 Inland Empire
14-15-16 . . .Lake Elsinore
17-18-19-20at Inland Empire
22-23-24 . . at Lake Elsinore
25-26-27-28. . Bakersfield
29-30 . . . . San Jose

MAY
1 . . . . San Jose
2-3-4 . . . . at Lake Elsinore
6-7-8 . . . . . . .at Lancaster
9-10-11. . . .Rancho Cuca.
12-13-14-15 . .at Bakersfield
16-17-18-19 at Rancho Cuca.
21-22-23-24 Inland Empire
25-26-27 . . .Rancho Cuca.
28-29-30-31 . . . at Stockton

JUNE
1-2-3-4 . . . . . . at Modesto
6-7-8-9 . . . .Lake Elsinore
10-11-12 . . .Rancho Cuca.
13-14-15 . . at Lake Elsinore
16-17-18 . . . . .at Lancaster
19-20-21 . . . . . .Stockton
26-27-28-29at Rancho Cuca.
30 . . . . Lancaster

JULY
1-2-3 . . . . Lancaster
4-5-6-7 . . .at Inland Empire
8-9-10-11 . .Rancho Cuca.
12-13-14 . . . . . .Modesto
16-17-18 . . at Rancho Cuca.
19-20-21 . . . . . Lancaster
22-23-24 . . Inland Empire
25-26-27 . . . . .at Lancaster
29-30-31 . . .Lake Elsinore

AUGUST
1-2-3 . . . .at Inland Empire
5-6-7 . . . . at Lake Elsinore
8-9-10. . . . Inland Empire
11-12-13 . . .Lake Elsinore
14-15-16 . . . . at Visalia
17-18-19 . . . . .at Lancaster
20-21-22. . . . . . . Visalia
23-24-25 . . . . . at San Jose
27-28-29 . . .Rancho Cuca.
30-31 . . . . at Lake Elsinore

SEPTEMBER
1 . . . . at Lake Elsinore

INLAND EMPIRE

APRIL
3-4-5-6 . . . . Visalia
7-8-9 . . . . Lancaster
10-11-12-13 . at High Desert
14-15-16. . . . . Visalia
17-18-19-20. .High Desert
22-23-24 . . . . at Visalia
25-26-27-28 . . . at San Jose
29-30 . . . . .Lake Elsinore

MAY
1 . . . . .Lake Elsinore
2-3-4 . . . . San Jose
6-7-8 . . . . at Rancho Cuca.
9-10-11 . . . . . .at Lancaster
12-13-14-15 Rancho Cuca.
16-17-18-19 Lake Elsinore
21-22-23-24 . at High Desert
25-26-27. . . . Bakersfield
28-29-30-31. . . Lancaster

JUNE
1-3-4-5 . . . at Lake Elsinore
6-7-8-9 . . . at Rancho Cuca.
10-11-12. . .Lake Elsinore
13-14-15 . . . . . at Stockton
16-17-18 . . . .at Bakersfield
19-20-21 . . .Rancho Cuca.
26-27-28-29 . . .at Lancaster
30 . . . . . . at Rancho Cuca.

JULY
1-2-3 . . . . at Rancho Cuca.
4-5-6-7 . . . . .High Desert
8-9-10-11 . . . . .Modesto
12-13-14 . . . . .at Lancaster
16-17-18 . . at Lake Elsinore
19-20-21 . . . . . .Stockton
22-23-24 . . . at High Desert
25-26-27 . . at Lake Elsinore
29-30-31 . . . . . Lancaster

AUGUST
1-2-3 . . . . . .High Desert
5-6-7 . . . . at Rancho Cuca.
8-9-10. . . . . at High Desert
11-12-13 . . . . . Lancaster
14-15-16 . . .Lake Elsinore
17-18-19 . . . . . at Modesto
20-21-22 . . .Lake Elsinore
23-24-25 . . .Rancho Cuca.
27-28-29 . . at Lake Elsinore
30-31 . . . . at Rancho Cuca.

SEPTEMBER
1 . . . . at Rancho Cuca.

LAKE ELSINORE

APRIL
3-4-5-6 . . . .Rancho Cuca.
7-8-9 . . . . Visalia
10-11-12-13 . . .at Lancaster
14-15-16 . . . at High Desert
17-18-19-20. . . .Modesto
22-23-24 . . . .High Desert
25-26-27-28 . . .at Lancaster
29-30 . . . .at Inland Empire
26-27-28-29 . . . at Stockton
30 . . . . at Visalia

MAY
1 . . . . . . .at Inland Empire
2-3-4 . . . . . .High Desert
6-7-8 . . . . at San Jose
9-10-11. . . . . . . at Modesto
12-13-14-15. . . .Stockton
16-17-18-19at Inland Empire
21-22-23-24 Rancho Cuca.
25-26-27 . . . . . Lancaster
28-29-30-31 at Rancho Cuca.

JUNE
1-3-4-5 . . . Inland Empire
6-7-8-9 . . . . at High Desert
10-11-12 . .at Inland Empire
13-14-15 . . . .High Desert
16-17-18 . . at Rancho Cuca.
19-20-21 . . . . . Lancaster
26-27-28-29 . . . at Stockton
30 . . . . at Visalia

JULY
1-2-3 . . . . at Visalia
4-5-6-7 . . . . . Bakersfield
8-9-10-11 . . . . Lancaster
12-13-14 . . at Rancho Cuca.
16-17-18 . . Inland Empire
19-20-21 . . .Rancho Cuca.
22-23-24 . . . . .at Lancaster
25-26-27 . . Inland Empire
29-30-31 . . . at High Desert

AUGUST
1-2-3 . . . . . .at Bakersfield
5-6-7 . . . . . .High Desert
8-9-10. . . . . San Jose
11-12-13 . . . at High Desert
14-15-16 . .at Inland Empire
17-18-19 . . .Rancho Cuca.
20-21-22 . .at Inland Empire
23-24-25 . . . .at Bakersfield
27-28-29 . . Inland Empire
30-31 . . . . . .High Desert

SEPTEMBER
1 . . . . .High Desert

LANCASTER

APRIL
3-4-5-6 . . . . at High Desert
7-8-9 . . . .at Inland Empire
10-11-12-13 Lake Elsinore
14-15-16. . . . . .Modesto
17-18-19-20 . .at Bakersfield
22-23-24 . . . . . at Modesto
25-26-27-28 Lake Elsinore
29-30 . . . . .Rancho Cuca.

MAY
1 . . . . .Rancho Cuca.
2-3-4 . . . . at Rancho Cuca.
6-7-8 . . . . . .High Desert
9-10-11. . . Inland Empire
12-13-14-15 . . . . . at Visalia
16-17-18-19. . Bakersfield
21-22-23-24. . . .Stockton
25-26-27 . . at Lake Elsinore
28-29-30-31at Inland Empire

JUNE
2-3-4-5 . . . .Rancho Cuca.
6-7-8-9 . . . . Visalia
10-11-12 . . . . . at San Jose
13-14-15 . . . . at Visalia
16-17-18 . . . .High Desert
19-20-21 . . at Lake Elsinore
26-27-28-29 Inland Empire
30 . . . . at High Desert

JULY
1-2-3 . . . . . at High Desert
4-5-6 . . . . .Stockton
8-9-10-11. . at Lake Elsinore

12-13-14 . . Inland Empire
16-17-18 . . . . . . San Jose
19-20-21 . . . at High Desert
22-23-24 . . . Lake Elsinore
25-26-27 . . . . High Desert
29-30-31 . . at Inland Empire

AUGUST
1-2-3 . . . . at Rancho Cuca.
5-6-7 . . . . . . Bakersfield
8-9-10. . . . .Rancho Cuca.
11-12-13 . . at Inland Empire
14-15-16 . . at Rancho Cuca.
17-18-19 . . . .High Desert
20-21-22 . . . . at Bakersfield
23-24-25 . . . . . . Modesto
26-27-28-29 . . . at Stockton
30-31 . . . . at San Jose

SEPTEMBER
1 . . . . at San Jose

MODESTO

APRIL
3-4-5-6 . . . . . . at Stockton
7-8-9 . . . . San Jose
10-11-12-13. . . .Stockton
14-15-16 . . . . .at Lancaster
17-18-19-20 at Lake Elsinore
22-23-24 . . . . . Lancaster
25-26-27-28. . . . . Visalia
29-30 . . . . . . at Bakersfield

MAY
1 . . . . .at Bakersfield
2-3-4 . . . . at Stockton
6-7-8 . . . . . . Bakersfield
9-10-11. . . .Lake Elsinore
12-13-14-15 . . . at San Jose
16-17-18-19 . . . . . at Visalia
21-22-23-24. . . . San Jose
25-26-27 . . . . Visalia
28-29-30-31 . . . at San Jose

JUNE
1-2-3-4 . . . . .High Desert
6-7-8-9 . . . . . . .Stockton
10-11-12 . . . . at Visalia
13-14-15 . . at Rancho Cuca.
16-17-18 . . . . Visalia
19-20-21 . . . .at Bakersfield
26-27-28-29. . . . San Jose
30 . . . . at Stockton

JULY
1-2-3 . . . . at Stockton
4-5-6-7 . . . . Visalia
8-9-10-11. .at Inland Empire
12-13-14 . . . at High Desert
16-17-18 . . . . Bakersfield
19-20-21 . . . . . at San Jose
22-23-24 . . . . at Visalia
25-26-27 . . . . . . San Jose
29-30-31 . . . . . .Stockton

AUGUST
1-2-3 . . . . at San Jose
5-6-7 . . . . at Stockton
8-9-10. . . . . . Bakersfield
11-12-13 . . .Rancho Cuca.
14-15-16 . . . .at Bakersfield
17-18-19 . . Inland Empire
20-21-22 . . . . . .Stockton
23-24-25 . . . . .at Lancaster
27-28-29 . . . . . . San Jose
30-31 . . . . . .at Bakersfield

SEPTEMBER
1 . . . . .at Bakersfield

RANCHO CUCA.

APRIL
3-4-5-6 . . . at Lake Elsinore
7-8-9 . . . . . .High Desert
10-11-12-13. . . . . Visalia
14-15-16 . . . .at Bakersfield
17-18-19-20 . . . at Stockton
22-23-24. . . . Bakersfield
25-26-27-28. . . .Stockton
29-30 . . . . . . .at Lancaster

MAY
1 . . . . .at Lancaster
2-3-4 . . . . Lancaster
6-7-8 . . . . Inland Empire
9-10-11 . . . . at High Desert
12-13-14-15at Inland Empire
16-17-18-19. .High Desert
21-22-23-24 at Lake Elsinore
25-26-27 . . . at High Desert
28-29-30-31 Lake Elsinore

JUNE
2-3-4-5 . . . . . .at Lancaster
6-7-8-9 . . . Inland Empire
10-11-12 . . . at High Desert
13-14-15 . . . . . .Modesto
16-17-18 . . .Lake Elsinore
19-20-21 . .at Inland Empire
26-27-28-29. .High Desert
30 . . . . . . Inland Empire

JULY
1-2-3 . . . . Inland Empire
4-5-6 . . . . at San Jose
8-9-10-11. . . at High Desert
12-13-14 . . .Lake Elsinore
16-17-18 . . . .High Desert
19-20-21 . . at Lake Elsinore
22-23-24 . . . . . .Stockton
25-26-27 . . . . at Visalia
28-29-30-31 . . . at San Jose

AUGUST
1-2-3 . . . . Lancaster
5-6-7 . . . . Inland Empire
8-9-10. . . . . . .at Lancaster
11-12-13 . . . . . at Modesto
14-15-16 . . . . . Lancaster
17-18-19 . . at Lake Elsinore
20-21-22 . . . . . . San Jose
23-24-25 . .at Inland Empire
27-28-29 . . . at High Desert
30-31 . . . . Inland Empire

SEPTEMBER
1 . . . . Inland Empire

SAN JOSE

APRIL
3-4-5-6 . . . . .at Bakersfield
7-8-9 . . . . at Modesto
10-11-12-13. . Bakersfield
14-15-16 . . . . .Stockton
17-18-19-20 . . . . . at Visalia
22-23-24 . . . . . at Stockton
25-26-27-28 Inland Empire
29-30 . . . . . at High Desert

MAY
1 . . . . at High Desert
2-3-4 . . . .at Inland Empire
6-7-8 . . . . .Lake Elsinore
9-10-11. . . . . Visalia
12-13-14-15. . . .Modesto
16-17-18-19 . . . at Stockton
21-22-23-24 . . . at Modesto
25-26 . . . . .Stockton
28-29-30-31. . . .Modesto

JUNE
1 . . . . .Stockton
2-3-4-5 . . . . at Visalia
6-7-8-9 . . . . . Bakersfield
10-11-12 . . . . . Lancaster
13-14-15 . . . .at Bakersfield
16-17-18 . . . . . at Stockton
19-20-21 . . . . Visalia
26-27-28-29 . . . at Modesto
30 . . . . .at Bakersfield

JULY
1-2-3 . . . . . .at Bakersfield
4-5-6 . . . . .Rancho Cuca.
8-9-10-11 . . . . . . Visalia
12-13-14 . . . . . at Stockton
16-17-18 . . . . .at Lancaster
19-20-21 . . . . . .Modesto
22-23-24 . . . . Bakersfield
25-26-27 . . . . . at Modesto
28-29-30-31 Rancho Cuca.

AUGUST
1-2-3 . . . . .Modesto
5-6-7 . . . . at Visalia
8-9-10. . . . at Lake Elsinore
11-12-13 . . . . Visalia
14-15-16 . . . . . .Stockton
17-18-19 . . . . at Visalia
20-21-22 . . at Rancho Cuca.
23-24-25 . . . .High Desert
27-28-29 . . . . . at Modesto
30-31 . . . . Lancaster

SEPTEMBER
1 . . . . Lancaster

STOCKTON

APRIL
3-4-5-6 . . . . . . .Modesto
7-8-9 . . . . . . Bakersfield
10-11-12-13 . . . at Modesto
14-15-16 . . . . . at San Jose
17-18-19-20 Rancho Cuca.
22-23-24 . . . . . . San Jose
25-26-27-28 at Rancho Cuca.
29-30 . . . . at Visalia

MAY
1 . . . . at Visalia
2-3-4 . . . . .Modesto
6-7-8 . . . . Visalia
9-10-11 . . . . .at Bakersfield
12-13-14-15 at Lake Elsinore
16-17-18-19. . . . San Jose
21-22-23-24 . . .at Lancaster
25-26 . . . . at San Jose
28-29-30-31. .High Desert

JUNE
1 . . . . at San Jose
2-3-4-5 . . . . . .at Bakersfield
6-7-8-9 . . . . at Modesto
10-11-12. . . . Bakersfield
13-14-15 . . Inland Empire
16-17-18 . . . . . . San Jose
19-20-21 . . . at High Desert
26-27-28-29 Lake Elsinore
30 . . . . .Modesto

JULY
1-2-3 . . . . .Modesto
4-5-6 . . . . . . .at Lancaster
8-9-10-11. . . .at Bakersfield
12-13-14 . . . . . . San Jose
16-17-18 . . . . Visalia
19-20-21 . .at Inland Empire
22-23-24 . . at Rancho Cuca.
25-26-27 . . . . Bakersfield
29-30-31 . . . . . at Modesto

AUGUST
1-2-3 . . . . at Visalia
5-6-7 . . . . .Modesto
8-9-10. . . . . Visalia
11-12-13 . . . .at Bakersfield
14-15-16 . . . . . at San Jose
17-18-19 . . . . Bakersfield
20-21-22 . . . . . at Modesto
23-24-25 . . . . at Visalia
26-27-28-29. . . Lancaster
30-31 . . . . Visalia

SEPTEMBER
1 . . . . Visalia

VISALIA

APRIL
3-4-5-6 . . .at Inland Empire
7-8-9 . . . . at Lake Elsinore
10-11-12-13at Rancho Cuca.
14-15-16 . .at Inland Empire
17-18-19-20. . . . San Jose
22-23-24 . . Inland Empire
25-26-27-28 . . . at Modesto
29-30 . . . . .Stockton

MAY
1 . . . . .Stockton
2-3-4 . . . . . . Bakersfield
6-7-8 . . . . at Stockton
9-10-11 . . . . . . at San Jose
12-13-14-15. . Lancaster
16-17-18-19. . . .Modesto
21-22-23-24 . .at Bakersfield
25-26-27 . . . . . at Modesto
28-29-30-31. . Bakersfield

JUNE
2-3-4-5 . . . . . . San Jose
6-7-8-9 . . . . . .at Lancaster
10-11-12 . . . . . .Modesto
13-14-15. . . . . Lancaster

16-17-18 . . . . . at Modesto
19-20-21 . . . . . at San Jose
26-27-28-29. . Bakersfield
30 . . . . Lake Elsinore

JULY
1-2-3 . . . . . Lake Elsinore
4-5-6-7 . . . . . . at Modesto
8-9-10-11. . . . . . at San Jose
12-13-14. . . . Bakersfield
16-17-18 . . . . . at Stockton
19-20-21 . . . . at Bakersfield
22-23-24 . . . . . . Modesto
25-26-27 . . . Rancho Cuca.
29-30-31 . . . . at Bakersfield

AUGUST
1-2-3 . . . . Stockton
5-6-7 . . . . San Jose
8-9-10. . . . . . . at Stockton
11-12-13 . . . . . at San Jose
14-15-16 . . . . High Desert
17-18-19 . . . . . . San Jose
20-21-22 . . . at High Desert
23-24-25 . . . . . . Stockton
27-28-29 . . . . Bakersfield
30-31 . . . . at Stockton

SEPTEMBER
1 . . . . at Stockton

CAROLINA LEAGUE

FREDERICK

APRIL
4-5-6 . . . . . . Lynchburg
8-9-10. . . . . at Kinston
11-12-13 . . at Myrtle Beach
14-15-16 . . . . Salem
17-18-19-20 . . . . at Winston
21-22-23 . . . . Wilmington
25-26-27 . . . . . . Potomac
28-29-30 . . . at Wilmington

MAY
1-2-3-4 . . . . . . at Potomac
5-6-7 . . . . Kinston
8-9-10-11. . . . at Lynchburg
12-13-14-15 . . . . . at Salem
16-17-18 . . . . Lynchburg
20-21-22. Winston-Salem
23-24-25 . . . Myrtle Beach
26-27-28-29 . . . . at Kinston
30-31 . . . . at Myrtle Beach

JUNE
1 . . . . at Myrtle Beach
2-3-4-5 . . . . Salem
6-7-8 . . . at Winston-Salem
9-10-11. . . . . Wilmington
12-13-14-15. . . . Potomac
17-18-19 . . . at Wilmington
20-21-22 . . . . . at Potomac
26-27-28 . . . . . . Kinston
29-30 . . . . . Myrtle Beach

JULY
1 . . . . Myrtle Beach
2-3-4 . . . at Winston-Salem
5-6-7 . . . . . . at Lynchburg
9-10-11. . Winston-Salem
12-13-14-15 Myrtle Beach
16 . . . . Lynchburg
17-18-19 . . . . . . at Kinston
20-21-22-23 at Myrtle Beach
25-26-27 . . . . . . Potomac
28-29-30 . . . . at Salem
31 . . . . Wilmington

AUGUST
1-2-3 . . . . . . Wilmington
4-5-6 . . . . Salem
7-8-9-10 . . . at Wilmington
11-12-13 . . . . . at Potomac
14-15-16-17. . . . Kinston
19-20-21 . . . . Lynchburg
22-23-24 . . . . at Salem
25-26-27 . . . . at Lynchburg
29-30-31 . Winston-Salem

SEPTEMBER
1 . . . . . . Winston-Salem

KINSTON

APRIL
4-5-6 . . . Winston-Salem
8-9-10. . . . . . . Frederick
11-12-13 . . . . . at Potomac
14-15-16 . . . at Wilmington
17-18-19-20 Myrtle Beach
21-22-23 . . . . Salem
24-25-26-27. . Lynchburg
28-29-30 . . . . at Salem

MAY
1-2-3 . . . . . . at Lynchburg
5-6-7 . . . . at Frederick
8-9-10-11 . . . . . Potomac
12-13-14-15. . Wilmington
16-17-18 . at Winston-Salem
20-21-22 . . at Myrtle Beach
23-24-25 . Winston-Salem
26-27-28-29. . . Frederick
30-31 . . . . at Potomac

JUNE
1 . . . . at Potomac
2-3-4-5 . . . . at Wilmington
6-7-8 . . . . . Myrtle Beach
9-10-11. . . . . at Salem
12-13-14-15 . . at Lynchburg
17-18-19 . . . . Lynchburg
20-21-22 . . . . Salem
26-27-28 . . . . . at Frederick
29-30 . . . . Potomac

JULY
1 . . . . Potomac
2-3-4 . . . . . . Wilmington
5-6-7 . . . at Winston-Salem
9-10-11 . . . . . at Lynchburg
12-13-14-15. . . . Winston
17-18-19 . . . . . Frederick
21-22-23-24 . . . at Potomac
25-26-27 . . . at Wilmington
28-29-30 . . . Myrtle Beach
31 . . . . at Salem

AUGUST
1-2-3 . . . . at Salem
4-5-6 . . . . at Myrtle Beach
7-8-9-10 . . . . Salem
11-12-13 . . . . Lynchburg
14-15-16-17 . . . at Frederick
18-19-20 . . . . . . Potomac
21-22-23 . . . . Wilmington
25-26-27-28 . . . .at Winston
29-30-31 . . at Myrtle Beach

SEPTEMBER
1 . . . . at Myrtle Beach

LYNCHBURG

APRIL
4-5-6 . . . . at Frederick
8-9-10. . . at Winston-Salem
11-12-13 . . . . Wilmington
14-15-16 . . . . . . Potomac
17-18-19-20 . . . . . at Salem
21-22-23 . . at Myrtle Beach
24-25-26-27 . . . . at Kinston
28-29-30 . . . Myrtle Beach

MAY
1-2-3 . . . . Kinston
5-6-7 . . . Winston-Salem
8-9-10-11 . . . . Frederick
12-13-14-15 . . . . at Winston-Salem
16-17-18 . . . . . at Frederick
20-21-22 . . . . Salem
23-24-25 . . . at Wilmington
26-27-28-29 . . . at Potomac
30-31 . . . . . . Wilmington

JUNE
1 . . . . Wilmington
2-3-4-5 . . . . Potomac
6-7-8 . . . . at Salem
9-10-11 . . . at Myrtle Beach
12-13-14-15. . . . Kinston
17-18-19 . . . . . . at Kinston
20-21-22 . . . Myrtle Beach
26-27-28 . Winston-Salem
29-30 . . . . . at Wilmington

JULY
1 . . . . at Wilmington
2-3-4 . . . . Salem
5-6-7 . . . . Frederick
9-10-11. . . . . . . Kinston
12-13-14-15 . at Wilmington
16 . . . . at Frederick
17-18-19 . . . . . at Potomac
20-21-22-23. . Wilmington
25-26-27 . . . . at Salem
28-29-30 . at Winston-Salem
31 . . . . . . at Myrtle Beach

AUGUST
1-2-3 . . . . at Myrtle Beach
4-5-6 . . . . Potomac
7-8-8-9 . . . . Myrtle Beach
11-12-13 . . . . . . at Kinston
14-15-16-17. . . . . Winston-Salem
19-20-21 . . . . . at Frederick
22-23-24 . . . . . at Potomac
25-26-27 . . . . . Frederick
29-30-31 . . . . Salem

SEPTEMBER
1 . . . . Salem

MYRTLE BEACH

APRIL
4-5-6-7 . . . at Wilmington
8-9-10. . . . . . at Potomac
11-12-13 . . . . . Frederick
14-15-16. Winston-Salem
17-18-19-20 . . . . at Kinston
21-22-23 . . . . Lynchburg
24-25-26 . . . . Salem
28-29-30 . . . . at Lynchburg

MAY
1-2-3-4 . . . . at Salem
5-6-7 . . . . Potomac
9-10-11 . . . . at Wilmington
12-13-14-15 . . . at Potomac
16-17-18 . . . . Wilmington
20-21-22 . . . . . . Kinston
23-24-25 . . . . . at Frederick
26-27-28-29 . . . . at Winston-Salem
30-31 . . . . Frederick

JUNE
1 . . . . Frederick
2-3-4-5 . . Winston-Salem
6-7-8 . . . . at Kinston
9-10-11. . . . . Lynchburg
12-13-14-15. . . . . . Salem
17-18-19 . . . . at Salem
20-21-22 . . . . at Lynchburg
26-27-28 . . . . . . Potomac
29-30 . . . . at Frederick

JULY
1 . . . . at Frederick
2-3-4 . . . . at Potomac
5-6-7 . . . . . . Wilmington
9-10-11. . . . . Salem
12-13-14-15 . . . at Frederick
17-18-19 . at Winston-Salem
20-21-22-23. . . Frederick
25-26-27 . Winston-Salem
28-29-30 . . . . . . at Kinston
31 . . . . Lynchburg

AUGUST
1-2-3 . . . . . . Lynchburg
4-5-6 . . . . Kinston
7-8-8-9 . . . . . at Lynchburg
11-12-13 . . . . at Salem
14-15-16-17. . . . Potomac
18-19-20 . . . at Wilmington
21-22-23 . at Winston-Salem
24-25-26-27. . Wilmington
29-30-31 . . . . . . Kinston

SEPTEMBER
1 . . . . Kinston

POTOMAC

APRIL
4-5-6 . . . . at Salem
8-9-10. . . . . Myrtle Beach
11-12-13 . . . . . . Kinston
14-15-16 . . . . at Lynchburg
17-18-19-20 . at Wilmington
21-22-23 . at Winston-Salem
25-26-27 . . . . . at Frederick
28-29-30 . Winston-Salem

MAY
1-2-3-4 . . . . . . Frederick
5-6-7 . . . . at Myrtle Beach
8-9-10-11. . . . . . at Kinston
12-13-14-15 Myrtle Beach
16-17-18 . . . . at Salem
20-21-22 . . . at Wilmington
23-24-25 . . . . .Salem
26-27-28-29. . Lynchburg
30-31 . . . . Kinston

JUNE
1 . . . . Kinston
2-3-4-5 . . . . . at Lynchburg
6-7-8 . . . . . .Wilmington
9-10-11. . Winston-Salem
12-13-14-15 . . . at Frederick
17-18-19 . at Winston-Salem
20-21-22 . . . . . Frederick
26-27-28 . . at Myrtle Beach
29-30 . . . . at Kinston

JULY
1 . . . . at Kinston
2-3-4 . . . . . Myrtle Beach
5-6-7 . . . . .Salem
9-10-11 . . . . at Wilmington
12-13-14-15 . . . . . at Salem
17-18-19 . . . . Lynchburg
21-22-23-24. . . . Kinston
25-26-27 . . . . . at Frederick
28-29-30 . . . .Wilmington
31 . . . . . Winston-Salem

AUGUST
1-2-3 . . . Winston-Salem
4-5-6 . . . . . . at Lynchburg
7-8-9-10 . at Winston-Salem
11-12-13 . . . . . Frederick
14-15-16-17 at Myrtle Beach
18-19-20 . . . . . . at Kinston
22-23-24 . . . . Lynchburg
25-26-27-28. . . . . .Salem
29-30-31 . . . at Wilmington

SEPTEMBER
1 . . . . at Wilmington

WILMINGTON

APRIL
4-5-6-7 . . . . Myrtle Beach
8-9-10. . . . . at Salem
11-12-13 . . . . at Lynchburg
14-15-16 . . . . . . Kinston
17-18-19-20. . . .Potomac
21-22-23 . . . . . at Frederick
25-26-27 . Winston-Salem
28-29-30 . . . . . Frederick

MAY
1-2-3-4 . . at Winston-Salem
5-6-7 . . . . .Salem
9-10-11. . . . Myrtle Beach
12-13-14-15 . . . . at Kinston
16-17-18 . . at Myrtle Beach
20-21-22 . . . . . .Potomac
23-24-25 . . . . Lynchburg
26-27-28-29 . . . . . at Salem
30-31 . . . . . . at Lynchburg

JUNE
1 . . . . at Lynchburg
2-3-4-5 . . . . Kinston
6-7-8 . . . . at Potomac
9-10-11 . . . . . . at Frederick
12-13-14-15. . . . Winston
17-18-19 . . . . . Frederick
20-21-22 . at Winston-Salem
26-27-28 . . . . .Salem
29-30 . . . . . . Lynchburg

JULY
1 . . . . Lynchburg
2-3-4 . . . . at Kinston
5-6-7 . . . . at Myrtle Beach
9-10-11. . . . . . . .Potomac
12-13-14-15. . Lynchburg
17-18-19 . . . . at Salem
20-21-22-23 . . at Lynchburg
25-26-27 . . . . . . Kinston
28-29-30 . . . . . at Potomac
31 . . . . at Frederick

AUGUST
1-2-3 . . . . at Frederick
4-5-6 . . . Winston-Salem
7-8-9-10 . . . . . Frederick
11-12-13 . at Winston-Salem
14-15-16-17. . . . . .Salem
18-19-20 . . . Myrtle Beach
21-22-23 . . . . . . at Kinston
24-25-26-27 at Myrtle Beach
29-30-31 . . . . . .Potomac

SEPTEMBER
1 . . . . .Potomac

SALEM

APRIL
4-5-6 . . . . .Potomac
8-9-10. . . . . .Wilmington
11-12-13 . at Winston-Salem
14-15-16 . . . . . at Frederick
17-18-19-20. . Lynchburg
21-22-23 . . . . . . at Kinston
24-25-26 . . at Myrtle Beach
28-29-30 . . . . . . Kinston

MAY
1-2-3-4 . . . . Myrtle Beach
5-6-7 . . . . . at Wilmington
8 . . . . . . Winston-Salem
9-10-11 . . at Winston-Salem
12-13-14-15. . . Frederick
16-17-18 . . . . . .Potomac
20-21-22 . . . . at Lynchburg
23-24-25 . . . . . at Potomac
26-27-28-29. .Wilmington
30-31 . . . Winston-Salem

JUNE
1 . . . . . . Winston-Salem
2-3-4-5 . . . . . . at Frederick
6-7-8 . . . . Lynchburg
9-10-11. . . . . Kinston
12-13-14-15 at Myrtle Beach
17-18-19 . . . Myrtle Beach
20-21-22 . . . . . . at Kinston
26-27-28 . . . at Wilmington
29-30 . . . Winston-Salem

JULY
1 . . . . . . Winston-Salem
2-3-4 . . . . . . at Lynchburg
5-6-7 . . . . at Potomac
9-10-11 . . . at Myrtle Beach
12-13-14-15. . . .Potomac
17-18-19 . . . .Wilmington
21-22-23-24 . . . . at Winston-Salem
25-26-27 . . . . Lynchburg
28-29-30 . . . . . Frederick
31 . . . . Kinston

AUGUST
1-2-3 . . . . Kinston
4-5-6 . . . . at Frederick
7-8-9-10 . . . . . . at Kinston
11-12-13 . . . Myrtle Beach
14-15-16-17 . at Wilmington
18-19-20 . Winston-Salem
22-23-24 . . . . . Frederick
25-26-27-28 . . . at Potomac
29-30-31 . . . . at Lynchburg

SEPTEMBER
1 . . . . at Lynchburg

WINSTON-SALEM

APRIL
4-5-6 . . . . at Kinston
8-9-10. . . . . . Lynchburg
11-12-13 . . . . .Salem
14-15-16 . . at Myrtle Beach
17-18-19-20. . . Frederick
21-22-23 . . . . . .Potomac
25-26-27 . . . at Wilmington
28-29-30 . . . . . at Potomac

MAY
1-2-3-4 . . . . . Wilmington
5-6-7 . . . . . . at Lynchburg
8 . . . . at Salem
9-10-11. . . . . .Salem
12-13-14-15. . Lynchburg
16-17-18 . . . . . . Kinston
20-21-22 . . . . . at Frederick
23-24-25 . . . . . . at Kinston
26-27-28-29 Myrtle Beach
30-31 . . . . at Salem

JUNE
1 . . . . at Salem
2-3-4-5 . . . at Myrtle Beach
6-7-8 . . . . Frederick
9-10-11 . . . . at Potomac
12-13-14-15 . at Wilmington
17-18-19 . . . . . .Potomac
20-21-22 . . . .Wilmington
26-27-28 . . . . at Lynchburg
29-30 . . . . at Salem

JULY
1 . . . . at Salem
2-3-4 . . . . Frederick
5-6-7 . . . . Kinston
9-10-11 . . . . . . at Frederick
12-13-14-15 . . . . at Kinston
17-18-19 . . . Myrtle Beach
21-22-23-24. . . . . .Salem
25-26-27 . . at Myrtle Beach
28-29-30 . . . . Lynchburg
31 . . . . at Potomac

AUGUST
1-2-3 . . . . at Potomac
4-5-6 . . . . . at Wilmington
7-8-9-10 . . . . . .Potomac
11-12-13 . . . .Wilmington
14-15-16-17 . . at Lynchburg
18-19-20 . . . . at Salem
21-22-23 . . . Myrtle Beach
25-26-27-28. . . . Kinston
29-30-31 . . . . . at Frederick

SEPTEMBER
1 . . . . at Frederick

FLORIDA STATE LEAGUE

BREVARD CO.

APRIL
3-4. . . . . at Daytona
5-6-7 . . . . . . Palm Beach
8-9-10. . . . . . . at St. Lucie
11-12-13 . . . at Palm Beach
15-16-17 . . . . . . St. Lucie
18-19 . . . . Daytona
20-21-22 . . . .at Vero Beach
23-24-25 . . . . Jupiter
26-27-28 . . . . Vero Beach
30 . . . . at Jupiter

MAY
1-2. . . . . at Jupiter
3-4-5-6 . . . . . at Clearwater
7-8-9-10 . . . . Tampa
12-13 . . . . at Daytona
14 . . . . Daytona
15-16-17 . . . . Jupiter
18-19-20-21. . . . Sarasota
22-23-24-25 . . . at Dunedin
26 . . . . at Daytona
28-29 . . . . Daytona
30-31 . . . . . . Vero Beach

JUNE
1 . . . . Vero Beach
2-3-4 . . . . at St. Lucie
5-6-7-8 . . . . . Fort Myers
9-10-11-12. . . . at Lakeland
16-17-18 . . . .at Vero Beach
19 . . . . at Daytona
20 . . . . Daytona
21 . . . . at Daytona
22-23-24-25. . . . Dunedin
26-27-28-29 . . at Fort Myers

JULY
1-2-3 . . . . at Jupiter
4-5-6 . . . . Daytona
7-8-9-10 . . . . . .Lakeland

11-12-13-14 . . . at Sarasota
16-17-18-19 . . Clearwater
20-21-22-23 . . . . at Tampa
24-25-26 . . . at Palm Beach
28-29-30 . . . . . . St. Lucie
31 . . . . Palm Beach

AUGUST

1-2. . . . . Palm Beach
3 . . . . Daytona
4 . . . . at Daytona
5-6-7 . . . . . . at Vero Beach
8-9. . . . . at Daytona
10-11-12 . . . . Vero Beach
13-14-15 . . . at Palm Beach
16-17-18 . . . . . . St. Lucie
20-21-22 . . . . . . at Jupiter
23-24-25 . . . . Palm Beach
26-27-28 . . . . Jupiter
29-30-31 . . . . . at St. Lucie

CLEARWATER

APRIL

3-4. . . . . Dunedin
5-6-7 . . . . at Lakeland
8-9-10. . . . . Fort Myers
11-12-13 . . . . . .Lakeland
15-16-17 . . . . at Fort Myers
18 . . . . Dunedin
19 . . . . at Dunedin
20-21-22 . . . . Tampa
23-24-25 . . . . . . Sarasota
26-27 . . . . .at Tampa
28 . . . . Tampa
30 . . . . at Fort Myers

MAY

1-2. . . . . at Fort Myers
3-4-5-6 . . . . . Brevard Co.
7-8-9-10 . . . . Jupiter
12-13-14 . . . . . at Dunedin
15-16-17 . . . . . . Sarasota
18-19-20-21 . . . at Daytona
22-23-24-25 . .at Vero Beach
27-28-29 . . . . . . Dunedin
30-31 . . . . at Sarasota

JUNE

1 . . . . at Sarasota
2 . . . . Tampa
3-4. . . . . .at Tampa
5-6-7-8 . . . . St. Lucie
9-10-11-12. . at Palm Beach
16 . . . . Tampa
17-18 . . . . .at Tampa
19 . . . . Dunedin
20 . . . . at Dunedin
21 . . . . Dunedin
22-23-24-25 . . Vero Beach
26-27-28-29 . . . at St. Lucie

JULY

1-2-3 . . . . .Lakeland
4-5-6 . . . . at Dunedin
7-8-9-10 . . . . Palm Beach
11-12-13-14 . . . . Daytona
16-17-18-19 . at Brevard Co.
20-21-22-23 . . . . at Jupiter
24-25-26 . . . . Fort Myers
28-29-30 . . . . . at Sarasota
31 . . . . at Fort Myers

AUGUST

1-2. . . . . at Fort Myers
3-4. . . . . Dunedin
5-6-7 . . . . at Lakeland
8-9-10. . . . . Tampa
11-12-13 . . . . . .Lakeland
14-15-16 . . . . .at Tampa
17-18 . . . . at Dunedin
20-21-22 . . . . . . Sarasota
23-24-25 . . . . Fort Myers
26-27-28 . . . . . at Sarasota
29-30-31 . . . . . . at Lakeland

DAYTONA

APRIL

3-4. . . . . Brevard Co.
5-6-7 . . . . . .at Vero Beach
8-9-10. . . . . . Palm Beach
11-12-14 . . . . Vero Beach
15-16-17 . . . at Palm Beach
18-19 . . . . . at Brevard Co.
20-21-22 . . . . Jupiter
23-24-25 . . . . . at St. Lucie
26-27-28 . . . . . . at Jupiter
30 . . . . St. Lucie

MAY

1-2. . . . . St. Lucie
3-4-5-6 . . . . . at Fort Myers
7-8-9-10 . . . . . at Sarasota
12-13 . . . . . . Brevard Co.
14 . . . . at Brevard Co.
15-16-17 . . . . . at St. Lucie
18-19-20-21 . . Clearwater
22-23-24-25 . . . . . Tampa
26 . . . . Brevard Co.
28-29 . . . . . at Brevard Co.
30-31 . . . . Jupiter

JUNE

1 . . . . Jupiter
2-3-4 . . . . . at Palm Beach
5-6-7-8 . . . . . . .Lakeland
9-10-11-12. . . . at Dunedin
16-17-18 . . . . Palm Beach
19 . . . . Brevard Co.
20 . . . . at Brevard Co.
21 . . . . Brevard Co.
22-23-24-25 . . . . .at Tampa
26-27-28-29 . . . at Lakeland

JULY

1-2-3 . . . . St. Lucie
4-5-6 . . . . . at Brevard Co.
7-8-9-10 . . . . . . Dunedin
11-12-13-14 . .at Clearwater
16-17-18-19 . . Fort Myers
20-21-22-23 . . . Sarasota
24-25-26 . . . .at Vero Beach
28-29-30 . . . . Palm Beach
31 . . . . Vero Beach

AUGUST

1-2. . . . . Vero Beach
3 . . . . at Brevard Co.
4 . . . . Brevard Co.
5-6-7 . . . . . at Palm Beach
8-9. . . . . Brevard Co.
10-11-12 . . . . . . at Jupiter
13-14-15 . . . . . . St. Lucie
16-17-18 . . . . Jupiter
20-21-22 . . . .at Vero Beach
23-24-25 . . . . . . at St. Lucie
26-27-28 . . . . Vero Beach
29-30-31 . . . . at Jupiter

DUNEDIN

APRIL

3-4. . . . . at Clearwater
5-6-7 . . . . . . Fort Myers
8-9-10. . . . . .at Tampa
11-12-13 . . . . at Fort Myers
15-16-17 . . . . Tampa
18 . . . . at Clearwater
19 . . . . Clearwater
20-21-22 . . . . . at Sarasota
23-24-25 . . . . . at Lakeland
26-27-28 . . . . . . Sarasota
30 . . . . .Lakeland

MAY

1-2. . . . . .Lakeland
3-4-5-6 . . . . .at Vero Beach
7-8-9-10 . . . at Palm Beach
12-13-14 . . . . Clearwater
15-16-17 . . . . . at Lakeland
18-19-20-21 . . . . St. Lucie
22-23-24-25 . . Brevard Co.
27-28-29 . . . .at Clearwater
30-31 . . . . .Lakeland

JUNE

1 . . . . .Lakeland
2-3-4 . . . . . . at Fort Myers
5-6-7-8 . . . . at Jupiter
9-10-11-12. . . . . Daytona
16-17-18 . . . . Fort Myers
19 . . . . at Clearwater
20 . . . . Clearwater
21 . . . . at Clearwater
22-23-24-25 . at Brevard Co.
26-27-28-29. . . . . Jupiter

JULY

1-2-3 . . . . at Sarasota
4-5-6 . . . . . . Clearwater
7-8-9-10 . . . . . at Daytona
11-12-13-14 . . . at St. Lucie
16-17-18-19. . Vero Beach
20-21-22-23. . Palm Beach
24-25-26 . . . . . . .at Tampa
27-28-29 . . . . Fort Myers
31 . . . . Tampa

AUGUST

1-2. . . . . Tampa
3-4. . . . . at Clearwater
5-6-7 . . . . Sarasota
8-9-10. . . . . . . at Lakeland
11-12-13 . . . . at Fort Myers
14-15-16 . . . . . . Sarasota
17-18 . . . . . . Clearwater
20-21-22 . . . . .at Tampa
23-24-25 . . . . . .Lakeland
26-27-28 . . . . Tampa
29-30-31 . . . . . at Sarasota

FORT MYERS

APRIL

3-4. . . . . Sarasota
5-6-7 . . . . at Dunedin
8-9-10. . . . . .at Clearwater
11-12-13 . . . . . . Dunedin
15-16-17 . . . . Clearwater
18-19 . . . . at Sarasota
20-21-22 . . . . . .Lakeland
23-24-25 . . . . .at Tampa
26-27-28 . . . . . at Lakeland
30 . . . . Clearwater

MAY

1-2. . . . . Clearwater
3-4-5-6 . . . . Daytona
8-9-10-11. . . . . at St. Lucie
12-13 . . . . at Sarasota
14 . . . . Sarasota
15-16-17 . . . . Tampa
18-19-20-21 . . . . at Jupiter
22-23-24-25 . . Palm Beach
27-28 . . . . Sarasota
29 . . . . at Sarasota
30-31 . . . . .at Tampa

JUNE

1 . . . . .at Tampa
2-3-4 . . . . Dunedin
5-6-7-8 . . . . at Brevard Co.
9-10-11-12. . . Vero Beach
16-17-18 . . . . . . at Dunedin
19-20-21 . . . . . . Sarasota
22-23-24-25 . at Palm Beach
26-27-28-29. . Brevard Co.

JULY

1-2-3 . . . . Tampa
4-5-6 . . . . at Lakeland
7-8-9-10 . . . .at Vero Beach
11-12-13-14. . . . . Jupiter
16-17-18-19 . . . at Daytona
20-21-22-23. . . . St. Lucie
24-25-26 . . . .at Clearwater
27-28-29 . . . . . at Dunedin
31 . . . . Clearwater

AUGUST

1-2. . . . . Clearwater
3-4. . . . . Sarasota
5-6-7 . . . . .at Tampa
8-9-10. . . . . . . at Sarasota
11-12-13 . . . . . . Dunedin
14-15-16 . . . . . .Lakeland
17-18 . . . . at Sarasota
20-21-22 . . . . . at Lakeland
23-24-25 . . . .at Clearwater
26-27-28 . . . . . .Lakeland
29-30-31 . . . . Tampa

JUPITER

APRIL

3-4. . . . . . . at Palm Beach
5-6-7 . . . . St. Lucie
8-9-10. . . . . . Vero Beach
11-12-13 . . . . . at St. Lucie
15-16-17 . . . .at Vero Beach
18-19 . . . . . . Palm Beach
20-21-22 . . . . . at Daytona
23-24-25 . . . at Brevard Co.
26-27-28 . . . . . . Daytona
30 . . . . Brevard Co.

MAY

1-2. . . . . Brevard Co.
3-4-5-6 . . . . .at Tampa
7-8-9-10 . . . .at Clearwater
12-13-14 . . . . Palm Beach
15-16-17 . . . at Brevard Co.
18-19-20-21 . . Fort Myers

22-23-24-25. . . .Lakeland
27-28 . . . . . at Palm Beach
29 . . . . Palm Beach
30-31 . . . . at Daytona

JUNE
1 . . . . at Daytona
2-3-4 . . . . . .at Vero Beach
5-6-7-8 . . . . Dunedin
9-10-11-12. . . . at Sarasota
16-17-18 . . . . . . St. Lucie
19 . . . . at Palm Beach
20-21 . . . . . . Palm Beach
22-23-24-25 . . . at Lakeland
26-27-28-29 . . . at Dunedin

JULY
1-2-3 . . . . . . Brevard Co.
4-5-6 . . . . . at Palm Beach
7-8-9-10 . . . . . . Sarasota
11-12-13-14 . . at Fort Myers
16-17-18-19. . . . . Tampa
20-21-22-23. . Clearwater
24-25-26 . . . . . at St. Lucie
28-29-30 . . . . Vero Beach
31 . . . . St. Lucie

AUGUST
1-2. . . . . St. Lucie
3-4. . . . . at Palm Beach
5-6-7 . . . . at St. Lucie
8-9. . . . . Palm Beach
10-11-12 . . . . . . Daytona
13-14-15 . . . .at Vero Beach
16-17-18 . . . . . at Daytona
20-21-22 . . . . Brevard Co.
23-24-25 . . . . Vero Beach
26-27-28 . . . at Brevard Co.
29-30-31 . . . . . . Daytona

LAKELAND

APRIL
3-4. . . . . .at Tampa
5-6-7 . . . . . . Clearwater
8-9-10. . . . . . . at Sarasota
11-12-13 . . . .at Clearwater
14-15-16 . . . . . . Sarasota
18 . . . . Tampa
19 . . . . .at Tampa
20-21-22 . . . . at Fort Myers
23-24-25 . . . . . . Dunedin
26-27-28 . . . . Fort Myers
30 . . . . at Dunedin

MAY
1-2. . . . . at Dunedin
3-4-5-6 . . . . . . at St. Lucie
7-8-9-10 . . . . Vero Beach
12-13-14 . . . . . . .at Tampa
15-16-17 . . . . . . Dunedin
18-19-20-21. . Palm Beach
22-23-24-25 . . . . at Jupiter
27-28-29 . . . . Tampa
30-31 . . . . at Dunedin

JUNE
1 . . . . at Dunedin
2-3-4 . . . . Sarasota
5-6-7-8 . . . . . . at Daytona
9-10-11-12. . . Brevard Co.
16-17-18 . . . . . at Sarasota
19 . . . . Tampa
20-21 . . . . .at Tampa
22-23-24-25. . . . . Jupiter
26-27-28-29 . . . . Daytona

JULY
1-2-3 . . . . . .at Clearwater
4-5-6 . . . . . . Fort Myers
7-8-9-10 . . . at Brevard Co.
11-12-13-14 . at Palm Beach
16-17-18-19. . . . St. Lucie
20-21-22-23 . .at Vero Beach
24-25-26 . . . . . . Sarasota
28-29-30 . . . . Tampa
31 . . . . at Sarasota

AUGUST
1-2. . . . . at Sarasota
3-4. . . . . .at Tampa
5-6-7 . . . . . . Clearwater
8-9-10. . . . . Dunedin
11-12-13 . . . .at Clearwater
14-15-16 . . . . at Fort Myers
17-18 . . . . Tampa
20-21-22. . . . Fort Myers
23-24-25 . . . . . at Dunedin
26-27-28 . . . . at Fort Myers
29-30-31. . . . Clearwater

PALM BEACH

APRIL
3-4. . . . . Jupiter
5-6-7 . . . . . at Brevard Co.
8-9-10. . . . . . . at Daytona
11-12-13 . . . . Brevard Co.
15-16-17 . . . . . . Daytona
18-19 . . . . at Jupiter
20-21-22 . . . . . . St. Lucie
23-24-25 . . . . Vero Beach
26-27-28 . . . . . at St. Lucie
30 . . . . .at Vero Beach

MAY
1-2. . . . . . . .at Vero Beach
3-4-5-6 . . . . Sarasota
7-8-9-10 . . . . . . Dunedin
12-13-14 . . . . . . at Jupiter
15-16-17 . . . . Vero Beach
18-19-20-21 . . . at Lakeland
22-23-24-25 . . at Fort Myers
27-28 . . . . Jupiter
29 . . . . at Jupiter
30-31 . . . . St. Lucie

JUNE
1 . . . . St. Lucie
2-3-4 . . . . Daytona
5-6-7-8 . . . . .at Tampa
9-10-11-12. . . Clearwater
16-17-18 . . . . . at Daytona
19 . . . . Jupiter
20-21 . . . . at Jupiter
22-23-24-25. . Fort Myers
27-28-29-30. . . . . Tampa

JULY
1-2-3 . . . . . .at Vero Beach
4-5-6 . . . . Jupiter
7-8-9-10 . . . .at Clearwater
11-12-13-14. . . .Lakeland
16-17-18-19. . . at Sarasota
20-21-22-23 . . . at Dunedin
24-25-26 . . . . Brevard Co.
28-29-30 . . . . . at Daytona
31 . . . . at Brevard Co.

AUGUST
1-2. . . . . . . at Brevard Co.
3-4. . . . . Jupiter
5-6-7 . . . . Daytona
8-9. . . . . at Jupiter
10-11-12 . . . . . at St. Lucie
13-14-15 . . . . Brevard Co.
16-17-18 . . . . Vero Beach
20-21-22 . . . . . at St. Lucie
23-24-25 . . . at Brevard Co.
26-27-28 . . . . . . St. Lucie
29-30-31 . . . .at Vero Beach

ST. LUCIE

APRIL
3 . . . . Vero Beach
4 . . . . .at Vero Beach
5-6-7 . . . . at Jupiter
8-9-10. . . . . Brevard Co.
11-12-13 . . . . Jupiter
15-16-17 . . . at Brevard Co.
18 . . . . .at Vero Beach
19 . . . . Vero Beach
20-21-22 . . . at Palm Beach
23-24-25 . . . . . . Daytona
26-27-28 . . . . Palm Beach
30 . . . . at Daytona

MAY
1-2. . . . . at Daytona
3-4-5-6 . . . . . . .Lakeland
8-9-10-11 . . . Fort Myers
12-13-14 . . . .at Vero Beach
15-16-17 . . . . . . Daytona
18-19-20-21 . . . at Dunedin
22-23-24-25 . . . at Sarasota
27-28-29 . . . . Vero Beach
30-31 . . . . . at Palm Beach

JUNE
1 . . . . at Palm Beach
2-3-4 . . . . . . Brevard Co.
5-6-7-8 . . . . .at Clearwater
9-10-11-12. . . . . . Tampa
16-17-18 . . . . . . at Jupiter
19-20-21 . . . .at Vero Beach
22-23-24-25. . . . Sarasota
26-27-28-29. . Clearwater

JULY
1-2-3 . . . . at Daytona
4-5-6 . . . . . . Vero Beach
7-8-9-10 . . . . . . .at Tampa
11-12-13-14. . . . Dunedin
16-17-18-19 . . . at Lakeland
20-21-22-23 . . at Fort Myers
24-25-26 . . . . Jupiter
28-29-30 . . . at Brevard Co.
31 . . . . at Jupiter

AUGUST
1-2. . . . . at Jupiter
3-4. . . . . Vero Beach
5-6-7 . . . . Jupiter
8-9. . . . . . . .at Vero Beach
10-11-12 . . . . Palm Beach
13-14-15 . . . . . at Daytona
16-17-18 . . . at Brevard Co.
20-21-22 . . . . Palm Beach
23-24-25 . . . . . . Daytona
26-27-28 . . . at Palm Beach
29-30-31 . . . . Brevard Co.

SARASOTA

APRIL
3-4. . . . . at Fort Myers
5-6-7 . . . . Tampa
8-9-10. . . . . . . .Lakeland
11-12-13 . . . . .at Tampa
14-15-16 . . . . . at Lakeland
18-19 . . . . . . Fort Myers
20-21-22 . . . . . . Dunedin
23-24-25 . . . .at Clearwater
26-27-28 . . . . . at Dunedin
30 . . . . Tampa

MAY
1-2. . . . . Tampa
3-4-5-6 . . . . at Palm Beach
7-8-9-10 . . . . . . Daytona
12-13 . . . . . . Fort Myers
14 . . . . at Fort Myers
15-16-17 . . . .at Clearwater
18-19-20-21 . at Brevard Co.
22-23-24-25. . . . St. Lucie
27-28 . . . . . . at Fort Myers
29 . . . . Fort Myers
30-31 . . . . . . Clearwater

JUNE
1 . . . . Clearwater
2-3-4 . . . . at Lakeland
5-6-7-8 . . . . .at Vero Beach
9-10-11-12. . . . . . Jupiter
16-17-18 . . . . . .Lakeland
19-20-21 . . . . at Fort Myers
22-23-24-25 . . . at St. Lucie
26-27-28-29. . Vero Beach

JULY
1-2-3 . . . . Dunedin
4-5-6 . . . . .at Tampa
7-8-9-10 . . . . at Jupiter
11-12-13-14. . Brevard Co.
16-17-18-19. . Palm Beach
20-21-22-23 . . . at Daytona
24-25-26 . . . . . at Lakeland
28-29-30 . . . . Clearwater
31 . . . . .Lakeland

AUGUST
1-2. . . . . .Lakeland
3-4. . . . . at Fort Myers
5-6-7 . . . . at Dunedin
8-9-10. . . . . . Fort Myers
11-12-13 . . . . Tampa
14-15-16 . . . . . at Dunedin
17-18 . . . . . . Fort Myers
20-21-22 . . . .at Clearwater
23-24-25 . . . . .at Tampa
26-27-28 . . . . Clearwater
29-30-31 . . . . . . Dunedin

TAMPA

APRIL

3-4 . . . . Lakeland
5-6-7 . . . . at Sarasota
8-9-10 . . . . Dunedin
11-12-13 . . . . . Sarasota
15-16-17 . . . . . at Dunedin
18 . . . . at Lakeland
19 . . . . Lakeland
20-21-22 . . . . at Clearwater
23-24-25 . . . . Fort Myers
26-27 . . . . . . Clearwater
28 . . . . at Clearwater
30 . . . . at Sarasota

MAY

1-2 . . . . at Sarasota
3-4-5-6 . . . . Jupiter
7-8-9-10 . . . at Brevard Co.
12-13-14 . . . . . Lakeland
15-16-17 . . . . at Fort Myers
18-19-20-21 . . Vero Beach
22-23-24-25 . . . at Daytona
27-28-29 . . . . . at Lakeland
30-31 . . . . . . Fort Myers

JUNE

1 . . . . Fort Myers
2 . . . . at Clearwater
3-4 . . . . Clearwater
5-6-7-8 . . . . . Palm Beach
9-10-11-12 . . . . at St. Lucie
16 . . . . at Clearwater
17-18 . . . . . . Clearwater
19 . . . . at Lakeland
20-21 . . . . Lakeland
22-23-24-25 . . . . Daytona
27-28-29-30 . at Palm Beach

JULY

1-2-3 . . . . . . at Fort Myers
4-5-6 . . . . Sarasota
7-8-9-10 . . . . . . St. Lucie
11-12-13-14 . . at Vero Beach
16-17-18-19 . . . . at Jupiter
20-21-22-23 . . Brevard Co.
24-25-26 . . . . . . Dunedin
28-29-30 . . . . . at Lakeland
31 . . . . at Dunedin

AUGUST

1-2 . . . . at Dunedin
3-4 . . . . Lakeland
5-6-7 . . . . . . Fort Myers
8-9-10 . . . . . . at Clearwater
11-12-13 . . . . . at Sarasota
14-15-16 . . . . Clearwater
17-18 . . . . at Lakeland
20-21-22 . . . . . . Dunedin
23-24-25 . . . . . . Sarasota
26-27-28 . . . . . at Dunedin
29-30-31 . . . . at Fort Myers

VERO BEACH

APRIL

3 . . . . at St. Lucie
4 . . . . St. Lucie
5-6-7 . . . . Daytona
8-9-10 . . . . at Jupiter
11-12-14 . . . . . at Daytona
15-16-17 . . . . Jupiter
18 . . . . St. Lucie
19 . . . . at St. Lucie
20-21-22 . . . . Brevard Co.
23-24-25 . . . at Palm Beach
26-27-28 . . . at Brevard Co.
30 . . . . Palm Beach

MAY

1-2 . . . . Palm Beach
3-4-5-6 . . . . Dunedin
7-8-9-10 . . . . . at Lakeland
12-13-14 . . . . . . St. Lucie
15-16-17 . . . at Palm Beach
18-19-20-21 . . . . . at Tampa
22-23-24-25 . . Clearwater
27-28-29 . . . . . at St. Lucie
30-31 . . . . . at Brevard Co.

JUNE

1 . . . . at Brevard Co.
2-3-4 . . . . Jupiter
5-6-7-8 . . . . Sarasota
9-10-11-12 . . . at Fort Myers
16-17-18 . . . . Brevard Co.
19-20-21 . . . . . . St. Lucie
22-23-24-25 . . at Clearwater
26-27-28-29 . . . at Sarasota

JULY

1-2-3 . . . . . . Palm Beach
4-5-6 . . . . at St. Lucie
7-8-9-10 . . . . Fort Myers
11-12-13-14 . . . . . Tampa
16-17-18-19 . . . at Dunedin
20-21-22-23 . . . . Lakeland
24-25-26 . . . . . . Daytona
28-29-30 . . . . . . at Jupiter
31 . . . . at Daytona

AUGUST

1-2 . . . . at Daytona
3-4 . . . . at St. Lucie
5-6-7 . . . . . . Brevard Co.
8-9 . . . . St. Lucie
10-11-12 . . . at Brevard Co.
13-14-15 . . . . Jupiter
16-17-18 . . . at Palm Beach
20-21-22 . . . . . . Daytona
23-24-25 . . . . . . at Jupiter
26-27-28 . . . . . at Daytona
29-30-31 . . . . Palm Beach

LOW CLASS A

MIDWEST LEAGUE

BELOIT

APRIL

3-4-5-6 . . . . Kane County
7-8-9-10 . . . . at Peoria
11-12-13 . . . . Fort Wayne
14-15-16 . . . . Dayton
18-19-20 . . . . . Wisconsin
21-22-23 . . . . at West Mich.
25-26-27 . . . . at Wisconsin
28-29-30 . . . . South Bend

MAY

1-2-3 . . . . . at Great Lakes
4-5-6 . . . . at Lansing
8-9-10-11 . . . . at Burlington
12-13-14-15 . . . . . Clinton
16-17-18 . . . . Peoria
19-20-21-22 . . . . at Clinton
23-24-25-26 . . Burlington
28-29-30-31 . . . . at Clinton

JUNE

1-2-3-4 . . . . . Quad Cities
5-6-7-8 . . . at Kane County
9-10-11-12 . . Cedar Rapids
13-14-15 . . . at Quad Cities
19-20-21-22 . . . . . at Peoria
23-24-25-26 . . . . at Clinton
27-28-29-30 Cedar Rapids

JULY

1-2-3-4 . . . . Clinton
5-6-7 . . . . at Wisconsin
9-10-11 . . . . . at Fort Wayne
12-13-14 . . . . at Dayton
16-17-18 . . . . West Mich.
19-20-21 . . . . . Wisconsin
23-24-25 . . . at South Bend
26-27-28 . . . . at Wisconsin
29-30-31 . . . . Great Lakes

AUGUST

1-2-3 . . . . Lansing
5-6-7-8 . . . at Kane County
9-10-11-12 . . . . . . Peoria
13-14-15 . . . . Quad Cities
16-17-18-19 at Cedar Rapids
21-22-23-24 . . at Burlington
25-26-27-28 Kane County
29-30-31 . . . . Burlington

SEPTEMBER

1 . . . . Burlington

BURLINGTON

APRIL

3-4-5-6 . . . . Peoria
7-8-9-10 . . at Kane County
11-12-13 . . . . Great Lakes
14-15-16 . . . . . . Lansing
18-19-20 . . . . at West Mich.
22-23-24 . . . at Quad Cities
25-26-27 . . . . South Bend
28-29-30 . . . Cedar Rapids

MAY

2-3-4 . . . . at Dayton
5-6-7 . . . . . . at Fort Wayne
8-9-10-11 . . . . Beloit
12-13-14-15 . . at Wisconsin
16-17-18 . . . . Quad Cities
19-20-21-22 Kane County
23-24-25-26 . . . . . at Beloit
28-29-30-31 . at Quad Cities

JUNE

1-2-3-4 . . . . Clinton
5-6-7-8 . . . at Cedar Rapids
9-10-11-12 . . . . Wisconsin
13-14-15 . . . . at Peoria
19-20-21-22 . . at Wisconsin
23-24-25-26 . . . . . Peoria
27-28-29-30 . . . Wisconsin

JULY

1-2-3-4 . . . at Kane County
5-6-7 . . . . Clinton
9-10-11 . . . . at Great Lakes
12-13-14 . . . . . . at Lansing
16-17-18 . . . at Quad Cities
19-20-21 . . . . West Mich.
23-24-25 . . . Cedar Rapids
26-27-28 . . . at South Bend
29-30-31 . . . . Dayton

AUGUST

1-2-3 . . . . . . Fort Wayne
5-6-7-8 . . . . at Peoria
9-10-11-12 . Cedar Rapids
13-14-15 . . . . . . at Clinton
16-17-18-19 . at Quad Cities
21-22-23-24 . . . . . . Beloit
25-26-27-28 . . Quad Cities
29-30-31 . . . . at Beloit

SEPTEMBER

1 . . . . at Beloit

CEDAR RAPIDS

APRIL

3-4-5-6 . . . . at Clinton
7-8-9-10 . . . . Quad Cities
11-12-13 . . . . . . Lansing
14-15-16 . . . . Great Lakes
18-19-20 . . . at South Bend
21-22-23 . . . . . . at Dayton
25-26-27 . . . . West Mich.
28-29-30 . . . . at Burlington

MAY

2-3-4 . . . . . . at Fort Wayne
5-6-7 . . . . Peoria
8-9-10-11 . . . . at Wisconsin
12-13-14-15 at Kane County
16-17-18 . . . . Clinton
19-20-21-22 . . . Wisconsin
23-24-25-26 . . . . . Clinton
28-29-30-31 . . . . . at Peoria

JUNE

1-2-3-4 . . . . Kane County
5-6-7-8 . . . . . Burlington
9-10-11-12 . . . . . . at Beloit
13-14-15 . . at Kane County
19-20-21-22 . . Quad Cities
23-24-25-26 . . . Wisconsin
27-28-29-30 . . . . . at Beloit

JULY

1-2-3-4 . . . . at Quad Cities
5-6-7 . . . . . Kane County

9-10-11 . . . at Lansing
12-13-14 . . . at Great Lakes
16-17-18 . . . Dayton
19-20-21 . . . South Bend
23-24-25 . . . at Burlington
26-27-28 . . . at West Mich.
29-30-31 . . . Fort Wayne

AUGUST

1-2-3 . . . Clinton
5-6-7-8 . . . Quad Cities
9-10-11-12 . . . at Burlington
13-14-15 . . . at Kane County
16-17-18-19 . . . Beloit
21-22-23-24 . . . at Peoria
25-26-27-28 . . . at Wisconsin
29-30-31 . . . Clinton

SEPTEMBER

1 . . . Clinton

CLINTON

APRIL

3-4-5-6 . . . Cedar Rapids
7-8-9-10 . . . at Wisconsin
11-12-13 . . . West Mich.
14-15-16 . . . Quad Cities
18-19-20 . . . at Dayton
21-22-23 . . . at Fort Wayne
25-26-27 . . . Lansing
28-29-30 . . . Great Lakes

MAY

2-3-4 . . . at Kane County
5-6-7 . . . at South Bend
8-9-10-11 . . . Peoria
12-13-14-15 . . . at Beloit
16-17-18 . . . at Cedar Rapids
19-20-21-22 . . . Beloit
23-24-25-26 at Cedar Rapids
28-29-30-31 . . . Beloit

JUNE

1-2-3-4 . . . at Burlington
5-6-7-8 . . . at Peoria
9-10-11-12 . . . Kane County
13-14-15 . . . Wisconsin
19-20-21-22 at Kane County
23-24-25-26 . . . Beloit
27-28-29-30 . . . Quad Cities

JULY

1-2-3-4 . . . at Beloit
5-6-7 . . . at Burlington
9-10-11 . . . at West Mich.
12-13-14 . . . Quad Cities
16-17-18 . . . Fort Wayne
19-20-21 . . . Dayton
23-24-25 . . . at Great Lakes
26-27-28 . . . at Lansing
29-30-31 . . . South Bend

AUGUST

1-2-3 . . . at Cedar Rapids
5-6-7-8 . . . Wisconsin
9-10-11-12 . . . at Quad Cities
13-14-15 . . . Burlington
16-17 . . . Peoria
18-19 . . . at Peoria
21-22-23-24 Kane County
25-26 . . . Peoria
27-28 . . . at Peoria
29-30-31 . . . at Cedar Rapids

SEPTEMBER

1 . . . at Cedar Rapids

DAYTON

APRIL

3-4-5-6 . . . at Great Lakes
7-8-9-10 . . . Fort Wayne
11-12-13 . . . at Wisconsin
14-15-16 . . . at Beloit
18-19-20 . . . Clinton
21-22-23 . . . Cedar Rapids
25-26-27 . . . at Kane County
28-29-30 . . . at Peoria

MAY

2-3-4 . . . Burlington
5-6-7 . . . Quad Cities
8-9-10-11 . . . Great Lakes
12-13-14-15 . . . at Lansing
16-17-18 . . . Great Lakes
19-20-21-22 . . . Lansing
23-24-25-26 . . . at West Mich.
28-29-30-31 . . . at Fort Wayne

JUNE

1-2-3-4 . . . West Mich.
5-6-7-8 . . . South Bend
9-10-11-12 . . . at Fort Wayne
13-14-15 . . . at South Bend
19-20-21-22 . . . Great Lakes
23-24-25-26 . . . South Bend
27-28-29-30 . . . at Fort Wayne

JULY

1-2-3-4 . . . at Great Lakes
5-6-7 . . . West Mich.
9-10-11 . . . Wisconsin
12-13-14 . . . Beloit
16-17-18 . . . at Cedar Rapids
19-20-21 . . . at Clinton
23-24-25 . . . Peoria
26-27-28 . . . Kane County
29-30-31 . . . at Burlington

AUGUST

1-2-3 . . . at Quad Cities
5-6-7-8 . . . Fort Wayne
9-10-11-12 . . . at Lansing
13-14-15 . . . at Great Lakes
16-17-18-19 . . . Great Lakes
21-22-23-24 . . . at West Mich.
25-26-27-28 . . . at Lansing
29-30-31 . . . West Mich.

SEPTEMBER

1 . . . West Mich.

FORT WAYNE

APRIL

3-4-5-6 . . . Lansing
7-8-9-10 . . . at Dayton
11-12-13 . . . at Beloit
14-15-16 . . . at Wisconsin
18-19-20 . . . Quad Cities
21-22-23 . . . Clinton
25-26-27 . . . at Peoria
28-29-30 . . . at Kane County

MAY

2-3-4 . . . Cedar Rapids
5-6-7 . . . Burlington
8-9-10-11 . . . at South Bend
12-13-14-15 . . . West Mich.
16-17-18 . . . South Bend
19-20-21-22 . at Great Lakes
23-24-25-26 . . . Great Lakes
28-29-30-31 . . . Dayton

JUNE

1-2-3-4 . . . at Great Lakes
5-6-7-8 . . . at Lansing
9-10-11-12 . . . Dayton
13-14-15 . . . at West Mich.
19-20-21-22 . . . at Lansing
23-24-25-26 . . West Mich.
27-28-29-30 . . . Dayton

JULY

1-2-3-4 . . . at West Mich.
5-6-7 . . . at South Bend
9-10-11 . . . Beloit
12-13-14 . . . Wisconsin
16-17-18 . . . at Clinton
19-20-21 . . . at Quad Cities
23-24-25 . . . Kane County
26-27-28 . . . Peoria
29-30-31 . . at Cedar Rapids

AUGUST

1-2-3 . . . at Burlington
5-6-7-8 . . . at Dayton
9-10-11-12 . . Great Lakes
13-14-15 . . . South Bend
16-17 . . . Lansing
19-20-21-22 . . . at Lansing
23-24 . . . Lansing
25-26-27-28 . . South Bend
29-30-31 . . . at Great Lakes

SEPTEMBER

1 . . . at Great Lakes

GREAT LAKES

APRIL

3-4-5-6 . . . Dayton
7-8-9-10 . . . at West Mich.
11-12-13 . . . at Burlington
14-15-16 . . at Cedar Rapids
18-19-20 . . . Peoria
21-22-23 . . . Kane County
25-26-27 . . . at Quad Cities
28-29-30 . . . at Clinton

MAY

1-2-3 . . . Beloit
4-5-6 . . . Wisconsin
8-9-10-11 . . . at Dayton
12-13-14-15 . . South Bend
16-17-18 . . . at Dayton
19-20-21-22 . . Fort Wayne
23-24-25-26 . at Fort Wayne
28-29-30-31 . . . at Lansing

JUNE

1-2-3-4 . . . Fort Wayne
5-6-7-8 . . . West Mich.
9-10-11-12 . . at South Bend
13-14-15 . . . Lansing
19-20-21-22 . . . at Dayton
23-24-25-26 . . . at Lansing
27-28-29-30 . . South Bend

JULY

1-2-3-4 . . . Dayton
5-6-7 . . . at Lansing
9-10-11 . . . Burlington
12-13-14 . . . Cedar Rapids
16-17-18 . . at Kane County
19-20-21 . . . at Peoria
23-24-25 . . . Clinton
26-27-28 . . . Quad Cities
29-30-31 . . . at Beloit

AUGUST

1-2-3 . . . at Wisconsin
5-6-7-8 . . . West Mich.
9-10-11-12 . . at Fort Wayne
13-14-15 . . . Dayton
16-17-18-19 . . . at Dayton
21-22-23-24 . . South Bend
25-26-27-28 . . at West Mich.
29-30-31 . . . Fort Wayne

SEPTEMBER

1 . . . Fort Wayne

KANE COUNTY

APRIL

3-4-5-6 . . . at Beloit
7-8-9-10 . . . Burlington
11-12-13 . . . at Peoria
14-15-16 . . . South Bend
17-18-19 . . . at Lansing
21-22-23 . . . at Great Lakes
25-26-27 . . . Dayton
28-29-30 . . . Fort Wayne

MAY

2-3-4 . . . Clinton
5-6-7 . . . at West Mich.
8-9-10-11 . . . at Quad Cities
12-13-14-15 Cedar Rapids
16-17-18 . . . at Wisconsin
19-20-21-22 . . at Burlington
23-24-25-26 . . Quad Cities
28-29-30-31 . . . Wisconsin

JUNE

1-2-3-4 . . . at Cedar Rapids
5-6-7-8 . . . Beloit
9-10-11-12 . . . at Clinton
13-14-15 . . . Cedar Rapids
19-20-21-22 . . . Clinton
23-24-25-26 . at Quad Cities
27-28-29-30 . . . at Peoria

JULY

1-2-3-4 . . . Burlington
5-6-7 . . . at Cedar Rapids
9-10-11 . . . Peoria
12-13-14 . . . at South Bend
16-17-18 . . . Great Lakes
19-20-21 . . . Lansing
23-24-25 . . . at Fort Wayne
26-27-28 . . . at Dayton
29-30-31 . . . at Peoria

AUGUST

1-2-3 . . . West Mich.
5-6-7-8 . . . Beloit
9-10-11-12 . . . at Wisconsin
13-14-15 . . . Cedar Rapids
16-17-18-19 . . . Wisconsin
21-22-23-24 . . . at Clinton
25-26-27-28 . . . at Beloit
29-30-31 . . . Peoria

SEPTEMBER

1 . . . Peoria

LANSING

APRIL

3-4-5-6 . . . . .at Fort Wayne
7-8-9-10 . . . . South Bend
11-12-13 . . at Cedar Rapids
14-15-16 . . . . at Burlington
17-18-19 . . . Kane County
21-22-23 . . . . Peoria
25-26-27 . . . . . . at Clinton
28-29-30 . . . at Quad Cities

MAY

1-2-3 . . . . Wisconsin
4-5-6 . . . . Beloit
8-9. . . . . West Mich.
10-11 . . . . at West Mich.
12-13-14-15. . . . . Dayton
16-17 . . . . . . at West Mich.
18 . . . . West Mich.
19-20-21-22 . . . . at Dayton
23-24-25-26. . South Bend
28-29-30-31. . Great Lakes

JUNE

1-2-3-4 . . . . at South Bend
5-6-7-8 . . . . . Fort Wayne
9-10-11-12. . . at West Mich.
13-14-15 . . . at Great Lakes
19-20-21-22. . Fort Wayne
23-24-25-26. . Great Lakes
27-28-29-30 . . at West Mich.

JULY

1-2-3-4 . . . . at South Bend
5-6-7 . . . . . . Great Lakes
9-10-11. . . . Cedar Rapids
12-13-14. . . . Burlington
16-17-18 . . . . at Peoria
19-20-21 . . at Kane County
23-24-25 . . . . Quad Cities
26-27-28 . . . . Clinton
29-30-31 . . . . at Wisconsin

AUGUST

1-2-3 . . . . at Beloit
5-6-7-8 . . . . at South Bend
9-10-11-12. . . . . . Dayton
13-14-15 . . . . at West Mich.
16-17 . . . . . . .at Fort Wayne
19-20-21-22. . Fort Wayne
23-24 . . . . . .at Fort Wayne
25-26-27-28. . . . . Dayton
29-30-31 . . . at South Bend

SEPTEMBER

1 . . . . at South Bend

PEORIA

APRIL

3-4-5-6 . . . . . at Burlington
7-8-9-10 . . . . Beloit
11-12-13 . . . Kane County
14-15-16 . . . . West Mich.
18-19-20 . . . at Great Lakes
21-22-23 . . . . . . at Lansing
25-26-27 . . . . Fort Wayne
28-29-30 . . . . Dayton

MAY

2-3-4 . . . . . . at South Bend
5-6-7 . . . . at Cedar Rapids
8-9-10-11. . . . . . at Clinton
12-13-14-15. . Quad Cities
16-17-18 . . . . at Beloit
19-20-21-22 . at Quad Cities
23-24-25-26. . . Wisconsin
28-29-30-31 Cedar Rapids

JUNE

1-2-3-4 . . . . . at Wisconsin
5-6-7-8 . . . . Clinton
9-10-11-12. . at Quad Cities
13-14-15 . . . . Burlington
19-20-21-22. . . . . . Beloit
23-24-25-26 . . at Burlington
27-28-29-30 Kane County

JULY

1-2-3-4 . . . . . at Wisconsin
5-6-7 . . . . . at Quad Cities
9-10-11 . . . at Kane County
12-13-14 . . . . at West Mich.
16-17-18 . . . . . . Lansing
19-20-21 . . . . Great Lakes
23-24-25 . . . . . . at Dayton
26-27-28 . . . .at Fort Wayne
29-30-31 . . . Kane County

AUGUST

1-2-3 . . . . . . South Bend
5-6-7-8 . . . . . Burlington
9-10-11-12. . . . . . at Beloit
13-14-15 . . . . . Wisconsin
16-17 . . . . at Clinton
18-19 . . . . Clinton
21-22-23-24 Cedar Rapids
25-26 . . . . at Clinton
27-28 . . . . Clinton
29-30-31 . . at Kane County

SEPTEMBER

1 . . . . at Kane County

QUAD CITIES

APRIL

3-4-5-6 . . . . . . Wisconsin
7-8-9-10 . . at Cedar Rapids
11-12-13 . . . . South Bend
14-15-16 . . . . . . at Clinton
18-19-20 . . . .at Fort Wayne
22-23-24 . . . . Burlington
25-26-27 . . . . Great Lakes
28-29-30 . . . . . . Lansing

MAY

2-3-4 . . . . . . at West Mich.
5-6-7 . . . . at Dayton
8-9-10-11 . . Kane County
12-13-14-15 . . . . . at Peoria
16-17-18 . . . . at Burlington
19-20-21-22. . . . . Peoria
23-24-25-26 at Kane County
28-29-30-31. . Burlington

JUNE

1-2-3-4 . . . . at Beloit
5-6-7-8 . . . . . at Wisconsin
9-10-11-12. . . . . . Peoria
13-14-15 . . . . Beloit
19-20-21-22 at Cedar Rapids
23-24-25-26 Kane County
27-28-29-30 . . . . at Clinton

JULY

1-2-3-4 . . . . Cedar Rapids
5-6-7 . . . . Peoria
9-10-11 . . . . at South Bend
12-13-14 . . . . . . at Clinton
16-17-18 . . . . Burlington
19-20-21 . . . . Fort Wayne
23-24-25 . . . . . . at Lansing
26-27-28 . . . at Great Lakes
29-30-31 . . . . West Mich.

AUGUST

1-2-3 . . . . Dayton
5-6-7-8 . . . at Cedar Rapids
9-10-11-12. . . . . . Clinton
13-14-15 . . . . at Beloit
16-17-18-19. . Burlington
21-22-23-24 . . at Wisconsin
25-26-27-28 . . at Burlington
29-30-31 . . . . . Wisconsin

SEPTEMBER

1 . . . . Wisconsin

SOUTH BEND

APRIL

3-4-5-6 . . . . . West Mich.
7-8-9-10 . . . . . . at Lansing
11-12-13 . . . at Quad Cities
14-15-16 . . at Kane County
18-19-20 . . . Cedar Rapids
21-22-23 . . . . . Wisconsin
25-26-27 . . . . at Burlington
28-29-30 . . . . at Beloit

MAY

2-3-4 . . . . Peoria
5-6-7 . . . . Clinton
8-9-10-11 . . . Fort Wayne
12-13-14-15 . at Great Lakes
16-17-18 . . . .at Fort Wayne
19-20-21-22. . West Mich.
23-24-25-26 . . . . at Lansing
28-29-30-31 . . at West Mich.

JUNE

1-2-3-4 . . . . Lansing
5-6-7-8 . . . . at Dayton
9-10-11-12. . . Great Lakes
13-14-15 . . . . Dayton
19-20-21-22. . West Mich.
23-24-25-26 . . . . at Dayton
27-28-29-30 . at Great Lakes

JULY

1-2-3-4 . . . . Lansing
5-6-7 . . . . . . Fort Wayne
9-10-11. . . . . Quad Cities
12-13-14 . . . Kane County
16-17-18 . . . . at Wisconsin
19-20-21 . . at Cedar Rapids
23-24-25 . . . . Beloit
26-27-28 . . . . Burlington
29-30-31 . . . . . . at Clinton

AUGUST

1-2-3 . . . . at Peoria
5-6-7-8 . . . . Lansing
9-10-11-12. . . at West Mich.
13-14-15 . . . .at Fort Wayne
16-17-18-19. . West Mich.
21-22-23-24 . at Great Lakes
25-26-27-28 . .at Fort Wayne
29-30-31 . . . . . . Lansing

SEPTEMBER

1 . . . . Lansing

WEST MICHIGAN

APRIL

3-4-5-6 . . . . at South Bend
7-8-9-10 . . . . Great Lakes
11-12-13 . . . . . . at Clinton
14-15-16 . . . . at Peoria
18-19-20 . . . . Burlington
21-22-23 . . . . Beloit
25-26-27 . . at Cedar Rapids
28-29-30 . . . . at Wisconsin

MAY

2-3-4 . . . . . . Quad Cities
5-6-7 . . . . . Kane County
8-9. . . . . at Lansing
10-11 . . . . Lansing
12-13-14-15 . .at Fort Wayne
16-17 . . . . Lansing
18 . . . . at Lansing
19-20-21-22 . at South Bend
23-24-25-26. . . . . Dayton
28-29-30-31. . South Bend

JUNE

1-2-3-4 . . . . at Dayton
5-6-7-8 . . . . at Great Lakes
9-10-11-12. . . . . Lansing
13-14-15 . . . . Fort Wayne
19-20-21-22 . at South Bend
23-24-25-26 . .at Fort Wayne
27-28-29-30. . . . Lansing

JULY

1-2-3-4 . . . . . Fort Wayne
5-6-7 . . . . at Dayton
9-10-11. . . . . Clinton
12-13-14 . . . . Peoria
16-17-18 . . . . at Beloit
19-20-21 . . . . at Burlington
23-24-25 . . . . . Wisconsin
26-27-28 . . . Cedar Rapids
29-30-31 . . . at Quad Cities

AUGUST

1-2-3 . . . . at Kane County
5-6-7-8 . . . . at Great Lakes
9-10-11-12. . . South Bend
13-14-15 . . . . . . Lansing
16-17-18-19 . at South Bend
21-22-23-24. . . . . Dayton
25-26-27-28. . Great Lakes
29-30-31 . . . . at Dayton

SEPTEMBER

1 . . . . at Dayton

WISCONSIN

APRIL
3-4-5-6 . . . . at Quad Cities
7-8-9-10 . . . . Clinton
11-12-13 . . . . Dayton
14-15-16 . . . . Fort Wayne
18-19-20 . . . . at Beloit
21-22-23 . . . at South Bend
25-26-27 . . . . Beloit
28-29-30 . . . . West Mich.

MAY
1-2-3 . . . . at Lansing
4-5-6 . . . . . at Great Lakes
8-9-10-11 . . Cedar Rapids
12-13-14-15 . . Burlington
16-17-18 . . . Kane County
19-20-21-22 at Cedar Rapids
23-24-25-26 . . . . . at Peoria
28-29-30-31 at Kane County

JUNE
1-2-3-4 . . . . Peoria
5-6-7-8 . . . . . Quad Cities
9-10-11-12 . . . at Burlington
13-14-15 . . . . . . at Clinton
19-20-21-22 . . Burlington
23-24-25-26 at Cedar Rapids
27-28-29-30 . . at Burlington

JULY
1-2-3-4 . . . . Peoria
5-6-7 . . . . Beloit
9-10-11 . . . . at Dayton
12-13-14 . . . . at Fort Wayne
16-17-18 . . . . South Bend
19-20-21 . . . . at Beloit
23-24-25 . . . . at West Mich.
26-27-28 . . . . Beloit
29-30-31 . . . . . . Lansing

AUGUST
1-2-3 . . . . . . Great Lakes
5-6-7-8 . . . . at Clinton
9-10-11-12 . . Kane County
13-14-15 . . . . at Peoria
16-17-18-19 at Kane County
21-22-23-24 . . Quad Cities
25-26-27-28 Cedar Rapids
29-30-31 . . . at Quad Cities

SEPTEMBER
1 . . . . at Quad Cities

SOUTH ATLANTIC LEAGUE

ASHEVILLE

APRIL
3-4-5-6 . . . . . . Lexington
7-8-9-10 . . . . at Kannapolis
11-12-13-14 . at Greensboro
15-16-17-18 West Virginia
19-20-21 . . . . . . Hickory
23-24-25 . . . . at Greenville
26-27-28 . . . . . at Augusta
29-30 . . . . . . at Columbus

MAY
1-2 . . . . at Columbus
3-4-5-6 . . . . . . Savannah
7-8-9-10 . . . . Charleston
12-13-14-15 . . at Savannah
16-17-18-19 . . at Charleston
20-21-22-23 . . . . . . Rome
24-25-26-27 . . . Columbus
29-30-31 . . . . at Rome

JUNE
1 . . . . at Rome
2-3 . . . . at Hickory
4-5 . . . . Hickory
6-7-8 . . . . Greenville
10-11-12 . . . . Augusta
13-14-15 . . . . . . at Hickory
19-20-21-22-23 . at Augusta
24-25-26 . . . . . . Hickory
27-28 . . . . Greenville
29-30 . . . . . . at Greenville

JULY
1 . . . . at Greenville
3-4-5-6 . . . . Rome
7-8-9-10 . . . at Hagerstown
11-12-13-14 . at Lake County
16-17-18-19 . . . Delmarva
20-21-22-23 . . . Lakewood
25-26-27-28 . . at Savannah
29-30-31 . . . . at Charleston

AUGUST
1 . . . . at Charleston
2-3-4-5 . . . . . . Columbus
7-8-9-10 . . . . at Lexington
11-12-13-14 . . Kannapolis
15-16-17-18 . . Greensboro
19-20-21-22 at West Virginia
23-24-25 . . . . . . at Hickory
27-28-29 . . . . . Greenville
30-31 . . . . Augusta

SEPTEMBER
1 . . . . Augusta

CHARLESTON

APRIL
3-4-5-6 . . . . at Rome
7-8-9-10 . . . . . Savannah
11-12-13-14 . . . . . . Rome
16-17 . . . . at Savannah
18-19-20-21 . . at Columbus
22-23 . . . . at Savannah
24-25-26-27 . . . Columbus
29-30 . . . . Augusta

MAY
1-2 . . . . Augusta
3-4-5-6 . . . . at Hickory
7-8-9-10 . . . . . at Asheville
12-13-14-15 . . . Greenville
16-17-18-19 . . . Asheville
20-21-22-23 . . at Greenville
24-25-26-27 . . . at Augusta
29-30-31 . . . . . . Hickory

JUNE
1 . . . . Hickory
2-3-4-5 . . . . Rome
6-7-8 . . . . at Savannah
9-10-11-12 . . . . . . at Rome
13-14-15 . . . . . Savannah
19-20-21-22 . . at Columbus
23-24 . . . . Rome
25-26-27 . . . . . Columbus
28-29 . . . . at Savannah
30 . . . . Savannah

JULY
1 . . . . Savannah
2-3-4-5 . . . . . . at Augusta
7-8-9-10 . . . . . Lexington
11-12-13-14 West Virginia
16-17-18-19 . . at Kannapolis
20-21-22-23 . at Greensboro
25-26-27-28 . . . . Hickory
29-30-31 . . . . . Asheville

AUGUST
1 . . . . Asheville
2-3-4-5 . . . . . at Greenville
6-7-8-9 . . . . Rome
11-12-13-14 . . . at Delmarva
15-16-17-18 . . at Lakewood
20-21-22-23-24 Columbus
25-26-27 . . . . . Savannah
28-29 . . . . at Rome
30-31 . . . . at Savannah

SEPTEMBER
1 . . . . at Savannah

AUGUSTA

APRIL
3-4-5-6 . . . . . Greensboro
7-8-9-10 . . at West Virginia
11-12-13-14 . . at Lexington
15-16-17-18 . . Kannapolis
19-20-21 . . . . . Greenville
23-24-25 . . . . . . at Hickory
26-27-28 . . . . . . Asheville
29-30 . . . . . . at Charleston

MAY
1-2 . . . . at Charleston
3-4-5-6 . . . . Rome
7-8-9-10 . . . . . . Columbus
12-13-14-15 . . . . . . at Rome
16-17-18-19 . . at Columbus
20-21-22-23 . . . Savannah
24-25-26-27 . . Charleston
29-30-31 . . . . . at Savannah

JUNE
1 . . . . at Savannah
2-3 . . . . Greenville
4-5 . . . . at Greenville
6-7-8 . . . . Hickory
10-11-12 . . . . . at Asheville
13-14-15 . . . . at Greenville
19-20-21-22-23 . Asheville
24-25-26 . . . . . Greenville
27-28-29-30 . . . . at Hickory

JULY
1 . . . . at Hickory
2-3-4-5 . . . . . Charleston
7-8-9-10 . . . . . at Lakewood
11-12-13-14 . . . at Delmarva
16-17-18-19. Hagerstown
20-21-22-23. Lake County
25-26-27-28 . . . . . . at Rome
29-30-31 . . . . . at Columbus

AUGUST
1 . . . . at Columbus
2-3-4-5 . . . . Savannah
7-8-9-10 . . . at Greensboro
11-12-13-14 West Virginia
15-16-17-18 . . . Lexington
19-20-21-22 . . at Kannapolis
23-24-25 . . . . at Greenville
27-28-29 . . . . . . Hickory
30-31 . . . . at Asheville

SEPTEMBER
1 . . . . at Asheville

COLUMBUS

APRIL
3-4-5-6 . . . . . . Savannah
7-8-9-10 . . . . at Rome
11-12-13-14 . . . at Savannah
15-16 . . . . Rome
18-19-20-21 . . Charleston
22-23 . . . . Rome
24-25-26-27 . . at Charleston
29-30 . . . . Asheville

MAY
1-2 . . . . Asheville
3-4-5-6 . . . . . at Greenville
7-8-9-10 . . . . . at Augusta
12-13-14-15 . . . . Hickory
16-17-18-19 . . . . . Augusta
20-21-22-23 . . . . at Hickory
24-25-26-27 . . . at Asheville
29-30-31 . . . . . Greenville

JUNE
1 . . . . Greenville
2-3-4-5 . . . . . . Savannah
6-7-8 . . . . at Rome
9-10-11-12 . . . . at Savannah
13-14-15 . . . . Rome
19-20-21-22 . . Charleston
23-24 . . . . at Savannah
25-26-27 . . . . at Charleston
28-29 . . . . Rome
30 . . . . at Rome

JULY
1 . . . . at Rome
2-3-4-5 . . . . at Hickory
7-8-9-10 . . . . Kannapolis
11-12-13-14 . . Greensboro
16-17-18-19 at West Virginia
20-21-22-23 . . at Lexington
25-26-27-28 . . . Greenville
29-30-31 . . . . Augusta

AUGUST
1 . . . . Augusta
2-3-4-5 . . . . . . at Asheville
6-7-8-9 . . . . . . at Savannah
11-12-13-14. Lake County
15-16-17-18. Hagerstown
20-21-22-23-24at Charleston
25-26-27 . . . . Rome
28-29 . . . . Savannah
30-31 . . . . at Rome

SEPTEMBER
1 . . . . at Rome

DELMARVA

APRIL
3-4-5-6 . . . . Hagerstown
8-9-10. . . . .at Lake County
11-12-13 . . . . at Lakewood
14-15 . . . . . Hagerstown
16-17 . . . . . at Hagerstown
18-19-20 . . . . at Lakewood
21-22-23 . . . Lake County
24-25-26-27 at West Virginia
29-30 . . . . Lexington

MAY
1-2. . . . . Lexington
3-4-5-6 . . . . West Virginia
8-9-10-11. . . . at Lexington
12-13-14-15 . .at Kannapolis
16-17-18-19. . Greensboro
20-21-22-23. . Kannapolis
24-25-26-27 . at Greensboro
28-29-30-31 . at Hagerstown

JUNE
2-3-4 . . . . . Lake County
5-6-7-8 . . . . . at Lakewood
9-10-11 . . . .at Lake County
12-13-14-15. . .Lakewood
19-20-21-22. Hagerstown
23-24-25 . . .at Lake County
26-27 . . . . . at Hagerstown
28-29 . . . . . . at Lakewood
30 . . . . Lake County

JULY
1 . . . . Lake County
3-4-5-6 . . . . at Greensboro
7-8-9-10 . . . . .Greenville
11-12-13-14 . . . . . Augusta
16-17-18-19 . . . at Asheville
20-21-22-23 . . . . at Hickory
25-26-27-28. . . Lexington
29-30-31 . . . . Kannapolis

AUGUST
1 . . . . Kannapolis
2-3-4-5 . . . at West Virginia
6-7-8-9 . . . .at Lake County
11-12-13-14. . Charleston
15-16-17-18. . . Savannah
20-21-22-23-24. . . . . . . at Hagerstown
25-26-27 . . . . at Lakewood
28-29 . . . . . Lake County
30-31 . . . . . . .Lakewood

SEPTEMBER
1 . . . . .Lakewood

GREENSBORO

APRIL
3-4-5-6 . . . . . . at Augusta
7-8-9-10 . . . . . . Hickory
11-12-13-14. . . .Asheville
15-16-17-18 . . at Greenville
19-20 . . . . . .at Kannapolis
22-23 . . . . . . Kannapolis
24-25-26-27. Hagerstown
29-30 . . . . .at Lake County

MAY
1-2. . . . . . . .at Lake County
3-4-5-6 . . . . at Hagerstown
8-9-10-11 . . Lake County
12-13-14-15. . .Lakewood
16-17-18-19 . . .at Delmarva
20-21-22-23 . . at Lakewood
24-25-26-27. . . Delmarva
29-30-31 . . . West Virginia

JUNE
1 . . . . West Virginia
2-3. . . . . .at Kannapolis
4-5-6 . . . . . . at Lexington
7-8. . . . . Kannapolis
9-10-11. . . . . .Lexington
12-13-14-15 at West Virginia
19-20-21-22-23 at Lexington
24-25 . . . . . West Virginia
26-27-28-29. . Kannapolis
30 . . . . . . at West Virginia

JULY
1 . . . . at West Virginia
3-4-5-6 . . . . . . Delmarva
7-8-9-10 . . . . at Rome
11-12-13-14 . . at Columbus
16-17-18-19. . . Savannah
20-21-22-23. . Charleston
25-26-27-28 . at Hagerstown
29-30-31 . . .at Lake County

AUGUST
1 . . . . .at Lake County
2-3-4-5 . . . . . . .Lakewood
7-8-9-10 . . . . Augusta
11-12-13-14 . . . . at Hickory
15-16-17-18 . . . at Asheville
19-20-21-22. . . Greenville
23-24-25-26 . .at Kannapolis
28-29-30-31. . . Lexington

SEPTEMBER
1 . . . . Lexington

GREENVILLE

APRIL
3-4-5-6 . . . . . Kannapolis
7-8-9-10 . . . . at Lexington
11-12-13-14 at West Virginia
15-16-17-18. .Greensboro
19-20-21 . . . . . at Augusta
23-24-25 . . . . . .Asheville
26-27-28 . . . . . . Hickory
29-30 . . . . at Rome

MAY
1-2. . . . . at Rome
3-4-5-6 . . . . . . Columbus
7-8-9-10 . . . . Rome
12-13-14-15 . . at Charleston
16-17-18-19. . .at Savannah
20-21-22-23. . Charleston
24-25-26-27. . . Savannah
29-30-31 . . . . at Columbus

JUNE
1 . . . . at Columbus
2-3. . . . . at Augusta
4-5. . . . . Augusta
6-7-8 . . . . at Asheville
10-11-12 . . . . . . at Hickory
13-14-15 . . . . Augusta
19-20-21-22-23. . Hickory
24-25-26 . . . . . at Augusta
27-28 . . . . at Asheville
29-30 . . . . Asheville

JULY
1 . . . . Asheville
2-3-4-5 . . . . . . Savannah
7-8-9-10 . . . . .at Delmarva
11-12-13-14 . . at Lakewood
16-17-18-19. Lake County
20-21-22-23. Hagerstown
25-26-27-28 . . at Columbus
29-30-31 . . . . at Rome

AUGUST
1 . . . . at Rome
2-3-4-5 . . . . . Charleston
7-8-9-10 . . . .at Kannapolis
11-12-13-14. . . Lexington
15-16-17-18 West Virginia
19-20-21-22 . at Greensboro
23-24-25 . . . . Augusta
27-28-29 . . . . . at Asheville
30-31 . . . . at Hickory

SEPTEMBER
1 . . . . at Hickory

HAGERSTOWN

APRIL
3-4-5-6 . . . . . .at Delmarva
8-9-10. . . . . . at Lakewood
11-12-13 . . . Lake County
14-15 . . . . . . .at Delmarva
16-17 . . . . Delmarva
18-19-20 . . .at Lake County
21-22-23 . . . . .Lakewood
24-25-26-27 . at Greensboro
29-30 . . . . . West Virginia

MAY
1-2. . . . . . . West Virginia
3-4-5-6 . . . . . Greensboro
8-9-10-11. . at West Virginia
12-13-14-15 . . at Lexington
16-17-18-19. . Kannapolis
20-21-22-23. . . Lexington
24-25-26-27 . .at Kannapolis
28-29-30-31. . . Delmarva

JUNE
2-3-4 . . . . . . at Lakewood
5-6-7-8 . . . . Lake County
9-10-11. . . . . .Lakewood
12-13-14-15 .at Lake County
19-20-21-22 . . .at Delmarva
23-24-25 . . . . .Lakewood
26-27 . . . . Delmarva
28-29 . . . . .at Lake County
30 . . . . Lakewood

JULY
1 . . . . Lakewood
3-4-5-6 . . . at West Virginia
7-8-9-10 . . . . . .Asheville
11-12-13-14. . . . Hickory
16-17-18-19 . . . at Augusta
20-21-22-23 . . at Greenville
25-26-27-28. . Greensboro
29-30-31 . . . . . Lexington

AUGUST
1 . . . . Lexington
2-3-4-5 . . . . .at Kannapolis
6-7-8-9 . . . . . . Lakewood
11-12-13-14 . . . . . at Rome
15-16-17-18 . . at Columbus
20-21-22-23-24. Delmarva
25-26-27 . . .at Lake County
28-29 . . . . at Lakewood
30-31 . . . . . Lake County

SEPTEMBER
1 . . . . Lake County

HICKORY

APRIL
3-4-5-6 . . . . West Virginia
7-8-9-10 . . . at Greensboro
11-12-13-14 . .at Kannapolis
15-15-16-17-18 Lexington
19-20-21 . . . . . at Asheville
23-24-25 . . . . Augusta
26-27-28 . . . . at Greenville
29-30 . . . . .at Savannah

MAY
1-2. . . . . .at Savannah
3-4-5-6 . . . . . Charleston
7-8-9-10 . . . . . Savannah
12-13-14-15 . . at Columbus
16-17-18-19 . . . . . at Rome
20-21-22-23. . . Columbus
24-25-26-27. . . . . . Rome
29-30-31 . . . . at Charleston

JUNE
1 . . . . .at Charleston
2-3. . . . . .Asheville
4-5. . . . . at Asheville
6-7-8 . . . . at Augusta
10-11-12 . . . . .Greenville
13-14-15 . . . . . .Asheville
19-20-21-22-23 at Greenville
24-25-26 . . . . . at Asheville
27-28-29-30 . . . . . Augusta

JULY
1 . . . . Augusta
2-3-4-5 . . . . . . Columbus
7-8-9-10 . . .at Lake County
11-12-13-14 . at Hagerstown
16-17-18-19. . .Lakewood
20-21-22-23. . . Delmarva
25-26-27-28 . . at Charleston
29-30-31 . . . . .at Savannah

AUGUST
1 . . . . .at Savannah
2-3-4-5 . . . . Rome
7-8-9-10 . . at West Virginia
11-12-13-14. .Greensboro
15-16-17-18. . Kannapolis
19-20-21-22 . . at Lexington
23-24-25 . . . . . .Asheville
27-28-29 . . . . . at Augusta
30-31 . . . . . . .Greenville

SEPTEMBER
1 . . . . .Greenville

KANNAPOLIS

APRIL
3-4-5-6 . . . . . at Greenville
7-8-9-10 . . . . . .Asheville
11-12-13-14. . . . Hickory
15-16-17-18 . . . at Augusta
19-20 . . . . . .Greensboro
22-23 . . . . . at Greensboro
24-25-26-27. Lake County
29-30 . . . . . . at Lakewood

MAY
1-2. . . . . at Lakewood
3-4-5-6 . . . .at Lake County
8-9-10-11 . . . .Lakewood
12-13-14-15. . . Delmarva
16-17-18-19 . at Hagerstown
20-21-22-23 . . .at Delmarva
24-25-26-27. Hagerstown
29-30-31 . . . . at Lexington

JUNE
1 . . . . at Lexington
2-3. . . . . . . .Greensboro
4-5-6 . . . . .West Virginia
7-8. . . . . . . at Greensboro
9-10-11 . . . at West Virginia
12-13-14-15. . . Lexington
19-20-21-22-23 W Virginia
24-25 . . . . . . at Lexington
26-27-28-29 . at Greensboro
30 . . . . .Lexington

JULY
1 . . . . .Lexington
2-3-4-5 . . . . Lake County
7-8-9-10 . . . . at Columbus
11-12-13-14 . . . . . at Rome
16-17-18-19. . Charleston
20-21-22-23. . . Savannah
25-26-27-28 . . at Lakewood
29-30-31 . . . . .at Delmarva

AUGUST
1 . . . . .at Delmarva
2-3-4-5 . . . . Hagerstown
7-8-9-10 . . . . .Greenville
11-12-13-14 . . . at Asheville
15-16-17-18 . . . . at Hickory
19-20-21-22 . . . . . Augusta
23-24-25-26. .Greensboro
28-29-30-31 at West Virginia

SEPTEMBER
1 . . . . at West Virginia

LAKE COUNTY

APRIL
3-4-5-6 . . . . . at Lakewood
8-9-10. . . . . . . Delmarva
11-12-13 . . . at Hagerstown
14-15 . . . . . . .Lakewood
16-17 . . . . . . at Lakewood
18-19-20 . . . Hagerstown
21-22-23 . . . . .at Delmarva
24-25-26-27 . .at Kannapolis
29-30 . . . . . .Greensboro

MAY
1-2. . . . . . . .Greensboro
3-4-5-6 . . . . . Kannapolis
8-9-10-11. . . at Greensboro
12-13-14-15 at West Virginia
16-17-18-19. . . Lexington
20-21-22-23 West Virginia
24-25-26-27 . . at Lexington
28-29-30-31. . .Lakewood

JUNE
2-3-4 . . . . . . .at Delmarva
5-6-7-8 . . . . at Hagerstown
9-10-11. . . . . . Delmarva
12-13-14-15. Hagerstown
19-20-21-22 . . at Lakewood
23-24-25 . . . . . Delmarva
26-27 . . . . . . .Lakewood
28-29 . . . . . Hagerstown
30 . . . . .at Delmarva

JULY
1 . . . . .at Delmarva
2-3-4-5 . . . . .at Kannapolis
7-8-9-10 . . . . . . Hickory
11-12-13-14. . . .Asheville
16-17-18-19. . at Greenville
20-21-22-23 . . . at Augusta
25-26-27-28 West Virginia
29-30-31 . . . .Greensboro

AUGUST
1 . . . . .Greensboro
2-3-4-5 . . . . . at Lexington
6-7-8-9 . . . . . . Delmarva
11-12-13-14 . . at Columbus
15-16-17-18 . . . . . at Rome
20-21-22-23-25 Lakewood
25-26-27 . . . Hagerstown
28-29 . . . . . . .at Delmarva
30-31 . . . . . at Hagerstown

SEPTEMBER
1 . . . . at Hagerstown

LAKEWOOD

APRIL
3-4-5-6 . . . . Lake County
8-9-10. . . . . Hagerstown
11-12-13 . . . . . Delmarva
14-15 . . . . .at Lake County
16-17 . . . . . Lake County
18-19-20 . . . . . Delmarva
21-22-23 . . . at Hagerstown
24-25-26-27 . . at Lexington
29-30 . . . . . . Kannapolis

MAY
1-2. . . . . Kannapolis
3-4-5-6 . . . . . . Lexington
8-9-10-11. . . .at Kannapolis
12-13-14-15 . at Greensboro
16-17-18-19 West Virginia
20-21-22-23. .Greensboro
24-25-26-27 at West Virginia
28-29-30-31 .at Lake County

JUNE
2-3-4 . . . . . Hagerstown
5-6-7-8 . . . . . . Delmarva
9-10-11 . . . . at Hagerstown
12-13-14-15 . . .at Delmarva
19-20-21-22. Lake County
23-24-25 . . . at Hagerstown
26-27 . . . . .at Lake County
28-29 . . . . Delmarva
30 . . . . at Hagerstown

JULY
1 . . . . at Hagerstown
2-3-4-5 . . . . . at Lexington
7-8-9-10 . . . . Augusta
11-12-13-14. . .Greenville
16-17-18-19 . . . . at Hickory
20-21-22-23 . . . at Asheville
25-26-27-28. . Kannapolis
29-30-31 . . . West Virginia

AUGUST
1 . . . . West Virginia
2-3-4-5 . . . . at Greensboro
6-7-8-9 . . . . at Hagerstown
11-12-13-14. . . Savannah
15-16-17-18. . Charleston
20-21-22-23-25 . at Lake Cty
25-26-27 . . . . . Delmarva
28-29 . . . . . Hagerstown
30-31 . . . . . . .at Delmarva

SEPTEMBER
1 . . . . .at Delmarva

LEXINGTON

APRIL
3-4-5-6 . . . . . . at Asheville
7-8-9-10 . . . . .Greenville
11-12-13-14 . . . . . Augusta
15-15-16-17-18. . at Hickory
19-20 . . . . at West Virginia
22-23 . . . . . West Virginia
24-25-26-27. . .Lakewood
29-30 . . . . . . .at Delmarva

MAY
1-2. . . . . .at Delmarva
3-4-5-6 . . . . . at Lakewood
8-9-10-11 . . . . Delmarva
12-13-14-15. Hagerstown
16-17-18-19 .at Lake County
20-21-22-23 . at Hagerstown
24-25-26-27. Lake County
29-30-31 . . . . Kannapolis

JUNE
1 . . . . Kannapolis
2-3. . . . . . at West Virginia
4-5-6 . . . . . .Greensboro
7-8. . . . . . . West Virginia
9-10-11 . . . . at Greensboro
12-13-14-15 . .at Kannapolis
19-20-21-22-23. Grnsboro
24-25 . . . . . . Kannapolis
26-27-28-29 at West Virginia
30 . . . . .at Kannapolis

JULY
1 . . . . .at Kannapolis
2-3-4-5 . . . . . .Lakewood
7-8-9-10 . . . .at Charleston
11-12-13-14 . . .at Savannah
16-17-18-19. . . . . .Rome
20-21-22-23. . . Columbus
25-26-27-28 . . .at Delmarva
29-30-31 . . . at Hagerstown

AUGUST
1 . . . . at Hagerstown
2-3-4-5 . . . . Lake County
7-8-9-10 . . . . . .Asheville
11-12-13-14 . . at Greenville
15-16-17-18 . . . at Augusta
19-20-21-22. . . . Hickory
23-24-25-26 West Virginia
28-29-30-31 . at Greensboro

SEPTEMBER
1 . . . . at Greensboro

ROME

APRIL
3-4-5-6 . . . . . Charleston
7-8-9-10 . . . . . Columbus
11-12-13-14 . .at Charleston
15-16 . . . . . . at Columbus
18-19-20-21. . . Savannah
22-23 . . . . . . at Columbus
24-25-26-27 . . .at Savannah
29-30 . . . . Greenville

MAY
1-2. . . . . .Greenville
3-4-5-6 . . . . . . at Augusta
7-8-9-10 . . . . at Greenville
12-13-14-15 . . . . . Augusta
16-17-18-19. . . . Hickory
20-21-22-23 . . . at Asheville
24-25-26-27 . . . . at Hickory
29-30-31 . . . . . .Asheville

JUNE
1 . . . . .Asheville
2-3-4-5 . . . . .at Charleston
6-7-8 . . . . Columbus
9-10-11-12. . . Charleston
13-14-15 . . . . at Columbus
19-20-21-22. . . Savannah
23-24 . . . . . . at Charleston
25-26-27 . . . . .at Savannah
28-29 . . . . . . at Columbus
30 . . . . Columbus

JULY
1 . . . . Columbus
3-4-5-6 . . . . . . at Asheville
7-8-9-10 . . . .Greensboro
11-12-13-14. . Kannapolis
16-17-18-19 . . at Lexington
20-21-22-23 at West Virginia
25-26-27-28 . . . . . Augusta
29-30-31 . . . . .Greenville

AUGUST
1 . . . . .Greenville
2-3-4-5 . . . . at Hickory
6-7-8-9 . . . . .at Charleston
11-12-13-14. Hagerstown
15-16-17-18. Lake County
20-21-22-23-24 at Savannah
25-26-27 . . . . at Columbus
28-29 . . . . . . Charleston
30-31 . . . . Columbus

SEPTEMBER
1 . . . . Columbus

SAVANNAH

APRIL

3-4-5-6 . . . . . at Columbus
7-8-9-10 . . . . at Charleston
11-12-13-14. . . Columbus
16-17 . . . . . . Charleston
18-19-20-21 . . . . . at Rome
22-23 . . . . . . Charleston
24-25-26-27. . . . . Rome
29-30 . . . . Hickory

MAY

1-2. . . . . Hickory
3-4-5-6 . . . . . . at Asheville
7-8-9-10 . . . . . . at Hickory
12-13-14-15. . . .Asheville
16-17-18-19. . . Greenville
20-21-22-23 . . . at Augusta
24-25-26-27 . . at Greenville
29-30-31 . . . . Augusta

JUNE

1 . . . . Augusta
2-3-4-5 . . . . . at Columbus
6-7-8 . . . . . . Charleston
9-10-11-12. . . . Columbus
13-14-15 . . . . at Charleston
19-20-21-22 . . . . . at Rome
23-24 . . . . Columbus
25-26-27 . . . . Rome
28-29 . . . . . . Charleston
30 . . . . at Charleston

JULY

1 . . . . at Charleston
2-3-4-5 . . . . . at Greenville
7-8-9-10 . . . West Virginia
11-12-13-14. . . Lexington
16-17-18-19 . at Greensboro
20-21-22-23 . .at Kannapolis
25-26-27-28. . . .Asheville
29-30-31 . . . . . . Hickory

AUGUST

1 . . . . Hickory
2-3-4-5 . . . . at Augusta
6-7-8-9 . . . . . . Columbus
11-12-13-14 . . at Lakewood
15-16-17-18 . . .at Delmarva
20-21-22-23-24. . . . Rome
25-26-27 . . . . at Charleston
28-29 . . . . at Columbus
30-31 . . . . . . Charleston

SEPTEMBER

1 . . . . Charleston

WEST VIRGINIA

APRIL

3-4-5-6 . . . . at Hickory
7-8-9-10 . . . . Augusta
11-12-13-14. . . Greenville
15-16-17-18 . . . at Asheville
19-20 . . . . Lexington
22-23 . . . . . . at Lexington
24-25-26-27. . . Delmarva
29-30 . . . . . at Hagerstown

MAY

1-2. . . . . . . at Hagerstown
3-4-5-6 . . . . . .at Delmarva
8-9-10-11 . . Hagerstown
12-13-14-15. Lake County
16-17-18-19 . . at Lakewood
20-21-22-23 . at Lake County
24-25-26-27. . . Lakewood
29-30-31 . . . at Greensboro

JUNE

1 . . . . at Greensboro
2-3. . . . . Lexington
4-5-6 . . . . . .at Kannapolis
7-8. . . . . at Lexington
9-10-11. . . . . Kannapolis
12-13-14-15. .Greensboro
19-20-21-22-23 . . . .at Kann
24-25 . . . . . at Greensboro
26-27-28-29. . . Lexington
30 . . . . .Greensboro

JULY

1 . . . . .Greensboro
3-4-5-6 . . . . Hagerstown
7-8-9-10 . . . . .at Savannah
11-12-13-14 . . at Charleston
16-17-18-19. . . Columbus
20-21-22-23. . . . . .Rome
25-26-27-28 . at Lake County
29-30-31 . . . . at Lakewood

AUGUST

1 . . . . at Lakewood
2-3-4-5 . . . . . . Delmarva
7-8-9-10 . . . . . . Hickory
11-12-13-14 . . . at Augusta
15-16-17-18 . . at Greenville
19-20-21-22. . . .Asheville
23-24-25-26 . . at Lexington
28-29-30-31. . Kannapolis

SEPTEMBER

1 . . . . Kannapolis

SHORT SEASON

NEW YORK-PENN LEAGUE

ABERDEEN

JUNE

17-18-19 . .at Hudson Valley
20-21-22. . . . . .Brooklyn
23-24-25 . . . Staten Island
26-27-28 . . . . . at Brooklyn
29-30 . . . . at Staten Island

JULY

1 . . . . at Staten Island
2-3-4 . . . . Lowell
5-6-7 . . . . .at Williamsport
9-10-11. . . . . . . .Auburn
12-13-14 . . . . . . at Batavia
16-17-18 . . . . Jamestown
19-20-21 . . Hudson Valley
22-23-24 at Mahoning Valley
25-26-27-28 at Hudson Valley
29-30-31 . . . . . . Oneonta

AUGUST

1-2-3-4 . . . Hudson Valley
6-7-8 . . . . at Tri-City
9-10-11. . . . State College
12-13-14 . . . . . at Vermont
15-16-17 . . . . . . .at Lowell
21-22-23. . . . . . . .Tri-City
24-25-26 . . . . . at Oneonta
27-28-29. . . . . . Vermont
30-31 . . . . . Staten Island

SEPTEMBER

1-2. . . . . .Brooklyn
3-4. . . . . . . at Staten Island
5-6. . . . . at Brooklyn

AUBURN

JUNE

17 . . . . .Batavia
18 . . . . at Batavia
19 . . . . .Batavia
20-21-22 . . at State College
23-24-25 Mahoning Valley
26-27-28. . . State College
29-30 . . at Mahoning Valley

JULY

1 . . . . . at Mahoning Valley
2-3-4 . . . . at Oneonta
5-6-7 . . . . . Staten Island
9-10-11 . . . . . at Aberdeen
12-13-14 . . . . Lowell
16-17-18 . .at Hudson Valley
19 . . . . .Batavia
20 . . . . at Batavia
21 . . . . .Batavia
22-23-24 . . . . Tri-City
25-26-27 . . . Williamsport
28-29-30 . . . at Jamestown
31 . . . . . . .at Williamsport

AUGUST

1-2. . . . . . .at Williamsport
3-4. . . . . Jamestown
6 . . . . at Batavia
7 . . . . .Batavia
8 . . . . at Batavia
9-10-11 . . . . . . at Vermont
12-13-14 . . . . . .Brooklyn
15 . . . . at Batavia
16 . . . . .Batavia
17 . . . . at Batavia
21-22 . . . . . Williamsport
23-24-25 . . . . Jamestown
26-27 . . . . .at Williamsport
28-29 . . . . . at Jamestown
30-31 . . . . . State College

SEPTEMBER

1-2. . . . Mahoning Valley
3-4. . . . . . at State College
5-6. . . . at Mahoning Valley

BATAVIA

JUNE

17 . . . . at Auburn
18 . . . . .Auburn
19 . . . . at Auburn
20-21-22 Mahoning Valley
23 . . . . Jamestown
24 . . . . at Jamestown
25 . . . . Jamestown
26-27-28 at Mahoning Valley
29 . . . . at Jamestown
30 . . . . Jamestown

JULY

1 . . . . at Jamestown
2-3-4 . . . . Hudson Valley
5-6-7 . . . . at Vermont
9-10-11. . . . . Lowell
12-13-14. . . . . . Aberdeen
16-17-18 . . at Staten Island
19 . . . . at Auburn
19 . . . . at Staten Island
20 . . . . .Auburn
21 . . . . at Auburn
22-23-24. . . . . . .Oneonta
25-26-27 . . at State College
28-29-30 . . .at Williamsport
31 . . . . State College

AUGUST

1-2. . . . . . . State College
3-4. . . . . . . Williamsport
6 . . . . .Auburn
7 . . . . at Auburn
8 . . . . .Auburn
9-10-11 . . . . . . at Brooklyn
12-13-14 . . . . . . at Tri-City
15 . . . . .Auburn
16 . . . . at Auburn
17 . . . . .Auburn
21-22 . . Mahoning Valley
23-24-25 . . . Williamsport
26-27 . . at Mahoning Valley
28-29 . . . . .at Williamsport
30 . . . . at Jamestown
31 . . . . Jamestown

SEPTEMBER

1-2. . . . . . at State College
3 . . . . at Jamestown
4 . . . . Jamestown
5-6. . . . . . . State College

BROOKLYN

JUNE

17 . . . . Staten Island
18 . . . . at Staten Island
19 . . . . Staten Island
20-21-22 . . . . at Aberdeen
23 . . . . . . Hudson Valley
24-25 . . . .at Hudson Valley
26-27-28 . . . . . Aberdeen
29-30 . . . . Hudson Valley

JULY
1 ... at Hudson Valley
2-3-4 ... at Williamsport
5-6-7 .. Mahoning Valley
9-10-11 ... at Jamestown
12-13-14 ... State College
16-17-18 ... at Oneonta
19 ... at Staten Island
20 ... Staten Island
21 ... at Staten Island
22-23-24 ... Vermont
25 ... Staten Island
26 ... at Staten Island
27 ... Staten Island
28 ... at Staten Island
29-30-31 ... at Vermont

AUGUST
1 ... at Staten Island
2 ... Staten Island
3 ... at Staten Island
4 ... Staten Island
6-7-8 ... at Lowell
9-10-11 ... Batavia
12-13-14 ... at Auburn
15-16-17 ... Tri-City
21-22-23 ... Lowell
24-25-26 ... at Tri-City
27-28-29 ... Oneonta
30 ... at Hudson Valley
31 ... Hudson Valley

SEPTEMBER
1-2 ... at Aberdeen
3 ... at Hudson Valley
4 ... Hudson Valley
5-6 ... Aberdeen

HUDSON VALLEY

JUNE
17-18-19 ... Aberdeen
20 ... at Staten Island
21 ... Staten Island
22 ... at Staten Island
23 ... at Brooklyn
24-25 ... Brooklyn
26 ... Staten Island
27 ... at Staten Island
28 ... Staten Island
29-30 ... at Brooklyn

JULY
1 ... Brooklyn
2-3-4 ... at Batavia
5-6-7 ... Tri-City
9-10-11 ... at State College
12-13-14 at Mahoning Valley
16-17-18 ... Auburn
19-20-21 ... at Aberdeen
22-23-24 ... Williamsport
25-26-27-28 ... Aberdeen
29-30-31 ... at Tri-City

AUGUST
1-2-3-4 ... at Aberdeen
6-7-8 ... Vermont
9-10-11 ... at Lowell
12-13-14 ... Jamestown
15-16-17 ... Oneonta
21-22-23 ... at Oneonta
24-25-26 ... at Vermont
27-28-29 ... Lowell
30 ... Brooklyn
31 ... at Brooklyn

SEPTEMBER
1 ... Staten Island
2 ... at Staten Island
3 ... Brooklyn
4 ... at Brooklyn
5 ... at Staten Island
6 ... Staten Island

JAMESTOWN

JUNE
17-18 ... State College
19 ... at State College
20-21-22 ... at Williamsport
23 ... at Batavia
24 ... Batavia
25 ... at Batavia
26-27-28 ... Williamsport
29 ... Batavia
30 ... at Batavia

JULY
1 ... Batavia
2-3-4 ... at Tri-City
5-6-7 ... at Lowell
9-10-11 ... Brooklyn
12-13-14 ... Vermont
16-17-18 ... at Aberdeen
19-20 ... at State College
21 ... State College
22-23-24 ... Staten Island
25-26-27 at Mahoning Valley
28-29-30 ... Auburn
31 ... Mahoning Valley

AUGUST
1-2 ... Mahoning Valley
3-4 ... at Auburn
6-7-8 .. Mahoning Valley
9-10-11 ... Oneonta
12-13-14 .. at Hudson Valley
15-16-17 at Mahoning Valley
21-22 ... at State College
23-24-25 ... at Auburn
26-27 ... State College
28-29 ... Auburn
30 ... Batavia
31 ... at Batavia

SEPTEMBER
1-2 ... at Williamsport
3 ... Batavia
4 ... at Batavia
5-6 ... Williamsport

LOWELL

JUNE
17-18-19 ... Tri-City
20-21-22 ... Vermont
23-24-25 ... at Oneonta
26-27-28 ... at Vermont
29-30 ... Oneonta

JULY
1 ... Oneonta
2-3-4 ... at Aberdeen
5-6-7 ... Jamestown
9-10-11 ... at Batavia
12-13-14 ... at Auburn
16-17-18 Mahoning Valley
19-20-21 ... at Tri-City
22-23-24 ... State College
25-26-27-28 ... at Vermont
29-30-31 ... Staten Island

AUGUST
1-2-3-4 ... Vermont
6-7-8 ... Brooklyn
9-10-11 ... Hudson Valley
12-13-14 ... at Williamsport
15-16-17 ... Aberdeen
21-22-23 ... at Brooklyn
24-25-26 .. at Staten Island
27-28-29 .. at Hudson Valley
30-31 ... Oneonta

SEPTEMBER
1-2 ... Tri-City
3-4 ... at Oneonta
5-6 ... at Tri-City

MAHONING VALLEY

JUNE
17-18-19 ... Williamsport
20-21-22 ... at Batavia
23-24-25 ... at Auburn
26-27-28 ... Batavia
29-30 ... Auburn

JULY
1 ... Auburn
2-3-4 ... at Staten Island
5-6-7 ... at Brooklyn
9-10-11 ... Vermont
12-13-14 .. Hudson Valley
16-17-18 ... at Lowell
19-20-21 ... at Williamsport
22-23-24 ... Aberdeen
25-26-27 ... Jamestown
28-29-30 .. at State College
31 ... at Jamestown

AUGUST
1-2 ... at Jamestown
3-4 ... State College
6-7-8 ... at Jamestown
9-10-11 ... Tri-City
12-13-14 ... at Oneonta
15-16-17 ... Jamestown
21-22 ... at Batavia
23-24-25 ... State College
26-27 ... Batavia
28-29 ... at State College
30-31 ... at Williamsport

SEPTEMBER
1-2 ... at Auburn
3-4 ... Williamsport
5-6 ... Auburn

ONEONTA

JUNE
17-18-19 ... at Vermont
20 ... at Tri-City
21 ... Tri-City
22 ... at Tri-City
23-24-25 ... Lowell
26 ... Tri-City
27 ... at Tri-City
28 ... Tri-City
29-30 ... at Lowell

JULY
1 ... at Lowell
2-3-4 ... Auburn
5-6-7 ... State College
9-10-11 ... at Staten Island
12-13-14 ... at Williamsport
16-17-18 ... Brooklyn
19-20-21 ... Vermont
22-23-24 ... at Batavia
25-26-27 ... Tri-City
28 ... at Tri-City
29-30-31 ... at Aberdeen

AUGUST
1-2-3 ... at Tri-City
4 ... Tri-City
6-7-8 ... Staten Island
9-10-11 ... at Jamestown
12-13-14 Mahoning Valley
15-16-17 .. at Hudson Valley
21-22-23 .. Hudson Valley
24-25-26 ... Aberdeen
27-28-29 ... at Brooklyn
30-31 ... at Lowell

SEPTEMBER
1-2 ... Vermont
3-4 ... Lowell
5-6 ... at Vermont

STATE COLLEGE

JUNE
17-18 ... at Jamestown
19 ... Jamestown
20-21-22 ... Auburn
23 ... at Williamsport
24 ... Williamsport
25 ... at Williamsport
26-27-28 ... at Auburn
29 ... Williamsport
30 ... at Williamsport

JULY
1 ... Williamsport
2-3-4 ... Vermont
5-6-7 ... at Oneonta
9-10-11 ... Hudson Valley
12-13-14 ... at Brooklyn
16-17-18 ... Tri-City
19-20 ... Jamestown
21 ... at Jamestown
22-23-24 ... at Lowell
25-26-27 ... Batavia
28-29-30 Mahoning Valley
31 ... at Batavia

AUGUST
1-2 ... at Batavia
3-4 ... at Mahoning Valley
6 ... Williamsport
7 ... at Williamsport

8 . . . . Williamsport
9-10-11 . . . . . at Aberdeen
12-13-14 . . . Staten Island
15-16 . . . . . at Williamsport
17 . . . . Williamsport
21-22 . . . . . . Jamestown
23-24-25 at Mahoning Valley
26-27 . . . . . at Jamestown
28-29 . . Mahoning Valley
30-31 . . . . at Auburn

SEPTEMBER

1-2 . . . . Batavia
3-4 . . . . Auburn
5-6 . . . . at Batavia

STATEN ISLAND

JUNE

17 . . . . at Brooklyn
18 . . . . Brooklyn
19 . . . . at Brooklyn
20 . . . . . . Hudson Valley
21 . . . . . . at Hudson Valley
22 . . . . . . Hudson Valley
23-24-25 . . . . at Aberdeen
26 . . . . . . at Hudson Valley
27 . . . . . . Hudson Valley
28 . . . . . . at Hudson Valley
29-30 . . . . Aberdeen

JULY

1 . . . . Aberdeen
2-3-4 . . Mahoning Valley
5-6-7 . . . . at Auburn
9-10-11 . . . . Oneonta
12-13-14 . . . . . . at Tri-City
16-17-18 . . . . Batavia
19 . . . . Brooklyn
20 . . . . at Brooklyn
21 . . . . Brooklyn
22-23-24 . . . at Jamestown
25 . . . . at Brooklyn
26 . . . . Brooklyn
27 . . . . at Brooklyn
28 . . . . Brooklyn
29-30-31 . . . . at Lowell

AUGUST

1 . . . . Brooklyn
2 . . . . at Brooklyn
3 . . . . Brooklyn
4 . . . . at Brooklyn
6-7-8 . . . . at Oneonta
9-10-11 . . . . Williamsport
12-13-14 . . at State College
15-16-17 . . . . . . Vermont
21-22-23 . . . . . at Vermont
24-25-26 . . . . Lowell
27-28-29 . . . . Tri-City
30-31 . . . . . . at Aberdeen

SEPTEMBER

1 . . . . at Hudson Valley
2 . . . . Hudson Valley
3-4 . . . . Aberdeen
5 . . . . Hudson Valley
6 . . . . at Hudson Valley

TRI-CITY

JUNE

17-18-19 . . . . at Lowell
20 . . . . Oneonta
21 . . . . at Oneonta
22 . . . . Oneonta
23-24-25 . . . . . at Vermont
26 . . . . at Oneonta
27 . . . . Oneonta
28 . . . . at Oneonta
29-30 . . . . Vermont

JULY

1 . . . . Vermont
2-3-4 . . . . . . Jamestown
5-6-7 . . . . at Hudson Valley
9-10-11 . . . . Williamsport
12-13-14 . . . Staten Island
16-17-18 . . at State College
19-20-21 . . . . Lowell
22-23-24 . . . . . . at Auburn
25-26-27 . . . . . at Oneonta
28 . . . . Oneonta
29-30-31 . . Hudson Valley

AUGUST

1-2-3 . . . . Oneonta
4 . . . . at Oneonta
6-7-8 . . . . Aberdeen
9-10-11 at Mahoning Valley
12-13-14 . . . . Batavia
15-16-17 . . . . . at Brooklyn
21-22-23 . . . . at Aberdeen
24-25-26 . . . . . . Brooklyn
27-28-29 . . at Staten Island
30-31 . . . . Vermont

SEPTEMBER

1-2 . . . . at Lowell
3-4 . . . . at Vermont
5-6 . . . . Lowell

VERMONT

JUNE

17-18-19 . . . . . . Oneonta
20-21-22 . . . . at Lowell
23-24-25 . . . . Tri-City
26-27-28 . . . . Lowell
29-30 . . . . at Tri-City

JULY

1 . . . . at Tri-City
2-3-4 . . . . at State College
5-6-7 . . . . Batavia
9-10-11 at Mahoning Valley
12-13-14 . . . at Jamestown
16-17-18 . . . Williamsport
19-20-21 . . . . . at Oneonta
22-23-24 . . . . . at Brooklyn
25-26-27-28 . . . . . Lowell
29-30-31 . . . . . Brooklyn

AUGUST

1-2-3-4 . . . . at Lowell
6-7-8 . . . . at Hudson Valley
9-10-11 . . . . Auburn
12-13-14 . . . . . Aberdeen
15-16-17 . . at Staten Island
21-22-23 . . . Staten Island
24-25-26 . . Hudson Valley
27-28-29 . . . . at Aberdeen
30-31 . . . . at Tri-City

SEPTEMBER

1-2 . . . . at Oneonta
3-4 . . . . Tri-City
5-6 . . . . Oneonta

WILLIAMSPORT

JUNE

17-18-19 at Mahoning Valley
20-21-22 . . . . Jamestown
23 . . . . State College
24 . . . . . . at State College
25 . . . . State College
26-27-28 . . . at Jamestown
29 . . . . . . at State College
30 . . . . State College

JULY

1 . . . . at State College
2-3-4 . . . . Brooklyn
5-6-7 . . . . Aberdeen
9-10-11 . . . . at Tri-City
12-13-14 . . . . . . Oneonta
16-17-18 . . . . . at Vermont
19-20-21 Mahoning Valley
22-23-24 . . at Hudson Valley
25-26-27 . . . . . . at Auburn
28-29-30 . . . . Batavia
31 . . . . Auburn

AUGUST

1-2 . . . . Auburn
3-4 . . . . at Batavia
6 . . . . at State College
7 . . . . State College
8 . . . . at State College
9-10-11 . . . at Staten Island
12-13-14 . . . . Lowell
15-16 . . . . . State College
17 . . . . at State College
21-22 . . . . at Auburn
23-24-25 . . . . . . at Batavia
26-27 . . . . Auburn
28-29 . . . . Batavia
30-31 . . Mahoning Valley

SEPTEMBER

1-2 . . . . Jamestown
3-4 . . . . at Mahoning Valley
5-6 . . . . at Jamestown

NORTHWEST LEAGUE

BOISE

JUNE

17-18-19-20-21 . . . Eugene
22-23-24-25-26 . . at Everett
27-28-29 . . . . Yakima
30 . . . . at Tri-City

JULY

1-2 . . . . at Tri-City
3-4-5-6-7 . . . . . Vancouver
9-10-11-12-13 . . . at Eugene
14-15-16 . . . . Tri-City
17-18-19 . . . . at Tri-City
20-21-22-23-24 . . . Everett
25-26-27-28-29 . at S.-Keizer
31 . . . . Tri-City

AUGUST

1-2 . . . . Tri-City
3-4-5 . . . . at Yakima
6-7-8-9-10 . . Salem-Keizer
11-12-13 . . . . Spokane
15-16-17-18-19 at Vancouver
20-21-22 . . . . . . at Spokane
23-24-25 . . . . at Yakima
26-27-28 . . . . Yakima
29-30-31 . . . . . . Spokane

SEPTEMBER

1-2-3 . . . . at Spokane

EUGENE

JUNE

17-18-19-20-21 . . . at Boise
22-23-24-25-26 . . Spokane
27-28-29 . . . . at Vancouver
30 . . . . Salem-Keizer

JULY

1-2 . . . . Salem-Keizer
3-4-5-6-7 . . . . . . at Spokane
9-10-11-12-13 . . . . Boise
14-15-16 . . . . at Everett
17-18-19 . . . . . Vancouver
20-21-22-23-24 . . . Tri-City
25-26-27-28-29 . . at Yakima
31 . . . . Everett

AUGUST

1-2 . . . . Everett
3-4-5 . . . . at Salem-Keizer
6-7-8-9-10 . . . . . . Yakima
11-12-13-14-15 . . at Tri-City
16-17-18 . . . . at Everett
20-21-22 . . . . . Vancouver
23-24-25 . . . Salem-Keizer
26-27-28 . . at Salem-Keizer
29-30-31 . . . . . at Vancouver

SEPTEMBER

1-2-3 . . . . Everett

EVERETT

JUNE

17-18-19-20-21 . at Spokane
22-23-24-25-26 . . . . Boise
27-28-29 . . at Salem-Keizer
30 . . . . at Vancouver

JULY

1-2 . . . . at Vancouver
3-4-5-6-7 . . . . Yakima
9-10-11-12-13 . . . at Tri-City
14-15-16 . . . . Eugene
17-18-19 . . at Salem-Keizer

20-21-22-23-24 . . . at Boise
25-26-27-28-29. . Spokane
31 . . . . at Eugene

AUGUST

1-2. . . . . at Eugene
3-4-5 . . . . . . .Vancouver
6-7-8-9-10 . . . . . .Tri-City
11-12-13-14-15. . at Yakima

16-17-18 . . . . . . .Eugene
20-21-22 . . . Salem-Keizer
23-24-25 . . . . at Vancouver
26-27-28 . . . . .Vancouver
29-30-31 . . . Salem-Keizer

SEPTEMBER

1-2-3 . . . . at Eugene

SALEM-KEIZER

JUNE

17-18-19-20-21. . . Yakima
22-23-24-25-26 . . at Tri-City
27-28-29 . . . . Everett
30 . . . . at Eugene

JULY

1-2. . . . . at Eugene
3-4-5-6-7. . . . . . . Tri-City
9-10-11-12-13. . . at Yakima
14-15-16 . . . . .Vancouver
17-18-19 . . . . Everett
20-21-22-23-24. at Spokane
25-26-27-28-29. . . . Boise

31 . . . . at Vancouver

AUGUST

1-2. . . . . at Vancouver
3-4-5 . . . . .Eugene
6-7-8-9-10 . . . . . . at Boise
12-13-14 . . . . at Vancouver
15-16-17-18-19. . Spokane
20-21-22 . . . . . . at Everett
23-24-25 . . . . . . at Eugene
26-27-28 . . . . . . .Eugene
29-30-31 . . . . . . at Everett

SEPTEMBER

1-2-3 . . . . . . .Vancouver

SPOKANE

JUNE

17-18-19-20-21. . . Everett
22-23-24-25-26 . . at Eugene
27-28-29 . . . . Tri-City
30 . . . . at Yakima

JULY

1-2. . . . . at Yakima
3-4-5-6-7. . . . . . . Eugene
9-10-11-12-13 at Vancouver
14-15-16 . . . . Yakima
17-18-19 . . . . . . at Yakima
20-21-22-23-24Salem-Keizer
25-26-27-28-29. . at Everett

31 . . . . Yakima

AUGUST

1-2. . . . . Yakima
3-4-5 . . . . at Tri-City
6-7-8-9-10 . . . .Vancouver
11-12-13 . . . . at Boise
15-16-17-18-19at Salem-Keizer
20-21-22 . . . . Boise
23-24-25 . . . . . . at Tri-City
26-27-28 . . . . Tri-City
29-30-31 . . . . at Boise

SEPTEMBER

1-2-3 . . . . Boise

TRI-CITY

JUNE

17-18-19-20-21at Vancouver
22-23-24-25-26Salem-Keizer
27-28-29 . . . . . at Spokane

30 . . . . Boise

JULY

1-2. . . . . Boise

3-4-5-6-7 . . at Salem-Keizer
9-10-11-12-13 . . . Everett
14-15-16 . . . . at Boise
17-18-19. . . . . Boise
20-21-22-23-24 . . at Eugene
25-26-27-28-29 Vancouver
31 . . . . at Boise

AUGUST

1-2. . . . . at Boise
3-4-5 . . . . Spokane
6-7-8-9-10 . . . . . at Everett
11-12-13-14-15. . .Eugene

16-17 . . . . Yakima
19-20 . . . . at Yakima
21 . . . . Yakima
22 . . . . at Yakima
23-24-25 . . . . . . Spokane
26-27-28 . . . . . at Spokane
29 . . . . Yakima
30 . . . . at Yakima
31 . . . . Yakima

SEPTEMBER

1-2. . . . . at Yakima
3 . . . . Yakima

VANCOUVER

JUNE

17-18-19-20-21. . . Tri-City
22-23-24-25-26 . . at Yakima
27-28-29 . . . . . . .Eugene
30 . . . . Everett

JULY

1-2. . . . . Everett
3-4-5-6-7 . . . . at Boise
9-10-11-12-13 . .Spokane
14-15-16 . . at Salem-Keizer
17-18-19 . . . . . . at Eugene
20-21-22-23-24. . . Yakima
25-26-27-28-29 . . at Tri-City

31 . . . . Salem-Keizer

AUGUST

1-2. . . . . . . Salem-Keizer
3-4-5 . . . . at Everett
6-7-8-9-10 . . . . at Spokane
12-13-14 . . . Salem-Keizer
15-16-17-18-19. . . . Boise
20-21-22 . . . . . . at Eugene
23-24-25 . . . . Everett
26-27-28 . . . . . . at Everett
29-30-31 . . . . . . .Eugene

SEPTEMBER

1-2-3 . . . . at Salem-Keizer

YAKIMA

JUNE

17-18-19-20-21 . . . . at Salem-Keizer
22-23-24-25-26 Vancouver
27-28-29 . . . . at Boise
30 . . . . Spokane

JULY

1-2. . . . . Spokane
3-4-5-6-7. . . . . . at Everett
9-10-11-12-13Salem-Keizer
14-15-16 . . . . . at Spokane
17-18-19. . . . . . Spokane
20-21-22-23-24at Vancouver
25-26-27-28-29. . .Eugene
31 . . . . at Spokane

AUGUST

1-2. . . . . at Spokane
3-4-5 . . . . Boise
6-7-8-9-10 . . . . . at Eugene
11-12-13-14-15. . . Everett
16-17 . . . . at Tri-City
19-20 . . . . Tri-City
21 . . . . at Tri-City
22 . . . . Tri-City
23-24-25 . . . . Boise
26-27-28 . . . . at Boise
29 . . . . at Tri-City
30 . . . . Tri-City
31 . . . . at Tri-City

SEPTEMBER

1-2. . . . . Tri-City
3 . . . . at Tri-City

ROOKIE

APPALACHIAN LEAGUE

BLUEFIELD

JUNE

17-18-19 . . .at Elizabethton
20-21-22 . . . . . Princeton
23-24-25 . . . Elizabethton
26-27-28 . . . . at Bristol
29-30 . . . . Kingsport

JULY

1 . . . . Kingsport
2 . . . . .at Princeton
3 . . . . Princeton
4-5-6 . . . . . . Greeneville
8-9-10. . . . . .at Danville
11-12-13 . . . . .at Princeton
14-15-16 . . . . Pulaski
17-18-19 . . . .at Greeneville

20-21-22 . . . . Burlington
23-24-25 . . . . . . Danville
26-27-28 . . . . at Burlington
30-31 . . . . at Kingsport

AUGUST

1 . . . . at Kingsport
2-3-4 . . . . .at Princeton
5-6-7 . . . . Danville
8-9-10. . . . . Pulaski
11-12-13 . . . . at Pulaski
14-15-16 . . . . at Burlington
18-19-20 . . . Johnson City
21-22-23. . . . . Bristol
24-25-26 . . at Johnson City

BRISTOL

JUNE

17-18-19 . . . Johnson City
20-21-22 . . . . at Burlington
23-24-25 . . . . . Kingsport
26-27-28 . . . . . .Bluefield
29 . . . . Pulaski
30 . . . . at Pulaski

JULY

1-2-3 . . . . at Pulaski
4-5-6 . . . . . Elizabethton
8-9-10. . . . . . . .at Princeton
11-12-13 . . . .at Greeneville
14-15-16 . . . . Danville
17-18-19 . . . Johnson City
20-21-22 . . . . . at Kingsport

23-24-25 . . at Johnson City
26 . . . . Greeneville
27-28 . . . . . .at Greeneville
30-31 . . . . Burlington

AUGUST

1 . . . . Burlington
2 . . . . .at Greeneville
3-4. . . . . Greeneville
5-6-7 . . . . .at Elizabethton
8-9-10. . . . . . . at Kingsport
11-12-13 . . . Elizabethton
14-15-16 . . . . . . Princeton
18-19-20 . . . . . . at Danville
21-22-23 . . . . . . at Bluefield
24-25-26 . . . . Pulaski

BURLINGTON

JUNE
17 . . . . Danville
18-19 . . . . .at Danville
20-21-22 . . . . Bristol
23-24-25 . . . . Pulaski
26-27-28 . . . . .at Princeton
29-30 . . . . . Elizabethton

JULY
1 . . . . Elizabethton
2-3. . . . . .at Danville
4-5-6 . . . . . Johnson City
8-9-10. . . . . .at Greeneville
11-12-13 . . . . . .at Danville
14-15-16 . . . . . Princeton
17-18-19 . . . . . Kingsport
20-21-22 . . . . . at Bluefield
23-24-25 . . . . . . at Pulaski
26-27-28 . . . . . .Bluefield
30-31 . . . . at Bristol

AUGUST
1 . . . . at Bristol
2-3-4 . . . . at Johnson City
5-6-7 . . . . . . Greeneville
8-9-10. . . . .at Elizabethton
11-12-13 . . . . . Princeton
14-15-16 . . . . . .Bluefield
18-19-20 . . . . at Kingsport
21-22-23 . . . . . . at Pulaski
24-25-26 . . . . . . Danville

DANVILLE

JUNE
17 . . . . at Burlington
18-19 . . . . . . Burlington
20-21-22 . . . .at Greeneville
23-24-25 . . . . .at Princeton
26-27-28 . . . . Greeneville
29-30 . . . . at Johnson City

JULY
1 . . . . at Johnson City
2-3. . . . . Burlington
4-5-6 . . . . . . at Kingsport
8-9-10. . . . . . . .Bluefield
11-12-13 . . . . Burlington
14-15-16 . . . . at Bristol
17-18-19 . . . . .at Princeton
20-21-22 . . . . Pulaski
23-24-25 . . . . . at Bluefield
26-27-28 . . . Johnson City
30-31 . . . . Pulaski

AUGUST
1 . . . . Pulaski
2-3-4 . . . . at Pulaski
5-6-7 . . . . at Bluefield
8-9-10. . . . . . . Princeton
11-12-13 . . . . . Kingsport
14-15-16 . . .at Elizabethton
18-19-20 . . . . Bristol
21-22-23 . . . Elizabethton
24-25-26 . . . . at Burlington

ELIZABETHTON

JUNE
17-18-19 . . . . . .Bluefield
20-21-22 . . . . . . at Pulaski
23-24-25 . . . . . at Bluefield
26-27-28 . . . Johnson City
29-30 . . . . . . at Burlington

JULY
1 . . . . at Burlington
2 . . . . Greeneville
3 . . . . .at Greeneville
4-5-6 . . . . at Bristol
8-9-10. . . . . . . Kingsport
11-12-13 . . at Johnson City
14-15-16 . . . . Greeneville
17-18-19 . . . . Pulaski
20-21-22 . . at Johnson City
23-24-25 . . . . Greeneville
26-27-28 . . . . . Kingsport
30-31 . . . . . .at Greeneville

AUGUST
1 . . . . .at Greeneville
2-3-4 . . . . . . at Kingsport
5-6-7 . . . . Bristol
8-9-10. . . . . . Burlington
11-12-13 . . . . at Bristol
14-15-16 . . . . . . Danville
18-19-20 . . . . .at Princeton
21-22-23 . . . . . .at Danville
24-25-26 . . . . . Princeton

GREENEVILLE

JUNE
17-18-19 . . . . at Kingsport
20-21-22 . . . . . . Danville
23-24-25 . . . Johnson City
26-27-28 . . . . . .at Danville
29-30 . . . . Princeton

JULY
1 . . . . Princeton
2 . . . . .at Elizabethton
3 . . . . Elizabethton
4-5-6 . . . . at Bluefield
8-9-10. . . . . . Burlington
11-12-13 . . . . Bristol
14-15-16 . . .at Elizabethton
17-18-19 . . . . . .Bluefield
20-21-22 . . . . .at Princeton
23-24-25 . . .at Elizabethton
26 . . . . at Bristol
27-28 . . . . Bristol
30-31 . . . . . Elizabethton

AUGUST
1 . . . . Elizabethton
2 . . . . Bristol
3-4. . . . . at Bristol
5-6-7 . . . . . . at Burlington
8-9-10. . . . at Johnson City
11-12-13 . . . Johnson City
14-15-16 . . . . Pulaski
18-19-20 . . . . . . at Pulaski
21-22-23 . . . . at Kingsport
24-25-26 . . . . . Kingsport

JOHNSON CITY

JUNE
17-18-19 . . . . at Bristol
20-21-22 . . . . . Kingsport
23-24-25 . . . .at Greeneville
26-27-28 . . .at Elizabethton
29-30 . . . . Danville

JULY
1 . . . . Danville
2 . . . . at Kingsport
3 . . . . Kingsport
4-5-6 . . . . . . at Burlington
8-9-10. . . . . Pulaski
11-12-13 . . . Elizabethton
14-15-16 . . . . at Kingsport
17-18-19 . . . . at Bristol
20-21-22 . . . Elizabethton
23-24-25 . . . . Bristol
26-27-28 . . . . . .at Danville
30-31 . . . . Princeton

AUGUST
1 . . . . Princeton
2-3-4 . . . . . . Burlington
5-6-7 . . . . at Pulaski
8-9-10. . . . . . Greeneville
11-12-13 . . . .at Greeneville
14-15-16 . . . . . Kingsport
18-19-20 . . . . . at Bluefield
21-22-23 . . . . .at Princeton
24-25-26 . . . . . .Bluefield

KINGSPORT

JUNE
17-18-19 . . . . Greeneville
20-21-22 . . at Johnson City
23-24-25 . . . . at Bristol
26-27-28 . . . . Pulaski
29-30 . . . . at Bluefield

JULY
1 . . . . at Bluefield
2 . . . . Johnson City
3 . . . . at Johnson City
4-5-6 . . . . Danville
8-9-10. . . . .at Elizabethton
11-12-13 . . . . at Pulaski
14-15-16 . . . Johnson City
17-18-19 . . . . at Burlington
20-21-22 . . . . Bristol
23-24-25 . . . . . Princeton
26-27-28 . . .at Elizabethton
30-31 . . . . .Bluefield

AUGUST
1 . . . . .Bluefield
2-3-4 . . . . . Elizabethton
5-6-7 . . . . .at Princeton
8-9-10. . . . . Bristol
11-12-13 . . . . . .at Danville
14-15-16 . . at Johnson City
18-19-20 . . . . Burlington
21-22-23 . . . . Greeneville
24-25-26 . . . .at Greeneville

PRINCETON

JUNE
17-18-19 . . . . Pulaski
20-21-22 . . . . . . at Bluefield
23-24-25 . . . . . . Danville
26-27-28 . . . . Burlington
29-30 . . . . . .at Greeneville

JULY
1 . . . . .at Greeneville
2 . . . . .Bluefield
3 . . . . at Bluefield
4-5-6 . . . . at Pulaski
8-9-10. . . . . Bristol
11-12-13 . . . . . . .Bluefield
14-15-16 . . . . at Burlington
17-18-19 . . . . . . Danville
20-21-22 . . . . Greeneville
23-24-25 . . . . at Kingsport
26-27-28 . . . . at Pulaski
30-31 . . . . at Johnson City

AUGUST
1 . . . . at Johnson City
2-3-4 . . . . .Bluefield
5-6-7 . . . . Kingsport
8-9-10. . . . . .at Danville
11-12-13 . . . . at Burlington
14-15-16 . . . . .at Bristol
18-19-20 . . . Elizabethton
21-22-23 . . . Johnson City
24-25-26 . . .at Elizabethton

PULASKI

JUNE
17-18-19 . . . . .at Princeton
20-21-22 . . . Elizabethton
23-24-25 . . . . at Burlington
26-27-28 . . . . at Kingsport
29 . . . . at Bristol
30 . . . . Bristol

JULY
1-2-3 . . . . Bristol
4-5-6 . . . . Princeton
8-9-10. . . . at Johnson City
11-12-13 . . . . . Kingsport
14-15-16 . . . . . at Bluefield
17-18-19 . . .at Elizabethton
20-21-22 . . . . . . .at Danville
23-24-25 . . . . Burlington
26-27-28 . . . . . Princeton
30-31 . . . . .at Danville

AUGUST
1 . . . . .at Danville
2-3-4 . . . . Danville
5-6-7 . . . . . Johnson City
8-9-10. . . . . . . at Bluefield
11-12-13 . . . . . . .Bluefield
14-15-16 . . . .at Greeneville
18-19-20 . . . . Greeneville
21-22-23 . . . . Burlington
24-25-26 . . . . .at Bristol

PIONEER LEAGUE

BILLINGS

JUNE
17-18-19 . . . at Missoula
20-21-22 . . . at Great Falls
23-24-25 . . . at Missoula
26-27 . . . at Helena
28-29-30 . . . at Great Falls

JULY
1-2-3 . . . Great Falls
4-5-6 . . . Helena
8-9-10-11 . . . at Ogden
12-13-14 . . . at Orem
16-17-18 . . . Ogden
19-20-21-22 . . . Orem
24-25 . . . at Helena
26-27-28 . . . Great Falls
29-30-31 . . . Missoula

AUGUST
1 . . . Missoula
2-3-4-5 . . . at Helena
7-8-9-10 . . . Idaho Falls
11-12-13 . . . Casper
14-15-16-17 . . . at Casper
18-19-20 . . . at Idaho Falls
22-23 . . . Helena
24-25-26-27 . . . Missoula
28-29 . . . at Great Falls
30-31 . . . at Missoula

SEPTEMBER
1-2 . . . Great Falls
3-4-5 . . . Helena

CASPER

JUNE
17-18-19 . . . at Idaho Falls
20-21-22 . . . Idaho Falls
23-24-25 . . . Orem
26-27 . . . at Idaho Falls
28-29-30 . . . at Orem

JULY
1-2-3 . . . at Ogden
4-5-6 . . . Ogden
8-9-10-11 . . . at Missoula
12-13-14 . . . at Helena
16-17-18 . . . Missoula
19-20-21-22 . . . Helena
24-25 . . . at Orem
26-27 . . . at Ogden
28-29-30 . . . at Idaho Falls
31 . . . Ogden

AUGUST
1-2 . . . Ogden
3-4-5 . . . Orem
7-8-9-10 . . . at Great Falls
11-12-13 . . . at Billings
14-15-16-17 . . . Billings
18-19-20 . . . Great Falls
22-23-24 . . . at Orem
25-26 . . . Orem
27-28 . . . Ogden
29-30-31 . . . at Ogden

SEPTEMBER
1-2-3-4-5 . . . Idaho Falls

GREAT FALLS

JUNE
17-18-19 . . . at Helena
20-21-22 . . . Billings
23-24-25 . . . Helena
26-27 . . . at Missoula
28-29-30 . . . Billings

JULY
1-2-3 . . . at Billings
4-5-6 . . . Missoula
8-9-10-11 . . . at Orem
12-13-14 . . . at Ogden
16-17-18 . . . Orem
19-20-21-22 . . . Ogden
24-25 . . . at Missoula
26-27-28 . . . at Billings
29-30-31 . . . Helena

AUGUST
1 . . . at Helena
2-3-4-5 . . . at Missoula
7-8-9-10 . . . Casper
11-12-13 . . . Idaho Falls
14-15-16-17 . . . at Idaho Falls
18-19-20 . . . at Casper
22-23 . . . Missoula
24-25 . . . Helena
26-27 . . . at Helena
28-29 . . . Billings
30-31 . . . at Helena

SEPTEMBER
1-2 . . . at Billings
3-4-5 . . . Missoula

HELENA

JUNE
17-18-19 . . . Great Falls
20-21-22 . . . Missoula
23-24-25 . . . at Great Falls
26-27 . . . Billings
28-29-30 . . . Missoula

JULY
1-2-3 . . . at Missoula
4-5-6 . . . at Billings
8-9-10-11 . . . Idaho Falls
12-13-14 . . . Casper
16-17-18 . . . at Idaho Falls
19-20-21-22 . . . at Casper
24-25 . . . Billings
26-27-28 . . . at Missoula
29-30-31 . . . at Great Falls

AUGUST
1 . . . Great Falls
2-3-4-5 . . . Billings
7-8-9 . . . at Orem
10-11-12-13 . . . at Ogden
14-15-16-17 . . . Orem
18-19-20 . . . Ogden
22-23 . . . at Billings
24-25 . . . at Great Falls
26-27 . . . Great Falls
28-29 . . . at Missoula
30-31 . . . Great Falls

SEPTEMBER
1-2 . . . Missoula
3-4-5 . . . at Billings

IDAHO FALLS

JUNE
17-18-19 . . . Casper
20-21-22 . . . at Casper
23-24-25 . . . at Ogden
26-27 . . . Casper
28-29-30 . . . Ogden

JULY
1-2-3 . . . at Orem
4-5-6 . . . Orem
8-9-10-11 . . . at Helena
12-13-14 . . . at Missoula
16-17-18 . . . Helena
19-20-21-22 . . . Missoula
24-25 . . . at Ogden
26-27 . . . at Orem
28-29-30 . . . Casper
31 . . . at Orem

AUGUST
1-2 . . . at Orem
3-4-5 . . . Ogden
7-8-9-10 . . . at Billings
11-12-13 . . . at Great Falls
14-15-16-17 . . . Great Falls
18-19-20 . . . Billings
22-23-24 . . . at Ogden
25-26 . . . Ogden
27-28-29-30-31 . . . Orem

SEPTEMBER
1-2-3-4-5 . . . at Casper

MISSOULA

JUNE
17-18-19 . . . Billings
20-21-22 . . . at Helena
23-24-25 . . . Billings
26-27 . . . Great Falls
28-29-30 . . . at Helena

JULY
1-2-3 . . . Helena
4-5-6 . . . at Great Falls
8-9-10-11 . . . Casper
12-13-14 . . . Idaho Falls
16-17-18 . . . at Casper
19-20-21-22 . . at Idaho Falls
24-25 . . . Great Falls
26-27-28 . . . Helena
29-30-31 . . . at Billings

AUGUST
1 . . . at Billings
2-3-4-5 . . . Great Falls
7-8-9 . . . at Ogden
10-11-12-13 . . . at Orem
14-15-16-17 . . . Ogden
18-19-20 . . . Orem
22-23 . . . at Great Falls
24-25-26-27 . . . at Billings
28-29 . . . Helena
30-31 . . . Billings

SEPTEMBER
1-2 . . . at Helena
3-4-5 . . . at Great Falls

OGDEN

JUNE
17-18 . . . at Orem
19-20 . . . Orem
21-22 . . . at Orem
23-24-25 . . . Idaho Falls
26-27 . . . Orem
28-29-30 . . . at Idaho Falls

JULY
1-2-3 . . . Casper
4-5-6 . . . at Casper
8-9-10-11 . . . Billings
12-13-14 . . . Great Falls
16-17-18 . . . at Billings
19-20-21-22 . . at Great Falls
24-25 . . . Idaho Falls
26-27 . . . Casper
28-29-30 . . . Orem
31 . . . at Casper

AUGUST
1-2 . . . at Casper
3-4-5 . . . at Idaho Falls
7-8-9 . . . Missoula
10-11-12-13 . . . Helena
14-15-16-17 . . . at Missoula
18-19-20 . . . at Helena
22-23-24 . . . Idaho Falls
25-26 . . . at Idaho Falls
27-28 . . . at Casper
29-30-31 . . . Casper

SEPTEMBER
1 . . . Orem
2-3-4-5 . . . at Orem

OREM

JUNE
17-18 . . . Ogden
19-20 . . . at Ogden
21-22 . . . Ogden
23-24-25 . . . at Casper
26-27 . . . at Ogden
28-29-30 . . . Casper

JULY
1-2-3 . . . Idaho Falls
4-5-6 . . . at Idaho Falls
8-9-10-11 . . . Great Falls
12-13-14 . . . Billings
16-17-18 . . . at Great Falls
19-20-21-22 . . . at Billings
24-25 . . . Casper
26-27 . . . Idaho Falls
28-29-30 . . . at Ogden
31 . . . Idaho Falls

AUGUST
1-2. . . . . Idaho Falls
3-4-5 . . . . at Casper
7-8-9 . . . . Helena
10-11-12-13. . . . Missoula
14-15-16-17 . . . . at Helena
18-19-20 . . . . . at Missoula
22-23-24 . . . . Casper
25-26 . . . . at Casper
27-28-29-30-31 at Idaho Falls

SEPTEMBER
1 . . . . at Ogden
2-3-4-5 . . . . Ogden

ARIZONA LEAGUE

HOME GAMES ONLY

ANGELS

JUNE
23 . . . . Mariners
26 . . . . Rangers
28 . . . . Cubs

JULY
1-21 . . . . Athletics
2-22 . . . . Padres
5-25 . . . . Giants
8-28 . . . . Brewers
10-30 . . . . Royals
13 . . . . Mariners
16 . . . . Rangers
18 . . . . Cubs

AUGUST
2-22 . . . . Mariners
5-25 . . . . Rangers
7 . . . . Cubs
10 . . . . Athletics
11-30 . . . . Padres
14 . . . . Giants
17-29 . . . . Brewers
19 . . . . Royals

ATHLETICS

JUNE
22 . . . . Giants
24 . . . . Royals
25 . . . . Padres
27 . . . . Angels
29 . . . . Mariners

JULY
2-22 . . . . Rangers
6-26 . . . . Padres
9-29 . . . . Cubs
11-31 . . . . Brewers
12 . . . . Giants
14 . . . . Royals
17 . . . . Angels
19 . . . . Mariners

AUGUST
1-21 . . . . Giants
3-23 . . . . Royals
6-26 . . . . Angels
8 . . . . Mariners
11 . . . . Rangers
15 . . . . Padres
18-30 . . . . Cubs
20 . . . . Brewers

BREWERS

JUNE
23 . . . . Athletics
26 . . . . Cubs
28 . . . . Mariners

JULY
1-21 . . . . Rangers
3-23 . . . . Angels
5-25 . . . . Royals
9-29 . . . . Giants
10-30 . . . . Padres
13 . . . . Athletics
16 . . . . Cubs
18 . . . . Mariners

AUGUST
2-22 . . . . Athletics
5-25 . . . . Cubs
7 . . . . Mariners
10-30 . . . . Rangers
12 . . . . Angels
14 . . . . Royals
18-27 . . . . Giants
19 . . . . Padres

CUBS

JUNE
22 . . . . Angels
24 . . . . Giants
27 . . . . Padres
29 . . . . Royals

JULY
2-22 . . . . Mariners
4-24 . . . . Athletics
6-26 . . . . Brewers
11-31 . . . . Rangers
12 . . . . Angels
14 . . . . Giants
17 . . . . Padres
19 . . . . Royals

AUGUST
1-21 . . . . Angels
3-23 . . . . Giants
6-28 . . . . Padres
8 . . . . Royals
11-26 . . . . Mariners
13 . . . . Athletics
15 . . . . Brewers
20 . . . . Rangers

GIANTS

JUNE
23 . . . . Rangers
25 . . . . Angels
28 . . . . Athletics
30 . . . . Padres

JULY
3-23 . . . . Mariners
4-24 . . . . Brewers
7-27 . . . . Cubs
8-28 . . . . Royals
13 . . . . Rangers
15 . . . . Angels
18 . . . . Athletics
20 . . . . Padres

AUGUST
2-22 . . . . Rangers
4-24 . . . . Angels
7 . . . . Athletics
9 . . . . Padres
12-28 . . . . Mariners
13 . . . . Brewers
16 . . . . Cubs
17-26 . . . . Royals

MARINERS

JUNE
22 . . . . Padres
25 . . . . Brewers
27 . . . . Royals
30 . . . . Angels

JULY
4-24 . . . . Rangers
7-27 . . . . Athletics
8-28 . . . . Cubs
10-30 . . . . Giants
12 . . . . Padres
15 . . . . Brewers
17 . . . . Royals
20 . . . . Angels

AUGUST
1-21 . . . . Padres
4-24 . . . . Brewers
6-29 . . . . Royals
9 . . . . Angels
13 . . . . Rangers
16-27 . . . . Athletics
17 . . . . Cubs
19 . . . . Giants

PADRES

JUNE
24 . . . . Brewers
26 . . . . Athletics
29 . . . . Giants

JULY
1-21 . . . . Cubs
4-24 . . . . Royals
5-25 . . . . Mariners
7-27 . . . . Rangers
11-31 . . . . Angels
14 . . . . Brewers
16 . . . . Athletics
19 . . . . Giants

AUGUST
3-23 . . . . Brewers
5-25 . . . . Athletics
8-29 . . . . Giants
10 . . . . Cubs
13 . . . . Royals
14 . . . . Mariners
16-26 . . . . Rangers
20 . . . . Angels

RANGERS

JUNE
22 . . . . Royals
24 . . . . Mariners
27 . . . . Giants
29 . . . . Brewers

JULY
3-23 . . . . Cubs
6-26 . . . . Angels
8-28 . . . . Athletics
9-29 . . . . Padres
12 . . . . Royals
14 . . . . Mariners
17 . . . . Giants
19 . . . . Brewers

AUGUST
1-21 . . . . Royals
3-23 . . . . Mariners
6 . . . . Giants
8 . . . . Brewers
12-27 . . . . Cubs
15 . . . . Angels
17-28 . . . . Athletics
18 . . . . Padres

ROYALS

JUNE
23 . . . . Cubs
25 . . . . Padres
28 . . . . Rangers
30 . . . . Brewers

JULY
2-22 . . . . Giants
3-23 . . . . Athletics
7-27 . . . . Angels
9-29 . . . . Mariners
13 . . . . Cubs
15 . . . . Padres
18 . . . . Rangers
20 . . . . Brewers

AUGUST
2-22 . . . . Cubs
4-24 . . . . Padres
7 . . . . Rangers
9-28 . . . . Brewers
11 . . . . Giants
12 . . . . Athletics
16-27 . . . . Angels
18 . . . . Mariner

GULF COAST LEAGUE

BLUE JAYS

JUNE
19 . . . . at Phillies
20 . . . . **Phillies**
21 . . . . at Braves
23 . . . . **Braves**
24 . . . . at Tigers
25 . . . . **Tigers**
26 . . . . at Yankees
27 . . . . **Yankees**
28 . . . . at Indians
30 . . . . **Indians**

JULY
1-14-24 . . . . **Phillies**
2-12-25 . . . . at Phillies
3-16-26 . . . . **Braves**
4-15-28 . . . . at Braves
5-18-29 . . . . **Tigers**
7-17-30 . . . . at Tigers
8-21-31 . . . . **Yankees**
9-19 . . . . at Yankees
10-22 . . . . **Indians**
11-23 . . . . at Indians

AUGUST
1-12-25 . . . . at Yankees
2-14-27 . . . . at Indians
4-15-26 . . . . **Indians**
5-18 . . . . at Phillies
6-16 . . . . **Phillies**
7-20 . . . . at Braves
8-19 . . . . **Braves**
9-22 . . . . at Tigers
11-21 . . . . **Tigers**
13-23 . . . . **Yankees**

BRAVES

JUNE
19 . . . . **Tigers**
20 . . . . at Tigers
21 . . . . **Blue Jays**
23 . . . . at Blue Jays
24 . . . . **Indians**
25 . . . . at Indians
26 . . . . **Phillies**
27 . . . . at Phillies
28 . . . . **Yankees**
30 . . . . **Braves**

JULY
1-14-24 . . . . at Tigers
2-12-25 . . . . **Tigers**
3-16-26 . . . . . . at Blue Jays
4-15-28 . . . . **Blue Jays**
5-18-29 . . . . at Indians
7-17-30 . . . . **Indians**
8-21-31 . . . . at Phillies
9-19 . . . . **Phillies**
10-23 . . . . at Yankees
11-22 . . . . **Yankees**

AUGUST
1-12-25 . . . . **Phillies**
2-15-26 . . . . at Yankees
4-14-27 . . . . **Yankees**
5-18 . . . . **Tigers**
6-16 . . . . at Tigers
7-20 . . . . **Blue Jays**
8-19 . . . . at Blue Jays
9-22 . . . . **Indians**
11-21 . . . . at Indians
13-23 . . . . at Phillies

CARDINALS

JUNE
19-29 . . . . **Marlins**
20-30 . . . . at Nationals
21 . . . . **Mets**
23-28 . . . . at Dodgers
24 . . . . at Marlins
25 . . . . **Nationals**
26 . . . . at Mets

JULY
1-11-21-31 . . . . **Mets**
3-8-13-28 . . . . **Dodgers**
4-14-19-24 . . . . . at Marlins
5-15-25 . . . . **Nationals**
6-16-26 . . . . at Mets
9-29 . . . . **Marlins**
10-20-30 . . . . . at Nationals
18-23 . . . . at Dodgers

AUGUST
2-17-22 . . . . **Dodgers**
3-13-23 . . . . at Marlins
4-14-24 . . . . **Nationals**
5-15-20 . . . . at Mets
7-12-27 . . . . at Dodgers
8-18 . . . . **Marlins**
9-19 . . . . at Nationals
10-25 . . . . **Mets**

DODGERS

JUNE
19-29 . . . . at Mets
21 . . . . **Nationals**
22 . . . . **Marlins**
23-28 . . . . **Cardinals**
24 . . . . **Mets**
26 . . . . at Nationals
27 . . . . at Marlins

JULY
1-11-21-31 . . . . . **Nationals**
2-12-22 . . . . at Marlins
3-8-13-28 . . . . . at Cardinals
4-14-24 . . . . **Mets**
6-16-26 . . . . . . at Nationals
7-17-27 . . . . **Marlins**
9-19-29 . . . . at Mets
18-23 . . . . **Cardinals**

AUGUST
1-11-21 . . . . at Marlins
2-17-22 . . . . at Cardinals
3-13-23 . . . . **Mets**
5-15-25 . . . . at Nationals
6-16-26 . . . . **Marlins**
7-12-27 . . . . **Cardinals**
8-18 . . . . at Mets
10-20 . . . . **Nationals**

INDIANS

JUNE
19 . . . . at Yankees
20 . . . . **Yankees**
21 . . . . at Phillies
23 . . . . **Phillies**
24 . . . . at Braves
25 . . . . **Braves**
26 . . . . at Tigers
27 . . . . **Tigers**
28 . . . . **Blue Jays**
30 . . . . at Blue Jays

JULY
1-14-24 . . . . **Yankees**
2-12-25 . . . . at Yankees
3-16-26 . . . . **Phillies**
4-15-28 . . . . at Phillies
5-18-29 . . . . **Braves**
7-17-30 . . . . at Braves
8-21-31 . . . . **Tigers**
9-19 . . . . at Tigers
10-22 . . . . at Blue Jays
11-23 . . . . **Blue Jays**

AUGUST
1-12-25 . . . . at Tigers
2-14-27 . . . . **Blue Jays**
4-15-26 . . . . . . at Blue Jays
5-18 . . . . at Yankees
6-16 . . . . **Yankees**
7-20 . . . . at Phillies
8-19 . . . . **Phillies**
9-22 . . . . at Braves
11-21 . . . . **Braves**
13-23 . . . . **Tigers**

MARLINS

JUNE
19-29 . . . . at Cardinals
20 . . . . **Mets**
22 . . . . at Dodgers
23-28 . . . . **Nationals**
24 . . . . **Cardinals**
25 . . . . at Mets
27 . . . . **Dodgers**
30 . . . . at Nationals

JULY
2-22 . . . . **Dodgers**
3-8-13 . . . . at Nationals
4-14 . . . . **Cardinals**
5-15-25 . . . . at Mets
7-11-17-27 . . . . . at Dodgers
9-19-24-29 . . . . at Cardinals
10-20-30 . . . . **Mets**
12-18-23-28 . . . . **Nationals**

AUGUST
1-11-21 . . . . **Dodgers**
2-17-22 . . . . . . at Nationals
3-13-23 . . . . **Cardinals**
4-14-24 . . . . at Mets
6-16-26 . . . . at Dodgers
7-12-27 . . . . **Nationals**
8-18 . . . . at Cardinals
9-19 . . . . **Mets**

METS

JUNE
19-29 . . . . **Dodgers**
20-30 . . . . at Marlins
21 . . . . at Cardinals
22 . . . . **Nationals**
24 . . . . at Dodgers
25 . . . . **Marlins**
26 . . . . **Cardinals**
27 . . . . at Nationals

JULY
1-11-21-31 . . . . at Cardinals
2-12-22 . . . . **Nationals**
4-14-24 . . . . at Dodgers
5-15-25 . . . . **Marlins**
6-16-26 . . . . **Cardinals**
7-17-27 . . . . . . at Nationals
9-19-29 . . . . **Dodgers**
10-20-30 . . . . at Marlins

AUGUST
1-11-21 . . . . **Nationals**
3-13-23 . . . . at Dodgers
4-14-24 . . . . **Marlins**
5-15-20 . . . . **Cardinals**
6-16-26 . . . . . . at Nationals
8-18 . . . . **Dodgers**
9-19 . . . . at Marlins
10-25 . . . . at Cardinals

NATIONALS

JUNE
20-30 . . . . **Cardinals**
21 . . . . at Dodgers
22 . . . . at Mets
23-28 . . . . at Marlins
25 . . . . at Cardinals
26 . . . . **Dodgers**
27 . . . . **Mets**

JULY
1-11-21-31 . . . . . at Dodgers
2-12-22 . . . . at Mets
3-8-13-28 . . . . **Marlins**
5-15-25 . . . . at Cardinals
6-16-26 . . . . **Dodgers**
7-17-27 . . . . **Mets**
10-20-30 . . . . **Cardinals**
18-23 . . . . at Marlins

AUGUST
1-11-21 . . . . at Mets
2-17-22 . . . . **Marlins**
4-14-24 . . . . at Cardinals
5-15-25 . . . . **Dodgers**
6-16-26 . . . . **Mets**
7-12-27 . . . . at Marlins
9-19 . . . . **Cardinals**
10-20 . . . . at Dodgers

ORIOLES

JUNE
19-29 . . . . at Reds
20-30 . . . . **Twins**
22 . . . . **Pirates**
23 . . . . at Red Sox
24 . . . . **Reds**
25 . . . . at Twins
27 . . . . at Pirates
28 . . . . **Red Sox**

JULY
2-12-22 . . . . **Pirates**
3-13-23 . . . . . . at Red Sox
4-14-19-24 . . . . **Reds**
5-15-25 . . . . at Twins
7-17-27 . . . . at Pirates
8-18-28 . . . . **Red Sox**
9-29 . . . . at Reds
10-20-30 . . . . **Twins**

AUGUST
1-11-21 . . . . **Pirates**
2-12-22 . . . . . . at Red Sox
3-8-18 . . . . at Reds
4-19 . . . . **Twins**
6-16-26 . . . . at Pirates
7-17-27 . . . . **Red Sox**
9-14-24 . . . . at Twins
13-23 . . . . **Reds**

PHILLIES

JUNE
19 . . . . **Blue Jays**
20 . . . . at Blue Jays
21 . . . . **Indians**
23 . . . . at Indians
24 . . . . **Yankees**
25 . . . . at Yankees
26 . . . . at Braves
27 . . . . **Braves**
28 . . . . **Tigers**
30 . . . . at Tigers

JULY
1-14-24 . . . . . . at Blue Jays
2-12-25 . . . . **Blue Jays**
3-16-26 . . . . at Indians
4-15-28 . . . . **Indians**
5-18-29 . . . . at Yankees
7-17-30 . . . . **Yankees**
8-21-31 . . . . **Braves**
9-19 . . . . at Braves
10-23 . . . . at Tigers
11-22 . . . . **Tigers**

AUGUST
1-12-25 . . . . at Braves
2-15-26 . . . . at Tigers
4-14-27 . . . . **Tigers**
5-18 . . . . **Blue Jays**
6-16 . . . . at Blue Jays
7-20 . . . . **Indians**
8-19 . . . . at Indians
9-22 . . . . **Yankees**
11-21 . . . . at Yankees
13-23 . . . . **Braves**

PIRATES

JUNE
19-29 . . . . at Twins
21 . . . . **Red Sox**
22 . . . . at Orioles
23 . . . . **Reds**
24 . . . . **Twins**
26 . . . . at Red Sox
27 . . . . **Orioles**
28 . . . . at Reds

JULY
1-11-21-26-31 . . . . **Red Sox**
2-12-22 . . . . at Orioles
3-13-23 . . . . **Reds**
4-14-24 . . . . **Twins**
6-16 . . . . at Red Sox
7-17-27 . . . . **Orioles**
8-18-28 . . . . at Reds
9-19-29 . . . . at Twins

AUGUST
1-11-21 . . . . at Orioles
2-12-22 . . . . **Reds**
3-13-23 . . . . **Twins**
5-10-15-25 . . . . . at Red Sox
6-16-26 . . . . **Orioles**
7-17-27 . . . . at Reds
8-18 . . . . at Twins
20 . . . . **Red Sox**

RED SOX

JUNE
20-30 . . . . **Reds**
21 . . . . at Pirates
22 . . . . at Twins
23 . . . . **Orioles**
25 . . . . at Reds
26 . . . . **Pirates**
27 . . . . **Twins**
28 . . . . at Orioles

JULY
1-11-21-26-31 . . . at Pirates
2-12-22 . . . . at Twins
3-13-23 . . . . **Orioles**
5-15-30 . . . . at Reds
6-16 . . . . **Pirates**
7-17-27 . . . . **Twins**
8-18-28 . . . . at Orioles
10-20-25 . . . . **Reds**

AUGUST
1-11-21 . . . . at Twins
2-12-22 . . . . **Orioles**
4-14-24 . . . . at Reds
5-10-15-25 . . . . **Pirates**
6-16-26 . . . . **Twins**
7-17-27 . . . . at Orioles
9-19 . . . . **Reds**
20 . . . . at Pirates

REDS

JUNE
19-29 . . . . **Orioles**
20-30 . . . . at Red Sox
21 . . . . **Twins**
23 . . . . at Pirates
24 . . . . at Orioles
25 . . . . **Red Sox**
26 . . . . at Twins
28 . . . . **Pirates**

JULY
1-11-16-31 . . . . **Twins**
3-13-23 . . . . at Pirates
4-14-19-24 . . . . . at Orioles
5-15-30 . . . . **Red Sox**
6-21-26 . . . . at Twins
8-18-28 . . . . **Pirates**
9-29 . . . . **Orioles**
10-20-25 . . . . . . at Red Sox

AUGUST
2-12-22 . . . . at Pirates
3-8-18 . . . . **Orioles**
4-14-24 . . . . **Red Sox**
5-15-25 . . . . at Twins
7-17-27 . . . . **Pirates**
9-19 . . . . at Red Sox
10-20 . . . . **Twins**
13-23 . . . . at Orioles

TIGERS

JUNE
19 . . . . at Braves
20 . . . . **Braves**
21 . . . . at Yankees
23 . . . . **Yankees**
24 . . . . **Blue Jays**
25 . . . . at Blue Jays
26 . . . . **Indians**
27 . . . . at Indians
28 . . . . at Phillies
30 . . . . **Phillies**

JULY
1-14-24 . . . . **Braves**
2-12-25 . . . . at Braves
3-16-26 . . . . **Yankees**
4-15-28 . . . . at Yankees
5-18-29 . . . . . . at Blue Jays
7-17-30 . . . . **Blue Jays**
8-21-31 . . . . at Indians
9-19 . . . . **Indians**
10-23 . . . . **Phillies**
11-22 . . . . at Phillies

AUGUST
1-12-25 . . . . **Indians**
2-15-26 . . . . **Phillies**
4-14-27 . . . . at Phillies
5-18 . . . . at Braves
6-16 . . . . **Braves**
7-20 . . . . at Yankees
8-19 . . . . **Yankees**
9-22 . . . . **Blue Jays**
11-21 . . . . at Blue Jays
13-23 . . . . at Indians

TWINS

JUNE
19-29 . . . . **Pirates**
20-30 . . . . at Orioles
21 . . . . at Reds
22 . . . . **Red Sox**
24 . . . . at Pirates
25 . . . . **Orioles**
26 . . . . **Reds**
27 . . . . at Red Sox

JULY
1-11-16-31 . . . . at Reds
2-12-22 . . . . **Red Sox**
4-14-24 . . . . at Pirates
5-15-25 . . . . **Orioles**
6-21-26 . . . . **Reds**
7-17-27 . . . . at Red Sox
9-19-29 . . . . **Pirates**
10-20-30 . . . . at Orioles

AUGUST
1-11-21 . . . . **Red Sox**
3-13-23 . . . . at Pirates
4-19 . . . . at Orioles
5-15-25 . . . . **Reds**
6-16-26 . . . . at Red Sox
8-18 . . . . **Pirates**
9-14-24 . . . . **Orioles**
10-20 . . . . at Reds

YANKEES

JUNE
19 . . . . **Indians**
20 . . . . at Indians
21 . . . . **Tigers**
23 . . . . at Tigers
24 . . . . at Phillies
25 . . . . **Phillies**
26 . . . . **Blue Jays**
27 . . . . at Blue Jays
28 . . . . at Braves
30 . . . . **Braves**

JULY
1-14-24 . . . . at Indians
2-12-25 . . . . **Indians**
3-16-26 . . . . at Tigers
4-15-28 . . . . **Tigers**
5-18-29 . . . . **Phillies**
7-17-30 . . . . at Phillies
8-21-31 . . . . at Blue Jays
9-19 . . . . **Blue Jays**
10-23 . . . . **Braves**
11-22 . . . . at Braves

AUGUST
1-12-25 . . . . **Blue Jays**
2-15-26 . . . . **Braves**
4-14-27 . . . . at Braves
5-18 . . . . **Indians**
6-16 . . . . at Indians
7-20 . . . . **Tigers**
8-19 . . . . at Tigers
9-22 . . . . at Phillies
11-21 . . . . **Phillies**
13-23 . . . . at Blue Jays

INDEPENDENT

AMERICAN ASSOCIATION

HOME GAMES ONLY

EL PASO

MAY
8-9-10-11. . . . . Shreveport
13-14-15 . . . . Wichita
27-28-29 . . . . St. Paul
30-31 . . . . Pensacola

JUNE
1 . . . . Pensacola
10-11-12 . . . . . Sioux Falls
13-14-15 . . . . . Shreveport
23-24-25 . . . . . . Pensacola
26-27-28 . . . . . Fort Worth

JULY
4-5-6 . . . . Shreveport
7-8-9-10 . . . . Grand Prairie
18-19-20 . . . . . Shreveport
27-28-29 . . . . Lincoln

AUGUST
7-8-9 . . . . . . Grand Prairie
10-11-12-13. . . . Pensacola
21-22-23 . . . . . Fort Worth

FORT WORTH

MAY
8-9-10-11. . . . . . Sioux Falls
12-13-14 . . . . Lincoln
26-27-28 . . . . . Shreveport
30-31 . . . . . . Grand Prairie

JUNE
1 . . . . Grand Prairie
6-7-8-9 . . . . El Paso
13-14-15 . . . . . . Pensacola
23-24-25 . . . . Grand Prairie

JULY
4-5-6 . . . . Wichita
7-8-9-10 . . . . . . Pensacola
15-16-17 . . . . Wichita
18-19-20 . . . . . . Pensacola
28-29-30 . . . . . Shreveport
31 . . . . Grand Prairie

AUGUST
1-2. . . . . Grand Prairie
14-15-16 . . . . El Paso
17-18-19 . . . . Grand Prairie

GRAND PRAIRIE

MAY
16-17-18 . . . . Wichita
19-20-21-22 . . . . . . El Paso
27-28-29 . . . . . . Pensacola

JUNE
3-4-5 . . . . El Paso
10-11-12. . . . . Fort Worth
13-14-15 . . . . . Sioux Falls
20-21-22 . . . . . Shreveport

JULY
1-2-3 . . . . El Paso
4-5-6 . . . . Pensacola
11-12-13 . . . . . Fort Worth
14-15-16 . . . . . Shreveport
23-24-25-26 . . . . . . El Paso

AUGUST
3-4-5 . . . . Pensacola
10-11-12-13. . . Shreveport
14-15-16 . . . . . . Sioux City

LINCOLN

MAY
16-17-18 . . . . . . Pensacola
20-21-22 . . . . . . Sioux Falls
23-24-25 . . . . Wichita

JUNE
3-4-5 . . . . St. Paul
6-7-8 . . . . Shreveport
17-18-19 . . . . El Paso
20-21-22 . . . . Sioux City
26-27-28-29 . . Grand Prairie

JULY
7-8-9-10 . . . . . . Sioux City
15-16-17 . . . . . . Sioux Falls
18-19-20 . . . . St. Paul
31 . . . . Sioux City

AUGUST
1-2. . . . . Sioux City
4-5-6 . . . . Wichita
10-11-12-13 . . . . . . St. Paul
14-15-16 . . . . . . Sioux Falls

PENSACOLA

MAY
8-9-10-11. . . . . Lincoln
19-20-21-22 . . . Shreveport
23-24-25 . . . . El Paso

JUNE
3-4-5 . . . . Fort Worth
6-7-8 . . . . . . Grand Prairie
16-17-18 . . . . Grand Prairie
19-20-21 . . . . . . Fort Worth

JULY
1-2-3 . . . . Wichita
11-12-13 . . . . St. Paul
14-15-16 . . . . El Paso
24-25-26-27 . . . . Fort Worth
28-29-30 . . . . Grand Prairie

AUGUST
6-7-8 . . . . Shreveport
17-18-19 . . . . . . Sioux City
21-22-23 . . . . Grand Prairie

ST. PAUL

MAY
8-9-10-11. . . . Grand Prairie
19-20-21-22 . . . . Sioux City
23-24-25 . . . . . . Fort Worth

JUNE
6-7-8 . . . . Wichita
9-10-11 . . . . Sioux City
20-21-22 . . . . . . Sioux Falls
23-24-25 . . . . Lincoln

JULY
1-2-3 . . . . Sioux Falls
4-5-6 . . . . Lincoln
15-16-17 . . . . . . Sioux City
23-24-25-26 . . . . . . Wichita

AUGUST
3-4-5 . . . . Sioux Falls
7-8-9 . . . . Lincoln
14-15-16 . . . . Wichita
18-19-20 . . . . Lincoln

SHREVEPORT

MAY
13-14-15 . . . . Grand Prairie
16-17-18 . . . . El Paso
23-24-25 . . . . Grand Prairie
30-31 . . . . St. Paul

JUNE
1 . . . . St. Paul
10-11-12 . . . . . . Pensacola
16-17-18 . . . . . Fort Worth
26-27-28-29 . . . . Pensacola

JULY
1-2-3 . . . . Fort Worth
7-8-9-10 . . . . St. Paul
11-12-13 . . . . El Paso
23-24-25-26 . . . . . . Lincoln
31 . . . . Pensacola

AUGUST
1-2. . . . . Pensacola
3-4-5 . . . . Fort Worth
14-15-16 . . . . . . Pensacola
17-18-19 . . . . El Paso

SIOUX CITY

MAY
10-11 . . . . Wichita
13-14-15 . . . . St. Paul
16-17-18 . . . . . Fort Worth
27-28-29 . . . . Lincoln

JUNE
3-4-5 . . . . Shreveport
6-7-8 . . . . Sioux Falls
13-14-15 . . . . Lincoln
16-17-18 . . . . St. Paul
27-28 . . . . Wichita

JULY
1-2-3 . . . . Lincoln
4 . . . . Sioux Falls
11-12 . . . . Sioux Falls
23-24-25-26 . . . . Sioux Falls

AUGUST
3-4-5 . . . . El Paso
7-8-9 . . . . Wichita
10-11-12-13 . . . . Fort Worth
21-22-23 . . . . St. Paul

SIOUX FALLS

MAY
13-14-15 . . . . . . Pensacola
16-17-18 . . . . St. Paul
23-24-25 . . . . . . Sioux City
30-31 . . . . Lincoln

JUNE
3-4-5 . . . . Wichita
17-18-19 . . . . Wichita
23-24-25 . . . . . . Sioux City
26-27-28-29 . . . . . . St. Paul

JULY
5-6. . . . . Sioux City
13 . . . . Sioux City
18-19-20 . . . . Grand Prairie
27-28-29 . . . . St. Paul
31 . . . . El Paso

AUGUST
1-2. . . . . El Paso
7-8-9 . . . . Lincoln
10-11-12-13. . . . . . Wichita
21-22-23 . . . . . Shreveport

WICHITA

MAY
7-8-9 . . . . Sioux City
19-20-21-22 . . . . Fort Worth
27-28-29 . . . . . . Sioux Falls
30-31 . . . . Sioux City

JUNE
1-2. . . . . Sioux City
10-11-12 . . . . Lincoln
13-14-15 . . . . St. Paul
20-21-22 . . . . El Paso
23-24-25 . . . . . Shreveport

JULY
7-8-9-10 . . . . . . Sioux Falls
11-12-13 . . . . Lincoln
18-19-20 . . . . . . Sioux City
27-28-29 . . . . . . Sioux City
30-31 . . . . St. Paul

AUGUST
17-18-19 . . . . . . Sioux Falls
21-22-23 . . . . Lincoln

ATLANTIC LEAGUE

HOME GAMES ONLY

BRIDGEPORT

MAY
2-3-4 . . . Somerset
5-6-7 . . . York
13-14-15 . . . So. Maryland
16-17-18 . . . Long Island
26-27-28-29 . . . Newark
30-31 . . . Camden

JUNE
1 . . . Camden
10-11-12 . . . Camden
13-14-15 . . . Somerset
23-24-25-26 . . . York
27-28-29 . . . Lancaster
30 . . . Southern Maryland

JULY
1-2 . . . Southern Maryland
8-9-10 . . . Lancaster
11-12-13 . . . Newark
24-25-26-27 . . . Camden

AUGUST
4-5-6-7 . Southern Maryland
8-9-10 . . . Long Island
18-19-20 . . . Newark
21-22-23-24 . . . Lancaster

SEPTEMBER
1-2-3 . . . York
4-5-6-7 . . . Somerset
18-19-20-21 . . . Long Island

CAMDEN

APRIL
25-26-27 . . . York
28-29-30 . . . Somerset

MAY
1 . . . Somerset
2-3-4 . . . Newark
8-9-10 . . . Bridgeport
13-14-15 . . . Long Island

JUNE
2-3-4 . . . Lancaster
5-6-7-8 . . . York
13-14-15 . . . So. Maryland
16-17-18 . . . Somerset
27-28-29 . . . Newark

JULY
8-9-10 . . . York
11-12-13 . . . Somerset
21-22-23 . . . Lancaster

AUGUST
1-2-3 . . Southern Maryland
4-5-6-7 . . . Long Island
15-16-17 . . . Bridgeport
26-27-28 . . . Bridgeport

SEPTEMBER
4-5-6-7 . . . Newark
8-9-10-11 . . . Lancaster
15-16-17 . . . Long Island
18-19-20-21 . . So. Maryland

LANCASTER

APRIL
25-26-27 . . . Bridgeport

MAY
5-6-7 . . . Camden
13-14-15 . . . Somerset
23-24-25 Southern Maryland
26-27-28-29 . . . Long Island

JUNE
5-6-7-8 . . . Bridgeport
13-14-15 . . . York
23-24-25-26 . . . Camden
30 . . . Somerset

JULY
1-2 . . . Somerset
3-4 . . . York
11-12-13 . . . Long Island
18-19-20 . . . So. Maryland
24-25-26-27 . . . Newark

AUGUST
1-2-3 . . . York
4-5-6-7 . . . Somerset
15-16-17 . . . Newark
18-19-20 . . . Camden
26-27-28 . . . Newark

SEPTEMBER
1-2-3 . . . Long Island
4-5-6-7 . Southern Maryland
12-13-14 . . . Bridgeport
20-21 . . . York

LONG ISLAND

APRIL
25-26-27 . . . Newark
29-30 . . . Lancaster

MAY
1 . . . Lancaster
8-9-10 . . Southern Maryland
19-20-21-22 . . . Camden
23-24-25 . . . Bridgeport

JUNE
2-3-4 . . . Somerset
5-6-7-8 . . . Newark
16-17-18 . . . Lancaster
19-20-21-22 . . . York
30 . . . Camden

JULY
1-2 . . . Camden
3-4-5-6 . . . Bridgeport
8-9-10 . . . Newark
18-19-20 . . . York
29-30-31 . . . Camden

AUGUST
1-2-3 . . . Bridgeport
11-12-13-14 . . . Lancaster
15-16-17 Southern Maryland
18-19-20 . . . Somerset
26-27-28 Southern Maryland

SEPTEMBER
8-9-10-11 . . . Somerset
12-13-14 . . . York

NEWARK

APRIL
29-30 . . . Bridgeport

MAY
1 . . . Bridgeport
8-9-10-11 . . . Lancaster
19-20-21-22 . . . York
23-24-25 . . . Somerset
30-31 . . . Lancaster

JUNE
1 . . . Lancaster
2-3-4 . . . Bridgeport
10-11-12 . . . Lancaster
13-14-15 . . . Long Island
19-20-21-22 . . . Camden
23-24-25-26 . . So. Maryland

JULY
18-19-20 . . . Camden
21-22-23 . . . So. Maryland
29-30-31 . . . York

AUGUST
8-9-10 . . . Somerset
11-12-13-14 . . . Bridgeport
21-22-23-24 . . . Long Island
29-30-31 . . . Long Island

SEPTEMBER
1-2-3 . . Southern Maryland
12-13-14 . . . Camden
15-16-17 . . . York
18-19-20-21 . . . Somerset

SOMERSET

APRIL
25-26-27 . . . So. Maryland

MAY
5-6-7 . . . Long Island
8-9-10-11 . . . York
16-17-18 . . . Newark
19-20-21-22 . . . Lancaster
27-28-29 . . . Camden

JUNE
5-6-7-8 . Southern Maryland
19-20-21-22 . . . Bridgeport
23-24-25-26 . . . Long Island

JULY
3-4-5-6 . . . Newark
18-19-20 . . . Bridgeport
21-22-23 . . . Long Island
29-30-31 . . . Lancaster

AUGUST
1-2-3 . . . Newark
11-12-13-14 . . . Camden
15-16-17 . . . York
26-27-28 . . . York
29-30-31 . . . Bridgeport

SEPTEMBER
1-2-3 . . . Camden
12-13-14 . . . So. Maryland
15-16-17 . . . Lancaster

SOUTHERN MARYLAND

MAY
2-3-4 . . . Lancaster
5-6-7 . . . Newark
16-17-18 . . . Camden
19-20-21-22 . . . Bridgeport
26-27-28-29 . . . York
30-31 . . . Long Island

JUNE
1 . . . Long Island
10-11-12 . . . Long Island
16-17-18 . . . Newark
19-20-21-22 . . . Lancaster
27-28-29 . . . Somerset

JULY
3-4-5-6 . . . Camden
8-9-10 . . . Somerset
11-12-13 . . . York
24-25-26-27 . . . Long Island
29-30-31 . . . Bridgeport

AUGUST
8-9-10 . . . Lancaster
18-19-20 . . . York
21-22-23-24 . . . Somerset
29-30-31 . . . Camden

SEPTEMBER
8-9-10-11 . . . Newark
15-16-17 . . . Bridgeport

YORK

APRIL
29-30 . . Southern Maryland

MAY
1 . . . Southern Maryland
2-3-4 . . . Long Island
13-14-15 . . . Newark
16-17-18 . . . Lancaster
23-24-25 . . . Camden
30-31 . . . Somerset

JUNE
1 . . . Somerset
2-3-4 . . Southern Maryland
10-11-12 . . . Somerset
16-17-18 . . . Bridgeport
27-28-29 . . . Long Island
30 . . . Newark

JULY
1-2 . . . Newark
5-6 . . . Lancaster
21-22-23 . . . Bridgeport
24-25-26-27 . . . Somerset

AUGUST
4-5-6-7 . . . Newark
8-9-10 . . . Camden

11-12-13-14 . . So. Maryland
21-22-23-24 . . . . . Camden

29-30-31 . . . . . . Lancaster

SEPTEMBER
4-5-6-7 . . . . . . Long Island

8-9-10-11. . . . . Bridgeport
18-19 . . . . Lancaster

CAN-AM LEAGUE

HOME GAMES ONLY

ATLANTIC CITY

MAY
26-27-28 . . . . .Ottawa
29-30-31 . . . . Quebec

JUNE
1 . . . . .Quebec
6-7-8 . . . . .Brockton
10-11-12 . . . . Sussex
20-21-22 . . . . . Worcester
23-24-25-26 . . . . . .Nashua

JULY
3-4-5-6 . . . . . . New Jersey
14-15-16 . . . . . New Jersey
25-26-27 . . . . Quebec
28-29-30-31 . . . . . .Ottawa

AUGUST
8-9-10. . . . . .Nashua
12-13-14 . . . . . . Worcester
19-20-21 . . . . . . .Brockton
29-30-31 . . . . Sussex

SEPTEMBER
1 . . . . Sussex

BROCKTON

MAY
24-25 . . . . .Nashua
26-27-28 . . . . Sussex

JUNE
10-11-12 . . . . .Ottawa
13-14-15 . . . . .Atlantic City
20-21-22 . . . . . New Jersey
23-24-25-26 . . . . . Quebec

JULY
4-5-6-7 . . . . Worcester
17-18-19-20 . . . . . . Sussex
22-23-24 . . . . .Nashua

AUGUST
1-2-3 . . . . . . .Atlantic City
4-5-6-7 . . . . Quebec
15-16-17 . . . . . . Worcester
25-26-27-28 . . . . . .Ottawa
29-30-31 . . . . . New Jersey

SEPTEMBER
1 . . . . New Jersey

NASHUA

MAY
22-23 . . . . .Brockton
27-28 . . . . Worcester
29-30-31 . . . . . . .Brockton

JUNE
1 . . . . .Brockton
9-10 . . . . New Jersey
12 . . . . New Jersey
13-14-15 . . . . Quebec
20-21-22 . . . . .Ottawa
30 . . . . .Atlantic City

JULY
1-2. . . . . .Atlantic City
7-8. . . . . Sussex
9 . . . . Worcester
17-18-19-20 . . . . . .Ottawa
27 . . . . Worcester
28-29-30-31 . . . . .Brockton

AUGUST
1-2. . . . . Worcester
12-13-14 . . . . . New Jersey
15-16-17 . . . . Sussex
22-23-24 . . . . Quebec
25-26-27-28 . . .Atlantic City

NEW JERSEY

MAY
29-30-31 . . . . .Ottawa

JUNE
1 . . . . .Ottawa
2-3-4 . . . . Quebec
13-14-15 . . . . Sussex
17-18-19 . . . . .Atlantic City
27-28-29 . . . . .Nashua
30 . . . . Worcester

JULY
1-2. . . . . Worcester
9-10-11-12. . . . . .Brockton
17-18-19-20 . . . . Worcester
22-23-24 . . . . Quebec

AUGUST
1-2-3 . . . . .Ottawa
4-5-6-7 . . . . .Nashua
15-16-17 . . . . .Atlantic City
22-23-24 . . . . . . .Brockton
25-26-27-28 . . . . . . Sussex

OTTAWA

MAY
22-23-24-25 . . . New Jersey

JUNE
3-4-5 . . . . .Nashua
6-7-8 . . . . Worcester
16-17-18 . . . . Quebec
23-24-25-26 . . . . . . Sussex
28-29-30 . . . . . . .Brockton

JULY
9-10-11-12. . . .Atlantic City
13-14-15 . . . . Quebec
21-22-23 . . . . .Atlantic City
25-26-27 . . . . . New Jersey

AUGUST
4-5-6-7 . . . . Sussex
8-9-10. . . . . .Brockton
19-20-21 . . . . .Nashua
29-30-31 . . . . . . Worcester

SEPTEMBER
1 . . . . Worcester

QUEBEC

MAY
22-23-24-25 . . .Atlantic City
26-27-28 . . . . . New Jersey

JUNE
6-7-8 . . . . .Nashua
9-10-11 . . . . Worcester
20-21-22 . . . . Sussex

JULY
1-2-3 . . . . .Brockton
4-5-6-7 . . . . .Ottawa
17-18-19-20 . . .Atlantic City
28-29-30-31 . . . New Jersey

AUGUST
1-2-3 . . . . Sussex
12-13-14 . . . . .Brockton
15-16-17 . . . . .Ottawa
26-27-28 . . . . . . Worcester
29-30-31 . . . . .Nashua

SEPTEMBER
1 . . . . .Nashua

SUSSEX

MAY
22-23-24-25 . . . . Worcester

JUNE
2-3-4 . . . . .Brockton
6-7-8 . . . . New Jersey
17-18-19 . . . . .Nashua
27-28-29 . . . . .Atlantic City

JULY
1-2-3 . . . . .Ottawa
4-5. . . . . .Nashua
9-10-11-12. . . . . . Quebec
14-15-16 . . . . .Nashua
25-26-27 . . . . . . .Brockton
28-29-30-31 . . . . Worcester

AUGUST
8-9-10. . . . . . . New Jersey
12-13-14 . . . . .Ottawa
19-20-21 . . . . Quebec
22-23-24 . . . . .Atlantic City

WORCESTER

MAY
29-30-31 . . . . Sussex

JUNE
1 . . . . Sussex
3-4-5 . . . . . . .Atlantic City
13-14-15 . . . . .Ottawa
17-18-19 . . . . . . .Brockton
23-24-25-26 . . . New Jersey
27-28-29 . . . . Quebec

JULY
3 . . . . .Nashua
10-11-12 . . . . .Nashua
14-15-16 . . . . .Brockton
21-22-23 . . . . Sussex
25-26 . . . . .Nashua

AUGUST
3 . . . . .Nashua
4-5-6-7 . . . . . .Atlantic City
8-9-10-11. . . . . . . Quebec
19-20-21 . . . . . New Jersey
22-23-24 . . . . .Ottawa

FRONTIER LEAGUE

HOME GAMES ONLY

CHILLICOTHE

MAY

21-22-23 . . . . Washington
27-28-29 . . . . Traverse City
30-31 . . . . Midwest

JUNE

1 . . . . Midwest
3-4-5 . . . . Gateway
6-7-8 . . . . Evansville
16-17-18 . . . . Midwest
19-20-21 . . . . Florence
25-26-27 . . . . . Kalamazoo
28-29-30 . . . . Washington

JULY

11-12-13 . . . . Rockford
21-22-23 . . . . Midwest
24-25-26 . . . . . Kalamazoo
30-31 . . . . River City

AUGUST

1 . . . . River City
8-9-10. . . . Southern Illinois
19-20-21 . . . . . Windy City
26-27-28 . . . . Midwest
29-30-31 . . . . Traverse City

SEPTEMBER

1-2-3 . . . . Florence

EVANSVILLE

MAY

21-22-23 . . . . . Windy City

JUNE

3-4-5 . . . . Florence
13-14-15 . . . . . . Chillicothe
19-20-21 . . . . Rockford
22-23-24 . . Southern Illinois

JULY

1-2-3 . . . . Southern Illinois
4-5-6 . . . . Rockford
8-9-10. . . . . Midwest
18-19-20 . . . . Gateway
27-28-29 . . . . . . River City
30-31 . . . . Kalamazoo

AUGUST

1 . . . . Kalamazoo
2-3-4 . . . . . . Traverse City
12-13-14 . . . . Gateway
19-20-21 . . . . Midwest
22-23-24 . . . . . Washington
29-30-31 . . . . . Windy City

SEPTEMBER

1-2-3 . . . . River City

FLORENCE

MAY

21-22-23 . . . . . Kalamazoo
24-25 . . . . Chillicothe
27-28-29 . . . . Midwest

JUNE

6-7-8 . . . . Gateway
9 . . . . Chillicothe
10-11-12 . . . . . . Evansville
16-17-18 . . . . . Washington
22-23-24 . . . . . Kalamazoo
25-26-27 . . . . Midwest
28-29-30 . . . . Traverse City

JULY

1-2-3 . . . . Chillicothe
8-9-10. . . . . Rockford
11-12-13 . . . . . Windy City
24-25-26 . . . . Midwest
30-31 . . . . Southern Illinois

AUGUST

1 . . . . Southern Illinois
2-3-4 . . . . River City
12-13-14 . . . . Midwest
15-16-17 . . . . Traverse City
29-30 . . . . Washington
31 . . . . River City

GATEWAY

MAY

17 . . . . River City
21-22-23 . . Southern Illinois
30-31 . . . . Evansville

JUNE

1 . . . . Evansville
10-11-12 . . . . . . Chillicothe
13-14-15 . . . . Florence
19-20-21 . . . . . Windy City
22-23-24 . . . . . . River City
25-26-27 . . . . . . Evansville

JULY

1-2-3 . . . . River City
11-12-13 . . . . Midwest
21-22-23 . . . . Rockford
27-28-29 . . . . . Windy City
30-31 . . . . . . Traverse City

AUGUST

1 . . . . Traverse City
2-3-4 . . . . Kalamazoo
19-20-21 . . . . . Washington
22-23-24 . . . . Midwest
29-30-31 . . . . Rockford

SEPTEMBER

1-2-3 . . . . Southern Illinois

KALAMAZOO

MAY

24-25-26 . . . . Midwest
27-28-29 . . . . . Washington

JUNE

3-4-5 . . . . Windy City
6-7-8 . . . . Rockford
16-17-18 . . . . Traverse City
19-20-21 . . . . Midwest
28-29-30 . . . . Midwest

JULY

1-2-3 . . . . . . Traverse City
4-5-6 . . . . Chillicothe
18-19-20 . . . . Florence
21-22-23 . . . . . Washington
27-28-29 . . . . Florence

AUGUST

5-6-7 . . . . Evansville
8-9-10. . . . . Gateway
15-16-17 . . . . . . Chillicothe
19-20-21 . . Southern Illinois
22-23-24 . . . . . . River City
29-30-31 . . . . Midwest

RIVER CITY

MAY

24-25-26 . . . . Gateway
27-28-29 . . . . Rockford

JUNE

3-4-5 . . . . Midwest
6-7-8 . . . . Washington
10-11-12 . . . . Midwest
16-17-18 . . . . . . Evansville
19-20-21 . . Southern Illinois
25-26-27 . . . . . Windy City
28-29-30 . . . . . . Evansville

JULY

8-9-10. . . . . . Traverse City
11-12-13 . . . . . Kalamazoo
21-22-23 . . Southern Illinois
24-25-26 . . . . . Windy City

AUGUST

5-6-7 . . . . Chillicothe
8-9-10. . . . . Florence
15-16-17 . . . . Rockford
26-27-28 . . . . Gateway

ROCKFORD

MAY

21-22-23 . . . . . . River City
24-25 . . . . Windy City
30-31 . . . . Southern Illinois

JUNE

1 . . . . Southern Illinois
2 . . . . Windy City
3-4-5 . . . . . . Traverse City
13-14-15 . . . . . Kalamazoo
16-17-18 . . . . Gateway
28-29-30 . . . . Gateway

JULY

1-2-3 . . . . Windy City
18-19-20 . . . . . . River City
24-25-26 . . . . . . Evansville
30-31 . . . . Washington

AUGUST

1 . . . . Washington
2-3-4 . . . . Midwest
8-9-10. . . . . Midwest
12-13-14 . . Southern Illinois
19-20-21 . . . . Florence
22-23-24 . . . . . . Chillicothe
26-27-28 . . . . . . Evansville

SOUTHERN ILINOIS

MAY

24-25-26 . . . . . . Evansville
27-28-29 . . . . Gateway

JUNE

3-4-5 . . . . Midwest
6-7-8 . . . . Washington
13-14-15 . . . . Midwest
16-17-18 . . . . . Windy City
25-26-27 . . . . Rockford

JULY

4-5-6 . . . . River City
8-9-10. . . . . . . Kalamazoo
11-12-13 . . . . Traverse City
24-25-26 . . . . Gateway
27-28-29 . . . . Rockford

AUGUST

2-3-4 . . . . Chillicothe
5-6-7 . . . . Florence
15-16-17 . . . . . . Evansville
26-27-28 . . . . . Windy City
29-30-31 . . . . . . River City

TRAVERSE CITY

MAY

21-22-23 . . . . Midwest
30-31 . . . . Kalamazoo

JUNE

1 . . . . Kalamazoo
10-11-12 . . . . Rockford
13-14-15 . . . . . Windy City
22-23-24 . . . . . Chillicothe
25-26-27 . . . . . Washington

JULY

4-5-6 . . . . Midwest
18-19-20 . . . . Midwest
21-22-23 . . . . Florence
24-25-26 . . . . . Washington
27-28-29 . . . . Midwest

AUGUST

5-6-7 . . . . Gateway
8-9-10. . . . . Evansville
12-13-14 . . . . . . Chillicothe
19-20-21 . . . . . . River City
22-23-24 . . Southern Illinois
26-27-28 . . . . Florence

SEPTEMBER

1-2-3 . . . . Kalamazoo

WASHINGTON

MAY
- 24-25-26 . . . . Traverse City
- 30-31 . . . . Florence

JUNE
- 1 . . . . Florence
- 10-11-12 . . Southern Illinois
- 13-14-15 . . . . . . River City
- 19-20-21 . . . . Traverse City
- 22-23-24 . . . . Midwest

JULY
- 2-3. . . . . Midwest
- 4-5-6 . . . . Florence
- 6 . . . . Rockford
- 8-9-10. . . . . Gateway
- 11-12-13 . . . . . . Evansville
- 18-19-20 . . . . . .Chillicothe
- 27-28-29 . . . . . .Chillicothe

AUGUST
- 5-6-7 . . . . .Rockford
- 8-9-10. . . . . . . Windy City
- 12-13-14 . . . . . Kalamazoo
- 15-16-17 . . . . Midwest
- 26-27-28 . . . . . Kalamazoo

SEPTEMBER
- 1-2-3 . . . . Midwest

WINDY CITY

MAY
- 27-28-29 . . . . . . Evansville
- 30-31 . . . . River City

JUNE
- 1 . . . . River City
- 6-7-8 . . . . . . Traverse City
- 10-11-12 . . . . . Kalamazoo
- 22-23-24 . . . . Rockford
- 28-29-30 . . Southern Illinois

JULY
- 4-5-6 . . . . Gateway
- 8-9-10. . . . . . . .Chillicothe
- 18-19-20 . . Southern Illinois
- 21-22-23 . . . . . . Evansville
- 30-31 . . . . Midwest

AUGUST
- 1 . . . . Midwest
- 2-3-4 . . . . . . .Washington
- 5-6-7 . . . . Midwest
- 12-13-14 . . . . . . River City
- 15-16-17 . . . . Gateway
- 22-23-24 . . . . Florence

SEPTEMBER
- 1-2-3 . . . . Rockford

GOLDEN LEAGUE

HOME GAMES ONLY

CALGARY

MAY
- 28-29-30-31 . . . .Edmonton

JUNE
- 1 . . . . .Edmonton
- 10-11-12 . . . . . .St. George
- 13-14-15 . . . . Chico
- 24-25-26 . . . . Reno
- 27-28-29 . . . . .Los Angeles

JULY
- 2-3. . . . . .Edmonton
- 17-18-19-20 . . . . Chico
- 21-22-23 . . . . Yuma

AUGUST
- 1-2-3 . . . . .Edmonton
- 5-6-7 . . . . . . .Los Angeles
- 8-9-10. . . . . Yuma
- 18-19-20-21 .Orange County
- 22-23-24 . . . . Reno
- 27-28 . . . . .Edmonton

CHICO

MAY
- 30-31 . . . . Long Beach

JUNE
- 1 . . . . Long Beach
- 2-3-4 . . . . .Orange County
- 6-7-8 . . . . Long Beach
- 17-18-19 . . . . .Calgary
- 20-21-22 . . . . . .Edmonton

JULY
- 4-5-6 . . . . Reno
- 7-8-9 . . . . .Orange County
- 11-12-13 . . . . Yuma
- 25-26-27 . . . . Reno

AUGUST
- 1-2-3 . . . . .Orange County
- 4-5-6-7 . . . . Reno
- 12-13-14 . . . . . . St. George
- 15-16-17 . . . . Yuma
- 29-30-31 . . . . . . St. George

EDMONTON

MAY
- 23-24-25-26 . . . . . .Calgary

JUNE
- 10-11-12 . . . . Chico
- 13-14-15 . . . . . .St. George
- 24-25-26 . . . . . Long Beach
- 27-28-29 . . . . Reno
- 30 . . . . .Calgary

JULY
- 1 . . . . .Calgary
- 11-12-13 . . . . .Calgary
- 17-18-19-20 . . . . Yuma
- 21-22-23 . . . . .Chico

AUGUST
- 5-6-7 . . . . Yuma
- 8-9-10-11. . . . . Long Beach
- 19-20-21 . . . . Reno
- 22-23-24 . . .Orange County
- 29-30-31 . . . . .Calgary

LONG BEACH

JUNE
- 13-14-15-16 . . . . Yuma
- 17-18 . . . . .St. George
- 20-21-22 . . .Orange County
- 25-26-27 . . . . .Calgary
- 28-29-30 . . . . . . .Edmonton

JULY
- 4-5-6 . . . . .Calgary
- 7-8-9-10 . . . . . . .Edmonton
- 11-12-13 . . . . Reno
- 17-18 . . . . .Orange County
- 20 . . . . . . .Orange County

AUGUST
- 12-13-14 . . . . .Calgary
- 15-16-17 . . . . . . .Edmonton
- 18-19-20-21 . . . . .Chico
- 26 . . . . . . .Orange County
- 29 . . . . . . .Orange County
- 31 . . . . . . .Orange County

ORANGE COUNTY

JUNE
- 10-11-12 . . . . Yuma
- 13-14 . . . . Reno
- 17-18-19 . . . . Yuma
- 23-24-25 . . . . Chico

JULY
- 1-2-3 . . . . Long Beach
- 4-5. . . . . .Edmonton
- 10-11-12 . . . . . .St. George
- 19 . . . . Long Beach
- 25-26 . . . . .Edmonton
- 28-29-30 . . . . . . .Edmonton

AUGUST
- 4-5-6-7-8 . . . . . .St. George
- 12-13-14 . . . . . . .Edmonton
- 15-16 . . . . .Calgary
- 27-28 . . . . Long Beach
- 30 . . . . Long Beach

RENO

MAY
- 23-24-25 . . .Orange County

JUNE
- 4-5. . . . . Long Beach
- 6-7. . . . . . .Orange County
- 10-11-12 . . . . . Long Beach
- 17-18-19 . . . . . .Edmonton
- 20-21-22 . . . . .Calgary
- 30 . . . . .Chico

JULY
- 1-2-3 . . . . Chico
- 8-9-10. . . . . Yuma
- 22-23-24 . . . . . Long Beach
- 28-29-30-31 . . . . Chico

AUGUST
- 1-2-3 . . . . .St. George
- 8-9-10. . . . . Chico
- 15-16-17 . . . . . .St. George
- 25-26-27-28 . . . .St. George

ST. GEORGE

MAY
- 22-23-24 . . . . . Long Beach
- 27-28-29-30-31 . . . . . Reno

JUNE
- 3-4-5 . . . . .Calgary
- 6-7. . . . . .Edmonton
- 23-24-25 . . . . Yuma
- 26-27-28 . . . . Chico

JULY
- 4-5. . . . . Yuma
- 7-8-9 . . . . .Calgary
- 17-18-19 . . . . Reno
- 21-22-23-24 .Orange County
- 25-26 . . . . .Edmonton
- 28-29-30 . . . . Yuma

AUGUST
- 9 . . . . .Orange County
- 11 . . . . . . .Orange County
- 19-20-21 . . . . Yuma
- 22-23 . . . . Chico

YUMA

MAY
- 22-23-24-25 . . . . Chico
- 28-29-30-31 .Orange County

JUNE
- 3-4-5 . . . . .Edmonton
- 6-7-8 . . . . .Calgary
- 20-21-22 . . . . . .St. George
- 27-28-29 . . .Orange County
- 30 . . . . .St. George

JULY
- 1-2-3 . . . . .St. George
- 25-26-27 . . . . . .St. George
- 31 . . . . Long Beach

AUGUST
- 1-2-3 . . . . Long Beach
- 11-12-13-14 . . . . Reno
- 22-23-24 . . . . . Long Beach
- 25-26-27 . . . . Chico
- 29-30-31 . . . . Reno

NORTHERN LEAGUE

HOME GAMES ONLY

FARGO-MOORHEAD

MAY
23-24-25-26 . . . . Gary
27-28-29 . . . . . . Winnipeg

JUNE
3-4-5 . . . . Joliet
11-12-13-14-15 Kansas City
20-21-22 . . . . . . Winnipeg

JULY
1-2-3 . . . . Kansas City
4-5-6 . . . . Gary
14-15-16-17 . . . . Gary
18-19-20 . . . . . . Winnipeg
25-26-27 . . . . Joliet

AUGUST
5-6-7 . . . . Winnipeg
8-9-10. . . . . . Schaumburg
20-21 . . . . Kansas City
22-23-24 . . . . Schaumburg
26-27-28 . . . . . . Winnipeg

GARY

MAY
15-16-17-18 . . . . Joliet
19-20-21 . . . . . Kansas City
30-31 . . . .Fargo-Moorhead

JUNE
1 . . . . . . .Fargo-Moorhead
6-7-8 . . . . Joliet
9-10 . . . . Schaumburg
20-21-22 . . . . Schaumburg
23-24-25 . .Fargo-Moorhead

JULY
1-2-3 . . . . Winnipeg
10-11 . . . . Kansas City
13 . . . . Kansas City
22-23-24 . .Fargo-Moorhead
25-26-27 . . . . . . Winnipeg

AUGUST
4-5-6 . . . . Joliet
8-9-10. . . . . . . Kansas City
20-21-22-23-24 . . . . . Joliet
26-27-28 . . . . Schaumburg

JOLIET

MAY
23-24-25-26 . . . . Winnipeg
27-28-29 . . . . Schaumburg

JUNE
11-12 . . . . Gary
13-14-15 . . . . . . Winnipeg
17-18-19 . .Fargo-Moorhead
24-25-26 . . . . Schaumburg
27-28-29 . . . . . Kansas City

JULY
4-5-6 . . . . Winnipeg
14-15-16-17 . . Schaumburg
18-19-20 . . . . Gary
29-30-31 . . . . Schaumburg

AUGUST
1-2-3 . . . .Fargo-Moorhead
12-13-14 . . . . . Kansas City
15-16-17 . .Fargo-Moorhead
18-19 . . . . Winnipeg
29-30-31 . . . . . . Winnipeg

KANSAS CITY

MAY
23-24-25-26 . . Schaumburg
27-28-29 . . . . Gary

JUNE
3-4-5 . . . . Winnipeg
6-7-8 . . . .Fargo-Moorhead
9-10 . . . . Joliet
17-18-19 . .Fargo-Moorhead
20-21-22 . . . . Joliet

JULY
4-5-6 . . . . . . Schaumburg
14-15-16-17 . . . . Winnipeg
18-19-20 . . . . Schaumburg
29-30-31 . .Fargo-Moorhead

AUGUST
1-2-3 . . . . Gary
15-16-17-18-19. . . . . . Gary
26-27-28 . . . . Joliet
29-30-31 . .Fargo-Moorhead

SCHAUMBURG

MAY
15-16-17-18 . . .Fargo-Moor.
19-20-21 . . . . Joliet
30-31 . . . . Kansas City

JUNE
1 . . . . Kansas City
3-4-5 . . . . Gary
11-12 . . . . Winnipeg
13-14-15 . . . . Gary
27-28-29 . . . . Gary

JULY
1-2-3 . . . . Joliet
10-11-12-13 . . .Fargo-Moor.
22-23-24 . . . . Joliet
25-26-27 . . . . . Kansas City

AUGUST
5-6-7 . . . . Kansas City
12-13-14 . . . . Gary
15-16-17 . . . . . . Winnipeg
18-19 . . . .Fargo-Moorhead
29-30-31 . . . . Gary

WINNIPEG

MAY
15-16-17-18 . . . Kansas City
19-20-21 . .Fargo-Moorhead
30-31 . . . . Joliet

JUNE
1 . . . . Joliet
6-7-8 . . . . . . Schaumburg
9-10 . . . . .Fargo-Moorhead
17-18-19 . . . . Gary
24-25-26 . . . . . Kansas City
27-28-29 . .Fargo-Moorhead

JULY
10-11-12-13 . . . . Joliet
22-23-24 . . . . . Kansas City
29-30-31 . . . . Gary

AUGUST
1-2-3 . . . . . . Schaumburg
8-9-10. . . . . Joliet
11-12-13 . .Fargo-Moorhead
20-21 . . . . . . Schaumburg
22-23-24 . . . . . Kansas City

UNITED LEAGUE

HOME GAMES ONLY

ALEXANDRIA

MAY
13-14-15 . . . . . . Harlingen
16-17-18 . . . . . San Angelo
27-28-29 . . . . Laredo

JUNE
5-6-7 . . . . .Edinburg
8-9-10. . . . . Harlingen
14-15-16 . . . . Amarillo
23-24-25 . . . . . San Angelo
26-27-28 . . . . Laredo

JULY
6-7-8 . . . . .Edinburg
9-10-11 . . . . Harlingen
21-22-23 . . . . . . .Edinburg
30-31 . . . . Amarillo

AUGUST
1 . . . . Amarillo
8-9-10. . . . . . . San Angelo
12-13-14 . . . . Amarillo
15-16-17 . . . . Laredo

AMARILLO

MAY
20-21-22 . . . . . .Alexandria
23-24-25 . . . . . . .Edinburg
27-28-29 . . . . . San Angelo

JUNE
2-3-4 . . . . .Alexandria
5-6-7 . . . . Laredo
17-18-19 . . . . . . .Edinburg
23-24-25 . . . . . . Harlingen

JULY
3-4-5 . . . . .Alexandria
6-7-8 . . . . Laredo
12-13 . . . . San Angelo
17-18-19-20 . . . San Angelo
24-25-26 . . . . Laredo

AUGUST
2-3-4 . . . . .Edinburg
8-9-10. . . . . Harlingen
15-16-17 . . . . . . Harlingen

EDINBURG

MAY
13-14-15 . . . . . San Angelo
16-17-18 . . . . Amarillo
27-28-29 . . . . . . Harlingen

JUNE
2-3-4 . . . . San Angelo
8-9-10. . . . . Amarillo
11-12-13 . . . . . . Harlingen
20-21-22 . . . . . .Alexandria
23-24-25 . . . . Laredo

JULY
3-4-5 . . . . San Angelo
9-10-11 . . . . Amarillo
12-13 . . . . Laredo
17-18-19 . . . . . . Harlingen
24-25-26 . . . . . .Alexandria

AUGUST
5-6-7 . . . . .Alexandria
8-9-10. . . . . Laredo

HARLINGEN

MAY
20-21-22 . . . . . . .Edinburg
23-24-25 . . . . Laredo
30-31 . . . . Amarillo

JUNE
1 . . . . Amarillo
5-6-7 . . . . San Angelo
14-15-16 . . . . Laredo
17-18-19 . . . . . .Alexandria
26-27-28 . . . . . . .Edinburg
29-30 . . . . Amarillo

JULY
1 . . . . Amarillo
6-7-8 . . . . San Angelo
12-13 . . . . .Alexandria
20 . . . . .Edinburg
21-22-23 . . . . Amarillo
27-28-29 . . . . . . .Edinburg
30-31 . . . . Laredo

AUGUST
1 . . . . Laredo
2-3-4 . . . . .Alexandria
12-13-14 . . . . . San Angelo

LAREDO

MAY
13-14-15 . . . . Amarillo
16-17-18 . . . . . . Harlingen
30-31 . . . . .Edinburg

JUNE
1 . . . . .Edinburg
2-3-4 . . . . Harlingen
11-12-13 . . . . . .Alexandria
17-18-19 . . . . . San Angelo
20-21-22 . . . . Amarillo
29-30 . . . . .Edinburg

JULY
1 . . . . .Edinburg
3-4-5 . . . . Harlingen
17-18-19-20 . . . .Alexandria
21-22-23 . . . . . San Angelo
27-28-29 . . . . . .Alexandria

AUGUST
2-3-4 . . . . San Angelo
5-6-7 . . . . Amarillo
12-13-14 . . . . . . .Edinburg

SAN ANGELO

MAY
20-21-22 . . . . Laredo
23-24-25 . . . . . .Alexandria
30-31 . . . . .Alexandria

JUNE
1 . . . . .Alexandria
8-9-10. . . . . Laredo
11-12-13 . . . . Amarillo
14-15-16 . . . . . . .Edinburg
20-21-22 . . . . . . Harlingen
26-27-28 . . . . Amarillo
29-30 . . . . .Alexandria

JULY
1 . . . . .Alexandria
9-10-11 . . . . Laredo
24-25-26 . . . . . . Harlingen
27-28-29 . . . . Amarillo
30-31 . . . . .Edinburg

AUGUST
1 . . . . .Edinburg
5-6-7 . . . . Harlingen
15-16-17 . . . . . . .Edinburg

COLLEGE

COLLEGE ORGANIZATIONS

NATIONAL COLLEGIATE ATHLETIC ASSOCIATION

Mailing Address: P.O. Box 6222, Indianapolis, IN 46206. **Telephone:** (317) 917-6222. **FAX:** (317) 917-6826 (championships), 917-6710 (baseball). **E-Mail Addresses:** dpoppe@ncaa.org (Dennis Poppe), rbuhr@ncaa.org (Randy Buhr), dleech@ncaa.org (Damani Leech), jhamilton@ncaa.org (J.D. Hamilton), ryurk@ncaa.org (Russ Yurk), kfasbender@ncaa.org (Kristen Fasbender). **Websites:** www.ncaa.org, www.ncaa.com.

President: Myles Brand. **Division I Managing Director, Baseball:** Dennis Poppe. **Director, Baseball:** Damani Leech. **Associate Director, Championships:** Randy Buhr. **Division II Assistant Director, Championships:** Russ Yurk. **Division III Associate Director, Championships:** Kristen Fasbender. **Media Contact, Division I College World Series:** J.D. Hamilton. **Contact, Statistics:** Sean Straziscar, Jeff Williams.

Chairman, Division I Baseball Committee: Larry Templeton (athletic director, Mississippi State). **Division I Baseball Committee:** John Anderson (head coach, Minnesota), Michael Cross (senior associate athletic director, Princeton), John D'Argenio (athletic director, Siena), Dave Heeke (athletic director, Central Michigan), Pat Murphy (head coach, Arizona State), Brian Quinn (athletic director, Cal State Fullerton), Bobby Staub (athletic director, Louisiana-Monroe), Larry Templeton (athletic director, Mississippi State), Tim Weiser (athletic director, Kansas State).

Chairman, Division II Baseball Committee: Wayne Riser (baseball coach, Shepherd). **Chairman, Division III Baseball Committee:** Malcolm Driggers Jr (baseball coach, McMurry).

2009 National Convention: Jan. 14-17 at Washington, D.C.

2008 CHAMPIONSHIP TOURNAMENTS

NCAA Division I

62nd College World Series	Omaha, Neb., June 14-24/25
Super Regionals (8)	Campus sites, June 6-9
Regionals (16)	Campus sites, May 30-June 2

NCAA Division II

41st World Series	Site TBA, May 24-31
Regionals (8)	Campus sites, May 15-18

NCAA Division III

31st World Series	Appleton, Wis., May 23-27
Regionals (8)	Campus sites, May 14-18

NATIONAL ASSOCIATION OF INTERCOLLEGIATE ATHLETICS

Mailing Address: 1200 Grand Blvd., Kansas City, MO 64106. **Telephone:** (816) 595-8000. **FAX:** (816) 595-8200. **Website:** www.naia.org.

President/CEO: Jim Carr. **Director, Championships:** Lori Thomas. **Manager, Championship Sports:** Scott McClure. **Director, Sports Information:** Chad Waller. **President, Coaches Association:** John Kolasinski.

2008 CHAMPIONSHIP TOURNAMENT

NAIA World Series	Lewiston, Idaho, May 23-29

NATIONAL JUNIOR COLLEGE ATHLETIC ASSOCIATION

Mailing Address: 1755 Telstar Dr., Suite 103, Colorado Springs, CO 80920. **Telephone:** (719) 590-9788. **FAX:** (719) 590-7324. **Website:** www.njcaa.org.

Executive Director: Wayne Baker. **Director, Division I Baseball Tournament:** Jamie Hamilton. **Director, Division II Baseball Tournament:** John Daigle. **Director, Division III Baseball Tournament:** Tim Drain. **Director, Media Relations:** Mark Krug.

2008 CHAMPIONSHIP TOURNAMENTS

Division I

World Series	Grand Junction, Colo., May 24-31

Division II

World Series	Millington, Tenn., May 24-30

Division III

World Series	Tyler, Texas, May 17-23

CALIFORNIA COMMUNITY COLLEGE COMMISSION ON ATHLETICS

Mailing Address: 2017 O St., Sacramento, CA 95814. **Telephone:** (916) 444-1600. **FAX:** (916) 444-2616. **E-Mail Address:** ccarter@coasports.org. **Website:** www.coasports.org.

Executive Director: Carlyle Carter. **Director, Marketing/Communications:** Unavailable. **Director, Championships:** Debra Wheeler.

2008 CHAMPIONSHIP TOURNAMENT

State Championship	Fresno, Calif., May 24-26

NORTHWEST ATHLETIC ASSOCIATION OF COMMUNITY COLLEGES

Mailing Address: Clark College PLS-033, 1933 Fort Vancouver Way, Vancouver, WA 98663-3598. **Telephone:** (360) 992-2833. **FAX:** (360) 696-6210. **Website:** www.nwaacc.org. **E-Mail Address:** nwaacc@clark.edu.

Executive Director: Dick McClain. **Executive Assistant:** Carol Hardin. **Director, Marketing:** Charlie Warner. **Sports Information Director:** Tracy Swisher.

2008 CHAMPIONSHIP TOURNAMENT

NWAACC Championship	Longview, Wash., May 22-26

AMERICAN BASEBALL COACHES ASSOCIATION

Office Address: 108 S. University Ave., Suite 3, Mount Pleasant, MI 48858-2327. **Telephone:** (989) 775-3300. **FAX:** (989) 775-3600. **E-Mail Address:** abca@abca.org. **Website:** www.abca.org.

Executive Director: Dave Keilitz. **Assistant to Executive Director:** Betty Rulong. **Membership/Convention Coordinator:** Nick Phillips. **Assistant Coordinator:** Juahn Clark.

Chairman: Glen Tuckett (Brigham Young). **President:** Steve Smith (Baylor).

2009 National Convention: Jan. 2-5 at San Diego (San Diego Convention Center).

NCAA DIVISION I CONFERENCES

AMERICA EAST CONFERENCE

Mailing Address: 10 High St., Suite 860, Boston, MA 02110. **Telephone:** (617) 695-6369. **Fax:** (617) 695-6385. **E-Mail Address:** cardinal@americaeast.com. **Website:** www.americaeast.com.

Baseball Members (First Year): Albany (2002), Binghamton (2002), Hartford (1990), Maine (1990), Maryland-Baltimore County (2004), Stony Brook (2002), Vermont (1990).

Director, Communications: K.J. Cardinal.

2008 Tournament: Four teams, double-elimination. May 22-24 at highest-seeded team with lights.

ATLANTIC COAST CONFERENCE

Office Address: 4512 Weybridge Lane, Greensboro, NC 27407. **Mailing Address:** P.O. Drawer ACC, Greensboro, NC 27417. **Telephone:** (336) 851-6062. **Fax:** (336) 854-8797. **E-Mail Address:** sbrown@theacc.org. **Website:** www.theacc.com.

Baseball Members (First Year): Boston College (2006), Clemson (1953), Duke (1953), Florida State (1992), Georgia Tech (1980), Maryland (1953), Miami (2005), North Carolina (1953), North Carolina State (1953), Virginia (1953), Virginia Tech (2005), Wake Forest (1953).

Assistant Director, Public Relations: Amy Yakola.

2008 Tournament: Eight teams, group play. May 21-25 at Jacksonville, Fla.

ATLANTIC SUN CONFERENCE

Mailing Address: 3370 Vineville Ave., Suite 108-B, Macon, GA 31204. **Telephone:** (478) 474-3394. **Fax:** (478) 474-4272. **E-Mail Address:** mwilson@atlanticsun.org. **Website:** www.atlanticsun.org.

Baseball Members (First Year): Belmont (2002), Campbell (1994), East Tennessee State (2006), Gardner-Webb (2003), Jacksonville (1999), Kennesaw State (2006), Lipscomb (1994), Mercer (1978), North Florida (2006), Stetson (1985).

Assistant Commissioner, Championships/Communications: Matt Wilson.

2008 Tournament: Eight teams, double-elimination. May 21-25 at DeLand, Fla. (Stetson).

ATLANTIC-10 CONFERENCE

Mailing Address: 230 S. Broad St., Suite 1700, Philadelphia, PA 19102. **Telephone:** (215) 545-6678. **Fax:** (215) 545-3342. **E-Mail Address:** shaug@atlantic10.org. **Website:** www.atlantic10.org.

Baseball Members (First Year): Charlotte (2006), Dayton (1996), Duquesne (1977), Fordham (1996), George Washington (1977), LaSalle (1996), Massachusetts (1977), Rhode Island (1981), Richmond (2002), St. Bonaventure (1980), Saint Joseph's (1983), Saint Louis (2006), Temple (1983), Xavier (1996).

Director, Baseball Communications: Stephen Haug.

2008 Tournament: Six teams. May 21-24 at Camden, NJ.

BIG EAST CONFERENCE

Mailing Address: 222 Richmond St., Suite 110, Providence, RI 02903. **Telephone:** (401) 453-0660. **Fax:** (401) 751-8540. **E-Mail Address:** jgust@bigeast.org. **Website:** www.bigeast.org.

Baseball Members (First Year): Cincinnati (2006), Connecticut (1985), Georgetown (1985), Louisville (2006), Notre Dame (1996), Pittsburgh (1985), Rutgers (1996), St. John's (1985), Seton Hall (1985), South Florida (2006), Villanova (1985), West Virginia (1996).

Director, Communications: John Gust.

2008 Championship: Eight teams, double-elimination. May 20-24 at Tampa, Fla. (South Florida).

BIG SOUTH CONFERENCE

Mailing Address: 7233 Pineville-Matthews Rd., Suite 100, Charlotte, NC 28226. **Telephone:** (704) 341-7990. **Fax:** (704) 341-7991. **E-Mail Address:** marks@bigsouth.org. **Website:** www.bigsouthsports.com.

Baseball Members (First Year): Charleston Southern (1983), Coastal Carolina (1983), High Point (1999), Liberty (1991), UNC Asheville (1985), Radford (1983), Virginia Military Institute (2004), Winthrop (1983).

Director, Public Relations: Mark Simpson.

2008 Tournament: Six teams, double-elimination. May 20-24 at Danville, Va.

BIG 10 CONFERENCE

Mailing Address: 1500 W. Higgins Rd., Park Ridge, IL 60068. **Telephone:** (847) 696-1010. **Fax:** (847) 696-1110. **E-Mail Addresses:** schipman@bigten.org; jsmith@bigten.org. **Website:** www.bigten.org.

Baseball Members (First Year): Illinois (1896), Indiana (1906), Iowa (1906), Michigan (1896), Michigan State (1950), Minnesota (1906), Northwestern (1898), Ohio State (1913), Penn State (1992), Purdue (1906).

Assistant Commissioner, Communications: Scott Chipman. **Assistant Director, Communications:** Jeff Smith.

2008 Tournament: Six teams, double-elimination. May 21-24 at regular-season champion.

BIG 12 CONFERENCE

Mailing Address: 2201 Stemmons Freeway, 28th Floor, Dallas, TX 75207. **Telephone:** (469) 524-1040. **Fax:** (469) 753-0145. **E-Mail Address:** kdavis@big12sports.com. **Website:** www.big12sports.com.

Baseball Members (First Year): Baylor (1997), Kansas (1997), Kansas State (1997), Missouri (1997), Nebraska (1997), Oklahoma (1997), Oklahoma State (1997), Texas (1997), Texas A&M (1997), Texas Tech (1997).

Sports Information Director: Katie Davis.

2008 Tournament: Eight teams, round-robin. May 21-25 at Oklahoma City.

BIG WEST CONFERENCE

Mailing Address: 2 Corporate Park, Suite 206, Irvine, CA 92606. **Telephone:** (949) 261-2525. **Fax:** (949) 261-2528. **E-Mail Address:** dcouch@bigwest.org. **Website:** www.bigwest.org.

Baseball Members (First Year): Cal Poly (1997), UC Davis (2004), UC Irvine (2002), UC Riverside (2002), UC Santa Barbara (1970), Cal State Fullerton (1975), Cal State Northridge (2001), Long Beach State (1970), Pacific (1972).

Assistant Director, Information: Darcy Couch.

2008 Tournament: None.

COLONIAL ATHLETIC ASSOCIATION

Mailing Address: 8625 Patterson Ave., Richmond, VA 23229. **Telephone:** (804) 754-1616. **Fax:** (804) 754-1830. **E-Mail Address:** rwashburn@caasports.com. **Website:** www.caasports.com.

Baseball Members (First Year): Delaware (2002), George Mason (1986), Georgia State (2006), Hofstra (2002), James Madison (1986), UNC Wilmington (1986), Northeastern (2006), Old Dominion (1992), Towson (2002), Virginia Commonwealth (1996), William & Mary (1986).

Sports Information Director: Rob Washburn.

2008 Tournament: Six teams, double-elimination. May 21-24 at Wilmington, N.C. (UNC Wilmington).

CONFERENCE USA

Mailing Address: 5201 N. O'Connor Blvd., Suite 300, Irving, TX 75039. **Telephone:** (214) 774-1300. **Fax:** (214) 496-0055. **E-Mail Address:** rdanderson@c-usa.org. **Website:** www.c-usasports.com.

Baseball Members (First Year): Alabama-Birmingham (1996), Central Florida (2006), East Carolina (2002), Houston (1997), Marshall (2006), Memphis (1996), Rice (2006), Southern Mississippi (1996), Tulane (1996).

Assistant Commissioner, Media Relations: Russell Anderson.

2008 Tournament: Eight teams, double-elimination. May 21-25 at New Orleans (Tulane).

HORIZON LEAGUE

Mailing Address: 201 S. Capitol Ave., Suite 500, Indianapolis, IN 46225. **Telephone:** (317) 237-5622. **Fax:** (317) 237-5620. **E-Mail Address:** rhester@horizonleague.org. **Website:** www.horizonleague.org.

Baseball Members (First Year): Butler (1979), Cleveland State (1994), Illinois-Chicago (1994), Wisconsin-Milwaukee (1994), Wright State (1994), Youngstown State (2002).

Director, Communications: Robert Hester.

2008 Tournament: Six teams, double-elimination. May 20-25 at Niles, Ohio (Youngstown State).

IVY LEAGUE

Mailing Address: 228 Alexander Rd., Second Floor, Princeton, NJ 08544. **Telephone:** (609) 258-6426. **Fax:** (609) 258-1690. **E-Mail Address:**info@ivyleaguesports.com. **Website:** www.ivyleaguesports.com.

Baseball Members (First Year): Rolfe—Brown (1948), Dartmouth (1930),Harvard (1948), Yale (1930). Gehrig—Columbia (1930), Cornell (1930), Pennsylvania (1930), Princeton (1930).

Assistant, Public Information: E.J. Crawford.

2008 Tournament: Best-of-three series between division champions. May 3-4 at team with best overall record.

METRO ATLANTIC ATHLETIC CONFERENCE

Mailing Address: 712 Amboy Ave., Edison, NJ 08837. **Telephone:** (732) 738-5455. **Fax:** (732) 738-8366. **E-Mail Address:** jill.skotarczak@maac.org. **Website:** www.maacsports.com.

Baseball Members (First Year): Canisius (1990), Fairfield (1982), Iona (1982), LeMoyne (1990), Manhattan (1982), Marist (1998), Niagara (1990), Rider (1998), St. Peter's (1982), Siena (1990).

Director, Media Relations: Jill Skotarczak.

2008 Tournament: Four teams, double-elimination. May 22-24 at Trenton, NJ (Rider).

MID-AMERICAN CONFERENCE

Mailing Address: 24 Public Square, 15th Floor, Cleveland, OH 44113. **Telephone:** (216) 566-4622. **Fax:** (216) 858-9622. **E-Mail Address:** jguy@mac-sports.com. **Website:** www.mac-sports.com.

Baseball Members (First Year): Akron (1992), Ball State (1973), Bowling Green State (1952), Buffalo (2001), Central Michigan (1971), Eastern Michigan (1971), Kent State (1951), Miami (1947), Northern Illinois (1997), Ohio (1946). Toledo (1950), Western Michigan (1947).

Associate Director, Media Relations: Jeremy Guy.

2008 Tournament: Six teams (top two in each division, two wild-card teams with next-best conference winning percentage), double-elimination. May 21-24 at regular season champion.

MID-EASTERN ATHLETIC CONFERENCE

Mailing Address: 222 Central Park Ave., Suite 1150, Virginia Beach, VA 23462. **Telephone:** (757) 416-7100. **Fax:** (757) 416-7109. **E-Mail Address:** jinksm@themeac.com; allemanm@themeac.com. **Website:** www.meacsports.com.

Baseball Members (First Year): Bethune-Cookman (1979), Coppin State (1985), Delaware State (1970), Florida A&M (1979), Maryland-Eastern Shore (1970), Norfolk State (1998), North Carolina A&T (1970).

Director, Media Relations: Michelle Jinks. **Baseball Contact:** Megan Alleman.

2008 Tournament: Seven teams, double-elimination. May 15-18 at Norfolk, Va. (Norfolk State).

MISSOURI VALLEY CONFERENCE

Mailing Address: 1818 Chouteau Ave., St. Louis, MO 63103. **Telephone:** (314) 421-0339. **Fax:** (314) 421-3505. **E-Mail Address:** fricke@mvc.org. **Website:** www.mvc.org.

Baseball Members (First Year): Bradley (1955), Creighton (1976), Evansville (1994), Illinois State (1980), Indiana State (1976), Missouri State (1990), Northern Iowa (1991), Southern Illinois (1974), Wichita State (1945).

Director, Communications: Erica Fricke.

2008 Tournament: Six teams, double-elimination. May 21-24 at Wichita, Kan.

MOUNTAIN WEST CONFERENCE

Mailing Address: 15455 Gleneagle Dr., Suite 200B, Colorado Springs, CO 80921. **Telephone:** (719) 488-4040. **Fax:** (719) 487-7241. **E-Mail Address:** medge@themwc.com. **Website:** www.themwc.com.

Baseball Members (First Year): Air Force (2000), Brigham Young (2000), Nevada-Las Vegas (2000), New Mexico (2000), San Diego State (2000), Texas Christian (2006), Utah (2000).

Assistant Director, Communications: Marlon Edge.

2008 Tournament: Six teams, double-elimination. May 20-24 at Fort Worth, Tex. (Texas Christian).

NORTHEAST CONFERENCE

Mailing Address: 200 Cottontail Lane, Vantage Court North, Somerset, NJ 08873. **Telephone:** (732) 469-0440. **Fax:** (732) 469-0744. **E-Mail Address:** rratner@northeastconference.org. **Website:** www.northeastconference.org.

Baseball Members (First Year): Central Connecticut State (1999), Fairleigh Dickinson (1981), Long Island (1981), Monmouth (1985), Mount St. Mary's (1989), Quinnipiac (1999), Sacred Heart (2000), St. Francis, N.Y. (1981), Wagner (1981).

Associate Commissioner: Ron Ratner.

2008 Tournament: Four teams, double-elimination. May 22-24 at Atlantic City, NJ.

OHIO VALLEY CONFERENCE

Mailing Address: 215 Centerview Dr., Suite 115, Brentwood, TN 37027. **Telephone:** (615) 371-1698. **Fax:** (615) 371-1788. **E-Mail Address:** kmelcher@ovc.org. **Website:** www.ovcsports.com.

Baseball Members (First Year): Austin Peay State (1962), Eastern Illinois (1996), Eastern Kentucky (1948), Jacksonville State (2003), Morehead State (1948), Murray State (1948), Samford (2003), Southeast Missouri State (1991), Tennessee-Martin (1992), Tennessee Tech (1949).

Assistant Commissioner: Kim Melcher.

2008 Tournament: Six teams, double-elimination. May 21-25 at Paducah, Ky.

PACIFIC-10 CONFERENCE

Mailing Address: 1350 Treat Blvd., Suite 500. **Telephone:** (925) 932-4411. **Fax:** (925) 932-4601. **Website:** www.pac-10.org.

Baseball Members (First Year): Arizona (1979), Arizona State (1979), California (1916), UCLA (1928), Oregon State (1916), Southern California (1923), Stanford (1918), Washington (1916), Washington State (1919).

Public Relations Intern: Katie Cavender.

2008 Tournament: None.

PATRIOT LEAGUE

Mailing Address: 3773 Corporate Pkwy., Suite 190, Center Valley, PA 18034. **Telephone:** (610) 289-1950. **Fax:** (610) 289-1952. **E-Mail Address:** jsiegel@patriotleague.com. **Website:** www.patriotleague.com.

Baseball Members (First Year): Army (1993), Bucknell (1991), Holy Cross (1991), Lafayette (1991), Lehigh (1991), Navy (1993).

Assistant Director, Media Relations: Jessica Siegel.

2008 Tournament: Four teams, May 10-11 and May 17-18 at site of higher seeds.

SOUTHEASTERN CONFERENCE

Mailing Address: 2201 Richard Arrington Blvd. N., Birmingham, AL 35203. **Telephone:** (205) 458-3000. **Fax:** (205) 458-3030. **E-Mail Address:** cdunlap@sec.org. **Website:** www.secsports.com.

Baseball Members (First Year): East—Florida (1933), Georgia (1933), Kentucky (1933), South Carolina (1992), Tennessee (1933), Vanderbilt (1933). West—Alabama (1933), Arkansas (1992), Auburn (1933), Louisiana State (1933), Mississippi (1933), Mississippi State (1933).

Assistant Director, Media Relations: Chuck Dunlap.

2008 Tournament: Eight teams, modified double-elimination. May 21-25 at Hoover, Ala.

SOUTHERN CONFERENCE

Mailing Address: 702 N. Pine St., Spartanburg, SC 29303. **Telephone:** (864) 591-5100. **Fax:** (864) 591-4282. **E-Mail Address:** bmcgowan@socon.org. **Website:** www.soconsports.com.

Baseball Members (First Year): Appalachian State (1971), Charleston (1998), The Citadel (1936), Davidson (1991), Elon (2004), Furman (1936), Georgia Southern (1991), UNC Greensboro (1997), Western Carolina (1976), Wofford (1997).

Assistant Commissioner, Public Affairs: Bryan McGowan.

2008 Tournament: Ten teams, double-elimination. May 20-25 at Charleston, S.C. (The Citadel).

SOUTHLAND CONFERENCE

Mailing Address: 1700 Alma Dr., **Suite 550, Plano, TX 75075. Telephone:** (972) 422-9500. **Fax:** (972) 422-9225. **E-Mail Address:** bludlow@southland.org. **Website:** www.southland.org.

Baseball Members (First Year): Lamar (1999), Louisiana-Monroe (1983), McNeese State (1973), Nicholls State (1992), Northwestern State (1988), Sam Houston State (1988), Southeastern Louisiana (1998), Stephen F. Austin (2006), Texas State (1988), Texas-Arlington (1964), Texas-San Antonio (1992).

Baseball Contact/Associate Commissioner: Bruce Ludlow.

2008 Tournament: Eight teams. May 21-24 at Huntsville, Texas.

SOUTHWESTERN ATHLETIC CONFERENCE

Mailing Address: A.G. Gaston Building, 1527 Fifth Ave. N., Birmingham, AL 35203. **Telephone:** (205) 252-7573, ext. **111. Fax:** (205) 252-9997. **E-Mail Address:** w.dooley@swac.org. **Website:** www.swac.org.

Baseball Members (First Year): East—Alabama A&M (2000), Alabama State (1982), Alcorn State (1962), Jackson State (1958), Mississippi Valley State (1968). West—Arkansas-Pine Bluff (1999), Grambling State (1958), Prairie View A&M (1920), Southern (1934), Texas Southern (1954).

Assistant Commissioner, Media Relations: Wallace Dooley.

2008 Tournament: Six teams, double-elimination. May 14-17 at Baton Rouge, La.

SUMMIT LEAGUE

Mailing Address: 340 W. Butterfield Rd., Suite 3-D, Elmhurst, IL 60126. **Telephone:** (630) 516-0661. **Fax:** (630) 516-0673. **E-Mail Address:** petersen@mid-con.com. **Website:** www.mid-con.com.

Baseball Members (First Year): Centenary (2004), Chicago State (1994), Oakland (2000), Oral Roberts (1998), Southern Utah (2000), Valparaiso (1984), Western Illinois (1984).

Director, Media Relations: Kristina Petersen.

2008 Tournament: Four teams, double-elimination. May 22-24 at Tulsa, Okla. (Oral Roberts).

SUN BELT CONFERENCE

Mailing Address: 601 Poydras St., Suite 2355, New Orleans, LA 70130. **Telephone:** (504) 299-9066. **Fax:** (504) 299-9068. **E-Mail Address:**broussard@sunbeltsports.org. **Website:** www.sunbeltsports.org.

Baseball Members (First Year): Arkansas-Little Rock (1991), Arkansas State (1991), Florida Atlantic (2007), Florida International (1999), Louisiana-Lafayette (1991), Louisiana-Monroe (2007), Middle Tennessee (2001), New Orleans (1976/1991), South Alabama (1976), Troy (2006), Western Kentucky (1982).

Director, Media Relations: Rob Broussard.

2008 Tournament: Eight teams, double-elimination. May 21-24 at Lafayette, La.

WEST COAST CONFERENCE

Mailing Address: 1250 Bayhill Dr., Suite 101, San Bruno, CA 94066. **Telephone:** (650) 873-8622. **Fax:** (650) 873-7846. **E-Mail Addresses:** jwilson@westcoast.org; wkiss@westcoast.org. **Website:** www.wccsports.com.

Baseball Members (First Year): Gonzaga (1996), Loyola Marymount (1968), Pepperdine (1968), Portland (1996), Saint Mary's (1968), San Diego (1979), San Francisco (1968), Santa Clara (1968).

Director, Communications: Jae Wilson. **Assistant Director, Communications:** Will Kiss.

2008 Tournament: Top two teams meet in best-of-three series at home of regular-season winner, May 23-25.

WESTERN ATHLETIC CONFERENCE

Mailing Address: 9250 East Costilla Ave., Suite 300, Englewood, CO 80112. **Telephone:** (303) 799-9221. **Fax:** (303) 799-3888. **E-Mail Address:** wac@wac.org. **Website:** www.wacsports.com.

Baseball Members (First Year): Fresno State (1993), Hawaii (1980), Louisiana Tech (2002), Nevada (2001), New Mexico

State (2006), Sacramento State (2006), San Jose State (1997).

Commissioner: Karl Benson. **Senior Associate Commissioner:** Jeff Hurd. **Director, Sports Information:** Dave Chaffin.

2008 Tournament: Six teams, double elimination. May 22-25 at Ruston, La. (Louisiana Tech).

NCAA DIVISION I TEAMS

* Recruiting coordinator

Provisional Division I status

AIR FORCE ACADEMY FALCONS

Conference: Mountain West.

Mailing Address: 2168 Field House Drive, USAF Academy, CO 80840. **Website:** goairforcefalcons.com.

Head Coach: Mike Hutcheon. **Assistant Coaches:** Scott Marchand, Mike Kazlausky, Chandler Rose. **Telephone:** (719) 333-0835. **Baseball SID:** Nick Arseniak. **Telephone:** (719) 333-9251. **Fax:** (719) 333-3798.

AKRON ZIPS

Conference: Mid-American (East).

Mailing Address: University of Akron, Rhodes Arena, Akron, OH 44325-5201. **Website:** www.GoZips.com.

Head Coach: Pat Bangtson. **Assistant Coaches:** *Brian Donohew, Ernest Simpson. **Telephone:** (330) 972-7290. **Baseball SID:** Paul Warner. **Telephone:** (330) 972-2677. **Fax:** (330) 374-8844.

Home Field: Lee Jackson Field. **Seating Capacity:** 1,500. **Outfield Dimension:** LF—330, CF—400, RF—330. **Press Box Telephone:** (330) 972-8896.

ALABAMA CRIMSON TIDE

Conference: Southeastern (East).

Mailing Address: PO Box 870391, Tuscaloosa, AL 35487. **Website:** www.rolltide.com.

Head Coach: Jim Wells. **Assistant Coaches:** B.J. Green, *Mitch Gaspard, Dax Norris. **Telephone:** (205) 348-6171. **Baseball SID:** Barry Allen. **Telephone:** (205) 348-6084. **Fax:** (205) 348-8840/8841.

Home Field: Sewell-Thomas Stadium. **Seating Capacity:** 6,118. **Outfield Dimension:** LF—325, CF—400, RF—325. **Press Box Telephone:** (205) 348-4927.

ALABAMA A&M BULLDOGS

Conference: Southwestern Athletic.

Mailing Address: PO Box 1597, Normal, AL 35762. **Website:** www.aamusports.com.

Head Coach: Jay Martin. **Assistant Coaches:** Jason Harrison, Demetris Jones, Bo Stevenson. **Telephone:** (256) 372-4004. **Baseball SID:** Thomas Galbraith. **Telephone:** (256) 372-4005. **Fax:** (256) 851-5919.

ALABAMA STATE HORNETS

Conference: Southwestern Athletic.

Mailing Address: 915 S. Jackson St., Montgomery, AL 36101. **Website:** www.bamastatesports.com.

Head Coach: Larry Watkins. **Assistant Coaches:** Anthony Hall, Tony Macon. **Telephone:** (334) 229-4228. **Baseball SID:** Kelvin Datcher. **Telephone:** (334) 229-4511. **Fax:** (334) 262-2971.

ALABAMA-BIRMINGHAM BLAZERS

Conference: Conference USA.

Mailing Address: 1530 Third Avenue South, BRTW 105, Birmingham, AL 35294-1160. **Website:** www.uabsports.com.

Head Coach: Brian Shoop. **Assistant Coaches:** *Doug Kovash, Perry Roth, Jared Walker. **Telephone:** (205) 934-7853. **Baseball SID:** Mark A. **Vellek. Telephone:** (205) 996-2576. **Fax:** (205) 934-7505.

Home Field: Young Memorial Field. **Seating Capacity:** 1,000. **Outfield Dimension:** LF—330, CF—400, RF—330. **Press Box Telephone:** (205) 934-0200.

ALBANY GREAT DANES

Conference: America East.

Mailing Address: 1400 Washington Ave., PE 123, Albany, NY 12222. **Website:** www.ualbanysports.com.

Head Coach: Jon Mueller. **Assistant Coaches:** Garett Baron, Tim Christman, Matt Quatraro. **Telephone:** (518) 442-2562. **Baseball SID:** Brianna LaBrecque. **Telephone:** (518) 442-5733. **Fax:** (518) 442-3139.

Home Field: Albany Field. **Seating Capacity:** 500. **Outfield Dimension:** LF—347, CF—375, RF—330.

ALCORN STATE BRAVES

Conference: Southwestern Athletic.

Mailing Address: 1000 ASU Drive, Alcorn State, MS 39096. **Website:** www.alcornsports.com.

Head Coach: Willie McGowan, Sr. **Assistant Coaches:** *Marqus Johnson, Rockiel Thompson. **Telephone:** (601) 877-6279. **Baseball SID:** LaToya Shields. **Telephone:** (601) 877-6466. **Fax:** (601) 877-3821.

APPALACHIAN STATE MOUNTAINEERS

Conference: Southern.

Mailing Address: PO Box 32024, Boone, NC 28608. **Website:** www.goasu.com.

Head Coach: Chris Pollard. **Assistant Coaches:** *Matt Boykin, Josh Jordan, Craig Scheffler. **Telephone:** (828) 262-6097. **Baseball SID:** Mike Flynn. **Telephone:** (828) 262-2845. **Fax:** (828) 262-4056.

Home Field: Beaver Field at Jim and Bettie Smith Stadium. **Seating Capacity:** 2,000. **Outfield Dimension:** LF—330, CF—400, RF—330. **Press Box Telephone:** (828) 262-6097.

ARIZONA WILDCATS

Conference: Pacific-10.

Mailing Address: McKale Memorial Center, 1 National Championship Dr. #253, Tucson, AZ 85716. **Website:** www.arizonaathletics.com.

Head Coach: Andy Lopez. **Assistant Coaches:** Jeff Casper, Keith Francis, *Mark Wasikowski. **Telephone:** (520) 621-4102. **Baseball SID:** Matt Rector. **Telephone:** (520) 621-0914. **Fax:** (520) 621-2681.

Home Field: Jerry Kindall Field/Frank Sancet Stadium. **Seating Capacity:** 6,000. **Outfield Dimension:** LF—360, CF—400, RF—360. **Press Box Telephone:** (520) 621-4440.

ARIZONA STATE SUN DEVILS

Conference: Pacific-10.

Mailing Address: 500 East Veteran's Way, Tempe, AZ 85287. **Website:** www.TheSunDevils.com.

Head Coach: Pat Murphy. **Assistant Coaches:** Tim Esmay, *Josh Holliday, Andy Stankiewicz. **Telephone:** (480) 965-1904. **Baseball SID:** Randy Policar. **Telephone:** (480) 965-6594. **Fax:** (480) 965-5408.

Home Field: Winkles Field-Packard Stadium at Brock Ballpark. **Seating Capacity:** 3,879. **Outfield Dimension:** LF—339, CF—395, RF—339. **Press Box Telephone:** (480) 727-7253.

ARKANSAS RAZORBACKS

Conference: Southeastern (West).

Mailing Address: 350 North Razorback Road, Fayetteville, AR 72701. **Website:** www.hogwired.com.

Head Coach: Dave Van Horn. **Assistant Coaches:** *Todd Butler, Dave Jorn, Stephin Robison, Brad Welker. **Telephone:** (479) 575-3655. **Baseball SID:** Josh Maxson. **Telephone:** (479) 575-6862. **Fax:** (479) 575-7481.

Home Field: Baum Stadium at George Cole Field. **Seating Capacity:** 10,737. **Outfield Dimension:** LF—320, CF—400, RF—320. **Press Box Telephone:** (479) 575-4141.

ARKANSAS-LITTLE ROCK TROJANS

Conference: Sun Belt.

Mailing Address: Jack Stephens Center, 2801 S. **University Ave, Little Rock, AR 72204. Website:** www.ualrtrojans.com.

Head Coach: Jim Lawler. **Assistant Coaches:** *Brian Grunzke, Tyler Herbst, Kyle Smith. **Telephone:** (501) 663-8095. **Baseball SID:** Joe Angolia. **Telephone:** (501) 569-3449. **Fax:** (501) 683-7002.

Home Field: Gary Hogan Field. **Seating Capacity:** 1,000. **Outfield Dimension:** LF—330, CF—400, RF—325. **Press Box Telephone:** (501) 351-1060.

ARKANSAS-PINE BLUFF GOLDEN LIONS

Conference: Southwestern Athletic.

Mailing Address: 1200 North University Drive, Mail Slot 4805, Pine Bluff, AR 71601. **Website:** www.uapb.edu/386_athletics.php.

Head Coach: Elbert Bennett. **Assistant Coaches:** Michael Bumpers. **Telephone:** (870) 575-8938. **Baseball SID:** Tamara Williams. **Telephone:** (870) 575-7174. **Fax:** (870) 543-4665.

ARKANSAS STATE INDIANS

Conference: Sun Belt.

Mailing Address: PO BOX 1000, State University, AR 72467. **Website:** www.asuindians.com.

Head Coach: Keith Kessinger. **Assistant Coaches:** Chris Cook, Justin Meccage, Steven Tharp. **Telephone:** (870) 972-2700. **Baseball SID:** Regina Bowman. **Telephone:** (870) 972-2541. **Fax:** (870) 972-3367.

ARMY BLACK KNIGHTS

Conference: Patriot.

Mailing Address: 639 Howard Road, West Point, NY 10996. **Website:** www.goarmysports.com.

Head Coach: Joe Sottolano. **Assistant Coaches:** Fritz Hamburg, Matt Reid. **Telephone:** (845) 938-3712. **Baseball SID:** Bob Beretta. **Telephone:** (845) 938-6416. **Fax:** (845) 446-2556.

Home Field: Johnson Stadium at Doubleday Field. **Seating Capacity:** 880.

AUBURN TIGERS

Conference: Southeastern (West).

Mailing Address: PO Box 351, Auburn, AL 36830. **Website:** www.auburntigers.com.

Head Coach: Tom Slater. **Assistant Coaches:** Bill Mosiello, *Butch Thompson. **Telephone:** (334) 844-4975. **Baseball SID:** Dan Froehlich. **Telephone:** (334) 844-9803. **Fax:** (334) 844-9807.

Home Field: Plainsman Park. **Seating Capacity:** 4,096. **Outfield Dimension:** LF—315, CF—385, RF—331. **Press Box Telephone:** (334) 844-4138.

AUSTIN PEAY STATE GOVERNORS

Conference: Ohio Valley.

Mailing Address: PO Box 4515, Clarksville, TN 37044. **Website:** www.apsu.edu/letsgopeay.

Head Coach: Gary McClure. **Assistant Coaches:** Seth Kenny, Jake Peterson. **Telephone:** (931) 221-6266. **Baseball SID:** Cody Bush. **Telephone:** (931) 221-7561. **Fax:** (931) 221-7562.

BALL STATE CARDINALS

Conference: Mid-American (West).

Mailing Address: HP 245, Muncie, IN 47306. **Website:** www.ballstatesports.com.

Head Coach: Greg Beals. **Assistant Coaches:** Alex Marconi, *Mike Stafford, C.J. Webb. **Telephone:** (765) 285-8226. **Baseball SID:** Tyson Matthews. **Telephone:** (765) 285-8242. **Fax:** (765) 285-8929.

Home Field: Ball Diamond. **Outfield Dimension:** LF—330, CF—400, RF—330.

BAYLOR BEARS

Conference: Big 12 (South).

Mailing Address: 1612 S. University Parks Dr., Waco, TX 76706. **Website:** www.baylorbears.com.

Head Coach: Steve Smith. **Assistant Coaches:** Chris Clemons, Steve Johnigan, *Mitch Thompson. **Telephone:** (254) 710-3029. **Baseball SID:** Larry Little. **Telephone:** (254) 710-4389. **Fax:** (254) 710-1369.

Home Field: Baylor Ballpark. **Seating Capacity:** 5,000. **Outfield Dimension:** LF—330, CF—400, RF—330. **Press Box Telephone:** (254) 754-5546.

BELMONT BRUINS

Conference: Atlantic Sun.

Mailing Address: 1900 Belmont Boulevard, Nashville, TN 37221. **Website:** www.belmontbruins.com/athletics.

Head Coach: Dave Jarvis. **Assistant Coaches:** Matt Barnett, *Jason Stein. **Telephone:** (615) 460-6166. **Baseball SID:** Greg Sage. **Telephone:** (615) 460-6698. **Fax:** (615) 460-5584.

BETHUNE-COOKMAN WILDCATS

Conference: Mid-Eastern Athletic.

Mailing Address: 640 Dr. Mary McLeod Bethune Blvd, Daytona Beach, FL 32114. **Website:** www.bccathletics.com.

Head Coach: Mervyl Melendez. **Assistant Coaches:** Brad Frick, *Joel Sanchez, Jose Vasquez. **Telephone:** (386) 481-2224. **Baseball SID:** Bryan Harvey. **Telephone:** (386) 481-2206. **Fax:** (386) 481-2238.

BINGHAMTON BEARCATS

Conference: America East.

Mailing Address: Binghamton University, Baseball Office, Events Center Office #110, Binghamton, NY 13902. **Website:** bubearcats.com.

Head Coach: Tim Sinicki. **Assistant Coaches:** Ed Folli, Ryan Hurba, Andy Hutchings. **Telephone:** (607) 777-2525. **Baseball SID:** John Hartrick. **Telephone:** (607) 777-6800. **Fax:** (607) 777-4597.

Home Field: Varsity Field. **Seating Capacity:** 1,000. **Outfield Dimension:** LF—315, CF—390, RF—315.

BOSTON COLLEGE EAGLES

Conference: Atlantic Coast (Atlantic).

Mailing Address: 140 Commonwealth Avenue, Chestnut Hill, MA 02467. **Website:** www.bceagles.com.

Head Coach: Mikio Aoki. **Assistant Coaches:** Jesse

Woods, Steve Englert, Joe Hastings. **Telephone:** (617) 552-2674. **Baseball SID:** Chris Cameron. **Telephone:** (617) 552-3004. **Fax:** (617) 552-4903.

BOWLING GREEN STATE FALCONS

Conference: Mid-American (East).

Mailing Address: 201 Doyt Perry Stadium East, Bowling Green, OH 43403. **Website:** www.bgsufalcons.com.

Head Coach: Danny Schmitz. **Assistant Coaches:** *Rick Blanc, Spencer Schmitz, Dave Whitmire. **Telephone:** (419) 372-7095. **Baseball SID:** J.D. **Campbell. Telephone:** (419) 372-7075. **Fax:** (419) 372-6015.

Home Field: Warren E. Stellar Field. **Seating Capacity:** 1,100. **Outfield Dimension:** LF—340, CF—400, RF—340. **Press Box Telephone:** (419) 372-1234.

BRADLEY BRAVES

Conference: Missouri Valley.

Mailing Address: 1501 West Bradley Ave, Peoria, IL 61625. **Website:** www.bubraves.com.

Head Coach: Dewey Kalmer. **Assistant Coaches:** Mike Dunne, *Marc Wagner. **Telephone:** (309) 677-2684. **Baseball SID:** Bobby Parker. **Telephone:** (309) 677-2624. **Fax:** (309) 677-2626.

BRIGHAM YOUNG COUGARS

Conference: Mountain West.

Mailing Address: 30 SFH, BYU, Provo, UT 84602. **Website:** www.byucougars.com.

Head Coach: Vance Law. **Assistant Coaches:** Bobby Applegate, Paul Bassett, *Ryan Roberts. **Telephone:** (801) 422-5049. **Baseball SID:** Ralph Zobell. **Telephone:** (801) 422-9769. **Fax:** (801) 422-0633.

Home Field: Larry H. Miller Field. **Seating Capacity:** 2,204. **Outfield Dimension:** LF—345, CF—400, RF—345. **Press Box Telephone:** (801) 422-4041.

BROWN BEARS

Conference: Ivy League (Rolfe).

Mailing Address: 235 Hope St., Providence, RI 02912. **Website:** www.BrownBears.com.

Head Coach: Marek Drabinski. **Assistant Coaches:** Bill Cilento, Jason Lefkowitz, Dave Cunningham. **Telephone:** (401) 863-3090. **Baseball SID:** Chris Hatfield. **Telephone:** (401) 863-6069. **Fax:** (401) 863-1436.

BUCKNELL BISON

Conference: Patriot.

Mailing Address: Bucknell University, Lewisburg, PA 17837. **Website:** www.bucknellbison.com.

Head Coach: Gene Depew. **Assistant Coaches:** Jim Gulden, *Scott Heather, Ben Krentzman. **Telephone:** (570) 577-3593. **Baseball SID:** Jillian Jakuba. **Telephone:** (570) 577-1835. **Fax:** (570) 577-1660.

BUFFALO BULLS

Conference: Mid-American (East).

Mailing Address: 175 Alumni Arena, Buffalo, NY 14260. **Website:** www.buffalobulls.com.

Head Coach: Ron Torgalski. **Assistant Coaches:** Joe Hesketh, Jim Koerner, Ryan Crotin. **Telephone:** (716) 645-6762. **Baseball SID:** John Fuller. **Telephone:** (716) 645-6762. **Fax:** (716) 645-6840.

BUTLER BULLDOGS

Conference: Horizon.

Mailing Address: 510 West 49th Street, Indianapolis, IN 46208. **Website:** butlersports.com.

Head Coach: Steve Farley. **Assistant Coaches:** Jeff Brown, Bob Keeney, Dan Gillin. **Telephone:** (317) 940-9721. **Baseball SID:** Jim McGrath. **Telephone:** (317) 940-9414. **Fax:** (317) 940-9808.

CALIFORNIA GOLDEN BEARS

Conference: Pacific-10.

Mailing Address: 210 Memorial Stadium, Berkeley, CA 94720. **Website:** www.calbears.com.

Head Coach: David Esquer. **Assistant Coaches:** *Dan Hubbs, Jon Zuber. **Telephone:** (510) 642-9026. **Baseball SID:** Scott Ball. **Telephone:** (510) 643-1741. **Fax:** (510) 643-7778.

Home Field: Evans Diamond. **Seating Capacity:** 2,500. **Outfield Dimension:** LF—320, CF—395, RF—320. **Press Box Telephone:** (510) 642-3098.

UC DAVIS AGGIES

Conference: Big West.

Mailing Address: One Shields Avenue, Davis, CA 95616. **Website:** ucdavisaggies.com.

Head Coach: Rex Peters. **Assistant Coaches:** Tony Schifano, Matt Vaughn, Jon Heuerman. **Telephone:** (530) 752-7513. **Baseball SID:** Wes Collins. **Telephone:** (530) 752-3505. **Fax:** (530) 754-5674.

UC IRVINE ANTEATERS

Conference: Big West.

Mailing Address: UC Irvine, Crawford Hall, Irvine, CA 92697. **Website:** www.ucirvinesports.com.

Head Coach: Mike Gillespie. **Assistant Coaches:** Bob Macaluso, *Pat Shine, Ted Silva. **Telephone:** (949) 824-4292. **Baseball SID:** Fumi Kimura. **Telephone:** (949) 824-9474. **Fax:** (949) 824-5260.

Home Field: Anteater Ballpark. **Seating Capacity:** 3,200. **Outfield Dimension:** LF—335, CF—405, RF—335. **Press Box Telephone:** (949) 824-9905.

UCLA BRUINS

Conference: Pacific-10.

Mailing Address: UCLA JD Morgan Center, PO Box 24044 Los Angeles, CA 90095. **Website:** www.uclabruins.com.

Head Coach: John Savage. **Assistant Coaches:** *Brian Green, Matt Jones, P.C. Shaw. **Telephone:** (310) 794-2470. **Baseball SID:** Alex Timiraos. **Telephone:** (310) 206-4008. **Fax:** (310) 825-8664.

Home Field: Jackie Robinson Stadium. **Seating Capacity:** 1,800. **Outfield Dimension:** LF—330, CF—395, RF—330. **Press Box Telephone:** (310) 794-8213.

UC RIVERSIDE HIGHLANDERS

Conference: Big West.

Mailing Address: Dept. of Athletics UC Riverside, Riverside, CA 92521. **Website:** www.ucr.edu/athletics.

Head Coach: Doug Smith. **Assistant Coaches:** Randy Betten, *Nathan Choate, Rusty McNamara. **Telephone:** (951) 827-5441. **Baseball SID:** Unavailable. **Telephone:** (951) 827-5438.

Home Field: UCR Sports Complex. **Seating Capacity:** 2,800. **Outfield Dimension:** LF—330, CF—400, RF—330.

UC SANTA BARBARA GAUCHOS

Conference: Big West.

Mailing Address: ICA Building, Santa Barbara, CA 93106-5200. **Website:** www.ucsbgauchos.com.

Head Coach: Bob Brontsema. **Assistant Coaches:** Brian Bowles, John Kirkgard, *Tom Myers. **Telephone:** (805) 893-3690. **Baseball SID:** Ryan Hall, Scott Flanders. **Telephone:** (805) 893-3428. **Fax:** (805) 893-4537.

Home Field: Caesar Uyesaka Stadium. **Seating Capacity:** 1,000. **Outfield Dimension:** LF—335, CF—400, RF—335. **Press Box Telephone:** (805) 893-4671.

CAL POLY MUSTANGS

Conference: Big West.

Mailing Address: Cal Poly, 1 Grand Avenue, San Luis Obispo, CA 93407-0388. **Website:** www.GoPoly.com.

Head Coach: Larry Lee. **Assistant Coaches:** Jaon Kelly, Jarek Krukow, *Jesse Zepeda. **Telephone:** (805) 756-6367. **Baseball SID:** Eric Burdick. **Telephone:** (805) 756-6550. **Fax:** (805) 756-2650.

Home Field: Baggett Stadium. **Seating Capacity:** 1,734. **Outfield Dimension:** LF—335, CF—405, RF—335. **Press Box Telephone:** (805) 756-7456.

CAL STATE FULLERTON TITANS

Conference: Big West.

Mailing Address: 800 N. State College Blvd., Fullerton, CA 92831. **Website:** fullertontitans.com.

Head Coach: Dave Serrano. **Assistant Coaches:** Greg Bergeron, *Sergio Brown, Brett Lindgren. **Telephone:** (714) 278-3081. **Baseball SID:** Michael Greenlee. **Telephone:** (714) 278-3081. **Fax:** (714) 278-3141.

Home Field: Goodwin Field. **Seating Capacity:** 3,500. **Outfield Dimension:** LF—330, CF—400, RF—330. **Press Box Telephone:** (714) 278-5327.

CAL STATE NORTHRIDGE MATADORS

Conference: Big West.

Mailing Address: 18111 Nordhoff Street, Northridge, CA 91330. **Website:** gomatadors.olinesports.com.

Head Coach: Steve Rousey. **Assistant Coaches:** Mark Kertenian, *Robert McKinley. **Telephone:** (818) 677-7055. **Baseball SID:** Miles David. **Telephone:** (818) 677-3860. **Fax:** (818) 677-2661.

CAMPBELL FIGHTING CAMELS

Conference: Atlantic Sun.

Mailing Address: PO BOX 10, Buies Creek, NC 27506. **Website:** www.gocamels.com.

Head Coach: Greg Goff. **Assistant Coaches:** Aubrey Blackwell, Justin Haire, John Caddell. **Telephone:** (910) 893-1354. **Baseball SID:** Quinn LeSage. **Telephone:** (910) 814-4367. **Fax:** (910) 893-1330.

CANISIUS GOLDEN GRIFFINS

Conference: Metro Atlantic.

Mailing Address: 2001 Main St., Koessler Athletic Center, Buffalo, NY 14208. **Website:** www.gogriffs.com.

Head Coach: Mike McRae. **Assistant Coaches:** *Mike Medici, Matt Mazurek, Jerry Shank. **Telephone:** (716) 888-3207. **Baseball SID:** Matt Lozar. **Telephone:** (716) 888-3756. **Fax:** (716) 888-3178.

Home Field: Demske Sports Complex. **Seating Capacity:** 1,000. **Outfield Dimension:** LF—320, CF—390, RF—320. **Press Box Telephone:** (440) 477-3777.

CENTENARY GENTS

Conference: Mid-Continent.

Mailing Address: 2911 Centenary Blvd., Shreveport, LA 71134. **Website:** www.gocentenary.com.

Head Coach: Ed McCann. **Assistant Coaches:** Mike Diaz, Jeff Poulin, Pat Holmes. **Telephone:** (318) 869-5298. **Baseball SID:** David Pratt. **Telephone:** (318) 869-5092. **Fax:** (318) 869-5128.

CENTRAL CONNECTICUT STATE BLUE DEVILS

Conference: Northeast.

Mailing Address: 16151 Stanley St., New Britain, CT 06050. **Website:** ccsubluedevils.com.

Head Coach: Charlie Hickey. **Assistant Coaches:** Tim D'Aquila, *Paul LaBella, Jim Ziogas. **Telephone:** (860) 832-3074. **Baseball SID:** Tom Pincince. **Telephone:** (860) 832-3089. **Fax:** (860) 832-3754.

CENTRAL FLORIDA GOLDEN KNIGHTS

Conference: Conference USA.

Mailing Address: 4000 Central Florida Blvd., Orlando, FL 32816. **Website:** ucfathletics.com.

Head Coach: Jay Bergman. **Assistant Coach:** *Craig Cozart, Bryan Peters. **Telephone:** (407) 823-0140. **Baseball SID:** Brian Ormiston. **Telephone:** (407) 823-2409. **Fax:** (407) 823-4296.

CENTRAL MICHIGAN CHIPPEWAS

Conference: Mid-American (West).

Mailing Address: Rose Center, Central Michigan University, Mount Pleasant, MI 48859. **Website:** www.cmuchippewas.com.

Head Coach: Steve Jaksa. **Assistant Coaches:** Dave Barkholz, *Mike Villano. **Telephone:** (989) 774-4392. **Baseball SID:** Scott Rex. **Telephone:** (989) 774-7323. **Fax:** (989) 774-7324.

Home Field: Theunissen Stadium. **Seating Capacity:** 2,046. **Outfield Dimension:** LF—330, CF—400, RF—330. **Press Box Telephone:** (989) 774-3594.

CHARLESTON COUGARS

Conference: Southern.

Mailing Address: 30 George St., Charleston, SC 29424. **Website:** www.cofcsports.com.

Head Coach: John Pawlowski. **Assistant Coaches:** *Scott Foxhall, Matt Heath, Chris Morris, Kevin Pratt. **Telephone:** (843) 953-5916. **Baseball SID:** Tony Ciuffo. **Telephone:** (843) 953-5465. **Fax:** (843) 953-6534.

Home Field: Patriots Point Field. **Seating Capacity:** 2,000. **Outfield Dimension:** LF—300, CF—400, RF—330. **Press Box Telephone:** (843) 953-9141/9142.

CHARLESTON SOUTHERN BUCCANEERS

Conference: Big South.

Mailing Address: PO Box 118087, 9200 University Blvd., North Charleston, SC 29406. **Website:** csusports.com.

Head Coach: Jason Murray. **Assistant Coaches:** *Tim Lau, David Wolfe. **Telephone:** (843) 863-7591. **Baseball SID:** Brendan Stevens. **Telephone:** (843) 863-7037. **Fax:** (843) 863-7676.

Home Field: Buccaneer Field. **Seating Capacity:** 500. **Outfield Dimension:** LF—330, CF—400, RF—330. **Press Box Telephone:** (843) 863-7764.

CHARLOTTE 49ERS

Conference: Atlantic 10.

Mailing Address: Wachovia Field House/9200 University City Blvd., **Charlotte, NC 28223. Website:** www.charlotte49ers.com.

Head Coach: Loren Hibbs. **Assistant Coaches:** Bo Durkac, *Brandon Hall, Brett Hall. **Telephone:** (704) 687-3935. **Baseball SID:** Ryan Rose. **Telephone:** (704) 687-6312. **Fax:** (704) 687-4918.

Home Field: Robert and Mariam Hayes Stadium. **Seating Capacity:** 3,000. **Outfield Dimension:** LF—330, CF—390, RF—330. **Press Box Telephone:** (704)-687-3148.

CHICAGO STATE COUGARS

Conference: Independent.

Mailing Address: 9501 S. King Dr, JDC 100E, Chicago, IL 60628. **Website:** www.csu.edu/athletics.

Head Coach: Husain Mahmoud. **Assistant Coaches:** Michael Caston, Dan Soria, Wallace Johnson. **Telephone:** (773) 995-3659. **Baseball SID:** Ruben Perez. **Telephone:** (773) 995-2217. **Fax:** (773) 995-3656.

CINCINNATI BEARCATS

Conference: Big East.

Mailing Address: 2751 O'Varsity Way, Richard E. Lindner Center, Cincinnati, OH 45221. **Website:** gobearcats.com.

Head Coach: Brian Cleary. **Assistant Coaches:** *Brad Meador, Chris Reilly, Brian Szarmach. **Telephone:** (513) 556-1577. **Baseball SID:** Unavailable. **Telephone:** (513) 556-5191. **Fax:** (513) 556-0619.

Home Field: Marge Schott Stadium. **Seating Capacity:** 3,085. **Outfield Dimension:** LF—325, CF—400, RF—325. **Press Box Telephone:** (513) 556-9645.

CITADEL BULLDOGS

Conference: Southern.

Mailing Address: 171 Moultire St., Charleston, SC 29409. **Website:** www.citadelsports.com.

Head Coach: Fred Jordan. **Assistant Coaches:** *David Beckley, Randy Carlson, Stuart Lake. **Telephone:** (843) 953-5901. **Baseball SID:** Noelle Orr Blaney. **Telephone:** (843) 953-5353. **Fax:** (843) 953-5058.

CLEMSON TIGERS

Conference: Atlantic Coast (Atlantic).

Mailing Address: 100 Perimeter Road, PO Box 31, Clemson, SC 29633. **Website:** clemsontigers.com.

Head Coach: Jack Leggett. **Assistant Coaches:** Toby Bicknell, Kyle Bunn, *Tom Riginos. **Telephone:** (864) 656-1947. **Baseball SID:** Brian Hennessey. **Telephone:** (864) 656-1921. **Fax:** (864) 656-0299.

Home Field: Doug Kingsmore Stadium. **Seating Capacity:** 6,127. **Outfield Dimension:** LF—320, CF—400, RF—330. **Press Box Telephone:** (864) 656-7731.

CLEVELAND STATE VIKINGS

Conference: Horizon.

Mailing Address: 2000 Prospect Ave., Cleveland, OH 44115. **Website:** www.csuvikings.com.

Head Coach: Kevin Kocks. **Assistant Coaches:** Rob Henry, Cliff Cook, Tim Spatz. **Telephone:** (216) 687-4822. **Baseball SID:** Brian McCann. **Telephone:** (216) 687-5115. **Fax:** (216) 523-7257.

COASTAL CAROLINA CHANTICLEERS

Conference: Big South.

Mailing Address: PO Box 261954 Conway, SC 29528. **Website:** www.GoCCUSports.com.

Head Coach: Gary Gilmore. **Assistant Coaches:** Brendan Dougherty, *Kevin Schnall, Drew Thomas. **Telephone:** (843) 349-2816. **Baseball SID:** Kent Reichert. **Telephone:** (843) 349-2840. **Fax:** (843) 349-2819.

Home Field: Charles L. **Watson Stadium/Vrooman Field. Seating Capacity:** 2,000. **Outfield Dimension:** LF—320, CF—390, RF—325. **Press Box Telephone:** (843) 421-8244.

COLUMBIA LIONS

Conference: Ivy League (Gehrig).

Mailing Address: Dodge Physical Fitness Center, 3030 Broadway, New York, NY 10027. **Website:** www.gocolumbialions.com.

Head Coach: Brett Boretti. **Assistant Coaches:** Pete Maki, Jay Quinn, Jim Walsh. **Telephone:** (212) 854-8448. **Baseball SID:** Todd Kennedy. **Telephone:** (212) 854-7141. **Fax:** (212) 854-8168.

CONNECTICUT HUSKIES

Conference: Big East.

Mailing Address: 2095 Hillside Rd., Storrs, CT 06269. **Website:** www.UConnHuskies.com

Head Coach: Jim Penders. **Assistant Coaches:** Justin Blood, Chris Podeszwa, Bruce Elliot. **Telephone:** (860) 486-4089. **Baseball SID:** Mike Enright. **Telephone:** (860) 486-3531. **Fax:** (860) 486-5085.

COPPIN STATE EAGLES

Conference: Mid-Eastern Athletic.

Mailing Address: 2500 W. North Ave., Baltimore, MD **21216. Website:** www.coppinstatesports.com.

Head Coach: Harvey Lee. **Telephone:** (410) 951-3740. **Baseball SID:** Roger McAfee. **Telephone:** (410) 951-3729. **Fax:** (410) 951-3718.

CORNELL BIG RED

Conference: Ivy League (Rolfe).

Mailing Address: Cornell University Baseball, Teagle Hall, Campus Road, Ithica, NY 14853. **Website:** cornellbigred.com.

Head Coach: Tom Ford. **Assistant Coaches:** Ryan Horning, Bill Kerry, *Scott Marsh. **Telephone:** (607) 255-6604. **Baseball SID:** Kevin Zeise. **Telephone:** (607) 255-5627. **Fax:** (607) 255-9791.

CREIGHTON BLUEJAYS

Conference: Missouri Valley.

Mailing Address: 2500 California Plaza, Omaha, NE 68178. **Website:** www.gocreighton.com.

Head Coach: Ed Servais. **Assistant Coaches:** Jason Shockey, *Rob Smith. **Telephone:** (402) 280-2483. **Baseball SID:** Brent Elsasser. **Telephone:** (402) 280-5801. **Fax:** (402) 280-2495.

Home Field: Creighton Sports Complex. **Seating Capacity:** 1,000. **Outfield Dimension:** LF—330, CF—400, RF—330. **Press Box Telephone:** (402) 280-2787 or (402) 380-1676.

DALLAS BAPTIST PATRIOTS

Conference: Independent.

Mailing Address: 3000 Mountain Creek Pkwy., Dallas, TX 75211. **Website:** www.dbu.edu/athletics.

Head Coach: Dan Heefner. **Assistant Coaches:** *Nate Frieling, Cody Montgomery, Travis Wyckoff. **Telephone:** (214) 333-5327. **Baseball SID:** Larry Northcut. **Telephone:** (214) 333-5349. **Fax:** (214) 333-5306.

Home Field: Wuksib Fuekd. **Seating Capacity:** 700. **Outfield Dimension:** LF—330, CF—388, RF—330.

DARTMOUTH BIG GREEN

Conference: Ivy League (Rolfe).

Mailing Address: 6083 Alumni Gym, Hanover, NH 03755. **Website:** dartmouthsports.com.

Head Coach: Bob Whalen. **Assistant Coaches:** Nicholas Enriquez, George Roig. **Telephone:** (603) 646-2477. **Baseball SID:** Heather Croze. **Telephone:** (603) 646-2468. **Fax:** (603) 646-1286.

DAVIDSON WILDCATS

Conference: Southern.

Mailing Address: Davidson College, Box 7158, Davidson, NC 28035. **Website:** www.davidsonwildcats.com.

Head Coach: Dick Cooke. **Assistant Coaches:** Jeff Arzonico, *Mike Zandler. **Telephone:** (704) 894-2368. **Baseball SID:** Mark Gignac. **Telephone:** (704) 894-2123. **Fax:** (704) 894-2636.

Home Field: Wilson Field. **Seating Capacity:** 700. **Outfield Dimension:** LF—320, CF—385, RF—325. **Press Box Telephone:** (704) 894-2740.

DAYTON FLYERS

Conference: Atlantic 10.

Mailing Address: 300 College Park, Dayton, OH 45469. **Website:** daytonflyers.com.

Head Coach: Tony Vittorio. **Assistant Coaches:** Terry Bell, Brian Harrison, *Todd Linklater. **Telephone:** (937) 229-4456. **Baseball SID:** Bill Thomas. **Telephone:** (937) 229-4419. **Fax:** (937) 229-4461.

Home Field: Time Warner Cable Stadium. **Seating Capacity:** 2,000. **Outfield Dimension:** LF—330, CF—400, RF—335.

DELAWARE BLUE HENS

Conference: Colonial Athletic.

Mailing Address: 631 South College Avenue, Newark, DE 19716. **Website:** udel.edu/sportsinfo.

Head Coach: Jim Sherman. **Assistant Coaches:** *Dan Hammer, Steve Harden, Brian Walker. **Telephone:** (302) 831-8596. **Baseball SID:** Kenny Kline. **Telephone:** (302) 831-2186. **Fax:** (302) 831-8653.

Home Field: Bob Hannah Stadium. **Seating Capacity:** 1,300. **Outfield Dimension:** LF—330, CF—400, RF—330. **Press Box Telephone:** (302) 831-4122.

DELAWARE STATE HORNETS

Conference: Mid-Eastern Athletic.

Mailing Address: 1200 N. Dupont Hwy, Dover, DE 19901. **Website:** www.dsuhornets.com.

Head Coach: J.P. Blandin. **Assistant Coach:** Michael August. **Telephone:** (302) 857-6035. **Baseball SID:** Dennis Jones. **Telephone:** (302) 857-6068. **Fax:** (302) 857-6069.

DUKE BLUE DEVILS

Conference: Atlantic Coast (Coastal).

Mailing Address: 115 Cameron Indoor Stadium, PO Box 90557, Durham, NC 27708. **Website:** www.goduke.com.

Head Coach: Sean McNally. **Assistant Coaches:** Jonathan Anderson, *Matthew Boggs, Sean Snedeker. **Telephone:** (919) 668-0255. **Baseball SID:** Chris Cook. **Telephone:** (919) 684-8708. **Fax:** (919) 684-2489.

Home Field: Jack Coombs Field. **Seating Capacity:** 2,000. **Outfield Dimension:** LF—330, CF—400, RF—330. **Press Box Telephone:** (919) 812-7141.

DUQUESNE DUKES

Conference: Atlantic 10.

Mailing Address: A.J. Palumbo Center, 600 Forbes Ave., Pittsburgh, PA 15282. **Website:** www.goduquesne.com.

Head Coach: Mike Wilson. **Assistant Coaches:** Jeff Minick, Jeff Stanek. **Telephone:** (412) 396-5245. **Baseball SID:** George Nieman. **Telephone:** (412) 396-5376. **Fax:** (412) 396-6210.

EAST CAROLINA PIRATES

Conference: Conference USA.

Mailing Address: Clark-LeClair Stadium, Greenville, NC 27858. **Website:** www.ecupirates.com.

Head Coach: Billy Godwin. **Assistant Coaches:** Bill Jarman, *Link Jarrett, Ben Sanderson, Brian Cavanaugh. **Telephone:** (252) 737-1985. **Baseball SID:** Malcolm Gray. **Telephone:** (252) 737-4523. **Fax:** (252) 737-4528.

Home Field: Clark-LeClair Stadium. **Seating Capacity:** 3,000. **Outfield Dimension:** LF—320, CF—390, RF—320. **Press Box Telephone:** (252) 328-0068.

EAST TENNESSEE STATE BUCCANEERS

Conference: Atlantic Sun.

Mailing Address: P.O. Box 70041, Johnson City, TN 37614. **Website:** www.etsubucs.com.

Head Coach: Tony Skole. **Assistant Coaches:** Reid Casey, *Clay Greene. **Telephone:** (423) 439-4496. **Baseball SID:** Michael White. **Telephone:** (423) 439-4220. **Fax:** (423) 439-6138.

EASTERN ILLINOIS PANTHERS

Conference: Ohio Valley.

Mailing Address: 600 Lincoln Avenue, Charleston, IL 61920. **Website:** www.EIUpanthers.com.

Head Coach: Jim Schmitz. **Assistant Coaches:** *Sean Lyons, Skylar Meade. **Telephone:** (217) 581-2522. **Baseball SID:** Ben Turner. **Telephone:** (217) 581-7020. **Fax:** (217) 581-6434.

Home Field: Coaches Stadium. **Seating Capacity:** 550. **Outfield Dimension:** LF—340, CF—380, RF—340. **Press Box Telephone:** (217) 581-8464.

EASTERN KENTUCKY COLONELS

Conference: Ohio Valley.

Mailing Address: 115 Alumni Coliseum, Richmond, KY 40475. **Website:** www.ekusports.com.

Head Coach: Elvis Dominguez. **Assistant Coaches:** *John Corbin, Cory Whitby. **Telephone:** (859) 622-2128. **Baseball SID:** Steve Fohl. **Telephone:** (859) 622-1253. **Fax:** (859) 622-5108.

EASTERN MICHIGAN EAGLES

Conference: Mid-American (West).

Mailing Address: 799 Hewitt Road, Ypsilianti, MI 48197. **Website:** www.emueagles.com.

Head Coach: Jake Boss. **Assistant Coaches:** Shane Davis, Del Young, Mark Van Ameyde. **Telephone:** (734) 487-0315. **Baseball SID:** Jim Streeter. **Telephone:** (734) 487-0317. **Fax:** (734) 485-3840.

ELON PHOENIX

Conference: Southern.

Mailing Address: 2500 Campus Box, Elon, NC 27244. **Website:** www.elonphoenix.com.

Head Coach: Mike Kennedy. **Assistant Coaches:** Robbie Huffstetler, Grant Rembert, *Greg Starbuck. **Telephone:** (336) 278-6741. **Baseball SID:** Chris Rash. **Telephone:** (336) 278-6712. **Fax:** (336) 278-6768.

EVANSVILLE PURPLE ACES

Conference: Missouri Valley.

Mailing Address: 1800 Lincoln Avenue, Evansville, IN 47722. **Website:** www.gopurpleaces.com.

Head Coach: David Seifert. **Assistant Coaches:** *Wes Carroll, Jacob Gill, Ryan Sowers. **Telephone:** (812) 488-1027. **Baseball SID:** Tom Benson. **Telephone:** (812) 488-1152. **Fax:** (812) 488-2090.

Home Field: Charles H. Braun Stadium. **Seating Capacity:** 1,500. **Outfield Dimension:** LF—330, CF—400, RF—330. **Press Box Telephone:** (812) 479-2587.

FAIRFIELD STAGS

Conference: Metro Atlantic.

Mailing Address: 1073 North Benson Rd., Fairfield, CT

6824. **Website:** www.fairfieldstags.com.

Head Coach: John Slosar. **Assistant Coaches:** *Patrick Hall, Kevin Huber, Dennis Whalen. **Telephone:** (203) 254-4000, ext. **2605. Baseball SID:** Kelly McCarthy. **Telephone:** (203) 254-4000, ext. **2877. Fax:** (203) 254-4117.

FAIRLEIGH DICKINSON KNIGHTS

Conference: Northeast.

Mailing Address: 1000 River Road, Teaneck, NJ 07666. **Website:** fduknights.com.

Head Coach: Jerry Defabbia. **Assistant Coaches:** Chris Bagley, Matt Born, Dan Gray. **Telephone:** (201) 692-2245. **Baseball SID:** Wes Heinel. **Telephone:** (201) 692-2149. **Fax:** (201) 692-9361.

FLORIDA GATORS

Conference: Southeastern (East).

Mailing Address: PO Box 14485, Gainesville, FL 32604. **Website:** www.GatorZone.com.

Head Coach: *Kevin O'Sullivan. **Assistant Coaches:** Craig Bell, Don Norris, Brad Weitzel. **Telephone:** (352) 375-4683, ext. 4457. **Baseball SID:** John Hines. **Telephone:** (352) 375-4683, ext. 6130. **Fax:** (352) 375-4809.

Home Field: McKethan Stadium. **Seating Capacity:** 5,500. **Outfield Dimension:** LF—329, CF—400, RF—325. **Press Box Telephone:** (352) 375-4683, ext. 4355.

FLORIDA A&M RATTLERS

Conference: Mid-Eastern Athletic.

Mailing Address: 1500 Wahnish Way, Tallahassee, FL 32307. **Website:** thefamurattlers.com.

Head Coach: Robert Lucas. **Assistant Coaches:** Brett Richardson, Kentaus Carter. **Telephone:** (850) 599-3202. **Baseball SID:** Ronnie Johnson. **Telephone:** (850) 561-2701. **Fax:** (850) 599-3206.

FLORIDA ATLANTIC OWLS

Conference: Atlantic Sun.

Mailing Address: 777 Glades Road, Boca Raton, FL 33431. **Website:** www.fausports.com.

Head Coach: Kevin Cooney. **Assistant Coaches:** Tony Fossas, Norberto Lopez, *John McCormack. **Telephone:** (561) 297-3956. **Baseball SID:** Justin Johnson. **Telephone:** (561) 297-3513. **Fax:** (561) 297-3963.

Home Field: FAU Stadium. **Seating Capacity:** 2,000. **Outfield Dimension:** LF—330, CF—400, RF—330. **Press Box Telephone:** (561) 297-3455.

FLORIDA INTERNATIONAL GOLDEN PANTHERS

Conference: Sun Belt.

Mailing Address: 11200 SW Eighth Street, Miami, FL 33199. **Website:** www.fiusports.com.

Head Coach: Turtle Thomas. **Assistant Coaches:** *Sean Allen, Felipe Suarez, Ray Marrero. **Telephone:** (305) 348-3166. **Baseball SID:** Evan Koch. **Telephone:** (305) 348-2084. **Fax:** (305) 348-2963.

Home Field: Golden Panther Stadium. **Seating Capacity:** 2,000. **Outfield Dimension:** LF—325, CF—400, RF—325. **Press Box Telephone:** (305) 348-3707.

FLORIDA STATE SEMINOLES

Conference: Atlantic Coast.

Mailing Address: 525 Stadium Drive West, Tallahassee, FL 32311. **Website:** www.seminoles.com.

Head Coach: Mike Martin. **Assistant Coaches:** Rod Delmonico, Mike Martin, Jr., *Jamey Shouppe. **Telephone:** (850) 644-1073. **Baseball SID:** Jason Leturmy. **Telephone:** (850) 644-5656. **Fax:** (850) 644-3920.

Home Field: Dick Howser Stadium. **Seating Capacity:** 6,700. **Outfield Dimension:** LF—340, CF—400, RF—320. **Press Box Telephone:** (850) 644-1553.

FORDHAM RAMS

Conference: Atlantic 10.

Mailing Address: 441 East Fordham Road, Bronx, NY 10458. **Website:** www.fordhamsports.com.

Head Coach: Nick Restaino. **Assistant Coaches:** Justin Ottman, *Kiko Reyes. **Telephone:** (718) 817-4292. **Baseball SID:** Scott Kwiatkowski. **Telephone:** (718) 817-4219. **Fax:** (718) 817-4244.

Home Field: Houlihan Park at Jack Coffey Field. **Seating Capacity:** 1,000. **Outfield Dimension:** LF—330, CF—400, RF—330. **Press Box Telephone:** (718) 817-0773.

FRESNO STATE BULLDOGS

Conference: Western Athletic.

Mailing Address: 5305 North Campus Drive, Room 153, Fresno, CA 93740. **Website:** gobulldogs.com.

Head Coach: Mike Batesole. **Assistant Coaches:** *Matt Curtis, Mike Mayne, Pat Wear. **Telephone:** (559) 278-2178. **Baseball SID:** Alyssa Chambers. **Telephone:** (559) 278-2509. **Fax:** (559) 278-4689.

Home Field: Beiden Field. **Seating Capacity:** 5,575. **Outfield Dimension:** LF—330, CF—400, RF—330. **Press Box Telephone:** (559) 278-7678.

FURMAN PALADINS

Conference: Southern.

Mailing Address: 3300 Poinsett Highway, Greenville, SC 29613. **Website:** furmanpaladins.com.

Head Coach: Ron Smith. **Assistant Coaches:** Tim Bright, *Brent Shade. **Telephone:** (864) 294-2146. **Baseball SID:** Hunter Reid. **Telephone:** (864) 294-2061. **Fax:** (864) 294-3061.

GARDNER-WEBB BULLDOGS

Conference: Atlantic Sun.

Mailing Address: P.O. Box 877, Boiling Springs, NC 28017. **Website:** www.gwusports.com.

Head Coach: Rusty Stroupe. **Assistant Coaches:** Jason Burke, *Kent Cox, Mike Lewis. **Telephone:** (704) 406-4421. **Baseball SID:** Marc Rabb. **Telephone:** (704) 406-4355. **Fax:** (704) 406-4739.

Home Field: Varsity Field. **Seating Capacity:** 800. **Outfield Dimension:** LF—325, CF—390, RF—335.

GEORGE MASON PATRIOTS

Conference: Colonial Athletic.

Mailing Address: 4400 University Drive, Fairfax, VA 22030. **Website:** gomason.com.

Head Coach: Bill Brown. **Assistant Coaches:** Steve Hay, *Jeff Palumbo. **Telephone:** (703) 993-3282. **Baseball SID:** Richard Coco. **Telephone:** (703) 993-3264. **Fax:** (703) 993-3593.

GEORGE WASHINGTON COLONIALS

Conference: Atlantic 10.

Mailing Address: 600 22nd Street NW, Washington, DC 20052. **Website:** gwsports.cstv.com.

Head Coach: Steve Mrowka. **Assistant Coaches:** *Dan Hodgson, Bob Smith, Pat O'Brien. **Telephone:** (202) 994-7399. **Baseball SID:** Ryan Hudson. **Telephone:** (202) 994-0339. **Fax:** (202) 994-2713.

Home Field: Barcroft Park. **Outfield Dimension:** LF—321, CF—370, RF—321. **Press Box Telephone:** (703) 400-5368.

GEORGETOWN HOYAS

Conference: Big East.

Mailing Address: McDonough Arena, 37th & O Streets NW, Washington, DC 20057. **Website:** guhoyas.com.

Head Coach: Pete Wilk. **Assistant Coaches:** Curtis Brown, J.J. Brock. **Telephone:** (202) 687-2462. **Baseball SID:** Ben Shove. **Telephone:** (202) 687-7155. **Fax:** (202) 687-2491.

GEORGIA BULLDOGS

Conference: Southeastern (East).

Mailing Address: PO Box 1472, Athens, GA 30603-1472. **Website:** www.georgiadogs.com.

Head Coach: David Perno. **Assistant Coaches:** *Jason Eller, Brady Wiederhold. **Telephone:** (706) 542-7993. **Baseball SID:** Christopher Lakos. **Telephone:** (706) 542-1621. **Fax:** (706) 542-7993.

Home Field: Foley Field. **Seating Capacity:** 3,291. **Outfield Dimension:** LF—350, CF—404, RF—314. **Press Box Telephone:** (706) 542-6161.

GEORGIA SOUTHERN EAGLES

Conference: Southern.

Mailing Address: PO BOX 8085, Statesboro, GA 30460. **Website:** www.georgiasoutherneagles.com.

Head Coach: Rodney Hennon. **Assistant Coaches:** Jason Beverlin, *Mike Tidick. **Telephone:** (912) 486-7360. **Baseball SID:** Patrick Osterman. **Telephone:** (912) 681-0352. **Fax:** (912) 681-0046.

GEORGIA STATE PANTHERS

Conference: Colonial Athletic.

Mailing Address: 125 Decatur St., Suite 201, Atlanta, GA 30303. **Website:** www.georgiastatesports.com.

Head Coach: Greg Frady. **Assistant Coaches:** Blaine McFerrin, *Brad Stromdahl. **Telephone:** (404) 413-4077. **Baseball SID:** Steven Ericson. **Telephone:** (404) 413-4033. **Fax:** (404) 651-0842.

GEORGIA TECH YELLOW JACKETS

Conference: Atlantic Coast.

Mailing Address: 150 Bobby Dodd Way, Atlanta, GA 30332. **Website:** www.ramblinwreck.com.

Head Coach: Danny Hall. **Assistant Coaches:** *Bryan Prince, Tom Kinkelaar. **Telephone:** (404) 894-5471. **Baseball SID:** Cheryl Watts. **Telephone:** (404) 894-5445. **Fax:** (404) 894-1248.

Home Field: Russ Chandler Stadium. **Seating Capacity:** 4,157. **Outfield Dimension:** LF—328, CF—400, RF—334. **Press Box Telephone:** (404) 894-3961.

GONZAGA BULLDOGS

Conference: West Coast.

Mailing Address: 502 East Boone Ave, Spokane, WA 99258. **Website:** gozags.com.

Head Coach: Mark Machtolf. **Assistant Coaches:** Steve Bennett, *Danny Evans, Gary Van Tol. **Telephone:** (509) 323-4209. **Baseball SID:** Rachel Engrissei. **Telephone:** (509) 323-4227. **Fax:** (509) 323-5730.

Home Field: Patterson Baseball Complex and Washington Trust Field. **Seating Capacity:** 1,500. **Outfield Dimension:** LF—328, CF—398, RF—328. **Press Box Telephone:** (509) 323-4224.

GRAMBLING STATE TIGERS

Conference: Southwestern Athletic.

Mailing Address: P.O. Box 868, Grambling, LA 71245. **Website:** www.gsutigers.com.

Head Coach: Barret Rey. **Assistant Coach:** Olen Parker. **Telephone:** (318) 274-6566. **Baseball SID:** Ryan McGinty. **Telephone:** (318) 274-6562. **Fax:** (318) 274-2761.

HARTFORD HAWKS

Conference: America East.

Mailing Address: Sports Center, 200 Bloomfield Ave., West Hartford, CT 6117. **Website:** www.hartfordhawks.com.

Head Coach: Jeff Calcaterra. **Assistant Coaches:** Inaki Ormeacha, *Mike Susi. **Telephone:** (860) 768-5760. **Baseball SID:** Dan Ruede. **Telephone:** (860) 768-4501. **Fax:** (860) 768-4068.

HARVARD CRIMSON

Conference: Ivy League (Rolfe).

Mailing Address: 65 North Harvard St, Boston, MA 02163. **Website:** www.gocrimson.com.

Head Coach: Joe Walsh. **Assistant Coaches:** Gary Donovan, Tom Lo Ricco. **Telephone:** (617) 495-2629. **Baseball SID:** Kurt Svoboda. **Telephone:** (617) 495-2206. **Fax:** (617) 495-2130.

HAWAII RAINBOWS

Conference: Western Athletic.

Mailing Address: 1337 Lower Campus Road, Honolulu, HI 96822. **Website:** uhathletics.hawaii.edu.

Head Coach: Mike Trapasso. **Assistant Coaches:** Keith Komeiji, *Chad Konishi. **Telephone:** (808) 956-6247. **Baseball SID:** Pakalani Bello. **Telephone:** (808) 956-7506. **Fax:** (808) 956-3543.

HAWAII-HILO VULCANS

Conference: Independent.

Mailing Address: 200 W. Kawili St., Hilo, HI 96720. **Website:** vulcans.uhh.hawaii.edu.

Head Coach: Joey Estrella. **Assistant Coaches:** John Matson, Clay Daugherty. **Telephone:** (808) 974-7700. **Baseball SID:** Kelly Leong. **Telephone:** (808) 974-7606. **Fax:** (808) 974-7711.

HIGH POINT PANTHERS

Conference: Big South.

Mailing Address: 833 Montlieu Avenue, High Point, NC 27262. **Website:** www.highpointpanthers.com.

Head Coach: Sal Bando. **Assistant Coaches:** Phil Maier, Justin Pinyan, Michael Lowman. **Telephone:** (336) 841-9190. **Baseball SID:** Brian Morgan. **Telephone:** (336) 841-4605. **Fax:** (336) 841-9182.

HOFSTRA PRIDE

Conference: Colonial Athletic.

Mailing Address: 230 Hofstra University PFC 223, Hempstead, NY 11549. **Website:** www.hofstra.edu/Athletics/index_Athletics.cfm.

Head Coach: Chris Dotolo. **Assistant Coaches:** Asa Grunewald, Josh Stewart. **Telephone:** (516) 463-5065. **Baseball SID:** Stephen Gorchov. **Telephone:** (516) 463-4933. **Fax:** (516) 463-5033.

HOLY CROSS CRUSADERS

Conference: Patriot.

Mailing Address: One College St., Worcester, MA 01610. **Website:** goholycross.com.

Head Coach: Greg DiCenzo. **Assistant Coaches:** Jeff Miller, Chris King, Kevin Gately. **Telephone:** (508) 793-2753. **Baseball SID:** Charles Bare. **Telephone:** (508) 793-2583. **Fax:** (508) 793-2309.

HOUSTON COUGARS

Conference: Conference USA.

Mailing Address: 3100 Cullen Blvd., Houston, TX 77204. **Website:** UHCougars.com.

Head Coach: Rayner Noble. **Assistant Coaches:** Abe Arguello, *Kirk Blount, Jorge Garza. **Telephone:** (713) 743-9396. **Baseball SID:** Jeff Conrad. **Telephone:** (713) 743-9410. **Fax:** (713) 743-9411.

Home Field: Cougar Field. **Seating Capacity:** 3,500. **Outfield Dimension:** LF—330, CF—390, RF—330. **Press Box Telephone:** (713) 743-0840.

ILLINOIS FIGHTING ILLINI

Conference: Big Ten.

Mailing Address: Bielfeldt Bldg. 1700 S. Fourth St., Champaign, IL 61820. **Website:** www.fightingillini.com.

Head Coach: Dan Hartleb. **Assistant Coaches:** Brett Herbison, *Eric Snider, Ken Westray. **Telephone:** (217) 333-8605. **Baseball SID:** Ben Taylor. **Telephone:** (217) 244-5045. **Fax:** (217) 333-5540.

Home Field: Illinois Field. **Seating Capacity:** 1,500. **Outfield Dimension:** LF—330, CF—400, RF—330. **Press Box Telephone:** (217) 333-1227.

ILLINOIS STATE REDBIRDS

Conference: Missouri Valley.

Mailing Address: Illinois State University, Athletics Media Relations, Campus Box 7130, Normal, IL 61790-7130. **Website:** GoRedbirds.com.

Head Coach: Jim Brownlee. **Assistant Coaches:** *Tim Brownlee, Mike Current. **Telephone:** (309) 438-5151. **Baseball SID:** John Sandberg. **Telephone:** (309) 438-3249. **Fax:** (309) 438-5634.

Home Field: Redbird Field. **Seating Capacity:** 1,500. **Outfield Dimension:** LF—330, CF—400, RF—330. **Press Box Telephone:** (309) 438-3504.

ILLINOIS-CHICAGO FLAMES

Conference: Horizon.

Mailing Address: 839 W. Roosevelt Road Mail Code 195, Chicago, IL 60608. **Website:** uicflames.cstv.com.

Head Coach: Mike Dee. **Assistant Coaches:** Mike Hughes, Sean McDermott, *Mike Nall. **Telephone:** (312) 996-8645. **Baseball SID:** John Jaramillo. **Telephone:** (312) 996-5880. **Fax:** (312) 996-8349.

Home Field: Les Miller Field. **Seating Capacity:** 1,000. **Outfield Dimension:** LF—331, CF—401, RF—331. **Press Box Telephone:** (312) 355-1190.

INDIANA HOOSIERS

Conference: Big Ten.

Mailing Address: 1001 East 17th St, Bloomington, IN 47408. **Website:** iuhoosiers.com.

Head Coach: Tracy Smith. **Assistant Coaches:** Ty Neal, *Sheldon Watkins. **Telephone:** (812) 855-1680. **Baseball SID:** Matt Brady. **Telephone:** (812) 856-0215. **Fax:** (812) 855-9399.

Home Field: Sembower Field. **Seating Capacity:** 1,000. **Outfield Dimension:** LF—333, CF—400, RF—333. **Press Box Telephone:** (812) 855-4787.

INDIANA STATE SYCAMORES

Conference: Missouri Valley.

Mailing Address: Baseball Office, Indiana State University, Terre Haute, IN 47809. **Website:** gosycamores.com.

Head Coach: Lindsay Meggs. **Assistant Coaches:** Brian Hoop, Chris Smart. **Telephone:** (812) 237-4051. **Baseball SID:** John Sherman. **Telephone:** (812) 237-4185. **Fax:** (812) 237-4157.

INDIANA-PURDUE UNIVERSITY-FORT WAYNE MASTODONS

Conference: Independent.

Mailing Address: 2101 Coliseum Blvd., Fort Wayne, IN 46805. **Website:** gomastodons.com.

Head Coach: Billy Gernon. **Assistant Coaches:** Brent Alwine, Caleb Smith. **Telephone:** (260) 481-5480. **Baseball SID:** Rudy Yovich. **Telephone:** (260) 481-6646. **Fax:** (260) 481-6002.

IONA GAELS

Conference: Metro Atlantic.

Mailing Address: 715 North Avenue, New Rochelle, NY 10801. **Website:** icgaels.com.

Head Coach: Pat Carey. **Assistant Coaches:** Brandon Mann, Chuck Todd. **Telephone:** (914) 633-2319. **Baseball SID:** Brian Beyrer. **Telephone:** (914) 633-2334. **Fax:** (914) 633-2072.

IOWA HAWKEYES

Conference: Big Ten.

Mailing Address: 232 Carver-Hawkeye Arena, Iowa City, IA 52242. **Website:** hawkeyesports.com.

Head Coach: Jack Dahm. **Assistant Coaches:** Ryan Brownlee, Nick Zumsande, Kris Welker. **Telephone:** (319) 335-9329. **Baseball SID:** Phil Haddy. **Telephone:** (319) 335-9411. **Fax:** (319) 335-9417.

JACKSON STATE TIGERS

Conference: Southwestern Athletic.

Mailing Address: 1400 John R. Lynch Street, Jackson, MS 39217. **Website:** www.jsutigers.com.

Head Coach: Omar Johnson. **Assistant Coach:** Eliseo Herrera. **Telephone:** (601) 979-3930. **Baseball SID:** Wesley Peterson. **Telephone:** (601) 979-5899. **Fax:** (601) 979-2000.

JACKSONVILLE DOLPHINS

Conference: Atlantic Sun.

Mailing Address: 2800 University Blvd North, Jacksonville, FL 32211. **Website:** judolphins.com.

Head Coach: Terry Alexander. **Assistant Coaches:** Chris Hayes, *Tim Montez, Les Wright. **Telephone:** (904) 256-7412. **Baseball SID:** Josh Ellis. **Telephone:** (904) 256-7402. **Fax:** (904) 256-7424.

JACKSONVILLE STATE GAMECOCKS

Conference: Ohio Valley.

Mailing Address: 700 Pelham Road North, Jacksonville, AL 36265. **Website:** www.jsugamecocksports.com.

Head Coach: Jim Case. **Assistant Coaches:** Steve Gillespie, Travis Janssen. **Telephone:** (256) 782-5367. **Baseball SID:** Greg Seitz. **Telephone:** (256) 782-5279. **Fax:** (256) 782-5958.

JAMES MADISON DUKES

Conference: Colonial Athletic.

Mailing Address: MSC 2301, James Madison University Baseball, Harrisonburg, VA 22807. **Website:** jmusports.com.

Head Coach: Joe "Spanky" McFarland. **Assistant Coaches:** Josiah Jones, *Jay Sullenger, Ted White. **Telephone:** (540) 568-3932. **Baseball SID:** Kevin Warner. **Telephone:** (540) 568-6154. **Fax:** (540) 568-3703.

Home Field: Long Field/Mauck Stadium. **Seating Capacity:** 1,200. **Outfield Dimension:** LF—340, CF—400, RF—320. **Press Box Telephone:** (540) 568-6545.

KANSAS JAYHAWKS

Conference: Big 12.

Mailing Address: Allen Fieldhouse, 1651 Naismith Drive, Lawrence, KS 66045. **Website:** www.kuathletics.com.

Head Coach: Ritch Price. **Assistant Coaches:** Kevin Frady, Ryan Graves, *Kevin Tucker. **Telephone:** (785) 864-7907. **Baseball SID:** Mike Cummings. **Telephone:** (785) 864-3575. **Fax:** (785) 864-7944.

Home Field: Hoglund Ballpark. **Seating Capacity:** 2,500. **Outfield Dimension:** LF—330, CF—392, RF—330. **Press Box Telephone:** (785) 864-4037.

KANSAS STATE WILDCATS

Conference: Big 12.

Mailing Address: KSU Baseball, 1800 College Avenue, Manhattan, KS 66501. **Website:** www.kstatesports.com.

Head Coach: Brad Hill. **Assistant Coaches:** Lane Burroughs, *Sean McCann, Craig Ringe. **Telephone:** (785) 532-5723. **Baseball SID:** Ryan Lackey. **Telephone:** (785) 532-7708. **Fax:** (785) 532-6093.

Home Field: Tointon Stadium. **Seating Capacity:** 2,331. **Outfield Dimension:** LF—340, CF—400, RF—325. **Press Box Telephone:** (785) 532-5801.

KENNESAW STATE OWLS

Conference: Atlantic Sun.

Mailing Address: 1000 Chastain Rd., Mailstop 0201, Kennesaw, GA 30144. **Website:** ksuowls.com

Head Coach: Mike Sansing. **Assistant Coaches:** Ryan Coe, Kevin Erminio. **Telephone:** (770) 423-6264. **Baseball SID:** Jason Hanes. **Telephone:** (678) 797-2562. **Fax:** (770) 423-6665

KENT STATE GOLDEN FLASHES

Conference: Mid-American (East).

Mailing Address: PO Box 5190, Kent, OH 44242. **Website:** www.kentstatesports.com.

Head Coach: Scott Stricklin. **Assistant Coaches:** Mike Birkbeck, *Scott Daeley. **Telephone:** (330) 672-8432. **Baseball SID:** Ty Linder. **Telephone:** (330) 672-2254. **Fax:** (330) 672-5978.

Home Field: Olga Mural Field at Schoonover Stadium. **Seating Capacity:** 1,148. **Outfield Dimension:** LF—330, CF—400, RF—320. **Press Box Telephone:** (330) 673-1447.

KENTUCKY WILDCATS

Conference: Southeastern (East).

Mailing Address: 338 Lexington Ave., Joe Craft Center, Lexington, KY 40506. **Website:** www.ukathletics.com.

Head Coach: John Cohen. **Assistant Coaches:** *Brad Bohannon, Gary Henderson, Keith Vorhoff. **Telephone:** (859) 257-8502. **Baseball SID:** Brent Ingram. **Telephone:** (859) 257-8504. **Fax:** (859) 323-4310.

Home Field: Cliff Hagan Stadium. **Seating Capacity:** 3,000. **Outfield Dimension:** LF—340, CF—395, RF—310. **Press Box Telephone:** (859) 257-9011.

LA SALLE EXPLORERS

Conference: Atlantic 10.

Mailing Address: 1900 West Olney Avenue, Box 805, Philadelphia, PA 19141. **Website:** www.goexplorers.com.

Head Coach: Mike Lake. **Assistant Coach:** Toby Fisher. **Telephone:** (215) 951-1995. **Baseball SID:** Marc Mullen. **Telephone:** (215) 951-1633. **Fax:** (215) 951-1694.

LAFAYETTE LEOPARDS

Conference: Patriot.

Mailing Address: Kirby Sports Center, Easton, PA 18042. **Website:** www.GoLeopards.com.

Head Coach: Joe Kinney. **Assistant Coaches:** Rick Clagett, Greg Durrah, Brandt Godshalk. **Telephone:** (610) 330-5476. **Baseball SID:** Phil LaBella. **Telephone:** (610) 330-5123. **Fax:** (610) 330-5519.

Home Field: Class of 1978 Stadium. **Seating Capacity:** 502. **Outfield Dimension:** LF—332, CF—403, RF—335.

LAMAR CARDINALS

Conference: Southland.

Mailing Address: Box 10066, Beaumont, TX 77710. **Website:** lamarcardinals.com.

Head Coach: Jim Galligan. **Assistant Coaches:** Scott Hatten, *Jim Ricklefsen. **Telephone:** (409) 880-8315. **Baseball SID:** Brian Henry. **Telephone:** (409) 880-8329. **Fax:** (409) 880-2338.

LE MOYNE DOLPHINS

Conference: Metro Atlantic.

Mailing Address: 1419 Salt Springs Road, Syracuse, NY 13214. **Website:** www.lemoynedolphins.com.

Head Coach: Steve Owens. **Assistant Coaches:** Peter Hoy, Scott Landers, Bob Nandin. **Telephone:** (315) 445-4415. **Baseball SID:** Kevin McNeill. **Telephone:** (315) 445-4412. **Fax:** (315) 445-4678.

LEHIGH MOUNTAIN HAWKS

Conference: Patriot.

Mailing Address: 641 Taylor St., Bethlehem, PA 18015. **Website:** www.lehighsports.com.

Head Coach: Sean Leary. **Assistant Coaches:** Kyle Collina, John Kochmansky, Bob Shebelsky. **Telephone:** (610) 758-4315. **Baseball SID:** Travis Collins. **Telephone:** (610) 758-5101. **Fax:** (610) 758-4407.

Home Field: Lehigh Baseball Field. **Seating Capacity:** 500. **Outfield Dimension:** LF—320, CF—400, RF—320.

LIBERTY FLAMES

Conference: Big South.

Mailing Address: 1971 University Blvd., Lynchburg, VA 24502. **Website:** www.LibertyFlames.com.

Head Coach: Jim Toman. **Assistant Coaches:** Jeremiah Boles, Scott Jackson, *Nick Schnabel. **Telephone:** (434) 582-2103. **Baseball SID:** Ryan Bomberger. **Telephone:** (434) 582-2292. **Fax:** (434) 582-2076.

Home Field: Worthington Stadium. **Seating Capacity:** 1,000. **Outfield Dimension:** LF—325, CF—390, RF—325. **Press Box Telephone:** (434) 582-2914.

LIPSCOMB BISONS

Conference: Atlantic Sun.

Mailing Address: 3901 Granny White Pike, Nashville, TN 37204. **Website:** lipscombsports.com.

Head Coach: Jeff Forehand. **Assistant Coaches:** Terence McClain, *Brian Ryman, Lantz Wheeler. **Telephone:** (615) 966-5716. **Baseball SID:** Mark McGee. **Telephone:** (615) 966-5862. **Fax:** (615) 966-1806.

LONG BEACH STATE 49ERS (DIRTBAGS)

Conference: Big West.

Mailing Address: 1250 Bellflower Blvd, Long Beach, CA 90840. **Website:** www.longbeachstate.com.

Head Coach: Mike Weathers. **Assistant Coaches:** T.J. Bruce, Jon Strauss, Andy Rojo. **Telephone:** (562) 985-7548. **Baseball SID:** Niall Adler. **Telephone:** (562) 985-7565. **Fax:** (562) 985-1549.

LONG ISLAND BLACKBIRDS

Conference: Northeast.

Mailing Address: One University Plaza, Brooklyn, NY 11201. **Website:** www.liuathletics.com.

Head Coach: Don Maines. **Assistant Coaches:** Josh MacDonald, *Craig Noto, Chris Reyes. **Telephone:** (718) 488-1538. **Baseball SID:** Shawn Sweeney. **Telephone:** (718) 488-1307. **Fax:** (718) 488-3302.

LONGWOOD UNIVERSITY LANCERS

Conference: Independent.

Mailing Address: 201 High Street, Farmville, VA 23909. **Website:** www.longwoodlancers.com.

Head Coach: Charles "Buddy" Bolding. **Assistant Coaches:** *Shawn Abell, Billy Daniels. **Telephone:** (434) 395-2352. **Baseball SID:** Greg Prouty. **Telephone:** (434) 395-2097. **Fax:** (434) 395-2568.

Home Field: Lancer Stadium. **Seating Capacity:** 500. **Outfield Dimension:** LF—335, CF—400, RF—335. **Press Box Telephone:** (434) 395-2710.

LOUISIANA STATE TIGERS

Conference: Southeastern (West).

Mailing Address: LSU Athletic Administration Bldg/ Nicholson Dr. at N. Stadium Dr./Baton Rouge, LA 70894. **Website:** www.LSUsports.net.

Head Coach: Paul Mainieri. **Assistant Coaches:** Cliff Godwin, *Terry Rooney, Javi Sanchez. **Telephone:** (225) 578-4148. **Baseball SID:** Bill Franques. **Telephone:** (225) 578-2527. **Fax:** (225) 578-1861.

Home Field: Alex Box Stadium. **Seating Capacity:** 7,760. **Outfield Dimension:** LF—330, CF—405, RF—330. **Press Box Telephone:** (225) 578-4149.

LOUISIANA TECH BULLDOGS

Conference: Western Athletic.

Mailing Address: 1650 W. Alabama Ave., Ruston, LA 71270. **Website:** www.latechsports.com.

Head Coach: Wade Simoneaux. **Assistant Coaches:** Fran Andermann, *Brian Rountree, Dr. David Szymanski. **Telephone:** (318) 257-4111. **Baseball SID:** Wes Todd. **Telephone:** (318) 257-3144. **Fax:** (318) 257-3757.

Home Field: J.C. **Love Field. Seating Capacity:** 3,000. **Outfield Dimension:** LF—315, CF—385, RF—325. **Press Box Telephone:** (318) 257-3144.

LOUISIANA-LAFAYETTE RAGIN' CAJUNS

Conference: Sun Belt.

Mailing Address: Cox Communications Athletic Center, 201 Reinhardt Drive, Lafayette, LA 70506. **Website:** www.ragincajuns.com.

Head Coach: Tony Robichaux. **Assistant Coaches:** Anthony Babineaux, Chris Domingue, Jason Krug, *John Szefc. **Telephone:** (337) 482-6189. **Baseball SID:** Chris Yandle. **Telephone:** (337) 482-6330. **Fax:** (337) 482-6529.

Home Field: M.L. "Tigue" Moore Field. **Seating Capacity:** 3,755. **Outfield Dimension:** LF—330, CF—400, RF—330. **Press Box Telephone:** (337) 851-2255.

LOUISIANA-MONROE WARHAWKS

Conference: Sun Belt.

Mailing Address: 308 Stadium Drive, Monroe, LA 71209. **Website:** ulmathletics.com.

Head Coach: Jeff Schexnaider. **Assistant Coaches:** Dax Leone, Mike Trahan, Phil Keifenheim. **Telephone:** (318) 342-3591. **Baseball SID:** Adam Prendergast. **Telephone:** (318) 342-5463. **Fax:** (318) 342-5464.

LOUISVILLE CARDINALS

Conference: Big East.

Mailing Address: University of Louisville, Baseball Office,215 Central Ave., Louisville, KY 40292. **Website:** www.UofLSports.com.

Head Coach: Dan McDonnell. **Assistant Coaches:** Xan Barksdale, *Chris Lemonis, Brian Mundorf, Roger Williams. **Telephone:** (502) 852-0103. **Baseball SID:** Sean Moth. **Telephone:** (502) 852-2159. **Fax:** (502) 852-7401.

Home Field: Jim Patterson Stadium. **Seating Capacity:** 2,500. **Outfield Dimension:** LF—330, CF—402, RF—330. **Press Box Telephone:** (502) 852-3700.

LOYOLA MARYMOUNT LIONS

Conference: West Coast.

Mailing Address: 1 LMU Drive, Athletics Department, Los Angeles, CA 90045. **Website:** LMULions.com.

Head Coach: Frank Cruz. **Assistant Coaches:** Scott Walter, Brady Koch. **Telephone:** (310) 338-2949. **Baseball SID:** Tyler Geivett. **Telephone:** (310) 338-7638. **Fax:** (310) 338-5915.

Home Field: George C. Page Stadium. **Seating Capacity:** 600. **Outfield Dimension:** LF—326, CF—413, RF—330. **Press Box Telephone:** (310) 338-3046.

MAINE BLACK BEARS

Conference: America East.

Mailing Address: 5747 Memorial Gym, Orono, ME 04469. **Website:** www.goblackbears.com.

Head Coach: Steve Trimper. **Assistant Coaches:** *Jared Holowaty, Aaron Izaryk, Mark Michaud. **Telephone:** (207) 581-1090. **Baseball SID:** Laura Reed. **Telephone:** (207) 581-3646. **Fax:** (207) 581-3297.

Home Field: Mahaney Diamond. **Seating Capacity:** 4,400. **Outfield Dimension:** LF—330, CF—400, RF—330. **Press Box Telephone:** (207) 581-1049.

MANHATTAN JASPERS

Conference: Metro Atlantic.

Mailing Address: 4513 Manhattan College Pkwy., Riverdale, NY 10471. **Website:** www.gojaspers.com.

Head Coach: Kevin Leighton. **Assistant Coaches:** *Mike Cole, Ryan Darcy, Shawn Tarkington. **Telephone:** (718) 862-7936. **Baseball SID:** Mike Antonaccio. **Telephone:** (718) 862-7228. **Fax:** (718) 862-8020.

Home Field: Van Cortlandt Park. **Seating Capacity:** 500. **Outfield Dimension:** LF—325, CF—398, RF—320.

MARIST RED FOXES

Conference: Metro Atlantic.

Mailing Address: 3399 North Road, Poughkeepsie, NY 12601. **Website:** goredfoxes.com.

Head Coach: Dennis Healy. **Assistant Coaches:** Steve Alhona, Chris Tracz. **Telephone:** (845) 575-3699, ext. 2570. **Baseball SID:** Mike Haase. **Telephone:** (914) 575-3699, ext. **6047. Fax:** (914) 471-0466.

MARSHALL THUNDERING HERD

Conference: Conference USA.

Mailing Address: P.O. Box 1360, Huntington, WV 25715. **Website:** herdzone.com.

Head Coach: Jeff Waggoner. **Assistant Coaches:** Tim Adkins, George Brumfield, Tim Donnelly. **Telephone:** (304) 696-5277. **Baseball SID:** Brandon Parro. **Telephone:** (304) 696-6525. **Fax:** (304) 696-2325.

MARYLAND TERRAPINS

Conference: Atlantic Coast (Atlantic).

Mailing Address: Comcast Center, Terrapin Trail, College Park, MD 20742. **Website:** umterps.com.

Head Coach: Terry Rupp. **Assistant Coaches:** Blaine Brown, Jim Farr. **Telephone:** (301) 314-7122. **Baseball SID:** Joey Flyntz. **Telephone:** (301) 314-8093. **Fax:** (301) 314-9094.

MARYLAND-BALTIMORE COUNTY RETRIEVERS

Conference: America East.

Mailing Address: 1000 Hilltop Cirlce, Baltimore, MD 21250. **Website:** www.umbcretrievers.com.

Head Coach: John Jancuska. **Assistant Coaches:** Joe Michalski, Bob Mumma. **Telephone:** (410) 455-2239. **Baseball SID:** Tim Conway. **Telephone:** (410) 455-1530. **Fax:** (410) 455-3994.

MARYLAND-EASTERN SHORE FIGHTING HAWKS

Conference: Mid-Eastern Athletic.

Mailing Address: William P. Hytch Athletic Center, Backbone Road, Princess Anne, MD 21853. **Website:** umeshawks.com.

Head Coach: William Gardner. **Assistant Coaches:** Mick Bigwood, Dustin Longchamps, Brandon McCabe. **Telephone:** (410) 651-8158. **Baseball SID:** Stan Bradley. **Telephone:** (410) 651-6499. **Fax:** (410) 651-7514.

MASSACHUSETTS MINUTEMEN

Conference: Atlantic 10.

Mailing Address: Baseball Office, 2 Boyden Building, Amherst, MA 01003. **Website:** umassathletics.com.

Head Coach: Mike Stone. **Assistant Coaches:** Ernie May, Mike Sweeney. **Telephone:** (413) 545-3120. **Baseball SID:** David Gunn. **Telephone:** (413) 545-5439. **Fax:** (413) 545-1556.

MCNEESE STATE COWBOYS

Conference: Southland.

Mailing Address: 700 East McNeese, Lake Charles, LA 70607. **Website:** mcneesesports.com.

Interim Head Coach: Terry Burrows. **Assistant Coach:** Jason Gonzales, Bubbs Merrill. **Telephone:** (337) 475-5484. **Baseball SID:** Louis Bonnette. **Telephone:** (337) 475-5207. **Fax:** (337) 475-5202.

MEMPHIS TIGERS

Conference: Conference USA.

Mailing Address: Athletic Office Building Room 207, 570 Normal, Memphis, TN 38152. **Website:** www.gotigersgo.com.

Head Coach: Daron Schoenrock. **Assistant Coaches:** Cory Barton, *Michael Federico, Al Woods, Jerry Zulli. **Telephone:** (901) 678-4137. **Baseball SID:** Jason C. Redd. **Telephone:** (901) 678-4640. **Fax:** (901) 678-4134.

Home Field: Nat Buring Stadium. **Seating Capacity:** 2,000. **Outfield Dimension:** LF—318, CF—379, RF—317. **Press Box Telephone:** 901-678-1301.

MERCER BEARS

Conference: Atlantic Sun.

Mailing Address: 1400 Coleman Ave, Macon, GA 31207. **Website:** www.mercerbears.com.

Head Coach: Craig Gibson. **Assistant Coaches:** Tim Boeth, Danny McMurtry, Ty McGehee. **Telephone:** (478) 301-2396. **Baseball SID:** Aimee Lind. **Telephone:** (478) 301-5218. **Fax:** (478) 301-2061.

MIAMI REDHAWKS

Conference: Mid-American (East).

Mailing Address: 120 Withrow Ct, Oxford, OH 45056. **Website:** www.muredhawks.com.

Head Coach: Dan Simonds. **Assistant Coaches:** *Ben Bachmann, Jeremy Ison, Nick Otte. **Telephone:** (513) 529-6631. **Baseball SID:** Mike Berry. **Telephone:** (513) 529-1601. **Fax:** (513) 529-6729.

Home Field: McKie Field at Hayden Park. **Seating Capacity:** 1,500. **Outfield Dimension:** LF—332, CF—400, RF—343. **Press Box Telephone:** (513) 529-4331.

MIAMI HURRICANES

Conference: Atlantic Coast.

Mailing Address: 5821 San Amaro Drive, Coral Gables, FL 33146. **Website:** www.hurricanesports.com.

Head Coach: Jim Morris. **Assistant Coaches:** J.D. Arteaga, *Gino DiMare, Joe Mercadante. **Telephone:** (305) 284-3248. **Baseball SID:** Kerwin Lonzo. **Telephone:** (305) 284-3248. **Fax:** (305) 284-2807.

Home Field: Mark Light Field. **Seating Capacity:** 3,000. **Outfield Dimension:** LF—330, CF—400, RF—330. **Press Box Telephone:** (305) 284-1231.

MICHIGAN WOLVERINES

Conference: Big Ten.

Mailing Address: 1000 South State Street, Ann Arbor, MI 48109. **Website:** www.mgoblue.com.

Head Coach: Rich Maloney. **Assistant Coaches:** Aaron Hepner, Bob Keller. **Telephone:** (734) 647-4550. **Baseball SID:** Jim Schneider. **Telephone:** (734) 763-4423. **Fax:** (734) 647-1188.

Home Field: Fischer Stadium at Wilpon Baseball Complex. **Seating Capacity:** 3,200. **Outfield Dimension:** LF—315, CF—390, RF—320. **Press Box Telephone:** 734-647-1283.

MICHIGAN STATE SPARTANS

Conference: Big Ten.

Mailing Address: 304 Jenison Fieldhouse, East Lansing, MI 48824. **Website:** msuspartans.com.

Head Coach: David Grewe. **Assistant Coaches:** *Tony Baldwin, Tom Lipari, Danny Lopaze. **Telephone:** (517) 355-4486. **Baseball SID:** Ben Pheglar. **Telephone:** (517) 432-8013. **Fax:** (517) 353-9636.

Home Field: Kobs Field/Oldsmobile Park. **Seating Capacity:** 4,000. **Press Box Telephone:** (517) 353-3009 (Kobs), (517) 485-5307 (Oldsmobile).

MIDDLE TENNESSEE STATE BLUE RAIDERS

Conference: Sun Belt.

Mailing Address: 1301 E. Main St., Murfreesboro, TN 37132. **Website:** GoBlueRaiders.com.

Head Coach: Steve Peterson. **Assistant Coaches:** *Jim McGuire, Mike McLaury. **Telephone:** (615) 898-2450. **Baseball SID:** Jo Jo Freeman. **Telephone:** (615) 898-5270. **Fax:** (615) 898-5626.

Home Field: Reese Smith Field. **Seating Capacity:** 2,600. **Outfield Dimension:** LF—330, CF—390, RF—330. **Press Box Telephone:** (615) 898-2117.

MINNESOTA GOLDEN GOPHERS

Conference: Big Ten.

Mailing Address: 516 15th Ave SE, Bierman Athletic Building, Minneapolis, MN 55455. **Website:** www.gophersports.com.

Head Coach: John Anderson. **Assistant Coaches:** *Rob Fornasiere, Todd Oakes, Lee Swenson. **Telephone:** (612) 625-1060. **Baseball SID:** Steven Geller. **Telephone:** (612) 624-9396. **Fax:** (612) 625-0359.

Home Field: Siebert Field. **Seating Capacity:** 1,100. **Outfield Dimension:** LF—330, CF—380, RF—330. **Press Box Telephone:** (612) 625-4031.

MISSISSIPPI REBELS

Conference: Southeastern (West).

Mailing Address: Ole Miss Baseball Office, University Place, University, MS 38677. **Website:** www.OleMissSports.com.

Head Coach: Mike Bianco. **Assistant Coaches:** Rob Francis, Carl Lafferty, Matt Mossberg, *Rob Reinstetle. **Telephone:** (662) 915-6634. **Baseball SID:** Bill Bunting. **Telephone:** (662) 915-1083. **Fax:** (662) 915-7006.

Home Field: Oxford University Stadium/Swayze Field. **Seating Capacity:** 5,000. **Outfield Dimension:** LF—330, CF—390, RF—330. **Press Box Telephone:** (662) 915-7858.

MISSISSIPPI STATE BULLDOGS

Conference: Southeastern (West).

Mailing Address: MSU Baseball, P.O. Box 5327, Starkville, MS 39762. **Website:** www.mstateathletics.com.

Head Coach: Ron Polk. **Assistant Coaches:** Greg Drye, Wade Hedges, Russ McNickle, *Tommy Raffo. **Telephone:** (662) 325-3597. **Baseball SID:** Joe Dier. **Telephone:** (662) 325-8040. **Fax:** (662) 325-3600.

Home Field: Dudy Noble Field, Polk-Dement Stadium. **Seating Capacity:** 15,000. **Outfield Dimension:** LF—330, CF—390, RF—326. **Press Box Telephone:** (662) 325-3776.

MISSISSIPPI VALLEY STATE DELTA DEVILS

Conference: Southwestern Athletic.

Mailing Address: 14000 Highway 82 West, No. 7246, Itta Bena, MS 38941. **Website:** www.mvsu.edu/athletics/.

Head Coach: Doug Shanks. **Assistant Coach:** Aaron Stevens. **Telephone:** (662) 254-3834. **Baseball SID:** Roderick Mosely. **Telephone:** (662) 254-3011. **Fax:** (662) 254-3639.

MISSOURI TIGERS

Conference: Big 12.

Mailing Address: 100 Mizzou Athletic Training Complex, Columbia, MO 65211. **Website:** mutigers.com.

Head Coach: Tim Jamieson. **Assistant Coaches:** Brian Delunas, Evan Pratte, *Tony Vitello. **Telephone:** (573) 882-0731. **Baseball SID:** Josh Murray. **Telephone:** (573) 882-0711. **Fax:** (573) 882-4720.

Home Field: Taylor Stadium. **Seating Capacity:** 3,000. **Outfield Dimension:** LF—340, CF—400, RF—340. **Press Box Telephone:** (573) 884-8912.

MISSOURI STATE BEARS

Conference: Missouri Valley.

Mailing Address: 901 South National Ave, Springfield, MO 65897. **Website:** www.missouristatebears.com.

Head Coach: Keith Guttin. **Assistant Coaches:** Paul Evans, *Brent Thomas. **Telephone:** (417) 836-5242. **Baseball SID:** Ben Adamson. **Telephone:** (417) 836-5402. **Fax:** (417) 836-4868.

Home Field: Hammons Field. **Seating Capacity:** 8,000. **Outfield Dimension:** LF—315, CF—400, RF—330. **Press Box Telephone:** (417) 832-3029.

MONMOUTH HAWKS

Conference: Northeast.

Mailing Address: 400 Cedar Ave, West Long Branch, NJ 07764. **Website:** www.gomuhawks.com.

Head Coach: Dean Ehehalt. **Assistant Coaches:** Jeff Barbalinardo, Mike Campagna, *Chuck Ristano. **Telephone:** (732) 263-5186. **Baseball SID:** Chris Tobin. **Telephone:** (732) 263-5180. **Fax:** (732) 571-3535.

Home Field: MU Baseball Field. **Outfield Dimension:** LF—325, CF—395, RF—325.

MOREHEAD STATE EAGLES

Conference: Ohio Valley.

Mailing Address: Allen Field, Morehead State University, Morehead, KY 40351. **Website:** www.msueagles.com.

Head Coach: Jay Sorg. **Assistant Coaches:** Rick Parr, Jason Neal. **Telephone:** (606) 783-2882. **Baseball SID:** Randy Stacy. **Telephone:** (606) 783-2500. **Fax:** (606) 783-2550.

MOUNT ST. MARY'S MOUNTAINEERS

Conference: Northeast.

Mailing Address: 16300 Old Emmitsburg Rd., Emmitsburg, MD 21727. **Website:** www.mountathletics.com.

Head Coach: Scott Thomson. **Assistant Coaches:** Tim Brown, Eric Haines, Eric Smith. **Telephone:** (301) 447-3806. **Baseball SID:** Mark Vandergrift. **Telephone:** (301) 447-5384. **Fax:** (301) 447-5300.

MURRAY STATE THOROUGHBREDS

Conference: Ohio Valley.

Mailing Address: 217 Stewart Stadium, Murray, KY 42071. **Website:** www.goracers.com.

Head Coach: Rob McDonald. **Assistant Coaches:** Luke Howard, *Paul Wyczawski. **Telephone:** (270) 809-4892. **Baseball SID:** David Snow. **Telephone:** (270) 809-3351. **Fax:** (270) 809-6814.

NAVY MIDSHIPMEN

Conference: Patriot.

Mailing Address: 566 Brownson Road, Annapolis, MD 21403. **Website:** navysports.com.

Head Coach: Paul Kostacopoulos. **Assistant Coaches:** *Scott Friedholm, Matt Reynolds, Jason Ronai. **Telephone:** (410) 293-5571. **Baseball SID:** Jonathan Maggart. **Telephone:** (410) 293-8771. **Fax:** (410) 293-8954.

Home Field: Terwilliger Brothers Field at Max Bishop Stadium. **Seating Capacity:** 1,500. **Outfield Dimension:** LF—323, CF—397, RF—304. **Press Box Telephone:** (410) 293-5430.

NEBREASKA CORNHUSKERS

Conference: Big 12.

Mailing Address: 403 Line Drive Circle, Lincoln, NE 68588-0123. **Website:** huskers.com.

Head Coach: Mike Anderson. **Assistant Coaches:** *Dave Bingham, Eric Newman, Nate Thompson. **Telephone:** (402) 472-9166. **Baseball SID:** Shamus McKnight. **Telephone:** (402) 472-7771. **Fax:** (402) 472-2005.

Home Field: Hawks Field at Haymarket Park. **Seating Capacity:** 8,486. **Outfield Dimension:** LF—330, CF—405, RF—330. **Press Box Telephone:** (402) 434-6861.

NEVADA WOLF PACK

Conference: Western Athletic.

Mailing Address: Legacy Hall/232, Reno, NV 89557. **Website:** www.nevadawolfpack.com.

Head Coach: Gary Powers. **Assistant Coaches:** Gary McNamara, *Stan Stolte, Jay Uhlman. **Telephone:** (775) 682-6978. **Baseball SID:** Jack Kuestermeyer. **Telephone:** (775) 682-6984. **Fax:** (775) 784-4386.

Home Field: Peccole Park. **Seating Capacity:** 3,000. **Outfield Dimension:** LF—340, CF—400, RF—340. **Press Box Telephone:** (775) 784-1585.

NEVADA-LAS VEGAS REBELS

Conference: Mountain West.

Mailing Address: 4505 Maryland Parkway, Las Vegas, NV 89154. **Website:** unlvrebels.com.

Head Coach: Buddy Gouldsmith. **Assistant Coaches:** Mike Kirby, David Martinez. **Telephone:** (702) 895-3499. **Baseball SID:** Bryan Haines. **Telephone:** (702) 895-3764. **Fax:** (702) 895-0989.

NEW MEXICO LOBOS

Conference: Mountain West.

Mailing Address: Athletic Department, MSC04 2680, 1 University of New Mexico, Albuquerque, NM 87131. **Website:** golobos.com.

Head Coach: Ray Birmingham. **Assistant Coaches:** Ken Jacome, Chad Tidwell. **Telephone:** (505) 925-5720. **Baseball SID:** Judy Willson. **Telephone:** (505) 925-5851. **Fax:** (505) 925-5529.

NEW MEXICO STATE AGGIES

Conference: Western Athletic.

Mailing Address: Regents Row Athletics Complex, MSC 3145, 1 Regents Row, Las Cruces, NM 88001. **Website:** nmstatesports.com.

Head Coach: Rocky Ward. **Assistant Coaches:** Chase Tidwell, Gary Ward. **Telephone:** (505) 646-5813. **Baseball SID:** Tyler Dunkel. **Telephone:** (505) 646-2927. **Fax:** (505) 646-2425.

NEW ORLEANS PRIVATEERS

Conference: Sun Belt.

Mailing Address: Lakefront Arena, New Orleans, LA 70148. **Website:** www.unoprivateers.com.

Head Coach: Tom Walter. **Assistant Coaches:** Kirk Bullinger, Bruce Peddie. **Telephone:** (504) 280-7021. **Baseball SID:** Rob Broussard. **Telephone:** (504) 280-7027. **Fax:** (504) 280-3977.

NEW YORK TECH BEARS

Conference: Independent.

Mailing Address: P.O. Box 8000, Old Westbury, NY 11568. **Website:** www.nyit.edu/athletics.

Head Coach: Bob Hirschfield. **Assistant Coaches:** Mike Caulfield, Ray Giannelli, Ron McKay. **Telephone:** (516) 686-7513. **Baseball SID:** Ben Arcuri. **Telephone:** (516) 686-7504. **Fax:** (516) 686-1219.

NIAGARA EAGLES

Conference: Metro Atlantic.

Mailing Address: P.O. Box 2009, Niagara University, NY 14109. **Website:** www.purpleeagles.com.

Head Coach: Chris Chernisky. **Assistant Coaches:** Rob McCoy, Devin McIntosh. **Telephone:** (716) 286-8624. **Baseball SID:** Ben Heckethorn. **Telephone:** (716) 286-8588. **Fax:** (716) 286-8609.

NICHOLLS STATE COLONELS

Conference: Southland.

Mailing Address: P.O. Box 2032, Thibodaux, LA 70301. **Website:** geauxcolonels.com.

Head Coach: Chip Durham. **Assistant Coaches:** Seth Thibodeaux, Chris Prothro, Ricky Newman. **Telephone:** (985) 448-4808. **Baseball SID:** Brandon Rizzuto. **Telephone:** (985) 448-4281. **Fax:** (985) 448-4924.

NORFOLK STATE SPARTANS

Conference: Mid-Eastern Athletic.

Mailing Address: 700 Park Avenue, Norfolk, VA 23504. **Website:** www.nsuspartans.com.

Head Coach: Claudell Clark. **Assistant Coaches:** Quentin Jones, A.J. Corbin. **Telephone:** (757) 823-8196. **Baseball SID:** Matt Michalec. **Telephone:** (757) 823-2628. **Fax:** (757) 823-8218.

NORTH CAROLINA TAR HEELS

Conference: Atlantic Coast.

Mailing Address: PO Box 2126, Chapel Hill, NC 27514. **Website:** tarheelblue.com.

Head Coach: Mike Fox. **Assistant Coaches:** Scott Forbes, *Chad Holbrook, Matt McCay. **Telephone:** (919) 962-4306. **Baseball SID:** John Martin. **Telephone:** (919) 962-0084. **Fax:** (919) 843-2309.

Home Field: USA Baseball Complex. **Outfield Dimension:** LF—335, CF—400, RF—335.

NORTH CAROLINA A&T AGGIES

Conference: Mid-Eastern Athletic.

Mailing Address: 1601 E. Market St., Moore Gym, Greensboro, NC 27411. **Website:** www.ncataggies.com.

Head Coach: Keith Shumate. **Assistant Coach:** Austin Love. **Telephone:** (336) 334-7371. **Baseball SID:** Brian Holloway. **Telephone:** (336) 334-7141. **Fax:** (336) 334-7181.

NORTH CAROLINA STATE WOLFPACK

Conference: Atlantic Coast.

Mailing Address: Box 8505, Raleigh, NC 27695-8505. **Website:** gopack.com.

Head Coach: Elliott Avent. **Assistant Coaches:** Chris Hart, *Tom Holliday, Brian Ward. **Telephone:** (919) 515-3613. **Baseball SID:** Bruce Winkworth. **Telephone:** (919) 515-1182. **Fax:** (919) 515-2898.

Home Field: Doak Field at Dail Park. **Seating Capacity:** 2,500. **Outfield Dimension:** LF—325, CF—400, RF—330. **Press Box Telephone:** (919) 513-0653.

UNC ASHEVILLE BULLDOGS

Conference: Big South.

Mailing Address: One University Heights, CPO 2600, Asheville, NC 28804. **Website:** www.uncabulldogs.com.

Head Coach: Willie Stewart. **Assistant Coaches:** Bob Fenn, *Tim Perry, Tommy Smith. **Telephone:** (828) 251-6920. **Baseball SID:** Everett Hutto. **Telephone:** (828) 251-6931. **Fax:** (828) 251-6386.

UNC GREENSBORO SPARTANS

Conference: Southern.

Mailing Address: PO Box 26168, Greensboro, NC 27402. **Website:** www.uncgspartans.com

Head Coach: Mike Gaski. **Assistant Coaches:** Chris Roberts, Jamie Athas. **Telephone:** (336) 334-3247. **Baseball SID:** Christy Kramer. **Telephone:** (336) 334-5615. **Fax:** (336) 334-8182.

Home Field: UNCG Baseball Stadium. **Seating Capacity:** 4,000. **Outfield Dimension:** LF—340, CF—405, RF—340. **Press Box Telephone:** (336) 334-5625.

UNC WILMINGTON SEAHAWKS

Conference: Colonial Athletic.

Mailing Address: 601 South College Road, Wilmington, NC 28403. **Website:** www.UNCWsports.com.

Head Coach: Mark Scalf. **Assistant Coaches:** *Randy Hood, Jason Howell, Aaron Smith. **Telephone:** (910) 962-3570. **Baseball SID:** Tom Riordan. **Telephone:** (910) 962-4099. **Fax:** (910) 962-3686.

Home Field: Brooks Field. **Seating Capacity:** 3,500. **Outfield Dimension:** LF—340, CF—380, RF—340. **Press Box Telephone:** (910) 395-5141.

NORTH DAKOTA STATE BISON

Conference: Independent.

Mailing Address: P.O. Box 8505, Raleigh, NC 27695. **Website:** www.gobison.com.

Head Coach: Tod Brown. **Assistant Coaches:** David Pearson, Steve Montgomery, Tyrus Powe. **Telephone:** (701) 231-8853. **Baseball SID:** Ryan Perreault. **Telephone:** (701) 231-8331. **Fax:** (701) 231-8022.

NORTH FLORIDA OSPREYS

Conference: Atlantic Sun.

Mailing Address: 4567 St. John's Bluff Rd. South, Jacksonville, FL 32224. **Website:** www.unfospreys.com.

Head Coach: Dusty Rhodes. **Assistant Coaches:** Damon Olinto, Greg Labbe, *Bob Shepherd. **Telephone:** (904) 620-1556. **Baseball SID:** Tom Strother. **Telephone:** (904) 620-4026. **Fax:** (904) 620-2836.

NORTHEASTERN HUSKIES

Conference: Colonial Athletic.

Mailing Address: 219 Cabot Center, 360 Huntington Ave, Boston, MA 02115. **Website:** www.gonu.com.

Head Coach: Neil McPhee. **Assistant Coaches:** Justin Gordon, Mike Glavine, Patrick Mason. **Telephone:** (617) 373-3657. **Baseball SID:** Jack Grinold. **Telephone:** (617) 373-2691. **Fax:** (617) 373-3152.

NORTHERN COLORADO BEARS

Conference: Independent.

Mailing Address: 251 Butler-Hancock Hall, Box 117, Greeley, CO 80639. **Website:** uncbears.com.

Head Coach: Kevin Smallcomb. **Assistant Coach:** Ryan Strain. **Telephone:** (970) 351-1714. **Baseball SID:** Heather Kennedy. **Telephone:** (970) 351-1065. **Fax:** (970) 351-1995.

NORTHERN ILLINOIS HUSKIES

Conference: Mid-American (West).

Mailing Address: Convocation Center, No. 224A, DeKalb, IL 60115. **Website:** niuhuskies.com.

Head Coach: Ed Mathey. **Assistant Coaches:** Steve Joslyn, Tom Carcione, Ray Napientek. **Telephone:** (815) 753-2225. **Baseball SID:** Donna Turner. **Telephone:** (815) 753-1706. **Fax:** (815) 753-9540.

NORTHERN IOWA PANTHERS

Conference: Missouri Valley.

Mailing Address: UNI-Dome NW Upper, Cedar Falls, IA 50614. **Website:** unipanthers.com.

Head Coach: Rick Heller. **Assistant Coaches:** Scott Brickman, Marty Sutherland. **Telephone:** (319) 273-6323. **Baseball SID:** Josh Lehman. **Telephone:** (319) 273-3642. **Fax:** (319) 273-3602.

NORTHWESTERN WILDCATS

Conference: Big Ten.

Mailing Address: 1501 Central St., Evanston, IL 60208. **Website:** nusports.com.

Head Coach: Paul Stevens. **Assistant Coaches:** Joe Keenan, Gabe RIbas, Tim Stoddard. **Telephone:** (847) 491-4652. **Baseball SID:** Mike Wolf. **Telephone:** (847) 491-7503. **Fax:** (847) 491-8818.

NORTHWESTERN STATE DEMONS

Conference: Southland.

Mailing Address: NSU Athletic Fieldhouse, Natchitoches, LA 71497. **Website:** www.nsudemons.com.

Head Coach: J.P. Davis. **Assistant Coaches:** Jeff McCannon, Bobby Barbier. **Telephone:** (318) 357-4139. **Baseball SID:** Matt Bonnette. **Telephone:** (318) 357-6467. **Fax:** (318) 357-4221.

NOTRE DAME FIGHTING IRISH

Conference: Big East.

Mailing Address: 112 Joyce Center, Notre Dame, IN 46556. **Website:** und.com.

Head Coach: Dave Schrage. **Assistant Coaches:** Sherard Clinkscales, *Scott Lawler, Graham Sikes. **Telephone:** (574) 631-6366. **Baseball SID:** Michael Bertsch. **Telephone:** (574) 631-7516. **Fax:** (574) 631-7941.

Home Field: Frank Eck Stadium. **Seating Capacity:** 2,500. **Outfield Dimension:** LF—331, CF—401, RF—331. **Press Box Telephone:** (574) 631-9018.

OAKLAND GOLDEN GRIZZLIES

Conference: Mid-Continent.

Mailing Address: Athletic Center Building, 2200 N. **Squirrel Rochester, MI 48309. Website:** www.ougrizzlies.com.

Head Coach: John Musachio. **Assistant Coaches:** Alec Moss, Aaron Hines. **Telephone:** (248) 370-4059. **Baseball SID:** Paul Smith. **Telephone:** (248) 370-4008. **Fax:** (248) 370-3056.

OHIO BOBCATS

Conference: Mid-American (East).

Mailing Address: Ohio University, Intercollegiate Athletics, Convocation Center, Athens, OH 45701. **Website:** www.ohiobobcats.com.

Head Coach: Joe Carbone. **Assistant Coaches:** Scott Malinowski, *Andrew See. **Telephone:** (740) 593-1180. **Baseball SID:** Wes Liles. **Telephone:** (740) 597-1784. **Fax:** (740) 597-1838.

Home Field: Bob Wren Stadium. **Seating Capacity:** 4,000. **Outfield Dimension:** LF—340, CF—405, RF—340. **Press Box Telephone:** (740) 593-0526.

OHIO STATE BUCKEYES

Conference: Big Ten.

Mailing Address: Room 124 St. John's Arena/410 Woody Hayes Drive, Columbus, OH 43210. **Website:** www.ohiostate-buckeyes.com.

Head Coach: Bob Todd. **Assistant Coaches:** *Greg Cypret, Eric Parker, Peter Jenkins. **Telephone:** (614) 292-1075. **Baseball SID:** Jerry Emig. **Telephone:** (614) 688-0343. **Fax:** (614) 292-8547.

Home Field: Bill Davis Stadium. **Seating Capacity:** 4,450. **Outfield Dimension:** LF—330, CF—400, RF—330. **Press Box Telephone:** (614) 292-0021.

OKLAHOMA SOONERS

Conference: Big 12.

Mailing Address: 401 W. Imhoff, Norman, OK 73019. **Website:** www.soonersports.com.

Head Coach: Sunny Golloway. **Assistant Coaches:** Mike Bell, *Tim Tadlock. **Telephone:** (405) 325-8354. **Baseball SID:** Craig Moran. **Telephone:** (405) 325-6449. **Fax:** (405) 325-7623.

Home Field: L. Dale Mitchell Ballpark. **Seating Capacity:** 2,700. **Outfield Dimension:** LF—335, CF—411, RF—335. **Press Box Telephone:** (405) 325-8363.

OKLAHOMA STATE COWBOYS

Conference: Big 12.

Mailing Address: 220 Athletics Center, Stillwater, OK 74078. **Website:** www.okstate.com.

Head Coach: Frank Anderson. **Assistant Coaches:** *Greg Evans, Billy Jones. **Telephone:** (405) 744-5849. **Baseball SID:** Wade McWhorter. **Telephone:** (405) 744-7853. **Fax:** (405) 744-7754.

Home Field: Allie P. Reynolds Stadium. **Seating Capacity:** 4,000. **Outfield Dimension:** LF—330, CF—398, RF—330. **Press Box Telephone:** (405) 744-5757.

OLD DOMINION MONCARCHS

Conference: Colonial Athletic.

Mailing Address: Athletic Admin. **Bldg, Norfolk, VA 23529-0201. Website:** www.odusports.com.

Head Coach: Jerry Meyers. **Assistant Coaches:** Nate Goulet, *Ryan Morris. **Telephone:** (757) 683-4230. **Baseball SID:** Carol Hudson Jr. **Telephone:** (757) 683-3395. **Fax:** (757) 683-3119.

Home Field: Bud Metheny Complex. **Seating Capacity:** 2,500. **Outfield Dimension:** LF—375, CF—395, RF—375. **Press Box Telephone:** (757) 683-5036/(757) 683-4142.

ORAL ROBERTS GOLDEN EAGLES

Conference: Mid-Continent.

Mailing Address: 7777 S. Lewis Avenue, Tulsa, OK 74147. **Website:** www.orugoldeneagles.com.

Head Coach: Rob Walton. **Assistant Coaches:** Ryan Folmar, Ryan Neill. Bryan Hickman, Ryan Neill. **Telephone:** (918) 495-7205. **Baseball SID:** Cliff Martin. **Telephone:** (918) 495-7094. **Fax:** (918) 495-7142.

Home Field: J.L. **Johnson Stadium. Seating Capacity:** 2,418. **Outfield Dimension:** LF—330, CF—400, RF—330. **Press Box Telephone:** (918) 495-7165.

OREGON STATE BEAVERS

Conference: Pacific-10.

Mailing Address: 114 Gill Coliseum, Corvallis, OR 97331. **Website:** www.osubeavers.com.

Head Coach: Pat Casey. **Assistant Coaches:** Pat Bailey, *Marty Lees, David Wong. **Telephone:** (541) 737-2825. **Baseball SID:** Hank Hager. **Telephone:** (541) 737-7472. **Fax:** (541) 737-3072.

Home Field: Goss Stadium at Coleman Field. **Seating Capacity:** 3,000. **Outfield Dimension:** LF—330, CF—400, RF—330. **Press Box Telephone:** (541) 737-7475.

PACIFIC TIGERS

Conference: Big West.

Mailing Address: 3601 Pacific Avenue, Stockton, CA 95211. **Website:** pacifictigers.com.

Head Coach: Ed Sprague. **Assistant Coaches:** *Steve Pearse, Jim Yanko. **Telephone:** (209) 946-7309. **Baseball SID:** Glen Sisk. **Telephone:** (209) 946-2289. **Fax:** (209) 946-2757.

Home Field: Klein Family Field. **Seating Capacity:** 2,500. **Outfield Dimension:** LF—317, CF—395, RF—325. **Press Box Telephone:** (209) 946-7668.

PENN STATE NITTANY LIONS

Conference: Big Ten.

Mailing Address: 112 Bryce Jordan Center, University Park, PA 16802. **Website:** www.goPSUsports.com.

Head Coach: Robbie Wine. **Assistant Coaches:** Jason Bell, Eric Folmar. **Telephone:** (814) 863-0239. **Baseball SID:** Matt Beltz. **Telephone:** (814) 865-1757. **Fax:** (814) 863-3165.

Home Field: J.L. Johnson Stadium. **Seating Capacity:** 2,418. **Outfield Dimension:** LF—330, CF—400, RF—330. **Press Box Telephone:** (918) 495-7165.

PENNSYLVANIA QUAKERS

Conference: Ivy League (Gehrig).

Mailing Address: 235 South 33rd Street, Weightman Hall, Philadelphia, PA 19104. **Website:** www.pennathletics.com.

Head Coach: John Cole. **Assistant Coaches:** John Yurkow, Jon Cross. **Telephone:** (215) 898-6282. **Baseball SID:** Chas Dorman. **Telephone:** (215) 898-6128. **Fax:** (215) 898-1747.

Home Field: Meiklejohn Stadium. **Seating Capacity:** 850. **Outfield Dimension:** LF—330, CF—380, RF—330. **Press Box Telephone:** Unavailable.

PEPPERDINE WAVES

Conference: West Coast.

Mailing Address: 24255 Pacific Coast Highway, Malibu, CA 90263. **Website:** www.PepperdineSports.com.

Head Coach: Steve Rodriguez. **Assistant Coaches:** *Rick Hirtensteiner, Sean Kenny. **Telephone:** (310) 506-4371. **Baseball SID:** Roger Horne. **Telephone:** (310) 506-4455. **Fax:** (310) 506-4322.

Home Field: Eddy D. Field Stadium. **Seating Capacity:** 1,800. **Outfield Dimension:** LF—330, CF—400, RF—330. **Press Box Telephone:** (310) 506-4598.

PITTSBURGH PANTHERS

Conference: Big East.

Mailing Address: Fitzgerald Field House, Allequippa and Darragh Street, Pittsburgh, PA 15261. **Website:** pittsburghpanthers.com.

Head Coach: Joe Jordano. **Assistant Coaches:** Joel Dombrowski, *Sean Moran. **Telephone:** (412) 648-8208. **Baseball SID:** Tim Will. **Telephone:** (412) 383-8650. **Fax:** (412) 648-8248.

Home Field: Trees Field. **Seating Capacity:** 500. **Outfield Dimension:** LF—302, CF—400, RF—328. **Press Box Telephone:** (814)242-7103.

PORTLAND PILOTS

Conference: West Coast.

Mailing Address: 5000 North Willamette Boulevard, Portland, OR 97203. **Website:** www.portlandpilots.com.

Head Coach: Chris Sperry. **Assistant Coaches:** Larry Casian, Matt Hollod, Jesse Rodgers. **Telephone:** (503) 943-7707. **Baseball SID:** Adam Linnman. **Telephone:** (503) 943-7731. **Fax:** (503) 943-7242.

PRAIRIE VIEW A&M PANTHERS

Conference: Southwestern Athletic.

Mailing Address: P.O. Box 97, Prairie View, TX 77446. **Website:** www.pvamu.edu/pages/104.asp.

Head Coach: Michael Robertson. **Assistant Coach:** Waskyla Cullivan. **Telephone:** (936) 261-9115. **Baseball SID:** Andrew Roberts. **Telephone:** (936) 261-9106. **Fax:** (936) 857-2395.

PRINCETON TIGERS

Conference: Ivy League (Gehrig).

Mailing Address: PO Box 71, Princeton, NJ 08542. **Website:** www.GoPrincetonTigers.com.

Head Coach: Scott Bradley. **Assistant Coaches:** *Lloyd Brewer, Kevin Leighton, Jeremy Meccage. **Telephone:** (609) 258-5059. **Baseball SID:** Yariv Amir. **Telephone:** (609) 258-5701. **Fax:** (609) 258-2399.

Home Field: Clarke Field. **Seating Capacity:** 2,000. **Outfield Dimension:** LF—325, CF—400, RF—315. **Press Box Telephone:** (609) 258-4849.

PURDUE BOILERMAKERS

Conference: Big Ten.

Mailing Address: Mollenkopf Athletic Center, 1225 Northwestern Avenue, West Lafayette, IN 47907. **Website:**

purduesports.com.

Head Coach: Doug Schreiber. **Assistant Coaches:** Spencer Allen, Jamie Sailors. **Telephone:** (765) 494-3998. **Baseball SID:** Mark Leddy. **Telephone:** (765) 494-3201. **Fax:** (765) 494-0554.

QUINNIPIAC BOBCATS

Conference: Northeast.

Mailing Address: 275 Mount Carmel Ave, Hamden, CT 06518. **Website:** quinnipiacbobcats.com.

Head Coach: Dan Gooley. **Assistant Coaches:** Marc Stonaha, Joe Tonelli. **Telephone:** (203) 582-8966. **Baseball SID:** Ken Sweeten. **Telephone:** (203) 582-8625. **Fax:** (203) 582-5385.

RADFORD HIGHLANDERS

Conference: Big South.

Mailing Address: P.O. Box 6913, Radford, VA 24142. **Website:** www.ruhighlanders.com.

Head Coach: Joe Raccuia. **Assistant Coaches:** Brian Anderson, Allen Rice, Mike Kunigonis. **Telephone:** (540) 831-5881. **Baseball SID:** Drew Dickerson. **Telephone:** (540) 831-5726. **Fax:** (540) 831-5556.

RHODE ISLAND RAMS

Conference: Atlantic 10.

Mailing Address: 3 Keaney Road, Suite One, Kingston, RI 02881. **Website:** gorhody.com.

Head Coach: Jim Foster. **Assistant Coaches:** Steve Breitbach, Eric Cirella. **Telephone:** (401) 874-4550. **Baseball SID:** Jodi Pontbriand. **Telephone:** (401) 874-5356. **Fax:** (401) 874-5354.

RICE OWLS

Conference: Conference USA.

Mailing Address: 6100 Main Street, Houston, TX 77006. **Website:** www.riceowls.com.

Head Coach: Wayne Graham. **Assistant Coaches:** Patrick Hallmark, *David Pierce, Mike Taylor. **Telephone:** (713) 348-8864. **Baseball SID:** John Sullivan. **Telephone:** (713) 348-5636. **Fax:** (713) 348-6019.

Home Field: Reckling Park. **Seating Capacity:** 4,800. **Outfield Dimension:** LF—330, CF—400, RF—330. **Press Box Telephone:** (713) 348-4931.

RICHMOND SPIDERS

Conference: Atlantic 10.

Mailing Address: Robins Center, University of Richmond, Richmond, VA 23173. **Website:** RichmondSpiders.com.

Head Coach: Mark McQueen. **Assistant Coaches:** Joe Frostick, Chad Oxendine, *Ryan Wheeler. **Telephone:** (804) 289-8391. **Baseball SID:** MIke DeGeorge. **Telephone:** (804) 287-6313. **Fax:** (804) 289-8820.

Home Field: Pitt Field. **Seating Capacity:** 600. **Outfield Dimension:** LF—328, CF—390, RF—328. **Press Box Telephone:** (804) 289-8714.

RIDER BRONCS

Conference: Metro Atlantic.

Mailing Address: 2083 Lawrenceville Road, Lawrenceville, NJ 08648. **Website:** www.gobroncs.com.

Head Coach: Barry Davis. **Assistant Coaches:** Jim Carone, Thomas Carr, Jim Maher. **Telephone:** (609) 896-5055. **Baseball SID:** Bud Focht. **Telephone:** (609) 896-5138. **Fax:** (609) 896-0341.

RUTGERS SCARLET KNIGHTS

Conference: Big East.

Mailing Address: 83 Rockafeller Road, Piscataway, NJ 08854. **Website:** www.scarletknights.com.

Head Coach: Fred Hill. **Assistant Coaches:** Jay Blackwell, Darren Fenster, Richard Freeman, Glen Gardner. **Telephone:** (732) 445-7834. **Baseball SID:** Doug Drabik. **Telephone:** (732) 445-4200. **Fax:** (732) 445-3065.

Home Field: Bainton Field. **Seating Capacity:** 1,500. **Outfield Dimension:** LF—330, CF—410, RF—320. **Press Box Telephone:** (732) 921-1067.

SACRAMENTO STATE HORNETS

Conference: Western Athletic.

Mailing Address: 6000 J Street, Sacramento, CA 95819-6099. **Website:** www.hornetsports.com.

Head Coach: John Smith. **Assistant Coaches:** *Don Barbara, Jim Barr, Matt Wilson. **Telephone:** (916) 278-7225. **Baseball SID:** Ryan Bjork. **Telephone:** (916) 278-6896. **Fax:** (916) 278-5429.

Home Field: Hornet Field. **Seating Capacity:** 1,267. **Outfield Dimension:** LF—330, CF—400, RF—330. **Press Box Telephone:** (916) 838-2346.

SACRED HEART PIONEERS

Conference: Northeast.

Mailing Address: 5151 Park Avenue, Fairfield, CT 6825. **Website:** www.sacredheartpioneers.com.

Head Coach: Nick Giaquinto. **Assistant Coaches:** Earl Mathison, Chris Aldrich, Wayne Mazzoni. **Telephone:** (203) 365-7632. **Baseball SID:** Gene Gumbs. **Telephone:** (203) 396-8127. **Fax:** (203) 371-7889.

ST. BONAVENTURE BONNIES

Conference: Atlantic 10.

Mailing Address: Reilly Center, P.O. Box G, St. Bonaventure, NY 14778. **Website:** gobonnies.com.

Head Coach: Larry Sudbrook. **Assistant Coaches:** Nick LaBella, Shane Sudbrook. **Telephone:** (716) 375-2641. **Baseball SID:** Patrick Pierson. **Telephone:** (716) 375-2575. **Fax:** (716) 375-2280.

ST. JOHN'S RED STORM

Conference: Big East.

Mailing Address: 8000 Utopia Parkway, Queens, NY 11439. **Website:** www.redstormsports.com.

Head Coach: Ed Blankmeyer. **Assistant Coaches:** Scott Brown, Mike Hampton, Julio Vega. **Telephone:** (718) 990-6148. **Baseball SID:** Mark Fratto. **Telephone:** (718) 990-6897. **Fax:** (718) 969-8468.

ST. JOSEPH'S HAWKS

Conference: Atlantic 10.

Mailing Address: 5600 City Avenue, Philadelphia, PA 19131. **Website:** sjuhawks.com.

Head Coach: Shawn Pender. **Assistant Coaches:** Aaron Barras, *Greg Manco, Lee Saverio. **Telephone:** (610) 660-1718. **Baseball SID:** Joe Greenwich. **Telephone:** (610) 660-1738. **Fax:** (610) 661-1724.

Home Field: Latshaw-McCarthy Field. **Seating Capacity:** 1,000. **Outfield Dimension:** LF—328, CF—393, RF—328. **Press Box Telephone:** (610) 278-7068 or (610) 637-8582.

ST. LOUIS BILLIKENS

Conference: Atlantic 10.

Mailing Address: 3672 West Pine Mall, St. Louis, MO 63108. **Website:** www.slubillikens.com.

Head Coach: Darin Hendrickson. **Assistant Coaches:** Will Bradley, Danny Jackson, *Kevin Moulder. **Telephone:** (314) 977-3172. **Baseball SID:** Brian Kunderman. **Telephone:** (314)

977-3346. **Fax:** (314) 977-7193.

Home Field: Billiken Sports Center. **Seating Capacity:** 1,000. **Outfield Dimension:** LF—330, CF—403, RF—330. **Press Box Telephone:** (314) 808-4868.

ST. MARY'S GAELS

Conference: West Coast Conference.

Mailing Address: 1928 St. Mary's Rd., Moraga, CA 94575. **Website:** www.smcgaels.com.

Head Coach: Jedd Soto. **Assistant Coaches:** Steve Roberts, Kevin Trochez, *Gabe Zappin. **Telephone:** (925) 631-4637. **Baseball SID:** Rich Davi. **Telephone:** (925) 631-4402. **Fax:** (925) 631-4405.

ST. PETER'S PEACOCKS

Conference: Metro Atlantic.

Mailing Address: 2641 John F. Kennedy Blvd, Jersey City, NJ 07306. **Website:** www.spc.edu/pages/408.asp.

Head Coach: Derek England. **Assistant Coaches:** Martin Craft, Tim Nagurka, Adam Myers. **Telephone:** (201) 761-7319. **Baseball SID:** Dan Drutz. **Telephone:** (201) 761-7316. **Fax:** (201) 761-7301.

SAM HOUSTON STATE BEARKATS

Conference: Southland.

Mailing Address: P.O. Box 2268, Huntsville, TX 77341. **Website:** gobearkats.com.

Head Coach: Mark Johnson. **Assistant Coaches:** Jim Blair, Chris Berry, Phillip Miller. **Telephone:** (936) 294-1731. **Baseball SID:** Paul Ridings. **Telephone:** (936) 294-1764. **Fax:** (936) 294-3538.

SAMFORD BULLDOGS

Conference: Ohio Valley.

Mailing Address: 800 Lakeshore Drive, Birmingham, AL 35229. **Website:** samfordsports.com.

Head Coach: Casey Dunn. **Assistant Coaches:** *Tony David, Mick Fieldbinder, Rucker Taylor. **Telephone:** (205) 726-2134. **Baseball SID:** Joey Mullins. **Telephone:** (205) 726-2799. **Fax:** (205) 726-2545.

Home Field: Joe Lee Griffin Field. **Seating Capacity:** 1,000. **Outfield Dimension:** LF—330, CF—390, RF—335. **Press Box Telephone:** (205) 726-4167.

SAN DIEGO TOREROS

Conference: West Coast.

Mailing Address: 5998 Alcala Park, San Diego, CA 92111. **Website:** www.usdtoreros.com.

Head Coach: Rich Hill. **Assistant Coaches:** Jay Johnson, *Eric Valenzuela, Mark Viramontes. **Telephone:** (619) 260-5953. **Baseball SID:** Chris Loucks. **Telephone:** (619) 260-7930. **Fax:** (619) 260-2990.

Home Field: Cunningham Stadium. **Seating Capacity:** 1,200. **Outfield Dimension:** LF—309, CF—395, RF—329. **Press Box Telephone:** (619) 260-8829.

SAN DIEGO STATE AZTECS

Conference: Mountain West.

Mailing Address: Athletic Department, San Diego, CA 92182. **Website:** www.goaztecs.com.

Head Coach: Tony Gwynn. **Assistant Coaches:** *Rusty Filter, Mark Martinez, Jody Stevens. **Telephone:** (619) 594-6889. **Baseball SID:** Dave Kuhn. **Telephone:** (619) 594-5242. **Fax:** (619) 582-6541.

Home Field: Tony Gwynn Stadium. **Seating Capacity:** 3,000. **Outfield Dimension:** LF—340, CF—410, RF—340. **Press Box Telephone:** (619) 594-4103.

SAN FRANCISCO DONS

Conference: West Coast.

Mailing Address: 2130 Fulton Street, San Francisco, CA 94117. **Website:** www.usfdons.com.

Head Coach: Nino Giarratano. **Assistant Coaches:** Joe Della Cella, *Greg Moore, Troy Nakamura. **Telephone:** (415) 422-2933. **Baseball SID:** Ryan McCrary. **Telephone:** (415) 422-6162. **Fax:** (415) 422-2510.

Home Field: Benedetti Diamond. **Seating Capacity:** 1,500. **Outfield Dimension:** LF—300, CF—400, RF—320.

SAN JOSE STATE SPARTANS

Conference: Western Athletic.

Mailing Address: 1393 South 7th Street, San Jose, CA 95112. **Website:** www.sjsuspartans.com.

Head Coach: Sam Piraro. **Assistant Coaches:** David Pierson, Jeff Pritchard, Justin Santich-Hughes. **Telephone:** (408) 924-1255. **Baseball SID:** Doga Gur. **Telephone:** (408) 924-1211. **Fax:** (408) 924-1291.

Home Field: San Jose Municipal Stadium. **Seating Capacity:** 5,200. **Outfield Dimension:** LF—320, CF—390, RF—320. **Press Box Telephone:** (408) 924-7276.

SANTA CLARA BRONCOS

Conference: West Coast.

Mailing Address: 500 El Camino Real, Santa Clara, CA 95053. **Website:** www.santaclarabroncos.com.

Head Coach: Mark O'Brien. **Assistant Coaches:** Chad Baum, Matt Daily, Shaun Epidendio, *Mike Zirelli. **Telephone:** (408) 554-5267. **Baseball SID:** Sabrina Polidoro. **Telephone:** (408) 554-4659. **Fax:** (408) 554-6942.

Home Field: Stephen Schott Stadium. **Seating Capacity:** 1,500. **Outfield Dimension:** LF—340, CF—402, RF—335. **Press Box Telephone:** (408) 554-5590.

SAVANNAH STATE TIGERS

Conference: Independent.

Mailing Address: 3219 College Street, Savannah, GA 31404. **Website:** www.savstate.edu/Athletics.

Head Coach: Carlton Hardy. **Assistant Coaches:** Tony Miner, Emmanuel Wheeler. **Telephone:** (912) 356-2801. **Baseball SID:** Opio Mashariki. **Telephone:** (912) 356-2446. **Fax:** (912) 353-5287.

SETON HALL PIRATES

Conference: Big East.

Mailing Address: 400 South Orange Ave, South Orange, NJ 07079. **Website:** www.shupirates.com.

Head Coach: Rob Sheppard. **Assistant Coaches:** Phil Cundari, Jim Duffy, Zach Porcello. **Telephone:** (973) 761-9557. **Baseball SID:** Matt Sweeney. **Telephone:** (973) 761-9493. **Fax:** (973) 761-9061.

SIENA SAINTS

Conference: Metro Atlantic.

Mailing Address: 515 Loudon Rd., Loudonville, NY 12211. **Website:** www.sienasaints.com.

Head Coach: Tony Rossi. **Assistant Coaches:** Idris Liasu, *Clint McAuley, Drew Pearce. **Telephone:** (518) 786-5044. **Baseball SID:** Jason Rich. **Telephone:** (518) 783-2411. **Fax:** (518) 783-2992.

Home Field: Siena Field. **Seating Capacity:** 500. **Outfield Dimension:** LF—340, CF—402, RF—325.

SOUTH ALABAMA JAGUARS

Conference: Sun Belt.

Mailing Address: 1209 Mitchell Center, Mobile, AL 36688.

Website: www.usajaguars.com.

Head Coach: Steve Kittrell. **Assistant Coaches:** *Jason Jackson, Alan Luckie, Seth VonBehren. **Telephone:** (251) 460-1397. **Baseball SID:** Jim Stephan. **Telephone:** (251) 454-8032. **Fax:** (251) 460-7297.

Home Field: Eddie Stanky Field. **Seating Capacity:** 4,000. **Outfield Dimension:** LF—330, CF—400, RF—330. **Press Box Telephone:** (251) 461-1842.

SOUTH CAROLINA GAMECOCKS

Conference: Southeastern (East).

Mailing Address: 1300 Rosewood Drive, Columbia, SC 29208. **Website:** www.gamecocksonline.com.

Head Coach: Ray Tanner. **Assistant Coaches:** Mark Calvi, Sammy Esposito, *Monte Lee. **Telephone:** (803) 777-0116. **Baseball SID:** Andrew Kitick. **Telephone:** (803) 777-5257. **Fax:** (803) 777-2967.

Home Field: Sarge Frye Field. **Seating Capacity:** 6,000. **Outfield Dimension:** LF—325, CF—390, RF—325. **Press Box Telephone:** (803) 777-6648.

SOUTH DAKOTA STATE JACKRABBITS

Conference: Independent.

Mailing Address: SDSU Box 2820, Stanley J. Marshall HPER Center, Brookings, SD 57007-1497. **Website:** gojacks.com.

Head Coach: Reggie Christiansen. **Assistant Coaches:** Ritchie Price, Aaron Swick. **Telephone:** (605) 688-5027. **Baseball SID:** Jason Hove. **Telephone:** (605) 688-4623. **Fax:** (605) 688-5999.

Home Field: Erv Huether Field. **Seating Capacity:** 1,000.

SOUTH FLORIDA BULLS

Conference: Big East.

Mailing Address: 4202 E. Fowler Ave., ATH 100, Tampa, FL 33620. **Website:** www.GoUSFBulls.com.

Head Coach: Lelo Prado. **Assistant Coaches:** *Lazer Collazo, Tino Martinez, Greg Parris, Bryant Ward. **Telephone:** (813) 974-2504. **Baseball SID:** Amy Woodruff. **Telephone:** (813) 974-4087. **Fax:** (813) 974-5328.

Home Field: Red McEwen Field. **Seating Capacity:** 1,500. **Outfield Dimension:** LF—340, CF—400, RF—340. **Press Box Telephone:** (813) 974-3604.

SOUTHEAST MISSOURI STATE REDHAWKS

Conference: Ohio Valley.

Mailing Address: One University Plaza, Cape Girardeau, MO 63701. **Website:** gosoutheast.com.

Head Coach: Mark Hogan. **Assistant Coaches:** Chris Cafalone, Jeff Dodson, J.C. Field. **Telephone:** (573) 651-2645. **Baseball SID:** Ron Hines. **Telephone:** (573) 651-2294. **Fax:** (573) 651-2810.

SOUTHEASTERN LOUISIANA LIONS

Conference: Southland.

Mailing Address: 800 Galloway Drive, Hammond, LA 70402. **Website:** www.lionsports.net.

Head Coach: Jay Artigues. **Assistant Coaches:** *Justin Hill, Matt Riser, Luke Weatherford. **Telephone:** (985) 549-3566. **Baseball SID:** Charlie Gillingham. **Telephone:** (985) 549-3774. **Fax:** (985) 549-5389.

Home Field: Alumni Field. **Seating Capacity:** 3,000. **Outfield Dimension:** LF—320, CF—400, RF—320.

SOUTHERN JAGUARS

Conference: Southwestern Athletic.

Mailing Address: P.O. Box 10850, Baton Rouge, LA 70813. **Website:** gojagsports.com.

Head Coach: Roger Cador. **Assistant Coaches:** Fernando Puebla, Russell Revere, Calvin Beal. **Telephone:** (225) 771-2513. **Baseball SID:** Kevin Manns. **Telephone:** (225) 771-2601. **Fax:** (225) 771-4400.

SOUTHERN CALIFORNIA TROJANS

Conference: Pacific-10.

Mailing Address: 3501 Watt Way, Los Angeles, CA 90089. **Website:** usctrojans.com.

Head Coach: Chad Kreuter. **Assistant Coaches:** *Tim Burton, Tom House, Doyle Wilson. **Telephone:** (213) 740-5762. **Baseball SID:** Jason Pommier. **Telephone:** (213) 740-3807. **Fax:** (213) 740-7584.

Home Field: Dedeaux Field. **Seating Capacity:** 2,500. **Outfield Dimension:** LF—335, CF—395, RF—335. **Press Box Telephone:** (213) 748-3449.

SOUTHERN ILLINOIS SALUKIS

Conference: Missouri Valley.

Mailing Address: Saluki Baseball Clubhouse, Southern Illinois University, Carbondale, IL 62901-6702. **Website:** siusalukis.com.

Head Coach: Dan Callahan. **Assistant Coaches:** Greg Andrews, Tim Dixon, *Ken Henderson. **Telephone:** (618) 453-2802. **Baseball SID:** Jeff Honza. **Telephone:** (618) 453-5470. **Fax:** (618) 453-2648.

Home Field: Abe Martin Field. **Seating Capacity:** 2,000. **Outfield Dimension:** LF—340, CF—390, RF—340. **Press Box Telephone:** (618) 453-3794.

SOUTHERN MISSISSIPPI GOLDEN EAGLES

Conference: Conference USA.

Mailing Address: 118 College Drive, No. 5017, Hattiesburg, MS 39406. **Website:** www.southernmiss.com.

Head Coach: Corky Palmer. **Assistant Coaches:** Scott Berry, *Chad Caillet, Graham Martin. **Telephone:** (601) 266-6542. **Baseball SID:** Jason Kirskey. **Telephone:** (601) 266-5332. **Fax:** (601) 266-4507.

Home Field: Pete Taylor Park at Hill Denson Field. **Seating Capacity:** 3,678. **Outfield Dimension:** LF—340, CF—400, RF—340. **Press Box Telephone:** (601) 266-5684.

SOUTHERN UTAH THUNDERBIRDS

Conference: Mid-Continent.

Mailing Address: 351 West University Blvd., Cedar City, UT 84720. **Website:** www.suubirds.com.

Head Coach: David Eldredge. **Assistant Coaches:** Mike Martin, Ryan Fecteau. **Telephone:** (435) 559-5314. **Baseball SID:** Kyle Cottam. **Telephone:** (435) 586-7752. **Fax:** (435) 865-8037.

STANFORD CARDINAL

Conference: Pacific-10.

Mailing Address: Stanford Athletics, Baseball Office, Argilla Family Sports Center, 641 East Campus Drive, Stanford, CA 94305. **Website:** gostanford.com.

Head Coach: Mark Marquess. **Assistant Coaches:** Jeff Austin, Dave Nakama, *Dean Stotz. **Telephone:** (650) 723-4528. **Baseball SID:** Kyle McRae. **Telephone:** (650) 725-2959. **Fax:** (650) 725-2957.

Home Field: Sunken Diamond. **Seating Capacity:** 4,000. **Outfield Dimension:** LF—335, CF—400, RF—335. **Press Box Telephone:** (650) 723-4629.

STEPHEN F. AUSTIN LUMBERJACKS

Conference: Southland.

Mailing Address: PO Box 13010, SFA Station, Nacogdoches, TX 75962. **Website:** www.sfajacks.com.

Head Coach: Donnie Watson. **Assistant Coaches:** *Johnny Cardenas, Chris Connally. **Telephone:** (936) 468-4599. **Baseball SID:** James Dixon. **Telephone:** (936) 468-2606. **Fax:** (936) 468-4593.

STETSON HATTERS

Conference: Atlantic Sun.

Mailing Address: 421 N. Woodland Blvd, Unit 8359, DeLand, FL 32724. **Website:** www.gohatters.com.

Head Coach: Pete Dunn. **Assistant Coaches:** Pat Leach, Mitch Markham, *Garrett Quinn. **Telephone:** (386) 822-8106. **Baseball SID:** Dean Watson. **Telephone:** (386) 822-8130. **Fax:** (386) 822-8132.

Home Field: Melching Field at Conrad Park. **Seating Capacity:** 3,000. **Outfield Dimension:** LF—335, CF—403, RF—335.

STONY BROOK SEAWOLVES

Conference: America East.

Mailing Address: Indoor Sports Complex, Stony Brook, NY 11794. **Website:** goseawolves.com.

Head Coach: Matt Senk. **Assistant Coaches:** *Joe Pennucci, Anthony Stutz. **Telephone:** (631) 632-9226. **Baseball SID:** Jeremy Cohen. **Telephone:** (631) 632-6328. **Fax:** (631) 632-8841.

TEMPLE OWLS

Conference: Atlantic 10.

Mailing Address: 1700 North Broad Street, Philadelphia, PA 19122. **Website:** www.owlsports.com.

Head Coach: Rob Valli. **Assistant Coaches:** Rob DiToma, *Casey Fahy, Joe Thomas. **Telephone:** (215) 204-8639. **Baseball SID:** Kevin Bonner. **Telephone:** (215) 204-9149. **Fax:** (215) 204-7499.

Home Field: Skip Wilson Field. **Seating Capacity:** 1,000. **Outfield Dimension:** LF—330, CF—400, RF—330. **Press Box Telephone:** (979) 458-3604.

TENNESSEE VOLUNTEERS

Conference: Southeastern (East).

Mailing Address: 1720 Volunteer Blvd., Knoxville, TN 37996. **Website:** www.UTsports.com.

Head Coach: Todd Raleigh. **Assistant Coaches:** Fred Corral, Nate Headley, *Bradley LeCroy. **Telephone:** (865) 974-2057. **Baseball SID:** Tom Satkowiak. **Telephone:** (865) 974-4947. **Fax:** (865) 974-1269.

Home Field: Lindsey Nelson Stadium. **Seating Capacity:** 3,712. **Outfield Dimension:** LF—320, CF—404, RF—330. **Press Box Telephone:** (865) 974-3376.

TENNESSEE TECH GOLDEN EAGLES

Conference: Ohio Valley.

Mailing Address: 100 McGee Blvd., Box 5057, Cookeville, TN 38505. **Website:** www.ttusports.com.

Head Coach: Matt Bragga. **Assistant Coaches:** Larry Bragga, Chris Cole, Ryan Haun. **Telephone:** (931) 372-3925. **Baseball SID:** Rob Schabert. **Telephone:** (931) 372-3088. **Fax:** (931) 372-3114.

TENNESSEE-MARTIN SKYHAWKS

Conference: Ohio Valley.

Mailing Address: 1037 Elam Center, Martin, TN 38238. **Website:** www.utmsports.com.

Head Coach: Bubba Cates. **Assistant Coaches:** Brad Goss, Joe Scarano. **Telephone:** (731) 881-7337. **Baseball SID:** Joe Lofaro. **Telephone:** (731) 881-7632. **Fax:** (731) 587-7624.

TEXAS LONGHORNS

Conference: Big 12.

Mailing Address: 2100 San Jacinto Boulevard, 327 Bellmont Hall, Austin, TX 78712. **Website:** www.TexasSports.com.

Head Coach: Augie Garrido. **Assistant Coaches:** *Tommy Harmon, Skip Johnson, Ben King, Clay Van Hook. **Telephone:** (512) 423-3396. **Baseball SID:** Thomas Dick. **Telephone:** (512) 471-6039. **Fax:** (512) 471-6040.

Home Field: UFCU Disch-Falk Field. **Seating Capacity:** 6,700. **Outfield Dimension:** LF—340, CF—400, RF—325. **Press Box Telephone:** (512) 471-1146.

TEXAS A&M AGGIES

Conference: Big 12.

Mailing Address: PO Box 30017, College Station, TX 77842-3017. **Website:** AggieAthletics.com.

Head Coach: Rob Childress. **Assistant Coaches:** Matt Deggs, *Jeremy Talbot, Andy Sawyers. **Telephone:** (979) 845-4810. **Baseball SID:** Matt Simon. **Telephone:** (979) 458-9240. **Fax:** (979) 845-0564.

Home Field: Olsen Field. **Seating Capacity:** 7,053. **Outfield Dimension:** LF—330, CF—400, RF—330. **Press Box Telephone:** (979) 458-3604.

TEXAS A&M CORPUS CHRISTI ISLANDERS

Conference: Independent.

Mailing Address: 6300 Ocean Drive, Unit 5719, Corpus Christi, TX 78412. **Website:** www.goislanders.com.

Head Coach: Scott Malone. **Assistant Coaches:** Jason Alamo, Rusty Miller, *Chris Ramirez. **Telephone:** (361) 825-3413. **Baseball SID:** Aaron Ames. **Telephone:** (361) 825-3411. **Fax:** (361) 825-3218.

Home Field: Chapman Field. **Seating Capacity:** 500.

TEXAS CHRISTIAN HORNED FROGS

Conference: Mountain West.

Mailing Address: 2900 Stadium Dr. Room 104, Forth Worth, TX 76129. **Website:** www.gofrogs.com.

Head Coach: Jim Schlossnagle. **Assistant Coaches:** Randy Mazey, Ryan Shotzberger, *Todd Whitting. **Telephone:** (817) 257-7985. **Baseball SID:** Brandie Davidson. **Telephone:** (817) 257-7969. **Fax:** (817) 257-5362.

Home Field: Lupton Stadium. **Seating Capacity:** 3,500. **Outfield Dimension:** LF—330, CF—400, RF—330. **Press Box Telephone:** (817) 257-7966.

TEXAS SOUTHERN TIGERS

Conference: Southwestern Athletic.

Mailing Address: 3100 Cleburne Street, Houston, TX 77004. **Website:** www.tsu.edu/athletics/index.asp.

Head Coach: Candy Robinson. **Assistant Coach:** Brian White. **Telephone:** (713) 313-7993. **Baseball SID:** Unavailable. **Telephone:** (713) 313-6829. **Fax:** (713) 313-1045.

TEXAS STATE BOBCATS

Conference: Southland.

Mailing Address: 601 University Drive, San Marcos, TX 78666. **Website:** txstatebobcats.com.

Head Coach: Ty Harrington. **Assistant Coaches:** Howard Bushong, Derek Matlock. **Telephone:** (512) 245-8395. **Baseball SID:** Chris Riley. **Telephone:** (512) 245-2988. **Fax:** (512) 245-2967.

TEXAS TECH RED RAIDERS

Conference: Big 12.

Mailing Address: PO Box 43021, Lubbock, TX 79409.

Website: www.texastech.com.

Head Coach: Larry Hays. **Assistant Coaches:** Lance Brown, Daren Hays, Dan Spencer, Trent Petrie. **Telephone:** (806) 742-3355. **Baseball SID:** Blayne Beal. **Telephone:** (806) 742-2770, ext. **270. Fax:** (806) 742-1970.

Home Field: Dan Law Field. **Seating Capacity:** 5,050. **Outfield Dimension:** LF—330, CF—405, RF—305. **Press Box Telephone:** (806) 742-3688.

TEXAS-ARLINGTON MAVERICKS

Conference: Southland.

Mailing Address: 1309 West Mitchell Street, Arlington, TX 76013. **Website:** utamavs.com.

Head Coach: Darin Thomas. **Assistant Coaches:** Jay Sirianni, Mark Flatten. **Telephone:** (817) 272-2542. **Baseball SID:** Darrin Scheid. **Telephone:** (817) 272-5706. **Fax:** (817) 272-5037.

TEXAS-PAN AMERICAN BRONCS

Conference: Independent.

Mailing Address: 1201 West University Drive, Edinburgh, TX 78541. **Website:** utpabroncs.com.

Head Coach: Willie Gawlik. **Assistant Coaches:** Gene Salazar, Patrick Hon. **Telephone:** (956) 381-2235. **Baseball SID:** Kristyna Mancias. **Telephone:** (956) 380-8799. **Fax:** (956) 381-2261.

TEXAS-SAN ANTONIO ROADRUNNERS

Conference: Southland.

Mailing Address: Physical Education Building, One UTSA Circle, San Antonio, TX 78249. **Website:** www.goutsa.com.

Head Coach: Sherman Corbett. **Assistant Coaches:** Mike Clement, Jason Marshall. **Telephone:** (210) 458-4805. **Baseball SID:** Carlos Valdez. **Telephone:** (210) 458-4930. **Fax:** (210) 458-4813.

TOLEDO ROCKETS

Conference: Mid-American (West).

Mailing Address: 2801 West Bancroft Street, Toledo, OH 43606. **Website:** utrockets.com.

Head Coach: Cory Mee. **Assistant Coaches:** Josh Bradford, Oliver Wolcott. **Telephone:** (419) 530-6263. **Baseball SID:** Brian DeBenedictis. **Telephone:** (419) 530-4919. **Fax:** (419) 530-4930.

TOWSON TIGERS

Conference: Colonial Athletic.

Mailing Address: 8000 York Road, Towson, MD 21252-0001. **Website:** www.towsontigers.com.

Head Coach: Mike Gottlieb. **Assistant Coaches:** Mel Bacon, Tony Quaranta, *Scott Roane. **Telephone:** (410) 704-3775. **Baseball SID:** Dan O'Connell. **Telephone:** (410) 704-3102. **Fax:** (410) 704-3861.

Home Field: Schuerholz Park. **Seating Capacity:** 700. **Outfield Dimension:** LF—312, CF—424, RF—302. **Press Box Telephone:** (410) 704-5810.

TROY TROJANS

Conference: Sun Belt.

Mailing Address: 5000 Veterans Stadium Drive, Troy, AL 36082. **Website:** www.TroyTrojans.com.

Head Coach: Bobby Pierce. **Assistant Coaches:** Jeff Crane, *Mark Smartt. **Telephone:** (334) 670-3489. **Baseball SID:** Jason Wright. **Telephone:** (334) 670-5834. **Fax:** (334) 670-5665.

Home Field: Riddle-Pace Field. **Seating Capacity:** 3,000. **Outfield Dimension:** LF—338, CF—400, RF—308. **Press Box Telephone:** (334) 670-5701.

TULANE GREEN WAVE

Conference: Conference USA.

Mailing Address: James W. Wilson, Jr. Center, New Orleans, LA 70118. **Website:** www.TulaneGreenWave.com.

Head Coach: Rick Jones. **Assistant Coaches:** *Mark Kingston, Billy Mohl, Chad Sutter. **Telephone:** (504) 862-8238. **Baseball SID:** Richie Weaver. **Telephone:** (504) 314-7232. **Fax:** (504) 865-5512.

Home Field: Greer Field at Turchin Stadium. **Seating Capacity:** 5,000. **Outfield Dimension:** LF—325, CF—400, RF—325. **Press Box Telephone:** (504) 862-8224.

UTAH UTES

Conference: Mountain West.

Mailing Address: 1825 E. South Campus Drive, Salt Lake City, UT 84112. **Website:** utahutes.com.

Head Coach: Bill Kinneberg. **Assistant Coaches:** Bryan Conger, Bryan Kinneberg, Nate Schlieman. **Telephone:** (801) 581-3526. **Baseball SID:** Andy Seeley. **Telephone:** (801) 581-3771. **Fax:** (801) 581-4358.

UTAH VALLEY STATE WOLVERINES

Conference: Independent.

Mailing Address: 800 W. University Parkway, Orem, UT 84058. **Website:** www.WolverineGreen.com.

Head Coach: Steve Gardner. **Assistant Coaches:** Jeremy Harris, *Eric Madsen. **Telephone:** (801) 863-8647. **Baseball SID:** Clint Burgi. **Telephone:** (801) 863-8644. **Fax:** (801) 863-8813.

Home Field: Wolverine Baseball Stadium. **Seating Capacity:** 5,000. **Outfield Dimension:** LF—312, CF—408, RF—315. **Press Box Telephone:** (801) 362-1548.

VALPARAISO CRUSADERS

Conference: Mid-Continent.

Mailing Address: Athletics-Recreation Center, 1009 Union Street, Valparaiso, IN 46383. **Website:** www.valpo.edu/athletics.

Head Coach: Tracy Woodson. **Assistant Coaches:** *Chris Maliszewski, Brian Schmack. **Telephone:** (219) 464-5239. **Baseball SID:** Ryan Wronkowicz. **Telephone:** (219) 465-5232. **Fax:** (219) 464-5762.

Home Field: Emory G. **Bauer Field. Seating Capacity:** 500. **Outfield Dimension:** LF—330, CF—400, RF—300. **Press Box Telephone:** (615) 320-0436.

VANDERBILT COMMODORES

Conference: Southeastern (East).

Mailing Address: 2601 Jess Neely Drive, Nashville, TN 37212. **Website:** www.vucommodores.com.

Head Coach: Tim Corbin. **Assistant Coaches:** *Erik Bakich, Derek Johnson. **Telephone:** (615) 322-7725. **Baseball SID:** Thomas Samuel. **Telephone:** (615) 343-0020. **Fax:** (615) 343-7064.

Home Field: Hawkins Field. **Seating Capacity:** 2,027. **Outfield Dimension:** LF—310, CF—400, RF—330. **Press Box Telephone:** (615) 320-0436.

VERMONT CATAMOUNTS

Conference: America East.

Mailing Address: 97 Spear St., Burlington, VT 05405. **Website:** www.uvmathletics.com.

Head Coach: Bill Currier. **Assistant Coaches:** *Anthony DeCicco, Jim Farrell. **Telephone:** (802) 656-7701. **Baseball SID:** Bruce Bosley. **Telephone:** (802) 656-1109. **Fax:** (802) 656-8328.

Home Field: Centennial Field. **Seating Capacity:** 4,400.

Outfield Dimension: LF—324, CF—405, RF—320. **Press Box Telephone:** (802) 324-8334.

VILLANOVA WILDCATS

Conference: Big East.

Mailing Address: Jake Nevin Field House, 800 Lancaster Avenue, Villanova, PA 19085. **Website:** villanova.com.

Head Coach: Joe Godri. **Assistant Coaches:** Chris Madonna, Matt Kirby. **Telephone:** (610) 519-4529. **Baseball SID:** David Berman. **Telephone:** (610) 519-4122. **Fax:** (610) 519-7323.

VIRGINIA CAVALIERS

Conference: Atlantic Coast (Coastal).

Mailing Address: PO Box 400828, Charlottesville, VA 22904-4848. **Website:** www.virginiasports.com.

Head Coach: Brian O'Connor. **Assistant Coaches:** Karl Kuhn, *Kevin McMullan, Kyle Werman. **Telephone:** (434) 982-4932. **Baseball SID:** Andy Fledderjohann. **Telephone:** (434) 982-5131. **Fax:** (434) 982-5525.

Home Field: Davenport Field. **Outfield Dimension:** LF—324, CF—405, RF—320. **Press Box Telephone:** (434) 244-4071.

VIRGINIA COMMONWEALTH RAMS

Conference: Colonial Athletic.

Mailing Address: 1300 W. Broad St., Richmond, VA 23284. **Website:** www.vcuathletics.com.

Head Coach: Paul Keyes. **Assistant Coaches:** Lucas Jones, Tim Haynes, *Shawn Stiffler. **Telephone:** (804) 828-4820. **Baseball SID:** Scott Day. **Telephone:** (804) 828-1727. **Fax:** (804) 828-9428.

Home Field: The Diamond. **Seating Capacity:** 12,134. **Outfield Dimension:** LF—330, CF—402, RF—330. **Press Box Telephone:** (302) 593-0115.

VIRGINIA MILITARY INSTITUTE KEYDETS

Conference: Big South.

Mailing Address: Virginia Military Institute, Lexington, VA 24450. **Website:** www.VMIKeydets.com.

Head Coach: Marlin Ikenberry. **Assistant Coaches:** *Ryan Mau, Barry Shelton. **Telephone:** (540) 464-7609. **Baseball SID:** Christian Hoffman. **Telephone:** (540) 464-7514. **Fax:** (540) 464-7583.

Home Field: Gray-Minor Stadium. **Seating Capacity:** 1,400. **Outfield Dimension:** LF—330, CF—395, RF—335. **Press Box Telephone:** (540) 460-6920.

VIRGINIA TECH HOKIES

Conference: Atlantic Coast (Coastal).

Mailing Address: Virginia Tech Athletics, 460 Jamerson Athletic Center (0502), Blacksburg, VA 24061. **Website:** www.hokiesports.com.

Head Coach: Pete Hughes. **Assistant Coaches:** *Mike Gambino, Tom Mackor, Dave Turgeon. **Telephone:** (540) 231-3671. **Baseball SID:** Matt Kovatch. **Telephone:** (540) 231-1894. **Fax:** (540) 231-6984.

Home Field: English Field. **Seating Capacity:** 1,500. **Outfield Dimension:** LF—330, CF—400, RF—330. **Press Box Telephone:** (540) 231-8974.

WAGNER SEAHAWKS

Conference: Northeast.

Mailing Address: One Campus Road, Staten Island, NY 10301. **Website:** wagnerathletics.com.

Head Coach: Joe Litterio. **Assistant Coach:** Jason Jurgens. **Telephone:** (718) 390-3154. **Baseball SID:** Kevin Ross. **Telephone:** (718) 390-3215. **Fax:** (718) 390-3347.

WAKE FOREST DEMON DEACONS

Conference: Atlantic Coast (Atlantic).

Mailing Address: Wake Forest Baseball, P.O. **Box 7346, Winston-Salem, NC 27109. Website:** wakeforestsports.com.

Head Coach: Rick Rembielak. **Assistant Coaches:** Greg Bauer, Marshall Canosa, *Jon Palmieri. **Telephone:** (336) 758-5570. **Baseball SID:** Scott Wortman. **Telephone:** (336) 758-6099. **Fax:** (336) 758-5140.

Home Field: Gene Hooks Stadium. **Seating Capacity:** 2,500. **Outfield Dimension:** LF—340, CF—400, RF—315. **Press Box Telephone:** (336) 758-3731.

WASHINGTON HUSKIES

Conference: Pacific-10.

Mailing Address: Graves Hall, Box 354070, Seattle, WA 98195. **Website:** www.gohuskies.com.

Head Coach: Ken Knutson. **Assistant Coaches:** Tighe Dickinson, Donny Harrel, *Joe Ross. **Telephone:** (206) 616-4335. **Baseball SID:** Jeff Bechthold. **Telephone:** (206) 685-7910. **Fax:** (206) 543-5000.

Home Field: Husky Ballpark. **Seating Capacity:** 1,500. **Outfield Dimension:** LF—327, CF—395, RF—317. **Press Box Telephone:** (206) 685-1994.

WASHINGTON STATE COUGARS

Conference: Pacific-10.

Mailing Address: PO Box 641602, Pullman, WA 99164. **Website:** wsu.edu.

Head Coach: Donnie Marbut. **Assistant Coaches:** Gabe Boruff, *Travis Jewett, Greg Swenson. **Baseball SID:** Craig Lawson.

Home Field: Bailey-Brayton Field. **Seating Capacity:** 3,500. **Outfield Dimension:** LF—340, CF—400, RF—315.

WEST VIRGINIA MOUNTAINEERS

Conference: Big East.

Mailing Address: P.O. **Box 0877, Morgantown, WV 26507. Website:** www.wvu.edu/~sports.

Head Coach: Greg Van Zant. **Assistant Coaches:** Bruce Cameron, Patrick Sherald, Casey Bowling. **Telephone:** (304) 293-2308. **Baseball SID:** Bryan Messerly. **Telephone:** (304) 293-2821. **Fax:** (304) 293-4105.

WESTERN CAROLINA CATAMOUNTS

Conference: Southern.

Mailing Address: Ramsey Center, Cullowhee, NC 28723. **Website:** catamountsports.com.

Head Coach: Bobby Moranda. **Assistant Coaches:** Grant Achilles, Dave Haverstick, Bruce Johnson, *Nick Mingione. **Telephone:** (828) 227-7338. **Baseball SID:** Daniel Hooker. **Telephone:** (828) 227-2339. **Fax:** (828) 227-7688.

Home Field: Childress Field at Hennon Stadium. **Seating Capacity:** 1,500. **Outfield Dimension:** LF—325, CF—390, RF—325. **Press Box Telephone:** (828) 227-7020.

WESTERN ILLINOIS LEATHERNECKS

Conference: Mid-Continent.

Mailing Address: 204 Western Hall, 1 University Circle, Macomb, IL 61455. **Website:** www.wiuathletics.com.

Head Coach: Stan Hyman. **Assistant Coaches:** Brock Bainter, Matt Newquist, *Tom Radz. **Telephone:** (309) 298-1521. **Baseball SID:** Brock Wissmiller. **Telephone:** (309) 298-1133. **Fax:** (309) 298-2060.

Home Field: Alfred D. **Boyer Stadium. Seating Capacity:** 4,000. **Outfield Dimension:** LF—330, CF—400, RF—330. **Press Box Telephone:** (630) 835-6284.

WESTERN KENTUCKY HILLTOPPERS

Conference: Sun Belt.

Mailing Address: 1605 Avenue of Champions, Bowling Green, KY 42101. **Website:** www.wkusports.com.

Head Coach: Chris Finwood. **Assistant Coaches:** Jonathan Haydra, Mike Hnytka, Matt Myers, *Andrew Slater. **Telephone:** (270) 745-2277. **Baseball SID:** Chris Glowacki. **Telephone:** (270) 745-5388. **Fax:** (270) 745-3444.

Home Field: Nick Denes Field. **Seating Capacity:** 2,000. **Outfield Dimension:** LF—330, CF—400, RF—330. **Press Box Telephone:** (270)745-4281.

WESTERN MICHIGAN BRONCOS

Conference: Mid-American (West).

Mailing Address: 1903 West Michigan Avenue, Kalamazoo, MI 49008. **Website:** www.wmubroncos.com.

Head Coach: Randy Ford. **Assistant Coaches:** Scott Demetral, Scott Bates. **Telephone:** (269) 276-3205. **Baseball SID:** Kristin Keirns. **Telephone:** (269) 387-4123. **Fax:** (269) 387-4139.

WICHITA STATE SHOCKERS

Conference: Missouri Valley.

Mailing Address: 1845 Fairmount, Campus Box 18, Wichita, KS 67260-0018. **Website:** www.goshockers.com.

Head Coach: Gene Stephenson. **Assistant Coaches:** Jerod Goodale, *Brent Kemnitz, Jim Thomas. **Telephone:** (316) 978-3636. **Baseball SID:** Tami Cutler. **Telephone:** (316) 978-5559. **Fax:** (316) 978-3336.

Home Field: Eck Stadium-Home of Tyler Field. **Seating Capacity:** 7,851. **Outfield Dimension:** LF—330, CF—390, RF—330. **Press Box Telephone:** (316) 978-3390.

WILLIAM & MARY TRIBE

Conference: Colonial Athletic.

Mailing Address: P.O. **Box 399, Williamsburg, VA 23187. Website:** www.tribeathletics.com.

Head Coach: Frank Leoni. **Assistant Coaches:** Jad Prachniak, Adam Taylor, Kyle Padgett. **Telephone:** (757) 221-3399. **Baseball SID:** Rob Turner. **Telephone:** (757) 221-3370. **Fax:** (757) 221-2989.

WINTHROP EAGLES

Conference: Big South.

Mailing Address: 1162 Eden Terrace Road, Rock Hill, SC 29733. **Website:** www.winthropeagles.com.

Head Coach: Joe Hudak. **Assistant Coaches:** Kyle DiEduardo, *Mike McGuire, Stas Swerdzewski. **Telephone:** (803) 323-2129. **Baseball SID:** Gustave Zanette. **Telephone:** (803) 323-2129. **Fax:** (803) 323-2433.

Home Field: Winthrop Ballpark. **Seating Capacity:** 2,000. **Outfield Dimension:** LF—325, CF—390, RF—325. **Press Box Telephone:** (803) 323-2155.

WISCONSIN-MILWAUKEE PANTHERS

Conference: Horizon.

Mailing Address: P.O. **Box 413, Milwaukee, WI 53201. Website:** uwmpanthers.com.

Head Coach: Scott Doffek. **Assistant Coaches:** Cory Bigler, Dean Haase, Blake Kangas. **Telephone:** (414) 229-5670. **Baseball SID:** Kevin O'Connor. **Telephone:** (414) 229-5674. **Fax:** (414) 229-5749.

WOFFORD TERRIERS

Conference: Southern.

Mailing Address: 429 N. **Church St, Spartanburg, SC 29303. Website:** WoffordTerriers.com.

Head Coach: *Todd Interdonato. **Assistant Coaches:** Dusty Blake, Anthony Dillenger, Nick Jaksa. **Telephone:** (864) 597-4497. **Baseball SID:** Brent Williamson. **Telephone:** (864) 597-4093. **Fax:** (864) 597-4129.

Home Field: Russel C. **King Field. Seating Capacity:** 3,000. **Outfield Dimension:** LF—325, CF—395, RF—325.

WRIGHT STATE RAIDERS

Conference: Horizon.

Mailing Address: 3640 Colonel Glenn HWY, Dayton, OH 45435. **Website:** wsuraiders.cstv.com.

Head Coach: Rob Cooper. **Assistant Coaches:** Kyle Geswein, Garret Holleran, *Greg Lovelady, Dick Molen. **Telephone:** (937) 775-2771. **Baseball SID:** Greg Campbell. **Telephone:** (937) 775-4687. **Fax:** (937) 775-2368.

Home Field: Nischwitz Stadium. **Seating Capacity:** 750. **Outfield Dimension:** LF—330, CF—400, RF—330. **Press Box Telephone:** (937) 602-0326.

XAVIER MUSKETEERS

Conference: Atlantic 10.

Mailing Address: 3800 Victory Parkway, Cincinnati, OH 45207-6114. **Website:** www.goxavier.com.

Head Coach: Scott Googins. **Assistant Coaches:** *J.D. Heilmann, Zach Schmidt. **Telephone:** (513) 745-2891. **Baseball SID:** Jake Linder. **Telephone:** (513) 745-3388. **Fax:** (513) 745-2058.

Home Field: Hayden Field. **Seating Capacity:** 500. **Outfield Dimension:** LF—310, CF—380, RF—310. **Press Box Telephone:** (513) 638-5304.

YALE BULLDOGS

Conference: Ivy League (Rolfe).

Mailing Address: P.O. **Box 208216, New Haven, CT 06520. Website:** yalebulldogs.com.

Head Coach: John Stuper. **Assistant Coaches:** Bill Asermely, John Dorman, Tucker Frawley. **Telephone:** (203) 432-1466. **Baseball SID:** Steve Conn. **Telephone:** (203) 432-1455. **Fax:** (203) 432-1454.

YOUNGSTOWN STATE PENGUINS

Conference: Horizon.

Mailing Address: 1 University Plaza, Youngstown, OH 44555. **Website:** www.ysusports.com.

Head Coach: Rich Pasquale. **Assistant Coaches:** Craig Antush. **Telephone:** (330) 941-3485. **Baseball SID:** John Vogel. **Telephone:** (330) 941-1480. **Fax:** (330) 941-3191.

Home Field: Eastwood Field. **Seating Capacity:** 6,000. **Outfield Dimension:** LF—335, CF—405, RF—335. **Press Box Telephone:** (330) 505-0000 ext. **229.**

AMATEUR & YOUTH

INTERNATIONAL ORGANIZATIONS

INTERNATIONAL OLYMPIC COMMITTEE

Mailing Address: Chateau de Vidy, 1007 Lausanne, Switzerland. **Telephone:** (41-21) 621-6111. **Fax:** (41-21) 621-6216. **Website:** www.olympic.org.

President: Jacques Rogge. **Director, Communications:** Giselle Davies.

Games of the XXIX Olympiad: Aug. 8-24, 2008, at Beijing, China.

U.S. OLYMPIC COMMITTEE

Mailing Address: One Olympic Plaza, Colorado Springs, CO 80909. **Telephone:** (719) 632-5551. **Fax:** (719) 866-4654. **Website:** www.usoc.org.

Chief Executive Officer: Jim Scherr. **Chief Communications Officer:** Darryl Seibel.

INTERNATIONAL BASEBALL FEDERATION

Mailing Address: Avenue de Mon-Repos 24, Case Postale 6099, 1002 Lausanne 5, Switzerland Telephone: (41-21) 318-8240. **Fax:** (41-21) 318-8241. **E-Mail Address:** ibaf@baseball.ch. **Website:** www.baseball.ch.

Year Founded: 1938.

Number of Affiliated National Federations: 116.

Acting President: Tom Peng (Taiwan). **Secretary General:** Eduardo De Bello (Panama). **Treasurer:** Alexander Ratner (Russia). **First Vice President:** Tom Peng (Taiwan). **Second Vice President:** Rodolfo Puente (Cuba). **Third Vice President:** Miguel Pozueta (Spain). **Members, At Large:** Mark Alexander (South Africa), Petr Ditrich (Czech Republic), Paul Seiler (United States). **Ex Officio Member:** Jianguo Hu (China).

Continental Vice Presidents: Africa—Ishola Williams (Nigeria). **America**—Hector Pereyra (Dominican Republic). **Asia**—Nae-Heun Lee (Korea). **Europe**—Martin Miller (Germany). **Oceania**—John Ostermeyer (Australia).

Executive Director: Miquel Ortin. **Communications Manager:** Enzo Di Gesu.

2007 Events

World Youth Championship	Venezuela, August
European Olympic Qualifier	Barcelona, Spain, Sept. 7-16
37th IBAF World Cup	Taiwan, Nov. 5-18
Asian Olympic Qualifier	Taiwan, Nov. 30-Dec. 2

CONTINENTAL ASSOCIATIONS

CONFEDERATION PAN AMERICANA DE BEISBOL (COPABE)

Mailing Address: Calle 3, Francisco Filos, Vista Hermosa, Edificio 74, Planta Baja Local No. 1, Panama City, Panama. **Telephone:** (507) 229-8684. **Fax:** Unavailable. **E-Mail Address:** copabe@sinfo.net.

President: Eduardo De Bello (Panama). **Secretary General:** Hector Pereyra (Dominican Republic).

2007 Events

Junior Championships	Aug. 24-Sept. 2
Olympic Qualifier-Americas	Havana, Cuba, Aug. 21-Sept. 3

AFRICAN BASEBALL/SOFTBALL ASSOCIATION

Mailing Address: Paiko Road, Changaga, Minna, Niger State, PMB 150, Nigeria. **Telephone:** (234-66) 224-555. **Fax:** (234-66) 224-555. **E-Mail Address:** absasecretariat@yahoo.com.

President: Ishola Williams (Nigeria). **Executive Director:** Friday Ichide (Nigeria). **Secretary General:** Fridah Shiroya (Kenya).

BASEBALL FEDERATION OF ASIA

Mailing Address: No. 946-16 Dogok-Dong, Kangnam-Gu, Seoul, 135-270 Korea. **Telephone:** (82-2) 572-8413. **Fax:** (82-2) 572-8416.

President: Nae-Heun Lee (Korea). **Secretary General:** Kyung-Hoon Minn (Korea).

EUROPEAN BASEBALL CONFEDERATION

Mailing Address: Zatopkova 100/2, P.O. Box 40, 160 17 Prague 6 (Czech Republic). **Telephone/Fax:** (420-2) 33017459. **E-Mail Address:** info@baseballeurope.com. **Website:** baseballeurope.com.

President: Martin Miller (Germany). **Secretary General:** Petr Ditrich (Czech Republic).

BASEBALL CONFERERATION OF OCEANIA

Mailing Address: 48 Partridge Way, Mooroolbark, Victoria 3138, Australia. **Telephone:** (61-2) 6214-1236. **Fax:** (61-3) 6214-1926. **E-Mail Address:** bcosecgeneral@baseballoceania.com. **Website:** www.baseballoceania.com.

President: John Ostermeyer (Australia). **Secretary General:** Chet Gray (Australia).

ORGANIZATIONS

INTERNATIONAL GOODWILL SERIES, INC.

Mailing Address: P.O. Box 213, Santa Rosa, CA 95402. **Telephone:** (707) 975-7894. **Fax:** (707) 525-0214. **E-Mail Address:** rwilliams@goodwillseries.org. **Website:** www.goodwillseries.org.

President, Goodwill Series, Inc.: Bob Williams.

17th International Friendship Series (16 and Under): Aug. **8-18, China. Goodwill Series:** Australia, Dec. **14-31.**

INTERNATIONAL SPORTS GROUP

Mailing Address: 11430 Kestrel Rd., Klamath Falls, OR 97601. **Telephone:** (541) 882-4293. **E-Mail Address:** isg-baseball@yahoo.com. **Website:** www.isgbaseball.com.

President: Jim Jones. **Vice President:** Tom O'Connell. **Secretary/Treasurer:** Randy Town.

NATIONAL ORGANIZATIONS

USA BASEBALL

Mailing Address, Corporate Headquarters: P.O. Box 1131, Durham, NC 27702. **Office Address:** 403 Blackwell St., **Durham, NC 27701 Telephone:** (919) 474-8721. **Fax:** (919) 474-8822. **E-Mail Address:** info@usabaseball.com. **Website:** www.usabaseball.com.

President: Mike Gaski. **Secretary General:** Jack Kelly. **Vice President, Treasurer:** Abraham Key. **Vice President, Administration:** Jerry Kindall. **Vice President, Secretary:** Elliott Hopkins. **General Counsel:** Lindsay Burbage.

Executive Director, Chief Executive Officer: Paul Seiler. **General Manager, National Teams:** Eric Campbell. **Director, Baseball Operations:** Ray Darwin. **Assistant Director, Baseball Operations:** Jeff Singer. **Director, Finance:** Miki Partridge. **Director, Marketing/Licensing:** David Perkins. **Director, Champions Program/14U National Team:** Rick Riccobono. **Program Coordinator, Marketing:** Matt Titus. **Program Coordinator, National Team:** Dave Palanzo.

National Members: Amateur Athletic Union (AAU), American Amateur Baseball Congress (AABC), American Baseball Coaches Association (ABCA), American Legion Baseball, Babe Ruth Baseball, Dixie Baseball, Little League Baseball, National Amateur Baseball Federation (NABF), National Association of Intercollegiate Athletics (NAIA), National Baseball Congress (NBC), National Collegiate Athletic Association (NCAA), National Federation of State High School Athletic Associations, National High School Baseball Coaches Association, National Junior College Athletic Association (NJCAA), Police Athletic League (PAL), PONY Baseball, T-Ball USA, United States Specialty Sports Association (USSSA), YMCAs of the USA.

2007 Events

Team USA—Professional Level

37th IBAF World Cup . . . . Taiwan, Nov. 6-18

Team USA—College Level

National Team Trials . . . . June 19-28, various sites
USA/Japan Collegiate Series . . . . July 4-9, Durham, NC
Pan American Games . . . . July 14-19, Rio de Janeiro, Brazil
World Port Tournament . . . . . . Aug. 3-12, The Netherlands

Team USA—Junior Level (18 and under)

Tournament of Stars . . . . June 18-25, Cary, NC
COPABE Championship . . . . August, Mexico

Team USA—Youth Level (16 and under)

Jr. Olympic Champ.—West . . Peoria/Surprise, AZ, June 22-30
Jr. Olympic Champ.—East . . . . Jupiter, FL, June 22-30
National Team Trials . . . . August 4-10, Cary, NC
IBAF World Champ. . . . San Cristobal, Venezuela, Aug. 17-26

BASEBALL CANADA

Mailing Address: 2212 Gladwin Cres., **Suite A7, Ottawa, Ontario K1B 5N1. Telephone:** (613) 748-5606. **FAX:** (613) 748-5767. **E-Mail Address:** info@baseball.ca. **Website:** www.baseball.ca.

Director General: Jim Baba. **Head Coach/Director, National Teams:** Greg Hamilton. **Manager, Baseball Operations:** Andre Lachance. **Manager, Media/Public Relations:** Andre Cormier. **Administrative Coordinator:** Denise Thomas.

2007 Events

Baseball Canada Cup (17 & under) Quebec City, Quebec, Aug. 8-13
COPABE Championship . . . . August, Mexico
2008 Olympic Qualifier . . . . March 2008, TBD

NATIONAL BASEBALL CONGRESS

Mailing Address: P.O. Box 1420, Wichita, KS 67201. **Telephone:** (316) 267-3372. **Fax:** (316) 267-3382.

Year Founded: 1931.

Assistant GM: Josh Robertson. **Tournament Director:** Jerry Taylor. **Sales Manager:** Justin Cole.

2007 NBC World Series (Collegiate, ex-professional, unlimited age): July 29-Aug. **12 at Wichita, KS (Lawrence Dumont Stadium).**

ATHLETES IN ACTION

Mailing Address: 651 Taylor Dr., Xenia, OH 45385. **Telephone:** (937) 352-1000. **Fax:** (937) 352-1245. **E-Mail Address:** baseball@aia.com. **Website:** www.aiabaseball.org.

Director, AIA Baseball: Jason Lester. **U.S. Teams Director:** Chris Beck. **International Teams Director:** John McLaughlin. **General Manager, Great Lakes:** Eddie Lang. **Recruiting Coordinator:** John Scholl. **Athletic Trainer:** Natalie McLaughlin.

SUMMER COLLEGE LEAGUES

NATIONAL ALLIANCE OF COLLEGE SUMMER BASEBALL

Telephone: (508) 801-8741. **E-Mail Address:** pgalop@comcast.net

Executive Director: Paul Galop (Cape Cod Baseball League). **Assistant Executive Directors:** Kim Lance (Great Lakes Summer Collegiate League), David Biery (Valley Baseball League). **Secretary:** Sara Whiting (Florida Collegiate Summer League). **Treasurer:** Jim Phillips (Valley Baseball League).

Member Leagues: Atlantic Collegiate Baseball League, Cape Cod Baseball League, Central Illinois Collegiate League, Florida Collegiate Summer League, Great Lakes Summer Collegiate League, New York Collegiate Baseball League, Southern Collegiate Baseball League, Valley Baseball League.

SUMMER COLLEGIATE BASEBALL ASSOCIATION

Mailing Address: 4900 Waters Edge Dr., Suite 201, Raleigh, NC 27606. **Telephone:** (919) 852-1960. **Fax:** 919-852-1973 E-Mail Address: info@summercollegiatebaseball.com. **Website:** www.summercollegiatebaseball.com.

Affiliated Leagues: Coastal Plain League, Northwoods League, West Coast Collegiate League.

ALASKA BASEBALL LEAGUE

Mailing Address: P.O. Box 240061, Anchorage, AK 99524. **Telephone:** (907) 283-6186.

Year Founded: 1974 (reunited, 1998).

President: Dennis Mattingly (Anchorage Bucs). **First Vice President/Secretary:** Chris Beck (AIA). **League Spokesman:** Mike Baxter. **League Stats:** Dick Lobdell.

Regular Season: 35 league games. **2008 Opening Date:** June 9. **Closing Date:** August 1.

Playoff Format: League champion and second-place finisher qualify for National Baseball Congress World Series.

Roster Limit: 24 plus exemption for Alaska residents. **Player Eligibility Rule:** Players with college eligibility, except drafted seniors.

ANCHORAGE BUCS

Mailing Address: P.O. Box 240061, Anchorage, AK 99524. **Telephone:** (907) 561-2827. **Fax:** (907) 561-2920. **E-Mail Address:** admin@anchoragebucs.com. **Website:** www.anchoragebucs.com. **General Manager:** Dennis Mattingly. **Head Coach:** Mike Garcia (Canada, Calif., **JC).**

ANCHORAGE GLACIER PILOTS

Mailing Address: 207 East Northern Lights Blvd., **Anchorage, AK 99503. Telephone:** (907) 274-3627. **Fax:** (907) 274-3628. **E-Mail Address:** gpilots@alaska.net. **Website:** www.glacierpilots.com. **General Manager:** Jon Dyson. **Head Coach:** Bob Miller (Cuesta, Calif., **JC).**

ATHLETES IN ACTION

Mailing Address: 651 Taylor Dr., Xenia, OH 45385. **Telephone:** (937) 352-1237. **Fax:** (937) 352-1245. **E-Mail Address:** chris.beck@aia.com. **Website:** www.aiabaseball.org. **General Manager:** Chris Beck. **Head Coach:** Chris Beck.

FAIRBANKS ALASKA GOLDPANNERS

Mailing Address: P.O. **Box 71154, Fairbanks, AK 99707. Telephone:** (907) 451-0095, (619) 561-4581. **Fax:** (907) 456-6429. **E-Mail Address:** addennis@cox.net. **Website:** www.goldpanners.com. **General Manager:** Don Dennis. **Head Coach:** Tim Gloyd (Yuba, Calif., **CC).**

MAT-SU MINERS

Mailing Address: P.O. **Box 2690, Palmer, AK 99645. Telephone:** (907) 746-4914. **Fax:** (907) 746-5068. **E-Mail Address:** generalmanager@matsuminers.org. **Website:** www.matsuminers.org. **General Manager:** Pete Christopher. **Head Coach:** Conor Bird (JC of Marin, Calif.).

PENINSULA OILERS

Mailing Address: 601 S. Main St., Kenai, AK 99611. **Telephone:** (907) 283-7133. **Fax:** (907) 283-3390. **E-Mail Address:** shawn@oilersbaseball.com. **Website:** www.oilersbaseball.com. **General Manager:** Shawn Maltby. **Head Coach:** Tom Myers (UC Santa Barbara).

ATLANTIC COLLEGIATE LEAGUE

Mailing Address: 1760 Joanne Drive, Quakertown, PA 18951. **Telephone:** 215-536-5777. **Fax:** 215-536-5177. **E-Mail:** tbonekemper@comcast.net. **Website:** www.acbl-online.com.

Year Founded: 1967.

Commissioner: Ralph Addonizio. **President:** Tom Bonekemper. **Secretary:** Ed Kull. **Treasurer:** Bob Hoffman.

Division Structure: Wolff—Jersey, Kutztown, Lehigh Valley, Quakertown. **Kaiser—**Hampton, Long Island, Metro New York, Peekskill.

Regular Season: 40 games. **2008 Opening Date:** June 1. **Closing Date:** Aug. **15.**

All-Star Game: July 14 at St. **John's University.**

Playoff Format: Top two teams in each division meet in best-of-three semifinals. Winners meet in one-game championship.

Roster Limit: 25 (college-eligible players only).

HAMPTON WHALERS

Mailing Address: P.O. Box 835, Montauk, NY 11954. **Telephone:** (631) 668-3901. **General Manager:** Mike Caulfield. **Head Coach:** Julio Vega..

JERSEY PILOTS

Mailing Address: 401 Timber Dr., Berkeley Heights, NJ 07922. **Telephone:** (908) 464-8042. **E-Mail Address:** jerseypilots1@aol.com. **President/General Manager:** Ben Smookler. **Head Coach:** Ross Trachtenberg.

KUTZTOWN ROCKIES

Mailing Address: 429 Baldy Rd., Kutztown, PA 19530. **Telephone:** (610) 683-5273. **E-Mail Address:** kutztownrockies@aol.com. **President/General Manager:** Jon Yeakel. **Head Coach:** Rich DeLucia.

LEHIGH VALLEY CATZ

Mailing Address: 103 Logan Dr., Easton, PA 18045. **Telephone:** (610) 533-9349. **E-Mail Address:** valleycatz@hotmail.com. **Website:** www.lvcatz.com. **General Manager:** Pat O'Connell. **Head Coach:** Adrian Yaguez.

LONG ISLAND MUSTANGS

Mailing Address: 825 East Gate Blvd., Suite 101, Garden City, NY 11530. **E-Mail Address:** phil.andriola@yahoo.com.

Website: www.limustangsbaseball.com. **General Manager:** Phillip Andriola. **Head Coach:** Bobby Cruz.

METRO NEW YORK CADETS

Mailing Address: 220-55 46 Ave., Bayside, NY 11361. **Telephone:** (917) 882-5904. **Fax:** (718) 225-5695. **E-Mail Address:** metronycadets@aol.com. **General Manager:** Charles Papetti. **Head Coach:** Frank DelGeorge.

PEEKSKILL ROBINS

Mailing Address: P.O. Box 113254, Stamford, CT 06911. **Telephone:** (203) 981-7516. **E-Mail Address:** michaelhalo3131@aol.com. **Website:** www.robinsbaseball.com. **General Manager:** Barry Schechtman. **Head Coach:** Luis Melendez.

QUAKERTOWN BLAZERS

Mailing Address: 510 Buttonwood St., Perkasie, PA 18944. **Telephone:** (215) 257-2645. **General Manager:** Todd Zartman. **Head Coach:** Dennis Robison.

CALIFORNIA COLLEGIATE LEAGUE

Mailing Address: 4299 Carpinteria Ave., Suite 201, Carpinteria, CA 93013. **Telephone:** (805) 684-0657. **Fax:** (805) 684-8596. **Website:** www.calsummerball.com.

Year Founded: 1993.

President: Bill Pintard (Santa Barbara Foresters).

Member Clubs: Clovis Outlaws, Conejo Oaks, Monterey Bay Sox, San Luis Obispo Blues, Santa Barbara Foresters.

Regular Season: 36 games. **2008 Opening Date:** May 31. **Closing Date:** July 29.

Playoff Format: League champion and runner-up advance to NBC World Series.

Roster Limit: 33.

CAL RIPKEN SR. COLLEGIATE LEAGUE

Address: P.O. Box 22471, Baltimore, MD 21203. **Telephone:** (410) 588-9900. **E-Mail:** athompson@crscbl.org. **Website:** www.ripkensrcollegebaseball.org.

Year Founded: 2005.

Commissioner: William Spencer. **Executive Director:** Alex Thompson.

Regular Season: 42 games. **2008 Opening Date:** June 6. **Closing Date:** July 27.

All-Star Game: Unavailable.

Playoff Format: Top two teams meet in championship series.

Roster Limit: 30 (college-eligible players 22 and under).

ALEXANDRIA ACES

Address: 6641 Wakefield Dr., Suite 618, Alexandria, VA 22307. **Telephone:** (202) 465-4830. **E-Mail:** pat@alexandriaaces.org. **Website:** www.alexandriaaces.org. **General Manager:** Brian Midkiff. **Head Coach:** Eric Williams.

BETHESDA BIG TRAIN

Address: P.O. Box 30306, Bethesda, MD 20824. **Telephone:** (301) 983-1006. **Fax:** (301) 652-0691. **E-Mail:** david@bigtrain.org. **Website:** www.bigtrain.org. **General Manager:** David Ireland. **Head Coach:** Sal Colangelo.

COLLEGE PARK BOMBERS

Address: 5033 56th Ave., Hyattsville, MD 20781. **Telephone:** (301) 674-7362. **Fax:** (301) 927-6997. **E-Mail:** collegeparkbombers@gmail.com. **Website:** www.collegeparkbombers.org. **President/Head Coach:** Gene Bovello. **General Manager:** Scott Weaver.

HERNDON BRAVES

Address: P.O. Box 631, Haymarket, VA 20168. **Telephone:** (703) 754-6808. **Fax:** (703) 783-1319. **E-Mail:** herndonbraves@cox.net. **Website:** www.herndonbraves.com. **Administrator:** Lauren Taggart. **Head Coach:** Chris Smith.

MARYLAND REDBIRDS

Address: 10819 Sandringham Rd., Cockeysville, MD 21030. **Telephone:** (410) 823-3399, ext. 118. **Fax:** (410) 823-4144. **E-Mail:** redbird1@hotmail.com. **Website:** www.mdredbirds.com. **General Manager:** Mark Russo. **Head Coach:** Pat Nagle.

ROCKVILLE EXPRESS

Address: P.O. Box 10188, Rockville, MD 20849. **Telephone:** (301) 928-6608. **Fax:** (240) 567-7586. **E-Mail:** shaffer048@hotmail.com. **Website:** www.rockvilleexpress.org. **General Manager:** Jim Kazunas. **Director, Baseball Operations:** Tom Shaffer.

SILVER SPRING-TAKOMA THUNDERBOLTS

Address: 326 Lincoln Ave., Takoma Park, MD 20912. **Telephone:** (301) 270-0598. **E-Mail:** tboltsbaseball@gmail.com. **Website:** www.tbolts.org. **President/General Manager:** Richard O'Connor. **Head Coach:** John Duffy.

YOUSE'S MARYLAND ORIOLES

Address: 6451 St. Phillips Rd., Linthicum, MD 21090. **Telephone:** (443) 690-6550. **E-Mail:** daalbany22@cablespeed.com. **General Manager/Head Coach:** Dean Albany.

CAPE COD LEAGUE

Mailing Address: P.O. Box 266, Harwich Port, MA 02646. **Telephone:** (508) 432-6909. **E-Mail:** info@capecodbaseball.org. **Website:** www.capecodbaseball.org.

Year Founded: 1885.

Commissioner: Paul Galop. **President:** Judy Walden Scarafile. **Senior Vice President:** Jim Higgins. **Vice Presidents:** Phil Edwards, Peter Ford. **Deputy Commissioner:** Richard Sullivan. **Deputy Commissioner/Director, Officiating:** Sol Yas. **Treasurer/Website Manager:** Steven Wilson. **Director, Public Relations/Broadcast Media:** John Garner. **Director, Communications:** Jim McGonigle. **Director, Publications:** Lou Barnicle.

Division Structure: East—Brewster, Chatham, Harwich, Orleans, Yarmouth-Dennis. **West**—Bourne, Cotuit, Falmouth, Hyannis, Wareham.

Regular Season: 44 games. **2008 Opening Date:** June 13. **Closing Date:** Aug. 15.

All-Star Game: July 26 at Chatham.

Playoff Format: Top two teams in each division meet in best-of-three semifinals. **Winners meet in best-of-three series for league championship.**

Roster Limit: 25 (college-eligible players only).

BOURNE BRAVES

Mailing Address: P.O. Box 895, Monument Beach, MA 02553. **Telephone:** (508) 345-1013; (508) 759-7711, ext. 224 **(pressbox in season). Fax:** (508) 759-4062. **E-Mail Address:** mcarrier@uppercapetech.org. **Website:** www.bournebraves.org. **President:** Thomas Fink. **General Manager:** Michael Carrier. **Head Coach:** Harvey Shapiro.

BREWSTER WHITE CAPS

Mailing Address: P.O. Box 2349, Brewster, MA 02631. **Telephone:** (508) 896-7442. **Fax:** (508) 896-9372. **E-Mail Address:** contact@brewsterwhitecaps.com, cgradone@hotmail.com. **Website:** www.brewsterwhitecaps.com. **President:** Claire Gradone. **General Manager:** Ned Monthie. **Head Coach:** Bob Macaluso (Cal State Los Angeles).

CHATHAM A'S

Mailing Address: P.O. Box 428, Chatham, MA 02633. **Telephone:** (508) 945-3841. **Fax:** (508) 945-4787. **E-Mail Address:** cthoms@verizon.net. **Website:** www.chathamas.com. **President:** Arthur Dunn. **General Manager:** Charles Thoms. **Head Coach:** John Schiffner.

COTUIT KETTLEERS

Mailing Address: P.O. Box 411, Cotuit, MA 02635. **Telephone:** (508) 428-3358. **Fax:** (508) 420-5584. **E-Mail Address:** info@kettleers.org. **Website:** www.kettleers.org. **President:** Martha Johnston. **General Manager:** Bruce Murphy. **Head Coach:** Mike Roberts.

FALMOUTH COMMODORES

Mailing Address: P.O. Box 808 Falmouth, MA 02541. **Telephone:** (508) 472-7922. **Fax:** (508) 862-6011. **E-Mail Address:** jreilly@falcommodores.org. **Website:** www.falcommodores.org. **President:** Jerry Reilly. **General Manager:** Dan Dunn. **Head Coach:** Jeff Trundy.

HARWICH MARINERS

Mailing Address: P.O. Box 201, Harwich Port, MA 02646. **Telephone:** (508) 432-2000. **Fax:** (508) 432-5357. **E-Mail Address:** mehendy@comcast.net. **Website:** www.harwichmariners.org. **President:** Mary Henderson. **General Manager:** John Reid. **Head Coach:** Steve Englert (Boston College).

HYANNIS METS

Mailing Address: P.O. Box 852, Hyannis, MA 02601. **Telephone:** (508) 420-0962. **Fax:** (508) 428-8199. **E-Mail Address:** billandmaura@comcast.net. **Website:** www.hyannismets.org. **General Manager:** Bill Bussiere. **Head Coach:** Unavailable.

ORLEANS CARDINALS

Mailning Address: P.O. Box 504, Orleans, MA 02653. **Telephone:** (508) 255-0793. **Fax:** (508) 255-2237. **Website:** www.orleanscardinals.com. **President:** Bob Korn. **General Manager:** Sue Horton. **Head Coach:** Kelly Nicholson.

WAREHAM GATEMEN

Mailing Address: 71 Towhee Rd., Wareham, MA 02571. **Telephone:** (508) 748-0287. **Fax:** (508) 880-2602. **E-Mail Address:** tom@ggflaw.com. **Website:** www.gatemen.org. **President:** John Wylde. **General Manager:** Tom Gay. **Head Coach:** Cooper Farris (Mississippi Gulf Coast CC).

YARMOUTH-DENNIS RED SOX

Mailing Address: P.O. Box 814, South Yarmouth, MA 02664. **Telephone:** (508) 394-9387. **Fax:** (508) 398-2239. **E-Mail Address:** jimmartin321@yahoo.com. **Website:** www.ydredsox.org. **President:** Bob Mayo. **General Manager:** Jim Martin. **Head Coach:** Scott Pickler (Cypress, Calif., **CC).**

CAROLINA VIRGINIA COLLEGIATE LEAGUE

Mailing Address: 155 Serenity Pointe Drive, Kernersville, NC 27284. **Telephone:** (336) 784-9122. **E-Mail Address:** cvcl@triad.rr.com. **Website:** www.cvscl.com.

Year Founded: 2006.

President: Thomas Eaton. **Treasurer:** Tom Dorzweiler.

Member Clubs: Carolina Hurricanes, Catawba Valley Stars, Fuquay-Varina Twins, Garner Orioles, Kernersville Bulldogs, Pulaski Pirates.

Regular Season: 36 games. **2008 Opening Date:** May 31. **Closing Date:** Aug. **11.**

All-Star Game: July 10 at Monroe, N.C.

Playoff Format: Double-elimination tournament.

CENTRAL ILLINOIS COLLEGIATE LEAGUE

Mailing Address: 15951 Thunderbird Ct. Bloomington, IL 61704. **Telephone:** (309) 828-4429. **E-Mail Address:** commissioner@ciclbaseball.com. **Website:** www.ciclbaseball.com.

Year Founded: 1963.

Acting Commissioner: Mike Woods.

Regular Season: 48 games. **2007 Opening Date:** June 7. **Closing Date:** Aug. **11.**

All-Star Game: July 23.

Playoff Format: Single-elimination tournament.

Roster Limit: 24 (college-eligible players only).

DANVILLE DANS

Mailing Address: PO Box 1041 Danville, IL 62834. **Telephone:** (217) 446-5521. **Fax:** (217) 446-9995. **E-Mail Address:** jc@cooketech.net. **General Manager:** Rick Kurth. **Assistant GM:** Jeanie Cooke. **Head Coach:** Pete Paciorek (Principia, Calif., **College).**

DUBOIS COUNTY BOMBERS

Mailing Address: P.O. Box 332, Huntingburg, IN 47542. **Telephone:** (812) 683-3700. **E-Mail Address:** dcbombes@psci.net. **General Manager:** John Bigness. **Head Coach:** Brian Smiley.

DUPAGE DRAGONS

Mailing Address: P.O. Box 3076, Lisle, IL 60532. **Telephone:** (630) 241-2255. **Fax:** (708) 784-1468. **E-Mail Address:** bob@dupagedragons.com. **Website:** www.dupagedragons.com. **General Manager:** Mike Thiessen. **Head Coach:** Mark Viramontes (San Diego).

QUINCY GEMS

Mailing Address: 300 Civic Center Plaza, Quincy, IL 62301. **Telephone:** (217) 223-1000. **Fax:** (217) 223-1330. **E-Mail Address:** mcveygr@quincy.edu. **Website:** www.quincygems.com. **General Manager:** Greg McVey. **Head Coach:** Chris Martin.

SPRINGFIELD SLIDERS

Mailing Address: 1415 North Grand Ave. E, Suite B. **Telephone:** (217) 679-3511. **E-Mail Address:** info@springfieldsliders.com. **Website:** www.springfieldsliders.com. **General Manager:** Darren Feller. **Head Coach:** Dylan Putnam.

CLARK GRIFFITH COLLEGIATE LEAGUE

Mailing Address: 10915 Howland Dr., Reston, VA 20191. **Telephone:** (703) 860-0946. **Fax:** (703) 860-0143. **E-Mail Address:** fannanfj@erols.com. **Website:** www.clarkgriffith-baseball.com.

Year Founded: 1945.

Executive Vice President: Frank Fannan. **Treasurer:** Tom Dellinger. **Vice President/Rules Enforcement:** Byron Zeigler. **Media Director:** Scott Elder.

Regular Season: 40 games. **2007 Opening Date:** June 1. **Closing Date:** July 28.

Playoff Format: Top four teams, double-elimination tournament.

Roster Limit: 25 (college-eligible players only).

BETHESDA BLUECAPS

Mailing Address: 6404 Ruffin Road, Chevy Chase, MD 20815. **Telephone:** (301) 461-0602. **E-Mail Address:** jonassinger@gmail.com. **Website:** www.bluecapsbaseball.com. **General Manager/Head Coach:** Jonas Singer.

DC GRAYS

Mailing Address: 1406-B Leslie Avenue, Alexandria, VA 22301. **Telephone:** (202) 315-6945. **Fax:** (703) 684-9702. **E-Mail Address:** antonio@dcgrays.net. **Website:** www.dcgrays.net. **General Manager:** Antonio Scott. **Head Coach:** Doug Remer.

FAIRFAX NATIONALS

Mailing Address: 1844 Horseback Trail, Vienna, VA 22182. **Telephone:** (703) 201-3346. **E-Mail Address:** garyboss@fairfaxnationals.com. **Website:** www.fairfaxnationals.com. **President:** Jim Beck. **General Manager:** Gary Boss. **Head Coach:** Billy Emerson.

MCLEAN RAIDERS

Mailing Address: 10915 Howland Dr., Herndon, VA 20191. **Telephone:** (301) 447-3806. **E-Mail Address:** dmnel1@verizon.net. **Website:** www.mcelanraiders.com. **General Manager:** Dan Nellum. **Head Coach:** Tim Brown.

VIENNA SENATORS

Mailing Address: 308 Hillwood Ave., Suite G2, Vienna, VA 22046. **Telephone:** (703) 534-5081. **Fax:** (703) 534-5085. **E-Mail Address:** cburr17@hotmail.com. **Website:** www.senatorbaseball.org. **President:** Bill McGillicuddy. **General Manager:** Bob Menefee. **Head Coach:** Chris Burr.

COASTAL PLAIN LEAGUE

Mailing Address: 4900 Waters Edge Dr., Suite 201, Raleigh, NC 27606. **Telephone:** (919) 852-1960. **Fax:** (919) 852-1973. **Website:** www.coastalplain.com.

Year Founded: 1997.

Chairman/CEO: Jerry Petitt. **President/Commissioner:** Pete Bock. **Assistant Commissioner:** Justin Sellers. **Director, Administration:** Cristi Solomon.

Division Structure: North—Edenton, Outer Banks, Peninsula, Petersburg. South—Columbia, Fayetteville, Florence, Wilmington, Wilson. West—Asheboro, Forest City, Gastonia, Martinsville, Thomasville, Wilson.

Regular Season: 56 games (split schedule). **2008 Opening Date:** May 28. **Closing Date:** Aug. 5.

All-Star Game: July 21 at Asheboro.

Playoff Format: Eight-team modified double-elimination tournament, Aug. **10-12.**

Roster Limit: 25 (college-eligible players only).

ASHEBORO COPPERHEADS

Mailing Address: P.O. Box 4006, Asheboro, NC 27204. **Telephone:** (336) 460-7018. **Fax:** (336) 629-2651. **E-Mail Address:** info@teamcopperhead.com. **Website:** www.teamcopperhead.com. **Owner:** Ronnie Pugh. **Co-General Managers:** Aaron Pugh, William Davis. **Head Coach:** Tim Murray.

COLUMBIA BLOWFISH

Mailing Address: P.O. Box 1328, Columbia, SC 29202. **Telephone:** (803) 254-4029. **Fax:** (803) 254-4482. **E-Mail Address:** skip@blowfishbaseball.com. **Website:** www.blowfishbaseball.com. **Owner:** HWS Baseball V (Michael Savit, Bill Shanahan). **General Manager:** Skip Anderson. **Head Coach:** Tim Medlin.

EDENTON STEAMERS

Mailing Address: P.O. Box 86, Edenton, NC 27932. **Telephone:** (252) 482-4080. **Fax:** (252) 482-1717. **E-Mail Address:** edentonsteamers@hotmail.com. **Website:** www.edentonsteamers.com. **Owner:** Edenton-Chowan Community Foundation Inc. **Vice President:** Jackie Laverty. **Head Coach:** Jason Krug (Louisiana-Lafayette).

FAYETTEVILLE SWAMPDOGS

Mailing Address: P.O. Box 64691, Fayetteville, NC 28306. **Telephone:** (910) 426-5900. **Fax:** (910) 426-3544. **E-Mail Address:** info@fayettevilleswampdogs.com. **Website:** www.goswampdogs.com. **Owner:** Lew Handelsman, Darrell Handelsman. **Head Coach/Director, Operations:** Darrell Handelsman.

FLORENCE REDWOLVES

Mailing Address: P.O. Box 809, Florence, SC 29503. **Telephone:** (843) 629-0700. **Fax:** (843) 629-0703. **E-Mail Address:** Jamie@florenceredwolves.com. **Website:** www.florenceredwolves.com. **President:** Kevin Barth. **General Manager:** Jamie Young. **Head Coach:** Wes Davis (UT Tyler).

FOREST CITY OWLS

Mailing Address: P.O. Box 1062, Forest City, NC 28043. **Telephone:** (828) 245-0000. **Fax:** (828) 245-6666. **E-Mail Address:** forestcitybaseball@yahoo.com. **Website:** www.forestcitybaseball.com. **President:** Ken Silver. **General Manager:** James Wolfe. **Head Coach:** Matt Hayes (Limestone, S.C.).

GASTONIA GRIZZLIES

Mailing Address: P.O. Box 177, Gastonia, NC 28053. **Telephone:** (704) 866-8622. **Fax:** (704) 864-6122. **E-Mail Address:** kevin@gastoniagrizzlies.com. **Website:** www.gastoniagrizzlies.com. **President:** Ken Silver. **General Manager:** Jesse Cole. **Head Coach:** Eli Benefield.

MARTINSVILLE MUSTANGS

Mailing Address: P.O. Box 1112, Martinsville, VA 24114. **Telephone:** (276) 632-9913. **Fax:** (276) 656-0404. **E-Mail Address:** mustangsgm28@aol.com. **Website:** www.martinsvillemustangs.com. **General Manager:** Doug Gibson. **Head Coach:** Barry Powell.

OUTER BANKS DAREDEVILS

Mailing Address: P.O. Box 7596, Kill Devil Hills, NC 27948. **Telephone:** (252) 202-1842. **Fax:** (252) 255-0702. **E-Mail Address:** obxdaredevils@yahoo.com. **Website:** www.obxdaredevils.com. **Owner:** Marcus Felton. **General Manager:** Karen Carlsen. **Head Coach:** Robbie Wilson (Francis Marion, S.C.)

PENINSULA PILOTS

Mailing Address: P.O. Box 7376, Hampton, VA 23666. **Telephone:** (757) 245-2222. **Fax:** (757) 245-8030. **E-Mail Address:** hank@peninsulapilots.com. **Website:** www.peninsulapilots.com. **Owner:** Henry Morgan. **General Manager:** Jeffrey Scott. **Head Coach:** Hank Morgan.

PETERSBURG GENERALS

Mailing Address: 1981 Midway Ave., Petersburg, VA 23803. **Telephone:** (804) 722-0141. **Fax:** (804) 733-7370. **E-Mail Address:** pbgenerals@aol.com. **Website:** www.petersburgsports.com/generals. **President:** Larry Toombs. **General Manager, Baseball Operations:** Jeremy Toombs. **Head Coach:** Dave Carfley (California, Pa.).

THOMASVILLE HI-TOMS

Mailing Address: P.O. Box 3035, Thomasville, NC 27360. **Telephone:** (336) 472-8667. **Fax:** (336) 472-7198. **E-Mail Address:** info@hitoms.com. **Website:** www.hitoms.com. **President:** Greg Suire. **General Manager:** Andrew Bradley. **Head Coach:** Matt McCay (North Carolina).

WILMINGTON SHARKS

Mailing Address: P.O. Box 15233, Wilmington, NC 28412. **Telephone:** (910) 343-5621. **Fax:** (910) 343-8932. **E-Mail Address:** info@wilmingtonsharks.com. **Website:** www.wilmingtonsharks.com. **Owners:** Lew Handelsman, Darrell Handelsman. **General Manager:** Chris Reavis. **Head Coach:** Daniel Hersey (St. Leo).

WILSON TOBS

Mailing Address: P.O. Box 633, Wilson, NC 27894. **Telephone:** (252) 291-8627. **Fax:** (252) 291-1224. **E-Mail Address:** wilsontobs@earthlink.net. **Website:** www.wilsontobs.com. **President:** Greg Turnage. **General Manager:** Ben Jones. **Head Coach:** Jeff Steele (Lubbock, Texas, Christian).

FLORIDA COLLEGIATE SUMMER LEAGUE

Mailing Address: 1778 N. Park Ave., Suite 201, Maitland, FL 32751. **Telephone:** (321) 206-9174. **Fax:** (407) 628-8535. **E-Mail Address:** info@floridaleague.com. **Website:** www.floridaleague.com.

Year Founded: 2004.

President: Sara Whiting. **Vice President:** Rob Sitz.

Division Structure: East—Sanford, Orlando, Winter Park. **West**—Clermont, Belleview, Leesburg.

Regular Season: 44 games. **2008 Opening Date:** June 4. **Closing Date:** July 29.

All-Star Game: July 20 at Sanford.

Playoff Format: Six-team, modified double-elimination tournament.

Roster Limit: 25 (college-eligible players only).

BELLEVIEW BULLDOGS

Operated through league office. **E-Mail Address:** belleviewbulldogs@floridaleague.com. **Head Coach:** Ricky Plante (Seminole, Fla., CC).

CLERMONT OUTLAWS

Operated through league office. **E-Mail Address:** clermontoutlaws@floridaleague.com. **President:** Tim Dye. **Head Coach:** Stephen Piercefield (Florida Southern).

LEESBURG LIGHTNING

Mailing Address: 318 South 2nd St., Leesburg, FL 34748 **Telephone:** (352) 728-9885. **E-Mail Address:** leesburglightning@floridaleague.com. **President:** Bruce Ericson. **Head Coach:** Frank Viola.

ORLANDO SUNS

Operated through league office. **E-Mail Address:** orlandosuns@floridaleague.com. **President:** Ken Gordon.. **Head Coach:** Scott Benedict.

SANFORD RIVER RATS

Operated through league office. **E-Mail Address:** sanfordriverrats@floridaleague.com. **President:** Charles Davis. **Head Coach:** Kenne Brown.

WINTER PARK DIAMOND DAWGS

Operated through league office. **E-Mail Address:** winterparkdiamonddawgs@floridaleague.com. **President:** Joe Russell. **Head Coach:** Derek Wolfe (Central Florida).

FLORIDA COLLEGIATE INSTRUCTIONAL LEAGUE

Mailing Address: IMG Academies/Bollettieri Campus, 5500 34th St. W., Bradenton, FL 34210. **Telephone:** (941) 739-7481. **Fax:** (941) 727-2962. **E-Mail Address:** tpluto@gte.net. **Website:** www.floridawoodbat.com.

Year Founded: 2001.

President: Tom Pluto. **Secretary:** Nick Phelps.

League Structure: Six teams play at IMG Academies and Pirate City sites in Brandenton, Fla.

Regular Season: 36 games (split schedule). **2008 Opening Date:** June 14. **Closing Date:** Aug. 3.

All-Star Game: July 14.

Playoff Format: One-game playoff between first- and second-half winners.

Roster Limit: Open. College-eligible players or graduating high school seniors who are recruited or recruited walk-on athletes.

GREAT LAKES LEAGUE

Mailing Address: 133 W. Winter St., Delaware, OH 43015. **Telephone:** (740) 368-3527. **Fax:** (740) 368-3999. **E-Mail Address:** kalance@greatlakesleague.org. **Website:** www.greatlakesleague.org.

Year Founded: 1986.

President, Commissioner: Kim Lance.

Regular Season: 40 games. **2008 Opening Date:** June 13.

Playoff Format: Top six teams meet in double-elimination tournament.

Roster Limit: 28 (college-eligible players only).

ANDERSON SERVANTS

Mailing Address: 8888 Fitness Lane, Fishers, IN, 46038. **Telephone:** (317) 842-2555. **Website:** www.servantsbaseball.com. **General Manager:** Greg Lymberopolous. **Head Coach:** Kyle Rail.

CINCINNATI STEAM

Mailing Address: 2745 Anderson Ferry Rd., Cincinnati, OH 45238. **Telephone:** (513) 922-4272. **Website:** www.cincinnatisteam.com. **General Manager:** Max McLeary. **Head Coach:** Unavailable.

COLUMBUS ALL-AMERICANS

Mailing Address: 50 West Broad St., Suite #700, Columbus, OH 43215. **Telephone:** (614) 620-1734. **Website:** www.all-americans.org. **General Manager/Head Coach:** Brian Mannino.

DELAWARE COWS

Mailing Address: 2379 Sherwood Rd., Bexley, OH 43209. **Telephone:** (614) 237-3837. **Website:** www.delawarecows.com. **General Manager:** Jay Sokol. **Head Coach:** Bruce Heine.

GRAND LAKE MARINERS

Mailing Address: 717 W. Walnut St., Coldwater, OH 45828. **Telephone:** (513) 207-5977. **Website:** www.grand-lakemariners.com. **General Manager:** Wayne Miller. **Head Coach:** Zach Schmidt.

LAKE ERIE MONARCHS

Mailing Address: 26670 Cranden Drive, Perrysburg, OH 43551. **Telephone:** (734) 626-1166. **Website:** www.lakeeriemonarchs.com. **General Manager:** Jim DeSana. **Head Coach:** Copley Gerdes.

LICKING COUNTY SETTLERS

Mailing Address: Department of Physical Education, Denison University, Granville, OH 43023. **Telephone:** (740) 344-1043. **Website:** www.settlersbaseball.com. **General Manager:** Dave Froelich. **Head Coach:** Kyle Sobecki.

LIMA LOCOS

Mailing Address: 3588 South Conant Rd., **Spencerville, OH 45887. Telephone:** (419) 647-5242. **Website:** www.limalocos.com. **General Manager:** Steve Meyer. **Head Coach:** Rob Livchak.

SOUTHERN OHIO COPPERHEADS

Mailing Address: P.O. Box 442, Athens, OH 45701. **Telephone:** (740) 541-9284. **Website:** www.copperheads-baseball.com. **General Manager:** David Palmer. **Head Coach:** Ted Tom.

STARK COUNTY TERRIERS

Mailing Address: 1019 35th St. Northwest, Canton, OH, 44709 **Telephone:** (330) 492-9220. **Website:** www.terriers-baseballclub.com. **General Manager:** Greg Trbovich. **Head Coach:** Eric Bunnell.

XENIA ATHLETES IN ACTION

Mailing Address: 651 Taylor Dr., Xenia, OH 45385. **Telephone:** (937) 352-1239. **E-Mail Address:** john.mclaugh-lin@aia.com. **Website:** www.aiabaseball.org. **General Manager:** John McLaughlin. **Head Coach:** Josh Hulin.

JAYHAWK LEAGUE

Mailing Address: 865 Fabrique, Wichita, KS 67218. **Telephone:** (316) 942-6333. **Fax:** (316) 942-2009. **Website:** www.jayhawkbaseballleague.org.

Year Founded: 1976.

Commissioner: Bob Considine. **President:** J.D. **Schneider. Vice President:** Curt Bieber. **Public Relations/Statistician:** Gary Karr. **Secretary:** Christi Billups.

Regular Season: 48 games. **2008 Opening Date:** Unavailable.

Playoff Format: Top two teams qualify for National Baseball Congress World Series in Wichita, KS.

Roster Limit: 30 to begin season; 28 at midseason.

DERBY TWINS

Mailing Address: 1245 N. Pine Grove, Wichita, KS 67212. **Telephone:** (316) 992-3623. **Fax:** 316-667-2286. **E-mail:** derbytwins@earthlink.net Website: www.derbytwins.com General Manager: Jeff Wells. **Head Coach:** Brandon Stover.

DODGE CITY A'S

Mailing Address: 2914 Center, Dodge City, KS 67801. **Telephone:** 620-339-5231. **E-mail:** no1teammom@hotmail.com General Managers: Mike and Debbie Setzkorn. **Head Coach:** Phil Stevenson.

EL DORADO BRONCOS

Mailing Address: 865 Fabrique, Wichita, KS 67218. **Telephone:** (316) 687-2309. **Fax:** (316) 942-2009. **Website:** www.eldoradobroncos.org. **General Manager:** J.D. **Schneider. Head Coach:** Steve Johnson.

HAYS LARKS

Mailing Address: 2715 Walnut., Hays, KS 67601. **Telephone:** (785) 259-1430. **Fax:** (630) 848-2236. **E-Mail Address:** cbieber@sbcglobal.net. **General Manager:** Curt Bieber. **Head Coach:** Frank Leo.

LIBERAL BEEJAYS

Mailing Address: P.O. Box 793, Liberal, KS 67901. **Telephone:** (620) 624-1904. **Fax:** (620) 624-1906. **General Manager:** Kim Snell.

NEVADA GRIFFONS

Mailing Address: 200 S. Alma, Nevada, MO 64772. **Telephone:** (417) 667-8308. **Fax:** (417) 667-8108. **General Manager:** Jason Meisenheimer.

SOUTHWEST SLASHERS

Mailing Address: 807 2nd Ave., Monett, MO 65708. **Telephone:** (417) 489-0629. **E-Mail:** swright@efcocorp.com. **Website:** www.southwestslashers.com General Manager: Scott Wright. **Head Coach:** Dennis Bilela.

M.I.N.K. LEAGUE

(Missouri, Iowa, Nebraska, Kansas)

Mailing Address: 3350 Chatham Avenue, St. Joseph, MO, 64506. **Telephone:** (660) 646-7484. **Fax:** (660) 646-2107. **Email Address:** jodo1986@aol.com. **Website:** www.min-kleaguebaseball.com.

Year Founded: 1995.

Commissioner: Linden Black. **President:** Ed Crawford. **Vice President:** Bob Steinkamp. **Secretary:** Jim Hamlin.

Regular Season: 30 games. **2008 Opening Date:** May 31. **Closing Date:** July 23.

Playoff Format: Top team qualifies for National Baseball Congress World Series in Wichita.

Roster Limit: None.

BEATRICE BRUINS

Mailing Address: P.O. Box 2, Beatrice, NE 68310. **Telephone:** (402) 223-3081. **E-Mail address:** ksteinkamp@alltel.net. **Website:** www.beatricebaseball.com. **General Manager/Head Coach:** Bob Steinkamp.

CHILLICOTHE MUDCATS

Mailing Address: P.O. Box 1155, Chillicothe, MO 64601.

Telephone: (660) 646-2165. **Fax:** (660) 646-6933. **E-Mail Address:** hitit@chillicothemudcats.com. **Website:** www.chillicothemudcats.com. **General Manager:** Liz Fechtig. **Head Coach:** Jud Kindle.

CLARINDA A'S

Mailing Address: 225 East Lincoln, Clarinda, IA 61632. **Telephone:** (712) 542-4272. **E-Mail Address:** memrse@heartland.net. **Website:** www.clarindaiowa-as-baseball.org. **General Manager:** Merle Eberly. **Head Coach:** Ryan Eberly.

FELLOWSHIP OF CHRISTIAN ATHLETES GRAYS

Mailing Address: FCA Baseball Office, 8701 Loeds Road, Kansas City, MO 64129. **Telephone:** (816) 876-2285. **Fax:** 816-921-8755. **E-Mail Address:** jreed@fca.org. **Website:** www.fcabaseball.org. **General Manager/Head Coach:** Joe Reed.

OZARK GENERALS

Mailing Address: 1336 West Plainview, Springfield, MO 65810. **Telephone:** (417) 881-2920. **Fax:** (417) 881-2982. **E-Mail Address:** rda160@excite.com. **Website:** www.generalsbaseballclub.com. **General Manager/Head Coach:** Rusty Aton.

TOPEKA GOLDEN GIANTS

Mailing Address: 3512 SE Colorado, Topeka, KS 66605. **Telephone:** (785) 266-7414. **E-Mail Address:** treb14@aol.com. **Website:** www.leaguelineup.com/goldengiants. **General Manager:** Brett Cowdin. **Head Coach:** Daniel Esposito.

MOUNTAIN COLLEGIATE LEAGUE

E-Mail Address: info@mcbl.net. **Website:** www.mcbl.net.

Year Founded: 2005.

Directors: Kurt Colicchio, Ron Kailey, Ray Klesh, Heidi Peterson, Ted Odle.

Regular Season: 48 games. **2008 Opening Date:** May 31. **Closing Date:** Aug. **4.**

Playoff Format: Second- and third-place teams meet in one-game playoff; winner advances to best-of-three championship series against first-place team.

Roster limit: 25 (college-eligible players only).

CHEYENNE GRIZZLIES

Telephone: (307) 631-7337. **E-Mail Address:** rkaide@aol.com. **Website:** www.cheyennegrizzlies.com. **Owner/General Manager:** Ron Kailey. **Head Coach:** Scott Laverty (Redlands, Calif.).

FORT COLLINS FOXES

Telephone: (970) 225-9564. **E-Mail Address:** info@fortcollinsfoxes.com. **Website:** www.fortcollinsfoxes.com. **Owner/General Manager:** Kurt Colicchio. **Head Coach:** Gherrett Levette.

GREELEY GRAYS

Telephone: (303) 870-2523. **E-Mail Address:** rklesh@earthlink.net. **Website:** www.greeleygrays.com. **Owner/General Manager:** Ray Klesh. **Head Coach:** Ryan Hodges (Indian Hills, Calif., **CC).**

LARAMIE COLTS

Telephone: (307) 742-2191. **E-Mail Address:** laramiecolts@msn.com. **Website:** www.laramiecolts.com. **General Manager:** Heidi Peterson. **Head Coach:** Ryan Goodwin (Northeastern, Colo., **JC).**

PARKER XPRESS

Telephone: Unavailable. **E-Mail Address:** tandmodle@msn.com. **Website:** www.parkerxpress.com. **Owner/General Manager:** Ted Odle. **Head Coach:** Bryan Sheppard (Northeastern, Colo., **JC).**

NEW ENGLAND COLLEGIATE LEAGUE

Mailing Address: 37 Grammar School Dr., Danbury, CT 06811. **Website:** www.necbl.com.

Year Founded: 1993.

Commissioner: Mario Tiani.

Division Structure: North—Holyoke, Keene, Lowell, North Shore, Sanford, Vermont. **South—**Danbury, Manchester, Newport, North Adams, Pittsfield, Torrington.

Regular Season: 42 games. **2008 Opening Date:** June 6. **Closing Date:** July 31.

All-Star Game: July 20 at Torrington.

Playoff Format: Top four teams in each division meet in best-of-three quarterfinals; winners meet in best-of-three divisional championship. **Winners meet in best-of-three final for league championship.**

Roster Limit: 25 (college-eligible players only).

DANBURY WESTERNERS

Mailing Address: 5 Old Hayrake Rd., Danbury, CT 06811. **Telephone:** (203) 797-0897. **Fax:** (203) 792-6177. **Website:** www.danburywesterners.com. **E-Mail Address:** westerners1@aol.com. **General Manager:** Terry Whalen.

HOLYOKE SOX

Mailing Address: Unavailable. **Telephone:** Unavailable. **Website:** www.holyokesox.com. **General Manager:** John Ferrara. **Head Coach:** Darryl Morhardt.

KEENE SWAMP BATS

Mailing Address: 31 W. Surry Rd., Keene, NH 03431. **Telephone:** (603) 357-5464. **Fax:** (603) 357-5090. **Website:** www.swampbats.com General Manager: Vicki Bacon. **Head Coach:** Mike Sweeney (Massachusetts).

LOWELL ALL-AMERICANS

Mailing Address: P.O. Box 2228, Lowell, MA 01851. **Telephone:** (978) 454-5058. **Fax:** (978) 251-1211. **E-Mail Address:** info@lowellallamericans.com. **Website:** www.lowellallamericans.com. **General Manager:** Harry Ayotte. **Head Coach:** Ken Connerty.

MANCHESTER SILKWORMS

Mailing Address: 16 West St., Manchester, CT 06040. **Telephone:** (860) 559-3126. **Fax:** (860) 432-1665. **Website:** www.manchestersilkworms.org. **General Manager:** Ed Slegeski. **Head Coach:** Al Leyva.

NEWPORT GULLS

Mailing Address: P.O. Box 777, Newport, RI 02840. **Telephone:** (401) 845-6832. **Website:** www.newportgulls.com General Manager: Chuck Paiva. **Head Coach:** Mike Coombs.

NORTH ADAMS STEEPLECATS

Mailing Address: P.O. Box 540, North Adams, MA 01247. **Telephone:** (413) 652-1031. **Website:** www.steeplecats.com. **General Manager:** Sean McGrath.

NORTH SHORE NAVIGATORS

Mailing Address: Frasier Field, Lynn, Mass. **Telephone:** Unavailable. **E-Mail Address:** philip@nsnavs.com. **Website:** www.nsnavs.com. **President:** Philip Rosenfield. **Head Coach:** Jason Falcon.

PITTSFIELD DUKES

Mailing Address: 75 S. Church St., Pittsfield, MA 01201. **Telephone:** (413) 447-3853. **Website:** www.pittsfielddukes.com. **President:** Dan Duquette. **Head Coach:** Mike Marron.

SANFORD MAINERS

Mailing Address: P.O. Box 26, Sanford, ME 04073. **Telephone:** (207) 324-0010. **Fax:** (207) 324-2227. **Website:** www.sanfordmainers.com. **General Manager:** Neil Olson. **Head Coach:** Joe Brown.

TORRINGTON TWISTERS

Mailing Address: 4 Blinkoff Ct., **Torrington, CT 06790. Telephone/Fax:** (860) 482-0450. **Website:** www.torringtontwisters.org. **General Manager:** Kirk Fredriksson. **Head Coach:** Gregg Hunt.

VERMONT MOUNTAINEERS

Mailing Address: P.O. Box 586, Montpelier, VT 05602. **Telephone:** (802) 223-5224. **Website:** www.thevermontmountaineers.com. **General Manager:** Brian Gallagher. **Head Coach:** John Russo.

NEW YORK COLLEGIATE LEAGUE

Summer Address: 28 Dunbridge Heights, Fairport, NY 14450. **Winter Address:** P.O. Box 2516, Tarpon Springs, FL 34688. **Telephone:** (585) 455-3667. **Website:** www.nycbl.com.

Year Founded: 1986.

Commissioner: Dave Chamberlain. **President:** Brian Spagnola. **Vice President:** Paul Welker. **Treasurer:** Dan Russo. **Secretary:** Ted Ford.

Member Clubs: East—Amsterdam Mohawks, Bennington Bombers, Glens Falls Golden Eagles, Little Falls Diamond Miners, Saratoga Phillies, Watertown Wizards. West—Alleghany County Nitros, Bolivar A's, Elmira Pioneers, Geneva Redwings, Genesee Valley River Bats, Hornell Dodgers, Niagra Falls Power, Webster Yankees.

Regular Season: 42 games. **2008 Opening Date:** June 8. **Closing Date:** Aug. **5.**

All-Star Game: July 6 at Amsterdam.

Playoff Format: Best-of-three championship series, matching winners of best-of-three division playoffs.

Roster Limit: 25 (college-eligible players only).

NORTHWOODS LEAGUE

Office Address: 2900 4th St. SW, Rochester, MN 55902. **Telephone:** (507) 536-4579. **Fax:** (507) 536-4597. **Website:** www.northwoodsleague.com.

Year Founded: 1994.

President: Dick Radatz Jr.

Division Structure: North—Alexandria, Brainerd, Duluth, Mankato, Rochester, St. Cloud, Thunder Bay. **South—B**attle Creek, Eau Claire, Green Bay, La Crosse, Madison, Rochester, Waterloo, Wisconsin.

Regular Season: 68 games (split schedule). **2008 Opening Date:** May 29. **Closing Date:** Aug. **17.**

All-Star Game: July 14 at Madison.

Playoff Format: First-half and second-half division winners meet in best-of-three series. Winners meet in best-of-three series for league championship.

Roster Limit: 26 (college-eligible players only).

ALEXANDRIA BEETLES

Mailing Address: 121 West 5th Street, Alexandria, MN 56308. **Telephone:** (320) 763-8151. **Fax:** (320) 763-8152. **E-Mail Address:** beetles@alexandriabeetles.com. **Website:** www.alexandriabeetles.com. **General Manager:** Shawn Reilly. **Head Coach:** Erik Maas (Tennessee Wesleyan).

BATTLE CREEK BOMBERS

Mailing Address: 189 Bridge Street, Battle Creek, MI 49017. **Telephone:** (269) 962-0735. **Fax:** (269) 962-0741. **Email Address:** info@battlecreekbombers.com Website: www.battlecreekbombers.com. **General Manager:** Rick Lindau. **Head Coach:** Brian Murphy.

BRAINERD BLUE THUNDER

Mailing Address: P.O. Box 1028, Brainerd, MN 56401. **Telephone:** (218) 828-2825. **Fax:** (218) 828-7857. **E-Mail Address:** pmarrplayball@yahoo.com. **Website:** www.brainerdbluethunder.com. **General Manager:** Tom Hice. **Head Coach:** Jason Huskey (Hutchinson, Kan., **CC).**

DULUTH HUSKIES

Mailing Address: 207 W. Superior St., Suite 206, Holiday Center Mall, Duluth, MN 55802. **Telephone:** (218) 786-9909. **Fax:** (218) 786-9001. **E-Mail Address:** huskies@duluthhuskies.com. **Website:** www.duluthhuskies.com. **General Manager:** Craig Smith. **Head Coach:** Adam Stahl.

EAU CLAIRE EXPRESS

Mailing Address: 108 E. Grand Ave., Eau Claire, WI 54701. **Telephone:** (715) 839-7788. **Fax:** (715) 839-7676. **E-Mail Address:** info@eauclaireexpress.com. **Website:** www.eauclaireexpress.com. **General Manager:** Jeff Jones. **Head Coach:** Dale Varsho.

GREEN BAY BULLFROGS

Mailing Address: 2121 South Oneida Street, Green Bay, WI 54304. **Telephone:** (920) 497-7225. **Fax:** (920) 497-7227. **Email Address:** info@greenbaybullfrogs.com. **Website:** www.greenbaybullfrogs.com General Manager: Mike Then. **Head Coach:** Elliott Strankman.

LA CROSSE LOGGERS

Mailing Address: 1223 Caledonia St., La Crosse, WI 54603. **Telephone:** (608) 796-9553. **Fax:** (608) 796-9032. **E-Mail Address:** info@lacrosseloggers.com. **Website:** www.lacrosseloggers.com. **General Manager:** Chris Goodell. **Director of Ballpark Operations:** Ben Kapanke. **Head Coach:** Rick Boyer.

MADISON MALLARDS

Mailing Address: 2920 N. **Sherman Ave., Madison, WI 53704. Telephone:** (608) 246-4277. **Fax:** (608) 246-4163. **E-Mail Address:** vern@mallardsbaseball.com. **Website:** www.mallardsbaseball.com. **General Manager:** Vern Stenman. **Head Coach:** C.J. **Thieleke (Madison Area Tech).**

MANKATO MOONDOGS

Mailing Address: 310 Belle Ave., Suite L-8, Mankato, MN 56001. **Telephone:** (507) 625-7047. **Fax:** (507) 625-7059. **E-Mail Address:** office@mankatomoondogs.com. **Website:** www.mankatomoondogs.com. **General Manager:** Kyle Mrozek. **Head Coach:** Jason Nell (Iowa Lakes CC).

ROCHESTER HONKERS

Office Address: 307 E. Center St., Rochester, MN 55904 **Stadium Address:** Mayo Field, 403 E. Center St., Rochester, MN 55904. **Mailing Address:** P.O. Box 482, Rochester, MN 55903. **Telephone:** (507) 289-1170. **Fax:** (507) 289-1866. **E-Mail Address:** honkers@rochesterhonkers.com. **Website:** www.rochesterhonkers.com. **General Manager:** Dan Litzinger. **Head Coach:** Greg Labbe (North Florida).

ST. CLOUD RIVER BATS

Office Address: Joe Faber Field, 5001 8th St. N., St. Cloud, MN 56303. **Mailing Address:** P.O. Box 5059, St. Cloud, MN 56302. **Telephone:** (320) 240-9798. **Fax:** (320) 255-5228. **E-Mail Address:** info@riverbats.com. **Website:** www.riverbats.com. **General Manager:** Marc Jerzak. **Head Coach:** Tony Arnerich (Sonoma, Calif., State).

THUNDER BAY BORDER CATS

Office Address: Port Arthur Stadium, 425 Winnipeg Ave., Thunder Bay, Ontario P7B 6P7. **Mailing Address:** P.O. Box 29105, Thunder Bay, Ontario P7B 6P9. **Telephone:** (807) 766-2287. **Fax:** (807) 345-8299. **E-Mail Address:** baseball@tbaytel.net. **Website:** www.bordercatsbaseball.com. **General Manager:** Greg Balec. **Head Coach:** Jared Manske (Viterbo, Wis.).

WATERLOO BUCKS

Office Address: Riverfront Stadium, 850 Park Rd., Waterloo, IA 50703. **Mailing Address:** P.O. Box 4124, Waterloo, IA 50704. **Telephone:** (319) 232-0500. **Fax:** (319) 232-0700. **E-Mail Address:** waterloobucks@waterloobucks.com. **Website:** www.waterloobucks.com. **General Manager:** Dan Corbin. **Head Coach:** Dan Fitzgerald (Des Moines Area CC).

WISCONSIN WOODCHUCKS

Office Address: Athletic Park, 300 Third St., Wausau, WI 54402. **Mailing Address:** P.O. Box 6157, Wausau, WI 54402. **Telephone:** (715) 845-5055. **Fax:** (715) 845-5015. **E-Mail Address:** info@woodchucks.com. **Website:** www.woodchucks.com. **General Manager:** Ryan Treu. **Head Coach:** Jim Gantner.

PACIFIC INTERNATIONAL LEAGUE

Mailing Address: 4400 26th Ave. W., Seattle, WA 98199. **Telephone:** (206) 623-8844. **Fax:** (206) 623-8361. **E-Mail Address:** spotter@potterprinting.com. **Website:** www.pacificinternationalleague.com.

Year Founded: 1992

President: Steve Konek. **Commissioner:** Brian Gooch. **Secretary:** Steve Potter. **Treasurer:** Mark Dow.

Member Clubs: BC Ballers, Everett Merchants, Seattle Studs, Skagit Eagles.

Regular Season: 28 league games. **2008 Opening Date:** Unavailable.

Playoff Format: Top three teams playoff; winner goes to NBC World Series in Wichita, Kan.

Roster Limit: 30; 25 eligible for games (players must be at least 18 years old).

SOUTHERN COLLEGIATE BASEBALL LEAGUE

Mailing Address: 9300 Fairway Ridge Road, Charlotte, NC 28277.

Telephone: (704) 847-5075. **Fax:** (704) 847-1455. **E-Mail Address:** SCBLCommissioner@aol.com. **Website:** www.scbl.org.

Year Founded: 1999.

Commissioner: Bill Capps. **President:** Jeff Carter. **Vice President:** Brian Swords. **Secretary:** Larry Tremitiere. **Treasurer:** Brenda Templin

Regular Season: 42 games. **2008 Opening Date:** June 4. **Closing Date:** July 28.

Playoff Format: No. 1 seed plays host to four-team, double-elimination tournament; begins July 25.

Roster Limit: 30 (College-eligible players only).

ASHEVILLE REDBIRDS

Mailing Address: P.O. Box 1515, Johnson City, TN 37605. **Telephone:** (828) 274-2272. **General Manager:** Bill Stewart. **Head Coach:** Robert Rudder (Blue Ridge, N.C., CC).

CAROLINA CHAOS

Mailing Address: 142 Orchard Drive, Liberty, SC 29657. **Telephone:** (864) 843-3232, (864) 901-4331. **E-Mail Address:** brian_swords@carolinachaos.com. **Website:** www.carolinachaos.com. **General Manager/Coach:** Brian Swords (Southern Wesleyan, S.C.).

CAROLINA SOX

Mailing Address: 1443 Wedgefield Drive, Rock Hill, SC 29732. **Telephone:** (803) 366-2207, (803) 517-6626. **Fax:** (803) 980-7438. **E-Mail Address:** Ltrem@comporium.net. **General Manager:** Larry Tremitiere. **Head Coach:** Kevin Durham.

DAVIDSON COPPERHEADS

Mailing Address: P.O. Box 928, Cornelius, NC 28031. **Telephone:** (704) 892-1041, (704) 564-9211. **E-Mail Address:** jcarter@standpointtech.com. **Website:** www.copperheadsports.org. **General Manager:** Jeff Carter. **Head Coach:** Derek Shoe (Pfeiffer, N.C.).

MORGANTON AGGIES

Mailing Address: P.O. Box 3448, Morganton, NC 28680. **Telephone:** (828) 438-5351. **Fax:** (828) 438-5350. **E-Mail Address:** gwleonhardt@aol.com. **General Manager:** Gary Leonhardt. **Head Coach:** Nick Jaksa (Eastern Illinois).

SPARTANBURG CRICKETS

Mailing Address: P.O. Box 1429, Cowpens, SC 29330. **Telephone:** (864) 266-1147. **E-Mail Address:** cricketsbb@bellsouth.net. **Owner/General Manager:** Steve Cunningham.

TENNESSEE TORNADO

Mailing Address: 1995 Roan Creek Road, Mountain City, TN 37683. **Telephone:** (423) 727-9111. **E-Mail Address:** tdr@maymead.com. **Owner:** Wiley Roark. **General Manager:** Tom Reese. **Head Coach:** Nathan Meade (Milligan, Tenn., College).

TAR HEEL SUMMER BASEBALL LEAGUE

Mailing Address: P.O. Box 2157, Indian Trail, NC 28079. **Telephone:** (704) 606-2492. **Fax:** (888) 501-7755. **E-Mail Address:** info@tarheelsbl.com. **Website:** www.tarheelsbl.com.

Year Founded: 2007.

President: Wesley Cook.

Member Clubs: Anson Rough Riders, Monroe

Channelcats, Charlotte Crowns, Pageland Red Roosters.

Regular Season: 50 games. **2008 Opening Date:** May 30. **Closing Date:** July 31.

All-Star Game: July 10 at Wingate University.

Roster Limit: 30 (college-eligible players only).

TEXAS COLLEGIATE LEAGUE

Mailing Address: 735 Plaza Blvd., Suite 200, Coppell, TX 75019. **Telephone:** (817) 339-9367. **Fax:** (817) 339-9309. **E-Mail Address:** info@texascollegiateleague.com. **Website:** www.texascollegiateleague.com.

Year Founded: 2004.

Commissioner: Darren Hall. **Supervisor, Umpires:** John Ausmus.

Regular Season: 48 games. **2008 Opening Date:** Unavailable.

Playoff Format: Top two teams in each division meet in best-of-three division series. Winners meet in best-of-three series for league championship.

Roster Limit: 25 (College-eligible players only).

BRAZOS VALLEY BOMBERS

Mailing Address: 405 Mitchell St., **Bryan, TX 77801. Telephone:** (979) 799-PLAY. **Fax:** (979) 779-2398. **E-Mail Address:** info@bvbombers.com. **Website:** www.bvbombers.com. **Owners:** Uri Geva, Kfir Jackson. **General Manager:** Mike Lieberman. **Head Coach:** Kevin Moulder (Central Missouri State).

COLLEYVILLE LONESTARS

Mailing Address: 4709 Colleyville Blvd., Colleyville, TX 76034. **Telephone:** (817) 354-0673. **E-Mail Address:** info@tcllonestars.com. **Website:** www.tcllonestars.com. **Owner:** Britt Britton. **Owner/President:** Stacey Hollinger. **Head Coach:** Rusty Greer.

COPPELL COPPERHEADS

Mailing Address: 509 W. Bethel Rd., Suite 100, Coppell, TX 75019. **Telephone:** (972) 745-2929. **E-Mail Address:** info@tclcopperheads.com. **Website:** www.tclcopperheads.com. **President:** Steve Pratt. **General Manager:** Chris Sorrels. **Head Coach:** Heath Autry.

DENTON OUTLAWS

Mailing Address: 16250 Dallas Pkwy., Suite 102, Dallas, TX 75248. **Telephone:** (940) 382-9396. **Website:** www.denton-outlaws.com. **Owners:** Jim Leslie, Todd Van Poppel. **General Manager:** Joby Raymond. **Head Coach:** Derek Matlock.

DUNCANVILLE DEPUTIES

Mailing Address: 407 North Cedar Ridge, Duncanville, TX 75116. **Telephone:** (972) 296-9700. **Fax:** (972) 296-9077. **Website:** www.duncanvilledeputies.com. **President:** Chris Najork. **General Manager:** Jeff Najork. **Head Coach:** Kyle Houser.

MCKINNEY MARSHALS

Mailing Address: 6151 Alma Rd., McKinney, TX 75070. **Telephone:** (972) 747-8248. **Fax:** (972) 747-9231. **E-Mail Address:** info@tclmarshals.com. **Website:** www.tclmarshals.com. **Owner:** David Craig. **Owner/President:** Mike Henneman. **Executive Vice President/General Manager:** Ray Ricchi. **Head Coach:** Kyle Hope.

MINERAL WELLS STEAM

Mailing Address: P.O. **Box 606, Mineral Wells, TX 76068.** **Telephone:** (937) 352-1240. **Fax:** (940) 445-4383. **E-Mail Address:** info@tclsteam.com. **Website:** www.aiabaseball.org/texas. **Owner:** Athletes in Action. **General Manager:** Jason Lester. **Head Coach:** Bernie Martinez.

WEATHERFORD WRANGLERS

Mailing Address: P.O. Box 2108, Weatherford, TX 76086. **Telephone:** (817) 771-8882. **Fax:** (817) 447-8637. **E-Mail Address:** info@tclwranglers.com. **Website:** www.tclwranglers.com. **Managing Partner:** Lonna Leach. **General Manager:** Misti Lightfoot. **Head Coach:** Jeff Lightfoot (Weatherford, Texas, JC).

WICHITA FALLS ROUGHNECKS

Mailing Address: 1416 Eighth Street, Wichita Falls, TX 76301. **Telephone:** (940) 687-4487. **E-Mail Address:** info@tclroughnecks.com. **Website:** www.tclroughnecks.com. **Owners:** Frank Beaman, J.W. **Oliver. General Manager:** Leslie Hawthorne. **Head Coach:** Johnny Cardenas (Stephen F. **Austin).**

VALLEY LEAGUE

Mailing Address: 58 Bethel Green Rd., Staunton, VA 24401. **Telephone:** (540) 885-8901. **Fax:** (540) 885-2068. **E-Mail Addresses:** dbiery@valleybaseballleague.com, kwarner@valleybaseballleague.com. **Website:** www.valleyleaguebaseball.com.

Year Founded: 1961.

President: David Biery. **Executive Vice President:** Todd Thompson. **Sports Information Director:** Kevin Warner.

Regular Season: 42 games. **2008 Opening Date:** May 31. **Closing Date:** July 27.

All-Star Game: July 6 at Covington.

Playoff Format: Eight teams; best-of-three quarterfinals and semifinals; best-of-five finals.

Roster Limit: 28 (college eligible players only).

COVINGTON LUMBERJACKS

Mailing Address: P.O. Box 171, Low Moor, VA 24457. **Telephone:** (540) 691-6351. **E-Mail Address:** covingtonlumberjacks@valleyleaguebaseball.com; jrh@alcovamortgage.com. **Website:** www.lumberjacksbaseball.com. **Owners:** Dizzy Garten, Jason Helmintoller. **Head Coach:** Andy Chalot.

FAQUIER GATORS

Mailing Address: PO Box 740 Warrenton, VA 20188. **Telephone:** (540) 341-3454. **Fax:** (540) 526-9444. **E-Mail Address:** gators@fauquiergators.org. **Website:** www.faquiergators.org. **Owners:** Alison Athey, Cecil Campbell. **Head Coach:** Paul Koch.

FRONT ROYAL CARDINALS

Mailing Address: P.O. Box 995, Front Royal, VA 22630. **Telephone:** (540) 636-1882, (540) 671-9184. **Fax:** (540) 635-8746. **E-Mail Address:** frontroyalcardinals@valleyleaguebaseball.com. **Website:** www.frcardinalbaseball.com. **President:** Linda Keen. **Head Coach:** Bob Brotherton.

HARRISONBURG TURKS

Mailing Address: 1489 S. **Main St., Harrisonburg, VA 22801. Telephone:** (540) 434-5919. **E-Mail Address:** turksbaseball@hotmail.com. **Website:** www.harrisonburgturks.com. **Operations Manager:** Teresa Wease. **GM/Head Coach:** Bob Wease.

HAYMARKET SENATORS

Mailing Address: 42020 Village Center Plaza, Suite 120-50, Stoneridge, VA 20105. **Telephone:** (703) 989-5009. **E-Mail Address:** haymarketsenators@valleyleaguebaseball.com. **Website:** www.haymarketbaseball.com. **President/General Manager:** Pat Malone. **Head Coach:** Billy Shields.

LURAY WRANGLERS

Mailing Address: 1203 E. Main St., Luray, VA 22835. **Telephone:** (540) 743-3338. **E-Mail Addresses:** luraywranglers@valleyleaguebaseball.com. **Website:** www.luraywranglers.com. **President:** Bill Turner. **General Manager:** Greg Moyer. **Head Coach:** Mike Bocock.

NEW MARKET REBELS

Mailing Address: P.O. Box 902, New Market, VA 22844. **Telephone:** (540) 740-4247, (540) 740-8569. **E-Mail Address:** nmrebels@shentel.net. **Website:** www.rebelsbaseball.biz. **President/General Manager:** Bruce Alger. **Executive Vice President:** Jim Weissenborn. **Head Coach:** Evan Brannon (Randolph Macon, Va.).

STAUNTON BRAVES

Mailing Address: 14 Shannon Place, Staunton, VA 24401. **Telephone:** (540) 886-0987. **Fax:** (540) 886-0905. **E-Mail Address:** stauntonbraves@valleyleaguebaseball.com. **Website:** www.stauntonbraves.com. **General Manager:** Steve Cox. **Director, Operations:** Kay Snyder. **Head Coach:** Lance Mauck (Anne Arundel, Md., **CC).**

WAYNESBORO GENERALS

Mailing Address: P.O. Box 615, Waynesboro, VA 22980. **Telephone:** (540) 949-0370, (540) 942-2474. **Fax:** (540) 949-0653. **E-Mail Address:** waynesborogenerals@valleyleaguebaseball.com. **Website:** www.waynesborogenerals.com. **Owner:** Jim Critzer. **Head Coach:** Lawrence Nesselrodt.

WINCHESTER ROYALS

Mailing Address: P.O. Box 2485, Winchester, VA 22604. **Telephone:** (540) 667-7677. **Fax:** (540) 662-1434. **E-Mail Addresses:** winchesterroyals@valleyleaguebaseball.com, jimphill@shentel.net. **Website:** www.winchesterroyals.com. **President:** Jim Shipp. **Vice President/General Manager:** Jim Phillips. **Head Coach:** John Lowery, Jr.

WOODSTOCK RIVER BANDITS

Mailing Address: 2115 Battlefield Run Ct., Richmond, VA 23231. **Telephone:** (804) 795-5128. **Fax:** (804) 226-8706. **E-Mail Address:** woodstockriverbandits@yahoo.com. **Website:** www.woodstockriverbandits.org. **Owner/President:** Stu Richardson. **Vice President:** Glenn Berger. **General Manager:** Jerry Walters. **Head Coach:** Donn Foltz.

WEST COAST COLLEGIATE LEAGUE

Mailing Address: 610 N. Mission St., #204, Wenatchee, WA 98801. **Telephone:** (509) 888-9378. **Website:** www.wccbl.com.

Year Founded: 2005.

Commissioner: Jim Dietz. **President:** Dan Segel. **Vice President:** Brent Kirwan.

Division Structure: East—Kelowna, Moses Lake, Spokane, Wenatchee. **West—Bellingham, Bend, Corvallis, Kitsap.**

Regular Season: 42 games. **2008 Opening Date:** June 12. **Closing Date:** Aug. **10.**

All-Star Game: July 22 at Moses Lake.

Playoff Format: First- and second-place teams in each division meet in best-of-three semifinal series; winners advance to best-of-three championship series.

Roster Limit: 28 (college-eligible players only).

BELLINGHAM BELLS

Mailing Address: 1732 Iowa St., Bellingham, WA 98226. **Telephone:** (253) 606-3670. **E-Mail Address:** info@bellinghambells.com. **Website:** www.bellinghambells.com. **General Manager:** Dave Lewis. **Head Coach:** Brandon Newell (Kansas).

BEND ELKS

Mailing Address: P.O. Box 9009, Bend, OR 97708. **Telephone:** (541) 312-9259. **E-Mail Address:** richardsj@bendcable.com. **Website:** www.bendelks.com. **Owner/General Manager:** Jim Richards. **Head Coach:** Ryan Thompson (Cuesta, Calif., **CC).**

CORVALLIS KNIGHTS

Mailing Address: P.O. Box 1356, Corvallis, OR 97339. **Telephone:** (541) 752-5656. **E-Mail Address:** dan.segel@corvallisknights.com. **Website:** www.corvallisknights.com. **President:** Dan Segel. **General Manager/Head Coach:** Brooke Knight.

KELOWNA FALCONS

Mailing Address: 201-1014 Glenmore Dr., Kelowna, B.C., V1Y 4P2. **Telephone:** (250) 763-4100. **E-Mail Address:** mark@kelownafalcons.com. **Website:** www.kelownafalcons.com. **General Manager:** Mark Nonis. **Head Coach:** Kevin Frady (Kansas).

KITSAP BLUEJACKETS

Mailing Address: P.O. Box 68, Silverdale, WA 98383. **Telephone:** (360) 692-5566. **E-Mail Address:** ricjansmith@comcast.net. **Website:** www.kitsapbluejackets.com. **Managing Partner/General Manager:** Rick Smith. **Head Coach:** Matt Acker (Green River, Wash., **CC).**

MOSES LAKE PIRATES

Mailing Address: 831 E. **Colonial Ave., Suite Arrr!, Moses Lake, WA 98837. Telephone:** (509) 764-8200. **E-Mail Address:** bkirwan@mlpirates.com. **Website:** www.mlpirates.com. **General Manager:** Brent Kirwan. **Head Coach:** Trevor Brown (Oklahoma State).

SPOKANE RIVERHAWKS

Mailing Address: P.O. **Box 19188, Spokane, WA 99219. Telephone:** (509) 747-4991. **E-Mail Address:** zakheim@zak.com. **Website:** www.spokaneriverhawks.com. **General Manager:** Steve Hertz. **Head Coach:** Barry Matthews (CC of Spokane, Wash.).

WENATCHEE APPLESOX

Mailing Address: P.O. **Box 5100, Wenatchee, WA 98807. Telephone:** (509) 665-6900. **E-Mail Address:** sales@applesox.com. **Website:** www.applesox.com. **Owner/General Manager:** Jim Corcoran. **Head Coach:** Ed Knaggs.

HIGH SCHOOL BASEBALL

NATIONAL FEDERATION OF STATE HIGH SCHOOL ASSOCIATIONS

Mailing Address: P.O. Box 690, Indianapolis, IN 46206. **Telephone:** (317) 972-6900. **Fax:** (317) 822-5700. **E-Mail Address:** baseball@nfhs.org. **Website:** www.nfhs.org.

Executive Director: Robert Kanaby. **Chief Operating Officer:** Bob Gardner. **Assistant Director/Baseball Rules Editor:** Elliot Hopkins. **Director, Publications/Communications:** Bruce Howard.

NATIONAL HIGH SCHOOL BASEBALL COACHES ASSOCIATION

Mailing Address: P.O. Box 12843, Tempe, AZ 85284. **Telephone:** (602) 615-0571. **Fax:** (480) 838-7133. **E-Mail Address:** rdavini@cox.net. **Website:** www.baseball-coaches.org. **Executive Director:** Ron Davini. **President:** Craig Anderson (Pine Island HS, Zumbrota, MN) First Vice President: Bill Seamon (Owensville, Mo.). **Second Vice President:** Garye LaFevers (Chaparral HS, Scottsdale, AZ).

2008 National Convention: Dec. 4-7, 2008 at Chicago, IL.

NATIONAL TOURNAMENTS

IN-SEASON

BASEBALL AT THE BEACH

Mailing Address: P.O. Box 1717, Georgetown, SC 29442. **Telephone:** (843) 448-7149. **E-mail:** tchristy@horrycountyschools.net **Website:** www.baseballatthebeach.com.

Tournament Director: Tim Christy

2008 Tournament: Feb. **28-March 1**

BATTLE AT THE RIDGE

Mailing Address: Southridge HS, 19355 SW 1114th Ave., **Miami, FL 33157. Telephone:** (305) 322-2255. **Fax:** (305) 253-4456. **E-Mail Address:** edoskow@dadeschools.net.

Tournament Director: Ed Doskow.

2008 Tournament: February 11-16 (three-game guarantee).

BLAZER SPORTCO SPRING BASH

Mailing Address: Durango HS, 7100 W. Dewey Dr., Las Vegas, NV 89113. **Telephone:** (702) 799-5850. **Fax:** (702) 799-1286. **E-Mail Address:** shknapp@interact.ccsd.net.

Tournament Director: Sam Knapp.

2008 Tournament: March 17-19 (26 teams).

FIRST BANK CLASSIC

Mailing Address: 8708 Savannah Ave., Lubbock, TX 79424. **Telephone:** (806) 535-4505. **Fax:** (806) 794-5306. **E-Mail Address:** scottgwinn@cox.net.

Tournament Director: Scott Gwinn.

2008 Tournament: March 8-10 (16 teams).

HORIZON CLEATS NATIONAL INVITATIONAL

Mailing Address: Horizon High School, 5653 Sandra Terrace, Scottsdale, AZ 85254. **Telephone:** (602) 867-9003. **E-mail:** huskycoach1@yahoo.com Website: www.horizonbaseball.com

Tournament Director: Eric Kibler.

2008 Tournament: March 17-20 (16 teams).

INTERNATIONAL PAPER CLASSIC

Mailing Address: 4775 Johnson Rd., Georgetown, SC 29440. **Telephone:** (843) 527-9606, (843) 546-3807. **Fax:** (843) 546-8521. **Website:** www.ipclassic.com.

Tournament Director: Alicia Johnson.

2008 Tournament: March 6-9 (eight teams).

LIONS INVITATIONAL

Mailing Address: 3502 Lark St., San Diego CA 92103. **Telephone:** (619) 602-8650. **Fax:** (619) 239-3539. **E-Mail Address:** peter.gallagher@sdcourt.ca.gov. **Website:** www.lionsbaseball.org

Tournament Director: Peter Gallagher.

2008 Tournament: March 17-20 (118 teams).

MIDLAND TOURNAMENT OF CHAMPIONS

Mailing Address: Midland High School, 906 W. Illinois Ave., Midland, TX 79701. **Telephone:** (432) 689-1337. **Fax:** (432) 689-1335. **E-Mail Address:** barryrussell@esc18.net.

Tournament Director: Barry Russell.

2008 Tournament: Feb. 28—March 1 (16 teams).

PHIL NEVIN NATIONAL CLASSIC

Mailing Address: P.O. Box 338, Placentia, CA 92870. **Telephone:** (714) 993-2838. **Fax:** (714) 993-5350. **E-Mail Address:** placentiamustang@aol.com. **Website:** national-classic.com

Tournament Director: Todd Rogers.

2008 Tournament: March 22-27 at Cal State Fullerton (16 teams).

USA CLASSIC

Mailing Address: 5900 Walnut Grove Rd., Memphis, TN 38120. **Telephone:** (901) 872-8326. **Fax:** (901) 681-9443. **Email:** jdaigle@bigriver.net Website: www.usabaseballstadium.org.

Tournament Organizers: John Daigle, Buster Kelso.

2008 Tournament: April 4-7 at USA Baseball Stadium, Millington, TN (16 teams).

POSTSEASON

SUNBELT BASEBALL CLASSIC SERIES

Mailing Address: 505 North Blvd., Edmond, OK 73034. **Telephone:** (405) 348-3839. **Fax:** (405) 340-7538. **Website:** www.geocities.com/baja/ravine/1976

Chairman: John Schwartz.

2008 Senior Series: Norman, OK, June 17-21

2008 Junior Series: McAlester and Wilburton, OK, June 6-11

2008 Sophomore Series: Edmond, OK, May 29-June 1

ALL-STAR GAMES/AWARDS

AFLAC HIGH SCHOOL ALL-AMERICA CLASSIC

Mailing Address: 10 S. Adams St., Rockville, MD 20850. **Telephone:** (301) 762-7188. **Fax:** (301) 762-1491. **Event Organizer:** Sports America, Inc. **President, Chief Executive Officer:** Robert Geoghan. **2008 Game:** Unavailable.

ALL-AMERICAN BASEBALL GAME

Mailing Address: 224 Stiger St., Hackettstown, NJ 07840. **Telephone:** (908) 684-5410. **Fax:** (908) 684-5415. **Event Organizer:** SportsLink, Inc. **President:** Rich McGuinness. **2008 Game:** Unavailable.

BASEBALL EXPRESS CAPE COD HIGH SCHOOL CLASSIC

Mailing Address: 9176 Red Branch Rd., Suite M, Columbia, MD 21045 **Telephone:** 410-715-5080. **E-Mail Address:** jason@baseballfactory.com. **Website:** baseballfactory.com/capecod.asp Event Organizers: Baseball Factory, Team One Baseball. **2008 Game:** July 27, Wareham, MA.

GATORADE CIRCLE OF CHAMPIONS

(National HS Player of the Year Award)

Mailing Address: The Gatorade Company, 321 N. Clark St., Suite 24-3, Chicago, IL, 60610 **Telephone:** 312-821-1000. **Website:** www.gatorade.com

SHOWCASE EVENTS

ALL-AMERICAN BASEBALL TALENT SHOWCASES

Mailing Address: 6 Bicentennial Ct., Erial, NJ 08081. **Telephone:** (856) 354-0201. **Fax:** (856) 354-0818. **E-Mail Address:** hitdoctor@thehitdoctor.com Website: thehitdoctor.com. **National Director:** Joe Barth.

AREA CODE GAMES

Mailing Address: 23954 Madison Street, Torrance, CA 90505. **Telephone:** (310) 791-1142 x 4424. **E-Mail Address:** andrew@studentsports.com. **Website:** www.studentsportsbaseball.com

Event Organizer: Andrew Drennen.

2008 Area Code Games: Aug. **5-10 at Long Beach, CA (Blair Field).**

ARIZONA FALL CLASSIC

Mailing Address: 6102 W. Maui Lane, Glendale, AZ 85306 **Telephone:** (602) 978-2929. **Fax:** (602) 439-4494. **E-Mail Address:** azbaseballted@msn.com. **Website:** www.azfallclassic.com.

Directors: Ted Heid, Tracy Heid.

2008 Events

Four Corner Classic (Open HS, 16 & under) Peoria, AZ, June 6-8
Prep National Classic (Summer HS Teams only). . . . . Peoria, AZ, June 28-July 5
Summer National Classic (2008 and Under) Peoria, AZ, July 6-12
National 16U Summer Classic . . . . Peoria, AZ, July 13-19
National 17U Summer Classic (2009 and Under). . . . . Peoria, AZ, July 20-26
National 14U Summer Classic . . . . Peoria, AZ, July 20-26
AZ Senior Fall Classic (HS seniors) . . . . Peoria, AZ, Oct. 16-19
AZ Junior Fall Classic (HS juniors) . . . . Peoria, AZ, Oct. 24-26
AZ Sophomore Fall Classic (HS sophomore and freshman) . . . Peoria, AZ, Oct. 31-Nov. 2

BASEBALL FACTORY

Office Address: 9176 Red Branch Rd., Suite M, Columbia, MD 21045. **Telephone:** (800) 641-4487, (410) 715-5080. **Fax:** (410) 715-1975. **E-Mail Address:** info@baseballfactory.com. **Website:** www.baseballfactory.com.

Chief Executive Officer: Steve Sclafani. **President:** Rob Naddelman. **Executive VP, Baseball Operations:** Steve Bernhardt.

Baseball Express Cape Cod High School Classic: July 27, Wareham, MA

National Tryouts and College Recruiting Program Video Sessions: Sites across the United States, Jan. 6-Dec. 28.

Under Armour Training and National Team Events: Sites across the United States, Jan. 20-Dec. 30.

BLUE-GREY CLASSIC

Mailing address: 68 Norfolk Road, Mills MA 02054. **Telephone:** (508) 376-1250. **Email address:** impactprospects@comcast.net. **Website:** www.impactprospects.com.

2008 events: July 18-20, Saint Petersburg, Fla; July 29-31 and Oct 24-26, Virginia Sports Complex.

COLLEGE SELECT BASEBALL

Mailing Address: P.O. Box 783, Manchester, CT 06040. **Telephone:** (800) 782-3672. **E-Mail Address:** TRhit@msn.com. **Website:** www.collegeselect.org.

Consulting Director: Tom Rizzi.

2008 Showcases: July 21-23, Norwich, CT; Aug. 4-6, Binghamton, NY, Aug. 18-21, Warwick, RI (Showcase team tournament).

IMPACT BASEBALL

Mailing Address: P.O. Box 47, Sedalia, NC 27342. **E-Mail Address:** andypartin@aol.com. **Website:** www.impactbaseball.com.

Operator: Andy Partin.

2008 Showcases: June 18-19, Appalachain State University; July 22-23, High Point University; Nov. 1-2, USA Baseball National Training Complex.

EAST COAST PROFESSIONAL SHOWCASE

Mailing Address: 2125 North Lake Avenue, Lakeland, FL 33805. **Telephone:** (863) 686-8075.

Tournament Directors: John Castleberry. **Tournament Coordinator:** Shannon Follett.

2008 Showcase: Aug. **1-4, Lakeland, FL.**

MID-AMERICA FIVE STAR BASEBALL SHOWCASE

Mailing Address: Champions Baseball Academy, 510 E. Business Way, Cincinnati, OH 45241. **Telephone:** (513) 247-9511. **Fax:** (513) 247-0040. **E-Mail Address:** champions510@yahoo.com. **Website:** www.championsbaseball.com.

Showcase contact: Mike Bricker

2008 Showcases: June 26-29 at Cincinnati, OH. **July 10-13 at Cincinnati, OH.**

PACIFIC NORTHWEST CHAMPIONSHIPS

Mailing Address: 42783 Deerhorn Road, Springfield, Or. 97478. **Telephone: (541) 896-0841. Email Address:** mckay@baseballnorthwest.com. **Tournament Organizer: Jeff McKay.**

2008 Events: August 16-20 in Portland, Or. State Prospect Games: Washington Northwest, June 30-July 3 at site TBA, Washington Metro, June 23-26 at Bellevue CC in Bellevue, Wa., Washington Southwest, July 21-24 at Lower Columbia CC in Longview, Wa., Oregon Metro, July 28-31 at Wilsonville HS in Wilsonville, Or., Oregon State, July 7-10 at Thurston HS, Springfield, Or., East Washington/Northern Idaho, July 14-17 at Columbia Basin CC in Pasco, Wa., Southern Idaho, June 16-19 at Twin Falls HS in Twin Falls, Id., Montana/Wyoming, June 9-12 at Luzenac Legion Field in Three Forks, Mt.

PERFECT GAME USA

Mailing Address: 1203 Rockford Road SW, Cedar Rapids, IA 52404. **Telephone:** (319) 298-2923 Fax: (319) 298-2924. **E-Mail Address:** jerry@perfectgame.org. **Website:** www.perfectgameusa.com.

President, Director: Jerry Ford. **Vice Presidents:** Andy Ford, Jason Gerst, Tyson Kimm. **International Director:** Kentaro Yasutake. **National Showcase Director:** Jim Arp. **Scouting Directors:** Kirk Gardner, Kyle Noesen, David Rawnsley (WWBA), Greg Sabers. **Baseball Championship Director:** Ben Ford. **WWBA Tournament Director:** Taylor McCollough. **League Director:** Steve James. **Director, Instruction:** Jim Van Scoyoc. **California Director:** Mike Spiers. **Mid-Atlantic Director:** Frank Fulton. **Northeast Director/State Showcase National Director:** Dan Kennedy. **Southeast Director:** Jeff Simpson. Georgia Supervisor: Billy Nicholson. **Director BaseballWebTV.com:** Tom Koerick Jr. **Supervisors BaseballWebTV.com:** Rick Stephenson, Matt Stephenson. **PGCrosschecker.com Director :** Allan Simpson. **PG National Academy Director:** Mike Chismar. **PerfectGameUSA.com writers:** Patrick Ebert, Jim McDonald, Jim Zellmann. **Vice President of Sales and Marketing:** Gary Keoppel. **Director of Sales and Marketing:** Austin Steines. **Merchandise Director:** Tom Jackson. **Merchandise Supervisor:** Dick Vaske. **Director of Information Technology:** David Mixon. **Building Manager:** Eric Oliver. **Business Manager:** Don Walser. **Office Managers:** Betty Ford, Nancy Lain.

2008 Showcase/Tournament Events: Sites across the United States, Jan. 5 – Dec. 30.

SELECTFEST BASEBALL

Mailing Address: 60 Franklin Pl., Morris Plains, NJ 07950. **Telephone:** (862) 222-6404. **E-Mail Address:** selectfest@optonline.net. **Website:** www.selectfestbaseball.org Camp Directors: Bruce Shatel.

2008 Showcase: June 27 at Jack Cust Baseball Academy; June 28-29 at Rutgers University.

TEAM ONE BASEBALL

(A division of Baseball Factory)

Office Address: 1000 Bristol Street North, Suite 17285, Newport Beach, CA 92660. **Telephone:** (800) 621-5452, (805) 451-8203. **Fax:** (949) 209-1829. **E-Mail Address:** jroswell@teamonebaseball.com. **Website:** www.teamonebaseball.com.

Senior Director: Justin Roswell. **Executive VP, Baseball Operations:** Steve Bernhardt. **Director of On-Field Sessions:** Jim Gemler.

2008 Showcases: West, June 29-July 1 in Costa Mesa, CA; South, July 5-7 in Atlanta; North, July 19-21 in Plymouth Meeting, PA.

2008 Under Armour Tournaments: Southeast Regional—June 7-11 in Jupiter, FL. **Southwest Regional**—July 31-Aug. 4 in Peoria, AZ. Fall Classic - Sept. 12-14 in Jupiter, FL. Winter Classic - Dec. 27-30 in Tucson, AZ.

TOP GUNS PROSPECT DEVELOPMENT CAMPS

Mailing Address: 9323 N Government Way #307, Hayden, ID 83835. **Telephone/Fax:** (208) 762-1100. **E-Mail Address:** topgunsbss@hotmail.com. **Website:** www.topgunsbaseball.com. **President:** Nick Rook.

2008 Camp: June 26-28, Las Vegas, NV

TPX TOP 96 COLLEGE COACHES CLINICS

Mailing Address: 6 Foley Dr. Southboro, MA 01772 **Telephone:** 508-481-5939

E-Mail Address: doug.henson@top96.com. **Website:** www.tpxtop96.com

Directors: Doug Henson, Dave Callum, Ken Hill

2008 Clinics: 44 clinics throughout the United States; see website for schedule.

YOUTH BASEBALL

ALL AMERICAN AMATEUR BASEBALL ASSOCIATION

Mailing Address: 331 Parkway Dr., Zanesville, OH 43701. **Telephone:** (740) 453-8531. **Fax:** (740) 453-8531. **E-Mail Address:** clw@aol.com. **Website:** www.aaaba.us.

Year Founded: 1944.

President: Doug Pollock. **Executive Director/ Secretary:** Bob Wolfe.

2008 Events: National Tournament (20 and under): Aug. 11-17 at Johnstown, PA (16 teams). **AAABA Regionals:** August 2-4 at Altoona, PA and Zanesville, OH.

AMATEUR ATHLETIC UNION OF THE UNITED STATES, INC.

Mailing Address: P.O. Box 22409, Lake Buena Vista, FL 32830. **Telephone:** (407) 934-7200. **Fax:** (407) 934-7242. **E-Mail Address:** dan@aausports.org, kristy@aausports.org. **Website:** www.aaubaseball.org.

Year Founded: 1982. **Sports Manager, Baseball:** Dan Stanley

AMERICAN AMATEUR BASEBALL CONGRESS

National Headquarters: 100 West Broadway, Farmington, NM 87401. **Telephone:** (505) 327-3120. **Fax:** (505) 327-3132. **E-Mail Address:** aabc@aabc.us. **Website:** www.aabc.us.

Year Founded: 1935.

President: Richard Neely.

AMERICAN AMATEUR YOUTH BASEBALL ALLIANCE

Mailing Address: 3851 Iris Lane, Bonne Terre, MO 63628. **Telephone:** (573) 518-0319. **Fax:** (314) 822-4974. **E-Mail Address:** clwjr28@aol.com. **Website:** www.aayba.com

President, Baseball Operations: Carroll Wood.

AMERICAN LEGION BASEBALL

National Headquarters: American Legion Baseball, 700 N. Pennsylvania St., Indianapolis, IN 46204. **Telephone:** (317) 630-1213. **Fax:** (317) 630-1369. **E-Mail Address:** baseball@legion.org Website: www.baseball.legion.org.

Year Founded: 1925.

Program Coordinator: Jim Quinlan.

2008 World Series (19 and under): Aug. 21-26 at Keeter Stadium, Shelby, NC (8 teams). **Mailing Address:** 810 Polkville Road, Shelby, NC 28150 Telephone: (704) 473-7865. **E-Mail Address:** holbrook@cleveland.cc.nc.us Website: www.2008worldseries.com

2008 Regional Tournaments (Aug. 13-18, 8 teams): Northeast—Bristol, CT; **Mid-Atlantic**—Colonial Heights, VA; **Southeast**—Shelby, NC; **Mid-South**—Enid, OK; **Great Lakes**—Chilicothe, OH; **Central Plains**—Minot, ND; **Northwest**—Bozeman, MT; **Western**—Surprise, AZ.

BABE RUTH BASEBALL

International Headquarters: 1770 Brunswick Pike, P.O. Box 5000, Trenton, NJ 08638. **Telephone:** (609) 695-1434. **Fax:** (609) 695-2505. **E-Mail Address:** info@baberuthleague.org. **Website:** www.baberuthleague.org.

Year Founded: 1951.

President, Chief Executive Officer: Steven Tellefsen.

BASEBALL CHAMPIONSHIP SERIES

(A Division of Perfect Game USA)

Mailing Address: 1203 Rockford Road SW, Cedar Rapids, IA 52404 Telephone: (319) 298-2923 Fax: (319) 298-2924 E-Mail Address: taylor@perfectgame.org. **Website:** www.perfectgame.org/bcs/

Year Founded: 2005.

President: Andy Ford. **National Director:** Taylor McCollough

CONTINENTAL AMATEUR BASEBALL ASSOCIATION

Mailing Address: 1173 French Court, Maineville, Ohio 45039. **Telephone:** (513) 677-1580. **Fax:** 513-677-2586 E-Mail Address: lredwine@cababaseball.com. **Website:** www.cababaseball.com.

Year Founded: 1984.

Executive Director: Larry Redwine.

Commissioner: John Mocny. **Executive Vice President:** Fran Pell.

DIXIE YOUTH BASEBALL

Mailing Address: P.O. Box 877, Marshall, TX 75671. **Telephone:** (903) 927-2255. **Fax:** (903) 927-1846. **E-Mail Address:** dyb@dixie.org. **Website:** www.dixie.org.

Year Founded: 1955.

Commissioner: Wes Skelton.

DIXIE BOYS BASEBALL

Commissioner/Chief Executive Officer: Sandy Jones, P.O. **Box 8263, Dothan, AL 36304. Telephone:** (334) 793-3331. **Office Manager:** Rhonda Skelton.

DIZZY DEAN BASEBALL

Mailing Address: P.O. Box 856, Hernando, MS 38632. **Telephone:** (662) 429-4365, (423) 596-1353 E-Mail Address: dizzydeanbaseball@yahoo.com. **Website:** www.dizzydeanbbinc.org.

Year Founded: 1962.

Commissioner: Danny Phillips. **Presdient:** Jimmy Wahl. **VP:** Bobby Dunn. **Secretary:** Billy Powell. **Treasurer:** D.B. **Stewart.**

HAP DUMONT YOUTH BASEBALL

(A Division of the National Baseball Congress)

Mailing Address: P.O. Box 83, Lexington, OK 73051. **Telephone:** (405) 899-7689. **E-Mail Address:** stevesmith@hapdumontbaseball.com. **Website:** www.hapdumontbaseball.com; www.oabf.net

Year Founded: 1974. **National Tournament Coordinator:** Steve Smith.

LITTLE LEAGUE BASEBALL

International Headquarters: P.O. Box 3485, Williamsport, PA 17701. **Telephone:** (570) 326-1921. **Fax:** (570) 326-1074. **E-Mail Address:** headquarters@LL.orgWebsite: www.littleleague.org.

Year Founded: 1939.

Chairman: Dennis Lewin.

President/Chief Executive Officer: Stephen D. Keener. **Chief Financial Officer:** David Houseknecht. **Vice President, Operations/Secretary:** Patrick Wilson.

Treasurer: Melissa Singer. **Senior Communications Executive:** Lance Van Auken. **Director, League Development:** Daniel Velte.

NATIONAL AMATEUR BASEBALL FEDERATION

Mailing Address: P.O. Box 705, Bowie, MD 20718. **Telephone:** (410) 721-4727. **Fax:** (410) 721-4940. **E-Mail Address:** nabf1914@aol.com. **Website:** www.nabf.com.

Year Founded: 1914.

Executive Director: Charles Blackburn.

NATIONAL ASSOCIATION OF POLICE ATHLETIC LEAGUES

Mailing Address: 658 W. Indiantown Road #201, Jupiter, FL 33458. **Telephone:** (561) 745-5535. **Fax:** (561) 745-3147. **E-Mail Address:** copnkid@nationalpal.org. **Website:** www.nationalpal.org.

Year Founded: 1914.

Executive Director: Mike Dillhyon. **National Program Manager:** Eric Widness.

PONY BASEBALL

International Headquarters: P.O. Box 225, Washington, PA 15301. **Telephone:** (724) 225-1060. **Fax:** (724) 225-9852. **E-Mail Address:** info@pony.org. **Website:** www.pony.org.

Year Founded: 1951.

President: Abraham Key. **Director.**

REVIVING BASEBALL IN INNER CITIES

Mailing Address: 245 Park Ave., **New York, NY 10167. Telephone:** (212) 931-7800. **Fax:** (212) 949-5695.

Year Founded: 1989. **Founder:** John Young. **Vice President, Community Affairs:** Thomas C. Brasuell.

Email: rbi@mlb.com. **Website:** www.mlb.com/rbi

SUPER SERIES BASEBALL OF AMERICA

National Headquarters: 3449 East Kael Street., Mesa, AZ 85213-1773. **Telephone:** (480) 664-2998. **Fax:** (480) 664-2997. **E-Mail Address:** info@superseriesbaseball.com. **Website:** www.superseriesbaseball.com.

President: Mark Mathew

TRIPLE CROWN SPORTS

Mailing Address: 3930 Automation Way, Fort Collins, CO 80525. **Telephone:** (970) 223-6644. **Fax:** (970) 223-3636. **Websites:** www.triplecrownsports.com. **E-mail:** thad@triplecrownsports.com, sean@triplecrownsports.com Director, Baseball Operations: Thad Anderson, Sean Hardy.

U.S. AMATEUR BASEBALL ASSOCIATION

Mailing Address: 7101 Lake Ballinger Way, Edmonds, WA 98026. **Telephone/Fax:** (425) 776-7130. **E-Mail Address:** usaba@usaba.com. **Website:** www.usaba.com.

Year Founded: 1969.

Executive Director: Al Rutledge. **Secretary:** Roberta Engelhart.

U.S. AMATEUR BASEBALL FEDERATION

Mailing Address: 389 Bryan Point Dr. Chula Vista, CA 91914. **Telephone:** (619) 934-2551. **Fax:** (619) 271-6659. **E-Mail Address:** usabf@cox.net. **Website:** www.usabf.com.

Year Founded: 1997.

Senior Chief Executive Officer/President: Tim Halbig.

UNITED STATES SPECIALTY SPORTS ASSOCIATION

Executive Vice President, Baseball: Joey Odom, 614 South Lake Court Dr., **Lake Charles, LA 70605. Telephone:** (337) 562-1251. **E-Mail Address:** joeyodom@aol.com.

Executive Vice President, Baseball Operations: Rick Fortuna, 6324 N. Chatham Ave., #136, Kansas City, MO 64151 **Telephone:** (816) 587-4545. **E-Mail Address:** rick@kcsports.org. **Website:** www.usssabaseball.org. **Year Founded:** 1965/Baseball 1996.

USA BASEBALL 16U CHAMPIONSHIP

Mailing Address: USA Baseball, 403 Blackwell St., **Durham, NC 27701. Telephone:** (919) 474-8721. **Fax:** (919) 474-8822. **E-Mail Address:** jeffsinger@usabaseball.com. **Website:** www.usabaseball.com.

Assistant Director, Baseball Operations: Jeff Singer.

WORLD WOOD BAT ASSOCIATION

(A Division of Perfect Game USA)

Mailing Address: 1203 Rockford Road SW, Cedar Rapids, IA 52404. **Telephone:** (319) 298-2923 Fax: (319) 298-2924. **E-Mail Address:** taylor@perfectgame.org Website: www.worldwoodbat.com.

Year Founded: 1997.

President: Andy Ford. **National Director:** Taylor McCollough. **Scouting Director:** David Rawnsley.

YOUTH BASEBALL TOURNAMENT CENTERS

BASEBALL USA

Mailing Address: 2626 W. Sam Houston Pkwy. N., Houston, TX 77043. **Telephone:** (713) 690-5055. **Fax:** (713) 690-9448. **E-Mail Address:** info@baseballusa.com. **Website:** www.baseballusa.com.

President: Charlie Maiorana. **Tournament Director:** Steve Olson. **Director, Marketing/Development:** Christina Yaya. **League Baseball:** Chip Nila. **Pro Shop Manager:** Don Lewis.

Activities: Camps, baseball/softball spring and fall leagues, instruction, indoor cage and field rentals, youth tournaments, World Series events, corporate days, summer college league, pro shop.

CALIFORNIA COMPETITIVE YOUTH BASEBALL

Mailing Address: P.O. Box 338, Placentia, CA 92870. **Telephone:** (714) 993-2838. **Fax:** (714) 961-6078. **E-Mail Address:** ccybnet@aol.com.

Tournament Director: Todd Rogers.

COCOA EXPO SPORTS CENTER

Mailing Address: 500 Friday Road, Cocoa, FL 32926. **Telephone:** (321) 639-3976. **Fax:** (321) 639-0598. **E-Mail Address:** athleticdirector@cocoaexpo.com. **Website:** www.cocoaexpo.com.

Athletic Director: Jeff Biddle.

Activities: Spring training program, instructional camps, team training camps, youth tournaments.

2008 Tournaments

President's Day Challenge, Feb. 16-18; Memorial Day Bash, May 24-26; Internationale, June 29-July 4; Cocoa Expo Summer Classic, July 29-Aug. 3; Labor Day Challenge, Aug. 30- Sep. 1; Fall Challenge Oct. 17 -19; Thanksgiving Classic Nov. 28-30.

COOPERSTOWN BASEBALL WORLD

Mailing Address: P.O. Box 530, Brick, NJ 08723. **Telephone:** (888) CBW-8750. **Fax:** (888) CBW-8720. **E-Mail:** cbw@cooperstownbaseballworld.com.

Complex Address: Cooperstown Baseball World, SUNY-Oneonta, Ravine Parkway, Oneonta, NY 13820.

President/Chairman: Eddie Einhorn. **Vice President:** Debra Sirianni.

2008 Tournaments (15 Teams Per Week): Open to 12U, 13U, 14U, 15U, 16U from June 23 through August 10.

COOPERSTOWN DREAMS PARK

Mailing Address: 330 S. Main St., Salisbury, NC 28144. **Telephone:** (704) 630-0050. **Fax:** (704) 630-0737. **E-Mail Address:** info@cooperstowndreamspark.com. **Website:** www.cooperstowndreamspark.com.

Complex Address: 4550 State Highway 28, Cooperstown, NY 13807.

Chief Executive Officer: Lou Presutti. **Program Director:** Dan Magnano.

2008 Tournaments: Weekly June 7–Aug. **29**

DISNEY'S WIDE WORLD OF SPORTS

Mailing Address: P.O. **Box 10000, Lake Buena Vista, FL 32830. Telephone:** (407) 938-3802. **Fax:** (407) 938-3442. **E-Mail Address:** wdw.sports.baseball@disney.com. **Website:** www.disneyworldsports.com.

Manager, Sports Events: Kevin Reynolds. **Sports Manager:** Brian Fling. **Tournament Director:** Al Schlazer. **Sales Manager, Baseball:** Rick Morris. **Sports Sales Coordinator, Baseball:** Kirk Stanley.

KC SPORTS TOURNAMENTS

Mailing Address: KC Sports, 6324 N. **Chatham Ave., No. 136, Kansas City, MO 64151. Telephone:** (816) 587-4545. **Fax:** (816) 587-4549. **E-Mail Addresses:** jay@kcsports.org, wally@kcsports.org Website: www.kcsports.org.

Activities: USSSA Youth tournaments (ages 6-18).

Tournament Organizers: Wally Fortuna, Jay Baxter.

U.S. AMATEUR BASEBALL FEDERATION (USABF)

Mailing Address: 389 Bryan Point Dr. Chula Vista, CA 91914. **Telephone:** (619) 934-2551. **Fax:** (619) 271-6659. **E-Mail Address:** usabf@cox.net. **Website:** www.usabf.com.

Year Founded: 1997. **Senior Chief Executive Officer/ President:** Tim Halbig.

INSTRUCTIONAL SCHOOLS/ PRIVATE CAMPS

ACADEMY OF PRO PLAYERS

Mailing Address: 140 5th Avenue, Hawthorne, NJ 07506. **Telephone:** (973) 772-3355. **Fax:** (973) 772-4839. **Website:** www.academypro.com. **Camp Director:** Dan Gilligan.

ALL-STAR BASEBALL ACADEMY

Mailing Addresses: 650 Parkway Blvd., Broomall, PA 19008; 52 Penn Oaks Dr., West Chester, PA 19382. **Telephone:** (610) 355-2411, (610) 399-8050. **Fax:** (610) 355-2414. **E-Mail Address:** basba@allstarbaseballacademy.com. **Website:** www.allstarbaseballacademy.com. **Directors:** Mike Manning, Jim Freeman.

AMERICAN BASEBALL FOUNDATION

Mailing Address: 2660 10th Ave. South, Suite 620, Birmingham, AL 35205. **Telephone:** (205) 558-4235. **Fax:** (205) 918-0800. **E-Mail Address:** abf@asmi.org. **Website:** www.americanbaseball.org. **Executive Director:** David Osinski. **Chairman of the Board:** James R. **Andrews, M.D.**

THE BASEBALL ACADEMY

Mailing Address: IMG Academies, 5500 34th St. W., Bradenton, FL 34210. **Telephone:** (941) 755-1000. **Fax:** (941) 739-7484. **Website:** www.imgworld.com.

BEN BOULWARE

Mailing Address: America's Baseball Camps, PO Box 2925, Hayden, ID 83865. **Telephone:** (208) 402-5003. **Fax:** (208) 762-4347. **E-Mail Address:** info@baseballcamps.com. **Website:** www.baseballcamps.com.

BUCKY DENT'S BASEBALL SCHOOL

Mailing Address: 490 Dotterel Road, Delray Beach, FL 33444. **Telephone:** (561) 265-0280. **Fax:** (561) 278-6679. **E-Mail Address:** staff@dentbaseball.com. **Website:** www.buckydentbaseballschool.com. **VP/GM:** Larry Hoskin.

DOYLE BASEBALL ACADEMY

Mailing Address: P.O. Box 9156, Winter Haven, FL 33883. **Telephone:** (863) 439-1000. **Fax:** (863) 294-8607. **E-Mail Address:** info@doylebaseball.com.

Website: www.doylebaseball.com. **President:** Denny Doyle. **Director:** Blake Doyle.

FROZEN ROPES TRAINING CENTERS

Mailing Address: 12 Elkay Dr., Chester, NY 10918. **Telephone:** (877) 846-5699. **Fax:** (845) 469-6742. **E-Mail Address:** info@frozenropes.com. **Website:** www.frozenropes.com. **Corporate Director:** Tony Abbatine. **Camp Director:** Dan Hummel.

MARK CRESSE BASEBALL SCHOOL

Mailing Address: 1188 N. Grove St., Suite C, Anaheim, CA 92806. **Telephone:** (714) 892-6145. **Fax:** (714) 892-1881. **E-Mail Address:** info@markcresse.com. **Website:** www.markcresse.com. **Owner/Founder:** Mark Cresse. **Executive Director:** Jeff Courvoisier.

MICKEY OWEN BASEBALL SCHOOL

Mailing Address: PO Box 4504, Springfield, MO 65808. **Telephone:** (417) 882-2799. **Fax:** (417) 889-6978. **E-Mail Address:** info@mickeyowen.com. **Website:** www.mickeyowen.com. **President:** Ken Rizzo. **Camp Director:** Tim Williams. **Clinician:** Tim Williams. **Advisor:** Howie Bedell.

MIKE DE SURVILLE

Mailing Address: US Sports Camps, 750 Lindaro Street, Suite 220, San Rafael, CA 94901. Telephone: (415) 479-6060. Fax: (415) 479-6061. E-Mail Address: baseball@ussportscamps.com. Website: www.ussportscamps.com.

NORTH CAROLINA BASEBALL ACADEMY

Mailing Address: 1137 Pleasant Ridge Road, Greensboro, NC 27409. **Telephone:** (336) 931-1118. **E-Mail Address:** info@ncbaseball.com. **Website:** www.ncbaseball.com.

Owner/Director: Scott Bankhead. **Assistant Director:** Chris Winterfeldt and Ben Barker. **Academy Director:** Ben Barker.

PENNSYLVANIA DIAMOND BUCKS

Mailing Address: 2320 Whitetail Court, Hellertown, PA 18055. **Telephone:** (610) 838-1219, (610) 442-6998. **E-Mail Address:** jciganick@moravian.edu. **Camp Director:** Jan Ciganick. **Head of Instruction:** Chuck Ciganick.

PROFESSIONAL BASEBALL INSTRUCTION

Mailing Address: 107 Pleasant Ave., Upper Saddle River, NJ 07458. **Telephone:** (800) 282-4638 (NY/NJ), (877) 448-2220 (rest of U.S.). **Fax:** (201) 760-8820. **E-Mail Address:** info@baseballclinics.com. **Website:** www.baseballclinics.com. **President:** Doug Cinnella.

RIPKEN BASEBALL CAMPS

Mailing Address: 1427 Clarkview Rd., **Suite 100, Baltimore, MD 21209. Telephone:** (800) 486-0850. **Fax:** (410) 823-0850. **E-Mail Address:** information@ripkenbaseball.com. **Website:** www.ripkenbaseball.com. **Director, Operations:** Adam Christ.

SHO-ME BASEBALL CAMP

Mailing Address: P.O. Box 2270, Branson West, MO 65737. **Telephone:** (800) 993-2267, (417) 338-5838. **Fax:** (417) 338-2610. **E-Mail Address:** info@shomebaseball.com. **Website:** www.shomebaseball.com. **Camp Director:** Christopher Schroeder. **Head of Instruction:** Dick Birmingham.

UTAH BASEBALL ACADEMY

Mailing Address: 389 West 10000 South, South Jordan, UT 84095. **Telephone:** (801) 561-1700. **Fax:** (801) 561-1762. **E-Mail Address:** kent@utahbaseballacademy.com. **Website:** www.utahbaseballacademy.com. **Director:** Bob Keyes

COLLEGE CAMPS

Almost all of the elite college baseball programs have summer/holiday instructional camps. Please consult the college section for listings.

SENIOR BASEBALL

MEN'S SENIOR BASEBALL LEAGUE

(25 and Over, 35 and Over, 45 and Over)

Mailing Address: One Huntington Quadrangle, Suite 3NO7, Melville, NY 11747. **Telephone:** (631) 753-6725. **Fax:** (631) 753-4031.

President: Steve Sigler. **Vice President:** Gary D'Ambrisi.

E-Mail Address: info@msblnational.com. **Website:** www.msblnational.com.

2008 Events: World Series: Oct. **14-Nov. 3, Phoenix, AZ (25-plus, 35-plus, 45-plus, 55-plus, 65-plus, Father/Son divisions). Fall Classic: Nov. 1-10, St. Petersburg, FL (25-plus, 35-plus, 45-plus, Father/Son Divisions).**

MEN'S ADULT BASEBALL LEAGUE

(18 and Over)

Mailing Address: One Huntington Quadrangle, Suite 3NO7, Melville, NY 11747. **Telephone:** (631) 753-6725. **Fax:** (631) 753-4031.

E-Mail Address: info@msblnational.com. **Website:** www.msblnational.com.

President: Steve Sigler. **Vice President:** Gary D'Ambrisi.

2008 Events: World Series: Oct. **17-21, Phoenix, AZ (four divisions). Fall Classic: Nov. 1-5, Clearwater, FL (two divisions).**

NATIONAL ADULT BASEBALL ASSOCIATION

Mailing Address: 3609 S. Wadsworth Blvd., Suite 135, Lakewood, CO 80235. **Telephone:** (800) 621-6479. **Fax:** (303) 639-6605. **E-Mail:** nabanational@aol.com. **Website:** www.dugout.org.

President: Shane Fugita.

2008 Events: Memorial Day Tournaments: 18 and over, 30 and over, 40 and over, 50 and over—May 26-28, Las Vegas, NV; 18 and over, 28 and over, 38 and over, May 26-28, Atlantic City, NJ. **Hall of Fame Tournament:** 18 and over, 28 and over, June 30-July 3, Cooperstown, NY. **Mile High Classic:** 18 and over, 28 and over, 38 and over, July 6-8, Denver, CO. **NABA World Championship Series:** 18 and over, 28 and over, 38 and over, 48 and over, 57 and over, Sept 29-Oct. 13, Phoenix, AZ. **NABA World Championship Series Florida:** 18 and over, 28 and over, 38 and over, 48 and over, 57 and over, Nov 8- Nov 13, Jupiter, FL. **NABA Over 50 Baseball National Tournament:** 48 and over, 58 and over, Oct. 22-27, Las Vegas, NV.

NATIONAL AMATEUR BASEBALL FEDERATION

Mailing Address: P.O. Box 705, Bowie, MD 20718. **Telephone:** (301) 464-5460. **Fax:** (301) 352-0214. **E-Mail Address:** nabf1914@aol.com. **Website:** www.nabf.com.

Year Founded: 1914.

Executive Director: Charles Blackburn. **Special Events Coordinator, NABF Classics:** Michael Felton.

2008 Events: College (22 and under), Rising Sun, MD, August 2-5; Major (unlimited), Louisville, KY, August 16-19.

ROY HOBBS BASEBALL

Open (28-over), Veterans (38-over), Masters (48-over), Legends (55-over),

Family Affairs Division, Classics (60-over), Seniors (65-over), Women's open

Mailing Address: 2048 Akron Peninsula Rd., Akron, OH 44313. **Telephone:** (330) 923-3400. **Fax:** (330) 923-1967. **E-Mail Address:** rhbb@royhobbs.com. **Website:** www.royhobbs.com.

President: Tom Giffen. **Vice President:** Ellen Giffen.

2008 Events: World Series (all in Fort Myers, FL): Oct. 20-27—Open Division; Oct. 27-Nov. 3—Veterans Division; Oct. 24-27—Women's Division; Nov. 3-10—Masters Division; Nov. 10-14—Father-Son Division; Nov. 10-17—Legends Division, Classics Division, Seniors Division.

ROY HOBBS WOMEN'S BASEBALL

Open Division (16 and over)

Mailing Address: 2048 Akron Peninsula Rd., Akron, OH 44313. **Telephone:** (330) 923-3400. **Fax:** (330) 923-1967. **E-Mail Address:** rhbb@royhobbs.com. **Website:** www.uswb.org.

President: Tom Giffen. **Vice President:** Ellen Giffen.

Youth Chairman: John Kovach. **Committee Members:** Adriane Adler, Chris Hill, Cherie Leatherwood.

2008 National Championship: Oct. 24-27 at Fort Myers, FL.

DIRECTORIES
AGENT
SERVICE

AGENT DIRECTORY

ACES, INC.

Seth Levinson, Esq.
Sam Levinson
Keith Miller
Peter Pedalino, Esq
Michael Zimmerman
188 Montague Street
Brooklyn, NY 11201
718-237-2900
Fax: 718-522-3906
acesinc2@aol.com

ALL-STAR SPORTS GROUP

Francis A. Marquez
Oscar Melendez
Jaime Guillemard
1302 Ponce De Leon Ave. Suite 302
San Juan, PR 00907
Fax: (787) 725-1339
www.asgbaseball.com
support@asgbaseball.com

ARLAND SPORTS

Jason Wood
2762 N. Lincoln Ave. Suite 305
Chicago, IL 60614
773-857-2078
Fax: 773-304-1919
www.arlandsports.com
jwood@arlandsports.com

ATHLETES FIRST

Camron Hahn
Brian Murphy
Mark Humenik
9140 Irvine Center Dr. Irvine, CA 92618
949-475-2222
Fax: 9494751006
www.athletesfirst.net
chahn@athletesfirst.net

CAPSTONE SPORTS GROUP

Chance J. Dennison
Jeremy J. Sanders
San Felipe Plaza
5847 San Felipe, 17th Floor
Houston, TX 77057
713-463-8985
Fax: 713-465-4060
www.capstone-sports.com
cdennison@capstone-sports.com

DAVID ABRAMSON, ESQ

Verrill Dana Sports Law Group
One Portland Square
Portland, ME 04112
207-774-4000
Fax: 207-774-7499
www.sportslaw.com
dabramson@verrilldana.com
dabramson@sportslaw.com

DETROIT SPORTS AND ENTERTAINMENT GROUP, LLC

Storm Kirschenbaum
Two Towne Square, Suite 800
Southfield, MI 48076
248-827-0510
Fax: 248-827-1002
skirschenbaum@sbcglobal.net

DIAMOND DIRECTORS SPORTS MANAGEMENT GROUP

CJ Stewart
358 Roswell Street, #2180
Marietta, GA 30060
404-867-4613
cj.stewart@diamonddirectorssmg.com
www.diamonddirectorssmg.com

DIAMOND STARS SPORTS MANAGEMENT

Lenard Sapp
5719 6th Avenue
Los Angeles, CA 90043
323-815-0722
Fax: 323-815-0827
diamondstarsagent@sbcglobal.net

DOUBLE DIAMOND SPORTS MANAGEMENT

Howard A Kusnick
Joshua A Kusnick
401 E. Las Olas Boulevard Suite 1650
Fort Lauderdale, FL 33301
954-527-8660
Fax: 954-315-7230
www.doublediamondsports
management.com
hkusnick@bellsouth.net

HARTLEY LAW FIRM

Jot Hartley
4150 S 100th E Ave., Ste. 200-I
Tulsa, OK 74146
918-244-0394
Fax: 918-256-2121
tjh@hartleylawfirm.com

IGLESIAS SPORTS MANAGEMENT

Juan C. Iglesias, President
Fernando Iglesias, Esq.
2655 LeJeune Rd. Suite 532
Coral Gables, FL 33134
305-446-9960
Fax: 305-446-9980
grndslm@aol.com

INTEGRITY SPORTS GROUP, LLC

Daniel Ferreira, Esq.
Alexander Sepulveda, Esq.
Jeff DeCaito
441 Summit Avenue
South Orange, NJ 07079
646-337-4547
www.integritysports.us
AL1906@aol.com

JET SPORTS MANAGEMENT

B.B. Abbott
Hank Sargent
Al Goetz
5136 W. San Jose St.
Tampa, FL 33629
813-902-9511
Fax: 813-902-0900
www.jetsportsmanagement.com
bbabbott@jetsportsmanagement.com
sarge@jetsportsmanagement.com
algoetz@jetsportsmanagement.com

KING & KING

Stanley O. King, Esquire
231 South Broad Street
Woodbury, NJ 08096
856-845-3001
Fax: 856-845-3079
stan@kinglaw.com

MONACO LAW OFFICE

Randell Monaco
660 Newport Beach Center Drive
Suite 400
Newport Beach, CA 92600
949-719-2669
Fax: 949-720-4111
randell@monacolawoffice.com

PETER E. GREENBERG & ASSOCIATES, LTD.

Peter E. Greenberg, Esq.
Edward L. Greenberg
Chris Leible
200 Madison Ave. Suite 2225
New York, NY 10016
212-334-6880
Fax: 212-334-6895

PLATINUM SPORTS & ENTERTAINMENT MANAGEMENT, LLC

Nick Brockmeyer –President
Bert Fulk
Chad McDermott
123 N. 5th Street
St. Charles, MO 63301
636-946-0960
Fax: 636-946-0283
www.pseagents.com
nbrockmeyer@psemagents.com

PRO AGENTS INC.

David P. Pepe
Billy Martin Jr.
90 Woodbridge Drive
Woodbridge, NJ 07095
800-795-3454
Fax: 732-726-6688
pepeda@wilentz.com

PROFESSIONAL SPORTS MANAGEMENT GROUP

Alan Meersand, President
Adam Karon
2100 N. Sepulveda Bvld. Ste. 23
Manhattan Beach, CA 90266
310-546-3400
Fax: 310-546-4046
meersand@aol.com

PROSPORT MANAGEMENT, INC.

James K. Krivacs
1831 N. Belcher Road, G-3
Clearwater, FL 33765
727-791-7556
Fax: 727-791-1489

PRO STAR MANAGEMENT

Joe Bick
Brett Bick
1600 Scripps Center 312 Walnut Street
Cincinnati, OH 45202
513-762-7676
Fax: 513-721-4628
www.prostarmanagement.com
prostar@fuse.net
prostar2@fuse.net

PRO-TALENT, INC.

3753 North Western Avenue
Chicago, IL 60618
773-583-3411
Fax: 773-583-4277
protalentchicago@aol.com

SOSNICK COBBE SPORTS

Matt Sosnick
Paul Cobbe
Matt Hofer
Adam Karon
Jim Munsey
Jonathan Pridie
Bryan Zahn
712 Bancroft Rd, #510
Walnut Creek, CA 94598
925-890-5283
925-476-0130
www.SosnickCobbeSports.com
MattSoz@aol.com
PaulCobbe@msn.com

THE SHOW

Andrew Mongelluzzi, Esq.
3040 Gulf to Bay Bvld
Clearwater, FL 33759
727-789-2109
Fax: 727-789-2109
www.theshow-baseball.com
nettie@theshow-baseball.com

THE SPARTA GROUP

Michael Nicotera
Gene Casaleggio
Sohail Shanpar, Esq.
140 Littleton Road Suite 100
Parsippany, NJ 07054
973-335-0550
Fax: 973-335-2148
www.thespartagroup.com
frontdesk@thespartagroup.com

STERLING SPORTS MANAGEMENT

Joe Speed
7650 River's Edge Drive
Columbus, OH 43235
513-227-6595
Fax: 614-846-2003
jspeed7@aol.com
www.sterlingsm.com

WEST COAST SPORTS MANAGEMENT

Dan Evans
Lenny Strelitz
Jim Lentine
Matt Shupper
Bill Shupper
369 South Fairoaks Ave.
Pasadena, CA 91105
626-683-4991
Fax: 626-844-1863
www.proballfirm.com
info@proballfirm.com

SERVICE DIRECTORY

ACCESSORIES

JKP SPORTS

PO Box 3126
Tualatin, OR 97062
800-547-6843
Fax 503-691-1100
www.jugssports.com

ACCOUNTING

RESNICK AMSTERDAM LESHNER P.C

653 Skippack Pike Suite 300
Blue Bell, PA 19422
215-628-8080
Fax 215-618-4752
www.baseballaccountants.com
sxr@ral-cpa.com

APPAREL

ALL-PRO SPORTS

5341 Derry Ave. Suite P
Agoura Hills, CA 91301
818-707-3180
www.allprosportshoes.com
allprosports@sbcglobal.net

CHSPORT

1400 Chamberlayne Ave.
Richmond, VA 23232
800-888-7606
Fax 804-643-4408
www.chsport.com
chouse601@aol.com

DINGER BATS

PO Box 88 109 Kimbro St.
Ridgway, IL 62979
866-9-Dinger
Fax 618-272-7253
www.dingerbats.com
info@dingerbats.com

MINOR LEAGUES, MINOR DREAMS

PO Box 6098
Anaheim, CA 92816
800-345-2421
Fax 714-939-0655
www.minorleagues.com
mlmd@minorleagues.com

RINGOR

7929 SW Burns Way
Wilsonville, OR 97070
800-524-1236
Fax 503-582-9899
www.ringor.com
contact@ringor.com

ROPES

Box 521
Southbury, CT 06488
888-767-3781
Fax 203-267-1825
www.ropesbaseball.com

UNDER ARMOUR

1020 Hull Street
Baltimore, MD 21230
888-4-ARMOUR
www.underarmour.com

BAGS

BRETT BROTHERS SPORTS INTERNATIONAL

East 9516 Montgomery St. Bldg #14
Spokane, WA 99206
509-891-6435
Fax 509-891-4156
www.brettbros.com
brettbats@aol.com

DIAMOND BASEBALL

11130 Warland Dr.
Cypress, CA 90630
800-366-2999
888-870-7555
diamond-sports.com

DINGER BATS

PO Box 88 109 Kimbro St.
Ridgway, IL 62979
866-9-Dinger
Fax 618-272-7253
www.dingerbats.com
info@dingerbats.com

GERRY COSBY AND CO. INC

3 Pennsylvania Plaza, Madison Square Garden
New York, NY 10001
877-563-6464
Fax 212-967-0876
www.cosbysports.com
gcsmsg@cosbysports.com

RINGOR

7929 SW Burns Way
Wilsonville, OR 97070
800-524-1236
Fax 503-582-9899
www.ringor.com
contact@ringor.com

BANNERS AND FLAGS

OLYMPUS FLAGS & BANNER

9000 W. Heather Ave
Milwaukee, WI 53224
414-355-2010
Fax 414-355-1931
www.olympus-flag.com
sales@olympus-flag.com

BASEBALL CARDS

GRANDSTAND CARDS

22647 Ventura Bvld. #192
Woodland Hills, CA 91364
818-992-5642
Fax 818-348-9122
gscards1@pacbell.net

BASEBALLS

DIAMOND BASEBALL

11130 Warland Dr.
Cypress, CA 90630
800-366-2999
888-870-7555
diamond-sports.com

JKP SPORTS

PO Box 3126
Tualatin, OR 97062
800-547-6843
Fax 503-691-1100
www.jugssports.com

BASES

BEACON ATHLETICS

2224 Pleasant View Rd. #6
Middleton, WI 53562
800-747-5985
Fax 608-836-0724
www.beaconathletics.com
info@beaconathletics.com

BATS

BRETT BROTHERS SPORTS INTERNATIONAL

East 9516 Montgomery St. Bldg #14
Spokane, WA 99206
509-891-6435
Fax 509-891-4156
www.brettbros.com
brettbats@aol.com

BWP BATS

80 Womel Dorf Lane
Brookville, PA 15825
814-849-4143
Fax 814-849-4143
www.bwpbats.com
sales@bwpbats.com

DEMARINI / WILSON SPORTING GOODS

8750 W. Bryn Mawr Avenue
Chicago, IL 60631
p: 800-333-8326
Fax: 773-714-4595
www.demarini.com

DINGER BATS

PO Box 88 109 Kimbro St.
Ridgway, IL 62979
866-9-Dinger
Fax 618-272-7253
www.dingerbats.com
info@dingerbats.com

EASTON SPORTS

7855 Haskell Avenue, Suite 200
Van Nuys, CA 91406
800-632-7866
www.eastonsports.com

LOUISVILLE SLUGGER

800 W. Main Street
Louisville, KY 40202
800-282-2287
502-585-1179
www.slugger.com

MATTINGLY BASEBALL

P.O. Box 2423
Shelton, CT 06484
866-627-2287
Fax 203-994-0284
www.mattinglybaseball.com
sales@mattinglybaseball.com

NIKE

One Bowerman Drive
Beaverton, OR 97005
800-806-6453
www.nike.com

OLD HICKORY BAT COMPANY

1735 Hwy 31 W
Goodlettsville, TN 37072
866-ProBats
Fax 615-285-0512
www.oldhickorybats.com
mail@oldhickorybats.com

PHOENIX BAT COMPANY

7801 Corporate Bvld. Suite E
Plain City, OH 43064
877-598-BATS
Fax 614-873-7796
www.phoenixbats.com
lefty@phoenixbats.com

RAWLINGS

510 Maryville University Drive
Suite 110
St. Louis, MO 63141
866-678-GEAR
www.rawlingsgear.com

REEBOK

1895 JW Foster Blvd.
Canton, MA 02021
800-934-3566
www.reebok.com

SSK CORPORATION

514 Sebastopol Ave.
Santa Rosa, CA 95401
707-318-3610
Fax 707-566-6997
www.ssksports.com/en/baseball
robwilliams10@yahoo.com

THE ORIGINAL MAPLE BAT COMPANY

93 Bayswater Ave.
Ottawa, Canada K1Y 2G2
613-724-2421
Fax 613-725-3299
www.sambat.com
bats@sambat.com

VERDERO

2417 Third Avenue Suite 207
Bronx, NY 10451
718-742-2751
Fax 718-742-2755
www.verdero.com
duke@verdero.com

BATTING CAGES

BEACON ATHLETICS

2224 Pleasant View Rd. #6
Middleton, WI 53562
800-747-5985
Fax 608-836-0724
www.beaconathletics.com
info@beaconathletics.com

C&H BASEBALL

2215 60th Drive East
Bradenton, FL 34203
941-727-1533
Fax 941-727-0588
www.chbaseball.com
danielle@chbaseball.com

JKP SPORTS

PO Box 3126
Tualatin, OR 97062
800-547-6843
Fax 503-691-1100
www.jugssports.com

LANIER BATTING CAGES

206 South Three Notch
Andalusia, AL 36420
334-222-9189
Fax 334-222-3323
alaweb.com/~battingcages
battingcages@alaweb.com

MILLER NET COMPANY

P.O. Box 18787
Memphis, TN 38181
800-423-6603
Fax 901-743-6580
www.millernets.com
miller@millernets.com

NATIONAL BATTING CAGES

3441 South 11th Avenue
Eldridge, IA 97116
800-547-8800
Fax 503-357-3727
www.nationalbattingcages.com
sales@nationalbattingcages.com

RUSSELL BATTING CAGES

626 Winwood Drive
Birmingham, AL 35226
888-RBC-CAGE
Fax: (205) 978-7161
russ@russellbattingcages.com
www.russellbattingcages.com

WEST COAST NETTING

5075 Flight Line Drive
Kingman, AZ 56401
928-692-1144/800-854-5741
Fax 918-652-1501
www.westcoastnetting.com
rthompson@westcoastnetting.com

BATTING GLOVES

ALL-PRO SPORTS

5341 Derry Ave. Suite P
Agoura Hills, CA 91301
818-707-3180
www.allprosportshoes.com
allprosports@sbcglobal.net

DINGER BATS

PO Box 88 109 Kimbro St.
Ridgway, IL 62979
866-9-Dinger
Fax 618-272-7253
www.dingerbats.com
info@dingerbats.com

LOUISVILLE SLUGGER

800 W. Main Street
Louisville, KY 40202
800-282-2287
502-585-1179
www.slugger.com

CAMPS/SCHOOLS

MICKEY OWEN BASEBALL SCHOOL

PO Box 4504
Springfield, MO 65808
417-882-2799
Fax 417-889-6978
www.mickeyowen.com
info@mickeyowen.com

THE BASEBALL ACADEMY

5500 34th St. West
Bradenton, FL 34210
800-872-6425
Fax 941-752-2531
www.imgacademies.com
netsales@imgworld.com

PROFESSIONAL BASEBALL INSTRUCTION

107 Pleasant Avenue
Upper Saddle River, NJ 07458
800-282-4638
Fax 201-760-8820
www.baseballclinics.com
info@baseballclinics.com

CAPS/HEADWEAR

MINOR LEAGUES, MINOR DREAMS

PO Box 6098
Anaheim, CA 92816
800-345-2421
Fax 714-939-0655
www.minorleagues.com
mlmd@minorleagues.com

OUTDOOR CAP COMPANY

1200 Melissa Drive
Bentonville, AR 72712
800-279-3216
Fax 479-273-2144
www.outdoorcap.com
sales@outdoorcap.com

ROPES

Box 521
Southbury, CT 06488
888-767-3781
Fax 203-267-1825
www.ropesbaseball.com

CLEATS/FOOTWEAR

ALL-PRO SPORTS

5341 Derry Ave. Suite P
Agoura Hills, CA 91301
818-707-3180
www.allprosportshoes.com
allprosports@sbcglobal.net

NIKE

One Bowerman Drive
Beaverton, OR 97005
800-806-6453
www.nike.com

REEBOK

1895 JW Foster Blvd.
Canton, MA 02021
800-934-3566
www.reebok.com

RINGOR

7929 SW Burns Way
Wilsonville, OR 97070
800-524-1236
Fax 503-582-9899
www.ringor.com
contact@ringor.com

UNDER ARMOUR

1020 Hull Street
Baltimore, MD 21230
888-4-ARMOUR
www.underarmour.com

CONCESSION OPERATIONS

CONCESSION SOLUTIONS INC

16022-26th Ave NE
Shoreline, WA 98155
206-440-9203
Fax 206-440-9213
www.concessionsolutions.com
theresa@concessionsolutions.com

CUP HOLDERS

CADDY PRODUCTS

73-850 Dinah Shore Drive, Unit 115
Palm Desert, CA 92211
760-770-7299/800-845-0591
Fax 760-1799
www.caddyproducts.com
info@caddyproducts.com

See our ad on the insde front cover!

ENTERTAINMENT

BIRDZERK!

P.O. Box 36061
Louisville, KY 40233
800-219-0899/502-458-4020
Fax 502-458-0867
www.birdzerk.com
dom@birdzerk.com

ZOOPERSTARS!

P.O. Box 36061
Louisville, KY 40233
800-219-0899/502-458-4020
Fax 502-458-0867
www.zooperstars.com
dom@birdzerk.com

FIELD EQUIPMENT

DIAMOND BASEBALL

11130 Warland Dr.
Cypress, CA 90630
800-366-2999
888-870-7555
diamond-sports.com

FIELD WALL PADDING

BEACON ATHLETICS

2224 Pleasant View Rd. #6
Middleton, WI 53562
800-747-5985
Fax 608-836-0724
www.beaconathletics.com
info@beaconathletics.com

C&H BASEBALL

2215 60th Drive East
Bradenton, FL 34203
941-727-1533
Fax 941-727-0588
www.chbaseball.com
danielle@chbaseball.com

COVERMASTER INC.

100 Westmore Dr, 11-D
Rexdale, ON M9V5C3
800-387-5808
416-742-6837
www.covermaster.com
info@covermaster.com

PROMATS

PO Box 508
Fort Collins, CO 80522
800-678-6287
970-482-7740
www.promats.com
ken@promats.com

FIELD COVERS/TARPS

BEACON ATHLETICS

2224 Pleasant View Rd. #6
Middleton, WI 53562
800-747-5985
Fax 608-836-0724
www.beaconathletics.com
info@beaconathletics.com

C&H BASEBALL

2215 60th Drive East
Bradenton, FL 34203
941-727-1533
Fax 941-727-0588
chbaseball.com
danielle@chbaseball.com

COVERMASTER INC.

100 Westmore Dr, 11-D
Rexdale, ON M9V5C3
800-387-5808
416-742-6837
www.covermaster.com
info@covermaster.com

FIREWORKS

ZAMBELLI FIREWORKS INT'L

PO Box 1463
New Castle, PA 16101
800-245-0397
Fax 724-658-8318
www.zambellifireworks.com
zambelli@zambellifireworks.com

GAMES

APBA GAMES

1001 Millersville Rd., 3rd Floor
Lancaster, PA 17603
800-334-2722
Fax 717-871-9959
custsupp@apbaintl.com
www.APBAgames.com

GLOVES

DINGER BATS

PO Box 88 109 Kimbro St.
Ridgway, IL 62979
866-9-Dinger
Fax 618-272-7253
www.dingerbats.com
info@dingerbats.com

OLD HICKORY BAT COMPANY

1735 Hwy 31 W
Goodlettsville, TN 37072
866-ProBats
Fax 615-285-0512
www.oldhickorybats.com
mail@oldhickorybats.com

RAWLINGS

510 Maryville University Drive
Suite 110
St. Louis, MO 63141
866-678-GEAR
www.rawlingsgear.com

REEBOK

1895 JW Foster Blvd.
Canton, MA 02021
800-934-3566
www.reebok.com

SSK CORPORATION

514 Sebastopol Ave.
Santa Rosa, CA 95401
707-318-3610
Fax 707-566-6997
www.ssksports.com/en/baseball
robwilliams10@yahoo.com

VERDERO

2417 Third Avenue Suite 207
Bronx, NY 10451
718-742-2751
Fax 718-742-2755
www.verdero.com
duke@verdero.com

WILSON SPORTING GOODS

8750 W. Bryn Mawr Avenue
Chicago, IL 60631
p: 800-333-8326
Fax 773-714-4595
www.wilson.com

GIVEAWAY ITEMS

GAMEOPS.COM

PO Box 77440
Lakewood, OH 44107
216-221-8242
Fax 978-418-0058
www.gameops.com
info@gameops.com

INSURANCE

K&K INSURANCE

PO Box 2338
Fort Wayne, IN 46801
866-554-4636
www.kandkinsurance.com

MASCOTS

OLYMPUS FLAGS & BANNER

9000 W. Heather Ave
Milwaukee, WI 53224
414-355-2010
Fax 414-355-1931
www.olympus-flag.com
sales@olympus-flag.com

SCOLLON PRODUCTIONS, INC.

PO Box 486
White Rock, SC 29177
803-345-3922 ext. 48
Fax 803-345-9313
www.scollon.com
rick@scollon.com

MINISTRY

C.A.P.S CHRISTIAN ATHLETES PERFECTING SPORTS

10315 Woodley Ave. Suite 104
Granada Hills, CA 91344
818-360-9600
Fax 818-360-9660
www.capsfoundation.org

MUSIC/SOUND EFFECTS

SOUND DIRECTOR

4380 SW Macadam Ave. Suite 540
Portland, OR 97239
503-963-3802
Fax 503-963-3822
www.sounddirector.com
jj@sounddirector.com

NETTING/POSTS

BEACON ATHLETICS

2224 Pleasant View Rd. #6
Middleton, WI 53562
800-747-5985
Fax 608-836-0724
www.beaconathletics.com
info@beaconathletics.com

C&H BASEBALL

2215 60th Drive East
Bradenton, FL 34203
941-727-1533
Fax 941-727-0588
www.chbaseball.com
danielle@chbaseball.com

MILLER NET COMPANY

P.O. Box 18787
Memphis, TN 38181
800-423-6603
Fax 901-743-6580
www.millernets.com
miller@millernets.com

WEST COAST NETTING

5075 Flight Line Drive
Kingman, AZ 56401
928-692-1144/800-854-5741
Fax 918-652-1501
www.westcoastnetting.com
rthompson@westcoastnetting.com

PENNANTS, FOAM FINGERS, AND NOVELTY GIFTS

RICO INDUSTRIES, INC./TAG EXPRESS

7000 N. Austin
Niles, IL 60714
800-423-5856
Fax 312-427-0190
www.ricoinc.com
jimz@ricoinc.com

PITCHING AIDS

PROFESSIONAL BASEBALL INSTRUCTION

107 Pleasant Avenue
Upper Saddle River, NJ 07458
800-282-4638
Fax 201-760-8820
www.baseballclinics.com
info@baseballclinics.com

PITCHING MACHINES

ATEC

655 Spice Island Drive
Sparks, NV 89431
p: (800) 998-2832
Fax: (800) 959-2832
www.atecsports.com

JKP SPORTS

PO Box 3126
Tualatin, OR 97062
800-547-6843
Fax 503-691-1100
www.jugssports.com

MASTER PITCHING MACHINES

4200 Northeast Birmingham Road
Kansas City, MO 64117
800-878-8228
www.masterpitch.com

PRO BATTER SPORTS

15 Old Gate Lane
Milford, CT 06460
203-874-2500
Fax 203-878-9019
www.probatter.com
info@probatter.com

SPORTS ATTACK, LLC

P.O. Box 1529 2805 U.S. 40
Verdi, NV 89439
Tel: 775.345.2882/800.717.4251
Fax:775.345.2883
www.sportsattack.com
info@sportsattack.com

See our ad on Page 7!

PITCHING TOES

ALL-PRO SPORTS

5341 Derry Ave. Suite P
Agoura Hills, CA 91301
818-707-3180
www.allprosportshoes.com
allprosports@sbcglobal.net

PLAYING FIELD PRODUCTS

BEAM CLAY

Kelsey Park
Great Meadows, NJ 07838
800-247-Beam
Fax 908-637-8421
www.beamclay.com
sales@partac.com

See our ad on Page 344!

DIAMOND PRO (TXI)

1341 West Mockingbird Lane
Dallas, TX 75247
800-228-2987
Fax 800-640-6735
www.diamondpro.com
diamondpro@txi.com

MOLTAN COMPANY

7125 Riverdale Bend Rd.
Memphis, TN 38125
901-755-5666
901-757-0546
www.moltan.com
jkitchens@moltan.com

PRO'S CHOICE

410 N. Michigan Suite 400
Chicago, IL 60611
800-648-1166
312-321-9525
www.proschoice1.com
proschoice@oildri.com

PROMOTIONAL ITEMS

GAMEOPS.COM

PO Box 770440
Lakewood, OH 44107
866-GAMEOPS
Fax 978-418-0058
www.gameops.com
info@gameops.com

PHOENIX SPORTS INC.

301 Boren Ave. North
Seattle, WA 98109
800-776-9229
Fax 800-776-4422
www.phoenixsportsinc.com
phoesports@aol.com

RICO INDUSTRIES, INC./TAG EXPRESS

7000 N. Austin
Niles, IL 60714
800-423-5856
Fax 312-427-0190
www.ricoinc.com
jimz@ricoinc.com

PROTECTIVE EQUIPMENT

DIAMOND BASEBALL

11130 Warland Dr.
Cypress, CA 90630
800-366-2999
Fax 888-870-7555
diamond-sports.com

RADAR EQUIPMENT

APPLIED CONCEPTS

2609 Technology Drive
Plano, TX 74074
800-Stalker
www.stalkerradar.com

See our ad on Page 2!

JKP SPORTS

PO Box 3126
Tualatin, OR 97062
800-547-6843
Fax 503-691-1100
www.jugssports.com

SPORTS SENSORS

1131 Embassy Drive
Cincinnati, OH 45240
888-542-9246
Fax 513-825-8532
adilz@cinci.rr.com

SCOUTING SERVICES

SOCAL GOLD SCOUTING SERVICE

254 E. Grand Ave Suite #201
Escondido, CA 92025
858-776-9361
Fax 760-738-8866
www.socalgoldscouting.com
rhabert@socalgoldscouting.com

SEATING

STURDISTEEL COMPANY

P.O. Box 2655
Waco, TX 76702
800-433-3116
Fax 254-666-4472
www.sturdisteel.com
rgroppe@sturdisteel.com

SHOWCASES/PLAYER DEVELOPMENT

BASEBALL FACTORY

9176 Red Branch Road, Suite M
Columbia, MD 21045
800-641-4487
Fax 410-715-1975
www.baseballfactory.com
info@baseballfactory.com

TEAM ONE BASEBALL

1000 Bristol Street N, Box 17285
Newport Beach, CA 92660
Ph- 800-621-5452
Fax- 949-209-1829
www.teamonebaseball.com
jroswell@teamonebaseball.com

SPORTING GOODS

ALL-PRO SPORTS

5341 Derry Ave. Suite P
Agoura Hills, CA 91301
818-707-3180
www.allprosportshoes.com
allprosports@sbcglobal.net

FRANK'S SPORT SHOP

430 East Tremont Avenue
New York, NY 10457
718-299-9628
Fax 718-583-1652
www.frankssportshop.com

See our ad after Page 16!

JUGHEAD SPORTS

107 Pleasant Avenue
Upper Saddle River, NJ 07458
800-282-4638
Fax 201-760-8820
www.jugheadsports.com

STADIUM ARCHITECTS

360 ARCHITECTURE

300 West 22nd St.
Kansas City, MO 64108
816-472-3360
www.360architects.com
clamberth@360architecture.com

STURDISTEEL COMPANY

P.O. Box 2655
Waco, TX 76702
800-433-3116
Fax 254-666-4472
www.sturdisteel.com
rgroppe@sturdisteel.com

STATISTICAL SERVICES

BASEBALL INFO SOLUTIONS

528 North New Street
Bethlehem, PA 18018
610-814-0107
Fax 610-814-0166
www.baseballinfosolutions.com
info@baseballinfosolutions.com

TICKETS

NATIONAL TICKET CO.

P.O. Box 547
Shamokin, PA 17872
800-829-0829
Fax 570-672-2999
www.nationalticket.com

TICKETING SOLUTIONS

ETIX.COM

909 Aviation Parkway Suite 900
Morrisville, NC 27560
919-653-0444
Fax 919-653-0580
www.etix.com
sales@etix.com

TRAVEL

BROACH BASEBALL TOURS

5821 Fairview Rd. Suite 118
Charlotte, NC 28209
800-849-6345
Fax 704-365-3800
www.baseballtoursusa.com
info@broachbaseballtours.com

TRAVEL, TEAM

WORLD SPORTS INTERNATIONAL TOURS

PO Box 661624
Los Angeles, CA 90495
800-496-8687
Fax 310-314-8872
www.worldsport-tours.com
Training Equipment

SPORTS SENSORS

1131 Embassy Drive
Cincinnati, OH 45240
888-542-9246
Fax 513-825-8532
adilz@cinci.rr.com

UNIFORMS

AIS

2202 Anderson Street
Vernon, CA 90058
800-666-2733
Fax 323-582-2831
www.aisuniforms.com
info@aisuniforms.com

OT SPORTS

172 Boone Street
Burlington, NC 27215
800-898-6285
Fax 336-227-3765
www.otsports.com
sales@otsports.com

WILSON SPORTING GOODS

8750 W. Bryn Mawr Avenue
Chicago, IL 60631
p: 800-333-8326
Fax 773-714-4595
www.wilson.com

WINDSCREENS

C&H BASEBALL

2215 60th Drive East
Bradenton, FL 34203
941-727-1533
Fax 941-727-0588
www.chbaseball.com
danielle@chbaseball.com

COVERMASTER INC.

100 Westmore Dr, 11-D
Rexdale, ON M9V5C3
800-387-5808
416-742-6837
www.covermaster.com
info@covermaster.com

BEACON ATHLETICS

2224 Pleasant View Rd. #6
Middleton, WI 53562
800-747-5985
Fax 608-836-0724
www.beaconathletics.com
info@beaconathletics.com

MILLER NET COMPANY

P.O. Box 18787
Memphis, TN 38181
800-423-6603
Fax 901-743-6580
www.millernets.com
miller@millernets.com

PROMATS

PO Box 508
Fort Collins, CO 80522
800-678-6287
Fax 970-482-7740
www.promats.com
ken@promats.com

WEST COAST NETTING

5075 Flight Line Drive
Kingman, AZ 56401
928-692-1144/800-854-5741
Fax 918-652-1501
www.westcoastnetting.com
rthompson@westcoastnetting.com

VIDEO PITCHING SIMULATORS

PRO BATTER SPORTS

15 Old Gate Lane
Milford, CT 06460
203-874-2500
Fax 203-878-9019
www.probatter.com
info@probatter.com

VINTAGE ATHLETIC CLOTHING

EBBETS FIELD FLANNELS

PO Box 4858
Seattle, WA 98104
888-896-2936
Fax 206-382-4411
www.ebbets.com

VISION TRAINING

ITRAC VISION TRAINING

1543 Abbott Drive
Wheeling, IL 60090
847-229-1554
Fax: 847-229-1039
www.itracvision.com
emaleski@itracvision.com

INDEX

MAJOR LEAGUE TEAMS

MINOR LEAGUE TEAMS

INDEPENDENT TEAMS

OTHER ORGANIZATIONS